DATE DUE

			PRINTED IN U.S.A.

Literature Criticism from 1400 to 1800

Guide to Gale Literary Criticism Series

When you need to review criticism of literary works, these are the Gale series to use:

If the author's death date is: | **You should turn to:**

After Dec. 31, 1959
(or author is still living)

CONTEMPORARY LITERARY CRITICISM

for example: Jorge Luis Borges, Anthony Burgess,
William Faulkner, Mary Gordon,
Ernest Hemingway, Iris Murdoch

1900 through 1959

TWENTIETH-CENTURY LITERARY CRITICISM

for example: Willa Cather, F. Scott Fitzgerald,
Henry James, Mark Twain, Virginia Woolf

1800 through 1899

NINETEENTH-CENTURY LITERATURE CRITICISM

for example: Fedor Dostoevski, Nathaniel Hawthorne,
George Sand, William Wordsworth

1400 through 1799

LITERATURE CRITICISM FROM 1400 TO 1800
(excluding Shakespeare)

for example: Anne Bradstreet, Daniel Defoe,
Alexander Pope, François Rabelais,
Jonathan Swift, Phillis Wheatley

SHAKESPEAREAN CRITICISM

Shakespeare's plays and poetry

Antiquity through 1399

CLASSICAL AND MEDIEVAL LITERATURE CRITICISM

for example: Dante, Homer, Plato, Sophocles, Vergil,
the Beowulf Poet

Gale also publishes related criticism series:

CHILDREN'S LITERATURE REVIEW

This series covers authors of all eras who have written for
the preschool through high school audience.

SHORT STORY CRITICISM

This series covers the major short fiction writers of all nationalities
and periods of literary history.

R

ISSN 0740-2880

Volume 12

Literature Criticism from 1400 to 1800

Excerpts from Criticism of the Works
of Fifteenth, Sixteenth, Seventeenth, and
Eighteenth-Century Novelists, Poets, Playwrights,
Philosophers, and Other Creative Writers, from
the First Published Critical Appraisals
to Current Evaluations

James P. Draper
James E. Person, Jr.
Editors

Shannon J. Young
Associate Editor

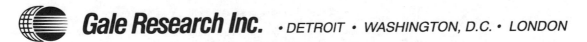 **Gale Research Inc.** · DETROIT · WASHINGTON, D.C. · LONDON

STAFF

...nes P. Draper, James E. Person, Jr., *Editors*

Shannon J. Young, *Associate Editor*

...el, Claudia Loomis, Allyson J. Wylie, *Assistant Editors*
Debra A. Wells, *Contributing Assistant Editor*

Jeanne A. Gough, *Permissions and Production Manager*

Linda M. Pugliese, *Production Supervisor*
Jennifer E. Gale, Suzanne Powers, Maureen A. Puhl, *Editorial Associates*
Donna Craft, David G. Oblender, Linda M. Ross, *Editorial Assistants*

Victoria B. Cariappa, *Research Supervisor*
Karen D. Kaus, Eric Priehs, Maureen R. Richards, Mary D. Wise, *Editorial Associates*
H. Nelson Fields, Judy L. Gale, Filomena Sgambati, *Editorial Assistants*

Sandra C. Davis, *Text Permissions Supervisor*
H. Diane Cooper, Kathy Grell, Josephine M. Keene, Kimberly F. Smilay, *Permissions Associates*
Maria L. Franklin, Lisa Lantz, Camille P. Robinson, Shalice Shah, Denise Singleton,
Permissions Assistants

Patricia A. Seefelt, *Permissions Supervisor (Pictures)*
Margaret A. Chamberlain, *Permissions Associate*
Pamela A. Hayes, Lillian Quickley, *Permissions Assistants*

Mary Beth Trimper, *Production Manager*
Shanna G. Philpott, *External Production Assistant*

Arthur Chartow, *Art Director*
C. J. Jonik, *Keyliner*

Laura Bryant, *Production Supervisor*
Louise Gagné, *Internal Production Associate*

Contents

Preface

The literature of the fifteenth through eighteenth centuries reflects a turbulent time of radical change that saw the rise of drama equal in critical stature to that of classical Greece, the birth of the novel and personal essay forms, the emergence of newspapers and periodicals, and significant achievements in poetry and philosophy. Much of modern literature reflects the influence of these centuries' developments. Thus the literature of this period, criticism of which appears in *Literature Criticism from 1400 to 1800 (LC)*, provides insight into the universal nature of human experience, as well as into the life and thought of the past.

Scope of the Series

LC is designed to serve as an introduction to the authors of the fifteenth through eighteenth centuries and to the most significant commentators on these authors. The works of the great poets, dramatists, novelists, essayists, and philosophers of those years are considered classics in every secondary school and college or university curriculum. Because criticism of this literature spans a period of up to six hundred years, an overwhelming amount of critical material confronts the student. To help students locate and select criticism of the works of authors who died between 1400 and 1800, *LC* presents significant passages from the most noteworthy published criticism of authors of these centuries. Each volume of *LC* is carefully compiled to represent the critical heritage of the most important writers from a variety of nationalities. In addition to major authors, *LC* also presents criticism of lesser-known writers whose significant contributions to literary history are reflected in continuing critical assessments of their works. Readers should note that there is a separate Gale reference series devoted to Shakespearean studies. For though belonging properly to the literary period covered in *LC*, William Shakespeare has inspired such a tremendous and ever-growing corpus of secondary material that the editors have deemed it best to give his works the extensive critical coverage best served by a separate series, *Shakespearean Criticism.*

The need for *LC* among students and teachers of literature of the fifteenth through eighteenth centuries was suggested by the proven usefulness of Gale's *Contemporary Literary Criticism (CLC), Twentieth-Century Literary Criticism (TCLC),* and *Nineteenth-Century Literature Criticism (NCLC),* which excerpt criticism of works by nineteenth- and twentieth-century authors. Because of the different time periods covered, there is no duplication of authors or critical material among any of Gale's literary criticism series. An author may appear more than once in the series because of the great quantity of critical material available or because of the aesthetic demands of the series's *new thematic organization.*

Thematic Approach

Beginning with Volume 12, roughly half the authors in each volume of *LC* are organized in a thematic scheme. Such themes include literary movements, literary reaction to political and historical events, significant eras in literary history, and the literature of cultures often overlooked by English-speaking readers. *LC* 12, for example, focuses upon the literary accomplishments of the Italian Humanist movement: the revival of classical letters that originated in Italy during the fourteenth and fifteenth centuries and which later spread throughout Europe. Future volumes of *LC* will devote substantial space to the authors of the Age of Charles I, the Age of Voltaire, and classical Russian literature, among many others. The remaining portion of each volume will be devoted to criticism of the works of authors not aligned with the selected thematic authors, and chosen from a variety of nationalities.

Organization of the Book

Each entry consists of the following elements: author or thematic heading, introduction, list of principal works (in author entries only), excerpts of criticism (each followed by a bibliographical citation), and a bibliography of further reading. Also, most author entries reproduce author portraits and other illustrations pertinent to the author's life and career.

- The *author heading* consists of the author's full name, followed by birth and death dates. The portion of the name not parenthesized denotes the form under which the author most commonly wrote. If an author wrote consistently under a pseudonym, the pseudonym will be used in the author heading, with the real name given in parentheses on the first line of the biographical and critical introduction. Also located at the beginning of the introduction to the author entry are any name variations under which an author wrote, including transliterated forms for authors whose native languages use nonroman alphabets. Uncertain birth or death dates are indicated by question marks. The *thematic heading* simply states the subject of the entry.

- The *biographical and critical introduction* contains background information designed to introduce the reader to an author and to the critical discussion surrounding his or her work. Parenthetical material following many of the introductions provides references to biographical and critical reference series published by Gale in which additional material on the author may be found. The thematic introduction briefly defines the subject of the entry and provides social and historical background important to understanding the criticism.

- Most *LC* author entries include *portraits* of the author. Many entries also contain illustrations of materials pertinent to an author's career, including selected author holographs, title pages, letters, or representations of important people, places, and events in an author's life.

- The *list of principal works* is chronological by date of first book publication and identifies the genre of each work. In the case of foreign authors whose works have been translated into English, the title and date of the first English-language edition are given in brackets following the foreign-language listing. Unless otherwise indicated, dramas are dated by first performance, not first publication.

- *Criticism* is arranged chronologically in each author entry to provide a useful perspective on changes in critical evaluation over the years. All titles by the author featured in the critical entry are printed in boldface type to enable the user to ascertain without difficulty the works being discussed. Also for purposes of easier identification, the critic's name and the composition or publication date of the critical work are given at the beginning of each excerpt. Unsigned criticism is preceded by the title of the source in which it appeared. Each critical entry attempts to present a historical survey of the critical response to the author's works. Early criticism is offered to indicate initial responses, later selections document any rise or decline in literary reputations and describe the effects of social or historical forces on the work of authors, and retrospective analyses provide students with modern views. The length of each author entry is intended to present the author's critical reception in English or foreign criticism in translation. Articles and books that have not been translated into English are therefore excluded. Every attempt has been made to identify and include excerpts from the seminal essays on each author's work and to include recent critical commentary providing modern perspectives. Publication information (such as publisher names and book prices) and parenthetical numerical references (such as footnotes or page and line references to specific editions of works) have been deleted at the editor's discretion to provide smoother reading of the text.

- Critical essays are prefaced by *annotations* as an additional aid to students using *LC*. These explanatory notes may provide several types of useful information, including: the reputation of a critic, the importance of a work of criticism, the specific type of criticism (biographical, psychoanalytic, structuralist, etc.), the intent of the criticism, and the growth of critical controversy or changes in critical trends regarding an author's work. In some cases, these notes cross-reference the work of critics who agree or disagree with each other.

- A complete *bibliographical citation* designed to facilitate location of the original essay or book by the reader follows each piece of criticism.

- The list of *further reading* appearing at the end of each author entry suggests resources for additional study of authors and themes. In a few rare cases it includes essays for which the editors could not obtain reprint rights.

Cumulative Indexes

Each volume of *LC* includes a cumulative index to authors listing all the authors that have appeared in *Contemporary Literary Criticism, Twentieth-Century Literary Criticism, Nineteenth-Century Literature Criticism, Literature Criticism from 1400 to 1800,* and *Classical and Medieval Literature Criticism,* along with cross-references to the Gale series *Short Story Criticism, Children's Literature Review, Authors in the News, Contemporary Authors, Contemporary Authors Autobiography Series, Contemporary Authors Bibliographical Series, Dictionary of Literary Biography, Concise Dictionary of Literary Biography, Something about the Author, Something about the Author Autobiography Series,* and *Yesterday's Authors of Books for Children.* Readers will welcome this cumulative author index as a useful tool for locating an author within the various series. The index, which includes authors' birth and death dates, is particularly valuable for those authors who are identified with a certain period but whose death dates cause them to be placed in another, or for those authors whose careers span two periods. For example, F. Scott Fitzgerald is found in *TCLC*, yet a writer often associated with him, Ernest Hemingway, is found in *CLC*.

Beginning with *LC* 12, this reference series will conform with the rest of Gale's Literary Criticism Series by including a cumulative topic index, which lists all literary themes and topics treated in *LC*, *NCLC* Topics volumes, *TCLC* Topics volumes, and the *CLC* Yearbook. Each volume of *LC* also includes a cumulative nationality index, in which authors' names are arranged alphabetically under their respective nationalities and followed by the numbers of the volumes in which they appear. In addition, each volume of *LC* includes a cumulative index to titles, an alphabetical listing of the literary works discussed in the series since its inception. Each title listing includes the corresponding volume and page numbers where criticism may be located. Foreign-language titles that have been translated are followed by the titles of the translations—for example, *El ingenioso hidalgo Don Quixote de la Mancha (Don Quixote)*. Page numbers following these translated titles refer to all pages on which any form of the titles, either foreign-language or translated, appear. Titles of novels, dramas, nonfiction books, and poetry, short story, or essay collections are printed in italics, while all individual poems, short stories, and essays are printed in roman type within quotation marks.

Suggestions Are Welcome

Readers who wish to suggest new features, themes, or authors to appear in future volumes, or who have other suggestions, are cordially invited to write the editors or call our toll-free number: 1-800-347-GALE.

Acknowledgments

The editors wish to thank the copyright holders of the excerpted criticism included in this volume, the permissions managers of many book and magazine publishing companies for assisting us in securing reprint rights, and Anthony Bogucki for assistance with copyright research. We are also grateful to the staffs of the Detroit Public Library, the Library of Congress, the University of Detroit Library, Wayne State University Purdy/Kresge Library Complex, and University of Michigan Libraries for making their resources available to us. Following is a list of the copyright holders who have granted us permission to reprint material in this volume of LC. Every effort has been made to trace copyright, but if omissions have been made, please let us know.

COPYRIGHTED EXCERPTS IN LC, VOLUME 12, WERE REPRINTED FROM THE FOLLOWING PERIODICALS:

American Imago, v. 29, Summer, 1972. Copyright 1972 by The Association for Applied Psychoanalysis, Inc. Reprinted by permission of the Wayne State University Press.—*Chinese Literature,* n. 2, February, 1962. Reprinted by permission of the publisher.—*English Literary Renaissance,* v. 2, Autumn, 1972. Copyright © 1972 by *English Literary Renaissance.* Reprinted by permission of the publisher.—*Fantasy Review,* v. 7, January, 1984 for "Three Kingdoms" by William F. Wu. Copyright © 1984 by the author. Reprinted by permission of the author.—*Italian Quarterly,* v. 10, Winter-Spring, 1966. Reprinted by permission of the publisher.—*Italica,* v. XL, June, 1963; v. XLI, September, 1964. Both reprinted by permission of the publisher.—*The Journal of Medieval and Renaissance Studies,* v. 18, Spring, 1988. Copyright © 1988 by Duke University Press. Reprinted by permission of the publisher.—*The New York Review of Books,* v. XXXVI, August 17, 1989. Copyright © 1989 Nyrev, Inc. Reprinted with permission from *The New York Review of Books.*—*The New York Times Book Review,* July 24, 1988. Copyright © 1988 by The New York Times Company. Reprinted by permission of the publisher.—*PMLA,* v. LXXXI, October, 1966. Copyright © 1966 by the Modern Language Association of America. Reprinted by permission of the Modern Language Association of America.—*Renaissance Quarterly,* v. XXXII, Autumn, 1979. Copyright © 1979 by the Renaissance Society of America, Inc. Reprinted by permission of the publisher.—*The Sewanee Review,* v. LXX, Winter, 1962. © 1962 by The University of the South. Reprinted by permission of the editor of *The Sewanee Review.*—*Western Humanities Review,* v. XVII, Winter, 1963. Copyright, 1963, University of Utah. Reprinted by permission of the publisher.

COPYRIGHTED EXCERPTS IN LC, VOLUME 12, WERE REPRINTED FROM THE FOLLOWING BOOKS:

Ackerman, James. From "Concluding Remarks: Science and Art in the Work of Leonardo," in *Leonardo's Legacy: An International Symposium.* Edited by C. D. O'Malley. University of California Press, 1969. © 1969 by The Regents of the University of California. Reprinted by permission of the publisher.—Allen, Michael J. B. From an introduction to *The "Philebus" Commentary.* By Marsilio Ficino, edited and translated by Michael J. B. Allen. University of California Press, 1975. Copyright © 1975 by The Regents of the University of California. Reprinted by permission of the publisher.—Altizer, Alma B. From *Self and Symbolism in the Poetry of Michelangelo, John Donne, and Agrippa D'Aubigné.* Martinus Nijhoff, 1973. © 1973 by Martinus Nijhoff, The Hague, Netherlands. All rights reserved. Reprinted by permission of Kluwer Academic Publishers.—Aretino, Pietro. From a letter in *Aretino: Selected Letters.* Translated by George Bull. Penguin Books, 1976. Introduction, translation and notes copyright © George Bull, 1976. Reproduced by permission of Penguin Books Ltd.—Arthos, John. From *Dante, Michelangelo, and Milton.* Routledge, 1963. Copyright © 1963 by John Arthos. Reprinted by permission of the publisher.—Bax, Clifford. From *Leonardo da Vinci.* D. Appleton and Company, 1932. Copyright, 1932, by D. Appleton and Company. Renewed 1960 by Clifford Bax. All rights reserved.—Berni, Francesco. From a poem in *The Divine Aretino.* By James Cleugh. Anthony Blond Ltd., 1965. Copyright © 1965 by James Cleugh. All rights reserved.—Bongiorno, Andrew. From an introduction to *Castelvetro on the Art of Poetry.* By Lodovico Castelvetro, edited and translated by Andrew Bongiorno. Medieval & Renaissance Texts & Studies, 1984. © Copyright Center for Early & Medieval Renaissance Studies 1984. Reprinted by permission of the publisher.—Bouwsma, William J. From "The Two Faces of Humanism: Stoicism and Augustinianism in Renaissance Thought," in *Itinerarium Italicum: The Profile of the Italian Renaissance in the Mirror of Its European Transformations.* Edited by Heiko A. Oberman with Thomas A. Brady, Jr. Brill, 1975. Copyright 1975 by E. J. Brill. All rights reserved. Reprinted by permission of the publisher.—Brandes, Georg. From *Michelangelo: His Life, His Times, His Era.* Translated by Heinz Norden. Revised edition. Frederick Ungar Publishing Co., 1967. Copyright © 1963, 1967 by The Ungar Publishing Company. Reprinted by permission of the publisher.—Bull, George. From an introduction to *Aretino: Selected Letters.* By Pietro Aretino, translated by George Bull. Penguin Books, 1976. Introduction, translation and notes copyright © George Bull, 1976. Reproduced by permission of Penguin Books Ltd.—Bull, George. From an introduction to *The Book of the Courtier.* By Baldesar Castiglione, translated by George Bull. Penguin Books, 1967. Copyright © George Bull, 1967. Reproduced by permission of Penguin Books Ltd.—Bull, George. From an introduction

Authors to Appear in Future Volumes

Abravenel, Isaac 1437-1508
Abravenel, Judah 1460-1535
Addison, Joseph 1672-1719
Agricola, Johannes 1494?-1566
Akenside, Mark 1721-1770
Alabaster, William 1567-1640
Alarcón y Mendoza, Juan Rúiz 1581-1634
Alberti, Leon Battista 1404-1472
Alembert, Jean Le Rond d' 1717-1783
Amory, Thomas 1691?-1788
Anton Ulrich, Duke of Brunswick 1633-1714
Ascham, Roger 1515-1568
Aubigne, Théodore Agrippa d' 1552-1630
Aubrey, John 1620-1697
Bâbur 1483-1530
Bacon, Sir Francis 1561-1626
Bale, John 1495-1563
Barber, Mary 1690-1757
Baretti, Giuseppi 1719-1789
Barker, Jane 1652-1727?
Bartas, Guillaume de Salluste du 1544-1590
Baxter, Richard 1615-1691
Bayle, Pierre 1647-1706
Beaumarchais, Pierre-Augustin Caron de 1732-1799
Beaumont, Francis 1584-1616
Belleau, Rémy 1528-1577
Berkeley, George 1685-1753
Bessarion, Johannes 1403-1472
Bijns, Anna 1493-1575
Bisticci, Vespasiano da 1421-1498
Blackmore, Sir Richard 1650-1729
Boccalini, Traiano 1556-1613
Bodin, Jean 1530-1596
Bolingbroke, Henry St. John 1678-1751
Boyle, Roger 1621-1679
Bradford, William 1590-1657
Brant, Sebastian 1457-1521
Bredero, Gerbrand Adriaanszoon 1585-1618
Breitinger, Johann Jakob 1701-1776
Breton, Nicholas 1545-1626
Broome, William 1689-1745
Brown, Thomas 1663-1704
Browne, Sir Thomas 1605-1682
Bruni, Leonardo 1370-1444
Bruno, Giordano 1548-1600
Buffon, George-Louis Leclerc, Comte de 1707-1788
Burgoyne, John 1722-1792
Burnet, Gilbert 1643-1715

Burton, Robert 1577-1640
Butler, Samuel 1612-1680
Byrd, William, II 1674-1744
Byrom, John 1692-1763
Calderón de la Barca, Pedro 1600-1681
Calvin, John 1509-1564
Camden, William 1551-1623
Campion, Thomas 1567-1620
Cantemir, Antioch Dmitrievich 1708-1744
Carew, Richard 1555-1620
Carew, Thomas 1594-1640
Carver, Jonathan 1710-1780
Casanova di Seingalt, Giacomo Girolamo 1725-1798
Castillejo, Cristobalde 1492-1550
Cavendish, William 1592-1676
Caxton, William 1421?-1491
Centlivre, Susanna 1667?-1723
Chapman, George 1560-1634
Charles I 1600-1649
Chartier, Alain 1390-1440
Chaucer, Geoffrey 1340?-1400
Cibber, Colley 1671-1757
Cleveland, John 1613-1658
Collyer, Mary 1716?-1763?
Colonna, Vittoria 1490-1547
Commynes, Philippe de 1445-1511
Condillac, Etienne Bonnot, Abbé de 1714?-1780
Cook, James 1728-1779
Corneille, Pierre 1606-1684
Cortés, Hernán 1485-1547
Cotton, John 1584-1652
Courtilz de Sandras, Gatiende 1644-1712
Cowley, Abraham 1618-1667
Cranmer, Thomas 1489-1556
Crashaw, Richard 1612-1649
Crébillon, Prosper Jolyot de 1674-1762
Cruden, Alexander 1701-1770
Curll, Edmund 1675-1747
D'Alembert, Jean le Rond 1717-1783
Dampier, William 1653-1715
Dancourt, Florent Carton 1661-1725
Daniel, Samuel 1562-1619
Davenant, Sir William 1606-1668
Davidson, John 1549?-1603
Day, John 1574-1640
Dekker, Thomas 1572-1632
Denham, Sir John 1615-1669
Deloney, Thomas 1543?-1600?
Descartes, René 1596-1650
Desfontaines, Pierre François Guyot, Abbé 1685-1745
Diaz del Castillo, Bernal 1492?-1584
Diderot, Denis 1713-1784

Douglas, Gavin 1475?-1522
Drummond, William 1585-1649
Du Guillet, Pernette 1520?-1545
Dunbar, William 1460?-1520?
Edwards, Richard 1523?-1566
Emin, Fedor ?-1770
Erasmus, Desiderius 1466-1536
Etherege, Sir George 1635-1691
Eusden, Laurence 1688-1730
Evelyn, John 1620-1706
Fabyan, Robert ?-1513
Fairfax, Thomas 1621-1671
Fanshawe, Sir Richard 1608-1666
Farquhar, George 1678-1707
Fénelon, François 1651-1715
Fergusson, Robert 1750-1774
Fletcher, John 1579-1625
Florian, Jean Pierre Claris de 1755-1794
Florio, John 1553?-1625
Fontaine, Charles 1514-1565
Fontenelle, Bernard Le Bovier de 1657-1757
Fonvizin, Denis Ivanovich 1745-1792
Ford, John 1586-1640
Foxe, John 1517-1587
Franklin, Benjamin 1706-1790
Frederick the Great 1712-1786
Froissart, Jean 1337-1404?
Fuller, Thomas 1608-1661
Galilei, Galileo 1564-1642
Garrick, David 1717-1779
Gascoigne, George 1530?-1577
Gay, John 1685-1732
Gibbon, Edward 1737-1794
Gildon, Charles 1665-1724
Glanvill, Joseph 1636-1680
Góngora y Argote, Luis de 1561-1627
Gosson, Stephen 1554-1624
Gottsched, Johann Christoph 1700-1766
Gower, John 1330?-1408
Gracian y Morales, Baltasar 1601-1658
Graham, Dougal 1724-1779
Greene, Robert 1558?-1592
Griffith, Elizabeth 1727?-1793
Guarini, Giambattista 1538-1612
Guicciardini, Francesco 1483-1540
Hakluyt, Richard 1553-1616
Hall, Edward 1498-1547
Harrington, James 1611-1677
Hartley, David 1705-1757
Helvetius, Claude Arien 1715-1771
Henryson, Robert 1430?-1506
Henslowe, Philip ?-1616
Herbert, George 1593-1633

Herrick, Robert 1591-1674
Heywood, Thomas 1574-1641
Hobbes, Thomas 1588-1679
Hoccleve, Thomas 1370?-1450
Hogarth, William 1697-1764
Holbach, Paul Heinrich Dietrich
 1723-1789
Holinshed, Raphael ?-1582?
Hooker, Richard 1544-1600
Hooker, Thomas 1586-1647
Howard, Henry, Earl of Surrey
 1517-1547
Howell, James 1593?-1666
Hung Sheng 1646-1704
Hutcheson, Francis 1694-1746
Ibn Khaldun, Abd al-Rahman ibn
 Muhammad 1332-1406
Iriarte, Tomas de 1750-1791
Isla y Rojo, José Francisco
 de 1703-1781
Ivan IV 1533-1584
James I, King of Scotland 1394-1437
Johnson, Samuel 1709-1784
King, William 1662-1712
Knox, John 1514?-1572
Kyd, Thomas 1558-1594
La Bruyére, Jean de 1645-1696
La Fontaine, Jean de 1621-1695
Langland, William 1330?-1400
La Rochefoucauld, Francois de
 1613-1680
Law, William 1686-1761
L'Estrange, Sir Roger 1616-1704
Let-we Thon-dara 1752-1783
Lipsius, Justus 1547-1606
Littleton, Sir Thomas 1422-1481
Lodge, Thomas 1558-1625
Lomonosov, Mikhail Vasilevich
 1711-1765
Lope de Vega 1562-1635
Lopez de Ayala, Pero 1332-1407?
Louis XIV 1638-1715
Lovelace, Richard 1618-1657
Loyola, Ignacio de 1491-1556
Lydgate, John 1370?-1452
Lyly, John 1554-1606
MacDomhnaill, Sean Clarach
 1691-1754
Macpherson, James 1736-1796
Maitland, Sir Richard 1496-1586
Mandeville, Bernard de 1670-1733
Marlowe, Christopher 1564-1593
Marston, John 1576-1634
Massinger, Philip 1583-1640
Mather, Cotton 1663-1728
Mather, Increase 1639-1723
Medwall, Henry 1462?-?
Mendelssohn, Moses 1729-1786

Metastasio, Pietro 1698-1782
Middleton, Thomas 1580-1627
Montfort, Hugo von 1357-1423
Morton, Thomas 1575-1647
Muret, Marc-Antoine de 1526-1585
Nashe, Thomas 1567-1601
Nawa i 1441-1501
Newton, Sir Isaac 1642-1727
North, Sir Thomas 1535?-1601?
Norton, Thomas 1532-1584
Oldham, John 1653-1683
Otway, Thomas 1652-1685
Pade-tha-ya-za 1684-1754
Painter, William 1540?-1594
Paracelsus, Philippus Aureolus 1493-1541
Parr, Catharine 1512-1548
Pascal, Blaise 1623-1662
Pasek, Jan Chryzostom 1636-1701
Peele, George 1556-1596
Pembroke, Mary Sidney, Countess of
 1561-1621
Penn, William 1644-1718
Pico della Mirandola, Giovanni
 1463-1494
Poliziano, Angelo 1454-1494
Prokopovich, Feofan 1681-1736
Quarles, Francis 1592-1644
Quevedo y Villegas, Francisco Gomez
 de 1580-1645
Racine, Jean 1639-1699
Raleigh, Sir Walter 1552-1618
Rapin, René 1621-1687
Regnard, Jean François 1655-1709
Reuter, Christian 1665-1712
Revius, Jacobus 1586-1658
Reynolds, Sir Joshua 1723-1792
Rochester, John Wilmot, Earl of
 1648-1680
Rojas Zorilla, Francisco de 1607-1648
Rousseau, Jean-Jacques 1712-1788
Rowe, Elizabeth 1674-1737
Rutherford, Samuel 1600?-1661
Sackville, Thomas 1536-1608
Saint-Simon, Louis de Rouvroy
 1675-1755
Santeuil, Jean Baptiste de 1630-1697
Savage, Richard 1696-1742
Savonarola, Girolamo 1452-1498
Scarron, Paul 1610-1660
Scott, Sarah 1723-1795
Selden, John 1584-1654
Sewall, Samuel 1652-1730
Shadwell, Thomas 1642-1692
Shaftesbury, Anthony Ashley Cooper,
 Earl of 1671-1713
Shenstone, William 1714-1763
Shirley, James 1596-1666
Sidney, Sir Philip 1554-1586

Skelton, John 1464?-1529
Smith, Adam 1723-1790
Sorsky, Nil 1433-1508
Spee, Friedrich von 1591-1635
Sprat, Thomas 1635-1713
Stanhope, Philip 1694-1773
Steele, Sir Richard 1672-1729
Suckling, Sir John 1609-1642
Sumarokov, Aleksandr Petrovich
 1718-1777
Swedenborg, Emanuel 1688-1772
Takeda Izumo 1690-1756
Tasso, Bernardo 1494-1569
Taylor, Jeremy 1613-1667
Temple, Sir William 1629-1699
Tencin, Madame de 1682-1749
Teresa de Jesús 1515-1582
Testi, Fulvio 1593-1646
Thomson, James 1700-1748
Tourneur, Cyril 1570-1626
Traherne, Thomas 1637-1674
Trai, Nguyen 1380-1442
Trediakovski, Vasili Kirilovich 1703-1769
Tristan 1601-1655
Tyndale, William 1494?-1536
Udall, Nicholas 1505-1556
Urquhart, Sir Thomas 1611-1660
Ussher, James 1581-1656
Vanbrugh, Sir John 1664?-1707
Vasari, Giorgio 1511-1574
Vaughan, Henry 1621-1695
Vaughan, Thomas 1622-1666
Vico, Giambattista 1668-1744
Villiers, George 1628-1687
Villon, François 1431-1463
Voltaire 1694-1778
Waller, Edmund 1606-1687
Walton, Izaak 1593-1683
Warburton, William 1698-1779
Warner, William 1558-1609
Warton, Thomas 1728-1790
Webster, John 1580-1638
Weise, Christian 1642-1708
Wesley, Charles 1701?-1788
Wesley, John 1703-1791
Wesley, Samuel 1662?-1735
Whetstone, George 1544?-1587?
White, Gilbert 1720-1793
Wigglesworth, Michael 1631-1705
Williams, Roger 1603-1683
Winckelman, Johann Joachim
 1717-1768
Winthrop, John 1588-1649
Wyatt, Sir Thomas 1503-1542
Yuan Mei 1716-1797
Zólkiewski, Stanislaw 1547-1620
Zrinyi, Miklos 1620-1664
Zwingli, Ulrich 1484-1531

Readers are cordially invited to suggest additional authors to the editors.

Pietro Aretino

1492-1556

Italian letter writer, dialogist, poet, dramatist, and biographer.

Considered by many to be a founder of modern journalism, Aretino was a sixteenth-century man of letters who rose from obscurity to become one of the most controversial literary figures of the Italian Renaissance. He was perhaps the first Italian to use his pen routinely to blackmail his contemporaries, and his success earned him both fear and admiration. Twentieth-century biographer James Cleugh concluded of Aretino: "Since the collapse of the civilisation of ancient Rome no private individual had exercised so considerable an influence on politics and social behaviour both by his written work and the force of his personality."

The biography of Aretino's life is replete with misinformation. Aretino himself often fabricated stories concerning his personal history, lying unabashedly in order to aggrandize his public image. Although he claimed to be the progeny of a nobleman and a courtesan, he was actually the legitimate son of a poor cobbler. Born in Arezzo in 1492, Aretino left his native village in 1505 for the larger metropolis of Perugia. While apprenticed to a bookbinder, he improved his meager education by studying the fine arts, particularly painting and poetry. Recognizing limits to his artistic talent, Aretino soon relinquished any hope of becoming a master painter. Instead, he devoted himself to his literary pursuits, and in 1512 published his first book of verse. According to legend, Aretino was expelled from Perugia in 1514 for the prank of painting a lute into the hands of a public fresco of Mary Magdalene. He thereafter journeyed to Rome, propagating the falsehood of his parentage to gain employment with a wealthy banker, Agostino Chigi. (Aretino evidently recognized that the bastard of a nobleman was much more likely to be hired as a domestic in an aristocratic household than the son of a shoemaker.) Years later when the truth was revealed, Aretino turned the potentially damaging information to his advantage, citing himself as an example of how a poor man could rise to become a scourge of wealthy men. "I who do not know the beginnings of A, B, C am teaching persons who know it to X, Y, Z," he boasted. Aretino's interest in painting increased after observing the artist Raphael at work in the Chigi household. Throughout his life Aretino had a passion for the visual arts, eventually becoming an influential and highly regarded art critic. Indeed, such masters as Titian and Jacopo Sansovino sought his advice, and he furthered the careers of other artists as well.

While working for Chigi, Aretino composed burlesque verses that amused his employer's wealthy guests and thus afforded him a peripheral position among the aristocratic society of Rome. Not content to remain on the fringes, Aretino wrote a comic elegy in 1516 on the death of Pope Leo X's pet elephant. The pope enjoyed the joke, inviting the brazen young satirist to court and extending to him the protection of the Medici family. Aretino quickly grew bolder, gaining favors from members of the papal court with threats of literary blackmail. Then, after Leo's sudden death in 1521, Aretino entered into the fray over the papal elections, attempting to secure the papal throne for his patron Cardinal Giulio de' Medici. Privy to court gossip, Aretino wrote a series of stinging pasquinades in which he slandered the cardinal's rivals and their supporters. Although the general public found the verses entertaining, the pasquinades earned Aretino many powerful, lifelong enemies. When his tactics failed and Adrian VI was elected Pope, Aretino fled the city. He returned only after Adrian died in 1523 and Giulio was named Pope Clement VII. Later that year Aretino was forced to flee Rome yet a second time after publishing *Sonetti lussuriosi*, sixteen obscene sonnets written to embellish a series of engravings by Giulio Romano that depict positions of lovemaking. Although the poet vehemently argued that his subject was a natural one and therefore appropriate, Clement disagreed. Aretino took refuge outside Rome until the pope's anger eventually subsided. The anger of another of the satirist's subjects, Giovanmetteo Giberti, did not let up, however. Furious at Aretino's repeated pillorying, Giberti ordered his enemy's assassination. Late one summer night in 1525, Aretino was dragged from his horse, stabbed repeatedly, and left for dead. He barely survived, suffering permanent damage to the tendons in his right hand. Commentators have expressed surprise that more such attempts were not made upon Aretino's life.

By 1527, Aretino was again in trouble. Angry at the pope's evident lack of interest in the stabbing, the satirist lashed out bitterly against him, finally calling Clement "a sorrier wretch than Adrian." Clement was infuriated by the name-calling and rescinded his patronage. Suddenly friendless and impoverished, Aretino traveled to Venice in search of new patrons. His strong personality and witty verses quickly commanded the attention of the Venetian public, as did his numerous letters. Soon he was afforded sumptuous surroundings, living the life of a wealthy, respected citizen in a distinguished, elegant society. He continued writing, and the majority of his works were printed during this time. In addition to maintaining his correspondence, he published all but one of his dramas, wrote his best known work, *Ragionamento della Nanna e della Antonia* (*Ragionamenti: The Harlot's Dialogues*), and completed several biographies of religious figures. The majority of his writings were well received and he was known throughout Venice. Despite his blackmailing practices, Aretino was also an extremely generous man, often giving away much of his wealth. Italian historian Francesco de Sanctis noted: "Pietro was not really a rogue by nature, but only a rogue deliberately and by necessity." Indeed Aretino's generosity made him an easy target, and he was taken advantage of on more than one occasion by unscrupulous acquaintances. Nevertheless, Aretino enjoyed a relatively peaceful existence for the most part, residing in Venice for the rest of his life. He died in 1556 of apoplexy. Enemies wishing to malign him circulated rumors that he died in a fit of laughter and had been refused a priest. Soon after his death, this scurrilous epitaph appeared: "Her Aretin enterr'd doth lye,/Whose Satire lash'd both High, and Low:/His God alone It spared; and why?/His God, he said, he did not know."

As Aretino openly acknowledged, he was motivated to write chiefly by the promise of material wealth. His literary canon is thus diverse and can be divided into several categories: dramas, poetry, letters, dialogues and sonnets treating sexual subjects, and religious writings. Most of his works were written in haste and many are considered of little literary value. His religious tracts and biographies of saints as well as his attempts at serious poetry have frequently been dismissed by critics. It is as journalist and letter writer that Aretino has garnered the most scholarly attention. He corresponded with numerous public figures, and his letters, though written in a polished style—everything Aretino wrote, he intended to publish—are free from the rigid rules adhered to by most of his contemporaries. In virtually all of his writings, Aretino rejected prevailing literary models in favor of a less formal style that he believed better conveyed life and living in Italy. Thus he rejected Petrarchan models in writing poetry and chose not to follow classical dramatic rules when writing his five prose comedies and verse tragedy. Aretino did borrow from Terence and Plautus for most of his plots and characters, though he also infused episodes of pure farce into his comedies. Scholars note that his comedies often parallel those of Shakespeare and Moliére in their natural tone and portrayal of contemporary life.

Aretino's personal reputation has frequently eclipsed his literary one. The reputation that gained him such wealth and prestige during his lifetime ultimately led to his posthumous literary demise. He was popularly known throughout Italy as "the Scourge of Princes," and his pen was both a source of fear and one of entertainment. Not surprisingly, within two years of his death, Aretino's enemies had his works officially banned in Italy. Aretino was fairly well-known in England and France during the sixteenth and seventeenth centuries. Most esteemed were his dramas—Ben Jonson borrowed from *Il marescalco* for his *Epicoene*, and Molière modeled his famous character Tartuffe on *Lo hipocrito*. In general, however, critical opinion of Aretino's works varied greatly. Some English writers praised him, but most later critics considered him a pornographer unworthy of critical notice. Indeed, in 1592 Gabriel Harvey classified the Italian as belonging to "that whole venomous and viperous brood, of old & new Raylers." In his *Areopagitica* (1644), John Milton echoed Harvey's negative conclusion, calling Aretino "that notorious ribald of Arezzo." Toward the end of the seventeenth century, interest in Aretino in any capacity had faded and his works were relegated to obscurity. With the exception of an occasional essay, little attention was paid to Aretino until the late nineteenth century when de Sanctis reassessed the satirist's life and literary achievements. In 1879 he wrote: "Pietro, as a man, is an important personage: any one who studies him will be drawn into the innermost centre of the Italian society of that time; he reflected it completely, in that mixture of his moral depravity and intellectual force and artistic feeling. . . . [As] a writer he is no less important."

Writing in 1905, Paul Van Dyke continued de Sanctis's efforts, noting that "the fame of Aretino, so vivid two centuries after his death, has declined until today many people of cultivation would know little more of him than his name." Van Dyke further added, "It is perhaps just as well not to know anything about Pietro Aretino, because up to the last few years it was difficult to know the truth about him." While Aretino's life and personality generally continue to be the focus of modern criticism, twentieth-century scholars have begun reevaluating his writings. In addition, biographers Edward Hutton and James Cleugh have done much to dispel myths and falsehoods surrounding Aretino's life. Recent literary criticism has focused primarily upon Aretino's dramas, letters, and sexual writings. He is considered an interesting, if minor, dramatist and satirist, who wielded much power through his pen. His distinct dramatic style is valued for its notable lack of pedantry and its departure from works modeled after classical dramas. Commentators concur that Aretino's dramas are valuable, though debate continues as to which are his best. Scholars have also noted the literary and historical value of Aretino's correspondence, citing his letters as an important source of information about sixteenth-century Italian life. According to Peter Stafford, "If Aretino's *Letters* were better known, their popularity would be equally assured and they would take their rightful place in the highest rank of literature."

Today, Aretino still survives more as a personality in literary history than as an accomplished writer. He had an extraordinary talent for advertising and advancing himself that both created and destroyed his literary reputation. Critics note that Aretino embodied the best and worst characteristics of the Italian Renaissance. Evaluating the nature of Aretino's career, Anna Maria Jardini wrote: "[Aretino] expressed with striking vigor the dominant tendencies of the Renaissance: the passion for beauty and life, the enjoyment of luxury and pleasure, the craving for the immortality of fame, the spirit of individualism."

PRINCIPAL WORKS

Sonetti lussuriosi (sonnets) 1523
Il marescalco (drama) 1526-27
   [*The Stablemaster,* 1978]
Cortigiana (drama) 1534
Ragionamento della Nanna e della Antonia (dialogues) 1534
   [*Ragionamenti: The Harlot's Dialogues,* 1966; also translated as *Sisters, Wives, and Courtesans,* 1967; also translated as *Aretino's Dialogues,* 1971]
La marfisa (verse) 1535
De le lettere di Pietro Aretino libro primo (letters) 1538
La vita di Catherina Vergine (biography) 1539
La vita di Maria Vergine (biography) 1539
Lo hipocrito (drama) 1542
Talanta (drama) 1542
Del primo libro de le lettere di Pietro Aretino editone seconda, con giunta de lettere XXXXIIII, scrittegli da i primi spirti del mondo. 6 vols. (letters) 1542-57
Comedia intitolata: Il filosofo (drama) 1546
L'horatia (drama) 1546
La prima (seconda) parte de ragionamenti (dialogue) 1584
Selected Letters (letters) 1976

FRANCESCO BERNI (poem date 1527)

[*A sixteenth-century Italian satirist and poet, Berni was Aretino's chief literary rival. After reading* Pax vobiscum, *a satire by Aretino upon the Roman Catholic church and the recent sack of Rome by the Imperial army of Charles V, Berni responded with a libellous poem commonly known as "Life of*

Aretino." In the following excerpt from this work, Berni paro-
dies his literary foe.]

You say so much and do so many things
with your foul tongue that has no salt of wit
that in the end a blade will silence it
sharper than that of Achille, with more stings.
The Pope's still Pope and you are a vile thief
nourished by others' bread and words of scorn.
You live in a brothel, in the slums were born,
O cripple ignorant and proud beyond belief!

Giovanmatteo and those men, his friends,
who, thanks to God, are living sound and sane,
one day in cesspool deep will drown your praise
unless, O filthy rogue, your life amends.
If you must chatter, of yourself complain
as on your head and chest and hands you gaze.

Like a dog's are your ways
which beaten strongly with most fierce endeavour
cringe and then whining are more tame than ever.

Will you shame never
O puffed-up monster, swine by fame unsung,
at whom are bitter words and hunger flung?

Know then a pile of dung
awaits you, scurvy wretch, whom scourges chide
when you shall die with sisters at your side,

those two who are the pride
of an Arezzo brothel, where they gain
applause for capers to lewd songs' refrain.

Of these, I tell you plain,
should be your stinking sonnets and low tales,
not of Sangallo, who had no such females.

From these, when your wit fails,
comes that from which you live in style so grand
and not from my lord Mantua's generous hand.

Since every place and land
you have polluted, man and beast make prayer,
God and the devil too, for your ill-fare.

Those ducal robes you wear,
of ducal thefts or ducal charities,
upon your back with such an awkward ease

to hard blows' melodies
shall be snatched off your shoulders ere you die
by reverend father hangman swung on high

to our great revelry
upon a gallows swaying to and fro
with quarterers attending down below

and sycophants you know
chanting for you the "May he rest in peace!"

So go, but pray decrease
your dirt till knife or well or noose
binds your vile tongue and never lets it loose. (pp. 126-28)

> *Francesco Berni, in a poem in* The Divine Aretino
> *by James Cleugh, 1965. Reprint by Stein and Day,*
> *Publishers, 1966, pp. 126-28.*

MICHELANGELO   (letter date 1538?)

[*Although best known as a painter, sculptor, and architect of*
the highest order, Michelangelo was also an accomplished poet,
madrigalist, and letter writter. In the following excerpt from

a letter apparently written in the early 1530s and likely pub-
lished by Aretino in 1538, he commends Aretino's skills as a
writer and art critic.]

Magnificent Messer Pietro, my master and brother, your letter gave me both pain and pleasure. I congratulated myself
because it came from you, who are unique in the world in
virtú, and at the same time I was very sorry that, having completed the great part of my picture, I could not use your imagination, which is so successful that if the day of judgment had
taken place and you had seen it, your words could not have
reproduced it better. I shall not only be glad to have you answer my letter, but I beg you to do so, because kings and emperors consider it the greatest of favors to be named by your
pen. Meantime, if I have anything which pleases you, I offer
it to you with my heart.

> *Michelangelo Buonarroti, in a letter to Pietro Areti-*
> *no in 1538?, in* Renaissance Portraits *by Paul Van*
> *Dyke, Charles Scribner's Sons, 1905, p. 76.*

MARQUIS DEL GUASTO   (letter date 1556?)

[*In the following excerpt from a letter written to Aretino some-*
time before 1556 and published in 1558, del Guasto advises his
friend to continue exposing the faults of others.]

Follow, I say, your usual manner; and, if you see any thing
faulty even in me your Friend, forget not to reprove me for
it, that I may profit by your Admonitions, and become better.
Persevere in Satire, I once more entreat you; that others may
blush at their Imperfections, and, by blushing, and growing
better, may fly from Vice to Virtue; and, being once reformed,
may be confirm'd in Good. What Advantages human Society
will from hence receive, let those judge, who understand it
better, than I am able to express it.

> *Marquis del Guasto, in an excerpt from a letter to*
> *Pietro Aretino in 1556, in* The Dictionary Historical
> and Critical of Mr. Peter Bayle, Vol. 1, *edited by*
> *Mr. Des Maizeaux, second edition, J. J. & P. Knap-*
> *ton and others, 1734, p. 436.*

BAPTISTA TORNIELLI   (letter date 1556?)

[*In the following excerpt from a letter written to Aretino some-*
time before 1556 and published in 1558, Tornielli praises Areti-
no's ability to influence great men through his writing.]

Are you not sensible, that, with Pen in hand, you have subdued more Princes, than ever the most powerful Monarch did
by force of Arms? To whom is not your Pen a Terror? To
whom is it not formidable? and who is not pleased with it,
when it has the Appearance of a Friend? With your Pen you
have, as it were, triumph'd over all the Princes in the World;
who are almost all tributary, and as it were feudatory, to you.
You merit the Titles of *Germannicus, Pannonicus, Gallicus,*
Hispanicus; Lastly, all the Titles given to the ancient *Roman*
Emperors, according to the Provinces they had conquer'd;
for that These shou'd subject Provinces by force of Arms, and
superior Power, is no wonder; it is much more surprizing,
that a private, unarm'd, Man should conquer numberless,
powerful, Men.

> *Baptista Tornielli, in an excerpt from a letter to*
> *Pietro Aretino in 1556?, in* The Dictionary Histori-
> cal and Critical of Mr. Peter Bayle, Vol. 1, *edited*

by Mr. Des Maizeaux, second edition, J. J. & P. Knapton and others, 1734, p. 436.

PIERRE BAYLE (essay date 1702)

[Bayle was a French philosopher and critic whose liberal Protestantism in an age of religious persecution compelled him to spend much of his life in exile. Although he wrote numerous works, it is upon his Dictionnaire historique et critique *(1697; rev. ed., 1702;* The Dictionary Historical and Critical of Mr. Peter Bayle, *1710) that his reputation rests. Composed of brief, pithy biographical articles, the* Dictionary *was influential, particularly in France, in shaping subsequent encyclopedic studies. In the following excerpt, incorporating notes and text from the entry on Aretino in the 1734 English edition of the* Dictionary, *Bayle examines the validity of various appraisals of the Italian's life and work.]*

[Aretino], renowned for his obscene and satirical Writings, lived in the XVIth Century. They, who desire to know what the Medal was, which it is said he struck, to inform the World how much the greatest Princes stood in fear of his Satires, may be informed by Mr *Moreri's Dictionary;* in which Medal *Aretin* values himself on having laid Those, to whom other Men pay Tributes and Imposts, under Contribution. This Tradition is so general, that he is as well known under the Title of *The Scourge of Princes,* as under the Name of *Aretin,* or That of *Peter Aretin.* He had another very glorious Appellation given him; the same, with which all Antiquity has honoured the great Merit of *Plato;* to wit, That of *Divine; il Divino Aretino:* He has been stiled on Medals, *Divus Petrus Aretinus.* Some have thought, that he gave himself this Title, to signify, that he performed the Office of a God upon Earth, by the Thunderbolts, which he darted at the most eminent Heads. He boasted, that his Libels were of more Benefit to the World, than Sermons. He was complimented, in Letters, with having subjected more Princes by his Pen, than the greatest Kings had ever subdued by their Arms [see excerpt by Tornielli dated 1556?]; and was exhorted to persevere in this kind of Writing, to the end, that Monarchs might learn to amend [see excerpt by del Guasto dated 1556?]. Our Age has produced as bold and virulent Satirists, as *Aretin* could be; and yet I believe none of them ever settled Contributions in an Enemy's Country. Some misinformed Writers make *Aretin* pass for the Author of the Book *De Tribus Impostoribus.* I cannot believe, that the Epitaph, mentioned by *Moreri,* was engraved on his Tomb, in St. *Luke's* Church, at *Venice.* The Author of this Epitaph, no doubt, exceeded his Commission. If there was reason to think, that *Aretin* did not *love* God, there was none to say, that he did not *know* him; his Works of Piety plainly testify the contrary. I do not believe, that any one Tenet of Atheism is to be found in his Writings; but, since many of his Libels severely lashed the Disorders of the Clergy, and described, in an impious and libertine Stile, the many Vices imputed to a Monastic Life, no wonder he is made to pass for an Atheist. Add to this, that a Man, who had any Respect for Religion and good Manners, would never have published Dialogues on such Subjects, as *Aretin* made choice of, nor express them in Language so obscene. It is easy to see, that I mean his **Ragionamenti** They are divided into Three Parts; the last of them, which treats of the Court, and Card-playing, is much more tolerable, than the others. The first treats of the disorderly Practices of Nuns, married Women, and Misses. It is sufficient to say, in general, that the Second is the Spirit and History of *Whoredom.* How abominable soever these Dialogues are, yet are they much less so, than the Book general-

ly ascribed to him, *de omnibus Veneris Schematibus.* They were printed in his Life-time; but it is difficult to discover the Year of their first Impression. We have Six Volumes of his *Letters,* which are but of little Value. [Notes Gilles Ménage of them:] There is nothing in them but Stile." One cannot convey a more expressive Idea of a Work, which is barren and dry; like an unfurnished House, or heathy, sandy, uncultivated Ground; for Mr *Ménage* knew how to make the most of his Reading, and had an happy Talent at varying his Application of it. [Aretino's] Works of Devotion were not much enquired after; yet they met with some, who gave them great Commendation. His Comedies in Prose are much better in their kind. . . . Observe, that This so satirical Poet was lavish of his Praises to excess. We find the most pompous Hyperboles, and extravagant Flatteries, in his Letters to Kings, Princes, Generals of Armies, Cardinals, and other eminent Men: So far are they from carrying the Air of an Author, who makes himself dreaded, or exacts Contributions, that, on the contrary, there appears in them the Meanness of a Writer, who humbly intreats for a Piece of Bread. He employs the most moving Expressions to represent his Poverty, so far as to use the Language of *Canaan,* I mean a Scripture-Cant, as likeliest to raise Compassion, and excite those to Charity, who expect a Reward of their good Works from God. It must not be forgot, that one of the Subjects of his Importunities was the Dowry of his dear Daughter *Adria.* He took a great deal of Pains to marry her; but saw her so unhappy in this State, that he heartily repented of his Impatience. A Fatality too common among Men! for how many things are there, which make us extremely uneasy, before they are accomplished, but much more so after Accomplishment? (pp. 435-42)

Pierre Bayle, "Aretin," in The Dictionary Historical and Critical of Mr. Peter Bayle, Vol. 1, *edited by Mr. Des Maizeaux, second edition, J. J. & P. Knapton and others, 1734, pp. 435-42.*

TAIT'S EDINBURGH MAGAZINE (essay date 1846)

[In the following excerpt, the anonymous critic sermonizes against Aretino's writings and style of living.]

Peter of Arezzo,—Pietro Aretino,—was known as "The Divine" and "the Scourge of Princes," and described himself in his title pages as "Peter the Truth-teller," and "Peter by the Grace of God a Free Man!" There was something grand in this. Pity that it was all pretence. But so the case was. It was all a lie. The Divine Peter was a literary man of the fourth or fifth rank. The Teller of Truth was an unscrupulous and malignant libeller, on all occasions when his venom could be spit out with safety to himself. The Free Man who Scourged Kings was a greedy sycophant. Alas for vaunting names! alas for the pride of letters! alas for fame so hollow and so rashly awarded! Yet there must have been some cause for so strange a phenomenon. An eminence such as this could not have been gained, but by a man possessing extraordinary qualities: and Pietro's voluminous correspondence, still extant, furnishes the means of detecting several of the springs which were most efficient in moving the machinery.

In settling at Venice he designed, as he tells us, to live by his literary labour,—"by the sweat of his ink." This design was formed by a man thirty-five years old, whose literary fame as yet lay wholly in expectancy: for down to this time his only published works were the infamous sonnets and a few occasional lyrics. The design was formed by a man debauched, and indolent, and ignorant; a man who, notwithstanding his excellent natural gifts, was yet disqualified, intellectually as well as morally, for executing any literary work really great. The design was formed by a man who, living in an age when literature could not subsist without the patronage of the great, avowed himself sick of the misery and degradation of dependance, and declared his resolution never again to submit to it. The design was formed, too, not by a man of few wants, to whom that might be competence which to others would be poverty, but by a man fond to excess of all sensual indulgences, an epicure, a profligate, and a fop; a man to whom wealth was indispensable, for the sake of the enjoyments which could not be purchased without it. Never was any scheme laid that seemed more thoroughly insane. Never was any scheme more triumphantly executed.

It is probable that his excessive self-esteem prevented him from seeing clearly the amount of the difficulty caused by his equivocal literary position. But he was quite justified in believing that he had considerable reputation, that great things were expected of him; and he took care not to leave unused any means (except one) for preserving and increasing the favourable opinion entertained of him. The one means which he did not use was, the performance of literary achievements justifying his reputation. This he did not do, because he could not. But as many of his hours of luxurious ease as he thought necessary for the purpose, were sacrificed to the composition of literary works, which might suffice to keep his name afloat so long as it was buoyed up also by other floaters. The only things he ever wrote that approached to goodness, were several plays; namely, comedies of exceeding cleverness, and a tragedy which has been praised by paradoxical modern critics. But none of these works seem to have been much looked to in his lifetime: nor was much more attention earned, or deserved, by his other poetical works, consisting of lyrics, occasional verses, pasquinades, and unfinished chivalrous poems. The villain even wrote theology, and was fitly rewarded by being placed in the Index Expurgatorius; a fate which (without having read the lucubrations) we may readily believe to have been well deserved by productions written simultaneously with libels, and with the disgusting and miserable *Dialogues.* But his chief literary works were his *Letters,* which indeed were mainly conducive to purposes not directly literary, but were secondarily intended for the press, just as plainly as Pope's, and are the most characteristic of his writings. He boasts in regard to them, quite justly, that they were the first Letters in the modern Italian language that were published in the lifetime of the author. Indeed we are probably right in believing, that this fashion of nonposthumous publication of correspondence (which it cost poor Pope so much intriguing to bring about) found its earliest precedent of any kind in no more respectable quarter than that which we are at present examining. Now, these and his other works show much native talent. Peter, if he had lived in a more cultivated and more moral age (say, in our own time, which in both respects is incalculably ahead of the boasted sixteenth century) would have made a prime magazine-writer, and an invaluable reviewer. Nay, he might even have aspired to the honours of the satirical or fashionable novel. "Cecil" is far below the pitch he would have attained to: we hold him quite capable of having, in proper circumstances, written "Coningsby" or "Vivian Grey." His writings are almost always what our writers of periodical criticisms call "racy," a word which, in sense as well as in sound, is something very like "rancid." The rancidity or raciness belongs to much of the matter: it per-

vades the mode of expression almost every where. The affectations of the seventeenth century of Italian style found in him one of their most instructive prototypes. His prose was of that hybrid kind which is called "poetical prose:" and the images which raise it to this equivocal rank are often of the strangest kind. He speaks of the caresses of sovereigns as being the mothers of hopes; of sounding the well of circumstances with the bucket of reflection; of fishing in the lake of reason with the hook of thought; of burying hope in the urn of lying promises; of the inability of the light of his ink to lull the wind of malignity or dispel the mist of envy. Yet, in regard to the *Letters,* it has been justly remarked, that "it would be possible to cull from them a large mass of sayings, sometimes false in taste or judgment, but all original and striking, and some of them very felicitous in expression as well as in thought." The criticisms on Art are the most successful things he ever did, except some of the scenes in his comedies: but even these criticisms are quite as remarkable for their presumption, as for their occasional acuteness of analysis, and their almost unfailing liveliness of sensibility to the beautiful. With matchless self-confidence, he announces to Michel Angelo his admiration of the Last Judgment, by sending him a description of the piece without having ever seen it: and the artist, in a highly characteristic answer, points out to the critic that which causes at once the chief excellencies and the chief faults in his descriptions of paintings; saying that even though Pietro had actually seen the Day of Judgment he could not have painted it better, if the painting were to be executed with words instead of colours.—In short, Peter maintained with great success the character with which he started, of being one who could do much better than he did. The kind of reputation is not unexampled in our own day.

For maintaining this character, however, he relied much less upon his published works than upon other exertions which cost him less. One of the most efficient of these was certainly his power of talking. He was not altogether earthy. Even in his mind, always polluted, and gradually more and more degraded, there dwelt a spark of diviner fire. He took great pleasure in the society of men intelligent and refined; and there is abundant proof that of such society he was capable of being, when he chose, a distinguished ornament. Indeed, it is not too much to attribute a considerable part of his reputation to the impression which his talents made on those who conversed with him. He possessed, in some degree, the taste and feelings of a poet; he possessed intensely the susceptibility of an artist. He delighted especially in contemplating and analyzing pictures, statues, and the masterpieces of architecture; and several passages in his writings show him to have had a fine eye for natural scenery. There is, in one of his letters to Titian, a gorgeous description of a sunset in Venice. All these powers were made, not only to furnish amusement for those of his idle hours which were not claimed by debauchery, but also to promote the chief means by which his great purpose was to be effected. Dryden says, in the prologue to one of his plays,

> The poet's bound to please, not to write well.

Peter Aretine's aim was to gain a reputation, not to deserve it. For this end, even more than for the pleasure it really gave him, he courted the society of literary men. He praised them unsparingly, that he might get praise in return, and that the praise might be reported to third parties. Nor did he cultivate less assiduously intercourse with persons who, although neither literary nor personally powerful, were yet likely to be influenced by the opinions of literary men, and whose position might enable them to convey those opinions to the quarters in which he desired to be thought well of. Such persons were, besides others, the Italian artists, among whom his acquaintance speedily became very extensive. (pp. 683-84)

The most cursory perusal of the *Letters* would disabuse us of a mistake almost universally current. Remembering Peter Aretine's common title, "The Scourge of Princes," we think of him as a person who visited the rulers of the earth with solemn warnings, or assailed them with vehement remonstrance or reproach. He really did nothing of the sort. In his direct addresses to monarchs he never went so far as even to threaten it. He wished the world to believe that he either did, or could, deal vengeance upon crowned heads: he expended innumerable artifices in insinuating indirectly, to those who sat upon the thrones, that their subjects thought him capable of shaking them from their seats. But, in his own approaches to royalty, he is nothing else than an abject sycophant. His letters to the great are couched in a strain of fulsome flattery. His attitude is a perpetual salaam. Indeed, with all his moral obstinacy of purpose, he had not physical courage enough to face personal danger: we may yet glance at one or two whimsical instances of his cowardice. His letters to princes, however, are not mere encomiums; they have been correctly described as being genuine begging letters. He gives it to be understood distinctly that his commendations have their price: he endeavours to convince his royal correspondents that the price is one which it would be worth while for them to pay. His expedients for putting the argument "ad crumenam," are amusingly diversified. Sometimes he strives directly to move compassion for his own alleged poverty. Sometimes he acts the part of frank bluntness; saying, for example, that he will never prostitute his pen to praise a king who does not possess liberality, the first of kingly virtues. On some occasions he plays off his patrons against each other, telling one of them what the rest have given. At one stage of the correspondence, he makes, in plain terms, a comically impudent offer to sell himself to the highest bidder; the two princes whom he wishes to incite to the competition being Charles V. and Francis I. He assumes his favourite appellation of "Peter the Truth-Teller!" To Francis, who required more pressing than his great rival, he offers to "tell the truth" about his great actions, as he had already "told the truth" about those of the emperor: but he adds, with great candour, that a poor man like him cannot afford to "tell the truth" for nothing; and that, unless furnished with the means of subsistence, he must remain silent. Unluckily for the chivalrous king of France, who had been one of the Truth-Teller's kindest patrons in early life, his gifts, though far from being scanty, were doled out irregularly: his imperial rival, a better man of business, in this as in more momentous things, was not content with assigning to the petitioner a stated pension, (the payments of which, however, were not always obtained without dunning,) but flattered his pensioner's vanity by showing him marked personal attentions. (pp. 686-87)

And now, gentle reader, what is it we have laid before thee? A ribald tale? A dull extract from the book of literary history? Neither, as we hope. In our own view, it is a sermon; and we devoutly trust thou hast derived, from every attendance of thine in church, as much instruction as this discourse of ours, if rightly understood and ripely digested, is well calculated to afford. Draw the practical application for thyself. We cannot do it for thee; our sand-glass shows the hour to have

run out. We draw but that one inference, in which we scribblers by profession are most directly interested. We thank heaven, that, bad as the world still is, it is better than it was three hundred years ago; we rejoice that literature is not now exposed to the degradations which it inevitably underwent while it lay at the feet of private patrons. Long live the Public! God save the Booksellers! (p. 688)

"Passages in the Life of a Literary Blackguard," in Tait's Edinburgh Magazine, *Vol. XIII, No. CLV, November, 1846, pp. 681-88.*

FRANCESCO DE SANCTIS   (essay date 1879)

[*De Sanctis was a nineteenth century Italian critic who regarded literature as the expression of a society's morals. His two-volume* Storia della letteratura italiana (History of Italian Literature), *first published in 1879 and translated in 1931, is a survey of Italian literature through the late nineteenth century. This work, recognized by modern critics as one of the best histories of a national literature, also traces the development of Italian culture. In the following excerpt from* History of Italian Literature, *De Sanctis offers a balanced assessment of Aretino's works.*]

How cynically [Aretino] speaks of his traffic in debauchery and human obscenity as though it were the most natural thing in the world! And he speculated in devotion, wrote obscene books and lives of saints—the *Ragionamento della Nanna* and the *Vita di santa Caterina da Siena,* the *Cortigiana errante* and the *Vita di Cristo*—all with the same indifference. And why not, since both of them brought him money? He used every material and every form: dialogues, romances, epopees, *capitoli,* comedies, and even a tragedy, his *Orazia.* We can imagine what sort of heroes his Horatii would be, and what sort of a heroine his Horatia, and what species of Romans would come from the pen of a Pietro Aretino! Yet this *Orazia* is the only work in which he had artistic intentions. He wrote it when he was old and satiated and had grown more greedy of fame than of money. It is a cold, abstract, pedestrian affair. The greatness and the simplicity of the Romans were beyond him. But in the works that he wrote for the pleasure of his public, to interest and capture them, to make his effects, we feel the man himself in the truth of his nature. He had a sort of moral market in his eye; he knew what kind of goods were in demand and easiest to deliver, and he knew how to sell them at the best price possible. He had an art that varied with the tastes of his master, the public. So he was the writer most in fashion, the one most appreciated by the people, and the best paid. His obscene books are the very perfection of the kind of literature that had invaded Europe under the name of "gallant stories." Ever since Boccaccio the piquant sauce of lubricity had been greatly in demand in Italy: here we get it in a ragout. His lives of saints are romances, a conglomeration of lies; he comes out with the most impossible stories, pandering to the imaginative and sentimental nature of his public. His verses are gross; his sonnets and *capitoli* are bitter and malignant and at the same time servile. Alluding to the munificence of Francis I, he says to Pier Luigi Farnese:

Impara tu, Pier Luigi ammorbato,
impara, ducarel da tre quattrini,
il costume da un re tanto onorato.
*   Ogni signore di trenta contadini*
e di una bicoccazza usurpar vuole
le cerimonie de' culti divini.

Learn, O thou maggoty Pier Luigi, learn, O thou little thrippenny duke, the customs of such an honoured king.
Every little squire of thirty bumpkins and a tumbledown hovel expects to be given the ceremonial of divine worship.

Pietro was not really a rogue by nature, but only a rogue deliberately and from necessity. He was in bad company from the beginning, with bad examples before him, and had no religion, home, or family. He was wholly lacking in moral sense, and had uncontrollable appetites and many intellectual means for satisfying them. The centre of his world was himself—he thought that the world existed to serve him. And he was logical: he perceived his means with perfect clearness and never scrupled to use them. He made no pretence about it, but gloried in what he did: he wanted people to know it, it was part of his power. And the rest of the world was rather like him; many would gladly have copied him, but they had not his brains, nor his diligence, nor his penetration, nor his versatility, nor his wit. So they admired him. He was the prince, the very perfection of the adventurer or soldier of fortune who was poisoning Italy at that time—vagabond people without principles or profession, looking for fortune at whatever cost. When Titian called him the "*condottiere* of literature," he was far from being offended at the name, but on the contrary was extremely proud of it. When he writes spontaneously, when not pushed by need of money or other motives, he shows some good qualities: he is gay, sociable, openhanded, indeed lordly, a proved, trusted friend and a grateful one, and an admirer of the great artists, such as Michelangelo and Titian. He had the logic of evil, but appreciated the good.

Pietro, as a man, is an important personage: any one who studies him will be drawn into the innermost centre of the Italian society of that time; he reflected it completely, in that mixture of his of moral depravity and intellectual force and artistic feeling. But as a writer he is no less important.

Culture in Italy was tending to become fixed and mechanized. People had ceased to argue as to whether the language to be used in writing should be the vulgar tongue or Latin: the vulgar tongue had conquered the field. What they argued about was its name—as to whether it should be called "Tuscan" or "Italian." And it was an argument not about words, but about things. Many of the writers were claiming that the correct language for literature was the tongue that was used in speaking, from one end of Italy to the other, and refused to be instructed by Florence; they preferred Latinizing to Tuscanizing. While accepting Boccaccio and Petrarch as models, they considered themselves free to choose in regard to the living language. To them the living language was the common language—the tongue that inclined towards Latin and Boccaccio. It was a mechanism generally accepted. There was only the exception of Florence, where the foundation of language was not the common tongue, which was mixed with local, Sicilian, Lombard, and Venetian elements, but was the Tuscan idiom as it was handled by the Tuscan writers. And Florence, exhausted by her intellectual production, raised the Columns of Hercules in her *Vocabolario della Crusca* and said: "Thus far shalt thou go, and no further." Bembo, and later Salviati, fixed the grammatical forms. And the rules for every form of writing were fixed in the "rhetorics," translations and rearrangements of Aristotle, Cicero, and Quintilian. At last it was actually possible for a writer, Giulio Camillo, to claim that he was able to impart the whole of knowledge by a mechanism of his own. It was the usual

thing: the tendency of art to become mechanized—the ordinary phenomenon when production has become exhausted and culture comes to a standstill, settles down into its forms and becomes crystallized.

Now Pietro, a man of extremely indifferent culture, looked on these rules as pedantry. His inner life, so rich in productive forces, was badly suited to them. He looked on pendantry as his enemy and met it in a hand-to-hand fight. And that manner of seeing things not directly and as they really are, but through the medium of ready-made ideas and rules taken from books, he saw as pedantry: he loathed the habit of wrapping up words and forms, pretending to a modesty one does not possess and preaching humility and decency, and all the time being just as bad as any one else. (pp. 607-10)

[Aretino] thought himself vastly superior to the others, and when literary men distilled their phraseology he usually dismissed them as pedants. A critical consciousness so direct, so decided, as Aretino's must have seemed a most extraordinary thing in those days. And he brought the same liberty and the same high judgment into art, for which he had the feeling. Writing to Michelangelo, he says: "I sigh for your merits, which are so great, and my own powers, which are so small." (p. 611)

[No] moral impression or elevation is produced by [Aretino's] feeling for living Nature, by its colours and its half-lights, but only a purely artistic admiration and wonder, typical of the Italy of that time. He looks at Nature across the brush of Titian, and of Vecellio, the landscape painter; but all the same he sees it, and gets it living and fresh; he has a feeling for art that we look for in vain in Vasari. In an era that produced such a great number of pedantic works on culture Aretino's letters are the first rays of the splendours of independent criticism, which passes beyond books and beyond traditions, and finds its basis in Nature.

What he was as a critic, such he was also as a writer. The last thing he thinks of is words. He welcomes them all, no matter where they come from, or what they are, whether Tuscan, local, or foreign, noble or plebeian, harsh or soft, humble or sonorous. And the result is a language that is spoken universally even today among the cultured classes in Italy. The period he abolishes entirely, breaks up the conjunctive sentences, dissolves the periphrases, smashes into every contrivance of the mechanism of "literary form," and draws near to the ordinary ways of natural speaking. In Lasca, in Cellini, in Machiavelli, we find an equal naturalness, but at the same time we feel the imprint of the Tuscan spirit, all grace. Pietro is an uneducated Tuscan, a child of Nature, who has lived away from his country; he uses every language, whichever seems best to him for expressing his thoughts. Tuscanizing he regards as pedantry, and avoids it, and grace is a thing he never thinks of at all. He aims entirely at expression and effectiveness; whatever word is useful for expressing the thing in his brain is a good word. But he never looks for it; so great is his facility that word and thing come to him together. The word is not always precise and not always suitable, because he often abuses his facility and scribbles instead of writing. His motto is, "It comes as it comes," and the result is a great inequality. He does not vex his brain by copying Boccaccio and Cicero, indeed he does the opposite; he does not seek the magnificence and breadth of form in which indolent brains rock themselves, but whatever form is the quickest and most convenient for his swift perceptions. Nor does he affect brevity, like Davanzati, whose brain, too indolent to look at the inside of things, is only interested in words and parenthetic clauses. Aretino does away with every mechanical process, and neglects the niceties and allurements of form. He writes and produces so easily, and his brain is so rich in concepts and images, that everything pours out of him impetuously, by the shortest way, without obstacles, digressions, or distractions. His style is as ready and decided as his life. Never was the saying that "the style is the man" so proved as in Aretino. He is the centre of his style in the same way that he is the centre of his universe. His world does not exist for itself, but for his personal benefit, and he treats it and handles it as though it were his own property—with the same caprice and liberty that Folengo brought to the world of his imagination. But Folengo was humorous because his world was imaginary, therefore he could treat it without seriousness and laugh at it, while Pietro's world is a real thing and he is clearly conscious of it, and exploits it, even at the cost of profaning it basely. Jesus Christ he treats as a knight errant, and speaking of the Virgin he says: "Poetic lies become evangelists when they are used for singing the praises of her who is the refuge of our hopes." Of his *Vita di santa Caterina* he says: "One can float almost anything by invention . . . but besides the fact that everything is accepted that turns to the glory of God, the subject, which in itself is but small worth, would be nothing at all without the help that I have given it by my reflections."

At times he is bored, his brain is empty, and all he does is to collect adjectives with a show and ostentation that show him to be the charlatan he is:

> The easy, religious, clear, graceful, noble, fervid, faithful, truthful, mild, good, salutary, holy, and sainted discourses of Catherine—of that sainted, holy, salutary, good, mild, limpid, truthful, faithful, fervid, noble, gracious, gentle, and religious woman—have seized on my mind in such a way, etc.

It is like a bell ringing in our ears, splitting them, deafening them. This was the style called "flowery"; he gives it to us when he has nothing better at hand. At times he really has something to say, but seems not to be in the vein for it, does not feel it at that moment, so he treats us to exaggerated metaphors and ridiculous subtleties, more especially in his eulogies, the work which paid him so well. He writes to the Duke of Urbino:

> As all the stars of the sky in their glory speak of your merits, my intelligence, which can almost be called a planet, moves me to depict the image of your soul by the medium of words, so that the true likeness of your virtue coveted by the world may be seen in each separate part. But the power of my intelligence is outstripped by the height of the subject; and notwithstanding the emotions that overcome me at the thought of it, I find myself powerless to describe how exactly it has come to pass that the goodness, the clemency, the strength, equally distributed in your nature, have inevitably, by the decree of fate, made you a prince.

This is a period à la Boccaccio, overstrained in conception and form. No question here of "as it comes, it comes," but rather of its not wanting to come at all, but being made to come whether it wants to or not. His panegyrics are all of them rhetorical, metaphorical, painted up, falsely pompous, and overinflated to the point of being ridiculous; they might almost be ironical caricatures posing as eulogies. Speaking ill of people comes easier than speaking well of them; in the for-

mer he is absolutely at home, and can spread himself with all the vigour of his cynical, sarcastic nature. But when he tries to speak well of people, somehow or other he gets an emphatic tone and makes use of far-fetched conceptions and out-of-the-way mannerisms; he gives us a refined language made of pearls, but of false ones—the sort of language that passed into France with Voiture and Balzac and was scourged by Molière, and in Italy became the hallmark of the literature of that time. (pp. all the time being just as bad as any one else. (pp. 607-10)

[Every] now and then this flowery and precious style is crossed by a flash of genius; original comparisons leap out at us, sudden and splendid images, new and daring conceptions, and incisive strokes of the pen. When the language is left to itself, and when the author is not bothering about effect, then the feeling and colours are true, as in the following extract from a letter, so simple and so touching:

> The blue and gold stockings that I received with one of your letters have made me weep as much as they have pleased me, because the girl who was to have enjoyed them was anointed with holy oil that very morning, and I cannot write to you for the pity they awaken in me.

The dissolution of literary mechanism means a form of writing nearer to ordinary speaking and free from every preconception, and the direct expression of what is in the mind; a style now flowery, now precious, the two forms of the decadence of art and letters: this is the significance of Pietro Aretino as a writer. And he had no small influence on his contemporaries. All around him were secretaries, pupils, and imitators of his manner, such as Franco, Dolce, Lando, Doni, and other journeyman writers. "I live by *Kyrie eleisons*," says Doni. "My books are written before they are composed, and read before they are printed." His *Libreria* is read to this day for a certain brio that belongs to it, and for curious bits of information.

And Pietro has a certain importance too as a writer of comedies. Comedy had become conventionalized; it was based on Plautus and Terence, with its accessories taken from the lower-class life of the day. The plot was centred in equivocal situations, cases of mistaken identity, and chance happenings that tickled the curiosity of the public. And the characters were conventionalized too. There was the usual parasite, and the greedy servant, and the courtesan, and the sly maidservant who acts as go-between, and the spendthrift son, and the miserly father who is made fun of, and the coward who pretends to be brave, and the pander, and the usurer. Any student who would like to pierce to the inner mysteries of Italian corruption could not do better than study the Italian writers of comedies. What he will find are broken family-ties, idle sons tricking their fathers and being baited in their turn by usurers and courtesans and panders, and the respectable public laughing at it all—the public that was a comedy itself, with its forms fixed and Latinized and punctuated with jokes and lubricity. The most prolific of the comic writers was Cecchi, who died in 1587. In less than ten days he could turn you out a comedy, a farce, a story, or a sacred play. He has the Florentine grace and liveliness of Lasca, but has less wit and less movement, indeed, he seems at times to be stuck in a quagmire. His characters and his world in general seem to have come from a repertory already fixed and classified, and he writes his works too hurriedly to give them colour, or flesh and blood. So he is often meagre and stagnant.

And here comes Pietro, smashing into the middle of this mechanism and breaking it up. Rules, traditions, theatrical usages, he rejects wholesale. In the prologue of his **Cortigiana** he says: "If I fail to observe the usual order that comedy demands, do not be surprised at it; because one lives in another manner in Rome than in Athens." According to the rules a character might not appear on the scene more than five times. Pietro makes fun of this rule with great wit. "If you see the personages coming on the scene more than five times, do not laugh at it, because the chains that hold the mills on the river would not be strong enough to hold the fools of today." He aims at effect, so he cuts the delays, does away with the obstacles, and avoids preparations, episodes, descriptions, declamations, and the frequent soliloquies. What he wants are action and movement, and when the curtain rises we are thrown at once into the very heart of his knavish world, vividly presented in detail. He has not the synthesis of Machiavelli, the sure eye that embraces a vast whole at a glance and binds it together and develops it with logical fatality as though it were a thesis. Pietro's talent is not of the speculative kind; he is a man of action, one of the characters of his own comedies. He sees the world only in bits and in mouthfuls: the whole escapes him. So the action of his play is not well arranged and carefully studied, like the action of the *Mandragola*. But together with Machiavelli he has a profound experience of the human heart and a profound understanding of the characters, who stand out very distinctly from the many accidental events, dominate the play, and create a number of piquant novelties and situations. And how we enjoy this rogue among all the rascally tricks he puts on the stage! For this comic world which he shows us is his own world, the place where he had put his malice to such good proof. His play is based on the conception that the world belongs to the person who knows how to take it, in a word, to the cunning and impudent. And woe to the stupid! Their share will be the hurt and the ridicule; they are abandoned to the laughter of the public, the comic material. His play the **Ipocrita** is the glorification of a rogue who manages to get rich by intrigue and malice, exactly like Aretino himself. His Talanta is a courtesan who deceives all her lovers and ends up rich and respected, married to an old and faithful suitor. In the "philosopher" we have a hero who studies Plato and Aristotle while his wife deceives him: and the good man forgives her. In the **Cortigiana** Messer Maco, who wants to be a cardinal, and Parabolano, who thanks to his riches imagines that every woman is at his feet, are baited through the whole of the play by courtesans and panders. The "marshal or groom of the stables" is afraid of displeasing his master, the Duke of Mantua, so consents to marry a woman he has never seen, though he hates women and hates marriage.

And this world is not in the least imaginary or subjective, but is the mirror of the society of that day, with all its customs, excellently shown in their finest shades and minutest details. And Pietro thoroughly enjoys himself in it, as though it were his element. Satires, eulogies, epigrams, knaveries, and indecencies spring from his brain with brio and ardour of movement, like fireworks. Some of his characters have passed into proverbs, but all are alive and true. A very original pleasantry is his "marshal," which Rabelais and Shakespeare both made use of. His Parabolano is proverbial: fatuous, vain men will be Parabolanos till the end of time. His Messer Maco is the original of Pourceaugnac. His "hypocrite" is a Tartuffe, but innocuous and put in a pleasant light; his "philosopher," whom he calls Plataristotile, is a skit on the Platonists of those times. (pp. 616-19)

The courtesan is his favourite subject. His Angelica is typical of the whole species, and his Nanna is the supreme specimen of her kind.

Such was the type of comedy that the century was able to produce, the last act of the *Decameron;* a shameless and cynical world, whose protagonists are courtiers and courtesans. Its centre was the court of Rome, which Aretino, safely intrenched in Venice as in a fortress, scourged unmercifully.

There is a popular tradition, and a very expressive one too, that Pietro died from excess of laughter, as Margutte died, and as Italy herself was dying at that moment. (p. 620)

> *Francesco de Sanctis, "Pietro Aretino," in his* History of Italian Literature, Vol. 2. *translated by Joan Redfern, Harcourt Brace Jovanovich, 1931, pp. 598-620.*

PAUL VAN DYKE (essay date 1905)

[*Van Dyke was an American cleric, academic, and essayist who wrote studies of European history. In the following excerpt from his* Renascence Portraits *(1905), he presents an in-depth look at Aretino's life and writing.*]

In the middle of the eighteenth century, Count Mazzuchelli, one of the most distinguished littérateurs of his day, published a life of Pietro Aretino. The preface to the second edition begins thus: "The name of Pietro Aretino has always been so famous in the world that it never could be hid from the knowledge of even the least learned." And Addison in a Spectator written at the beginning of the century, declines to tell the career of Aretino as an illustration of his point because he is "too trite an instance. Everyone knows that all the Kings of Europe were his tributaries."

Neither of these sentences would be written now. The fame of Aretino, so vivid two centuries after his death, has declined until today many people of cultivation would know little more of him than his name. It is perhaps just as well not to know anything about Pietro Aretino, because up to the last few years it was difficult to know the truth about him. Pietro's life was written by enemies. And as his contemporary, Cranmer, said of his own foes,—"They dragged him out of the dunghill." The scandal mongers of later generations enlarged their invectives into the following story, and features of the disreputable career thus created appear in every mention of Pietro Aretino except those of a few Italian writers of the last dozen years.

He was the illegitimate son of a gentleman of Arezzo and a notoriously bad woman. After such an upbringing as might be expected from his parentage, he fled from Arezzo because of an impious poem (a variation of the legend makes him steal from his mother). He made a living in Perugia as a bookbinder and picked up his education by reading the books he handled. There was a picture in the city representing the Madonna at the foot of the cross. Aretino painted a lute in her outstretched arms. After this sacrilege he fled to Rome, where he became a servant in the house of Chigi, the great banker. He stole a silver cup from his master and fled to Venice, where he led a life of extraordinary debauchery and won an evil reputation as an atheist and writer of pornographic literature. He was fatally hurt by falling over backward from his seat in a fit of laughter at an anecdote about a dishonorable adventure of one of his sisters, whose lives were worse than his mother's. And this scene was painted in 1854 by the

German painter Feuerbach. Finally he died uttering one of the most profane sayings in the annals of blasphemy. In addition to this unsavory life history, entirely false, Aretino has been labeled with a larger number of strong epithets than any other man in the history of literature,—"The ignominy of his century," "The Cæsar Borgia of literature," "Perverter of morals and letters," "The synonym for all infamies." These are a few of the judgments that have been passed upon him.

To know Pietro Aretino in the four thousand letters from and to him, which have survived in print, is to recognize that he had great capacities and some amiable qualities which won him many ardent admirers and a number of warm friends. But it is also to perceive that he was essentially selfish and corrupt. In spite of the strain of religiosity in Pietro's character, it is hard to raise any very strong objections to the epitaph falsely supposed to have stood on his tomb,—"Here lies Pietro Aretino, who spoke evil of everyone except God. He never spoke evil of God simply because he never knew him."

If, then, the epitaph is just, why trouble to retell correctly the story of a bad life? Simply because to put Pietro Aretino aside labeled and classified by an absolute moral judgment,—to make him a scapegoat for the sins of his times—is to miss knowing a vivid and illuminating personality. To judge him sympathetically, to see his career as it appeared to himself and to many of his contemporaries, is to throw upon the society of the late Renascence in Italy gleams of light comparable in revealing power to those which shine from the pages of Benvenuto Cellini. If this cobbler's son, who in an age of pedantry gained fame and fortune by an untrained pen, whom Titian painted out of close friendship, whose head San Savino cast on the bronze doors of Saint Mark, of whom Ariosto wrote in Orlando Furioso,—"Behold the scourge of Princes, the divine Pietro Aretino"—to whom his native city gave the title Salvator Patriae, and the King of France sent a gold chain of eight pounds' weight, whom the Pope rose from his seat to receive with a kiss of welcome and who by command rode in a stately procession in the post of honour at the Emperor's right hand,—if this man be a degenerate type, his degeneration cannot be diagnosed by a fixed moral judgment—for his character and career are symptomatic of the disease of his times.

Pietro was born in Arezzo in 1492, of a poor shoemaker, and his wife. He always had a very tender memory of his mother. Years afterward he got his friend and fellow-townsman, Vasari, to copy the Virgin in an annunciation over the door of a church in Arezzo, for which she had served as a model, and was delighted to trace a resemblance to the picture in the face of his little daughter. He left his birth-place to seek his fortune and went to Perugia, where probably he studied painting without success. When about twenty-five years old he went to Rome. There he found a patron in Agostino Chigi. This descendant of an influential Siennese family inherited from his father the business of a banker. His skill and success gained enormous wealth. And this joined to his personal qualities made him the friend of the Pope. He became papal banker, and to a certain extent finance minister. His social position was even more imposing than his standing in the business world. He was permitted by Julius II to take the coat of arms of the della Rovere, which made him a sort of adopted relative to that Pope. He was a great friend and patron of the study of Greek literature, a most liberal and skillful connoisseur of art. The best creators of beautiful things in Rome, Sodoma, Peruzzi, Viti, Raphael, worked for him and gathered

round his table. The poets, scholars and wits flocked to his house, where his entertainments displayed the insolence of wealth amid the graces of literature and art. At a banquet he gave to celebrate the signing of his will the tables were laid in front of the frescoes where Raphael's hand has told the story of Psyche. The courses rivaled in their strangeness and profusion the days of Heliogabalus. And at the end of each service the gold and silver dishes were flung out of the window into the river; though in order to save his pocket book without lowering his pride the Pope's host had nets stretched beneath the waters to catch them. In such a household the wit and literary talent of young Pietro could find the stimulus of applause. His natural edacity and insolence would grow by what it fed upon.

From the house of Chigi, Pietro passed to the Court of Leo X, that Pope who "enjoyed the papacy God had given him," spent eight thousand ducats a year on his kitchen, a hundred thousand in gaming and presents to Court favorites, gave Michael Angelo six thousand for painting the Sistine Chapel and showed equal zest for a hunting trip, a fresco of Raphael, an indecent comedy, a discussion between Bembo and Bibbiena or the elaborate farce of a wild practical joke. In the cultivated company gathered in Leo's palace, Pietro soon made a place for himself among the best—not by learning, for he had none, but by the vigour of his language. A poet known for skill in reciting improvised verses to the lute mentions him among the famous men of Leo's Court, Bembo, Castiglione, Sadolet and others, as "a singer sweet and free, whose lithe tongue had the mastery both of praise and blame." But, either because the men he knew were not laudable or because his spirit was acrid, blaming evidently came easier to him than praising. A pastoral dialogue of the time makes one speaker advise the other,—"Try your best to have Aretino for your friend because he is a bad enemy to make. God guard every one from his tongue." (pp. 33-8)

[Aretino] never cared for the fashionable style and methods of the trained littérateurs of his day. His bent took him into unbeaten paths. Six times in his life he gave to a literary form, as yet but little used, power and vogue. In this way he made, while fighting for his patron, the beginning of fame which could be called Italian. Pietro Aretino was, so far as we know, the first man whose name became noted outside of Rome as a writer of pasquinades. (p. 40)

After colour and form in the plastic arts, the Italians of the early sixteenth century seem to have found most pleasure in satire, and Aretino had shown himself able to give them a satire suited to their taste, suggesting no ideals, hoping no reforms,—so local and personal that it is hard for another generation to read and understand it; no bitter passion of the soul but just a delicate morsel for the intense "schadenfreude" of the day. They called on him not to stop his career. What stood for the public of our time demanded something from his pen. So a poet wrote in a dialogue between a Traveller and Marforio, a gossip of Pasquino:

> TRAVELLER. Marforio, since the day when this Pope was elected, your brother Pasquino is grown almost dumb and Aretino no longer reproves vice. What have you to say about it?
> MARFORIO. Why, don't you know that Armellino has cut short Pasquino by giving him to understand that if he makes a sound they'll slit his tongue for him, so the poor chap doesn't dare to breathe, much less talk.
> WAY. Pietro Aretino, who is in such high favor,

was taken with a mouthful of bait like a frog, and now he sings but he doesn't want to touch the court. That would be a mistake, because it is giving him means to play the swell like a baron, etc.

But it was difficult for Aretino to keep his pen still, and he used it in a kind of writing which, though it occupied but a small part of his works, has fixed the attention of posterity to the neglect of all the rest. Giulio Romano, one of the most distinguished painters of the day, painted a series of sixteen pictures and Marc Antonio Raimondi engraved them. The plates have fortunately perished but descriptions are enough to tell us that in English-speaking countries printer and seller of such plates would now be sent to the penitentiary. At the instance of the Datario, his most trusted counsellor, the Pope put Raimondi in prison. But Aretino appealed to the Pope to set him free and was successful. Then Aretino proceeded to write for the series, sixteen sonnets which matched the pictures. The Datario was indignant and Aretino found it best to retire from Rome to Arezzo. That the disgrace was not very serious is shown by two letters from Giovanni de' Medici, addressed just at this time to "The Stupendous Pietro Aretino, my true friend," and to "Pietro Aretino, Miracle of Nature." And in a short time we find him back at Rome in high favor with Clement VII, who made him a Knight of Rhodes.

One of the most distinguished littérateurs of the day, whose presence was sought by every cultivated court of Italy, was Bernado Accolti, the reasons for whose great esteem among his contemporaries do not appear in any of his verses which have survived. He was known everywhere by the title of L'Unico Aretino, because he had been born in Arezzo. This recognized model and authority in the poetic art on one occasion turned to Pietro, in the presence of the Pope and the whole court, assembled to hear him recite his verses, and said:—"Holy Shepherd, I rejoice in your presence because I leave behind me another self from my own city."

Pietro's thanks for the renewed favour and increased reputation he received at the Court of Clement VII, appeared in verses praising the Datario and the Pope, than whom,—"Christ could not find today a better Vicar." For that praise he also found another expression in a literary form to which he gave new force and vigour. In the first of his comedies, which showed less dependence upon the form and method of Roman comedy than any of the few which had previously been written in Italian, he interpolated into the dialogue, somewhat after the fashion of the modern "gag," complimentary references to the Pope and his Court. But this sort of writing did not satisfy either himself or his admirers. (pp. 44-7)

It had long been the part of every finished man of the world to have some taste in art and to be ready to express a judgment upon a statue or a picture, but Aretino has the best possible claim to be regarded as the father of that *genre* of literature which is known as art criticism. His skill in this was so clearly recognized that his contemporary Lodovico Dolce, writing a Dialogue on Painting, makes Aretino the chief speaker. Any artist seems to have been glad to work for him. Half a dozen different medalists modeled his head, some of them several times. Six of the leading art collections of the world, Munich, Windsor, the Belvedere, Berlin, the Pitti, the Hermitage, possess his portrait, so frequently reproduced by the engraver that the Bibliothèque Nationale has thirty-eight different prints of him. These favors seem to have cost Aretino no money. He was able fully to repay them by the constant advertisement he gave to his friends. He never misses a chance of mentioning and praising the work of artists he approves. (pp. 76-7)

Aretino was not content with advancing the reputation of his artist friends. He did everything in his power to foster the taste for art among those who paid for it. He makes the characters of his comedies discuss noted pictures and buildings and the glory of those who built them. His letters speak continually of art, and in one he touches with master hand the strongest motive of most of its patrons in the Renascence:

> The prince, who reigns solely because he is made in the image of God, ought to imitate the maker of all things, whose power, according to the model of his will, built Paradise for the angels and the world for men, placing on the facade of the great edifice of heaven, as it were, his coat of arms painted by the brush of nature—a sun of gold with its infinite stars and a moon of silver in a broad field of bright blue. And just as every one of us who is born, as soon as he opens the eyes of consciousness is astonished looking now at the heaven and now at the earth, giving thanks to Him who made one and created the other, so the descendants of your Excellency, wondering at the magnitude of the edifices begun and finished by you, will bless the generous providence of their magnanimous predecessor with the blessing given to the mind of the ancients embodied in stone in their theaters and amphitheaters by one who sees the pride of the ruins of Rome—whose wonders show what were the habitations of the conquerors of the universe.

Aretino judged in the taste of the day and wrote in its style. He told Vasari in regard to some drapery, "Raphael has drawn things of the same sort. He has not surpassed you so much that you need regret it." He wrote to Giulio Romano that if Apelles and Vitruvius could see the buildings and paintings he was doing in Mantua, "they would approve the judgment of the world which preferred him for originality and charm to any one who had ever touched compass or brush." But in regard to one of his friends Aretino's enthusiasm was guided by knowledge and skill. Those who knew Titian best are most ready to admit that they do not understand the secrets of his art better than Aretino. The comments he has left touch the finest points of his friend's pictures. The angel of the annunciation "filling everything with light and shining in the air with fresh radiance, bending gently with a reverence which makes us believe he is really in the presence of Maria;" the portrait of the little girl of Roberto Strozzi, so true that if "art should say it was not real, nature would swear it was not imitation;" the lamb in the arms of the little St. John, "so natural that a ewe would bleat at sight of it"—these are not vague praises. The words come not only from the lips but the eyes. And it would be hard to find a better phrase than that by which he places Titian in a sonnet alongside of the two most celebrated artists Italy had produced.

"Divine in beauty was Raphael, and Michael Angelo was more divine than human in his stupendous design—but Titian has in his brush *the sense of things.*" (pp. 79-81)

On the other hand, Titian does not fail to tell of the triumphs his friend has won by the pen. He writes from Rome that in the highest society of the court one hears nothing but, "This is what Aretino said." He writes from Ratisbon to say that the Duke of Alva talks of the divine Aretino every day and the Emperor showed every sign of pleasure when he was told that all Italy believes that the Pope is going to make Aretino a cardinal.

For during his life at Venice, Aretino vastly increased the literary reputation he brought there and made himself an acknowledged power in the world. His work may be summed up under six heads,—poetry, tragedy, comedy, letters, pornographic writings, religious writings.

His non-dramatic poetry may for the purposes of this essay be dismissed in a few lines. He wrote great quantities of it, but except where verse was the medium for his satiric verve, it is hard to understand why it was esteemed highly in a day when everybody composed poetry. Most of it was never printed and the loss to the world is not thought to be great by any of his commentators except Bertani, who seems to consider Aretino in all respects one of the great lights of Italian literature. His tragedy of Horace was the most carefully composed of all his works, and the only one which is approved by those who wrote of him up to the last ten or fifteen years. A French critic considers it superior to Corneille and an Italian historian of literature ranks it with Shakespeare. Such judgments came rather from the ardor of discoverers than from the sobriety of critics. But the most esteemed of all general historians of Italian literature, Professor Gaspary, considers it "absolutely the most important tragedy of the sixteenth century." One merit it certainly had, the merit of a new method of treatment. The few tragedies in the vernacular which preceded it were imitations of the Greek writers. Aretino did not, like Shakespeare, cast off entirely the fetters of the classic unities, but he tried to write like an Italian of the sixteenth century and not like a Greek of the fifth or a Latin of the first. And therefore he is certainly not unworthy of honour among the predecessors of the great modern, who, ceasing to imitate the ancient giants, won a place among them.

Even more original are his comedies. The three or four comedies worthy of mention which were in existence when he wrote the first of his were, to a great extent, imitations of Plautus and Terence, introducing the stock characters of the Roman stage. Aretino, who could not read Latin, was more inclined to draw from life as he saw it. He knew life on the shady side and the comic force of his scenes is coarse. But he made the characters who tread his stage out of his own recollections of men he had known. And to read his scenes is to know them too. The street urchin of Mantua tying fireworks to the school teacher's coat tail; Messer Maco, of Siena, come up to Rome to fulfil the wish of his father that he should become a cardinal, and the hawks into whose claws he flutters; the hypocrite, a parasite cloaking his greed with piety instead of flattery—these and a score of others are real people. They move against a background vile with the vileness Aretino had learned at the courts and in the streets of the cities where he had lived. But obscenity was then considered a necessary element of comedy, and the atmosphere which surrounds the characters of Aretino's comedies is less turpid than that of the Suppositi by Ariosto, acted in the castle of San Angelo with scenery by Raphael and to the delight of Leo X.

The distinctively pornographic works of Aretino, aside from the sonnets already alluded to, consist of the two first parts of a book entitled *Ragionamenti.* Competent judges who have read them hazard the opinion that they earn for Aretino the primacy of that long succession of writers through all the ages of the history of literature who have sold their pens to the service of the goddess of lubricity. There are times when

the imagination of a generation seems to be poisoned by a mephitic miasma and impelled to dwell with insane persistence on the shames of life. The result of such a diseased bias in our own literature may be seen in the dialogue of the dramatists of the Restoration, and page after page written in Italy during the first half of the sixteenth century reeks with the same stuff.

It is true indeed that coarseness of language is not the measure of corruption. Habits of speech change in the course of centuries. Shakespeare puts jests in the mouths of gentlemen and ladies which seem strangely out of place in the modern theatre. In the Latin reading book Erasmus wrote for boys, there are jokes of the kind that circulate in low drinking places. Queen Anne of France asked an ex-ambassador to teach her a few phrases of Spanish to greet the Spanish ambassador. He taught her some indecent expressions, which she conscientiously repeated until she had learned them by heart. When he told the King what he had done Louis XII, it is true, warned the Queen, but roared with laughter over what he thought an excellent piece of wit.

Soiled waters do not come from a pure spring and that with which the heart is full runs over on the lips, but still it will not do to confound manners with morals, nor forget certain modern writers who have pandered to depraved instincts with a perfumed diction and the subtlest refinements of style.

We should keep in mind also the satiric intent of much of the writing of Aretino's day. It was frequently asserted that the best way to save people from vice was to show it to them. Both these extenuations, of social custom and the prevalent methods of satire may be pled for Aretino. One of the coarsest of his letters (most of which are not at all coarse) was written to a noble lady and printed in the collection to do her honour. And Aretino claimed that his dialogues were a warning to virtue and an exposure of vice. It is not possible, however, that he could have been unaware that such an exposure is never a warning. He ranked his dialogues in honour among his other works and in telling a dream where the gods on Parnassus presented him with a basket of wreaths, alongside "one of thorns for his Christian writings" and "one of laurel for his verses on love and war," was one "of rue for his lascivious writings." All of his modern critics agree that they are a shame to literature.

The assertion is made nowadays that such an absolute moral judgment has no place in history—that to see life truly in the perspective of the ages we must forget our own measures of right and wrong. But knowledge does not require us to limit conscience to the domain of conduct. Conscience has rights also in the realm of reason. The surrender of fixed principle is not the necessary preparation for sympathetic observation of men living or dead. History puts her students in no such perilous position between the risk of surrendering their moral heritage to obsolete barbarisms or of enslaving their moral judgment to decadent opinion. There is a righteousness against which we have the right to measure the past as well as the present. But every man lives not only under the eternal heavens but also in the changing horizon. To see Aretino as his admirers saw him, we must see him in his horizon, and in that horizon public opinion did not force license to wear the cloak of secrecy nor compel vice to find a decorous appearance convenient. There are tales of Boccaccio which seem as bad as possible until one opens the novels of some of Aretino's contemporaries. Two clergymen he knew, popular romancers, put on many of their pages scenes which could now be recited only in the secret sittings of the police court. One of them received praise and reward for reciting some of his stories before Pope Clement VII. The other in his later years was the temporary incumbent of a bishopric in France.

The age bore with pleasure the empire of corrupt imagination; Aretino defended the rights of that rule which he did more than any other to confirm; to make him the scapegoat of the vileness of his people is not to do any particular injustice to him but it is to fail to see mirrored in his life the age in which he lived. The pornographic writings of Aretino did not make him infamous in his own day—they did not even make him famous. They were published before his death less often than his other prose works, and contemporary imprints of them are so rare that, in 1693, Bayle had some trouble in finding out whether they had been printed during the life of their author [see excerpt dated 1702]. It was subsequent generations who found in them his chief claim to be read, and attributed to him a number of similar works by other writers. Among all his works they have had the most continuous life in print. They have been translated into four languages and recently, re-translated into French and English, they have been issued in sumptuous editions. The type which gives vogue to such dialogues in the nineteenth century is more immoral than the pen which wrote them in the sixteenth century. Conscience has its rights in the realm of judgment but history cannot be read in the spirit of the Pharisee, and zeal in blackening by denunciation the dark spots in the lives of the dead is apt to lighten too much by contrast the vile shadows that lurk around the most brilliant centres of our modern civilization.

Judged by the statistics of the press, the most popular of Aretino's writings were his religious books. Eight editions of his *Penitential Psalms* appeared during his lifetime, eight of his *Life of Christ,* five of his *Genesis* and *Vision of Noah,* five of his *Life of Saint Catherine,* three of his *Life of Saint Thomas Aquinas,* two of his *Life of the Virgin.* Their character can best be judged by a specimen extract. He dilutes the first verse of the fifty-first psalm,—"Have mercy upon me, O God, according to Thy loving kindness; according unto the multitude of Thy tender mercies blot out my transgressions," into the following,—

> Have mercy on me, O God, not according to the small merit of my fasting, my prayers, my wearing of hair shirts, my weeping, but according to Thy great mercy with which Thou dost surpass in greatness the vault of heaven, the breast of the mountains, the bosom of the sea, the lap of the earth, the bottom of the abyss and the measure of immensity, and beside which any fault whatever is less than a tiny point marked in the center of the largest circle. Although the poison which iniquity generates in sin sometimes makes it swell up so that, moving Thee to anger, it turns to rise on wings until it seems to desire to equal the very summit of the height of that pity of Thine before which, because I am certain that it conquers in Thyself the severity of Thy justice, I have not despaired of my faults. . . .

(pp. 83-9)

The *Humanity of Christ* is a life of Christ written to suit the taste of the age. The fact that it was translated into French and the quick succession of reprints show that Pietro succeeded in what he tried to do. He was not able to base his work, as the authors of the large number of lives of Christ which have been written in our own day all profess to have done,—upon a careful criticism of the value of the records of that life. Nor if he had been able would he have thought of doing it. For to begin any historical criticism of the documents of the life of Christ would have raised a charge of heresy so radical and profound that no writer, orthodox or schismatic, would have had the moral courage to face it. Out of the mass of all those stories about Jesus Christ which anyone had ever believed to be true, whether they were found in the canon or apocryphal writings, he takes what suits him, arranges his material in a series of interesting pictures and ornaments them with imaginary details to make them appear real. He carries this so far that he does not scruple to put into the mouth of Christ long harangues which, like the speeches of the heroes of the classic histories, are entirely invented. By these means he made a life of Christ very popular, and about as much like the gospels as the sacred pictures of the painters of his own day,—such a work as the editor of a magazine is said to have recently demanded of a well-known writer, a "Life of Christ up to date and snappy."

He sketches into the picture with rapid strokes the popular stories of the apocryphal gospel of the infancy, like the birds of clay made to fly by the Infant Jesus. He tells in detail the story of Christ's descent into the under world. He expands the incidents which seem apt to excite the interest of his readers. He gives a description of the feast of the marriage at Cana and reports a long discourse of Christ to the young couple on the dangers of the married state. He is particularly pleased with the incident of Mary Magdalen, describes a splendid banquet served in her house and gives two pages to a full description of the toilet she makes when persuaded by her good sister to go and see Christ. The Master receives her with a speech precisely like a paragraph from the sermon of one of the popular preachers of the day; several of whom Aretino admired very much. Some of the sayings of our Lord recorded in the gospels, Aretino reproduced clearly and with vigour. Indeed, the vivid and nervous style he occasionally uses in his letters and comedies, was well fitted to translate the gospels. Aretino had found it where Luther found the words for his translation of the gospels, in the mouths of the common people who "heard Christ gladly." But Aretino tries to emphasize Christ's words by diluting them into his other style—the style of his complimentary letters to the scholars of the time like Bembo and Molza, or to the kings and captains who paid him. Here, for instance, is the way he begins the Sermon on the Mount,—"Blessed are they whose spirit, poor in power of argument, is content in Thy belief, considers what it sees, what it hopes and what it possesses as the gift of God and does not make confusion for itself in doubt suggested by the temerity of the sciences. The Kingdom of Heaven is of him who nourishes the intellect with the simplicity of faith. Blessed are they in whose bosom beats the heart of a lamb and not of a lion, because meekness is the manna of the soul, and pride is the poison which puffs up the body. The meek have power to make the earth fertile with blessings. Therefore their humility surpasses the heights of the mountains." Here is the way he makes Christ begin the model prayer,—"Our father who art in heaven, our country for we travel like pilgrims in these bodies until the hour Thou dost appoint for us takes us from this vale of tears, and, recalling us from earthly exile, replaces us in the bosom of paradise; hallowed by Thy name in everything that comes to pass. Because whether we are called by Thee through grace, or punished by Thee through justice, both results are to Thy glory," etc.

Instead of illustrations the book is provided with little reproductions in words of such pictures as the artist friends of the author were painting from the Life of Christ; the Nativity, with the background of "the ruin of an ancient edifice with broken columns and many pieces of living stone which storms and ivy taking their own way had made their own;" or the Descent from the Cross, with the fall of the limbs of the dead body and the muscular action of those lowering it minutely described from canvases Aretino remembered; or the Angel descending from Heaven to comfort Christ in the Garden, "his wings coloured like the rainbow letting him sink to earth gently as a pigeon into its nest." In all these features the book appealed to the taste of the day, and although of far less literary value than his comedies, his pious writings were equally admired. Religious literature suited to popular tastes was as yet little known in Italy, and in it the famous satirist scored a great success. Nor is there anything in this *Life of Christ,* judged by lasting standards, more foreign to the spirit of the gospels or more shocking to taste, than that paragraph of one of the most celebrated lives of Christ of our own day, which makes "the vision of a lovesick woman give to a world a risen God." Everything indicates that Aretino had no sense of incongruity in publishing during the same year the *Life of Christ* and the *Ragionamenti.* He prints the dedicatory letters to his *Ragionamenti,* his *Sonnets* on Marc Antonio's engravings and his *Life of Christ* side by side in the first volume of his letters. Nor did any of the thirty odd Cardinals to whom he wrote or from whom he received letters, suggest that the collocation was infelicitous.

In the publication of his letters Aretino showed again his originality. He was the first Italian to print his own letters in the vulgar tongue and a crowd of imitators proved the success of the experiment. Five years after their appearance he spoke of plenty of volumes of "learned elegances of all the best wits of the century," being in print. But he comforted himself for the poor showing his might make among these learned imitators, by the reflection that, though "the types of Aldus are like pearls, one would much sooner have made the first rude characters which began the art of printing."

The men of the sixteenth century seem to have been ceaselessly engaged in correspondence. More than three thousand of Aretino's letters have survived. And there is every reason to believe him when he says that a number at least as great has perished. The conscientious reader is often tempted to wish that time had been a little more severe. For the scattered pages in which, with quick and sure strokes, he draws pictures full of life, are surrounded by interminable successions of pompous and complimentary phrases, laboriously repeating the same idea. As the reader can see by the extracts already given, Aretino could write straightforwardly and naturally. But, to please his public, he uses for most of his letters the sort of writing he employed in his religious works. The decadence of taste which was to show itself in the love of baroque art was beginning to appear in a liking for the bombastic in literature, and Aretino fed this nascent liking to the full in foretastes of the sort of rhetoric Shakespeare parodied in *Love's Labour's Lost.* In sentences fairly smothered in the exuberance of their own rhetoric he reiterates his thanks for gifts or letters, his excuses for not having written before, his sense of unworthiness of such favours, and rises above the pitch of Japanese politeness in compliment and self abasement. According to his own account he burst into tears of joy on receiving many letters. He cannot force himself to the impertinence of writing to one who has deigned to notice him.

For example, he tells the Cardinal Pisani,—"If the vileness of my condition could approach as close to the nobility of yours as the nobility of yours is superior to the vileness of mine, I would say that the astonishment I have felt in finding myself obliged to write to you, would be equal to that you will feel at sight of the letter I address to you." He tells Messer Ugolino Martelli that he loves him because he has "the tree of genius entirely covered with the flowers which produce the fruits that the sun of glory ripens."

It is difficult to see why there was any demand for hundreds of pages of this sort of collocation of words, and future generations may wonder at the vogue of writers who appear to us perfect. One thing is certain, Aretino wrote in this way not because of the infection of literary fashion, but from choice. We can tell this because his style is direct, whenever he sets it free, and because of the flashes of shrewd common sense which break into the long drawn passages of rhetoric. If at one time he spends a page of strained eloquence praising the virtues of clemency and its usefulness in government, he is able to condense it all into a phrase when he writes—"the city of Perugia is like a hard-mouthed horse which, ridden with an easy hand, seems to be quite gentle."

He is full of contempt for the two most powerful literary affectations of his day, the idea of the Pedants that the perfect writers of classic antiquity had left nothing for succeeding ages except comment or imitation, and the similar idea of the Petrarchists that all possibilities of Italian style and diction were contained in the poetry of Petrarch and the prose of Boccaccio. He frankly confesses more than once that he cannot read Latin,—"I hardly understand the language with which I was born and I talk in it and write in it, and so Plato and Aristotle, Demosthenes and Cicero, Homer and Virgil talked and wrote in their native idioms." "If the soul of Petrarch and Boccaccio," he burst out in disgust, "are tormented in the other world as their works are in this, they ought to deny their baptism." For we find two kinds of writing among Aretino's letters; one which frankly expresses what he thought and felt at the moment, the other related to the chief purpose for which he wrote half his letters and printed them all. That purpose was to coin his fame into gold. (pp. 89-95)

[In] hiring himself out as a giver of immortality, Aretino was playing on the common weakness of the men of his day, an insatiable desire for fame. This craving for glory, which possessed the age like an infectious disease, was not the desire to be praised by those who knew, for doing well things worth doing,—but a passion largely vulgar,—a thirst to be known among one's fellows for anything and everything, a material pride that made all ears itch for even the coarsest flattery. This liking for applause beset the men of the Renascence. One has only to glance at a book which shows the best side of the society of the first generation of the sixteenth century, the *Cortigiano* of Castiglione, to see that he advises the perfect gentleman to be always, in every act of his life, playing to the gallery.

Aretino has given perhaps the most striking description of this characteristic passion of his age—this thirst and hunger for praise which made fame seem almost like a material thing to be eaten and drunk. "I do not know the pleasure misers feel in the sound of the gold they count, but I know well that the blessed spirits do not hear music which is more grateful than the harmony which comes out of one's own praises. One feeds on it as in paradise the souls feed on the vision of God." (p. 102)

The passion for fame had another side, and the audacious cleverness of Aretino's scheme for coining his reputation cannot be appreciated until we have looked at it. The love of flattery seldom fails to breed an extreme touchiness. The man greedy of adulation, shrinks with an agony of dislike from dispraise. If the Italian of the Renascence was apt for satiric speech, he paid for his evil tongue by a thin skin, sensitive to every malicious breath. Even to-day among the Latin races where the Renascence flourished in its vigour, there is a lasting sense of wrong for verbal insult "injures," "oltraggi," which the English-speaking race, used to a word and a blow, or to words forgotten, finds it hard to appreciate. And Aretino counted on this shrinking hatred of mordant words to bring in his tribute from those who thought the price of his praise too high.

When he came to Venice he had won by his pasquinades and his comedy a great reputation, and his specialty was "maldicentia." It was admitted that he had the worst tongue in Italy. In . . . his running comment on events, his irregular newspaper mixing news with editorials, he found a field for his power of satire. It became the object of every prince in Italy to keep out of the giudizi the facts of his career or the traits of his character which would bring cynical laughter instead of applause. From the time he went to Venice until his death, Aretino asserted that he had a divine mission,—to punish the vices of princes and expose the hypocrisy of priests. This is what he meant by calling himself "the fifth evangelist."

One cannot turn over five pages of his letters without finding vague allusions to the crimes which haunt princely courts, and the vileness by which prelates rose to power at Rome. For example, promising to write regularly, he adds,—"And in case I fail, put it down to the fault of a certain beastly desire to resemble princes. And not being able to do so with any other mask than that of lies, it may be that I make this promise keeping it in the way they keep theirs." Asked by a preacher to define "charity," he answers,—"A friar's hood, because the shadow of its sanctity covers the multitude of the vile progeny of your hypocritical actions." A certain transaction, he says, would be dishonest "even among cardinals." "If," he writes to the Spaniard Don Luigi d'Avila, "from being Italian one could change into a Spaniard, as from being a Christian one can change into a priest," etc. Through all his letters runs a stream of such allusions to the meanness and bad faith of princes or to the hypocrisy of all ranks in the church. These allusions in his published letters are for the most part vague. Occasionally, indeed, where the pay of one of his patrons had been too long delayed, he becomes more pointed. . . . And sometimes he names prelates who for him incarnate the hypocrisy he denounces in the church. But these passages, though not few among his published letters, would hardly have maintained, amidst the strong competition of the day, his reputation of having the most dangerous tongue in the world. This reputation, absolutely necessary for keeping at its highest figure the income he drew from his profession, he maintained in his Giudizi, his satiric verses and in unpublished letters; pieces circulated for the most part in manuscript. By these less public writings he could cause fear without giving deadly offense. If necessary, he could disavow them.

The choice which Aretino presented to kings and great men was a very simple one. An eulogistic letter assured them of his desire to spread their fame and make them immortal. Not to accept the offer was to run the risk of being pilloried for

the laughter of Italy. This literary mill, whose upper stone was flattery and its lower satire, squeezed from the vanity of men a steady stream of gold for its ingenious author. The plan was not entirely original. In the fifteenth century the sale of eulogy and invective had been common among the humanists, but Aretino first assembled and arranged the rude and elementary devices of his predecessors. And he drew from his machine a large income which enabled him to live in far better style than Erasmus, the acknowledged king of letters.

From the seventeenth century on, writers have expanded in severe epithets on the infamy of this system. One obvious thing seems to have escaped them. If the system had seemed in its own day too infamous it could not have been so successful. The utterances of a ribald blackmailer, looked down on by all honest men as infamous, could not have steadily flattered pride nor stirred fear. Nor did Aretino try to hide his practices. On the contrary, he made so clear an explanation of his system in letters he printed that we trace it entirely in them. (pp. 103-07)

He thought he had done a great service to literature in systematizing this commercial use of invective and eulogy, and calls himself the "Redeemer of Genius who has restored her to her ancient place!" "Her glory was dimmed by the shadows of the avarice of men of power, and before I began to lacerate their names, men of genius begged the honest necessaries of life. And if some one rose above the pressure of necessity, he did it as a buffoon and not as a person of merit. My pen armed with its terrors has brought matters to such a pass that the Signori, coming to themselves, have cherished great intellects with enforced 'cortesia.' "

Conscious of this great service, he was convinced that the world owed him the splendid living he drew from the vices and merits he praised or blamed. For he naively writes in thanking the new Duke of Florence for money,—"The cortesia shown me is an augury of felicity for the reign of his Excellency, because none give to me but true princes who reign by the choice of God and by the counsel of good men."

This easy conscience about his work is the more emphasized by the pious phrases which run through his letters. Aretino considers himself an excellent churchman and a good Christian. To attack the corruptions of the clergy and the Roman court was not of course in the least incompatible with piety and orthodoxy. Some of the saints had done it in the past; some of the apologetes of the Church against schism did it in his own day. Heresy Aretino always hated. He makes many hostile allusions to Luther. (pp. 109-10)

These various traits of Aretino, his lack of shame for pornographic writing, the brutal immorality of his life, his sense of high moral service to the world, his thanks to God for the gifts he used in that service, his interest in religion, his self complacency and his frank exposition of willingness to praise the virtues of the princes who paid him not to denounce their vices, are hard to unite into a consistent character. And most writers have solved the problem in portraiture by the easy device of labeling him a blatant hypocrite. But to see him set forth in his own letters as we can see Benvenuto Cellini in his autobiography, is to perceive that Aretino, while not without a tinge of hypocrisy, took himself on the whole at his own high valuation—and one who does not believe that this may be true, has not begun to know the men of the Renascence. (p. 113)

To account for the success of Aretino's masterly organization of the crude methods of the humanists for the sale of eulogies and invectives, writers have pointed out that there is a resemblance between his Giudizi and the modern newspaper. It is suggested that Charles V, who paid Aretino more than he paid Titian, knew what he was about in subsidising a rising power—the power of the press. It would be easy to spend several malicious and partly true pages, suggesting certain similarities between Aretino's methods and style and those of some newspapers, and there is truth in the comparison, but not enough to make us attribute too much force to the motive. Charles V may have shrewdly calculated that the pen of Aretino might arouse or allay certain hostilities to his policy, but we know that when his ambassador first advised him to put Aretino on a pension, it was for fear he might publish a particular private scandal about the Emperor's life which was already talked about and thought to be true.

And in addition, the power of the press has risen with the power of democracy. Now, while Aretino was living at Venice, the democracy everywhere throughout Italy was either dying or dead. Public opinion in the sense of a general moral judgment producing political effects, did not exist in the Peninsula. Charles V, who made a bastard Medici Duke of Florence, and built a fortress in Siena to hold a Spanish garrison, had little reason to fear the political effect of public opinion.

Aretino's letters did not always bring golden answers. Little unpleasantnesses occasionally arose. He found it hard to hold his insolent tongue even about his patrons. His greed kept him in intermittent irritation over the smallness or delay of their payments, and they resented things he said not intended for their ears. (pp. 114-15)

[The subtlest trait of Aretino's] art in wielding an evil tongue was that he rarely lied. Luzio, who has tested the statements of the only one of his Giudizi which has survived, says,—"The Archives of the Gonzaga prove that Aretino rarely calumniates and invents. Ninety-nine times out of a hundred he does nothing but propagate accepted scandals, put in circulation malignant assertions of others, giving them a sharp and striking form." When one of the characters in Aretino's Cortigiana asks: "How can I best say evil of men?" he receives the answer,—"By telling the truth—by telling the truth." For Aretino discovered very early that in his business of literary blackmail truthfulness was the best policy. This crafty truthfulness gave him a great superiority over his adversaries. And he further disarmed them by proclaiming as virtues those things in his life they denounced as infamous. It was useless for Franco to call him "an angry cur to whom men fling bones in order not to be bitten." Aretino had already in letters and medals proudly announced himself the Scourge of Princes, drawing tribute from their fears by denouncing their vices. And the boasts had not checked the intimacy of great artists, dropping into his house as if they belonged to the family, nor prevented his aristocratic neighbours from sending fruit and flowers from their gardens, nor stopped the rain of gold chains that fell upon his neck from all quarters of the world.

It is not to be supposed that Aretino's manipulation of vanity was invariably successful. In Michael Angelo, for instance, he found a difficult subject. (pp. 122-23)

In another direction also, Aretino's system of literary blackmail failed to work to his satisfaction. All through his writings runs a series of damaging and denunciatory allusions to the Papal court, the clergy and monks. These allusions are vague and general, and not at all incompatible with his equally continuous professions of loyalty to the orthodox faith and the ancient church. They do not prevent the exchange of highly complimentary letters with a large number of prelates and monks nor the receipt of favours from popes. His attacks are generally by way of slurs, as when he writes to the Cardinal of Trent that "he is as truthful as every other man of his habit is full of lies," or says that a certain thing "would be shameful even among cardinals let alone among cavaliers," or tells Cardinal Hippolito de' Medici "that as others show the honours, incomes and favours gained in the Roman court by their vices, he will show the offenses he has received for his virtues." Sometimes he repeated a story like that of Julius II rushing out of his room in fury at five o'clock in the morning to pursue a careless singer in the corridors of the palace, not heeding one of his attendants, who kept calling "Holy Father, go to bed," and finally giving a terrible rap over the head to his luckless steward who came to see what the row was and was taken for the rash musician.

But on occasions he made more direct and deadly assaults. Just after the sack of Rome, he wrote a satiric address to the Roman clergy, called the *Pax Vobiscum.* The scorching sentences struck Pope Clement in the midst of his ruined city so cruelly that he let the book fall from his hands and burst into tears. In the presence of Aretino's friend, the painter Sebastiano del Piombo, he said with a sigh, when in the castle of Saint Angelo,—"If Pietro had been with me I should not be here worse than a prisoner," and went on to explain that the representatives of the Emperor would not dare to treat him so shamefully if the dreaded pen of Pietro were on his side.

In this attack as in others, Pietro was cleverly using for ignoble ends what was generally thought to be the truth. It was the universal opinion, expressed by many whose fidelity to the Church could not be questioned, that the sack of Rome was the divine judgment on the sins of the Curia. But the impelling motive of Pietro's criticism of the Church was not prophetic wrath, nor were his temporary reconciliations with the popes entirely the result of that readiness to forgive injuries of which he often boasts, and not without truth. In the case of the corruptions of the Church, as in the case of the corruptions of princely courts, he was using, sometimes without being conscious of it at the moment, a not altogether ungenuine indignation to gratify revenge and greed. And the man to whom that seems impossible does not know the curious anomalies of character that flourished in the air of the Italian Renascence. (pp. 125-27)

It was during the bitterest part of [Aretino's] attacks on the papal court, that this bravo of the pen received his hardest and most damaging blow. It came from the same household that furnished the assassin's dagger that drove him from Rome. The Datario Ghiberti, afterwards bishop of Verona, had as secretary Francesco Berni, who wrote burlesque poetry with such success that he has given his name to the Bernesque style which Byron used in Beppo and Don Juan. Soon after the publication of the *Pax Vobiscum,* Berni wrote a famous sonnet in answer [see excerpt dated 1527]. It contained at least one malicious libel, the story about Aretino's sister, and enables the reader to judge of the malodorous flowers that bloomed in the controversial pages of Aretino and many of his contemporaries. (p. 130)

It is a typical instance of the way in which Aretino has been made the scapegoat of his time, that Berni's biographer, Virgili, who cannot be stern enough about the coarseness and irresponsibility of Aretino, should speak of this sonnet as a "frank and loyal" attack on that unique monster of wickedness. (p. 132)

When death had removed [Aretino] from attack, war was made on his works. Ten years before his death, an attempt had been made to persuade the Pope to have his religious works burnt. The year after his death some of his writings, two years after, all, were placed by the Church on the index of prohibited books. The need of stopping their circulation if they were heretical, is suggested by one account of the officers of the Inquisition. They seized the stock of Cappello, a bookseller of Naples, who was agent for Gabriel Giolito, a publisher and bookseller of Venice with shops in Bologna, Ferrara and Naples. In the stock of seven hundred and twenty-nine books, one hundred and twenty-six were by Aretino; the next best selling author, if we can test by this standard, was Erasmus, of whose works seventy-one copies were found. There were in stock thirty-nine copies of Aretino's dramatic works, thirty copies of his letters and forty copies of his religious books. Of his pornographic writings only nine copies were found.

It has been assumed that Aretino's works were put upon the index, because of his pornographic writings. This assumption seems to be mistaken; the very slight references which have survived to suggest the motives for that condemnation refer to heretical tendencies. There are things in his religious writings on which a charge of departure from orthodoxy could have been based. And when the influence of the Council of Trent was being felt in reforming the abuses and restoring the discipline of the church, Aretino's freedom in criticising the clergy became offensive. (p. 135)

Aretino was condemned not for obscenity but for heresy, and more particularly because of the sneers and derogatory remarks against the clergy, which were scattered so freely through his works.

He was buried in the church of San Luca, but his tomb was destroyed when the level of the floor was changed. His epitaph was not the fabled one which accused him of never having known God, but probably the one a German traveller reports at the end of the sixteenth century:—

"From a lowly origin, Pietro Aretino rose to such height by denouncing impure vice that, through the fear he inspired, he levied tribute from those to whom the world paid tribute." (p. 137)

> Paul Van Dyke, "Pietro Aretino," in his Renaissance Portraits, *Charles Scribner's Sons, 1905, pp. 33-137.*

L. E. ROBINSON (essay date 1906)

[*In the following excerpt, Robinson chronicles Aretino's career and literary achievements.*]

[Aretino's] importance as an illustration of the spirit of the later Italian Renascence is very great. Well known to Englishmen in Addison's day, the fame, or rather the ill-fame, of this remarkable sycophant gradually lapsed into obscurity, until to-day, even among the educated, he is scarcely known by name. The researches of Italian scholars have recently made the writings of this erstwhile "Perverter of morals and letters" accessible to the extent to which they have survived,

so that it is now possible to study Aretino soberly in the light of the diseased age in which he lived.

Aretino spent the last thirty years of his life in Venice, where he died in 1557. Unaided by a knowledge of the humanities, he developed in the vernacular a style of expression remarkable for its facility and power. His mastery of pasquinade made him in truth the "Scourge of Princes." He reduced invective and eulogy to a successful commercial system. The dread or pleasure which his pen inspired became a continual source of revenue from the official incumbents of both church and state. His knowledge of the crimes and rumors of crimes chargeable to the priests and princes of Europe made it desirable for them to keep the facts of their careers out of his Giudizi, periodically circulated and eagerly read. On the principle that offenders hate publicity, he demanded gifts from promising victims as a condition of his silence or eulogy. Henry VIII., Francis I., and Charles V. were among those who pensioned him; such was the power of the press in its incipiency! He was always ready to confer immortality for a subsidy—an exchange of "servitu" for "cortesia." In return for generous treatment, he thus writes to Barbarossa, pirate prince of Algiers: "The sun envies you because the glory of the fame which crowns you with eternal praise goes into those parts of the world where the light of the flame which he offers cannot go." Henry VIII.'s liberality is rewarded by similar grandiloquence of praise. An instance of Aretino's failure of reward is afforded in Michaelangelo's admirable indifference to his request for some sketches; but the great artist was punished by a seriously phrased denunciation of the nudities in the "Last Judgment."

In hiring himself out as a giver of immortality, Aretino illustrates the "common weakness of the men of that day, an insatiable desire for fame." His own words best express this "characteristic passion of the age": "I do not know the pleasures misers feel in the sound of the gold they count, but I know well that the blessed spirits do not hear music which is more grateful than the harmony that comes out of one's own praises. One feeds on it as in Paradise the souls feed on the vision of God."

As a writer, Aretino was prolific and versatile. His works include comedies, obscene sonnets, and pornographic dialogues which he maintained were "a warning to virtue and an exposure of vice." His religious writings include a life of Christ and the lives of several mediæval saints. Presumably he wrote about six thousand letters, of which more than half have survived. (pp. 13-14)

> L. E. Robinson, "Three Men of the Renaissance," in The Dial, *Chicago, Vol. XLI, No. 481, July 1, 1906, pp. 13-15.*

EDWARD HUTTON (essay date 1922)

[*In the following excerpt from his biography of Aretino, Hutton praises the Italian for his rejection of pedantry.*]

Had Aretino lived in our day he would have established a journal, humorous, social, political, satirical, and, even as he did in the sixteenth century, would have made a fortune out of it. But such a statement by no means sums up Aretino: it takes into account less than half his achievement and largely disregards what he actually was.

Who, then, was this Pietro Aretino—*Il Divino—Flagello dei*

principi? He was what Titian called him, the *Condottiere* of Literature: and above all a production of his time. Indeed, the spirit of that age of decadence and dissolution, not of Italy alone, but of all Europe as Europe, is very completely represented in Italy by Ariosto, Machiavelli and Aretino—the perfection of form, the hardness and security of the intellect, and the moral anarchy and complete egoism in which the soul is its own prisoner corrupting itself, and in which cynicism takes the place of that charity of which St. Paul speaks; death, of life. And it is in Aretino rather than in Ariosto or Machiavelli, for he is more complete than either and more vital, that we can best understand that tragic and disastrous moment in which the destiny of Europe was decided: its mixture of moral depravity, intellectual force and artistic sentiment.

Any egoist can say with Aretino: "If I was born to live thus, who will prevent me from living thus? What are you going to do about it?" But few egoists have his enormous appetite: it is one of the really valid things about him. "Why do you spend so much," you say to me? I answer: "Because royal souls show themselves in spending inordinately."

But if he had a great and an omnivorous appetite, he had great energy too, a body of iron, a serene soul, the hide of a rhinoceros and perfect health. Look at his portraits by Titian. He is all there.

It is this man who is a great writer, for it is as a writer that Aretino is really important and not merely interesting. He found letters in Italy dying of pedantry, wholly artificial, and imitative of classical or Tuscan models, Virgil, Plautus, Terence, Petrarca, Boccaccio. Bembo was even attempting to fix the grammatical forms, and the manner of writing had become mechanical, a matter of rule: one would soon write Italian precisely as one writes Latin, without regard to the living and spoken language. Well, Aretino's whole effect as a writer was to smash up all that pedantry. There is scarcely a page in his six volumes of **Letters** that does not hold the pedants up to scorn. He was, if any writer ever was, free, spontaneous and full of life. For this cause, if for no other, he should be forgiven all his sins, which for the most part were almost necessary defects of these qualities. But these qualities were invaluable.

What does he mean by pedantry? This: seeing things through the eyes of others, through a veil of preconception, and not directly for oneself; the mistaking of words for things, till the mere expression comes to seem to have the value of an act. He states, and states truly, that it was this pedantry, "this assassination of the dead" that "provoked the heresy against our Faith by the mouth of Luther the worst pedant of all."

Again and again he asserts that poetry cannot be written by pedantry, by imitating Petrarca and Boccaccio:

> O unstable folk, I tell you and I tell you again, that poetry is a fancy, a whim, a child of Nature in its happiness, and, unless it is that, it becomes a tinkling cymbal and a bell without music.

Just there we seem to perceive a critic direct and decisive and certainly unique in his day. And this great gift of criticism was applied by him almost as securely to the art of painting as to the art of literature. It is no doubt one of the many attractions he had for Titian, Michelangelo and Sansovino.

As for his love of Nature, "Nature mistress of all masters," we have only to read his letter to Titian describing Venice from his window to feel its enthusiasm and sincerity. Yet, so great a critic as De Sanctis can ask why his admiration and love of Nature did not awake in him "any moral impression or elevation" [see excerpt dated 1879]. It certainly did not: but why should it? It awoke in him as in any other artist a sheer delight. Surely that was enough? He was not a pantheist to worship Nature, nor, perhaps, would he have cared for the Lesser Celandine. Let us leave the moral elevation to Vasari, and only regret that Vasari was totally lacking in Aretino's critical judgment and artistic appreciation of painting; and let us acknowledge in Aretino the first critic of modern art, in painting and letters, who refers us not to the classics but to nature and to life.

This is his value; and he realised what he preached. Every line he wrote came out of his head and his heart, quite spontaneously, in its anger, contempt and derision, its enthusiasm, greed and simplicity. If one feels much the same in regard to Machiavelli and Cellini, their directness and simplicity, one feels too a certain quality in their work not wholly their own: they too seem to invoke the dead. Aretino invoked no one but himself. He was a child of nature and of life; he continually appealed to them and to them only, and almost without culture as he was, he makes up—far more than makes up—in spontaneity what he lacks in scholarship.

If his work is thus without urbanity and certainly without grace, he sought always expression, action, movement—in a word, life. And with what swiftness, with what directness he achieves his end! He has so much energy and facility, such a wealth of ideas and feelings; and he pours them out with the freshness and the impetus of an inexhaustible spring; and as with such a source, the secret and centre of the whole is in himself, Pietro Aretino.

He seems too, enclosed as he is in the prison of his egoism, to measure all things by himself and not to know that anything can exist for him in itself or apart from its relations to him; it only exists as he is aware of it.

And if this be so, those panegyrics of his, are they panegyrics, or only furious and subtle ironies, almost passionate in their cynicism and absurdity? It may be, he found it easier to speak evil than to speak good, to condemn than to praise; and when we consider the age he lived in, we need not wonder too much: he seems always to have come to bless and remained to curse and castigate.

And everywhere in all his work the style is the man in its sheer genius for expression, its final expressiveness, and again and again in its simplicity. He thanks his benefactors (who often go in fear of that winged pen) for clothes, for food, for jewels, again and again for money, with the simplicity of a child; and this, if we read him without pedantry, continually moves us.

In now turning very briefly to his works one by one, I shall have nothing to say of the earliest of them, those **Sonetti Lussuriosi** which have become famous, as Voltaire said of Dante, because they are so little read. At the same time let us stay long enough in reach of these obscenities to note their characteristic marks—their spontaneity and their irony. He tells us himself that he saw the works of Raimondi, and "when I saw them I was touched by the spirit that moved Giulio Romano to design them." As for their irony he explains it himself in his letter of defence; it is part of his defence: "the beasts are more free than we."

Of the pasquinades, too, I have said enough . . . and will

only note here the really valid quality in them: namely, that they dealt with life and that it was Aretino who, with them, took Pasquin out of the hands of the pedants and grammarians and gave him life, made him the most popular figure in Rome and through him published what everyone wished to read.

In both these works, in the sonnets as well as in the pasquinades, we see at once a work of rebellion. This rebellion is instinctive; and we feel this quite as much in what is perhaps his most important achievement, his dramatic works, his *Teatro,* his comedies and tragedy, as in the sonnets and pasquinades. He refuses here above all, where all men were imitators and copyists and pedants, to be anything but himself. Of all the writers of comedies in his day he is the only one, except perhaps Machiavelli, who forgets Plautus and writes what is in his head.

His comedies are among the very best written in Italian before Goldoni; and his *Orazia* written in verse, the best tragedy in the Italian language. Spontaneous and full of the life that he saw about him, as works of art it must be confessed they are too volatile and spoiled by levity and superficiality. If they are full of life, the life he shows us is common and base and his characters wholly without nobility of any sort. They live while they move across the scene but they leave us no memory of themselves. Yet nothing can be more lively and vivid than many of his scenes. Take this street scene from the *Cortigiana,* for instance:

> FURFANTE. (*selling loose fly-sheets of stories and verses*). MESSER MACO and a SIENESE. Scene: a Street in Rome.
> FUR. Fine stories. Fine stories.
> MAC. Be quiet. What is that fellow crying?
> SIENESE. He must be mad.
> FUR. Fine stories, fine stories; the Turkish war in Hungary, the sermons of Fra Martino, the Council, stories, stories, the English affair, the Pomp of the Pope and the Emperor, the Circumcision of the Vaivoda, the Sack of Rome, the Siege of Florence, the Conference of Marseilles with the conclusion: stories, stories.
> MAC. Run, fly, hurry, Sienese! Here is a *giulio,* buy me the Leggenda dei Cortigiani, that I may make myself courtier before the master comes: but don't you make yourself courtier before me, you know.
> SIENESE. No, the devil! O there, books, speeches, cards. . . . He has turned the corner. I will run after him.
> MAC. Run, I say run. O what streets, what streets! I see up there in that window a beautiful lady: she must be the Duchess of Rome. I feel myself falling in love. If I become Cardinal, if I become Courtier she shall not escape me. She is looking at me, she is staring at me. . . .

That short scene, like so many others, is full of life and altogether different from anything else written at this time: it gives you the very streets of Rome, and its comedy is full of irony and comment upon the affairs of the day. How often Aretino writes thus and yet it is, we feel, good as it is and far better than anyone else in Italy could achieve, not nearly good enough. It is too light and too superficial. In all these comedies there is no living character, no human being whom we know as an individual: never for a moment is Aretino within measurable distance of creating a Falstaff or a Jourdain, yet he had matter made to his hand. Consider what he makes of Marescalco and what Shakespeare made of Malvolio—a thing eternally living and exquisite: think what

he made of Ipocrito and what Molière made of Tartuffe. His work suffers with even the best Italian work of all ages in this, that it cannot build with character or create living human beings who live in and by themselves and endure for ever. He cannot create, he can only give us at his best what he sees and is able to understand. It is amusing to compare the *Marescalco* with *Twelfth Night,* to remember that both were written in the *Cinquecento,* to place this ridiculous and hideous figure of the Marescalco—who is a pederast and hates women and is driven half mad because he has been gulled into believing that the Duke of Mantua is going to get him married—with Malvolio; and then to listen to an Italian critic telling you that Shakespeare was a barbarian, and English unlike Italian, not a humanistic but a commercial language.

For the *Cortigiana* and the *Marescalco* are probably the best Italian comedies before Goldoni (1740-60). Though published in 1534, the year after the publication not only of the *Marescalco,* but of the *Filosofo,* the *Cortigiana* is the earliest of his plays and in some ways the best, the most vivid and living. It, with the *Marescalco* and *Filosofo,* form a first and distinctive part of Aretino's *Teatro;* the *Ipocrito* and the *Talanta,* written later and published in 1540 and 1542 respectively, are different in manner and perhaps less vital, certainly less modern, original and amusing.

The *Cortigiana,* really without plot, consists of a series of scenes in which we are given a picture of the life of Rome in the time of the Medici popes, full of bitter irony and scorn. Of the *Marescalco* I have already spoken; both these comedies have a passionate and personal note which is lacking in the rest, in which are to be found hints from Boccaccio (in the two principal incidents of the *Filosofo*), from Sacchetti in two incidents in the *Talanta* (those of Messer Necessitas and of the Pizzicagnolo), and from Boiardo, Terence and Plautus in both.

The *Ipocrito,* as its name implies, deals with a hypocrite and parasite, indifferent alike to good and bad, who only thinks of filling his pockets by the most servile subservience, cunning contrivance and exploitation of others, chiefly women. He is not, however, the chief comic figure of the play: this is Messer Liseo, an old man who, not knowing what to do to remedy the ills of his life in the person of a despotic wife and five daughters whom he cannot marry, turns for advice and help to the Ipocrito, who counsels him to resign himself and to comfort himself with philosophy. The wretched being ends by becoming utterly indifferent and stupid, exclaiming, *"todos es nada . . . nada es todos."*

When Aretino was already an old man it is said he turned his mind to the production of a work of art for its own sake and wrote his only tragedy, *La Orazia.* This has been compared with the work of Shakespeare by critics who cannot have understood what Shakespeare's work really was. The only likeness in any sense to the work of Shakespeare lies in the choice of a story of ancient Rome, the part the crowd plays in the action, and the fact that a certain comic element relieves the tragedy. This is very much but it is all merely superficial. *La Orazia* shows nothing of the genius of Shakespeare, his poetry, his apprehension of life, his power of creating living men and women. It is, in fact, less alive than anything else of Aretino's, and certainly less characteristic and less within his reach than anything he set his hand to.

It is strange to pass from the wholly irresponsible comedies, often gross enough and vulgar enough to have won infinite applause, to the religious works which he must have been writing much about the same time and which were certainly not less popular. But even in his lifetime he was bitterly attacked for daring to use such a pen as his to write of divine things, and the seventeenth and eighteenth centuries which appreciated his ribaldry could not bear his religious works. They, with many of his contemporaries, regarded him as a profaner of holy things, and though many appreciated them, more perhaps thought they ought to be burnt.

The first of these works *L' Humanità di Christo,* of which *La Passione di Gesù* is but the last part, was dedicated to the Emperor; the *Sette Salmi* to Antonio De Leyva, the *Genesis* to the Emperor's brother Ferdinand; the Lives of the Virgin and of St. Catherine to Marchese del Vasto. Were these works but another means then of obtaining money from patrons? He certainly seems to have written ascetic and obscene works together and with equal indifference. Well, the *Ragionamento della Nanna* and the life of St. Catherine of Alexandria were both romances, but what can we say of the *Cortigiana* and the *Life of Christ?* However, according to De Sanctis he draws Christ as a Knight Errant. But was Aretino in these works really as devoid of sincerity as has been thought? I think he was.

He was trying to make a name and a fortune in a certain way. We may regard all his letters as a journal, a humoristic-social-politico-financial journal. Well, these religious works were a part of it.

We have seen the same thing in our own day. A man will make a fortune by running and writing a paper which exists on a sort of libel and abuse, political, personal, financial; in which the people and the poor and half educated—those who will buy his paper—are carefully catered for and exploited, their intelligence, such as it is, exploited without scruple. On Sunday, in a Sunday paper he will write about Christ or the Sermon on the Mount. In Italy he would write about the Blessed Virgin and the Saints. That is exactly what Aretino did. We must regard these "religious" works as articles in his journal, in his review, which never appeared as such but which existed none the less for that. His letters form the main part of this review; they are the "articles." Well, the religious works are the articles "for Sunday" as we should say. They probably gulled a larger, and perhaps not less important "public" and they no doubt impressed the "princes" whose screw he was, as well. They have, however, their value, not indeed for any religious quality, but as mirrors of a part of that obscure soul.

Let us turn now to the *Ragionamenti,* those curious and obscene *Dialoghi* which appear to have been written at the same time as the religious works, the first being published in 1534. These strange works consist of two parts, each divided into three dialogues filling three days. The First Part contains the Dialogues on the Life of Nuns, the Life of Married Women, and the Life of Courtesans, and is wittily and maliciously dedicated by the author to his monkey. The Second Part contains the dialogues entitled "Pippa's Education," "The Wiles of Men" and "The Bawd's Trade," and is dedicated to Bernardo Valdaura.

Two years after the publication of the Second Part of the *Ragionamenti,* Aretino issued, in 1538, a *Ragionamento de le Corti* in which he attacks the Court of Rome; and in 1543 he published the *Dialogo del Pietro Aretino nel quale si parla del gioco con moralità piacevole,* which has for its subjects

games of cards. Neither of these two dialogues has anything to do with the *Ragionamenti* proper—the *Capricci,* as he sometimes calls them in his letters,—The Six Days. They do not form a third part to the *Capricci* as they appear to do in Melagrano's edition of 1589. Bandello, in his *Novelle,* makes a similar mistake when he attributes the *Raffaella* to Aretino. Bandello was a contemporary of Aretino's and a scholar, yet he seems to have had no sense of Aretino's inimitable style, since he can attribute such a work as the *Raffaella* to him. Nothing would seem to be easier than to reject confidently such a work, which with the *Puttana Errante* and the *Ragionamento del Zoppino* has nothing but its obscenity in common with the work of Aretino. Aretino's page is full of life, hard to read, spontaneous and yet packed tight, worked upon and forged, full of queer instances and odd comparisons, glittering with wit and every sort of comic exaggeration. Such work does not exist outside his pages. His successor was Rabelais; but also Molière. He has the robust joy of the one, but something of the intellectual charm of the other. He takes us not only in spite of ourselves, but in spite of his own animalism and coarseness. He fascinates us with his good-for-nothing but candid women who are so pretty and so amusing, and yet as we know all the time such lamentable, mournful, and even nauseating beings. What sluts he shows us in that mirror he holds up to nature! For his work is a mirror, though it may distort much in malice. He is a realist. The "Dialogue of the Life of Nuns," for instance—we can believe it: even two centuries later Casanova and Rousseau give us only a less brutal picture. And if it shocks and disgusts us we cannot but be astonished at the robustness of a world which could survive such animalism and confusion, which could not only indulge its appetites so unselfconsciously, but which had such appetites to indulge. There is something valid there at any rate; and if it is impossible for us to realise the scenes he gives us as having actually happened, though we are obviously the gainers, we are losers, too, in that we have lost something of that energy, that zest, which made such an abundance of life delightful even in its rudest expression.

For all these dialogues, obscene as they are, are not lascivious, they have the vigour of life and are filled with action. One could not find a work less "cerebral," as the jargon of to-day has it, than these dialogues. Wholly without atmosphere, naked and dramatic in their objectivity, they leave us cold as ice, and since they expose, and at the top of the voice, the brutal corruption of the time—the time which saw the break-up of Europe, the failure of that philosophical system which had built up Europe, and the domination of the barbarian—they may even have served a useful if not a moral purpose; though it is the last thing their tone seems to hint at, at least to modern ears. "I have spoken the truth": it is Aretino's continual cry as it was Boccaccio's, and now as in their own day no one can be found to believe them. It is perhaps unnatural to love the truth for its own sake. We think the truth, if it must be spoken, should be uttered with more seriousness, more modesty and with less inordinate joy: not in a shout of laughter, but with severity and sorrow. It is not perhaps our hypocrisy, but our nerves which insist upon this. We are less robust than they, we know as little of their huge laughter as of their enormous and violent gestures: we take our pleasures—and among them the rebuking of sin—sadly. We are no longer capable of their enormities, their spontaneous lusts as of young animals at play: their nakedness seems a little brutal to us who have hidden our own under the daintiest of *lingerie.* But we are still capable of much, and I doubt if there be anything in the Sack of Rome as described in the Second Day of the

Second Part of the *Ragionamenti* which we have not matched and overmatched in the late war, and we shall find nothing in the sixteenth century to equal in horror much that was done quite coldly and as a matter of course in the last few years.

But what is so amusing in the *Ragionamenti* is the strange quality they seem to have; a sort of devilish glee, a malignity and malice of observation which find expression in an exuberance of sarcastic particulars, of picturesque expressions, of comic detail, and comparisons. They are, too, filled with a wonderful variety of people and of characteristic scenes, both drawn swiftly from life. Like the *Decameron,* they are full of anecdotes, witty sayings, noisy mirth and enormous laughs, so that if their whole subject were not become impossible to us they might be as universally appreciated as *Pickwick,* or, at any rate, as the books of Rabelais, for as a product of human energy they are surely not less astonishing or less true or less full of life or less in artistic achievement.

In regard to the life-work of their author they have their own place. In the great review or journal which he ran, which never appeared as such, but which existed nevertheless, if the Letters are the articles, the religious works the articles for Sunday, the *Ragionamenti* are the *feuilletons,* and, as must often be the case, by no means the least read or the least popular part of the paper. (pp. 235-56)

It is perhaps astonishing that the influence of Aretino upon Italian literature has been much less than, seeing his energy and vitality, we might have expected: and this is unfortunate, for whatever we may think of his subject-matter, he had the root of all good literature in him, in his freedom from pedantry and his closeness to life. His influence in France was much greater, and both Rabelais and Molière, to name only the greatest, would seem to owe him much. In England his work seems to have been altogether ineffective. Perhaps at that time, and indeed at any time, we needed it less than any other people. The only translation into English of any of his works is *The Crafty Whore,* published in London in 1658, which is partly from the *Ragionamenti,* while Mr. A. Esdaile of the British Museum has pointed out to me that Sir Thomas Wyatt's *Penitential Psalms* were in their earlier part translated and in their later imitated from the *Sette Salmi* of Aretino. It is the only case of Aretino's non-obscene work being translated or ever noticed in English, and it is, unhappily, very dull stuff.

References to Aretino in English works of the sixteenth century are fairly numerous, but they are all the same; they treat him as the great exemplar of the obscene, and to make an "Aretino allusion book" would be very monotonous and profitless.

It is only in our day that something of the significance of this robust and spontaneous writer has been understood. We find in him among much else, not certainly the first obscene writer in literature, but the first journalist, the first writer to see and to use to the utmost the Press, the power of publicity; and we may think of him as the first of those "Napoleons of the Press" who so largely inspire and control public opinion in the world to-day. As such he has for us an unique interest, for it is well to study any disease, anything that has become so dangerous, in its genesis.

A great journalist of genius, then, is that what Pietro Aretino comes to? He was this, but he was more than this, as I have tried to show. He seems, as I have said, with Ariosto and Ma-

chiavelli to sum up the Italy of his time in a way that no other journalist has ever come to do for any other country at any other time. He is the utter end of the Renaissance, and in a sense its negation. He prophesies. He seems to dismiss the whole past of his country and of civilization with contempt, he cares nothing for long tradition or gentle convention, but engulphs them all in a brutal, malicious and enormous laugh which only the universal elements of life can endure, in which all the flowers of the spirit shrivel and perish. Is it the modern world he thus ushers in with all its more brutal realities, its contempt for beauty, its insistence upon mere life? He seems to thrust a newspaper into our hands and therewith to banish for ever all that was most quiet, holy and of good report. In his rude and irreverent and irrefutable voice we may catch the first accents of the Revolution, in his establishment and success the first glimpse of our Democracy. (pp. 264-68)

> *Edward Hutton, in his* Pietro Aretino: The Scourge of Princes, *Houghton Mifflin Company, 1922, 268 p.*

SAMUEL PUTNAM   (essay date 1926)

[*Putnam was a prominent American translator, poet, essayist, and editor. In the following excerpt from the introduction to his translation of a selection of Aretino's works, he deems Aretino "the first modern realist of importance."*]

Aretino today is barely a name. He is chiefly known in Europe, and in America by a few collectors of *erotica,* as the author of certain obscene *Dialogues* and obscener *Sonnets.* True, some years ago, a couple of addle-pated college boys got hold of him, went completely out of their heads and—well, the criminal case that ensued, attended by world-wide notoriety, familiarized the public for a fleeting moment with at least the name; and Hearst newspapers even dug up one of Titian's bearded portraits of the "Scourge of Princes." All this, doubtless, has been long since forgotten by the man in the street, and Aretino remains a name for a few Romance professors to conjure with, while if he has any other readers outside the *curiosa* hounds, they are a few pale-handed youths with mildly decadent ambitions who go abrousing in campus libraries.

Sic transit.

If Aretino had been a non-literary personality, the oblivion thus thrust upon him might be understandable. The public may have heard of Machiavelli and the Borgias, for the reason that these names, in a manner, have passed into schoolboy language as classy synonyms or flossy references; Cellini, too, may be fairly well known by those more or less directly concerned with the arts, or who have been told that his *Autobiography* is first-rate reading; but how many would be able to state, for example, who Guicciardini was?

But though most of those who collect and read him—the smut-hounds who trail him down, along with the *Venus in Furs* or Pierre Louys' *Aphrodite*—have no suspicion of the fact, Aretino was something a good deal more than a mere picturesque figure in a picturesque age. He was, among other things, the first modern realist of importance, the first writer who dared to break away from the old, dead and deadening, hide-bound traditions of the classicists and the academicians and to write in the language of the people, the language of the street and the market place, even that of the brothel. He was, in a way, the Ring Lardner of his day (plus, of course, much more frankness than our twentieth-century Puritan America permits). Or, we might call him the H L. Mencken (with all scruples removed) or, possibly, the Ben Hecht of his time. (His defense of his *Sonetti lussuriosi* reads strangely like Hecht's flauntingly youthful preface to *Fantazius Mallare*.) It would not be wholly improper to term him the Rabelais of the *cinquecento,* though he lacks the gargantuan, cosmic vitality of François of blessed memory. As a matter of fact, he is the antecedent of Rabelais, his contemporary in years, and of Molière, both of whom would seem to owe him no little, as do, also, Shakespeare and Balzac.

Aretino is not only the first modern realist; he is the first modern journalist. The founder and "first great Adventurer of the Press" Edward Hutton, in his scholarly and lonesome English biography, calls him. In his *Pasquinades,* his *giudizii* and his letters, as Hutton points out, Aretino really conducted what corresponds to a great modern newspaper, in which scheme, his religious writings (the *prose sacre*) are the pompous, inflated editorials. He is, in a sense, in his "yellow" proclivities, the forerunner of Mr. Hearst, Lord Northcliffe and others, while he is also the father of the awful tribe of modern press agents, who, when they wish to put on airs, become "publicists." It is his boast that "throughout the world, Fame is sold by me." He had to have publicity; it was his living; and he certainly knew how to set about to get it.

He is more than this, however. He is also the first modern critic of the arts—of painting, as of literature. Indeed, he seems to have had, as will be shown later, even more feeling for painting than for literature. His genius was essentially a plastic one, and there was a reason for his almost life-long intimacy with Titian. Like Titian, he was a realist of the senses. De Sanctis, in the role of moralizing professor, finds fault with him for not drawing any "moral impression or elevation of soul" from his contemplation of and love for nature [see excerpt dated 1879]. The kick which Aretino got was a purely sensuous, purely aesthetic one; and in this, he is truly a modernist.

Here, then, we have a man who may be called, in point of chronology, the first literary realist, the first journalist, the first publicist, the first art critic. Surely, such a man has his importance. Is a first-hand knowledge of that importance to be confined to a few Romance instructors and their scattered seminars, for which only a handful of bespectacled graduate students ever enroll? Is the public to know Aretino only as the purveyor of smut, as a writer who is on the *Index expurgatorius* of the contemporary Puritan, and who must, therefore, be smuggled past the customs as a contraband?

Why is this? Why is it that Aretino, for four centuries, has been the victim of a world-wide conspiracy of *shush?* Even the prurient virtue of our combined comstockeries is scarcely enough to account for this, since, with the mouldering influence of time, a bad boy of literature usually puts on the more or less sacrosanct garb of a "classic" and, thenceforth, is looked upon as naughty but, for the sake of art, as comparatively innocuous. Rabelais is a case in point. The *Maitre* is now seldom bothered on the metropolitan stalls. He hardly could be sold, it is true, in Dayton, Tenn., but in Chicago, the Committee of Fifteen does not stay up nights tracking him down. And yet, Aretino, as has been stated, is the godfather of Gargantua and Pantagruel. Why, then, all the animus against Pietro?

The answer is, Aretino is a bad example, not on the sexual side, but in his attitude toward life.

He is capable of being, upon occasion, the most tremendous hypocrite, as in his official and semi-official letters and in his *"laudi,"* those cringing, knuckling sonnets that he wrote to order. In this, he was conforming, outwardly and for his own shrewd purposes, to the custom of the age; it was a part of his game. In reality, he is a hardened, ingrown and parading cynic, and that is one thing your Babbitt will never forgive.

Hutton calls Aretino "the negation of the Renaissance" [see excerpt dated 1922]. He is more than that. He is the living negation of all the copybook maxims. He knows that early to bed and early to rise may make a man healthy, but that it will never make him wealthy or wise. Get all you can while the getting's good is, rather, his motto, as it is that of the American big business man; only, the latter will never, never stand for a formulation of his practice. Aretino, like the captain of industry, started at the bottom and worked his way up. But how? And to what? He should have ended on the gallows, but as it was, he came near being made a prince of the church. In other words, he beat the game, and that is, of all things, unforgivable; it is worse than breaking the bank at Monte Carlo.

Aretino has no illusions about himself or, above all, about humanity. He knows human lusts and meanesses and depravations, and speculates in them; they are his stock in trade. He is a non-conformist. He lives his own life, amid his harem of beautiful women and his art treasures, and remarks, with a sneer, "Who's going to keep me from it?" He prefers a talk with Titian or an interview with a lady of fortune to going to mass. When, on his death bed, he is given the holy oils, he bursts forth, to the horror of the pious ones about him, with "Now that I'm all greased up, don't let the rats get me." And he is the man who, according to tradition, had for epitaph:

> Here lies Aretino, the Tuscan poet, Who slandered every one but God, and said: Sorry, but if I ever met him, I did not know it.

No, Aretino is not, precisely, a Sunday school lad. He was no worse, probably, than Machiavelli, Guicciardini or a hundred others of his day; but Machiavelli and Guicciardini, putting on the cloak of political necessity, have acquired a certain respectability in their *diablerie.* What is wrong for an individual may be, it seems, right for a nation. Aretino merely applies the *Principe* and the *Ricordi politici* to private life; but that is always dangerous. It is doubly dangerous in a democracy. Every republic is replete with Aretinos, but they stay under cover and disguise their depradations under moralistic croakings. To speak out, to be frank with one's self and others, is the unpardonable sin. It is to be doubted if, after all, Aretino ever could have existed elsewhere than in such an oligarchy as that which flourished in Venice under the Medici.

This is the real reason for the conspiracy of silence against him. This is the reason the world has chosen to overlook his undeniable contributions to literature, art and the spirit of modernity. It is time, in the name of scholarship, that the veil were lifted. Let us take the man as he was and, giving him his dues, good and bad, endeavor to place him as accurately as possible. In the course of the process, there are a few of us, it is to be hoped, confirmed amoralists, who love color and take it where we find it, who will be content to rejoice in the vivid reds of the picture and to leave the rest to priests and pedants.

Aretino, like Baudelaire, has been the victim of a legend, a legend which he encouraged, rather than discouraged. When they accused him of being the son of a prostitute, he admitted it. When it was found that he was, really, the son of a shoe-maker (*acconciator di scarpe*), which was far more damning, he trumpeted the fact to the world in a letter to the Duke of Medici. Like Baudelaire, he was quite willing to do anything *pour èpater la bourgeoisie,* and, like the author of *Les Fleurs du mal,* he paid the penalty. Baudelaire had his Maxime du Camp, of whom Huneker so effectually disposes (see his "The Baudelaire Legend" in *Egoists*); Aretino had his pseudo-Berni. And the resulting legend, in each case, has displayed a surprising persistence, and resistance to the discoveries of scholars.

Nevertheless, despite all legends and overthrowings of legends, the man himself remains a miracle of vividness. The names and titles that were conferred upon him during his life time are an indication of this. Ariosto won Aretino's undying gratitude by referring to him, in the *Orlando Furioso,* as "the divine Pietro Aretino, the Scourge of Princes." The "Scourge," as Hutton remarks, might more aptly have been called "the Screw of Princes." *"Buffone, cativo"* his own townsman, Meforo Nucci, calls him. He was looked upon, in turn, as a magician and a "prophet" (*propheta divino*). He was the Ward McAllister of his day and refers to himself as *"censor del mondo altero."* Coming to bless and remaining to curse, he stands forth as a "charlatan of genius." Francis I sends him a chain of gold, with vermilion-colored serpents' tongues, bearing the exergue: *"Lingua eius loquetur mendacium"* ("His tongue speaks lies"). Aretino is delighted and is never seen without the chain thereafter; it appears in all his portraits. And yet, this man, whom the mighty college of cardinals could not silence, boasts always that "I speak the truth," insisting that therein lies his strength. De Sanctis implies that he is a "poltroon," but it is still Aretino's vaunt that "With a goose-quill and a bottle of ink, I mock myself of the universe." (pp. 11-17)

This, then, was . . . Pietro Aretino, the first modern journalist, perhaps the greatest blackmailer in all history, the first truly modern exponent of the "poison pen," to lift one of the pet phrases of our own brethren of the yellow press. There is a constant temptation, in the case of Aretino, to pile up names and adjectives; he lends himself to it so readily. But when the adjectives and the picturesque and picaresque titles have been sifted, what remains?

Edward Hutton calls him "the founder of the European press" and adds that he "used the hitherto unsuspected weapon of publicity with an incomparable appreciation of its power." For "European press," one might read "modern press."

"And if we add to this," continues the Englishman, in the introduction to his biography, "that he contrived a weapon for his own ends which has in our day come to be more poweful than any established government or elected parliament or hereditary monarchy—publicity, the press—there is more than sufficient excuse for this book. . . . Aretino's virtues . . . are always those of a journalist, never those of a man of letters. His strength is in his spontaneity, his ability to write what is in his head almost without a second thought."

And, it may here be parenthesized, is not this the prime virtue of the modern newspaper man—his spontaneity? Your present-day reporter also writes "what is in his head, almost with-

out a second thought;" and if he does not happen, usually, to have a head, it is that which accounts for the poor quality of our contemporary journalism. Aretino, who, in his more pompous letters, is the prototype of the twentieth-century editorial-writer, in his *giudizii* and his Pasquinades is, frequently, the antecedent of the rewrite-man; while in his **Ragionamenti,** he is the Ring Lardner, risen out of the local room.

Yes, Aretino was the first of the tribe of "yellow" journalists. He told the truth, not lies—*"per finger no, ma per predire il vero,"* he assures us in one of his sonnets—and he strutted all over the shop about it; but so, too, does Mr. Hearst. Something, it is to be presumed, may depend on the manner in which the truth is told, and the act of telling it may readily become the worst form of blackmail. In any event, the man who goes in for it makes the discovery of a certain power; he makes powerful friends and powerful enemies; and that is what Aretino did. If the latter were living today, there is not much doubt that he would be one of our "Napoleons of the Press."

It is interesting to note that modern journalism grew out of the Renaissance, in the person of Pietro Aretino, the greatest of the Renaissance decadents. Aretino revolutionized the character of two of the nearest approaches to the thing that the Revival of Learning had sported: the Pasquinade and the *giudizio.*

Pasquin was a fifteenth-century schoolmaster. Like many schoolmasters, he had a scurrilous tongue. The Pasquinade, therefore, retains the qualities of its nominal founder: scholasticism and scurrility.

"Pasquin, indeed," says Hutton, "is of the modern world and is a sign of the return of free satire, anonymous and violent and often as vulgar and salacious as anything in antiquity. He is not really of the people: he is the creation of the learned, of scholars and men of letters. He is part of the Renaissance, and, in the age of Aretino, was bound to be abused. But he was already famous before Aretino transformed him for his own purposes during the election of Pope Adrian VI."

The Pasquinades were originally attached to the statue of Pasquino, but they seem very early to have been distributed in the form of fly-sheets, in the manner of the *istorie* or "extras" which are cried in the first act of **La Cortigiana.** The first Pasquinades were extremely pedantic; they were of the scholars, not of the people. Aretino transformed these exercises and made them popular, for his own purpose, which at the time happened to be the advancement of Cardinal de' Medici's claim to the papal throne. Aretino turned out his Pasquinades, furiously and daily. The fact that he "lost the election" mattered little; he had made himself famous—and infamous. It was at this time that amazement was expressed at the college of cardinals' not being able to silence him. It was the old order against the new; the latter had shown its teeth and won, even in the temporary victory of the old.

And when, later, the Doge of Venice interfered to make peace between Aretino and the Pope, it was but another sign that the press had been recognized and had to be tolerated, whether the powers that be liked it, altogether, or not. A new social entity had been discovered, public opinion, the new tyrant of the new democracies. The same might be said of Francis I.'s chain of gold; kings as well as doges bowed.

Aretino revolutionized the *giudizio,* as well as the Pasquinade. The former, before his time, had been an *Old Moore's*

Almanac. Pietro cut out the astrology and the weather and, as the modern journalist would say, "played up the news," putting in, often, even a little more "punch" than would get by the average copy desk of today. The *giudizii* had at first appeared once a year, but who ever heard of a once-a-year newspaper? Aretino issued one whenever he felt the need of self-expression or money, particularly the latter.

Indeed, Aretino's writings as a whole constitute a sort of daily journal of his times. Their quality, with the exception of the **Ragionamenti** and his plays, is essentially ephemeral. It is because their author so sums up his age, the chromatic *cinquecento*, that they are worth preserving and worth reading.

Aretino is not only the first modern journalist; he is the first modern critic of painting.

Like Baudelaire, whom Courbet taught to mix a palette, Pietro, it is likely, studied painting in his youth, and like Baudelaire, he retained a keen interest in the art all his life, while his dearest and closest friendships lay among painters. We know, at any rate, that he was lampooned by his enemies as having been formerly a painter; but if it was the fact that he had been, there was in it nothing strange. Many a writer has walked through the studio, returned to it and remained to chat. Aretino's chattings (*"ciancie,"* he would have called them) are our first modern art criticism.

Speaking of this, Eugenio Camerini says:

> The truth is, Aretino, in his writings, displays sometimes the desire to compete with the rich palette of his painter friends. His familiarity with Titian and his affection for the art helped him sufficiently. Certainly, the best colorists among French writers of today have served their apprenticeship to art, either as students or as admirers. Dante drew. Aretino was fond of decoration and color-harmony, both in his habits of thought and in his person; *dissonance appeared only in his actions.*

The italics here are the present writer's own; they are employed to stress what impresses him as being an important point in any "psyching" which may be attempted of Pietro.

The fact would seem to be, Aretino had a natural inclination toward the art of painting, which was piqued by association. When a man is found consorting with painters or writers, barbers or plumbers, as a class, it generally means that he has some predilection for one pursuit or the other. In Rome, we find Aretino, with Raimondi and Giulio Romano, getting into a scrape over the artists' designs and Pietro's **Sonnets.** When he goes to Venice, his friend, Sansovino, makes him acquainted with Titian, and the three set up their "triumvirate." The triple friendship, so far as we are able to judge, was a very genuine one on all sides. It is easy to point out that Aretino was useful to both Titian and Sansovino in the capacity of press agent. In a way, he *was* their press agent. He introduced Titian to Charles V. and put himself out of the way to procure commissions for his painter friend. We have seen that he was accused of taking a "rake-off" on these orders. But there was, in this three-sided friendship, something far deeper than this. Any one who doubts it has but to read Aretino's letters to Titian. They are, by far, the sincerest he ever penned. In these, he is human, not pompous, and at least one of them, the one describing the view from his window in Venice, has a true plastic quality.

In these letters, too, we glimpse a total absence of "side" between the men. Titian, like the women he painted, had a good, lusty appetite for life that almost rivaled Aretino's own. We see him as a chap who liked a good bottle of wine, a pretty girl and a well-cooked thrush. Highest compliment of all, Titian often painted in the *casa Aretina,* the walls of which he decorated with his brush. And Aretino sought the painter's opinion on everything from the character of his daughter Adria's face to the color qualities of a landscape. He took a keen interest in his friend's work, and his description of the "Annunciation," now lost to us, is a bit of verbal coloring in the master's own style.

No, there would seem to be some deeper explanation of this triumvirate than mere utility. (pp. 41-6)

Aretino had a real *flair* for painting criticism. In his criticism, he is a pure realist, of the school of Titian. He has no suspicion that painting may have any other end. He would not have appreciated the Byzantines or other primitives. But in this, he was true to his age. It is only within the last century that something beyond realism has come into painting.

We should be grateful for one thing, and that is, that he was not a moralist in his criticism. De Sanctis finds fault with him on this score, but De Sanctis is wrong. There is no reason why the sight of a beautiful landscape should awake "any moral impression or any elevation of soul." Aretino was not a nature-worshiper or a theorist of any sort. He was a pure sensualist in his reactions, and this it was that would have made him an excellent critic of the art of painting at any time from his own century to, let us say, the advent of Manet.

What, finally, is the literary significance, the literary importance of Pietro Aretino? This question has been answered, to a degree, at the outset of this paper; the answer is the justification of the present translation of Aretino's representative works. But a few details remain to be sketched in.

In the first place, Pietro had few if any illusions with regard to his own literary quality. Just as he made capital of his lack of academic knowledge by turning on the pedants, so he sometimes bragged about the manner in which he "got by," as we would say, in a literary way. In his sonnet, *Togli il lauro,* he tells us, quite frankly, *"Non son poeta"*—"I am not a poet"—and boasts that, while "neither a poet nor an emperor," he yet has filched the laurels from Homer's and from Caesar's brow. In this sonnet also he asserts that his style has been his star, and that his reputation is due, not to fictionizing (*per finger no*) but to speaking the truth. We know that, while with unwise worldlings, he sometimes passed as a "learned man," he himself had no such illusions; and we know, too, that he had a vast and slightly overweening respect for writers and men of letters; these latter were the only ones towards whom he seems to have cherished a salutary fear; a mere prince of the earth might be cast down by the thunder of the famed Aretino pen, but a minor pedant, through the employment of a similar weapon, might work his ruin.

What was this "Aretino style?" Aretino himself tells us that the phrase was coined through "the hairsplittings of pedants," but he nourished the legend. Speaking of Aretino's style, Hutton is worth quoting once more:

> Aretino's page is full of life, hard to read, spontaneous and yet packed tight, worked upon and forged, full of queer instances and odd comparisons, glittering with wit and every sort of comic exaggera-

tion. Such work does not exist outside his pages. His successor was Rabelais; but also Molière. He has the robust joy of the one, but something of the intellectual charm of the other.

On the whole, Hutton finds him "the most significant and certainly the nearest to life of any Italian writer of his day."

Aretino's greatest contribution lies in the breath of realism which, in his revolt against pedantry and academicism, he brought to literature. As his British biographer remarks, his work has "the smell of the city" and "the odour of life." It has all the futile turmoil, all the grandiloquent and sterile gestures of the metropolis.

But Aretino was not always, by any means, the realist and the modernist. As a matter of fact, by far the greater bulk of his prose work, if we take his pompously inflated letters (many of them) and his turgidly pietistic religious writings over against his ***Ragionamenti*** and his plays, is of the old, rather than of the newer school.

Among the severer of Aretino's critics were the Frenchmen, Bayle and Montaigne. The former wrote [see excerpt dated 1702]:

> This man, who is so satiric a poet, is prodigal of his praises to the last degree. We find the most pompous hyperboles and the most rampant flatteries in those letters which he wrote to kings and princes, to the generals of armies, to cardinals and to the other great ones of the world. To such an extent is this true that one sees in him the airs of an amateur, who is endeavoring to make himself feared or to extort favors, and all the baseness of an author who is demanding, very humbly, a morsel of bread. He draws upon the most touching expressions to depict his poverty; and he resorts even to the language of Canaan—makes use of devout phrases, that is—the better to excite compassion and to move to charity those persons who look to God for the recompense of their good works.

Bayle then goes on to speak of the letters.

"We have," he says, "six volumes of the letters, which are not worth a great deal (*qui ne valent pas grand' chose*) . . . It is a dry work, and one very like an unfurnished house in a waste and sandy place."

Mènage also has something to say on the subject.

"I have read," he says, "all the letters of Pietro Aretino, without finding in them anything which I was able to make use of in any of my books. There is nothing but the style to be had from their reading."

While Mènage praises the style, Montaigne condemns it as: "A fashion of speaking that is puffed and gushy, made up of ingenious points, in truth, but far-fetched and fantastic." The author of the *Essays*, nevertheless, concedes Aretino a "certain eloquence."

Commenting on such passages as these, Camerini makes what impresses one as being a very good criticism of Aretino's critics.

"Bayle and Montaigne," he says, "were not able to savor Aretino's style, for the reason that the one was not looking for and the other did not grasp that species of erudition which is to be found in Aretino's writings: an erudition based, not upon ancient standards or solemn facts, but upon a feeling for life, the same erudition that Macaulay was to transform into a splendid picture of the life of nations."

And this, finally, is Aretino's contribution: that, breaking the chains of a tradition that had become slavery, he was the first to declare war on the tribe of pedants, whom, like the poor, we have always with us. The fact that his revolt was motivated by purely selfish reasons means, simply, that it was a vital matter with him.

And yet, Aretino's direct influence, even upon his own literature, has been surprisingly small. He may have had "the root of all good literature in him, in his freedom from pedantry and closeness to life," but it was slow in telling. His influence was greater in France than in Italy. It is generally conceded that Rabelais owes him a distinct debt, as does Molière, particularly in his Tartuffe. We do not know just how direct Shakespeare's indirect debt was, but Aretino's Marescalco would appear to have been the antecedent of Malvolio, though it cannot compare with the Elizabethan character in full-flavored richness. But the Venice of Pietro *was* the Venice of Shakespeare's early plays, from whatever source the English poet got them.

Otherwise, Aretino's influence in English has been almost entirely negligible. Sir Thomas Wyatt, in his *Penitential Psalms,* owes Aretino something; the early part of Sir Thomas' work was translated, and the latter part imitated, from the Italian writer's ***Sette Psalmi.*** One agrees with Hutton, however, that Sir Thomas is "very dull stuff."

We also find Thomas Nash referred to by Lodge as "the true English Aretino." This seems to have been due, chiefly, to the fact that Nash, like Aretino, employed the vernacular for comic effect and was given to the coining of "boisterous" words from other languages. Aside from this, there is not much in common between the two.

Here, it may be remarked that Shakespeare also shares these same qualities with Aretino, and it was only a few years later that he was to perform his own experiments in the use of the vernacular (also for "comic relief").

References to Aretino in the sixteenth century are fairly numerous. Hutton cites a number from Gabriel Harvey's *Marginalia* [see Further Reading]. . . . (pp. 47-51)

As to translations, Aretino, as stated, has been practically untouched in English. Hutton says that the only translation into English of any of his works was ***The Crafty Whore,*** published in London in 1658 and taken partly from the ***Ragionamenti.*** This is not precisely correct. There is a translation of the ***Dialogues,*** made by I do not know whom, that is sold by the "bookleggers" at an exorbitant price. There is also a very lewd rendering of the ***Sonetti lussuriosi,*** by "an English poet," rumored to be from the pen of Oscar Wilde, but which, those who have read it assure me, Oscar undoubtedly never saw. At the time I write this, I have not been able to get hold of either of these translations. That of the ***Dialogues*** is, probably, the 6-volume one published by Isodore Liseux in 1889.

There would seem, then, to be room for a translation of at least the representative works, not for the smut-hounds, whose exclusive property Aretino has been in the past, but for the general cultivated reader, as well as for scholars whose working language happens to be English.

Aretino's ultimate importance lies, not so much in what he wrote as in what he was, what he stood for. With Ariosto, Titian and Machiavelli, he *is* the *cinquecento.* But the others, even Cellini, invoked the past; Aretino insulted it—insulted it, wholesomely.

His archetypal enemy is Luther, from whose half-baked pedantry has sprung the unlovely phenomenon of Protestantism, which achieves a horrible culmination in the barren and ugly little frame meeting house of the American prairies. Luther appealed to the individual conscience and, by so doing, set up a new tyranny, the tyranny of the illiterate. Aretino appealed only to—Pietro Aretino and his will; but in the course of the process, he set in motion the tyranny of the modern press.

Hutton calls Aretino "the negation of the Renaissance." He was, if we take "Renaissance" in its narrower sense, that of the Revival of Classical Learning; but this, as any undergraduate student of history knows, was not the whole Renaissance; it was merely one side of the Renascence. Let us say that Aretino was, rather, the Renaissance on its last legs, the Renaissance gone to seed. He represents the well known phenomenon of decadence. There is no need to get out our Paul Bourget and our Havelock Ellis to tell us this. What a glorious red rag he would have been to that Philistine bull, Max Nordau!

The trouble is, the word decadence is too frequently garbled to imply something naughty, like the *Fleurs du mal.* Suppose we take it, for once, in its true technical sense, as a process of breaking up and breaking down—as an expansion, a pushing out and back of the limits of language, life and thought. In this process, the old becomes a manure-heap to fertilize the growth of the new. But from this rich and decomposing earth there sometimes spring strange poisonous flowers, like the mandragora. Of such was Pietro Aretino, the nightshade of the sixteenth century. (pp. 51-3)

> Samuel Putnam, *"Pietro Aretino: Poison-Flower of the Renaissance,"* in The Works of Aretino, Vol. 1 *by Pietro Aretino, translated by Samuel Putnam, 1926. Reprint by Covici-Friede, Publishers, 1933, pp. 9-53.*

JEFFERSON BUTLER FLETCHER   (essay date 1934)

[*Fletcher was an American educator and poet best known for his critical studies of Dante and of the Italian Renaissance. In the following excerpt from* Literature of the Italian Renaissance *(1934), he briefly assesses Aretino's* Orazio *and* Ragionamenti.]

Neither as man-of-letters nor as man was Pietro Aretino all bad. It seems he could not have been, and been the intimate friend he was with Titian, whose magnificent portrait of him hangs in the Palazzo Chigi at Rome. He made his money often vilely, but spent it generously and charitably. He was always ready to help the needy, especially struggling artists. His private life was dissolute; but it is said that, before discarding his mistresses, he married them off well, and saw to it that their husbands were faithful. He was a tender father to at least two of his illegitimate children,—daughters whom he named, as became his international importance, Adria and Austria. Once he really loved,—a young girl who deserted him for a younger lover, was herself deserted, and returned to die in Aretino's arms.

Similar contradictions appear in his writings. Himself unlearned, and proud of it, he ridiculed the purism and academicism of the day. He hated Luther as a good Catholic, but

even more for his pedantries,—*"Lutero pedantissimo!"* he exclaimed. He would have no books in his study, only pen, paper and ink. Yet by common consent of critics, he wrote in his *Orazia* the best regular tragedy of the age, the only one with life in it. His comedies, too,—of which Gabriel Harvey spoke so highly to Edmund Spenser,—followed, though with certain licences, the prescribed formula of the Roman comedy—as indeed Harvey remarked.

The last irony of Aretino's singular career and reputation is the fact that, although he wrote much and in many kinds and sometimes well, the one of his works to survive today—outside of classrooms and literary histories—is the most infamous one, the so-called *Ragionamenti.* It is, conservatively speaking, the nastiest book ever written, and still fetches, for that reason, a high price among pornographic collectors. (pp. 274-75)

> Jefferson Butler Fletcher, *"Benvenuto Cellini—Pietro Aretino,"* in his Literature of the Italian Renaissance, *The Macmillan Company, 1934, pp. 268-75.*

ERNEST HATCH WILKINS   (essay date 1954)

[*Wilkins was a distinguished American authority on Italian Renaissance literature. In the following excerpt from his 1954* History of Italian Literature, *he briefly assesses Aretino's dramas.*]

In contemporary opinion Pietro Aretino (1492-1556) would probably have been regarded as the leading man of letters of the period, after Bembo. Born in Arezzo, he lived in Rome under Leo X and through the first years of Clement VII: from 1527 on he lived in Venice. He called one of his portraits by his friend Titian (the one in the Pitti Gallery) *una terribile maraviglia:* he was himself a terrible marvel, not only in semblance but in reality. He was terrible in the viciousness of his life and of his writing, especially in the extraordinary system of blackmail that underlies his voluminous correspondence. He was called "the scourge of princes": even the Emperor was among his victims. He was marvelous in the extent to which he imposed himself upon the fearful but admiring imagination of his contemporaries, and in the extent to which, despite his viciousness, he retained the tolerance or the at least apparent friendship of many decent people; and he was marvelous in his polygraphic fertility.

In addition to his letters (of which he collected some three thousand for publication) he wrote pasquinades; lyrics of many different kinds; satires; four unfinished epics; prose dialogues; the *Giudizi,* annually issued prognostications of what would befall certain persons and certain places in the year ahead; a treatise "On the Humanity of Christ"; an exposition of Biblical mysteries; pious lives of Mary, of St. Thomas Aquinas, and of St. Catherine of Siena; a prose paraphrase of the Penitential Psalms; various miscellaneous compositions; five comedies; and a tragedy.

The earliest of his comedies, *La cortigiana, Life at Court,* was (in its first form) written in Rome in 1525; the second, *Il marescalco, The Farrier,* was written in 1526 or 1527 for the court of Mantua; and the rest were written in Venice, *La Talanta* (a personal name) in 1541, *Lo ipocrito* in 1542, and *Il filosofo* in 1544. All are in prose and in five acts; all have twenty or more characters; all except the *Marescalco* are confusingly intricate; and all breathe corruption. Their dialogue is vivacious; and they offer picturesque glimpses of everyday street life, in which such folk as a fishmonger, a peddler of trinkets, an old-clothes man, and a vender of chapbooks mingle with the inevitable parasites, pedants, braggart soldiers, and rascally servants. The *Cortigiana* presents a devastating picture of the lower levels of life in papal Rome, and sets forth in some detail the means of obtaining advancement in the papal court. The Hypocrite, an unctuous and unscrupulous friar who is constantly mouthing *carità,* serves at least to anticipate the far greater figure of Tartuffe. The Philosopher rejoices in the name Plataristotele.

Two years after the writing of the *Filosofo* Aretino entered the field of tragedy with his *Orazia, The Tragedy of the Horatii,* which is Senecan rather than Greek in its general character. The story is Livy's familiar story of the combat of the Horatii and the Curiatii, of the bitter lamentations of the Horatian sister wedded to one of the Curiatii, of the fatal wrath of the triumphant Horatius against his sister, and of the final clement punishment of Horatius. Aretino, writing in this instance with more artistic patience than usual, attains a considerable degree of tragic dignity: the central situation, in which a relentless patriotism slays an unyielding love, is well handled. But the moralizing dialogues are too many and too long; too much of the essential action is reported by witnesses; and the final *deus ex machina* is very mechanical indeed. With all its limitations, however, the *Orazia* is the best Italian tragedy of the sixteenth century. (pp. 240-41)

Ernest Hatch Wilkins, "Comedy and Tragedy," in his A History of Italian Literature, *edited by Thomas G. Bergin, revised edition, Cambridge, Mass.: Harvard University Press, 1974, pp. 237-43.*

MARVIN T. HERRICK (essay date 1960)

[*Herrick was an American dramatist and essayist. In the following excerpt from his* Italian Comedy in the Renaissance *(1960), he examines Aretino's comedies, comparing them with those of Ben Jonson.*]

Between 1525 and 1542 the great satirist Pietro Aretino wrote five comedies in prose, two of which, *La cortigiana* (*The Courtesan*) and *Il marescalco* (*The Horse Doctor*), are among the most remarkable plays of the century.

Although his plays reflect many characteristic qualities of the learned comedy, Aretino was not a typical learned dramatist; he was more like Ruzzante, the great writer of farces. Both the *Cortigiana* and the *Marescalco* are essentially farces extended to five acts. Both Aretino and Ruzzante were naturalists, both rebelled at the constraint of classical models, both were contemptuous of "literary" drama. Ruzzante excelled in the representation of peasant life, Aretino in the representation of urban life. Ruzzante, it may be recalled, repeatedly scoffed at classical and neoclassical rules, and Aretino made his position clear in the prologue to his first play, the *Cortigiana:* "If you see the characters enter on the stage more than five times, don't laugh, because the chains that hold the mills on the river would never hold the madmen of today. Moreover, don't wonder if the comic style is not observed as ordinarily required, because we in Rome live in another manner than that of Athens."

The symmetry, the restraint, the economy that distinguish Machiavelli's masterpieces are not to be found in Aretino's rollicking comedies. Aretino could and did borrow from the ancients, and probably from Machiavelli as well, but he went his own boisterous way, ever ready to sacrifice continuity of plot for a good belly laugh, a jibe at an enemy, or a flattering tribute to friend or patron. Most readers will not quarrel with these digressions, for they are often the most colorful scenes in his plays. Occasionally his discussions of politics, of arts and letters, are tiresome and add little or nothing to the play.

Since he was a very astute man, Aretino was well aware of the liberties he took with the conventional dramaturgy. He was aware, for example, that his *Cortigiana* was too long and too loose—it has 106 scenes—and he made the lackey Rosso comment on this quality at the very end of the play: "Folks, whoever would blame the length of our sermon is little used to the court, because if he knew that the fashion in Rome was to run to great length he would not expect us to do otherwise; he will praise our long babblings, because these goings-on could not be recounted in *saecula saeculorum.*" Aretino justified his own composition, as other writers have done, on the grounds of naturalism.

The farcical plot of the *Cortigiana* is relatively simple; it is the gulling of two silly men, a Roman courtier and a visitor from Siena. The two actions run more or less parallel, being loosely connected by the mechanical device of mutual acquaintanceship. The courtier Parabolano (chatterer) fancies himself desperately in love with a young lady who doesn't even know that he exists. His knavish lackey Rosso connives with a bawd named Alvigia to palm off a baker's wife in place of the divine Donna Livia. The Sienese Maco is made the butt of a more outrageous prank. Maco has come to Rome to learn how to become a cardinal. He at once falls into the hands of a waggish painter, Maestro Andrea, who promises to make him a courtier first and then a cardinal. Maco is put through the full treatment reserved for simple-minded well-to-do yokels. The plot, however, often seems incidental to the scenes of local color, the satire on the papal court, and the exhibition of extravagant characters.

A good example of the naturalistic yet highly colored episodes comes early in the play, a cross section of street life in sixteenth-century Italy. Maco, accompanied by his servant Sanese, has just arrived in Rome. He has already met Maestro Andrea, who has promised to make him an accomplished courtier. Maco is very anxious to begin his training at once.

SANESE. Say "your worship." Now listen to the master, what he would say: "I commend myself to your worship."
MACO. I commend myself to your worship. With cap in hand, no?
SANESE. Yes, Signor. Draw yourself up, straighten your mantle in the back, speak roundly and carefully. Walk solemnly. Good, very good!
(*Enter a wandering rogue who sells histories* [*istorie*].)
ROGUE. Fine histories, fine histories! The war with the Turk in Hungary, the sermons of Fra Martino, the Church Council, histories, histories, the English affair, the parade of the pope and the emperor, the circumcision of the Hungarian governor, the sack of Rome, the siege of Florence, the Marseilles Conference with its result, histories, histories!
MACO. Run, fly, trot, here's sixpence, buy me the *Book of the Courtier,* which will make me a courtier before the maestro comes. But don't you become a courtier before me, you understand?
SANESE. The devil no. You want books, orations,

documents? O there, O you! May you break your
neck! He has turned the corner; I must go after him.
MACO. Go, I say, go!

There are frequent attacks on the corrupt life at the papal
court. Usually this satire is fitted to the situation and the
characters, but sometimes it seems to be brought in merely
to give the author another chance to vent his spleen.

When Maestro Andrea gives Maco his first lesson in the art
of the courtier he outlines the fundamentals: "The main thing
the courtier needs to know is how to swear; he should be a
gambler, spiteful, a whoremonger, a heretic, a flatterer, slan-
derous, ungrateful, ignorant, an ass; he should know how to
boast, to be a fop, and to be both active and patient." Maco
takes so readily to these lessons that Andrea soon regards
him as a star pupil: "I am of the opinion that this fellow, since
he is a fool, a very rich simpleton, and a twenty-four-carat
gull, may become the greatest favorite in the court."

Sometimes the satire has a more serious tone, as in the complaints of Flamminio, one of Parabolano's chamberlains.
Flamminio advises old Sempronio against introducing his
son at court; he paints such an appalling picture of the courtier's life that the old man changes his plans.

> SEMPRONIO. Go with God. It is clear, then, that
> nowadays it is better to be in hell than in the court.
> FLAMMINIO. A hundred times better, because in
> hell the soul is tormented and in the court both soul
> and body.
> SEMPRONIO. We'll speak of this again; and I'm de-
> termined to strangle Camillo with my own hands
> before I send him to court.

Flamminio himself has spent a lifetime trying to get ahead in
the world of fashion and has nothing to show for his labors
but a wasted body and a despairing mind: "When I stand before a mirror and see my white beard, tears come to my eyes
from the great pity I have for myself, who have nothing to
live for. Ah me! Unhappy me! How many knaves, how many
grooms, how many ignoramuses, how many gluttons do I
know who are rich, and I am a beggar! Go to, I am determined to go away to die; and I am sick at heart that I came
here young and go away old, that I came here all dressed up
and go away naked, that I came here satisfied and leave in
despair."

But Flamminio has no place to go, for the rest of Italy is
scarcely better than Rome, where, as his friend Valerio says,
there is at least Ippolito de' Medici. Flamminio, however, has
had enough of Rome: "Perhaps I shall go to Venice, where
I have already been, and enrich my poverty with her liberty,
which there at least is not at the whim of a favorite; nor does
every favorite there assassinate poor wretches; for only Venice holds the scale of justice in balance, and there alone fear
of disgrace does not force you to flatter one who yesterday
was a louse."

This serious tone, resembling the tone of Jonson's *Volpone*,
is more than counterbalanced by the mad gaiety of most
scenes. Maco, Parabolano, the bawd Alvigia, and lackey
Rosso are especially diverting.

Maco is finally made a courtier by being parboiled and
purged in a huge kettle. When he recovers himself after this
ordeal he is perfectly convinced that the treatment is successful. (pp. 85-8)

Signor Parabolano is described by his lackey thus: "Our mas-

ter is the kindest hangman, the most excellent knave, and the
most venerable ass in all Italy." The courtier is not quite so
bad as Rosso depicts him; his worst qualities are ignorance
and gullibility, and all of his troubles in the play arise from
his silly vanity, which leads him to believe that all women
must find him irresistible. Of course he is encouraged in his
foppery by Rosso, who delights in mischief. Like Lovewit in
Jonson's *Alchemist*, Parabolano is easygoing and good-
natured. He readily forgives his rascally servant in the end
although he has good reason to punish him severely: "I also
pardon you, Rosso, because you're a Greek and have behaved
like a Greek, with the craftiness of a Greek."

Rosso is a descendant of the Roman *servus*, but thoroughly
brought up to date. While he is scheming to make a fool of
his master he yet finds time for other mischief. In the first act
he dickers for some eels, gets cheated, informs a sacristan that
the fishmonger's wife is bewitched and that the man himself
is half mad. Thereupon the sacristan has the poor fellow arrested and flogged. In the fourth act Rosso cheats a Jewish
peddler out of a cloak and then hands him over to the police,
who put him in the stocks. Rosso is jealous of his fellow servants and contemptuous of his betters. When Alvigia, in response to his request for help, proposes that they palm off the
baker's wife on Parabolano in place of Donna Livia, he sees
no reason why the fraud should fail: "Let us suppose that
Togna is ugly and worthless, she will still appear an angel to
the signor, because gentlemen have less taste than a corpse;
they drink the worst wines and eat the vilest food that is
found, thinking them the best and the most precious."

The fraud does fail, however, though its failure owes more to
Togna's jealous husband than to the perception of Parabolano. Togna, believing that her husband is drunk as usual,
puts on his clothes and sneaks out of the house to keep the
assignation arranged by Alvigia. For once, however, Arcolano is sober; he watches his wife dress and sneak out. Then
he gets up, puts on his wife's clothes because she has taken
his, follows her, and overtakes her.

Then follows one of the most ridiculous scenes in the play.
Arcolano, who sports a heavy beard, is dressed in his wife's
petticoats.

> ARCOLANO. I've caught you, I've found you. And
> you, you treacherous old hag, you're here? I'll kill
> both of you. Don't hold me, good sir.
> PARABOLANO. Stand back.
> ARCOLANO. Let me punish my wife and this evil
> old bawd.
> VALERIO. Be quiet. Ha, ha, ha!
> ARCOLANO. Trick me, you whore? Trick me, you
> bawd?
> VALERIO. Ha, ha, ha!
> TOGNA. You lie, you loafer.
> ALVIGIA. Signor Arcolano, be fair.
> PARABOLANO. Is this one your wife?
> ARCOLANO. Yes, Signor.
> PARABOLANO. She looks to me like your husband.
> Ha, ha, ha! Drop that knife! It would be a shame
> if such a fine comedy ended in tragedy.

Alvigia is Aretino's most triumphant characterization and
the most memorable bawd among a host of such creatures on
the Italian stage. She describes herself in the third act:

> In my day neither Lorenzina, nor Beatricicca, nor
> Angioletta of Naples, nor Beatrice, nor Madrema
> mattered, nor was the great empress herself fit to

lace my shoes. The fashions, the masks, the fine houses, the bullfights, the cavalcades, the sables with gold trim, the parrots, the monkeys, and the scores of chamberlains and maidservants were just trifles to me, and the hordes of gentlemen and lords and ambassadors. Ha, ha! I laugh when I recall how I snatched a bishop's miter and put it on the head of one of my maids, mocking the poor man. And a sugar merchant left his stock with me, and for a while everything at my house was seasoned with sugar. Then I caught a disease, the name of which no one knew, yet we treated it as though it were the French evil, and thanks to so many medicines I became an old woman.

A more revealing portrait emerges in the next act, when Alvigia is trying to arrange an assignation for the baker's wife while the baker himself is standing by. (pp. 89-90)

One more specimen of the many ridiculous scenes in this extraordinary comedy will have to suffice. This scene involves Alvigia, Rosso, and Parabolano, and it shows that Aretino was willing to make use of ancient devices when they suited his purpose—in this instance the aside.

> ALVIGIA. I'm ashamed to talk with such a great master in so sorry a gown.
> PARABOLANO. This necklace will brighten it.
> ROSSO. Didn't I tell you that he makes no more of giving a hundred *scudi* than a lawyer of stealing a thousand? (He would strangle a bedbug to drink its blood.)
> ALVIGIA. His countenance shows it.
> ROSSO. He gives us a bale of clothes every year. (Oh, if he would only pay our salaries!)
> ALVIGIA. What a gentleman!
> ROSSO. It's always carnival in the servants' hall. (We're dying of hunger.)
> ALVIGIA. So everyone says.
> ROSSO. We are all his comrades. (So long as he has breath he'll never show a good face to anyone.)
> ALVIGIA. The duty of a great master.
> ROSSO. He would even speak to the pope for the humblest in his household. (If he saw the halter about our throats he wouldn't say a word.)
> ALVIGIA. Don't swear to it.
> ROSSO. He loves us like a father. (He'd sooner see us dead of the plague.)
> PARABOLANO. Rosso knows my nature.

The *Marescalco* was written at Mantua in 1526-27. Also an extended farce, it is not so loosely constructed as the *Courtesan,* perhaps because it used only one prank instead of two. The argument, doubtless suggested by the *Casina* of Plautus or by Machiavelli's *Clizia,* is a practical joke played by the courtiers of Mantua on a young man who is a confirmed woman hater. After Marescalco learns that he must accept a young wife selected by the duke he is assailed from two sides. His old nurse, a pedant, and Messer Jacopo try to convince him that marriage is a comfortable and joyful state, but Ambrogio points out the miseries and evils brought by a wife. An impudent boy named Giannicco further torments him by drumming the baleful word "wife" in his ears at every opportunity. This baiting of the woman hater continues for nearly five acts. (pp. 91-2)

Like the *Cortigiana,* this comedy has naturalistic scenes of local color and brings in several characters, such as a Jewish peddler and a jeweler, that have little to do with the progress of the action. One typical episode is an exchange between the peddler and the boy Giannicco at the beginning of the third act. (pp. 92-3)

Both of these Italian comedies suggest parallels with Ben Jonson's comedy, and the *Marescalco* in particular very probably exercised a direct influence upon the *Silent Woman.* Both Aretino and Jonson may have been indebted to the *Casina* of Plautus, but both of their comedies are in prose, not in verse, and both use the prank of the youth dressed as a bride as the main action, while in the Roman comedy it is merely another prank.

Marescalco and Jonson's Morose, while years apart in age, are so desperately anxious to escape being tied to a wife that they both claim to be impotent at the last moment before the ceremony. Morose is fanatically opposed to noise, any kind of noise, street sounds, bells, horns, the babbling of men as well as the babbling of women. While Marescalco betrays no aversion to any noise except the chattering of a wife, in this particular he is as fanatical as Morose. Another parallel that has not been emphasized, so far as I know, is the very close similarity between the characters of Aretino's Carlo and Jonson's Epicoene. When Epicoene first meets Morose "she" is very demure and speaks so softly, and so little, that Morose, to his delight, can scarcely hear her. When Carlo first appears, he-she, too, is the very pattern of modesty. Jonson's scene is very good, but Aretino's is funnier and better theater. (p. 94)

There are no such close parallels between the *Cortigiana* and any one Jonsonian comedy, yet here some general similarities are even more striking. Aretino's merciless exposure, in the *Cortigiana,* of the corruption of mankind in general, of courtiers, politicians, and churchmen in particular, is certainly comparable to Jonson's exposure of corruption and folly among the courtiers, politicians, merchants, lawyers, and dissenting clergymen in *Volpone,* the *Alchemist,* and *Bartholomew Fair.* Aretino's Maco, for example, with his voluptuous dreams of enjoying all the luxuries of Rome, especially her beautiful women, after he becomes a cardinal, is very like Sir Epicure Mammon in the *Alchemist,* who plans to run riot in similar delights when he becomes rich.

> MAMMON.   I do mean
> To have a list of wives and concubines
> Equal with Solomon. . . .
> I will have all my beds blown up, not stuffed;
> Down is too hard. And then mine oval room
> Filled with such pictures as Tiberius took
> From Elephantis, and dull Aretine
> But coldly imitated.

Some important differences between Aretino and Jonson should be mentioned, of course. Although Rosso ironically refers to the *Cortigiana* as a "sermon," Aretino apparently had no patience with any talk about the didactic function of comedy, while Jonson repeatedly emphasized the moral lessons contained in his lashings of folly and vice. Moreover, the moral Jonson was seldom if ever coarse or bawdy for the fun of it. Aretino was often coarse and bawdy because he himself enjoyed being so. Finally, Jonson was a good poet, and poetic comedies like *Volpone* and the *Alchemist* have qualities of the imagination, as well as the qualities of verse, that do not exist in the naturalistic prose of the "Courtesan."

If Aretino had never written the *Cortigiana* and the *Marescalco,* he would still be an important dramatist because of his *Ipocrito,* which adds highly romantic elements to the conventional matter of neoclassical comedy. With one of the most involved plots in all sixteenth-century drama, the **Hypocrite** starts out like a learned comedy and pursues a regular course with its first action, which is a variation of the twin-brothers situation that stems originally from the *Menaechmi* of Plautus. In addition there is a serious romantic action suggested by an episode in Boiardo's *Orlando innamorato*. The result of combining two such actions, plus some minor actions, is a rapidly moving play that runs from fun to pathos and back to fun.

When the play opens Liseo is fretting over his domestic troubles, which include five daughters, a wife with a mind of her own, and a twin brother who has been missing for years but may still be alive and likely to return at any moment to put another burden on the household. The harassed head of the family turns to Ipocrito for advice. This situation is comparable to that in Molière's *Tartuffe;* Liseo is very like Orgon in some ways and Ipocrito is as hypocritical as Tartuffe though not so vicious. Ipocrito's rule for life indicates the whole pattern of his behavior: "He who does not know how to feign doesn't know how to live, for simulation is a shield that blunts every weapon, or rather a weapon that shatters every shield." Many of the characters, including the servants, detest the pious fraud, but Liseo admires him. At the very peak of his vexations Liseo exclaims, "If the goodness of Ipocrito had not taught me how to live, I would be dead today."

The twin brother, Brizio, returns home in the first act, and from then on there is the usual ridiculous series of mistaken identities. Even Brizio's own son cannot distinguish him from the uncle (Liseo). The romantic action is introduced in the second act. Of Liseo's five daughters, Tansilla is already married to Artico, who has deserted her. Now Liseo is arranging a second marriage for her with Tranquillo. Porfiria is betrothed to Prelio, whom she has sent abroad to fetch some feathers from the fabulous phoenix. Since Prelio has not returned from this fantastic quest, she is now engaged to Corebo. Another young man, Zefiro, is courting another daughter, Annetta. There are the usual gossiping servants and a bawd. About all that is missing from the regular cast of a learned comedy is the braggart soldier.

As soon as the serious action is introduced the dialogue shifts abruptly from wit and humor to romantic sentiment. For example, there is a balcony scene early in the second act. Corebo, like Romeo, is below on the street, Porfiria-Juliet is above.

> COREBO. You observe the decorum that befits the grandeur of your soul, whereby I refresh myself with the breath of words that issue from your mouth.
> PORFIRIA. Heart of mine, be merry, for if that man who for love of me is journeying all over the world does not return this evening within three hours, I promise you I will at once console you.

Did the author of the **Courtesan** and the **Horse Doctor** write these speeches? He must have had his tongue in his cheek. But more such speeches followed them.

Porfiria's first lover, Prelio, does return within three hours. He has been successful in his mission, but is somewhat disillusioned about the life of a romantic lover. "No one," he says, "should undertake to serve [Cupid] who does not have valor and patience, because he is a god that is nourished no less on nobility and hard labor than on laughter and tears, and this I can testify, who to execute Porfiria's vow have traversed be-

yond the course of the sun, flaunting the wrath of the sea, the horrors of the forest, and the crests of mountains."

Within a very short time—Aretino carefully preserved the unities of time and place—Tansilla's husband Artico returns home, to the consternation of her new lover Tranquillo, who learns that Artico means to keep his wife at all costs. Tranquillo's consternation is nothing, however, compared with the flurry of Porfiria when Prelio knocks on her door. Porfiria is a very impulsive young woman, her head stuffed with romantic notions, and she resolves to make a heroic escape from the coil of troubles. She gets some rat poison from a friendly physician. Then she summons Corebo and announces her intention to commit suicide. Corebo argues with her, but gets nowhere, and finally offers reluctantly to share the poison with her.

The first scene in Act 5 is highly emotional. Porfiria tells Prelio that she has taken poison as the only solution to their unhappy triangle. When Prelio declares his wish to join the suicides Porfiria is delighted; in fact, she is in an ecstasy of romantic triumph: "The gulfs will be overcome with admiration when the glowing specters of three lovers soon appear among their flames." The good physician soon brings Prelio back to his senses by informing him that the poison is a harmless sleeping potion and by advising him to behave like a generous man. Prelio tells Corebo the good news and surrenders all claim to Porfiria. He is consoled by another of Liseo's daughters, and the play ends in the usual marriage feast.

The two remaining comedies of Aretino, **La Talanta** and **Il filosofo,** are less original than the other three. The "Philosopher," which satirizes pedantry in the person of Plataristotile, is the least successful of the lot. The **Talanta** is an elaborate adaptation of Terence's *Eunuch.* In it three men compete for the favors of the courtesan Talanta. Orfino gives her a gold chain, Captain Tinca gives her a Moorish girl who has been a companion to his daughter, Messer Vergolo gives her a Saracen boy who has been a companion to his son. It is discovered that the Moorish girl is actually a young man and that the Saracen boy is actually a girl. These young people have been hoodwinking their fathers for some time. Messer Blando obligingly turns up in Rome to claim the sham Moor and the sham Saracen as his own children and so patches up the scandal. The most notable character in the play, and one of the best braggart soldiers in Renaissance drama, is Captain Tinca. Aretino transformed Terence's Thraso into an Italian mercenary, giving him up-to-date manners and speech and reducing him to poverty. In so doing he prepared the way for Shakespeare's Falstaff and Jonson's Bobadill. (pp. 95-8)

> *Marvin T. Herrick, "The Learned Comedy," in his* Italian Comedy in the Renaissance, *University of Illinois Press, 1960, pp. 60-111.*

PETER STAFFORD (essay date 1970)

[*In the following excerpt from the introduction to his translation of* The Ragionamenti, *Stafford examines Aretino's career, chronicling the Italian's personal and literary reputations in subsequent centuries as well.*]

The great blackmailer [Aretino] was, without doubt, a great writer. Apart from Machiavelli's *Mandragora,* he wrote the best comedies of the Renaissance. With very slight changes, they are all suitable for modern performance and far less offensive than most of our contemporary plays. I cannot defend

Aretino's poetry. He was a better 'poet in prose'. He succeeded only in a few of his poems—chiefly two satirical parodies called *Capitoli,* the first directed against Albicante, a fifth-rate poetaster, the second against an Italian prince. His many sonnets have little literary value. The six volumes of the *Letters* give an incredibly sharp picture of sixteenth-century social, artistic and political life and fall into an entirely different category from the rest of his works. Much has been ascribed to him, by the way, which was certainly not the product of his pen.

Two good autobiographies survive from sixteenth-century Italy; those of Cellini and Cardano. The first achieves its great success by its charming bragging and unconscious, self-betraying sincerity. The second hardly interests anybody except doctors and medical experts. But if Aretino's *Letters* were better known, their popularity would be equally assured and they would take their rightful place in the highest rank of literature.

Sixteenth-century Italy, by and large, admired him—and those of his contemporaries who hated and abused him could still not deny his literary talent. The hostility which they displayed was almost always a cover for envy. But a hundred years later, as we have seen, there was no critic or historian who did not try to bury Aretino under mountains of vituperation and contempt. It was only after 1880 that very slowly a literate public began to re-discover—thanks to the labours of a small, elect band of the learned and the curious—some of his works. Among them the *Dialogues* stood in the first place; even though some fourteen years earlier, the 1866 edition of the great Larousse Encyclopaedia did not even mention the *Ragionamenti* in the column-long article on Aretino.

Yet, as Pascal Pia pointed out in the 1958 French edition of the book, this is the most endurable, perhaps the most important part of Aretino's literary legacy. 'No other work', writes Pia, 'manifests more vividly his talents of observation, his knowledge of morals—and especially of immorality—his malice and his natural gift for satire'. Because he had a wicked tongue and a brilliant pen, because he was certainly a man of considerable sexual appetite, it was only natural that posterity elected Aretino to the role of the Great Pornographer. Since his death innumerable works have been published under his name that had nothing to do with him. There are few posthumous editions of the *Dialogues* themselves that have not been enlarged if not embellished by prose and verse additions.

The first volume of this work carried the following title-page: *Ragionamento de la Nanna at de la Antonia fatto a Rome sette una ficaia: composto dal divino Aretino per suo capricio a corretione de i tre stati delle donne.* (Conversation of Nanna and Antonia carried on at Rome under a fig-tree; composed by the divine Aretino as a whim, for the improvement of the three states of women). The date on this title-page was 1534 which is probably correct—though the place of the printing was given as Paris, an obvious falsehood. Both volumes were without doubt printed in Venice where Aretino had settled in 1527. In this book as we shall see, Nanna comments for Antonia who is less experienced on the *tre stati delle donne,* the three estates or conditions of women. The dialogue continues for three days, the first of which is devoted to the lives of nuns, the second to that of married women and the final one to the lives of courtesans.

The second volume published in 1535 (with a pretended

Turin imprint) covered a further three days. Therein, Nanna gave her daughter Pippa instruction on the first day how to be a whore; on the second she warned her against the wicked ruses and rogueries of men; and then, together with her, listened to a dialogue between a good wife and a nurse about procuring.

Freedom of literary expression was greater in sixteenth-century Italy than ever before—and certainly since then until our own permissive days. Only those authors ran real risks who were opposed to the established dogma of the Church or tried to upset the authority of the princes. In other words: sexual freedom and erotic licence were practically unlimited. It would be quite wrong to think that at the time of their publication in 1534 and 1536 the *Ragionamenti* were considered as particularly immoral or obscene. In order to understand in what spirit the first readers of this book approached it, one must be familiar with their education, their upbringing. In the sixteenth century those who could read were very much in the minority. And among the literate only comparatively few read anything but the catechism or the equivalent of Old Moore's Almanack. Those who did were certain to read, write and even speak Latin as a living language. And in Latin the words, the four-letter or all-too-graphic words that have caused so much trouble to the D. H. Lawrences and Henry Millers, were as little shocking as any normal, natural expressions which they met in Horace, Catullus, Martial and Juvenal.

But the *Dialogues* must not be classified with the erotic or pornographic writings of the same epoch—just as his open letters to the sovereigns of Europe, his satirical prophecies, his comedies, his biting satires are totally different from the run-of-the-mill production of late Renaissance poetasters. Aretino had an immense vivacity and exuberance that surmounts even the barriers of the centuries—and, far more difficult, the sea-change that any translation causes the original to suffer. Throughout the *Ragionamenti,* as Alcide Bonneau said in the Liseux edition of 1879, 'You find the same irrepressible verve, the same maliciousness of observation and that abundance of piquant details, picturesque expressions, unusual comparison, that extraordinary variety of types caught on the wing, those characteristic scenes, that profusion of spirited exchanges and of irresistibly gay sallies which place Aretino among the first rank of writers, the equal of the greatest comic authors and fully justify the fame he won while he was alive'.

Gradually Aretino's reputation as a 'pornographer' underwent a change. A few years before the First World War Guillaume Apollinaire published two new editions of the cobbler's son. He edited a new version of the *Ragionamenti* in the Bibliothèque des Curieux and compiled an anthology of Aretino's writings in a series which Remy de Gourmont directed for the Mercure de France. Slowly Aretino took his place (at least in France) beside Boccaccio, the *Célestine* of Rojas, the Restoration playwrights of England. Readers and critics discovered that though he did not have the sweeping richness of Rabelais, at least he had the same appetite for life, the same verve. French literary historians began to trace his considerable influence upon the satirical poets of the age of Henri IV.

Aretino could never become 'respectable'. He was too disrespectful, too unashamedly sensual for that. But he entered into the halls of world literature not as a universal genius yet as a major figure. (pp. xiii-xvii)

Peter Stafford, in an introduction to The Ragionamenti: The Lives of Nuns, The Lives of Married Women, The Lives of Courtesans *by Pietro Aretino, translated by Peter Stafford, The Odyssey Press, 1970, pp. v-xvii.*

RAYMOND ROSENTHAL (essay date 1972)

[*In the following excerpt, Rosenthal examines the satirical and sexual content of Aretino's* Dialogues.]

Pietro Aretino is a complicated writer, steeped in both the health and corruption of the last phase of the Italian Renaissance of which he is rightly considered a representative figure, and the famous or notorious *Dialogues* is a highly complicated work. It has called forth greatly divergent responses from its critics. (I leave aside, as not worth discussing, all those who turned from it in horror due to its outspokenness.) At one extreme are those who see it as a body blow to sexual hypocrisy, a cool account of what men and women do to and with each other in the pursuit of their pleasure, an underground book that became such because it told the truth without fuss or equivocation. At the other extreme are those who see it as the anguished cry of a stifled moralist and preacher, who, after a lifetime of flattering and blackmailing the great and powerful and the society they embodied, suddenly loosed the floodgates of his disgust and told the truth, invoking the image of mercenary love to express his deepest feelings about the greed and bestiality of his times.

In the first instance, the *Dialogues* would appear to be a work of rather straightforward realism, embellished to be sure with verbal fireworks and curious digressions, yet essentially documentary in tone and purpose and speaking straight from the salutary heart of the best Humanist tradition. In the second view, it takes on the slashing, ironic accents of a satire; its subject matter becomes a weird, gloomy masquerade, a depiction of human misery whose most grotesque expression is the act of human copulation, which is immersed in the stink given off by limbs destined to putrefy. His men are goaded to love-making by gross and vulgar lust; his women do not have even this excuse, but do it out of simple greed, for the money. That lust and that greed provide the basis for the deceptive, entrapping machinery of the social world, in which money, ambition, and cynical power rule. Aretino, a nihilist before his time, defies his age by showing it its own miserable and distorted face in the mirror of its most degraded characters and their acts.

I have brought forward these two views of Aretino's book because the book itself is varied and commodious enough to contain both, at least partially. The first view surely has less to recommend it. It is a typical example of the firmly ideological mind at work—the ideological mind of the fighter for sexual freedom—finding what it intends to find at all costs. True enough, Aretino does strike a blow against sexual hypocrisy, but it is a glancing blow, hardly a forthright wallop. Aretino's sexual frankness is at best an ambiguous affair, mixed up with other concerns and muddied by a satiric humor which has much different targets in view. Indeed, in speaking of freedom, we should realize that nobody suffers more from the tyranny of sex in its crudest aspects than the chief characters in the dialogues—Nanna admits to having robbed, lied, swindled, and murdered because of sex, while Antonia bears on her body the boils and scars left by syphilis, contracted in the practice of her profession as a prostitute.

So what is left of Aretino the liberator from oppressive convention, the celebrator of sexual joy? Not very much. If anything, simply the tone of his work as a whole, which, being plebeian, is per force crude and frank. As for pleasure, enjoyment? These things Aretino hardly ever associated with sex; on the contrary, when feelings of tenderness or peace manage to steal onto the scene—in the interludes that suddenly, inexplicably crop up between the bouts of raging invective and scorn—they are most often produced or evoked by some conscious piece of artistry or fabrication, such as a musical concert, a dancer's performance, a beautiful dinner table set by two devoted nuns, a hermitage built by an eccentric monk. Aretino is much too conscious an opponent of the reigning Humanist conception of Platonic love promulgated by the philosophers and the poet Petrarch to allow his sexual partners even a modicum of tenderness and affection.

I believe that there is more to support the second view of Aretino as a moral-minded satirist in the book's tone and texture, though certainly not in its overall form and intellectual design. It is a satire in the original sense of the word, that is *satura,* a hash or mélange. For when critics accuse Aretino of lacking a lofty intellectual purpose, a controlling conception, they are only reporting the facts of the case. Aretino is an improviser of genius, but still only an improviser. Out of this genius comes a verbal exuberance, a talent for malign observation, a gift for piling up sarcastic details—an innocence of eye and spirit, so improbably conjoined with sophistication and cynicism, that produces the astonishing profusion which, as Northrop Frye has pointed out, typifies satire in one of its most characteristic moods.

As Frye also says, the satirist must "bear down his opponent by sheer weight of words, and hence be a master of that technique of torrential abuse which we call invective." That is the art brought to a dazzling polish by the Elizabethans Nashe, Dekker, and Urquhart—the "art of verbal tempest, the tremendous outpouring of words in catalogues, abusive epithets, and erudite technicalities." In this art, too, Aretino can be considered a master, although often his effects are somewhat muffled by the demands of the dramatic form he has adopted. He can also carry off those "weirdly logical fantasies of debauch, dream and delirium" which, as so often in satire, counterpose the bewildering variety and breadth of the practical world to the neat but faulty abstractions of philosophers and sages; and he can approximate "the riotous chaos of Rabelais, Petronius and Apuleius [where] satire plunges through to its final victory over common sense." But the victory is never quite final, perhaps because Aretino is too Italian and too hard-headed, loath to inflate his images beyond the bounds of credibility. Nanna rules her fantastic, depraved world, and in ruling it employs the same brutal devices used by the rulers in the palaces—but that intellectual ingredient necessary to satire, an explicit or implicit counterposition of the good to the bad, is never sufficiently there and imaginatively present to lift the *Dialogues* to the level of true and completely satisfactory satire.

Once its satiric content is suggested, however, Aretino's book immediately assumes another, deeper aspect. It was an Italian critic, Massimo Bontempelli, who first advanced the idea, and he seems to have been impelled to it by his appreciation of how much in Aretino's work was a criticism of the age in which he lived and flourished. Bontempelli's is perhaps too sweeping a rehabilitation of the "infamous Aretino," too peremptory an attempt to give him a moral standpoint; and yet to any attentive reader of this book it becomes immediately apparent that such an interpretation is borne out by a thousand details and a pervasive rhythm and texture. Nanna, Antonia, and Pippa are always on the verge of becoming the monstrous, inflated puppets of some gigantic, obscene charade that intends to display "the blasted world of repulsiveness and idiocy, a world without pity and without hope"; but, again, something holds Aretino back from this final leap into the satiric other-world inhabited by such masterpieces as *Gulliver's Travels* and *Volpone*.

It was, I believe, a very human love for his main characters that got in Aretino's way. For this ferocious satirist of human folly and greed is also a great innocent, a kind of prehensile but mild animal—we see him in Titian's overpowering portraits—who can describe a glass of water, a distracted lover, an absent-minded professor as though all these things and persons were being seen for the first time. It is this quality also that distinguishes his erotic writing from the manufactured pornography of the modern era, which is so patently addressed to the weakness and vices of the individual, lone and alienated. Aretino's eroticism has the vigor and health of a public spectacle—a sort of morality play for the populace—which thereby divests it of any perverse or sickly intention. Not only was it the first erotic book in the Christian world to be written in the vulgar tongue of ordinary speech—the speech which, as De Sanctis, the great Italian literary critic, said, was to become that of all educated Italians—it was also, paradoxically, the last erotic book to describe the "filth" of commercial love without, itself, being filthy or vicious. Indeed this is Aretino's true genius, the sheer capacity for sensual good spirits which somehow touches his most revolting scenes with freshness and charm. (pp. 6-10)

> *Raymond Rosenthal, in a preface to* Aretino's Dialogues *by Pietro Aretino, translated by Raymond Rosenthal, Stein and Day Publishers, 1972, pp. 6-10.*

GEORGE BULL   (essay date 1976)

[*A well-known American writer and journalist, Bull has translated the works of such Italian Renaissance authors as Benvenuto Cellini, Niccolò Machiavelli, and Giorgio Vasari. In the following excerpt from the introduction to his 1976 translation of the letters of Aretino, he examines the author's life and literary accomplishments.*]

Pietro Aretino finally selected over 3,000 letters for publication in book form, and they illumine innumerable facets of Italian life during the first half of the sixteenth century. His literary versatility was extraordinary, as both the generous sweep of his other writings and the letters chosen for this translation demonstrate by their variations in mood and style while they range over art and politics, war, sport and religion, and city life or country pleasures of every sort. This diversity of subject-matter has helped to characterize Aretino as the first journalist. He made his money and reputation by the high-speed production, for a wide, educated public, of letters or broadsheets that may be seen as the Renaissance equivalent of the leaders, features, art criticism, gossip columns and eye-witness reporting of modern times. His prolific output (as well as his notoriety as a pornographer) for centuries after his death obscured his merits as a writer of genius. Today his journalistic immediacy seems the very quality to re-awaken interest in him, not only as a wonderfully evocative observer of his times but also, at his best, as a stylist who was among the most inventive, intelligent and original prose writers of the Italian Renaissance during its final, transitional years.

Pietro Aretino lived from 1492 to 1556, born and dying, coincidentally, in two highly critical decades at either end of the half century. During this period, the cultural, religious and moral values of Italians were shaken in a ferment of ideological conflict and disillusionment. Between the 'golden age' of Florentine humanism and the era of Roman reform, discipline and fervour, the first half of the sixteenth century witnessed a succession of fierce conflicts. Among individuals, the tensions were seen in their intensely competitive motivations and constant personal violence. Among the states of Europe, they erupted in frequent war for reasons of personal princely greed and dynastic ambition.

The half century during which Aretino lived has left for history the impression of a thousand impetuous gestures of violence and brutality amidst scenes of contrasted splendour and squalor in the streets and courts as well as on the battlefields of Europe. Idealized pictures of the courtiers of Urbino discoursing about Platonic love with the gentle Pietro Bembo are crowded out, especially during the years to 1530, by the more insistent images of personal rivalry and violence: the strangling of Cesare Borgia's comrades-in-arms at Senigallia; Niccolò Machiavelli suffering six sharp turns of the rack; the broken-nosed Michelangelo Buonarroti, in a terrible fury, shouting defiance at Pope Julius from the scaffolding in the Sistine Chapel; Benvenuto Cellini plunging a Pistoian dagger into the neck of his brother's assassin.

The elements of conflict and competitiveness in the Italian character were strongly marked before the lifetime of Aretino; but in his time they were undoubtedly coarsened by the effects of years of plague, war and foreign invasion which started at the end of the fifteenth century. In 1492 the death of Lorenzo de' Medici undermined the stable government of Florence and upset the balanced political structure of Italy. It was followed by the invasions of Charles VIII and Louis XII of France; the involvement in fighting in the peninsula of the Empire and Spain under Maximilian, Charles V and Philip II; the desperation of the rulers of Italy as they formed and broke alliances in angry but ineffectual attempts to maintain their own local independence and restore Italian self-respect. The first half of the sixteenth century in Italy was remarkable for its concentration of genius in literature and the arts. Italy was also the laboratory for testing new military systems, and weapons using gunpowder, in the continual invasions and internecine strife recalled by such names as Fornovo, Seminara, Barletta, Cerignola, Garigliano, Agnadello, Ravenna, Marignano and Pavia.

During these years, Venice was stripped for a while of her mainland empire by French, German and Papal armies. Florence finally shed her republican government after a series of military humiliations and *coups d'état*. Naples was overrun temporarily by the French and finally by the Spaniards. Milan and her rich lands suffered a similar fate. The Papacy for most of the period sent armies into the field like any secular state and—under the Borgia Pope Alexander VI—almost became a dynastic possession. Its greatest horror came in 1527, when Rome was atrociously sacked by Imperial troops.

The political instability and violence of the time, moreover, was accompanied by the traumatic shock of religious revolt against the Papacy, which began with symbolic gestures of violence (the nailing up of Martin Luther's ninety-five theses, the burning of the Bull *Exsurge Domine*), fed some heretical movements in Italy, and embittered theological opinion within the Catholic Church.

Before mid-century, the river of Italy's history was flowing less wildly. In 1559, three years after the death of Aretino, the Peace of Cateau-Cambrésis ended the Habsburg-Valois dynastic wars from which the Italian states had been the chief sufferers: the greater part of Italy was to stay fast under Austrian and Spanish rule for over two hundred years. In the same year, the first general Roman Index of Prohibited Books, drawn up by the Congregation of the Inquisition, was approved and published by Pope Paul IV. Among the authors cited was Aretino—*Opera omnia*—and the event marked a profound revulsion against the relative intellectual freedom of the Renaissance as well as its licentiousness.

The struggles for power, possessions and wealth in Italy during the first half of the sixteenth century took place in almost every area of life and at every level. Among artists, for example, the quest for patronage and fame was intensely competitive. (One of the notable features of Vasari's *Lives of the Artists* is the institutionalized channelling of rivalry between painters, sculptors and architects, who seem to have thrived on it both emotionally and materially.) Between the rulers of the two great European powers of the time—the Empire and France—rivalry flared up constantly over territorial possessions, political influence and personal reputation, especially in Italy. The Italian rulers themselves, of Urbino, Mantua, Ferrara, Bologna or Florence, were avid both for dynastic security and territorial expansion, and for fame if not immortality through the fruits of their patronage of artists and writers. On a grand scale, the craving of Europe's rulers for publicity, adulation and fame came to be met by the new court festivals and spectacles and by propagandist writers in the service of single princes or dynasties.

The letters written by Aretino provide their own highly individual and intelligent commentary on European and Italian politics of the Renaissance. They show a path or two through the maze of contemporary political and artistic propaganda. Most important of all, they were written by an immensely respected writer whose arrogance and venality tarnish but do not destroy his value.

In his complex character and talents, Aretino is a clear mirror of his time; in return, the times help to explain his flawed character and the conflicts within him which found such forceful expression in his work. Specifically, the composition and publication of the works of Aretino, and particularly the **Letters,** would have been impossible outside the context of Venetian history during the first half of the century. (pp. 13-16)

Venice provided Aretino with visual and cultural inspiration, with protection and sustenance, and with a network of friends and acquaintances in high life and low, extending to Andrea Gritti, head of state. But it was not until 1527, when he was thirty-five, that Aretino came to Venice where he was to settle for life. From his earliest years he had been a wanderer among the courts of Italy, living off his wits and often in danger of his life, but acquiring the sharp insights into human nature and the intimate knowledge of the realities of all levels of Italian life that provided the substance for his most notable letters and books.

Aretino was born in Arezzo, a dependency of Florence, in Tuscany, the night of 19-20 April 1492. The details of his family background, which were to be imaginatively supplied in lurid colours by his enemies, are uncertain, but his father was a shoemaker called either Andrea or Luca del Tura. More is known about his mother, Tita or Margherita Bonci, whom his father abandoned while her four children (a brother and two sisters to Pietro) were still young. She was apparently noted for her beauty, enjoyed good family connections, and was befriended by a local nobleman, Luigi Bacci, with whose children Pietro was brought up. Probably because of family dispute and neglect, Pietro's childhood seems to have been rebellious and his education neglected. He was said to have had to flee from Arezzo when he was ten for writing a sonnet against indulgences. Whatever the truth of this, well before he was eighteen he was living in Perugia in the care of the humanist Francesco Bontempi. He grew friendly with a circle of poets and painters and tried his hand as an artist and writer.

After an apparently happy stay at Siena, Aretino moved about 1517 to Rome where he was a member of the household of the wealthy Sienese financier, Agostino Chigi. Ambitious, self-confident, clever, witty and already demonstrably able as a writer, Aretino found in the Rome of Pope Leo X the excitement and stimulus of the most talented court in Europe and the most catholic and corrupt of cities. Elected in 1513, the Medici Pope Leo X, although less coarse than the Borgias, was utterly worldly in his pleasures and pursuits, which embraced fishing, music and the munificent patronage of scholars such as Pomponazzi, writers such as Ariosto, and artists, including notably Raphael of Urbino. For the new pontiff Raphael continued the great frescoes for the Stanze of the Vatican; he designed the tapestry cartoons intended for the Sistine Chapel; he painted his remarkable portrait of the Pope himself; and (with other members of his circle such as Sebastiano del Piombo and Jacopo Sansovino) he befriended the young and amusing Aretino and helped him to enjoy the experiences of Roman life to the full. One can imagine him at the kind of gatherings enjoyed at the time by Benvenuto Cellini, who refers to a twice-weekly meeting for talk and supper of a band of friends living in Rome, including painters, sculptors and goldsmiths, and the famous Giulio Romano.

Aretino's growing fascination with power politics and gift for satire found a notable outlet on the death of Pope Leo in 1521. He threw himself enthusiastically into the campaign for the election of the next Pope, and wrote propaganda for his friend and patron Cardinal Giulio de' Medici. Aretino's *pasquinate* or lampoons—some of which he later reproduced in his plays and referred to in his letters—attacked other candidates for the Papal throne in a highly indecent and irreverent fashion. When the cardinals chose a high-minded and good-living Dutchman—Adrian of Utrecht—instead of the Medici candidate, Aretino enhanced his own literary and satirical reputation beyond Rome with more attacks, and then discreetly left the city in 1522. (pp. 18-20)

During the months Aretino was away from Rome—visiting Arezzo and then Fano on the Adriatic, where Giovanni delle Bande Nere was encamped—he was presented to one of his greatest future benefactors, Francis I. The French king, a great huntsman and humanist, was in Lombardy in command of a huge French army striking into Italy against the Imperialist forces, and temporarily in alliance with the Papacy. Somehow reconciled with the Pope, Aretino was back in Rome by the early winter of 1524, writing verse in praise of

Giovanni de' Medici, of Clement, and even of Giberti, being honoured and paid by the Pope but inwardly brooding over the repulsive indignities and hypocrisies of court life. The evidence for this is in Aretino's first prose comedy, *La cortigiana (Comedy about Life at Court),* written early in 1525. This is an exuberant sexual farce heavily seasoned with satire against the Papacy. ('The principal thing a courtier must know is how to swear, how to be a gambler, how to be spiteful, a whoremonger, a heretic, a flatterer, a slanderer, an ingrate, an ignoramus, an ass, and he must know how to trick people, mince around, and be either the doer or the done . . .' says the courtier Andrea explaining his profession.)

The farce displays Aretino's ingenuity, defiant literary and verbal freedom, forcefulness and robustness of expression in full spate. The violence caught in the action of the play was soon acted out in Aretino's own life, when he was attacked and stabbed in chest and right hand by a certain Achille Della Volta whose mistress he is reputed to have seduced, but who was also in the service of Giberti, lately enraged by a fresh volley of lampoons directed against himself and his policies. Aretino's hand was maimed for the rest of his life; his pride was badly bruised; and the protection of the Pope clearly withdrawn.

This time he left Rome for good, in October 1525. It was eight months after the Imperial victory at Pavia, the unhorsing and capture of the French king, and the tightening of the German and Spanish hold on Italy.

Aretino went first briefly to Mantua, and then to the camp of Giovanni de' Medici, who had recovered from a leg wound that had kept him out of action during the Battle of Pavia and whose troops were skirmishing against the Imperialists. Aretino stayed with Giovanni until his death on the last day of November 1526. Machiavelli had wanted to see Giovanni leading Italian forces in place of the inept Francesco della Rovere, Duke of Urbino; he had been impressed personally by his bravery and ambition and won his friendship on a visit to him earlier in the year. Francesco Guicciardini, who as the Pope's Lieutenant-General had been in close contact with him for several years, also admired Giovanni's personal courage but still more his skills in training and leading his troops. Aretino's affection and admiration went deeper still. After Giovanni was shot in the thigh and carried to Mantua for treatment, Aretino was with him when he died, and he recorded the event in the most eloquent of his letters in which the admiration for Italy's fiercest man of action paradoxically inspires great delicacy of sentiment and style. Throughout his life, he was to remember and recall his friendship with Giovanni delle Bande Nere.

Aretino stayed in Mantua at Federico Gonzaga's invitation until March 1527. He enjoyed months of almost febrile literary activity, during which, according to a letter from Gonzaga to Guicciardini, he wrote more things in verse and prose than 'all the best talents of Italy had composed in ten years. . . .' They included sharply satirical sonnets and epigrams, and the draft of another comedy, *Il marescalco* or *The Stablemaster.*

Published in 1533, the play is developed around the consequences of a practical joke played on the master of horse of the Duke of Mantua—a misogynist whom the courtiers convince that he has to marry at the Duke's orders and whose relief comes after five acts of debate, suspense and farce, when the 'bride' turns out to be a boy. It has some splendid mo-

ments of wit and bawdy, but is remarkable chiefly for its colourful depiction of local life in a north Italian town of the Renaissance and the acute good-humoured observation of character disguised by the stock appellations of Nurse, Pedant, Knight and so forth.

Aretino's spleen went into verses attacking the Papal court, especially after Gonzaga's intercession on his behalf proved fruitless. His invective was developed and honed in a series of *pronostici* and *giudizi* modelled on the traditional form of popular predictions but adapted by Aretino to his own purposes of blackmail, self-advertisement and display, spite and bravado. Published in loose sheets, the *giudizi* were written for Aretino's growing and ever-attentive public at the courts of Italy. One *giudizio,* in particular, composed at the end of 1526, attacked the Pope and prelates of Rome, forecast a terrible fate for the city, and led to a suggestion from the Mantuan ambassador at Rome that the Marquis would be wise to ban Aretino from Mantua. Federico seemingly replied with an offer to have Aretino assassinated if that were thought to be desirable.

In March 1527, Aretino left Mantua for ever, with his memories of the indulgence and treachery of its prince, of his own infatuations with a girl named Isabella Sforza and shortly afterwards with a Mantuan boy, and with plans for an epic poem in honour of the House of Gonzaga. This was the *Marfisa* (finally dedicated to the Marchese del Vasto), written in emulation and continuation of Ariosto's *Orlando furioso,* planned at first to run to 3,000 stanzas but of which Aretino published only 215 stanzas in two cantos, to no one's great loss. (pp. 22-5)

In 1533-4 Aretino launched an ambitious range of new work sweeping well beyond the occasional verse, letters and *pronostici* of previous years. The *Marescalco* was published in 1533. In April 1534 appeared the first part of Aretino's *Ragionamenti* or *Sei giornate,* namely the *Ragionamento della Nanna e della Antonia.* In June, he published *La Passione di Gesù,* part of the forthcoming work on the *Humanity of Christ (Umanità di Cristo);* in August the revised *Cortigiana;* and in November, *I sette salmi de la penitenzia di David,* the *Seven Penetential Psalms of David.*

Among the remarkable aspects of this burst of literary activity were both its decisive enlargement of Aretino's range of subject-matter and also its experimental nature. Despite his little Latin and less Greek, Aretino was no rogue elephant of literature. There are particularly fine passages of dramatic descriptive writings in his religious works, which were praised by the devout Vittoria Colonna. His acute responsiveness to the social and literary trends of the age was demonstrated by his borrowings (as from Boccaccio), by his fondness for parody (as of Pietro Bembo) and by his spirit of contradiction. All these tendencies were evident in the work of 1534.

La cortigiana, for example, yields more if it is read with an awareness of the influence of The Book of the Courtier, the idealized portrait of court life which was circulated to Baldesar Castiglione's friends, including Pietro Bembo, before publication in 1528. *The Passion of Jesus* (Aretino's first published 'sacred' work which, he claimed, made him the Fifth Evangelist) grew naturally out of the triumph of the vernacular in Italian literature in the first quarter of the century and—like his imaginative and poetical translation of the Psalms—was also an appropriate Catholic response to the literary militancy of Lutheranism.

The *Ragionamento* of the *Sei giornate* was in structure a parody of the Platonic dialogue that was so popular during the High Renaissance, caricaturing with brutal and uproarious sensuality and carnality the passionate and spiritual abstractions of the humanists. More than simply a devastating parody, the *Ragionamento* takes its place along with the *Life* of Benvenuto Cellini as a fantastically exaggerated but vivid and convincing portrayal of the seamy side of Italian life in the towns and villages, streets and piazzas, churches and convents of an age when restraint was being thrown aside. The first Goyaesque dialogue took the form of a leisurely three-day conversation, exploiting the colourful colloquialisms of sexual innuendo and euphemism, between an old and a young prostitute about the lives of nuns, wives and whores. A richly erotic work, its lubricity is far from being a simple plea for sexual freedom although it makes its own case for freedom of sexual expression. Overtly, Aretino neither approves nor disapproves of the gross sexual encounters and escapades which he describes so zestfully.

Like Machiavelli, claiming in *The Prince* that he will write otherwise than those who had dreamed up imaginary republics and principalities and will 'represent things as they are in real truth', through the mouth of the prostitute Nanna, Aretino says that, in contrast to Boccaccio's, his tales will be real and not feigned. His passion for realism contends with his obsessive delight in fantasy and invective and verbal extravagance to produce a sprawling Rabelaisian compendium with not a few passages of unexpected tenderness, psychological insight and fresh descriptive brilliance.

In 1534, Clement VII was succeeded by the Farnese Pope, Paul III, and in 1536 there was a renewal of the war between France and the Empire. During the 1530s and early 1540s, in the shadow of the growth of Imperial power and the Counter-Reformation, Aretino continued his series of richly contrasted religious and erotic works: the second part of the *Sei giornate*—the *Dialogo nel quale la Nanna insegna a la Pippa*—in 1536; various other dialogues including one on the Court of Rome in 1538-9; his *Genesis* in 1538; the *Life of the Virgin Mary* in 1539; the *Life of St Catherine* in 1540; and the *Life of St Thomas* in 1543. Four new plays—*Lo ipocrito* (*The Hypocrite*) and *La talenta, Il filosofo* (*The Philosopher*) and *L'Orazia* (*The Horatii*) were published between 1542 and 1546.

The three comedies continued in the vein of intricately plotted farce and realism previously explored in the *Cortigiana* and the *Marescalco:* they still further established Aretino's theatrical credentials, in the succession to Plautus and Terence and in turn influencing possibly Shakespeare and Jonson. The *Orazia* was his first and only tragedy, but arguably the best Italian tragedy of the century. More important by far than the completion of the plays or the outpouring of a mass of immensely varied verse was the progress made by Aretino during these years with preparation and publication of his letters. Just as Aretino's encounter with the Emperor in 1543 marked the summit of his social and political success, so the publication between 1537 and 1542 of the first two books of the *Letters* marked the apogee of his literary achievement. In this most flexible and sensitive form of self-expression, Aretino also most convincingly and compellingly conveyed the rich texture and complex spirit of his age. The first volume of the letters created an appetite for more that lasted till after his death. Those to whom the letters were addressed mostly formed an impressive gallery of the 'establishment' of the

time, as did many of the signatories of the letters sent in return to Aretino, and published in Venice in 1551.

The books of Pietro Aretino were cited in the first draft for the Index of prohibited books in 1557, and indeed during the last decade of Aretino's life intellectual and literary freedom was under assault in Italy. Even so, the circumspection detectable in Aretino's later plays, the Papal knighthood and pension conferred on him in 1550 by Julius III, and the fame and fortune by which he was lapped were interrupted by occasional flashes of contention and violence. Thus the second book of his *Letters* had been dedicated to King Henry VIII of England. (pp. 30-3)

Publication of the first book of Aretino's *Letters* marked a new peak of his literary and social success. The second book appeared in 1542 (the same year as Marcolini's explicitly recorded second edition of the first book and a year before his triumphant encounter with the Emperor). Further books were published in 1546, 1550 (two volumes) and, just posthumously, in 1557.

The *Letters* of Aretino in their contents and style best represent the many aspects of his literary skill as well as the texture of the age in which he lived. All his works, for example, are adorned with memorable verbal pictures of contemporary scenes and events. Among the most notable, in the *Sei giornate,* is his description of the Sack of Rome. The *Letters* abound with passages which bring before our eyes with great immediacy the vivid spectacle of Renaissance life in Venice: a crowd pressing forward for the lottery; the Grand Canal alive with gondolas and barges and the markets teeming with fish and vegetables; a summer day in the countryside.

Aretino's painter's eye fixes almost pictorially the image and movement of life at court, of soldiers in camp or of ordinary men and women at table or in bed. To these studies of physical life and movement, the letters add rich psychological insights into the mood and preoccupations of the period: its ribald anti-clericalism, its earthy and ambiguous sexuality; its sense of tension between political cynicism (the failure of the Italian princes) and idealism (the superiority of Italy over the barbarians, the war against the infidel). Too great a lover of comfort and fame to press his questioning of the rules of society, or those of literature, to the extreme, Aretino constantly reflected the self-questioning of his Italian contemporaries, which grew so sharp after the physical and psychological upheaval of the first quarter of the sixteenth century. For the study of Renaissance art, the letters also provide technical and psychological insight.

At least 600 of his published letters deal in one way or another with art and artists. The chief interest focuses on Aretino's relationship with Titian, and although he died before the latter reached his full stature as a painter, he influenced Titian's acceptance of Roman and classical ideals of grandeur and fidelity to nature. One of the most appealing of the letters, full of movement and colour, shows how Aretino learned to see the world, and describe it, as Titian saw and painted it; his writing—and we must remember the warmth and duration of his friendship with Titian—may be taken as interpreting the aims of the painter in a manner the latter would have accepted and approved.

In several letters, Aretino manifested his grasp of the essential qualities of Venetian painting, with its intensity of colour and magnificent rendering of light and air. Although he quarrelled shamefully with Michelangelo and attacked him for the indecency of his nudes in the Sistine Chapel (on the grounds of their inappropriateness in such surroundings) Aretino understood and appreciated too the elements of fury and awesomeness and experiment in his style, which he prompted Titian to study and emulate. In Lodovico Dolce's *Dialogue on Painting* of 1557, Aretino is reported as rather tiresomely expounding the case for the superior quality of Raphael's painting as compared with that of Michelangelo, but his appreciation is shown in what he wrote about the ceiling of the Sistine Chapel and in the fine judgement that *'il mondo ha molti re e un solo Michelangelo',* 'the world has many kings but only one Michelangelo'. Aretino's artistic sensibilities embraced architecture and sculpture as well as painting, in an age when the unity of the arts was generally accepted and a man of letters or a humanist was believed perfectly able to be an expositor and connoisseur of all three.

In the dedication to the **Dialogue** of the **Sei giornate,** Aretino relates his own style to painting in the following revealing passage:

> . . . I force myself to portray people's characters with the vivacity with which the marvellous Titian portrays this or that countenance; and just as good painters appreciate greatly a fine collection of drawings and sketches, so I let my works be printed just as they are, and I am not in the slightest concerned to embellish what I write: this is because all the effort goes into the design, and although the colours may be beautiful in themselves, the cartoons remain what they are, namely cartoons; everything else is nonsense, except to work quickly and your own way. Here then are my *Psalms,* here is the *History of Christ,* here are my *Comedies,* here is the *Dialogue,* here are religious and light-hearted books, depending on the subject-matter; and I have given birth to each work almost in a day. . . .

Then follows his persistent claim which is not belied even by the flattery of so many of his letters, exaggerated more often by his love of hyperbole than by sycophancy. '. . . I deserve some particle of glory for having thrust the truth into the bedrooms and the ears of the powerful instead of lies and adulation.'

Aretino's concern with the arts went far beyond his function as a patron and publicist and included his use of them as a means of extending the range of his own literary criticism. There are correspondences, for example, between descriptive passages in the architectural criticism of Sebastiano Serlio and the descriptive and critical work of Aretino.

Aretino's occasional use of architectural metaphors when describing physical appearance or, more important, personality and character is a feature of various letters written from 1537. In his mid-forties, he was then at the age when if a writer's invention and energy are sustained, confidence and sheer literary competence are often at their height. He had long secured social poise and financial success; he told his publisher, for example, that he had no wish to lower himself by wanting to earn money from the sale of his books. He knew the power of his invective and his flattery to infuriate or delight important people, whether they were rulers or artists. He was fascinated by his own reputation as a man who told the truth, however terrible it might be. He was of an age and status to express his own feelings more uninhibitedly than ever, to want still to exercise influence on contemporary life, but also to philosophize and reminisce. He was also feeling the years a little, and the toll taken by writing: he used to write forty

stanzas every morning, he wrote to a friend in the spring of 1537, and take ten days to finish a play, and now he wrote only a few letters. The letters, as it happened, were the perfect form for his middle-aged talent. At this juncture he published the first selection and he found they were successful beyond all his expectations. These letters (the earliest to be published being dated 1525 but the bulk of them being written during and after 1537) were, against this background, the perfect vehicle for his confident exercises in several styles of writing, as extraordinarily varied as the personality of the man himself. The consequences of his dialogue with Serlio on the style of some of them is only one instance of his versatility and experimentation.

The first experiment, to some extent, was his use of Italian (perforce) rather than Latin, for the purposes of published correspondence. By 1537, the influence of Bembo's Ciceronianism had waned and the strength of the vernacular for literary works increased with the appearance of such works as Castiglione's *Book of the Courtier* (1528), Machiavelli's *Prince* (written 1513), and Ariosto's *Orlando furioso* (1516). Nonetheless, Latin would still have been the more obvious choice among the educated for a book of letters published in the late 1530s. Many of the letters were written at great speed, and both in this context and in other works, Aretino scathingly criticized and lampooned the 'pedants' of his time: either the half-educated schoolmasters who spattered their speech with Latin words and phrases (like the pedant in his own play, **The Stablemaster**) or the writers who believed, with Bembo, that the best language and style should spring from the imitation of Italy's fourteenth-century Florentine writers and preeminently Petrarch and Boccaccio. Aretino gives specific examples to mock writers who prefer to imitate archaic usages rather than write in a contemporary and popular style. All the same—and one has only to read a page of his to know it—for all his fury and spontaneity, Aretino was most thoughtful and scrupulous in his choice of words. He worked painstakingly for his effects, not only when his pen was gliding or spluttering over the page but through all the experiences and reflections of his life that preceded any particular literary work. In a letter of 1542, he recorded that he wrote 'only in Tuscan, taught to me in Arezzo where I was born and brought up'. (Just so Michelangelo, as Vasari, another Aretine, tells us, boasted he had got his good brains from the pure air of the countryside of Arezzo where he sucked in hammers and chisels with his mother's milk.)

Basically, Aretino is writing in Tuscan, the language of Machiavelli whose lucidity and economy he often rivals (and whose political writings could almost be paralleled by a treatise put together from the shrewd counsel and observation on political affairs scattered throughout Aretino's letters and plays), but he is also writing in the living language of the courts and the streets and of an Italy bombarded by foreign cultural and linguistic as well as military forces. So his greedily receptive ear and memory—as well as his intellectual extravagance and fantasy—produce in the letters a language that is rooted in Tuscan but embraces the eclectic usage of the courts, and is veined with foreign (e.g. Spanish) words, rich varieties of specialist jargon and the vivid slang of Rome, Mantua and Venice. This flexible language he deploys in a highly personal style which is capable of tremendous range and diversity and in which he invariably succeeds in achieving perfectly the effects at which he is aiming. In the **Letters** he forges a new style in opposition to the rigidities of the humanists, whose rules he breaks with careful effect.

The *Letters* are studded with memorable phrases which concisely express a dramatic event, the key feature of a man's personality or fame, or a beautiful scene in nature. In *The Prince,* Machiavelli expressed his contempt for mercenary troops in words which simultaneously summed up his view of the history of the period in the phrase: *'tanto che gli hanno condotta Italia stiava e vituperata',* 'they have captained Italy into slavery and ignominy'. Aretino frequently achieves the same striking economy and forcefulness and in no instance more nobly than in his letter on the death of Giovanni delle Bande Nere who during his sleep *'fu occupato de la morte',* 'was occupied by death'. Erasmus, he writes in another letter, 'has enlarged the confines of human genius'. The letter on Giovanni's death, using a calm and detached tone of voice, succeeds in conveying the deep emotional commitment of the writer, in delineating the essential features of the character of Giovanni, and in creating suspense and grief in the mind of the reader, while bringing before his eyes a vivid picture of the camp where the tragedy was enacted. The style is plain and relatively unadorned, and in this particular letter provides a prime example of Aretino's descriptive powers and psychological insight. A few pages were enough for his moving tribute to Giovanni delle Bande Nere; elsewhere in the *Letters* a few lines or words bring an event, character or scene convincingly to life, as when he describes the grotesque old courtier Pietro Piccardo, or a boatload of German merchants spilling over into the Grand Canal, or a gift of salad from the country. The shifting moods and tensions in Aretino's personal world, however, constantly erupt into his letters in the form of invective, wit or fantasy. In these instances, the tone and structure of his writing are often less controlled and he indulges in idiosyncrasies of style that may sometimes be tiresome but often stretch the language to its brilliant limits.

His tricks of style include the frequent use of adjectives in place of nouns, e.g. *'il semplice de la fede'* for 'the simplicity (*semplicità*) of faith' or *'il perpetuo de la memoria'* for 'the perpetuity (*perpetuità*) of memory'; and an excessive fondness for alliteration, antithesis and euphuism. Such contrivances sometimes work extremely well. The letter in which Aretino denounces the treachery of Nicolò Franco, for example, ingeniously controls and sustains its rage and uses a startling series of menagerie terms in a strong vocabulary of abuse. This kind of invective is in the tradition of humanism but here Aretino characteristically adapts literary tradition to his down-to-earth purposes. The simplicity of many of his letters and the images they contain—descriptions of food or of the seasons, for instance—are matched by the unexpected and yet perfectly natural tenderness of his emotions expressed in gentle language on occasions of grief or nostalgia over the lost friendships of youth or over the fears that a father feels for his children. Sometimes his words overload the thinness of his thoughts. His instinct for synonym, hyperbole and fantasy is never far from the tip of his pen. When he wants to flatter Charles V, for instance, he writes that in comparison with his Majesty, infinity seems short and immensity seems tiny (*'lo infinito par breve e lo immenso poco'*). In the letter to Meo Franci, containing a marvellous description of a slobbering monkey, he finds a dozen synonyms for the word 'mob'.

Justifying his defence of the indecent pictures by Giulio Romano, his love of fantasy produces a masterpiece of ridiculous and indelicate irony. In one of his most extraordinary and densely packed letters, about his dream of Parnassus, all these elements of baroque, fantasy and wit, spiteful invective and perceptive observation fuse into several pages of inventive literary surrealism. Aretino's letters may disclose noble emotions only too rarely, but there is scarcely one that does not confirm his humanity. (His metaphors, taken from life rather than from literature, spring from his profound satisfaction with ordinary sensual pleasures, which he describes with refreshing wonder, very convincingly, for instance, in his letter on winter.)

Humanity, too, was the unifying feature of Aretino's complex soul. He was very human himself, and he seemed to find nothing that was human—except hypocrisy and pedantry—really repugnant. Perhaps his failure to discriminate (as well as his egotism and lust) has done most to earn him the censure of critics and moralists through the centuries, where this has not arisen simply from ill repute. Francesco de Sanctis castigated the 'moral dissolution' of an Aretino 'without conscience and without remorse'. Modern sensibilities make it easier to understand Aretino's sensuality and professed defiance of the rules of literature and society; but it would be an injustice to him to reduce his immorality to some kind of gently rebellious agnosticism like Bernard Shaw's, just as it is wrong to smooth down the exuberance and bombast of his language too much in translation. Nearer to the mark, in oblique judgement of the elemental force of Aretino's nature, were the words of Hazlitt in his comments on the Titian portrait: 'The large colossal profile of Peter Aretine is the only likeness of the kind that has the effect of conversing with "the mighty dead"; and this is truly spectral, ghastly, necromantic.' Aretino's letters have this effect. (pp. 38-46)

> *George Bull, in an introduction to* Aretino: Selected Letters *by Pietro Aretino, translated by George Bull, Penguin Books, 1976, pp. 13-48.*

FURTHER READING

Chubb, Thomas Caldecot. *The Letters of Pietro Aretino.* Archon Books, 1967, 362 p.
    Introduction to Aretino's correspondence.

Cleugh, James. *The Divine Aretino.* New York: Stein and Day, 1966, 256 p.
    Critical biography.

Hartley, K. H. "Pietro Aretino and Molière." *AUMLA,* No. 20 (November 1963): 309-17.
    Compares Aretino's *Lo hipocrito* with Molière's *Tartuffe,* asserting that the French dramatist borrowed heavily from his Italian predecessor.

Harvey, Gabriel. *Gabriel Harvey's Marginalia,* edited by G. C. Moore Smith, pp. 91ff. Stratford-upon-Avon: Shakespeare Head Press, 1913.
    Marginalia written by sixteenth-century English poet Harvey at various times after 1567, favorably assessing Aretino.

Haynes, Alan. "Pietro Aretino." *History Today* XXII, No. 5 (May 1972): 321-28.
    Biographical essay.

Lothian, John M. "Shakespeare's Knowledge of Aretino's Plays." *Modern Language Review* XXV, No. 4 (October 1930): 415-24.
    Offers evidence that Shakespeare borrowed from Aretino's comedy *Il marescalco.*

Mitchell, Gene. "Our Man from Arezzo." *Mankind* VI, No. 5 (May 1979): 22-4, 32, 34, 36.
  Deems Aretino "the symbol of the dark side of the Renaissance."

The Nation 63, No. 1634 (22 October 1896): 314-16.
  Defends Aretino against critics who treat him as "one of the world's scapegoats."

Walsh, Maurice N. "Some Character Aspects of the Satirist (Pietro Aretino)." *The American Imago* 18, No. 3 (Fall 1961): 235-62.
  Psychosexual analysis of Aretino's life and writings.

Lodovico Castelvetro

1505-1571

(Also Ludovico) Italian essayist, dramatist, and critic.

Castelvetro was a sixteenth-century Italian humanist who wrote critical commentaries on such literary figures as Aristotle, Petrarch, and Dante. He is most remembered as the first to give full expression to the three unities of drama: a body of principles involving action, time, and place often erroneously attributed to Aristotle. The theory states that a drama should adhere to three basic rules: it should have a beginning, middle, and end, with a causal relationship in its different parts; its action should take place within a limited time-frame; and the action should exist in a limited place. The three unities had a profound impact on Italian and French neoclassical drama until they were largely discredited in the eighteenth century.

Castelvetro was born in Modena in 1505. Encouraged by his parents, he proved an able student, taking courses at the universities of Bologna, Ferrara, Padua, and Siena. While pursuing a law degree, Castelvetro nurtured a desire to learn more about the humanities, particularly literature and philosophy. Upon completing his law studies at Siena, Castelvetro was sent to Rome to live with his uncle, Giovanni Maria della Porta. Maria della Porta was influential among the Roman nobility, and Castelvetro was well positioned for a lucrative court appointment. Arriving around the time of the Sack of Rome in 1527, Castelvetro became immediately disillusioned with the state of affairs in the city, so he journeyed back to Siena. At the university, he once again undertook the study of literature as well as Greek, Latin, and Italian.

In 1529 Castelvetro returned to Modena, where he quickly became a prominent figure in the local literary circle. He and a friend, Giovanni Grillenzono, formed an exclusive academy, the Accademia Modenese, dedicated to classical literature and humanist culture. The Accademia flourished under Castelvetro's leadership and attracted many disciples of humanism to Modena. Problems arose in 1541, however, when the Accademia was rumored to have Protestant leanings. When orders were sent from Rome to suppress the alleged heretics, the members of the Accademia signed a document affirming their Catholic faith. The issue was put to rest until 1545 when a member of the Accademia, Pelligrino degli Erri, became incensed when his colleagues played a joke on him. Desiring revenge, he appealed to Rome, accusing his fellow members of the Accademia of heresy. This accusation proved the death knell for the Accademia Modenese, for the members were prohibited from further engaging in any joint activity whatsoever.

Throughout these initial conflicts with the Catholic church, Castelvetro's reputation remained untarnished. His personal problems began in 1553, however, when he became embroiled in a literary dispute with Annibale Caro, a secretary to Cardinal Alessandro Farnese. Although Castelvetro was a respected scholar, he was also considered tactless and impolite, and he often infuriated his contemporaries. Such was the case with Annibale Caro. Caro had recently published a canzone in honor of Cardinal Farnese entitled *Venite all'ombra de'*

gran gigli d'oro (1553). This poem was harshly criticized by Castelvetro, causing Caro much embarrassment. Intent on revenge, Caro began a propaganda and pamphlet war with Castelvetro that culminated in Caro's writing of the *Apologia degli Academici di Bianchi di Roma contra M. Lodovico Castelvetro* in 1558. In the *Apologia,* Caro accused Castelvetro of heresy, which resulted in his being summoned before the Sacred Inquisition in Rome. During a preliminary hearing in 1560, Castelvetro's examiner, Tomaso da Vigevana, threatened him with torture if he was found guilty. Fearing for his life, Castelvetro fled from Rome, whereupon he was immediately pronounced guilty and excommunicated from the Catholic church. Forced into exile, Castelvetro settled in the village of Chiavenna on the border of Switzerland and Italy. He stayed there for two years, writing commentaries and appealing to the Inquisition Council for his case to be heard. When his entreaties to Rome failed around 1563 or 1564, Castelvetro moved to Lyons, where he lived until 1567. While in Lyons, misfortune plagued Castelvetro again. At the time, Huguenots and Catholics were struggling violently for control of the city. During one outbreak, Castelvetro's house was looted and burned. Among the books and manuscripts written by Castelvetro said to have been lost in the fire were a book on Italian grammar, a commentary on the dialogues of Plato, a critique of the comedies of Plautus and Terence, remarks on Dante's *Divina Commedia,* and a translation of the New Testament. Today, only fragments of these works exist in a collection entitled *Opere Varie Critiche di Lodovico Castelvetro.* From Lyons, Castelvetro moved to Geneva, Chiavenna, and finally Vienna, where he was welcomed by Maximilian II. Under Maximilian's patronage, Castelvetro published his *Poetica d'Aristotele vulgarizzata et sposta per Lodovico Castelvetro* in 1570. The same year, Vienna was struck by plague, and Castelvetro returned to Chiavenna to avoid the pestilence. He intended to spend the winter in Chiavenna before moving on to Basel, but he died in February 1571 before completing his journey to Switzerland.

Castelvetro's most important work is *Poetica d'Aristotele vulgarizzata et sposta per Lodovico Castelvetro.* Including both the Greek text and an Italian translation of Aristotle's *Poetics,* this commentary addresses many of the issues set forth by the Greek philosopher. Scholars have noted that Castelvetro's approach to *Poetics* differed from that of previous critics, many of whom had merely accepted the work as a masterpiece. In contrast, Castelvetro questioned many of the issues raised by Aristotle, reinterpreting points that he felt Aristotle did not express adequately. Castelvetro addressed the nature and function of poetry, the relationship between history and poetry, and the role of divine inspiration in the composition of poetry. *Poetica d'Aristotele* also presented the theory of the three dramatic unities—time, place, and action. Castelvetro's lesser works include *Gl'ingannati, Giunta fatta al ragionamento di Messer Pietro Bembo, "Le Rime" del Petrarca brevemente esposte per Lodovico Castelvetro, Opere varie critiche di Lodovico Castelvetro,* and *Sposizione di Lodovico Castelvetro a XXIX canti dell'Inferno. Gl'ingannati,* a comedy, was produced in 1550. It has been attributed to Castelvetro, though some scholars have questioned his authorship. *Giunta, "Le Rime,"* and *Sposizione* are critical commentaries on eminent Italian literary figures. *Opere* is primarily a collection of Castelvetro's fragmented works.

Although Castelvetro has been studied by pre-twentieth-century critics writing in Italian, little has been translated into English. In fact, almost no English criticism exists from before the end of the nineteenth century. The earliest comprehensive essay in English on Castelvetro, by Richard Bentley, was published in 1699. In this work, Bentley defended Castelvetro against a critical attack waged by Charles Boyd in his *Phalaridas Agrigentinorum Tyranni Epistolae* (1695). Addressing Boyd's claim that Castelvetro was "an Italian pedant, famous for his snarling faculty, and contradicting Great Men upon very slight grounds," Bentley countered by praising Castelvetro as "one of the most ingenious and judicious and learned Writers of his Age; and his Books have at this present such a mighty Reputation, that they are sold for their weight in Silver in most countries of *Europe*." Castelvetro was next examined in detail in 1899 by J. E. Spingarn, who devoted part of his study of Renaissance criticism, *A History of Literary Criticism in the Renaissance,* to early controversy surrounding Castelvetro's *Poetica d'Aristotele.* Soon after, in 1903, George Saintsbury briefly discussed Castelvetro's literary theories as well as their impact on European drama for two centuries after his death. Critical interest in Castelvetro's work continued in 1913 with the publication of H. B. Charlton's *Castelvetro's Theory of Poetry.*

Little criticism of Castelvetro's work was written in English during the next forty years. In 1952, Bernard Weinberg, an authority on Renaissance criticism, wrote a detailed essay on Castelvetro's *Poetica d'Aristotele.* Weinberg argued that although Castlevetro's theories were grounded in Aristotelian thought, many of his conclusions were "un-Aristotelian." Later, in 1962, Baxter Hathaway maintained that Castelvetro "struck out in untried directions, motivated, if one were to judge by his contemporaries, simply by an invincible obtuseness of spirit. The clue to understanding Castelvetro's method was his willingness to follow down any avenue of thought, whether or not he had any reason to believe that it would lead him anywhere." More recently, critics writing in English have treated three further issues concerning Castelvetro. His annotations to the *Inferno* have been closely studied, his anti-Horatian stance in *Poetica* has been examined, and a translation of *Poetica* with a critical introduction was published in 1984.

Castelvetro's writings helped usher in the neoclassical period in Europe, particularly in France, where the principles he enumerated in *Poetica d'Aristotele* were embraced by poets and dramatists. Today, Castelvetro is recognized as a penetrating and original critic, one who helped define the meaning and purpose of literature to his own and a later age. According to Baxter Hathaway "[the] art of poetry according to Castelvetro is something that each poet works out for himself, more or less consciously, following the nature of things. Genius is needed, but genius is needed for all original activity."

PRINCIPAL WORKS

Gl'ingannati (drama) 1550
Giunta fatta al ragionamento di Messer Pietro Bembo (criticism) 1563
Poetica d'Aristotele vulgarizzata et sposta per Lodovico Castel-

vetro (criticism) 1570
[*Castelvetro on the Art of Poetry* [abridged edition], 1984]
"Le Rime" del Petrarca brevemente esposte per Lodovico Castelvetro (criticism) 1582
Opere varie critiche di Lodovico Castelvetro (essays and criticism) 1727
Sposizione di Lodovico Castelvetro a XXIX canti dell'Inferno (criticism) 1886

*The authorship of this anonymously published work is disputed.

FRANCESCO BUONAMICI   (essay date 1597)

[*Francesco Buonamici was a sixteenth-century Italian scientist. His lectures on physics at the University of Pisa are said to have dramatically influenced Galileo, one of his students, when he later wrote his* Juvenilia. *Buonamici's most significant work,* De motu libri X *(1591), is considered a Renaissance masterpiece heavily influenced by the humanist tradition. In the excerpt below from his* Discorsi poetici nella Accademia Fiorentina in difesa d'Aristotile, *Buonamici criticizes Castelvetro for not crediting the common audience with much imagination.*]

[By not distinguishing between an imitated action and the real thing] Castelvetro generates confusion, and he also confuses the nature of the thing represented with the nature of the thing representing. . . . And he gives little credit to the intelligence of the auditor of the representation, if the latter cannot discern the time of the representation from that represented. Finally, he does not distinguish those people who are a part of the action from the spectators.

> *Francesco Buonamici, in an extract in* A History of Literary Criticism in the Italian Renaissance, *Vol. II by Bernard Weinberg, The University of Chicago Press, 1961, p. 695.*

RICHARD BENTLEY   (essay date 1699)

[*A seventeenth- and eighteenth-century English classicist and theologian, Bentley was renowned for his literary genius as well as his incisive wit. His clashes with contemporary literary critics were so frequent that he was satirized in both Jonathan Swift's* Battle of the Books *(1697) and Alexander Pope's* Dunciad *(1727). In addition to his* Dissertation upon the Epistles of Phalaris *(1699), Bentley wrote* Epistola ad Millium *(1691) and prepared editions of Horace, Manilius, and Terence. In the excerpt below from the preface to the* Dissertation, *Bentley defends Castelvetro against a critical attack upon his character mounted by Charles Boyd in his 1695 essay* Phalaridas Agrigentinorum Tyranni Epistolae.]

Mr. *B.* [Charles Boyd] is pleas'd to bestow his next favour upon *Lodovico Castelvetro;* whom he calls *an Italian Pedant, famous for his snarling faculty, and contradicting Great Men upon very slight grounds;* and he thinks *Balzac says very well of him, That he was a public Enemy.* But whether some body else will not be *infamous for His snarling faculty,* we may predict from this very instance. This *Pedant,* as our modest Author calls him, was one of the most ingenious and judicious and learned Writers of his Age; and his Books have at this present such a mighty Reputation, that they are sold for their weight in Silver in most Countries of *Europe.* I will mention but Three Testimonies of him; the famous *Lilius Giraldus* says, He had seen some of his pieces, which fully satisfied him, that he was *Judicio sane quam acerrimo, & eruditione non vulgari.* Henricus Stephanus dedicated a Book to him, and, says he, I refer the Censure of a piece of Poetry, *Sagaciæ & emunctæ tuæ nari, Ludovice* χριτιχώτατε *&* ποι ητιχώτατε. And he has this character given him by *Menagius; Ludovicus Castelvetrius in Commentariis illis suis eruditissimis & acutissimis;* and again, *Omnium optime acutissimus Castelvetrius.* I am persuaded our Examiner has never read one line of this Author, whom he abuses thus out of *Balzac,* a Writer, without undervaluing him, many degrees inferiour to *Castelvetro.* I had the fortune some years ago to meet with most of the Pieces of *Castelvetro* and his Antagonists; and I find that the sole occasion of all his Troubles in *Italy* was a Copy of Verses made by *Annibal Caro* in praise of the *House of France:* so that the very subject of it was enough to bypass the Judgments of *Balzac* and some others of that Nation. These Verses were dispers'd over *Italy* and *France,* and receiv'd with mighty applause; and being sent to *Castelvetro* by a private Friend at *Rome,* who desir'd his Judgment of them, he return'd him some short Censures, desiring they should neither be publish'd, nor shown to any one as His. But by chance they got abroad and were printed, and brought such a violent Faction against him, as made the poor man weary of *Italy.* The very first Lines of *Caro's* Verses are

> Venite à l'ombra de' gran Gigli d'oro,
> Care Muse, devote a' miei Giacinti:

Where the Muses are invited to come under the shadow of Flower-de-luces. Upon which *Castelvetro* remark'd; That the Muses must be less than Pygmies, if they could be shadow'd by Flower-de-luces which were scarce shelter enough for little Insects. Who can have the folly to deny, that this Censure was just? *Quis tam Lucili fautor ineptus Ut neget hoc?* And yet this fault, and others as plain as this, were stoutly maintain'd by *Caro* and his Party. For the advantage of *Caro* was, That he was Member of an *Academy,* and a whole College was engag'd for him; and when neither Reason nor Truth was of their side, they confided in their Numbers,

> Defendit numerus, junctœque umbone phalanges.

Their way of refuting *Castelvetro,* was by Pasquils, Lampoons, Burlesque Dialogues, Public Speeches in the Academy, Declamations of School-boys, and in the close of all, *A short Account of Messer Lodovico Castelvetro by way of Index,* full of the most virulent Abuses. These were the fair and honourable methods of managing their Controversie: and though their Adversary, while he liv'd, suffer'd much from their malice; yet Posterity has been just to him, and has set an extraordinary value upon all his Performances; while Theirs upon this Argument (for in other things they were men of some worth) have nothing that now makes them enquir'd after, but the great Reputation of the man they abuse. And such a man will never be call'd *an Italian Pedant,* but by those that copy after his Adversaries in their infamous way of writing. (pp. 63-5)

> *Richard Bentley, in a preface to his "A Dissertation upon the Epistles of Phalaris," in* Dr. Richard Bentley's Dissertations upon the Epistles of Phalaris, Themistocles, Socrates, Euripides, and upon the Fables of Aesop, *edited by Wilhelm Wagner, S. Calvary and Co., 1874, pp. 3-70.*

A NEW AND GENERAL BIOGRAPHICAL DICTIONARY
(essay date 1784)

[*In the excerpt below, the anonymous critic relates an anecdote concerning the significance of Castelvetro's* Poetica d'Aristotele.]

We learn from the Menagiana, that Castelvetro's house being on fire at Lyons, he cried out *al poetica,* "Save my *Poetics!*" which shews, that he considered this work as the best of his performances. Indeed it ought to be so, if what is said be true, that it cost him half his life in composing. His other pieces are inferior to his *Poetics;* and his posthumous works want the greatest part of that perfection, which, if he had lived to correct them, he would probably have given them. (p. 197)

> *An excerpt in* A New and General Biographical Dictionary, Vol. III, *revised edition, W. Strahan and others, 1784, pp. 196-97.*

J. E. SPINGARN   (essay date 1899)

[*Spingarn was a turn-of-the-century American literary critic, author, and editor. In the following excerpt from a work first published in 1899, he offers a critical summary of controversial points from Castelvetro's commentary on Aristotle's* Poetics.]

The treatment of Castelvetro, in his commentary on the *Poetics* (1570), is at times much more in accord with the true Aristotelian conception than most of the other Renaissance writers. While following Aristotle in asserting that verse is not of the essence of poetry, he shows that Aristotle himself by no means intended to class as poetry works that imitated in prose, for this was not the custom of Hellenic art. Prose is not suited to imitative or imaginative subjects, for we expect themes treated in prose to be actual facts. "Verse does not distinguish poetry," says Castelvetro, "but clothes and adorns it; and it is as improper for poetry to be written in prose, or history in verse, as it is for women to use the garments of men, and for men to wear the garments of women." The test of poetry therefore is not the metre but the material. This approximates to Aristotle's own view; since while imitation is what distinguishes the poetic art, Aristotle, by limiting it to the imitation of human life was, after all, making the matter the test of poetry.

Castelvetro, however, arrives at this conclusion on different grounds. Science he regards as not suitable material for poetry, and accordingly such writers as Lucretius and Fracastoro are not poets. They are good artists, perhaps, or good philosophers, but not poets; for the poet does not attempt to discover the truth of nature, but to imitate the deeds of men, and to bring delight to his audience by means of this imitation. Moreover, poetry, as will be seen later, is intended to give delight to the populace, the untrained multitude, to whom the sciences and the arts are dead letters; if we concede these to be fit themes for poetry, then poetry is either not meant to delight, or not meant for the ordinary people, but is intended for instruction and for those only who are versed in sciences and arts. Moreover, comparing poetry with history, Castelvetro finds that they resemble each other in many points, but are not identical. Poetry follows, as it were, in the footsteps of history, but differs from it in that history deals with what has happened, poetry with what is probable; and things that have happened, though probable, are never considered in poetry as probable, but always as things that have happened. History, accordingly, does not regard verisimilitude or necessity, but only truth; poetry must take care to establish the probability of its subject in verisimilitude and necessity, since it cannot regard truth. Castelvetro in common with most of the critics of the Renaissance seems to misconceive the full meaning of ideal truth; for to the Renaissance—nay, even to Shakespeare, if we are to consider as his own various phrases which he has put into the mouths of his dramatic characters—truth was regarded as coincident with fact; and nothing that was not actual fact, however subordinated to the laws of probability and necessity, was ever called truth.

It is in keeping with this conception of the relations between history and poetry, that Castelvetro should differ not only from Aristotle, but from most of the critics of his own time, in asserting that the order of the poetic narrative may be the same as that of historical narrative. "In telling a story," he says, "we need not trouble ourselves whether it has beginning, middle, and end, but only whether it is fitted to its true purpose, that is, to delight its auditors by the narration of certain circumstances which could possibly happen but have not actually happened." Here the only vital distinction between history and poetry is that the incidents recounted in history have once happened, while those recounted in poetry have never actually happened, or the matter will not be regarded as poetry. Aristotle's fundamental requirement of the unity of the fable is regarded as unessential, and is simply observed in order to show the poet's ingenuity. This notion of poetic ingenuity is constant throughout Castelvetro's commentary. Thus he explains Aristotle's statement that poetry is more philosophic than history—more philosophic, according to Castelvetro, in the sense of requiring more thought, more speculation in its composition—by showing that it is a more difficult and more ingenious labor to invent things that could possibly happen, than merely to repeat things that have actually happened. (pp. 44-7)

For Castelvetro . . . , the end of poetry is delight, and delight alone. This, he asserts, is the position of Aristotle, and if utility is to be conceded to poetry at all, it is merely as an accident, as in the tragic purgation of terror and compassion. But he goes further than Aristotle would have been willing to go; for poetry, according to Castelvetro, is intended not merely to please, but to please the populace, in fact everybody, even the vulgar mob. On this he insists throughout his commentary; indeed, as will be seen later, it is on this conception that his theory of the drama is primarily based. But it may be confidently asserted that Aristotle would have willingly echoed the conclusion of Shakespeare, as expressed in *Hamlet*, that the censure of one of the judicious must o'erweigh a whole theatre of others. At the same time, Castelvetro's conception is in keeping with a certain modern feeling in regard to the meaning of poetic art. Thus a recent writer [Hutcheson Macaulay Posnett] regards literature as aiming "at the pleasure of the greatest possible number of the nation rather than instruction and practical effects," and as applying "to general rather than specialized knowledge." There is, then, in Castelvetro's argument this modicum of truth, that poetry appeals to no specialized knowledge, but that its function is, as Coleridge says, to give a definite and immediate pleasure. (pp. 55-6)

Castelvetro's theory of the drama was based entirely upon the notion of stage representation. All the essentials of dramatic literature are thus fixed by the exigencies of the stage. The stage is a circumscribed space, and the play must be performed upon it within a period of time limited by the physical

necessities of the spectators. It is from these two facts that Castelvetro deduces the unities of time and place. While asserting that Aristotle held it as *cosa fermissima e verissima* that the tragic action cannot exceed the length of an artificial day of twelve hours, he does not think that Aristotle himself understood the real reason of this limitation. In the seventh chapter of the *Poetics* Aristotle says that the length of the plot is limited by the possibility of its being carried in the memory of the spectator conveniently at one time. But this, it is urged, would restrict the epic as well as the tragic fable to one day. The difference between epic and dramatic poetry in this respect is to be found in the essential difference between the conditions of narrative and scenic poetry. Narrative poetry can in a short time narrate things that happen in many days or months or even years; but scenic poetry, which spends as many hours in representing things as it actually takes to do them in life, does quite otherwise. In epic poetry words can present to our intellect things distant in space and time; but in dramatic poetry the whole action occurs before our eyes, and is accordingly limited to what we can actually see with our own senses, that is, to that brief duration of time and to that small amount of space in which the actors are occupied in acting, and not any other time or place. But as the restricted place is the stage, so the restricted time is that in which the spectators can at their ease remain sitting through a continuous performance; and this time, on account of the physical necessities of the spectators, such as eating, drinking, and sleeping, cannot well go beyond the duration of one revolution of the sun. So that not only is the unity of time an essential dramatic requirement, but it is in fact impossible for the dramatist to do otherwise even should he desire to do so—a conclusion which is of course the *reductio ad absurdum* of the whole argument.

In another place Castelvetro more briefly formulates the law of the unities in the definitive form in which it was to remain throughout the period of classicism: "La mutatione tragica non può tirar con esso seco se non una giornata e un luogo." The unities of time and place are for Castelvetro so very important that the unity of action, which is for Aristotle the only essential of the drama, is entirely subordinated to them. In fact, Castelvetro specifically says that the unity of action is not essential to the drama, but is merely made expedient by the requirements of time and place. "In comedy and tragedy," he says, "there is usually one action, not because the fable is unfitted to contain more than one action, but because the restricted space in which the action is represented, and the limited time, twelve hours at the very most, do not permit of a multitude of actions." In a similar manner Castelvetro applies the law of the unities to epic poetry. Although the epic action can be accomplished in many places and at diverse times, yet as it is more commendable and pleasurable to have a single action, so it is better for the action to confine itself to a short time and to but few places. In other words, the more the epic attempts to restrict itself to the unities of place and time, the better, according to Castelvetro, it will be. Moreover, Castelvetro was not merely the first one to formulate the unities in their definitive form, but he was also the first to insist upon them as inviolable laws of the drama; and he refers to them over and over again in the pages of his commentary on the *Poetics*.

This then is the origin of the unities. . . . It may be said, therefore, that just as the unity of action is *par excellence* the Aristotelian unity, so the unities of time and place are beyond a doubt the Italian unities. They enter the critical literature of Europe from the time of Castelvetro, and may almost be said to be the last contributions of Italy to literary criticism. (pp. 98-101)

J. E. Spingarn, "The General Theory of Poetry in the Italian Renaissance" and "The Theory of the Drama," in his A History of Literary Criticism in the Renaissance, *revised edition, 1908. Reprint by Columbia University Press, 1925, pp. 24-59, 60-106.*

GEORGE SAINTSBURY (essay date 1902)

[*Saintsbury was a late nineteenth- and early twentieth-century English literary historian and critic. In the excerpt below, he commends Castelvetro for proposing methods by which the epic might be liberated from Aristotelian restrictions.*]

[Castelvetro's] most important work appeared late, the famous edition and translation, with commentary, of the *Poetics* not being published till a year before his death. "He was of his nature choleric" . . . , and he bestowed a good deal of this choler not merely upon Caro, but upon the majestic Bembo and others. Yet Castelvetro was a very remarkable critic, and perhaps deserved the ascription of actual critical genius better than any man who has yet been mentioned in this volume. It is but for chequered righteousness that his practically certain formulation of the Three Unities can be counted to him; but, as we shall see, he has other claims, from which it is not necessary to write off anything.

His impartial attachment to both classical and vulgar tongues ranks him, of itself, in a higher sphere than that of Scaliger; and a certain impetuous, incalculable, *prime-sautier* genius puts him higher still. Even contemporaries seem to have recognised this in him, though they sometimes shook their heads over its pronouncements. It may, indeed, sometimes seem that these pronouncements are, if not inconsistent, difficult to connect by any central tie-beam of critical theory. But this is almost inevitable in the case of a critic whose work takes the form, not of regular treatises on large subjects, nor even of connected essays on separate authors and books, but of commentaries and *adversaria,* where the passage immediately under consideration is uppermost in the writer's mind, and may—not illegitimately in a fashion—induce him to display a facet of his thought which does not seem logically connected with other facets. This peculiarity is perhaps the only excuse for the depreciation of Dacier, who, reinforcing his native dulness with the superciliousness of a Frenchman in the later years of Louis XIV., accused Castelvetro of ignorance, and even of contradiction of Aristotle. The fact is, that Castelvetro is first of all an independent critic, and that, though there are few less common, there are no more valuable critical qualities than independence, even when it is sometimes pushed to the verge of eccentricity, providing only that it is sincere, and not ill-informed. It seems to me uncharitable, if not flagrantly unjust, to deny Castelvetro sincerity, and either impudent or ignorant to deny him information.

But he had also acuteness and taste. I do not know a better example in little of the latter quality at the time than his short and scornful description of a preposterous comparison by another critic, Bartolommeo Riccio, between the "Sparrow" of Catullus and a pretty but commonplace poem of Navagero on a dog. One may sigh over the ruling passion, not to say the original sin, of critical man, on passing from this to a tangle of recrimination and "that's *my* thunder" which follows with reference to Riccio and Pigna and Cinthio. But this

passes again into a solid discussion on the material and form of poetry, and on the office of the Muses. Many of these animadversions are, as we should expect, purely verbal, sometimes not beyond the powers of the *grammaticuccio,* of whom Castelvetro himself not unfrequently talks with piquant scorn. But the comfort of finding annotations on Virgil alternating with discourses on Dante, like that of placing a quarto on Petrarch side by side with one on Aristotle, more than atones for any occasional hair-splitting. We are at last in the Jerusalem of general Literature which is the mother of us all, which is free and universal; not in this or that separatist Samaria or exclusive Hebron. The Platonic annotations, which are numerous, are important, because they show just the other side of Castelvetro's talent from the merely verbal one—almost the whole of them being devoted to the exposition and illustration of meaning. It is a great pity that he did not work his notes on the *Gorgias* (which he regards expressly as Plato's *Rhetoric*) into a regular treatise of contrast and comparison on this subject between Aristotle and Plato. But all these notes show us the qualification of the commentator to deal with so difficult a subject as the *Poetics.* (pp. 80-2)

No analysis of a book of such a size, so necessarily parasitic or satellitic on another in general run, and yet branching and winding with such a self-willed originality of its own, is possible. One might easily write a folio on Castelvetro's quarto. Here we can only, as in most other cases now, except those of books or parts of books at once epoch-making in character and moderate in bulk, give an idea of the author's most important views on general and particular points. It was necessary, since Castelvetro is revolving round Aristotle, that the greater part of his treatise should deal with the drama: and perhaps nowhere is that originality which has been praised more visible than here, whether it lead him wrong or right. He has undoubtedly made a step, from the mathematical towards the æsthetic view of literature, in conditioning, as he does, his view of the Drama by a consideration of the stage. To literary *a-priorists* this is of course horrible; to those who take the facts of literature, as they take the facts of life, it is a welcome and reconciling discovery. The conditions of the Greek stage were admittedly such as can never be naturally reproduced, and therefore, however great and perfect the Greek Tragedy may be in its own way, it cannot usurp the position of "best in all ways"; and can still less pretend to dictate to other kinds that they shall not be good at all in ways different from its own.

If the details of Castelvetro's theory do not always correspond in excellence to the sense and novelty of the general view, this is because he adulterates his notion of stage requirements with that unlucky "verisimilitude" misunderstood, which is the curse of all the neo-classic critics, and which comes from neglect of the Aristotelian preference of the probable-impossible to the improbable-possible. The huge Mysteries of the Middle Ages, which ranged from Heaven to Hell, which took weeks to act, and covered millennia in their action, did at least this good to the English and some other theatres—that they familiarised the mind with the neglect of this verisimilitude. But Castelvetro would have none of such neglect. His play must be adjusted, not merely in Action, but in Space and Time, as nearly as possible to the actual capacity of the stage, the actual duration of the performance. And so the Fatal Three, the Weird Sisters of dramatic criticism, the vampires that sucked the blood out of nearly all European tragedy, save in England and Spain, for three centuries, make their appearance. They "enter the critical literature of Europe," as Mr. Spingarn has very truly laid it down, "from the time of Castelvetro" [see excerpt dated 1899].

But to balance this enslaving of the Drama (in which he far exceeds Aristotle), Castelvetro frees the Epic from Aristotelian restrictions in an almost equally important manner. From his references in the **Opere Varie** to Cinthio and Pigna, it would appear that he claimed, if not priority, an even portion with them in the consideration of the subject of Epic Poetry. And though not agreeing with them altogether, he certainly agrees with them in enlarging the domains of the Epic. Poetry, he says in effect, may do anything that History can do; and, like the latter, it may deal, not only with one action of one man, but with his life-actions, or with many actions of many men.

With Castelvetro, however,—and it is probably the cause why pedants like Dacier undervalue him,—both the character of his compositions, and probably also the character of his mind, draw him much more to independent, though by no means always or often isolated, critical *aperçus* and judgments, than to theoretical discourses, with or without illustration. To put it differently, while there is usually a theory at the back of his appreciations, the appreciation generally stands in front of the theory. But however this may be, that quality of "unexpectedness," in which some æsthetic theorists have found such a charm, belongs to him as it does to few critics. One might, for instance, give half-a-dozen guesses to a tolerably ingenious person without his hitting on Castelvetro's objection to the story of Ricciardetto and Fiordispina in the *Orlando.* That objection is not moral: not on the ground of what is ordinarily called decorum: not on that of digression, on that of improbability generally, on any other that is likely to occur. It is, if you please, that as Fiordispina was a Mahometan, and Ricciardetto a Christian, and as Christians and Mahometans do not believe in the same kind of Fauns and Fairies, as, further, Fauns do not eat ladies or goddesses, whether alive or dead, Ricciardetto's explanation of his alleged transformation of sex is not credible. In a modern writer this would look like an absolute absence of humour, or like a clumsy attempt at it; and I am not prepared to say that humour was a strong point with these Italian critics as a rule. But Castelvetro strikes me as being by no means exceptionally unprovided with it: and such a glaring lapse as this is probably due to the intense seriousness with which these critical questions, new as they were, presented themselves to him and to his class.

They get, as was once said, "into logical coaches"; and are perfectly content to be driven over no matter what minor precipices, and into no matter what sloughs of despond, so long as they are not actually thrown out. Yet Castelvetro at least is never dull. At one time he compares the "somnolent indecorum," the *sconvenevolezza sonnachiosa,* of Homer to the practice of German innkeepers (whether observed by himself in his exile, or taken from Erasmus, one cannot say) in putting the worst wines and viands on the table first, and the best later. Elsewhere he gives a very curious reason against that other *sconvenevolezza* (this sonorous word is a great favourite with him) which he too saw in the use of prose for tragedy—namely, that in reciting verse the speaker *naturally* raises his voice, and so makes it more audible to the audience. He has been blamed for adopting the notion of rank being necessary to tragic characters, but on this see *ante.*

His irreverent independence in regard to Virgil is noticeable in a critic of his time, and of course especially so if one comes

to him straight from Scaliger. It would not be fair to represent him as a "Virgiliomastix," but his finer critical sense enables him to perceive the superiority of Homer, in respect of whom he goes so far as to say that Virgil "is not a poet." But this—*per se,* of course, excessive—had been provoked by the extravagance of Maronolatry from Vida downwards: and Castelvetro does not scruple to praise the Mantuan for his grasp, his variety of phrase, and other good things. He has an extremely sensible passage—not novel to us, but by no means a truism to his contemporaries or to a good many poets still—on what he who publishes miscellaneous poetry has to expect. By the publication, says this other Messer Lodovico, of a thing which nobody asked him for (*cosa non richiesta*) without any necessity, he publishes at the same time his confidence in himself, and affirms that the thing is good. "Which thing," goes on Castelvetro in his pitiless critical manner, "if it be found to be faulty (*rea*) and blame-worthy, it convicts him who publishes it either of malice or of folly." Alas! for the minor bard.

His attitude to the everlastingly vexed question of the connection of verse and poetry is very sensible, and practically anticipates, with less reluctant circumlocution, that of Coleridge, who in more things than one comes close to Castelvetro, and who probably knew him. He does not here contradict Aristotle by denying that verse is un*essential* to poetry. But he insists—and points out the undoubted truth that Aristotle's practice, whatever his theory may do, admits this—that Verse is a kind of inseparable accident of poetry,—that it is the appropriate garb and uniform thereof, which cannot be abandoned without impropriety. And he takes up this attitude still more emphatically in regard to the closely connected, and still more important, question of the *end* of Poetry. Here, as we have seen, the great Master of Criticism temporised. He did not doubt that this end was Delight: but in deference to idols, partly of the Cavern, partly of the Marketplace, he yokes and hampers this end with moral improvement, with Imitation, itself for itself, and so on. Castelvetro is much more uncompromising. One shudders, almost as much as one rejoices, at the audacity of a critic who in mid-sixteenth-century calmly says, "What do beginning, middle, and end matter in a poem, provided it delights?" Nay, Castelvetro has reached a point of view which has since been attained by very few critics, and which some who thought they had gained this peak in Darien first may be mildly chagrined to find occupied by him—the view that there are different *qualities* of poetry, suited to delight different qualities of persons and of mind.

How seldom this view has been taken all critics ought to know, if they do not. Even now he who climbs the peak must lay his account with stone-throwing from the garrisons of other points. That Burns administers, and has a right to administer, one delight to one class of mind, Shelley another to another; that Béranger is not to be denied the wine of poetry because his vintage is not the vintage of Hugo: that Longfellow, and Cowper, and George Herbert are not to be sneered at because their delight is the delight of cheering but not of intoxication; that Keble is not intrinsically the less a poet because he is not Beddoes, or Charles Wesley because he is not Charles Baudelaire—or *vice versa* in all the cases—these are propositions which not every critic—which perhaps not very many critics—will admit even in the abstract, and which in practice almost every critic falsifies and renounces at some time or other. But they are propositions which follow fairly, and indeed inevitably, from Castelvetro's theory of the necessary end, Delight, and the varying adjustment of the delighting agent to the patient's faculty of being delighted.

He is perhaps less sound in his absolute condemnation of "knowledge" as material for poetry. He is right in black-marking Fracastoro from this point of view: but he is certainly not right in extending the black mark to Lucretius. The fact is, that even he could not wrench himself sufficiently free from the trammels of old time to see that in the treatment lies the faculty of delighting, and that therefore, on his own scheme, the treatment is the poetry.

There are few writers to be dealt with in this volume—none, I think, already dealt with—to whom it would be more satisfactory to devote the minutest handling than to Castelvetro. He has been called by Mr. Spingarn "revolutionary." The term, in an American mouth, probably has no unfavourable connotation; but waiving that connotation altogether, I should be inclined to demur to it. Even the *Vehmgericht* (if one may rely on the leading case of *Vgr.* v. *Philipson,* reported by Sir Walter Scott) acquitted of High Treason those who had spoken evil of it in countries where its authority was not acknowledged, and indeed its name hardly known. Now, Castelvetro was dealing—as we must, for his honour as well as for our comprehension of him, remember that he dealt—with modern as well as with ancient literature at once, and instead of adopting the injudicious though natural separation of Minturno, or the one-sided treatment of Scaliger, was constantly exploring, and always more or less keeping in view, territories not merely in which Aristotle's writ did not run, but which in Aristotle's time were No Man's Land and *terra incognita.* He can no more be regarded as a revolutionary or a rebel, in framing new laws for the new facts, than a man could be regarded in either light for disregarding the Curfew Law at the North Pole, or for disobeying sumptuary regulations as to the use of woollen in the tropics. His *ethos* is really that of the self-reliant, resourceful, and adventurous explorer, as he has been called—of the experimenter in new material and under new conditions. That the paths he strikes out sometimes lead to *culs-de-sac*—that the experiments he makes sometimes fail, is nothing more than is natural, than is inevitable in the circumstances.

More generally his value is great, and we may forgive him (especially since he did *us* little or no harm) the binding of the Unities on the necks of Frenchmen and Italians, in consideration of the inestimable service which he did in standing up for Epic—that is, Romantic—Unity of a different kind, and in formulating, in a "No Surrender" fashion, the doctrine of Delight as the Poetic Criterion. By doing this he not merely fought for the freedom of the long narrative poem (which, as it happens, has been a matter of minor importance, save at rare intervals, since his time), but he unknowingly safeguarded the freedom of the long narrative prose romance or novel, which was to be the most important new contribution of modern times to literature. Nor may it be amiss once more to draw attention to a more general merit still, the inestimable *indifference* with which he continually handles ancient and modern examples. Only by this—the wisest "indifference of the wise"—can true criticism be reached. It is an indifference which neglects no change of condition, which takes count of all features and circumstances, but which, for that very reason, declines to allow ancient literature to prescribe unconditionally to modern, or modern to ancient, or either to mediæval. As to this last, Castelvetro has, and could be expected to have, nothing to say: as to the others, he is more

eloquent in practice than in express theory. But his practice speaks his conviction, and it is the practice by which, and by which alone, the serene temples of the really Higher Criticism can be reached. (pp. 83-9)

George Saintsbury, "Scaliger, Castelvetro, and the Later Italian Critics of the Sixteenth Century," in his A History of Criticism and Literary Taste in Europe from the Earliest Texts to the Present Day, *Vol. II, William Blackwood & Sons Ltd., 1902, pp. 69-108.*

H. B. CHARLTON   (essay date 1913)

[*In the following excerpt, Charlton appraises Castelvetro's theories as profound discoveries in their own time but outdated and flawed after centuries of critical scrutiny.*]

Bearing in mind the facts that Castelvetro's chief work is a commentary on the *Poetics,* and that it follows this closely in order and in subject, we may anticipate some of the more general qualities of his doctrine. Like Aristotle, he has no complete theory of art: he has no theory of the beautiful. The word 'bellezza' occurs but once or twice throughout the *Poetica;* and from one or two allusions, it is evident that Castelvetro holds to the formal beauty of the early Greek philosophers; indeed, he specifically defines the beautiful as "restricted within the limits of proportionate lines, measures, and colours." Still, by virtue of greater length alone, Castelvetro is more explicit than is Aristotle. He has interesting references to the other fine arts, many to painting, one or two to sculpture and architecture. It is doubtful, however, if Castelvetro's conception of painting would justify its inclusion amongst the fine arts. He has no idea of its artistic function; to him, its end is in photographic reproduction—"nell' evidentemente rassomigliare," "in making similar to the true, the living, and the natural." At most, the artist may imitate beauty if his model is a beautiful woman; but the formal conception of beauty, mentioned above, modifies this to futility.

Further, Castelvetro's treatise runs to a great length; in arrangement, his method lends itself to prolixity, and in content, his wide survey of literature includes references to Hebrew, Greek, Latin, and Italian letters, epic and drama, prose and verse, with a special penchant for Boccaccio, for most of which riches he has an admiration, never, like Vida, an idolatry. Yet despite this width of outlook and length of treatment, it remains true that Castelvetro's most apparent and keenest interest is in the drama, or rather, in tragedy. But perhaps this study will show that his main contribution to poetic theory, is not to that of tragedy, nor indeed to that of drama, but to the inclusive idea of poetry as a fine art. Like Aristotle, he deals with comedy, but only in so far as a dramatic theorist cannot entirely neglect this species. Like Aristotle, he treats of the epic, but only sporadically; that is, if a sporadic and incidental treatment is possible to a 16th century commentator. Like Aristotle, he neglects the theory of lyric poetry almost entirely; in the *Opere Varie Critiche,* the canzoni of Petrarch and Dante are brought under notice, but only to the extent of explanatory and textual annotations. Like that of the Aristotle's *Poetics,* his main theme is a consideration of tragedy. And even here, a further limitation may be made. Castelvetro's interest is not primarily philosophical and in the idea of drama. It is more practically dramaturgic, with a view to the repertoire of the future stage. Yet Castelvetro had a keen speculative insight, he was "the most subtle of all the Commentators," says Rapin, and so, avowedly practical and particular as he is, he is always guided by a philosophic conception of the idea of drama, or of the idea of poetry. If he has no clear vision of these ideas as themselves components of and subordinate to the supreme idea of art, it is because his genius was not so universal as Aristotle's. And that is no damnatory admission. (pp. 16-18)

In an age when criticism was a legislation whose first and last sanction was the authority of the old world, Castelvetro stands forth as a critic of refreshingly open mind and independence of judgment. Art is justified by its end, by something, if not precisely inherent, yet directly immediate to itself, and not by a phrase of any the greatest philosopher of the world. Its end is an immediate consequence of its immanent nature, and is ever present with us. To look back through the ages to imitate the practice or follow the precepts of the ancients, forgetting the spirit of the day that is here, is inartistic and annihilatory. For art is always new and original, a perpetual youth rivalling nature in its creative force. But Aristotle's theory of imitation had misled the critics of the Renaissance. . . . (pp. 173-74)

[There] is in the Renaissance, as perhaps in Aristotle himself, a confusion of two ideas under the term 'imitation': there is the idea of a static imitation which expresses the relation of the work of art to its prototype in the ideal, and there is the idea of a dynamic imitation, denoting psychologically the artistic process by which genius creates a work of art according to the ideal: the static imitation is a term which would be applied to a work of art considered as a thing in relation to another thing, namely to its ideal, and the dynamic imitation is a term which would be applied to the kind of energy involved in the creation of a work of art. Of neither of these ideas of imitation have the Renaissance critics in general a true conception. Confusion is further confounded by their doctrine of the imitation of the ancients, in accordance with which the prototype is not in the ideal, but is a concrete instance of ancient poetry, and following from this, the process one merely of mechanical copying. By the importation of idealism alone is the theory of imitation valuable, and only thus is it cut apart from its radical suggestion of copying: for we generally imply by a copy, a consideration of a concrete prototype, and a technical means of reproduction. A truer name than imitation is necessary for artistic idealisation. That Castelvetro realised. But to Renaissance critics generally, artistic imitation is imitation of the ancients. (pp. 175-76)

That Castelvetro, in the face of all his contemporaries, will have none of the imitation of the ancients, is a blow struck for the emancipation of art, and for its eternal good, even although the specific reasons he alleges for the rejection of this noxious dogma are no more than specious: he rejects it because reproduction in the sense of copying involves no artistic difficulty overcome.

This brings us to one of the central pillars on which Castelvetro's art of poetry is built, the notion of the *difficulté vaincue*, the fatigue to be endured by the artist, of which the flagrant signs are a witness to his originality. This idea, more than that of verisimilitude, pertains to the essence of Castelvetro's theory. For the uncultured mob recognises art by the clear marks of the difficulty of its production: these to them are the positive sign of art: the verisimility is not so obviously apparent, being more negatively so, rather in the breach than in the observance.

The proclamation of the true poet is the sign of the difficulty overcome. This is a most dangerous doctrine: but Castelvetro fits it in with his theory of conscious, as opposed to inspired, art, and further still, with his theory of the appeal of art primarily to the "moltitudine rozza." For it is the apparent sign of wonderful skill which first excites the untrained observer. (p. 178)

To fix the eye on the artist is a tacit declaration that the substance of art is immaterial. Cleverness can be shown in the painting of a flower vase as well as in the portrayal of a Monna Lisa: but not genius. Hence, the failure to satisfy our artistic sense in the greater part of the Dutch school of still life: the Berlin Gallery has a huge canvas on which the painter of the Laughing Cavalier dissipated his time and degraded his genius to copy an exquisitely wrought chalice of gold; and this type of work has the approbation of the difficulty overcome, though it would not be justified by Castelvetro's full theory of art, for he insists on a human substance. It may be true . . . that a pleasure is derived by the artist himself from the sense of conquered difficulty: but it certainly is not true in most cases. To set over against his opinion is that of a greater artist than he. . . . True art is untrammelled, a thing of inspiration. The process of its birth, if not entirely hidden, is not primarily apparent; it does not enter into the immediate pleasure. The realised genius confronting the senses is the art, and the art alone. The purely intellectual interest is a secondary pleasure outside the scope of pure æsthetics. It is not part of the philosophy of the beautiful as a thing of beauty, but is a contribution to the science of the psychology of genius. And in a concrete work of the highest art, the artist is forgotten. He only emerges at the call of after-consideration, when art is being regarded in its human, philosophical or historical aspects: and though these questions are essential to a universal culture, where art is at one with the manifold expressions of life in full, yet they are an excrescence of art, and not of its essence. The difficulty overcome is no true æsthetic pleasure. But it is presumption to write where Ruskin has written before.

> The skill of the artist and the perfection of his art are never proved until both are forgotten. The artist has done nothing till he has concealed himself, the art is imperfect which is visible, the feelings are but feebly touched if they permit us to reason on the methods of their excitement. . . . The power of the the masters is shown by their self-annihilation. It is commensurate with the degree in which they themselves appear not in their work. The harp of the minstrel is untruly touched if his own glory is all that it records. Every great writer may be at once known by his guiding the mind far from himself to the beauty which is not of his creation, and the knowledge which is past his finding out.

One of Dante's arguments for the choice of the vulgar tongue as the language of poetry, is its "prontezza di liberalità"; all humanity, the vulgar and the learned, the peasant and the noble are within the radiance of its largess universal as the sun. The Renaissance, however, was essentially aristocratic, and its aristocracy was one of learning more than one of blood. Hence the tendency for poetry to be academic, the pleasure of the select. In Castelvetro there is the reaction. Poetry is by its nature an appeal to the mass of the people, and their pleasure alone is its function. This attitude is thoroughly typical of Castelvetro. He sees the error of his times, and sets himself against it: but in the reaction, he drives too far, and passes the point where impartiality would halt. In a similar way he protests rightly that poetry is not history: he ends wrongly by denying that the matter of history can be the matter of poetry. In this way, also, he raises his voice against the literary trickery and the codified artifices which a Horatian and Virgilian idolatry had sanctified as the sole instruments of poetry; he will have no compulsion of Horace's artificial order in the epic, "in medias res non secus ac notas, auditorem rapit": but in the rejection, he falls into a dogmatism almost as dangerous; the poet must follow the strict order of history. That is, in casting out artificiality, Castelvetro often leaves little room for art.

And so too, in this case of the function of poetry. Dante's universality of the appeal of art is limited by Castelvetro to the pleasure of the mob. As a contribution to æsthetic theory, this is ultimately unsatisfactory: as an immediate counterblast to the pedantry of his own times, it is incomparably salutary. Art had its origin in human nature, says Aristotle, because it is a human necessity. The baby is crooned to sleep by a lullaby: youth is stirred to battle by a martial ballad: man is borne to his gràve to the solemnity of a *marche funèbre.* "Even among the most barbarous and simple Indians," Sidney assures us, "where no writing is, yet have they their poets, who make and sing songs which they call Areytos, both of their ancestors' deeds and the praises of their gods." Wherever there is life, there is art: for life is the impulse for expression, and its ultimate expression is art. But not only have we the crude gods of the Chinese pagoda and the uncouth songs of the aborigines; not only have we this art which is the spontaneous expression of emotional necessity: we have also the paintings of Italy, the sculptures of Greece, and the dramas of Shakespeare; we have an art in the creation of which necessity has yielded to genius. And yet their nature is the same. One is the confused cry of the heart of men: the other is the ideal voice of one in whose soul the essence of humanity has sublimed itself. One is the cry of the emotions, uttered instinctively for the relief of the utterance: the other is their song, sung for its music alone. But both have their being in and for the emotions. When the minstrel refines the subtleties of his lays forgetful of the feelings of his listeners, his art has become artificial: the Meistersinger has ousted the Minnesinger. And these feelings are common to all men. Wherever there is human nature, there is potential susceptibility to art; for she moves her hearers not in so far as they are kings or scholars or mobs, but in so far as they are men.

Romanticism—and there is much of the Romantic in Castelvetro—turns back from the cities which man made to the woods which are old as the hills. Wordsworth held that the diction of poetry should be a selection of the language of men of humble and rustic life. But Wordsworth only meant that the fundamental human instincts and human passions, with the words which are their visible symbols, are more evident on the native hills of the rustic than in the crowded streets of his more civilised fellow, so that the poet who seeks to express our stark humanity by the throb of vital language finds his best material and his best means in rustic life. Wordsworth never for a moment meant that the peasant is more susceptible to the humanity of art. For art does not impinge on the feelings like a mountain wind: it is only seen and felt through a medium. Bare nature is blind to this. The eye must be taught to see, the ear to hear, and the mind to understand the old world in the new form to which the limbec of the poet's art has transmuted it. But with this reservation, the most instinctive and most unsophisticated nature is the one that feels the fulness of art. Emotional existence has there its

primitive strength: culture alone is necessary to give it width of range. But artistic culture seeks only to open the eyes of the blind: it seeks only to develop natural instincts. It never attempts to add to nature an extraneous accomplishment. For art strikes straight to the native passions: and these are as stunted by the necessities of a sordid existence in the mob as they are smothered by the dust of the bookshelves and the fumes of the midnight oil in a pedant's study.

But pedants had been constituted arbiters of poetry; the curse of a finical intellectuality had descended on art. By referring the ultimate appeal to the mob, Castelvetro removed the bane of scholastic eccentricity: but he substituted that of superficial sensationalism. Again, he has preached to his fellows the error of their ways; and again, his fanaticism has passed beyond the truth. Eclecticism became vulgarity instead of halting at universality. (pp. 180-85)

There is another point which is closely associated with Castelvetro's view of the direction of the poetic appeal, and in accord with the logical harmony of his whole theory. He asserts the position firmly that poetry has only pleasure as its function, and going further, he attempts a definition of the pleasure in psychological terms. He finds it, as we have seen, in the 'maraviglia.' Tragedy loves the unexpected, the surprising: dramatic critics and dramatic poets are particularly liable to lay stress on the marvellous. The underlying notion would seem to be that fear is intensified by conjunction with the effect of the marvellous: in Castelvetro's words, "la maraviglia è il colmo dello spavento." (pp. 187-88)

What Castelvetro meant precisely by his 'maraviglia' is not clear. At any rate, the 'verisimile' prevented any wild flights. But any theory which propounds the effect of the marvellous as the primary æsthetic function is false, and has the manifold dangers of all falsity. Its place is in the art of melodrama, not in the art of poetry. The Heroic drama which dazzled almost all Europe in the seventeenth century is its offspring; and under the power of its enchantment, Corneille turned from such masterpieces as the *Cid* and *Horace,* to produce monstrous imbroglios like *Rodogune.*

Castelvetro's conception of the art of poetry needs little criticism. Nobody believes now that the poet is just a man as other men. Despite Castelvetro, the artist has in him some sparks of divine inspiration. Theory may not prove this in syllogism: but experience testifies to it in fact. . . . We can dismiss Castelvetro's idea of a poet-producing art of poetry as false and antiquated. If we are to seek in criticism a positive aid to creation, we must find it rather in the maintenance of a current of ideas than in the formulation of a specific technical cyclopædia. We must follow Matthew Arnold rather than Castelvetro. And perhaps we must not follow him too closely.

Of Castelvetro's theory in general, the fundamental fallacy is the insufficiency of the premises from which it is developed. He takes one form of poetic art, namely the drama, and the conditions pertaining to it. His conclusions are thus based on particular limitations. Yet he often gives them universal validity. One example will be sufficient illustration. Drama must be acted on the public stage: therefore it must appeal to a public audience, that is, says Castelvetro, to the mob. But then, with reminiscences of the ancient bards and gleemen, he proceeds to generalise his conclusion: all poetry must have this specific aim. Such a method can obviously only be logical when the limiting conditions are not peculiar to the form of art under immediate notice, but hold good in all artistic species. For instance, all art is the transference of some form to a substance alien from it by nature. Sculpture gives to marble the form of man: music gives to sound the form of melody: poetry gives to words the form of rhythm: drama gives to actors the form of a life other than their own. Hence the necessity in all art of an æsthetic semblance by means of which the incongruity between the material and the ideal form of the matter is overcome. This is Aristotle's doctrine of verisimilitude. But verisimilitude is absolutely of no account in a consideration of the relation of matter to form: that is a question not of the semblance of truth but of truth itself, not of coincidence but of identity. The only validity of the principle of the 'verisimile' is in the adjustment of the material to the matter in its ideal form.

But in drama the material is of the concrete things of life: drama, as Castelvetro points out, not only imitates words by words, but also things by things. And its ideal form is an image of life. The common term leads to the unwarranted presumption of identity. The identical laws conditioning the things by which the representation is made also condition the things in their natural form, which are to be represented in an ideal form: and so the representation, that is, the matter in its ideal form, is shackled with the laws which govern the thing represented and the means of representation. Art is to obey the laws of time and space incident to natural life. The stage with its effects, that is, part of the material of the dramatic art, has become coincident with its matter: and both are thus to be in the same sense verisimilar. So verisimilitude produces the unities, but it is a verisimilitude which has ceased to be æsthetic.

Castelvetro's theory of the unities must be rejected. Still in his defence of them he stands above his contemporaries. With him they are part of a theory, namely, that of verisimilitude. And moreover, as we have tried to show, there is a verisimilitude which is a necessary constituent of æsthetic theory. It is not, however, the verisimility of pure reason, but that of imaginative reason. Even Coleridge's "willing suspension of disbelief" seems to point to a misconception of the really æsthetic verisimilitude: for it implies a process in which pure reason is free to exercise its function according to the criteria of reality. In no other way could 'disbelief' arise to require a 'willing suspension.' The truer account seems to be that pure reason makes neither positive nor negative decision, having no function in the æsthetic judgment, which is within the scope of the imaginative reason alone. (pp. 191-94)

[We] make no claim that Castelvetro is a Hegel, a Kant, or an Aristotle. We have endeavoured to show that he has a firmer hold on æsthetic truth than have his immediate forerunners; that as a theorist of poetry, he is above Tasso, as a theorist of æsthetics, at least his equal; that as an expositor of the idea of drama and particularly of tragedy he is unique in a long period of time when the epic dominated critical attention; and that above all he is the man of his age "from whom," in Rapin's words, "most may be learnt." He stands for openness of mind, and a disposition to enquire into the root of the matter, for an insight which pierces to the radical error. His method and genius lead him to such fundamental truths as the assertion of the true function of art, the originality of the artist, and the rejection of conventional trickery: and all this in the sixteenth century. On the other hand, he is responsible for the ushering of the unities into dramatic criticism, and for the theory of the difficulty overcome. Unfortunately, these were the parts of his doctrine which had

the most apparent and immediate influence on his successors. But take him for all in all, he is the most illuminating critic of the art of poetry between Longinus and Dryden; one, with whom to err, is a liberal critical education. (pp. 211-12)

> *H. B. Charlton, in his* Castelvetro's Theory of Poetry, *Manchester at the University Press, 1913, 221 p.*

THE NATION   (essay date 1914)

[*In the following excerpt, the anonymous critic praises Castelvetro for his unprecedented study of aesthetic theory and philology.*]

The mentality of Lodovico Castelvetro has been the subject of continuous admiration from his own time to the present. There has been less willingness since the time of Vico to credit him with much else. De Sanctis, who read him a half century and more ago, did not reconstitute his personality. From America, in fact, came, in the work of Spingarn, the first definite appreciation of Castelvetro's real distinction. Croce, Cavazzuti, Bertoni, Vivaldi, and Trabalza have taken up successively his case. To-day we may say that his work is present in all essential traits before us. As a commentator on Aristotle's *Poetics,* Castelvetro stands out in modern times with Butcher and St. Hilaire. In certain details he sees the real import of Aristotle's ideas more clearly than Aristotle himself; in every respect he has a juster notion of the *Poetics* than all of his contemporaries. In æsthetic theory itself Castelvetro's case seems irretrievable. He never attained to solid fundamental principles; he fluctuates and gropes, showing moments of keen vision and moments of absurdity. Here he is extraordinarily interesting, and that is all, in relation to many specific problems of literary history.

When we pass to philology, on the other hand, the situation is different. It is not enough to recognize him as the greatest of his period; he leads in this department not only his own age, but all before the rise of modern philological science in the nineteenth century. At the base of his method lie the two foundations of phonetics and, in morphology, of analogy. Leaving aside the capricious guesses of his contemporaries in etymology, he lays Vulgar Latin at the basis of Romance studies, and proceeds with a comparative method and with the same categories that are in use to-day. . . .

If Castelvetro had no notion of the expressive nature of art, he was original in his time in substituting pleasure for didacticism as the function of poetry, and his hedonism has a superficial if not a radical democratic outlook. He was original, too, in seeing the futility of classic imitation in literature; and thus coming back to the insistence on original invention in art, he was at the threshold of real discovery, only to lose himself in the problem of "historicity" and fantasy, of "beautiful" and "ugly," and in details of perceptual formalism. (p. 19)

> *A review of, "Castelvetro's Theory of Poetry," in* The Nation, *New York, Vol. XCIX, No. 2557, July 2, 1914, pp. 19-20.*

ALLAN H. GILBERT   (essay date 1940)

[*In the following excerpt, Gilbert offers a succinct critical description of Castelvetro's* Poetica d'Aristotele.]

It is not an accident that in recent times Lodovico Castelvetro has attracted perhaps more attention than any other Italian critic of the Renaissance, certainly more than any other who is not both poet and critic. His commentary on Aristotle is full, explicit, and painstaking, and yet often acute; he is, moreover, not afraid to take what in his day were unpopular positions, as in his assertions that pleasure is the end of poetry and that the poet need not be a learned man. Yet his abilities were recognized to such an extent that the references of six-teenth-century writers to critics and commentators are likely to include him or to refer to him alone. It is not strange that in the next century Milton thought of him as one of the chief expositors of Aristotle's *Poetics*. Notwithstanding his well-deserved reputation, he is not without faults, usually those of the scholar. He is unnecessarily prolix, and though willing to revolt against the thought of his own age, he is under the au-thority of Aristotle. Though familiar with Italian literature, he yet regards it through the eyes of former critics rather than seeing it as something not quite amenable to Greek princi-ples. Thoroughgoing in his rationalism, he has the unenviable distinction of having formulated the so-called unities of place and time. Yet within his limits he is admirable; he sees how Aristotle can be applied, and few important ideas in the liter-ary thought of his age escape his analysis. . . . (p. 304)

Allan H. Gilbert, "Lodovico Castelvetro," in his Lit-erary Criticism: Plato to Dryden, *American Book Company, 1940, pp. 304-57.*

BERNARD WEINBERG (essay date 1952)

[*In the excerpt below, Weinberg asserts that although Castelve-tro's poetic theories are based upon Aristotle's* Poetics, *many of his conclusions are "un-Aristotelian."*]

In the history of modern literary criticism Lodovico Castel-vetro figures as the man who invented the three pseudo-Aristotelian unities of time, place, and action. Or at least he is credited with having given the first complete expression to the time-place-action complex and with having thus exerted an important influence on the development of the classical doctrine. This is perhaps a correct estimate of his contribu-tion. But it does not emphasize as fully as it should his real position in the movement away from the text of Aristotle and toward the theory of the French classicists. That position is not so much a matter of the incidental question of the unities as it is of his total philosophical approach, of his general treatment of poetic matters, of his method of analysis. For Castelvetro, whose **Poetica d'Aristotele vulgarizzata et sposta** dates from 1570, represents in a sense a culmination of the tendencies already manifest in the first commentary on Aristotle's *Poetics*, Robortello's *In librum Aristotelis De arte poetica explicationes* of 1548. He incorporates in his discus-sion the accretion of the intervening years; and what he pro-duces, since it is more extreme, is much farther away from the text of Aristotle and much closer to the point of view of French classicism.

The first notable difference between Robortello and Castelve-tro is to be found in their attitude toward Aristotle himself. For Robortello, the text which he is expounding is a master-piece of clarity and logic. He pauses frequently to point out the excellence of its construction, to defend it against those who hold that it is fragmentary, imperfect, or erroneous. His intention is to justify and accept integrally the text of Aristot-le; if he comes up with an essentially un-Aristotelian analysis, it is because of his incapacity to understand the text and be-cause of long-standing habits of textual exposition, and not through any intention to disagree. With Castelvetro, the point of departure is a basic scorn for the text of the *Poetics*. The *Poetics* is not a complete work, but "a collection of poetic materials from which an art might be written"; it includes re-marks which Aristotle meant later to refute or reject; many passages are out of place; and there are obvious contradic-tions. But these are merely matters of organization; Castelve-tro's contempt goes farther. He does not hesitate to charac-terize certain ideas of Aristotle's as false: "Aristotle here and elsewhere is of the opinion that the same pleasure is derived from tragedy through reading it as through seeing it and hearing it recited in action; which thing I esteem to be false"; "Now, according to Aristotle, poetry always imitates one of the three things indicated by him. . . . This does not seem true to me, simply speaking"; "Now Aristotle assumes as simply true a thing which is not so at all." He rejects Aristot-le's ideas when they seem inadequately supported: "I should wish this to be shown to me otherwise than on his authority, since he seems to say and repeat several times this same thing without adducing a single reason of any value." He goes so far as to ask the question, given the uselessness of Aristotle's precepts to the art of history: "What will prevent us, follow-ing the strength of this argument, from being constrained to say that these precepts are neither proper nor useful to poetry itself?"

Nothing is farther from Castelvetro's mind, then, than to at-tempt a justification of the Aristotelian text. He tries to ex-plain it when he can, to point out what he thinks Aristotle meant. But generally he uses it as a point of departure for the development of his own theories. His favorite device is to take a given passage in the *Poetics*, show how and why the distinc-tions made are incomplete and incorrect, and then proceed to his own set of distinctions on the same subject. We may take as an example his treatment of *Poetics* 1460a26, on the impossible probable:

> Now, if I am not mistaken, this question would have been better understood, and greater light would have been shed upon the things which need to be said, if three divisions had been made, in each one of which would be the virtue to be followed and the vice to be avoided. And the first would be that of possibility and impossibility, and the second would be that of credibility and incredibility; these two divisions have been discussed so far. And the third would be that of usefulness and of uselessness to the constitution of the plot.

From this point he proceeds to a development of the distinc-tion, to a subdivision into eight possible combinations, to the statement that the first and second divisions belong "to na-ture, or to civil and human reason," whereas the third is the proper province of the poet. There are a score or more of sim-ilar passages. Castelvetro's real aim seems, then, to be the substitution of his own ideas for Aristotle's and the develop-ment of a set of statements which may properly be called "Castelvetro's theory of poetics."

I

Among those tendencies which, already in Robortello, marked a departure from the spirit of the *Poetics*, the most significant methodologically is the removal of the principal emphasis from the poem to the audience. Such a transforma-tion means that all aspects of poetry are considered not in terms of the artistic exigencies of the poem itself but in terms of the needs or demands of a specifically characterized audience. Now in Castelvetro this tendency is pushed to the extreme: the audience is very carefully delimited and restricted, and every phase of the poetic art is considered in relationship to this audience. In the first place, Castelvetro assumes that Aristotle treats only such genres as were susceptible of public performance and that hence his audience is the "common people": "poetry was invented for the pleasure of the ignorant multitude and of the common people, and not for the pleasure of the educated"; "for purposes of the common people, and for the pleasure alone of the rough crowd, was invented the stage and the representative [or dramatic] manner." Any audience of the elite is specifically excluded: "it is not true that in poetic imitations one must pay greater attention to the distaste of the intelligent spectators than to the joy of the ignorant spectators." At times, special segments or special conditions of the audience will have to be taken into account: its political complexion will determine its reactions to given works, and those members of the audience who are parents will have a peculiar attitude toward given plots.

Since the elite and the educated are thus rigorously excluded, certain qualities of the mind will be denied the audience:

> poetry [was] invented exclusively to delight and give recreation, I say to delight and give recreation to the minds of the rough crowd and of the common people, which does not understand the reasons, or the distinctions, or the arguments—subtle and distant from the usage of the ignorant—which philosophers use in investigating the truth of things and artists in establishing the rules of the arts; and, since it does not understand them, it must, when someone speaks of them, feel annoyance and displeasure.

"They are not, and cannot be capable of understanding scientific and artistic disputes, but they are able only to understand the events of the world which depend upon chance." The audience will be almost completely lacking in imagination and will believe only the evidence of its senses: "Nor is it possible to make them believe that several days and nights have passed when they know through their senses that only a few hours have passed, *since no deception can take place in them which the senses recognize as such.*" In matters not reducible to the senses, it will be incapable of going beyond what historical fact it knows—"We cannot imagine a king who did not exist, nor attribute any action to him"—or beyond certain opinions which it holds as true; e.g., "the common people, which believes that God rules the world and has a knowledge of all particular things and a special care of them, also has the opinion that he does all things justly, and directs all things to his glory, and to the utility of his believers." The consequences of this complete lack of imagination will be seen later; but it is immediately apparent that the poet who must take it into account will be seriously restricted in his creative activity. In a similar way this audience will have a memory of limited capacity, and such technical devices as the division of tragedy into five acts will exist "to help the memory of the spectators to keep in mind an action which is not at all brief." Conversely, an action which is related too succinctly will not be understood, and hence such a plot should be expanded.

In addition to these limitations, the physical comfort and the convenience of the audience will need to be considered. We are speaking of poems presented before an assembled crowd; we must not ask the crowd to assemble for a poem so short that it would not be worth its while, nor must we expect it to remain beyond a certain limit of physical endurance. Strangely enough, that limit is broadly conceived as extending up to twelve hours:

> the restricted time is that during which the spectators can comfortably remain seated in the theater, which, as far as I can see, cannot exceed the revolution of the sun, as Aristotle says, that is, twelve hours; for because of the necessities of the body, such as eating, drinking, excreting the superfluous burdens of the belly and the bladder, sleeping, and because of other necessities, the people cannot continue its stay in the theater beyond the aforementioned time.

Finally, this audience has as one of its characteristics the capacity to be pleased by certain things and to be displeased by others. Castelvetro studies this capacity in detail and finds several bases for pleasure and displeasure. One is knowledge: the audience takes pleasure in learning, "especially those things which it thought could not come about"; contrariwise, it dislikes stories from which it cannot learn anything, those which present commonplace events and rapidly lead to satiety. Second, its hopes (or *volontà*): the audience is pleased by events which happen in accordance with its wishes, displeased by those which do not. Third, the audience will relate the events of a poem to the fortunes of its own life; it will enjoy seeing the good happy and the wicked unhappy, since the case of the former will lead it to expect happiness from its own goodness and the case of the latter will give it a sense of security and of justice. On the other hand, if the good are unhappy, it will experience fear and pity, and if the wicked are happy, it will feel envy and scorn; but these will be only temporary displeasures, since they will give way to feelings of self-righteousness and of justice, which will be ultimately pleasurable. With pleasure and displeasure will also be associated certain sentiments of a moral nature which will make the audience blush at "dishonest" actions, and hence reject them.

Such is the audience for which Castelvetro's poet must write—ignorant, unlettered, lacking in imagination and memory, attentive to its creature comforts, bound by certain selfish considerations which limit its possibilities of pleasure.

What is more, the poet is not to attempt to improve this audience in any sense; Castelvetro specifically rejects any profit or utility as the end of poetry. The sole end of poetry, as far as the audience is concerned, is to delight, to give pleasure and recreation. Castelvetro summarizes his position in the following passage:

> if we were to concede that the materials of the sciences and the arts could be the subject of poetry, we should also concede that poetry either was not invented to give pleasure, or that it was not invented for the uncultured crowd, but rather to teach and for persons initiated into letters and disputations; all of which will be seen to be false by the proofs that I shall now give. Now, since poetry was invented, as I say, to delight and give recreation to the common people, it must have as its subject those things which can be understood by the common people and, once understood, can make it joyous.

The position is reiterated on several occasions, notably in his discussion of purgation in tragedy; he finds Aristotle in agreement with him on the matter of pleasure and sees the utilitarian notion of purgation (as he interprets it) as a contradiction on Aristotle's part:

> For if poetry was invented principally for pleasure, and not for utility, as he demonstrated in the passage where he spoke of the origin of poetry in general, why should he now insist that tragedy, which is a part of poetry, should seek utility above all else? Why should it not seek mainly pleasure without paying attention to utility?

Again, the contention of Plato or of his followers that poetry must serve the purposes of the state is attacked; no such end exists for it:

> Moreover, the end of the government of the city is different from the end of poetry. For the end of the government of the city concerns living harmoniously together for the greater comfort and utility of the body and of the spirit, and the end of poetry concerns the mere pleasure and recreation of the auditors.

In connection with pleasure, the question of purgation seems a very knotty one to Castelvetro. He explains it as an answer on the part of Aristotle to Plato's banishment of the poets on moral grounds; here, insists Aristotle, is a moral use for poetry. The utility lies in the diminution of the passions of pity and fear in the audience or their expulsion. But if it is admitted as a utility, this is only incidental to the real end of pleasure:

> Those who insist that poetry was invented mainly to profit, or to profit and delight together, let them be aware lest they oppose the authority of Aristotle who here [*Poetics* 1459a21] and elsewhere seems to assign nothing but pleasure to it; and if, indeed, he concedes some utility to it, he concedes it accidentally, as is the case with the purgation of fear and of pity by means of tragedy.

As a matter of fact, Castelvetro believes that purgation itself may be considered as a source of pleasure; thus he affirms that "Aristotle meant by the word ἡδονὴν [1453b11] the purgation and the expulsion of fear and of pity from human souls," and he goes on to explain how it can be pleasurable:

> it comes about when, feeling displeasure at the unhappiness of another unjustly suffered, we recognize that we ourselves are good, since unjust things displease us, which recognition—because of the natural love that we have for ourselves—is a source of great pleasure to us. To which pleasure is joined still another, not at all inconsiderable, that when we see the excessive tribulations which happen to others, and which could happen to us and to those like us, we learn in a quiet and hidden way how subject we are to many misfortunes, and how we should not put faith in the calm course of the events of this world; and this pleases us much more than if another, as a teacher and openly in words, should teach us the same thing.

Note that the pleasures involved fit into the pattern of the capacities of the audience for pleasure and displeasure: the act of learning, the sentiment of self-righteousness. The other sources of delight and sadness indicated for tragedy and comedy belong to the same categories; the "novelty of the case" contributes to knowledge, and to the tendency to relate poetic actions to one's own life will belong such feelings as these: the joy, in tragedy, at the cessation of the danger of death and, in comedy, at the revenge for some insult; the sadness, in tragedy, at the coming of death and, in comedy, at the suffering of some such insult. In each case the spectator will identify the hero with himself or with someone dear to him.

If the end of pleasure and its achievement are related to certain characteristics of the audience, the means by which the end is to be achieved are similarly related. Here the main consideration is the lack of imagination on the part of the audience. In sum, the argument runs as follows: the audience will derive pleasure only if it identifies itself with the characters and the events; this identification is possible only if the audience believes in their reality; its belief in their reality will depend upon the credibility—the verisimilitude—of the presentation. It is here that imagination enters. If the audience were endowed with great capacities of imagination, it would "believe" things far removed from the conditions of "real life"; since it is not, it will "believe" only what seems to it to be in the realm of its own experience, to be "true." Since the argument is complex and since the real crux of Castelvetro's poetic system resides here, I shall examine it in some detail.

For Castelvetro, all considerations of verisimilitude oscillate between two poles: the impossibility of pleasure, on one side, without credibility, and, on the other side, the inadequacy of credibility, by itself, to produce pleasure. Credibility is the *sine qua non,* but it is only a beginning. If the audience is to experience the pleasure to be derived from learning, what is merely credible must be supplemented by what is rare, extraordinary, marvelous—in a word, by the incredible. The precise point at which the "incredible" becomes "inverisimilar" is a matter of subtle and difficult determination by the poet. The demand for both credibility and the marvelous is insistently made by Castelvetro throughout the text. First, credibility:

> all [the spectators] do not know whether the action or the names are true or invented, but those who do not know it believe that the action is true and that the royal names are true, and therefore these things give them pleasure; and if they knew that they were invented, they would feel displeasure in the same way as one who, having received a jewel and thinking it to be good, enjoys it, but, learning later that it is false, he becomes sad, and especially if it was sold to him for genuine.

Just as in painting, so in poetry:

> a monstrous thing, and which has never been, or is not, accepted by the common opinion of the people as possible to come about, or as probable—such a thing put into poetry cannot delight us, as far as the pleasure to be derived from resemblance is concerned.

Whether the action be a true one or not, then, the spectator or the reader must believe it to be such, must see in it a resemblance to the reality which he believes exists. Next, the marvelous, which seems to be contained in the very definition of pleasure:

> Now, since someone might ask for what reason the marvelous was required in tragedy, and was required in proportionately greater quantity in the epic, I answer that the end of poetry, as has been said, is pleasure and that the marvelous produces pleasure, and thus the marvelous is properly required in tragedy and in the epic, in order that the poem may achieve its own proper end in these types of poetry.

The end of poetry, as has been said several times, is pleasure, and the marvelous especially produces pleasure; therefore, the tragic poet should, as much as he can, seek the marvelous, and the epic poet, because of the ease that he has in so doing, must produce it to a much greater extent.

As a matter of fact, these two ingredients—the credible and the marvelous—are not entirely distinct; for the marvelous itself must be credible if it is to produce the proper pleasure:

> And it is said [by Aristotle] that the invention of in-credible things is permitted the poet if these incred-ible things bring about the end more marvelously than credible things would. And I myself say that incredible things cannot produce the marvelous. As, for example, if I hold it to be incredible that Daedalus should fly, I cannot marvel at the fact that he is said to fly, since I do not believe that he does fly. . . . For it is absolutely necessary that we have credible things if the marvelous is to be pro-duced.

As a result, in various incidental definitions of poetry, both ingredients are included, directly or indirectly expressed: "the proper function of poetics consists in the imitation, through harmonious words, of a human action which could possibly happen, pleasurable through the novelty of the case"; plot is "a discovery of an action which has never yet happened, in whole or in part, but which could possibly hap-pen and which is worthy of being remembered."

If we would understand these distinctions of terms, we must examine Castelvetro's treatment of the general question of possibility. He divides the whole realm of possible actions ac-cording to the following schema:

> I. Possible actions, *which have actually happened*
>   A. Natural
>   1. According to the course of nature
>   2. Contrary to the course of nature (i.e., mon-strous or miraculous happenings)
>   B. Accidental
>   1. Resulting from chance or fortune
>   2. Resulting from the will of men
> II. Possible actions, *which have not yet happened*
>   A. and B. as above

Now Category I, since it includes accomplished actions, is es-sentially the province of history; it corresponds to Aristotle's τὰ γενόμενα and is limited to particular actions, per-formed by specific persons. Actions of this kind are essential in tragedy and epic, which, since they deal with royal per-sons, cannot dispense with a historical basis; we, the audi-ence, are incapable of imagining kings who did not exist, etc. But no poem may be composed entirely of such actions, since then it would be a history and not a poem at all. Comedy, of course, needs no component of historical events, since its per-sons and their actions are private and obscure.

Category II, on the other hand, is coequal with Aristotle's τὰ δυνατά; it is the realm of the universal, since the actions are possible for many persons; it is thus the realm of poetry. All poems must possess some component of actions which have not actually happened. But whereas in the first category the question of credibility does not arise, in the second it is of pri-mary importance. In order that credibility may be assured (and hence verisimilitude) and that the necessary ingredient of the marvelous may nevertheless be present, the following three requisites are established for possible actions:

a) They must be similar to those actions which have actually happened
b) They must be similar to those actions which had the least probability of happening, but which did actually happen
c) The parts or parcels of such actions must individ-ually be similar to those parts of actions which happened in various cases to various people

The matter of verisimilitude is further clarified by a later dis-tinction between possibility and credibility: possibility is a po-tential of the action itself, which contains no impediment that would prevent the action from coming to realization; credi-bility is a suitability (a *convenevolezza*) of the action to the ex-pectations of the audience, "by which a person may be led to believe that that action was brought to realization."

With respect to credibility, then, it may be assured by several means: first, by the use of a historical basis for the action in certain genres; second, by a close adherence, in invented ac-tions, to the conditions of "real" or "true" actions. At this point, the expectations of the audience again impinge upon the poet in a very important way, for the audience is the touchstone of natural probability and it will believe whatever conforms to its conceptions of reality. The case is especially clear with the comic poet, who invents everything:

> But let nobody believe for this reason that the cre-ator of the comic plot has liberty to invent either new cities imagined by himself, or rivers, or moun-tains, or kingdoms, or customs, or laws, or to change the course of the things of nature, making it snow in summer and having men reap in winter, and so forth; for it is necessary for him to follow history and truth.

The whole story of Oedipus runs against this natural proba-bility, "for a private citizen who kills the legitimate king should be most sharply punished and not rewarded, nor should the queen be given him to wed and the kingdom as a dowry." In the same way, certain apparitions of the ancient gods are unacceptable to the modern audience's conceptions:

> For you must know that the common people be-lieve that God in the present day rules the world in a different way from what he did in ancient times. For the opinion is that in our times he rules it si-lently without showing himself in person through inspirations, through signs, or through visions, through admonitions to his servants, and through other means not understood nor considered by the coarse crowd; just as, on the other hand, the opin-ion is that in the first ancient centuries, in the time of the demigods, God intervened directly in the af-fairs of the world, by appearing personally and speaking with men.

The natural probabilities so considered became a function of a given audience in a given time, losing any universal quality.

In this way the second means of assuring credibility comes to be very close to the third, which is the observance of deco-rum. A norm of *convenevolezza* is proposed. Again, the case of the comic poet is the most instructive. He may invent names for his personages: "But in so doing the poet must nev-ertheless pay attention to the usage of the place and the time when and where the action is supposed to have taken place, so that the names will not be exceptional for the given place and time."

So for the conception of character:

For we know that the poet must follow what is appropriate [*il conueneuole*] in representing not only the persons under the sway of passions but the other persons, also, and the actions; which appropriateness is derived by the poet not from that which is in himself or from that which has happened to himself but rather from what is commonly found in that type of person similar to the one who is being represented, full attention being paid to the place, and the time, and the other circumstances; and from what usually happens to such a person.

Such a notion of appropriateness is applied not only to persons of a given character (where it is related at once to the ἁρμόττοντα of Aristotle and to the Horatian decorum) but also to certain kinds of actions. If you speak of prophecy, for example, it must be in the light of invariable conventions. Vergil, here, has erred:

> Vergil sins in the decorum of prophecy, which does not usually descend to the use of proper names, nor to things so clear and so particular; but, withholding names, it usually indicates the persons and their actions with somewhat obscure figures of speech, as we see observed in the prophecies of Holy Scripture and in the *Alexandra* of Lycophron.

If restrictive conventions of this type are multiplied not only with respect to characters but also with respect to actions, the possibilities of "invention" on the part of the poet soon disappear; this is indeed the case with Castelvetro.

But the multiplication of these commonplaces and these conventions would also tend to make the poem completely uninteresting to the audience itself; the cause of credibility would be perfectly served, yet the resulting poem would be thoroughly dull. The antidote to this danger is the cultivation of the marvelous. Castelvetro, since he is unwilling to admit any improbability, conceives of the marvelous as a kind of infrequent probability:

> There are two kinds of probabilities [*verisimili*], one of which represents the truths which most frequently occur according to the fixed course of nature, and the other of which represents the truths which occasionally depart from the usual course; as, for example, it is probable that a clever, wicked man should deceive and not be deceived, and that a powerful man should vanquish and not be vanquished, since truly we usually see things come to pass in this way. And it is, moreover, probable that a clever, wicked man, wishing to deceive, should on occasion be deceived, and that a powerful man, wishing to conquer, should at times be conquered. So that one of these probabilities concerns the "many times" of truth, and the other the "few times" of truth, and thus the one like the other is probable. But the second, because of its rarity, is more marvelous and is said to be probable outside of probability only because of its rarity and because it turns aside from the path of the first probability.

On various occasions he points out that what happens more frequently is less marvelous, hence less desirable in poetry; thus a recognition which could easily come about, through the will of the person recognized, is less to be sought than one which would be more difficult. In a similar way, as regards purgation, what happens less frequently is more pitiable and more horrible. The admission of this kind of improbable probability makes way for the acceptance of certain brands of "impossibility" in poetry. Of the four varieties of impossi-

bilities which he distinguishes, two are forbidden the poet; these are actions impossible for God and for men and actions impossible for men alone. The other two may be used by the poets; they comprise actions not impossible to God, such as miracles, and actions which seem impossible to men because of their rarity. Both of these are recommended to the poet whenever he can find a justification for using them:

> And it is a sufficiently evident matter why poetic fiction can and should receive these two kinds of impossibilities used in this way and justified by reason, since the poet seeks to move the reader or the listener to admiration [*marauiglia*], which proceeds principally from miraculous doings and from those doings which happen only very rarely.

I should insist at this point that all degrees of probability as Castelvetro conceives them are natural probability rather than aesthetic probability; that is, probability is established in a work not by reference to the conditions of the work itself or to preliminary statements within the work, but by reference outside of the work to the operations of nature. This is especially clear in the example he uses for distinguishing between necessity and verisimilitude. Actions of both kinds are possible, hence admissible into poetry. If a man is wounded on the head, it is "verisimilar" or probable that he will die; hence the poet may represent his death. If a man is wounded in the heart, it is "necessary" that he die; hence the poet may represent his death. Similarly for actions springing from character, all of which are really matters of decorum: it is "necessary" that a mother who resolves to kill her innocent children (cf. Medea) do so only with great perturbation of her soul (this is presumably because of the eternal character of mothers as mothers); it is "probable" or verisimilar that a person who has been full of fear in the past will continue to be so (this is presumably a matter of consistency).

In all such considerations of historical truth or natural probability or necessity and verisimilitude, the primary aim is not the imitation of nature for the sake of making the poem resemble nature but rather the resemblance to nature for the sake of obtaining the credence of the audience. Credibility remains the ultimate touchstone.

II

A poetics which in this way seeks to give pleasure to an audience of limited imaginative capacities presents a very special and a very difficult problem to the poet. The problem is not to produce a beautiful work of art through the ordering of all the parts to an artistically perfect structure. Questions of beauty rarely concern Castelvetro. Rather, it is the task of the poet to find some way of entertaining the audience while he keeps it convinced that what it sees (or reads) is true, that is, of striking a proper balance between the probable and the marvelous. "The greatest praise of a poet is that he makes the uncertain seem certain through every means of which he is capable."

The first means to the achievement of this end is the proper selection and assorting of materials. In the tragic and epic genres this necessitates the choice of a historical subject, to assure credibility, and the addition to that subject of episodes or variations or developments that will make of it a new and interesting plot. This latter is the difficult part; for it is only in so far as he expands or embroiders upon his historical *données* that a poet is an inventor, hence a poet. "Invention is the most difficult thing that the poet has to do, and the thing from which it seems that he derives his name, that is πoιητησ." It is in connection with this demand for invention that Castelvetro introduces a criterion of originality:

> For a poet cannot compose a plot already composed by another poet, for this would either be history or a plagiarism. For example, if one should wish to arrange in a plot the events by which Orestes killed his mother, it would not be proper to follow any story of a son who killed his mother in the way in which she was killed in the plot composed on the subject by Aeschylus, or by Euripides, or by Sophocles. But it would be necessary that, setting aside all historical and poetical resemblances, he should give himself over to subtle searching and with his own wit to finding how that event might be made to come about in another way, which had not yet been narrated or written by anybody, just as those other poets had done.

Here, apparently, only the central action would be historical; the rest would be up to the poet. Put in another way,

> the plot of tragedy and of the epic can be constituted only of things which have actually happened and are known, the royal estate upon which it is founded making this necessary. These historical events must nevertheless be known only summarily, so that the poet may exercise and demonstrate his own genius and find the particular things and the means by which that action was brought to its conclusion.

Either the historical subject itself or the decorations provided by the poet must, in part at least, partake of the nature of the marvelous.

A second means to convincing and amusing the audience is the disposition of these materials in accordance with the unities of time, place, and action. We have already seen, early in the discussion, how the physical comforts of the audience and its lack of imagination have to be taken into account by the poet; these two factors lead, respectively, to the unities of time and of place. With respect to time, the clearest statement is found in the comparison of tragedy and the epic:

> Now, just as the perceptible end of tragedy has found its proper compass within the revolution of the sun over the earth without going beyond this limit, in order to put an end to the discomfort of the audience and the expense of the actors, so the perceptible end of the epic has found its proper compass in being able to be extended over several days, since neither the discomfort of the listener nor harm or expense connected with the reciter took this possibility away from it.

Essentially, then, the basic factor is that the audience can remain within the theater (for tragedy and comedy) only for a given time—maximum, twelve hours. Besides, the action before its eyes will take place on a single spot, the stage. Hence two unities: "tragedy . . . must have as its subject an action accomplished in a small area of place and in a small space of time, that is, in that place and in that time where and when the actors remain engaged in acting, and not in any other place or in any other time." For the imagination of the audience, limited to the witness of its senses, will not permit it to believe that the action takes place in more than one locality—"restricted not only to a city, or a town, or a country place, or some such site, but even to that view which alone can pres-

ent itself to the eyes of a person"—or in a time in excess of that of the performance:

> But as for the magnitude of the plot, which is subjected to the senses and is taken in by sight and hearing together, I must say that it should be as long as would be an actual event, depending upon fortune and worthy of being written down in history that might come to pass, it being necessary that this imagined event of the plot should occupy as much time . . . as was occupied or would be occupied by a similar event if it really happened or were to happen.

Ideally, then, the invented action should occupy no more time than a real action, and this time should not exceed the time of performance; the place should remain unchanged and be contained within the space visible to a person who himself did not move.

The extent to which the senses, especially sight, are a governing factor in this theory of the unities is indicated by the change in requirements when the epic is considered. For the events of the epic do not actually appear before the eyes of the spectator. Instead, they are narrated to him. Since he does not see them, he can admit broad variations of place and a discrepancy between time of performance and time of action. Castelvetro draws a distinction between perceptible time (*il sensibile*, that distinguished by the senses) and intellectual time (*lo'ntellettuale*, that conceived of by the mind). In tragedy, the two must be identical; in epic, there may be a wide divergency between them.

As for the unity of action, which for Aristotle is the only important one and which for him is of the very essence of the work of art, Castelvetro's treatment of it is highly revelatory of his general attitude toward poetics. To begin with, he denies any necessity—in the nature of things—for limitation of a poem to a single action; as so frequently, he takes issue sharply with Aristotle here:

> For there is no doubt that, if in history one may relate in a single narrative several actions of a single person, . . . in poetry it will be possible in a single plot to narrate without being blamed for it several actions of a single person, just as similarly in poetry one may relate without being blamed for it a single action of a whole people, for history does this with much praise. . . . And, indeed, in poetry not only a single action of a whole people may be narrated, but even several actions of a people. . . . And even if it were conceded to poetry to relate many actions of many persons or of many peoples, I do not see that any blame should come to it for this reason.

Moreover, the presentation of a double or even a multiple plot would more readily serve the end of pleasure sought by the poet:

> we should not marvel at all if several actions of one person or one action of a people or several actions of several persons delight us and make us attentive to listen, since such a plot carries with it, through the multitude of the actions, through the variety, through the new events, and through the multitude of persons and of the people, both pleasure and greatness and magnificence.

Why, then, does Aristotle insist upon unity, and why does Castelvetro recommend it? The reason is different for the different genres. For tragedy and comedy, unity of action is a consequence of the unities of time and of place; it would not be possible to crowd, into a restricted space and into twelve hours, more than one action; indeed, sometimes one of these plays will contain only a part of an action. For the epic, where this "necessity" does not exist, unity of action is sought for two other reasons: first, because such a unified plot is more "beautiful," less likely to satiate the spectator with an abundance of different things, and, second, because such a plot demonstrates the ingenuity and the excellence of the poet:

> In the narration of the single action of one person, which at first glance would not seem to have the capacity of keeping the minds of the auditors listening with delight, one discovers the judgment and the industry of the poet, who achieves that with one action of one person which others can hardly achieve with many actions and of many persons.

What is symptomatic about this position is its abandonment of any concern with the structural or formal beauties of the work and its insistence upon two such nonartistic considerations as the comfort and character of the audience and the glory of the poet.

A third means to the achievement of the ends with respect to the audience is what we might call, roughly, the total excellence of the work. This is in a way related to the unity of plot just discussed; a certain admiration, a certain sense of the marvelous, will result from the perfect execution of the poem. There might seem to be here an independent criterion of beauty, were it not for the fact that beauty is itself reduced to qualities already considered: "so that it [the plot] may turn out to be beautiful, that is, marvelous and probable." Or, negatively, beauty is reduced to an absence of flaws from a form large enough to permit the perception of such flaws:

> For that thing is really beautiful in which no ugliness is discovered but in which, if there were any, it would be discovered; and that is really not beautiful which, being ugly, seems beautiful because for some reason its ugliness does not become apparent.

The first consequence of this essentially negative criterion is that larger poems will be preferable to smaller; Dante is greater than Petrarch, since his poem is so "grande e magnifico" that, were there any errors in it, they would immediately be visible. As far as the audience is concerned, such a poem shows the artifice of the poet and is a source of admiration. A second consequence is that magnitude of form will be accompanied by multiplicity of parts and by variety of developments, and that multiplicity and that variety, in turn, will be sources of pleasure. These are major excellences of the poem, and they are to be sought in preference to such minor excellences as purity of diction, ornamentation through figures, and the sound of the verses. These latter may indeed supply pleasure, but it will be inferior to the pleasure derived from imitation. Again with respect to total excellence, it should be noted that it is not an absolute quality but one discovered by comparison with other works: "for nothing reveals better the goodness or the badness of anything whatsoever than comparison." The poet who would gain the admiration of his audience must therefore keep in mind all the precepts and "apply them so excellently that his poem will surpass in all things the poems of past poets."

III

These indications of the ways by which the art of poetry achieves its ends—ends with respect to the audience and ends with respect to the poet—may be taken as preliminary steps toward a definition of the art itself. If we would further approach such a definition, the best means is to examine the relationships that Castelvetro establishes between poetry and the other arts.

The art to which poetry is most closely akin is the art of history. Indeed, their kinship is so intimate that, if we possessed an adequate art of history, it would be unnecessary to write an art of poetry, "since poetry derives all its light from the light of history." Such an art of history would tell us

> what things were memorable in greater and in lesser degree and worthy of having a place in history, and, on the other hand, which ones were not memorable and unworthy of being touched upon by the historian. And then it would tell us what things should be narrated briefly and summarily and which ones at length and in particular; and afterward what order and disposition should be followed in recounting the events. And, besides, it would not fail to tell us when and where should be intercalated digressions, and descriptions of a place or of a person or of other things. And then it would decide whether it is permissible to the author of the history to offer a judgment on things that he relates, blaming or praising them, and adapting them to the instruction and utility of the reader and to his conduct as a citizen. And similarly it would decide if it is proper and possible for the historian to present some matters by narration, others by dramatic representation, as the poet does, or whether, indeed, this is a prerogative of poetry alone. And, finally, it would tell us what kinds of words suit history in general and what kinds do not, and which particularly in certain places and which not.

Precepts of this kind, were they properly presented in an art of history, would not have to be repeated in an art of poetry, being common to both arts. Now if we examine in detail these precepts, we discover that they do, in fact, cover the primary preoccupations of Castelvetro throughout his treatment of poetry: choice of subject matter (sufficiently noteworthy to be marvelous); distinction between central plot and episodes; ordering of the plot, digressions, moral conclusions from the plot; use of the *récit* in tragedy and of dramatic scenes in the epic; and the general problem of diction. The two arts differ in two respects only: history presents events which actually happened, poetry those which have not occurred but which might occur, and poetry uses verse whereas history uses prose. Otherwise they are so much alike that poetry may be defined as "a resemblance or imitation of history."

Aristotle's likening of poetry to painting, thinks Castelvetro, is essentially erroneous; for there are more dissimilarities than similarities between the two arts. They are unlike, first, in the kinds of things which they represent. Painting (like history) depicts true things—the "cosa certa & conosciuta"—whereas poetry imitates probable things—the "cosa incerta & sconosciuta." Moreover, whereas poetry represents actions, painting at its best represents objects (historical painting is a definitely inferior genre). They are unlike, second, in the relationship to be expected between the imitation and the object; in painting, exact resemblance is to be demanded: "the slightest dissimilarity between the image and the man depicted can be blamed and condemned as bad art"; in poetry, the imitation is an expansion, an embellishment, an idealization of whatever real events may have been taken as a starting point. Third, the sources of pleasure in the two are unlike.

Painting, appealing to the eye, delights precisely through this exact resemblance, which in poetry is displeasing; on the other hand, the imitation in poetry of an unknown, probable action "delights us beyond all measure." This is explained on the basis of the difficulty involved for the artist. For the painter, faithful rendering is the hardest procedure, shows the greatest talent, evokes the most unlimited admiration. For the poet, such rendering makes him a simple historian; it is the introduction of the "unreal," of the "invented," of the "marvelous," that constitutes his greatest glory. Castelvetro himself sees only one basis of comparison between the two arts, and that is on the score of the *convenevole,* which here means the representation of things as they should be; but I see no attempt on his part to reconcile this with the requirement, for painting, that things be represented as they are.

In the light of the close affinity which other theorists, such as Robortello, saw between poetry and rhetoric, we are compelled to ask whether Castelvetro also treats the two arts as cognate. We discover immediately that he does not. He makes a number of references to Aristotle's *Rhetoric,* largely on matters of diction, the passions, and thought, but does not proceed from them to the indication of a general similitude between poetic and rhetoric. This is all the more remarkable, since, as we have seen, in its broadest lines Castelvetro's system is essentially rhetorical. Perhaps the explanation may be found in his insistence on declaring the close relationship between poetry and history, on treating poetic as if it were a branch of the historical art, and on eliminating—by denial or by silence—any other art which might be set up as a contender to history. In the last analysis, this wedding of poetry to history may constitute one of the most original features of Castelvetro's system.

As a result of this likening of poetry to history, some of the usual preoccupations of Renaissance arts of poetry disappear. The poet himself does not need to be divinely inspired, to write under the influence of the *furor poeticus,* to feel himself the passions which he incorporates in his characters; these are superstitions fostered by the poets to improve their credit with the ignorant masses. Instead, he is a careful and deliberate artisan, who follows the precepts of the art so as to achieve, immediately, the pleasure of his audience and, ultimately, his own glory. We have already seen how these precepts relate to the choice, the disposition, and the embellishment of his materials. Castelvetro treats the moot question of the relationship of the poem to nature only summarily and indirectly. The notion of imitation as introducing differences between an object in nature and that object as represented in a work of art is completely absent; indeed, in a work which is a commentary on Aristotle, none of the implications of the Aristotelian concept of imitation are present. So completely are these implications lost that imitation (*rassomiglianza*) is said not to be present when true or historical events are treated and to be present only in the details and embellishments "invented" by the poet—in accordance with probability, of course. Still, in relationship to imitation, the distinction between $\pi\rho\alpha\xi\epsilon\omega\sigma$ and $\delta\rho\omega\nu\tau\omega\nu$ is wrested from its meaning in such a way that the thing represented becomes the action of the poem and the person representing becomes the poet (e.g., the *Aeneid* and Vergil).

With the popular conception of the poet as divinely inspired now discarded, with all notions of the poem as an imitation of nature either distorted or abandoned, with the resemblance to painting specifically denied, Castelvetro's poetic system becomes a very special system for his times. Poetics turns out to be a branch of history, but with the special feature of a history that attempts to please its audience and bring glory to its author. Whatever in a poem relates to the necessities of credibility derives its characteristics and its criteria from the science of history; whatever relates to the necessities of pleasing an audience whose character is very carefully delimited derives its characteristics and its criteria from the art of rhetoric. If there is any proper role for an art of poetry—and at times this is practically denied—it is in the combination of the precepts supplied by these two parent-arts, in the filling of gaps where, as in the case of the unities, the other arts do not afford specific recommendations. Or, to state the case more accurately, the poet considers himself as a kind of historian and relies openly on the teachings of history to guide him in his writing of poems; but there are places where these teachings are inadequate, and here the poet—even though he may not recognize the fact—has recourse to the fundamental relationships existing between a work using language and the audience to which it is directed. This second kind of activity leads him to formulate for himself—or to take over from the previous formulations of such theorists as Castelvetro—a set of special conventions or rules or practices which, taken together, compose an art of poetry. But that art is never an independent art, bearing always the traces of its origins in history and rhetoric. It has, therefore, very little to do with the "art" of Aristotle. Anyone who would adopt it, theorist or poet, would thus be committing himself to an essentially un-Aristotelian system of poetics, one which was even farther removed from the presuppositions of the original text than had been the theory contained in the commentary of Robortello. (pp. 349-71)

Bernard Weinberg, "Castelvetro's Theory of Poetics," in Critics and Criticism: Ancient and Modern *by R. S. Crane and others, edited by R. S. Crane, The University of Chicago Press, 1952, pp. 349-71.*

ERNEST HATCH WILKINS   (essay date 1954)

[*Wilkins was an American educator and scholar of Italian literature. In the following excerpt from his* History of Italian Literature *(1954), he offers a brief summary of critical issues in Castelvetro's* Poetica d'Aristotele.]

The most acute of all the treatises of the period on the art of poetry is the voluminous commentary on the *Poetics* by Ludovico Castelvetro (1505-1571) of Modena, published, with the Greek text and an Italian translation, in 1570. Castelvetro was an able scholar, and did his own thinking. He was, however, one of the most contradictious of men: he had no respect for the opinions of his contemporaries, and frequently pointed out their errors. . . . His interpretation of Aristotle is more penetrating than that of any of his predecessors; but his emphases and some of his deductions are his own. Earlier theorists had in general failed to make any distinction between the art of poetry and the art of rhetoric: that distinction is clear in Castelvetro. Earlier theorists had maintained that poetry has two functions, to give pleasure and to give moral instruction—a doctrine based on Horace, and reënforced, as regards the moral function, by the pressures of the Counter Reformation. Castelvetro maintains, on the contrary, that the single function of poetry is to give pleasure, and that the provision of instruction is none of its proper business: any utility that may spring from poetry is merely incidental. The range of auditors, moreover, to whom poetry should purvey its pleasure is not limited, as earlier theorists had generally assumed, to persons of cultivation, but includes "the crude multitude." There is nothing mysterious about the poetic art: the idea that poets are possessed with a divine fury is nonsense: it originated in ignorant admiration, and has been fostered, for selfish reasons, by poets themselves. But though Castelvetro was capable of liberalizing ideas such as these, he was capable also of trivialities, and of pronouncements which, however logical in their derivation, were in effect restrictive. It was he who first, in a concise and authoritative formula, consecrated the unities of time and place:

> La mutatione tragica non puo tirar con esso seco
> se non vna giornata e vn luogo—

> The tragic process cannot cover more than one day
> and one place.

He was indeed so much concerned with these two minor unities that he regarded the major unity of action as being relatively unimportant. With all his limitations, he wins from H. B. Charlton the verdict that "he is the most illuminating critic of the art of poetry between Longinus and Dryden." (pp. 258-59)

> Ernest Hatch Wilkins, "Prose of the Mid-Sixteenth Century," in his A History of Italian Literature, revised edition, edited by Thomas G. Bergin, Cambridge, Mass.: Harvard University Press, 1974, pp. 251-62.

BAXTER HATHAWAY (essay date 1962)

[In the excerpt below from three sections of his Age of Criticism: The Late Renaissance in Italy, Hathaway presents a critical overview of Castelvetro's Poetica d'Aristotele, noting also critical reactions of Castelvetro's contemporaries to the work.]

In innumerable points of doctrine, Ludovico Castelvetro's commentary on Aristotle's Poetics was a landmark or turning point in the development of literary criticism in the sixteenth century. On the subject of Aristotle's classifications of kinds of imitation he had much to say that was subtle and important, even though here as elsewhere he infuriated his readers by his method as often as he enlightened them. The non-Aristotelians were angered by his close adherence to Aristotle's main lines of thought; the Aristotelians were angered by his eagerness to show that in the working out of the details Aristotle either was wrong or did not say enough. His introduction to the subject was strictly Aristotelian; he said that the general mode of poetry is imitation, and of imitations there are three genera: according to object, according to medium, and according to manner. But he believed Aristotle needed more differentia to show how imitation in poetry corresponds to imitation in painting and sculpture. Poetry, he said, is imitation having for its object "men as better than they are, or worse, or as they are; for its medium language, rhythm, and harmony; and for its mode narration and drama." His usual refinement upon Aristotle was not, however, long in following. Castelvetro said: "And yet Aristotle could have explained the modes of poetry more precisely if he had not used the example of painting as his point of departure, and had used the following argument instead. Poetry represents a possible action either by using words to represent words and things to represent things, or by using words to represent both words and things." Castelvetro's "words to represent words and things to represent things" is the imita-

tion of life found in the stage presentation of dramatic poetry. "Words to represent both words and things" is narrative imitation. Castelvetro continued: "Of these two modes of representing an action, the first gives the more lifelike representation. We have an analogous phenomenon in painting, which represents objects either by their natural colors or by light and shade, the second kind of representations being called by the Greeks $\mu o\nu\acute{o}\chi\rho\omega\mu\alpha$. Monochromes, as regards their mode, are like narrative poetry, which uses only words to represent both words and things; and paintings in color, as regards their mode again, are like dramatic poetry, which uses words to represent words, and things to represent things."

Genres of poetry should be determined by subject matter and by meter, Castelvetro said. He had a minor quarrel with Aristotle on this point, for he understood Aristotle to have said that kinds of poets are determined by the kinds of subjects they treat rather than by diction or meter. Distinction on the basis of diction Castelvetro especially refused, since he claimed that a poet is not a poet when he uses nonpoetic diction.

Castelvetro carped at Aristotle also for not giving a precise list of the kinds of possible imitations. He reasoned that since there are three objects of imitation (better, same, worse), five media, and three modes, even without compounding these Aristotle should have described eleven species of imitation. By compounding them he calculated that the largest possible number of species would be ninety-five; but he decided that a more realistic number would be fifty-five species, since some of the items would not combine well with some of the others. He did not tell how he arrived at the number fifty-five. Addressing himself to questions that were creating more stir in his own day, he distinguished between modes of imitation in which speeches are summarized or paraphrased and those with direct discourse and indirect imitation of the descriptive items of the situation. But when he came to constitute the three main genres of poetic imitation, these idiosyncrasies did not prevent him from achieving a list that was in the main traditional. Instead of the two kinds he had defined in his paralleling poetry with painting, he listed the classes as narrative, dramatic, and similitudinary, without making clear how his similitudinary class was distinct from the other two. When we find him saying that the similitudinary kind uses words and things to resemble words and things, we can be puzzled to determine how it differs from the dramatic and can therefore be puzzled to find him offering the Iliad as an example of the similitudinary kind. If by using "things to represent things" Castelvetro meant that Homer gave descriptions of objects, why is the result not simply narrative? Furthermore, on the same page Castelvetro claimed that one of the subclasses of the narrative mode actually belonged in the similitudinary category. The narrative mode, he said, can be compared to chiaroscuro. In this mode, the writer, "in expressing words stored in his memory," may follow one of three methods, two of which are direct and one is oblique:

> First direct kind—the poet or the narrator used speaks throughout in his own person.
> Oblique kind—the action is presented in indirect discourse.
> Second direct kind—the poet presents speeches of his characters verbatim. It is this kind that belongs to the similitudinary category, according to Castelvetro's assertion.

Aside from Castelvetro's claim that the similitudinary kind

uses words and things to resemble words and things, this is simply the usual list of narrative, dramatic, and mixed kinds. Tasso often followed the ideas of Castelvetro and sometimes clarified Castelvetro's distinctions in objecting to them. But all does not come clear when Tasso says that imitation should not be defined as a resemblance since some resemblances occur accidentally; imitation should be thought of as a similitude even though only those similitudes that are intentionally created by study and art should be called imitations. "I say," remarked Tasso, "that imitation is artful similitude, and imitating is the intention of resembling, and what does not exist cannot be imitated or resembled." In Castelvetro's interpretation of poetic imitation the outstanding feature is the latitude he gave to narrative, but he was far less specific in this regard than many of his contemporaries. He argued that gnomic poetry could legitimately be called poetry because wise sayings have affinities with oracular sayings and so have something of the divine in them. Consequently, it would seem that for him not all poetry was imitative.

If Castelvetro's basis of classification remains somewhat confused, one can nevertheless feel the cogency of some of his comments on the separate modes. The narrative mode can be subdivided, he said, in terms of whether or not the poet slants his material. Still another way of dividing it is to distinguish between universalized narrative and particularized narrative. Universalized narrative concerns classes, species, or wholes, whereas particularized narratives concern individuals or units. This distinction would no doubt remain entirely unclear had Castelvetro not added that the *Aeneid* is a generalized narrative, whereas the *Odyssey* and *Iliad* are particularized. This distinction was primarily a rhetorical one originating from distinctions of style. . . . (pp. 37-9)

In spite of the fact that some of Castelvetro's comments on the nature of the dramatic mode have been cited as the first insistence on the unities of place and time and hence the significant beginning of the rigidities of the Neoclassic attitudes toward drama and hence a prime instance of his wrongheadedness, taken in context of the making of distinctions between the narrative and the dramatic modes of imitating, they seem to make rather good sense. The dramatic mode, Castelvetro said, can move about less easily in time and space than can the narrative mode. It can represent only the visible and the audible, whereas the narrative mode can more easily bring into play states of consciousness and internal promptings. The dramatic mode stirs emotions more than narrative but gives a simpler and less full-bodied account of the nature of the events since some aspects of the action cannot be directly or fully represented on a stage. This is the kind of analysis of the limitations of certain media such as we make today when we decide what can be done in motion pictures that can be done only less well on the stage or in novels. When Castelvetro said further that "the dramatic mode represents actions as occurring in the time in which they would naturally occur" and that for this reason the length of a comedy or tragedy is limited by the comfort of the audience and "cannot represent more things than those which can occur in the space of time which it takes to present the drama," he did, it is true, limit the drama to what is simply imitative. The concept of poetic imitation held in the Renaissance was capable of extension to include expressive poems as well as poems that are content to mirror externals, but Castelvetro—as well as some of the others—was trapped by his own logic to assume that no special case had to be made for drama as direct imitation and that consequently the nature of drama was to imitate wholly

and directly. For such reasons an expressive theater like that of Shakespeare came to be excluded from the Neoclassic world.

On the other hand, Castelvetro was led by the literalness of his mind to argue that the dramatic mode must present feigned or imaginary events that could happen, presumably because it is impossible to conceive of the staged event as an imitation of itself as a historical action. Cicero delivering an oration is not an imitation. A stage presentation of an oration delivered by Cicero would have to be imaginary. But Castelvetro allowed the narrative mode to treat both what has actually happened and what is in the realm of the possible; that is to say, it can be either a rendition of actuality or a rendition of something feigned which is made to look like actuality. Who can tell why he did not see the possibility of a stage rendering of actuality? But Castelvetro claimed that his restriction of the stage to imaginary actions was due not to its inability to handle actual happenings but to a tradition handed down by the Ancients. Passion plays are a violation of this principle.

Castelvetro gave some insight into the nature of his similitudinary mode in asserting that the dramatic mode is to the similitudinary as a metaphor is to a simile—a remark Mazzoni was to repeat a few years later. The similitudinary, Castelvetro continued, is usually accompanied by narrative but is found separate and alone in works like Ovid's *Heroides*—a series of letters supposedly written by famous women of antiquity—and in epigrams involving a speaker other than the poet. Richardson's *Pamela* or *Clarissa* he would no doubt have called similitudinary, or Browning's dramatic monologues. He said, however, that the true similitudinary poem demands some words by the author to set the scene for the simile. All in all, Castelvetro claimed that there are seven ways of representing speech: three simple and four compound. Precisely what these are he did not say, but they were probably included among his fifty-five kinds of imitation.

Although Castelvetro seemingly consented to a division of poetic imitation into three principal modes—the dramatic, the narrative, and the similitudinary—he did not, in his main discussions of the modes of imitation, patently indicate that all narrative should be thought of as imitation. Near the end of his commentary, in his discussion of Aristotle's treatment of the modes of narrative in epic poetry, he showed more plainly his reluctance to consider as imitation narrative in which a poet speaks in his own person. The epic poet's manner of introducing characters to speak in direct discourse is not really representational but similitudinary, he said. When words are represented with words we have imitation (*rassomigliare*), but we do not have this direct resembling when words have to represent things. So he argued that if words cannot represent actions in some manner epic poetry is not imitation. Following this line of reasoning, he decided that only presentation of characters on a stage is truly imitative and that the other two modes, the narrative and the similitudinary, are so only to a lesser degree. He revealed his methods of defining in saying:

> Moreover, following this line of reasoning, we can say that, comparatively, that instrument by means of which the action is best imitated is the only imitative one, in contrast to those instruments by means of which one imitates less, and that these latter in comparison and in contrast to it are not imitative; from this reasoning we can be secure in say-

ing that speech is the only imitative instrument, in relation to dance and melody, which in contrast to it can be called nonimitative instruments, since they do not imitate as fully as speech does.

Since the dramatic mode of speech is the most imitative mode, it follows that for Castelvetro it was also the only truly imitative one. The same relative principle he applied to the distinctions between particularized and generalized narratives and between biased and unbiased narratives. He said: "For since the poet imitates more fully in narrating the particularized material of the action than the universalized, it follows that only the particularized material of the action can be called imitable if we consider it alongside of the universalized, which can be called nonimitable." The result was that Castelvetro considered Homer more an imitator than Virgil not only because he introduced characters speaking more often and allotted them longer speeches but also because he particularized more in describing actions.

Even less is a poet an imitator, according to Castelvetro's view, to the extent that he introduces expository comment upon the material supposedly being imitated. Castelvetro's analysis was:

> If the poet in that part of the epic in which he narrates only and recounts the action and does not introduce characters speaking is not an imitator according to Aristotle and consequently is not a poet, what shall we say about a poet in that part of his epic in which he neither narrates action nor introduces a character to speak but passes judgment on the things narrated, either blaming or praising them or deriving from them common utility or instructions about civil life or the good life? Surely no other than that he is not an imitator by reason of the mode, since he does not introduce any character to speak—that is, any character among those who intervene in the fable—or by reason of the material of the fable, since that material is separate from the fable and arises from the feeling of the poet toward the action. Now if he is not imitator either because of the mode or of the material, it follows that he is not a poet in any way.

By-products of adding judgments to narrative presentations, in Castelvetro's view of things, were that we recognize the poet to be partisan and hence not to be trusted and that he makes himself hateful to us by adopting a stance of superiority to us "in revealing a certain pride and confidence in his own goodness when in putting aside the office of narrator which was rightfully his he takes on the office of preacher and corrector of behavior out of reason, into which error Homer never falls but Virgil on occasion does." Since Castelvetro broadly considered poetry an imitation of history, it was characteristic of him to apply the historian's prohibition against bias to the poet. Furthermore, since he believed that the pleasure of poetry comes largely from our admiration for the poet's artistry, there need be no surprise to find him advocating the writing of the more purely imitative modes of poetry because he thought introducing characters to speak requires more skill and acuteness of wit than simple narration. (pp. 39-43)

[Castelvetro's] plain intention was to agree with Aristotle that no art or science is fit subject matter for poetry. Castelvetro remarked that Aristotle's insistence on this point had perplexed the literary minds of his time since it refused the name of poet to many good writers and encouraged some critics to

reject Aristotle entirely. Since Castelvetro stressed invention, the important point for him was that a poet is not doing anything original when he uses scientific or philosophic materials. This belief of Castelvetro's squares only partly with his subsequent assertion that poets dealing with philosophic or scientific subject matter may be good philosophers or scientists but not good poets, for if a poet is a good philosopher or scientist he presumably has an original over-all comprehension of his material. Castelvetro resolved this dubiety by resorting to the belief that the poet's function, unlike the philosopher's or scientist's, is to "imitate faithfully the fortuitous events of the world," to give delight by means of imitations, and to leave the discovery of truth to philosophers and scientists. The poet should stay in his own province and benefit or delight men in his own way. Finally, however, Castelvetro made use of the principle of gradation. He claimed Aristotle did not say that Empedocles was in no way a poet. Instead, Castelvetro argued that the scientific poet could be said to bear "some of the outward marks of the poet, just as a wolf in sheep's clothing remains a wolf but could be said to bear some resemblance to a sheep." This is not, to be sure, much of a concession! He felt that Cicero, Horace, and Quintilian proved that they did not understand Aristotle by calling Empedocles a good poet. The Renaissance critics consistently refused to believe that the text of Aristotle's *Poetics* was not available to all classical writers. (pp. 71-2)

[In Aristotle's system, Castelvetro said, a] man's true moral nature is always discernible since his morals determine his actions, but Castelvetro denied that poets imitate men in action in order to reveal their moral stances. He argued:

> If that were true, poetry would be an imitation chiefly of morals, and of goodness and wickedness, which Aristotle firmly denies it to be. . . . Poetry, on the contrary, is the imitation of men in action, that is, it is the imitation of a story which is in general like history but differs from it in that it has never happened, though it is always within the realm of the possible. . . . Now these stories are told not to reveal the goodness or wickedness of the persons imitated but to delight the common people as much as possible with the novelty of the events represented, events which give them more pleasure than do the exposition of philosophers, the portrayal of character, the exposition of doctrines concerning the arts and sciences, or the representation of events which possess no novelty.

Since effects of novelty are not limited to human action, Castelvetro could not well have argued in this way had he not limited his concept of poetry almost entirely to narrative and dramatic forms. The real problem with the limitation of poetry to human action came in connection with the other genres, and aside from these idiosyncrasies, Castelvetro's explanation was conventional. Common to all men are five things, he said: mind, will, fortune, station, and action, of which mind and will are essential whereas the other three are external or accidental. Questions of mind embrace distinctions between intelligence and stupidity, those of will between goodness and wickedness, those of fortune between happiness and unhappiness, those of station between royal and private situation, and those of action between philosophical and political activity. Now any of these except philosophical activity can be a subject of poetic imitation. Genres, however, Castelvetro distinguished by differences in station and made matters of will relatively unimportant. He thought that stupidity is more likely to be found in low station and intelligence in high and that "the nobility or humbleness of a person is not revealed by his virtue or his wickedness but by his deportment." Gentility or rusticity—these proceed from intelligence or stupidity, not from morals. In barring philosophical activity from poetry, Castelvetro rejected Tasso's "actions of contemplation." Otherwise, his approach was negative: he accepted the definition of poetry as the imitation of human actions, but not because these revealed the moral nature of mankind. He did nevertheless envision the possibility of imitations in poetry of five kinds of beings, of which human beings were only one: (1) men and women; (2) gods and supernatural beings, a possibility only because the common people think anthropomorphologically; (3) personified moral traits and human abstractions such as wealth, poverty, glory, infamy, and so on (these would seem to encroach upon philosophical activity); (4) animals such as are found in Aesop's fables; and (5) senseless animals and plants (Castelvetro did not make clear what he meant here or how seriously he took this category). The main drift of this classification is that anything can be imitated that can be personified. (pp. 82-3)

Castelvetro should . . . be called a fence straddler, even though he maintained stoutly that verse forms are the proper instruments for expressing fictions and prose for expressing truths. . . . [He] was at pains to decide whether the mimes of Sophron and Xenarchus and the dialogues of Plato, granted that they ought to be considered poems, should be classed with epic poems or with drama. By drama Castelvetro thought Aristotle meant only those poetic forms using language, harmony, and rhythm. He found evidence in Plutarch that after Aristotle's time certain dialogues of Plato were presented as dramas for children, but he also knew that Athenaeus had classed the dialogues of Plato with epic poems. In general, Castelvetro condemned medleys of prose and poetry like *The Consolation of Philosophy* of Boethius, but he did divide them into three categories and made some distinctions among them. His categories were: (1) those works which develop their subjects with both prose and poetry, such as the *Satyricon* of Petronius Arbiter, the first part of the *Golden Ass* of Apuleius, Boethius, the *Philologia* of Martianus Capella, and the *Arcadia* of Sannazaro; (2) verse with introductions in prose—the *Silvae* of Statius and the *Epigrams* of Martial; (3) works that are mainly prose but with some illustrative verse, as in the *Decameron* or in some writings of Cicero. Of these Castelvetro called the first two classes monstrous, especially the first.

The classification of dialogues also preyed upon Castelvetro's mind. He recognized the existence of three kinds of dialogues in antiquity: (1) those that were presented on the stage, (2) those for which stage presentation was impossible since the writers wrote in a historian's manner, as in some of Cicero's dialogues, and (3) those that combine the first two methods, in which the author first speaks in his own person and then presents his characters dramatically. Castelvetro asserted that dialogues are often defective when they are written in prose. He said: "Now an author should never write in prose unless his subject is truth and not fiction, and never in verse unless . . . his subject is fiction and not truth." His conclusion was that since dialogues are fictions they should be written in verse. A special argument was that prose dialogues like Plato's are not suited to the stage because prose utterance calls for speaking in a low voice, whereas verse is utterance designed to be spoken in a loud voice. This idea of Castelvetro's was debated at some length throughout the rest of the century. On the basis of it Castelvetro decided that contem-

porary dramatists should not write in prose. Furthermore, he found that dialogues with a narrator have the defect of faulty verisimilitude, because if they are thought of as history it is highly improbable that the narrator could remember all the speeches recorded or because they are trivialities since history deals with memorable events and these would be the mere opinions of someone on the matters of the arts and sciences, as in Bembo's *Prose* or in some of Cicero's dialogues.

Castelvetro made a strange but, for him, understandable exception for dialogues containing conversations of animals and plants, as in Aesop or Hesiod, since these dialogues are purely imaginary, dealing only with "lies," whereas the other kinds are true or probable. He added:

> It must be borne in mind, however, that the presence of lies in these dialogues does not render them contemptible, for the lies are both delightful and instructive. Dialogues of this kind are to be classed with allegories and with the figures called prosopoeias, to which they doubtless owe their origin and their form. Now the subjects of these dialogues delight us for their universal and miraculous novelty, and we are delighted with them for the same reason that we are delighted not only with miraculous things but with prosopoeias as well. Moreover, we derive no small pleasure from being kept in suspense before we see the end and aim of the dialogue, which is to teach us sound morals or to induce us to do or to avoid doing some particular thing.

The only pertinent conclusion to be drawn from this mélange of opinions is that Castelvetro did not really make up his mind whether poetry could be written in prose or not. His handling of this question was all too typical of his method, for his slow, grinding exploration of possibilities led him as often to chaotic inconclusiveness as to brilliancy. (pp. 95-6)

• • • • •

Many writers of the cinquecento in attempting to fit poetry into their categories of logical discourse interpreted it as proof by means of example, even though, in the tradition they inherited from the Age of Scholasticism, Thomas Aquinas had established that proof by example was the weakest of all kinds of proof and had consequently given poetry the lowest position in his scale. The Humanists in reversing this order of nobility retained the idea that poetry functioned through example. Mario Equicola, who said that "we esteem poets to excel all other writers," also said that poetry "reduces to our use the examples of many things." Varchi fully discussed the use of example in poetry, calling example poetry's logical instrument and asserting, in support of his main claim that the function of poetry was to make mankind blessed and perfect, that the poet's "office is to imitate—that is, feign—things that render man good and virtuous, and as a consequence happy." His two ways of doing this were by removing mankind's vices or by injecting virtues, and both methods called for the use of clear examples arranged so that not only the acts but also their consequences were understandable. Once again, buried under the pile of ideas, are to be found the principles of demonstrative rhetoric. Other discussions of poetry regarded as a mode of proof by use of example can be found in Speroni, Lionardi, Capriano, Luisino, Robortelli's treatise on history, Viperano and Bodin on the writing of history, Patrizi's treatise on history, Castelvetro, Tasso, Mazzoni, Summo, Buonamici, and Beni, but to follow this side road would take us too far afield. To be sure, it is evident that the line of reasoning which turned poetry into proof by example did not inevitably lead to proof by example through the selection by the poet of perfectly virtuous heroes. Principally, in Tasso's literary speculation, it was the hero of a heroic poem only who should be the perfect exemplar of all virtues.

Castelvetro's objection was the proper one. The equivalent of the Platonic Idea (that which should be perfect) in poetry, he believed, should be found in the structure of action, not in a static character. His most pertinent passage in this connection is:

> Moreover, it is not true that the poet should keep in mind an idea of perfect virtue and perfect vice, which he ought to contemplate to compose a good poem. What he ought to keep in mind, in my opinion, is an idea of the most perfect and delightful history, from which his mind must never swerve when he is engaged in composing a poem.

As a corollary to this proposition, Castelvetro advanced the idea that characters could fulfill their functions fully without being perfect exemplars. "To make the poem perfect and like that idea," he said, "he will have to introduce persons of different kinds, sometimes perfectly valiant men, sometimes perfect cowards, and sometimes men who are means between these two extremes; otherwise his story will be only slightly possible or slightly marvelous." Furthermore, Castelvetro was even willing that his principle be used to call into question the method of Zeuxis and to argue that "the art of painting does not consist in creating a figure beautiful or ugly in the highest degree, but in making one that resembles the real, the living, and the natural."

In his *Poetica,* Castelvetro returned often to expression of doubts about the *ut pictura poesis* formula. Aristotle had said that painters ought to find perfect examples of beauty. Here was an opportunity of the kind Castelvetro was always looking for, the chance to show that Aristotle's judgment was far from impeccable. Castelvetro thought that Aristotle's advice to poets to follow the painter's method was useless unless he could in addition specifically tell how perfection was formed. Castelvetro wanted no rigid concept of perfection; he said that when we are dealing with the diversity of human nature we can find even more ideas about what perfection is than among those who try to decide what ideal feminine beauty is. (pp. 146-48)

The besetting sin of Castelvetro was his willingness to compromise his own set of beliefs in order to win a point against established authority. His intent in this particular argument was to destroy the imputed parallel between poetry and painting, and to do so he had to use arguments that played into the hands of his opponents who wanted perfect exemplars used in poetry, for he tried to show that the painter's job is to represent goodness of body, which is beauty, while the poet's job is to represent goodness of mind, that is, good character traits; so that the work of the two kinds of artificers is not really comparable. To be consistent with his theoretical system, he should have said that poets use characters whose actions will constitute a good fable. The terms "goodness of mind" and "beauty of mind" are presumably interchangeable, and goodness of mind is not the mere heightening of any moral quality, good or bad. But Castelvetro partly protected himself by his argument that "goodness" can be manifested in many different ways in the world of particulars. And he added a significant corollary to his meaning when he stated that the painter's perfection does not lie in creating perfect beauty but in creating a likeness since if this were not so all

the subjects of all excellent painters would look alike. Castelvetro was close to important insights when he remarked that we can readily observe that statues do look more alike than the real-life people around us do, but the mark of a beginning painter is that he may find himself creating imitations that are like statues and not like people. Undaunted by the doubts he had raised, he concluded this particular argument by returning to his original line of attack. Why, he asked, did Aristotle not say a poet should have in mind a perfect example of a fable, "since it is just as possible to find a perfect example of a fable as a perfect example of a character trait"? Characters exist for action, not action for character.

Modern literary critics, it would seem, should applaud Castelvetro's having taken this stand, for he probed some of the chief weaknesses of the thought structure of his age. But H. B. Charlton scolded Castelvetro for his opposition to "idealization" (that is, the creation of perfect exemplars) [see excerpt dated 1913]. Charlton's belief was, "Art is not nature to advantage dressed, but by art nature is drawn to its ideal." Charlton's master poet was one who looked always for the perfect example of beauty and in that way made the ideal and the actual interdependent. At the same time, Charlton commended Castelvetro for realizing that the moral interpretation, which he thought Castelvetro was duped into accepting, is irrelevant in aesthetic criticism. But what should be apparent is that Castelvetro was unwilling to commit himself fully to Platonic ideas of beauty. (pp. 149-50)

[Castelvetro] struck out in untried directions, motivated, if one were to judge by his contemporaries, simply by an invincible obtuseness of spirit. The clue to the understanding of Castelvetro's method was his willingness to follow down any avenue of thought, whether or not he had any reason to believe that it would lead him anywhere. He was a gold hunter who worked over every square yard of his territory. As a result, even his most valuable ideas seem to have been arrived at by accident.

In his principal accounts of the relationship of poetry and history, the question of the universality of the one and the particularity of the other was an irrelevancy. For he believed that poetry is an invented imitation of history in which the poet by means of his skill at invention attempts to make his poem as lifelike and convincing as a history would be. He said, "Now the matter of poetry must resemble and imitate the matter of history, but it must not be identical with the matter of history," for if it were identical it would not imitate history but would be history. The poet would not have to labor to show his inventiveness if he merely had to follow history; it is his inventive faculty that makes him more like a god than like a man. In addition to not inventing his subject matter, the historian uses a diction that is like ordinary speech, whereas the poet in handling his invented material uses a diction unlike ordinary speech.

But the idea of Castelvetro's that was starkly novel was that we first must know what the art of history is before we can know anything about the art of poetry, since before an imitation is possible the thing to be imitated must be understood. The crux of Castelvetro's problem was the old question of what is truth and what is reality. From his comments it would follow that truth pertains not to the raw datum, the individual fact, but to the assembling of facts according to some general principle. History he defined as "the story of memorable actions that have been actually accomplished, and its distinguishing quality is truthfulness," and poetry as "the story of memorable human actions that may be accomplished, and its distinguishing quality [is] verisimilitude." The attribute "memorable" does not so much distinguish poetry from history as it limits and conditions the nature of the truthful facts of history.

A series of passages will reveal the full scope of Castelvetro's argument:

> If either Aristotle or another had written a book on the art of history before one on the art of poetry—and the art of history should have been treated first—and if his treatment of the subject had been adequate, we are certain that we should either have found the present booklet of Aristotle's of even greater service to us in writing poems, or should have found it unnecessary.

For

> truth, by nature, came before verisimilitude, and, by nature also, the thing represented before the representation. It therefore follows that verisimilitude depends entirely upon the truth, and models itself after it, and the representation depends entirely upon the thing represented, and models itself after it. And since we cannot have a right knowledge of dependent and modeled things unless we have first a knowledge of the things upon which they depend and are modeled, it follows that we cannot acquire the faculty of judging aright if verisimilitude and the representation are accurate or do not accord, unless we have first a complete and correct knowledge of the truth and the thing represented.

His conclusion was that "no art of poetry that has been written hitherto or may be written in the future can give us a complete and distinct knowledge of the art of poetry unless we have first a complete and distinct knowledge of the art of history."

This novel reasoning of Castelvetro's can be readily taken either as the work of a crank or a complete fool or as an act of real penetration. It seems to prevent the poet from taking the much-celebrated short cut to knowledge in the modifying of Plato's placing poetry at two removes from truth by allowing the poet to turn from the world of sense and mere things directly to the creation of Ideas of transcendental truth. For in Castelvetro's system, truth was not the truth of particulars, but an ideal truth, the method of arriving at which was to be described in the books on the art of history that he called for. This was another way of showing that when the poet creates Ideas he has no way of assuring himself and others that what he has concocted has real being and is not merely a chimera. But since no art of history of the kind described by Castelvetro existed, or indeed can exist, his reasoning had the effect only of casting doubt upon the poet's ability to create transcendent Ideas. Poetry, he said, "borrows its light from history, a light that does not yet burn or at least not as brightly as it should, and, unable to borrow it, poetry must wander in great darkness." At bottom, this reasoning was a slap at humanistic Neoplatonism which had tended to glorify the poet for his ability to create higher universals directly.

Granted, it is hard to tell whether Castelvetro was thinking of the modes of gaining knowledge or more simply of the arts of poetry and history as matters of technique or disposition. His key word was "memorable." His art of history would tell us what kinds of things were more or less "memorable and worthy of a place in history." Memorability can be equated

with value, and value for Castelvetro, as for almost all writers of his century, led to the rhetorician's "praise and blame." The rhetorician was interested in knowing how his ethical effects could be achieved technically. And so Castelvetro stated that his desired art of history would go on to tell us

> what things should be told briefly and summarily, and what elaborately and in detail; what order should be followed in narrating events; when and where digressions should be introduced, and descriptions of places, of persons, or of other things; that it would have determined for us whether the historian may or may not be allowed to pass judgment upon the things that he narrates, praising one thing and condemning another, and to draw from them lessons useful to his readers and to political life.

If the higher uses of the Jamesian "point of view" in fiction or Allen Tate's concept of "authority" were in any way appropriated in Castelvetro's aesthetics, it was at this point, at this conversion of epistemological problems to technical problems. The chances are that Castelvetro was not unconscious of what he was doing.

However, some hundreds of pages later in his commentaries Castelvetro attacked the problem differently and considered the "universal" part of a narrative poem to be the general outline of the plot, much as Malatesta Porta did later. Here the taking-off point was the problem of how different poets could create differing tragedies on the base of the same legend of history. Castelvetro first assumed that Aristotle meant this was done by varying the episodes; later he decided Aristotle did not mean variation to consist only in a rearrangement of the accidents of a story (as, for instance, in the way the particulars of the death of Clytemnestra and Aegisthus had been varied) but meant instead that we reduce fables to their universal form by changing time and place and not using the same particular characters. From this idea, Castelvetro was led back to renewed stress upon poetry as invention. He said:

> So he [Aristotle] was of the opinion, as we saw above, that not only can imaginary names be given to the characters of the tragedy by a poet but also the material of which the fable is composed can be imagined, since we are obliged to believe that he wanted to teach how to imagine matter for forming similar fables.

Although Castelvetro did leave room for the use of historical subjects, particularly in tragedy, he made this concession grudgingly at the expense of his usual demand for poetry defined in terms of invention.

Especially noticeable in Castelvetro's treatment of universals is his handling of them as stock-plot patterns. He delved deeper into this aspect of the broad problem and more copiously illustrated his idea than his contemporaries had done. In reducing any given fable to its universal form, he said, we should make the original specific situations and characters no longer recognizable. So the episodes, that is,

> the particular ways by which it is recognizable, are taken out and in their place other and different ones are inserted. And if perchance Aristotle holds this view and understands universality in this way here, subjects for poetry can then be taken not only from tragedies and epic poems that we and others have already made but also from comedies and histories, since they can be differentiated by episodes to the

point of being no longer recognizable as having come from them, and have been universalized, whether they are tragedies, epic poems, comedies, or histories.

For instance, he added, let us consider the basic plot situation of an ardent lover who, unable to reveal his love, shuts himself up prepared to die of his love pangs, so that his friends have to invent a scheme whereby he can enjoy his mistress. This is the plot of Seleucus, Antiochus, and Stratonice universalized, but it can be changed so that it applies to a Tito, Gisippo, and Sofronia or to Boccaccio's story of Giachetto and Gianetta. "And because we do not recognize this universal to pertain more to the latter than to the former, we can use it in forming other fables, but we cannot in other fables use the particulars by which we recognize the universal as pertaining to certain persons. And if a certain particular is used there, it will deservedly be blamed as stolen goods." Castelvetro cited a particular incident in which Boccaccio duplicated too exactly a set of incidents he had previously used; he argued that a poet must create for himself the particular ways and means of expressing the universal.

Doubts arose in his mind when he tried to apply his principle to the Iphigenia story. He concluded:

> For however much any one of the things told universally about Iphigenia can happen to other persons, when they are taken all together it seems that they so particularize this universal that we recognize it as pertaining only to Iphigenia and not to another character. And if this is how things stand, Aristotle has not taught us how we should reduce a fable to the universal, nor has he given us any norm or adequate or suitable example.

At what point, in other words, can the particulars be changed and give the effect of newness to a basic plot when some basic plots are already closely identified with particular situations? In this connection, Castelvetro said positively that all particulars that tend to identify the basic situation with any particular character should be discarded.

It must be remembered that Castelvetro believed the function of poetry was to give delight, not profit, to the "rude multitude." This basic tenet of his is hard to match with his notions of universality and the relations between history and poetry. Quite possibly the word "universal" had two distinct meanings in Castelvetro's vocabulary, one philosophic and one popular. At the time when he discussed Aristotle's exclusion of Empedocles and his like from the roles of poets, Castelvetro asserted that a poet making use of scientific or philosophic material would not be engaging in original creation and so would not be a poet. He foresaw the need to answer the objection that if a poet happened to be a good original philosopher or scientist he would presumably create a good part of his own material, and he responded that the poet's function, unlike the philosopher's or scientist's, is "to imitate faithfully the fortuitous events of the world" and by means of his imitations to give delight to his listeners, leaving the discovery of the truths hidden in natural or accidental phenomena to philosophers and artists, who have their own way (one different from that of the poets) of delighting or benefiting men. These remarks can be used as evidence to show that Castelvetro broke sharply with Aristotle over the differences between history and poetry and reinforced his belief that no satisfactory art of poetry could be written until an art of history had been worked out. For Aristotle had distinctly made poetry not an imitation of the fortuitous events of the world. But it should be clear that Castelvetro's theories never achieved final coherence. And yet at this point he was quite conscious that he differed from Aristotle, even though a scant page before he had scolded writers bold enough to challenge Aristotle— "whom we cannot contradict without shame." Nevertheless, he assured his readers that poetry does not differ from history, as Aristotle had said, by being more philosophical (that is, more universal, in the usual critical vocabulary of the sixteenth century) than history but by being an invented imitation of history. The significant difference between Castelvetro and his contemporaries was that he envisioned a Platonic Idea in a composed action and not in a static character. The kind of universality that he consistently failed to find in poetry was the perfect exemplar of character.

In the years following the publication of Castelvetro's commentary on the *Poetics,* a storm of protest arose against his ideas, and one of the incitements was his giving precedence to the art of history. Tasso, who often did accept novel ideas from Castelvetro, objected but partly misunderstood what Castelvetro had said. Tasso denied that history preceded poetry in origin—Castelvetro had never said that it did—or that truth must precede verisimilitude. Poetry, Tasso insisted, was several centuries older than history, and he argued that a poet therefore could hardly have needed to learn an art that was developed later. He supposed Castelvetro to have meant that history came first by nature even though not in time, but he responded firmly that "the poet considers the verisimilar only as it is universal." An art of universality should be learned before the art of particularity. Tasso held that Aristotle obviously thought that the art of history was simpler than the art of poetry and that the rules of rhetoric should be adequate for the writing of it (unless there was some truth in the belief of Demetrius Phalereus that history writers followed a few distinct principles of their own).

Patrizi, who was no lover of Aristotle, took Castelvetro to task for following Aristotle too closely, and so his quarrel was really with Aristotle. He argued that the notions of Castelvetro on the differences between poetry and history were based upon Aristotle's dismissal of Herodotus as a poet and on his statement that poetry tells what should have been done and history what was done. The fallacy in the logic here, according to Patrizi, was that the fault to be found with Herodotus should have been his failure to achieve unity of action, not verisimilitude and necessity as Aristotle said. Furthermore, since countless poets had written history in verse form before Aristotle's day, the accounting of a difference on the basis of verisimilitude and necessity carried little force. Patrizi was a consistent descriptivist: he asserted always that if rules for poetry were to be formulated they should be based upon the range of actual practice. For him, the existence of histories written in verse was proof that histories could be made poetic. Scrutiny of actual practice, he claimed, would show that poets usually differed from historians in dealing with fantastic improbabilities rather than with idealized constructions. Poetry is that which is handled poetically. The poetic substance of minor poetry Patrizi identified with the rhetorical principle of *enargeia* (vividness) or "evidence," and he thought that the historian could use this principle as well as the poet. He also said the historian imitates in telling what has happened: he can compose his action so that it becomes a fable; the parts can hang together in necessary connection. So what difference is there according to these criteria between poetry and history? Surely none at all. And if none, why are not the historian and the poet one and the same according to these precepts? After fighting this battle Patrizi felt that Tasso's notion of the hero of an epic poem as Idea or perfect exemplar still needed leveling, and this he proceeded to do.

Francesco Buonamici turned a large part of his *Discorsi poetici* (1597) into a rebuttal against Castelvetro. His first discourse was a complex study of the determinants generally used in the classification of the arts and sciences for the purpose of showing how senseless and confusing were Castelvetro's theses about the relations between the arts of poetry and history in terms of classical methodology. An art, he said, differs from a science in that a science contemplates only, and an art must carry science over into practice. Art can be divided into theory and practice. The theoretical aspect of an art is actually a science and submits to the same conditions as science. When it is reduced to practice, it should function with the right reason derived from the theoretic; but practice depends upon the material used as well as on the theory employed, and the material can impede the intention. But although poetry is more like philosophy than like history since both poetry and philosophy deal with universals and history with particulars, Castelvetro was guilty of a shift of terms by comparing poetry and history and not poetics and history in saying poetry bases its shadow images of the true on what really is true.

Buonamici assumed that poetry is subordinate to politics since he found that both Plato and Aristotle said so. The two principal parts of poetry are metrics and hypocritics, that is, verse forms and the explication of concepts. Hypocritics, he said, consist of "the explication of its concepts with modes not signifying what is true, as affirmations and negations do, but with modes signifying affective traits such as imperatives, prayers, and desideratives." Buonamici was not unlike a modern semanticist. Poetry, he added, makes use of rhetoric in several ways. But he made the distinction between the true and the verisimilar fundamental to definitions of poetry, for he allowed logic and metaphysics to be concerned with what is true, dialectic with the probable ("which is a semblance of the truth"), rhetoric with the persuasible, and poetry with the verisimilar (which "shows how it ought to be done"). Buonamici's classification here, however, was subject to further distinctions between what is true in itself and what is true conditionally and between complex and uncomplex truth, even though his initial classification was standard in his time.

Buonamici made use of these general remarks in determining that for both the orator and the poet "the theoretic part concerns the true and the other part formally and as secondary intention and, leaving consideration of essences to the metaphysician or logician, addresses itself more to giving rules showing how they can be obtained, as, for instance, the poetic method uses sweetness of verse as guide and inducement; so that when one comes to practice, the former [rhetors] to debates and the latter [poets] to poetizing, the [essences] are dealt with according to what is true or verisimilar, not in universal form but made appropriate to some one situation by means of the fable," as in the particular condition of Aeneas' meeting Dido at a time when her political position was insecure.

The argument came to a head when Buonamici said that an art of history is then not necessary or important for an art of poetry. He pointed out that Aristotle made many cross references among poetics, metrics, rhetoric, and hypocritics, but since he made no such references to an art of history the clear implication is that he found such references unnecessary. History should be thought of as a kind of writing of value principally in oratory and politics "since the good orator has to be a historian in order to have copious examples at hand, and a politician [has to be one] in order to base his discourses on experience." No art is necessary for the knowledge of history.

The final principal contender against Castelvetro on this score was Paolo Beni, in the early years of the seventeenth century, when the ghost of Castelvetro's irregularities should by then have been laid. And in actuality Beni used some of Castelvetro's arguments in the attempt to upset Castelvetro. He said that the reason Castelvetro was led to argue both that poetry should be derived from history and that it is useless to try to determine precepts for writing poetry without first determining the rules for writing history was that the poet tries so hard to make us forget we are dealing with feigned materials that he convinces us an actual event is unrolling before our eyes. Beni, like Castelvetro, emphasized invention, but although their beliefs seem similar, Beni's assertions conformed more to the usual set of doctrine of his time than did Castelvetro's. Beni continued: "Thence it cannot be readily conceded that a poet imitates things which have happened, since he either invents everything, as in comedy, or varies, changes, and makes additions, as in epic poetry or tragedy." And later he added: "For if he borrows some things from the monuments of history, he does not represent them as they have been done but as they should have been done. He refers everything back as if to Ideas." Consequently, the poet does not so much imitate what has actually happened as he tries *not* to imitate them just as they happened. For the historian the highest praise comes from following truth. "In poetry the highest praise is in deceiving eyes and minds and in making the auditors mistake the false for the true." As a result, poetry is not at all the mere shadow image of history.

When the extremity of Beni's position as a defender of Tasso's idealized heroes is considered, it becomes a matter of wonder that he could have moved so close to Castelvetro's position. What he and Castelvetro stressed in common was the doctrine of verisimilitude. Beni was interested in a poem with historical subject matter universalized away from strict adherence to history but still resembling history. Castelvetro wanted invented stories that seemed as true to life as history, and he had relatively little to say about universality. Beni could concede that

> just as a shadow follows a body and seemingly comes out from it fable and poetry follow history and entirely flow out from it. Thus, while the historian is concerning himself with things men have done and pursues the deeds and saying of mortals, here is poetry for you which represents the deeds of heroes and powerful leaders, and the misfortunes and fates of kings and of men in high places, and the loves, laughter, frauds, brawls, in both deeds and sayings, of citizens and populace. . . . In this respect, poetry seems to be merely the shadow and image of history, and in this connection it can be said that poetry is feigned history and history is true poetry.

But the poet refers the true events of history to the Ideas, which are superficially false. Truth or falsehood in poetry is unimportant, Beni said, as long as the poetry is verisimilar. It is better that a poet avoid the true and necessary than the verisimilar. (pp. 177-86)

The critical speculation in the sixteenth century on the differences between poetry and history, although acquiring special impetus from the theories of Castelvetro, was caused primarily by Aristotle's pronouncements, and it was because of Aristotle that the differentiation involved the problem of universality and particularity. Castelvetro's principal importance was in describing a type of universality based on general significance of action rather than of stock character. (p. 188)

• • • • •

[Since art, according to Antonio Minturno in his *L'arte poetica* (1563),] is an imitation of nature, a pure reflection of it, and since, according to Castelvetro, art reproduces nature, the reactions of the two to the question seem to be more alike than the differences of their stances in general would suggest. What we do not find in Castelvetro is the unresolved opposition, and the lack of interest in finding a resolution, of the terms of furor and art. As his rejection of furor has revealed, Castelvetro was all on the side of art. In his view of the situation, the sedulous aping of one's predecessors is outside of the area of art, and herein lies one of Castelvetro's more original distinctions. Castelvetro wanted writers to think and invent, not merely follow a tradition. Art for him was the road to originality. There are, he said, two kinds of artists, just as there are in general two kinds of men: (1) those capable of discovering by and for themselves the essential principles of their arts and (2) those who are forced by their nature to follow the precepts and examples left by others. Castelvetro noted that Petrarch, in a letter to Tommaso da Messina, put himself in this second class, that is, in the class of those who follow the traditional precepts for writing poetry and who imitate their forerunners. Using the standard Humanist's analogy, Petrarch called poets of the first class silkworms and those of the second class bees. Castelvetro, however, took a stand that for his day was unusual and seemingly anti-Humanist, arguing for the silkworm and against the bees. The honey gatherers, he claimed, do not use reason but merely follow tradition blindly. But who can tell whether Castelvetro saw a real opposition between Humanism and rationalism? His primary object here was to undermine the authority of Aristotle, and to his way of thinking Aristotle was responsible for the theory of imitating one's predecessors. Since Castelvetro's contemporaries had often distinguished clearly between the two concepts of imitation, the reasons for the retrogression implied in his confusing them again are not self-evident, except that he needed to lump together the blind following of Aristotle as an authority in the matter of poetics and the poets' blind following of classical poets.

These are three conclusions Castelvetro arrived at which were at variance, he thought, with Aristotle:

(1) Imitation is not one of the causes of poetry, for imitation "functions without the guidance of reason, following contemporary models or tradition." The poet should, instead, sharpen his own wits and invent a new version of poetry; otherwise, he is a plagiarist.

(2) It can be said that "the kind of imitation required by poetry is not natural to man" as Aristotle said it was. (But Castelvetro here identified imitation of reality with the monkey's kind of imitation and believed—along with the better Aristotelians—that a sharp distinction should be made between simian imitation and positive creation. Simian imitation may be natural to man, but real creative activity is not.)

(3) Even primitive poetry was not produced without premeditation, without cognition. Poetry would not be marvelous if its creation were as easy and as natural as Aristotle implied. "Nothing can be produced without forethought except by those who have had long practice in it and have formed the proper habits," Castelvetro insisted.

It follows, he said, that the imitation that is natural to man is one thing, and the imitation required in making poetry is quite another; for natural imitation is merely "following blindly the example of others." The real poet is the one who "does things quite different from anything done in previous days and sets examples, so to speak, for others to follow." He must know the reason for everything that he does. In a larger sense, he does not really imitate at all, for there is a competition between him and the "course of mundane events to see which will produce the more wonderful event," so that the poet is a kind of second deity. But Castelvetro did not take this competition very seriously. When he moved to the more specific question posed by Horace of whether a poet profits more from nature or from art, he answered that the opinions of Horace and Quintilian need correcting, "for art is not a different thing from nature, nor can it go beyond the limits of nature, and it aims at doing the same thing as nature." The simple answer to Horace's question is that it is more important to have a perfect mastery of the poetic art than to have the greatest genius. The radical, but rationalist, Castelvetro thus reversed not only the usual art-furor ratio of his time but also the usual art-nature ratio.

H. B. Charlton was no doubt right in claiming that Castelvetro, unlike Scaliger, Minturno, and Tasso, rejected "the formation of a kind of poetical stockroom of metaphors and figures, regulation poetic devices and tricks for the production to order of epic, tragedy, sonnet, or epigram." But he was wrong in saying that in Castelvetro's kind of art of poetry "criticism is mere prescription-writing; its object is legislative and executive at once; judicial hardly at all." The art of poetry according to Castelvetro is something that each poet works out for himself, more or less consciously, following the nature of things. Genius is needed, but genius is needed for all original activity. The upshot was that Castelvetro and Minturno were quite unlike. The key difference was that between the classicist bees and the rationalist silkworms, the honey gatherers as opposed to those who spin out of their own substance. For Minturno had said that the imitator should be like the bees that convert the sweetness of the flowers into honey. Even with him the poet must make borrowed material his own, so that it seems to have grown in his garden and not merely have been transplanted there. The difference is between Minturno's "seeming-to-be" native and Castelvetro's "actually-being" native. But widely divergent ontologies lie behind this difference that seems slight on the surface. What can puzzle us in the subsequent history of the Neoclassical period, when the contrasts between the bees and the silkworms (or the bees and the spiders, as Swift had it) continued to be made and when the temper of rationalism was overtly dominant, is that the bees continued to flourish, especially in literary creation. However, strong belief in originality belonged on the rationalist side in Castelvetro's body of ideas and was connected with the validity of art.

As we move toward the end of the century, the answer we encounter more commonly than Castelvetro's is the compromise that nature must be developed by study and art, which is practically what Horace had said in the beginning. Luisino did little more than expand upon Horace, in acknowledging that the question was a much-debated one and in citing Isocrates and Diogenes Laërtius. The stalwart Florentine academician, Lorenzo Giacomini, speaking of humane learning in general, said, in 1583, that the human being needs three qualities to arrive at his highest state of perfection—apt wit, doctrine, and exercise; "wit is given to us by God alone, without any doing on our part; but for doctrine and exercise we need industry, labor, and diligence, since we must learn the sciences from written books and from the words of those who know and since we must exercise ourselves in those things in the knowing of which we wish to habituate the intellect." Habit, in the Renaissance scheme of things, made the world go around. (pp. 448-51)

> *Baxter Hathaway, in his* The Age of Criticism: The Late Renaissance in Italy, *Cornell University Press, 1962, 473 p.*

ROBERT C. MELZI   (essay date 1963)

[*In the excerpt below, Melzi examines Castelvetro's* Chiose: *annotations to Dante's* Inferno.]

The fortune of Lodovico Castelvetro rests mainly upon his commentary on Aristotle's *Poetics,* and his place in history is quite secure because of this famous book and, to a lesser extent, because of his commentary on Petrarch's *Rime Diverse.* Castelvetro's activity as a commentator of Dante has been largely overshadowed by his works on Aristotle and Petrarch, in spite of the praise that the dean of Dante's interpreters, Michele Barbi, bestowed upon his exegesis of the *Inferno.* When referring to Castelvetro, Barbi had in mind the **Sposizione ai primi XXIX canti dell'Inferno dantesco** that Franciosi had just edited in Modena. This commentary, however, is by no means the only treatise on Dante that Messer Lodovico ever wrote. If we trust the almost always reliable testimony of Muratori, Castelvetro wrote not only a commentary to the first twenty-nine cantos of the *Inferno,* but he actually annotated the entire *Commedia.* This work was lost in Lyons in 1567, when our commentator had to flee for his life and leave behind most of his precious manuscripts.

In addition, a mention of a different work appears in Tiraboschi who, in describing the loss of the manuscript in Lyons, observes that Castelvetro had not only written a commentary on the first twenty-nine cantos but had also annotated an *Inferno* in its entirety. These marginal notes, he adds, appear on an incunabulum owned by Ferdinando Cepelli. Tiraboschi concludes that, since these two works seem to be of a different nature, Castelvetro must have composed two separate sets of commentaries, one to the first twenty-nine cantos and the other one to the entire Inferno. (p. 306)

When writing his preface to the edition of the commentary to the first twenty-nine cantos of the *Inferno,* G. Franciosi observed that the marginal notes in the Landinian Dante owned by the Cepelli family were not the work of Castelvetro because of what he called "la natura intima di quelle postille affatto diversa dall'indole del Comento." It seems, however, that Franciosi's opinion is not substantiated by facts; first of all, the supporting documents owned by the Biblioteca Estense point to a definite Castelvetrian paternity; we have then the

testimony of Giammaria Castelvetro (Lodovico's nephew and editor of some of his work), who cautions us against seeking too close a resemblance between his famous uncle's early works and his more mature ones. Third, a graphological comparison points to a common authorship, and finally a comparison between the marginal notes and the Modenese's later books reveals many similarities of interest and clearly points out that the *Chiose* are the working copy used by Castelvetro to prepare some of his most famous books. (p. 307)

How can we explain the divergence in literary outlook that has prompted Franciosi to declare that "la natura intima delle postille" in the *Chiose* is altogether different than that of the **Sposizione**? To find an answer we should bear in mind the time and place of composition of these two works. The **Sposizione** was written in Vienna while Castelvetro was gravely ill; deprived of his dear books, he had to quote mostly from memory, a fact that he lamented several times. The **Chiose** were written over a much longer period of time, probably during the period of the *Accademia Modenese,* and if in them the author shows a greater feeling for art and beauty, this is due to the fact that the young Castelvetro has not yet felt the humiliation and bitterness of the exile. The more serene outlook shown by our commentator in the **Chiose,** where he is, indeed, already searching into the very depths of Dante's innermost thoughts, without however assuming the fierce countenance shown in the **Sposizione** cannot simply be dismissed as the product of youth versus old age. The loss of feeling for beauty is the result of an unjust accusation, a prolonged trial, a flight, an exile, all factors that can change the outlook on life of the most serene individual. (pp. 312-13)

Two questions arise then: the first concerning the date of composition, the second one concerning the place that the **Chiose** occupy in the stream of Castelvetro's literary production. The **Chiose** were probably composed in the decennium between 1548 and 1558 that represents the best period in our commentator's creative life. The "terminus a quo" must necessarily be the year 1532, since the quotations from Ariosto that we find in folio 14 were taken from the *Furioso*'s 1532 edition. As a further proof that the **Chiose** were annotated in the late period of the *Accademia Modenese,* we notice Castelvetro's apologetic attitude when he is confronted with the high opinion that Landino had of Plato. It does not surprise us to find that Landino had a greater opinion of Plato than he had of Aristotle and that he seeks Petrarch's authority as a comfort for his opinion. In the period of the Florentine Platonism Landino does not even remotely consider the possibility that his statement might be interpreted as heterodox. Castelvetro, on the other hand, when he writes his *Chiose,* some fifty years later, is careful to observe that, in his opinion, there is nothing improper in extolling Plato's preexcellence and that "non par sconvenevole a cristiano preporre Aristotele a Platone perchè nelle cose trattate da Plat[on]e habbiamo più eccellente authore." These words obviously suggest that the stern hand of the Counterreformation was being felt at the time Castelvetro was annotating the *Chiose.* (pp. 313-14)

If we cannot find in the *Chiose* references to any of his books that were already in print, we can, on the other hand, find countless references to other books that our Modenese was to compose in the future. In addition to the **Sposizione** that we have already mentioned, we find copious references to another important book by our commentator, the **Giunte** to Bembo's *Prose della volgar lingua.* This book had originally been printed in Venice in 1525 and had been reedited in 1548 by Varchi. This is the edition Castelvetro had in front of him when he was jotting down his philological observation in the *Chiose.* He also had before him Aldus' 1514 edition of Petrarch's *Rime* and, whenever he came upon a verse that suggested a Dantesque origin, he jotted down the Petrarchan cross-reference in the *Chiose.* The result of this careful annotation was **Le Rime del Petrarca brevemente sposte per Ludovico Castelvetro** which was to be printed posthumously in Basel in 1576. The *Chiose* were also preparatory to a commentary to the entire *Commedia* that, as we mentioned, was lost in the flight from Lyons.

The *Chiose* is then a working copy, a collection of thoughts of literary, philological and critical nature destined to form two of our commentator's best works. The *Chiose* stands "a cavallo" between Landino's Platonism and the Aristotelianism of the *Trattatisti* that will become apparent in the *Sposizione* to the first XXIX cantos of the *Inferno* and in the commentary to the *Poetics.* Not only does the Modenese slowly detach himself from the older predecessors allegorical exegesis but he consciously leans toward a more literal interpretation. This is, however, but one sign of the change; other symptoms can be detected in the search for a better manuscript, in the attempt to establish that which Castelvetro calls "il vero testo" and in his preference for Aldus' text. These symptoms bespeak the new critic who is no longer satisfied with the heritage that has been bequeathed to him by his predecessors, but is aware of the necessity to improve their results. In this respect no contribution can be called more significant and more modern than Castelvetro's attempt to interpret Dante through Dante himself, consonant with his later interpretation of Petrarch with Petrarch's own verses. Especially progressive is the very unusual fashion in which the Modenese arranges some of Dante's most important ideas under a common heading, thus anticipating Apollonio's recent attempt to group Dante's concepts according to great topics such as "la lode, la morte, etc."

The other point to observe is that Castelvetro's main contribution is of a philological nature. If the Modenese's critical comments on the *Inferno* are important, they remain, however, fragmentary in nature and they are sometimes of a negative, rather than of a constructive character. In the observations of linguistic interest, on the other hand, the true master is evident; even in the casual form of marginal notes the *Chiose* contain observation of philological import that are sufficient to pave the way for the great work that was to follow, the *Giunte.* (pp. 314-16)

[From Castelvetro's] marginal notes we can learn that he knew French, Provençal and Hebrew, but we can also observe that he used these languages as a help in deriving etymologies from Latin. Not only does he show a great deal of philological acumen, but he is not afraid, at times, to depart from the interpretation of the older commentators. This was going to be one of Castelvetro's greatest virtues, that of not being awed by the authority of any of his predecessors or contemporaries. It is true that this virtue brought upon him the animosity of most of his "confrères" and that, in the field of criticism, it forced him to cavil rather than to seek the truth; but in the field of philology it had to be his greatest asset. His commentary is always engagingly fresh, and his language, because of the very nature of the *Chiose,* is as direct and unsophisticated as a page of Cellini. The very fact that he was addressing himself, as it were, in preparation for future works, rather than addressing the scholarly world, gave his speech

a force and an immediacy that none of his future books was ever going to possess again.

The study of the *Chiose* will then help us in many respects. First it will provide us with many new and refreshing interpretations on important passages of the *Inferno,* just as well as it will shed further light upon the genesis of the non allegorical type of interpretation that had to characterize his later works. In the field of Petrarchan studies, the *Chiose* will enable us to search with him into the complex problem of the relationship between Dante and Petrarch. By shedding further light upon the heretofore confused figure of Castelvetro, the *Chiose* enable us to put him into a much better perspective. They suggest that, rather than focusing our attention on his activity as a commentator of the *Poetics,* we should pay more attention to his role as a literary critic and, especially, as a philologist. His figure will then emerge as that of one of the Renaissance's greatest philologists, one who was cognizant of his own power and who knew how much ahead of the times he really was. (pp. 317-18)

> *Robert C. Melzi, "Castelvetro's Annotations to the 'Inferno': A Second Look at a Scarcely Known Manuscript," in* Italica, *Vol. XL, No. 2, June, 1963, pp. 306-19.*

PHILLIPS SALMAN   (essay date 1979)

[In the following excerpt, Salman addresses Castelvetro's claim that poetry should give pleasure, not instruction.]

[As Bernard Weinberg has shown in his *Trattati di poetice e retorica del cinquecento* (1970)], there are rival Horatian and Aristotelian strains in the sixteenth century, one focusing on a text's style and the other on its ethical content as it produces an effect on an audience. Weinberg argues that the pleasure derived from a text is regarded as 'moral pleasure,' a phrase which he does not define but which seems to imply a relation between instruction and pleasure. These stylistic and ethical concerns are accompanied by a third, which we may call the oratorical or, with M. H. Abrams, the 'pragmatic.' Here the interest is in the effect of the text on its audience. All three show a shift away from a stress in the medieval period on the product of reading toward a stress on the process of reading.

The interest in the process seems related to a shift from religious to secular concerns. Although a critic's orientation may be generally religious, his discussions of literature are usually secular; hence, the nature and function of didacticism are defined more in human than in theological terms. The kind of man Pico celebrates in his *Oration* and that Hamlet despairs of becomes, together with sublunary creation, a source of wonder and pleasure. It is also difficult to find a critic who is explicit, complete, and coherent about the faculty psychology. Instead, we find critics relying on a reader's knowledge of it and referring to delight or instruction separately and to the operations and pleasures of one or more of the faculties. It is not until the seventeenth century, when the faculty psychology is under attack, that we again find it completely described. The effect of these differences on the theory of instruction and delight in literature may be seen in assertions suggesting that a text may give pleasure in itself and in new assumptions that a faculty may be activated and pleasured without either that activity or that pleasure being related directly to one's last end. Renaissance critics accept the notion that we may derive instruction and delight from representations of the ethical, not the theological, from fictions showing prudence informed by wisdom, and they move toward elaborating the notion of a purely aesthetic response to literature. (pp. 316-17)

Ludovico Castelvetro's *Poetica d'Aristotele vulgarizzata et sposta* provides an example of the concern with ethical content. Castelvetro relies on a psychology of motion and rest, but the psychology is visible only in the way he interprets the *Poetics* on certain issues. He seems to find little need to explicate amply the operations of appetency in his assumed audience, yet they appear in the kind of interpretation he has that audience make. Castelvetro frequently works out his notion of Aristotle's position on some point and then states the response of the audience. In that response we can glimpse instruction both in terms of ethical content and psychological operations.

A typical, much-cited instance is Castelvetro's assertion that the end of poetry is only delight—a delight, at that, enjoyed by the *rozza moltitudine,* the rude multitude. He distinguishes between the delight experienced by the philosopher and that experienced by the mob; and although we might expect him to define the delights of the mob as purely sensual or as boorish, instead we find him applying a religious conception of the delights of the will. In discussing the heroes and malefactors of tragedy, Castelvetro says,

> If we see a representation of someone good whose actions will be fortunate, we feel a tacit pleasure (*piacere*) born in us that will make us mirthful, both in respect of ourselves and in respect of the fortune of the good man. Through this a hope is born in us that through our being similar or not much dissimilar in goodness we might also obtain similar happiness, and a desire is also born to enjoy with him his fortune by making him know that we enjoy his having fulfilled his desire.

Castelvetro goes on to explain the converse desire to see the malefactor punished and he argues that we delight in seeing the divine justice assert itself. These pleasures he divides into a *diletto oblico* for tragedy and a *diletto diritto* for epic and comedy. Representation leads to a satisfying of the wills of an audience. The audience sees and therefore learns that the divine judge is concerned with terrestrial justice. Other passages operate similarly and to the same effect. The treatment of deception as the source of comedy locates the cause in the response of our corrupted natures, which laugh at any misfortune derived from the denigration of reason, 'in which men are nearest to God and greatly superior to all the other animals.' Tragedy purges by inuring us to the sufferings of others. Actions worthy of pity and fear move us less and less for two reasons: (1) having escaped, we assume God is protecting us and (2) seeing the frequent occurrences of terrible things makes them lose their novelty for us. It is evident not only that Castelvetro assumes a universal order, but also that his vocabulary, while occasionally hinting at the cosmological metaphors we have been noticing, derives from the faculty psychology and unmistakably associates delight with volition. Since we find ourselves akin to God by reason of intellectual superiority or protection, we attain a desirable object. In seeing a drama, we rationalize our position in relation to the characters, and our wills move and are satisfied by seeing on stage the working out of the desires of characters better or worse than we. A good action for a poet to imitate, therefore, is the actualizing of the potentiality of a character's will to unite with its object.

Poetry as instructor becomes a problem for Castelvetro in his translation and exposition of Aristotle's fourth chapter. This is a difficult place for Castelvetro because it holds that we delight in imitation and that we both learn from imitations and delight in learning. The passage challenges him on poetry as serving only to delight. Aristotle says, using the verbs ($\mu\alpha\nu\theta\dot{\alpha}\nu\omega$) and ($\sigma\upsilon\lambda\lambda\omicron\gamma\iota\zeta\omega$), that the reason we enjoy seeing likeness is that as we look, we learn and infer what each likeness represents by comparing the likeness to the original. Castelvetro's translation shows his acquaintance with Aristotle's distinction. 'Likenesses' ($\epsilon\dot{\iota}\kappa\dot{\omega}\nu$) becomes *imagini* (likenesses or images) and the rest, *considerandole [si] imparino & comprendano per sillogismo, che sia ciascuna cosa* (considering the likenesses, one learns and understands by means of syllogisms what each is). Castelvetro's translation, at least, commits him to a process of instruction in which the observer imagines what is before him and compares it by means of the faculty of reason to a likeness presumably in the memory. It is a process in which the observer moves from particulars to generals. We might expect Castelvetro's subsequent exposition somehow to side-step his translation's disruption of his view of the purpose of poetry. Instead, Castelvetro handles the problem by ignoring it and straight-forwardly showing that the reason makes identifications by comparing likeness with original and sorting out similarities and differences, with a resulting delight in the recognition of similarities. Towards the end of this discussion, he commits himself further to a view of instruction by means of a telling metaphor. The one who is not comparing original with likeness, he says, but is dealing with likeness only, does not 'derive this delight rising from the fountain of recognizing resemblances.' That such recognition should be a fountain suggests that Castelvetro grasps very well Aristotle's notions on the process of learning about the tragedies of others. In his treatment of that form of pleasure, Castelvetro shows it to be 'the purgation and removal of fear from human minds,' which 'ought properly to be called utility, since it is health of mind acquired through very bitter medicine' and a form of learning by experience. Apparently, becoming inured to the sufferings of others is a form of comparing likeness with original.

However cynical he may be about our natures, Castelvetro's account of our responses to an imitation rests on a notion of instruction as well as of delight. In the passages cited, delight is implicitly a function of the poet's representation of the audience's interpretation. Silently, and in contradiction to his claim for delight, he brings instruction in by the back door. For an audience to make these interpretations is essentially for it to instruct itself in its ethical situation by means of a verbal artifact. The purpose of poetry cannot be only to delight, even if instruction is viewed as a means to an end.

Both Bembo and Castelvetro accept the text as a fit object for the sense organs and other faculties to work with. Bembo's argument is important because it assumes that the act of intellectual closure and its consequent delight need go no further than the particular text. Contrasted with Augustine's way of reading, Bembo's may seem heretical; for Bembo precisely loves the text itself and not for its higher signification. Similarly, Castelvetro implies that one's pleasure and instruction in seeing the operations of the divine justice are valid for the here and now. Neither the Horatian Bembo nor the Aristotelian Castelvetro, furthermore, seems to feel that the focus on the present in any way detracts from his concern with his last end. They awaken, rather, the sense that they have learned to give the temporal pleasures their proper weight and have learned to see them as unidolatrous even if earthly. (pp. 320-24)

Phillips Salman, "Instruction and Delight in Medieval and Renaissance Criticism," in Renaissance Quarterly, Vol. XXXII, No. 3, Autumn, 1979, pp. 303-32.

ANDREW BONGIORNO (essay date 1984)

[*In the excerpt below, Bongiorno examines the* Poetica d'Aristotele *as a departure from the critical works of Castelvetro's Aristotelian contemporaries.*]

In his dedicatory epistle to the Emperor Maximilian II, Castelvetro offers several reasons for undertaking to expound the *Poetics* of Aristotle after that work had been translated or expounded or both translated and expounded by Averroes, Giorgio Valla, Alessandro de' Pazzi, Francesco Robortello, Vincenzo Maggi, Pier Vettori, and Bernardo Segni. One of them is that for all their intellectual acumen and great learning those worthy men had not succeeded in "removing all the difficulties and making smooth all the rough places with which [that] little book abounds," so that without "doing a second time what they had done and repeating what they had said," he could still exercise "the feeble powers" of his own intellect to do much of what they had left undone. Another and perhaps more compelling reason is that all his predecessors, without exception, had mistaken the *Poetics* for a complete art of poetry and had not felt called upon "to do more than explain what they had found written there." Castelvetro, on the other hand, had come to the awareness—he boasts of it as his discovery (*io mi [sono] aveduto*)—that the *Poetics* is not really a book but the "rough, unfinished, and unpolished" draft of one which, having failed to satisfy its author, was laid aside to serve him at a later time as a repository from which to draw materials for the two books of his *Treatise on the Art of Poetry,* an item in the catalogue of his works at the end of Diogenes Laertius' life of Aristotle. That discovery opened his eyes to the opportunity of doing more than had ever been attempted to serve the needs of both the poets and the critics. . . . His program, then, would include not only the expansion of the little that Aristotle had written on all the matters touched upon in his "little book," but also the introduction of much new matter of a kind not found there. The resulting work would be only in part a commentary on the *Poetics*; the additional matter would make the complete work an approximation of the lost *Treatise on the Art of Poetry.* Castelvetro's great ambition to recreate Aristotle's lost work is one of the two causes of the extraordinary length of his book (911 pages in Romani's edition). The other is the extraordinary prolixity of his style.

An acquaintance with Castelvetro's ambition could easily predispose a reader to look in his book for a complete and recognizably Aristotelian art of poetry. But any reader so predisposed would soon be disillusioned. Castelvetro's exposition of Aristotle's text bears little resemblance to the one published ten years earlier by Pier Vettori, the only one of his contemporaries whom he frequently refers to by name (and usually to discredit him). Vettori's commentary is the work of a man who possessed not only the scholar's learning and methods but also the will to search out the true meaning of his author's text. To turn from Vettori's commentary to Castelvetro's is to leave "the quiet and still air of delightful studies" for the turbulent atmosphere of acrid controversy.

Castelvetro is by temperament less the scholar and critic than the controversialist. He can speak with sincerity of Aristotle, as he does in the dedicatory epistle, as a philosopher supreme among philosophers (*sommo philosopho*) and extol his intellect as not less than superhuman; and in the commentary he can admonish critics who dared challenge his authority that he is honored by the world as an oracle of truth (*philosopho verace*) and "cannot be contradicted without diffidence." But Castelvetro is no less sincerely himself when, having said that the pleasure produced by tragic actions is of three kinds, he adds that "once we have duly examined them we shall know how little Aristotle understands the nature of tragic pleasure." Castelvetro undertook the labor of composing his commentary not as a humble and dispassionate investigator but as an assured master of the art of poetry, and in his eagerness to expound that art he welcomed every occasion for exposing what he took to be fallacies in Aristotle's arguments and refuting all ideas that did not square with his own. In the end the doctrines he recommends to would-be poets and critics are rarely Aristotle's. The elements of his system are recognizably Aristotelian; he plainly owes his conception of poetry as imitation and his view of the end of poetry as pleasure to Aristotle, but as he develops those ideas they assume a form that Aristotle could never have found acceptable. They are unlike Aristotle's, and they are unlike most poetic orthodoxies of his time. In a century in which the end of poetry was universally understood to be utility as well as pleasure and Virgil was worshiped as the prince of poets, Castelvetro could stubbornly deny that poetry had any other end than pleasure and could dare vilify Virgil as a thief, a liar and finally a non-poet. He was unique among his contemporaries, and the praise he would have relished most would have been the world's recognition of his uniqueness. (pp. xiii-xv)

Castelvetro consistently speaks of poetry as an invention. It would be no extravagance to say that he speaks of it as an invention like the wheel and that like the wheel it was invented to perform a specific function. For poetry that function was to provide "pleasure and recreation . . . to the souls of the common people and the rude multitude." Considered as a sixteenth-century formulation this statement is heretical on two counts: it designates pleasure as the sole end of poetry, and it singles out the common people as the audience which poetry must be designed to please. To the literary world of Castelvetro's century it was almost self-evident that poetry was a learned art designed for a learned audience and that its end was not only to please but also to teach.

That pleasing and teaching were the dual end of poetry was one of the firmest literary orthodoxies of the Graeco-Roman critical theory. In Aristophanes' *Frogs,* Euripides says (line 1009) that the only praiseworthy poets were those whose sage counsels made better citizens, and Aeschylus (lines 1054-55) that boys are taught by schoolmasters and men by the poets. But sixteenth-century Europe owed its generally accepted formulation of the poet's whole duty to Horace, who in his *Ars Poetica* had said (lines 333-34) that the intention of all poets (*volunt poetae*) is to improve their readers or to please them (*aut prodesse . . . aut delectare*) or both to improve and please them, adding (line 343) that the most honored poet is the one who has combined utility with delight (*qui miscuit utile dulci*). (p. xvii)

Castelvetro's rejection of half of Horace's doctrine is absolute, and he rejects it all the more confidently because the likes of it had been tacitly rejected by Aristotle, who teaches that every species of poetry affords its peculiar pleasure but never mentions a peculiar utility. To be sure, Aristotle is not consistent throughout. Castelvetro observes that in his effort to contradict Plato, who would have banished tragic and other poets from his ideal commonwealth for the pernicious moral effects of their poems, Aristotle would have given his approval to the kind of tragedy that "in his opinion effects the moral improvement of the people (*la quale è di pro a costumare il popolo*) by purging their souls of pity and fear." This, to Castelvetro, represents a departure from the true doctrine advanced in the earlier pages of the *Poetics* and also in a later one, for when a remark of Aristotle's gives him the occasion for returning to the subject he says that if Aristotle ever concedes that tragedy may have a certain utility he regards it "as an incidental thing, like the purgation of pity and fear." Surprisingly, Castelvetro himself did not succeed in avoiding this very concession that he attributes to Aristotle, once when he speaks with tacit approval of the magistrates who forbid the performance of tragedies and the recitation of epic poems for moral reasons and praises princes and popes for bestowing the laurel crown on poets whose works were judged to be models of moral soundness and technical proficiency, and again when he states it as a fact that "tragedy is of very great utility to the common people and is greatly favored by democracies, confirming their citizens in the resolve to preserve their liberty and to hate tyrants as unjust men displeasing to God." And he regards as morally beneficial the witnessing of both the unjust sufferings of the good and the fall of the wicked because the first spectacle may teach that all men "are subject to many misfortunes and that no man should rest his trust on the tranquil course of the things of this world" and the second may serve to confirm the virtuous in the pursuit of virtue.

But Castelvetro never plainly affirms that poetry has any other end than that of pleasure. On the subject of utility he is no more Ciceronian than he is Horatian. In his commentary he enlarges upon Aristotle's few remarks on rhetoric in the *Poetics* by drawing freely upon Cicero's (as well as Aristotle's and Quintilian's) rhetorical works for his discussion of thought as the third of the qualitative parts of tragedy, but his study of Cicero never converted him to the view that the poet is closely related to the orator or that the poem is by nature a rhetorical example and can perform the function of one. These ideas are not refuted by him; they are simply ignored. Yet the world's nearly universal insistence on the utility of all poetry finally succeeded in drawing from him the admission that poetry may be said to have an *incidental* function which can be called its utility. Castelvetro perhaps never rejected the idea of poetic utility more resolutely than on a page in the posthumous **Opere Varie Critiche,** where he accuses Giovan Battista Pigna of having incorporated into his book on *romanzi* three ideas of his without naming him as their author, the second of them being, in his own words (*con mie parole, tralasciando le sue*) "that though poetry may on occasion have its utility, it may nevertheless be confidently affirmed that it never provides utility except incidentally (*per accidente*), but that when it does so the utility proceeds from outside the poem and from the reader's acute discernment and not from within it and the poet's intention." Castelvetro's pronouncement is of considerable value for two reasons. It is intended to state unequivocally that authentic poetry pleases but does not teach, that it moves to pleasure but not to virtuous words or deeds, that it arouses a person's emotions directly, without, so to speak, first passing through his mind, that it adds nothing to the sum of his knowledge and

wisdom. And yet here, as in his defense of Aristotle as the exponent of a purely hedonistic poetry, an incidental moral effect is not denied to poetry; the denial of utility is not unqualified by the admission that even when the poem is designed to purvey no more than pleasure, utility may prove to be one of its incidental ends. This may explain why no poems—not Aeschylus' *Oresteia* or Dante's *Divine Comedy*—is ever judged by him to be an inferior poem by reason of its utility. (pp. xviii-xix)

The reader of Castelvetro's [*Poetica d'Aristotele vulgarizzata et sposta*] cannot fail to be impressed by the frequency with which Castelvetro expounds a principle of the art of poetry by referring, for comparison or contrast, to some principle of the art of history. The precedent for this procedure was set by Aristotle, who finds it illuminating, when defining the matter of poetry as "what may happen", to contrast it with the matter of history which he defines as "what has happened", and when considering the proper structure of an epic poem to contrast the unity of a poem, which consists of the unity of the action it imitates, with that of history, which consists of a variety of actions brought together by the fortuitous fact that they happened in a single period of time. Aristotle seems to be impressed by the contrasting features of poetry and history. One cannot imagine him endorsing Castelvetro's pronouncement that "poetry borrows all its light from history" or that "if we already had an art of history we could have refrained from the labor of writing a complete art of poetry." Castelvetro understands that poetry differs from history in that the matter of poetry is invented by the poet and the matter of history is not invented by the historian, and he even goes so far as to insist that "history cannot and should not with impunity be written in verse and poetry in prose any more than women can or should dress as men and men as women," adding that Lucian should have written his dialogues and Boccaccio his *Decameron* in verse and Fracastoro his *Joseph* in prose. But by and large Castelvetro regards poetry and history as sister arts. The fact that between Aristotle's time and his own no one had written an art of history does not inhibit him from writing an art of poetry in the light of historiographical principles which he himself formulates. Castelvetro is not defeated, as he professes to be, by the absence of a necessary guide; he does not "wander in great darkness"; to read his art of poetry, to grow acquainted with what to his mind constitutes a good poem, is at the same time to grow acquainted with what to his mind constitutes a good history. (p. xxv)

The poet at work, Castelvetro has said, should strive to excel the dispositions of fortune and the course of human events by making his imitations of them more delightful than they and also more marvelous. The implication here is plainly that the marvelous is not the peculiar property of poetic inventions but is to be observed in the life of the world that is the general object of the poet's imitations; and since historians are bound by the nature of their art to offer a true account of what has happened, descriptions of the marvelous will not be absent from their histories. That being so, the poet cannot choose to slight the marvelous; its presence must be felt in every one of his poems. A poem which fails to astound will fail to do what poetry was invented to do, which is to give pleasure. "The end of poetry," Castelvetro says, "is pleasure; and since the marvelous is especially capable of giving pleasure, it follows that the tragic poet must do his utmost to achieve the marvelous, and the epic poet, because of his greater opportunities, to achieve it in a much higher degree." This injunction Castelvetro lays upon the poet not only on his own authority but also on Aristotle's, whose definition of tragedy implies, in Castelvetro's reading of it, that "the plot must be marvelous, for Aristotle's definition of it says that 'through pity and fear [tragedy] effects the purgation of such emotions,' and a plot cannot arouse pity and fear unless it astounds us." Castelvetro never undertakes to define the marvelous. He categorically denies that it can be identified with the miraculous, reasoning that since all things are possible to God, divine interventions are miraculous but not marvelous. (p. xxviii)

A poet who has succeeded in producing a truly marvelous action could have done so only by the strenuous exercise of a genius schooled in all the doctrines that constitute a perfect art of poetry. The poem that produces its effect from the stage or the platform is the result of expertly directed labor. "Labor" (*fatica*) is a prominent idea throughout Castelvetro's commentary, almost as prominent as the idea of pleasure. It is to the poet's *fatica,* the indefatigable application of all his knowledge and skills, that the audience owes the appropriate pleasure it receives from each of the species of poetry. A poem's worth can in part be judged by the amount of labor that must have gone into its making; the competent critic possesses the capability of discerning the number and the magnitude of the difficulties that the poet overcame in making his poem. The poet who gives the world a versified version of a particular history known in great detail is morally culpable of having shirked the labor of invention. The true poet possesses not only the art but the moral energy to poetize acceptably. (pp. xxix-xxx)

Speaking of the difference in length between the epic poem and tragedy Aristotle says that "tragedy endeavors to stay as much as possible under one revolution of the sun, or to vary from it only a little." In the commentary Castelvetro expands Aristotle's statement and says that the length of tragedies is limited to "the period [of time] within which the audience may sit in the theatre without discomfort, and this period, as Aristotle tell us and I myself believe, cannot be longer than one revolution of the sun, or twelve hours." Aristotle's statement is intended as no more than a generalization on the customary length of the tragedies of his and earlier times; Castelvetro not only reduces Aristotle's "under one revolution of the sun" to twelve hours, which he frequently interprets as the time taken by the sun to run its course above our hemisphere, but establishes the twelve hours as the limit which no tragedy or comedy may ever legitimately exceed. The apparently arbitrary distortion of Aristotle's thought is to be accounted for by Castelvetro's conception of dramatic imitation and of the dramatic audience. A tragedy or comedy "represents words directly with words and things with things," and, that being so, "it must of necessity (*di necessita*) fill as many hours on the stage as the imaginary action it represents would have filled or would fill in the world if it had actually occurred or were to occur there." In analogical terms a tragedy is to the possible event it imitates as "a portrait is to its original when the latter's dimensions are preserved." And even if a tragic poet should succeed, against what Castelvetro conceived to be the nature of things, in compressing an imaginary action of some days into a few hours, the audience could never "be deceived into believing that the action extends over a number of days and nights when they can tell by the testimony of their senses that they have been sitting in the theatre for only a few hours." In the circumstances it remains for the tragic (or comic) poet to imitate

only actions that can be seen and heard in their entirety in a reasonable number of hours, not so few "that the public [would] resent having been lured to the theatre with great inconvenience to itself for one hour or even two" nor so many that it would be subject to severe discomfort, "for people cannot go without food, drink, and sleep, and without relieving their bowels and their bladders and attending to other bodily needs for longer than twelve hours." Tragic poets could, to be sure, emulate poets and construct their tragedies in such a way that one part of them after another could be performed at intervals over a period of time. But to do so would be to ignore the fact that "with the end of the first day and the coming of night the characters continue to speak and act and that what they say and do would not be seen and heard by the audience, who by then will have returned to their homes." Castelvetro names Plautus and Terence as having written comedies "in which the action fills more than a single day" and again Euripides, together with Plautus "and others," for committing the same offense. The offending plays are not named, but two of them are Plautus' *The Captives,* in which Philocrates travels to Elis from Anatolia and returns with Philopolemus before the end of the comedy, and Euripides' *Suppliants,* in which Theseus leaves Athens with an army to fight a battle in Thebes before a short hemichorus and a messenger enters at the end of it to announce his victory. Julius Caesar Scaliger takes note of these facts and condemns both as offenses against verisimilitude. The third seems to be Terence's *Self-Tormentor,* which begins on one day and ends on the next, an irregularity that Scaliger finds excusable because the comedy was performed at the Ludi Megalenses, which lasted for seven days.

The twelve-hour limit—the "unity of time"—has been arrived at through deliberations that took into account Aristotle's authority and what Castelvetro conceived to be the peculiar nature of dramatic imitation and the physiological and psychological constitution of its audience. No authoritative statement by Aristotle and no deliberation of any sort precedes the enunciation of the "unity of place;" it is simply handed down as an injunction and not as a reasoned conclusion. Perhaps Castelvetro assumed as self-evident that if an audience believes that the time which a dramatic representation fills on the stage is neither longer nor shorter than that which it would fill if it were happening in the world, it can also believe that a stage which is represented as a particular place in the first scene cannot be accepted as a different place in a later one. And so it becomes mandatory upon the dramatist to restrict the space in which the action occurs "not only to a single city, village, field, etc., but to as much of them as can be seen by the eyes of a single person"; more precisely, that the action "must be set in a place no larger than the stage on which the actors perform."

As for the plot, it too has its unity. Aristotle says that it must imitate not more than a single action, though Castelvetro takes him to say "the single action of a single person." Having mistaken Aristotle's meaning Castelvetro rejects it by stating it as a matter of fact that every well-constructed tragedy and comedy contains not one action but two and that the two actions are sometimes so loosely related that it would seem possible to stage them separately. Of Euripides' *Hercules Furens* he says that "no one is so blind as not to see that [it] contains two actions." The same could be said for a comedy, Terence's *Andria.* But having as much as said that all tragedies and all comedies are constructed like the *Hercules Furens* and the *Andria,* he retreats to a position from which he can proceed to "the whole truth" of the matter in hand. It is the position from which he can see poetry as "the imitation of history" and as constantly following in its footsteps. Once that is known, we can see that the truth about poetic unity is to be found by considering the practice of the historians. What has that practice been? Plutarch and others have brought into one history "a number of actions of a single person;" Sallust, "who wrote the history of Rome's war against Jugurtha," can be said to have written "the single action of a whole people;" Livy and others have written histories containing "a number of actions of a whole people;" and Trogus Pompeius and many others have written "many actions of many persons or of many peoples." What the historians have done the dramatic poets should, considering the nature of their art, be bound to do. But certain practical considerations will not permit them to follow that course.

> A tragic or comic plot should contain a single action or two so interrelated that they may be accounted one, and of one person rather than of a whole people, not because it cannot by nature hold more, but because limitations of time [twelve hours] and place under which tragedies and comedies are performed will not permit the representation of many actions or of a single action of a whole people, and quite frequently not even the whole of a single action if it is somewhat long. This, not Aristotle's, is the principal and most compelling reason why tragic and comic plots should contain only a single action of a single person or two actions that may be accounted one because of their interdependence.

The proper tragic or comic plot, then, observes the unities of plot, of time, and of place. (pp. xxxviii-xl)

The tyranny which the doctrine of the three unities exercised on the European dramaturgy of two centuries invites an inquiry into the considerations that could have induced Castelvetro to conceive of the dramatic poem as a single action every part of which must be represented as occurring in a single place and lasting no longer than twelve hours. [In his *History of Literary Criticism in the Italian Renaissance* (1961), Bernard Weinberg] attributes Castelvetro's formulation of the doctrine to the limitations of the gross minds and lethargic imaginations of the peculiar audience for whom all poetry, as Castelvetro believed, was invented. If the audience was to know the pleasure which dramatic poetry is capable of giving, then no drama could be said to have been properly designed that had not taken those limitations into account. "The audience's demand for comfort," Weinberg says, "introduced the requirement of a 'unity' of time. . . . " The time limit imposed by Castelvetro is twelve hours; that limit is necessary because at the end of twelve hours in the theatre the people must return to their homes to attend to their physical needs. But would Castelvetro have prescribed a period longer or shorter than twelve hours if the audience had been composed of a social and intellectual élite? "Its lack of imagination," Weinberg continues, "adds the 'unity' of place." Actually, Castelvetro formulates no rationale for the 'unity' of place; he simply imposes it on the dramatist, never explaining that the unity is designed to meet the psychological needs of a popular, and therefore unimaginative, audience.

Castelvetro generally speaks as one who understands that the rude and ignorant multitude cannot be effectively reached by a poetry that is not designed to suit their limited intellectual capacities. The required poetry was, to his mind, neither more nor less than fictitious history, a kind of fiction that faithfully represents, with metrical language as its medium, persons and actions and scenes observable in daily life. The unities, which lend to fiction the appearance of history, can therefore be said to have been invented to serve the Castelvetrian audience, which has been represented as incapable, in Coleridge's words, of "that willing suspension of disbelief for the moment, which constitutes poetic faith." But the lack of poetic faith is possibly more characteristic of Castelvetro than of his audience. The first poetic theory formulated by him is that poetry is an imitation of history. His word for imitation is *rassomiglianza:* resemblance. By 1570 the accepted Italian translation of Aristotle's *mimesis* was *imitatione.* Castelvetro's departure from contemporary usage may well signify that to his mind *imitatione* failed to denote with sufficient exactness the required fidelity of the well-made representation to the thing represented. The poet for whom he reserves the highest praise is the one who "employs every means at his command to give fiction the appearance of fact." (pp. xli-xlii)

[The] Castelvetrian poem was an exotic growth in the critical milieu of sixteenth-century Italy, where Virgil reigned more securely than he had ever reigned before or would ever again. It is a poem that could not have been conceived but by a critic who not only admired the particularized narrative style of Homer more than the generalized style of Virgil, but may well have judged Boccaccio's tales superior as *rassomiglianze* to the Homeric epics. (Even so, he believed that those tales would have greatly gained in verisimilitude if Boccaccio "had given his seven ladies names like Francesca and Giovanna, which were common in the Florence of their day, instead of resorting to Greek names.") In the company of Vida and Scaliger, Castelvetro was destined to preside over the emergence and development of the French classical drama, contributing to it, most conspicuously, the inflexible doctrine of the unities. The seventeenth was to be the century of his greatest eminence. After the decline of French classicism he ceased to be an active influence on the literature of Europe and became a critic read by other critics and the historians of literary criticism. But if his doctrines (other than that of the unities) had acquired a new authority and had been rightly understood, their effect on the development of modern drama and the modern novel would surely have been that of reducing the distance between the world, the things "commonly encountered in daily life," and the verbal representations of them. Castelvetro often says, echoing Aristotle, that tragic and epic actions are magnificent actions; but when speaking for himself of poetic subjects in general he can say of them, like the anti-Aristotelian he often is, that they are of a kind suited to the understanding of the multitude, more specifically that they are like "the everyday happenings that are talked about among the people, the kind that resemble those reported in any one day's news and in histories." The formulation of that statement appears to be that of a critic whose thoughts were more often than not of a poetry less exalted than that which had formed the tastes of the Renaissance humanists. It is for this reason that the pages which he devotes to thought tend to minimize the value of ancient rhetoric to the poets of his own time. But the critic who repudiates the magniloquence which ancient rhetoric contemplates is at the same time the critic by whom that rhetoric is never renounced. Castelvetro no sooner recognizes that the oratory of the ancient rhetoricians is "different in nature from that suited to narrative and dramatic poetry" than he adds that "the art of rhetoric as we know it is not without its value to the poet, for it can offer him part of what he needs to know to frame the less-than-magniloquent utterances suited to his characters." The rhetorical works of Aristotle, Cicero, and Quintilian, then, must not be cast away; properly studied they will yield doctrines that duly mastered will qualify the poet to invent a new rhetoric, a rhetoric by which he will successfully imitate the utterances of persons in typically poetic situations, as when they are soliloquizing, conversing, bewailing some misfortune, offering a prayer, giving encouragement to others or striking fear into them. The gain that the new rhetoric will bring to narrative and dramatic poetry will be greater naturalness and appropriateness—the naturalness no less premeditated than the appropriateness—of thought and language. Castelvetro concludes a paragraph on the necessity of natural and appropriate thought and speech with the condemnation of a sonnet by Francesco Maria Molza in which the speaker, though a shepherd, speaks in a manner indistinguishable from Molza's own. That judgment, which condemns a single sonnet, effectively condemns the corpus of Renaissance pastoral poetry and strongly suggests that Castelvetro would not have approved without serious reservations the French classical drama, which owed much of its peculiar character to some of his own doctrines. It is not fanciful to suppose that Castelvetro would not have been scandalized to meet in a tragedy a drunken porter uttering the sentiments of a drunken porter in language natural and appropriate to his kind.

Castelvetro would have every component of a poem—its characters and their thoughts and words and actions—represented with an immediacy not to be found in Virgil but present in Homer and even more conspicuously in Boccaccio. That immediacy was not unknown in the literatures of Europe in the two centuries between Castelvetro's death and the rise of Romanticism. But thanks to developments which were not wholly literary and owed nothing to Castelvetro's doctrines, Castelvetro's ideal poem (minus unities and meter) came into its own only after the decline of the Romantic movement and the emergence in those literatures of realism, naturalism, and *verismo.* (pp. xlvi-xlviii)

> *Andrew Bongiorno, in an introduction to* Castelvetro on the Art of Poetry *by Lodovico Castelvetro, edited and translated by Andrew Bongiorno, Medieval & Renaissance Texts & Studies, 1984, 384 p.*

FURTHER READING

Clark, John R. Review of *Castelvetro on the Art of Poetry,* by Andrew Bongiorno. *Manuscripta* XXIX, No. 3 (November 1985): 199-201.
    Offers brief critical remarks about Castelvetro's theory of poetics.

Melzi, Robert C. *Castelvetro's Annotations to the Inferno.* The Hague: Mouton & Co., Publishers, 1966, 189 p.
    Examines Castelvetro's annotations to the *Inferno* in relation to his larger works.

——. "Giuntini's Correspondence with 'Il Dubbioso Accademico' and Observations on Editorial Principles of the Renaissance in Italy and France." *Library Chronicle* 45, Nos. 1-2 (1981): 30-43.
    Attempts to link Castelvetro with the pseudonymous sixteenth-century epistler known as "Dubbioso Accademico."

Baldassare Castiglione

1478-1529

(Also Baldassar, Baldesar, and Balthasar) Italian prose writer and poet.

Castiglione is remembered for *Il libro del cortegiano* (*The Book of The Courtier*), a series of prose dialogues which delineates the author's conception of the ideal courtier and the norms of courtesy in a cultured society. Highly influential throughout Renaissance Europe for its comprehensive code of social refinement, *The Courtier* is today regarded as a brilliant historical document and a noted literary achievement.

Castiglione was born in Casatico, Mantua to an ancient aristocratic family. As a youth, he received a traditionally humanist education from the best classical scholars. From 1496 to 1499 he served at the court of the Milanese duke Ludovico Sforza, and subsequently under Francesco Gonzaga, Duke of Mantua. In 1503 he visited the cities of Rome and Urbino on his way south, where he participated in Gonzaga's unsuccessful campaign against the Spanish invasion of Naples. He afterwards requested and was granted a transfer to the court of Guidobaldo da Montefeltro at Urbino.

Here Castiglione experienced his greatest fulfillment. Because he won the duke's confidence, he was entrusted with numerous important embassies, among them one which led to an entrée into the court of Pope Julius II, where he became a fast friend of Italian artist Raphael. In 1506 he was sent to England in the duke's behalf to receive the Order of the Garter from Henry VII. Most importantly, he enjoyed the company of many leading humanists of the day, who assembled at court as much for philosophical exchange as social intercourse. The literary and intellectual activities at Urbino were the inspiration for Castiglione's *magnum opus, The Courtier.* While he began the work in 1507, it was most extensively written and revised between 1513 and 1518 and was published in 1528.

After Guidobaldo's death in 1508, Castiglione was retained by his nephew, Francesco Maria della Rovere. The author married in 1516 but was widowed four years later, then joined the clergy in 1521. Made papal nuncio to Spain in 1524, he was sent by Pope Clement VII to arbitrate conflicting contentions between the papacy and Charles V. His mission failed and, after Rome was sacked by imperial troops in 1527, Clement accused him of treacherous intent. Castiglione cleared himself of Clement's charges and died shortly thereafter in Toledo, Spain, in 1529.

As if transpiring at Urbino in March, 1507, *The Courtier* unfolds a dialogue between nineteen men and four women, guests of the duke and duchess. The speakers are authentic persons, most of them well-known humanists—including Giuliano de' Medici, l'Unico Aretino, and Pietro Bembo—who either lived at court or visited there between 1506 and 1507. The work is divided into four books intended to represent four consecutive evenings. Each treats a subject that is distinct but has bearing on the others, and the common aim is the verbal construction of an ideal courtier. The first book defines qualities essential to a courtier and means by which these attributes may be nurtured; the second book explores

the ideal courtier's behavior in varied—some of them potentially compromising—situations; the third fashions an ideal court lady whose function is to refine and complement her male counterpart; the final book enlarges and summarizes the author's vision of courtiership. Interspersed throughout are debates unrelated to the main topic but of decided contemporary interest, such as the advisability of a pure Italian language, the character of women, and the nature of Platonic love (the last rapturously depicted by Pietro Bembo at *The Courtier's* conclusion). The fundamental complexity and gravity of the work are frequently relieved by anecdote and witty repartee. Above all, discourse and argument are skillfully arranged to impart an impression of realism to the fictional conversations at Urbino.

Both as a model for courtly conduct and a source of philosophical exposition, *The Courtier* was successful immediately after publication, in Italy and throughout Europe. More than eighty editions and translations appeared between 1528 and 1619. Perhaps the most significant of these was Sir Thomas Hoby's rendering of the text into English in 1561. Scholars have traced its literary and social imprint on the writings of such renowned Elizabethans as Edmund Spenser, Ben Jonson, Sir Philip Sidney, and William Shakespeare. *The Courtier* is credited with having inspired several practical guidebooks for noble comportment. Even after the waning of courtly influence, the book was popular for its vivid portrayal of aristocratic life in Renaissance Italy and superb reflection of Renaissance values in general. Turn-of-the-century critic and essayist Walter Raleigh avowed that, were a single work "to be taken for an abstract or epitome of the chief moral and social ideas of the [Renaissance], that one must be *The Courtier*."

Yet *The Courtier*'s reputation has not been without dissention. Some commentators have questioned the work's unity, finding that, while eloquent, Bembo's famous discourse is a philosophically inadequate conclusion to the preceding material and, further, that the book itself has no real philosophical development. Others have examined the author's dialectical method—patterned after but not identical to the method employed in Plato's works—and, like Lawrence Lipking, have determined that "*The Courtier* is not a philosophical confrontation, immersed in the perpetual refinement and modification of an abstraction, so much as it is a linear presentation of the ideal courtier, a list of his qualities and attributes." A few critics have, moreover, skeptically regarded Castiglione's realization of the courtier's role in Renaissance society, at times perceiving it to be unduly incumbent upon speciousness and opportunism. However, as George Bull has observed, if "*The Courtier* offends modern sensibilities," it "cannot be so easily dismissed. It is historically significant and instructive. It is, at the very least, an entertaining book. Most of all, it is a work of substantial literary achievement."

While its historical and literary importance remain unchallenged, *The Courtier*'s intrinsic interest to the current reader has been deemed negligible. Those vigorous ideals that governed Renaissance life have seemed to many irrelevant in the contemporary world. Yet, according to Peter Bondanella, despite its customary status "as a monument to a particular view of civilization," Castiglione's work may ultimately be seen "as an alternative vision of humanity to that of the specialist and technician which has come to dominate our own era."

PRINCIPAL WORKS

Tirsi (dramatic eclogue) 1506
Il libro del cortegiano (prose) 1528
    [*The Book of the Courtier,* 1561]
Poesie volgari e latine (poetry) 1760
Lettere. 2 vols. (letters) 1769-71

BALDESAR CASTIGLIONE (letter date 1528)

[*In the following excerpt from the dedicatory epistle to Don Michel de Silva that precedes the text, Castiglione laments the passing of individuals represented in* The Courtier *and defends the idioms he has used in the work.*]

When signor Guidobaldo of Montefeltro, Duke of Urbino, departed this life, I, together with several other gentlemen who had served him, remained in the service of Duke Francesco Maria della Rovere, his heir and successor in the state. And, as the savor of Duke Guido's virtues was fresh in my mind, and the delight that in those years I had felt in the loving company of such excellent persons as then frequented the Court of Urbino, I was moved by the memory thereof to write these books of the *Courtier*: which I did in but a few days, meaning in time to correct those errors which had resulted from my desire to pay this debt quickly. But Fortune for many years now has kept me ever oppressed by such constant travail that I could never find the leisure to bring these books to a point where my weak judgment was satisfied with them.

Now being in Spain, and being informed from Italy that signora Vittoria della Colonna, Marchioness of Pescara, to whom I had already given a copy of the book, had, contrary to her promise, caused a large part of it to be transcribed, I could not but feel a certain annoyance, fearing the considerable mischief that can arise in such cases. Nevertheless, I trusted that the wisdom and prudence of that lady (whose virtue I have always held in veneration as something divine) would avail to prevent any wrong from befalling me for having obeyed her commands. In the end I learned that that part of the book was in Naples, in the hands of many persons; and, as men are always avid of new things, it appeared that certain of these persons were trying to have it printed. Wherefore, alarmed at this danger, I decided to revise at once such small part of the book as time would permit, with the intention of publishing it, thinking it better to let it be seen even slightly corrected by my own hand than much mutilated by the hands of others.

And so, to carry out this thought, I started to reread it; and immediately, at the very outset, by reason of the dedication, I was seized by no little sadness (which greatly grew as I proceeded), when I remembered that the greater part of those persons who are introduced in the conversations were already dead; for, besides those who are mentioned in the proem of the last Book, even messer Alfonso Ariosto, to whom the book is dedicated, is dead: an affable youth, prudent, abounding in the gentlest manners, and apt in everything befitting a man who lives at court. Likewise Duke Giuliano de' Medici, whose goodness and noble courtesy deserved to be enjoyed longer by the world. Messer Bernardo, Cardinal of Santa Maria in Pòrtico, who for his keen and entertaining readiness of wit was the delight of all who knew him, he too is dead. Dead also is signor Ottaviano Fregoso, a most rare man in our times: magnanimous, devout, full of goodness, talent, prudence, and courtesy, and truly a lover of honor and worth, and so deserving of praise that his very enemies were always obliged to praise him; and those misfortunes which he so firmly endured were indeed enough to prove that fortune, as she ever was, is, even in these days, the enemy of virtue. Dead, too, are many others named in the book, to whom nature seemed to promise very long life.

But what should not be told without tears is that the Duchess, too, is dead. And if my mind is troubled at the loss of so many friends and lords, who have left me in this life as in a desert full of woes, it is understandable that I should feel sorrow far more bitter for the death of the Duchess than for any of the others, because she was worth more than the others, and I was much more bound to her than to all the rest. Therefore, in order not to delay paying what I owe to the memory of so excellent a lady, and to that of the others who are no more, and moved too by the threat to my book, I have had it printed and published in such form as the brevity of time permitted.

And since, while they lived, you did not know the Duchess

or the others who are dead (except Duke Giuliano and the Cardinal of Santa Maria in Pòrtico), in order to make you acquainted with them, in so far as I can, after their death, I send you this book as a portrait of the Court of Urbino, not by the hand of Raphael or Michelangelo, but by that of a lowly painter and one who only knows how to draw the main lines, without adorning the truth with pretty colors or making, by perspective art, that which is not seem to be. And, although I have endeavored to show in these conversations the qualities and conditions of those who are named therein, I confess that I have not even suggested, let alone expressed, the virtues of the Duchess, because not only is my style incapable of expressing them, but my mind cannot even conceive them; and if I be censured for this or for any other thing deserving of censure (and well do I know that such things are not wanting in the book), I shall not be gainsaying the truth.

But as men sometimes take so much delight in censuring that they censure even what does not deserve it, to those who blame me because I have not imitated Boccaccio or bound myself to the usage of Tuscan speech in our own day, I shall not refrain from saying that, even though Boccaccio had a fine talent by the standards of his time, and wrote some things with discrimination and care, still he wrote much better when he let himself be guided solely by his natural genius and instinct, without care or concern to polish his writings, than when he attempted with diligence and labor to be more refined and correct. For this reason his own partisans declare that he erred greatly in judging of his own works, esteeming those little that have done him honor, and those much that are without worth. If, then, I had imitated that style of writing for which he is censured by those who otherwise praise him, I should certainly not have escaped the same blame as is leveled at him in this regard; and I would have deserved it the more in that he made his mistake thinking that he did well, whereas I would now be making mine knowing that I did ill. Moreover, if I had imitated that manner which many think good, and which he esteemed least, it would have seemed to me, by such imitation, to show that my judgment was at variance with that of the author I was imitating: which thing I thought unseemly. And even if this concern had not moved me, I could not imitate him in subject matter, since he never wrote anything at all like these books of the *Courtier*; nor did it seem to me that I ought to imitate him in the matter of language, because the power and true rule of good speech consists more in usage than in anything else, and it is always bad to employ words that are not in use. Therefore it was not fitting that I should use many of those words of Boccaccio, which were used in his time and are not now used by the Tuscans themselves. Nor have I wished to bind myself to follow the Tuscan speech of today, because intercourse among different nations has always had the effect of transporting new words from one country to another, like articles of merchandise, which words endure or fall away according as usage accepts or rejects them. And this, besides being attested by the ancients, is clearly seen in Boccaccio, in whom there are so many French, Spanish, and Provençal words, as well as some perhaps not very intelligible to Tuscans today, that it would much reduce his book if these were all taken away. And because, to my mind, we should not wholly despise the idiom of the other noble cities of Italy where men gather who are wise, talented, and eloquent, and who discourse on great matters pertaining to the governing of states, as well as on letters, war, and business, I deem that among the words which are current in the speech of these places, I have been justified in using those which have grace in them-

selves, and elegance when pronounced, and which are commonly held to be good and expressive, even though they may not be Tuscan, and may even come from outside Italy. Moreover, in Tuscany they use many words which are evident corruptions of the Latin; which same words in Lombardy and in other parts of Italy have remained intact and without change whatever, and are so universally used by everyone that they are admitted by the nobility to be good, and are understood by the people without difficulty. (pp. 1-5)

[Since] this is sufficiently discussed in the first Book, I shall say no more, save that, to forestall all debate, I confess to my critics that I do not know this Tuscan speech of theirs, so difficult and recondite; and I affirm that I have written in my own, just as I speak, and for those who speak as I do. And thus I do believe that I have not wronged anyone: for, in my opinion, no one is forbidden to write and speak in his own language. Nor is anyone bound to read or listen to what does not please him. Therefore, if such persons do not choose to read my *Courtier,* I shall not consider myself to be offended by them in the least.

Others say that since it is so difficult, and well-nigh impossible, to find a man as perfect as I wish the Courtier to be, it was wasted effort to write of him, because it is useless to try to teach what cannot be learned. To such as these I answer (without wishing to get into any dispute about the Intelligible World or the Ideas) that I am content to have erred with Plato, Xenophon, and Marcus Tullius; and just as, according to these authors, there is the Idea of the perfect Republic, the perfect King, and the perfect Orator, so likewise there is that of the perfect Courtier. And if I have been unable to approach the image of the latter, in my style, then courtiers will find it so much the easier to approach in their deeds the end and goal which my writing sets before them. And if, for all that, they are unable to attain to that perfection, such as it is, that I have tried to express, the one who comes the nearest to it will be the most perfect; as when many archers shoot at a target and none of them hits the bull's eye, the one who comes the closest is surely better than all the rest.

Still others say I have thought to take myself as a model, on the persuasion that the qualities which I attribute to the Courtier are all in me. To these persons I will not deny having tried to set down everything that I could wish the Courtier to know; and I think that anyone who did not have some knowledge of the things that are spoken of in the book, however erudite he might be, could not well have written of them; but I am not so wanting in judgment and self-knowledge as to presume to know all that I could wish to know.

Thus all defense against these charges, and perhaps many others, I leave for the present to the tribunal of public opinion; because more often than not the many, even without perfect knowledge, know by natural instinct the certain savor of good and bad, and, without being able to give any reason for it, enjoy and love one thing and reject and detest another. Hence, if my book pleases in a general way, I shall take it to be good, and I shall think that it is to survive. If, instead, it should not please, I shall take it to be bad and shall at once believe that the memory of it must needs be lost. And if my censors be not yet satisfied with this verdict of public opinion, then let them be content at least with that of time, which reveals the hidden defects of all things, and, being the father of truth and a judge without passion, is wont to pronounce always, on all writing, a just sentence of life or death. (pp. 6-8)

Baldesar Castiglione, in a letter to Don Michel de Silva in 1528, in his The Book of the Courtier, *translated by Charles S. Singleton, Doubleday & Company, Inc., 1959, pp. 1-8.*

THOMAS SACKEVYLL   (poem date 1561)

[*Sackevyll (or, more commonly, Sackville) was an English poet, dramatist, and statesman. In the following commendatory verse included in the prefatory material of Hoby's 1561 translation of* The Courtier, *he compares Castiglione's work to the riches of royalty.*]

These royall kinges, that reare up to the skye
Their pallace tops, and deck them all with gold:
With rare and curious workes they feede the eye:
And shew what riches here great Princes hold.
A rarer worke and richer far in worth,
Castilios hand presenteth here to thee.
No proude, ne golden Court doth he set forth,
But what in Court a Courtier ought to be.
The prince he raiseth huge and mightie walles,
Castilio frames a wight of noble fame:
The king with gorgeous Tissue clads his halles,
The Count with golden vertue deckes the same,
Whose passing skill, lo Hobbies pen displaies
To Britaine folke, a worke of worthy praise.

Thomas Sackevyll, "Thomas Sackevyll in Commendation of the Worke," in The Book of the Courtier *by Baldassare Castiglione, translated by Thomas Hoby, J. M. Dent & Sons Ltd., 1928, p. 1.*

THOMAS HOBBY   (letter date 1561)

[*Hobby (or, more commonly, Hoby) was an English diplomat and translator whose 1561 translation of* The Courtier *was highly influential in courtly and literary circles. In the following excerpt from the dedicatory epistle that precedes his translation of Castiglione's work, he extols* The Courtier *and commends its reception in England to his patron, Lord Henry Hastings.*]

Themistocles the noble Athenian in his banishment entertained most honorably with king of Persia, willed upon a time to tell his cause by a spokesman, compared it to a peece of Tapistrie, that being spread abroad, discloseth the beautie of the workmanship, but foulded together, hydeth it, and therefore demaunded respite to learne the Persian tongue to tell his owne cause: Right so (Honorable Lord) this *Courtier* hath long strayed about this Realme, and the fruite of him either little, or unperfectly received to the common benefite: for either men skilful in this tongue have delighted in him for their owne private commoditie, or else he hath eftsones spoken in peecemeale by an interpreter to such as desired to know his mind, and to practice his principles: the which how unperfect a thing it is, Themistocles and experience teach. But now, though late in deede, yet for all that at length, beside the principall languages, in the which he hath a long time haunted all the Courtes of Christendom, he is become an Englishman (which many a long time have wished, but fewe attempted, and none atchived) and willing to dwell in the Court of England, and in plight to tell his owne cause. In whose commendation I shall not neede to use any long processe of wordes, for he can so well speake for himselfe, and answere to the opinion that men have a long time conceyved of him, that whatsoever I should write therein, were but labour in wast, and rather a diminishing, than a setting forth of his wor-

thines, and a great deale better it were to passe it over with silence, then to use briefnesse. Onely for the litle acquaintance I have with him, and for the generall profit is in him, my desire is, hee should now at his first arrivall, a new man in his kind of trade, be well entertained and much honored. And for somuch as none, but onely a young Gentleman, and trayned up all his life time in Court, and of worthy qualities, is meete to receive and entertaine so worthie a *Courtier,* that like may felowship and get estimation with his like, I do dedicate him unto your good Lordship, that through your meanes, and under your patronage he may be common to a great meany. And this doe I not, for that I suppose you stand in neede of any of his instructions, but partly because you may see him confirme with reason the Courtly fashions, comely exercises, and noble vertues, that unawares have from time to time crept into you and alreadie with practise and learning taken custome in you: And partly to get him the more authoritie and credit through so honorable a Patrone. For no doubt, if you be seene willingly to embrace him, other young and Courtly gentlemen will not shun his companie: And so both he shall get him the reputation now here in England which he hath had a good while since beyond the sea, in Italy, Spaine and Fraunce, and I shall thinke my small travaile well imployed and sufficiently recompensed. The honour and entertainment that your noble Auncestours shewed Castilio the maker, when he was in this Realme to be installed knight of the Order, for the Duke his Maister, was not so much as presently both he, and this his handy worke shall receive of you. Generally ought this to be in estimation with all degrees of men: For to Princes and great men, it is a rule, to rule themselves that rule others, and one of the bookes that a noble philosopher exhorted a certaine king to provide him, and diligently to search, for in them he should find written such matters, that friendes durst not utter unto kings. To men growen in yeares, a pathway to the beholding and musing of the mind, and to whatsoever else is meete for that age: To young Gentlemen, and encouraging to garnish their minds with morall vertues, and their bodies with comely exercises, and both the one and the other with honest qualities to attaine unto their noble end. To Ladies and Gentlewomen, a mirrour to decke and trimme themselves with vertuous conditions, comely behaviours and honest entertainment toward all men: And to them all in generall, a storehouse of most necessarie implements for the conversation, use, and trayning up of mans life with Courtly demeaners. Were it not that the ancientnes of time, the degree of a Consul, and the eloquence of Latin stile in these our dayes beare a great stroke, I know not whither in the invention and disposition of the matter, as Castilio hath folowed Cicero, and applyed to his purpose sundrie examples and pithie sentences out of him, so he may in feat conveyance and like trade of wryting, be compared to him: But wel I wot, for renowme among the Italians, he is not inferiour to him. Cicero an excellent Oratour, in three bookes of an Oratour unto his brother, fashioneth such a one as never was, nor yet is like to be: Castilio an excellent Courtier, in three bookes of a *Courtier* unto his deare friend, fashioneth such a one as is hard to find, and perhaps unpossible. Cicero bringeth in to dispute of an Oratour, Crassus, Scevola, Antonius, Cotta, Sulpitius, Catullus, and Cesar his brother, the noblest and chiefest Oratours in those daies. Castilio, to reason of a *Courtier,* the Lord Octavian Fregoso, Sir Frideric his brother, the Lord Julian de Medecis, the Lord Cesar Gonzaga, the L. Frances comaria Della Rovere, Count Lewis of Canossa, the Lord Gaspar Pallavisin, Bembo, Bibiena, and other most excellent Courtiers, and of the noblest families in these daies in Italie. Which all afterwarde became Princes, Cardinalles, Bishops and great Lordes, and some yet in life. Both Cicero and Castilio professe, they folow not any certaine appointed order of precepts or rules, as is used in the instruction of youth, but call to rehearsall, matters debated in their times too and fro in the disputation of most eloquent men and excellent wittes in every worthy qualitie, the one company in the olde time assembled in Tusculane, and the other of late yeares in the new Pallace of Urbin, where many most excellent wittes in this Realme have made no lesse of this booke, than the Great Alexander did of Homer. I cannot sufficiently wonder that they have not all this while from time to time done a common benefite to profit others as well as themselves. . . . (pp. 1-4)

> *Thomas Hobby, in a letter to Lord Henry Hastings in 1561, in* The Book of the Courtier *by Baldassare Castiglione, translated by Thomas Hoby, J. M. Dent & Sons Ltd., 1928, pp. 1-7.*

ROGER ASCHAM   (essay date 1568?)

[*Ascham was an English diplomat, scholar, and private tutor to Lady (afterwards Queen) Elizabeth I. He is best known for his posthumously published essay* The Scholemaster *(1570), a popular treatise on education. In the following excerpt from that work, he affirms* The Courtier's *instructive value.*]

To ioyne learnyng with cumlie exercises, *Conte Baldesar Castiglione* in his booke, **Cortegiano,** doth trimlie teache: which booke, aduisedlie read, and diligentlie folowed, but one yeare at home in England, would do a yong ientleman more good, I wisse, then three yeares trauell abrode spent in *Italie*. And I meruell this booke, is no more read in the Court, than it is, seying it is so well translated into English by a worthie Ientleman Syr *Th. Hobbie*, who was many wayes well furnished with learnyng, and very expert in knowledge of diuers tonges. (p. 119)

> *Roger Ascham, in an excerpt in his* The Scholemaster, *edited by John E. B. Mayor, George Bell and Sons, 1907, p. 119.*

ROBERT SAMBER   (letter date 1724)

[*In the following excerpt from the dedicatory epistle to the Duke of Montagu that precedes his 1724 translation of* The Courtier, *Samber richly praises Castiglione's work.*]

The ensuing Pages were written originally in *Italian*, by one of the finest Wits of *Italy*, the incomparable *Balthasar*, Count *Castiglione*, who, in *Henry VIIth's* Reign, resided here in *England* as Ambassador, or Envoy, from *Francis Gonzaga*, Marquis of *Mantua*; and to which Prince he afterwards carried the Ensigns of the Garter. How much this Book [*The Courtier*] was praised and valued heretofore by Princes and great Men, there can be no greater and more honourable Proof and Argument, than the many Translations it bore by Men of the greatest Erudition into various Languages.

The **Courtier** was too great to be confined within the narrow Limits of *Italy*: He soon travelled into *Spain, France* and *England*; nor was it sufficient that he was read, loved and admired by the most celebrated Courts in the Universe, unless, in order to become more familiar to them, they might dress him in the Habit proper to each Country. (pp. iv-v)

Of the rare Abilities, and fine Esprit of *Castiglione*, . . . your *Grace* will sufficiently discover the Excellency and high Merit by perusing the following Sheets. . . . (p. ix)

> *Robert Samber, in a preface to* The Courtier *by Balthasar Castiglione, translated by Robert Samber, A. Bettesworth and others, 1724, pp. iii-xxi.*

TINSLEY'S MAGAZINE   (essay date 1880)

[*In the following excerpt, an anonymous critic probes* The Courtier's *didactic worth.*]

At all periods in the history of mankind, their vices and virtues have presented such a strangely-interwoven fabric as often to baffle the attempts of the student to separate the one from the other; and perhaps of no time can this be so truly stated as of the transition period of the fifteenth century, with all the tangled elements, political, social, and literary, of the Italian Renaissance.

While Machiavelli, on the one hand, was teaching princes to govern by dissimulation, strategy, and selfishness, his contemporary, Baldassare Castiglione, was instilling into the minds of courtiers that the good-will of princes could be obtained by integrity, nobility of conduct, and uniform honesty of purpose. It appears strange that in our day the works of Machiavelli are studied by many with unabating interest, while to as many the **Cortegiano** of Castiglione is unknown even by name. Yet students are beginning to discover that the latter, presenting, as it does, a new and nobler phase of Italian court life, is quite as valuable to the historian as the works of Machiavelli. (p. 390)

I must endeavour to give some idea of the book that remains as index to the mind of the man. The work is divided into four parts, the first of which treats of the qualities and attainments indispensable to a courtier—and in those days all gentlemen were courtiers, though the inverse no more held good at that time than at the present. The society outside the court was not such as a well-bred gentleman could mix in, the shades being much less delicately blended than in the present day. The courtier having the list of necessary attainments given in the first part of the book is instructed how to make the best of them in the other three divisions; and here it strikes one that the division is very much what has always been observed in the education of our youth—one-fourth to the attainment of all necessary acquirements, and three-fourths to spreading them out to make the greatest possible effect. First and foremost in the list of virtues Castiglione places bravery: 'It is as indispensable to man,' he declares, 'as purity to a woman. But a man must be amiable as well as brave, he must be able as well to please and amuse in the *salon* as to fight on the field of battle. Yet should his desire to please never interfere with or lessen his dignity. He must not degenerate into the trifler or buffoon. Above all, he must be natural, simple, easy; for whatever is affected is detestable.' Beyond the outward polish of manner Castiglione demands that his courtier's mind be as well furnished as his natural abilities and circumstances will allow. He must be a man of great mental culture, a poet and a historian, as well as a soldier and gentleman. He should excel in languages, and know enough about the fine arts to be able to appreciate and criticise, even if he is no painter or singer himself. (p. 392)

Castiglione was no pessimist, although there was enough in the state of Italy, in the fifteenth century, to make a thoughtful man take a desponding view of things. He believed firmly that, 'somehow, good shall be the final goal of ill;' that the world, in spite of many seeming retrogressions, gets better, and not worse. He had little patience with those people who are perpetually talking of 'the good old days,' and wishing the past back again. 'Such men,' he says, 'are like lovers who stand gazing at the window where their innamorata's face used to appear. The window is closed now, and she is no longer to be seen; but they can only remember that she was once there, and the spot possesses an interest for them that it lacks in the eyes of others. We may pity such men, but we must not accept their views; there is no returning to an un-returning past.' 'Besides,' he adds, 'many things that these people condemn in the present are merely matters of taste or custom, not of principle. There have been bad people in every age, and every period has its own peculiar drawbacks and disadvantages; but to these dwellers in the past the hills look so purple in the distance, that they forget how steep they found them to climb.'

Castiglione, though he disapproved of an undue leaning towards the past, never spoke slightingly of it. On the contrary, he knew well how to recognise and appreciate its merits, political, social, and literary. He was a good classical scholar, and his own work shows the colour of the leaf on which he fed.

Between Castiglione and Rochefoucauld there is a resemblance in their mutual dread of ridicule and admiration of tact. But there the similarity ends, for the Italian, whatever be his shortcomings, is thorough. He demands that his courtier should *be* what he aims at appearing, and his standard is a high one in spite of the accusations made against him that he merely inculcated pagan virtues, and that all the good he advocated began and ended with self—self-respect, self-improvement. For what more truly elevates the character of the mass than the careful culture of the individual parts? The courtier is also addressed with respect to his duties to society, and the inculcation of social virtues was sorely needed in Christian Italy of the fifteenth century. Thackeray himself never lashed more severely the flatterer, the toady, or the man who is ashamed of his poor friends when in the company of the rich, than did Castiglione. He had, too, a thorough contempt for him who sacrificed dignity and self-respect to pander to the vices and follies of the great. The true courtier should be, he maintained, above such conduct. 'Should the king demand of his vassal to commit an act of cruelty or treachery, the latter is not only not bound to do it, but he is bound not to do it. He must refuse as much for his sovereign's sake as his own; for he has no right to commit an act of baseness himself, nor to be the instrument by which another commits it.' After reading such words as these, it is surely not just to say that Castiglione only inculcated the selfish virtues. The man who, while he preached the high duty a subject owes to his king, insisted upon the still higher duty that he owes to his conscience, scarcely deserves the criticism passed upon him by a French writer, that he 'frittered away morality and substituted mere politeness.'

Perhaps the best chapter in *Il Cortegiano* is the one in which the author makes Giuliano de' Medici undertake to depict woman as she should be, and to stand forth as the vindicator of her rights, the redresser of her wrongs. He is sneered at for so doing by Bernardo Accolti and Gaspar Pallavicino; but he bravely holds his own, and maintains his cause in spite of the aspersions cast upon the sex by his two opponents.

In nothing does Castiglione show himself more truly a courteous gentleman beyond the courtiers of his age than in his views respecting woman. He assigns to her her true place in the world as the representative of the grace, purity, and refinement of life, and as the true helpmeet of man. He would never have allowed her to be 'a lesser man,' 'a beautiful mistake of Nature's making,' as a later writer has termed her. He makes Giuliano de' Medici vindicate in strong terms her courage and constancy. 'You talk of woman's weakness and instability,' cries Giuliano, in answer to the aspersions of Accolti and Pallavicino; 'have you never remarked the firmness she displays when her affections are concerned?' 'O yes, she can be obstinate,' they admit that. 'But obstinacy in a good cause is firmness, and women are less apt to espouse a wrong cause than we men; and as to calling them imperfect men,' he adds indignantly, 'what approximation to perfection in life would there be without them? How morose, how coarse, how ferocious we should become without their softening influence!' Three centuries later, Chateaubriand, in writing upon this same subject, uses almost Castiglione's own words; and there are passages in *L'Ecole des Maris,* and also in *L'Ecole des Femmes,* that lead us to suspect strongly that Molière has studied, we will not say borrowed from, *Il Cortegiano.* With all his generosity and kindly disposition towards them, Castiglione was no blind admirer of the sex; he neither said nor thought that all women are objects of adoration or worthy of honour. But when praise was impossible, gentle pity was ever at hand, 'for those who fall are worthy of the profoundest compassion (*somo degne di molta compassione*)'. The Italian proverb, 'Si non caste, tamen cante,' was utterly abhorrent to his nature. As he forbad men to transgress duty to please a prince, so he adjured them never to sacrifice honour to love. No! he was certainly no 'fritterer away of morality.' His opinions, his maxims, and his actions were the opinions, actions, and maxims of an honest man; and if his motives to duty are not always such as we consider the highest, at least he assigns to duty its proper place in life—the first and foremost. (pp. 393-94)

"'Baldassare Castiglione': Courtier, Diplomatist, and Philosopher," in Tinsley's Magazine, v. XXVI, January-June, 1880, pp. 390-94.

JOHN ADDINGTON SYMONDS   (essay date 1881)

[*Symonds was an English poet, historian, and critic who wrote extensively on Greek and Italian history and culture; he also rendered several highly praised translations of Greek poetry and literature of the Italian Renaissance. In the following excerpt from a work originally published in 1881, he discusses* The Courtier's *merits, focusing on its style.*]

Bembo was a power in literature, the exact force of which it is difficult to estimate without taking his personal influence into consideration. Distinguished by great physical beauty, gifted with a noble presence, cultivated in the commerce of the best society, he added to his insight and his mental energy all the charm that belongs to a man of fashion and persuasive eloquence in conversation. He was untiring in his literary industry, unfailing in his courtesy to scholars, punctual in correspondence, and generous in the use he made of his considerable wealth. At Urbino, at Venice, at Rome, and at Padua, his study was the meeting-place of learned men, who found the graces of the highest aristocracy combined in him with genial enthusiasm for the common interests of letters. Thus the man did even more than the author to promote the revolution he had at heart. This is brought home to us with force when we consider the place assigned to him in Castiglione's *Cortegiano*—a masterpiece of composition transcending, in my opinion, all the efforts made by Bembo to conquer the difficulties of style. Castiglione is no less correct than the dictator strove to be; but at the same time he is far more natural. He treats the same topics with greater ease, and with a warmth of feeling and conviction which endears him to the heart of those who read his golden periods. Yet Castiglione gives the honours of his dialogue to the author of the *Asolani,* when he puts into the mouth of Bembo that glowing panegyric of Platonic love, which forms the close and climax of his dialogue upon the qualities of a true gentleman.

The crowning merit of the **Cortegiano** is an air of good breeding and disengagement from pedantic prejudices. This urbanity renders it a book to read with profit and instruction through all time. Castiglione's culture was the result of a large experience of men and books, ripened by intercourse with good society in all its forms. His sense and breadth of view are peculiarly valuable when he discusses a subject like that which forms the topic of the present chapter [style]. There is one passage in his book, relating to the problem of Italian style, which, had it been treated with the attention it deserved, might have saved his fellow-countrymen from the rigours of pedagogical despotism.

Starting from his cardinal axiom that good manners demand freedom from all affectation, he deprecates the use in speech or writing of those antiquated Tuscan words the purists loved. As usual, he hits the very centre of the subject in his comments on this theme. 'It seems to me, therefore, exceedingly strange to employ words in writing which we avoid in all the common usages of conversation. Writing is nothing but a form of speaking, which continues to exist after a man has spoken, and is, as it were, an image or rather the life of the words he utters. Therefore in speech, which, as soon as the voice has issued from the mouth, is lost, some things may be tolerated that are not admissible in composition, because writing preserves the words, subjects them to the criticism of the reader, and allows time for their mature consideration. It is consequently reasonable to use greater diligence with a view to making what we write more polished and correct, yet not to do this so that the written words shall differ from the spoken, but only so that the best in spoken use shall be selected for our composition.' After touching on the need of lucidity, he proceeds: 'I therefore should approve of a man's not only avoiding antiquated Tuscan phrases, but also being careful to employ such as are in present use in Tuscany and other parts of Italy, provided they have a certain grace and harmony.' At this point another interlocutor in the dialogue observes that Italy possesses no common language. In the difficulty of knowing whether to follow the custom of Florence or of Bergamo, it is desirable to recognise a classical standard of style. Petrarch and Boccaccio should be selected as models. To refuse to imitate them is mere presumption. Here Castiglione states the position of the school he combats. In his answer to their argument he makes Giuliano de' Medici, one of the company, declare that he, a Tuscan of the Tuscans as he is, should never think of employing any words of Petrarch or Boccaccio which were obsolete in good society. Then the thread of exposition is resumed. The Italian language, in spite of its long past, may still be called young and unformed. When the Roman Empire decayed, spoken Latin suffered from the corruptions introduced by barbarian invaders. It retained greater purity in Tuscany than elsewhere. Yet other districts of Italy preserved certain elements of the ancient language that have a right to be incorporated with the living tongue; nor is it reasonable to suppose that a modern dialect should at a certain moment have reached perfection any more than Latin did. The true rule to follow is to see that a man has something good to say. 'Making a division between thoughts and words is much the same as separating soul and body. In order, therefore, to speak or write well, our courtier must have knowledge; for he who has none, and whose mind is void of matter worthy to be apprehended, has nought to say or write.' He must be careful to clothe his thoughts in select and fitting words, but above all things to use such 'as are still upon the lips of the people.' He need not shun foreign phrases, if there be a special force in them above their synonyms in his own language. Nor is there cause to fear lest the vulgar tongue should prove deficient in resources when examined by grammarians and stylists. 'Even though it be not ancient Tuscan of the purest water, it will be Italian, common to the nation, copious and varied, like a delicious garden full of divers fruits and flowers.' Here Castiglione quotes the precedent of Greek, showing that each of its dialects contributed something to the common stock, though Attic was recognised as sovereign for its polish. Among the Romans likewise, Livy was not tabooed because of his patavinity, nor Virgil because the Romans recognised a something in him of rusticity. 'We, meanwhile, far more severe than the ancients, impose upon ourselves certain new-fangled laws that have no true relation to the object. With a beaten track before our eyes, we try to walk in bypaths. We take a wilful pleasure in obscurity, though our language, like all others, is only meant to express our thoughts with force and clearness. While we call it the popular speech, we plume ourselves on using phrases that are not only unknown to the people, but unintelligible to men of birth and learning, and which have fallen out of conversation in every district of the land.' If Petrarch and Boccaccio were living at our epoch, they would certainly omit words that have fallen out of fashion since their days; and it is mere impertinence for a purist to tell me that I ought to say *Campidoglio* instead of *Capitolio* and so forth, because some elder Tuscan author wrote it, or the peasants of the Tuscan district speak it so. You argue that only pride prevents our imitating Petrarch and Boccaccio. But pray inform me whom they imitated? To model Latin poems upon Virgil or Catullus is necessary, because Latin is a dead language. But since Italian is alive and spoken, let us write it as we use it, with due attention to artistic elegance. 'The final master of style is genius, and the ultimate guide is a sound natural judgment.' Do we require all our painters to follow one precedent? Lionardo, Mantegna, Raphael, Michelangelo, Giorgione have struck out different paths of excellence in art. Writers should claim the same liberty of choice, the same spontaneity of inspiration. 'I cannot comprehend how it should be right, instead of enriching Italian and giving it spirit, dignity and lustre, to make it poor, attenuated, humble and obscure, and so to pen it up within fixed limits as that everyone should have to copy Petrarch and Boccaccio. Why should we, for example, not put equal faith in Poliziano, Lorenzo de' Medici, Francesco Diaceto, and others who are Tuscan too, and possibly of no less learning and discretion than were Petrarch and Boccaccio? However, there are certain scrupulous persons abroad nowadays, who make a religion and ineffable mystery of their Tuscan tongue, frightening those who listen to them, to the length of preventing many noble and lettered men from opening their lips, and forcing them to admit they do not know how to talk the language they learned from their nurses in the cradle.' (pp. 230-34)

John Addington Symonds, "The Purists," in his Renaissance in Italy: Italian Literature, Part II, *1888. Reprint by Smith, Elder, & Co., 1904, pp. 214-68.*

WALTER RALEIGH (essay date 1900)

[*Raleigh was an English scholar and essayist regarded by his contemporaries as a major authority on English literature. In the following excerpt from an essay originally published as the introduction to a 1900 translation of* The Courtier, *he outlines Castiglione's work as one representative of its age.*]

No single book can serve as a guide to the Renaissance, or as an index to all that is embraced by 'the comprehensive energy of that significant appellation'. But if one, rather than another, is to be taken for an abstract or epitome of the chief moral and social ideas of the age, that one must be *The Courtier.* It is far indeed from being the greatest book of its time; it is hardly among the greatest. But it is in many ways the most representative. That dominant note of the Renaissance, the individualism which subordinated all institutions to the free development of human faculty, finds full expression in *The Courtier*—nowhere with a stronger, simpler, and less conscious emphasis than in the high exordium: 'Let us therefore at length settle oure selves to begin that is oure purpose and drifte, and (if it be possible) let us facion such a Courtier, as the Prince that shalbe worthye to have him in his servyce, although hys state be but small, maye notwythstandynge be called a mightye Lorde.' The almost idolatrous reverence for classical precedent, for the deeds and words of the noble Grecians and Romans, which pervades Renaissance literature, has left its mark on every page of *The Courtier,* and has, moreover, by a happy inspiration, been allowed to determine the very form in which the book is cast. Many of the matters discussed by the writers of his time in separate treatises are dealt with by Castiglione in those interwoven digressions which are permitted to break the monotony of his continued theme. Thus, for instance, the discourse on jests and jesting, introduced into the second book, compares creditably enough with the *Facetiae* of Poggio the Florentine, Secretary of the Apostolic See, or with the *Detti e Fatti, piacevoli e gravi, di diversi Principi, Filosofi e Cortigiani,* compiled and 'reduced to morality' by the sober Guicciardini, or with any other in the estimable and prolific family of Renaissance jestbooks. The discussion in the first book on the true standards of vernacular literature, the use of archaisms, and the relation between writing and speech, is the author's contribution to a question which had been broached by Dante in his treatise *De Vulgari Eloquentia,* and which was hotly debated during the sixteenth century, on the one side and the other, by writers as considerable as Trissino, Machiavel, and Bembo. By his own age and the next, Castiglione rather than Dante was accepted as the most distinguished champion, against the Tuscan purists, of a courtly speech common to all Italy. The passionate monologue, again, in praise of Platonic love, which is assigned by the author to Bembo in the fourth book of *The Courtier,* finds its precedent and parallel in the works wherein Ficino and Pico treated the same subject at large. And the lighter pieces of dialectic, the debates, dramatically interrupted, on the comparative worthiness of the sexes and of the fine arts, deal with topics which constantly exercised the wit and the imagination of Renaissance society and Renaissance literature. Take it for all in all, the *Book of the Courtier* reflects as in a mirror the age that gave it birth.

But rather than in these diversions and digressions Castiglione's title to memory is to be found in his treatment of his main theme, his admirable presentment of an ideal perhaps the most valuable and potent of those bequeathed to us by the Renaissance. The idea of the 'scholar-gentleman' is nowhere set forth with more likelihood and consistency of detail, nowhere analysed with a finer skill, than in *The Courtier.* (pp. 42-4)

Walter Raleigh, "Sir Thomas Hoby," in his Some Authors: A Collection of Literary Essays, 1896-1916, *Oxford at the Clarendon Press, 1923, pp. 41-121.*

GEORGE SAINTSBURY (essay date 1901)

[*Saintsbury was a turn-of-the-century English literary historian and critic. Hugely prolific, he wrote histories of English and European literature as well as critical works on individual authors. In the following excerpt, he presents a mixed appraisal of* The Courtier.]

[Castiglione] wrote Italian as well as Latin poetry, and was a diplomatist of some importance in his day. But for none of these things can he be said to have any real share in the general European memory, though undoubtedly he has such a share. His title is the famous *Cortegiano,* which was printed in 1528, but had been written some twelve years earlier, which spread itself rapidly over Europe, reaching England (under the care of Sir Thomas Hoby) in 1561, and which has been selected and praised by good wits as a sort of Bible of the Renaissance—a summary of its creed as to almost all things noble and of good report.

That the book is itself a noble one there need not be the least hesitation in granting; and, for once, there seems to be little if any doubt that the preacher recked his own rede. None of the distinguished Italians of the time has a less questionable record than Castiglione. His book is not in the least exposed to the imputation sometimes made against it, of being a mere manual of etiquette, a successor of the "Babee's Books" of the Middle Ages, and a predecessor of the more trivial part of Chesterfield's *Letters.* The *Galateo* of La Casa, which came a little later, is obnoxious to this charge; the *Courtier* is not. Nor, further, can it be denied that the tone of the book represents an ideal which the Renaissance saw afar off and approved of too often platonically, or after the Ovidian fashion rather.

The scheme of it is but a variation on that which the genius of Boccaccio, if it had not exactly invented, had made canonical in Italy for a very large part of lighter and even of graver literary work—the scheme of conversation between a party of noble, or gentle, or learned men and women. The scene is the Court of Urbino, where Castiglione actually abode for a considerable time, and the central figure—not speaking much, but addressed by all and guiding everything—is its Duchess, whom, from the unmistakable sincerity of his lament over her death in the later-written Introduction [see excerpt dated 1528], the author would seem to have regarded with no small share of the fantastic but generous adoration which he inculcates in his book. The subject is sufficiently close to the title on the whole—dealing with the qualities and qualifications of courtiers of both sexes. But the author permits himself considerable expatiations, though he usually brings them round to the point. Thus the Second Book is mainly occupied with jests of one kind or another, sometimes not too strait-laced, though never outstepping the decency which is the note of the whole book. A great deal of space, too, is occupied by a repetition or variation of the old slanders on women by some of the characters, and a long and vigorous defence of them by Frederico Fregoso and Giuliano de' Medici. In the earlier part there are some remarks on the vexed question of Tuscanism, which played only too large a part in Italian Criticism, and the whole piece ends by a discourse on love, in the highest Platonic altitudes, by no less a person than Pietro Bembo. On the whole, no one can deny that Castiglione does his best to outline the "very perfect gentle knight" of his own times in a spirit at once of delicate accomplishment, of manly proficiency in sport and war, and of high ethical and intellectual, though scarcely religious, sentiment. It is almost enough to say that there is no man of the century who fulfils the ideal of *The Courtier* so well as Sir Philip Sidney, and that there is not the slightest reason for doubting that Sidney himself had *The Courtier* and its ideal constantly before him.

This is very high praise, and it may be supplemented and enlarged for English readers. Very much of the best distinctive character of our Elizabethan period generally, from its earlier, more homely, and more prosaic foreshadowings in Ascham to its perfect flower of poetry and philosophy in Spenser, is closely connected with Castiglione's temper and teachings. Whatsoever evil the "Italianation" of Englishmen may have done must be regarded as compensated handsomely by the holding up of this pattern, which, by the way (we may something pride ourselves upon the fact), was nowhere welcomed and developed to such an extent as with us. Germany was too coarse and too distracted; France, though there is more than a touch of *The Courtier* in the exquisite passage—satire softening at the thing satirised—on the Court of Quintessence in Rabelais, was too confused and too careless of morality to serve as good culture for this germ. In Spain, indeed, it found a not uncongenial home: Don Quixote is a spiritual son of Castiglione, who, by the way, seems to have had not a little of the Don's guilelessness as well as of his chivalry, and was admired and cheated by Charles V. on Spanish ground itself. But England alone received the seed in a thoroughly kindly soil, and brought the flower and fruit to perfection. All the gentler and nobler side of the great Elizabethan heroes reflects *The Courtier* within its own century, and after half another had nearly passed, the typical Cavalier is the Courtier himself, ennobled and strengthened a little, that he may "keep the bird in his bosom" against a worsening world, and die with it still there. Nay, Milton on the other side, though of temper in part opposed to the ideal, still has much of it.

But in speaking of a book which is so famous, and has been so much and to a great extent so justly praised, it is necessary also to give the other side. That the atmosphere of *The Courtier* is extremely artificial—that it is hardly adapted for any but a very small section of the human race in a somewhat accidental condition of society, possessing a very large number of comparatively small courts, at which most of the men of birth or sons of learning congregate—is no fatal objection. The conditions, though complicated and artificial, were real for a considerable time, and in more than one country, and might very conceivably become real again; while it would not be destructive to the book if they were as fantastic as those

of Brobdingnag or Utopia. A much more serious objection is the singular, or rather, in the Italian Renaissance, not singular but ordinary, limitation of the ethical element, and the almost entire elimination of the religious. The Elizabethans, as we have seen, supplied the gaps, and thus made the ideal both a nobler and a more practical one. But the actual Courtier, however accomplished as a courtier, is distinctly rudimentary as a man. He is to have justice, wisdom, temperance, and so forth, just as he is to be good at the jereed and in the tiltyard, and to speak French and Spanish. But Sidney's action with the water *n'est pas dans son rollet.* And the devotion which is as ardent and as sincere in the *Faerie Queene* as in the *Lancelot,* sends neither glance nor glow through any page of the volume, unless somebody good-naturedly discovers it in Bembo's Platonic raptures.

The last name, too, brings us to another head of the Devil's Advocate's brief. We have no reason, as has been said, to question Castiglione's own character; and if his time simply had not lived up to the shining pattern he put before it, it would not be the only time which has "sinned its mercies" in such a kind. But the contrast of the book and the time is almost *too* glaring. In the book itself the highest praise is given to Ippolito of Este, a worse than fratricide from the point of view of morality, and from the point of view of taste the author (in some form or other to all but certainty) of the description of the greatest poem of the time, and one of the greatest poems of the world, as a "pack of rubbish." When Aretino and Machiavelli write they may shock us or not, but they are certainly expressing the spirit of their age and country. When Castiglione writes he may have expressed a spirit which animated himself, and Michelangelo, and Vittoria Colonna, and a few more elect souls, but which certainly animated few others. There is hardly in all literature a passage of bitterer irony than the enthusiastic anticipations of what Henry VIII., Francis I., and Charles V. are to be and to do, when we remember what each one of the three actually was, actually did. Indeed from a certain point of view *The Courtier* is the counterpart and the explanation of *The Prince.* When goodness was so limited and so unpractical, practicalness must almost be excused for being so unlimitedly bad. (pp. 169-74)

George Saintsbury, "The Zenith of the Cinquecento," in his The Earlier Renaissance, *William Blackwood and Sons, 1901, pp. 103-75.*

[J. E. SPINGARN] (essay date 1902)

[*Spingarn was an American author, educator, and literary critic. In the following excerpt from an anonymously published essay, he assesses* The Courtier *as an expression of Renaissance ideals.*]

If the literary tastes of an age are as typical of it as its creative impulses or the great works of literature which mirror its various life, the future historian may find it not unworthy of his notice to consider the attractiveness of the Renaissance for the more exquisite of contemporary minds. . . . The aristocratic temper of the times, the taste for luxury, the growth of the courtly spirit, and the new scientific ardor—all marking a reaction against the democratic ideas of the Revolution—have found in the period alike of Ariosto and Titian, of Machiavelli and Galileo, a reinforcement of their most intimate spiritual and æsthetic needs. Some of the typical books of the Renaissance have assumed anew the splendor and fame of classics, and of none is this more true than of the *Cortegiano* of Castiglione. (p. 330)

The *Cortegiano* is a dialogue, in which the family and the retinue of the Duke of Urbino discuss the qualities of the perfect courtier. What is a courtier? What accomplishments should he possess? What is the purpose or aim of courtiership? These are the questions which the courtly interlocutors, the sprightly Emilia Pia, the Duchess Elisabeth Gonzaga, Giuliano de' Medici, Bembo, and a score of others, discuss and argue after dinner. Here the dialogue form is no mere Platonic or Ciceronian convention of the age, but gives the required opportunities for individual characterization, for *nuances* of thought and expression, and, in short, for all the artistic qualities which make of a mere social treatise a delicate and permanent work of art. These qualities are apparent in the most cursory perusal of the book itself, but some historical explanation is essential before the general reader can assume the point of view of the interlocutors, and find a more than perfunctory interest in a discussion of the courtier and of courtiership.

Each age, considering the eternal problem of the individual's relation to his social environment, develops its own ideal of perfect manhood, and more often leaves to a critical age the problem of formulating it. For secular society in the Middle Ages this problem is simple. There knighthood expresses the highest aspirations of social life. The infinite gradations of feudal society offered no common basis for individual perfection, and in the knight mediæval chivalry developed a visible symbol of ideal manhood. Forming part of a warrior class, the knight's virtues are martial virtues, courage, magnanimity, loyalty, courtesy; and of all these honor was the touchstone. But, being a child of his age, and therefore of the Church, the knight was not merely a soldier but a Christian soldier, and chivalry borrowed from religion some of its external rites and some of its sanctified spirit. By his profession called to all parts of the world, he was essentially a wanderer, and hence arose the bastard forms of knight-errantry; but his home life was passed at the feudal courts, and from this social life there sprang the finer developments of courtesy and the system of courtly love.

Here we find the point of departure for the ideal of the next age. Feudalism, with its innumerable courts and varying gradations of society, had disintegrated through internal corruption and external action. Political concentration was the result, and the countless castles of feudal lords ceased to be important social and military centres. The life of every state was focussed on a single prince and a single court, and here alone were the opportunities for individual preferment. These are historical commonplaces, but they indicate, as is well known, the conditions under which the courtier, the ideal man of the Renaissance, gradually developed. No longer merely a warrior like the knight, the courtier yet inherited some of the martial virtues of chivalry; and the knight's amusements, which had naturally been martial, became the fashionable amusements of the courtier. With more leisure, and a single centre of interest, it followed that the courtly graces, courtesy, chivalrous love, and the like, were still further developed, and loyalty to the prince took the place of devotion to a cause. The religious element was eliminated, and, more important still, Humanism added the further grace of culture, and fused the ideal of honor with the classical ideal of glory.

As knighthood had virtually been the creation of mediæval France, so courtiership was a product of Renaissance Italy, and of this ideal the *Cortegiano* is the complete and certainly

the noblest expression. The courtier, according to Castiglione, must be proficient in letters and arms, and in all the graces and accomplishments which form part of a refined and cultivated society. He must be a lover, for love is one of the highest virtues. All this and more he must be, not solely for the sake of his own individual *virtù,* but more especially for the sake of the prince at whose court he is a courtier. This is the ideal element in Castiglione's conception—that virtues and accomplishments alike are nothing unless, working through the prince, they accomplish moral ends. But this is perhaps the dream of an idealist, and the courtier as a type is rather a man in the universal cultivation of his accomplishments, like Castiglione himself—soldier, poet, courtier, and diplomat. (pp. 330-31)

J. E. Spingarn, in a review of "Cortegiano," in The Nation, *New York, Vol. 74, No. 1921, April 24, 1902, pp. 330-31.*

JEFFERSON BUTLER FLETCHER (essay date 1934)

[*Fletcher was an American educator and poet best known for his critical studies of Dante and of the Italian Renaissance. In the following excerpt, he provides an overview of* The Courtier *and its historical influence.*]

From Machiavelli we may construct in our minds the Renaissance state. If in ultimate ideal a *republic,* the state prescribed by Machiavelli for Italy and for the near and predictable future was *monarchical,*—later to become perhaps constitutional. In fact, the whole movement of the Renaissance was towards monarchical government, consolidated nationally in France, Spain and England, in Italy multiplied into petty duchies and principalities. The concentrated aristocratic oligarchy of Venice, for all that it preserved some form and semblance of a republic, is hardly an exception.

The gentleman of the *Cinquecento* is, therefore, naturally the courtier, companion and adviser of the Prince. The root of gentility is courtesy, and courtesy is of the Court. So Edmund Spenser:

> Of Court, it seemes, men Courtesie doe call,
> For that it there most useth to abound;
> And well beseemeth that in Princes hall
> That vertue should be plentifully found,
> Which of all goodly manners is the ground,
> And roote of civill conversation.

So the Conte Baldassare Castiglione, himself a perfect courtier after his own noble pattern, in his *Cortegiano* portrays the "goodly manners" and "civill conversation" of the Court of the Duchy of Urbino. Nay more: he is the *arbiter elegantiarum* for all Renaissance Europe.

Italian culture had become conscious of itself, interested to define itself to itself. The interest was not merely curious; it was the zeal of the artist to formulate for himself the methods and ends of his art so that he may be the better artist. For never perhaps so much as in the Italian Renaissance have human institutions, the state and society itself, been regarded as works of self-conscious art. The idea was more completely possible then, before the formulation of theories of historical evolution, of slow complex growth, of the past living inevitably on into the present. As yet it seemed quite possible to wipe clean the slate, and to write on it altogether new figures. Petrarch could not see why Rienzi's shaky little republic at Rome should not legislate out of existence all that had happened since Julius Caesar, and so continue on where Caesar left off. For Dante language—at least, language fit for gentlemen and poets—was not a growth but an art, a "grammar." The Renaissance held to the notion, if at times modifying its terms. I take two illustrations at hazard; but the idea was everywhere. There were, however, special reasons why social life should be theorized about, as if it were potter's clay capable of being softened out of its existing forms, and remodelled at once on a new pattern.

As far back as Guinizelli and Dante, Italians were already calling in question the claims of blood-nobility so absolute in the feudal north. Revived influence of ancient writers gave further authority for the doubt in the fifteenth century; and the many mushroom despotisms springing up from the ruins of the communes naturally encouraged indifference to birth and family tradition. Most of the *Quattrocento* despots were self-made men, if not bastards. "But," as Burckhardt says, "in proportion as distinctions of birth ceased to confer any special privilege, was the individual himself compelled to make the most of his personal qualities, and society to find its worth and charm in itself. The demeanour of individuals, and all the higher forms of social intercourse, became ends pursued with a deliberate and artistic purpose." Cultivated Italians conceived, and within certain limited circles realized, social living as a fine art.

A large conception of a society so artistically ordered, and at the same time a remarkably brilliant picture of a social circle actual and actually so artistically ordered is given by a member of the circle itself, Count Baldassare Castiglione, in his dialogue *Il Cortegiano,* "The Courtier." The dialogue, or rather conversation,—for the term *dialogue* suggests something too bookish and set,—is carried on in the drawing-room of the gracious Duchess of Urbino, Elizabetta Gonzaga, where she, assisted by her vivacious and witty cousin, the lady Emilia Pia, entertains a group of some of the most distinguished men of the day—churchmen of high rank, diplomats, men-of-letters, artists, statesmen. The theme is the character of a right Courtier; this first, and then the portrait of a Court-Lady fit to match and inspire him. There is nothing dull or didactic in the talk: definitions, qualifications, applications emerge spontaneously from thrust and counterthrust in the debate; there are sallies of wit, phrases of sentiment; the argument grows warm, but no one gets heated; all aspects of life are touched on from boudoir and drawing-room to cabinet and throne; there is no mincing but no indelicacy. For these people are consummate artists; they possess what is declared to be the essence of social refinement—grace, *grazia,* the trained instinct which can do or say difficult things with apparent ease. A word more specific to social intercourse itself would be *tact.* But for all that they take the amenities of life so seriously, neither are the men fops or dawdlers, nor the women unwomanly. Eighteenth century "Belinda" and "Sir Fopling Flutter" are still unborn. After all, as is concluded in the dialogue, the principal interest and profession of the Courtier is that of arms. Castiglione himself was one of the foremost diplomats and soldiers in Europe. It is reported that, on hearing of Castiglione's death, Charles V said: "I tell you there has died one of the knightliest men in the world." If Castiglione would have his perfect courtier of noble birth, it is only because he believed in—and himself lived up to—the maxim of *noblesse oblige.* The Duchess Elizabetta was a devoted wife and capable consort as well as a social leader and a highly educated woman. She was neither the meek *Quattrocento* housewife sketched with approval by Leo Bat-

tista Alberti in his essay *On the Family,* or illustrated in the flesh by Lorenzo de'Medici's Clarice, nor yet the mannish *virago,* the executive woman like Caterina Sforza who so long held Forlì against the terrible Cesare Borgia himself. Elizabetta is the modern woman of society—in the best sense.

In the Courtier—the *gentleman* of the Renaissance— Cicero's *humanitas* is almost perfectly revived, even to the courtier's supreme virtue as adviser of state. The connection is not mere coincidence, for Cicero is constantly quoted by Castiglione. But I say the revival of Ciceronian *humanitas* is *almost* perfect. The self-made Roman, a vain and weak man for all his intellectual genius, was incapable of feeling or inculcating the aristocratic Italian's chivalry, at once sensitive and courageous. There is another important difference. Castiglione's courtier has all the virtues that Cicero attributes to his gentle-man; all his faculties are likewise developed to the full; he is in his degree the "universal man"; but the chief influence making him all this, drawing out the best in him, is an influence unknown to the gentleman of ancient Rome,— or at least unrecognized by his portrayer, Cicero. It is the influence of a beautiful woman.

When the company at Urbino have drawn the right courtier full-length and four-square, they raise the question—*What is he good for?* Well, of course he has many functions, being by definition a many-sided man; but his last and supreme function is to be counsellor of state, adviser to his Prince. To that end he must be much experienced, naturally; but he must be high-minded as well as broad-minded, and there is no real high-mindedness which is not based on religious faith.

Now so far Cicero might have spoken,—in fact, did so speak. And, curiously, for the religious faith, the creed, of his gentleman, Cicero anticipates Castiglione in turning to Plato, a mysticized Plato,—but a Plato with no woman in the case.

The faith of Castiglione's courtier is in the Beautiful,—one might say in Fine Art, in the divine art which made the world beautiful, and all things in it, and more especially beautiful women. But his attitude towards these last is that . . . prescribed by the Platonist Benivieni. Approach to perfection is by the "ladder of love." But to get started, the courtier must be in love. And here is where the court-lady comes in. Dante's angelic lady descends to earth to become a social force, an agent of spiritual development in the courtier, a refiner of the brutal sex. To her, as artist of the beautiful, the courtier will be able to say, as the poet-dean, Dr. John Donne, said to a great lady of the court of James I:

> Madam:
> You have refined me, and to worthiest things.

Castiglione was well aware that in recommending love, however "platonic," for a beautiful woman as a medicine for the soul, he was dealing, as it were, with a high explosive. The Platonist defined his love as the friendship of souls. But if two souls have bodies of different sex, their friendship is also a little different. So Byron, for instance, notes:

> No doubt the secret influence of the sex
> Will there . . .
> An innocent predominance annex,
> And tune the concord to a finer mood.

But that the concord may keep in tune, the man, though something more than a *friend,* must also be less than a *lover.* There is perhaps wisdom as well as flippancy in Byron's conclusion:

The Palace of Urbino, setting of the dialogues of The Book of the Courtier.

No friend like to a woman earth discovers,
So that you have not been nor will be lovers.

In any case, it is the Platonist's conclusion. The balance between platonic and profane love is a nice one; and Castiglione puts it into the court-lady's keeping. She must accordingly, for her medication by love of the courtier, have developed *"una certa mediocrità difficile," "*a certain golden mean of reserve,"—must be not a wanton, nor yet a prude. She must be gracious, but not too gracious; not "easy," and yet not *difficile*. In a word, she must have the *tact* to draw out the bashful, but to check the overbold. Edmund Spenser has drawn her allegorical portrait in his Medina. Medina has two sisters, Elissa and Perissa, who fail to appreciate her nicely balanced courtesy:

> One thought her cheare too little, th'other thought too
> much.

Elissa and the sour-faced Huddibras just sit stupidly staring at each other. Perissa and "the bold Sansloy" overstep all bounds of propriety. Medina plays the part of moderator:

> That forward paire she ever would asswage,
> When they would strive dew reason to exceed:
> But that same froward twaine would accorage,
> And of her plenty adde unto their need:
> So kept she them in order, and her selfe in heed.

Now while there are ladies like Elissa and Perissa, the prude and the wanton, there will be lovers like Huddibras and Sansloy, the precisian and the lawless. A Medina will call to, and call forth, a Sir Guyon of knightly temperance. And like Medina and Sir Guyon are Castiglione's court-lady and courtier. Their loves will be gentle because they themselves are gentlefolk. "If," declares the *Magnifico* Giuliano de'Medici at the last, "beauty, demeanour, wit, goodness, knowledge, modesty, and all the other virtuous parts we have allotted to our lady, shall be the occasion of the courtier's love towards her, necessarily will the end of that love be also virtuous; and if nobility of soul, valour in arms, accomplishment in arts and letters, in music,—if courtesy, charm of speech, grace in conversation, shall be the means whereby the courtier wins the love of that lady, it must needs be that the end of his love is of the qualities through which it attains its end."

On these foundations—and who can doubt their sufficiency if they are anywhere to be found?—the elegant churchman and poet, later Cardinal Pietro Bembo raises again the six-runged Ladder of Love. Castiglione's choice of him for the spiritual guide of the courtier was not arbitrary. Already, in 1505, Bembo had published his dialogues *Gli Asolani,* a Renaissance courtly imitation of Plato's *Symposium.* The scene is laid in the residence of Caterina Cornaro, once Queen of Cyprus, at Castello di Asolo. Three youths and three maidens debate upon the worth of Love, its evils and excellences, joys and sorrows, until finally one of the youths, supposedly reporting a wise hermit,—as Socrates reports the wise woman of Mantineia,—exalts as true love desire of eternal Beauty, of which earthly beauty is only a pale reflection.

These Platonic dialogues of Bembo were widely read, and certainly would be present to the minds of Castiglione's audience. It is also true that Bembo lent his counsel toward the composition of the *Courtier* itself. And his formulation in that work of the Platonic creed is then a virtual summary of his own dialogues. "True love leads the soul," he says, "from the particular beauty of one body to the universal beauty of all bodies, and so in the last grade of perfection from the particular mind to the universal mind. And thence the soul, kindling in the sacred fire of the love truly divine, soars to union with the angelic nature, and not only altogether leaves sense behind, but even no longer has need of the discoursings of reason; for, transformed into an angel, it comprehends all things intelligible, and through not any veil or cloud, beholds the wide sea of the pure divine beauty, and is filled with it, and enjoys that supreme felicity which to the senses is incomprehensible." And the orator thereupon bursts into an apostrophe to sacred Love of such pious fervency that he seems fairly transported and entranced. He comes down from the ecstatic vision he has himself evoked like a second Moses returned from Sinai. "He seemed," reports Castiglione, "as if transported and spellbound, and stood mute and immobile, as if he were distraught; until the Lady Emilia . . . took him by the hem of his garment, and plucking it gently, said: 'Have a care, Messer Pietro, lest with these thoughts your own spirit be reft away from the body.' 'Madam,' answered Messer Pietro, 'nor would that be the first miracle which Love hath wrought in me.' " In vain the company urges him to tell more of this wondrous Love. He has told, he protests, what the "fury divine" has dictated. The frenzy has passed: Love would not have his further secrets revealed. It will be remembered that Benivieni ended his ode of Love with the same enforced reticence.

Bembo's pious and mystic protestations do not—to my ear, at least—ring quite true. That gallant retort—"Madam, nor would that be the first miracle which Love hath wrought in me"!—betrays the pose, the make-believe, the play-acting in this courtly religion of Beauty. The genuine mystic, "the deep transported mind" that has "at Heaven's door look's in," is not the next minute ready with a witty phrase, a *mot* of the *salon*. Bembo's mysticism, like all else in this ardent but artificial Renaissance society, is religion become a fine art of living, *savoir vivre*. The Platonist and Petrarchist who speaks is rather the new *arbiter elegantiarum* than the priest. I do not mean that Bembo or Castiglione was consciously insincere in professing a religion of Beauty, of living as a fine art. Even if the new Platonic piety were partly make-believe, the new Platonic homage to ladies partly pose, the make-believe and the pose might yet have a pragmatic value. Treated as true, the cult might be in its effect as good as true. By it womanhood might be exalted, manhood ennobled and refined, society enriched and purified. Had not the divine Plato commended just such "medicinal lies?"

In any case, not Italy alone, but all Europe listened to Castiglione, applauded, and followed. The *Courtier* was read, translated, imitated in every country. Austere Roger Ascham, tutor and secretary to two English Queens, he who found in Italian society itself only a "Circe's Court," and in nine days saw, he says, in one Italian city "more libertie to

sinne, than ever I heard tell of in our noble city of London in nine years,"—he who condemns "these bookes, made in Italie, and translated in England" for opening, "not fond and common wayes to vice, but such subtle, cunnyng, new, and diverse shiftes to carry yong willes to vanitie, and yong wittes to mischief . . . as the simple head of an Englishman is not hable to invent, nor never was hard of in England before,"—yet this same censor of things Italian praises, and urges to be "advisedlie read, and diligentlie folowed" Castiglione's *Courtier*, "an excellent booke for a gentleman" [see excerpt dated 1568?]. Sir Philip Sidney, that very perfect gentleman, is said to have shaped his life upon it. Upon it Spenser modelled in principle his Knight of Courtesy. Meanwhile, great ladies, and small, were everywhere administering that "medicinal lie" of charming men into worthiness. (pp. 193-202)

> *Jefferson Butler Fletcher, "Castiglione," in his* Literature of the Italian Renaissance, *The Macmillan Company, 1934, pp. 193-202.*

WILHELM SCHENK   (essay date 1949)

[*In the following excerpt, Schenk challenges claims for* The Courtier's *preeminence.*]

We are often told that English Literature owes a great debt to Castiglione's *Libro del Cortegiano* (*The Book of the Courtier*); this is, indeed, normally regarded as one of the outstanding examples of England's general debt to the Italian Renaissance. That such an influence existed and that it was great, is beyond doubt. But the value of this influence is not beyond doubt; it is the aim of this paper to raise this question. (p. 93)

[There are] some fundamental flaws in the polite and glittering world of Urbino. The philosophy of these courtiers, we cannot help concluding, was a lie; sensual pleasure, so far from being despised, was in fact the mainspring of their lives. And more than that: not only was there a gulf between ideal and reality (there always is), but the ideal itself is highly questionable. This is not to suggest that good manners and conviviality are to be despised. But here they became divorced from life which, after all, is not a permanent sherry-party. Castiglione's courtier, and Bembo in particular, is the true precursor of a cultural type well-known among the educated classes of our own day: the sophisticated dilettante constantly searching for amusement, as if to conceal from himself and from the world his inner emptiness. (A good translation of *Il Cortegiano* might be: *The New Statesman*). The conception of 'courtesy' itself, so far from being enriched by the *Courtier*, became in face debased. It lost the fuller meaning contained for example in Dante's unforgettable line: 'O anima cortese Mantovana' (Inf. II, 58: Beatrice's address to Virgil), or again in a significant sentence from Dame Julian of Norwich: 'Our curtes Lord will that we ben as homley with him as herte may thinke or soule may desiren'. Courtesy, in those contexts, denotes a quality of the soul.

It is not surprising to find that Castiglione is unaware of the more serious functions of art. Poetry, he lays down, should be practised by the courtier because of the enjoyment that it brings to himself and because 'he shall by this means never want pleasant entertainments with women which ordinarily love such matters'. One may also be a little sceptical about the *Cortegiano*'s appreciation of other arts. True, Raffael and Michelangelo are mentioned with approval, but in music homophonic songs to the viol or lute are preferred to the much more valuable polyphonic works of the period, which include the best works of Josquin de Près, one of the greatest composers of all times. The Cortegiani may have applauded, but cannot have understood, Michelangelo's intensely serious and self-sacrificing striving after artistic perfection.

Much of the courtiers' conversation in Castiglione's book turns on problems of language, and it must be admitted that in this connection some common sense is put forward. One of the main questions concerns the use of archaic words; after a very long argument the following sensible view seems to carry the day: 'The good use of speech ariseth of men that have wit, and with learning and practice have gotten a good judgment, and agree to receive the words they think good, which are known by a certain natural judgment, and not by any artificial rule'. But one of the contributions to the discussion deserves special mention: 'Words', says Bernardo Bibbiena, 'that are no more in use in Florence do still continue among the men of the country, and are refused of the gentlemen for words corrupt and decayed by antiquity'. This hint is not taken up by the company; once again we must turn to Bembo for a view that was undoubtedly taken for granted by the courtiers of Urbino.

In his long and very influential treatise 'Della Volgar Lingua', Bembo makes a clear distinction between the language of the courtiers ('la Cortegiana lingua') and the language of the people ('quell altra che rimane in bocca del popolo'). He leaves us in no doubt about his view that, in poetry at least, popular language has to be avoided: 'Do you believe', he writes, 'that Petrarca could have written such beautiful, such exquisite, such noble poems in the language of the people? You are wrong if you believe that'. (It is characteristic that Dante is not mentioned in this context). The Cortegiano's poetry, it is clear, has to rely on the poetic diction provided by the refined 'lingua Cortegiana'.

This linguistic question provides us with the most convenient transition from the Italian Renaissance to its English counterpart. The *Cortegiano* exercised a great influence in England; Bembo's Petrarchism was much imitated; many Englishmen become thoroughly Italianate (to the pious horror of the traditionalists). But we know that the greatest writers of the English Renaissance did not despise the popular language; they made in fact constant use of the traditional idioms and the speech-rhythms of the people. Ben Jonson demands that the poet's language, though it 'differ from the vulgar somewhat, shall not fly from all humanity'. And in fact Jonson's English, as L. C. Knights reminds us, 'is not "polite"; it is, very largely, the popular English of an agricultural country'. Bembo would have condemned as unrefined such lines as these of Wyatt's:

> They flee from me, that sometime did me seek
> With naked foot stalking in my chamber.

And much of Shakespeare and Donne he would have regarded as utterly barbarous.

This attitude has all too often been echoed by English critics. Here, for example, is what the Victorian critic Richard Garnett had to say, in 1898, of England's relation to Italy: 'A little while yet, and it would be needful to look beyond Alp and sea for the true Italy, and find her in Shakespeare, Spenser, and Sidney'. The lumping together of these names is still quite customary, and the search for the 'true Italy' has not been abandoned yet. This 'search' is, of course, connected

with major issues which F. R. Leavis has often discussed: the cult of 'form' and 'style'; the inflated reputations of Spenser and Milton; Tennyson's ambition 'to bring English as near to the Italian as possible'; the whole question, in fact, of the English poetical tradition—all this is involved. For my present purpose I must confine myself to the following statement of the case. The culture of Castiglione's Italy tended to remain esoteric and precious; its leaders formed, on the whole, an artificial and self-conscious group. The people have no place at all in the Cortegiano's scheme of things. In the English Renaissance, on the other hand, many successful attempts were made to combine refinement with genuinely popular culture; its greatest achievements, as well as many of the minor ones, reflect the experiences and problems of a great people with its roots in the remote past. Tradition was being challenged by a new spirit, but the response often combined elements of both.

One of the earliest works of the English Renaissance is itself an interesting counterpart to Castiglione's *Cortegiano:* it is Sir Thomas Elyot's *Book of the Governor* (published in 1531, three years after Castiglione's work). *The Governor,* according to Elyot, is the man who bears any authority in the state, from the local magistrate upwards, and Elyot's book discusses the qualities and formation of that man. Here, for example, is what Elyot wishes his 'governors' to consider on appointment to office: 'First, and above all thing, let them consider that from God only proceedeth all honour, and that neither noble progeny, succession, nor election be of such force, that by them any estate or dignity may be so established that God being stirred to vengeance shall not shortly resume it, and perchance translate it where it shall like him . . . They shall not think how much honour they receive, but how much care and burden . . . Let them think the greater dominion they have, that thereby they sustain the more care and study. And that therefore they must have the less solace and pastime, and to sensual pleasures less opportunity'. The moral seriousness of Elyot's approach is borne out by the context of his thought. He was a follower of Erasmus—'the famous Erasmus', as he says, 'whom all gentle wits are bound to thank and support'. Erasmus' own ideal of the good life, though different from Elyot's 'vita activa', is yet nearer to it than to the world of Castiglione—the ideal of a life lived in serious intercourse with friends, simple yet civilized, beautiful yet devout. Elyot was also a friend of Thomas Moore—the man who tried to combine the Erasmian life with the duties of a 'governor'. It was in Thomas More's circle that the foundations were laid of the characteristically English contribution to the Renaissance. Thomas More was a courtier, certainly, and he was open to new influences, but he was also firmly rooted in the popular culture of the Middle Ages. (pp. 97-100)

In the course of the sixteenth century the smooth Italian sonnets and the accomplishments of the Cortegiano reached England. The court of 'Gloriana' modelled itself on the famous company of Urbino, and many of its members wrote the appropriate sonnets. Like the Italian courts, their English counterpart proved all but irresistible to many of the potential leaders of culture; we need only remind ourselves what a fascination the Court exercised over such great men of letters as Donne, Bacon, and George Herbert.

Apart from this alluring court-world (a world of seemingly autonomous secular values) there existed an older world in the parish-communities all over the country, in many a gentleman's household, in schools and vicarages, in guilds and fraternities. This was a world of traditional morality, a world where religion (no doubt, intermingled with superstition) tended to be taken seriously; in all essentials a mediæval world. . . . Here was the home of the popular tunes and the racy idioms; here also the awareness, however dim and inarticulate, of a supernaturally sanctioned natural order which man could violate only at the price of his undoing. This was an all-embracing order: all spheres of life (politics, economics, sexual relations, etc.) were within its orbit. It was this order which most of the artists and thinkers of the period assimilated in their youth. During their lives they came to experience the conflict between the two co-existing worlds.

We cannot pursue this subject in the present context. Perhaps we can just venture the suggestion that this complexity is among the causes of the dramatic and polyphonic nature of the best works of the English Renaissance. L. C. Knights has analysed this complexity in the case of Ben Jonson and has pointed to the co-existence in Jonson's work of a 'naïve delight in splendour' with a 'clear-sighted recognition of its insignificance judged by fundamental human, or divine, standards'. The greatest artists of the English Renaissance were able to transcend the world of the *Cortegiano* and to achieve a critical attitude towards it. (pp. 101-02)

It may be that here we have come across one of the two common-places of the English Renaissance. It was of course a mediæval heritage—here is Langland's statement of it: 'For all we are Christ's creatures, and of his coffers rich, And brethren as of one blood, as well beggars as earls'. . . .

When the social critics and reformers from More onwards, inveigh against the evils of their age, they appealed to an underlying idea of equality which, in an important sense, outweighs all inequalities without obliterating them. Paradise was traditionally noted for the absence of gentlemen; so was the Golden Age; and 'state of nature' and 'status innocentiæ' seem to have merged into one. A specifically English version of the Golden Age was represented by the image of pre-Conquest England. The well-known anti-Normanism of some Civil War radicals was not without precedent: many of the Elizabethan chroniclers, for example, were surprisingly anti-Norman. 'Primitivism', in one form or another, was a good antidote against the claim of the ruling class for adulation.

Perhaps it was partly because of all this that so many of the works of the English Renaissance are both 'refined' and 'popular'. It will not be apparent that 'refinement' and 'popularity' are not, as is often believed, mutually exclusive; it may well be that the vitality of a civilization depends on a certain balance between them. However that may be, we are perhaps allowed to conclude from our survey that the good manners and social graces of the *Cortegiano* must not be too readily identified with the real civilization of the Renaissance. The great achievements of that civilization transcend the court-world in every way, and there is a sense in which they came about not because, but in spite, of the polished society that assembled in Urbino and in all the other would-be Urbinos of that age. (p. 103)

Wilhelm Schenk. "The 'Cortegiano' and the Civilization of the Renaissance." in Scrutiny, *Vol. XVI, No. 2, June, 1949, pp. 93-103.*

KENNETH BURKE (essay date 1950)

[*Burke is a prolific American poet and critic whose critical works focus on language and the underlying assumptions of its interpretation. In the following excerpt from one such study,* A Rhetoric of Motives *(1950), he establishes a series of connections between courtship and education in Castiglione's handbook.*]

[By its gradations, ***The Book of the Courtier***] builds a ladder of courtship dialectically, into a grand design that, in its ultimate stage, would transcend the social mystery, ending Platonically on a mystic, mythic vision of celestial mystery. The work is usually studied as a handbook of manners, or book of etiquette, which had a strong influence on the courtly style of Elizabethan poets. But we would stress rather its nature as a series of formal operations for the dialectical purifying of a rhetorical motive. When viewed thus formally, it is seen to contain a range of persuasiveness usually found but in fragments. And by observing its various kinds of persuasion thus brought together in a unity, we can better detect their significance where they are found only in fragments.

The book tells of four dialogues that supposedly took place on four successive evenings at the Court of the Duke of Urbino, in 1507. The duke being absent, the conversations are held in the presence of the duchess. A dozen members of the court participate in the dialogue. At first they talk of discussing, as a "pastime," the "sweet disdains" that the lover suffers "in the person beloved"; but it is finally decided "to shape in words a good courtier, specifying all such conditions and particular qualities, as of necessity must be in him that deserveth this name."

The first book lists the major endowments which the perfect courtier must have. Here are such items as noble birth, good fortune, skill at arms, good horsemanship, gracefulness, ability to "laugh, dally, jest, and dance," to speak and write well, to play musical instruments (particularly since at court the women's "tender and soft breasts are soon pierced with melody, and filled with sweetness"); the courtier should also be accomplished in drawing and painting (one speaker remarks that in Greece painting had been "received in the first degree of liberal arts, afterwards openly enacted not to be taught to servants and bondmen").

Objections are raised to some of these points. For instance, one speaker having said that the courtier should consider arms the most important thing of all, with "the other good qualities for an ornament thereof," Cardinal Peter Bembo replies that arms and all other gifts should be considered "an ornament of letters," letters being "in dignity so much above arms, as the mind is above the body." Cardinal Bembo's position will come into its own at the end of Book IV. Meanwhile, we need note only that the courtier's endowments are preëminently those of *appeal* (to this extent being rhetorical in essence); and, in keeping, his prime motive is to be "glory," a strongly addressed motive, that seeks to live in the good opinion of others.

The first dialogue closes with "every man taking his leave reverently" of the duchess.

In the second book, the rhetorical motive becomes still more obvious. This chapter deals with the tactics of address, the art of appearing to best advantage. Thus, when the courtier is "at skirmish, or assault, or battle upon the land, or in such other places of enterprise," he should "work the matter wisely in separating himself from the multitude." Whatever "notable and bold feats" he does, he should undertake them "with as little company as he can, and in the sight of noble men that be of most estimation in the camp, and especially in the presence and (if it were possible) before the very eyes of his king or great personage he is in service withal; for indeed it is meet to set forth to the show things well done."

Note that in this way of bearing witness, the courtier's relation to his social superior is as martyr to God, as writer to public, as actor to audience. Much that now goes under the name of "exhibitionism" might thus be placed as a species of the rhetorical motive. We recall a related maxim in La Rochefoucauld: *"Les véritables mortifications sont celles qui ne sont point connues; la vanité rend les autres faciles."* La Rochefoucauld is explicitly contrasting the pure rhetoric of religious appeal with the mere appeal to vanity. Mortifications *must* be witnessed; they are evidence, presented to an invisible divine audience. Martyrdom (bearing witness) is so essentially rhetorical, it even gets its name from the law courts. However, it is vanity when addressed not to the Absolute Witness, but to human onlookers. Martyrdom would be but a severe kind of "epideictic oratory," were it not for the supernatural witness which it postulates (the Christian persuasion being so essentially a rhetoric, that Cicero's thoroughness in rhetoric made him seem essentially Christian).

La Rochefoucauld was discussing a rhetorical situation where the testimony supposedly addressed to a supermundane principle was in actuality addressed to the *haut monde*. But *The Book of the Courtier* is discussing testimony explicitly addressed to a worldly principle. (With regard to the way in which the two realms rhetorically impinge upon each other, making social and religious reverence interchangable, we might recall an editor's reference to an early English book on manners instructing the youth to kneel on one knee before their worldly sovereign, on both knees to God. And when Edmund Burke said that European civilization depended "upon two principles—the spirit of a gentleman and the spirit of religion," his statement suggests the possibility that these "two principles" can be one principle named in two different orders of vocabulary. It is the magical confusion that allows spontaneously for the rhetorical use of religion as an instrument of politics, in keeping with the frank paganism of the old feudal expression, "your Worship.")

We thus confront three kinds of address: bearing witness to God, bearing witness to the sovereign, bearing witness to one's peers under the guise of bearing witness to God. If you bring them all together, and think of "glory" as both heavenly and courtly motive, do you not see the rhetorical ingredient in "conscience" itself, exacting a kind of conduct addressed to the ideal spirit of the community? (pp. 221-23)

Returning to the dialogue itself, we should note that at this stage, in Book II, it is concerned mainly with courtly ways of appearing to good advantage. Thus, one speaker questions the propriety of wrestling with men of low social status, for if the man of noble rank wins, his gain is small, "and his loss in being overcome very great." There are warnings against too incessant a display of one's talent, as with those who, if they are good at music, speak as though they were on the verge of breaking into song, or as when you meet a fencer in the market place and he greets you with "a gesture as though he would play at fence." A useful ironic device is suggested for a courtier wearing a mask. Let him disguise himself as someone of inferior rank, such as an uncouth shepherd; then, if he performs superbly on horseback, the show will be doubly

effective, since the horseman so greatly outstrips the expectations of the onlookers. The courtier is exhorted "to love and (as it were) to reverence the prince he serveth above all other things, and in his will, manners and fashions, to be altogether pliable to please him." (The transference of this principle from the courtier-sovereign relation to the relation between the courtier and world's judgment generally, is seen in the injunction "to use continually, and especially abroad, the reverence and respect that becometh the servant toward the master.")

The courtier is warned against asking favors for himself directly, lest they either be denied or, what is worse, granted with displeasure. And one eager "to purchase favor at great men's hands" should not "press into the chamber or other secret places where his Lord is withdrawn"; for when great men are alone, they often "love a certain liberty to speak and do what they please," and may resent being surprised. And if the courtier, engaged in important matters for his lord, happens to be "secretly in chamber with him," the courtier "ought to change his coat, and to defer grave matters till another time and place," watching "that he be not cumbrous to him." The courtier should rather "look to have favor and promotion offered him, than crave it so openly in the face of the world, as many do." He should not be like those who, "if they happen to enter into favor, then passing a mean, they are so drunken on it, that they know not what to do for joy," and "are ready to call company to behold them, and to rejoice with them, as a matter they have not been accustomed withal." For though a courtier should "esteem favor and promotion," he should not give the impression that he could not live without it, nor "show himself new or strange in it." On the other hand, he should not refuse it "as some, that for very ignorance receive it not, and so make men believe that they acknowledge themselves unworthy of it." The courtier should thus be neither too forward not too retiring but should always:

> humble himself somewhat under his degree, and
> not receive favor and promotions so easily as they
> be offered him, but refuse them modestly, showing
> he much esteemeth them, and after such a sort, that
> he may give him an occasion that offereth them, to
> offer them with a great deal more instance.

The courtier should remember that favors and promotions, when received with modesty, seem to be more deserved—whereupon the speaker gives a Biblical parallel strong in hierarchic thought: "When thou art bid to a marriage, go and sit thee down in the lowest room, that when he cometh that bid thee, he may say, Friend come hither, and so it shall be an honor for thee in the sight of the guests." But we have cited enough to illustrate the "addressed" quality (hence the rhetorical element) in the courtier's ways, as they are treated in this opening section of Book II.

After a series of transitions, warning among other things against both rowdyism and the tendency to tell jokes at one's own expense, the chapter turns to another kind of address, making an almost systematic study of the things "which make men laugh," comic devices valued for their effect upon audiences (though no formal theater was needed since, in the pageantry of their self-absorbed society, the courtiers were audience for one another).

The cult of laughter is suited to the "courtly psychosis" on many counts: first, it is "liberal," befitting a class of freemen (the Rabelaisian motive); it is "humane," since only humans laugh (hence it is probably a function of "rationality," which confronts reality by the roundabout route of symbols). Impropriety can provoke laughter only because at one remove it reaffirms the very propriety it violates; and the explosive laughter of surprise is made possible by the sudden violation of expectancies—hence the "merry jest" could in a free way reaffirm the courtier's code. In displaying his sense of the "right" things to laugh at, the courtier thereby displayed the marks of his class. And in proving himself equal to the tests of merriment, he gave evidence that he was not being outclassed. While superiority to fools and boors draws strongly upon the hierarchic principle, it can readily couple such superiority with a sense of personal misgivings, through subterfuges whereby the laugher subtly identifies himself with the very victim to whom he is superior; for in laughter there can be a transcending of the distinction between laughing-at and laughing-with. Comedy is much more pronouncedly *addressed* than tragedy, as is evident from the ease with which the comedian on the stage can take the audience into his confidence without breaking the frame of the fiction, whereas in tragedy even an aside expressly inserted for the audience's benefit must be spoken rather as though the actor were talking to himself.

The "invidious" element in laughter could deflect into less serious channels all competition for the sovereign's favors. It could thus allow for a kind of solidarity among the courtiers as a professional class. It was like a fraternal meeting of business competitors, a commodity made all the stronger when members of a lower class were chosen as butt of the joke.

The discussion ends on the subject of the "merry prank," which we are told relies on the same "places" as the jest for its effect. Boccaccio's tales being cited as an example, we can thus glimpse behind them an appeal not just as stories, but as a mark of rank. And once the hierarchic relation is firmly established, the mystery can become so subtilized that, as the duchess says, smiling:

> It is not against good manner sometime to use merry pranks with great men also. And I have heard of many that have been played to Duke Frederick, to King Alphonsus of Aragon, to Queen Isabel of Spain, and to many other great Princes, and not only they took it not in ill part, but rewarded very largely them that played them those parts.

Where the irreverence of laughter is thus directed against the very Principle of Courtly Favor itself, it must be so carefully qualified that it signalizes reverence too—whereat the "sacrificial king" need not grow wrathful to restore his dignity, but is grand in exercising with good humor his powers of munificence.

The primary thing to note about *The Book of the Courtier,* from the standpoint of dialectic, is the great change in the quality of motivation that occurs as one turns from the third book to the last. The third book has some inklings of the final transcendence, since it deals with the code of courtly intercourse between men and women. It thus introduces the theme of sexual love which Cardinal Bembo will platonically transform at the ecstatic, sermonlike close of the work. But though there are occasional signs of a new stirring, in general men and women here confront each other as classes, considering questions of advantage, in a war of the sexes reduced to dance steps.

Book III begins with a recipe of traits deemed appealing in

women, discusses such related matters as comparative prowess in feats of continence on the part of the two sexes; pathetic sorrow at loss of maidenhood due to forcing; situations that follow from the code of honor, one speaker saying, "in a thousand years I could not repeat all the crafts that men use to frame women to their wills"; and another, who has been complaining that women are cruel to him, is accused of using such complaints "as a certain kind of discretion," to "cloak the favors, contentations and pleasures" he had "received in love," and to assure other women that, if they reward him he will keep the secret. Among other things, the woman's code at court requires that, when invited to dance or play, like the courtier receiving favors, "she ought to be brought to it with suffering her self somewhat to be prayed"—and in innuendo, she should seem to miss the point.

In general, the chapter might have for its device this statement by Lord Cesar Gonzaga:

> Like as no Court, how great soever it be, can have any sightliness or brightness in it, or mirth without women, nor any Courtier can be gracious, pleasant or hardy, nor at any time take any gallant enterprise of Chivalry, unless he be stirred with the conversation and with the love and contentation of women, even so in like case, the Courtier's talk is most unperfect evermore, if the entercourse of women given them not a part of the grace wherewithall they make perfect and deck out their playing the Courtier.

And for the equating of love and war, we are told that "Who so could gather an army of lovers that should fight in the presence of the Ladies they love, should subdue the whole world, unless against it on the contrary part there were an other army likewise in love."

Through these first three books, though the quest of advantage has taken several forms, the motive of "reverence" has been kept within the realm of manners, as related to the sovereign and to the object of courtly sexual love. It has been manifested roundabout, through the perversities of the jest and the merry prank. And much has been said about the properties that make men and women appealing in courtly situations. We now turn to higher orders of persuasion. This fourth book is not less rhetorical than the other three. But the advantages to which it would persuade transcend those of the preceding chapters.

Fittingly, the change in the quality of motives is signalized at the start of the last book by a deathy note. Though the talks were supposedly held on four successive nights, as the author prepares to write out the record of the fourth discourse a "bitter thought" causes him to remember "that not long after these reasonings were had, cruel death bereaved our house of three most rare gentlemen, when in their prosperous age and forwardness of honor they most flourished."

The device is perhaps borrowed from Cicero, who uses it similarly to make the final section of his *De Oratore* more solemn. The justification for it seems greater in this case (in accordance with the puns whereby finality can mean either purpose or demise), since this concluding book is to deal with "the end . . . of a perfect Courtier." It is to discuss the ultimate purpose of courtship. So, in introducing it with thoughts of great courtiers who have died, the author reënforces one kind of finality by topics belonging to the other kind (leads into the discussion of end in the philosophic sense through mention of end in the biologic sense). And we might even glimpse a subtler propriety in this opening talk of courtiers' deaths: henceforth the many variants of acquisitive advantage are to be abandoned for efforts more sacrificial.

Above the transitional matter, two themes stand out. The first concerns a rhetoric of *education,* considering the powers of the courtier as *informant* to the prince. In this context the courtier would be winsome for the advancement not of himself personally, but of human relations in general. He would seek ways whereby he can impart even unpalatable truths to his sovereign, "to dissuade him from every ill purpose, and to set him in the way of virtue," in contrast with those who, "to curry favor and to purchase good will," tell their lord only what he would most like to hear ("because among many vices that we see now a days in many of our Princes, the greatest are ignorance and self-liking," yet "there is no treasure that doth so universally hurt, as an ill Prince"). In sum: As the training in "pleasant fashions" is "the flower of Courtliness," so the fruit of it is in "the training and helping forward of the Prince to goodness, and the fearing him from evil."

For our purposes it is not necessary to consider the details of the argument, or even the theory of psychology that goes with it, beyond noting the customary identification of reason with authority: As reason rules over the affections of the body, so it "is chiefly requisite in Princes." The important consideration for our purposes is that this treatise on education grows out of the theories on courtship. Though, according to the hierarchic order in its perfection, the prince would rather be the exemplar for the courtiers, the unsettled nature of the times brought to the fore many princes new to the courtly tradition. Hence, the courtiers, as a special professional class, might find themselves in the role of educators to the prince, initiating him into the mysteries of their code. The situation is not unlike that of scientists today, who are hired to serve the interests of local financial or industrial sovereigns. As hirelings, they should be interested in the tactics of advancement; but as a class of scientific specialists, they represent, with varying degrees of honesty and obsequiousness, a purely professional interest in truth, not identical with the preferences of the "sovereign."

But there is a profounder connection here between courtship and education than derives from the accident of the times. It is an element inborn to the dialectic method itself, as . . . [may be seen by considering] the Socratic erotic, "loving" truth, beauty, and goodness pedagogically (a cult that had its variants of courtship, as with Socrates' gallantry when cajoling and enticing young men into the dialectical path of the Absolute).

The imagery of courtship in the Socratic education is to be interpreted mythically. Its primary motives are not positive, but dialectical. And education dialectically approached could not be reduced to sexual terms in the positivist sense. Nor, by the same token, could education dialectically approached be properly reduced to positivist terms of a mere job. It would have a mythic glow, as it would be a form of "pure persuasion," the rhetorical motive dialectically made ultimate. But it would gravitate about the imagery of courtship, since it would be a kind of courtship, as . . . in the *Phaedrus.* And variants of the same motive are seen in Castiglione's fourth book, where we are told that "to become the instructor of a Prince, were the end of a Courtier," quite as Aristotle and Plato "practiced the deeds of Courtiership, and gave them-

selves to this end, the one with the great Alexander, the other with the kings of Sicilia."

After the pages on the courtier as educator of the prince, by appropriate transitions the work rises to its exhilarating close, the oration by Cardinal Bembo, on Beauty as "an influence of the heavenly bountifulness." By the time the cardinal is finished, we have gone from the image of beauty to the pure idea of beauty (from sense to intellect); we have united ideal beauty with truth, utility, and goodness; we have heard objections that "the possessing of this beauty which he praiseth so much, without the body, is a dream"; there has been talk of a transcendent insemination (putting the seeds of virtue into a mind, "the right engendering and imprinting of beauty in beauty," though the opposition claims that this should be done by "the engendering of a beautiful child in a beautiful woman"); a penetrating has been advised, but through eye and ear (the least sensual senses), and by the union of mouths, a bond called the "opening of an entry to the souls" (since an ecclesiastical orator is speaking, we may think of the oral as figuring not only the primary gratification of feeding, but also the vocation of prayer); imagination has been praised for its power to fashion "that beauty much more fair than it is in deed," to use perception of one beauty as a stair for climbing to a "universal conceit" for "meddling all beauty together"; then "by reason of the agreement that the fancies have with the body," even this stage must be transcended, until beauty is "seen only with the eyes of the mind," and the soul is turned "to the beholding of her own substance," which is angelic; whereupon the soul is kindled by the desire to partake of the heavenly nature, so that with images of burning, and mounting, and coupling, we end on a prayer to "the father of true pleasures, of grace, peace, lowliness, and good will," and on talk of hopes to "smell those spiritual savors," and of ultimate arrival through bodily death—whereat the cardinal pauses, "ravished and beside himself," having given to the others "a certain sparkle of that godly love that pricked him." It is discovered that the company has talked until dawn. And in contrast with our thoughts of journeys to the end of night, and our tracts foretelling a universal heat-death, "they saw already in the East a fair morning like unto the color of roses, and all stars voided, saving only the sweet Governess of heaven, Venus which keepeth the bounds of the night and day, from which appeared to blow a sweet blast, that filling the air with a biting cold, began to quicken the tunable notes of the pretty birds, among the hushing woods of the hills."

Is it not obvious why we could use this work as a paradigm, when looking for respects in which the rhetoric of persuasion leads dialectically to an ultimate of pure persuasion? The hierarchic principle of courtship sets a pattern of communication between "lower" and "higher" classes (or kinds). This can be universalized in terms of a climbing from body to soul, from senses through reason to understanding, from worldly to the angelic to God, from woman to beauty in general to transcendent desire for Absolute union. Or the communication may be between merely "different" kinds, where the relative grading is not established by general agreement. And, of course, when one analyzes a given case of such "courtship," one can also expect to find ambiguities whereby, even if a set scale is recognized, the roles become reversed, the superior in one respect becomes the inferior in another, or the superior must court the underling.

In making "beauty" both courtly and religious, *The Book of the Courtier* makes religion courtly, thereby "mystically" fusing social and religious "reverence." "Even as in the firmament the sun and the moon and the other stars show to the world (as it were) in a glass, a certain likeness of God: So upon the earth a much more liker image of God are those good Princes that love and worship him, and show unto the people the clear light of his justice." And by being so explicit in its way of advancing from a worldly to a celestial hierarchy, it gives us insight into situations where the "mystery of divinity" inspirits relations that, on their face, call for purely mundane motives.

Such an identification may be present in the man who cannot become a social rebel without becoming an atheist. And conversely, with some the cult of religion can be so grounded in class courtship that explicit instruction in the terms of theological hierarchy implicitly coaches obedience to one particular social hierarchy. Where such motives are formally denied (as with the pragmatic terminologies of technology, finance, and political administration), we are at least admonished to look for persuasive vestiges of them, or perhaps for their emergence in new guises.

For if man, as symbol-using animal, is *homo dialecticus,* and if the use of symbols is a kind of *transcendence,* then such a rounded instance of dialectical transcendence as we find in **The Book of the Courtier** may contain the overt expression of elements that elsewhere exist covertly, and in fragments. The work might thus make precise our understanding of the purely dialectical motives (ultimate verbal motives) behind the rhetorical convertibility between terms for social hierarchy and terms for theologic hierarchy. Here is a source of "mystery" grounded in the very perfection of formal thinking, with worldly and transcendent "reverence" each drawing sustenance from the other (and with all the variants of these, even to the rebel snapping of the continuity). (pp. 224-33)

> *Kenneth Burke, "The Paradigm of Courtship: Castiglione," in his* A Rhetoric of Motives, *Prentice-Hall, Inc., 1950, pp. 221-33.*

ERNEST HATCH WILKINS   (essay date 1954)

[In the following excerpt from a work originally published in 1954, Wilkins commends The Courtier *and briefly outlines its historical influence.]*

In style, in design, and in tone the *Cortegiano,* itself a courtly creation, is free from affectation, and maintains faithfully "a certain honorable mean." The style is a mean between the commonplace and the elevated: its naturalness and simplicity are those of cultured speech. The book as a whole has a governing plan; but that plan is not so forced upon the reader as to produce a feeling of undue formality: the transitions are handled so well that the sequence of thought appears to spring naturally from the easy flow of conversation. Similarly, while many of the speeches of the discussion leaders are of some length, the technique of interruption is used with such great skill that the reader is never oppressed by any sense of monotony. The material of the book is serious in itself, and is developed with a serious thoughtfulness; but the seriousness is constantly controlled and relieved by touches of humor.

Humor indeed pervades the book, appearing not only in the section devoted to jests, but as a constant unifying grace. Yet one is aware of a deep underlying sadness in Castiglione's own spirit. Most clearly perceptible in certain pages of the dedicatory letter and of the introduction to the fourth Book (pages in which he mourns the loss of several of the interlocutors who had been dear friends of his), his sadness is yet deepest in his consciousness of the discrepancy between his own ideals and the surrounding reality, and in his presentiment that the graciousness of the court life he had loved and championed was destined all too soon to vanish.

Ideally, the four Books should be read on four successive long and leisurely evenings. If that is done, the reader will retain the sense that he has been for a time in a truly courtly company of men and women, well worth his acquaintance and his memory. And there will form gradually in his mind a sense of companionship with Baldassare Castiglione, who in his own day and ever since has seemed, to his princes, his friends, and his readers, to be himself the perfect courtier. In his portrait in the Louvre one may see him as Raphael saw him.

The *Cortegiano,* in the original Italian and in translations, brought to Spain and France and England a code of social refinement, touched with the glamor of Italy, which greatly influenced both literature and life. The *caballero,* the *honnête homme,* and the *gentleman* owed much to Castiglione's perfect courtier; and their ladies owed not a little to Castiglione's Duchess and Emilia Pia. Castiglione's Bembo was, moreover, for France and England, one of the main expositors of the concept of Platonic love. In literature the influence of the **Cortegiano** was in part immediate and in part diffused through the life it had already influenced. Don Quixote, as he instructs the governor-designate Sancho Panza, is mindful of the first part of the fourth Book; Rabelais borrows a jest; and Corneille's conception of character reflects knowledge either of the **Cortegiano** itself or of courtly ideals derived therefrom. In England the **Cortegiano** was well presented in the translation of Thomas Hoby, who says of it, in his dedicatory letter:

> to Princes and Greate men, it is a rule to rule themselves that rule others . . . To men growen in yeres, a pathway to the beholding' and musing of the minde, and to whatsoever elles is meete for that age: To yonge Gentlemen, an encouraging to garnishe their minde with morall vertues, and their bodye with comely exercises, and both the one and the other with honest qualities to attaine unto their noble ende: To Ladyes and Gentlewomen a mirrour to decke and trimme themselves with vertuous condicions, comely behaviours and honest enterteinment toward al men: And to them all in general, a storehouse of most necessary implements for the conversacion, use, and training up of mans life with Courtly demeaners [see excerpt by Hobby dated 1561].

Ascham was one of the earlier sponsors of the **Courtier.** The writers who for their own varying purposes drew from it most deeply were Spenser, Lyly, Sidney, and Burton. (pp. 230-31)

> *Ernest Hatch Wilkins, "Castiglione and Other Prose Writers," in his* A History of Italian Literature, *Cambridge, Mass.: Harvard University Press, 1954, pp. 226-36.*

JOSEPH ANTHONY MAZZEO (essay date 1965)

[*In the following excerpt, Mazzeo provides a thematic explication of* The Courtier.]

It is said that Charles V kept three books by his bedside: Machiavelli's *Prince,* Castiglione's **Courtier,** and the Bible. Whether Charles ever saw any difficulty in relating these three disparate universes is unknown, but the pomp and splendor of his court, the realism of his politics and his final retirement to a monastery, whatever disappointments drove him there, would seem to indicate that he did not. Like other great figures of the Renaissance he was quite able to be a Machiavellian Centaur, the man of power who lives in divided and distinguished worlds of humanity and animality, and who, indeed, must live there if he is to retain both his power and his humanity. He has Machiavelli for his guide when he must employ force or fraud, the arts of the lion and the fox, Castiglione when he moves in the social world, the world of "small morals" or manners, and the Bible for the times when even Caesar becomes burdened by those things which are his.

I need hardly mention how much commentary and scholarship surrounds the Bible, and Machiavelli has attracted, I suppose, as much scholarly and critical attention as any secular author of equivalent stature. It is a little surprising to discover that Castiglione (1478-1529) has been relatively neglected. Most of the literature about him is of a philological or biographical character. Works of interpretation are few but surprisingly diverse for what appears to be a relatively simple text even if one of the most widely read books in the history of our culture. (p. 131)

It was largely in Italy and in his own times that Castiglione enjoyed the reputation of a major writer, in the narrower sense of that word, that is, as a master of the language and a revealer of its resources. His great influence outside his own country and in subsequent generations, both in and out of Italy, was cultural. In the past, and even now, the most widespread reading of Castiglione's work was as a normative book on education. This is certainly the view that all of his English scholars and critics have taken, from Hoby, to Dr. Johnson, who called it "the best book ever written on good breeding," to Sir Walter Raleigh in more recent times. For most of its readers, the **Courtier** has been a breviary of *savoir-faire* or *savoir-vivre,* a code of good society, a book concerned with manners in the most exalted sense of that word, with manners as "minor morals" dealing with that range of conduct which must be both ethical and beautiful at the same time, the kind of behavior which eases and graces the conduct of life. Another way of stating this interpretation of the *Courtier* is to say that, while it is in part a continuation and adaptation of the best elements of the chivalric tradition, it incorporates the revived ideals of ancient Greek *kalokagathia,* the conception of the gentleman as both an ethical agent and an artistically structured self, the man in whose actions there is no separation of what is good from what is beautiful.

Another reading of the **Courtier,** which overlaps this one, is as a "moral" work, in the French sense of the word: a work concerned with *mores,* with the customs and habits of man. On the whole, and with significant exceptions including Vittorio Cian, the leading Castiglione scholar of recent times, this is an Italian view of the book, and Italians like Leopardi have read Castiglione in much the same way some Frenchmen have read Montaigne: for his reflections and maxims, for his observations on the various manifestations of the individual's character in society, and for suggestions as to the proper way of manipulating the self in society.

These two have been what we might call the "serious" readings of the **Courtier,** the way people read the book when it was felt to be of vital social, intellectual, or moral use, and both of them more or less correspond with Castiglione's intention *de formar con parole un perfetto Cortegiano.* It is only in relatively modern times, when both the world and ideals of Castiglione have come to seem distant, that the utility of the work has been largely reduced to that of a faithful portrait of the conversations and diversions of the Court of Urbino, to a valuable but remote historical document.

Given the expressed political intention of Castiglione—the task of the perfect courtier is in the last analysis that of giving political advice to his ruler—some readers have pointed to the fact that Castiglione is remarkably unrealistic or unconcerned about the way affairs of state are actually conducted. After all, he lived in the same chaotic Italy that Machiavelli inhabited and he too was a diplomat with ample opportunity to see the same truths. This sort of objection can really have no force once we understand that Castiglione's task is that of delineating a *perfect* Courtier, an ideal type, and not that of drafting a program of action to be implemented at every point. His book is a kind of Utopia, or better, an Arcadia, for it begins with a lament for the deaths of so many of the beautiful and charming people who graced the court of Urbino and created that perfect moment, now gone forever, of which the **Courtier** is an imaginative representation. Whether the events and people of the book ever existed as Castiglione gives them to us is less important than it is for us to understand that they were able to inspire a nostalgic vision of a perfect small society vitally concerned with perfection of the self.

The intention of delineating the perfect courtier links Castiglione to one of the important cultural impulses of his time. The Renaissance abounds with books on ideal commonwealths and ideal modes of personal, social, and professional existence. Books like More's *Utopia,* Alberti's *Della Famiglia,* Palmieri's *Della vita civile,* and Pontano's *De principe* are some among many of the books delineating one ideal or another of perfection. And human perfection, if I understand Castiglione's book correctly, is realizable in the life of the courtier and is the result of the harmonious relation of normally opposed impulses, the binding in a balanced unity of what, in a state of nature, are warring tendencies within the person. In other words, perfection lies in the development and mastery of the major capacities of human nature, a mastery which can only be achieved by the discipline, not by the suppression, of any important human potentiality, and by developing no single human function at an excessive charge against another one. This requires specially endowed people and a receptive society so that Castiglione does not posit his ideal of perfection as an easily obtainable one. In this he agrees with other Renaissance delineators of ideal types or roles. Such portraits really express Platonic forms, "ideas" which may serve as final causes, as the goals toward which men and societies may strive. Like all things in Aristotle's sublunary world, man may strive to reach perfection, as does the rest of nature, but he can never quite reach it even when he draws very near.

Castiglione's conception of human perfection is stated explicitly in the form of instruction and precept, but it is perhaps best disclosed in the very character of the conversations which comprise the book. They never lose their social, indeed playful, tone. All the speakers carefully shy away from every occasion for pedantry, although they possess ample erudition, and time after time they delicately and gracefully refuse to elaborate and define certain ideas thoroughly. Their statements tend, rather, to supplement each other even when some of the ironies of their dialectical interchanges remain unresolved. This tone does not suggest, however, any frivolity or irresponsibility about whatever it is they think or believe, even when the disagreements that crop up are plainly contrived by the protagonists for comic effect, as in the protracted discussion over women in Book III. On the contrary, Castiglione manages to convey the underlying cultural, social, and human harmonies which support their debates, the identity of context in which their discourse takes place, the similarity of their assumptions and allusions. In other words, the perfection they reveal is of a "prudential" rather than an absolute character. For them, dialogue does not end in salvation or damnation but is the primary mode of self-realization. They reveal themselves as people possessing the highest capacity for making modulated choices and capable of the highest degree of flexible rationality. No one is driven or drives himself to absolute identification with the views of another.

The perfection that Castiglione presents is of the active life. Earlier, the active life had found very able defenders among the so-called "civic humanists," who contributed to a whole body of debate literature which has since come to be referred to as the *vita activa* controversy. The vigorous political life of the free citizens of the city-state republics in fifteenth-century Italy called forth equally vigorous defenders of the active life of the citizen against those who still maintained a philosophico-religious contemplative ideal of human perfection. Some defenders of the active life practically identified it with economic activity in the classical sense of the word, that sense which includes family and related social concerns as well as strictly economic ones.

With the rise of the tyrannical princedoms of the later Renaissance there was a subsequent shift from civic humanism—the last great voices of it are heard in the writings of Machiavelli and Guicciardini—to a courtly culture ideologically structured by Neoplatonism. The terms, then, of the *vita activa* controversy shifted, and although Castiglione finds some place for consideration of the contemplative ideal in his thought, he does not regard it as antithetical to the active life, nor does he use it in its classical meaning—the undisturbed pursuit of understanding. In fact, what Castiglione means by the contemplative ideal is theoretical knowledge of how to rule, of what good commands are, and the ability to see that they are executed. These abilities belong to the ruler and not to his courtiers, so that it is only the ruler who shares in Castiglione's version of the contemplative ideal, although, to be sure, he is also more deeply engaged in the active life. This conception of the contemplative ideal is really the active life colored by a weak version of the Platonic conception of the philosopher-king. (pp. 133-37)

One of the most interesting ironies of Italian cultural history is that the development of a courtly culture in Italy turned Italian writers back to a tradition of medieval chivalric, feudal, and aristocratic ideas of love and war which had not ever really been rooted in Italian soil. The values of courtly and erotic chivalry came to Italy from Provence and were almost immediately transformed into expressions of spiritual nobility. This, of course, was the work of Dante and his forerunners, especially Guido Guinicelli. Nobility and gentility were

moralized and virtually made into synonyms of goodness. Like a good bourgeois, Dante insists that nobility is not really hereditary. In contrast, there is a protracted and almost inconclusive debate in Book I of Castiglione's **Courtier** on whether or not nobility is inherited nobility, but he did not toss off the weight of tradition descending from Dante through the humanists which attacked the notion that gentlemen are ever born and which offered instead a conception of the gentlemen as the creation of a particular kind of moral education and discipline. Castiglione settles the problem by suggesting that gentle birth confers certain advantages even if it is not indispensable: certainly, universal regard and the probable inheritance of those good qualities and aptitudes which will enable the born nobleman to become the ideal courtier with maximum ease.

Castiglione's chivalric ideals are really of a nostalgic character—a nostalgia, by the way, which had become traditional and can be found in Boccaccio and Sacchetti decades earlier—not only for a romantic feudal past but for the values of that more recent past which had added connotations of self-culture and self-conquest to the medieval ideals of nobility. While Boiardo, Ariosto, and Tasso lament the virtual absence of chivalry and nobility in the courts of their time, Castiglione was able to find it completely incarnated in one court of his own time, at least for a while, and to create the most complete and imaginative ideal portrait of courtly perfection. Castiglione's nostalgia would seem to indicate that he had little hope for the reflowering of true chivalry and courtliness, but the existence of his book would show that he nourished some expectation that a beautiful model of courtliness might lure men back to the lost ideals or arrest their decay. (pp. 138-39)

The core of Castiglione's thought and of his originality is perceptible in a cluster of related and virtually untranslatable concepts: *grazia, gravità, sprezzatura* and *leggiadria*. We can best define them through indirection, starting with the simplest one first.

Gravità is virtually synonomous with dignity, and Castiglione identifies it with the culture of Spain. The Spaniards possess a *gravità riposata,* a quiet majesty of bearing which is reflected not only in the physical posture of the person but in his choice of clothes and the materials they are made of. It suggests the kind of impression difficult for us to generate in an age which has seen the virtually complete democratization of men's clothing and in which we can even see signs of the desexualization of appearances. Perhaps what Castiglione meant by *gravità* can be illustrated by Raphael's magnificent portrait of him, in which the figure's expression and clothing reveal a harmonious balance between self-revelation and reticence, between modest simplicity and assertive decoration. (pp. 143-44)

Although Castiglione is indeed elegantly posed he also appears to be unposed, simply because Raphael somehow conveys the impression that Castiglione is always much the way that he has been painted, always presentable, as it were, always in possession of a modest or measured greatness, a greatness which is not insistent and which appears to be unstudied and "artless." We should not equate this ideal manner with that which goes with habitual understatement, precisely because modern understatement implies inevitably a false humility if only because of the shrill self-assertiveness of the age. What Castiglione—and Raphael—had in mind was that a true gentleman, in their society at any rate, did things with an almost accidental air. He *need* not insist on himself if he wished to convey his own magnificence in a truly human mode. Therefore the possessor of *gravità riposata* did not do anything in haste or anxiously. He avoided fast dances and when he rode, presumably even to war, he did so in a relaxed way, something by the way impossible for a man wearing the heavy armor of the medieval knight. (pp. 144-45)

Sprezzatura and *leggiadria* are both purely social virtues which find their essential manifestation in conversation and in play. *Sprezzatura* is the art of concealing art, of giving to whatever is said and done a certain effortless and unpremediated quality. The root of the word is from the verb *sprezzare*, "to disdain" or "to hold in contempt," and this sense is vaguely present in Castiglione's concept, although without pejorative connotations. A synonym for *sprezzatura* is *disinvoltura* which means "ease," "simplicity of manner," "aplomb" but also can mean "coolness," "cheek" and "impudence." Again we find the elimination of negative connotations, and he uses them both together in the phrase *sprezzata disinvoltura*. *Sprezzatura* and *disinvoltura*, with their suggestions of hauteur and disdain, are meant to convey an attitude toward one's own behavior which will save it from affectation, whether the source of that affectation is an excessive haste or eagerness or an excessive artificiality, both avoidable only through a kind of disengagement or detachment. They point to the proper attitude to have if one is to observe the "mean" in one's manner. The "mean" does not imply being blasé, but the manifestation of a kind of rational appropriateness in all of one's conduct. Indeed, *sprezzatura* increases "grace" and is, in a sense, the external manifestation of that grace.

Leggiadria is close to *sprezzatura* in its meaning, if not identical to it, although it was also used as a synonym for *grazia*, by Della Casa and Firenzuola. While Castiglione does not give a definition of it, he applies it often to women in reference to what we would have to translate as grace or charm.

Grazia is the most important term of value in the *Courtier*. Grace or the potentiality to acquire it is a gift of nature. In reality it cannot be taught. It can only be learned if the potential courtier—or his lady, for women may also possess it—has at least the germ of it and if he is able to receive proper instruction. While it is virtually impossible to define, it can be reached in a flight from affectation, in the use of *sprezzatura* as a kind of easy way of doing difficult things, and it flows from good judgment. It is an elusive quality which would disappear in any deliberate effort to obtain it, and is not reducible to any of the more teachable and describable properties of the educated and civilized man. It springs, as we have seen, from *sprezzatura*, from a kind of "recklessness," an unstudied but skillful spontaneity. Grace is, indeed, "beyond the reach of art" and even beyond critical intelligence. It implies what the eighteenth century meant by "felicity," whether of style, phrase, or manner.

Like Machiavelli's *virtù*, Castiglione's *grazia* is essentially ambiguous because both terms finally refer to the conditions of conduct or action, to the intuition, judgment, and skill required if we are to apply general principles to specific situations. The habit of right action like the habit of right manner in conduct requires that practical wisdom possessed by Aristotle's truly ethical man who really can adapt the general principle of conduct to the endlessly varied specific situations of experience.

Grazia, further, can only be the result of the kind of education which avoids what the French call *déformation professionelle*, that degree of expertise in any field which overdevelops one human function or talent at the cost of leaving others in a raw state. *Grazia* is a quality actualized, if at all, only in a self which, like a great work of art, is truly a harmony of parts. This is why, in the careful program of education outlined in Book I of the *Courtier*, there is such insistence on what we would call the "amateur spirit." By all means learn to play chess but don't try to be an expert. Learn Greek and Latin but don't be a pedant. Castiglione's "amateurism" is not to be understood in the somewhat contemptuous sense we would now give to the word. Since the courtier must advise his ruler, it is necessary for him to be free from any angularity of vision, to be able to adopt a plurality of points of view and not be dominated by any single one of them. The word "amateur" has come to have a bad sense for us because we think of it in connection with artistic work which must, of course, aim at perfection. But Castiglione's amateur is a man in a society, one who must come to know and love many things if he is to function properly in that society. Whatever differentiation and complexity he develops in one region of his personality must not proceed too far and must also be carried over into others, and this process should go on in the service of unifying the heterogeneous elements of the self. The striving for wholeness and a kind of universality is, after all, still the ideal of humanistic education, even if the humanistic temper, its concern for refinement of feeling rather than efficiency of action, its spatial and aesthetic rather than temporal mode of awareness, would seem to have less and less place in the contemporary world.

The attention Castiglione gives to gesture, manner, games, jokes, and anecdotes might seem to some of his readers an extraordinary trivialization of the ideals of true education. But we are the products of years of education in which almost no attention is given to nonverbal modes of communication and expression, or to the nonreferential uses of language. The result is the production of "experts" with extraordinary capacities in certain well-defined areas and no grasp of the meaning of human actions, activities, gestures, or of the varieties of emotional expression. Such are those who cannot distinguish between what men say and do and what they mean by what they say and do, who cannot truly understand speech because speech is much more than the words it uses. What the modern reader may see as trivia in Castiglione's program of education are after all the vehicles of those subtle and feeling interchanges between people which do as much as anything to give them the sense that they are really alive. Castiglione knew that gestures, actions, and objects—the clothes you wear, for example—are modes of language, ways of making statements, and that these languages are not substitutes for one another. It has become essential for modern mass societies to create in all of us the sense that we live in a verbal world, for the governing of such societies demands the incessant generation of verbal messages, laws, edicts, regulations, and promises. Castiglione's society was not tempted to confuse statements with events, nor had the floods of words manufactured by the so-called mass media become the primary instruments of political control and social discipline.

Modern civilization with its tendency toward uniform dress and uniform recreations has severely limited expression to verbal statement and has tended to denigrate action language, object language, or sign language. This has had the result of blocking whole ranges of emotional experience simply because what can be said in one such language cannot be said in another. I am not attributing this analysis to Castiglione as his conscious possession any more than it was the conscious possession of any other exponents of the great tradition of humanistic education. It was, rather, so deeply held a presupposition of their thought that only we, who have lost it, can be fully aware of it.

Grace presides over all the activities of man, whether important or trivial, and it is grace which makes the self into a work of art. It is no accident that in the generation after Castiglione, Vasari made the concept of grace central to his art criticism. It had been applied to painting before Vasari, but largely as a synonym for beauty or to describe a quality differing from beauty only in degree. Vasari not only distinguished grace and beauty, but at times he drew a really strong contrast between them. Grace was a quality impossible to define but which was a function of the artist's judgment, of, as it were, his "eye," while beauty was a quality a painting might possess as a result of the artist's carefree observance of the rules or the "science" of his art. (pp. 145-48)

Castiglione, I think, can be said to offer us an image of self as both various and comprehensively whole. The aim of education is to develop our consciousness, to make us aware of a wide range of different kinds of human possibilities and activities, and to unify thought and action, learning and feeling, by imposing on them, as it were, *a common style.* This remains a unique human possibility because only in man are contradictory impulses and disparate, fragmented experiences brought together in a single consciousness, only man can impose those relations, rhythms, accents, and symmetries on experience that are the essence of style itself. As men may turn the contents of consciousness into works of art, so may they manipulate and form themselves into works of art.

The only alternative to style of life is to be the prisoner of convention, and I mean by convention not that indispensable set of social habits we all need to exist in the world, but those ritualistic, rigid, and stereotyped patterns of response to the multiplicity of experience which finally serve to deny it. Style is, of course, social and must be if it is to be meaningful. Nevertheless, it is finally intensely personal, the possession of a unique personality, capable of infinite variations within its overarching patterns of order.

A man with style in Castiglione's sense will be most various yet recognizably one in all the contingencies of life. He will be morally solvent, as it were, able to handle any transactions of life in such a way that morals and manners will be one thing. He is *kalokagathos* in that he grasps that no moral act is ugly, and that flexibility and variety of response will not endanger his identity.

I suppose that every age presents us with its own version of the true gentleman as well as with the mock gentleman, the one the subject of epic and romance, the other the butt of the satirist. So too, Castiglione throughout the work has his characters distinguish the true coin from the false. I think we can say that, for Castiglione, the true gentleman is finally marked by that sense of personal dignity and value of which all his actions have become the vehicle. (pp. 150-51)

Joseph Anthony Mazzeo, "Castiglione's 'Courtier': The Self as a Work of Art," in his Renaissance and Revolution: The Remaking of European Thought, *Pantheon Books, 1966, pp. 131-60.*

LAWRENCE LIPKING (essay date 1966)

[*In the following excerpt, Lipking traces variations of Plato's dialectical tradition in* The Courtier.]

The Book of the Courtier, by the overwhelming weight of its reputation and influence, comes to us as a handbook of the courtly virtues, or, more historically considered, as a treatise on the education of a Renaissance courtier. It is reasonable that it should. Castiglione himself announced his intention of teaching "what manner of man he must be who deserves the name of perfect Courtier, without defect of any kind", and his division of his work into four books which treat successively and compendiously the personal qualities, the conduct, the female counterpart, and the utility and aspirations of the courtier emphasizes its appearance of being a handbook. One can hardly refute, therefore, those writers who use *The Courtier* as an encyclopaedia of courteous manners, or even those who find in it a manual of Renaissance philosophy. Few works of the Renaissance have a more genuine documentary value.

Yet the form of *The Courtier* is not that of the handbook. The lessons of the work are unfolded in a series of conversations, precisely set in a particular time and place, cast with real people of decided personality, and fashioned through the point and counterpoint of argument. *The Courtier,* that is to say, is not only a text, but a dialogue; and because we receive the ideas of the text only in the state to which they have been tempered by the dialectical drama through which they pass, even someone interested primarily in the work's didactic statement must attempt to understand how Castiglione's dialogue presents and modifies his ideas. The elegant precepts of *The Courtier* are enfolded in a context that develops from page to page, through the give and take of four long nights. To follow Castiglione's principles of courtesy, we must first follow his principles of art; we must ask what sort of dialogue he chooses to employ, with what refinements and to what ends he uses his form.

When Castiglione resolved to put his instructions into the mouths of speakers, he had his choice of many models. Cicero, Ficino, Pico, Bembo; all could have lent him a form. Beyond them all, however, was the master of those who speak together: Plato, the epitome and the virtuoso of dialectical tradition. Here a harmonious pattern and a philosophy of dialectic lay ready for use. In dialogues like the *Symposium* and the *Phaedrus,* paradigms of the form, we can see the concept of love being passed through multiple perspectives, modified by the rhetoric, profession, or personality of each speaker, until it mounts to the dramatic and philosophical climax of Socrates' oration. The argument spirals, and each turn of the spiral brings a refinement or redefinition of the idea of love which lends, in context, significance to each speech beyond its individual significance. Philosophers have devoted much attention to the relationship between form and content in Plato, to the process by which Platonic argument ascends from image to definition to essence to principle. Formally considered, the philosophy of Plato can be seen to emerge only through the struggle of dialectical confrontation; some philosophers would go still further, and claim that the complicated procedure by which truth frees itself from the false values which imperil it on every level of discourse is not only the method, but the subject, of Plato. At any rate, whether or not the form and content of Platonic dialogue are identical, there is no denying their intricate union.

If, keeping in mind Plato, or even his disciple Ficino, as a master of dialectical method, we turn to Castiglione looking for something similar, we are bound to be disappointed. *The Courtier* is not a philosophical confrontation, immersed in the perpetual refinement and modification of an abstraction, so much as it is a linear presentation of the ideal courtier, a list of his qualities and attributes. Each of the four books deals with a segment of courtiership that is kept largely discrete, or adds new material without revaluating the old. Thus the discussion in the second book of the courtier's manner of employing his gifts does not force us to change our notions about those gifts themselves; the court lady of Book Three complements and adorns, but does not revise, her gentleman. The struggle of thought against half-truth, the sense that truth can be arrived at only through arduous conflict with its opposites, are conspicuously lacking in *The Courtier.*

Nevertheless, there seems to be a trace of Plato's spiral even in Castiglione's relatively linear treatment of dialectic. When we read in the fourth book that "the aim of the perfect Courtier, which we have not spoken of up to now, is so to win for himself, by means of the accomplishments ascribed to him by these gentlemen, the favor and mind of the prince whom he serves that he may be able to tell him, and always will tell him, the truth about everything he needs to know, without fear or risk of displeasing him; and . . . to dissuade him of every evil intent and bring him to the path of virtue" our picture of the courtier takes on a different coloring: his dominant personal charm has become ancillary to his function of statesmanship. In Ottaviano's discourse, the strands of the courtier's manifold accomplishments are gathered into a unity, and that unity is seen to be greater than the sum of its parts.

Even here, however, the effect is not quite "spiral," for acquaintance with the aims of a courtier supplements our knowledge of his qualities, rather than refining or subtly changing it. We are told that the courtier must be what he is in order to become something still better, like a chrysalis harboring a butterfly; which is not at all the same as a Socratic argument that the courtier, while from one point of view he may appear to be one sort of thing, will be revealed from another point of view to be something else and something better, when our eyes pierce the mask of the cocoon and see at once all the stages and potentialities of butterfly essence. The dialogues of Plato, seamless fabrics, yield their meaning only as wholes, when the illumination provided by Socrates casts new light upon every thread in the pattern. The first three books of *The Courtier* do not fulfill Castiglione's ideal, but they are sufficient of their kind; if the author had not lived to finish his work, we should still be able to discuss its parts without misrepresentation. *The Courtier* is certainly much enhanced by its concluding book, but it is not dialectically transformed.

Similarly the interruptions and interlocutions in *The Courtier* have some appearance of producing dialectical modifications of the argument, but seldom go beyond that mere appearance. Most of the time an attack upon the speaker only leads him to explain himself or to develop some line of thought more easily. Thus Federico's quarrel with Count Ludovico on matters of language is no more than the means of prompting Ludovico to his lengthy review of linguistics, which closely follows Castiglione's own opinions expressly delivered in the author's epistle. Not strictly pertinent to the description of the courtier (" 'Madam,' replied the Count, 'I think the thread is broken' "), this discussion, of evident in-

Elisabetta Gonzaga, Duchess of Urbino, by Giovanni Francesco Caroto.

terest to Castiglione, could not very gracefully have been introduced without the mechanism of interruption. The continual challenges offered by Gasparo throughout the third and fourth books are of the same order. Gasparo, only in his twentieth year in 1506, the year of the conversations at Urbino, clearly enjoys twitting, flirting, provoking, and playing at logic, yet his remarks rarely cut deep; frequently he is a mere convenience or pause of breath for the speaker ("Then signor Gasparo said: 'The discreet and virtuous, and those who are not by nature slaves, in what mode are they to be ruled?' Signor Ottaviano replied: 'By the gentle kind of rule, kingly and civic' "); frequently he is exercising the young man's privilege of exuberance, thus standing surrogate for ingenuous readers. So casual a use of the maneuvers of dialogue is hardly dialectical in a Platonic, or any philosophical, sense.

A closer approximation to the Plato of the *Symposium* or *Phaedrus* seems to be suggested by what has often been called the difference in *tone* which distinguishes Castiglione's fourth book from his first three. Does *The Courtier,* taken as a sequence of arguments and moods, mount to any higher plane of discourse than that on which it begins? Certainly many readers have received such an impression, for Bembo's memorable flight on love brings the game into the realm of the ethereal just before its close, and thoughts of such mundane matters as when to tell a joke or how to mount a horse seem to have been effaced beneath a new sublimity: "Therefore let us direct all the thoughts and powers of our souls to this most holy light, that shows us the path leading to heaven." Under the spell of Bembo's eloquence, we, like his listeners, may well be ravished into believing that at last the essential spirit of the courtier has been revealed to us, that the various discussions have here been distilled into their purest form. Regarded in this light, *The Courtier* can be consistently interpreted as an ever-progressing series of opinions about real life and the ideal in which Castiglione and his characters win through to an increased spirituality; only at the very end is the harmony of the conception made manifest.

When read as this sort of consequential argument, the didactic lesson of *The Courtier* can be outlined with great success, but unfortunately *The Courtier* itself seems to fail. It fails twice over: first, artistically, because one speech, however eloquent, has not enough weight to bring into balance all that has gone before, and the work seems to end suddenly just at the moment when it has begun to free itself from triviality; second, intellectually, because the ideas of love in the resolution have no specific relevance to the idea of the courtier in his services as courtier. Even if we were to accept logically Bembo's espousal of spiritual love as the condition in which man fulfills himself, as the soul "flies to unite itself with the angelic nature," we should not understand why that fulfillment must be more appropriate to the courtier than to other men. Indeed, when considered as a dialectical conclusion to *The Courtier,* Bembo's ideal is at best destructive of the attempt to isolate the specific nature of the subject of the work, at worst, he transports all ideas and all reality into a nebulous and shadowy emotion (" 'it seems to me that to possess this beauty which he so much praises, without the body, is a fantasy' "). If Bembo's speech is truly the last link in the argument of *The Courtier,* then the whole chain of thought must come under suspicion.

Yet there seems in fact to be little reason to accept Bembo's elevated discourse as a dialectical resolution of the *ideas* of Castiglione's work. Love is only one among many occupations and activities of the courtier, an activity, to be sure, of surpassing interest, since besides occupying much of the gentleman's time and most of the lady's it transfers to the emotional sphere that ideal of service which looms so large in the courtier's professional and intellectual career, but nevertheless a single activity which neither validates nor invalidates the many other occupations carefully pursued by the court through four full nights of conversation. Precisely how has Bembo summarized or metamorphosed Castiglione's argument? By his superior rhetoric? his infectious idealism? or simply his position at the conclusion? All of these may lend him authority, yet none seems enough to enable him to forge a reconciliation of opposing ideas, or to win a conclusive victory for the idealism he voices over more superficial or realistic viewpoints. The courtiers of Urbino are entranced by Bembo, but there is no sign that they are about to vote him or his system into power.

The nature of the dialectical authority conferred upon Bembo can be approached in a significantly different way. The majority of Plato's dialogues, despite the widely varying dialectical methods they employ, are very obviously alike in one respect: the use of Socrates as a sort of hero whose function is to assist truth in the struggle against its enemies. So much is Socrates the master of debate that many Platonic dialogues can be said to have two authors, one who directs the argument from without, one who controls it from within. To what extent, we

may ask, can Bembo similarly be identified, either in his opinions or in his powers of controlling the discussion, with Castiglione? In spite of the real Bembo's revision of *The Courtier* before its publication, in spite of his influence upon Castiglione as well as upon the conversations, the answer is not difficult: Bembo's role in *The Courtier* as a whole, however memorable, is too slight for us to believe that he commands the group either practically or intellectually. His ideas are worthy of respect, but other fine courtiers also dwell at Urbino, and only the Duchess has the power to tell them when to dance and when to speak.

Indeed, for a proper perspective upon Bembo's concluding eloquence we must consider his place generally in *The Courtier.* From this point of view, it must be admitted that good messer Pietro seems prey to a certain (albeit gracious) over-refinement or over-intellectuality not only at the moment when signora Emilia plucks his robe to draw his soul back into his body, but even at his first appearance, when he proposes for sport that "each should tell, if she whom he loves must be angry with him, where he would wish the cause of her anger to lie, in her or in himself." This proposal, as subtle as a thesis topic, not surprisingly stirs little enthusiasm in a company assembled in party mood. A similar charming pedantry is displayed by Bembo when, coyly declining for a moment to speak of love, he slips in a reference to his own work [*Gli Asolani*]: "Truly, Madam, if I am to talk about this matter, I should have to go and ask counsel of my Lavinello's hermit." Only with his closing words and seizure of inspiration does Bembo move to the center of the courtier's spirit and of our attention.

As soon as we begin to consider Bembo this way, in terms of his dramatic function rather than his dialectical authority, many things become clear about the structure of *The Courtier.* If the philosophical basis for ending the conversations with a prayer for spiritual love seems dubious, its dramatic basis can hardly be questioned: the eloquent intensity of the prayer, which brooks no argument and indeed presumes a level of emotional abandonment where argument or disputation cannot live, is precisely the right note on which to put an end to all discussion. Much calculation has gone into this effect. Castiglione has deliberately refrained from introducing the praise of intellectual love where it might have seemed more appropriate, in the conversations about love in Book Three; he has economically withheld Bembo from any earlier display of his powers; he has separated Ottaviano's dignified discourse from Bembo's final peroration by some comparatively trivial arguments which enhance by contrast the beauty of the conclusion. The calculation is successful, the effect conclusive. No one who has approached *The Courtier* without expecting to find in it some confirmation of his own theories of philosophy, history, or morality, has ever found it less than an elegant and moving work of art. Though *The Courtier*'s structure does not satisfy criteria for Platonic dialectic, it has a satisfactory logic of its own. The nature of that logic must be sought, not in our preconceived expectations about dialogue form, but in the particular dramatic and intellectual effects which Castiglione contrived. (pp. 355-58)

Lawrence Lipking, "The Dialectic of 'Il Cortegiano'," in PMLA, *Vol. LXXXI, No. 5, October, 1966, pp. 355-62.*

GEORGE BULL   (essay date 1967)

[*Bull is an English author, editor, and translator who has written widely on figures of the Italian Renaissance. In the following excerpt from the introduction to his translation of* The Courtier, *he offers a balanced assessment of Castiglione's work.*]

It is hard, indeed, to think of any work more opposed to the spirit of the modern age [than *The Courtier*]. At an obvious level, its preoccupation with social distinction and outward forms of polite behaviour creates an intense atmosphere of artificiality and insincerity. (When James Joyce first read *The Courtier* his brother told him he had become more polite but less sincere.)

The great virtues it proposes for a gentleman are discretion and decorum, nonchalance and gracefulness. As Luigi Barzini comments in his satirical book on the modern Italian, quoting Castiglione as the model, the 'show' is all. The courtier must watch his dress, his speech, his gestures chiefly because of their effect on his reputation. If he fights well in battle, he must make sure his commander sees him do so. He has to consider earnestly whether it is correct behaviour to take part in sport with the common people or even to perform in front of them. In love, he must conquer where he can; whereas the women he most admires are those who regard dishonour as a fate worse than death. And then, even when the discussions in *The Courtier* take a more serious turn, and shallow values are repudiated, notably in the Fourth Book with Bembo's melding of Platonic love with Christian theology, the language and sentiments seem inflated and occasionally grotesque.

The combination of intense and selfish individualism with appalling snobbery naturally repels the modern reader, and also the modern historian, who is suspicious of the assumption that history consists in the exploits of the ruling class and the favoured few, and who is anxious to know less about the way gifted amateurs danced at Court and more about the mortality rate in the villages down the hill.

More seriously, *The Courtier* offends modern susceptibilities because it is a flight from the truth. Throughout the book, to be sure, there runs a vein of natural melancholy, partly attributable to Castiglione's constant awareness of the fickleness of Fortune and the inevitability of death. But by its very nature it is a book which turns aside from the realities of life to its idealization. War—which Castiglione experienced and disliked—is glorified; the criminal behaviour of some of the gay companions he knew at Urbino is glossed over or ignored; the crudeness of Court life in sixteenth century Italy—an earlier version of *The Courtier* was far nearer in this respect to the historical reality—is refined away. The political discussions—using the language and concepts of the ancient world with regard to the rule of the one, the best or the many—are totally unrealistic. When Machiavelli wrote *The Prince,* in all innocence he shocked the world for several hundred years because he set out to 'represent things as they are in real truth, rather than as they are imagined'. Machiavelli had the humanists very much in mind when he wrote this—'Many have dreamed up republics and principalities which have never in truth been known to exist. . . .' And the cap fits Castiglione, who purported to be teaching people how to behave and recording life as it was, and not writing a Utopia. Machiavelli, indeed, has come into his own in the modern world which understands and appreciates the unabashed language of power;

whereas Castiglione's pretences—in the context of normal social behaviour or high politics—are remote.

As a handbook for gentlemen, *The Courtier* conceals the most shameless opportunism under the cloak of a tiresome refinement; as a memoir of life at the Court of Urbino, it touches up history to the point of distortion. None the less, even though many of Castiglione's values are questionable (though for their time they shone out in an uncouth world), *The Courtier* cannot be so easily dismissed. It is historically significant and instructive. It is, at the very least, an entertaining book. Most of all, it is a work of substantial literary achievement.

The historical value of *The Courtier,* apart from its influence outside Italy, is twofold. It is first and foremost a compendium of Renaissance thought. Not only does it provide the best illustration of the Renaissance preoccupation with the *uomo universale,* the many-sided man; it also touches, however briefly, on all the themes, great and trivial, pursued in contemporary Italian literature and thought, from the importance of study and imitation of the classical world to the role of Fortune in human affairs. Moreover, it sets before us the ideals of the Renaissance; and in this way it corrects and complements the picture of how Renaissance men did behave—as drawn, say, by Cellini—with an account of the moral and aesthetic standards to which many of them at least aspired.

As for its entertainment value, the reader fresh to *The Courtier* can judge for himself. The discussions concerning what constitutes the perfect courtier, taking place during four evenings in spring between an intimate circle of cultivated women, men of the world, scholars and buffoons, lead to the exploration of topics which in varying degrees still retain their interest and might even spark off conversation in a senior common room or a television studio: the importance of correct speech; the essential prerequisites for a gentleman, including good breeding and good looks; the superiority of the skilled amateur to the tedious professional; the kinds of witticism and practical joke that are really funny; the qualities men look for in their women; the duties of a good government; and, finally, the true nature of love.

The style, very Latin and sonorous, skilfully catches the tone of the conversations and the mood of the speakers: simple and direct in argumentative dialogue, sometimes like comedians' cross-talk; matter of fact, cutting and even coarse in the interjections, involved and elevated in the occasional rhetorical flights. The pace is generally brisk and confident (though now and then Castiglione rides a hobby-horse of his own too long) and the transitions from one subject or mood to another are smooth and natural. When the talk grows too pompous, Castiglione hurriedly dispels the gloom with a dramatic interruption or a joke. One of his most attractive aspects, indeed, is his obvious fear of boring anyone or seeming too serious. Gaiety keeps breaking in—and sometimes with disconcerting bathos, as at the very end of *The Courtier* when, after Bembo's invocation to Love has struck the whole company dumb, Emilia Pia brings them abruptly back to earth with a matter of fact remark about the next day's debate. This, incidentally, throws fresh light on her character which, like those of the others taking part in the conversations, is portrayed with notable economy and effect. Gaspare Pallavicino, Count Lodovico da Canossa, Pietro Bembo, Elisabetta Gonzaga, Emilia Pia are clearly revealed through their words as misogynist, nobleman, scholar, duchess and shrew, respectively, but also as living persons, with whose complex attitudes and temperament the reader becomes increasingly familiar and whom he even learns to like.

Castiglione's sensitivity to character and atmosphere and his ability to recreate them convincingly, his delicate psychological perception and his powers of narrative and description betray, in fact, the novelist and the poet. *The Courtier* may be approached as a romance rather than as an historical record. The story is in the past, almost in the golden days of Italy before the full force of the foreign invasions made themselves felt. Castiglione over the years changed what had been a memoir into a fiction. The first shrewd device was to pretend that he himself had been away in England when the conversations were held: 'as our Castiglione writes from England', remarks Ottaviano in the Fourth Book, 'promising to tell us much more on his return . . .'. The Palace of Urbino is transformed from the local habitation of a petty Italian ruler into a model for all time. First, it is described, with a touch of realism, as being in a city 'surrounded by hills which are perhaps not as agreeable as those found in many other places'; when the conversations end, the abstract beauty described by Bembo is complemented by a final look at the beauty of Urbino itself, where dawn has just come to the east, a delicate breeze is blowing, and the birds are breaking into song. It was beyond his power, Castiglione protested, to do a portrait of Urbino as ambitiously as Raphael or Michelangelo, since he knew only how to draw the outlines and could not adorn the truth with pretty colours or use perspective to deceive the eye. And yet there are passages in *The Courtier* which do nothing so much as suggest a scene by a great painter of the High Renaissance, as when, on the first evening, as Cesare Gonzaga begins to speak there was heard 'the noise of a great tramping of feet, and, as everyone turned to see what was happening, there appeared at the door a blaze of torches preceding the arrival of the Perfect, with a large and noble escort . . .'

By the time *The Courtier* was finished it had become, too, a work of piety towards not only Duke Guidobaldo but also all the other 'outstanding men and women who used to frequent the Court of Urbino'. For, as Castiglione sighed, as he read his manuscript, 'I recalled that most of those introduced in the conversations were already dead. . . .' And so they too were idealized in this glowing account of the last days of Italian chivalry: Castiglione's remembrance of things past. (pp. 15-19)

> *George Bull, in an introduction to* The Book of the Courtier *by Baldesar Castiglione, translated by George Bull, Penguin Books, 1967, pp. 9-19.*

DAIN A. TRAFTON (essay date 1972)

[*In the following essay, Trafton seeks to demonstrate that the books of* The Courtier *are linked by a logical progression.*]

Bembo's discourse on love at the end of Castiglione's *Book of the Courtier* has been much admired. It is one of the clearest and briefest as well as one of the most influential expressions of Renaissance Platonic love, and within *The Courtier* as a whole the passage stands out by virtue of its elevated intensity of thought and feeling. Beyond questions of influence and intrinsic beauty, however, lies the question of Bembo's function in relation to the rest of the work; and here there has been less unanimity of response. To many readers, Bembo's words, coming as they do with special emphasis in the closing

moments, mark a climax and provide an appropriate and powerful conclusion to all that has gone before. Other readers, however, have disagreed. Some, for example, have objected that the discussion of Platonic love lies outside the limits of the work's proper subject, courtiership, and therefore has the effect of destroying the focus of the discussions rather than of completing them. Still others, stressing the looseness and heterogeneity of *The Courtier*'s overall structure, have contended that no final discourse, no matter how cogent or impassioned in itself, could tie together and properly conclude the varied themes that Castiglione introduces. And the most recent contribution to the debate argues that while Bembo's doctrines may provide a conclusion that is satisfying from a "dramatic" point of view, they are philosophically quite inadequate. According to this most recent view, *The Courtier* has no true philosophic conclusion because it has no philosophic development. Unlike Platonic dialogue which builds through constant "refinement and modification" of its central ideas, the discussions of *The Courtier* are "linear" and in the end amount to little more than an accumulated "list" of the courtier's qualities. Platonic love is no conclusion, then; it is just the last item on the list.

As the case now stands, the last and best word seems to belong to this latter point of view. The arguments that tend to disintegrate *The Courtier* by denying the philosophic appropriateness of its conclusion have never been met by any thoroughgoing demonstration of its structural integrity. Even the most extensive recent analyses of the book, which seem to take for granted that it does possess fundamental structural integrity, are fragmentary, deal at length with particular ideas or themes, but never rise to a comprehensive view except in the most general terms. The purpose of the present essay is to sketch the outlines of a new reading of *The Courtier* which will be both comprehensive and precise and which will describe the coherent development of its various parts, both philosophic and dramatic, towards their proper conclusion in Bembo's discourse. As I read it, *The Courtier* reveals Castiglione's close understanding and imitation of Platonic dialogue. Castiglione's aim is not to compile a mere list of courtly attributes, but rather to lead the reader gradually through "refinement and modification" of the earlier ideas of the courtier to the fullest possible understanding at the end. In its first three and a half books, *The Courtier* examines a number of views of courtiership, all of which finally expose their inadequacy. It is the thorough examination of all these flawed views, the progressive exploration of the problems inherent in them, that constitutes the structural design by which Castiglione leads us to recognize the necessity for Bembo's doctrines at the dialogue's conclusion.

The first view of courtiership comes to light at the beginning of the first book. Castiglione explains that he wrote *The Courtier* because a friend, Alfonso Ariosto, asked him to express his opinion about "the form of courtiership most befitting a gentleman living at the courts of princes, by which he is able and knows how to serve them perfectly in every reasonable thing, thereby acquiring grace from them and praise from others; in short what sort of man he ought to be who is worthy to be called a perfect courtier." Castiglione's restatement of his friend's request focuses our attention at the very outset on the main concerns of courtly life—reasonable service and the acquisition of grace and praise—around which much of the discussion in *The Courtier* and its most serious issues in fact develop. Moreover, through his precise wording Castiglione makes Ariosto the spokesman within the work for a particular interpretation of those concerns, the spokesman for a particular view of the proper relationship between service and grace. By asking to learn how courtiers can serve princes "perfectly in every reasonable thing," Ariosto seems to imply that unreasonable service is of course incompatible with perfect courtiership; and the syntax connecting the clause "thereby acquiring . . . from others" to the rest of the sentence implies further that reasonable service will of course suffice to win the grace and praise that the courtier desires. Of the courtier's two main concerns, then, Ariosto's request implies that reasonable service must be primary; it merits attention for its own sake, and it is also the proper and sufficient means to acquire grace and praise.

Thus, Castiglione raises an expectation about the contents of his book. Since the book is addressed to Ariosto, and since he is described in its opening sentence as a "most dear" friend, one might expect that it would reflect his opinions, that it would express a rather high-minded and optimistic view of courtiership, stressing reasonable service as at once the only morally acceptable and the most effective course for the courtier to follow. More precisely, one might expect the bulk of the book to be devoted to discussions of reasonable service, to inquiry into the peculiar problems that face a man who seeks to be guided by reason through the complex social and political pressures of the courtly world. This expectation is soon disappointed, however; as the first book develops, the unproblematic relationship between reasonable service and the acquisition of grace and praise that Ariosto's request assumes is called into doubt, and attention consequently turns to other means of acquiring grace and praise. In the process, moreover, it becomes increasingly clear that for many of the courtiers in the dialogue the acquisition of grace and praise rather than reasonable service constitutes the primary concern of courtiership. And the inevitable effect of these two developments is that concern for reasonable service, although never entirely lost, fades into the background. Ariosto's high-minded and optimistic view of courtiership is replaced by a different, more realistic view.

It is in fact Castiglione himself, speaking in his own voice, who first raises doubts about Ariosto's view. Immediately after restating his friend's seminal request, Castiglione explains that he was at first reluctant to comply because he feared being thought rash by "all those who know how difficult it is, among so great a variety of customs as are practiced in the courts of Christendom, to choose the most perfect form and, as it were, the flower of courtiership." The variety of customs leads him to reflect on their power and finally to conclude rather pessimistically "that usage is more powerful than reason in introducing new things among us and in blotting out old things." "Us" may no doubt be taken generally, to refer to all men, but more specifically, in the context, "us" means those who live at courts. Custom and usage, Castiglione would have us understand, are more powerful than reason in courts. We can hardly be as confident as Ariosto, then, that a courtier's reasonable service will surely be recognized and rewarded.

Thus, with a courtly kind of irony devoid of bluntness, Castiglione suggests that his friend's optimism about court life may be unjustified and naïve. Within the context of *The Courtier* as a whole, moreover, this suggestion is supported by a recurrent stress upon the irrationality and unpredictableness of life and especially of court life. This stress is not restricted to one character or to one part of the book; it is a pervasive theme coloring the attitudes of many characters and the discussions of every major topic, encompassing references to broken promises and the perversity of human judgment, amorous folly and the harsh reality of politics, and summed up darkly in the many comments upon the malign power of time, Fortune, and death. Moreover, Ludovico da Canossa's admission that high birth and false reputation have enabled "dull witted and maladroit" courtiers to fool the courtiers of Urbino themselves "for many days" indicates that even the court that Castiglione holds up as an example to the world is under the sway of irrational custom. We should not be surprised, then, that when Ludovico, to whom the task of describing the perfect courtier first falls, turns to the problem of acquiring grace and praise, his emphasis is not on reasonable service but on a technique of calling attention to oneself, a technique for insuring, in a world ruled by the prejudices of custom and usage, that one's services will be recognized. This technique Ludovico sums up in a "new word": *sprezzatura*. To win grace and praise, one must

> use in everything a certain *sprezzatura* which hides art and makes whatever is done and said appear to be without effort and almost without any thought about it. From this, I believe, comes much grace: because everyone knows the difficulty of things that are rare and well done; wherefore facility in these things causes the greatest wonder; and, on the other hand, to labor and, as they say, to drag forth by the hair of the head causes the greatest disgrace and makes everything to be esteemed lightly, no matter how great it may be.

Ludovico's doctrine of *sprezzatura,* his "new word" about how to acquire grace, is based squarely on the cynical assumption that those whose judgment the courtier values, especially princes, are more likely to be impressed by the manner of a courtier's service than by its reasonableness. Great deeds will not be admired if the courtier is observed to work too hard at accomplishing them, while the appearance of facility in a difficult achievement will cause it to be considered of more worth than the same achievement without the show of facility. Taking into account the fact that the courtly world is a world of custom and usage rather than of reason, a world dominated more by apparent than by real worth, *sprezzatura* offers the courtier a way to free himself from an uncertain dependence upon the unadorned merit of reasonable service alone. To gain recognition, he must learn the art of concealing art. *Sprezzatura* is essentially a kind of dissimulation that enables the courtier to show off without seeming to. Thus, Ludovico's doctrine of *sprezzatura* suggests a new view of courtiership, more calculating but also apparently more realistic in its understanding of courtly life than Ariosto's optimism.

But what about Ariosto's high-mindedness? Must it be abandoned along with his optimism? Apparently not. It seems to be taken for granted by most of the participants in the dialogue that the cultivated dissimulation involved in the exercise of *sprezzatura* does not preclude a high-minded view of the courtier himself. As far as one can tell from the first book at least, all the courtiers present seem to assume that the necessity for the dissimulation involved in *sprezzatura* derives solely from the unreasonableness of the world and does not imply any deficiency in the courtier's own soul. The essentially reasonable quality of his service will not be tainted by the dissimulation necessary to make that service pleasing. Consequently, no objections are raised when, not long after the discussion of *sprezzatura,* Ludovico contends that the courtier must not only practice *sprezzatura* but also be a "true moral philosopher who wishes to be good."

In spite of the fact that no one objects, however, we may wonder how harmonious the cultivation of *sprezzatura* and goodness would prove in practice, for Castiglione contrives, through the arguments and explanations of Ludovico himself and through the development of the dialogue generally, to suggest how easily a concern for recognition through *sprezzatura* might conflict with virtue and reasonable service. At one point in the elucidation of his new doctrine, for example, Ludovico reveals that its usefulness is not only to make the courtier's reasonable service look attractive but also to suggest that his accomplishments are greater than in fact they are. According to Ludovico, *sprezzatura* can make "any human action, however small," appear "much greater than it really is, since it impresses upon the minds of the onlookers the opinion that he who performs well with so much facility must know how to do more than he actually does, and that, if he were to devote care and effort to what he does, he would be able to do it far better." Simply knowing how to strike an easy pose while handling weapons will make people believe that one is expert in using them; a single graceful step can suggest that one is an excellent dancer; and a few well-chosen notes or one elegantly drawn line can give the impression that one knows the arts of music and painting. That such impressions can be false is obvious, and more than one passage in *The Courtier* (many of the jokes in the second book come to mind immediately) attests to the fact that one can learn the gestures and poses of an activity or of virtue itself without knowing that activity thoroughly or without being truly virtuous. From a moral point of view, then, the doctrine of *sprezzatura* is potentially dangerous. By teaching the gestures and poses that are able to make a small action look great, *sprezzatura* goes beyond the mere embellishment of reasonable service and offers courtiers a way to win grace and praise for appearances that are not backed by any substance. In spite of Ludovico's apparent intentions, his words suggest how *sprezzatura* might become a substitute for, rather than an adornment of, reasonable service.

In presenting the doctrine of *sprezzatura,* then, as when he disengaged himself from the optimism of his friend Ariosto, Castiglione works through irony and implication, leaving the reader to draw the explicit conclusions. Ludovico is no less Castiglione's friend than Ariosto, but by the same token Ludovico is no more than Ariosto to be taken uncritically as Castiglione's spokesman. *The Courtier* takes its ideas seriously, but its presentation, like that of Platonic dialogue, is essentially dramatic; it requires our careful and critical participation before it becomes fully intelligible. The first book of *The Courtier* is designed to leave one with an essentially problematic view of courtiership. The high-minded and optimistic view associated with Alfonso Ariosto at the book's beginning has been found wanting in its understanding of the world and has given way to Ludovico's more realistic doctrines. But Ludovico's doctrines in turn have revealed a serious problem of coherence and a vulnerability to exploitation. The relation between his demand for reasonable service and the temptations implicit in his doctrine of *sprezzatura* seems precarious.

It is a significant aspect of *The Courtier*'s dramatic structure, moreover, that the conduct of the courtiers of Urbino themselves forces upon us a sense of this precariousness. If the danger that *sprezzatura* might function as a substitute for,

rather than as an adornment of, reasonable service is to be averted, it is clear that desire for grace and praise must be subordinate to the ideal of service in the courtier's conception of his role. But if one compares the amount of time and ingenuity in the first book devoted to *sprezzatura* with the amount devoted to reasonable service, one cannot avoid the impression that in the best court that Castiglione knows interest in the arts of pleasing takes precedence over interest in the problems of service. The second book confirms and strengthens this impression. Federico Fregoso sets the tone at the very outset when he justifies further discussion on the ground that it is not easy for a courtier to know how "to refrain from praising himself on the wrong occasion, or from indulging in tiresome presumption, or from saying something which he thinks will provoke laughter but which, because said at the wrong time, turns out to be cold and without grace." In all of these examples Federico's concern is with pleasing manners rather than service, and under his direction the discussion focuses quite frankly on the courtier's means of making an impression: on how to look best in battle, even though this may be incompatible with the common effort, how to dress, how to employ skill to give the impression of possessing even greater skill, and how to tell jokes.

Of course the second book does not allow the reader to lose sight entirely of the courtier's need for virtue. When accused, for example, of turning the courtier into little more than "a noble flatterer," Federico hastens to add that the courtier must please princes only in their "wishes that are reasonable and honest." And in another passage he insists that the courtier ought to refuse to serve a wicked prince. On the whole, however, these reminders of the courtier's higher obligations arouse little interest; they are introduced from time to time, hastily agreed to, and then passed over without any real attempt to square those obligations with the predominant concern for the projection of an effective image through *sprezzatura.* As reminders, nevertheless, they serve to keep us aware of what is being neglected and thus illuminate ironically the second book's almost exclusive preoccupation with appearances, a preoccupation that leads the courtiers of Urbino finally and appropriately into the joke fest with which the book concludes. The art of telling the right joke in the right way at the right time represents *sprezzatura* as the most trivial kind of ingratiation. Neither the jokes nor the advice about joking at the end of the second book aim at anything more than the passing amusement of the drawing room, and the courtiers of Urbino who devote so much of their discussion to this lowest form of pleasing seem a prophecy of those later courtiers who, as glorified valets and court jesters, were to throng the courts of the Grand Dukes of Tuscany, of the Bourbon kings of Naples and Spain, of Charles II, of Louis XIV, and of others like them. Of course an art that enables a courtier to seem more virtuous than he is might be used to more sinister ends. For an ambitious man, an Edmund rather than an Osric, the first two books of *The Courtier* might complement *The Prince.* Charles V is said to have kept the two works together at his bedside, along with the Bible. Nevertheless, Castiglione chooses to conclude his examination of *sprezzatura* with an image of triviality, and thus provides a further ironically amusing comment upon the court of Urbino. Perhaps it is one sign of that court's goodness that there are no potential princes among those of its courtiers who do not rise above a concern for mere *sprezzatura.*

If within the dramatic structure of *The Courtier* as a whole the section on joking is Castiglione's representation of the nadir of courtiership devoted to mere *sprezzatura,* it also serves ironically to lead the courtiers quite unexpectedly back to more serious matters. In spite of the prevailing lightness of tone, there are jokes here and throughout the section which unmistakably suggest to the reader more searching reflections about human nature and human affairs than the jokers intend. And as the emphasis at the end of the section turns to jokes involving women, real moral questions persistently arise. "Why was it not as permissible for Ricciardo Minutolo to deceive Filipello's wife and cause her to go to that bathhouse as it was for Beatrice to make her husband Egano get out of bed and get a sound beating from Anichino, when she has been lying with the latter long since?" Why should a courtier's joking show more respect for women's honor than for men's? Are women less capable of moral virtue than men? Does a lover seek to possess the mind of his beloved or only the body? These are questions which raise serious moral issues whether certain courtiers wish to recognize them or not. Thus the joking about women, which is obviously introduced to provide a transition to the subject of the third book—the court lady—serves in addition to reintroduce a note of moral seriousness to the discussions. And this renewal of moral seriousness also looks forward to the third book; by contrast with the second, it exhibits a convincing concern for goodness.

It may have been surprising to many would-be courtiers in the book's early audience, especially to those who shared Gaspar Pallavicino's attitudes towards women, to discover that the discussion of the qualities of the court lady serves to introduce for the first time a sustained and serious concern for virtue, both moral and political, but such is the irony with which Castiglione confronts us. Giuliano de' Medici, who initiates the discussion in the third book, acknowledges at the outset that the lady must "know how to gain and keep the grace of her mistress and of all others, to perform well and gracefully all the exercises that are suitable for women." But moral philosophy is clearly more interesting to him than *sprezzatura.* Consequently, a question about the relative merits of men and women, a question which, like the whole question of women itself, could easily lend itself to trivial *jeux d'esprit,* in fact raises for Giuliano the very serious problem of what is essentially human, the body or the mind. And this discussion in turn leads to discussions of the role of sexual differentiation in nature, of the psychology of love, and finally to analyses of the virtues of temperance and courage that are far more searching than anything earlier. Although necessarily brief, these discussions and others like them in the third book stand in sharp contrast to the earlier spirit of mere *sprezzatura,* and they express a serious concern for the virtues upon which rational courtly service could be founded.

The passage which makes Giuliano's opposition to mere *sprezzatura* clearest, however, is the one in which he castigates hypocrites

> who—forgetful, or rather scornful, of Christ's teaching, which requires a man to anoint his face when he fasts in order that he may not be known to fast, and commands that prayers, alms, and other good works shall be done, not in the public square nor in synagogues, but in secret, so that the left hand shall not know what the right hand does—affirm that there is no better thing in the world than setting a good example: and so, with head bent to one side and with downcast eyes, letting it be known they do not wish to speak to women or eat anything save raw herbs—grimy, with their habits all torn, they deceive the simple.

Nothing could be further from the spirit of *sprezzatura* than the teaching of Christ to which Giuliano refers here. The courtier as described by Ludovico and Federico, whose constant concern is to perform in as conspicuous a manner as possible, certainly does not want the left hand to be ignorant of what the right hand is doing. On the contrary, he learns through *sprezzatura* to advertise himself by calculating every gesture; sometimes he may even, by leading men to believe that he possesses virtues that he does not, "deceive the simple."

Thus, under the influence of Giuliano, the discussions of the third book begin to exemplify that subordination of *sprezzatura* to virtue that we have seen is necessary to prevent courtiership from degenerating into deception and triviality, and we should not be surprised that a high moral seriousness informs the stories about women which fill nearly half the book. It is significant that these stories have nothing to do with *sprezzatura.* None of them teaches the art of showing oneself off to the best advantage. Rather, they exemplify almost all the virtues. Chastity is, as we should expect, the most common subject, but the other virtues are discussed as well. The story of Alessandra, wife of Alessandro, king of the Jews, for example, exhibits her tough and resourceful political prudence. Epicari and Leona are types of constancy. Aspasi and Diotima represent wisdom. Justice is praised in Anne of France and in Margherita, the daughter of the Emperor Maximilian. And Isabella of Castile is said to have possessed all the virtues, including that of extending her dominions, in the highest degree. Structurally, these stories and the many others with them form a parallel to the jokes that take up half of the second book; but the point of the parallelism is a contrast, to mark the radical change in moral tone between the two books.

As examples of virtue, however, Giuliano's stories shed little light on the specific problems of courtiership. His heroines are simply good women drawn from all walks of life; and it remains for Ottaviano Fregoso, at the beginning of the fourth book, to make explicit the significance of this shift in moral tone and to direct the discussion of virtue specifically into a discussion of the courtier's reasonable service. Ottaviano functions partly as a choric figure who puts into explicit language the judgments that have emerged implicitly from the dialogue of the first three books. Thus he condemns as "frivolities and vanities" many of the accomplishments which have been attributed to the courtier by Ludovico and Federico, "such as dancing, merrymaking, singing, and playing," unless they are employed as means to the end of reasonable service. According to Ottaviano, the acquisition of grace and praise should be important to the courtier mainly because it enables him to lead his prince to virtue:

> I think that the end of the perfect courtier, which we have not spoken of up to now, is to win for himself, by means of the accomplishments ascribed to him by these gentlemen, the benevolence and the mind of the prince whom he serves that he may be able to tell him and always will tell him the truth about everything that he needs to know, without fear or risk of displeasing him; and that when he sees the mind of his prince inclined to a wrong action, he may dare to oppose him, and in a gentle manner avail himself of the grace acquired by his good accomplishments, so as to dissuade him of every evil intent and bring him to the path of virtue.

Once Ottaviano's choric function has become clear, once the

implicit limitations of the earlier concerns have been made explicit and the conception of the courtier has been reinvigorated with a high-minded concern for reasonable service, one might expect the book to end. That it does not, however, indicates the fullness and complexity of presentation that make it a great book. One more step is necessary to complete the intellectual and dramatic design. For, although Ottaviano elevates the idea of courtiership and introduces the serious topics with which courtiers dedicated to reasonable service should be concerned, the specific discussions that he initiates raise more problems than they solve. Throughout the opening passages of the fourth book, Castiglione introduces characters who question and oppose Ottaviano on specific issues, and although Ottaviano usually has the last word he often fails to meet the arguments of his opponents fully and convincingly. Thus his account of the Socratic idea that if one truly knows the good one will never do wrong is simply not full enough to dispel the problem raised by Bembo's commonsensical objection that we often act badly in spite of the fact that we know better; nor, to take another example, is Ottaviano's defense of monarchy sufficient to answer the claims of republicanism put forward by Bembo. Ottaviano always makes a good case, but so do his opponents, especially Bembo, and the result is an inconclusiveness that runs throughout the first two-thirds of the book and points to the necessity for further thought. The discussions under Ottaviano's leadership exemplify how courtiers ought to proceed, what questions they ought to ask if they are to become true moral philosophers and learn to serve reasonably, but the answers to those questions, the content of true moral philosophy and the precise nature of reasonable service, remain unrevealed.

Ottaviano's earnestness, then, is not enough. Moral and political earnestness must be enlightened by real understanding, by wisdom, and if the courtier takes seriously the injunction to reasonable service he must be prepared to search for the truth by going beyond the discussions of the opening section of the fourth book. Within *The Courtier* itself, this further search for truth is expressed by Bembo's concluding discourse. Ostensibly Bembo sets out to show how the courtier can be a lover of women as well as a prudent counselor, but in fact his account of the lover's ascent by a ladder of love to divine beauty transforms the courtier from a lover of women into a lover of wisdom, a philosopher in the root sense of the word. For the divine beauty to which the lover aspires as a result of the progressive discovery of the inadequacy of lower kinds of beauty is indistinguishable from the highest truth: "This is that beauty which is indistinguishable from the highest good, which by its light calls and draws all things unto itself, and not only gives intellect to intellectual things, reason to rational things, sense and appetite for life to sensual things, but to plants also and to stones it communicates motion and the natural instinct proper to them, as an imprint of itself." The inconclusiveness of the earlier discussions leads to the recognition that reasonable service depends upon knowledge. Only by the light of that ultimate divine truth and beauty by which all things are seen in their proper perspective will the answers to the particular and immediate questions of moral philosophy and reasonable service, questions such as Ottaviano raises but does not answer, fall into place.

Thus Bembo's discourse completes the presentation of courtiership by making us aware of the proper relationship between two ways of life—the active and the contemplative—that the Renaissance was accustomed to considering mainly in terms of opposition. The active life of courtly service must be founded upon the contemplative ascent to divine truth and beauty. In an explicit discussion of these two ways of life which occurs earlier in *The Courtier,* Ottaviano asserted that the prince ought to live so that he can participate in both activity and contemplation. Bembo indicates that this rule obtains for the courtier too. But he also indicates that the contemplative life should not be seen only or even primarily as the means to solving political and moral problems. For it stands as an end in itself, higher in kind even than the ends of activity. Indeed, contemplation appears to be the highest end for man, for in it "we shall find a most happy end to our desires, true rest from labors, sure remedy for miseries, most wholesome medicine for illnesses, safest refuge from the whirling storms of this life's tempestuous sea."

The double vision of divine truth and beauty, both as the only means to virtue and reasonable service and as man's highest end in and for itself, confronts the reader with a perplexing sense of the courtier's situation at the end of the book. What will draw him back to the world of courtly service once he has glimpsed a better home in contemplation, safe from "the whirling storms of life's tempestuous seas," safe from those forces of irrationality and disorder whose power is a recurrent theme throughout *The Courtier?* The courtier would seem to be left in the position of the philosopher at the beginning of the seventh book of *The Republic* who has escaped from the cave but who must return to it and direct its affairs in spite of the fact that he would prefer to stay entirely in the sun. What compulsion brings this philosopher back is not entirely clear, but he must return, and so, apparently, must the courtier. We know that Bembo, who must be acquainted with the vision he describes, is living as a courtier in Urbino; and we know that Castiglione's own life was steadily devoted to active service. Perhaps we can conclude that both lives, the active and the contemplative, are good in a way and necessary in a way; the contemplative is higher but the active is also noble and necessary. Bembo expresses the balance and complexity of his view most beautifully when he describes the experience of divine love paradoxically as "the beginning and end of all good": "Thou art father of true pleasures, of the graces, of peace, of gentleness and benevolence, enemy of boorish savagery and baseness—in short, the beginning and end of all good." Divine truth and beauty are the beginning and the end; the contemplation of them is the highest end of human life, but that contemplation is also to be understood as a beginning, the beginning of true courtiership, the beginning of a life of active service filled with grace, peace, gentleness, and benevolence, and free from boorish savagery and baseness.

Bembo's discourse, too, is both an end and a beginning; it provides a conclusion to the pattern of the work, and it also leaves its readers and the courtiers of Urbino poised at the beginning of the intellectual and spiritual ascent that they must make both for its own sake and to become perfect courtiers. Does Castiglione wish us to assume, then, that Bembo's listeners are in fact about to set out upon the most beautiful ascent? Apparently he does not. No doubt the mood of awed eagerness and expectancy that holds the group when Bembo stops speaking is sincerely felt, but it is also important that *The Courtier* does not end precisely at this high point. Instead, the elevated mood that Bembo has created is gradually allowed to dissipate in the last three sections of the book: as Emilia Pia plucks Bembo by the robe with a kind of mockery to break the spell of his words, as other courtiers add their comments, as the old, rather trivial quarrel over the relative merits of men and women returns to the surface, and as the sun comes up, a symbol of the light that Bembo's discourse has shed upon all the preceding discussions but also a reminder of mundane reality and the fact that it is past time to go to bed. With the great good humor and sense of comic irony that is characteristic of the whole book, these final sections impress upon us Castiglione's firm grasp of the dramatic reality of his characters. He is too shrewd not to know that men like Ludovico and Federico are not to be transformed into philosophers, into seekers after divine truth, by a single speech, no matter how eloquent. He is too honest and too keenly aware, as the first two books demonstrate, of the limitations of even the best group of courtiers to try to persuade us that they have been miraculously changed for the better. They have been moved, but Bembo's elevation and intensity are too much to sustain for a group in which concern for mere *sprezzatura* runs so deep. Ludovico's opinion notwithstanding, virtue is not easy to attain. *The Courtier* points out the path to perfection to those courtiers who are able to see it and willing to follow it, but at the same time the book leaves us with a clear and unsentimental image of the gap that in reality separates most courtiers from this path. (pp. 283-97)

Dain A. Trafton, "Structure and Meaning in 'The Courtier'," in English Literary Renaissance, *Vol. 2, No. 3, Autumn, 1972, pp. 283-97.*

RICHARD A. LANHAM   (essay date 1976)

[*Lanham is an American educator and essayist on rhetoric and literature. In the following excerpt, he examines* The Courtier *as a work written in a style that juxtaposes two otherwise distinct orchestrations of reality: the "rhetorical" and the "serious" worldviews.*]

The conversation [in *Il libro del Cortegiano*] is built upon a series of speeches, and takes its meaning from their relation to the layers of context enclosing them. The book is self-conscious about language from the beginning; style and usage are discussed as such, transcended also in a final, or perhaps semifinal, sublime *Altitudo.* Castiglione employs generic layering to prohibit any single-orchestration coziness. He leads us in several directions at once. *The Courtier,* though obviously in the mirror-of-princes tradition, displaces the stress slightly—with a tacit shrug at real princes—from the prince onto his courtier, and then displaces it further by discussing the court lady sympathetically. Castiglione invokes the shade of ideal *res publica* too, of Plato's *Republic* as well as Xenophon's mirror, the *Cyropaedia.* He stands, as well, self-consciously in the Ciceronian shadow of *De Oratore*—fairly enough, considering his debt to it. Thus he offers a rhetorical treatise, too. Much of the Ciceronian borrowing comes in a section on comedy which recalls the joke book. But a persistent philosophic concern balances this frivolity, moves *The Courtier* toward Platonic dialogue. The anatomy of love and sexuality recalls the *Symposium* especially. Indeed, Castiglione's structural thinking may have started there. A philosophical treatise, then, as well as a political and educational one, it is also a basic etiquette handbook, superficial only in theorizing about the social surface. So often has *The Courtier* been called aristocratic that we might stress this last bourgeois purpose, concern with getting the social surface right. An aristocrat does not ponder the surface so. He floats on it. Again generic tension: aristocratic lightness contends with bourgeois didacticism. Castiglione casts himself as a social

historian too. His book portrays an Urbino vanished, an Urbino almost golden. All the basic historiographic questions— what we can know of the past, how and why we know it— suggest themselves and find implicit answers. *The Courtier* becomes, considered as history, almost a "faction," a fiction from real life, halfway between life and art. Past and present, self and city, poetic and historic reality, all work together.

The basic preoccupations of the commentary . . . indicate a document built on the rhetorical view of life: tone, seriousness, structure. How are we to take such a book? When is it serious? How does Bembo's sublimity follow from the frivolities preceding? Castiglione invokes the broadest range of serious topics and considers them in a frivolous temper and tempo. He makes, as with *Gargantua and Pantagruel,* a book which is no one single thing, he calculates a form which prohibits specialization. Yet the subject is clear and clearly in the title, an exercise in definition: all things lead toward defining the courtier. Castiglione reveals his theme by placing the whole of *The Courtier* in a matrix of game. Seriousness, thus deliberately posed, must become the main concern. It is all a game—"the best game that could possibly be played." But, since "game" is never defined, neither is the tone of what follows. Motive, sublimity, love, decorum, all come to share a common ontological peril. And the courtier they create—is he the image of Western man or a social butterfly? Can Castiglione have posed this question by accident? He seems deliberately to juxtapose two fundamentally opposed orchestrations of reality, the two conceptions of man we have been considering, rhetorical man and serious man, the rhetorical and the serious views of the world. His strategy juxtaposes them to create a new definition of seriousness, a model of motive for a renewedly self-conscious Western man.

The Courtier reports a game. We can think of games as essentially separate from life (comment on, preparation for, whatever) or as quintessential, human culture itself a game. The first is a serious view, obviously, and the second rhetorical. We can read *The Courtier* with either assumption. In the first, the game will remain just that, a game. The possibilities for the courtier will remain exercises in possibility. No opinion, however serious in itself, will be advanced seriously. All figure as counters in a debating game. The aim will be not truth but rhetorical victory. All motives will be game motives, rhetorical, *ad hoc* and *ad hominem.* The grand design strives but to pass time, to entertain, please, embroider an idle hour. Castiglione means to urge this view upon us. The courtier game is not the first game suggested. The game begins with a game to select the worthiest game, the game "piú degno di celebrarsi in questa compagnia." Emilia's motives for suggesting *her* game are suitably rhetorical and self-interested: little blame and less labor. And the object of the game is suitably ludic: to suggest the game worthiest to be played, most entertaining. Thus the *motive* for the proposals is ludic, to win the game of suggesting the game. The suggestions, like everything else in *The Courtier,* run the gamut from Cesare Gonzaga's moralizing, "Let each confess a characteristic folly," to fra Serafino's demande, "onde è che le donne quasi tutte hanno in odio i ratti, ed aman le serpi"— why all women hate rats and love snakes.

After Ottaviano's suggestion halfway between, Federico Fregoso advances the winner—forming the perfect courtier, "esplicando tutte le condizioni e particular qualità che si richieggono a chi merita questo nome." It pleases Emilia and the Duchess—whereupon everyone agrees that this is the best game that could be played ("il piú bel gioco che far si potesse"). **The Courtier** is rich in such subtle qualifications. They like the game because the Duchess and Emilia like it. And why do these two ladies like it? Because it flatters them. **The Courtier** can tell us how to flatter without seeming to, and no better illustration than here. The game is the best, because the most *flattering*, the most narcissistic, that could possibly be played. They will *always*, whatever they say, talk of themselves.

Thus motive has been qualified at two removes before the game begins. Emilia, to start it, qualifies motive yet further. Ludovico is selected as master of ceremonies, πατηρ λογου, for rhetorical rather than serious purposes, because he will certainly be contentious ("perché, dicendo ogni cosa al contrario, come speramo che farete, il gioco sarà piú bello"). He accepts in just this spirit. He will not put off his task a night and think. That would constitute the wrong kind of challenge, tax diligence rather than quickness of wit. Instead he will improvise. If with approval, he will have won a bigger bet unprepared; if not, he will be excused by not having given the matter previous thought.

He continues, in a remarkable speech, to push the matter even further into the game sphere: "dico, che in ogni cosa tanto è difficil conoscer la vera perfezion, che quasi è impossibile; e questo per la varietà dé guidicii." An ideal is impossible and it is not, and anyway it is all a matter of opinion. People differ not only with each other but with themselves: "Né io già contrasterò che 'l mio sia migliore che 'l vostro; ché non solamente a voi po parer una cosa ed a me un'altra, ma a me stesso poría parer or una cosa ed ora un'altra." The matter could not well be rendered more conjectural and frivolous than this extended and involved narrative machinery renders it.

The rhetorical context perseveres. We never forget that each speaker speaks in attack or defense, from egotism. Everyone impugns everyone else's motives as a matter of course as well as of jest. Nearly every speech begins or ends with laughter, and most aim to evoke it. Arguments are held lightly, as counters, shields, weapons. Much debate has contested what Castiglione "really thought" about the issues at stake. Manifestly such an environment makes it impossible to know what *anyone* really thinks. This is a game, not life. Nobody is serious, except perhaps Bembo, who loses control and floats upward like a gas-filled balloon.

If we come to **The Courtier** with a serious referent reality then, and a serious referent self, we shall find a narrative carefully prepared and consistently sustained as a game, a rhetorical contest. The behavior *within* the game is completely rhetorical, of course. Pose, not central self, victory not truth, pleasure not improvement, prevail. Pleasure is the presiding deity. Every time the discussion, silly or significant, threatens boredom, Emilia or the Duchess cuts it off. We are free, of course, to take the opinions expressed as seriously as we choose. But the narrative, by definition of the game, can offer no help. If you want to take a game seriously, that is your probably tedious business.

If we approach **The Courtier** with rhetorical coordinates, however, a curious transformation comes over it. The game of courtier, far from being one they "have never played," becomes one that they play every day. The game becomes *realistic*, a straightforward mimesis of a dramatic reality. Now Castiglione encourages us to apply rhetorical coordinates as

much as he encourages serious ones. **The Courtier** is, after all, a portrait of aristocratic Urbino. Games are taken to be its most characteristic reality. Urbino succeeds at these things much better than other places. Clearly Urbino's ideality in some way emerges from the idea of game. Serious life, war, and politics aim at creating the climate of aristocratic leisure in which such activities flourish. They provide the justifying activity for the state. Furthermore, the very narcissism of the game encourages us to apply rhetorical coordinates. The players talk about themselves, about the ideal forms which they wish their lives to approximate, and these all amount to a dramatic reality and a dramatic self. Their game is reflexive, an anatomy of their everyday lives, a game about a game. Thus, paradoxically, we come to take the arguments themselves *seriously*. There is no "as if" about them. We are being admitted behind the scenes. This game is special. As Castiglione emphasizes at the beginning, a special mood of festivity prevails. We might call it group confessional, therapy. So emerges the special typicality, as it were, of this game, and the reason why a game is chosen as Urbino's characteristic activity: the game symbolizes the kind of seriousness Castiglione sees Urbino as representing, the characteristic seriousness, he suggests, of human life.

We are invited, then, to read **The Courtier** in two ways at once. The two ways stand fundamentally opposed. Castiglione's narrative strategy aims to bring all that he discusses under this double gaze. Can we hold both ways of seeing in the mind at once? **The Courtier** trains us. It does so by rapid temporal alternation, by continually switching back and forth. The speeches in **The Courtier** are often long, long enough at least to catch us up in matter rather than rhetorical stance. Then we are pulled back into the argument, laughed at, scorned, whatever. We recoil into a rhetorical world, only to be caught up again in serious reality. Thus on a small scale the oscillation works—if we read seriously. If rhetorically, the opposite happens. We are always returned to seriousness when we return to rhetorical interchange, to game when we return to matter. Castiglione has taken the speech-narrative-speech alternation and superencrypted two contrary patterns of expectation above it. . . . As a result, we move continually in and out of seriousness, stay always in motion. We never adopt one relation to the world without lively awareness that we might have adopted the other.

Such a narrative method by nature discourages static analysis. You can see only half the process at once. You must keep moving. And the whole process will be isomorphic only with the whole book. (This is one reason why Castiglione wants the structure open-ended and repetitive, and ends by recalling *another* conversation the following night.) If you isolate a part of it, fail to reckon in the whole narrative context, you will not understand that part. It is a long book and the duration of real time required to read it, as with *The Faerie Queene* or *Clarissa*, makes a difference. It takes time to train us as we pass through. For we are asked to learn not a pattern of concepts—of whatever sort—but a skill. Reading **The Courtier** is like learning to ride a bicycle, not like learning about Renaissance Platonism. Critical analysis, though needed, defeats its own purpose and **The Courtier**'s. Worry about *how* you ride a bicycle and you fall off. So, here, Castiglione tries to teach us a skill, an intuitive not a conscious, considered response. No surprise, this. The theme of intuitive judgment, intuitive response, runs through **The Courtier** from first to last. To think about response inevitably spoils it. Yet it must be thought on. Castiglione solves the paradox by putting it in motion, alternating nature and nurture concurrently. No real syncretism is involved. That would degrade the interaction. Oscillation is recommended, not blending. Such a process wars with logic, of course, as it is intuition's business to do. As we read we are not always to remember how we read it. Again like *The Faerie Queene*, *The Courtier* requests a selective forgetting. And to be understood, it demands our repeated experience of itself. It trains us in intuitive knowing, in a skill. What is known is not a collection of objects but a corresponding process. Thus *The Courtier* is by design no one thing. Castiglione seeks to build a dynamic not a static model of man and his society. And so the problem of structure, of narrative context, looms so large. Here is where, how, the process is created.

We become, put through Castiglione's course, the prime pupils of Western literature. The two fundamental categories this literature seeks to express here find their fundamental, alternating pattern. Our experience in reading is designed to parallel the courtier's experience at court. We too alternate serious and rhetorical views, learn and forget, pose spontaneously, develop a talent for, a skill in, living.

Castiglione makes this clear enough. He bludgeons us at the beginning with his central concept—*sprezzatura*. The term's manifest absurdity—a certain carefully rehearsed and prepared spontaneous unrehearsedness—disappears if it describes a process taking place over time. A skill. The company is talking about grace. Cesare Gonzaga asks Count Ludovico how it can be acquired. The Count replies by invoking rhetorical coordinates: "Obligato non son io . . . ad insegnarvi a diventar aggraziati, né altro; ma solamente a dimostrarvi qual abbia ad essere un perfetto Cortegiano." He has undertaken not to teach grace but only to model a perfect courtier. Having reinvoked the rhetorical coordinates he transcends them to discuss seriously how to teach grace, or rather whom to steal it from: "così il nostro Cortegiano averà da rubare questa grazia da que' che a lui parerà che la tenghino. . . ." Then comes the famous passage on sprezzatura, the art of concealing art, of unaffected affectation:

> But having thought often already about where this grace comes from, excluding those who were born with it, I find one universal rule, which seems valid to me above all others in human affairs, whether in acting or speaking. That is to flee as much as you can—as if it were a very rough, perilous rock—affectation. And, to coin a new word perhaps, to observe in all behavior a certain *sprezzatura*, so that art is hidden and whatever is said and done seems without effort or forethought. From this, I believe, a great deal of grace comes. Everyone knows the difficulty of unusual, well done things, and so ability in such things causes very great wonder. To labor, on the other hand and, as who should say, to drag forth by the hair of the head, seems most ungraceful and makes us disesteem something, however marvelous it may be.

A rationale for hypocrisy certainly, within serious coordinates at least. Rhetorically, it is honest posing. Castiglione wants both. Affectation is not to be banished for romantic sincerity. In that sense, he obviously thought *nothing* natural to man. The alternative is a fully learned, complete possession of an attribute. We make it ours through the repeated acting out which naturalizes it, makes it a completely learned skill. No paradox haunts spontaneity's being a skill. What else can it be?

Castiglione sets out in *The Courtier* to describe the courtier's "parts," catalog his attributes. At the beginning, he is careful to specify how they are to be possessed, the spirit in which they are to be exercised. Sprezzatura retains the force of its parent verb. It involves disdain. It declares, brags about, successful enselfment, a permanent incorporation in, addition to, the self. It satisfies because it publicly declares an enlarged self. One has *acquired* an area of *instinctive* response. And the audience response certifies it, makes it real. Thus the self is enriched, amplified, and as sign of amplification comes the effortlessness, the sprezzatura. What Castiglione has done here is to model the growth of the self, a growth equally narcissistic, equally dependent on audience, on, as G. H. Mead puts it, a "generalized other." Such a growth, as Mead describes it in *Mind, Self, and Society,* indeed involves a process, a continual interchange. Each individual must learn, in addition to a symbolic vocabulary of word and gesture, how to read his own gestures as others read them. He must, as he grows up, through the repeated dramatic interchanges of socialization learn how to reenact both the roles which constitute his own self and the roles of others which respond to his own. He must grow up, that is, as a miniature narcissistic drama. The success his self will find, the fullness, the joy, will depend on how well he has deposited the dramatic reality of his society within his own personality. The hoary issues of sincerity fail to arise here because the model is dynamic not static, process not entity. The self at any time comprises a series of experiences and potential experiences, drama enacted and yet to be. If Castiglione is a behaviorist, he is Mead's kind of behaviorist, a dynamic one. Man cannot know naive response. Our attention starts out selective, nature and nurture in dynamic alternation.

It follows that we cannot cut our selves loose from the society which creates and sustains them. The pressure to do so persists, to be sure, never more than now. Castiglione must come to terms with it too, as we see in Bembo's Platonic sublimity. But the model of self Castiglione invokes by his discussion and dramatization of sprezzatura denies such radical sublimity, such an independent self. It is not forbidden. It is impossible.

Identity, the self, in such a theory proves then both process and skill. No eleatic substance informs it. A process, a drama, as Castiglione saw it, a game. Thus *The Courtier*'s narcissistic form is not simply a happy choice. Given what Castiglione had to say, it is inevitable. If Mead is right, the creation of the self means continuous drama, and drama sustains the self once created. Such a conception of self does not advocate hypocrisy. It simply places it, shows it as part of a larger process. . . . Sincerity, then, full expression of the self, depends on the opportunities for expression society affords it. And so Urbino becomes the main character in *The Courtier.* Like the self, it emerges as process not entity. Its history must be literary, dramatic. Its essence can be preserved no other way.

Urbino is sustained by the same kind of skill which sustains the selves who compose it. The courtier game is played with sprezzatura, and the game sustains the state. The game enshrines the state's ultimate purpose, an ideal individual. The game supplies an ideal toward which the state moves, and, since the ideal is social, by implication an ideal state as well. But priority matters: Plato talks of a state; Castiglione talks of an individual. Again, stasis and dynamism. Plato's ideal commonwealth, like More's, strives for an ideal stasis. A conception of self like Castiglione's—genesis and continuance—prohibits such a stasis. Things must continue to change in order to continue to exist. The state, like the individual, must develop in order to continue being itself. As Ortega reminds us in *La rebelión de las masas,* "La nación está siempre o haciéndose o deshaciéndose. *Tertium non datur."* The process must be reasoned upon, self-consciously entertained, yet spontaneous—inevitably a game and entertained as such. Yet its citizens must be committed to it, citizens, not visiting anthropologists. Citizenship, ideally, emerges from **The Courtier** as a skill much like selfhood. The same technique is required—holding opposite worlds in the mind at once. When the conversation turns to serious themes, as it seems, in book four, Ottaviano poses the hard question. Is the courtier useful, or an ornamental butterfly? Castiglione's bitterness threatens to overflow the fictional measure just here. He casts the princes of his time as symbols of human corruption, . . . and to their allegory of fallen man the courtier must play an allegorical poet. Ottaviano's argument, as he develops it, insists that the courtier will affect politics by playing poet-of-the-public-life, by connecting the good with the pleasurable and thus bridging the gap in our fallen nature. Castiglione has not been sufficiently praised for thus prophetically charting the dramatistic ingredient in the politics of a self-conscious state. Whether Castiglione was monarchist or republican seems irrelevant. Either form of government must make terms with pleasure-loving sinful man. The crucial issue remains, how? Artful, well-directed flattery. No reader of **The Courtier** ought be surprised. Artful flattery holds Urbino together. People continually stroke each other, put the best construction on events. They often, too, apply the worst construction—and then soften this with flattery. The serious reader demands a more vigorous accounting—moral confrontation, satiric scorn at least. Castiglione never allows it. He writes about style as ingratiation. The courtier cannot change reality. It will be a drama of some sort. He must become expert in drama, in stylistic manipulation, so that it will be convincing drama.

The politician, then, will play both poet and critic by turns, acting and assessing the acting of others. Such purely rhetorical coordinates observe no difference between being and doing, between active and contemplative life. In such a process, the need for an either/or distinction evaporates and both poet and critic assume their essential places in the state. Their roles, though, reverse what proverbial wisdom requires. Poets supply the day-to-day expertise, the needful conversions to pleasure; the practical serious men design the Utopias, tell the state where to go. Art is a necessity for man, but a practical not a theoretical or ornamental one.

A poetic lurks in all of this, as in all political theory. Obviously enough, it centers on pleasure. Literature's job, like the job of **The Courtier** itself, seems to be reality-maintenance. Literature maintains reality by continually rehearsing it. We are led to conclude with Castiglione that politics is most often played for its own sake, for fun, just to assure us that we are alive. Politics is as literary as life, perhaps more so. It seldom "debates the issues" because the real "issue" is the act of debating. Literature creates a similar reality but does not pretend so often to purposeful action. The politician as poet and critic must stay alert, skillful, in continually moving from purpose to game, serious to rhetorical coordinates, as circumstances require. He must know in his bones what to take seriously, when to play and maintain reality, or to be serious and destroy in order to rebuild it. The game sphere provides the

home of pleasure. The job of literature, like the job of politics, is to harmonize and space these journeys home and to fructify them. For both literature and politics, the self represents a more efficient version of the state. The back-and-forth motion is quicker. In this respect, indeed, we might parallel art and self. Both embody condensed, more efficient versions of the public polity, the process on a reduced scale. We must beware of thinking the individual stabler, less a process, than the state because on a smaller scale. The self is no more or less an entity than the state.

The self emerges from **The Courtier,** then, as aesthetic rather than moral entity, as a matter, finally, of taste. Castiglione depicts a self built from the outside in. To know people, we argue from the surface back, from the allegory of clothes and gesture, from the psychopathology of everyday life that men are largely known by. . . . We are not born with an authentic central self. We try to create one. The central self is a skill, instinctive good drama. This does not imply a naive behaviorism—we are merely roles. We are a process which has its genesis in roles, but grows into a characteristically human combination of self-consciousness and skill. The central self is not a substance but an effect, successful process. Castiglione's comparison of this effect with grace exposes the point. We cannot strive for authenticity, for a real self. Like happiness, it seems to come *en passant.* We act in the world inevitably within a matrix of our own interests. We hope these will yield a genuine self, but no inevitability governs the process.

What misleads us are the occupational psychoses our purposes create in each of us. We are formed by our purposes, become the creation of our desires. Surely here emerges the morality in Castiglione's study of the surface. He wants to reverse the process, recommend purposes which will yield a central self. He becomes, seen thus, not scorner of the central self, but a chief defender and prophet. The whole courtier portrait is calculated to yield a central self, not, of course, through naive experience—in Castiglione's view there isn't any naive experience—but through knowledge of the surface. The central self is to be sought through self-consciousness, not around it. So Castiglione proceeds to rearrange purposive life to yield the rich self he wishes to portray. Resources for converting purposive life into game, and thus allowing it to create and reinforce a self, crowd around us. Man will not use them. He wants desperately to return to naive experience, to be a first Adam.

It is, then, a profound mistake to consider Urbino a leisure-class state. Urbino knows no leisure at all, just as self-conscious man knows no leisure in the world. He is either making or unmaking himself. *Tertium non datur.* What Urbino aristocrats *can* do is confront this calculus more directly than most of us do. But the calculus itself is undeniable: They have nothing to do but play games. Pure leisure. They make up games. The best game that can be played? The creation of an ideal self. They must then—*to be more themselves,* to raise the temperature of reality—imitate the ideal. Farewell leisure. It is of course an artificial goal, and narcissistic. But are our own "practical" purposes not both these to a fantastic degree? "O reason not the need," Lear agonizes under the whips of usefulness. We can, then, refute the charge that **The Courtier** presents a decorative, narcissistic, useless theory of identity simply by accepting this theory as a realistic imitation of life. Our purposes are more decorative and narcissistic, less purposive, than we want to admit. In a sense such narcissistic decoration is the most purposive of all. It sustains

Autograph of Castiglione.

reality. Again, we don't want to admit this. Reality is *just there,* like the *self.* It needs no maintenance. Castiglione was not so soft-headed.

He thus plots out a full cycle of address to the world, a model for motive. We begin in pure play. We have nothing to do. We invent games to amuse ourselves. But the appetite comes in eating. These games grow purposive. We have become committed to purposes and these change us, form our self, invigorate it or deny it, stunt it. If the game maximizes our pleasures, enriches the self and fulfills it, renders it capable of genuine moral choice, it will be in truth the best game that could possibly be played. For goodness in Castiglione's world is an action too, process, not reified substance. Goodness must be enacted. It must form part of us, a skill not an external ethic. Castiglione wishes to internalize ethics, to transfer its domain, make it grow with the self rather than against it. He comes to terms with pleasure and he finds the final source of pleasure to be progressive enrichment of the self. I have been glossing a dictum of Whitehead's: "Style is the ultimate morality of mind." Castiglione chronicled the social surface but he also pondered it. He saw clearly that for self-conscious man ethics was, initially if not entirely, a matter of style. It would have to orchestrate ornament before it could plead to essentials because only by the orchestration of ornament could it create the essentials it would plead to.

Castiglione merits admiration not least for his steady resistance to satire, his reluctance to debunk. Material lies ready to hand in *The Courtier* for radical exposure of "real" motive, backstage debunking of Urbino. Castiglione sees further. He refuses to accept any single range of motive as referential, to interpret all others as only a disguised version of the referent, be this economic, psychoanalytical, religious. One might almost call him a "rebunker," concerned as he is to show how different ranges of motive can reinforce one another. All things can be known in terms of other things—and only thus. . . . Part of his redefinition of seriousness comes as an understated, implicit war on dogmatism, on the robust confidence that life within a single orchestration engenders. He wants to credit the other fellow's reality, stands ready to embrace customs radically different from his own. He thus verifies rhetorical motive while he exposes it.

It follows, incidentally, from this willingness to entertain alternate realities that *The Courtier*'s comedy must be an unconventional kind. Theories of comedy fall into two categories, absolute and normative. In absolute theories, comedy is created by measuring, by whatever manipulation of time and space scale, an aberrant performance against "reality." This is serious comedy in its pure form and it can be serious indeed. All such theories depend on a preexistent serious reality and central self, and on a referent motive-system depending from them. Such a theory might be Fielding's theory, as expressed in the preface to *Joseph Andrews:* comedy exposes pretended motive. Or Bergson's: the real nature of man is elastic and so inelasticity seems comic. But what if no set of motives is more real than another? What if inelasticity is as natural to man as elasticity—or anything else? What happens to comedy without a referent reality? When it is denied its redefining complementary, tragedy?

Obviously it then invents a temporary god's-eye view, usually called decorum, contingent external sanction, social norm. The reasoning back to norm can remain the same and, since day-to-day dealings with reality remain largely normative, comic power remains unimpaired. Castiglione's characters entertain a number of normative arguments, exhortations to observe *una certa onesta mediocrità.* But the mean is not an entity. It constitutes an empty category. It balances extremes, a moment of poise. It cannot be discussed except in terms of the extremes creating it. Again, process, oscillation. It thus needs comic excess in order to exist. The long section on comedy in **The Courtier** exemplifies as much as it theorizes. The comic corrective the extremes supply does not reveal the norm, it creates it. Folly is not just a diversion. It is a necessity. The middle path is then a skill like the self, a path among follies. So in **The Courtier** folly is almost cherished. A dynamic rather than a static model of the self inevitably produces this effect, throws the defining locus outward toward the defining extremes. The decorous norm is a *path,* hedged by the extremes at every point.

The Courtier, then, contains two theories of comedy corresponding to its two conceptions of reality. For serious reality, comedy is a corrective and the measure by a preexisting norm. Rhetorical comedy makes the process two-way. It accepts the measurement against norms. More fun lies that way. Comedy in **The Courtier** is fundamentally therapeutic, aims to *esilarar l'animo* and make us forget our troubles. The laughter emerges from a process of comparison circular, inevitable, and partly disingenuous. We reify the norm because it is more fun to do so, it puts more zest into our laughter. But we can—and at some stage should—reverse the polarity and admit the extremes as referent preexisting reality. The theory of comedy thus parallels in structure a theory of normative clarity in verbal utterance.

An apologist for rhetorical comedy would then stress comedy as pleasure rather than ethical restorative. Whether the comic theory be based on superiority, ambiguity, incongruity, or sudden deliverance, what takes our interest is the pleasure of the change. A norm may be inverted, that is, for pleasure rather than ethical measurement. A balanced view, a seriousness both rhetorical and serious, would alternate the two emphases, stress norm as product of both search for truth and search for pleasure. Normative judgments recur more commonly because they give more pleasure. Some such awareness may explain the lightness of Castiglione's touch, his reluctance to laugh aggressively. He is trying to establish a norm—and so by definition reform—but he wants to marshal the resources of social pleasure as well.

We can extract from the book's thinking about comedy a sketch not simply of a single norm, but of how to hold norms of any kind. Clearly, for Castiglione, language and behavior can be considered in the same terms. In both a norm, but a dynamic norm, ought to prevail. So the conversation on antique diction in book one suggests that Tuscan words should be known but seldom used. Extremes should enter as suggestive shadow, suggest meaning by their absence. Ludovico specifies for the courtier full and traditional verbal skills, which is to say fundamentally contradictory and confusing ones. So he insists that antique diction by itself cannot avail. We must have thought: "for to separate thoughts from words is to separate soul from body." Yet there must be good words and in good order, and with suitable gesture. Yet not too heavy, but expressed "sensibly in everything, with readiness and a lucid fullness . . . making every ambiguity clear and plain." Yet metaphorical when necessary, coined words if need be. Yet not so as to dazzle. And so on. We confront again the paradoxes of normative clarity. The style Ludovico describes is the successful style. It possesses no formal content at all. Anything can be permitted that works. Both the courtier and his speech come forward as normative portraits formed by extremes, and teachable only by imitation. Both advance a paradoxical ideal, visible invisibility. The style must be seen in order to work. In order to work, it must not be noticed. What Castiglione has done is to define the middle style, to show it as dynamic rather than empty. He emerges as the great apologist for the middle style. If the successful self consists of a process, a dynamic interchange, so does the middle style. It has no discrete formal content. It is an attitude, a skill. The oscillation from one kind of self to another finds parallel here in the oscillation from word to concept and back. Just as the successful self has built into its creative apparatus a "generalized other," so the mature stylist has internalized his own sense of decorum, poise between extremes. Sprezzatura means the same thing for both verbal style and life-style. It means success. Like verbal clarity, it is an artificial state, projects an idiosyncratic moment of poise. Just so with successfully presenting a public self. Oddly enough, what has seemed central to seriousness for verbal style has seemed frivolity itself for life-style, yet "sincerity" means the same thing in both: successful illusion.

So close stand the two kinds of style that Castiglione may be used to exemplify a typical Renaissance process: personality theory formed on the analogy of rhetorical theory. Or, put another way, the progressive realization that all rhetorical theory implied—close under the surface—a theory of personality. The style was indeed the man. And the man was less a work of art, as Burckhardt thought him, than a work of rhetoric. The parts of speech and the "parts" of a man could be discussed with the same vocabulary, within the same theory of decoration. For both man and speech, Castiglione provided, in addition to a set of specific ornaments, a theory of ornament. He showed how, working inward from the circumference, ornament defines an essential man, supplies a center.

But the self can be authenticated in the opposite way, by positing a center through sublime exaltation. Castiglione's decision to include this choice has puzzled posterity. What relation does Bembo's soaring hymn to love bear to the sophisticated comedy preceding? As with the *Phaedrus,* how can we connect the discussion of style with that of love? The obvious answer talks about the styles of love. Such talk exists in **The Courtier** but it does not interest Bembo. It is just this he flees. He yearns for a retreat from, transcendence of, all style. He wants to confront essence rather than process, pure subject.

We are left on our own in assessing Bembo's sudden inspiration. He is heard with profound attention but also with comic interruption, Signor Morello playing that role stoutly by insisting that old men can still make love. Bembo is not challenged as to his arguments, except by the whole of **The Courtier** preceding. The speech ends **The Courtier** but it does not end the debate. That will resume the next night, and continue, presumably—since the debate allegorizes culture, represents our self-reflexive efforts to understand ourselves—forever. We are left to construe Bembo's oration as we choose; we can soar with him or stay on the ground. To soar is tempting. *The Courtier* then becomes something like a complete spectrum of human involvement in the world, our full model for motive. We begin in pure play, at leisure, debating for the fun of it. We get progressively more caught up in the game. It becomes ever more serious, modulating from surface ornaments to essential attributes of self, politics and the public life, love and the private. The self becomes ever more serious, finally moving from the game sphere to sublimity, from process to essence. The book and the enselfing process the book describes thus find a proper conclusion, end in apotheosis. A parallel development in style moves from early preoccupation with surface to final transcendence of it, moves from the world's mortal beauty to an indwelling immanence beyond style. The ritual of love serves here as paradigm for the whole stylistic address toward life. The book then moves from a closed circle of play to a certification of self beyond it. It carries us as far as words can go and then, like Bembo, leaves the remaining rungs of the ladder to each of us alone. The concluding mysticism is designedly ecumenical, equal parts Christianity and Platonism. It absolves us of self-consciousness, pours the self into a union beyond human contrivance. It leads us out of the wilderness of game.

We may thus think of Bembo's mysticism as completing what has gone before or as contradicting it. Castiglione takes pains not to force the issue. If we want a god's-eye view, a perspective from the eighth sphere, he provides one, takes us at least as far as man can. If we doubt such a perspective exists, we are free to view Bembo as the author of *Gli Asolani,* an outstanding spokesman of fashionable Platonism—another spokesman for another style. *The Courtier* is a game in which people entertain theories because the theories entertain them. Platonism earns no exemption. If Bembo wants to heat his mind with incredibilities, the conversational framework proves wide enough to contain him. But it does not certify him, any more than it certifies any other attitude. Bembo's search for the center may lead to heaven or to heavenly sentimentality. We choose our own compass points. *The Courtier* shows us how to leave process for essence, but, like Chaucer's *Troilus,* it does not itself do so. Sublimity can be thought of as a skill as well as a transport. It may lead back to game as well as out of it.

Castiglione frames his book in a context which intensifies our choice rather than simplifying it. He characterizes his task, in the opening letter to Don Michel de Silva [see excerpt dated 1528], as erecting a pious memorial to Urbino, and at the beginning of each book he includes a proleptic necrology. Castiglione frames the whole *Courtier* in the pathos of death and time. Here is a final seriousness if you like. (pp. 144-63)

Castiglione seems a decorative rather than an essential Platonist. Bembo may be right, but perhaps he is not, perhaps the only finality is old age, death, and the sadness they bring. Carefully, then, as Castiglione imitates the structure of the *Symposium,* he finally chooses an opposite strategy: the seriousness of *The Courtier* remains man-made. It finds less the footprint of God Bembo seeks than the ambiguous, posing, and imposing footprints of man. (p. 164)

Richard A. Lanham, "The Self as Middle Style: 'Cortegiano',"in his The Motives of Eloquence: Literary Rhetoric in the Renaissance, *Yale University Press, 1976, pp. 144-64.*

J. R. WOODHOUSE   (essay date 1978)

[*In the following excerpt, Woodhouse places* The Courtier *within its historical and cultural context as an educational handbook in the Renaissance humanist tradition.*]

One of the glories of Castiglione's native city was the tradition of humanist education instituted by Vittorino Rambaldino da Feltre (1378-1446) under the patronage of Gianfrancesco Gonzaga, first marquis of Mantua. Vittorino had studied at Padua under Giovanni di Conversino da Ravenna (1343-1408); among his fellow-students had been Pier Paolo Vergerio (1370-1444), whose treatise on education, the *De ingenuis moribus,* was to prove one of the most popular handbooks of the Renaissance. In his youth Castiglione had not been immune to that educational revolution and his letters home on the subject of his son's education, as well as the variety of training and accomplishments of his courtier, reflect the influence of that great tradition. At this point then, it would seem fitting to consider more fully to what extent Castiglione's opinions coincided with the educational aspirations of the Renaissance humanists. Such a survey might appropriately begin with one of the most important discoveries of the early Renaissance—the twelve Books of Quintilian's *De institutione oratoria (On the education of the Orator),* which formed the theoretic basis for many of the reforms of Vergerio and his successors.

Marcus Fabius Quintilianus (c.A.D. 35-c. 95) had been renowned among his contemporaries as something more than a guide to oratory, and though modern Classical scholarship tends to value highly his literary critical opinions, the Renaissance, rather like his own contemporary and fellow-Spaniard, Martial, regarded him as the 'supreme guide of wayward youth'. The breadth and wisdom of the views he expressed (particularly in Books I, II and XII of the *Institutio*) were especially influential for the humanist educational ideal. They find an echo throughout the *Cortegiano,* either as the result of Castiglione's personal acquaintance with Quintilian or as the filtered product of a century of educational theory based in large part on his work. (p. 38)

Quintilian had used Cicero's *Orator* and the *De oratore* as sources for some of his comments; indeed, his debt to Cicero is acknowledged at many points. The rediscovery of the *De oratore,* therefore, in 1422, reinforced humanist appreciation of Quintilian's great precepts, and the humanists even more readily seized upon his purpose—to provide an all-round education which was designed to produce not pedants but men of high moral character and general culture. That need is stressed particularly in Book II of the *Institutio,* which also discusses the qualifications of the good teacher and the proper treatment of pupils. The early education of the future 'orator' is dealt with in Book I, which contains a discussion of the home environment, the influence on the pupil of those persons most likely to come into contact with him, such as nurse, parents, and the slave, who would be, in a very literal sense, his 'pedagogue' or $\pi\alpha\iota\delta\alpha\gamma\omega\gamma\sigma\delta$. There, too, is underlined the importance of a thorough study of Latin and the need for a knowledge of Greek. The same preoccupations are later to be displayed in Castiglione's correspondence with his mother on the education of his son, Camillo. (pp. 39-40)

There are striking similarities of tone between Quintilian and Castiglione. Just as Castiglione's final book rises to a pitch of enthusiasm which approaches Christian gospelling, so Quintilian's paean of praise to his *orator perfectus* becomes almost religious. And both men recall in their words the Aristotelean type of eulogy to the very human ideal which all should emulate. . . . 'Let us strive to this end with all our mental powers and let us work at this task. We may even attain to our ideal. For, if Nature does not prohibit the combination of moral and rhetorical perfection, why may one single man not achieve both ideals?' (*Institutio,* XII, i, 31). But, although this seems an idealistic conclusion, the practicality of Quintilian's purpose for the tormented Renaissance (and for the uncertainties of life at court) is borne out by his stoic and contemplative, and more personal conclusion: 'Now secluded and venerated, free from envy, far from controversy, his fame will be safe, and he will receive, in his own lifetime, that reverence which is usually reserved for his posthumous reputation, and he will see how his own posterity will assess him' (ibid.). The words have an uncanny relevance for Castiglione.

The early humanists had defended their love of the new learning with all the subtlety they knew. Coluccio Salutati (1331-1406), for example, justified the study of poetry on the grounds that the whole of the Bible was a great poem. More specifically, in a letter of 1401, he tells Giovanni Dominici (1357-1419) how a deeper knowledge of the Classics aids towards more accurate interpretations of the Bible and Church Fathers, and how an acquaintance with allegory and symbolism is almost a prerequisite for scholars hoping to understand, for instance, the secrets of the Apocalypse. The debate on the usefulness or morality of Classical studies, as opposed to the revealed truth of Christianity often finds echoes in the early humanist educators. Thus Leonardo Bruni (1369-1444) in his *De studiis et litteris,* pays lip-service to the need for the educated woman to study the Scriptures, but emphasises above all the moral benefits which may be simultaneously derived from reading the Classics. And, conversely, San Bernardino (1380-1444), while he stresses the need for Christian faith in whatever training a person undergoes, and while he enjoins upon his flock the avoidance of blatantly 'immoral' texts (such as Ovid or the Boccaccio visible in the *Corbaccio*), nevertheless has an attitude to the past not dissimilar to Machiavelli's, and suggests that by reading the Apostles and Church Fathers, one can communicate directly with them. 'Wouldn't you find immense pleasure in seeing or hearing Jesus Christ preaching? Immense indeed! Does the same apply for St Paul, St Augustine, St Gregory, St Jerome and St Ambrose, and the other holy doctors? Of course! Then go and read their books . . . and you will speak with them and they with you; they will hear you and you them, and you will derive great delight from it' (San Bernardino, *Prediche,* III). And in Bernardino's eulogy of education and learning we see a hint of the universal man, qualified to do anything, go anywhere, able to overcome the blows of fortune. Education or study for Bernardino was useful to the individual for benefiting his family, his city and his friends. Through study he would then be able to show his face in every country in the world and before every and any lord, and become a Man (while without study he would be a nonentity) (ibid.). Significantly the same Sermon preaches, as a necessary precondition for the attainment of such freedom-through-study, the need for tranquillity—freedom, that is, from fear and from presumption, the avoidance of dissipating one's energies in frivolity or in melancholy, the avoidance of excessive love of anything except study, and the avoidance of hatred of all

things. The catalogue begins to sound like a plea for the Aristotelean Golden Mean, an impression confirmed by the physical Means adduced—eat and sleep in moderation, etc., all extremes are vicious.

Those ideas are to recur throughout the history of educational theory and practice, both among Bernardino's contemporaries and during the following decades, notably in the *De educatione liberorum clarisque eorum moribus* of Maffeo Vegio (1407-58). Indeed, so closely are educational and humanistic ideals bound up during the fifteenth century that it would be an artificial distinction to separate out those treatises, such as the *De ingenuis moribus* of Pier Paolo Vergerio, from the more general political, economic or social preoccupations of his time.

Vergerio's treatise enjoyed enormous popularity for the two hundred years following its composition, not only because of its erudite good sense, but also because of its practical nature and its concise and quickly assimilated pieces of advice. . . . Vergerio, perhaps concerned more with his diplomatic ambitions, certainly concerned more with being diplomatic, dwells upon this aspect. The 'liberal' life-style and education require, for Vergerio, contemplative and active life, study and meditation and action and social commitment. Later in his book he condemns the purely speculative and contemplative individual, who, he says, will be of little use to himself or to his city. The sentiment echoes that expressed by Bruni in his *Vita di Dante,* where there is to be found harsh criticism of the pure contemplative—'Such scholars don't know more than three letters,' remarks Bruni. . . . Castiglione is willing to concede, to the well-qualified but non-noble man, equal status with his courtier, but he is only too well aware that the non-noble needs to work much harder at his qualifications than the noble, whose simple accident of birth gives him automatic advantages in the eyes of the world, however mediocre his true character. Castiglione has an eye, as ever, to the practicalities of court life, while Vergerio (and his contemporaries) could still permit themselves the luxury of allowing such potential to every virtuous man. (pp. 41-3)

Vergerio saw, in the death of rhetorical training, the death of truth. More precisely, he regretted the demise of the rhetorical ideal, not for any nostalgia, it would seem, for the Ciceronian ideal *per se,* but rather because no other training seemed so clearly to posit distinctions between Truth and Falsehood. He regretted the passing of the clarity of rhetorical argument, and he tried to compensate for it by an oft-stated preference for the debating method. It 'sharpened the mind, made for eloquence, reinforced the memory and added self-confidence'. The dialogue form which enjoyed such enormous popularity during the rest of the Renaissance, reaching its apogee with Castiglione, is an example of Vergerio's preference at work, as well as being a straight imitation of the Classical dialogue. Almost every educational writer seemed to emphasise the need for clear discernment and truth (the need for 'truthful' readings of the Classics was to lead to such brilliant textual criticism as has hardly been surpassed since. (p. 44)

Vergerio devotes some space in his treatise to less profound considerations, such as his cautions against paying overmuch attention to personal appearance. Too much care of this kind carries with it, he suggests, the danger of appearing foppish, of being accused of vanity and of having an effeminate mind. Proper attention to such details is covered by a general admonition, stated early in the book, that the Golden Mean should be a key ambition. In this context he quotes from Terence's *Andria* (I, i, 60), advocating moderate actions and avoidance of excesses. He particularises in various instances, such as in social relationships, which should not be rudely austere, nor yet ridiculously frivolous. That commonplace is to be repeated throughout the Renaissance and will surface again in the *Cortegiano.* But, continuing in now less serious vein, Vergerio concedes the pleasure which may be obtained through the playing of musical instruments (though preferably not wind instruments!) and through dancing. Indeed, he sees a certain utilitarian value in dancing, in encouraging exercise and in enabling the body to acquire greater agility. On the whole, however, he is against the potential dangers of corruption and vanity which he fears that dancing may bring. Music may also have a practical use in moderating excited passions and 'tempering' the mind, another possible example of the Mean, imitated from many Classical sources, and repeated *inter alios* by Castiglione. Vergerio also quotes Aristotle (*Politics,* VIII, 3,2, and VIII, 2,6) on the need to know about the techniques of figurative art, and his motives for that advice combine aesthetics (such knowledge teaches men to distinguish the beautiful from the ugly) with economics (with such expertise men are less likely to be cheated over the price of a work of art!).

In the field of civic education, Vergerio, following Aristotle again, states clearly that it is in the interests of the state to provide an education, since the usefulness of such an education will redound to the benefit of the state or the city as a whole, as well as upon the individual who is thus trained. Parents (and the home environment) tended, according to Vergerio, to spoil children—hence they were best educated by friends, or away from home. Castiglione . . . was educated in Milan, away from his close family, though his suggestions for the education of his son, Camillo, seem to indicate that he preferred the boy to remain with his mother and grandmother, and be taught by a pedagogue in Mantua. And, Vergerio insists, the richest gift a parent can give to his son is to ensure that he is taught '*bonae artes, honestae artes, liberales disciplinae, honestae disciplinae*'. Such training, says Vergerio, would provide fame for an obscure house, and a glory for one's place of origin if it were humble. The idea is one which Alberti will amplify in his *Della famiglia* and the personal nature of Vergerio's advice, which here seems directed at the betterment of the individual and his household, rather than at any ideals of perfection in behaviour, may be a glimpse between the lines of something less universal than the civically beneficent education which he is normally considered as advocating. Despite that personal note, Vergerio pays a very subtle compliment to his possible masters. Dante had urged that his monarch should possess all and so desire nothing; Vergerio confessed himself frankly astonished that potentates could be decent men (*bonus et sapiens*), since their positions of power, surrounded by everything they could possibly desire and besieged by parasitic acolytes, 'who make fools into madmen', seemed to leave little room for reason and right judgement; and the end of the first Book echoes Plato's *Gorgias* (526a): 'Surrounded by so many opportunities for sinning, it is doubly praiseworthy for a prince to live as a just man.'

There are other general hints which Vergerio offers. He is not slow, for instance, to urge his pupil to keep his own counsel, an attitude visible in Castiglione's restriction of friendship to one well-trusted man, and brought to a peak in the way Niccolò Strozzi (1590-1655) cautions against trusting anyone at all. Vergerio also points to the value of ethics to teach men moral goodness, a lesson that goes hand in hand with the study of history, which teaches men the proper behaviour on given occasions. The use of historical exemplars to bolster moral precepts (often Aristotelean precepts) is to be a feature of the Renaissance humanistic treatise, and Castiglione's *Cortegiano* is no exception to that rule. Among Vergerio's general remarks about moral (and good) exemplars, particularly significant in view of what Castiglione will have to say about the moral examples of both courtier and prince in Book IV, is his argument that the best way to arouse love of virtue and honest moral conduct in a person, is to provide him with a living example of a good, honest man. On his part, too, the pupil should make a positive effort to select someone worthy of his veneration, in order to imitate his behaviour. The idea was not new, and Vergerio probably took it over from Quintilian, but his words help keep alive the tradition which is still visible in Castiglione.

If Vergerio's treatise was the theoretic basis for most educational institutions during the Renaissance, the practical basis was provided by the two great pedagogues, Vittorino da Feltre and Guarino da Verona (1374-1460), whose names we may briefly join here in considering their methods. Not that those methods seemed wholly to Castiglione's taste, but their two schools (at Mantua and Ferrara) kept alive and passed on, through a whole series of fine teachers, the precepts of Quintilian and other great educators. Both men began their careers as university lecturers. At a time when the glories of the Latin Classics were first being discovered, when manuscripts and documents were rare (and printing yet to be invented), the exegetic method of a man like Giovanni di Conversino da Ravenna, who taught both Vittorino and Guarino, was appropriate and economical, travelling around Italy as he did, and spreading the new gospel. Parallels with the publicity given by St Paul to the message of Christianity are extraordinarily close, and Manuel Chrysoloras (c. 1350-1415) and Francesco Filelfo (1398-1481) were among similar publicising disciples of the new learning. It was Giovanni di Conversino's Chair at Padua which Vittorino eventually inherited for a brief period. The peripatetic teacher, then, usually attracted by a rich patron (or municipality) to a temporary position as public lecturer, had been one feature of the system by which the noble and bourgeois public were educated during the fifteenth century.

Another major element which here requires mention was the patronage of great dynasties, such as the Medici in Florence, who encouraged select groups of intelligent and cultured individuals to join together in informal groups, sometimes referred to as academies, where the new learning might be discussed, commented upon and perhaps adapted to meet the contemporary situation. A very informal group of this kind is the one imagined as gathering at the Urbino court in the *Cortegiano,* where social graces and conversation impose an added informality upon the academic discussion. The smaller size of such gatherings would inevitably lead to less formal exegesis and to a friendlier social atmosphere, such as that which characterised the Platonic Academy, for instance, centred around Marsilio Ficino (1433-99). The academicians saw their own activities as reflections of their Classical precursors in the Athenian agora, and celebrated, in the case of the Florentine academy, the 'anniversary' of Plato's birth (and death) with almost mystic rituals which implied for them direct continuation of the ancient traditions.

Similar groups sprang up at all the major courts and centres of learning in Italy. An early portrait of the kind of group which came together and a description of the discussions which they held is given in the *Disputationes Camaldulenses* of Cristoforo Landino (1424-92), composed in 1475 in the form of a dialogue in which the author imagines a group of Florentines, including Leonbattista Alberti (1404-72) and Lorenzo de'Medici (1449-92), who have withdrawn from the heat of the city to a Camaldolite monastery in the Apennines. There they discuss, over a four-day period, the relative merits of the contemplative and active life. That theme is one which Castiglione himself will treat, and the discussions described by Landino, themselves based on Classical dialogues, such as those of Cicero's *Tusculanae disputationes,* are similar to the conversations which form the body of the **Cortegiano.** The advantages of the cut and thrust of dialectic argument, which Vergerio admired in the Classical authors and imitation of which he advocated, are seen there to great advantage. In Castiglione's treatise a leading figure, not necessarily an expert, in a particular field, starts off a discussion (on wit—Canossa and Bibbiena; on the role of women—Giuliano de'Medici; on politics—Federico Fregoso; on Platonic love—Bembo, etc). The company then join in to discuss, contradict or confirm the views expressed, leaving the resolution of the problem under discussion clearly indicated by the dominance of one speaker (often underwritten by the approval of the ladies present) or by the positing of the Golden Mean. The elements of earlier educational dialogues are easily discernible in Castiglione's work.

To complete the picture we need to consider briefly those unwritten precepts which characterised the teaching of Vittorino and Guarino. Although Castiglione seemed to want his son educated at home in Mantua (aware perhaps of the benefits he himself had missed by spending so much of his life among strangers, and remembering perhaps with nostalgia the two happiest years of his life, spent with his wife during their first years of marriage in Mantua) the appropriateness of their methods is nonetheless implicitly recognised in the advice offered in parts of the **Cortegiano.**

Guarino's teaching method seems to have consisted essentially in the graduated reading of Classical authors, with critical comments of a linguistic and historical nature upon the texts. He appears to have encouraged physical exercise in order to maintain an equilibrium of physical health similar to that advocated by Aristotle. Similar methods were being practised by Vittorino in Mantua at the *ca'zoiosa* ('house of joy', the name given to his school). Guarino, it should also be noted, was unusual among the earliest pedagogues for his ability as a Greek scholar. He had spent five years (1403-8) in Constantinople learning the language, and for several years Vittorino and he exchanged lessons of Latin and Greek. In middle life, Guarino spent his years as a lecturer, in Florence, Venice and Verona, before transferring his talents to Ferrara in 1429, where he was, first of all, like Vittorino, the head of his own school, and then private tutor to Lionello d'Este. Vittorino was more of the dedicated schoolmaster, though his attention to readings of the original texts of the Classics, and the regime he devised for his pupils was, more or less, the same as Guarino's. We can glean such information from contemporary witnesses, such as Vespasiano da Bisticci (1421-98).

Aristotle's explanation of the distinction between body and soul, and between instinct and reason had led him to advocate in the *Politics* a discipline which trained the mind in a

way not dissimilar from that adopted and perpetuated by the two great pedagogues. The kind of physical exercise which seems to have formed an integral part of Vittorino's system, trained the body (and by maintaining its fitness kept the humours in equilibrium and ensured tranquillity.) The moral edification of Vittorino's pupils would be inculcated by habit and personal example (and Vespasiano makes much of this last in his biography of Vittorino), while intellectual rigour is obtained from the study of Classical authors. The similarities between the practice of Vittorino and Guarino and the theories put forward by Vergerio are clear. The custom of using pupil-teachers, who taught the material they were learning, was an amalgam closer still to Vergerio's idea that the pupil should model himself upon virtuous exemplars. . . . [One] of the most significant influences exerted by the two schools was to help create in the young a personality untrammelled by previous conditioning, an individual able to think for himself. The old compendia of learning gave way under the new schoolmasters to a study of the original texts of the Classics, and an imitation not only of their style, but also of their way of thinking. By growing up with an appreciation of the 'pagan' texts, a series of new generations arose, to whom a defence of the Classics, such as the apology of Salutati, would seem utterly superfluous. The removal of education from the hands of the Church was complete, and the possibility of the free-thinking, autonomous individual, able to develop himself as highly as he was humanly capable, was now no longer a concept visible only in the historical past.

Although the wheel had turned full circle by the time Castiglione's career reached its peak, and although, under totalitarian regimes, that old individualism and freedom no longer had the dynamic potential which they had had a century before, nevertheless Castiglione had the advantage of the store of experience and knowledge laid up by the previous century. By drawing upon that inheritance he was better able to formulate for his own times a solution which, within the limits imposed, could ensure some approximation to the *uomo universale* of the previous century. For the next two hundred years or more of Italian history after the publication of the **Cortegiano,** every outstanding individual had to pay a price for being allowed to practise, even in a limited way, his art or profession. Some paid with their liberty, some with their lives, others by prostituting their artistic or professional offspring. But if a line were drawn between the more successful survivors and the more unfortunate (if often 'greater') failures, then the former would be seen as coming closer to Castiglione's norm. The teacher had himself been a pupil, learning in a harsh school the material he now promulgated to others. (pp. 44-9)

Castiglione's supreme achievement was to grasp the new situation. He was young enough in 1499, when he realised change was coming, and that, for instance, a court like that of Ludovico *il Moro,* the pearl of Europe, could never be the same again, to condition himself to the new circumstances. He was still young enough in 1508 to be able to adapt himself to what he saw would be an inevitably changed regime of life, after the removal of that decent man, his protector, Guidubaldo da Montefeltro. *Virtù* for him no longer implied simply the heroic qualities which had characterised earlier writers on the subject. His strategy was that of the waiting game. The complexity of new political alignments and the internal problems of court diplomacy, required the subtlety of chess rather than the brusqueness of a duel or a tourney (now reduced largely to a ceremonial role). Castiglione's experience showed him that the acquisition, in some measure, of all possible virtues (qualifications or qualities) was more important for survival than the injunction of the early educationists: the acquisition of as many excellences as possible with a special qualification in one's *forte*. Francesco Guicciardini (1483-1540) had mused in his *Ricordi* on the 'trifles' (*leggiadrie*) which he had 'mocked as a young man' because they seemed unnecessary social trivia. Later he came to recognise that 'to have an abundance of all accomplishments (*tutti gli intrattenimenti*) opens the way to the favour of princes, and the man who has this abundance sometimes finds it the prelude to great profit and exaltation, for the world and its princes are no longer formed as they should be, but as they are' (ibid., CLXXIX). Guicciardini's remarks are lent greater point by his personal situation—out of favour with the Medici and in exile from his beloved Florence. Being prepared to take fortune's offerings now meant advocating something closer to Guicciardini's reflections than to Machiavelli's heroic exhortations on dominating destiny. This was Castiglione's new course and new message.

The advantages of what Castiglione considers his particular educational suggestions are shown in the 'list of successes' which precedes the main business of Book IV. The catalogue is impressive—two Dukes, a Cardinal, a Doge of Genoa, a Papal Secretary, an Archbishop and a Bishop, all of whom 'graduated', so to speak, from his school in the course of ten years or so (IV,ii). The other noble spirits (who had died before attaining such high honours) would, Castiglione suggests, have reached similar heights and 'would thus have provided for all who knew them a clear proof (*argomento*) of the praiseworthy qualities of the Urbino court and of its adornment by so many noble gentlemen. Such proof has been provided by almost all the other gentlemen who have been *created* in that court (*che in essa creati si sono*)' (ibid.). The theme is taken up in the eulogy of Francesco Maria della Rovere, for whose elevation 'greater praise is to be accorded to the [Montefeltro] household in which he was brought up (*la casa ove nutrito fu*) . . . than to his accession to the Duchy of Urbino' (ibid.). And between the two important statements is an aside which may seem awkward to us today, but which would have been very familiar to his contemporaries, namely that, 'truly so many lords and captains, so outstanding for their virtues and held in such universally high esteem, never came out of the Trojan Horse'. The allusion is to a simile in the *De oratore* of Cicero, referring to the school of Isocrates (436-338 B.C.): 'From his school, as from the Trojan Horse, came out innumerable men of the first rank.' Isocrates was well known to the Renaissance educationists: Vergerio quoted from him, Guarino translated his works, Vittorino included him as set reading for his pupils and Chrysoloras transcribed his writings. Castiglione evidently regarded the court (and particularly the Urbino court) as his *school,* an institution with a record of practical successes proved by its distinguished 'graduates'.

The reputation which Urbino had for producing great men (and great rulers) allows Castiglione to 'hope that good fortune should continue to so favour these virtuous works (*queste opere virtuose*) . . . that house and state . . . continue to prosper'. Eleonora Gonzaga, wife of Francesco Maria, is praised for her qualities of 'learning, grace, beauty, intelligence, good breeding, humanity and other polite attributes, qualities which would ensure a continuation of the prosperity of the Duchy'. And yet Castiglione *knew* that the Duchy, par-

Castiglione, after a work by Raphael.

ticularly after the depredations of Pope Leo in 1517, was destined for anything but prosperity. But he left the pre-1517 version of that eulogy as it stood. Educationally, if not historically, his injunctions were valid, and they and his auguries were meant for all time. He believed, in other words, that such a school of behaviour trained the best elements in society and that fortune usually favoured such high qualifications. On a more personal level, the man who is willing to train and qualify himself so 'universally', even though he may not necessarily be inclined or destined for high office (though that was where maximum self-determination lay), nevertheless affords himself far more possibilities of finding freedom in society by making his many talents desirable. And such freedom—for instance to move from court to court—was the best that most men could expect, the best way most men had of controlling their fortune, during the 1520s.

The notion of the **Cortegiano** as an educational handbook does not stop here. One of the most significant changes between the *Seconda redazione* and the final edition of 1528 is the relinquishing, in the new Book IV, of the title *cortegiano* in favour of *institutor del principe*: 'If you do not want to call him *courtier,* I am unconcerned,' says Ottaviano Fregoso (IV,xlvii). . . . [To] the epithet *institutor* at that point in the book are added other qualifications. The courtier, for instance, should instruct his prince as Aristotle and Plato had done. To this Cesare Gonzaga adds the interjection, 'You would deserve, rather, the name of a good schoolmaster (*maestro di scola*) than good courtier [if that be true]' (IV, xxxvi). As becomes clear from that fourth Book, Castiglione regards it as part of the courtier's duties, to society as much as to his prince, to instruct his lord as best he can, and this is his principal role and purpose. At the same time, such a powerful and intimate counsellor, by definition, would be in his master's good graces and secure in his court employment—as tranquil and as fulfilled a situation as an individual could hope for. Further, he could use his influence to help create a more tranquil environment for his fellow men. All these conclusions may be applied to Castiglione's own position at the court of Charles V. Aristotle and Plato had been, in addition to their function as tutors to princes, preceptors to other 'courtiers' (and citizens). It is probable that, as author of the **Cortegiano** and as Papal Nuncio to the Imperial court, Castiglione viewed his own role in the same dual fashion—effectively and potentially adviser to princes, and, in the final version of his treatise, educational adviser to others who might hold similar positions. The idea would not seem unfamiliar to a society used to the schools, like Vittorino's, which turned out both princely rulers, such as Federigo da Montefeltro, alongside great scholars and lecturers—Lorenzo Valla (1407-1457) was a pupil of Vittorino's—and great pedagogues—Vittorino himself was a pupil of another great pedagogue, Gasparino Barzizza (1360?-1421)—who were often regarded as official or supernumerary court advisers. (pp. 55-8)

> *J. R. Woodhouse, in his* Baldesar Castiglione: A Reassessment of "The Courtier," *Edinburgh University Press, 1978, 217 p.*

WAYNE A. REBHORN   (essay date 1978)

[*In the following excerpt, Rebhorn investigates the nostalgia that colors Castiglione's role as memoirist in* The Courtier.]

Throughout the prologues to his four books and the dedicatory letter which prefaces the entire work [see excerpt dated 1528], Castiglione speaks to his readers *in propria persona,* creating a distinct image of himself as a complex, emotional character who is by far the most real and moving personality in **The Courtier.** Speaking directly to the reader in his own person did not mean for him, or for any other Renaissance author, either indulgence in maudlin confession or romantic self-dramatization. Whether he wrote a treatise or a novel, a satire or an epic, the Renaissance writer obeyed the rules of decorum. Consciously or unconsciously, he adopted an authorial persona, a mask (*persona* in Latin), appropriate both to the genre and the subject matter of his work. When creating this persona, he was not required to exclude totally all details from his personal life; rather, he made a careful selection of feelings, opinions, and experience generally consistent with the generic mask he inherited from tradition and adapted to the particular needs of his work. Moreover, no genre or subject matter restricted him to just a single persona. In writing satire, for instance, he could adopt the more urbane satyr mask of Horace or the rougher one of Juvenal, while in love lyrics he could play the lady's suffering servant along with Petrarch or the detached, erotic ironist with Ovid. Nor was he necessarily prevented from refashioning a traditional mask to suit his own purposes, just as Dante and Milton were to do, in their different ways, with the persona of the epic bard. He might actually combine masks from several different genres, especially if his work, like so many in the Renaissance, was itself a hybrid, the union of many different traditions and genres. For instance, the character of the fisherman in Izaak Walton's *Compleat Angler* derives its features from the pastoral, the georgic, and the philosophical dialogue. Similarly, Castiglione creates a most complex self-image for himself in his **Cortegiano,** a blend of ideal courtier modelled after Cicero's ideal orator, devoted memorialist seeking to immortalize the people of Urbino with his art, and nostalgic shepherd, a role Castiglione knew well from classical and Renaissance pastoral and which allowed him to articulate the profound yearning he felt over the loss of his ideal court.

In the first place, although Castiglione translates Cicero's personal statements from the *Orator* and the *De Oratore* in his first and last prologues, he does not simply ape Cicero's character. Rather, he assimilates it into his own, courtly mask, just as he appropriates many features of Cicero's ideal orator when fashioning his ideal courtier. What he really seems to have learned from Cicero is less a matter of imitating particular features when creating a persona in a philosophical dialogue than the aesthetic desirability of harmonizing that persona with the subject of the work. In the *De Oratore,* Cicero deliberately structured his image to reflect the features of his ideal: he stressed his life-long public role as orator; he supplied evidence from his own life of the encyclopedic learning and public, political involvement prescribed for the ideal; and he demonstrated in his masterful style the desired command of rhetoric. Inspired by Cicero's example, Castiglione presents himself to the reader in the role of ideal courtier, exhibiting in his style, his praise for the men and women of Urbino, and his tactful treatment of Alfonso Ariosto, Michel de Silva, and others, many of the qualities defining the ideal courtier of his book. Fully conscious of the role he chooses to play, Castiglione disclaims in the dedicatory letter that he modelled the ideal after his own image, but his modest disclaimer is just more proof that Carlos V accurately pronounced Castiglione "uno de los mejores caballeros del mundo."

That Castiglione makes his mask reflect the qualities prescribed for the ideal courtier is most immediately evident in the carefully controlled, artfully complex, yet clear style with which he speaks. Far from sharing the random movement of real speech or even the relative spontaneity of his characters' exchanges, the statements he makes *in propria persona* are distinguished by quite different stylistic qualities, which begin to manifest themselves from the very first sentence of the book. . . . In the first place, Castiglione creates the impression of dignified formality, conscious deliberation, and even solemnity in the slow, measured pace of this sentence, an effect he achieves by placing lengthy subordinate clauses before the main ones, inserting appositive constructions, incidental phrases, and even clauses into the interstices of the sentence, and separating grammatical elements that would normally follow one another closely. . . . Secondly, his precise use of grammar, tense sequences, and conjunctions keeps the structure of the sentence clear and bears witness to the rational mind behind it. Finally, by expanding the end of each period through the addition of phrases and clauses after the main verbs, he balances the weight of subordinate clauses placed at the beginning, thus giving the sentence a feeling of static balance and equilibrium.

As Castiglione employs similar techniques whenever he speaks *in propria persona,* the slow-paced formality of his style creates the impression of a person who, like the ideal courtier, possesses a reserved dignity. Its fundamental clarity and balance testify to that easy mastery of things the ideal courtier manifests by means of his *sprezzatura.* Again, like his ideal figure, Castiglione uses his style to suggest that he knows a great deal more than he says directly. Through his constant allusions to classical and contemporary authors, his abbreviated considerations of language and elements of Aristotle's philosophy, and of course, the command of Neoplatonic doctrine revealed in Bembo's bravura performance, Castiglione hints at depths of untapped learning while demonstrating his courtly sense of propriety by avoiding excessively detailed, pedantic expositions. Thus in many ways, and with singular appropriateness, the courtly author of *Il Cortegiano* shows his readers how to speak in a courtly style. (pp. 91-4)

Even more than presenting himself in the role of a perfect courtier, Castiglione also undertakes to play the role of memorialist for the court of Urbino. He identifies his primary purpose in writing his *Cortegiano* as a desire to preserve from oblivion the memory of the court and its people, and as he carries out this labor of love, he not only paints a flattering portrait of the court in his dialogues but uses his four prologues explicitly to justify his admiration for it and to extol its virtues and accomplishments directly and unambiguously. Moreover, as he progresses from one prologue to the next, his praise progresses as well, rising to increasingly lofty heights. Thus where the prologue to the first book describes the beauties of Urbino's palazzo and the noble character of its rulers, the prologue to the second argues for the court's superiority in comparison with all courts past and present. The prologue to Book III goes even further, equating Urbino's superior stature to Hercules' superior size and thus actually relating it to the more than human world of heroes. In his last prologue, Castiglione consummates this particular development, as Urbino becomes an epic realm in his imagination and metamorphoses into the Trojan horse, a gigantic receptacle for the greatest heroes of ancient Greece. Appropriately enough, while in the first prologue he merely listed the names of all those courtiers associated with Urbino, in this last one he sings the praises of their "heroic" accomplishments, eulogizing the dead for their dramatic struggle against hostile fortune and celebrating the living for the distinguished offices they held and the noble ranks to which they rose. (pp. 95-6)

Castiglione does not compose his memorial to Urbino simply in order to prove himself an ideal courtier; rather, his book rises out of its author's profound nostalgia for the court of good Duke Guidobaldo's days and from his tragic experience of loss and isolation. His nostalgia and sense of loss color every statement he utters about Urbino and its people, but they are especially strong at the very start of his book, and their presence there effectively establishes them as the most affecting and memorable traits in Castiglione's courtly persona. With great skill, Castiglione begins the dedicatory letter to Don Michel de Silva that opens his book by quietly recounting how, after Duke Guidobaldo's death, he remembered the happiness he had enjoyed at the court and was stimulated by his memories to begin writing. His first impulse to write, as he recalls it, is unmistakably triggered by his exposure to death and by a nostalgia for the past. As yet, however, there is no suggestion of urgency, no compelling sense of loss that drives him to bring his work to its completion. As he recounts his first decision to write *Il Cortegiano,* the motivation his narrative suggests is simply the wish of a grateful, devoted courtier to pay homage to his fallen lord, and to recall a period he described in earlier versions of his book as "il fior della vita mia." Castiglione continues the narrative of his dedicatory letter, however, in order to explain how Vittoria Colonna's intervention led him to complete his manuscript. He recounts that many years after he had put it aside, he took it in hand

again, and was, as he reread it, filled with a much more profound, more total nostalgia for the past. . . . What Castiglione remembers here is not past happiness as much as the painful *loss* of that happiness through the deaths of so many people. Alfonso Ariosto, Giuliano de' Medici, Ottaviano Fregoso—one by one he mourns for them in a powerful crescendo of lament, transforming the opening of his book into an elegy that reaches its climax only when he recalls the greatest loss of all [the Duchess]. (pp. 96-8)

Once firmly established at the start of the dedicatory letter, Castiglione's sense of loss, his sad isolation in a universe of death, and his yearning for a happier past exercise a decisive influence on the reader's reaction to all that follows, complementing and magnifying the nostalgic elements that are continually present in Castiglione's response to his experience. (p. 98)

[Nostalgia] involves more than mere remembrance of things past. It is a sense that the past was qualitatively superior to the present, that it would be desirable to resurrect it, but that, except in the memory, the past is separated from the present by an unbridgeable chasm. Nostalgia originates as a response to a feeling of lost youth and vitality, innocence, and freshness. Characteristically, it projects this yearning into the recollection of the past, envisioning it as a happy, fulfilling world of communal harmony and personal pleasure. Often, since nostalgia involves a fundamental feeling of loss, it goes beyond mere yearning for a supposedly more perfect past and generates a strong contrast between that past and a distinctly diminished present. Consequently critics have claimed, with some justice, that nostalgia underlies the myths of a paradise lost and a vanished Golden Age, and that it is the typical emotion behind the pastoral, manifested in the shepherd-poet's longing for that strange and distant, yet familiar and satisfying realm which Virgil immortalized as Arcadia.

Although he does not use the word "nostalgia," when he is defending his claims for Urbino's superiority at the start of his second book Castiglione nevertheless demonstrates a genuine understanding both of nostalgia's pyschological origin and the characteristic way it shapes each individual's perceptions of past and present. As he attacks the old men for condemning the courts of the present indiscriminately while praising without qualification those of their youth, he describes perfectly how nostalgia operates in shaping one's memory of the past. . . .

> . . . and [the mind] retains of past pleasures merely a lingering memory and the image of that precious time of tender youth in which (while we are enjoying it), wherever we look, heaven and earth and everything appear merry and smiling, and the sweet springtime of happiness seems to flower in our thoughts as in a delightful and lovely garden.

Castiglione goes on to berate the old men for not realizing that it is they who have changed, not the courts, that they mourn their own loss of youth, power, and vitality without realizing it, and that their powerful feelings of nostalgia make them misperceive the truth about both past and present.

If Castiglione denounces the old men's nostalgia, isn't he equally vulnerable to the same criticisms? Doesn't his own nostalgia for Duke Guido's court lead him to a distorted presentation of its image? To some degree, it certainly does, for even a reader unfamiliar with the real history and people of Urbino may suspect that Castiglione sees his all-too-ideal court through rose-colored glasses. Nevertheless, his nostalgia differs from that of the old men in two major ways. First, Castiglione establishes an implicit set of contrasts between his own character and that of the nostalgic old men he attacks. Where they are presented as giving in to their feelings and irrationally condemning the present without exception, Castiglione presents himself as a much more balanced and reasonable judge who wisely contends that no age, past or present, can be wholly good or wholly evil. Where the old men attack mere changes in customs as signs of moral degeneration, Castiglione shows himself able to discriminate between morally indifferent matters like dress and things of real, moral significance. Finally, where the old men are scolded for being unaware of how their nostalgia affects their perceptions of past and present, that very scolding demonstrates Castiglione's own self-consciousness about it. The effect of all these contrasts is not to deny the latter's nostalgia, which colors his entire work from its powerful, affecting first pages, but to show that it has not blinded him to reality or perverted his judgment. Castiglione places his nostalgia within the context of a reasonable, discriminating, self-conscious personality and thus makes himself a difficult target for the mockery and censure he directs at the old men.

Castiglione's nostalgia differs from theirs in yet another respect. While both he and they yearn for a more beautiful, fulfilling past, he refrains absolutely from projecting his sense of loss into a moralistic condemnation of the present. Instead of contrasting Urbino's past glory with its subsequent decline, he chooses to contrast it with his own very personal isolation, and he refuses to interpret the separation between his past and his present as a symptom of moral decay or historical degeneration. As a result, his nostalgia differs substantially not only from that of the moralistic old men, but from that of the more historically oriented Cicero, who offered Castiglione at least a partial model for his nostalgia in the prologues to the *De Oratore.*

In their prologues, both Cicero and Castiglione celebrate historical figures whose supposedly real conversations their dialogues record and whose deaths they eloquently mourn. Both authors also firmly establish their own personal relationship to the figures and events described, and both depict themselves as looking back from an unhappy present to a happier world in the past. Here, however, the resemblances cease, for Castiglione seems much less concerned with the complex, concrete historical situation of his beloved Urbino when compared to Cicero, who carefully relates the characters and events he describes, as well as his own situation, to the larger developments of Roman history. The latter specifically sets his dialogues at a crucial turning point in Roman history, a time just before the first serious explosions of violence and revolution that would eventually lead to the Augustan *imperium.* (pp. 99-101)

By contrast, Castiglione ignores much of Urbino's history and is especially vague when alluding to historical events involving its relationships to other Italian states. He never explains what enemies Duke Federico triumphed over or who was responsible for Duke Guidobaldo's many misfortunes. Moreover, he selects a date just after Pope Julius II's visit in 1506 as the time when his dialogues supposedly took place, not because he wishes to call attention to its historical significance, but because the visit allows him to account for the particularly festive mood of his courtiers' conversations. Finally, where Cicero has an intense, personal involvement in histori-

cal events, Castiglione says nothing about his own historically quite significant diplomatic activities, which brought him into direct contact with the most powerful European rulers of his age. He also remains somewhat vague about what happened to the court of Urbino during the time he was writing and revising his *Book of the Courtier,* and he is equally vague about his own personal relationship to it. The dedicatory letter raises a series of puzzling questions: Did the court of Urbino cease to exist when the duchess and her courtiers died? Is Francesco Maria no longer its ruler as he was when Castiglione composed the prologue to Book IV? Has Castiglione himself left the duke's service, and is he still in Spain as he was when he sent the manuscript of *Il Cortegiano* to Vittoria Colonna? To all these questions concerning his own and Urbino's history, Castiglione's reply is silence. Deprived of any historical framework, his separation from what he might call his sweet, springtime garden of Urbino becomes a mysterious process: a mythical fall from innocence, an inexplicably sinless expulsion from a paradise of delights into a bleak universe held thrall to death.

Castiglione's mysterious separation from Urbino as well as his nostalgic lament over death and loss also suggestively invoke similar elements in the pastoral tradition that may well have strongly influenced him as he wrote his book. The courtly society to which Castiglione belonged and which he celebrated in his *Cortegiano* particularly affected the pastoral. In works of that literary mode, courtly poets could fabricate an illusory world of innocence and nature which was simultaneously and paradoxically extremely sophisticated and artificial. Utilizing the most transparent allegories, they could flatter the powerful by making shepherds and shepherdesses sing the praises of figures easily identifiable as their lords and ladies. Thus, Renaissance poets from Poliziano and Sannazaro to Sidney and Jonson wrote pastoral verse, masques, plays, and novels in which the roles of shepherd and courtier merged and the pastoral world was supplied with all the aristocratic hierarchies, urbane manners, and sophisticated characters associated with the court. Castiglione himself, with his cousin Cesare Gonzaga, wrote a pastoral masque called *Tirsi* for the carnival of 1506 at Urbino. While its characters are "simple" shepherds, they are clearly disguised courtiers; their manners are refined and graceful, and their language is highly sophisticated, a pastiche of translations from Virgil and quotations from Poliziano and Sannazaro. Moreover, not only do its characters speak like courtiers, but they are actively engaged in courtship during their performance, one singing a love complaint to an obdurate nymph, and the other hymning the praises of the shepherds' goddess, an allegorical figure representing the duchess Elisabetta Gonzaga. The contrast between these two courtship songs is a contrast between inferior courtship directed at an unsuitable object and superior courtship directed at a stable, benevolent figure; and it thus provides the theme of Castiglione's work, which is a revelation of the nature of true courtship. *Tirsi* offers a clear demonstration of the total interpenetration of courtly and pastoral worlds in the minds of its author and the members of his society. Consequently if Castiglione, like most of his contemporaries, felt no reluctance to transport the court into the pastoral bower, he could also simply reverse the process in his *Courtier* and give its courtly world and his own courtly role some of the chief characteristics of pastoral. (pp. 103-04)

Although *Il Cortegiano* contains many features that link it to Sannazaro's *Arcadia* and to countless bucolic works from classical antiquity and the Renaissance, Castiglione's brooding response to death, which has overwhelmed his Arcadian Urbino, involves a fundamental horror that profoundly differentiates his work from the entire pastoral tradition. To be sure, death lurks in the shades of shepherds' bowers just as it does in Urbino's halls, but there it is treated as a fact of nature, part of the natural cycle that offers the mourning shepherd the consolation of seasonal, if not personal, rebirth, and thus softens death's potentially brutal impact. Death is transmuted into an affirmation of the wholeness and inviolability of nature, and by providing material for the shepherd's enjoyable, sad songs, it even becomes an ally of pleasure in his bower.

At some points in his *Book of the Courtier,* Castiglione seems to embrace this pastoral view of death; he seems to imagine time moving through an organic cycle in which death occupies the last phase as a fitting and natural terminus of life and guarantees some form of rebirth and renewed existence. Although *Il Cortegiano* contains no detailed treatment of history and does not adumbrate an explicit scheme for it, there are many indications that Castiglione implicitly shared with his humanist predecessors and contemporaries a basically organic, cyclical view: culture flourished in antiquity, faded and died in the Middle Ages, and was reborn in the time of Dante, Petrarch, and Boccaccio, reaching its new maturity during Castiglione's own age. Thus, when addressing himself to the old men who attack contemporary courts, he insists on the progress that has been made in civilized life when early, crude beginnings are compared to the heights reached at Urbino, where the best men and customs were in flower. (pp. 106-07)

The fundamental experience of death to which Castiglione was exposed and which he records in *Il Cortegiano* is clearly not the pastoral vision of natural consummation; for him, death is a sudden, unexpected interruption of life. Unnatural, arbitrary, irrational, and unjust, it did not allow the inhabitants of Urbino to grow to maturity and then slip gently away into the peaceful sleep of eternity, but struck them down without warning just when they were beginning the most productive phases of their careers. . . . Arbitrary, perverse, irresistible, death and fortune are the ultimate powers in Castiglione's universe; they reduce cosmos to chaos and negate the very possibility of forming any scheme, any order at all. The tragedy of Urbino is thus not simply that its inhabitants have died, but that their premature deaths have destroyed Castiglione's sense that any universal form of order and justice exists in the world about him.

While Castiglione's horrified vision of a universe overwhelmed by the absolute tyranny of death and fortune separates him from the pastoral tradition, it also helps explain why he refused to follow Cicero's lead and establish a historical scheme in which to embrace the deaths of his protagonists. For Castiglione, man's life is not lived within the framework of history, but rather in the context of his personal struggle against the universal forces of time, fortune, and mortality. Instructively, although Cicero also laments the deaths of his protagonists in the *De Oratore* as examples of the power and mutability of fortune . . . , such general reflections hardly prevent him from carefully relating those deaths to the tragic development of Roman history, from claiming that when a certain Gaius Julius died, the Republic died with him. . . . (pp. 111-12)

Although Castiglione does not share either the pastoral poet's complacency or Cicero's historical vision, it might be expected that, faced with the horror of death and the chaos

it makes of human life, he would turn to Christianity, just as Milton did in *Lycidas,* and seek in the order of an eternal, heavenly existence some compensation for the inadequacies of this earthly one. In fact, such a compensation must have suggested itself to Castiglione in his life, for he was a serious, pious Christian whose decision to take holy orders in 1521 testifies to the depth of his religious concern. Nevertheless, in response to the horrors of death, nowhere in *Il Cortegiano* does he hold out clearly the possibility of Christian redemption. Strikingly, in his vision of the human condition as a frail bark helpless before the destructive storms of fortune, he actually constructs a sort of Christian commonplace *manqué.* In a fully Christian version of the commonplace, man may be buffeted about by the storms of time and fortune, but he also has a sure port in heaven toward which he can successfully steer his course. In the first passage where Castiglione develops this image, the only port mentioned is the one left behind at the journey's beginning, and in the second, while he does speak of a port to which man attempts to sail, the context makes it clear that that port is an earthly harbor of material success and worldly fame. In neither case is there any hint of a pious hope that heaven awaits man as his true port, a secure haven after the storms and sufferings of his earthly journey. To be sure, Castiglione's passages do not specifically exclude Christian readings, and there is every reason to believe that the man who was awarded the bishopric of Ávila would approve pious interpretations. Nevertheless, he completely refrains from inviting them himself, and throughout *Il Cortegiano* he presents a stark and tragic vision of the human condition which renders his nostalgia for the vanished Arcadia of Urbino all the more poignant and understandable.

In response to the horror of death, which swallowed up all of Urbino's gentle shepherds and shepherdesses, Castiglione does more than simply yearn nostalgically for the happy, innocent world from which he has been cut off definitively. As he contemplates his Arcadian landscape littered with the tombstones of those he loved so well, he does what he did when Falcone, the friend of his youth, died: he sets out to write an elegy, to compose a fitting and enduring memorial for the dead. Rather than brood passively and helplessly about the past, Castiglione is spurred into action by his recollections, and like Cicero in the *De Oratore,* he recreates the vanished world of the past, making his book into a monument for those who left behind them few traces of their earthly passage. Castiglione would save his friends from the ultimate anonymity of *mortal oblivione,* from remaining nameless and unremembered throughout the brief duration of human history. Like that greater master of nostalgia, Marcel Proust, Castiglione also turns to art, not religion, in his attempt to recapture lost time, to resurrect a dead past, and to achieve for himself, perhaps, a momentary intimation of immortality. Cast into a solitary universe of death, the nostalgic courtier engages himself and his art in a heroic struggle to create a sense of meaning, justice, and order in life which untimely death has denied. In this desperate battle against the forces of time and fortune, only art has a chance of prevailing. Even so, there can be no real certainty of success in Castiglione's enterprise, only the hope beyond hope that he can transform the painful recollection of his vanished past into the enduring memorial of his art. (pp. 113-15)

Wayne A. Rebhorn, in his Courtly Performances: Making and Festivity in Castiglione's "Book of the Courtier", *Wayne State University Press, 1978, 238 p.*

DAIN A. TRAFTON (essay date 1983)

[In the following excerpt, Trafton reveals the political orientation underlying the third book of The Courtier.*]*

The sixteenth century in Europe was one of reduced political options. Monarchy was in the ascendant almost everywhere. Here and there, older traditions of feudal aristocracy, civic autonomy, and republicanism retained some vigor, but the pressures tending to focus power in the figure of a strong central monarch and his court dominated the age. As a result, a young man of political virtue and ambition, taking his bearings around 1500 in Milan, Naples, Vienna, Paris, or London (and a bit later in Madrid), saw two main paths open before him: to become a prince or a courtier. Only a rare young man, obviously, found in circumstances or in himself what it took to become a prince. For him the century produced, by its second decade, a book of instruction that stands out above all other such books written before or after: Machiavelli's *Prince.* For the others—the young men of ambition whose virtue had not been transformed into *virtù* or whose spirit was simply of a different order—there appeared, about the same time as the *Prince,* another preeminent guide to conduct: Castiglione's **Book of the Courtier.** It is said that the Emperor Charles V, who seems to have grasped as well as anyone the peculiar character of the age, kept both these books along with the Bible by his bedside. Perhaps he thought of the *Prince* and the **Courtier** as repositories of an essential political wisdom analogous to the spiritual wisdom of Holy Scripture. Indeed, the **Courtier** and the *Prince* might be considered the fundamental political testaments of the sixteenth century.

That the **Courtier** is in some sense a political book will be readily granted; it instructs in the arts of getting along at court and thus reflects the political realities of the age. But can the book be described as political in the strict sense of the word? Does Castiglione offer more than a superficial examination of the essential fact of sixteenth-century politics: princely rule itselfc? Does he provide any truly practical suggestions about how courtiers ought to participate in that rule? The **Courtier** invites these questions. At the beginning of the fourth book we are told that the courtier's highest duty consists in teaching his prince to be a better ruler. We are told further that the courtier must couch his teaching in a cautious, oblique style. What the content of that teaching should be, however, remains disappointingly vague. Beyond a few pious generalities—a prince must be temperate and virtuous, must participate in the contemplative as well as the active life, must obey the laws and set a good example, and must reward the good while punishing the bad—book 4 has nothing to say about the actual business of ruling. Such truisms hardly constitute an adequate guide to the slippery and dangerous world of Cesare Borgia and Julius II. Must we conclude, then, that the preeminent book about courtiers is radically deficient, that it fails precisely when it comes to the most important matter, to the courtier's function as political counselor? I think not. In this essay I shall try to demonstrate that the **Courtier** does in fact supply practical political instruction aimed at preparing courtiers who must guide princes. I intend to assert Castiglione's claim as a serious writer of political doctrine.

My approach will be to focus on what might at first seem an unlikely element in the **Courtier**'s structure: the discussion of women in the third book. One might expect the attempt to describe the court lady, which induces the company to turn away from the courtier himself at the end of the second book,

Castiglione's tomb.

to lead to something quite different from politics—to the social graces, perhaps, or chastity, or courtly love. While touching on all these matters, however, the third book also contains an extended commentary on rule. Indeed, it is the most truly political of the **Courtier**'s four books. It goes directly to the heart of sixteenth-century politics and raises the most searching question about the courtier's function. Beneath the camouflage of the court lady and assorted tales of good women, the third book reveals the fundamental orientation of Castiglione's political thought. As we shall see, that thought is not so different from Machiavelli's as most commentators have concluded or assumed. The **Courtier**'s political doctrine cannot be reduced to dully edifying platitudes; it is informed by a spirit of boldness, flexibility, and pragmatism. At the same time, book 3 enables us to establish some important distinctions between Castiglione's boldness and pragmatism and those of his less moderate Florentine contemporary. Castiglione's readiness to fight evil on its own terms, "to make good use of the beast as well as the man," is restrained by a firmly traditional sense of limits. Because his affinity with Machiavelli has not been understood, the originality and vigor of Castiglione's allegiance to tradition have also been missed. (pp. 29-31)

After some preliminary uncertainty, discussion on the third night settles into the Magnifico Giuliano de' Medici's attempt to describe a court lady who can be considered the equal of the courtier as he has emerged from the first two books. Initially the description proceeds along familiar lines established during the previous nights. The Magnifico makes passing reference to practically every virtue known to moral and political philosophy but locates the court lady's specific excellence in "a certain-pleasing affability . . . whereby she will be able to entertain graciously every kind of man with agreeable and comely conversation suited to the time and place and to the station of the person with whom she speaks." Challenges from Gaspar Pallavicino, however, soon force abandonment of this neatly limited approach. Some of these challenges simply reflect Gaspar's role, which he obviously relishes, as the group's sacrificial misogynist but others cannot be so easily dismissed. At one point, drawing attention to the disparity between the Magnifico's casual references to the highest virtues and his stress on "affability," Gaspar remarks, "Since you have granted letters and continence and magnanimity and temperance to women, I am quite surprised that you do not wish them to govern cities, make laws, lead armies, and let the men stay home to cook and spin." The Magnifico promptly replies, "Perhaps that would not be so bad either," and finds himself drawn rapidly into a discussion that cuts through mere affability to serious intellectual, moral, and political issues.

At first the discussion takes the form of an abstract and almost scholastic debate over the nature of women. Gaspar unlimbers some of the big guns in the arsenal of traditional misogyny: woman is a "defect" or "accident" of nature; man can be compared to "form" and woman to "matter," and since "form" is superior to "matter" man must be considered superior to woman; men are by temperament warm, women cold, and "warmth is far more noble and more perfect than cold." To each of these and other similar points, the Magnifico offers a careful and thoroughly convincing rebuttal. There can be no doubt that here and elsewhere the *Courtier* asserts the dignity of women and their essential equality with men. In itself, of course, this assertion amounts to a political teaching of great consequence, and among the *Courtier*'s many influences on later European civilization, its contribution to an increasing recognition of, and respect for, women might be traced. Within the dramatic economy of the dialogue, moreover, the Magnifico's skillful rebuttal of misogyny serves to raise him above the general run of Urbino's courtiers. We see for the first time the qualities of mind that establish him in the course of book 3 as one of Castiglione's chief spokesmen—a figure comparable in authority to Ottaviano Fregoso or Pietro Bembo. In addition, the Magnifico's demonstration that both sexes must be considered equally capable of virtue serves as a necessary preparation for what follows: his elaboration of a series of tales about good women into a vehicle for political ideas intended to have a general applicability to both sexes.

Between the demonstration and the tales, however, the Magnifico introduces a digression that is of great importance for understanding the design of book 3. Lamenting the plight of women whose goodness remains unknown "because the poor creatures are kept shut in," the Magnifico suddenly launches into a tirade against a certain group of "accursed hypocrites among men," who by their wiles win a false reputation for piety and virtue. These hypocrites make a show of holiness, going about with bowed heads and ragged habits, while in fact they are bent upon seductions, forgeries, murders, treacheries, and "every sort of villainy." The Magnifico refrains from naming the group he means but his unstated point is not lost upon Emilia Pia. She promptly identifies the object of his attack as the friars and reproaches him for speaking ill of them. "Then," Castiglione tells us, "the Magnifico laughed

and said: 'How, Madam, have you guessed so well that I was speaking of friars when I did not name them?' " Through this digression Castiglione alerts us to a dimension of the Magnifico's rhetoric that is essential to an interpretation of his stories about women. He knows how to speak through hints and implications; he does not always make his main point explicit. To catch his full intention we must, like Emilia Pia, be prepared to perceive what is implied clearly enough even when it is not named.

Of the Magnifico's stories of good women, some amount to little more than the citation of a famous name; others are presented in enough detail to be understood even by a reader unfamiliar with their sources. The latter are the more revealing. Although all support the contention that women are capable of the highest virtue, the more fully developed stories illustrate the particular qualities that not only women, but men too, need in order to rule and function as advisers to rulers. In the very first of these stories the Magnifico confronts the young courtier abruptly with the political world that awaits him beyond the sheltering walls of the palace. In compiling a list of women who "have been as worthy of praise as the great men whose wives or sisters or daughters they were," the Magnifico first names several well-known Roman ladies and then extols at length the "prudence" of Alexandra, wife of Alexander, King of the Jews. After the death of the tyrannical Alexander, the people rose in arms, eager to revenge themselves by killing his children. Grasping the danger, Alexandra acted promptly, boldly, and effectively. She had her husband's body thrown into the public square and addressed the mob, commiserating with them, inviting them to tear her husband to pieces and feed him to the dogs but begging them "to have mercy on her innocent children." Her words "were so effective that the fierce wrath prevailing in the minds of all the people was at once mitigated and converted to such a feeling of pity that with one accord they not only chose those children as their rulers, but they even gave a most honorable burial to the body of the dead man." Alexandra's story carries with it the bracing odor of the real world of power and violence—an odor that pervades the *Prince* but that has been for the most part absent from the *Courtier* up to this point. Alexandra is faced not with the obstreperousness of a Gaspar but with an enraged mob, out for her children's and perhaps her own, blood. And she triumphs not through learned wit and charming raillery but by confronting ruthlessness with ruthlessness, by boldly and impiously encouraging a mob to desecrate her husband's body in the hope that this will satisfy their passions and win them to her side. Her bold impiety, which the Magnifico characterizes as "prudence," succeeds. Here is a tale to be pondered by courtiers who would instruct princes. The Magnifico does not call attention to the fact that his very first extended example of a virtuous woman introduces a new and more realistic tone into the discussion. As in his description of the friars, he lets the style and substance of his account speak for themselves. At least one of his reasons for such indirectness can be readily understood. Speaking ill of friars may arouse Emilia; to describe as "prudence" Alexandra's throwing her husband's body to the mob (even granting that he was a tyrant) might be considered much more subversive. It implies that ordinary decency may be irrelevant and even a hindrance to the real business of ruling.

Many of the stories that follow prompt similar reflections. A thread of political realism and pragmatism runs throughout the Magnifico's examples, distinguishing book 3 from the rest of the *Courtier* as well as from conventional handbooks of politics and courtesy. When the Magnifico recounts how the Trojan women with Aeneas "helped in the founding of Rome," his tale stresses not only their benefaction but also the trickery by which it was achieved. The fugitives from Troy had landed near the mouth of the Tiber. While the men were away in search of provisions, the women, who were weary of traveling and had remained behind, burned the ships so that their husbands would not be able to reembark. Thus the men were forced to accede to the wishes of the women and to found the city that became Rome. In fact, the Magnifico asserts, following Plutarch, the very name of the city honors a certain Roma, the leader of this female meeting. From an act of conjugal deception, an act that would be blameworthy on moral grounds, it appears that salutary political consequences as well as fame may result. A student of the ways in which courtiers should deal with princes might also remark in this story about women the implication that such deception can be especially helpful when the weak seek to influence the strong. (pp. 32-6)

Behind these and the Magnifico's other stories in book 3 lies, it is true, no systematic political program—no blueprint for uniting Italy against the barbarians, no scheme for revitalizing Italian arms, not even a comprehensive list of the virtues necessary for rule. Rather, the Magnifico's political teaching seems to aim at the inculcation of certain fundamental insights and attitudes essential to political success. Above all, it seems, the courtier, and the prince whom he instructs, must not allow the elegant, civilized sublimations of the court to obscure the fact that cruder passions and ugly dangers inform the outside world of politics; those passions and those dangers cannot be laughed away with raillery but must be subdued by bold cunning and force. Both the courtier and the prince must know how to confront brutality on its own terms; they must be prepared to fight ruthlessness with ruthlessness, to counter strength with strength, or with deception, to make the best of indecent necessities, and to depend upon themselves instead of Providence. They must cultivate freedom from too fastidious a morality and from the potential enervation of piety.

In view of the bold and potentially shocking character of this political teaching, Castiglione's decision to camouflage it in the rhetoric of a character adept at speaking obliquely is understandable. To express such ideas openly would have been imprudent for a man who was himself a courtier moving in the highest circles and who was serving, at the time of the book's publication, as papal nuncio to the court of Charles V. Self-protection, however, does not provide a complete explanation of the third book's subtle art. Castiglione's indirection also reflects the essential conservatism that informs the *Courtier* as a whole—the love of style, the respect for the decorous and decent, and the idealism that are such striking features of the work's surface texture. Unlike Machiavelli, Castiglione does not revel in the harsh, ugly, and shocking facts of life. He is fully aware of those facts and realizes that they must be understood by courtiers who advise rulers, but he refuses to engage in an assault upon traditional values and pieties in the name of realism. By concealing rather than trumpeting his view that those traditional vaues and pieties are sometimes politically inadequate, Castiglione upholds them, albeit in a qualified manner. Praise of constancy, love, continence, chastity, and the values of the classical-Christian synthesis carries a dominant weight throughout book 3 and the rest of the *Courtier,* in spite of the Magnifico's indications that a darker knowledge too is needful. Machiavelli takes his

political bearings by the extreme cases of brutality—Romulus's murder of Remus, Hannibal's "inhuman cruelty," and Cesare Borgia's *virtù* at Sinigaglia; Castiglione wants courtiers to meditate upon such cases and grasp their implications for the problem of ruling but not to make them an excuse for the abandonment of established values. For Castiglione virtù appears to complement, but does not replace, virtue. (pp. 38-40)

One wonders what Charles V thought as he reflected upon the Magnifico's tales of good women. If that prince penetrated the third book's veiled political doctrine, perhaps he recognized the benign as well as the self-protective motive behind the veiling. Perhaps his own experience and position made him sympathetic to the political temper of a man who looked unflinchingly at the base facts that absorbed Machiavelli, who acknowledged the necessity implicit in those facts, but who still preserved an allegiance to the humane ideals of tradition. Of course there is no way to know exactly what Charles made of the *Courtier,* but if we bear in mind the dimension of the book that has been described here, we may discover a special poignancy in the eulogy that we are told the emperor pronounced upon learning of Castiglione's death: "Yo vos digo que es muerto uno de los mejores caballeros del mundo" ["I tell you that he who is dead was one of the greatest gentlemen in the world"]. (pp. 42-3)

> *Dain A. Trafton, "Politics and the Praise of Women: Political Doctrine in the 'Courtier's' Third Book," in* Castiglione: The Ideal and the Real in Renaissance Culture, *edited by Robert W. Hanning and David Rosand, Yale University Press, 1983, pp. 29-44.*

RICHARD L. REGOSIN (essay date 1988)

[*In the following excerpt, Regosin explores the complex relationship between art and life in* The Courtier.]

From its use as a direct sourcebook for manuals of manners in the Renaissance to its more complex modern reading as the expression of an exemplary human and social ideal, Castiglione's **Book of the Courtier** has been read as an urbane and elegant portrayal of courtiership intended for its reader's imitation. While the text appears to transform ordinary life gracefully and elegantly into art, these readings through the centuries have sought to invert the process and transform this art into a civil and decorous life. Art and life have thus been treated as if they exist in a comfortable and mutually hospitable relationship in which each can form the basis for the other, transform it or be transformed, without introducing difference or creating disruption. Castiglione's text appears to demonstrate that life can be modeled on art and can be a model for it; the models hold out the promise of their stability—and of the stability of their relationship—and give imitation integrity.

Myth and ritual have always, of course, linked life and art; ceremony and spectacle with their theatrical elements distinguish human cultures from the earliest times. In the Renaissance, the carefully delineated boundaries of traditional ritual and play appear to open up to allow the self-conscious engagement in life as art and to foster conviction in a malleable and mobile self, which, within received cultural and social patterns, could be shaped by individual will like the raw material of the artist. Although specific authors vary considerably in the faith they appear to place in individual will or in human potential, from Pico della Mirandola's conception of moral transformation through the social and cultural fashioning of a Machiavelli, a Montaigne or a Shakespeare, we have found the expression of an implicit confidence in the potential of life and art to reproduce each other, or to be reproduced in each other. The *Book of the Courtier* appears to take its place as a particularly polished and eloquent statement of what we have read as a Renaissance commonplace.

In recent years we have become aware that Castiglione's text does not sit entirely comfortably in that place. As part of what might be considered a broad revisionist reading of the Renaissance that is lately taking place, critical studies have begun to emphasize conflict and tensions in the work: between a violent and threatening real world and the harmonious, artful world of the court; between destructive time and the desire to memorialize through art; between the fixed written word and speech's evanescence. But while we have made a place in our reading of the *Book of the Courtier* for opposition and paradox (even for a certain opposition between life and art), we have found it more difficult to abandon our belief in art's transformative power. With all of the caveats that our recent insights have produced, we continue to evince a faith in the ultimate ability of art and the aesthetic to allow us to reconcile or to transcend life's contingency and to overcome difference. Our reading tends still to emphasize how Castiglione turns life (at the court) into the art of his book and how that (bookish) art can be re-turned into life.

More is at stake, however, in our understanding of *The Book of the Courtier* than a higher tolerance for tension and conflict or our greater willingness to acknowledge that life in the everyday world places limits on the art of self-fashioning. Central to the work are questions of the nature and status of art itself and of its problematical relationship to life. Castiglione's book reflects self-consciously on its own textuality and on its functioning as a system of linguistic signs and draws our attention to the disturbing implications of all fashioning—of text, self, or world—as forming with words ("formar con parole"). The interlocutors make their explicit concern "forming with words a perfect courtier," and this too is Castiglione's project ("let us form . . . a courtier," he responds to Ariosto before opening the dialogue); words give form to the court and to the courtier and are given form, they form the interlocutors themselves and the courtier which is *their* project. The text announces itself as a linguistic construct but it also announces its courtier(s) as linguistic constructs, as functions of a game (*gioco*) of a name which forms an oxymoron, a "living likeness" of both courtier and court, a figure who arises from speech but always also a figure of speech formed and fashioned with words.

But though I have been arguing against the comfortable interaction of art and life, there is also a danger that this focus on textuality—the troping of Castiglione and his interlocutors, and the status of the courtier as a trope—might lead to a reading that separates art from life altogether and declares the absolute self-reflexivity of the text. There is much in *The Book of the Courtier* that would support that reading. The portrait of the perfect and harmonious court of Urbino seems so remote from life and impervious to it. The game of the name proceeds according to its own rules of decorum and dialogue and generates its own movement. It exists in its own time and creates its own space as the interlocutors sit in a circle facing each other (with their backs to the world) to speak their circular dialogue and to represent with their words the courtier as an ideal reflection of self. And yet, beyond itself

as art or game, as pastime playing with words, the *Courtier* also reflects in its introductory frameworks and within the dialogues themselves the world of the transitory and the contingent, of disorder and disruption. We are reminded that *The Book of the Courtier* never completely closes the text in upon itself, never allows the work to refer *only* to itself and be completely its own source to the exclusion of all that is not "textuality."

Any reading of *The Book of the Courtier,* then, must take seriously into account *both* a life that calls for an artful response or transformation and an art that forms the courtier as a trope. What is at stake in Castiglione's book is the complex nature of the work of art—both as literature and as life—and its problematical status as it seeks to make life over or to give itself life. The text discloses art's effort to transcend the limitations of factitiousness, to show itself as that which "by nature" it cannot be. But at the same time the text appears to recognize the need to oppose transcendence, to affirm the necessity for art to announce itself, to sustain its tension with life and to enact the paradoxical status of the oxymoron. This is the curious, and precarious, situation of the courtier acting with *sprezzatura* (the artless art), the art which must expose itself so that the prowess of the artist can be recognized and praised and the art which must deny itself to appear natural and unaffected. The courtier is thus that which forms itself through its art—with words or with other signs, as we shall see—and that which performs itself to earn the name of courtier. Courtiership is not a state or a mode of being but an attribution, a name given—and taken away—by a public which judges the performance; it is not a signified but a signifier that must be continually renamed just as the performance must be continually replayed. *The Book of the Courtier* cannot in any simple way be a model for life since it must always reflect its own artfulness, and that of courtiership itself, nor can it completely transcend that artfulness to become life since it must draw attention to its own instrumentality, its own medium and to the nature of its operations. Castiglione's text both portrays and enacts the game of the name of "courtier," the game situated on the border of both art and life, implicated in each and implicating each in the other. The game of the name/the name of the game: the chiasmus whose own instability performs the problematic status of the courtier on the border of life and art.

The structure of *The Book of the Courtier* juxtaposes three different modes of discourse to set discourse itself in relief and to disclose its function in art *and* life. The dedicatory epistle to De Silva, with which the work opens, appears to stand outside the "properly" literary text, unambiguously representing life. It is spatially removed as preface, temporally distinguished as the present tense of publication, and generically distinct as letter, authentically referential, signed by the author and addressed to a designated historical reader. The introduction to each of the books, as the second form of discourse, reiterates that authorial voice within the literary context in proximity to the artful pastime. Cast in the present tense of the transcription of the dialogue, the first-person voice—which also addresses an historical reader—in each case creates a temporal frame which discloses that all has passed, that the scene at its center and the figures it represents are the likenesses of a distant, and absent, time. At the center, the third discourse, the dialogue of the courtiers, performs the self-conscious game, itself a work of art, self-contained and functioning according to its own rules. The present tense of the dialogue imputes a presence to the interlocutors and claims its own truthfulness and authenticity.

These three modes of discourse might be said to distinguish between an "outside" historical reality and an "inside" of art. The authorial voice and its world appear to lie beyond the perfect circle of the dialogue where the speakers, with their backs literally turned on all that is not their own perfection, inhabit the ordered and harmonious place of art. Only outside, in the apparently real space of the author and his readers (De Silva, Ariosto, us) do contingency, mutability, death, and time itself hold sway. But this spatial distinction, like the temporal distinction between present and past, is not stable in the *Courtier.* Just as each discourse must be read simultaneously as present *and* past, as a present which by juxtaposition with the other "presents" becomes a past, so each complicates the simple opposition between outside and inside, the "real" and art. The dedicatory letter, for example, the ostensible outside, reiterates the artfulness of the inside by its own rhetorical turns and by its expression of the author's *sprezzatura,* the artless art by which he modestly dissimulates the work's claim to truth. Within the dialogue itself, the outside intrudes in the form of topics potentially disturbing to the perfect order of art, topics which variously challenge the privilege of birth, question the status of (noble) women, suggest the emptiness of courtiership and reveal the contradiction between the virtuous courtly ideal and the reality of service to an evil prince. These discussions are cut short because they threaten to reveal the inadmissible discrepancy between ideal values and real practices and to upset that self-contentment which allows the circle to mirror and model itself. Occasional personal aggressivity is tamed by laughter and transformed into a socially accepted register. The game, by its very self-contained nature, must protect itself against intrusion, but the tensions between art's perfect invention and life's disruptive intervention surface throughout.

More significantly, perhaps, the "outside" inheres in the dialogue in the inescapable presence of the narrative voice which sets the artful presentation in relief. In the Platonic dialogue, the direct discourse of the interlocutors presents itself as unmediated, except for the unobtrusive designation of the speakers, so that the written would appear paradoxically to efface itself in the immediate presence of the oral. Castiglione's dialogue, by contrast, constructs its own outside and inside through the irresistible effects of narration. The voice of the writer intervenes in the verbal exchanges to narrate in the past tense, to describe actions and reactions, and to introduce the speakers. The fiction that the dialogue has already gone through intermediaries—Castiglione's account of the conversations having been recounted to him and here recalled from memory as his book—prepares what we might call the "reality" of its mediation, that is, the reader's ready awareness of the written and its secondary status as a text. The actuality of the spoken word is contaminated by a narrator on whom it depends for its re-presentation: the dialogue is a function of *recitare* and features alongside its interlocutors him who re-cites it, who is the source of this "feigned" presence.

In this complex of multiple and interacting discourses, dialogue plays out its own art. The speakers explicitly draw attention to its functioning as plural (and competing) voices by their commitment to the give and take of difference defined as *contradire.* Federico suggests this as a rule of the game when he proposes that the evening be spent forming the perfect courtier in words; everyone should be free to challenge

(*contradire*) in the manner of philosophical debate. Canossa is chosen as the opening speaker because, as the Lady Emilia says, he is contrary-minded, and speaking thus (*al contrario*), the game will be better, for it will provoke response. There is no danger, he replies sarcastically, of a lack of contradiction (*contradizione*) as long as the Lady Emilia is present. Sexually different voices generate exchange just as voices speaking of the difference of the sexes produce the ongoing debate on the nature and status of women. When Gonzaga seeks a short while later to ask a question, he excuses himself for not following the rules of the game ("demandando e non contradicendo"). At the end of the second book when Magnifico is charged with presenting the next day's topic, the forming of a gentlewoman of the court, he reiterates the dialogic formula: that anyone may challenge him (*contradirmi*); that in his case he will consider it help rather than contradiction ("non contradizione, ma aiuto"), and that perhaps in correcting his errors they all will discover the perfection of the woman which they seek.

Dire and *contradire* are the point and counterpoint of Castiglione's dialogue. To what extent are they functional elements in dialectical argumentation as Federico's reference to philosophical debate would imply? Magnifico's hope that error would be corrected suggests that the discussion is modified by its movement, that exchange between speakers clarifies and redresses, and shapes a progression which discloses (*scoprire*) truth in its permanence and stability. Canossa had indicated his belief that true perfection was unknowable, given the diversity of men's judgment, but he appears nonetheless to affirm a certain faith in rational discussion and thus to lend weight to the dialogic process about to begin: "Still I do think that there is a perfection for everything, even though it be hidden; and that this perfection can be determined by someone reasoning about it ('con ragionevoli discorsi') who has knowledge of the subject."

Yet, as Lipking has pointed out [see excerpt dated 1966], the interruptions and interlocutions mostly produce the *appearance* of dialectical modifications of the argument. The dialogue does not seem to transcend *dire* and *contradire* as questioning, defining, and refining so that the untenable cedes before the irresistible weight of logic and truth. *Contradire* is to attack, to disagree, to take exception to what is said; it cannot produce synthesis or resolution because difference and irresolution are embedded in the form itself. There is no privileged speaker in *The Book of the Courtier*—as there is in Platonic dialogue—and thus no privileged perspective, not even that of the author or narrator, who can only construct the *appearance* of resolution. The argument moves forward, but through accretion, through the juxtaposition of often heterogeneous elements until a broadly brushed portrait of the courtier is completed. Should the courtier be of noble birth? Both sides of the argument are presented (Pallavicino argues against Canossa's view of the importance of noble birth because the form of the game agreed upon demands that *contradire* be respected); Canossa then speaks again to reiterate his position before introducing another aspect of courtiership, expertise in arms. Like so many questions debated by the interlocutors, closure is not absolute or stable; debaters do not acquiesce to superior reasoning nor do they abandon or reformulate their positions. The speaker who speaks last on a subject literally has the last word, and the discussion moves on.

Lady Emilia had suggested another justification of "speaking against" when she chose Canossa to begin the discussion: the game would be better because everyone would have a chance to respond ("il gioco sarà più bello, ché agnun averà che respondervi"). Philosophical argumentation is alien to this notion of a better game because here "better" predicates only fuller participation, livelier exchange and, one understands, dialogue's more elaborate and abundant development. The conversation functions not only as movement towards an end—the formation of the courtier—but as movement which becomes its own end. Thus the challenges and disagreements might be problematical in strictly dialectical terms—as elements of a verbal exchange that leads to resolution—but as elements of the exchange itself of the verb they guarantee its plenitude by filling out the game and filling in the pastime. The dialogue thus displays and enacts its own nature. It widens through the numbers taking part and through its formal structure of counter-statement, which is often as prolific as statement itself and which in turn necessitates further response to develop the encounter. The interlocutors provide each other with occasions for reiteration, elaboration and illustration, and they build up their conversation by opening to diverse and often digressive subject matters. Through *contradire* as its formal and structural principle, the game perpetuates itself in the prevalence of multiple voices. A rhetorical purpose displaces a philosophical one, copiousness fulfills the function of art, of self-invention as forming with words.

Rhetorically speaking, the interlocutors are engaged in *definitio,* in creating the form of the courtier by delineating the verbal bounds (*definire:* to set bounds) which give shape by inclusion and exclusion. The notion of bounds is central to *The Book of the Courtier* and to the plural levels of its art. The little society at Urbino operates within the strictest bounds of civility and courtesy—the implicit rules of the game of courtiership—and is extremely sensitive to the possibility of transgression. The interlocutors artfully employ shifts in conversation, intercessions and laughter to mark social boundaries and deflect tension so that interaction remains within its accepted limits (*i termini,*). The performance of *sprezzatura* is also a question of bounds to be respected, for there is a fine line which the perfect courtier cannot exceed without crossing into affectation. Excess tips the delicate balance between art and artlessness, reveals the artless art as an oxymoron *and* as artifice, and undoes the perfection of courtiership. But the process of defining the courtier through the dialogue is even more complex, for if the act of definition is that of limiting and thus delineating, its function as a pastime requires that it proliferate so as to fill that time. Within the game, the limits of definition must be overrun so that the conversation can be copious and endure. The text thus enacts the tension of the boundary to produce that accretion of courtly characteristics and diversity of subject matter which constitute its abundance. What are commonly considered digressions in subject matter from the purpose of forming the courtier—the debate on women, the discussion on language, the practice of jests and Bembo's disquisition on love—are among other things expressions of that amplitude which the dialogue requires if it is to fulfill its definition as pastime.

Another way to view this question of definition is to reiterate that the meaning of courtiership is not only articulated but exemplified by the speakers. In their comfortably feigned modesty and carefully controlled and self-conscious display of knowledge they enact their art to illustrate the very definition in question. (pp. 21-30)

The courtiers perform the tension between copious speech and an inflation which discloses its emptiness; they signal their awareness of the infinite richness of possibility in verbal display and seek to realize the dictum of fullness through judicious action, by continuing to speak, for example, only when urged to do so. Words serve for self-display, for exhibiting that natural ability (*ingegno*) which, as the artless art, defines them as perfect courtiers. But this language also opens up the precarious pitfalls of loquacity and the fatal flaw of affectation, that excessive display of art which is the sign of imperfection. In that excess, art reveals that it does not refer beyond itself, that like inflated money or cheap talk, it has no backing. The "fiction" which *The Book of the Courtier* seeks to impose (and which it exposes at the same time), which the courtier and art (language) itself in the text seek to perpetrate, is that nature does indeed substantiate art, that signs and their referents do coincide, that representation has integrity and authenticity. (p. 32)

Since *The Book of the Courtier* is a text, and a dialogue, the linguistic sign, the word, gets most play; for Castiglione and his interlocutors, language is like action, the means by which the speakers interact and act upon each other (*conversare* is both to associate and to converse, to associate through conversation). But it is equally true that in the *Courtier* action, and life itself, is like language; courtiership is a performance that seeks to impose itself as the sign of perfection. All that the courtier does impresses the onlooker/listener as so many signs whose significance must be determined. Courtiership calls for a semiotics of courtly behavior, of decorum, of gestures, demeanor and attitude so that meaning may be attributed and praise and approbation conferred. The ubiquitous lover of the *Courtier* engages above all else in a semiotic experience, confronting signs of affection or of rejection in every look, every sigh, every word of the lady and seeking to give witness to his own posture in love. So too does the gentlewoman of the court whose perfection depends on her ability to discern the most certain and sure signs ("i più certi e sicuri segni") in order to distinguish true love from false. Love functions as a metonymic figure for courtiership; what is at stake is the status of signs (*segni*), of evidence (*testimonio*) and its interpretation.

All aspects of the aspiring courtier, even his noble birth, are signs which impose upon his audience and cause them to attribute or withhold grace and approbation. In courtly circles, one would have expected nobility to be the stable, universal sign of worth, the lamp of truth as Canossa would have it. But Pallavicino, in the spirit of *contradire,* raises the possibility of nobility's deceptiveness; nobles may be mean-spirited, he claims, and those of ordinary birth may through nature or fortune have outstanding characters. Although the issue is not pursued for obvious reasons, and Canossa proposes that the group accept noble birth because it inclines others in one's favor (at least at first), Pallavicino's remarks undermine the integrity of the "natural order" as a mark of distinction. No sign demonstrates its value unequivocally, not even that by which the courtiers set most store. Without the guarantee of birth, nature or the accepted order of things, the state is set for perfect courtiership to become a matter of performance.

Once again the polysemous sign leads back to art. There is art which must be acquired because study and effort are essential to enhance and embellish nature. And there is art which must be dissimulated so that study and effort are made to look natural. *Il studio* and *la fatica* are necessary in all things that are to be done well, Federico says in Book II. On the other hand, the lesson of *sprezzatura* is to hide that what one says and does is artful (*nascondere l'arte*) and to disclose (*dimostrare*) that what one says and does has come about without effort and without premeditation. Facility (*la facilità*) makes the audience marvel; things done simply (*simplicissimamente*) suggest their source in nature and truth rather than in effort and art ("il studio e l'arte"). Herein lies the paradoxical status of perfect courtiership and the complexity of its sign. *Sprezzatura*—which proclaims that true art is that which does not appear to be art—thus signifies simultaneously that (i) there is no art; the speech or action is natural, unaffected; (ii) there is art but it is so well hidden that it does not show, and (iii) if there were art, the actor could do even better than he has done. The multi-faceted sign plays on deception and sleight-of-hand to make something be esteemed for much more than it really is. It cunningly holds in tension the mysterious presence and absence of art and skillfully invents the oxymoron of the artless art which is the name of the game (or the game of the name). (pp. 36-7)

The Book of the Courtier thus sets before courtier and reader, actor and audience, the shifting sign in all its multiplicity and the perplexing task of interpretation. And it sets before them the irreconcilable complexities of deception itself because perfection (*sprezzatura*) signifies only through dissimulation (by the actor) and misreading (by the audience). Pallavicino is sensitive to this paradox and argues for the absolute coincidence of worth and its signifiers. In response to Federico's elaboration of the art of appearing better than one is (an obvious application of *sprezzatura*), he exclaims, "This seems to me to be not an art, but an actual deceit; and I do not think it seemly for anyone who wishes to be a man of honor ever to deceive." Federico rejects the moralizing attack in favor of that aestheticizing of life which characterizes the entire enterprise of the *Courtier.* By a series of well-chosen metaphors he transfers from art to deceit the characteristics of skill, style, and effective audience response. Like the effect produced by the jewel set by the master goldsmith, grace and beauty issue from the manipulative (and judicious) sleight-of-hand of the courtier and so redeem the artful deceit. But if Pallavicino's reaction underscores the moral deficiency of *sprezzatura* and implicates the courtier in its inevitable duplicity, Federico's justification highlights the equally disquieting issue of its linguistic instability, sliding between nature and art, art and deception, nature/art and affectation. The sign is no more firmly grounded in real worth than it is in real nobility, and while one might espouse the position that external things often bear witness to internal things, there is no guarantee of their relationship in the world of the *Courtier.* (p. 38)

The dialogue of Castiglione's last book of the *Courtier* appears to overcome these limitations by shifting the register of the conversation from the aesthetic to the moral and by imposing Bembo's transcendent vision of neo-Platonic love. Apparently leaving behind considerations of art and of appearance at the court—which Ottaviano dismisses as "lightness and vanity"—the interlocutors discuss the proper and virtuous role of the courtier as advisor to the prince. The courtier would no longer be concerned with producing the signs of his courtliness and with the problems relating to their interpretation but would justify his name in unequivocal service for the good. The nagging issue of deception, although not disappearing altogether, would be finessed as deception itself be-

came an instrument serving virtuous action, the prince and the state (the interlocutors do not pursue the question of virtue's contamination in this context). And in Bembo's final rapture, the conflict between appearance and reality, between surface and depth, between the sign and its truth would be resolved; outward beauty becomes the authentic sign of inner goodness ("la bellezza estrinseca è vero segno della bontà intrinseca") as the soul mounts beyond the world of contingency to union with God. (pp. 39-40)

Bembo's discourse may differ in degree from the discourse of the other interlocutors of **The Book of the Courtier** but it does not differ in kind; like theirs, it enacts the oxymoron, the artless art. All dialogue in the **Courtier** is *ex tempore* because dialogue is the paradigmatic performance of improvisation just as improvised speech is the paradigm of performance. Thus all speech is the result of study and effort, the enactment of artful strategies designed to produce the effect of the natural. Bembo has the last word, as it were, because his discourse goes further than the others—it strives to become an event, to present itself as unmediated voice, as the sign of nature and the expression of authenticity, but he does not exceed the bounds imposed by the game of the name, *formar con parole*. Even as his presentation itself seems to disclaim any connection with art, its rhetorical underpinnings show themselves (as they must) in order to display his own perfection as a courtier.

If we demystify Bembo's rapture in this way, we expose transcendence as the most prestigious (*praestigiosus,* full of tricks, deceitful) of the **Courtier**'s many rhetorical games. At the same time we underscore the stunning effects of artful discourse, its ability to overwhelm and to capture the mind of the listener, to mark it with its sign. It may be, as one critic has remarked, that Bembo's words "are about nothing at all," but the reaction of his audience clearly indicates that they are not without significance; they are the sign of the performance of perfect courtiership, the enactment of the role which earns the name of perfect courtier. . . . As in all other cases of courtly perfection, the truth of the performance is academic; what matters is its authenticity, the degree to which it approaches the artless art. Does Bembo really experience some kind of transcendence, as the response of the others seems to indicate, or is he merely carried away with his own words, borne off by the sound of his own voice, as the Lady Emilia's tug at his sleeve might imply? Does inspired nature produce genuine discourse or do ingenuity and eloquence promote artful speech? This is the question on which turns the problematic status of the perfect courtier and it implicates Bembo, as it does all the other interlocutors, in the game of the name. (pp. 45-6)

Richard L. Regosin, "The Name of the Game/the Game of the Name: Sign and Self in Castiglione's 'Book of the Courtier'," in The Journal of Medieval and Renaissance Studies, *Vol. 18, No. 1, Spring, 1988, pp. 21-47.*

FURTHER READING

Amelia, William. "Castiglione and *The Courtier*." *History Today* XXVIII (September 1978): 580-88.
Overview of *The Courtier*'s literary and historical significance.

Bonadeo, Alfredo. "The Function and Purpose of the Courtier in *The Book of the Courtier* by Castiglione." *Philological Quarterly* L, No. 1 (January 1971): 36-46.
Probes the courtier's political and moral efficacy within the framework of Castiglione's handbook.

Cartwright, Julia. *Baldassare Castiglione, the Perfect Courtier: His Life and Letters, 1478-1529*, Vols. I & II. London: John Murray, 1908, 460 p., 507 p.
Comprehensive biography of the author.

Greene, Thomas M. "*Il Cortegiano* and the Choice of a Game." *Renaissance Quarterly* XXXII, No. 2 (Summer 1979): 173-86.
Proposes that the game of creating an ideal courtier implies self-examination for its participants.

Grudin, Robert. "Renaissance Laughter: The Jests in Castiglione's *Il Cortegiano*." *Neophilologus* LVIII, No. 2 (April 1974): 199-204.
Reveals an interaction of extremes in *The Courtier*, exemplified by its blend of levity and profound observation.

Hale, J. R. "Castiglione's Military Career." *Italian Studies* XXXVI (1981): 41-57.
Suggests that the author's military experience shaped ideals delineated in his work.

Hanning, Robert W., and Rosand, David, eds. *Castiglione: The Ideal and the Real in Renaissance Culture*. New Haven: Yale University Press, 1983, 215 p.
Collection of discursive essays on Castiglione.

Harrison, Thomas Perrin, Jr. "The Latin Pastorals of Milton and Castiglione." *PMLA* L, No. 2 (June 1935): 480-93.
Establishes parallels between John Milton's *Epitaphium Damonis* and Castiglione's little-known elegy, *Alcon*.

Lanham, Richard A. "More, Castiglione, and the Humanist Choice of Utopias." In *Acts of Interpretation: The Text in Its Contexts, 700-1600: Essays on Medieval and Renaissance Literature in Honor of E. Talbot Donaldson*, edited by Mary J. Carruthers and Elizabeth D. Kirk, pp. 327-43. Norman, Okla.: Pilgrim Books, 1982.
Compares the author's behavioral norms with those espoused in *Utopia* by his English contemporary, Sir Thomas More.

Menut, Alfred D. "Castiglione and the Nicomachean Ethics." *PMLA* LVIII, No. 2 (June 1943): 309-21.
Claims that Castiglione patterned the moral philosophy of his courtier after virtues outlined in Aristotle's *Nicomachean Ethics*.

Paul, David. "A Book of Behaviour." *The Cornhill Magazine* 161, No. 966 (December 1945): 474-78.
Vignette on the author and his work.

Pugliese, Olga Zorzi. "Variations on Ficino's *De Amore*: The Hymns to Love by Benivieni and Castiglione." In *Ficino and Renaissance Neoplatonism*, edited by Konrad Eisenbichler and Olga Zorzi Pugliese, pp. 113-21. Ottawa: Dovehouse Editions Canada, 1986.
Asserts the influence of Italian humanist Marsilio Ficino on treatments of love in *The Courtier* and Girolamo Benivieni's "Canzona d'amore."

Rebhorn, Wayne A. "Ottaviano's Interruption: Book IV and the Problem of Unity in *Il Libro del Cortegiano*." *MLN* 87, No. 1 (January 1972): 37-59.
Attributes cohesion of *The Courtier*'s books to their form.

————. "The Enduring Word: Language, Time and History in *Il Libro del Cortegiano*." *MLN* 96, No. 1 (January 1981): 23-40.
Explores numerous paradoxes fundamental to *The Courtier* as a work of art.

Roeder, Ralph. *The Man of the Renaissance: Four Lawgivers: Savonarola, Machiavelli, Castiglione, Aretino*. New York: Viking Press, 1933, 540 p.
Creates a composite of the Renaissance man from the varied attributes of Castiglione and three Italian contemporaries.

Ryan, Lawrence V. "Book Four of Castiglione's *Courtier*: Climax or Afterthought?" *Studies in the Renaissance* XIX (1972): 156-79.
Admits *The Courtier*'s inconsistencies, but maintains its ultimate success in "resolving the apparent contradiction between the active and the contemplative lives."

Saccone, Eduardo. "The Portrait of the Courtier in Castiglione." *Italica* 64, No. 1 (Spring 1987): 1-18.
Disputes the critical contention that the author's work presents ideals of courtiers or court life.

Salamon, Linda Bradley. "*The Courtier* and *The Scholemaster*." *Comparative Literature* XXV, No. 1 (Winter 1973): 17-36.
Notes similarities between *The Courtier* and sixteenth-century English scholar Roger Ascham's *The Scholemaster*.

Schnerr, Walter J. "Two Courtiers: Castiglione and Rodrigues Lôbo." *Comparative Literature* XIII, No. 2 (Spring 1961): 138-53.
Contrasts *The Courtier* with a prose work of sixteenth-century Portuguese author Francisco Rodrigues Lôbo.

Shapiro, Marianne. "Mirror and Portrait: The Structure of *Il libro del Cortegiano*." *The Journal of Medieval and Renaissance Studies* 5, No. 1 (Spring 1975): 37-61.
Emphasizes the relationship of play to reality in *The Courtier*.

Stewart, James T. "Renaissance Psychology and the Ladder of Love in Castiglione and Spenser." *The Journal of English and Germanic Philology* LVI (April 1957): 225-30.
Links *The Courtier* to Edmund Spenser's *Fowre Hymnes* (1596), noting their similar expressions of the Renaissance conception of love.

Tetel, Marcel. "The Humanistic Situation: Montaigne and Castiglione." *The Sixteenth Century Journal* X, No. 3 (Fall 1979): 69-84.
Maintains that Castiglione and sixteenth-century French essayist Michel de Montaigne confront human transience with similar dialectic advances.

Williamson, Edward. "The Concept of Grace in the Work of Raphael and Castiglione." *Italica* XXIV, No. 4 (December 1947): 316-24.
Finds *The Courtier*'s notion of grace to have been executed in the paintings of Italian Renaissance artist Raphael.

Woodhouse, J. R. "Book Four of Castiglione's *Cortegiano*—A Pragmatic Approach." *The Modern Language Review* 74, No. 1 (January 1979): 62-8.
Argues of *The Courtier* that its author "was forced into writing Book IV and into publishing the whole work in order to vindicate his position as a serious-minded diplomat, a worthy Papal Nuncio and a potential cardinal."

Young, Ruth Elizabeth. "Introduction to Castiglione and His Courtier." *Smith College Studies in Modern Languages* XXI, Nos. 1-4 (October 1938-July 1940): 240-57.
Biographical and critical sketch of the author.

Mary (Granville Pendarves) Delany

1700-1788

English epistler and autobiographer.

Delany was an eighteenth-century English epistler who wrote thousands of letters about her experiences at court and among various social circles of the day. While her letters focus chiefly on gossip and small talk, commentators note that they help shed much light on details of eighteenth-century English daily life not otherwise well recorded. Although Delany expressly forbade any publication of her letters and even burned some of them, a selection covering the years 1779-88 was issued in 1820, and six massive volumes of her correspondence were published by her great-great-niece, Lady Llanover, in 1861-62. To future generations of readers who have valued the work for its social and literary merit, Mrs. Delany's *Autobiography and Correspondence* offers a comprehensive retrospective of life in the eighteenth century.

Mary Granville Pendarves Delany was born in 1700 in Coulston, Wiltshire, the daughter of Colonel Bernard and Mary Granville. The Granville family was prominent among the nobility and had close ties to the monarchy, but because the colonel was a second son, he was relatively poor. Owing to his prestigious name, however, Colonel Granville enjoyed many aristocratic privileges, including the opportunity to have his daughter Mary appointed maid of honor to Queen Anne. To prepare Mary for this position, Colonel Granville placed her in a private academy reserved for the daughters of the most powerful families in England. Her education began at the age of six under the tutelage of Mlle. Puelle, a French refugee. While at the academy, Mary studied such disciplines as mathematics, grammar, French, and music until at the age of eight she moved to Whitehall with her uncle and aunt, Sir John and Lady Stanley.

Mary's preparation for life at court continued for several years until Queen Anne's death in 1714 brought an end to the Stuart royal line. With the succession of George I and the House of Hanover, Mary's claim to the position of maid of honor was denied. At this time, the Granvilles moved to the country estate of Buckland in Gloucestershire. While at Buckland, Mary, now an attractive young lady, became the object of the amorous advances of a Mr. Twyford. Twyford proposed to Mary, but his parents refused to permit his marriage into such a poor family. In order to avoid further problems with the young lovers, Mary was sent to live with her uncle, Lord Lansdowne, at Longleat, his seat in Wiltshire. At Longleat, Lord Lansdowne took it upon himself to match Mary with a more promising suitor, one who would secure a fortune for her. The man selected for this marriage of convenience, Lansdowne's good friend Alexander Pendarves, was sixty years old, whereas Mary was only seventeen. As Mary described him in one of her letters, "he was excessively fat, of a brown complexion, negligent in his dress, and took a vast quantity of snuff which gave him a dirty look . . . altogether a person rather disgusting than engaging." At first, Mary desperately fought her uncle's decision, but when he became furious at her disobedience, she acquiesced. Regardless of the ill feelings that surrounded the whole affair, Alex-

ander Pendarves and Mary Granville were married on 17 February 1718. After the wedding, Pendarves took Mary back to his lonely country estate in Cornwall where she spent several unhappy years with him until his death in 1724. Unfortunately for Mary, Pendarves did not leave a will. Most of his possessions were therefore bequeathed to his blood relatives. As a result, the widow settled in London with only a modest pension from Pendarves's estate, not the fortune her uncle had envisioned.

Comfortable with her newfound freedom, Delany rejected the advances of many suitors during the next several years. She was deeply affected by a courtship with Lord Baltimore, however, which lasted nearly five years, only to end bitterly when the lovers could not agree on a committment of marriage. In a state of distress, Delany went on an extended trip to Ireland from 1731 to 1733. There she became closely acquainted with Anglo-Irish satirist Jonathan Swift, with whom she carried on a correspondence for nearly four years after her return to England. She also met Dr. Patrick Delany, an Irish scholar and clergyman, on her long journey. Her admiration for Dr. Delany was apparent when she first heard one of his sermons. She wrote, "Dr. Delany is as agreeable a companion as I ever met with, and one who condescends to converse with women and treat them like reasonable creatures. . . . These are the sort of men I find myself inclined to like, and wish I had such a set in England."

Upon her return to London, Mrs. Delany continued to associate with aristocratic friends and relatives. She often stayed with her uncle, Sir John Stanley, at Somerset House. She also spent time with her good friend Margaret Cavendish Harley, Duchess of Portland, whose husband owned a country estate, Bulstrode, outside of London. In 1743, Dr. Delany came to England and asked Mary to marry him. Mary accepted Delany's proposal, even though her family considered him to be from a lower social class. The Delanys lived happily together for the next twenty-five years, spending much of their time in Ireland while making several extended trips to England so Mary could visit her friends. In May 1768, while he and Mrs. Delany were visiting friends in Bath, Dr. Delany died at the age of eighty-three.

Widowed once again, Delany settled in a house in Thatched House Court in London, but she spent most of her time as a guest of the Duchess of Portland at Bulstrode. Through the duchess, Delany met George III and Queen Charlotte, who frequently came to Bulstrode for tea. During one visit, the monarchs evinced fascination with an art form that Delany had created at the age of seventy-two. Deemed by her "flora" or "paper mosaic," it entailed the recreation of flowers by layering colored pieces of paper on top of one another. Delany became so adept at her new art form that many people mistook her creations for real flowers, and she became quite famous. Over the next ten years, Delany created nearly one thousand "paper mosaics," stopping at the age of eighty-three because her weakening eyesight compromised her accuracy. During this time, such a bond of friendship grew between Delany and the king and queen that when the Duchess of Portland died in 1785, George III provided Delany with a house near Windsor Castle. He also gave her a pension of £300 per year to ensure that his "dear Mrs. Delany" could continue to live comfortably. Delany lived at the house, welcomed as an intimate friend of the royal family, until her death on April 15, 1788.

Delany's collected correspondence was published posthumously in two versions. The first, the short collection *Letters from Mrs. Delany (Widow of Doctor Patrick Delany,) to Mrs. Frances Hamilton,* was published in 1820. This collection focused not so much upon Delany as upon her intimate anecdotes concerning George III and the royal family. The second version, consisting of six volumes of letters and brief autobiographical sketches, was published in 1861-62 by Lady Llanover. Known as the *Autobiography and Correspondence,* it is Delany's principal work and the one most often discussed by critics of her writings. Delany did not write her letters with the intention of entertaining a large audience. Her letters were merely personal communications to relatives, friends, and acquaintances. Most of them were written to her younger sister, Anne Granville Dewes, to whom Delany was very close. After Anne's death in 1761, however, the Duchess of Portland, as well as Anne's daughter, Mary Dewes, became her intimate correspondents and remained so for the next twenty years. Other correspondents of note include the founder of Methodism, John Wesley, and Delany's friend from Ireland, Jonathan Swift. Commentators agree that Delany's letters are not written in a literary style worthy of special attention, nor do they give a first-hand account of the significant political changes Delany witnessed in her lifetime. They do, however, provide contemporary gossip, fashion

trends, etc., adding a social dimension to the copiously documented political events of the eighteenth century. These details, scholars note, focusing as they do on quotidian life as opposed to events in the literary sphere, are exactly what one would expect to find in the correspondence of an eighteenth-century woman who had no aspirations to become a famous literary figure. As such, Delany's *Autobiography and Correspondence* creates a more complete perspective from which to view the eighteenth century.

All of Delany's contemporary critics, chiefly consisting of her various correspondents, considered her a remarkable woman, one worthy of high praise. To Swift and Wesley, she was the ideal of faultlessness and purity. Fanny Burney considered it a "blessing" to be in her presence. Hannah More described her as "a living library of knowledge." To have received such respect from so many influential eighteenth-century figures is a strong indication of Delany's overall significance, critics have noted. Detailed aesthetic criticism of her *Autobiography and Correspondence,* however, was not available until Lady Llanover's edition was published in 1861-62. Almost all of the critics from this period agree that a greater understanding of eighteenth-century life may be gained from the *Autobiography and Correspondence.* One critic, however, took a decided stand against this observation, issuing a warning to "the unwary wight who may be entrapped by a title into reading a farrago of nostrums, fashions, and chit-chat. . . ." Lady Llanover herself received much negative criticism for her role as the editor of the *Autobiography and Correspondence.* Charges ranged from her alleged use of footnotes intentionally biased against early detractors of Delany to her haphazard approach toward the compilation of material.

With the publication of an abridged edition of Delany's letters by Emily Morse Symonds (writing under the pseudonym George Paston) in 1900, critics reaffirmed the historical significance of the letters while commending Symonds for organizing and condensing the *Autobiography and Correspondence* into one volume. Since the turn of the century, critics have attempted to examine Delany as not just a witness of eighteenth-century daily life, but also as an interesting personality. In 1925, E. Beresford Chancellor commented on Delany's artistic talents, highlighting such accomplishments as her exquisite needlework, oil painting reproduction, and "paper mosaics." In his 1940 biography of Delany, John Saint Clair Muriel, writing as "Simon Dewes," emphasized a further quality of her letters. The critic wrote: "That her letters are such a joy, that they give an unparalleled portrait of the life of a leisured lady in a leisured age is because they were written only to her intimate friends. They were *private* letters. They were for no eyes but those of the person to whom they were addressed." Essentially, Muriel argued that critical condemnation of Delany's letters as mere gossip and chitchat fails to recognize that she never intended her correspondence for publication, for exposure to a wide audience. Another critical essay, written by Robert Manson Myers in 1946, focuses on Delany's close friendship with German-born composer George Frideric Handel, particularly their collaboration on an oratorio based on John Milton's *Paradise Lost.* Only with recent growth of interest in literature by women has there been an attempt to create a psychological profile of Delany. In 1988, Patricia Meyer Spacks examined Delany's letters as the work of a socially restricted woman. Spacks argued that like many other women of her time, Delany combatted repression by using letter-writing as a vehicle for self-discovery. Spacks's approach to Delany's letters, combined with a variety of studies ranging over nearly two hundred years, confirms for critics Delany's importance as a witness of events great and small.

Although she was a woman of no major historical significance, Delany nevertheless played a leading role in eighteenth-century English society. Thus, her *Autobiography and Correspondence,* in which she fashioned a detailed account of her experiences at court and in reigning social circles, offers a colorful picture of what life was really like for the eighteenth-century leisure class. Wrote Dr. Richard Hurd, Bishop of Worcester, in Delany's epitaph: "She was a lady of singular ingenuity and politeness, and of unaffected piety. These qualities endeared her through life to many noble and excellent persons, and made the close of it illustrious by procuring for her many signal marks of grace and favour from their Majesties."

PRINCIPAL WORKS

Letters from Mrs. Delany (Widow of Doctor Patrick Delany,) to Mrs. Frances Hamilton, from the Year 1779, to the Year 1788; Comprising Many Unpublished and Interesting Anecdotes of Their Late Majesties and the Royal Family (letters) 1820
The Autobiography and Correspondence of Mary Granville (Mrs. Delany), with Interesting Reminiscences of King George the Third and Queen Charlotte. 6 vols. (letters) 1861-62
"An Essay on Propriety" (essay) 1925; published in *Mrs. Delany At Court and Among the Wits*

*This work was written in 1777.

JOHN WESLEY   (letter date 1731)

[*As cofounder (with his brother Charles) of Methodism, Wesley had a profound impact on life in eighteenth-century England. Ministering to the spiritual and social needs of thousands of people, Wesley and his Methodist creed stimulated a wave of religious fervor throughout the country. Because of its emphasis on emotion rather than ritual and on intuitive rather than analytic thought, Methodism has been called the religious counterpart of the Romantic movement in literature. Wesley wrote tirelessly, producing numerous volumes on the history of the church, biblical commentaries, educational treatises, and translations from the classics. He also edited the works of John Bunyan, William Law, and Henry Brooke. Wesley and Delany (then Mrs. Pendarves) met in Stanton, England through mutual friends in 1730. Although some scholars believe that a courtship took place, the content of their letters gives no indication that they were anything more than good friends. After their departure from Stanton, Wesley and Delany maintained a correspondence for the next four years, adopting the pseudonyms Cyrus and Aspasia. In his letters to Aspasia, Wesley expressed many of the spiritual and intellectual ideas which later became integral components of Methodism. In the following excerpt from a 1731 letter to Delany, Wesley praises "Aspasia" for her spiritual purity.*]

Far be it from me to think that any circumstance of life shall ever give the enemy an advantage over Aspasia. Though she walk through the vale of the shadow of death, where sin and vanity are on every side; where vice and folly appear in so fair a light as to deceive, if it were possible, the very elect; where the utmost skill of the world and the prince of it join to tear up humility, the root of Christian virtue, and consideration, which alone (under God) is able to give it any increase,—even there her footsteps shall not slide; she shall fear and shall find no evil: He who hath overcome the world and its prince shall give His angels charge over her to keep her in all her ways. (pp. 80-1)

> *John Wesley, in a letter to Mrs. Pendarves on April 14, 1731, in* The Letters of the Rev. John Wesley, *Vol. I, edited by John Telford, The Epworth Press, 1931, pp. 80-2.*

MARY PENDARVES DELANY   (letter date 1733)

[*In the following excerpt from a 1733 letter to Anglo-Irish satirist Jonathan Swift, Delany responds to Swift's assessment of her skills as a grammarian and invites further criticism of her writing.*]

I am resolved to be even with you for what you say about my writing, and will henceforward write to you as carelessly as I can; and, if it is not legible, thank yourself. I do not wonder at the envy of the ladies, when you are pleased to speak of me with some regard: I give them leave to exercise their malice on an occasion that does me so much honour. I protest I am not afraid of you, and would appear quite natural to you, in the hopes of your rewarding my openness and sincerity by correcting what you disapprove of; and, since I have not now an opportunity of receiving your favours of pinching and beating, make me amends by *chiding* me for every word that is *false-spelt* and for my *bad English.* You see what you are like to suffer. If this promises you too much trouble do not give me so much encouragement in your next letter, for upon something in your last I have almost persuaded myself that, by your assistance and my own most earnest desire, I may in time become worthy of your care. Vanity stands at my elbow all this while, and animates me by a thousand agreeable promises: without her encouragement I should never have presumed to correspond with the Dean of St. Patrick's. You must not be angry with me for keeping her company, for I had very little acquaintance with her till I had received some marks of your favour. (pp. 79-80)

> *Mary Pendarves Delany, in an excerpt from a letter to Jonathan Swift on July 21, 1733, in her* Mrs. Delany (Mary Granville): A Memoir, 1700-1788, *edited by George Paston, Grant Richards, 1900, pp. 79-81.*

JONATHAN SWIFT   (letter date 1734)

[*Swift is considered the foremost satirist in the English language and one of the greatest in world literature. He was also an accomplished poet, a master of political journalism, and a leader of the Anglican church in Ireland. Swift was in his mid-sixties and employed as the Dean of Saint Patrick's Cathedral in Dublin when he first met Delany (then Mrs. Pendarves). She was in Ireland on a protracted visit after her unsuccessful courtship with Lord Baltimore in London. Upon meeting at a dinner party in January 1733, Swift and Delany began an intellectual flirtation—Swift assuming the role of Mary's literary "master"—which lasted the two months they spent together before Delany went back to England. Thereafter, their relationship continued through a series of elaborately complimentary letters. At issue in many of Swift's letters was a desire to lure Delany back to Ireland, thereby enabling him to discover some "fault" in her all the more easily. Equally, Delany sought to convince Swift to come to England so she could be closer to her "master," who, she often noted, could teach her how to improve herself. Swift and Delany's correspondence proved a great source of entertainment to both parties until Swift began to lose his faculties in 1736. At this point, correspondence between the two friends ceased. In the following excerpt from a 1734 letter to Delany, Swift compliments his correspondent on her fault-lessness.*]

Nothing vexes me so much with relation to you, as that with all my disposition to find faults, I was never once able to fix upon anything that I could find amiss, although I watched you narrowly; for when I found we were to lose you soon, I kept my eyes and ears always upon you, in hopes that you would make some *boutade*. It is, you know, a French word, and signifies a sudden jerk from a horse's hinder feet which you did not expect, because you thought him for some months a sober animal, and this hath been my case with several ladies whom I chose for friends: in a week, a month, or a year, hardly one of them failed to give me a *boutade;* therefore I command you will obey my orders, in coming over hither for one whole year, after which, upon the first *boutade you make,* I will give you my pass to be gone. (p. 259)

> *Jonathan Swift, in a letter to Mrs. Pendarves on October 7, 1734, in* The Correspondence of Jonathan Swift: 1732-1736, Vol. IV, *edited by Harold Williams, Oxford at the Clarendon Press, 1965, pp. 257-60.*

JONATHAN SWIFT   (letter date 1735)

[*In the following excerpt from a 1735 letter, originally published in the* Monthly Mirror *in March 1797 under the heading "Letter from Dean Swift to the Celebrated Mrs. Delany," Swift expresses his fondness for Delany while challenging her self-criticism in the postscript of one of her own letters.*]

Madam, I have had one great, and not very usual, misfortune in my life, which was to come to a kingdom where I was utterly a stranger, when it was too late to make new friendships; every body worth knowing being already bespoke. As to the *many* friends I left in England when I first came over, they are either banished or dead, or by a tacit agreement we have dropt correspondence; and the *few* remaining, my ill health hath condemned me never to see again. Another ill circumstance is, that years have not hardened me; and therefore, when I lament my absence from those I love and esteem, I fly for a remedy to ill-nature: I recollect whatever I found amiss in them; one was positive, another was a bad listener; a third talked too much, and a fourth was too silent, and so on. For these reasons, I would give half my goods that I had known you five times more than I did; and had the forecast to watch all your behaviour till I could have found something that was wrong, though it was in the least significant part of your conduct; and upon that one point I would have forced my memory and observation to dwell, as some little cure for the vexation of despairing ever to see you again. Pray, Madam, will you be pleased, in mere mercy, to send me the names and places of abode of your enemies and censurers (for God forbid you should want either): after which, I will desire a commerce of letters with them, whereof you shall be the subject; and then I shall be able to talk ill of you to myself, as well as to other people, without being believed by either. As you are in doubt whether you would have me sick or neglect you, so, for the sake of those who come to visit you, I might be in doubt whether I could wish your eyes were well or not; because ten thousand may suffer in the first case, and only one in the second. My concern is only that they should give you no pain, whatever they may do to the fine gentlemen twenty miles round, who, ten to one, are such coxcombs as to think they only make you handsomer, without considering that they discover almost every good quality of your mind. I do not remember that I called you a fool; but as to your being a knave, there may be some probability. You have forsaken your friend Mrs. Donnellan; you ran away with five hundred and fourteen hearts, to which you had no other claim than power tyrannical; not to mention that of the Killala parson; for which all the clergy of the kingdom, and principally myself, look upon you as a mortal enemy to the church. My partiality for you forceth me to congratulate you on your sister's recovery. I hope she is like you in every thing, but the hardness of her heart. However, as we gave you the government of this kingdom, we desire you will send her over, as your deputy, to tyrannize in your stead. Whose fault it is that you lose Mrs. Donnellan? Or how can you pretend to lose any thing that you know at any time where to find? And we heartily wish that the distress you complain of, on her account, were five hundred times greater than it is. I have visited Mrs. Donnellan but once since her arrival: she is in the family of a person with whom I have no acquaintance, nor am likely to have any; so that she is of no more comfort to me than to you. . . . The apology you make in the post[s]cript is, in few words, a compound of falsehood and affectation. You are ashamed, you say, of your blunders: and I cannot observe one. I suppose it is a civil way of reproaching mine; for my ill head makes me always mistake syllables, letters, words, and sometimes half sentences; you may see how often I am forced to interline. Pray God preserve you! I am with the truest respect and great esteem, Madam, your most obedient humble servant. . . . (pp. 548-49)

> *Jonathan Swift, "An Uncollected Letter from Swift to Mrs. (Pendarves) Delany," in* Notes and Queries, *n.s. Vol. 26, No. 6, December, 1979, pp. 548-49.*

PATRICK DELANY   (essay date 1757)

[*In the following excerpt from "Mrs. Delany: A Character," an essay written in 1757 but not published at the time, Dr. Patrick Delany presents Mary, here styled "Maria," as an example of the ideal toward which all fashionable ladies should strive. "Arabella" and "Lucelia," to whom Dr. Delany refers in his essay, had earlier been portrayed in the doctor's short-lived weekly paper, the* Humanist, *as examples "to inspire the fashionable ladies of the day with emulation."*]

The next extraordinary woman that hath yet come within the compass of my acquaintance, is Maria. She came into the world with all, indeed more than all, the united advantages of Arabella and Lucelia. She was nobly descended, and most advantageously educated. Both her parents pious, intelligent, and polite, to a very distinguished degree; early initiated in every art, with elegance and erudition, that could form her into a fine lady, a good woman, and a good Christian. She read and wrote two languages correctly and judiciously; she soon became a mistress of her pen, in every art to which a pen could be applied. She wrote a fine hand in the most masterly manner. She drew, she designed with amazing correctness and ability! the noblest and most varied landscapes came as easily and exactly under the mastery of her imagination and

Dr. Patrick Delany.

eyes, as the meanest objects into those of another, and she could delineate them, in the utmost perfection of drawing, with more dispatch than a common hand could scrawl or scribble. (p. xxviii)

Her letters were written in a natural freedom of style, but with ease and elegance; while at the same time she displayed such enlarged charity, liberality, nobleness, and integrity of heart, as did honour to human nature. (p. xxx)

> *Patrick Delany, "Mrs. Delany: 'A Character'," in* Mrs. Delany at Court and among the Wits, *Stanley Paul & Co. Ltd., 1925, pp. xxvii-xxxii.*

HANNAH MORE   (letter date 1776)

[*More was an eighteenth-century English essayist, novelist, dramatist, religious reformer, and philanthropist. Among her works are two tragedies,* Percy (1777) *and* The Fatal Falsehood (1779), *several essays, including* Cheap Repository Tracts (1795-98), *which led to the founding of the Religious Tract Society, and a popular novel entitled* Coelebs in Search of a Wife (1808). *In the following excerpt from a 1776 letter written to her friend Mrs. Gwatkin, More describes her first meeting with Delany, praising her as "a living library of knowledge."*]

Yesterday, good and dear Mrs. Boscawen came herself to fetch me to meet at dinner a lady I have long wished to see. This was Mrs. Delany. She was a Granville, and niece to the celebrated poet Lord Lansdowne. She was the friend and intimate of Swift. She tells a thousand pleasant anecdotes relative

to the publication of the *Tatler.* As to the *Spectator,* it is almost too modern for her to speak of it. She was in the next room, and heard the cries of alarm when Guiscard stabbed Lord Oxford. In short, she is a living library of knowledge; and time, which has so highly matured her judgment, has taken very little from her graces or her liveliness. She has invited me to visit her; a singular favour from one of her years and character. (pp. 52-3)

> *Hannah More, in an excerpt from a letter to Mrs. Gwatkin in 1776, in her* The Letters of Hannah More, *edited by R. Brimley Johnson, John Lane, 1925, pp. 52-3.*

HANNAH MORE   (poem date 1778)

[*In the following excerpt from her 1778 poem "Sensibility," an extended paean to her contemporaries, More accords Delany much praise for wisdom and virtue.*]

> Delany too is ours, serenely bright,
> Wisdom's strong ray, and virtue's milder light:
> And she who bless'd the friend, and grae'd the lays
> Of poignant Swift, still gilds our social days;
> Long, long protract thy light, O star benign!
> Whose setting beams with milder lustre shine.
>
> (p. 33)

> *Hannah More, "Sensibility: An Epistle to the Honourable Mrs. Boscawen," in her* The Works of Hannah More, *Vol. I, Harper & Brothers, 1835, pp. 32-6.*

LETTERS FROM MRS. DELANY TO MRS. FRANCES HAMILTON   (essay date 1820)

[*In the following excerpt from the preface to the 1820 edition of Delany's letters,* Letters from Mrs. Delany (Widow of Doctor Patrick Delany,) to Mrs. Frances Hamilton, *the anonymous editor maintains that Delany's intimate portrayal of court life in her letters defies any claim that her correspondence is merely a record of trivial events.*]

At a moment like this, when the recent loss of our beloved Monarch has excited interest towards every circumstance illustrative of his private life and character, it is thought that [the **Letters from Mrs. Delany (Widow of Doctor Patrick Delany,) to Mrs. Frances Hamilton**], unaffectedly displaying the domestic happiness that reigned at Windsor Castle, and recording many traits which do honour to the head and the heart of the Sovereign, and of his Consort, would not prove uninteresting to the public. Who, indeed, would not rejoice to learn that *"true happiness,"* characterised by a great author [Addison], as "arising from the enjoyment of one's self, and from the friendship and conversation of a few select companions," should have so eminently existed, where least likely to be found; in the centre of a Court, on the very throne of the greatest and most powerful empire of Europe.

Many of the anecdotes will, perhaps, be thought by some readers too trivial and unimportant for public notice: did they concern private individuals the objection would be readily admitted; but the most trifling circumstance acquires dignity and interest, when it refers to departed worth and greatness; and the mind dwells with more satisfaction upon the recollection of George the Third, as the exemplary character in every social relation of life, than it does upon the splendour of his regal state. Critical accuracy may detect some careless phraseology, and even grammatical inaccuracies, which might easily have been corrected in preparing the letters for the press; but it was thought advisable to leave them in their original unpretending, unstudied form; and the internal *evidence* they bear of the *sincerity* and *truth* in which they were written, will, perhaps, give them greater interest, than often is derived from more correct, or even elaborate compositions.

Some passages, referring to private transactions, and which would have been wholly uninteresting to the public, have been expunged. The excellent person to whom these letters (with the exception of the first,) were addressed, had, some time previous to her death, expressed a wish that they should be published. It was, therefore, in contemplation to produce them immediately after the demise of Her late Majesty; but circumstances arose, which prevented the fulfilment of that intention. At the present moment, however, it is hoped, they will appear as acceptable as they could have been at any former period. (pp. vi-viii)

> *A preface to* Letters from Mrs. Delany (Widow of Doctor Patrick Delany,) to Mrs. Frances Hamilton *by Mrs. Delany, Longman, Hurst, Rees, Orme, and Brown, 1820, pp. v-viii.*

THE EDINBURGH MONTHLY REVIEW (essay date 1820)

[*In the excerpt below from a review of the 1820 edition of Delany's letters, the anonymous critic considers the value of Delany's correspondence as a record of English court life.*]

The insincerity of courts has been a very ancient and popular topic of animadversion and complaint. The splendour necessarily connected with their imposing scenes, and the pomp and forms which regulate the intercourse of those who move in them, have been pronounced not only unpropitious, but irreconcileable to the exercise of the kind affections, and are supposed alike to repel every effusion of friendship, and to wither every generous emotion of the heart. While it is obviously unfair to make such sweeping and confident averments respecting any individuals, founded merely on the circumstances in which they are placed, it must at the same time be allowed, that the situation of kings and those who are immediately around them, is not favourable to the free interchange of sentiment and unrestrained expression of feeling, which are of spontaneous and natural occurrence among the less elevated ranks of society. (p. 379)

It is to this curiosity, accordingly, that we must refer the extreme avidity with which all anecdotes respecting persons in the most exalted station are received by the public; of which there can be no stronger proof than the extensive circulation of various recent publications, in every form, of numerous incidents illustrative of the character and habits of our late excellent and much-revered sovereign. The anecdotes to which we allude, all bear the same gratifying and unequivocal testimony to the unaffected piety and lofty moral feeling, which preeminently distinguished that illustrious individual; but, besides their relating chiefly to the more advanced period of his life, they are also, as having been gleaned from various casual sources, of a detached and insulated description. The little volume before us [*Letters from Mrs. Delany, Widow of Dr. Patrick Delany, to Mrs. Frances Hamilton*] on the other hand, we consider to be more peculiarly interesting, as it exhibits a view of the domestic habits of their late Majesties when in the prime of life, in the midst of their children then young, and for a series of years, during which an intercourse

with the royal family, of a nature the most easy and unceremonious, was enjoyed by the writer of the letters of which the volume is composed.

Mrs. Delany, the author of them, was a lady of respectable family, the daughter of Barnard Granville, Esq. of Wiltshire, and niece of George, afterwards Lord Granville, a poet and literary man, and the friend of Pope, Swift, and other eminent writers of that day. Her first husband was a gentleman of large property in Cornwall, who died and left her a widow at an early age. After a considerable interval, she was married to Dr. Delany, well known as the friend and intimate of Swift, and as a literary character of some celebrity.—She was a person of cultivated understanding, fine taste, and elegant accomplishments, and was honoured by the distinguished esteem of many eminent individuals. After the decease of Dr. Delany, she intended to fix her residence in Bath, but was prevailed upon to take up her abode with the late Duchess Dowager of Portland, mother of the late Duke, a lady who had a particular friendship and value for her; after which her time was spent with her Grace, between her country seat of Bulstrode and London. The letters, which are written in the confidence of friendship, are addressed to the Hon. Mrs. Hamilton in Ireland, widow of the Hon. and Rev. Francis Hamilton, son of James Earl of Abercorn, and embrace a period from 1779 to 1788, when the writer, who was born in 1700, had attained a goodly old age. They form part of a course of regular correspondence with her friend; and the notices which they contain respecting the royal family, were intended to gratify that friend's expressed curiosity on the subject. The purpose of giving them to the world, as stated in the preface, being to preserve some interesting accounts of the late king and the royal family, such letters only are inserted as refer to them, and even from these, every passage relating to other matters is excluded. It is but fair to explain these circumstances in order to avert any impression as to egotism and vanity on the part of the writer, which the sameness of the topics might make on the mind of a reader.

The incidents narrated in the correspondence occurred during the period of the regular annual residence of the royal family at Windsor, in the neighborhood of which was the country seat of the Duchess Dowager of Portland, and to this it is owing that there are such chasms between the dates of some of the communications.

In [*Letters from Mrs. Delany . . . to Mrs. Frances Hamilton*] . . . there is exhibited much of domestic happiness, simple manners, and unaffected friendship, blended together with a harmony of colouring so delightful as is rarely to be discovered amid the ordinary aspects of society, and grouped in a felicitous combination that has been commonly imagined to form the exclusive and appropriate distinction of the humbler and more secluded walks of life. (pp. 380-82)

> *A review of "Letters from Mrs. Delany, Widow of Dr. Patrick Delany, to Mrs. Frances Hamilton," in* The Edinburgh Monthly Review, *Vol. IV, No. IV, October, 1820, pp. 379-82.*

LITTELL'S LIVING AGE (essay date 1861)

[*In the following excerpt from an anonymously published 1861 review of Volumes 1-3 of Lady Llanover's edition of Delany's letters, the critic comments favorably on Delany's simple, candid letter-writing style.*]

[*The Autobiography and Correspondence of Mary Granville, Mrs. Delany*] gives us a real old picture without any of the touching and varnishing employed too often by editors of memoirs, who consider themselves as artists bound to present a glossy portrait of the person whose living features they propose to represent. Lady Llanover has represented the life of her kinswoman, Mrs. Delany, as detailed by herself in her correspondence with her sister and most intimate friends. Here we have "the familiar matter, joy and pain," which makes up daily life in every century, and which can be written and spoken of only in the innocent unreserve of domestic intercourse. We are admitted to the privilege of intimacy and relationship with one who is almost an ideal Englishwoman. Mrs. Delany's letters were not meant for any eyes except those of the dear sister to whom chiefly they are addressed. They have the charm of a perfect unconsciousness, the modest unreserve which had no secrets except those which come of innate good sense and reverence for all that is pure. There is a dignified reticence upon subjects about which mere talk is undesirable, affording healthy contrast to the morbid self-analysis of which examples are not few. These letters contain simple, natural, and living words; the reader is taken by them into the heart of life and manners as they were a hundred and sixty years ago, and finds in it nothing stiff or old-fashioned. We may look at old portraits of great-grandmothers, and wonder where their human nature was, when we see only the cumbrous embroidery and the uncomfortable fashions of their clothes. In these volumes women, whom we know only as great-grandmothers, live in the freshness of their youth and beauty, coming out in new fashions, stirring, gossiping, and amusing themselves. The work illustrates that English life of the last century which is best known to us through Tom Jones, and Sir Charles Grandison. . . .

The three volumes now before us only reach halfway through Mrs. Delany's life—to the first break in the chain of her domestic ties, the death of her dear and only sister, Mrs. d'Ewes, to whom most of her letters are addressed. Illustrations of her life with the Court of George the Third and Queen Charlotte, are yet to come. One fitness there is in the prolixity of detail illustrative of a private lady's life in the last century. The life itself of those days was very much slower than it is at present, and it would have been difficult, without thus covering time and space, to convey an idea of the stately coach-and-six movement with which all business was in those days transacted. (p. 29)

One of the most curious and entertaining portions of the Memoirs is the autobiography addressed in letters to Mrs. Delany's early and life-long friend, the celebrated Duchess of Portland. It is written with fictitious names, to which, however, we have the key given us. The style is singularly simple and flowing. There is no attempt at fine writing or effect, and the result is an excitement of the strongest interest. One of the first remarkable events that befell her was finding, when she awoke one morning, two soldiers with guns in their hands standing beside her bed! They had come to arrest the whole family on a Secretary of State's warrant, granted on suspicion that her father was about to leave England on the Pretender's business. All the Granvilles had hereditary affection for the House of Stuart. (p. 30)

Always noble and tender, a true heroine, English Mrs. Delany was; as unlike the heroine of a French novel or drama as if she had belonged to another race of beings. We com-

mend her history to the attentive study of all fidgety *femmes incomprises*. (p. 31)

A review of "The Autobiography and Correspondence of Mary Granville, Mrs. Delany," in Littell's Living Age, Vol. 69, No. 879, April, 1861, pp. 29-31.

LITTELL'S LIVING AGE   (essay date 1861)

[*In the following excerpt from an anonymously published 1861 review, the critic evaluates the importance of Delany's* Autobiography and Correspondence *as a record of daily life in eighteenth-century England, noting as well its value as a historical complement of Hester Lynch Thrale Piozzi's own letters.*]

There is at least an apparent propriety in taking the works at the head of our article together [*Autobiography and Correspondence of Mrs. Delany* and *Autobiography, Letters, and Literary Remains of Mrs. Piozzi*]. They belong to the same class of literature, and thus seem to give one another importance and a purpose. They may be said exactly to divide the gossip of the eighteenth century between them, and to give us a picture of its social life, such as only women can give, and which very materially adds to our power of realizing its tone and aspect; by turns modifying, correcting, and strengthening our previous impressions, and giving life to the whole. Diffuse and often trifling as both works are, full of superfluous and unnecessary matter, they yet leave us with ideas enlarged; we feel that we have learned something; yet both seem to require apology, and need to be accounted for. We are disposed of each in turn to ask why it is published now. What circumstances then can at the same time have brought to light letters and documents which, having slumbered so long, might seem to have passed the period of possible resuscitation? Each editor has no doubt a good and different reason to give for the intrusion upon the latter half of our century of a name of such mild lustre even in her own day as Mrs. Delany's, and of such questionable celebrity as that of Mrs. Piozzi, and may establish a distinct claim on public attention; but one thing is certain, that if the obsolete system of buying books before we read them still prevailed we should have no such coincidence. Neither of these old ladies could possibly have appeared again upon the scene. Public libraries generally, and Mr. Mudie in particular, must be the occasion of such publications as those before us; and we recognize something even judicial in the three enormous volumes, two thousand ample pages in all, which embody Mrs. Delany's experience. It must be for Mr. Mudie's sins that a woman's private letters of more than a hundred years old should be given to the world in such unmeasured unexampled profusion. No person whose name and family does not occur in the select and aristocratic circle of her friends and intimates, would dream of buying a mass of correspondence, half of which was devoted to trifles so perfectly immaterial and unimportant at the time, except to the person addressed, that no lapse of years can make it curious, or give it adventitious value. But every reader of the literature of the day will want to see the books which hold in solution a great deal that is both curious and interesting. It is just the work to be in universal demand; not to be read through, page by page,—though after all that is the best way if people have the art of reading quickly,—but to be dipped into for the chance of a well-known name, a telling anecdote, a trait of obsolete manners, a glimpse of old-world splendors. Mr. Mudie is pledged to a supply in proportion to the demand wherever his sectarian convictions do not interfere with the liberality of his scheme—he must therefore have had to order a very large and costly supply of Mrs. Delany's correspondence. Again the prestige that still attends Dr. Johnson's name makes it a necessity that every one should know the last facts that can possibly be told of him from a reliable, or at any rate a genuine source, if it can be done without loading our shelves with more books about him; for his sake therefore the reader willingly skims the poor remains and gleanings of long-ago gathered recollections; and submits to follow the details of Mrs. Piozzi's sprightly, but not very reverent old age, for the chance of passing allusions and fresh combinations of names whose sole interest now lies in their association with the great social wonder of his time. Probably these volumes will lie but a short time within each one's reach—the suggestions therefore of a more systematic reading may supply some of the deficiencies of a passing and careless perusal.

The attempt to revive the more than half-forgotten names of two old ladies, will at least have a temporary success. Both books are suggestive, as the picture of any life whatever must be, but these had both a distinctness and a vigor in their several ways, and were passed under such circumstances of note and observation as fit them particularly for subjects of speculation. Regarding life not as a probation, but as a performance, they show us some of the elements of success and of failure in a marked manner. While a certain parallel may be drawn between the external position of these two women, the events of their lives, the place they once held, the notice and admiration they once excited, and the intellectual superiority attributed to them; the mode in which they used the advantages and met the difficulties of their lot, constitute as strong a difference as can well be found. Their portraits as old women, which stand at the opening of their works, prefigure and define this difference—though thirty years' distance in date may possibly diminish its full significance. Mrs. Delany, in coif and hood, comely and venerable, model of a wise, pious, decorous, acquiescent old age: Mrs. Piozzi, at nearly the same time of life, in hat and plumes, and false flaxen curls, to which her chronicler in candor bids us add, cheeks violently rouged. Each face is the type of a character and a career: in Mrs. Delany, of a harmony which is the characteristic of her life, adapting her to every successive stage of existence, causing her to fit in with every change and be always in keeping with the seasons of life as they came and passed by, from the tearful April and glowing May of her youth to the fall of Autumn and December snows: in Mrs. Piozzi's of exactly opposite characteristics—of a total want of this harmony and of the resolute hitch in her nature which disturbed all proportions; telling of a precocious womanhood, a girlish middle life, and a frivolous and fantastic old age. The one picture represents the gift of self-government, founded on a calm and modest self-reliance, the other that total incapacity for self-guidance, which so often is seen where vanity holds possession in the place of self-respect—the craving for the approbation or admiration of others rather than a wish to satisfy the individual judgment.

We are not attributing these differences wholly to an intrinsic superiority in one over the other. Circumstances seem to have been in the elder lady's favor, as they were against Mrs. Piozzi. It is not many people who know how to manage a borrowed and reflected consequence, or who, being once raised above their merits, can either be judicious under the fictitious elevation, or descend gracefully into obscurity. Probably Mrs. Delany's view of what she owed to herself, would under any circumstances have withheld her from devoting herself

to a great name or a great man of any kind; she would not have disorganized her household, or deranged her hours, or broken her habits, for any colossus under the sun. She would have fully estimated Dr. Johnson, and given him a fair share of her respect, time, and affection; but no monopoly, nothing to derange the completeness and consistency of her own life, as to detract from the rights of other friends and other claims. (pp. 323-24)

[In Mrs. Delany's course] there are no mistakes, no lapses, no blunders. She never shocked her friends by a departure from their previous conception. Indeed, a certain halo played round her which we hardly understand. Ballard, for instance, chose her as the woman in England to whom to dedicate his "British Ladies," without any personal knowledge, simply from her reputation as fulfilling the ideal woman of her own time. And here we recognize that good fortune which distinguishes her from Mrs. Piozzi. Her qualities essentially fitted her for her own age; she could hardly have made so great a stir in ours, though such a nature would adapt itself to all circumstances. She was one of those wise persons who make the best of their own times, without too violent an effort to mend them. Reformers are a very useful and necessary class, but they do not attract the praise and veneration of those who have most to do with them, and they are apt to acquire embarrassing and provoking habits, if they do not start with them. There are, it is true, in these volumes mild protests against the vices of the time; we find excellent reflections on its peculiar vanities and follies: but she, nevertheless, takes the general view of things for granted, and makes the best of it, as of all the circumstances arising out of this view which befall herself, which, in her opening life, were very trying and awkward indeed. But she was was always able to see them exactly for what they were. She had no romance to exaggerate evil, or to raise impossible schemes for emancipation. She could, in the heyday of youth, take the good with the bad, and make the best of compensations. She never felt herself the sport of circumstances, as impulsive natures under misfortune are apt to do. She had self-possession in the fullest sense of the word, and was mistress of herself; realizing herself as something separate, distinct, her own—which no one could take from her—which she must defend, protect, and develop; not, of course, that she knew or thought all this, but she acted upon a class of impressions which belong to some persons, and not to others—which constitute a very marked, fundamental difference in those who are actuated by them. (p. 325)

[Mrs. Delany's] letters give us a glimpse of the society, and especially of the women, of the period between the respective dates of the "Spectator," and "Rambler," and Richardson's novels, as far as we can accept the last as a picture of fashionable life.

There is an impression of sweetness and choiceness thrown over the coterie who form her immediate friends and allies which is very attractive: they group themselves into fine combinations—the magnificence in which they lived or shared sets them off. We are convinced that they were lovely, graceful, elegant, after a distinct and distinguished fashion which our more levelling days will not admit of. Gorgeous to look upon, in their hours of state they wore their glittering attire with a sweeping grace which no width of crinoline can achieve now. To be observed and admired, to drive in coaches and six, to be attended by a bevy of devoted fine gentlemen, was so much their birthright, that notice influenced and moulded every movement, without making them vain. In this

A letter from Queen Charlotte to Delany, dated 15 December 1781.

particular set, under Mrs. Pendarves' genial pen, we find no envy, jealousy, or meanness: they enhance one another's charms by a mutual adoration; they seek one another's society with constant friendship; they write volumes in absence; they consult one another's interest, and further each other's ends; they pursue pretty labors together; they sympathize, are merry, and sad together. There is no apparent affectation,—it was before the age of bluestockings,—no straining after what is not theirs; but the serene content, the undoubting repose, induced by the knowledge that all that the world or society has to give is theirs already. They are evidently a set, a clique; they have names, grotesque, fanciful, or poetical, for themselves, and a cipher to express the outer world of their acquaintance. "Penny," "Pipkin," "Colly," "Fidget," the "Twopennies," are the Duchess of Portland's names for her friends and children. The "Pearl" and "Pearlydews" are the epithets for Mrs. Delany's darling sister, Mrs. Dewes, to whom her letters are mainly addressed. Her cousins are, "Violet," "Primrose," "Daisy;" while the pretty, clever, lively, accomplished Duchess of Portland, the centre of this group, is "Our duchess," "Our sweet duchess," "Our well-beloved duchess," "Our lovely queen." Herein, however, Mrs. Delany rather conforms to a fashion than invents one; for, except under the pressure of some unusual excitement, her style is grave; she treats what are now called trifles seriously. For she, no doubt, perceived that they were very far from trifles in the influences they possessed over the success of society

and of individuals. The topic of dress, for instance, is treated with the gravity which its importance no doubt demanded, but which in our times no woman would have the courage to use. She might say as much about it, and betray a deeper personal interest, but she would disguise it by an affectation of contempt for her theme. The subject of *"clothes"* with Mrs. Delany never meets with this injustice. It was, in fact, with her one of the fine arts. She had, probably, an exquisite taste in it, and in her early days, like the hapless Clarissa, exercised her invention, and struck out new thoughts. We see by the short and distinct directions she gives her sister in the country, that her judgment was final, and her authority law, as far as ladies' attire was concerned; for she says—and it is characteristic of her main sympathies lying with her own sex—she never can remember men's clothes which made quite as bold a claim to attention in brightness of colors and splendor of material; sometimes dismissing them summarily with "The men in general not remarkably fine," or the reverse.

When ladies by their *head* meant not the throne of intellect and the seat of expression, but the bit of lace that surmounted and presided over them, we can hardly wonder that the vocabulary of the art generally should be weighty. "Gauze heads," we are told, "are now the top mode;" and our prudent heroine does not think she is wasting her money when she gives fifty pounds, which would teach a language or an accomplishment, for a "Brussels head." There are pages of elaborate description of brocades of gold, and silver, and flowers, which read like more than mortal splendor, always written with the quiet conviction that they are as well worth describing as a fine picture. The very term *clothes* is a sort of voucher. "He saw my clothes," she writes of a beau who calls on her,—"The queen commended my clothes,"—"My clothes were grave, a great pennyworth I happened to meet with; they cost me seventeen pounds,"—"There were many old clothes at court." Very rarely is there allusion to the effect of her magnificent get-up on others. She dresses in the mode due to herself and to the occasion. (pp. 326-27)

The picture of this lady and her family, which these letters present, is certainly a very agreeable one. The mixture of splendor and simplicity of manners could hardly be in our time, and characterizes an age. Rank, in some respects, was a more evident and glaring possession then. Great people had monopolies of certain sensations; they figured in a more particular way before men's eyes; they, as it were, *wore* their coronets. Thus, when the Duke of Portland and his family migrated from Bulstrode to London, which they would now do by rail no faster, and in no greater privacy, than their neighbors, Mrs. Pendarves, who accompanied them, writes:—

> We set out from Bulstrode at eleven, and were in town by half an hour after two, over fields of snow and heaps of ice, but our horses flew as if each had been a Pegasus; four coaches and six with twelve horsemen attending, besides apothecaries, bakers, and butchers that joined in the procession to escort us part of the way.

A certain retinue, state, and publicity accompanies all their acts and movements; but the occupation of time and the family life is all simple and domestic—the children are brought up under the mother's eye; their education and dispositions are constantly in her mind. In the midst of constant necessary company, entertained with due splendor, the duchess is always busy with her own little schemes of fancy and usefulness. Her mind is stored with recipes and nostrums. She delights in being out of doors. She observes flowers and mosses and insects, and contrives all manner of devices to indulge her innate turn for work and invention. She and her friends are indeed alike in this, all are active spirits, full of business, occupied in their own affairs, taking a part in all the work going on about them, contriving, directing, managing, exhibiting the especial virtue of "notableness" so often commended, and uniting in their persons "the excellence of a good economist with the elegance of a fine lady," both qualities alike indispensable. It is wonderful where the good ladies of these books, but more especially Mrs. Delany, found time for all they did; but it was before the intellectual and dreaming age. Reading was not regarded by any of them as the business of life: it came in by the by. They were read to now and then, or they reserved certain evening hours, between tea and cards; but the prime hours of the day, such as were not passed with the visitors who came early and stayed long, and which were devoted to sitting at all, were spent in painting, *turning,* which was the duchess' hobby, and needlework, which was one of Mrs. Delany's numerous specialities, as well as spinning, which seems to have been a favorite occupation with her and her mother; the fineness of the thread testifying to the quality of the spinster. We cannot doubt that if the claims of rank and society had not stood in the way, these ladies, in our own time, would have made a bevy of authoresses. All the cravings after expression which found satisfaction in painting and shell work, and feather work, and grottoes, and quilts, and beds, and curtains, and fringes, and patterns, and

neat and appetizing bills of fare (an admitted subject for arrangement and invention), would have found another vent—would have resulted in tales—moral, didactic, romantic—in poems, in essays, in scientific dialogues, in educational treatises, in tracts, by which the ladies of our own time confer such benefits on the world. (pp. 328-29)

[Mrs. Delany] owns to ranking a good manner, in her own sex at least, next to religion and pure morals, and perhaps *the* lesson to to be learned from this book is the value and importance of good manners. We feel that we have been to school. There is no doubt that (according to the approved phrase), we rise from its perusal with an added sense of the desirableness and pleasantness of being well mannered ourselves, and of all our friends being so gifted. We see a moral in a courteous and gracious deportment, and have an insight into the education that forms it. It is a subject on which Mrs. Delany thought a good deal: she practised all she preached, and no doubt was herself an authority. It enters into her primary ideas of education. (p. 332)

[Mrs. Delany] was one of the people made for friendship rather than more absorbing emotions. She had a reserve and self-reliance, which led her to choose the confidence and companionship of her own sex, and to repose on the calmer domestic affections, the love of family and home; such influences as offered no disturbing forces to the natural development of her own nature. These volumes show us a temper perhaps a good deal rarer than we would at first sight suppose, one which we are apt to assume for ourselves, as a matter of course—we mean the affectionate temper; that is, really a nature in which there is such a harmony of engaging qualities, of warmth, tenderness, kindness, indulgence, unselfishness, fidelity, and discretion, as may lead to the formation of many real attachments, and constancy in them. Most people can be affectionate to those immediately about them and belonging to them, as parts of themselves; or they can be affectionate so long as there is an identity of interests or frequency of intercourse; but it belongs to few to go on loving with unwavering regard—in spite of changes of place and fortune, and inevitable changes of character (we speak of change, not deterioration)—the same people throughout a life; to hold by the friends of youth to old age. We all must admit that it implies habitual forbearance, toleration, and justice, a constant sense of others' claims and submission of our own, a freedom from jealousy, and a general right balance of mind, to maintain friendships unimpaired through the innumerable trials and vicissitudes to which they are exposed, as it needs expansiveness and warmth of heart to form them. It is a subject which might be pursued to great length: we consider Mrs. Delany an example of the virtue, though the circumstances of her day befriended this natural capability.

In her day a large number of separating causes did not exist which affect us now. The grades of society were more fixed, opinion in religion and politics was more fixed, people were more tolerant, they more needed each other's society, and had ways of entertaining themselves which kept them clear of intellectual excitement. It is curious, in this vast mass of correspondence, how few sore subjects, or disputed points, or differences of opinion, are touched upon. And when they occur it is no personal matter, but some case in which the warmth and generosity of her friendship leads her from the usual calm charity of judgment. Minds now-a-days, separated by circumstances, are apt to drift from one another in spite of themselves; there are so many questions on which friends may split, such rapid transitions, so many opportunities for divergence; such a feverish activity of thought circulates about us, of which there is little indication in these volumes. We infer that an intellectual age, in which people are always probing into the depths of their own and other people's minds, does not encourage habits of friendly, sociable, affectionate constancy. But that, even in Mrs. Delany's day, the temper we have attributed to her needed guidance and self-restraint is evident, in the following early counsel to her sister:—

> I am of your opinion, that nothing requires more penetration than to be able to find out other people's characters; too candid, or too severe a way of judging, is apt to mislead one, though the first occasions less mischief than the latter. *That talent* seems to me as much a genius as music, or poetry, etc.: it may possibly *be acquired* by much experience and observation, but not often. I think one ought to be very cautious in declaring one's opinion either to the prejudice or advantage of any one; for if you commended upon a slight acquaintance, and they afterwards prove unworthy of it, one's judgment will certainly be called in question. I need not give you any caution against censure, for no one is less apt to run into it; but I find, upon the whole, that a proper silence gives one more the *character* of wisdom than speaking one's sentiments too openly, though ever so well expressed.

She had not only caution but this knowledge of character, and an instinct of perceiving who and what she liked; for we find her pronouncing, for once on a slight acquaintance, a certain Mrs. Hamilton, "as one that I should always feel happy to have within my reach," who, twenty years after, when she was within reach, exactly fulfilled her expectation, was a much valued neighbor, with whom she held constant, delightful intercourse. To account in some degree for this felicity, it must be observed that she had an absolute accordance with her own age; she was visited by no obstinate questionings; she served her friends in the approved way, as well as with zeal. And after all, zeal does a great deal more, and is a much firmer ally when it goes with the times than against them. These good ladies, for instance, had none of them any scruples about places and sinecures. Their notions of politics are circumscribed; they value statesmen as they can get from them pensions and appointments for their friends. If they fail in finding a husband for some fair cousin, they try to make her a maid of honor, or to get her a pension; and when success attends these efforts, the congratulation and applause are without a suspicion or a doubt of the intrinsic merit of the transaction. (pp. 339-40)

[In Mrs. Delany's letters there is] constant mention of Handel, who was on terms of friendship with her brother Mr. Granville, and patronized by her family. She was an enthusiast for his music, and attends every opera and oratorio, but we learn nothing new about the man. She knew Hogarth and the leading artists of the day, but only names occur. She corresponded with Swift, with whom she became acquainted only a short time before his loss of reason. His letters convey a favorable impression as far as they go; his compliments are not so unmeaning as the compliments of the time generally are, and there is too much spirit, point, and style in all that he writes for him ever to degenerate into that wonderful form of composition, the complimentary letter of the eighteenth century, which is a thing *sui generis*. We have in these volumes innumerable examples of them from all sorts of people,

but not one conveys any idea beyond a certain cloudy incense of homage, not one contains a fact or a statement—any thing so definite as either would be felt to be an impertinence. It is eating in a dream, groping in the dark, fume, flourish, and emptiness. Fortunately, it is only a state dress, kept for state occasions. Mrs. Delany assumes it now and then, when her style is nearly as pompous, turgid, and destitute of interest as Dr. Young's of the *Night Thoughts* himself, and we might almost add, John Wesley. . . . Her ordinary style is more modern than her age, and singularly free from affectation, telling what she wants to say in few words and in the simplest manner. It was regarded as a model and wonder of grammatical propriety and elegance in her own time, when many women of fashion could hardly spell, and when Swift told her he could remember fine court ladies writing to him with the "scrawl and the spelling of a Wapping wench." (p. 341)

A review of, " *'Autobiography and Correspondence of Mrs. Delany' and 'Autobiography, Letters, and Literary Remains of Mrs. Piozzi','* " *in* Littell's Living Age, *Vol. LXIX, No. 884, May 11, 1861, pp. 323-48.*

[MARGARET OLIPHANT] (essay date 1862)

[*Oliphant was a prolific nineteenth-century Scottish novelist, critic, biographer, and historian. A regular contributor to* Blackwood's Magazine, *she published nearly one hundred novels, many of them popular tales of English and Scottish provincial life, including her best-known work, the series of novels entitled* Chronicles of Carlingford (1863-76). *In the excerpt below, Oliphant reviews Lady Llanover's edition of Delany's* Autobiography and Correspondence.]

Few questions, incapable of direct demonstration, have given the world so much trouble, or, at least, have occasioned so much discussion and expenditure of words, as that most evident, yet most subtle difference between men and women, which most rational people are thoroughly conscious of, but which very few, on either side, have managed to define without rising into arbitrary judgment or falling into misty vagueness. To discriminate the real difference which lies between them, yet to acknowledge and allow for the broader human identity which often temporarily confounds that difference, is matter apparently too difficult for ordinary observers. A distinction so delicate, so important, so apparent, yet so indescribable, is precisely such as tempts the superficial philosopher into making sharp lines of division which have no existence in nature. All of us know very well by actual experience that there are women whose hard lot lies in the heat of the life-battle, and whose hands are burdened with the heaviest labours and responsibilities proper to a man's career in the world—all of us know that there are men almost more tender, charitable, and beneficent than it is a woman's vocation to prove herself. The line of separation is confused by many an anomaly, and often lost, not only in the contradictoriness of life, but in the sweeping tide of universal human nature which by times floods over all distinctions. Nevertheless, there it remains, always reasserting itself. We are aware of a different atmosphere when we step out of that world of men where popular admiration finds its heroes, into the smaller and daintier hemisphere where—altogether independent of act and deed, possessors of a more ethereal reputation—are congregated those women who have outlived contemporary applauses, and received enfeoffment into the homage of the world.

Of such, yet of the very opposite extremities of such, as different from each other as it is possible to imagine two human creatures living at the same time to be, are the two women, Mrs. Delany and Mrs. Thrale, who have lately been represented to the public. Whether we are ever likely to come to an end of the domestic and personal records of their long-winded century, it seems impossible to predict; but here, out of that age, so short a way removed from us in reality, but so utterly far off—further off than the Gothic distances of medieval times—have just arisen, in a clearer personality than before, these two recognisable figures, already by name and character as well known to us as if they had been country neighbours or fellow-townsfolk of our immediate sphere. Many an English family which lives in contented and total ignorance of its neighbour family next door, knows Mrs. Delany almost as well as if she had been gossip at its christenings and lent her authority to its social ambitions; and scores of persons, ignorant enough of their own kith and kin, would blush to be supposed unacquainted with the lady of Streatham, the afflicted wife and gay widow, whose second marriage still awakens among us almost as keen a discussion as though we had all entered personally into the squabble, and warned and denounced the culprit. If this intimate acquaintance with posterity is in any sense to be called fame, it has come to these two ladies without any special effort on their part. They were not women of genius; they were not "working" women; they neither wrote books nor organised public movements. On the face of things they had no personal claim whatever to the recognition of any, even the contemporary age which enjoyed their sprightly conversations, admired their good looks, and criticised their follies. It is not even enough to say that it was their association with distinguished men which brought them out so clearly before the eyes of the world, for others of the same circle have passed out of human ken, and even Fanny Burney, whose history helps to throw light upon theirs, has not been able to interest the world in her own personal chronicle, and becomes unrecognisable under the name of her marriage, to know the particulars of which no human creature cares two straws. But we were all born into acquaintance with those two other women who were not authoresses. We have all known from our cradle the benign old lady at Windsor with whom old King George and his virtuous Queen drank tea and heard the echoes of that hubbub through which the brewer's widow hastened to her second nuptials. It would be difficult to tell upon what grounds this permanent reputation has been built. But the fact is undeniable; and it forms a remarkable illustration of the nature of female fame. Nobody will deny that women have now and then, especially within the last hundred years, snatched scanty bays out of the hands of time. But it is not greatness of intellect, nor power of production, nor genius in any demonstration, which raises such a star as that of Mrs. Delany into the historical firmament. She did nothing but pretty efforts of female ingenuity—said nothing very distinctly brilliant—yet there she shines calmly over the heads of the Carters, Rowes, and Montagus, in tender, individual celebrity. Is it that some natural instinct of humanity points out as the perfection of her sex, the appreciative sympathetic woman, whose business it is to comprehend, to perceive, to quicken the eye and ear of society with that bright and sweet intelligence which in the most subtle, imperceptible way, leads, and forms, and refines public opinion, and brings genius and excellence into fashion? or is it, as some fond female fanatics would have us believe, that the jealousy of man, which keeps down the gifted among women, gladly com-

pounds by elevating now and then a feminine celebrity whose claims can never come into rivalry with his own? Most people will believe the first solution of the mystery to be the true one, though it is somewhat at war with modern conclusions; and to make the problem the clearer, here stands forth Lady Llanover to convince us, once for all, that the reputation of her venerable relative sprang, not from genius or commanding gifts of any kind, but was the spontaneous tribute of one generation's love, admiration, and homage, handed down to posterity with a certain indescribable independence of any actual foundation—differing in some ineffable fashion not to be put into words from the hard-earned renown of heroes and great men, yet warm with a tender personal sentiment beyond the reach of loftier laurels, the quintessence of female fame. (pp. 401-03)

An Englishwoman, born in 1800 instead of 1700, could not, or would not, have chronicled such a history [as that presented in the *Autobiography and Correspondence of Mary Granville, Mrs. Delany*]; but for a contemporary and correspondent of Swift, it is natural; and it throws another distinct personal light upon the Frenchest of all English ages—the grand epoch of gossip and scandal, of fineness and of brutality.

Curious lights gleam on every side from this female book, upon the questions in which women have the strongest interest. Here love—which is the chief business of a woman's life, according to most modern authorities—has scarcely a recognised place at all amid the crowd of gaieties and festive assemblies supposed to be most conducive to it. When it appears at all in honour, it is when some mad boy of twenty sets his foolish heart upon a full-blown beauty old enough to be his mother, or when some old man, equally mad, mumbles adoration to a reluctant girl. These fair, virtuous, cultivated women, the flower of their generation, have little to say to the doubtful divinity. When they are suitably married, it is with a mild equanimity and friendship that they regard the partner of their life. He is *mon ami* to his calm consort. She addresses her female friends with passionate regard, but composes herself in the presence of her lord. It is true that the young widow, when she has escaped the loathsome bonds of her first marriage, implies with delicate touches a silent preference for a certain dangling lord, who haunts her steps for a number of years, and keeps her on that tiptoe of expectation for the always deferred *eclaircissement,* which has lately been found of so much use in the construction of three-volume novels. But it is with the most fastidious reticence that Mrs. Delany tells the story of this unlucky and protracted flirtation, which never came to anything; and she is the only one of her virtuous and amiable coterie who owns to any such weakness. In those loving letters which continually pass among them, the *grande passion* is clearly at a discount. Amid unlimited gossip, and talk about a crowd of personages often disguised in nicknames, not one of all these female letterwriters divulges any tender secret to the ear of her bosom friend. When Anne Granville, Mrs. Delany's sister, begins to think of changing her condition, she writes, with laudable prudence and good sense to inquire into the character and estate of the bridegroom who has been recommended to her, and at no time professes to expect more than *an equality of sentiments and mutual good opinion* between herself and her future husband. This lady, evidently a woman of sense and spirit, calmly declares that she "thinks a *chez nous* with a man of sense and worth preferable to the unsettled life she now leads, and being continually divided in her heart what friend to remain with;"

Longleat from the south, by Jan Sieberechts. Delany lived here for a time with her uncle, Lord Lansdowne.

and on this placid basis, being at the time unacquainted with the equally calm candidate for her hand, proceeds to build her domestic happiness. Such were the sentiments a hundred years ago of the innermost heart of society. Yet the good people seem to have been happy in their way—happy enough to bear banishment into the country, and absence from all the drums, ridottos, and other fashionable diversions to which, under other circumstances, they honestly, and without any affectation of indifference, devoted themselves. Kindness, mild friendship, and affection, equality of sentiments, whatever that may signify, and mutual good opinion, reigned between the placid pairs; while the wife, whom modern ideas and interpreters would represent as wretched in this meagre union—the wife found in a circle of enthusiastic female friends, that passionate and tender love which had nothing to do with those commonplace matrimonial bonds. What, on the other hand, the husband might do for the refreshment of his heart, is not entered upon in this book, which is essentially a female book, the record not of one, but of several lives of women. No fictitious representation of the age, no mere general history, could give so fair an insight into that world within the world, that secret influence and impulse of society. In these early volumes there rises before us a female clique, not to be despised in any point of view; some five or six women, the best of their age, unblamable, sweethearted, students and scholars in their way, full in the current of life, knowing and meeting on equal terms the leading spirits of the time. They rise distinct, one by one, in Lady Llanover's gatherings; their letters now and then dignified by quaint artificial reflections, by far the most part filled, like the park, or one of their own

assembly rooms, with crowds of passing figures—my lord this and my lady that; or, more quaintly still, with mysterious mummers, under incomprehensible names, moving in inarticulate dumb show across the crowded canvass, communicating nothing except the general scope of the writer's mind and fashion of the time to the bewildered reader. The correspondence of a couple of schoolgirls writing harmless secrets to each other of their own friends and lovers, under childish nicknames, would, it is impossible to deny, be quite as edifying and as intelligible as many of the Duchess of Portland's affectionate epistles, which perhaps Lady Llanover had some occult reason, not visible to the ordinary reader, for dragging into unprovoked print. But these innocent communications, as well as the more characteristic letters of Mrs. Delany and her sister, open out the detail of the astonishing picture. It is not scandal which circulates among the gentle sisterhood; it is *news,* genuine and undiluted—news such as, alas! with newspaper correspondents in every region of the world, and a *Times* every morning to breakfast, has become an impossible and unhoped for luxury. And it is wonderful to look out of this rude human atmosphere, thrilling with troubles and momentary joys, into that calm cheerful old world, where passion and agony are unknown, and where gentle emotions, too well bred to disturb any existing decorum, go velvet shod over the carpeted universe. The Duchess and her ladies are far from being hard-hearted. They are, on the contrary, Lady Bountifuls, each in her sphere; good wives, good mothers, loving friends; but the composure of the gentle souls is exemplary. Few tears gleam through those records of years; when they lose the dearest of their relations, they write that they have too much confidence in each other's reason to doubt a speedy recovery of the disturbed tranquillity. The sorest disappointment that afflicts them is when their Kitty's letters do not turn up on the appointed morning; the warmest delight they feel is when that beloved Kitty herself is likely to visit her longing friends. Few motherly raptures break into those mild epistles, and no foolish wifely triumph in public success or domestic tenderness ever lights them up. Friendship alone attunes their placid voices to a warmer strain; and when vulgar love is to be represented in the best light, it is the perfect friendship to be found in marriage upon which the writer insists; though that perfect friendship seems a matter-of-fact affair enough in comparison with the tender passion which every Kitty lavishes upon her Nanelia, the friend of her bosom. How they praise each other, that fair female band! how they live in each other's smiles! how they communicate patterns and sentiments, and the news, which is so honestly dear to all!

The correspondence in Lady Llanover's first series of vast volumes, concentrates in the communications which pass between Mrs. Pendarves, her sister, Mrs. Dewes, the Duchess of Portland, and Lady Throckmorton, all of them at the height of life and apparent happiness, and as little abstract or philosophical as could be desired. Their lively talk, their perpetual occupation, the crowd of gentle interests and ingenious labours which keep them happy, might be studied with advantage by the morbid heroines of modern days; but admirable and exemplary as is the whole, it is impossible to restrain a little wonder at the amazing tranquillity of these gentle lives. (pp. 405-08)

[Respecting the later period] of Mrs. Delany's life, Lady Llanover makes a passing onslaught upon poor Fanny Burney, that unlucky autobiographist whom recent critics have cut to pieces so unsparingly, that it is to be hoped a reaction of charity will shortly take place in her favour. The Duchess of Portland, whom the clever self-admiring authoress had declared *very anxious to see her,* had, on the contrary, as Lady Llanover informs us, "a prejudice against female novel-writers which almost amounted to a *horror of them,*" and the poor author of *Evelina* was presented to her benevolently by Mrs. Delany by way of "diminishing the prejudice of her friend against the class which she then considered so undesirable as acquaintance in private life;" an opinion which her ladyship states with so much warmth that, alas for female authors! one almost fears Lady Llanover herself, notwithstanding the honour she has done the sisterhood by almost joining it, must concur in her Grace's sentiments; which, considering how universal female authorship is nowadays, would be a sad thing for literature. Miss Burney's misstatements otherwise, though enough to rouse a good deal of family indignation, seem to convey nothing but a false impression that Mrs. Delany was, in some respects, dependant upon her dear Duchess, and to ignore partially her own obligation to Mrs. Delany for the countenance and patronage which that lady afforded her. Mrs. Delany herself, however, seems to have had no fault to find with the grateful and pretty-behaved Fanny, whose personal bearing was always as respectful and affectionate as any patroness could desire, and who, after all, correct or incorrect, gives a more lively and attractive picture of the delightful old lady than is conveyed even by her own letters, or by the world of letters addressed to her, here laboriously collected by Lady Llanover. This autobiography, so called, is indeed entirely marred by over-doing. The interest is frittered away from Mrs. Delany upon a crowd of other personages,

two or three generations in fact, who throng into the well-filled pages in groups, appearing for a vivacious moment, as young ladies will, in exuberant letters and affectionate good offices, but vanishing thereafter into such change of name and circumstance, as totally puzzles and puts out the most conscientious reader. With much trouble and difficulty we indeed drive into our memory the fact that the "Sally" of one volume is the Mrs. Sandford of the next, and that these are the Lady Harriets and Bettys of the Bulstrode nursery, who appear afterwards communicating details of their daughters' marriages to the long-lived woman who connects so many generations. But the marriages of these daughters have nothing in the world to do with Mrs. Delany's history. Scores of letters in which she is scarcely mentioned occur throughout the book; and not content with the introduction of half of the veritable persons of the day, Lady Llanover takes the most conscientious pains to make us acquainted at least with the birth, marriage, and death of every individual name which appears during the course of that world of antiquated gossip which she has given to the public,—even going so far as to identify Sebastian Bourdon and other painters whose works had the honour and happiness of being copied by Mrs. Delany. The passion for big books never had a more remarkable development. This story of the life of a most good and pure English gentlewoman, to whom in all her long existence nothing particular ever happened, who was entirely unconnected with the great events of the day, and did nothing more remarkable than exquisite needlework, occupies *six* huge volumes, the index to which alone takes up nearly a hundred pages! Perhaps, had they been condensed into one by skillful hands, the result might have been a biography not much less exquisite than one of Mrs. Delany's embroideries; as it is, we fish up the relics of her life from an engulphing ocean, and have to set the fragments in order for ourselves.

She died in her old age at eighty-eight, among ministrations of love and universal lamentation, having loved, consulted, amused, and protected three or four generations of kindred and friends, and accomplished her fair career in all that delicate honour and causeless celebrity which is the highest tribute that can be paid to a woman. She did nothing all her blameless days to conquer the applause of the world, and left no result behind her on which to challenge the admiration of posterity, which does not care two straws for the Granvilles, nor reckon the distinguished place they have held for centuries as any prognostic of personal fame. But while nobody could tell how she came by it, the spotless gentlewoman takes her sweet place in history, and so far justifies the evident sentiment of superiority, with which her biographer proves her to have kept herself detached from all the literary coteries of the time, as character is ever superior even to genius. The feminine world has its own rules, different from, yet not inharmonious with, the wider laws of the universe; and we are content to agree with Lady Llanover that Mrs. Delany's reputation possesses a sweeter charm than if she had worked for her laurels and won them. On her and such as her the world bestows spontaneously, and of grace, such tender myrtle crowns as neither toil nor talent can win. (pp. 411-12)

[Margaret Oliphant], "The Lives of Two Ladies," in Blackwood's Edinburgh Magazine, *Vol. DLVIII, No. XCI, April, 1862, pp. 401-23.*

THE WESTMINSTER AND FOREIGN QUARTERLY REVIEW (essay date 1862)

[*In the following excerpt, the anonymous critic offers a generally unfavorable review of the six-volume edition of Delany's* Autobiography and Correspondence, *finding particular fault with the editor, Lady Llanover.*]

However good, accomplished, and beautiful a woman may be, her chief sphere is still her own home, and there is scarce one in a thousand for whom it is not the truest and most feminine glory to pass through life unnoticed, and in death to be forgotten when the last of her immediate circle passes away. Extraneous circumstances only, or an exceptional position, can make her actual appearance before the public either graceful or appropriate, and seldom indeed can her life be interesting to posterity, unless its thread has been interwoven with that of some world-hero, as the inspirer to win whose smile great deeds were enacted, or the consoler whose sympathy made even defeat not wholly unwelcome. Well may we wish to know more of such a one, whose tale is too often to be summed up in six words, she lived, she loved, and died; but here we rather ask, of what crime was Mrs. Delany guilty, that after sleeping seventy years in peace, she should at length be dragged forth to court a publicity which, if any faith is to be given to her own words, was the last thing she would have wished for in her lifetime. She was not the mother, nor the daughter, the wife, nor the sister, of any hero; for children she had none, her father was an officer of broken fortunes, her first husband a squire from Cornwall, her second an Irish dean, her brother a fine gentleman, her brother-in-law a lawyer; and though she did happen to be godmother to Garrett Wesley, father of the Duke of Wellington, that spiritual relationship alone can scarcely suffice to account for her memoirs being printed [*The Autobiography and Correspondence of Mary Granville (Mrs. Delany), with Interesting Reminiscences of King George the Third and Queen Charlotte*], and however willing we may be to believe that she was admired in youth, and beloved in age, we trust the same is true of so many, that were the correspondence of all published in as voluminous a shape, we should apprehend a scarcity of paper when required for more useful purposes, and an overflow in the receptacles whence housemaids take materials for lighting their fires. Thus much we have said by way of a general protest, but the reasons we should have thought conclusive against this publication not having appeared so to the family into whose hands these letters had fallen, we must proceed with our duty to our readers. . . . (pp. 375-76)

Connected directly by birth, or by the marriage of her numerous cousins, with many of the leading aristocracy, [Mrs. Delany] made London her home, alternating it with visits to her relatives in the country, and those who lived with, and at the court, her associates, until her second marriage removed her to Ireland, between which country and her own she oscillated, until again at liberty to settle on this side St. George's Channel. Her story is told in innumerable letters—for she seems to have loved writing, and no wonder, since she possessed considerable command of language, and could spell, an accomplishment by no means universal among the women of her day—addressed chiefly to her family or near connexions, and that of her early days is developed in autobiographical fragments, written at the request of her most intimate friend, the Duchess of Portland (Margaret Harley), who, being considerably younger, appears to have wished for details of events she had no personal knowledge of. There are also inserted, as if purposely to swell the size of this work—an

object we should not have thought desirable—many letters from different persons, addressed not only to Mrs. Delany herself, but to different members of her family, and now fallen into the possession of her heirs, who must all have been particularly addicted to the preservation of old papers, and whose stories, placed in chronological order, afforded the materials for the present work. The possibility of such proceedings should be a lesson to ladies, and teach them, even when answering a mere invitation to tea, to be careful of the rules of grammar and orthography, since even if they count on the secrecy of their correspondent, they may yet not be secure from posthumous indiscretion, while those who receive notes may learn, that it is not enough to refrain from improperly showing them, since it is here proved that the fire alone is a confidant who never betrays his trust.

It is as well to gather this lesson as we pass, since the theatre on which Mrs. Delany played her part precludes us at once from all hope of finding in her pages any of those vivid pictures of the impression produced by coeval events, by which Lady Mary Wortley Montagu might still instruct us. She made no journey to Constantinople, and therefore cannot teach us to compare the then almost insuperable difficulty of passing through Hungary, with the ease with which we can now steam down the Danube, or by painting in more vivid colours than the solemnity of history will admit of, the power of the Grand Seignor, render the present abasement of Turkey still more significant; but we did hope, on opening her volumes, to learn something of the political and social state of England and Ireland during the past century. We should have thought it impossible for a lady of certainly not less than average abilities, to have lived for eighty-eight years in the best society, the associate of statesmen and bishops, of fine ladies and wits, a correspondent of Swift, whom Richardson visited, and on whose harpsichord Handel frequently played, not to have left in her correspondence some valuable contributions to the history of her day. We did expect to have found some youthful reminiscences of the impression produced in London by the march of the Pretender to Derby, and a riper remembrance of the Rebellion of 1745, or some hint as to the opinions entertained in his own day as to the mysterious personality of Junius.

We were, however, soon obliged to renounce all such delusive hopes. Mrs. Delany appears to have hated the very name of politics, and far more interesting matters absorbed her attention. This correspondence duly records in successive years, the bill of health of a certain magnolia tree belonging to the Dowager Countess Gower, and also the number of blossoms it bore, how many layers were taken off, whom they were bestowed upon, and how they flourished. We can quite believe that each of these offshoots had its own importance in the eyes of its proprietor, and the original plant in those of all, at a time when it would seem to have been a rarity; but it strikes us that the fact of a magnolia having bloomed out of doors in England nearly a century ago being once ascertained, even the most zealous devotee of gardening would have preferred hearing no more of it, and we cannot help being surprised that even in its own day "Mag the Great" should not have been once eclipsed by the Letters of Junius, although so loyal a subject had only mentioned them to express her abhorrence. But from this very silence, we may, perhaps, deduce a lesson little flattering to the vanity of those who think to shake the world, but none the less true on that account. Historians gravely weigh the influence this anonymous pamphleteer exerted on the politics of his day, volumes have been written in the vain attempt to establish his identity; and here we have a lady, living in the very circles we might suppose most chafed by his attacks, who does not even once allude to his existence! Still more astonishing is it to find that, though Mrs. Delany lived on terms of intimacy with the Earl and Countess of Bute, and, in the last years of her life, with George III. and his Queen, the relations between that nobleman and his sovereign are not once mentioned, and were all other cotemporary records swept away, and this correspondence alone preserved, we should never be able to suspect the incessant intrigues and prevarications, by which the king and his favourite contrived to drive his ministers nearly distracted.

"Variety is the soul of wit," and therefore lest our readers should grow weary of an uninterrupted enumeration of subjects that Mrs. Delany does not introduce, we will, before proceeding further, note one curious instance of the manners of that day, and also of the change which fashion worked in them in the course of a single life. Formality in all relations of life was as characteristic of the eighteenth century as powdered heads or stiff hoops, and it is possible that the primness of deportment necessary to keep the latter in order, may have contributed to the ceremonious behaviour which, even between those most closely connected, was far greater than what we should now deem becoming towards the veriest stranger. Parents were treated with an outward respect, little less than what we might suppose due to a divinity; but it is more strange to observe the terms in which those who might almost be supposed to stand in their place, addressed a younger member of their family. The language in which Mrs. Delany corresponds with her mother, although it seems to us incompatible with either affection or confidence, is not surprising, when we remember the implicit obedience exacted from children; but it is singular to see her uncle, Lord Lansdowne, who had just set aside with contempt her strong objections to the alliance with Mr. Pendarves, subscribing himself, in letters written immediately afterwards, as "her most faithful and humble servant." And this antiquated form strikes us the more, as, nearly seventy years afterwards, we find Viscountess Weymouth, a lady very much her junior, signing her letter, "very affectionately yours."

We should not perhaps have made so much of this small mite of information, had we found it in any other work, but while perusing this we are like a mariner cast away on a desert island, who collects for food substances he would have disdained under any other circumstances, and are fain to make the most of what is given by noting as a matter of relative importance, illustrating the progress this country has made during the last century, that a person desirous of crossing over to Dublin was then encouraged by the announcement that the voyage "seldom lasted *more* than forty hours;" and that whereas our ports are open to the products of the whole world, Irish poplins and gloves were contraband articles, that could not be introduced into the sister island without violating the regulations of the custom-house.

The life of Mary Granville naturally divides itself into two parts, of greatly different character. From seventeen to forty-three, as Mrs. Pendarves, she was essentially a fine lady, more cautious in her behaviour and refined in her tastes than the greater part of her cotemporaries perhaps, but still her heart was in dress and dancing, operas and court balls; whereas, after her second marriage, she appears to have adapted herself to her new position with marvellous facility, and to have

become as clerical in her demeanour and way of thought as an orthodox dean's wife ought to be. We may cite as an example of this, that she who had corresponded with Swift in terms of extravagant compliment, could scarcely find censure unmitigated enough for the author of *Tristram Shandy*. Now it is certainly no wish of ours to be severe on the Dean of St. Patrick's, but we do maintain that one who professed to admire and venerate him who wrote the "Tale of a Tub," had no right to denounce poor Sterne as an enemy to all morality and religion, especially when, as she herself confesses, with an unfairness truly ecclesiastical, she had never read his work, nor had any intention of doing so. The admiration expressed in the first case, may have been homage to *bon ton,* since it is matter of notoriety that Swift was well received in fashionable society, and the friend of statesmen and nobles, of Oxford and Bolingbroke; but in any case, this example of inconsistency or intolerance, not to say both, is so glaring, that we must refuse assent to the claim to almost infallible sagacity put forth by the editor on behalf of Mrs. Delany, even though she was the friend of that Mrs. Chapone, whose moral work Sheridan makes Lydia Languish substitute for *Peregrine Pickle* on the approach of her aunt.

It would almost appear, that to write a good biography is the most difficult task that any one can undertake, and if the intending editor be a relation, natural partiality makes the obstacles to success almost insuperable. Piles of letters and papers are heaped before and around him, and while turning from one to the other, bewildered with the task of selection and arrangement, he is but too apt to forget that a correspondence, which may be highly entertaining when read aloud from the manuscript to a family circle, or a small number of friends, whom oral tradition or their own memory has made acquainted with the writers, loses the greater part, if not the whole, of its interest when printed and placed before a public, in whose eyes the persons addressed or alluded to appear far more shadowy than the heroes and heroines of Bulwer's or Dickens' last novel; and whereas a few letters, judiciously chosen, might really please, a multitude, in which the same names and ideas continually recur, are rather likely, especially when there is no connexion with great public events to enable us to establish a certain co-relation between what we already know and are then reading about, to produce a sense of bewilderment, and thus render what is essentially light literature as difficult to wade through as a parliamentary blue-book on education.

Redundance, however, is not the only fault into which editors of family papers are almost invariably betrayed. An old story tells us of a sculptor who fell in love with the statue he had just carved; this passion was an unfortunate one for him, no doubt, but at least it did no harm to any one else. When editors become enamoured of the figure that has formed itself before them out of the dust of old papers, their love is not of the most discreet, and seldom indeed can they refrain from taking hold of the opportunity given them when appending a note, or an explanation of some obscure point, to foist in an eulogy of the writer of the preceding letter, and this in a form peculiarly offensive to perverse human nature, since, however the sentence may be turned, its sense almost always says to the reader, See how much better the lady (or gentleman) was than people in general, and you in particular!

Numerous instances of both these errors must strike every reader of the memoirs before us. The first is perhaps the one least to be complained of, for the remedy is to a certain extent in our own hands. Any one but the unfortunate reviewer, whose lay conscience will not allow him to criticise what he has not read, may skip over a score or so of pages until he finds something likely to interest him, and rejoice at the rapidity with which he will thus reach the end of the volume; but those only who decline reading at all can escape the sting of the second. It is bad enough when we are called upon to peruse the letters of two contemporaries, writing to each other in a labyrinth of eulogium, which reminds us of the old joke of the man saying to his comrade, "My dear fellow, I am modest, I cannot praise myself; but do you butter me, and I will butter you." But when a posthumous editor, who has not even the excuse of bidding for a return in kind, claims for one object of idolatry the exclusive possession of all virtues and accomplishments, it is time for us to protest. We make no doubt that Mrs. Delany was a highly virtuous and accomplished person; an agreeable inmate her acquaintance must undoubtedly have deemed her, or she would not have had more invitations to country houses than she could possibly accept; we have every reason to believe her industrious, since, besides writing letters so numerous that we might have thought they alone would have occupied the whole of her time, she found leisure to execute with her brush, her needle, and her scissors, the long list of works enumerated in the appendix; but when we are desired to wonder at her good sense, Christian principles, and pious resignation, as if such qualities had never flourished in the world either before or since, there arises within us an inveterate inclination to cavil. If we are to regard her as the oracle of correctness in the past century, we are bound to scrutinize her opinions and judgments far more closely than we should do those of a lady who merely poured out her own thoughts in unrestrained correspondence with her sister or her friends, and this it was that induced us to take notice of the injustice of her censure on *Tristram Shandy,* which is the more provoking since *Roderick Random* passes muster without an observation. As the author of one of the most original works ever written, Sterne and his reputation are part of the literary inheritance of England, and though we cannot of course pretend that the best of books should meet with unanimous approval, we must protest against any being condemned unread, and cannot allow this verdict to go forth unchallenged—the more so as we may note in the same sentence the admission, highly creditable to the taste of England in 1760, that *Tristram Shandy* was almost universally read, and nearly as extensively admired.

As we read the letters written by Mary Granville as Mrs. Pendarves, we are always on the point of exclaiming with Hudibras—

> And what, alas! is it to us,
> If in the moon men thus and thus
> Do eat their porridge, cut their corns,
> Or whether they wear tails and horns?

As a crabbed critic we must expect to be told that we know nothing of the matter, still, while we are quite ready to believe that the day after a drawing-room many ladies find those columns of the *Morning Post* in which the dresses there displayed are described, the most interesting part of the morning paper, and that in order to keep up with the spirit of the age it is necessary daily to study the first column of the *Times,* we take leave to doubt if these records will have much interest in the year 1962; and however much a lady to whom the Queen addressed a few gracious words at a court ball might be justified in thinking a report of them would highly interest her country correspondent, time and an absence of interest

in the person so honoured, divests even royal phrases of a portion of their value. Now, for nearly twenty years the letters of Mary Granville resemble nothing so much as a jumble of the two newspapers to which we have alluded. The lists of births, deaths, and marriages that constantly occur are almost interminable; but, as regards the latter, the first column of the *Times* has this advantage over her, that, as the chronicler of what has taken place, its record is at least exact, whereas she, writing of reports, often announces matches never intended, or afterwards broken off, as may be seen by reference to any old *Peerage.*

Then, as for toilettes. No doubt Anne Granville, living at Gloucester, with little amusement, liked to hear what "nightclothes" (by this term evening dress was then designated) Mrs. Pendarves wore on any grand occasion; and while she was ready to pore over the comparative merits of white lutestring and blue paduasoy, it was kind and sisterly to inform her at length, and to make her the envy of her neighbours, by enabling her to report with accuracy what the Queen said, how the Princess Royal looked, and what coloured velvet the Prince of Wales wore at the last drawing-room. But for us the intrinsic charm of these descriptions has gone by. As contributions to a treatise on the costume of the last century, Mrs. Delany's descriptions of the finery worn at birthdays and balls may possess a value of their own. It may possibly be interesting to some to learn from the directions given to her sister how long mourning was then worn for a second cousin, and how long for an uncle; that grey poplin was considered deeper than black silk, or when white gloves might be resumed without offence; others may take pleasure in observing that even the vulgar no longer deem the wearing of a necklace of bloodstones a sure preservative against violent bleedings, and heralds find instruction in comparing the ceremonial of the marriage of the Princess Royal, daughter of George II., with that observed at the last similar occasion. But is it possible for the general public to take an interest in the clothes or jewels worn by persons they never heard of, in the diamonds bestowed by unknown gentlemen on forgotten brides, or even in the fact that it was then usual for ladies to go to court bedecked in the ornaments of their friends?

We would not, however, be misunderstood. We by no means wish to imply that the records of a court are necessarily dull. Were we to hazard such an assertion, Lord Hervey's memoirs, relating to the very same period, would suffice to confute us, for however little it may raise our opinion of either royal or ministerial morality, it must always be amusing to trace the intricacies of the combination to govern the King, which made Sir Robert Walpole bribe Lord Hervey to retain his post about the Queen that his influence might persuade her to exert that which she in turn possessed over Lady Suffolk, to induce the favourite to coax George II. into a temper of compliance with the designs of his minister. We confess we should have preferred some report of the gossip that must have been current in London concerning so singular an arrangement, from the pen of an indifferent bystander, or some details as to that association called the "Hellfire Club," of which both men and women appear to have been members, and which met for purposes by no means pious, since they acted plays ridiculing the Scriptures, in which the Virgin Mary was brought forward as one of the *dramatis personae,* to the most minute description of the mantle of Lady Sunderland or the headgear of Mrs. Spencer. We cannot even say that it is necessary to take part in court intrigues in order to write letters amusing to posterity; the shade of Madame de

Sévigné would protest against such a verdict; but it is indispensable to possess a talent which would seem to have rarely flourished out of the atmosphere of Paris. Either matter or form may make memoirs entertaining, but if they deal with every-day affairs, the writer must make us acquainted, as it were, with the persons whose names are constantly recurring. A few lines, rapidly and vigorously sketching in their chief characteristics, may often make us feel we know them as well as if we had met them every day for the last twelvemonth, and we then grow to sympathize alike with their pleasures and their pains.

For a clever person, it strikes us that Mary Granville was peculiarly deficient in the art of word-painting. Her most intimate friends never seem to return to life in her writings. Even when her letters are not disfigured by the introduction of assumed names, which excite in us an impression of unreality that no editorial explanations suffice to remove, or initials and innuendoes which, however clear to her correspondent, by no means enlighten us,—and we purposely refrain from more than alluding to the letters of the Duchess of Portland to Miss Collingwood, introduced here for no purpose that our utmost ingenuity can discover, in which this defect is so glaring as to render them perfectly unintelligible—her figures move before us with as ghostly a tread as that of the dead men with whom Gulliver met after escaping from the flying island of Laputa. . . . (pp. 377-85)

Why it should be so, we are at a loss to explain, but it does appear that intercourse with royal personages has a charm of its own, quite irrespective of their individual qualities, for here we find Mrs. Delany, a lady of high attainments, used to live among the most intelligent people of her day, whose understanding was not clouded by the novelty of finding herself in such exalted society, recording in various letters gestures and phrases, which she would have thought very insignificant if emanating from any other source. Can we possibly care to know in what order the carriages drove up to Bulstrode, who were the attendants in waiting, that King George brought her a chair, or that Queen Charlotte chose herself to replace, when empty, the teacup which the Duchess of Portland had presented to her on a silver salver? Yet pages and pages in the last two volumes are filled with such details; or else we read that on the return visits to Windsor, the King and the Bishop of Lichfield came to receive the ladies at the door; how the chairs in the drawing-room were placed, what music was played by the band in the adjoining saloon, and what was said by the principal parties concerned, reports which, as far as they go, seem to us to prove that the conversation was very much of the same calibre as what goes on at any non-regal evening party. That Queen Charlotte was a lady in the truest sense, we did not need Mrs. Delany to tell us, while many still alive can testify to the amiable qualities and charming manners the princesses inherited from her, and we see no reason to doubt that George III. loved his children, especially while they were too young to give him umbrage, but though not the slightest allusion is here made to the qualities which rendered him so bad a sovereign, we confess that the perusal of these memoirs does not tend to raise him in any degree in our esteem. As a private gentleman, there would be nothing against him, but the conduct of every individual should be regulated by the position to which he is born; a king should be king-like, and though nothing but the most genuine kindness could have suggested the gift of a house at Windsor to Mrs. Delany, when the death of the Duchess of Portland deprived her of her usual summer home at Bulstrode, or the

manner in which the Queen herself undertook the payment of the pension granted her to meet the expenses thus entailed upon her, we feel there was something incongruous in a king acting overseer of repairs, and that Louis XIV. isolating himself in his pomp, had a truer sense of the obligations of his rank, than George III. going day after day to drink tea with a subject.

The familiarity of the intercourse thus established, is to us something almost incomprehensible. The King did honour to himself in showing it to a lady of the high birth and venerable age of Mrs. Delany; and far from thinking there was anything strange in his offering her his arm, or placing her on a sofa next the Queen, we should have deemed him very ill-bred had he ever kept her standing, but there is a great difference between this and the suppression of all ceremony. However frequent the visits to Bulstrode, there was still a certain becoming distance preserved, and a summons from the palace always preceded a visit there not required by etiquette; but after Mrs. Delany was established at Windsor, her royal neighbours visited her at all hours unattended and unexpected, and she was desired to come to them as often as she felt well enough. All this may have been very pleasant at the time, and still afford a kind of secondhand satisfaction to those nearly connected with the object of such attentions; but for our own part, we are free to confess that these accounts are as little edifying to us as the grammar of two notes of George III. here inserted, though, strange to say, we have the same fault to find with a note from Horace Walpole, less excusable, since while clipping his English, the King might think he was dealing with what was his own.

But we must not ourselves fall into the fault of prolixity that we blame in others, nor complain of the length of these memoirs in a review proportionately as long. The sojourn at Windsor was the last stage of Mrs. Delany's career; and the gradual failure both of sight and hearing rendered her daily more unfit to profit by the constant attention of her friends. To the last, however, her mental faculties were unimpaired, and she felt the liveliest interest in the welfare of those about her. There is something very beautiful in lively sympathy between youth and age, and the strongest feeling of Mary Granville's latter days seems to have been affection for her great-niece, Miss Port, who from the age of seven had been her pupil, and almost her friend. Her letters to and concerning this child are interesting, from the vivacious youthfulness of mind which they display. Her amusements and her studies were watched over alike with the most sympathetic care, and though some of Mrs. Delany's ideas now appear strange and antiquated, and we are disposed to lay less stress than she did on the importance of continually reading the moral work of Mrs. Chapone, we cannot but be struck with the general soundness and wisdom of her views on education, and the household matters whereon she consulted with her niece.

We do not wonder that an aunt so gifted and so kind should have been deeply regretted when she at length died a few weeks before the completion of her eighty-eighth year, more from the debilitating effects of constant bleeding and blistering, continued up to the very last moment, than of any positive illness, nor that the tradition of respect for her memory should have been handed down in her family. But the very intensity of this feeling should have put the editor more upon her guard, and have made her reflect that for the sake of producing a good effect she should have taken greater care not to weary the attention of the public she wished to attract. All

A letter written by Delany, dated 28 June 1779.

long-suffering has its limits: even the Emperor of the French may some day grow weary of protecting an ungrateful Pope; and we have heard of a prisoner who, being offered his choice, preferred, after a fair trial, to spend ten years as a galley slave rather than read through the Italian history of Guicciardini.

It is not for us to decide whether any criminal would prefer working out his time under Sir Joshua Jebb to the perusal of these volumes, but we do think that whosoever has for any motive attempted the latter task must have often felt tempted to leave off and exclaim, "Enough is as good as a feast." Not that we are by any means prepared to say that *no* memoirs of Mrs. Delany should have been published. Her life was a connecting link between different periods. She formed the centre of which but for her might always have remained apart, and an interesting life story has often been woven from far less promising materials. Scattered up and down in these volumes, there are many curious and instructive anecdotes illustrative of the general or individual manners of the last century; as for instance, those concerning the trial for bigamy of the notorious Duchess of Kingston and the history of Mrs. Anastasia Robinson; but in the multitude of words they are as ill searching for as a needle in a bottle of hay. The editor should also have taken to heart the wishes and feelings of Mrs. Delany herself, for these very volumes clearly indicate what she would have thought on such a point. Her letters testify that on the death of her brother Bernard Granville, she repeatedly desired that her own letters to him should be returned; and as they have not been found, the editor is forced to conclude that the object of this demand was to destroy them, and her personal attendant bears witness that when her failing health made her view her own death as an event not

long to be delayed, she caused hundreds of letters to be burnt; and on the remark that their publication would make the fortune of any one into whose hands they might fall, she answered, "That is exactly what I want to prevent." (pp. 393-96)

To pour on the heads of the public such a flood of nonsense as is contained in the volumes before us, without even attempting to embank the stream, or to garner up the stray planks of instructive or amusing anecdote that are floating on the surface, is, in our eyes, a double crime, being not only an offence against the unwary wight who may be entrapped by a title into reading a farrago of nostrums, fashions, and chit-chat, for which he cares nothing, served up as a sauce to a registrar-general-like report of polite society in the past age, but a still greater one against a worthy and very unoffending person, whose most careless effusions are shown up to the probable damage of whatever reputation for taste or talent he or she may previously have enjoyed. In the present case, had but one half of the pains and research which the editor has evidently bestowed on the task of informing us, through the notes, of the exact epoch of the birth, marriage, and death of nearly every person even casually mentioned in these letters, been devoted to the far more necessary duty of sifting and analysing the correspondence itself, we should have been able to report the appearance in general literature of a pleasant and readable book; but the execution of the latter task would have required thought, taste, and a correct knowledge of the history and manners of the last century, whereas the former could be accomplished by consulting annual registers, old *Peerages,* and works of the same nature relating to the untitled nobles of England, and thus it has happened that the memoirs before us merit little less than unqualified condemnation, in all save the style of production, for which we presume our passing compliments are due to Mr. Bentley. As far as lay in our power, we have endeavoured to disentangle the really pleasing characteristics of Mrs. Delany from amid the mass of words with which they are here overgrown, but we fear few will have the patience to perform the like task for themselves, and that if she is to be remembered at all in days to come, her reputation had better have been left even to the tender mercies of Madame D'Arblay. (pp. 398-99)

> *"Mrs. Delany," in* The Westminster and Foreign Quarterly Review, *n.s. Vol. XXI, No. II, April 1, 1862, pp. 374-99.*

LUCY H. M. SOULSBY   (essay date 1884)

[*In the following excerpt, Soulsby offers a summary review of the content of Delany's letters.*]

[Mary Delany's] *Life and Correspondence* have been given to the world by her great-great-niece, Lady Llanover, in six fascinating large octavo volumes; but as few in these hurrying days lead lives of sufficient leisure to permit the luxury of reading so long a book, I hope that a slight sketch of it will not be wholly "impertinent," to use the word in the sense that Mrs. Delany herself would have done.

To one imbued with the spirit of these volumes, the present times do indeed appear sadly hurrying. Things have changed since Mrs. Delany, in the midst of a gay London life and a daily correspondence with her sister, found time for a series of autobiographical letters to her life-long friend, the Duchess of Portland, in which the personages mentioned are designated by fictitious names, the key to which was on a separate sheet of paper. She found time for a thousand and one such thoughtful contrivances, many of them, it must be confessed, wholly useless; but, nevertheless, worthy of a regretful sigh in these days of rushing through books, when we are so far from exercising *any* thought, that to speak of the "former" and the "latter" is enough to upset the calculations of the ordinary reader. The letters of those old days were written with a care and thought to which the penny post has made us strangers; the most trivial compliments of Mrs. Thrale and Fanny Burney are neatly turned with a thoughtful reference to the thing in question, that in no way reminds us of the epistles placed on our own breakfast tables. People had time for politeness in those days, and made their very backbiting more courteous and stately than we do our compliments. Mrs. Delany, recalling her childish recollections of her aunt, Lady Stanley, instead of saying that Lady Stanley was a great Turk, remarks suavely, "I could ill bear the frequent checks I met with, which I too easily interpreted into indignities, and have not been able wholly to reconcile to any other character." Her father objected to Sally Kirkham, one of her young friends (afterwards mother-in-law to *the* Mrs. Chapone), as being bold and masculine: in her review of her young days, she allows that his strictures were well-grounded by politely saying: "From the improvements she has since made, I see she was not at my first acquaintance the perfect creature I then thought her." Very possibly dueling may fairly claim the credit of this old-world ceremoniousness which was reflected in the ladies' letters. People had to think twice before they spoke, for fear of accidents, and consequently things were implied, not said. There is an eminently cautious tone about Mary Granville's letters, and a lady-like reticence in the un-

charitable passages, indicative of much culture. Thus, she describes their Gloucestershire parson (under the name of Tranio), intimating that he was, as we should say in these blunter days, a thorough boor, but her severest remark is: "He used to say he had a familiar who always advised him how to act. As much as I can remember of Tranio's conduct, I think it did not do much honor to his familiar." (p. 284)

[In her letters Mrs. Delany] writes *bouts-rimés,* tells court gossip, and in general gives the news of the day. She goes to the Lord Mayor's feast, and dances with Michaiah Perry, "an alderman, a married man, and as blind as a beetle." She is also at George II.'s coronation and Handel's operas, and excuses herself (most unnecessarily) for not writing longer letters, saying that breakfast is not over till twelve; their toilette till two or three; then comes dinner, and then she is "liable to impertinent visits, or is engaged to go abroad."

However, in spite of all this she finds time to read as well as write, and her little dissertations on friendship are supported by quotations from Epicurus, though she observes that she has "no vast opinion" of that philosopher herself, and she is agreeably surprised to find that Cicero confutes his "sensual and false notions," in *Tully of Moral Ends,* which happens to be her book in hand. Tully seems to have remained in hand some time, as her next mention of a book is eighteen months later, when she recommends her sister only to hire, not to buy, as "'tis indifferently done," the *Life of Congreve. . . .*

The demarcation between town and country life, or rather, between London and the Provinces, was, in the matter of frivolity, more strongly marked then than now. While Mrs. Pendarves led a butterfly existence, diversified by occasional classics and astronomy, Anne Granville and Sally Chapone (*née* Kirkham) led solid, useful lives, like Lucinda in Hannah More's *Cœlebs,* a good type of a nice country girl who spent her time in district visiting and self-improvement, confining what diversion she had to the evening. It is true that one winter's day we find Mrs. Pendarves and her friends playing "My Lady's Hole" and "Puss in the Corner" to warm themselves; but, except for that, the only games we hear of are the evening ones of Pope Joan, Commerce, and Quadrille. Now-a-days girls who wish to waste their time have much more opportunity for so doing. But girls were kept in wholesome discipline in Mrs. Delany's days. (p. 286)

[One detects in Mrs. Delany's letters] a curious feeling that she owed it to society—or rather (as she always puts things on a high ground), to Providence—to enjoy herself; for instance, she meets with some one who talks of her mother after the latter's death, and "raised a tender recollection that is rather more than my spirits can at this time well bear; but as I think it wrong to indulge what may prejudice one's health, I intend going about this morning to see fine pictures, and dine at Whitehall (the Portlands'), where I shall meet the Duchess of Queensberry." One hardly gets the impression from her letters that her health was in any danger from a tendency to brood over the past: she might have been more lovable if it had suffered a little more from that, and if she had had less personal experience of the efficacy of the recipe she frequently sends to bereaved friends, namely, "a little cheerful society." Her life was divided into such distinct portions that it gave full scope for the exercise of this peculiarity of ignoring what had been; it is curious how she never seems to think of her past—or rather, her pasts. When living in Little Brook Street during her first widowhood, she never alludes to Gromio except when she finds irregularity in the remittance of her jointure. At Delville she seems to have no interests but Irish ones, and first and foremost D. D.'s health. No sooner is she established in London as a widow for the second time, than poor Pat and his house and garden vanish from the scene like smoke. True, she kept a sort of remembrance of him, for when Mr. Granville sent to borrow one of his books she replies that "the author had been under the impression that Mr. G. possessed all his works." Still, "the author" is a cautious, not to say distant, way of mentioning a husband, even though he may have been dead for some years, and we cannot infer from her remark with any certainty that she remembered the precise relationship in which he had stood towards her. Mrs. Delany's one passion in life seems to have been her sister, and in after years that sister's daughter, for the mother's sake. This freedom from unregulated affection must have been largely influential in preserving her to such a good old age, and also in making her so generally beloved—for, not being especially attached to any one, she had a mind at leisure to be charming to all. (p. 296)

Lucy H. M. Soulsby, "Mrs. Delany," in Overland Monthly, *Vol. III, No. 3, March, 1884, pp. 283-99.*

THE ATHENAEUM (essay date 1900)

[*In the excerpt below, the anonymous critic discusses Delany's place among eighteenth-century English men and women of letters.*]

It is now nearly forty years since Lady Llanover's edition of Mrs. Delany's *Autobiography and Correspondence* appeared and was duly noticed in these columns. The work was of a bulk proportioned to the length of years which it covered, the two series (1861-2) occupying no fewer than six volumes. . . .

It is true that the chief value of the papers consists in the complete picture which they present of the social life of the eighteenth century, from the earliest Hanoverian days. Mrs. Delany was no politician, but was almost everything else. She drew, she played the spinet, she read learned works, she did most beautiful needlework, and she invented the art of floral mosaic. But more than all these, she was, in Burke's words, "a truly great woman of fashion," "the highest bred woman in the world, and the woman of fashion of all ages." The standpoint which she took up, so truly typical of the best minds of her century, is indicated in a letter of advice about her niece:—

> There is nothing I wish so much for Mary, next to right religious principles, as a proper knowledge of the polite world. It is the only means of keeping her safe from an immoderate love of its vanities and follies, and of giving her that sensible kind of reserve which great retirement converts either into awkward sheepishness or forward pertness.

During her long life of eighty-eight years she was more or less acquainted with most of the best of her contemporaries—Swift, Handel, Chesterfield, Richardson, Sir Joseph Banks, Horace Walpole, Fanny Burney, not to mention the learned ladies Mrs. Montagu, Mrs. Carter, and Hannah More. Dr. Johnson and Mrs. Thrale she, for some reason or other, was unwilling to meet. She witnessed the marriages of George II., his son Frederick, and his grandson George III.; she was complimented by Queen Caroline, and made an intimate friend of by Queen Charlotte. Devoted to Handel, she heard

the 'Messiah' in its early days at Dublin, and was present at the first commemoration in Westminster Abbey, some forty years later. Always interested in painting, she did much to help forward Opie (whose portrait of her is at Hampton Court), and lived long enough to patronize Lawrence. According to an old servant, Mrs. Astley, she used to procure preferment for deserving clergy of her acquaintance, and "had the first interest in the kingdom." The same authority says that she caused to be destroyed in her last years a large box of letters, some of them "written by the first people in the world"; and when Mrs. Astley observed that these would have been worth a fortune to any one were they published, she replied, "That is what I want to prevent." (p. 524)

Mrs. Delany's position towards the bluestockings was that she was with them, but not of them. She sympathized with their aspirations after female education, but was never guilty of their extravagances. She had a sense of humour and a sense of proportion. She is seldom or never stilted or bombastic, and she expresses well-bred surprise at the "room of Cupidons" where that mature wit Mrs. Montagu received her foreigners, *literati*, and macaronies—"unless she looks upon herself as the wife of old Vulcan, and mother of all these little loves." Yet the *femmes savantes* delighted to do her honour in dedications, literary portraits, and the like. In truth, she saw no reason why, if a woman was interested in literature, art, or even philosophy and the rights of her sex, she should demean herself as though she were a thing apart.

Mrs. Delany's literary and artistic judgments display no extraordinary insight, though much one-sided appreciation. She admired Hogarth, but thought Gainsborough's canvases "splendid impositions." Horace Walpole sent her a copy of a new issue of his *Anecdotes of Painting*, in which he had inserted a reference to herself as the inventor of a new form of art, and he inscribed her epitaph on the frame which he designed for Lady Bute's Opie portrait of her. Her deliverance on the subject of Rousseau for the benefit of her niece, who had fallen under his glamour, is highly characteristic, but is somewhat spoilt by the admission that she was but little acquainted with his writings,

> as I avoid engaging in books from whose subtlety I might perhaps receive some prejudice, and I always take an alarm when virtue in general terms is the idol, without the support of religion.

Her opinion of Chesterfield's letters is what one might expect, but it is disappointing to find her taking the common view of the correspondent of her youth, John Wesley. Richardson was, of course, her favourite novelist; she found her Sir Charles Grandison in Lord Dartmouth. With regard to Fielding, she put *Tom Jones,* and even *Joseph Andrews,* above *Amelia;* but it is not surprising that she refused to have any parleyings with Sterne. As is well known, she admired Fanny Burney; and she also took up another of the rising generation in Hannah More. In 1770 Mrs. Delany and the Duchess of Portland paid a visit to the Garricks at their riverside residence, and were much pleased with it.

The great friendship of the closing years of the old lady's life was that with George III. and Queen Charlotte, whom she first met at Bulstrode. After the death of the duchess the king and queen gave her a house at Windsor and also an income of 300*l.* a year, which the queen was accustomed to bring herself to prevent it being docked by the tax-collector. Curiously enough, one of Mrs. Delany's earliest recollections had been the arrest of her uncle, Lord Lansdowne, after the death of Queen Anne, on suspicion of Jacobitism. But even as early as the Forty-five we see her to have been a staunch Hanoverian. She won the heart of George III. by procuring for him a catalogue of her brother Bernard Granville's collection of Handel's music, one fruit of the commission being the autograph letter:—

> The king hopes when the spring is far enough advanced that he may have the pleasure of having that song performed at the queen's house to the satisfaction of Mrs. Delany, not forgetting to have it introduced by the overture to 'Radamistus.'— GEORGE R.

(pp. 524-25)

A review of "Mrs. Delany: A Memoir, 1700-1788," in The Athenaeum, *No. 3783, April 28, 1900, pp. 524-25.*

GEORGE PASTON [PSEUDONYM OF EMILY MORSE SYMONDS] (essay date 1900)

[*In the excerpt below, Symonds, writing as "George Paston," examines Delany as an ordinary woman who accomplished extraordinary things.*]

Two portraits of Mrs. Delany were painted by Opie—one for the King, and the other for Lady Bute. Of the former Horace Walpole said that it was 'pronounced' like a Rembrandt, and told Mrs. Delany that it did not make her look older than she *was,* but older than she *did.* For Lady Bute's portrait, an elaborately-carved frame was designed by Horace Walpole, the principal ornaments being emblematic of Mrs. Delany's particular accomplishments, such as easel, palette, pencil, and musical instruments. On the palette was the following inscription, also the work of Horace Walpole:

> Mary Granville, niece of Lord Lansdown, correspondent of Swift, widow of Mr. Pendarves and of Dr. Delany, Dean of Down. Her piety and virtues, her excellent understanding, and her talents and taste in music and painting were not only the merits, ornaments, and comfort of an uniform life, but the blessings that crowned and closed the termination of her existence at the uncommon age of eighty-eight.

Stilted epitaphs, however, render but inadequate testimony to the worth of this 'honourable woman' compared with that which may be read between the lines of her letters and recollections. The fact that she attained so great a celebrity in her own day, and that her name is still revered, must be regarded as one of the rare triumphs of personal character over the more dazzling attributes of genius. She was no professional wit, no publicly toasted beauty; she never published a book, exhibited a picture, nor even made herself the heroine of a scandal. Her artistic productions, though admirable of their kind, were avowedly the work of an amateur, and were only known among her own circle of friends. Why, then, was she famous? For it seems to be still regarded as a slight achievement for a woman to be virtuous, cultivated, and charming, though there may come a time when genius in the art of living may be held deserving of greener and more glorious laurels than genius in the arts of music, painting, or poetry.

In an interesting and sympathetic article on Mrs. Delany in *Blackwood's Magazine* for April 1862 [see excerpt by Margaret Oliphant dated 1862], the writer seeks to solve the problem why Mrs. Delany, who never achieved nor even attempted any public success, should shine serenely over the heads of the Carters, Rowes, and Montagus in tender individual celebrity. 'Is it,' he inquires, 'that some natural instinct of humanity points out as the perfection of her sex the appreciative, sympathetic woman, whose business it is to perceive, to comprehend, to quicken the ear and eye of society with that bright and sweet intelligence which, in the most subtle, imperceptible way, leads, forms, and refines public opinion, and brings genius and excellence into fashion?' The reviewer is of opinion that Mrs. Delany's reputation was the spontaneous tribute of one generation's love, admiration, and homage, handed down to posterity with a certain indescribable independence of any actual foundation—differing in some ineffable fashion from the hard-earned renown of heroes and great men, yet warm with a tender personal sentiment beyond the reach of loftier laurels, the quintessence of feminine fame.

'On her and such as her the world bestows spontaneously and of grace such tender myrtle crowns as neither toil nor talent can obtain.' (pp. 273-75)

• • • • •

It seems probable that Lady Llanover had long in contemplation the publication of Mrs. Delany's *Correspondence,* and had collected materials from other members of the family; but it is not until the late 'fifties' that we find her regularly at work upon the book, selecting, arranging, and annotating the vast mass of material. In 1857 she spent three months in London, going daily to the British Museum, accompanied by her assistants, for purposes of research and verification. In 1861 the first series appeared in three substantial volumes, ornamented with numerous engravings from family portraits, and enriched by voluminous notes. This was followed, in 1862, by the second series, also consisting of three volumes, with an index covering nearly a hundred pages. (p. 282)

[In mid-nineteenth-century France], Taine and the De Goncourts, in their historical essays, were doing brilliant work on the lines of reconstruction. The latter, more especially in their vivid pictures of society in France under the Republic and the First Empire, had forsaken the dry-as-dust records beloved of their colleagues, and had relied for their material upon 'living documents' in the shape of newspapers, letters, diaries, squibs, almanacs, and other contemporary ephemerides. They had indeed gone so far as to assert that 'un temps dont on n'a pas un échantillon de robe et un menu de dîner, l'histoire ne le voit pas vivre.' It is easy to imagine the avidity with which the brothers would have fallen upon the correspondence of Mrs. Delany had she been their compatriot, more especially when we remember their theory that the old lady's tub-chair (*tonneau*) was the social pillar of the eighteenth century; and their testimony to the historical value of these 'living memories' in mob cap and spectacles, who held the traditions of the past in their wrinkled hands, and exercised so gentle yet potent an influence on those who came after them.

The *Blackwood* reviewer observes that the Delany Correspondence is essentially 'a female book,' an 'ill phrase,' but it will pass. We know he meant that the book presented the woman's point of view; that it was, in short, a feminine commentary upon the people and events of the period, written frankly, freely, carelessly, and intended only for the eyes of relations or intimate friends. But the fact that it is so completely a 'female book' will hardly lessen its value in the eyes of reflecting persons. Since the first dawn of civilisation we have been made familiar with the man's point of view; but, with few exceptions, the woman's thoughts, feelings, opinions, have been buried with her, and the half of human history is left a blank. What would we not give nowadays for the Travels of a Lady Mandeville, the Familiar Letters of a Mrs. Howell, the Diary of a Mrs. Evelyn, or a Mrs. Pepys?

By the critics and public of 1861 a biographical work appears to have been judged upon its merits as a 'story' rather than as a document for the elucidation of history. There was a decided impatience of gossiping records and of the repetition of trivial incidents which had no direct bearing upon the life-drama of hero or heroine. It was not yet generally realised that the chronicles of small beer improve, like many other things, with keeping, and that even 'female gossip' which is upwards of a century old acquires the same kind of pathetic interest as a woman's work-bag or a child's plaything that has come down to us out of a remote past. We could better spare better things than, for instance, the gossip of a Dame Margaret Paston, or of certain ladies of the Verney family. Splendidly as the eighteenth century has been illustrated for us by the literary and political correspondence of a Pope or a Swift, a Burke or a Bolingbroke, by the vivid character-portraits of a Hervey, and the witty chronicles of a Walpole or Wortley Montagu, the picture would still be incomplete without those details of the *vie intime* of the period which are painted with Dutch fidelity by Mrs. Delany. From her we know exactly how life appeared to a well-bred, well-educated woman in the reigns of the first three Georges. Nothing is hid from us. We are the confidantes of her love-affairs, we assist at her toilettes, we accompany her to weddings and christenings, to operas and masquerades, we look over her shoulder when she reads or works, we help her to carry out her shopping commissions for country correspondents, we are privy to her little acts of charity, we share her tender anxiety for sick or absent friends. It is these familiar trifles of everyday life that put marrow into the dry bones of history, and blood into its flaccid veins. (pp. 286-88)

> *George Paston [pseudonym of Emily Morse Symonds], in* Mrs. Delany (Mary Granville): A Memoir, 1700-1788, *edited by George Paston, Grant Richards, 1900, 310 p.*

AUSTIN DOBSON (essay date 1902)

[*Dobson, an English poet and man of letters, wrote a number of biographical prose works showing a close knowledge of eighteenth-century English society and literature. He is best remembered as the author of* Eighteenth Century Vignettes (1892-96) *and* Poems on Several Occasions (1889). *In the excerpt below, Dobson extols Delany's letters for their richly anecdotal character.*]

Among Mrs. Delany's chief attractions must certainly have been her many accomplishments; and it was no doubt owing to her unvarying amiability and well-bred amenity that she was such a universal favourite. One feels that she must have been good to look at and to live with; and that she must have represented in all its soothing perfection that leisured and measured old-world mode of address and conversation which has departed with the advent of telegrams and snap-shot portraits. It is easy to conceive her as the 'Dear Mrs. Delany' of her environment,—as the handsome and wonderful old lady whom every one delighted to fondle and make much of (including the Royal Family!); who was so sympathetic and so

lovable, and whose endless fund of anecdotes of Swift and Pope, coupled with her extraordinary achievements in needle work and cut paper (at her *age* too!) made her almost a curiosity. Nor must it be forgotten that, besides being cultivated and accomplished when these things were rare, she seems to have also been what was rarer still, a woman of unblemished character in a decidedly difficult society, and after an unobtrusive fashion sincerely religious.

Her life has been said to have more of anecdote—in the Johnsonian sense—than actual incident. Nevertheless the two series of her ***Autobiography and Correspondence,*** as edited by the late Lady Llanover, occupy no fewer than six bulky volumes. Apart from the gradual disclosure of [their author's] singularly composed and even-blooded nature . . . , they abound in valuable details of the social life of the eighteenth century. But their material is by no means of the kind which can be lightly summarised in a short paper. There are too many names and too many occurrences to be scheduled effectively. Here it is a little picture of Rousseau's ante-chamber at Paris, 'filled with bird-cages,' and guarded by Thérèse Levasseur, vigilant to protect *mon Mari* from inconvenient visitors; here a reference to Handel's blindness, or Mrs. Woffington's admirable acting of Lady Townly, despite her 'disagreeable voice' and 'ungainly' arms, or Mrs. Montagu's 'Room of Cupidons' at Hill Street, which must have been even more remarkable than the famous 'Feather Hangings,' of which Cowper was the laureate. 'How such a *genius* at her *age,* and so *circumstanced,* could think of painting the walls of her dressing-room with bowers of roses and jessamins entirely inhabited by little Cupids in all their little wanton ways, is astonishing!' Another page shall give you an excellent report of a visit to Garrick at Hampton, with a drinking of tea in Shakespeare's temple, under Roubillac's statue, and in close proximity to the famous Stratford chair designed by Hogarth; or a description of a *fête champêtre* at Lord Stanley's, worthy to pair off with Walpole's *festinos* at Strawberry or with that notable entertainment given by Miss Pelham at Esher Place to his Grace the Duc de Nivernais. Not the least interesting of the records, as may be anticipated, relate to bygone pastimes and costumes, in which latter the vagaries of the Duchess of Kingston naturally find a mention. In October, 1772, she was flaunting it in 'a sack sometimes white, sometimes other colours, trimmed with roses of ribbon, in each a large diamond, no cap, and diamonds in her hair, and some gewgaws hovering over head; a tucker edged with diamonds, a little twist with a jewel dangling, and no more of a tippet than serves to make her fair bosom conspicuous rather than to hide it.' Elsewhere there is an account of Lady Coventry's coiffure, 'a French cap that just covered the top of her head, of blond, and stood in the form of a butterfly, with its wings not quite extended, frilled sort of lappets crossing under her chin, and tied with pink and green ribbon—a head-dress that would have charmed a *shepherd!*' Some of the designs described are extraordinary. That the Duchess of Queensberry's attire should have successfully simulated a landscape, with 'brown hills,' tree-stumps gilded by the sunlight, and other picturesque accessories, is quite in keeping with what we know of the lady whom Walpole named 'Sa Singularité.' We must, however, invite the reader to guess to whom the following extract refers: 'Her petticoat was black velvet embroidered with chenille, the pattern a *large stone vase* filled with *ramping flowers* [the italics, as always, are in the original] that spread almost over a breadth . . . from the bottom to the top; between each vase of flowers was a pattern of gold shells, and foliage embossed and most heavily rich.' *'Je vous le donne en* *quatre, je vous le donne en dix, je vous le donne en cent,'*—as Mme. de Sévigné would say. The person who sported this 'most laboured piece of finery' was Selina Hastings, Countess of Huntingdon, afterwards the respected head of a special Methodist connection, with George Whitefield to her Chaplain. (pp. 125-29)

> Austin Dobson, " 'Dear Mrs. Delany'," in his Side-Walk Studies, *Humphrey Milford, 1924, pp. 110-29.*

E. BERESFORD CHANCELLOR (essay date 1925)

[*In the excerpt below, Chancellor examines Delany's achievement as a letter-writer and describes her relationships with literary, artistic, and royal figures of the day.*]

The "dear Mrs. Delany" of George III and Queen Charlotte, whom Burke once described as the finest example of a *grande dame* he had ever met, and whose name is so familiar to readers of Fanny Burney's diary, has become something of a legendary figure. Students of the eighteenth century know her as that anomaly to foreigners, a great lady without an ennobling title; as a *persona gratissima* of the reigning family; as the writer of an autobiography and letters which form one of the staple sources of information on the social life of a supremely interesting period in our annals. Those who have won through the six massive volumes, edited by Lady Llanover in 1861, which comprise Mrs. Delany's records, realise that she was a woman of considerable judgment, of much observation, of no little literary ability, of a kind but forceful nature, and, above all, one who possessed in a marked degree what has been called the genius for friendship.

To the majority, however, her name and the portraits of her, by Opie, which hang in the National Portrait Gallery and Kensington Palace are practically all that are known about a lady who occupied for so many years almost a unique position in the social life of her time; for she was not a bluestocking like Mrs. Montagu nor a successful novelist like Fanny Burney; she was no classical scholar like Mrs. Carter nor a kind of professional letter writer as was Mrs. Chapone; unlike the Duchess of Devonshire, she took no conspicuous part in politics, and she did not, as did the Duchess of Queensberry, make a reputation by petting literary men and snubbing her sovereign. She must have been undeniably handsome, but her beauty, although it helped to procure her many offers of marriage, was hardly of the striking character of that of Mary Lepel or the lovely Bellenden. In a word, she was that rather rare product of eighteenth-century society, a normal woman, and the influence she exercised and the fame she attained must therefore be traced to her inherent common sense and her calm and equable temperament.

Mrs. Delany's autobiography and letters not only form a complement to the better known diary of Fanny Burney and the correspondence of Horace Walpole, but it is probable that without her records we should only know half of the picture, in the more brilliant output of these famous contemporaries. She was both in and of the society of her time as was Walpole, but, unlike him, she exhibits a serious outlook on current topics, and she does not seem, as he always does notwithstanding the art that conceals art in his letters, to have had one eye on subsequent publication. High-born but poor, she occupies a position more familiar in French social life than in our own, where money has to so large an extent always covered a multitude of shortcomings.

Delany as a young woman.

Born two years before the accession of Queen Anne, Mrs. Delany died when George III had been on the throne twenty-eight years. Her life thus covered a period in which this country entered on a new phase of its career, and Europe passed through a state of existence which was not only significant in itself, but was the prelude to such drastic changes as were without parallel in its history.

Marlborough was winning his victories when Mary Granville, as she then was, was a child; she was eighteen when Charles XII fell by "a dubious hand," and twenty-seven when Catherine the Great finished her tempestuous career; and when she died Napoleon and Wellington were entering on manhood. What she could remember included such stirring events as the Sacheverell riots, the risings of the two Pretenders, the rise and fall of Sir Robert Walpole, the disaster of the South Sea Bubble, the inauguration of Methodism, Clive's successes in India, the ministry of Chatham and the commencement of the trial of Warren Hastings. Pepys died when she was three, and she survived Johnson by four years; Sir Joshua Reynolds outlived her four years, and Sir Christopher Wren died when she was twenty-three.

It is thus obvious that even a very cursory acquaintance with the political, literary, and artistic annals of those eighty-eight years will enable us to estimate the importance of the period through which Mrs. Delany lived; its importance to one of so impressionable a nature as hers was doubly significant.

Living in, and being of, that section of society which consisted of the governing classes, she came in contact with many of the most illustrious men and women of her time, and although she had none of the advanced aspirations of Mrs. Montagu, or even of her own relative, Mrs. Pendarves, or the literary qualities of Mrs. Chapone, who we know on great authority corresponded with Miss Pinkerton, yet she possessed a *seeing* mind and a retentive memory, and thus much that she records is of particular value, and even that portion of her reminiscences which is concerned with the gossip of the time and the thousand and one trivial details which made up the daily life of a lady of quality has its peculiar significance. (pp. 504-06)

[In 1768, Mary Delany] settled down to a calm old age in London (her house was off St. James's Street, in what was then called Catherine Wheel Lane, its back looking on to the Duke of Bridgewater's garden), corresponding largely, visiting much, and still occupied with her artistic resources, among which began now to be numbered that "paper mosaic" for which she became famous. In her letters the various events, some of them of great significance, others of merely ephemeral interest, which marked this period are noted in that easy manner which betokens the woman of the world, and are not infrequently characterised by that deeper insight which indicates the reflective mind: the institution of Almack's, "the first female club"; a notable visit to Garrick at his villa at Hampton, and others to the studios of "the great Mr. West" and Angelica Kauffmann; the opening of the Pantheon in Oxford Street in 1772; meetings at Bulstrode with Sir Joseph Banks and Dr. Solander; amusing references to the notorious Duchess of Kingston, whose vagaries were the talk of the town at this period; a description of Mrs. Montagu's then new "palace" in Portman Square; and the publication of "Lord Chesterfield's letters," all find a place in her discursive pages.

The "paper mosaic" I have just referred to, besides being mentioned with admiration by such men as Banks and Reynolds, Horace Walpole and Dr. Darwin, who celebrates it in his *Botanical Garden,* has become so identified with Mrs. Delany's name that the following description of its inception must necessarily find a place in any account of that lady:

> Having a piece of Chinese paper on the table of bright scarlet, a scarlet geranium of the same colour caught Mrs. Delany's eye; and, taking out her scissors, she amused herself with cutting out each flower in the paper which resembled its hue; she laid the paper petals on a black ground, and was so pleased with the effect that she proceeded to cut out the calyx, stalks and leaves in different shades of green, and pasted them down. After she had completed a sprig of geranium in this way, the Duchess of Portland came in and exclaimed: 'What are you doing with that geranium?' having taken the paper imitation for the real flower. Mrs. Delany replied that if the Duchess really thought it so like the original, a new work was begun from that moment.

For upwards of ten years this labour was continued, and at the close, when her eyesight gave way and caused her to abandon the work, Mrs. Delany had filled her "Flora," as she called it, with over a thousand imitations of flowers. (pp. 513-14)

Hardly does Mrs. Papendiek, or Fanny Burney, who, by the by, first met Queen Charlotte at Mrs. Delany's, give a more vivid account of the family side of the royal circle, than is to be found in Mrs. Delany's correspondence. Queen Charlotte sent her a lock of her hair accompanied by one of those gracious notes which make us forget the plainfaced Queen in the well-bred lady; and George III was never happier than when talking to Mrs. Delany and listening to her reminiscences. It was by the royal command that Opie painted the portrait which is now at Kensington Palace; and some years later the King gave Mrs. Delany a residence at Windsor, where he seems to have been fond of dropping in in the most unceremonious way, one of which occasions Fanny Burney describes in a well-known passage in her Diary. So insistent were the King and Queen on having their old friend about them that, even when they went for their fortnightly visits to Kew, they not infrequently commanded her presence in that once rural spot.

Mrs. Delany holds a unique position in the history of the eighteenth century, and it is rather extraordinary that she does so. She was undoubtedly a clever woman, but many cleverer are forgotten; she was artistic, musical, and generally accomplished, but in no special degree could she be said to excel in any of these directions; she was a high-born lady, but how many of her equals in this respect are to-day remembered? The fact that she was essentially a womanly woman, notwithstanding her gifts and her strong mind, seems to differentiate her from those of her contemporaries who, because they knew a little, never quite realised how little they knew; and it is this that has perhaps succeeded in perpetuating her name. (pp. 514-15)

> *E. Beresford Chancellor, "Mrs. Delany," in* The English Review, *Vol. XL, April, 1925, pp. 504-15.*

SIMON DEWES [PSEUDONYM OF **JOHN SAINT CLAIR MURIEL**] **(essay date 1940)**

[*In the excerpt below, Muriel, writing as "Simon Dewes," maintains that while occasionally given to embracing public action, Delany was essentially a private person whose concerns seldom reached beyond her intimate social sphere.*]

Life at Court, balls and dances were never enough for [Mary Pendarves Delany]: and when, in the fever following the appearance of Captain Jenkins's ear in a bottle, the galleries of the House of Lords were closed to the public and reserved for the Members of the House of Commons, Mary, in company with "a tribe of dames resolved to show that neither men nor laws could resist them", invaded the House and demanded admittance.

They did it for excitement. But it was not long before their friends had persuaded them that their aims were higher than that. Lady Mary Wortley Montague called them "the boldest assertors and most resigned sufferers for liberty that ever I heard of ". Mrs. Pendarves, writing to [her sister] Ann, tells her that she has embarked on "a sea of troubles".

It was *most* satisfactory. It was most delightful to be able to impress Ann with one's interest in politics and to assert that one was fighting for the liberty of the subject: and soon the adventure had become quite famous and all London talked of it and the ladies were pointed out by the common people who cheered them . . . and they were quite convinced that they had struck a great blow for liberty. (pp. 150-51)

[Mary] was and she remained essentially a *private* individual.

Her life, during which she moved endlessly among public figures, remained essentially a private life, the life of a woman who hated publicity, who was alarmed and distressed and even angry when her affairs became public, who could not bring herself to writing other than a stilted letter to a celebrity whose correspondence might one day be the hunting ground of a biographer.

That her own letters are such a joy, that they give an unparalleled portrait of the life of a leisured lady in a leisured age is because they were written only to her intimate friends. They were *private* letters. They were meant for no eyes but those of the person to whom they were addressed. They would have been, had she had it in her power to do so, destroyed as soon as they had been read.

That they were not all destroyed is almost a miracle. That many of them were is a tragedy. Fanny Burney, the devoted and rather pathetic little friend of old age, probably burned many. Lady Llanover, the nineteenth century editor, probably edited with a natural eye on the proprieties. At any rate, the letters of Wesley are not printed in Lady Llanover's volumes. Probably Mrs. Wesley was considered too sacred a subject for such frivolous affairs as concerts of music on Sunday evening.

But, the assault on the House of Lords accomplished, Lady Montague supplied with material to make her boast about the emancipation of women, Mary retired from even such elegant public life as that. (p. 154)

> *Simon Dewes [pseudonym of John Saint Clair Muriel], in his* Mrs. Delany, *Rich & Cowan, Ltd., 1940, 320 p.*

ROBERT MANSON MYERS (essay date 1946)

[*In the excerpt below, Myers briefly characterizes Delany's correspondence as "a social and literary document of peculiar significance."*]

In the six enormous volumes of her autobiography and correspondence Mrs. Delany produced a social and literary document of peculiar significance. Her autobiography consists actually of only a few fragments, but the voluminous correspondence involves most of the fashionable and literary figures of 18th-century England. No other collection of letters paints a more animated picture of polite society under the Georges, or illuminates in more brilliant detail the exquisite graces of Augustan England as seen through the eyes of a true "lady of quality". Of these letters many hundreds were addressed to her sister Anne Granville (Mrs. Dewes), and here Mrs. Delany reveals the astonishing energy and zeal of her manifold cultural pursuits. With the temperament, taste, and executive skill of a genuine artist she was intense in her acquisition of knowledge till the end of her life, and her strong taste for art and study led her not only into literature, painting, and music, but even into natural philosophy and the sciences. She was a painter of no mean skill, a botanist, an accomplished musician. She read widely, and her comments upon contemporary literature are sound and illuminating. With an harmonious sense of proportion that put equal emphasis upon good sense, sincerity, intellect, and social life, she eagerly absorbed everything she touched, and commented on all in the sprightly observation and lively confession of her witty, informal letters. (pp. 12-13)

> *Robert Manson Myers, "Mrs. Delany: An Eigh-*

teenth-Century Handelian," in The Musical Quarterly, *Vol. XXXII, No. 1, January, 1946, pp. 12-36.*

ALICE ANDERSON HUFSTADER (essay date 1978)

[*In the excerpt below, Hufstader argues that Delany's accomplishments belie critical claims that she was a superficial woman.*]

The two versions of Mrs. Delany's life and correspondence [Lady Llanover's *Autobiography and Correspondence* and George Paston's *Mrs. Delany: A Memoir*] fulfill in a lesser way the function of Pepys's *Diary*. In the latter we have nine years of middle-class life in Restoration London. In the former we experience the patrician world of Georgian England and Ireland as it was relished by a great lady of exuberance, compassion and versatility.

Mrs. Delany was a creative conformist. She participated in the social routines of her class and times without sacrifice of her many talents. It would be unfair to accuse her, as a person or an artist, of superficiality. Her attainments, however, were in breadth rather than depth. She excelled in music and in the applied arts. She loved sea shells, from which she made "lustres." Moralist that she was, she admired the didactic painting of Hogarth, writing in 1731 that "there is more sense in it than any I have seen." Her own drawing interested him sufficiently to proffer "some instructions about drawing that will be of great use . . . some rules of his own that he says will improve me more in a day than a year's learning in the common way." Armed with these precepts, she made numerous copies from the old masters and, during her years of residing in Ireland, sketched the landscape of County Down, an Irish harper playing at her side to heighten local color. Her embroideries, of which only photographs remain, were detailed by Lady Llanover as examples of the superior feminine skills of the eighteenth century. (p. 146)

Ireland was to provide Mrs. Pendarves with a powerful stimulus to her chief literary gift. She possessed to a high degree the ability to describe her environment, whether it was that of the countryside, the theatre or the drawing room. With personalities she was less expert. The general social scene she captured because she had a flair for occasion and ceremony. The complexities of human motivation were either beyond her or a matter of indifference. She was not, where individual persons were concerned, analytical. Like her mentor, Hogarth, she possessed a photographic sense and, like him, her concern was with society "in the round." (p. 152)

Although Mrs. Delany's literary abilities did not equal her skill in the applied arts, her exhaustive correspondence supplies an invaluable picture of the day-to-day activities, concerns, convictions and even limitations of her class and times. Some of the immediacy of her letters and those of her friends is owing to the fact that they were written by amateurs. Style seldom competes with news. We are never diverted from a ballroom or a recipe by rhetoric. Like her sometime tutor, Hogarth, her interest was in the general human scene. She loved her life, her friends and her projects. In recording them, she remains witness to a vanished world. (pp. 194-95)

> *Alice Anderson Hufstader, "The Artist" in her* Sisters of the Quill, *Dodd, Mead & Company, 1978, pp. 142-95.*

PATRICIA MEYER SPACKS (essay date 1988)

[*In the following excerpt, Spacks views Delany's* Autobiography and Correspondence *as the writer's attempt to discover herself through the act of letter-writing—a process not uncommon, Spacks claims, in the letters of many eighteenth-century women.*]

Eighteenth-century letters by women reflect and elucidate the conflict between the desire for self-assertion and the need for self-suppression, and they demonstrate strategies of deflection. Lady Mary Wortley Montagu, Mary Delany, and Elizabeth Carter . . . all conducted voluminous correspondences in which they worked out ways of understanding themselves: each set of letters reveals its own dominant theme of self-elucidation. But the writers also find ways to avoid the troubling threat of egotism. Female correspondence, their letters suggest, supplies means of evasive self-definition, and the sex of women letter writers informs their use of the epistolary form.

The twentieth-century reputations of Lady Mary, Delany, and Carter confirm the women's avoidance of excessive personal claims. Most people who now recognize the name of Elizabeth Carter dimly recollect Johnson's praise of her as one who could make good puddings as well as translate Greek. Lady Mary Wortley Montagu survives in present-day consciousness because Pope attacked her. The entry for Mary Delany in the *Concise Dictionary of National Biography* begins, "Friend of Swift." All three women lived prolonged lives (Carter died at eighty-nine, Delany at eighty-eight, Lady Mary at seventy-three) of various accomplishment: among other things, Carter translated Epictetus; Delany invented the paper mosaic, a mode of representing flowers with accuracy and beauty by layered shapes of colored paper; Lady Mary introduced small-pox inoculation into England. But their modern fame, such as it is, rests largely on their associations with distinguished men.

The women's published letters exist in different states of completeness and accuracy. . . . Lady Llanover, a descendant of Mary Granville Delany's sister Ann, produced six volumes of Delany's letters, each more than six hundred pages long, in 1861. The reverential tone of her preface conveys her high regard for her subject (born in 1700), but the editor fails to explain her editorial principles; we cannot know what has been silently omitted. (pp. 177-78)

In an early letter to [her sister Ann], Delany complains about another correspondent who adopts too "cramped" and obscure an epistolary style. "The beauty of writing (in my opinion)," she concludes, "consists in telling our sentiments in an easy natural way" (14 Mar. 1728-29). Almost a quarter of a century later, she complains because Ann has shown Samuel Richardson some of Delany's letters to her. "Indeed, such careless and incorrect letters as mine are to you, should not be exposed: were they put in the best dress I could put them into, they have nothing to recommend them but the warm overflowing of a most affectionate heart, which can only give pleasure to the partial friend they are addressed to" (17 Nov. 1750). Stressing the importance of epistolary style, these comments also differentiate appropriate styles in relation to levels of intimacy. The "easy and natural" mode desirable in letters between friends provides an appropriate "dress" for the telling of sentiments—meaning, epistolary practice suggests, the expression of views about such matters as books and current political happenings. Only between extreme intimates can feeling be allowed simply to overflow, justifying

"careless and incorrect" style, but also shaping letters inappropriate for any audience but the intended recipient. From a modern perspective, even Delany's most intimate letters sound highly controlled, sharply restraining their expression of personal feeling. But she manifestly experiences more freedom in writing her sister than in other correspondences; in that context she allows herself at least the possibility of focusing on her own emotions.

The conventions of female correspondence resemble those dominating its male counterpart. Women's letters almost ritualistically apologize for their own length; they reiterate ardent professions of friendship. Pope and Swift do the same thing, but because the women often apparently have less to write about, their conventional protestations assume a larger place in their letters. In her old age, Delany would offer lessons in "propriety" to her little grandniece, pointing out that propriety amounts to thoughtfulness, a way to demonstrate concern for others. The stylized aspects her letters share with those of other women express their status as communications dominated by consciousness of *the other*. Hence the special importance of self-subordination: concern for self must not be allowed to block sensitivity to the imagined needs of the recipient. Hence the insistent recurrence, within these texts, of rituals of politeness.

The ideology of self-subordination implies, among other things, suppression of narrative about the self. Even when these letter writers experience their own emotional dramas, they frequently fail to report them directly. Lady Mary, in her premarital letters to Wortley and in her later passionate correspondence with the young Italian Algarotti, with whom she fell in love in her middle age (he, bisexual in orientation, apparently preferred Lord Hervey), expresses herself rather like a literary heroine; she calls attention to the analogy between her situation and Clarissa's in a letter written late in her life. But she elides the aftermath of her romantic predicaments, hardly hinting at her unhappiness with her husband in letters to intimates and never revealing what has happened with Algarotti, much less how she feels about it. Delany, for some years during her first widowhood, participated in a flirtation? a courtship? *some* kind of relationship with Lord Baltimore. She probably wished to marry him; certainly she expected him to propose. Like Lovelace in *Clarissa,* he finally proposed in terms that made it impossible for her immediately to accept him; then for some years he disappeared from her life. One deduces this story not from Delany's letters, which largely ignore it, but from Llanover's editorial comments. Carter received at least one proposal of marriage during the years of the Talbot correspondence; she hints at more. She tells the story of the proposal in a comic mode, and quickly. Of psychosexual drama in her life, she says nothing.

Why should a modern reader feel interested in women who avoid self-revelation and personal narrative, concern themselves obsessively with stylistic propriety, and fill their letters with courteous protestation? One may note in such phenomena evidence of familiar social attitudes toward women and of the internalization of these attitudes by the women themselves; that once said, why bother? In fact, these letters create an impression of vitality and emotional tension comparable to that generated by the fictional letters conveying the drama of such novels as *Pamela* and *Clarissa*. If real female letter writers eschew narratives focused on themselves and avoid direct outpourings of emotion, they nonetheless find ways of indirect self-dramatization, codes for revealing the self.

In her first letter to Wortley after their marriage, Lady Mary describes the family in which she is living—five children, a mother, and a father. Then she remarks, "I don't know whether you will presently find out that this seeming Impertinent Account is the tenderest expressions [*sic*] of my Love to you, but it furnishes my imagination with agreeable pictures of our future life, and I flatter my self with the hope of one day enjoying with you the same satisfactions" (22 Oct. [1722]). She thus suggests that anecdotes about other people supply metaphors for her desire. Carter's and Delany's letters as well as Lady Mary's abound in stories serving comparable functions.

The stories, however, rarely concern domestic bliss. Lady Mary's anecdotes more often dwell on the corruptions of high life with gusto and with brilliant detail. In her letters, as in Delany's, rich young men commit public suicide, footmen rape peeresses, men try successfully or futilely to obtain divorces in order to enact their lustful desires with younger women, randy middle-aged women entice young men to their beds. A particularly delicious narrative concerns an unmarried aristocratic couple, interrupted in an assignation by "a tall, musical, silly, ugly thing, . . . call'd Miss Leigh." They urge her to play the harpsichord for them; when she begins, they "decamp'd to the Bed Chamber," returning to invite her to perform another piece, only to disappear once more. Finally, at the third repetition, Miss Leigh leaves in a rage, telling everyone in town what has happened; "and poor Edgcombe met with nothing where ever he went but compliments about his third tune, which is reckon'd very handsome in a Lover past forty" (to Lady Mar [23 June 1727]).

At the end of this same letter, Lady Mary observes, "I send you a novell instead of a letter." She thus calls attention to the flavor of fictionality in her most compelling narratives. The stories she sketches resemble in substance the novels she and her contemporaries read. (By "novell," in 1727, Lady Mary of course meant something more like what we now call "romance.") More than a quarter century later, she reports to her daughter a scandalous-sentimental narrative which, she says, "in Richardson's hands would serve very well to furnish out 7 or 8 volumes" (8 Dec. [1754]). Like Carter and Delany, she finds the stuff of fiction in the world she knows.

Lady Mary states most directly a theme implicit in the stories all three women tell. Sounding like Mr. Bennet in *Pride and Prejudice,* she writes her sister, "I own I enjoy vast delight in the Folly of Mankind, and God be prais'd that is an inexhaustible Source of Entertainment" ([Sept. 1725]). The narrative energy of these female letters often derives from their loving rendition of mankind's—and womankind's—folly:

> What a sad story of that vile Miss T. who has run away with Mr. O., and poor Mrs. O *run mad,* and gone into the Bedlam! An intrigue was discovered last year, and hushed up, and Miss T. was more circumspect in her behavior, and it made no noise, but about a month ago she left her father's house under pretence of going to see her mother, she took her maid in the post-chaise with her, all her jewels, her best clothes, and £700, and went off to France; she was pursued but not overtaken. (Delany to Mrs. Dewes, undated)

Delany loves such episodes; she reports many of them. Even Carter, despite her "insignificancy" ("I often secretly exult in the privileges that attend one's being suffered to go in and out of a room with as much silence, and as little ceremony as the cat" [14 Sept. 1754]), and despite her editor's excisions, relates, for example, the tale of a rich man who shut himself up in his house, running to lock the door if he spied a human being nearby, and associating only with six "conversible" hogs (23 Jan. 1744).

Such narratives substitute for narratives of the self—most strikingly, perhaps, in Delany's reports of her association with King George III and Queen Charlotte. Day after day, she renders in loving detail everything said and done at court and during royal visits, suppressing the fact of her own presence as much as possible, while yet emphasizing her powerful role as observer and narrator. In most of the anecdotes told by the other women, the tellers have not actually witnessed the events they report. Yet all, like Delany, assert by their narratives the traditional resources of women: to notice, to interpret, to tell.

The often scandalous stories incorporated in female correspondences help to define their reporters by the principle of differentiation—the women tell of lives led by other values and based on other assumptions than their own. They also satisfy forbidden wishes by brief vicarious excitement, reminding themselves of possibilities for the unconventional—if also, often, of the likelihood of retribution for deviation. And, of course, they enjoy the power of their knowledge and their telling, of being able to convey titillating information that their correspondent lacks. But their stories of male and female enactments of desire most forcefully convey their musings on the relative positions and possibilities accessible to men and women in their society. Their expedients for self-definition involve reflection on the same compelling subject. (pp. 180-84)

In her reflections about women, Lady Mary expresses the dilemmas of her own sense of specialness, her desire to declare her difference, and then her need at last to find what she shares with others of her kind. Mary Delany, compliant where Lady Mary was rebellious and leading a conventional rather than an ostentatiously original life, makes community her theme from the beginning—a more indirect way of thinking about women and of thinking about herself. Even her earliest letters to her sister emphasize the importance of "friendship." "I am convinced," the then Mrs. Pendarves writes her sister in 1727, after the death of her first husband,

> there is no real happiness but in a faithful friend. As Doctor Swift says to his Vanessa, it is a *"rational delight,"* it fills the mind with generous motives, and I must have a mean opinion of those that call it *romantic:* it is the most improper name for it in the world, for the foundation of a worthy friendship is truth. People may fancy themselves in love, and work up their imagination to such a pitch as to really believe themselves possessed of that passion, but I never yet heard of anybody's carrying friendship on by mere imagination. (25 Nov. 1727)

This is her fullest and most explicit explanation of what she means by "friendship," an important ideal of her period, a noun Delany applies consistently to her relation with her sister, a term of transcendent value. Despite her disclaimer, imagination plays its part in her friendships, particularly the one with her sister. "Though so many hills and vales separate our bodies, thought (that is free and unlimited) makes up in some measure that misfortune, and though my eyes are shut, I see my dearest sister in my dreams. I talked with you all last night and was mortified when the vision fled" (30 May 1724).

A view of St. James's Square, London, dated 1768. Delany spent her last years living in a house on St. James's Place.

The human connection between Delany and her sister, like that between her and her other female intimates, feels more solidly based than alliances with men. As a widow, after her miserable marriage at her uncle's behest, she expresses vehement distaste for marriage as an institution:

> Matrimony! I marry! Yes, there's a blessed scene before my eyes of the comforts of that state.—A sick husband, squalling brats, a cross mother-in-law, and a thousand unavoidable impertinences . . . : but stop my rage! be not too fierce. I may be dashed on the very rock I endeavour to avoid, and therefore I will say no more against a station of life which in the opinion of some people is not in our power to prevent. (19 Mar. 1727/8)

She often writes of male-female union in comparably negative terms. When her beloved sister marries, Delany observes to a friend that "marriage *is serious and hazardous*" (to Lady Throckmorton, 5 Dec. 1740). Like Lady Mary Wortley Montagu, Mary Pendarves comments on the persistence with which men interpret women to the disadvantage of her sex; she complains that men lead women astray and then blame them for their weakness. Men are not to be trusted; to trust women, on the other hand, makes the happiness of her life. She says this, one way and another, again and again.

Finally she marries happily—marries a man so dedicated to virtue, so supportive of all her endeavors, that he possesses the qualities Mrs. Delany more consistently found in women. Even during her second marriage, however, she continues to defend the notion that women should possess the choice of remaining single (see letter to Ann Dewes, 31 Mar. 1759). Her vision of good marriage more and more approximates her notion of friendship: "we are worthy of being their [men's] companions, their friends, *their advisors,* as well as *they ours*" (to Mrs. Dewes, 14 Apr. 1759).

As Delany ages, as friends and relatives in increasing numbers die, she realizes the moral problem implicit in commitment to human connection. Such commitment involves valuing the things of this world, whereas one's thoughts and feelings should properly direct themselves to preparing for the afterlife. On the other hand, at the age of eighty-six she writes to a friend: "Time and absence, I think, rather increase than diminish affection, when we from time to time communicate that mutual remembrance and regard which *had lasted so many years!*" (to Mrs. F. Hamilton, 24 Sept. 1786). "Tho' I dayly feel a decay of my faculties," she tells her niece, "there is none in my affection" (to Mrs. Port, 21 Dec. 1785). Her central preoccupation continued to dominate her letters until her death. (pp. 185-87)

> *Patricia Meyer Spacks, "Female Rhetorics," in* The Private Self: Theory and Practice of Women's Autobiographical Writings, *edited by Shari Benstock, The University of North Carolina Press, 1988, pp. 177-91.*

FURTHER READING

Hayden, Ruth. *Mrs. Delany: Her Life and Her Flowers.* London: British Museum Publications Ltd., 1980, 176 p.

  A detailed study of Delany's creative talents, with a biographical and critical introduction and several illustrations of her handiwork.

"Mrs. Delany in Ireland." *Littell's Living Age* XLIII, No. 2040 (28 July 1883): 240-49.

  Examines Delany's years in Ireland.

Review of *Mrs. Delany (Mary Granville): A Memoir,* by George Paston. *The Nation* 71, No. 1840 (4 October 1900): 275.

> A review of George Paston's *Mrs. Delany (Mary Granville): A Memoir,* with references to the historical components of the *Autobiography and Correspondence.*

Newton, Stella Mary. "Mrs. Delany and Her Handiwork." *Antiques* XCVI, No. 1 (July 1969): 100-105.

> A brief biographical survey of Delany. Newton focuses chiefly on such creative skills of Delany's as needlework, painting, and paper mosaics.

Pain, Nesta. *George III at Home.* London: Eyre Methuen, 1975, 191 p.

> Examines the domestic life of George III, offering scattered references to Delany.

Scott, Walter S. *The Bluestocking Ladies.* London: John Green & Co., 1947, 212 p.

> A history of the origin of the Bluestockings, with a chapter on Delany's involvement in the group.

Soulsby, Lucy H. M. "Mrs. Delany. II." *The Overland Monthly* n.s. III, No. 4 (April 1884): 394-408.

> Biography of Delany constructed around excerpts from her letters.

Vulliamy, Colwyn Edward. *Aspasia: The Life and Letters of Mary Granville, Mrs. Delany.* London: Geoffrey Bles, 1935, 289 p.

> Examines Delany's life as it is documented in her letters and in other historical material.

Marsilio Ficino

1433-1499

Italian philosopher and translator.

Called "the second Plato" by his contemporaries, Ficino is remembered for a lifelong devotion to Greek philosophy, one evidenced in an unprecedented reconciliation of Greek thought with other philosophical and religious teachings, particularly Christianity. Throughout a literary canon ably represented by a celebrated magnum opus, *Platonica theologia de immortalitate animorum,* Ficino integrated philosophical principles long considered naturally contrary and significantly broadened the scope of Renaissance humanism.

Ficino was born in Figline, the son of the personal physician to powerful Florentine statesman Cosimo de' Medici. Young Marsilio's potential for learning was early recognized. Cosimo supplied the means for his primary education and later sent him to the universities of Bologna, Pisa, and Florence, where he studied philosophy and humane letters. At about eighteen Ficino was received into the Medici household. Here he was exposed to the great humanists of the day, including the Byzantine Platonic scholar Georgius Gemistus Pletho, whose ambition was to establish a learning academy in Florence equal to that of ancient Athens. With his impressive knowledge of Latin and classical literature, Ficino was designated the official Platonist of a loosely knit, informal circle that came to be known as the Platonic Academy.

Beginning in 1459, Ficino mastered Greek and began the task of translating into Latin the works of Plato and other Greek writers. Cosimo provided him with instructors, manuscripts, and a comfortable villa at Careggi where he might work undisturbed. Ficino repaid his patron's generosity with singleminded and diligent dedication. Aside from translations of Neoplatonic and early Christian writings and of the works of such ancients as Homer, Hesiod, and Proclus, he rendered complete translations of Plotinus and Plato. The last—begun in 1463, completed around 1470, and published in 1484 and 1485—was the earliest complete translation of Plato into a Western tongue. It is recognized as Ficino's most distinguished achievement as a translator and, like his translation of Plotinus, was considered an authoritative source into the eighteenth century. Ficino also furnished Latin commentaries on some of the works he translated, including a 1469 discourse on Plato's *Symposium* in which he promoted the author's celebrated dialogue on love as the essence of Platonism. His Italian translation of the treatise—*Il libro dello amore*—published in 1474, was instrumental in disseminating the Renaissance conception of Platonic love throughout Italy and the rest of Europe.

Outside of his work and friendships with many of the leading scholars of his day, Ficino's life was uneventful. During his youth and up to about the age of forty, Ficino is said to have struggled with conflicts between the pagan philosophies of his studies and his orthodox Catholic background. Around 1473 he took religious orders and was ordained a canon of Florence cathedral, an office he held until his death. Ficino's original writings detail his resolution of religious doubts and rec-

onciliation of Platonic principles with Christian tenets. Among other studies, he published *Platonica theologia de immortalitate animorum* in 1482, his chief philosophical work. In this exposition of the existence and immortality of the soul, Ficino unified ancient, medieval, and Christian doctrine in systematic arguments that were to influence humanist thought throughout the sixteenth century. Ficino retired in 1494 after the expulsion of the Medici, his long-standing patrons, from Florence. He died at Careggi in 1499.

Jefferson Butler Fletcher noted that Ficino "examined historic creeds, not to prove all but one wrong, but rather to see if all might not be at one fundamentally." The open-minded, generous spirit that informs each of Ficino's works is particularly evident in *Platonica theologia* ("Platonic Theology"), acknowledged his greatest and most comprehensive achievement. Against a medieval background of lingering philosophical rigidity and partisanship, *Platonic Theology* stands as a bold directive in the advancement of Italian humanism. The use of Platonic arguments to support Christian beliefs was not, in itself, an innovation, as this had been accepted practice from the earliest church writings. However, these dialectics were often strained or diluted to support specific doctrines for which they were clearly unintended and with which they were sometimes even demonstrably at odds. Moreover, an essential divisiveness between Platonism and Christianity remained up to Ficino's time, typified by the authoritarian teachings of St. Augustine, who, while conceding that some Platonic tenets might be compatible with Christian thought, maintained that their overall tenor was not. By contrast, *Platonic Theology* justifies belief in the divine inspiration of Platonic tradition and demonstrates not only its parity with the Christian faith but also its capacity to confirm Christianity to skeptical intellects by way of reason. As Josephine L. Burroughs has observed of *Platonic Theology*, "philosophy is no longer taken to be an activity separated from religion, whether as rival or 'handmaid.' Both are manifestations of spiritual life and, as such, have a single aim—the attainment of the highest good. Each is required by the other, for religion saves philosophy from an inferior notion of this highest good, while philosophy saves religion from ignorance, and without knowledge the goal cannot be reached. Thus for Ficino philosophy must be religious, religion philosophical."

As its full Latin title implies, *Platonic Theology* treats the immortality of the soul by way of typically Platonic queries. In the first four books of the treatise, Ficino distinguishes types of being from the lowest to highest, designating the soul as one of middle nature which may rise or descend and which similarly assumes different stages in an instinctive drive towards the ultimate good that is God. The fifth book substantiates the immortality of the soul, and subsequent books refute contrary opinions. The entire work is designed as an ordered analysis of Plato's writings in its revelation of Platonic mysteries and their conformity with Christian teachings. Critics have been perplexed by Ficino's approach, finding some of his hypotheses shaky and questioning the existence of a formal system governing their exposition. Yet, though "single propositions tend to stand or fall on the truth or adequacy of a few a priori assumptions," as Michael J. B. Allen has indicated, "this has one overwhelming advantage: the commentary is more than a series of scholarly notes for it explores propositions with endless ramifications—something it shares with other Neoplatonic and scholastic commentaries derivative in appearance but often containing truly original insights." With others, Allen has also pointed to Ficino's extensive borrowings from various sources and his general eclecticism. George Boas considered the author "a typical eclectic, taking what pleased him, rejecting what displeased him." Boas added, however, that "Ficino laid down as a philosophical principle that there was truth in apparently contradictory philosophies, such as those of Plato and Aristotle, the apparent contradiction lying in the words in which they were expressed. Thus no philosophy would seem to be wholly false; the scholar's problem was to discover and unearth that which was true in it." This enterprise has been deemed no less than monumental. Within the scope of its essentially Platonic framework, *Platonic Theology* accommodates not only certain Aristotelian precepts which had formerly been rejected by many humanists, but diverse Augustinian, Thomist, and other elements as well. Paul Oskar Kristeller remarked that, insofar as "Ficino attempted to express the new ideas of the humanists in a strictly speculative metaphysical form, he may be called the first philosopher of the Italian Renaissance."

While less a literary showpiece than *Platonic Theology*, Ficino's commentary on Plato's *Symposium* influenced humanist thought in ways directly traceable to its author. *Il libro dello amore* is a series of dialogues designed to mirror Plato's exposition on love, in which guests at a banquet discourse in turn on that subject and Socrates provides the culminating speech. The work commemorates yearly celebrations of Plato's birthday at the Careggi villa, which Ficino and others of the Platonic Academy made traditional. *Il libro dello amore* is Ficino's own interpretation of Platonic or Socratic love, predicated on the human desire for beauty in general and, ultimately, for the beauty of God. According to the author, the love one individual bears another is tantamount to love of the beauty of God as reflected in the recipient. As with *Platonic Theology*'s stages of the soul, human love advances from love of the visible beauty of a particular person through love of ideals of physical beauty, of moral and intellectual virtues, and of angelic beauty. Ultimately, this advance may encompass the love of God's infinite beauty. Critics have cited *Il libro dello amore* as the main source of the literary Platonism that flourished throughout Renaissance Europe. Its contents were summarized in a *canzone* by Florentine poet Girolamo Benvieni, which verse was then expounded in a treatise by Pico della Mirandola, a disciple of Ficino. Ficino's work or its derivatives were then adopted by Pietro Bembo, Baldassare Castiglione, and other Italian writers. Commentators have recognized the imprint of *Il libro dello amore* on poet Edmund Spenser's *Fowre Hymnes* (1596) and on George Chapman's verse.

Ficino's influence as a forward thinker has at times been so profound as to render his achievements indistinguishable from those of his successors. According to modern scholars, such assimilation might have gratified rather than antagonized the author, whose philosophical mission was, as he saw it, the coalescence of knowledge. Yet, within even the expansive realm of his own epoch, Ficino and his legacy remain distinctive. Nesca A. Robb has concluded: "He has some claim to be regarded as one of the saints of humanism. He stands out from the other men of letters of the age by his singular disinterestedness. His work, which he looked upon as a sacred charge, was carried on unflinchingly throughout a lifetime of ill-health. In his personal life he was almost an ascetic, but his gentle and affectionate nature won him the love and veneration of the most divergent types of his fellow citizens."

PRINCIPAL WORKS

Il libro dello amore (treatise) 1474
Platonica theologia de immortalitate animorum (treatise) 1482
De Christiana religione (treatise) 1484
Prohemium Marsilii Ficini Florentini in libros Platonis ad Laurentium Medicem Virum Magnanimum. Marsilii argumentum in Hipparchum. [translator] (treatises) 1484-85
Prohemium M. Ficini Florentini in Plotinum &c. Plotini vita composita a Porphyrio traducta vera a M. Ficino. Plotini liber primus [translator] (treatises) 1492
Epistolae familiares (letters) 1495
De triplici vita (treatise) 1496
Opera omnia. 2 vols. (treatises, essays, and letters) 1561
Opera omnia. 2 vols. (treatises, essays, and letters) 1641
Supplementum Ficinianum—Marsilii Ficini Florentini opuscula inedita et dispersa. 2 vols. (treatises and essays) 1937
The Letters of Marsilio Ficino. 3 vols. (letters) 1975-81

*The initial collected works contains the first publication in Latin of Ficino's commentary on Plato's *Symposium, Commen-*

tarium . . . in convivium Platonis de amore, originally published in Italian as *Il libro dello amore* in 1474.

MARSILIO FICINO (letter date 1457-76)

[In the following excerpt from a letter written sometime between 1457 and 1476, Ficino enumerates his works at the request of Angelo Poliziano, a poet and man of letters eminent in the Medicean circle.]

Why do you ask so often for the titles of my books, Angelo? Is it perhaps so that you can praise me in your verse? However, there is no praise in number, but in selection; there is no goodness in quantity, but in quality. Or is it that you may have with you all that is mine? Whatever the reasons, take what you ask, since everything is common among friends.

I have translated from Greek into Latin the *Physics* and *Elements of Theology* of the Platonist Proclus and the four books by Iamblichus of Chalcis about the Pythagorean School, the *Mathematics* of Theo of Smyrna, the *Platonic Definitions* of Speusippus, the *Epitome of Platonism* by Alcinous, the book by Xenocrates on the *Consolation of Death,* the *Hymns* and *Symbols* of Pythagoras, the work of Hermes Trismegistus on the *Power and Wisdom of God,* all the works of Plato.

I have written a commentary on the Gospels, one on Plato's *Phaedrus,* one on his *Philebus,* about the Highest Good, and one on the *Symposium* about love. I have written a book on *Physiogonomy* and on the *Principles of Platonic discipline* to Cristoforo Landino, which I later amended; also a compendium on *The Opinions of the Philosophers on God and the Soul,* on *Economics,* on *Pleasure,* on *The Four Schools of Philosophy,* on *Magnanimity, Happiness, Justice, Divine Frenzy,* on *Consolation for Parents on the Death of a Son,* on *Desire,* a *Theological Prayer to God,* a *Theological Dialogue between God and the Soul,* a *Theology on the Immortality of Souls* in 18 books, a work on *The Christian Religion, Arguments against the Opinions of Astrologers,* on the *Rapture of Paul into the Third Heaven,* on *Light, The Principles of Platonic Theology, The Life and Teaching of Plato, Five Questions about Mind,* and a volume of *Philosophic Letters.*

Angelo, would that I had written well as I have written copiously! Would that my works might please others as much as I do you, and you me! (pp. 59-60)

> *Marsilio Ficino, in a letter to Angelo Poliziano, in* The Letters of Marsilio Ficino, Vol. I, *translated by various translators, Shepheard-Walwyn, 1975, pp. 59-60.*

MARSILIO FICINO (letter date 1474?)

[In the following excerpt from the introductory letter to the author's commentary on Plato's Philebus, *written, scholars believe, no later than 1474, Ficino imparts the nature of philosophy and philosophers to Giovanni Francesco Ippoliti, his friend and fellow humanist.]*

Since philosophy is defined by all men as love of wisdom (the very name introduced by Pythagoras supports this) and wisdom is the contemplation of the divine, then certainly the purpose of philosophy is knowledge of the divine. This our

Plato testifies in the seventh book of *The Republic,* where he says that true philosophy is the ascent from the things which flow and rise and fall, to those which truly are, and always remain the same. Therefore philosophy has as many parts and ministering powers as it has steps by which it is climbed from the very lowest level to the highest. These steps are determined partly by the nature and partly by the diligence of men. For, as Plato teaches in the sixth book of *The Republic,* whoever is to become a philosopher should be so endowed by Nature that, in the first place, he is willing and prepared to enter upon all manner of disciplines; thereafter that he is truthful by nature, completely opposed to all falsehood; in the third place that, having scorned all that is subject to corruption, he directs his mind to that which remains always the same. He must be magnanimous and courageous, so that he neither fears death nor longs for empty glory. Over and above this, he should be born with something of an even temperament, and from nature he should receive already under control those parts of the mind which are usually carried away by the feelings. For whoever longs for the truth turns his mind to contemplation of the divine and sets little value on the pleasures of the body. Beyond this, a philosopher should be of liberal mind. And in fact the prizing of worthless things is opposed to this and completely counter to the way of a man intending to contemplate the truth of things. Above this his will chooses justice, since he is utterly devoted to truth, moderation and liberality. But most of all, it seems that he needs sharp insight, memory and magnanimity.

What is more, these three gifts of nature, namely sharp insight, memory and magnanimity, when discipline and a proper education have been added, produce a man perfect in virtue. But if they are neglected, they are said by Plato to be the cause of the greatest crimes. Therefore, this nature must be given man's greatest care, so that he who is thus shaped by Nature, from his childhood, learns letters, the elements of all knowledge. And indeed the unordered mind of this person must be put in order by use of the lyre; the body must be exercised by gymnastic games, so that, coming into a good condition itself, it offers service to the studies of philosophy. Meanwhile the precepts of the best laws should be heard by him and fixed in his mind. Thus the mind of the young man should be formed by honest encouragement, so that it is rendered temperate and peaceful. This moral education, men in fact call Ethics.

In truth, when the mind is freed from the disturbance of desire by these means of which we have spoken, it will already have begun to be loosed from the body; then it must be given knowledge of mathematics, which concerns number, plane figures, and whole forms, and their manifold movements. Indeed, since numbers and figures and the principles of movement belong to the faculty of thought rather than the outer senses, the mind, by the study of these, is separated not only from the appetites of the body, but from its senses also, and applies itself to inner reflection. This is indeed to meditate on death which, Plato writes in *Phaedo,* is the duty of one practising philosophy. Through this we are restored to the likeness of God, as is taught in *Phaedrus* and *Theaetetus.*

However, according to the Platonists, in the thorough understanding of these things there is this order: Geometry follows Arithmetic; Stereometry, Geometry; Astronomy follows this, and lastly Music follows Astronomy. For numbers are before figures, plane figures are before whole forms, but bodies are whole before they are set in motion. The order and ratios of sounds follow movement. Therefore let Arithmetic, which concerns number, come first. Let Geometry, which deals with plane figures, follow. Let Stereometry, which considers whole bodies, follow after this. Let the fourth place be held by Astronomy which raises the sight to the movements of whole bodies, that is, the movements of the spheres. Let Music, which investigates the order of sounds born out of motion, be last.

When these have been thoroughly understood, Plato gives dialectic, that is, knowledge of how truth is made manifest. But he means by dialectic not only that logic which teaches the first and most detailed rules of reasoning, but also the profound skill of the mind freed to comprehend the true and pure substance of each thing, first by physical, then by metaphysical principles. Thus the reason for anything can be made known and finally the light of the mind may be perceived beyond the nature of senses and bodies; and the incorporeal forms of things, which we call ideas, may be understood. By means of these, the same one source of all species, the origin and light of minds and souls, the beginning and end of all, which Plato calls the good itself, may be inwardly perceived. The contemplation of this is wisdom, love of which is most correctly defined as philosophy.

In truth, once the mind of a man practising philosophy has contemplated the good itself, and thence judges what things in human affairs are good, what bad, what dishonourable or honourable, harmful or useful, he organizes human affairs as a model of the good itself. He leads them away from evil, directs them to the good, and by this wise governance he manages personal, family and public affairs, and he teaches the laws and principles of good management. From this laws have their beginning.

For this reason in *Timaeus* Plato asserts that philosophy is a gift of God, and nothing more excellent has ever been granted us by God than this. For the good itself, which is God, could bestow nothing better on a man than a complete likeness of its own divinity, as near as possible. Indeed, who would doubt that God is truth unconfined by the body and providing for all? But the philosopher, by moral instruction and that early education of which we have spoken, frees the mind from desire and the sense of the body, attains truth by dialectic, and makes provision for men by teaching them citizenship. Thus it comes about that philosophy is a gift, a likeness, and a most happy imitation of God. If anyone is endowed with philosophy, then out of his likeness to God he will be the same in earth as He who is God in heaven. For a philosopher is the intermediary between God and men; to God he is a man, to men God. Through his truthfulness he is a friend of God, through his freedom he is possessor of himself, through his knowledge of citizenship he is a leader of all other men. Indeed it is said that the golden age once existed because of such a ruler and Plato prophesied that it will return only when power and wisdom come together in the same mind.

According to Plato, the minds of those practising philosophy, having recovered their wings through wisdom and justice, as soon as they have left the body, fly back to the heavenly kingdom. In heaven they perform the same duties as on earth. United with God in truth, they rejoice. United with each other in freedom, they give thanks. They watch over men dutifully, and as interpreters of God and as prophets, what they have set in motion here they complete there. They turn the minds of men towards God. They interpret the secret mysteries of God to human minds. On this account the ancient theologians justly honoured the minds of those practising philosophy as soon as they were released from the body, just as they honoured the thirty thousand divinities of Hesiod as demigods, heroes and blessed spirits.

Thus philosophy, to express it in a few words, is the ascent of the mind from the lower regions to the highest, and from darkness to light. Its origin is an impulse of the divine mind; its middle steps are the faculties and the disciplines which we have described; and its end is the possession of the highest good. Finally, its fruit is the right government of men. (pp. 28-31)

> *Marsilio Ficino, in a letter to Giovanni Francesco in 1474? in* The Letters of Marsilio Ficino, Vol. 3, *translated by various translators, Shepheard-Walwyn, 1981, pp. 28-31.*

MARSILIO FICINO   (essay date 1495)

[*In the following excerpt from the preface to the first book of the 1495 printing of his letters, Ficino salutes Giuliano de' Medici, a grandson of Cosimo and member of the Platonic Academy.*]

Magnanimous Giuliano: the great Cosimo, your grandfather and my patron, often spoke these words of Plato: that in undertaking important affairs, nothing is more profitable than the good-will of prudent and learned men. And there is no clearer evidence of justice and prudence in such affairs than if friends of this kind are present; nor of injustice and imprudence than if they are absent. This is the golden rule of Plato. Cosimo throughout the whole of his life proved it by what he did, much more than by what he said. He was certainly an exceptionally wealthy man; rich in money, far richer in men and most rich in prudence and justice. And what is most rare and wonderful, he left a son and grandchildren who inherit this treasure. So it is that in my Giuliano I recognise that old man, on whom alone, after God, my welfare totally depended.

> *Marsilio Ficino, in a letter to Giuliano de' Medici in 1495, in* The Letters of Marsilio Ficino, Vol. I, *translated by various translators, Shepheard-Walwyn, 1975, p. 29.*

J. LEMPRIERE   (essay date 1808)

[*Lemprière was an English scholar, biographer, and classicist. He is best known as the author of* Bibliotheca Classica; or, a Classical Dictionary *(1788), still acknowledged a notable reference source on the ancient world, and* Universal Biography *(1808), issued as a companion piece to this volume. In the following excerpt from the latter work, Lemprière briefly surveys Ficino's life and career.*]

[Ficino was] a learned Italian, born at Florence 1433, and educated at the expense of Lorenzo de Medicis, to whom his father was physician. He distinguished himself as an able scholar, a great philosopher, physician, and divine, and under the patronage of his friends Lorenzo and Cosmo de Medicis, he restored in the West the study of the platonic philosophy, and translated not only his favorite author Plato, but also Plotinus, Proclus, Iamblicus, Porphyrius, &c. Though originally a sceptic, the eloquent preaching of Savanorola brought him to a due sense of religion and of religious duties, but like many of the learned of his time he still remained devoted to astrology. By care and a proper regimen he supported his naturally feeble constitution to the age of 66. He died at Correggio 1499, and soon after, as Baronius gravely affirms, appeared according to his promise to his friend Michael Mercatus, to prove thus the immortality of the soul.

J. Lempriere, in an excerpt in his Universal Biography, Vol. I, *E. Sargeant, 1808.*

ALEXANDER CHALMERS (essay date 1814)

[*A Scottish biographer and miscellaneous writer, Chalmers is known chiefly as the editor of* The General Biographical Dictionary (1812-17). *In the following excerpt from that work, he evinces some skepticism at Ficino's achievement as a philosopher.*]

As a philosopher, much cannot now be said in favour of Ficinus, and the high encomiums to which he appeared entitled in the fifteenth century, will not all bear the test of modern criticism. His works afford abundant proofs how deeply he was influenced by the reveries of judicial astrology. His principal want was vigour and accuracy of judgment, with which if he had been furnished, he would have avoided the superstitious attachment manifested by him to the "Platonismus Alexandrinus," than which, Brucker observes, no philosophical reveries could possibly be more ridiculous; and he would have evinced more sagacity in detecting the sophisms of this sect. He was devoid also of the more splendid and exterior graces of a well cultivated understanding; his style is pronounced inelegant, and his language confused. He was a Platonist even in his correspondence, and some of his letters are enigmatical and mysterious. Brucker also accuses him of being of a timid and servile spirit, which would naturally lead him to accommodate his version to the judgment of his patron. He entertained the notion which prevailed among the Christian fathers, that the doctrine of Plato was, in some sort, of divine origin, and might be fairly construed into a perfect agreement with that of divine revelation. From these causes, Ficinus is very far from adhering with strictness to his author's meaning; in many instances he rather expresses his own conceptions than those of Plato, and often gives his interpretation a bias towards the Alexandrian or Christian doctrine, for which he has no sufficient authority in the original. On the whole, Brucker is of opinion, that Ficinus was rather an industrious than a judicious translator, and that his version of Plato should be read with caution. (pp. 272-73)

Alexander Chalmers, "Ficinus (Marsilius)," in The General Biographical Dictionary, Vol. XIV, *edited by Alexander Chalmers, revised edition, J. Nichols and Son, 1814, pp. 271-73.*

CHARLES KNIGHT (essay date 1866)

[*Knight was an English author and publisher who promoted popular instruction by publishing inexpensive but informative periodicals, encyclopedias, and histories, some of which he also wrote. The following excerpt from one of his compilations,* The English Cyclopædia (1854-70), *offers a sketch of Ficino's career.*]

[Marsilo Ficino] was the son of Ficino, the physician of Cosmo de Medici, who perceiving the happy dispositions of the youth, generously provided for his education. Ficino studied Greek, and applied himself especially to the works of Plato, which he translated into Latin. He afterwards translated Plotinus, Jambichus, Proclus, and Porphyrius, and became a great admirer of the late Platonicians of the Alexandrian school. He was one of the preceptors of young Lorenzo, Cosmo's grandson. Cosmo appointed him president of the literary society which he assembled at his house, and which was called Academia Platonica, having for its object to explain the doctrines of the Platonists. Its meetings, which were greatly encouraged by Lorenzo, were cheered by symposia, or annual banquets, on the anniversary of Plato's birthday, of one of which, held at the villa of Careggi, Ficino has given an interesting description. (pp. 908-09)

At the age of forty Ficino resolved to devote himself to the church, and being ordained, his patron Lorenzo conferred upon him a canonry in the cathedral of Florence. He now made an attempt to amalgamate the theology of Plato with Christianity, and in so doing was carried by his zeal beyond the limits of sound judgment or propriety. He is said however to have been sincere and singleminded, exemplary in his private conduct, mild and moderate in his temper, and averse from literary feuds and polemics. But his writings savour everywhere a great deal more of the heathen philosopher than of the Christian divine. Being of a diminutive size, and of very precarious health, he says himself that he hardly passed a day without bodily pain, and yet he constantly applied to study. Much of his time was spent at the various country residences of the Medici near Florence, in which he composed his works. He died on the 1st of October, 1499, and his countrymen raised to him a monument in the cathedral of Florence, with his bust, and an epitaph written by his friend Poliziano. (p. 909)

Charles Knight, in an excerpt in Biography; or, Third Division of "The English Encyclopaedia," Vol. I, *edited by Charles Knight, Bradbury, Evans, & Co., 1866, pp. 908-09.*

JOHN ADDINGTON SYMONDS (essay date 1910)

[*Symonds was an English poet, historian, and critic who wrote extensively on Greek and Italian history and culture. He also rendered several highly regarded translations of Greek poetry and literature of the Italian Renaissance. In the following excerpt, Symonds evaluates Ficino's literary career and personal life.*]

It is not easy to value the services of Marsilio Ficino at their proper worth. As a philosopher, he can advance no claim to originality, his laborious treatise on Platonic theology being little better than a mass of ill-digested erudition. As a scholar, he failed to recognize the distinctions between different periods of antiquity and various schools of thought. As an exponent of Plato he suffered from the fatal error of confounding Plato with the later Platonists. It is true that in this respect he did not differ widely from the mass of his contemporaries. Lorenzo Valla and Angelo Poliziano, almost alone among the scholars of that age, showed a true critical perception. For the rest, it was enough that an author should be ancient to secure their admiration. The whole of antiquity seemed precious in the eyes of its discoverers; and even a thinker so acute as Pico di Mirandola dreamed of the possibility of extracting the essence of philosophical truth by indiscriminate collation of the most divergent doctrines. Ficino was, moreover, a firm believer in planetary influences. He could not separate his philosophical from his astrological studies, and caught eagerly at any fragment of antiquity which seemed to support his cherished delusions. It may here be incidentally mentioned that this superstition brought him into trouble with the Roman Church. In 1489 he was accused of magic before Pope Innocent VIII., and had to secure the good offices of Francesco Soderini, Ermolao Barbaro, and the archbishop Rinaldo Orsini, in order to purge himself of a most perilous imputation. What Ficino achieved of really solid, was his translation. The value of that work cannot be denied; the impulse which it gave to Platonic studies in Italy, and through them to the formation of the new philosophy in Europe, is indisputable. Ficino differed from the majority of his contemporaries in this that, while he felt the influence of antiquity no less strongly than they did, he never lost his faith in Christianity, or contaminated his morals by contact with paganism. For him, as for Petrarch, St Augustine was the model of a Christian student. The cardinal point of his doctrine was the identity of religion and philosophy. He held that philosophy consists in the study of truth and wisdom, and that God alone is truth and wisdom,—so that philosophy is but religion, and true religion is genuine philosophy. Religion, indeed, is common to all men, but its pure form is that revealed through Christ; and the teaching of Christ is sufficient to a man in all circumstances of life. Yet it cannot be expected that every man should accept the faith without reasoning; and here Ficino found a place for Platonism. He maintained that the Platonic doctrine was providentially made to harmonize with Christianity, in order that by its means speculative intellects might be led to Christ. The transition from this point of view to an almost superstitious adoration of Plato was natural; and Ficino, we know, joined in the hymns and celebrations with which the Florentine Academy honoured their great master on the day of his birth and death. Those famous festivals in which Lorenzo de' Medici delighted had indeed a pagan tone appropriate to the sentiment of the Renaissance; nor were all the worshippers of the Athenian sage so true to Christianity as his devoted student.

Of Ficino's personal life there is but little to be said. In order that he might have leisure for uninterrupted study, Cosimo de' Medici gave him a house near S. Maria Nuova in Florence, and a little farm at Montevecchio, not far from the villa of Careggi. Ficino, like nearly all the scholars of that age in Italy, delighted in country life. At Montevecchio he lived contentedly among his books, in the neighbourhood of his two friends, Pico at Querceto, and Poliziano at Fiesole, cheering his solitude by playing on the lute, and corresponding with the most illustrious men of Italy. His letters, extending over the years 1474-1494, have been published, both separately and in his collected works. From these it may be gathered that nearly every living scholar of note was included in the list of his friends, and that the subjects which interested him were by no means confined to his Platonic studies. As instances of his close intimacy with illustrious Florentine families, it may be mentioned that he held the young Francesco Guicciardini at the font, and that he helped to cast the horoscope of the Casa Strozzi in the Via Tornabuoni.

At the age of forty Ficino took orders, and was honoured with a canonry of S. Lorenzo. He was henceforth assiduous in the performance of his duties, preaching in his cure of Novoli, and also in the cathedral and the church of the Angeli at Florence. He used to say that no man was better than a good priest, and none worse than a bad one. His life corresponded in all points to his principles. It was the life of a sincere Christian and a real sage,—of one who found the best fruits of philosophy in the practice of the Christian virtues.

A more amiable and a more harmless man never lived; and this was much in that age of discordant passions and lawless license. In spite of his weak health, he was indefatigably industrious. His tastes were of the simplest; and while scholars like Filelfo were intent on extracting money from their patrons by flattery and threats, he remained so poor that he owed the publication of all his many works to private munificence. For his old patrons of the house of Medici Ficino always cherished sentiments of the liveliest gratitude. Cosimo he called his second father, saying that Ficino had given him life, but Cosimo new birth,—the one had devoted him to Galen, the other to the divine Plato,—the one was physician of the body, the other of the soul. With Lorenzo he lived on terms of familiar, affectionate, almost parental intimacy. He had seen the young prince grow up in the palace of the Via Larga, and had helped in the development of his rare intellect. In later years he did not shrink from uttering a word of warning and advice, when he thought that the master of the Florentine republic was too much inclined to yield to pleasure. A characteristic proof of his attachment to the house of Medici was furnished by a yearly custom which he practised at his farm at Montevecchio. He used to invite the contadini who had served Cosimo to a banquet on the day of Saints Cosimo and Damiano (the patron saints of the Medici), and entertained them with music and singing. This affection was amply returned. Cosimo employed almost the last hours of his life in listening to Ficino's reading of a treatise on the highest good; while Lorenzo, in a poem on true happiness, described him as the mirror of the world, the nursling of sacred muses, the harmonizer of wisdom and beauty in complete accord. Ficino died at Florence in 1499.

Besides the works already noticed, Ficino composed a treatise on the Christian religion, which was first given to the world in 1476, a translation into Italian of Dante's *De monarchia,* a life of Plato, and numerous essays on ethical and semi-philosophical subjects. Vigour of reasoning and originality of view were not his characteristics as a writer; nor will the student who has raked these dust-heaps of miscellaneous learning and old-fashioned mysticism discover more than a few sentences of genuine enthusiasm and simple-hearted aspiration to repay his trouble and reward his patience. Only in familiar letters, prolegomena, and prefaces do we find the man Ficino, and learn to known his thoughts and sentiments unclouded by a mist of citations; these minor compositions have therefore a certain permanent value, and will continually be studied for the light they throw upon the learned circle gathered round Lorenzo in the golden age of humanism. (p. 318)

> *John Addington Symonds, in an excerpt in* The Encyclopaedia Britannica, Vol. X, *edited by Hugh Chisolm, eleventh edition, Cambridge at the University Press, 1910, pp. 317-19.*

JEFFERSON BUTLER FLETCHER   (essay date 1934)

[*Fletcher was an eminent American authority on the Italian Renaissance. Among his works are* Dante (1916), Symbolism of the Divine Comedy (1921), *and* Literature of the Italian Renaissance (1934). *In the following excerpt from the last-named study, he broadly characterizes Ficino as man and philosopher.*]

[Marsilio Ficino was an] eager truth-seeker, the modest master of learning, the lovable and inspiring teacher. His own master was Plato, and he inherited much of the serene tolerance and humanity of the Greek sage.

More lastingly significant than the doctrine he formulated and taught was indeed Ficino's temper of mind towards all sincere truth-seeking. . . . Ficino's attitude of mind was one less of hard rationalism than of "sweet reasonableness"—in Matthew Arnold's sense. He examined historic creeds, not to prove all but one wrong, but rather to see if all might not be at one fundamentally. It was in principle the position Emerson took. And to a large extent, Ficino gave immediate inspiration to the enlightened Englishman, John Colet, Dean of St. Paul's, who in a time of bitterly warring creeds, offered for guidance the simple question,—"Why should we try to narrow what Christ has made so broad?"

Doctrinally, Ficino's master, and accepted "master of them that know," is Plato. He actualizes, so to speak, the poetic prescience of Petrarch, in whose *Triumph of Fame* Plato marches ahead of Aristotle. But Ficino read his Plato in the mystic light of Plato's Alexandrian disciple Plotinus. The *Enneads* of Plotinus are for Ficino climax and consummation of a development starting with almost the first dawn of truth-seeking. In one of Ficino's *Epistles* we read: "Once among the Persians under Zoroaster, and among the Egyptians under Mercury, a certain devout philosophy was born, the one consonant with the other. Then among the Thracians under Orpheus and Aglaophemus this philosophy was nursed. Under Pythagoras among the Greeks and Italians it attained its youth. Finally by the divine Plato at Athens it reached full maturity . . . Plotinus, however, first and alone stripped theology of these veils,"—i.e. of myth and fable and allegory.

I must not exaggerate. This passage is hardly a foreshadowing of the modern comparative study of religions,—unless indeed in the fashion that Bronson Alcott conceived it. The methods of Ficino and his followers were very far from what would today be regarded as critical. Profoundly influenced by the Cabbala and by degenerate contemporary Byzantine Neo-Platonism, they saw almost all prior "scriptures," to use Emerson's word, as carrying not only allegories but also cryptograms and other secret codes. Thus Ficino's most illustrious disciple, the amazingly precocious and gifted Pico della Mirandola decodes the opening verse of the Hebrew *Genesis,* and discovers in it a full and doctrinal proclamation of the Trinitarian creed. (pp. 102-03)

Our present concern, however, is not with the merits or demerits of this Florentine school of thought as a philosophical system, but with its literary effects. (p. 105)

In 1438-9 representatives of the Greek and Roman Catholic Churches met at Ferrara and Florence to seek a compounding of their differences. With the Greek mission came philosophers of the Neo-Platonic school still dominant at Byzantium and in the Peloponnesus. Especially distinguished were a certain Gemistho Pletho, a man of great if unmerited repute as a philosopher, and the Bessarion who remained to become a Roman Cardinal, and narrowly missed being made Pope. These men, especially these two, aroused a lively interest in Florentine intellectual circles. And whether in response to this new concern with Plato or his own personal interest or perhaps to both considerations, Cosmo de'Medici, patron and untitled prince of Florence, took under his protection the eighteen-year-old Marsilio Ficino, son of his physician, and had him trained in Greek language and philosophy that he might translate and interpret Plato. A quarter of a century later Ficino fulfilled the trust, and for good measure translat-

ed the works of Plotinus also. He also wrote an elaborate commentary, and other translations.

Ficino's life-aim was wider than merely interpreting and translating Plato. It was to harmonize Platonism with Christianity. Indeed, St. Augustine himself had declared Platonists to be near-Christians. And, reading Plato in the light of the mystical and trinitarian Plotinus, and freely interpreting the myths and mythology of the Dialogues as allegories, Ficino found no serious difficulty in his way. His disciple, the brilliant young Giovanni Pico della Mirandola, attempted a still more ambitious synthesis.

Even more than Plotinus, Ficino stressed the *Symposium* as containing the core of the Platonic system. In it is presented as the supreme mover and motive Love,—love of the Beauty, Goodness, Truth, which as one and in one is God. Indeed, Plato's *Symposium* may be taken as an expanded commentary on the Gospel text: "Thou shalt love the Lord thy God with all thy heart, and with all thy soul, and with all thy mind, and with all thy strength." For in the *Symposium,* the Wise Woman of Mantineia, Diotima, reveals the doctrinal significance of these specifications. She explains how God, seen by the mortal eye in all things beautiful, awakens vague but ardent longings in the *heart;* how these longings then move the *soul* instinctively to shape its life also in symmetry and harmony; and how at last the *mind* recognizes the heart's true object of longing as the Beauty, Goodness, Truth in one, which is God. To actualize such love is indeed to love "with all thy strength." So in the Christian Gospel precept is implied the Platonic "ladder of love" with here the three rungs of desire of sense (the *heart*), desire of will (the *soul*), desire of intellect (the *mind*). From this first and great commandment of Christ may thus be developed the whole system of Plato—according to the Florentines. (pp. 105-06)

Jefferson Butler Fletcher, "Valla—Ficino—Beniviene," in his Literature of the Italian Renaissance, *The Macmillan Company, 1934, pp. 97-113.*

PAUL OSKAR KRISTELLER   (essay date 1943)

[*Kristeller is a German-born American educator, editor, and scholar. According to C. B. Schmitt, he exerted influence "on the philosophico-intellectual side of Renaissance studies . . . greater than that of any of his contemporaries." Among his works are* The Classics and Renaissance Thought (*1955*), Studies in Renaissance Thought and Letters (*1956*), *and several full-length studies of Ficino, including* The Philosophy of Marsilio Ficino. *In the following excerpt from the last-named work, completed in German in 1937, translated into Italian in 1938, but first published, with revisions, in English in 1943, Kristeller discusses Ficino's connection with the Italian humanist movement and comments on the moral, aesthetic, and religious implications of his Platonic philosophy.*]

Since the brilliant work of J. Burckhardt the term "Renaissance" has come to stand for a distinctive period in European history and civilization. Its temporal limits coincide, roughly speaking, with the fifteenth and sixteenth centuries, and its main characteristic in the field of literature is classical humanism—in other words, the study, imitation, and revival of Greek and Roman antiquity. Recent studies have considerably modified our conception of the Renaissance. Many new details have been discovered: in particular it has become increasingly clear that there was more continuity between the Middle Ages and the Renaissance than most humanists or their modern interpreters care to admit. However, we cannot eliminate the concept itself as some modern scholars are inclined to do. We must rather be ready to adjust our concept of the Renaissance to the complexity of the known historical facts, instead of expecting the facts to agree with our artificial notions.

Whereas Burckhardt and most of his followers among the historians paid slight attention to the philosophy of the period, other scholars, such as Fiorentino, Dilthey, and Cassirer, began to speak of a "philosophy of the Renaissance." This does not merely mean that certain thinkers happened to live during that period; it means, rather, that those thinkers gave philosophical expression to the prevailing intellectual tendencies of the age and that underlying all differences between various schools and traditions there were certain characteristic problems common to all philosophers of the Renaissance. The attempt to give a concrete and conclusive definition of the philosophy of the Renaissance involves considerable difficulty. But the concept, as such, is fruitful and indispensable—especially when we do not take it for granted, but use it as a guiding principle for further research. In the earlier part of the fifteenth century we find that in Italy there was a rather complex and obscure situation with respect to philosophical studies. Most teachers of philosophy at the various universities, such as Bologna, Pavia, and especially Padua, were developing a particular type of Aristotelianism, which was by no means uniform and was to reach its most mature conclusions in the sixteenth century. The roots of this Aristotelianism lie in the fourteenth century, its orientation is medical rather than theological, and its chief interest is in the fields of logic and natural philosophy. On the other hand, the humanists were writing a number of treatises and dialogues in the Ciceronian manner, which often dealt with more-or-less philosophical subjects. The humanists were either men in public office or, more often, teachers of grammar, rhetoric, and the classics at the universities, as well as in the secondary schools of various cities. They continued the traditions of medieval grammar and rhetoric, but they received a new impulse and inspiration from Petrarch. Their philosophical interest was limited to ethics, political theory, and education, but of even greater, though indirect, importance was their philological study of the ancient thinkers. The humanists tended to be slightly amateurish in their philosophical works, but in compensation they were inclined to give direct expression to the modern ideas of the age. The theological writers of the time represent a third group which has not yet been sufficiently investigated. While the authors of the more popular devotional literature continued the tradition of medieval Augustinianism, the more scientific theologians followed the line of Thomas Aquinas or that of Duns Scotus. In the period with which we are concerned many of these theologians were partly influenced both by the more recent type of Aristotelianism and by classical humanism. Most of them were connected with the flourishing schools of the various religious orders. Their influence in the Italian universities was at first very slight, but it increased gradually during the fifteenth and sixteenth centuries. Since its foundation in the fourteenth century, the university of Florence, alone, had been a stronghold of the theologians and it retained that characteristic far into the fifteenth century. The foreign scholars living in Italy during that period represent a fourth group of philosophical writers. Nicholas of Cusa, probably the most vigorous thinker of the fifteenth century, spent much of his later life in Italy and counted numerous friends and pupils among the Italians. Even more important were the Byzantine scholars who came to Italy in increasing numbers after 1397. The famous polem-

ic between Greek Platonists and Aristotelians took place, for the most part, in Italy during the fifteenth century. Though the Italians did not take a very active part in this discussion, the Byzantine scholars helped to popularize the knowledge of ancient Greek philosophy through their teaching and their writings, a knowledge based on the original text and on ancient interpretations rather than on medieval translations and commentaries.

It is against this background that we must understand the Platonic Academy of Florence and the philosophy of its founder and leader, Marsilio Ficino. In so far as Ficino attempted to express the new ideas of the humanists in a strictly speculative metaphysical form, he may be called the first philosopher of the Italian Renaissance.

Ficino's close connection with the humanistic movement is obvious. Born and brought up in Florence, which was one of the most important centers of humanism, Ficino moved in the same social and cultural circles as the earlier humanists. Among his friends and correspondents we find many representatives of contemporary literature and educated society. His Latin style reflects the formal education of the humanistic school and a tendency to imitate the classical writers. Furthermore, he was an assiduous letter writer, collecting his correspondence for publication after the fashion of the earlier humanists. Ficino's correspondence is rhetorical in form, but it is also a direct reflection of his personal life and sentiments. Following a particular trend of Florentine humanism in his day, he was interested in the old Tuscan poets, translated Dante's *De monarchia* and some of his own works into Italian, and even wrote certain tracts in the vernacular. Through his translations and commentaries Ficino did for Plato, Plotinus, and other ancient philosophers what the other humanists did for the ancient Greek orators, poets, and historians. His revival of Platonism may be considered the realization of an old humanistic dream. Even since the days of Petrarch many humanists had made a point of praising Plato at the expense of Aristotle, the great authority of the Middle Ages— for the most part without much direct knowledge of Plato's works. Many of Ficino's philosophical problems originated in the modern tendencies of humanistic thought and owed their wide influence to that fact. This is particularly true of his theory of love, his doctrine of the dignity of man, and above all of the emphasis he gives to the position of man, who now becames the center of the universe, in contrast to the medieval emphasis on God.

On the other hand, we find in Ficino a strong and definite element of medieval Aristotelianism, a point generally less emphasized by modern scholars. Traces of the logical tradition, which goes back to Suiseth's *Calculationes,* appear in the doctrine of the "primum in aliquo genere." The polemic against Averroism, as developed in the fifteenth book of the ***Theologia Platonica,*** shows his acquaintance with the teachings of his opponents. Elsewhere he quotes Aristotle and the Arabic Aristotelians with great respect, and he never launched a general attack against Aristotelianism or scholasticism, as so many humanists did. Some of Ficino's earliest works are largely Aristotelian and scholastic in form and content and are written in the typical form of "Quaestiones." His principal work, the ***Theologia Platonica,*** preserves the form of a "Summa de immortalitate animorum" and follows throughout the scholastic method of demonstration, enumerating many successive arguments for or against a given statement. Certain important concepts, such as "essentia" and "esse," "perfection," and "hierarchy of being," are derived directly from the Scholastics, while other important theories, such as the "primum in aliquo genere" and the "appetitus naturalis," clearly contain scholastic elements. Hence we may conclude that Ficino owed to humanism his literary form and his preference for certain problems; to medieval Aristotelianism his metaphysical terminology and his logical method of argumentation.

The influences which Ficino felt from the Aristotelian philosophers of his time were apparently strengthened by, and combined with, theological influences. A reliable tradition mentions St. Antoninus, the famous Thomist, as one who exerted a personal influence on Ficino in his youth. In any case, the influence of Thomas Aquinas and of Augustine is very strong in Ficino's work, and we are inclined to attribute this to the theological environment at Florence. Many metaphysical statements and arguments show a close relationship to Thomas, especially to his *Summa contra Gentiles.* Even more profound is the influence of Augustine, from whose works Ficino quotes entire pages. Augustine is Ficino's guide and model in his attempt to reconcile Platonism with Christianity. Many of Ficino's shorter treatises are Augustinian in style. His emphasis on the relation between the Soul and God is also due to Augustinian inspiration.

Ficino mentions Nicholas of Cusa in one letter, but the evidence of a direct philosophical relationship is not very clear. It is possible that Ficino's theory of the infinity of the human mind may have been derived from Cusa. Of much greater importance was the work of the Byzantine Platonists, especially of Pletho. Ficino tells us in the Preface to his translation of Plotinus that Pletho's lectures given at Florence in 1438 inspired Cosimo de' Medici with the idea of founding the Platonic Academy. We cannot doubt that Pletho's personal appearance left some traces in Florence. Yet his direct influence on Ficino is less tangible than the quoted statement suggests. Ficino was still a child when Pletho came to Florence. By the time he had entered into correspondence with Pletho's pupil Bessarion, Ficino had already elaborated his own philosophy. There is also a basic difference between Pletho's position and that of Ficino. Pletho was primarily a political reformer, using Platonic philosophy to combat Christian theology and to give an allegorical interpretation of ancient Greek mythology. Ficino was not interested in political problems and always sought to maintain harmony between the Platonic philosophy and the Christian dogma. However, Ficino obviously derived at least one characteristic idea from Pletho—the idea of an ancient tradition of pagan theology that led directly from Zoroaster, Hermes Trismegistus, Orpheus, and Pythagoras to Plato and his followers.

A final important factor for Ficino's doctrine was, of course, his direct contact with Plato and the ancient Neoplatonists, whom he studied and translated. Many of his central concepts are derived directly from those ancient sources, for example, the theory of Ideas, the hierarchical series of forms, and the concept of Soul and of its ascent to God. It would, however, be a mistake to say that Ficino's Platonism is a mere repetition of Plotinus or of other Neoplatonists. Many factors render this impossible: among others, the great span of intervening time, the medieval and Renaissance elements in Ficino's thought, and his own quality as a thinker of wide interests and of remarkable speculative force. Ficino did not repeat Platonic theories just because he translated Plato and Plotinus. As his early tracts show clearly, he was rather led

to study and to translate these thinkers because he had first become interested in their ideas. In restating their thought he could not fail to combine it with the original impulses of his own philosophy. (pp. 10-16)

[Here] we must pause and ask ourselves by what right and in what sense Ficino chose to attach himself to ancient Platonism in particular, among the various trends of philosophical tradition, and sought to bring about a revival of that Platonism. At first we may answer that from the beginning of Renaissance humanism some philosophical writings of the Greeks had gradually become better known, along with many other works of ancient literature. In this process the humanists emphasized, not so much the internal unity of ancient philosophy, as the differences between the four major schools that had developed in the Hellenistic age. Just as the humanists sought to imitate ancient models in every field, so in that period all those philosophical schools found new followers. Ficino's adherence to the Platonic school, therefore, appears to be merely a personal preference, a supposition confirmed by some of his earlier works in which he limits himself to reporting the positions of all four schools. In his later development, however, Ficino tends to give a more profound and also more independent foundation to his Platonism.

The scholastic theology of the Middle Ages sought to confirm doctrines based on the ecclesiastical tradition, in other words, on the "auctoritas" of the Bible and of the church fathers, by means of "ratio," that is, of independent philosophical reflection. Ficino, who was himself a convinced Christian and wished to avoid any scandal in the Church, found himself confronted with a similar task. "I believe," he says in the Preface to his ***Theologia Platonica,*** "and this belief is not fallacious, that divine Providence has decided that the perverse minds of many persons who do not easily yield to the authority of the divine law alone, should be satisfied at least by Platonic arguments that are brought to the aid of religion." In this way he consciously compares the "rationes platonicae," or as he says elsewhere, the "ratio platonica" with the authority of the divine law. Ficino here replaces Aristotle, who prevailed in the preceding period, with Plato (a choice made possible only through the recently acquired knowledge of ancient literature), basing his decision on the agreement between the Platonic doctrine and the Christian religion and on the judgment of St. Augustine and of the other church fathers. "Confiding in them," he writes to the Archbishop of Amalfi, "I thought it worth while—it being necessary to philosophize—to philosophize rather in the Academy," in other words, in the Platonic tradition. It is significant that the medieval principle of "ratio" in general appears in Ficino with the special qualification of "ratio platonica." In this way Plato's name is identified with independent philosophical consideration and the difference between "ratio" and "auctoritas" is repeated within the field of "ratio" itself. Ficino therefore says of the Neoplatonists (and not incidentally) that "they rely mainly on two principles, their own reason and Platonic authority." And in a letter to Johannes Pannonius he writes that "divine Providence at present supports the Christian religion with philosophical authority and reason." Plato's authority thus acquires for Ficino a value similar to that of the Bible, and in one place he uses the characteristic expression: "the Platonic doctrine is related to divine law . . . as the moon to the sun."

It is obvious that Ficino's conviction of the truth of the Platonic doctrine excludes, in his opinion, any basic contrast between the authority of the doctrine and his own opinion. On the other hand, however, it is important to note his effort to give a historical explanation concerning the authority of Plato and the Platonists and his judgment of their relation to the Christian tradition in particular. To Ficino, Plato is not only an admirable philosophical thinker, he is also the exponent and perfecter of an old tradition of "theology." The writings attributed to the ancient wise men and now recognized by modern criticism as the apocryphal products of a later period are for Ficino authentic testimony of that venerable tradition. (pp. 23-5)

Though Platonic philosophy has its own authority and tradition, it is in no way opposed to Christian doctrine and tradition. More than any other system it is able to give Christian doctrine a philosophical confirmation. The Platonic doctrine is a religious philosophy. It guarantees the accord between philosophy and religion and may therefore even be called "theology," as the title of Ficino's principal work indicates. As to the intimate affinity of Platonism with the Mosaic and the Christian doctrines, Ficino quotes Numenius and Augustine again and again, even writing two small tracts to prove the agreement between the Mosaic and the Platonic doctrines and between the Socratic and the Christian conduct of life. He considers "religious philosophers" such as Pythagoras, Socrates, and Plato precursors of Christianity and allows them a share in eternal salvation, along with the prophets of the Old Testament. In the same sense he assigns to Platonic philosophy the task of furthering religion and of bringing men back to the Christian faith. Anyone who has had a philosophical education and as a result is wont to follow reason alone, can find the way to religion and to eternal salvation only through a religious philosophy, in other words, through Platonic reason (*ratio platonica*). Along with and in accord with the Christian tradition, therefore, the Platonic tradition fulfills a mission necessary to the divine scheme of world history. As a follower and renewer of that tradition Ficino does not hesitate to consider himself an instrument of divine Providence. (pp. 27-8)

[As for] the phenomena of moral life, we must keep in mind from the outset that Ficino has no real system of morals. We are therefore obliged to interpret the basic tendency of his doctrine from a number of scattered sentences and opinions. The perfection of the human Soul . . . is entirely bound up with its spiritual ascent and with the contemplative attitude. "The deeper the mind is merged with this body, the more defective it is; and the farther it withdraws from it, the more progress it makes." Consequently, the empirical distinction between the various virtues, as developed by Ficino in his early treatise *De magnificentia,* loses all significance in the light of a more accurate philosophical analysis. Hence the particular virtues in the *Theologia Platonica* are directly related to the two "genera" of speculative and moral virtue, which express the dualism of intellect and will and are consistently defined as their perfect attitudes.

> What else is speculative virtue but the clarity of the intellect? What else is moral virtue but the stable ardor of appetite kindled by the clarity of the intellect? . . . What is the end of virtue? The end of moral virtue is to purify and to separate the Soul from the divisible body; that of speculative virtue, to grasp the incorporeal and universal concepts of things, whose locus is far from divisible bodies.

Virtue is therefore equivalent to the spiritual ascent of the Soul. This idea corresponds to the doctrine of the four degrees of virtue, which has belonged, since Porphyry, to philosophical tradition and is explicitly restated by Ficino as follows: passing through the civic virtues, the purifying virtues, the virtues of the purified Soul, and the exemplar virtues, the Soul arrives at the union with God.

No less clearly does Ficino identify the second important doctrine of ancient ethics—that of happiness and the highest good—with the inner or spiritual ascent of the Soul and with the knowledge of God. The idea is briefly developed in the *Argumentum de summo bono* and at somewhat greater length in the *Epistola de felicitate,* which was written as a result of a discussion with Lorenzo de' Medici who on the same occasion composed his poem *L'altercazione.* Ficino starts with the well-known distinction between external, corporeal, and spiritual blessings, and he tries to reach the concept of happiness by gradually eliminating all imperfect blessings. So external and corporeal blessings are first rejected as defective, then among the blessings of the Soul those belonging to the irrational Soul, afterward the natural blessings of the rational Soul and the moral virtues which are fatiguing and so cannot represent the goal of our desire. Happiness, therefore, can consist only in the speculative virtue—that is, in contemplation. Above all, it consists in that knowledge of God which the Soul attains after separation from the body and in the joy connected with it.

The contemplative attitude not only receives a kind of moral interpretation in such abstract reasonings about virtue and happiness but it is also directly offered to men as a valid norm and goal of their life in a series of exhortatory treatises.

> Separate the Soul from the body [we read in a letter to mankind] and reason from the passions of the senses . . . Seek yourself outside of the world, but in order to seek and to find yourself outside, fly outside, or rather look outside. . . . Leave behind the narrowness of this shadow and look within yourself.

And in a similar exhortation:

> If you want rest, do not seek rest through movement, but halt the movement; if you want domination, command yourself through reason; if liberty, serve reason; if you wish to avoid pain, flee pleasure, the lure of the evils.

Accordingly, Ficino exhorts his friends to take refuge in God alone.

> O Friends, let us stay in that which never leaves, and we shall remain. Let us serve only the Lord of all things, who serves no one, that we may not serve anyone, but may command all. Let us enjoy Him if we can, and we can if we wish . . . let us enjoy, I say, only that which spreads itself throughout the infinite; only so shall we be entirely fulfilled, only so shall we truly and fully enjoy.
>
> (pp. 289-91)

[Ficino's] criticism on the stupidity of outward life, which only a mind spiritually awakened can make, is clearly symbolized in the figures of the laughing philosopher and the crying philosopher, well known to ancient tradition.

> Why did Democritus laugh so much? Why did Heraclitus mourn? One at the stupidity of men, I believe, the other, at their misery. Stupidity seems to be ridiculous, misery lamentable.

Since we exercise virtues falsely, but vices actually,
we shall become falsely happy and actually miserable in so far as we ourselves are concerned. This is
what Democritus laughed at, what Heraclitus deplored, what Socrates desired to cure, and what
God can cure.

This symbol of the two philosophers seemed to Ficino so significant that he had it painted in his villa in Careggi for the
exhortation of his friends and disciples. (p. 294)

The contrast between the contemplative and the sensuous life
is reflected in a characteristic way in the notion of time. The
corporeal world, in so far as it has movement, is bound to the
attribute of time, while the intelligible world is superior to
time and movement and characterized by the attribute of
eternity. "The theologians measure rest by eternity; the natural philosophers measure movement by time." Consequently,
the human Soul, located midway between corporeal and intelligible things, participates equally in time and in eternity.
"The rational Soul . . . is placed on the horizon, that is, on
the borderline between eternity and time, since it possesses
an intermediate nature between eternal and temporal
things." This relationship finds concrete expression in human
life. The sensuous life, dedicated to the outer world, is subject
to the rule of time. So long as man always turns toward new
ends and gives up the present for the sake of the future, he
never really comes to rest and the perpetual loss of time is the
mark of his worldly and inwardly empty existence. On the
other hand, the contemplative life has a part in eternity; and
since eternity is nothing but a pure present, without past and
future, time is overcome in any moment of real fulfillment as
in a pure actual present, and the ascent to eternity is accomplished. In this sense Ficino exhorts men to ascend from tomorrow toward today, from the flux of time to the pure present. "Learn well," he writes to Antonio de' Pazzi, "and please
learn today; he who learns tomorrow, never learns." (p. 295)

The moral relation of man to the world, however, is not limited to the simple contrast between sensuous and contemplative life. The man internally awakened is still subject to the
outward course of events. Although he can free himself from
it in a spiritual sense and with the higher part of his self, he
is in fact forced by his lower self to compromise with it. Ficino discussed these problems in connection with the idea of
fortune. The idea of the blind goddess of fortune who according to her arbitrary caprice guides men from nothing up to
the peak of power and wealth and throws them back again
into misery occupied a large space in the popular thought of
the Renaissance and found expression in many mottos and
allegorical pictures. Ficino did not entirely accept this conception, but he discussed it. It is consistent with his system
for him to assign to fortune a certain power over the outward
life of men and at the same time to require that the spiritual
man shall inwardly overcome this power and with the essential part of his self withdraw from its sphere of action. A preliminary discussion of the problem, in which the solution is
but vaguely indicated, is found in the early letter **Della fortuna,** occasioned by a question of Giovanni Rucellai. Experience teaches, Ficino concludes, that, not the ordinary masses,
but only the wise man is able to resist changes of fortune. Prudence, however, cannot be acquired by human effort; it is a
gift of nature, or rather of God. For whatever is natural in
us depends on nature; whatever is spiritual in us, on God. So
it is really God Himself who gives man power against fortune. And as so-called "good fortune" in reality goes back to
nature and God, so the human force of resistance comes from

the same source. Ficino therefore arrives at the following rule
of life:

It is good to fight against fortune with the arms of
prudence, patience, and generosity. It is better to
withdraw and to flee from such a war, in which but
a few achieve victory at the cost of insufferable
trouble and extreme sweat. The best thing to do is
to make peace or a truce with it, adjusting our will
to it, and to go willingly where it indicates, in order
that it may not drag us by force.

Ficino does not attribute an unlimited power to fortune, but
from the outset subordinates it to nature and God. Moreover,
he gives human prudence, which affirms itself in the active
life, a certain sphere of action, apparently compromising on
that point with the views of his correspondent. But at the end
he indicates the contemplative solution, suggesting that we
conclude internal peace with fortune and withdraw from the
hopeless struggle. (pp. 297-98)

Ficino's moral theories, as we see, are based essentially on the
experience of contemplation. We may now understand why
he connects philosophical knowledge so closely with the
moral life. For him philosophy is no mere theoretical doctrine whose truth can be learned and understood solely by
reason. Instead he follows the true Platonic tradition, according to which knowledge can be acquired only by a profound
moral and spiritual regeneration of the entire person. Ficino
therefore ranks the philosopher first among those who arrive
at a higher insight through a temporary separation of the
Soul from the body (*abstractio*), and he mentions several examples of this contemplative rapture.

After Plato had frequently withdrawn far from the
body through the effort of contemplation, he finally
left the bonds of the body entirely in this rapture
(*abstractio*). His disciple Xenocrates was separated
from the body for a whole hour each day. . . . Porphyry the disciple of Plotinus writes that Plotinus
was accustomed to be freed from the body frequently, to change face and at that time to discover
admirable things which, afterwards, he wrote
down.

There are some persons, though very few such are
found, who, subduing their pleasures and neglecting public affairs, conduct their life in such a way
that they burn with eagerness to attain truth; but
they do not have faith that it can be investigated
through its human traces, in which the ambiguous
minds of most natural philosophers are accustomed
to trust. Therefore they give themselves to God and
do not attempt anything by themselves. With open
and purified eyes they wait for what may be shown
by God, and this is what Socrates is said to have
taught and to have done.

Not only is the inward rapture in contemplation peculiar to
the philosopher, but also the moral purification achieved in
the inner ascent is, according to Ficino, the necessary condition for any philosophy. (pp. 300-01)

Philosophy is here conceived as an active and living force
guiding men by means of knowledge toward their real goal.
We must go back to antiquity to find such a sublime yet concrete conception of philosophy. Ficino also tries to illustrate
the connection between philosophy and inner experience by
arranging the individual philosophical disciplines and their
objects in a fixed hierarchical order and identifying the gradual course of knowledge through these disciplines with the

gradual ascent of the mind toward God. In the *Laus philosophiae* he describes this ascent: the Soul is first purified by morals from the dross of sensible things, then ascends with the help of physics from the lowest bodies to heaven, afterward passes, under the guidance of mathematics, through the celestial spheres, and finally, under the guidance of metaphysics, elevates itself to God Himself. The same four degrees are listed in the fourteenth book of the *Theologia*. In the treatise on the nature of the philosopher he gives a similar, but slightly different, version, mentioning the same four disciplines, but putting mathmatics, with its partial fields, in the second place and uniting physics and metaphysics into one discipline under the name "dialectics." This difference, probably originating in the desire to reconcile different traditional schemes, makes completely clear (what is in any event obvious enough) that the correlation between the philosophical disciplines and the grades of contemplative ascent by no means corresponds to inner experience itself, but comes rather from a secondary need of speculation. This need arises from the identification of philosophical knowledge with contemplative experience.

If we pass now from moral phenomena to a consideration of art and artistic creation, we must again confess that there is no real system of aesthetics in Ficino; so the task of interpretation is confined to a significant collection of isolated passages. Moreover, in order to understand the particular character and limitations of Ficino's conception we must keep in mind that the idea of "pure art," as opposed to science, handicraft, and practical activity, has been developed only in comparatively recent times. Classical antiquity and the Middle Ages made no such clear distinction; they understood by "arts" any kind of human activity. Ficino also conceives "art" in that broad meaning when he sees in the variety and free exercise of the arts one of the essential privileges of man. For the animals either live without art or possess only one art each, prescribed to them by nature. For example, the swallows build their nests, the bees their hives, the spiders their cobwebs. On the contrary, by his own power man invents the most diverse arts and so proves himself the master of nature. For he works with all materials, dominates all elements and natural creatures, elevates himself through his spirit to the heavens and even beyond the heavens, and finally gives his own life a rational order in the family and in the state. For Ficino this whole system of arts is based on the contemplative experience, since every creative work in an art is made possible by an act of internal concentration and elevation. Only when the Soul has freed itself from the body can it approach the inwardly accessible sphere of truth and then bring to reality in the corporeal world the contemplated object or communicate it in words to other men.

> All those who have invented anything great in any of the nobler arts did so especially when they took refuge in the citadel of the Soul, withdrawing from the body. . . . Therefore Aristotle writes that all outstanding men in any art were of melancholy temper, either born so or having become so by continual meditation. I think this comes from the fact that the nature of the melancholy humor follows the quality of earth, which is never spread widely like the other elements, but always withdrawn closely into itself. So the melancholy humor invites and helps the Soul to gather itself into itself.

> Why should we wonder that Homer and Didymus and many other persons who were blind by nature or from their childhood could write in such a way

that they seem to have seen everything clearly? Why should we wonder that Zoroaster and other inventors of wisdom have produced a knowledge of all things merely by long solitude and by the conversion of the whole Soul toward the mind alone?

Among the arts those called "arts" in the modern sense constitute a particular group, recognizable, it is true, but not clearly separated from other activities. If we try, however, to describe briefly Ficino's "aesthetic" position and begin with the fine arts, we must not expect too much. For what the leading thinker of the early Renaissance, who was a personal friend of men like Alberti and Pollaiuolo, has to say about painting and architecture is surprisingly insignificant. The notion of visible beauty, which has some importance for Ficino and might have been a starting point for aesthetic analysis, is entirely orientated toward the theory of love. . . . The essence of that beauty, as illustrated primarily in the human body, but valid for works of art as well, consists for Ficino, according to the ancient doctrine, in proportion—that is, in the symmetric and pleasant relationship of the individual parts. For example, the round figure is considered pleasant; likewise in buildings the quadratical ground plan, the equality of the walls, the disposition of stones, the opposition of angles, the figure and disposition of windows. Accordingly, two windows placed beside each other must be of equal size, while two windows placed above each other may have a different size. This difference is a matter of choice when there are only two windows; in the case of three, the eye requires a homogeneous gradation of size. These and similar views are especially effective in judging given works of art. Ficino tries to show explicitly that human reason finds such a measure of equality in itself and through it is related to the divine mind. In other words, in the case of the aesthetic approval of a visible proportion, the external object is related to the inner conception and through that to the divine Idea of equality. . . .

This is a conception which played a role in so-called Middle Platonism. Ficino probably learned it from Cicero and Seneca. He did not utilize it as a theory of the fine arts or develop it further in a metaphysical sense, and the precise relationship between the "Ideas" of the artist and the divine Ideas is left entirely undetermined.

Ficino certainly had a deeper interest in music than in the other arts. We know that he played an instrument himself and gave frequent performances before large circles of friends. In the *De amore* he places the beauty of sounds on an equal plane with that of visible forms and thoughts; he speaks with great conviction about the effect of music on the Soul and even dedicates several short treatises to the praise of this art. Even here, however, he does not develop any genuine aesthetic theory, but simply voices a few isolated thoughts, most of which go back to tradition. The essence of the beauty of sounds consists in consonance, which he analyzes in a special treatise and which he relates explicitly to the concept of proportion. It is a remarkable fact that he recognizes the third interval as consonant, which is contrary to classical tradition. Consonance is a criterion almost analogous to the principle of optic symmetry or equality, and Ficino consequently relates the judgment of vocal harmony through a cause inherent in the Soul to God Himself. . . . However, music consists not only in the corporeal phenomenon of the sound; it has its origin in the Soul of the musician and can therefore act on the Soul of the listener.

> Since song and sound come from the thought of the

mind, from the impulse of the imagination, and from the passion of the heart and, together with the broken and formed air, move the air-like spirit of the listener, which is the bond of Soul and body, it easily moves the imagination, affects the heart, and penetrates the innermost sanctuary of the mind.

Serious music preserves and restores the consonance of the parts of the Soul, as Plato and Aristotle say and as we have experienced frequently.

But to say something about your Marsilio, I frequently dedicate myself to the more serious strings and songs after the study of theology or medicine, in order to neglect the other pleasures of the senses, to expel the troubles of Soul and body, and to elevate the mind as much as possible to sublime things and God.

To emphasize the metaphysical meaning and origin of music, Ficino sometimes reverted to the Pythagorean doctrine of the harmony of the spheres. The celestial spheres, attuned to each other according to the rules of consonance, produce a divine music imperceptible to us; and human music, being an earthly imitation of the celestial sounds, through its admirable effect induces the Soul to elevate itself into the realm of celestial harmony. "Through the ears of the Soul perceives certain sweet harmonies and rhythms, and through these images it is exhorted and excited to consider the divine music with a more ardent and intimate sense of the mind."

Ficino treats of poetry in close connection with music, since poetry also appeals to the ear and, in addition to using words, often incorporates melody and always has rhythm. But poetry is superior to music, since through the words it speaks not only to the ear but also directly to the mind. Therefore its origin is not in the harmony of the spheres, but rather in the music of the divine mind itself, and through its effect it can lead the listener directly to God Himself. For a more profound interpretation of poetic creation in comparison with the other arts, Ficino used Plato's theory of divine madness and inspiration. The true poet does not follow the arbitrary impulse of his human thoughts, but is inspired by God—in other words, he composes on the basis of what he has seen in a state of inner or spiritual elevation and rapture. Hence, in the thirteenth book of the *Theologia,* Ficino puts the poet in second place, following the philosopher, among those who separate themselves from the body during life. For the theory of divine madness he quotes Plato's *Ion* and *Phaedrus* and gives three arguments: first, poets, in their works, reveal a knowledge of all the arts, whereas men as a rule acquire the individual arts slowly and with effort.

Secondly, in their madness they sing many admirable things which afterward, when their fury has lessened, they do not well understand themselves, as if they had not themselves made the utterance, but God had announced it through them as through trumpets. Moreover, the great poets were often insane and uneducated. Consequently, poetry is a gift of heaven. In the *Phaedrus* Plato gives as a sign of it that no one was ever outstanding in poetry, though most industrious and erudite in all the arts, if to these qualities there was not added that more ardent excitement of the Soul which we feel when God is in us. We become warm because of His incitement. That impulse contains the germs of the sacred mind.

Poetry originates in the inner or spiritual elevation of the mind. Therefore it is consistent to say that true poetry is given only to a pure mind and that the true poet who receives his art from God must also return to God and take Him as the object of his poetry. All these considerations, it is true, make no new contribution to a theory of art; but the interpretation of poetry shows once more that artistic activity, like other manifestations of spiritual life, is based upon the certainty of contemplation.

Passing from the arts to the consideration of religious life, we shall analyze first the special phenomena of prophecy and of supernatural influence. The phenomena of prophecy have had an important part in the tradition of all religions, and a philosophical interpretation of "mantics" was attempted again and again, especially in late antiquity. Ficino continued this tradition, not by chance or caprice, but because he was convinced of the reality and significance of predictions through personal, direct experience. He relates that his mother, Alessandra, frequently foresaw a death or an accident among her relatives and that his father, Ficino, was called in a dream to heal a hitherto hopeless patient. Ficino himself apparently inherited the gift from his mother, and during a grave illness he received the announcement of his recovery in a dream. In 1477, a miracle having occurred in connection with some relics, he prophesied the war and pestilence of the following year; in 1480 he warned Lorenzo de' Medici against a dangerous constellation; in 1489 he indicated to Filippo Strozzi the right hour for laying the cornerstone of his palace; and he repeatedly read the horoscope for his friends.

If we would understand the philosophical theory behind these predictions, we must distinguish astrology from all other forms of prophecy, since it pretends to be a definite science, based on rules verified by experience. Ficino's attitude toward astrology was somewhat wavering and uncertain. In his unfinished *Disputatio contra iudicium astrologorum,* written in 1477, he attacked astrology with a number of arguments, and in 1486 he inserted part of these arguments almost literally into his commentary on Plotinus. But in the third book of his *De vita,* written in 1489 and originally intended as a chapter of the same commentary on Plotinus, he uses astrology in a positive way for the purposes of medicine. Finally, in 1494, when Pico wrote his huge work against astrology, Ficino announced his agreement in a letter to Poliziano and then tried to make his previous statements in the *De vita* seem consistent with his (and Pico's) view. However, his justification was somewhat artificial and was received with skepticism by Poliziano. In reality Ficino's own practice during his whole lifetime, especially in his later period, shows that he was not at all opposed to astrology. This uncertain attitude of Ficino toward astrology certainly constitutes a problem that deserves a more accurate re-examination. Meanwhile, it is better not to assume inconsistency or weakness in Ficino. We should try rather to understand the contrasting intellectual motives which drove him in various directions. On the one hand, the professional astrologers upheld the complete dependence of all human destiny upon the course of the stars, a thesis which Ficino could not accept and rejected consistently at all times. For since the human mind excels the whole corporeal world, it cannot be subject to the influence of the stars; and just as we are superior to the play of fortune, through our real selves, so we are superior to the fate imposed by the stars. This is the real and ultimate reason why Ficino attacked astrology in the *Disputatio* and in the commentary on Plotinus. On the other hand, he never denied that the stars have a natural influence upon earthly creatures and hence upon the human body, since each higher entity in the world can act upon the lower entities. This "contradiction," which in reality merely reflects the difference between nature and spirit, is stated in a remarkable formula expressed in the ninth book of the *Theologia* and repeated in the *Disputatio:* "The heavens do not move our will through the instinct of nature, but they do move our body." The view of the *De vita,* in which the care of the human body itself is treated, is therefore fully justified. But Ficino, following the example of Plotinus, took still another step toward astrology, stating that many facts may be predicted by means of the stars in their character of divine signs, without being caused by the stars. This device helps to justify astrological practice in spite of all basic objections, and so astrology is conceived as a form of prediction, characterized by a particular method and "scientific" procedure.

While astrology rests on art and experience, prophecy proper, to which a divine origin is attributed, is based on inspiration and hence referred, as in the case of poetry, to an inner or spiritual elevation of the Soul. Consequently, in the thirteenth book of *Theologia* Ficino, speaking of those who withdraw temporarily from the body, mentions last the soothsayers and prophets and states explicitly that their predictions are made without reflection and art, whereas those of the astrologers, augurs, and so forth, require an experienced mind. In defense of these prophecies he refers to the ancient seers and sibyls, to the prophets of the Bible, to the testimonials of Platonic philosophers, and to the experience of dreams.

> The minds of all these [prophets] searched through many places and comprehended the three parts of time in one when they separated themselves from the body. . . . Or rather such a Soul by its nature is almost everywhere and always. It is not obliged to go outside itself in order to look at many and distant places and to recall the whole past and to anticipate the future. Its achievements are won by leaving the body behind and by returning into itself, either because its nature is everywhere and always, as the Egyptians believe, or because when retiring into its own nature it is at once united with the divinity which includes all limits of places and times.

Ficino explains at length the phenomenon of inspiration in terms of a theory of the three orders of the universe which he calls nature, fate, and providence, to which man belongs through his body, lower Soul, and mind, respectively. Since our mind lives in perpetual contact with the divine intelligences, it is moved by them by a kind of sympathy, but this impulse penetrates our consciousness only when received by the middle part of our Souls, which is called reason. Among the other forms of prophecy dreams are especially emphasized by Ficino. Since sleep is a form of *vacatio,* that is, a state in which the Soul withdraws from the body, during sleep the Soul is immediately accessible to divine influence, particularly the Soul of a man who has been previously purified and directed toward God. "While these men are awake their Souls are freer [from the body] than those of all others, and while they sleep, [their Souls] are completely free, therefore the higher impulse is easily perceived by them." A genuine dream, therefore, is also a divine inspiration, given only to those who have already elevated themselves above the body while awake. All dreams which do not fulfill this condition cannot pretend to be true or of divine origin, but are derived from the influence of the senses, of the imagination, and of finite thought. But genuine dreams, like all predictions, need interpretation, and in general the prophet and the interpreter

are two different persons. For the gift of prophecy and prophetic dream is superior to reason, but interpretation requires art and acuteness.

Just as in the case of predictions, Ficino did not take the doctrine of supernatural influences merely from the religious tradition: he attached it to his personal, immediate experience. He mentions repeatedly the miracles performed by a relic of St. Peter on Christmas, 1477, in Volterra, and in the *De religione christiana* he reports a miraculous cure accomplished in 1470 in Ancona. Ficino himself made two real exorcisms, in 1493 and in 1494, as he reports with a certain self-conceit in his commentary on Plato's *Timaeus.*

In his theory concerning these extraordinary phenomena we must distinguish between various kinds or groups with Ficino, since the supernatural effect, produced with or without human co-operation, is due to natural forces, to demons, or to God. So-called "natural magic" consists merely in "conveniently subjecting to natural causes natural matters which are to be formed by them in a miraculous way." In other words, the expert can conduct certain hidden forces of nature into an object and so produce talismans or effective remedies. This type of magic is a kind of art, and Ficino makes extensive use of it for medical purposes in the third book *De vita.* Another type of magic is connected with the activity of demons. Since demons have a certain influence over men and things, through a special ritual man may obtain their help and so perform miraculous works. Ficino basically rejects this kind of magic as incompatible with the Christian religion: but he does not deny its possibility. The exorcism of demons as he practiced it is directed against demons, but obviously belongs to the same type of action. The truest and most perfect form of supernatural influence, which is a miracle in the proper sense, consists in the power of a man as the instrument of God to change the natural course of things. In this sense Ficino considers the miracles of Christ and of His disciples as a genuine proof of their divine mission, and in the thirteenth book of the *Theologia* he gives a remarkable philosophical explanation of miracles. The human Soul, which by its nature is superior to the body, may become an instrument of God and perform miracles when it frees itself inwardly from the body and ascends toward God.

> When reason is fixed upon God with the whole intention of the Soul to seek a benefit, it sometimes gives a benefit to its own body or to a foreign body toward which it is turned. . . . But let us return to those Souls through which God performs miracles as through instruments. How does the temperate state of the body help them in that privilege? Because their reason is freer, not being disturbed by any trouble of excessive humors. How does moderate and pure living help them? Because the Soul is not aggravated by the burden of its body. How does honest and pious education? Because [the Soul] desires goods for men and being similar to God is helped by God, or rather is guided by God as an instrument.

The Soul can therefore free itself from its own body and act upon others.

> What Soul does this? That which stills the imagination and, while burning with desire for the higher divinity, does not trust the usual procedures of natural reason, but lives through the mind alone, becomes an angel, and receives God with its whole breast.

Among religious activities that do not transcend the natural sphere, Ficino emphasizes especially prayer, which constitutes, so to speak, the intellectual element of worship, and which may be considered as a kind of miracle when it is heard by God and so indirectly produces the desired effect. To Ficino, following a Neoplatonic conception, prayer is nothing but an inner conversion of the Soul toward God. Prayer is heard when the Soul becomes unified with God and so participates in His activity.

> The prayers of a saintly man, especially when the prayers of the people concur with him, connect Souls with God in such an admirable way that the action of God and that of the Soul become one in a certain sense, but that of God after the manner of an artist, that of the Soul after the manner of a divine instrument.

(pp. 303-16)

Having considered the phenomena of prophecy, miracle, and prayer, we must turn to the theory of religion. Though Ficino has no systematic philosophy of religion, just as he has no ethics or aesthetics, religion has a basic significance for his world system. Religion in all its forms is equivalent to the worship of God (*cultus Dei*).

> Nothing displeases God more than to be despised, nothing pleases Him more than to be worshiped. . . . Therefore divine Providence does not permit any region of the world at any time to be entirely without religion, though it does permit different rites of worship to be observed in various places and at various times. This variety ordered by God does, perhaps, produce admirable beauty in the universe.

We must notice two aspects in particular in this concept of religion. First, any given form of religion, however primitive, is related, though unconsciously, to the one, true God. Secondly, all rites and ceremonies of religion are but different expressions of an internal relation to God which is called worship and coincides essentially with divine love. (pp. 316-17)

Religion is not only natural for man and therefore common to all men but also a privilege which distinguishes man from all other animals. Artistic ability, as Ficino shows in detail, is not peculiar to man, for beasts also share in it. Likewise, beasts possess at least a substitute for language. If we consider reason the privilege of man, we have to distinguish its individual parts. For active reason and the rational contemplation of natural things is not entirely absent in beasts. Only the contemplation of divine things, that is, religion, remains peculiar to man, and in it beasts have no share.

> If man is the most perfect of the animals, as is confirmed by many reasons, he is perfect especially because of that part and potency which he has as peculiar to himself and not in common with other animals. But this is in religion alone. For the more clever beasts seem to have some traces of reason, but no sign of religion.

Since, therefore, religion is peculiar to man alone, and since it has God for its object, there is a particular link between man and God, and it is this participation in God which distinguishes the existence and life of man from that of beasts and compensates him for the many defects and weaknesses of his nature.

I think if we take away divine worship, the human genus will be unhappier than all the animals.

It is impossible that man, who through the worship of God comes closer than any mortal creature to God, the author of happienss, should be the most unhappy among them all.

It is not right that the human genus, which through divine worship comes very close to God, who is highest happiness, should always be unhappier than brute animals which are very far removed from God, since they are deprived of such worship.

Though Ficino bases his considerations on natural religion, a concept which seems to place Christianity on the same level with other cults, since he is a convinced Christian he upholds the superiority of the Christian religion to all others. In fact, if the natural or common religion is considered a kind of genus, comprising the Christian religion and the other positive religions as species, this does not exclude a hierarchical difference between these species and a resulting superiority of Christianity. . . . From this conviction Ficino comes to believe in the possibility of constructing a Christian theology upon his premises. He himself made this attempt in the apologetic **De Christiana religione** and in the fragmentary commentary on St. Paul. An accurate interpretation would be needed to show to what extent he actually succeeded in reconciling his philosophical doctrine with traditional Christian theology.

In any case, Ficino raised the question of the relation of philosophy to religion and believed that he could answer it by establishing an inner congruence and harmony between them. It cannot be denied that there may be conflicts between particular philosophical and religious doctrines and that there have been such conflicts in history. But true philosophy and true religion, in other words, Platonism and Christianity, must necessarily agree, since they both have their origin in the same source: in contemplative experience or the inner relationship with God. The co-existence of philosophy and religion may be explained on the basis of the dualism of intellect and will or of knowledge and love: they are two manifestations of the same internal process. Philosophical doctrine is therefore destined to prove the truths of religion by rational means and thus to make it convincing even to the unbelievers. Ficino, the renewer and reviver of the Platonic doctrine, believing himself to be an instrument of divine Providence, considered participation in this task as his life work. He states these facts clearly in the prefaces to some of his principal works. Among ancient peoples, we read in the Preface to the **De religione,** the same men were both philosophers and priests:

> And that was right. For since the Soul, as our Plato believes, can fly back to the celestial father and fatherland only on two wings, namely, intellect and will, and since the philosopher depends mainly on the intellect, the priest on the will . . . it is obvious that those who by their intelligence were the first either to find divine things by themselves or to attain them with divine help were also the first to worship rightly divine things through their will and to spread their right worship and their way of worshiping among others.

Not till much later, to the great disadvantage of mankind, did the separation of faith and knowledge begin, whereby religion was profaned by ignorance and philosophy by impiety.

O men, citizens of the celestial fatherland and habitants of the earth, let us at last free philosophy, the sacred gift of God, from impiety . . . and let us redeem the sacred religion from detestable ignorance as much as possible.

Accordingly, in the Preface of the *Theologia,* Ficino says:

I believe, and this belief is not vain, that it was decided by divine Providence that even the perverse minds of many people who do not easily give in to the authority of divine law should at least acquiesce to the Platonic reasons which come to the aid of religion and that all those who too impiously separate the study of philosophy from sacred religion shall recognize some day that they are going astray, just as if someone should separate love of wisdom from the honor of wisdom itself or true intelligence from right will.

Ficino, therefore, emphasizes again and again the union of philosophy and religion, using especially the example of the old wise men. To emphasize the congruence between Platonic philosophy and Christian religion, he collected in short treatises analogies of the doctrines of Plato and Moses and of the life of Socrates and Christ. With open satisfaction he gave his philosophical lectures in a church. In a letter to Pico he praised the Platonic doctrine as a fish net with which the incredulous minds are caught and converted to the Christian faith. This program also explains the title of his principal work, *Theologia Platonica,* taken from Proclus. Since, according to Ficino, Platonism is the true philosophy, Platonic theology is equivalent to a philosophical theology and is the complement of the religious, Christian theology with which it agrees in content, but from which it is distinguished by its form. This alliance with religion is essential for philosophy in so far as it is based on the original inner or spiritual relation of man with God.

If philosophy is defined by all as the love and study of truth and wisdom [he says in the *Laus philosophiae*] and if truth and wisdom itself is God alone, consequently legitimate philosophy is nothing else than true religion and legitimate religion is nothing else than true philosophy.

Ficino expresses this relation emphatically in the title of a letter: **"Philosophy and Religion Are Sisters."** One is reminded just here of the scholastic formula that calls philosophy "the handmaid of theology," and though we must not overestimate the value of that formula, since the Scholastics did not always apply it, the comparison indicates Ficino's intellectual purposes and tendencies. Ficino obviously abandons the subordination and dependency of philosophy as it was upheld throughout the Middle Ages. Philosophy stands free and equal beside religion, but it neither can nor may conflict with religion, because their agreement is guaranteed by a common origin and content. This is no doubt one of those concepts with which Ficino pointed the way to the future, clearly announcing, if not actually determining, the course of later developments. (pp. 318-23)

> *Paul Oskar Kristeller, in his* The Philosophy of
> Marsilio Ficino, *translated by Virginia Conant, Co-*
> *lumbia University Press, 1943, 441 p.*

JOSEPHINE L. BURROUGHS   (essay date 1948)

[*In the following excerpt, Burroughs highlights distinguishing*

features of Ficino's Platonic philosophy, chiefly as evidenced in the treatise Five Questions Concerning the Mind.]

As the most influential exponent of Platonism in Italy during the fifteenth century, Marsilio Ficino belongs both to the history of the diverse fortunes of that ancient philosophy and to the evolution of those ideas and attitudes which we term "modern," He was born near Florence in 1433, and the Humnanistic influences of this environment did much to shape both the style of his writings and the problems with which he was concerned. Under the patronage of Cosimo de' Medici, he devoted himself to the task of reviving Platonism in Italy, not only as a distinct philosophical doctrine, but also as an intellectual movement with the same vitality and community of interest which characterized the ancient school. The first part of this task consisted in making the source material of Platonism easily accessible through Latin translations. Of these, the translation of the *Corpus Hermeticum* was completed in 1463, that of Plato's dialogues in 1468, some writings of Porphyry and Proclus in 1489, and those of Dionysius the Areopagite and Plotinus in 1492.

In 1462 Cosimo established what has since been called the Platonic Academy of Florence. Although "academy" only in name, the villa at Careggi gave Ficino an opportunity to promote the study of Platonism among a congenial group of thinkers, artists, and literary men and also to present the fruits of his own thought to a sympathetic and enthusiastic audience. Through this "teaching" at Careggi and through his own writings, particularly his major work, the *Theologia Platonica,* and the short treatises which comprise the *Letters,* Ficino was able to inspire a new attitude toward the Platonic material as a comprehensive framework within which the dominant ideas of Humanism might be expressed and its dominant problems resolved. It is this attitude and the character of the doctrine which resulted from it, rather than the revival of Platonism as such, which accounts for the popularity and diverse influence of Ficino's work.

What, then, are the distinguishing characteristics of Ficino's Platonic philosophy? According to his own statements, the choice of Platonism as source and framework for a philosophic system was determined by the harmony he believed to exist between it and the Christian faith. The use of Platonic concepts and arguments to support and develop religious beliefs was, of course, not an innovation but rather a return to the tendency of the early Church Fathers. Ficino himself cites Augustine as his guide in judging Platonism to be superior to all other philosophies. However, the earlier writers had either used particular Platonic doctrines divorced from their context or absorbed Platonic ideas in a diluted form from others. Ficino deliberately set out to combine the Platonic doctrine as a whole with the Christian doctrine, itself the result of centuries of incremental development. Such an attempt was possible only after the recovery of the complete and original texts of the Platonic writers. Furthermore, it depends upon a fundamental difference between the earlier evaluation of Platonism and that which is characteristic of Ficino. For instance, in *De doctrina Christiana* Augustine advises that if the Platonists have "by chance" taught anything that is "true and in harmony with our faith," this part of their teaching should be appropriated by the Christian, who must, nevertheless, "separate himself in spirit from the miserable company of these men." Ficino, on the other hand, regards the Platonic doctrine as an authority comparable to that of the divine law and contrasts it, like the latter, to independent philosophical reasoning. Not only is the Platonic tradition itself divinely inspired; its revival is necessary in order that the Christian religion may be confirmed and rendered sufficiently ratonal to satisfy the skeptical and atheistical minds of the age.

This change reveals a new conception of the unity and universality of human aspiration, a conception in terms of which certain important characteristics of Ficino's thought may be stated. First, philosophy is no longer taken to be an activity separated from religion, whether as rival or "handmaid." Both are manifestations of spiritual life and, as such, have a single aim—the attainment of the highest good. Each is required by the other, for religion saves philosophy from an inferior notion of this highest good, while philosophy saves religion from ignorance, and without knowledge the goal cannot be reached. Thus for Ficino philosophy must be religious, religion philosophical. Being philosophical, Ficino's system is constructed through the application of universal principles to all levels of being. At the same time, being religious, it is ultimately concerned with a system of the universe only because in that system the glorification of the human soul can be justified and its ability to attain the *summum bonum* can be demonstrated. This concentration of interest upon the unique nature and destiny of the human soul is inherent in the religious tradition. The desire to develop this notion in relation to nature as a whole springs from the tendencies of the new Humanism. The insistence that this be substantiated by rational arguments, as part of a system of speculative thought, shows that in Ficino the religious heritage and the new Humanism have together taken on philosophic form.

Second, the assertion that Platonism is of divine origin is related to the Humanistic belief in the universal ability of man to envision and attain the highest good. The truth and superiority of the Christian religion is not questioned in Ficino's writings, but this truth and superiority does not depend upon a unique revelation. Rather, Christianity could not be regarded as the true religion unless all men in all times had a desire for and a capacity to attain that same goal, the pursuit of which it defines as the only way to salvation. It could not be regarded as superior unless it perfected and facilitated the attainment of such a natural aim. Therefore Ficino must find in the nature of man himself a basis for the identification of the highest good with the knowledge and enjoyment of God. The assertion that there is such a basis may then obtain support from the opinions of thinkers of other cultures and of other times. For instance, in the treatise [*Five Questions concerning the Mind*] Ficino uses the agreement of the Hermetic, Peripatetic, Platonic, and Persian writers as an argument. In accordance with this, it cannot be said that Ficino as Humanist and Platonist opposes either the Scholastic thinkers or Aristotle and the Aristotelian school. On the contrary, he does not hesitate to use the methods of the former and the ideas of both. For example, the principles of *primum in aliquo genere* and *appetitus naturalis* are directly related to the medieval Aristotelian tradition. Many of his technical terms are taken from the Scholastic writers without substantial change in signification, and a number of his treatises, including the present one, preserve the form of *quaestiones*.

In *Five Questions concerning the Mind* Ficino sets out to demonstrate that the ultimate end of all human desire and activity can be no other than "boundless truth and goodness," that is, God; and that the soul must be able to reach this end and enjoy it forever. The assertion that the soul must be di-

rected toward some end peculiar to it, and be able to attain that end, depends upon the theory of natural movement, or natural desire, *appetitus naturalis*. The assertion that this end of the soul is infinite truth and goodness and that it can be attained only in the after-life depends upon the unique nature of the soul, its universality and dual inclination.

The theory of *appetitus naturalis* is, for Ficino, both a necessary explanation of the observed facts of orderly change and a consequence of the perfection of God and of His relation to the universe. The observed order of created things results from a tendency or desire inherent in the essence characteristic of each species, a tendency to proceed toward a particular end identified with the good of that species. The origin of any motion is thus found in the essence of the moving thing; the end, in the perfection of that thing. These tendencies are called "natural" because they are directly dependent upon the essence and common to all members of a species at all times. Further, as dependent upon essence, every natural tendency is ultimately related to God. The relation between particular goods and the highest good and that between the order found in particular things and God as the one source of order illustrates the general ontological principle of *primum in aliquo genere*.

According to this principle, there is in every genus a highest member, or *primum,* which contains through itself the essence characteristic of that genus, whereas all other members must be referred back to the *primum* as cause and source of the attributes they share. The members of every genus are thus organized into a definite hierarchy, from the *primum* which is pure and complete, through descending degrees which participate in the defining essence only partially, and contain other qualities which are alien to that essence. This principle is applied to any plurality of entities which share certain attributes and differ in the possession of others. For instance, the five degrees of Ficino's order of Being are related successively as cause and effect, so that each degree below God resembles the one above it in some way, differs from it in another; and each is passive in respect to those above it and active in respect to those below it.

Since the totality of Being is conceived as a kind of genus, God, as Being itself and Goodness itself, may be called the *primum* of that genus. Thus all things below God receive being and goodness from Him. From this it follows that all natural desires are related to God, both with respect to origin and to end. God as the cause of all being is the source of the essence upon which the desire of each created thing is based. The end of every desire is a good, and God is Goodness itself, so that all desire "takes its beginning" from God as the highest end. Finally, since order is the result of natural desire, order of any kind is derived from God.

The attainment of the appropriate end is guaranteed by this relationship between God and created being. Just as the order and goodness found in particular things is ultimately dependent upon God, so the perfection of the whole order is a necessary consequence of the perfection of God. No created thing can exist which does not contribute to the order and good of the whole. A natural desire unaccompanied by the power to achieve its proper end would be worthless in this respect and therefore contrary to the "order of nature."

Since all less perfect things are directed toward ends in which they are perfected, the soul must likewise possess a natural desire for an end identified with its good. This desire, like all others, must be grounded in the nature of the desiring thing. Therefore, the specification of the ultimate end and good of the soul is based upon the doctrine of the unique metaphysical position of the soul, and the characteristics which result from this position. In Ficino's hierarchy of Being the soul is the third or middle essence and the "fountain of motion." Because of its central position, it has an affinity with all things above and below it; because of its self-motion, it is able to move in either direction. Therefore, through the intellect the soul strives to know all things; through the will it strives to enjoy all things. This desire for all truth and goodness cannot be satisfied except by the possession of that infinite truth and goodness which is the source of all others, that is, God.

Like all other things, the soul must be able to attain this desired end. Unlike all others, its attainment of this end does not follow inevitably from the presence of its natural desire. By virtue of its central position, the soul of man is of a dual nature. With lower forms of life man shares the powers of generation, nutrition, and sensation, and these comprise the lower or irrational soul. The higher soul includes both the power of contemplation ("mind" in the strict sense), which man shares with the angels and God, and the discursive power of reason which is peculiar to him alone. In accordance with this, the soul itself has two tendencies, one toward the body and associated with sense, the other toward God and associated with the rational soul. Because human reason is free, it can either oppose the senses or be misled by them; but in neither case can it attain its own end and good or let the lower soul find satisfaction. The result of this is the paradox which Ficino expresses through the Humanistic interpretation of the myth of Prometheus. Because of reason, the nature or essence of man is more perfect than that of all other beings below God and the angels, that is, of all things characterized by motion, and thus possessing some determinate desire. Also because of reason, man is unable to attain happiness, that is, final perfection. This conclusion not only compromises the perfection of man but also contradicts the general ontological principle that no natural desire can be in vain. Therefore, referring to this principle, Ficino asserts that the human soul must attain knowledge and enjoyment of God, if not in this life, then in the after-life. However, in thus attaining the end of one inclination, that toward God, the soul cannot abandon the other, that toward the body, for this is also "natural." The final end, therefore, can be attained only when this second inclination is satisfied through the possession of its own body "made everlasting." In this most natural condition the soul finds eternal rest. (pp. 185-92)

> *Josephine L. Burroughs, "Marsilio Ficino: Introduction," in* The Renaissance Philosophy of Man, *Ernst Cassirer, Paul Oskar Kristeller, John Herman Randall, Jr., eds., in collaboration with Hans Nachod and others, The University of Chicago Press, 1948, pp. 185-92.*

ERNEST HATCH WILKINS (essay date 1954)

[*Wilkins was an American educator and the author of several critical studies devoted to writers of the Italian Renaissance. In the following excerpt from one such work,* A History of Italian Literature, *originally published in 1954, Wilkins offers an overview of Ficino's work.*]

Marsilio Ficino (1433-1499) was drawn in his youth, by his meditative and idealistic nature, to the study of philosophy, and in particular to the study of Platonic doctrines as set forth by the Latin Neoplatonists. Soon he was studying Greek, and giving evidence, through minor writings, of eager productivity. Cosimo de' Medici became much interested in him, and with an extraordinary combination of foresight and generosity established his life time scholarly program and his lifetime scholarly security by giving him, in 1462, a large supply of Greek Platonic and Neoplatonic manuscripts and a villa at Careggi. There Ficino lived and wrote prolifically; and his villa became a familiar gathering place for men interested in philosophic discussion under Ficino's guidance. His primary task was to make the works of Plato and the Neoplatonists available in complete and reliable Latin translations. He wrote commentaries, also, on many Platonic and Neoplatonic texts; and he wrote many original works, nearly all of them Platonic, or Neoplatonic, in the distinctive character of their thought.

His *Commentary on the Symposium,* the most important, from the point of view of literary history, of all his works, was first written in Latin in 1469: in or before 1474 Ficino translated it into Italian, calling it *Il libro dello amore.* The *Symposium* itself has the form of an account of a banquet at which the guests speak in succession on the subject of love, the culminating speech being that of Socrates. Ficino's *Commentary* is case in a corresponding form: the preface states that on the initiative of Lorenzo de' Medici a banquet was held, on an anniversary of Plato's birth and death, in the Medici villa at Careggi, Landino and Ficino being among the guests. After dinner one of the guests reads the *Symposium* aloud, and asks the others, except Ficino, to expound, one by one, the several speeches. As a commentary on Plato the work has little value; but in spite of its conformity with the sequence of Plato's speeches the *Libro dello amore* is in reality an exposition of Ficino's own conception of the nature of what he calls Socratic love. Socratic love, for Ficino, is always the desire of beauty; and the beauty desired is always, ultimately, the beauty of God. The Socratic love that one particular person bears to another is love of the beauty of God as reflected in that other person. Such love has nothing to do with sex, or with any sense except the senses of sight and hearing. A man, therefore, may bear it either to a man or to a woman. The particular form of love that Ficino seems to have most constantly in mind is the love of an older man for a younger man, the older man seeking, through his love, to educate the younger man in virtue. Ficino's version of the ascent of love, corresponding to that described to Socrates by the wise Diotima, has in its five stages these several objects:

> Love of the visible beauty of a single person.
> Love of the synthetic idea of perfect visible beauty.
> Love of beauty of the soul, manifested in the moral and intellectual virtues, which are various forms of truth.
> Love of angelic beauty, which is spaceless and eternal, but differentiated.
> Love of the infinite and unitary beauty of God.

The *Libro dello amore* is the main source of the literary Platonism of the late fifteenth century and the sixteenth century. In Italy it was summarized in a *canzone* by Benivieni; that *canzone* was then expounded in a prose commentary by Pico della Mirandola; and from Ficino's work itself or from one of its derivatives its ideas were transmitted to Bembo, to Castiglione, and to other writers. In England Spenser's *Foure Hymnes* appear to reflect specifically the *canzone* of Benivieni and the commentary of Pico. Chapman drew directly on the

Latin text of Ficino's commentary for passages in four of his poems.

The most massive of the original works of Ficino is his ***Theologia platonica de immortalitate animorum.*** The main purpose of human life, he argues, is contemplation, by which he means a progressive spiritual experience culminating in the immediate vision of God; such contemplation can be attained in this life only rarely and momentarily; therefore the soul must have before it an immortal life in which the attainment may be perpetual. The hierarchy of being, as here set forth, consists of five essences, which Ficino calls God, the Angelic Mind, the Rational Soul, Quality, and Body. The soul, then, is the central and linking essence:

> This is the greatest of all the miracles of nature. For everything else under God is in itself one single being, but the soul is, at one and the same time, all things. It has in itself the images of the divine things from which it is itself derived, and the ideas and patterns of the lower things which in its turn it, in a sense, produces. And since it is the center of all things it partakes of the powers of all things . . . so that it may rightly be called the center of nature, the middle term of all things, the series of the world, the likeness of all things, the know and the bond of the universe.

Ficino was conscious of a double consecration: he was consecrated to Platonism (which for him always included Neoplatonism) not only by his commitments to Cosimo de' Medici, but also by his firm belief in the dignity of man and by his ardent conviction that Platonism was rich in religious truth and power; and he was consecrated to Christianity not only formally—he took holy orders in 1473—but by a strong sense of mission, springing from his desire to win men to the love of God. Quite naturally, then, he sought to weave his Platonism and his Christianity together into a single system, and to enrich and reënforce Christianity by the introduction of all elements of Platonism that were in his judgment consonant with it. In a sense, he undertook to do for Christianity and Platonism what Thomas Aquinas had done for Christianity and Aristotelianism. But Ficino's Platonic theology, despite its philosophic earnestness and its poetic enthusiasm, was too esoteric to have lasting religious influence. Yet whenever one turns to him one has the rewarding sense of being in the presence of a fine mind and a pure and loving spirit. (pp. 149-51)

> *Ernest Hatch Wilkins, "Florentine Humanists," in his* A History of Italian Literature, *edited by Thomas G. Bergin, revised edition, Cambridge, Mass.: Harvard University Press, 1974, pp. 148-57.*

GEORGE BOAS (essay date 1957)

[*Boas was an American educator and author who wrote widely on aesthetics and philosophy. In the following excerpt, he summarizes Ficino's philosophical principles.*]

Readers of Shakespeare's sonnets, of the *Faerie Queen,* and of the works of Milton, Shelley, Keats, Tennyson, and Swinburne have absorbed, whether they are aware of it or not, echoes of a philosophy which found its first modern expression at the end of the fifteenth century in Florence. This philosophy, which is usually called Platonism, is a mixture of Platonic themes and neo-Platonic interpretations of them. Apologies and defenses of poetry, hymns to intellectual beauty, statements of the Divine Ideas in accordance with which this world was created, praises of heavenly love, idealizations of

friendship, ideal communities, along with a score of other themes, derive ultimately from a few Florentine writers, outstanding among whom are Marsilio Ficino, Pico della Mirandola, and Leone Ebreo. Their influence spread well beyond the Alps and well beyond literature. We find it, as such scholars as Panofsky and his former colleagues in the Warburg Institute have so well shown, in painting and sculpture. In fact, it is likely that the original interest in perspective, which did so much to change the form of painting—to say nothing of the subject matter—was attributable to the Platonic interest in geometry. Even Galileo, whose empiricism . . . culminated in a kind of anti-Platonism, developed an idea which had its origin in the *Timaeus;* I refer to his statement that the world must be interpreted in terms of circles, triangles, and other geometrical figures.

It is usually assumed with some reason that knowledge of Platonism came into Florence with the arrival of Gemisthus Pletho, a Byzantine philosopher who came to Italy about 1440 to negotiate the reunion of the Eastern and Western Churches. But in an account as short as ours we must consider Marsilio Ficino to be the originator of the school. That the group who made up the famous Academy in Florence, men like Poliziano, Landino, Pico, Alberti, Michelangelo, were representative of both art and science at the end of the fifteenth century, surely needs no proof. With the exception of Leonardo da Vinci, they may also be said to be the minds who set the pattern of high Renaissance thought, and it is a question how widely Leonardo's thoughts could have been known. For it must be remembered that most of his ideas were not only kept in private notebooks but also written in a kind of cipher. He does not seem to have been one who wished to teach others. But Ficino and his associate, Pico della Mirandola, were both avid students and zealous teachers, and in their case we need have no hesitation in setting them up as the sources of later Platonism.

Marsilio Ficino (1433-99) both developed a philosophy of his own and translated the works of Plato and Plotinus as well as the Hermetica into Latin. Before the knowledge of Greek became common, men read these translations much as their forefathers of the Middle Ages had read Chalcidius's translation of the *Timaeus* and as we read Jowett. It must also be pointed out that the translations were amply provided with explanatory glosses which were freely used when readers found passages too difficult to understand by their own means. As for his own writings, we find him producing juvenilia on Epicurus and on Pleasure, and later, a more mature work on the immortality of the soul [***Platonica theologia***] and the Christian religion [***De Christiana religione***]. He was a typical eclectic, taking what pleased him, rejecting what displeased him. But after all none of us is without his intellectual ancestors. Yet Ficino laid down as a philosophical principle that there was truth in apparently contradictory philosophies, such as those of Plato and Aristotle, the apparent contradiction lying in the words in which they were expressed. Thus no philosophy would seem to be wholly false; the scholar's problem was to discover and unearth that which was true in it.

This rested upon an assumption which was to eventuate in the philosophy of common sense, though that philosophy differed widely from what Ficino believed. To him there were certain truths, which could be called either religious or metaphysical, revealed in the Bible and expounded rationally in the writings of the philosophers, both pagan and Christian,

Eastern and Western. There could thus be no real contradiction between philosophy and revelation. The trouble obviously lay in the adjective "real." But at least as early as Philo it had been believed that the correct interpretation of the Scriptures was allegorical, and by the thirteenth century the number of possible interpretations had grown to four: the literal or historical, the allegorical, the tropological, and the anagogical. This was all very well and usually succeeded in preserving the truth of any statement, however bizarre, that one wanted to believe was true. But behind it lay the greater problem of how one could verify the various interpretations. In practice tradition did the work, and tradition could only be that part of the entire tradition which was known to the interpreter himself. Sometimes the theory of multiple interpretations was based upon Christ's use of parables. Sometimes it was based on the curious idea that symbols, allegories, enigmas were used to prevent the vulgar crowd from penetrating into mysteries of which they were unworthy. It is indeed strange that knowledge, which was supposed to redeem and sanctify us all, should have been concealed from those most in need of it.

That the ancient philosophies were a preparation for the reception of the Gospels was an idea which had been expressed in very early times and it is one which has survived into our own time. Furthermore, Plato's *Timaeus* with its creation story was an ideal presentation of a philosophy which could be made harmonious with parts of Genesis and had been so used during the Patristic and medieval periods. Moreover, Plato himself and the Neo-Platonists had made use of myths for many purposes, and the latter had even given allegorical interpretations of both traditional myths and quasi-historical legends such as appear in the poems of Homer. As a matter of cold fact, the practice is not much different from the interpretations now current of the plays of Shakespeare, especially of *Hamlet,* in which the poet is seen as revealing in symbolic form things of which he would have been ashamed to speak openly, things which the Collective Unconscious permitted to appear only in disguise, or even things of which it would not have been prudent to speak overtly because of political restrictions.

Whenever an allegory is interpreted, and I use the word "allegory" loosely, there must be a key and, by the nature of the process, the key at least must be a set of literal statements. For Ficino Platonism was that key. But before the key could be utilized, faith was needed in that which was held to be the meaning of the allegory. The old motto *credo ut intelligam* meant simply that one was going to use one's intellect to make one's faith intelligible, as one might today hold that one was going to justify the way of God to man or to give a defense of naïve realism. The difficulty arose when one was asked in what precisely one had faith. For were one to answer that question, one could not reply in terms of the allegory, but must have recourse to its interpretation. For the sake of argument, let us suppose with Tertullian that the doctrine of the Incarnation is logically absurd. Then clearly it can be stated only in terms of inner contradiction until it has been rephrased in literal language. Tertullian, of course, believed that no such paraphrase was possible. But it is conceivable that some philosopher would attempt to put in rational language that which up to the date of his struggles had existed only in allegorical language. Such a man would first have to know what the dogma meant before he could succeed. But he could only acquire such knowledge if he had access to the very goal which he himself was attempting to reach before he

set out to reach it. But if one has already assumed that the human race—or at least the elite—has a common store of knowledge and that over a thousand years of illuminating that knowledge are in one's library, then the task of interpreting the allegory is easier. If Ficino had not accepted Neo-Platonic philosophy as the truth and then assumed that the truth was one and unique, he could not have concluded that the apparently different truth of Christianity was the same in meaning as the truth of what he believed to be Platonism.

But in that case Ficino was almost forced to maintain that the source of philosophy was also the source of religious insight. Fortunately for him there was an authority, Justin Martyr, who had maintained that the Logos had inspired Plato as it or He had inspired the Apostles. Both had seen the same thing. What they had seen was the dialectical fertility of The Word. The notion that by an inner force ideas flow out of a fountainhead, that they proceed like light which pours forth from a single source and spreads into darkness, was at least as old as Plotinus. But there must be some power which impels us to seek that source of light. In the *Symposium,* Plato had made Socrates relate a speech of a seeress Diotima, in which she speeaks of the scale of Beauty, running from corporeal beauties to absolute ideal beauty, from the many particular instances of beautiful things to the Idea of Beauty itself. One can mount this ladder only if one is attracted upwards by Love of Beauty. In Plotinus love arises by the attraction which the soul experiences upon seeing its reflection in others. The soul is the idea of the human being, beauty is the idea of whatever is beautiful, its form in Aristotle's term, that for which it exists. But since in Plato, as in St. Paul, the human being was a duality of soul and body, each might have its form or idea and a person might easily be attracted to the form of the body instead of to the soul. Plato's theory of love is not intended to be a description in psychological terms of man's erotic experiences. It is a corrective of them. It is a plea that men turn from love of the body to love of the soul, union with which will procreate not other bodies but minds. The role of the teacher in Plato is that of the midwife who brings perfect minds into the world, but since there was always the danger that the earthly Venus would prevail over the heavenly, an act of will was needed to turn one away from the former to the latter. And also there was needed an act of faith that the latter was nobler than the former.

To fortify the notion that the force of love was of an importance transcending human affairs was the statement of Aristotle that the Prime Mover moves the world as the beloved moves the lover. The cosmos is attracted to its First Cause, not pushed by it, and thus when the Prime Mover turns into God, God is interpreted as the goal of all our striving. There was, hence, nothing novel in the idea when the Florentine Platonists took it up. It had been expressed in scores of mystical writings, in such works as Dante's *Convivio,* and of course in numerous medieval hymns. And since Love, as *Caritas,* had always been one of the Christian virtues, the Platonic discourses seemed merely to bolster a theory which was at the very heart of orthodox Christianity. But Love is a feeling which anyone, philosopher or not, can feel in one form or another, and therefore all the philosopher had to do was to clarify its significance, to give a rational account of its role in the universe. For one loves without knowing why, and thus the simplest soul may share with the most learned man the experience of what the latter would have called the essential mystery of life. But this is precisely what religion was looking for. Throughout the Middle Ages there had been a search for a rational account of the religious experience, an account which need not be understood before having that experience. The Platonic tradition seemed to Ficino and his fellows, as for that matter it did to St. Augustine, to provide it.

The Italian historian of philosophy, Eugenio Garin, has rightly emphasized the Franciscan element in this attitude. If "love can penetrate where no science can go," then science is needed, to be sure, for philosophy, but not for religion. We shall see this motif recurring later. When religious philosophers emphasize that religion operates through an act of will, rather than of reason, they are probably trying to express the same thought. But even the will, even love itself, is unfortunately bound in some way to the body. This way may be only in what the Platonists would have called the lower levels, but the metaphor of levels is not of much help. For our knowledge of love begins, at any rate, with corporeal love and, as for the will, it begins with moving the body. Ficino's problem is to find some way of decorporealizing both, for, to begin with, the body is perishable and its functions must cease with it. There is no need to point out why he wants a soul which will not perish. Aristotle had given some ground for the belief that it was man's active reason which was immortal, but that would not do for Ficino. For the reason, whether active or not, was the one psychic faculty which was alike in all men— even the least religious philosophers clung to that. . . . Moreover, there had been Arabian metaphysicians who had seen in the universality of the reason evidence for the soul's loss of individuality after death. The will, however, is individual and remains individual in all its activity. Even if two men love and desire the same thing, they retain their individuality and do not merge into the object of their desire. Thus if the essence of the soul is its love of God, the soul is not lost in God, as the mystics maintained, but is purified by the object of its love while still retaining its separateness from other wills. Ficino is striving to describe a community of souls adoring the Supreme Being; and his fundamental problem, especially in view of the doctrine that it was matter that individuated things, is to account for individuals who have no matter. Plotinus had already laid down the principle that human souls were replicas of the Divine Mind (the *Nous*) and thus were individuated before their incorporation. Ficino could not accept the idea that we had existed in another world before birth and that our birth was "but a sleep and a forgetting," for that would have been in conflict with Christian dogma. But he could maintain that just as the source of light sends out individual rays, so our souls may maintain their individuality even though coming from a single source and returning to that source.

The soul then is, regardless of its incorporation, an individual. It is not the form of the body in the sense that the body determines its nature or its individuation, but is the body's form as that for which the body exists. In Plotinus's system the soul's work in the universe is to govern a body and one might almost say—though one would be wrong if the "almost" were omitted—that the soul individuated the body. The human being is an irreconcilable duality. Human life is a battle between two contrary natures, temporarily linked together for moral purposes. The body may conquer the soul, to be sure, but the purpose of the soul is to conquer the body. It is freed from its task at death; but unlike Plotinus, Ficino did not believe that it had an infinite number of opportunities to try again. Its position in the body is that of the Soul of the World (*anima mundi*) in the universe. The Soul of the World served the Platonists as an explanation of the activity of the

cosmos. It seemed clear that if there was order in the universe, there must be more than brute matter in it. Clearly this order came ultimately from God, but by removing God from all possibility of contagion with multiplicity and time, one removed Him also from all effective contact with His creation. As the *ens realissimum* He had lost all describable characters; He could be spoken of only in negative terms. One might some day look upon Him, but one even then could not describe Him. In Plotinus there was a Trinity of three hypostases, the One, the *Nous*, and the Soul of the World. There had been heretical suggestions in the Middle Ages, one for which Abelard was condemned, that the Soul of the World was the Holy Spirit. Ficino did not fall into this heresy, but he did revive the idea that all beings owed their orderliness, life, and perhaps their beauty to their participation in the universal soul. It must be remembered that, until the time of Galileo, matter was believed to be completely inert. Movement was always imposed upon it. And force was immaterial. The Soul of the World was the being ideally fitted to provide that force and to act in relation to the universe as a whole—and of course it was believed to be a whole—as the human soul behaved toward the human body.

Finally we have in Ficino a theory of beauty which was to dominate the European imagination until our times, the theory that the beautiful is the idea in corporeal form. A statue of a man is not just a literal representation of a given individual, but an incorporation of the ideal of humanity; a portrait must present not merely the peculiar features of the individual portrayed, but the ideal for which he stands; a sacred picture must be an emblem of the theme symbolized in the story which it illustrates. In the sixteenth century this program was to be used by Cardinal Bellori against such a "naturalistic" painter as Caravaggio. But how was one to attain a vision of the ideal? By the inner eye, not the outer. The latter could give one only the material and sensuous appearance of things; only the former could give that of which the outer appearance was a hint. It must not be forgotten that the young Michelangelo was a member of the Florentine Academy, nor will it be forgotten by those who have read his sonnets. Should anyone doubt the influence of Platonism on his powerful imagination, conviction will probably arise through reading the various studies which Erwin Panofsky has made of his works and thoughts. But the movement was not terminated at the end of the sixteenth century, and well into the nineteenth painters were speaking of the *beau idéal*, though far from clear about how one reached it. The most practical advice on the subject was probably that of Reynolds in his *Discourses* when he maintained that ideal beauty was found in something like the statistical mean.

However strange this may seem to eyes accustomed to the naturalistic school of art, for generations—ever since the days of Theophrastus in literature and perhaps from those of the Humoralists in medicine and psychology—it had been believed that men were of certain types or characters. Consistency of character, as it was called, was logical consistency. If Achilles was to be always Achilles, as the followers of Horace asserted, then there must be an Achilles-type whose behavior could be predicted rationally. The ritualization of themes, gestures, facial expressions, dialogue, depended in the last analysis upon the theory that people "stood for" something, were not simply themselves, but incorporated ideal traits, whether these traits were those of the miser, the hypocrite, and the flatterer; or the hero, the gentleman, and the perfect lover. It was not until our own times, after all the preliminary work of writers like Zola and painters like Courbet, that it was possible to see people as individuals, not of a piece, not always brave and strong, but sometimes also fearful and weak; not always truthful and courageous, but sometimes also mendacious and cowardly. What we have gained in realism we have lost in intelligibility. But to the aesthetic idealist all nature became intelligible for the very reason that it became standardized. This is not meant to imply that Zola first read Ficino, or even Bellori, and then rejected them. But it does mean that the tradition which Ficino and his fellows revived lasted in various expressions well into our own times. (pp. 50-8)

George Boas, "Italian Platonism," in his Dominant Themes of Modern Philosophy: A History, *The Ronald Press Company, 1957, pp. 50-69.*

GRETCHEN LUDKE FINNEY (essay date 1960)

[*Finney is an American educator and author who has written extensively on music theory. In the following excerpt, she delineates Ficino's perception of celestial music and its cosmic influence.*]

When Orpheus descended into Hades and revealed his power to give life to the dead, or when by his song he moved trees and rocks or tamed wild beasts, and when Arion caused stones to build the walls of Thebes, they performed miracles that gave many future centuries cause to wonder. If certain philosophers agreed with Clement of Alexandria that Orpheus and the Theban, too, "under cover of music . . . outraged human life, being influenced by daemons, through some artful sorcery," occult philosophers argued that demons and magic are not necessarily evil. At all events, Orpheus and Arion demonstrated that music could cause not only ecstatic death but could restore life, and the Renaissance philosopher was not one to let such a miracle go unexplained.

He had at his disposal several explanations of how music might give life to dead things, but the two most common ones—if explanation was considered necessary—had to do with various kinds of "spirit." One originated, to an important degree, in Hermetic philosophy, that body of literature so filled with astrological, cabalistic, alchemical, and neoplatonic notions that was compiled during the first few centuries after Christ and attributed to Hermes Trismegistus. The other seemed to be dictated by common sense.

Hermetic writings were translated, studied, and brought into prominence by the Renaissance neoplatonists, especially by Ficino and Pico della Mirandola. It was certainly Ficino who developed the occult spirit-theory of music into one that had wide acceptance. According to this theory, music worked on the "spirits" of man. Spirits, in a medical sense, were believed to be (in Robert Burton's words) "a most subtle vapour expressed from the blood." By means of spirits, soul controlled body and body reached to soul; thus spirits carried out all the functions that we today attribute to the nervous system. But Ficino, in this connection, broadened the concept of spirits from their medical meaning to a cosmic one in which the whole universe was believed to be filled and animated by spirit, a spirit that linked lowest stone to purest angel.

This expansion of meaning did not, however, originate in Ficino. From Aristotle, from the Stoics, and from Hermetic philosophy came the idea of spirit, or *pneuma,* which pervaded the universe and gave life and motion to everything; it ce-

mented all parts into a whole. The word *spiritus* or *pneuma,* in ancient science, meant literally *breath,* and " . . . could be applied to a vapor, a gas, a disembodied spirit or even to the Holy Ghost." This conception was not incompatible with Christian belief: the "Spirit of God" moving "upon the face of the waters" (Genesis 1:2) gave life and form to the world. World spirit was sometimes equated with the soul of the universe, the Platonic *anima mundi,* though it was usually thought to be different. It was the median between the soul and body of the world, just as spirits in man were the knot of his soul and body. (pp. 179-80)

But since the spirits in man resembled, or were a part of, world spirit, it did not seem unreasonable to suppose that his spirits . . . might be altered or replaced by spirit finer than his own. The distillation of alcoholic spirits, called *aqua vitae* (life-giving water), obviously had curative effects. This alcoholic spirit combined with spirit drawn from plants (which received their growth from stellar spirit and thus carried stellar influences) explains, probably, the early monastic production of liqueurs. Many an eminent philosopher devoted his life to an attempt to capture the purest world spirit and infuse it into a philosopher's stone which could then be used to cure all human ills.

But music, as well as plants or stones or talismans, was thought to transmit celestial spirit and influence. On this assumption, Ficino projected what a recent scholar calls his "Music-Spirit Theory" [see D. P. Walker entry in Further Reading]. His belief in the efficacy of music to carry celestial influence was based on the ancient Pythagorean and Platonic theory of a musically and mathematically ordered universe, an ordering whose mathematical proportions were similar to those of heard music. This universe, according to Ficino's conception, was animated by spirit, and since the universe is fundamentally musical, its spirit must be musical. "Undoubtedly the world lives and breathes," he wrote in the *De Vita,* and its breath is music.

It was by a "personalizing" of world spirit that Ficino, in his *Commentary* on Plato's *Symposium,* explained the musical sirens of the spheres and the demons that inhabit every element—an idea frequently attributed to Plato, as it was by Milton. Since the whole body of the world lives, every one of its parts must live, and since it lives, must have soul. These spirits, which have soul, appear in heaven as Angels, in spheres as sirens, in elements as demons, through the world as genii, man's tutelary spirits. And all are musical. (pp. 181-82)

The spirit of music, according to Ficino (and innumerable other writers) reflected the mood or emotion of the planet by which it was especially influenced. Each planet had the characteristics of the god whose name it bore, and sounded a music that possessed those characteristics. The music of the sun was thought to be grave and earnest, that of Venus voluptuous. Saturn, Mars, and the Moon have only voices, not music. These moods were imitated in musical modes. Because the spirit of music shares in world spirit, and because music imitates the proportions and the moods of heavenly bodies, it is uniquely efficacious, Ficino believed, in transmitting celestial spirit and stellar influence to man, whose spirits respond to it by natural sympathy. (p. 184)

By means of astrologically powerful music, then, Ficino thought it possible to transmit both stellar influence and cosmic spirit to the spirit of man, to alter his temperament, and to govern his emotions. The breath of celestial spirit could revive man's spirit. By infusion of world spirit, even material objects could be given life:

> One can attract into and retain in, a material object 'something vital from the soul of the world and the souls of the spheres and stars,' that is, celestial spirit, if the object is of a material which reflects the celestial source of the spirit in question.

For these purposes, Ficino composed and sang songs, which he called, for various reasons, "Orphic." They were intended to be like those sung by Orpheus and to possess similar powers. The words were those of the Orphic *Hymns.* The meaning of the text, it must be emphasized, was for Ficino of prime importance, for that alone, he wrote, reaches the mind. The mode fitted that of a particular planet, and attention was given to the daily position and aspect of the stars. They were delivered in the monodic style made popular later in the century by the proponents of the new musical style that was used in *melodrama,* now called "opera."

This notion was not an isolated aberration of a single mind. Its origins were in the past; its influence was a powerful one throughout the 16th century and into the 17th. It explained for many the use of music for prophetic possession (a practice, still, among primitive people), for, as Sylvester translated Du Bartas:

> O! what is it that *Musick* cannot doo!
> Sith th'all-inspiring Spirit it conquers too:
> And makes the same down from th'Empyreall Pole
> Descend to Earth into a Prophets soule.

It explained the origin of the emotions apparently in music that could sway man even against his will; it explained how music could elevate the soul and why it "breathed" and revealed heaven. "Musicke breathes heaven, nay more, it doth disclose it," wrote Thomas Palmer in "An Epigram" to Elway Bevin "upon his Canons of three parts in one."

Music might, then, refine the soul to ecstasy, but according to this theory, it was usually not man who was carried to heaven, but heaven that was brought to man. It was by influx of divine spirit, not withdrawal of soul or spirit, that man was made celestial. (pp. 185-86)

Authority for this use of music to infuse prophetic spirit, or to give life where none was before, was to be found in the writings of early neoplatonists, such as Proclus and Iamblichus. However, Mr. D. P. Walker believes that Ficino's chief sources were Plotinus and the Hermetic *Asclepius,* a work Ficino had translated. It was in the *Asclepius* that he found an account of the alchemical infusion of soul into matter: "Our first ancestors invented the art of making gods." Having made a statue or an image, "they evoked the souls of demons or angels, and put them into images with holy and divine rites." This they did by means of ". . . herbs, stones and aromas, which have in them a natural divine power"; and by means of "hymns and praises and sweet sounds concerted like the harmony of the heavens," they retained these spirits. This passage Ficino considered the source of an idea in the *Enneads* of Plotinus, which he interpreted to mean that by music " . . . one can attract into, and retain in, a material object 'something vital from the soul of the world and the souls of the spheres and stars.' "

Ficino avoided the idolatry inherent in Hermes' statement. Demons and genii, like angels, were world spirits, but they were personalized world spirits, and because they were personalized, they were thought to have soul. Ficino was firm in his insistence that talismans, odors, music, and the like infuse only impersonal world spirit, which has no soul, and that they affect not the soul of man but his spirits. He disclaimed any use of "demonic magic"—the "black magic" condemned by the Church because there was always the danger that bad demons as well as good might be invoked. The air was thought to be full of spirits which could course through the spirits of man. The eminent physician, Levinus Lemnius, referred to these " . . . externall spirites recoursing into his [man's] bodye and mynde," the good angels imparting a "pleasant sweet inspiration," the bad angels breathing out "a pestiferous poyson." The Devil, wrote Alsted, uses filthy music " . . . as his Vehicle, by which he slideth himself into the minds of men." Ficino had no intention of encouraging possession by demons and angels. It was "natural magic," not demonic, that he hoped to employ. Music was used, according to tradition, to drive *out* evil spirits, but that is another story. Giovanni Pico agreed with Ficino in postulating a world spirit that could be controlled by natural magic and by use of which man could be made celestial. He wrote (in a passage quoted by Henry Reynolds in his *Mythomystes* in 1633):

> In natural magic nothing is more efficacious than the Hymns of Orpheus, if there be applied to them the suitable music, the disposition of the soul, and the other circumstances known to the wise.

> (pp. 187-88)

Ficino's ideas were repeated—with some variation—in the *Occult Philosophy* of Cornelius Agrippa. The universe is pervaded by spirit, wrote Agrippa, the same in the universe as in man, which carries to man the influences of the stars:

> For this is the band, and continuity of nature, that all superior vertue doth flow through every inferiour with a long, and continued series, dispersing its rayes even to the very last things; . . . as a certain string stretched out, to the lowermost things of all, of which string if one end be touched, the whole doth presently shake, and such a touch doth sound to the other end. . . .

This spirit, which is warm and generative, the source of all life, may be infused by music, for "Musical harmony is not destitute of the gifts of the Stars":

> . . . there is in Sounds a vertue to receive the heavenly gifts. It is a most powerful imaginer of all things, which whilst it follows opportunely the Celestial bodies, doth wonderfully allure the Celestial influence.

In a section *Concerning the agreement of them* [voices] *with the celestial bodies, and what harmony and sound is correspondent of every star,* he attributed to each planet a particular musical tone and mood and quality of sound. Music can thus alter dispositions of bodies and souls, and music, he wrote, is not used in vain to restore the mind "to wholesome manners untill they make a man suitable to the Celestial Harmony and make him wholly Celestial."

In the works of Pomponazzi, of Francesco Giorgi, and many other writers, theories for the magical power of music recur, as Mr. Walker points out. As late as 1589 the theme of neoplatonic magic was given prominence by Fabio Paolini, a professor of Greek at Venice, in his *Hebdomades,* in which he referred again to the *Asclepius* statutes' being animated by "herbs, stones and celestial music." He regretted that the church frowned on such notions, but he clung to them nevertheless. He quoted Ficino's rules for composing planetary music in imitation of the Orphic Hymns, which contains "divine Mysteries." A discussion of the power of Orpheus' music to inspire life became a violent issue during a series of lectures given by Paolini in the *Accademia degli Uranici* (of which Tasso was a member), the seriousness of which it is difficult for a modern reader to imagine. As influential a philosopher as Campanella believed that music, among other things, could be used for "breathing in the Spirit of the World." (pp. 189-90)

Gretchen Ludke Finney, "Music: The Breath of Life," in The Centennial Review of Arts & Science, Vol. IV, Spring, 1960, pp. 179-205.

FRANTIŠEK NOVOTNÝ   (essay date 1964?)

[*In the following excerpt from a work completed sometime before the critic's death in 1964 and first published in 1970, Novotný surveys Ficino's works and comments on his Platonism.*]

[Ficino] believed that philosophic minds come to Christ through Plato—in a letter to Braccio Martellus he examines Plato's dialogues and shows what a Christian can find in them to strengthen his faith—and he believed that it was possible to convert philosophic infidels to religion through Platonism and that he himself was led to translate Plato and later also Plotinus through divine providence. In this belief he wrote within five years (1469-1474) the extensive treatise (in 18 books) *Theologica Platonica de immortalitate animarum,* which with the *De Christiana religione,* written in 1474, is his fundamental systematic work. The title itself discloses that he deals here particularly with the immortality of the soul. Were the soul not immortal, he says at the beginning, no living creature would be more unhappy than man. Other Platonic questions are treated here from the Christian point of view. Ficino distinguishes here five kinds of being, from the lowest which is multiform and changeable to the highest which is one and unchangeable. The soul is a being of a middle nature which may rise or descend. There are also different stages of the soul: first, the world-soul, second, the soul of the spheres, third, the souls of live beings within the spheres. This is the content of the first four books of this work. In the fifth book the evidence for the immortality of the soul is set out and in the others contrary opinions are refuted. In truth, Ficino was here expounding his own philosophical system under the name of Platonic theology. But at the same time he wished to remain an orthodox Christian and therefore he added a conditional clause that only such of the opinions he expressed were to be considered as his own, as were approved by the Church.

This work was intended to be a systematic commentary on Plato's writings, to reveal the Platonic mysteries and to prove that they agree with Christian teaching and can thus serve to support it against infidel philosophers. There are three kinds of these: the Epicureans or Lucretians, the Peripatetics of Alexandria and the Peripatetics who are followers of Averroës. The weapon which may be used against them is the Neo-Platonic tradition, starting with six theologians—they were Zoroaster, Hermes, Orpheus, Aglaophemus, Pythagoras, Plato—and complemented and explained by later philosophers divided into six academies: the Old Academy of Xenoc-

rates, the Middle Academy of Arcesilaus, the New Academy of Carneades, the Egyptian Academy of Ammonius, the Roman Academy of Plotinus and Proclus' Academy. In this work Ficino used the Platonic philosophy—Plato's and the Neo-Platonists'—conceived as the continuation and completion of the doctrines of the ancient theologians Zoroaster, Hermes and Orpheus as a means for learning the substance of God, man and the world. "Let us, I beg", he writes at the beginning, "as celestial souls who long for our celestial country, break as quickly as we may the bonds of our earthly fetters, that, borne up by Plato's wings and guided by God, we may the more easily fly to our ethereal dwelling-place, where we shall happily contemplate the excellence of our race". The two concepts "on Plato's wings" and "guided by God" are fused in Ficino's philosophy into one indivisible unity. Like Plato, Ficino here conceives the cosmos as an organism composed of body and soul and containing in itself all kinds of beings. However, he categorises these beings in a manner partly his own, for he distinguishes *corpus* (body, i. e. the indefinite "first matter", capable of quantitative formation in four elements), *qualitas* (quality by which Ficino means the dynamic faculty of the body), *anima* (the soul, composed of potential being), *essentia* (and real existence, *esse*), *mens* (the mind, i. e. angels, spirits, demons in the Neo-Platonic sense), *Deus* (God, the one, first, infinite being, the source of all activity, the creator and the preserver of the world).

His theory of cognition is also from Plato and is founded upon the doctrine that immutable ideas are the models of things. In discussing the problem of the process of cognition he also considers the noetic exposition in Plato's 7th epistle. Man arrives at the highest knowledge through intuition assisted by reason and the power of the will, if his mind is enlightened by the divine mind. This addition of will-power is obviously due to Christian influence, we might call it Augustinean, as the acceptance of the mystical ecstasy shows the influence of the "Chaldean prophecies".

Ficino's ethics are also based on Platonism, for he holds that the chief end of man is to become like God, the highest being. In political theory he stresses that it is desirable that the philosopher should take part in legislation and government.

Ficino wrote *De Christiana religione* as a token of gratitude to Lorenzo for his appointment as the rector of the church S. Cristofano. He shows here how unfortunate is the separation of philosophy from religion, to which it is due that in his age there are infidel philosophers and ignorant priests, and he attempts to reunite them. Here too he allots a great part to Plato. Plato's writings, he says, contain the whole of pagan theology. Plato prophesies in the *Epistles* that its mysteries will be revealed only after many centuries. This is what happened indeed, for it was in the times of Philo and Numenius, immediately after the preaching of the apostles and their disciples, that the teaching of the old theologians, which was preserved in Plato's writings, was first understood. The Platonists used the divine light of the Christians to expound the divine Plato. On the authority of Plato's *Epinomis* Ficino thinks that the antique theology originated in Syria. He regards Abraham as its founder, and from him originated the three kindred religious doctrines of Antiquity, the Chaldean, Hebrew and Egyptian. From these developed on the one hand Judaism, on the other Greek theology, two systems which prepared the way for Christianity and merged with Christianity into one whole. Christianity appears thus as the perfection of antique theology, a stage in the history of religion, but by no means the last stage. Ficino regards the Sibyls as a significant factor in the history of the Antique religious tradition for they acted as intermediaries between the Eastern doctrines and the Graeco-Roman theology.

By the year 1477 Ficino had finished the revision of his translation of Plato, written the contents of each dialogue and completed his work on Plato with a biography of him. He then sent all these works to Lorenzo de' Medici with a special dedication. In Plato's biography he accepted and indeed stressed the legendary characteristics with which tradition had adorned Plato's image and tried to present Plato as a true philosopher. He also uses here the horoscope which was cast for Plato by Firmicus Maternus and deduced from it Plato's eloquence and his sense of the mystery of God.

The translation of Plato's writings was published in print in the year 1484 in Florence (explicit: *Impressum Florentiae per Laurentium Venetum*). The cost of this publication was paid by the Florentine nobleman Filippo Valori, Ficino's friend. The Valori family, politically rather important, were next to the Medici family the greatest supporters of the Florentine Renaissance Platonism. Ficino writes gratefully about them in the dedication of his commentaries on Plato to one of them, to Nicolò. Only the second Florentine edition, published in the year 1491, was paid for by Lorenzo de' Medici, to whom it is dedicated.

Ficino emphasises in his dedicatory introduction the task, which divine providence has given to philosophy to ensure that religion "which is the only path to happiness", should be common both to simple folk and to men of learning. "And therefore almighty God at a time of his choosing sent down from the height the divine spirit of Plato, marvellous in his life, in his genius, in his eloquence, who was to explain holy religion among all peoples". Cosimo Medici then decided to diffuse Platonic light among the Latins and chose for this purpose Ficino. "I, though from my earliest years I had reverenced Plato's name, undertook so weighty a task under the prosperous auspices of your grandfather Cosimo rather than my own, hoping that divine assistance would not be refused to a service so necessary and so pious". He then goes on to describe how the translation progressed during the life-time of Cosimo, then under Piero, and how he finally returned to it after a certain lapse of time and succeeded under his patronage and with his help in finishing it. "I do not claim that I have completely reproduced Plato's style in these books, nor do I believe that it could ever be reproduced by any man, though far more learned than I. I should call his style liker to an oracle of God than to human speech, often loftily thundering, often again flowing with the sweetness of nectar, but always containing heavenly secrets. For as the world is provided with three great advantages, utility, order, and ornament, which prove to us the existence of its divine maker, so the style of Plato, which contains the whole universe, abounds especially in these three: the philosophical utility of the opinions, the rhetorical order of the arrangement and expression, and the ornament of poetical phraseology. Throughout his works he invokes divine testimony and himself gives the most certain testimony of God, the architect of the world". Plato's writings are not intended for uninitiated beginners and are not suitable for the education of young people. Plato should be studied by people already educated who gain from it not a knowledge of those fundamentals which are taught to children, but divine secrets. Sometimes Plato deliberately conceals his true meaning and than it may seem that

he is joking. "But the jests and games of Plato are graver than the earnest of the Stoics". He intermingles the useful with the pleasing. Often also he invents tales in the manner of poets and his style seems more poetical than philosophical. "Sometimes he rages and wanders in his speech like a prophet and then he follows divine and prophetic rules rather than human rules of composition, acting not as a teacher but as a priest or prophet, sometimes maddened, sometimes purifying others and bringing them to the same divine madness". He writes everything in the dialogue form "so that living speech may bring before our eyes the persons who speak, may persuade us more effectually and move us more strongly".

In his more general reflections Ficino—by combining the Greek mythology with the personification used in the *Book of Proverbs* 8,22, 35—describes the service done by Plato to Philosophy, the daughter of Wisdom, born from Jupiter's head, who is happy only in the Academy, the best school for all, be they young or old, poets, orators, lawyers, politicians, philosophers, scholars or priests. "Come hither then, I pray you, all who follow the liberal arts, for you will receive them here, and liberty of life besides. Assemble here, all of you who are fired with the perpetual ardour to attain truth and blessedness. Here by God's inspiration you shall attain to the truth and felicity which you desire". Ficino concludes his appeal to the readers with the admonition that they should judge "Platonic or rather divine matters" after thorough consideration and that they should bestow their favour both upon Plato and upon his translator who "labours with all his strength for the common good of all, not only translating the words but explaining the sense".

Ficino concludes this introduction by recommending himself and Filippo Valori to Lorenzo's favour.

Thus a work was finished which was the first to introduce Plato fully and systematically into the culture of the Latin world. Ficino had assistents, both his own countrymen and aliens, whom he mentions gratefully in the preface, especially the Greek Demetrius—it was Demetrius Chalcondyles († 1511), a Platonist from Pletho's school but not blinded by his prejudice, Reuchlin's teacher—"Attic not less by his philosophy and eloquence than by his birth". These, however, were only occasional advisers. Otherwise he did all this great work himself, and he did it well. There are passages in his translation—as in any other translation of Plato's—which could be corrected and improved, but on the whole it is philologically fairly accurate—he also frequently supplements the manuscript tradition of the original text by using manuscripts which are unknown to us—and as a rule give the correct reading. But it has always had its critics, and already certain contemporaries of Ficino received it with reservations. But it is nevertheless possible to say that it fully deserved to be printed as late as in the 19th century, when there were other translations available—with a few corrections—in Immanuel Bekker's edition of Plato.

The value of Ficino's translation is increased by his introductions to each dialogue, describing in most cases their content (*argumentum* or *epitome*) and containing, as far as two, the *Symposium* and the *Timaeus,* are concerned, also an analysis of them and Ficino's own reflections. The commentary on the *Symposium* is a memorable piece of work. It introduced the men of the Renaissance to Plato's philosophy of love as Ficino himself conceived it.

The extant commentary dedicated to Lorenzo is the second

version and was written in the years 1474-1475. Ficino commented the *Symposium* for the first time at the instigation of Giovanni Cavalcanti in 1467. The first version also contained a short biography of Plato and a concise survey of his philosophical system. For Lorenzo and on his advice he made a change and dealt successively in his commentary with the themes of the seven speeches which were delivered at that Platonic feast which did really take place in Careggi, but instead of attempting to reproduce the actual speeches that were made, he gave his own contemplations on the themes of the Symposium. The commentary thus arranged, the ***Commentarium in convivium Platonis,*** he then translated into Italian.

Instead of a simple interpretation of Plato's dialogue, the commentary on the *Symposium* contains a complete philosophical system, wherein Eros is studied and understood from the standpoint of natural sciences, cosmology, theology, ethics and aesthetics. Plato's thoughts are ingeniously combined with those of the orphic *Argonautica,* with the teaching of Hermes Trismegistus, with the mystic theology of Dionysius the Areopagite—whose Eros has quite a definite influence here—and also with the orthodox teaching of the Church. The summit of all being and its sun, which with Plato is the good, is here God the creator. The ideas are the patterns of things in his mind. God created a three-fold world: *mentem angelicam* (the angelic mind, the angels and demons), *mundi animam* (the world-soul), *mundi corpus* (the world-body). In God are goodness, beauty and justice, divine beauty, which emanates from the divine goodness and whose rays penetrate the spiritual and material world and inspires love. The lover of beauty proceeds from the beauty perceived by sense to the contemplation and love of God. It is thus that Ficino interprets the discourses in the *Symposium* employing allegorical interpretation where necessary, as it is in Aristophanes' speech, in order to give the speech a unified spiritual content. In his interpretation of Socrates' speeches he distinguishes three kinds of love which correspond to three kinds of people. Every love starts with gazing. But the love of a "contemplative" person rises from the sight to the mind, the love of a "voluptuous" person descends from sight to touch, and the love of an "active" person consists unchanged in gazing. The love of the first turns more to the highest demon than to the lowest, the love of the second deviates to the lower rather than to the highest demon, and the love of the third keeps the same distance from both. This threefold love has a threefold name: the love of a contemplative person is called divine, the love of the active one human, and the love of a voluptuous person animal. The stages through which Diotima leads Socrates correspond here to the three worlds created by God: above the body is the soul, above the soul the angel, and above the angel God. *"Fons totius pulchritudinis Deus est, fons totius amoris Deus est"* ("the source of all beauty is God, the source of all love is God").

Whereas the pre-Renaissance Platonists were mainly interested in the cosmology of the *Timaeus,* the Renaissance placed in the foreground Plato's concept of beauty and love and also his theory of the perfect state. This revolution was effected by Ficino. (pp. 365-72)

His contemporaries called Ficino "the second Plato". Gaudenzio Paganini, professor of eloquence in Pisa, said about him with humanistic elegance after more than a hundred years: "It might have seemed that the soul of Plato himself had entered Ficino, had not the Pythagorean transmigration

of soul been disproved by the Christian religion". Ficino, no doubt deserved to be linked with Plato, for Plato was for him after God his main guide throughout his life. By his work he gave Plato a further lease of posthumous life in the history of European culture, for his influence reached to the cultural centres of Italy and to other centres beyond the Italian frontiers, in France, Germany, England, Poland, Bohemia and also Hungary. Ficino kept up an extensive correspondence with the whole learned world of Latin culture. Pope Sixtus IV invited him to lecture on Platonism at the University of Rome, and king Matthias Corvinus asked him to come to Hungary, who had at his court three zealous friends of Ficino's doctrine, Francesco Bandini, Filippo Valori and Filippo Buonaccorsi. At the University in Paris lectures were delivered upon his books. His writings were also read by some learned Greeks in Constantinople. The German Humanist Conrad Celtes stayed with him for some time, and later after he had also got to know the Roman Academy of Pomponius Laetus he founded similar learned circles in the transalpean countries: in Poland, where he was in touch with Filippo Buonaccorsi, called Callimachus, he founded the *Sodalitas litteraria Vistulana,* in Hungary the *Sodalitas litteraria Hungarorum,* which was later called *Danubiana,* in Mainz the *Societas litteraria Rhenana.* All these societies also studied Plato. In Poland the author of the dialogue *De mentis saluberrima persuasione,* Laurentius Corvinus, was attracted to the study of Platonism by the influence of Celtes. In Florence also the German Humanist Johann Reuchlin attended Ficino's lectures, but Pico della Mirandola exercised a greater influence upon his opinions and interests.

When after Lorenzo's death Ficino's life also was slowly declining, Plato's supporter could derive pleasure from letters such as the one he received, to give a single example, in 1496 from Robert Gaguin, the rector of the University in Paris who wrote to him: "Your virtue and wisdom, Ficino, are widely known and appreciated especially in our Academy in Paris, so that your name is loved and praised in the society of the most learned men as well as in the class-rooms of young boys. The witnesses of your merits are the exemplary efforts you made to render Plato into Latin. Your fame is augmented by your translation of the Platonist Plotinus. Apart from this other volumes of your work and your letters to your friends are read and highly esteemed. On account of this many members of our school are filled with the desire to make your personal acquaintance and to see the man, who created works of such exquisite learning".

However, the Florentine Academy ceased to exist. Although Francesco Gattani, whom Ficino had recommended to his disciples before his death as his successor, continued to expound Plato and Platonism at the public University in Florence, these were lectures and not free discussions, there were teachers and disciples rather than a society of friends leading a sociable life like that of a club. Not even the later meetings of the higher Florentine society in the gardens of Orti Oricellari belonging to the Rucellai family, in which Michel Angelo also took part, can be considered as a continuation of Ficino's Academy in Careggi. There is no evidence that Plato's philosophy was cultivated there, and the discussions were more concerned with history, politics and especially the Italian language and literature.

The later attempts to revive the Platonic Academy, which were made in the 16th century by Francesco de Vieri (Franciscus Verinus Secondus), the author of the Latin *Apology of* the Philosophy (Romae 1586) and of the writing *Vere conclusioni di Platoni conformi alla Dottrina Christiana et a quella d'Aristotile* (Firenze 1590), in the 17th century by the cardinal Leopoldo de' Medici and in the 18th century by the marquis Francesco Castiglioni, were futile. They did not meet the spiritual needs of their time and lacked the stimulating personality of Marsilio Ficino.

In spite of this the work which had been done by Ficino and his Academy lasted, although the Academy ceased to exist. Its philosophy, the Renaissance Platonism, in which Plato and Plotinus were almost merged into a single individual, became firmly rooted in the thought of that time and remained an important element of European culture. (pp. 376-78)

> František Novotný, "Marsilio Ficino: The Florentine Academy," in his The Posthumous Life of Plato, translated by Jana Fábryová, Academia Prague, 1977, pp. 355-78.

CHARLES TRINKAUS (essay date 1970)

[*Trinkaus is an American educator and Renaissance scholar. His two-volume opus,* In Our Image and Likeness: Humanity and Divinity in Italian Humanist Thought *(1970), is considered an authoritative treatment of religious theory of the quattrocento. In the following excerpt from that work, he discusses providential design and the supremacy of Christianity as expounded in Ficino's* On the Christian Religion.]

[Gianozzo] Manetti, prompted by his need to come to terms with the very Judaic religious tradition with which his humanistic study of Hebrew confronted him, composed his defence of Christianity and critique of paganism and Judaism in the 1440s and '50s. Roughly twenty years later (*ca.* 1476) Marsilio Ficino wrote his work *On the Christian Religion*, prompted, perhaps also, by the need to settle in his own mind the relationship of the ideas he had encountered in Plato and the Neoplatonists with Christianity and his own Christian faith. Although he had entitled his great work on the immortality of the soul, *Theologia platonica*, and professed not to recognise a distinction between theology and philosophy, he did see that there was a difference between *sapientia* and *religio*, and between the philosopher and the priest. Although he entitled the proem to this work 'That there is the greatest kinship between Wisdom and Religion', this does not imply identity. The two mental states derived from the distinction within the human soul between intellect and will by which the soul

> as it pleases our Plato can, as though by two wings (that is by intellect and will) fly back to the heavenly Father and fatherland, and the philosopher relies on the intellect and the priest especially leans on the will, the intellect illumines the will and the will kindles the intellect, . . .

The wise and holy men of all nations were philosophers and priests. The Hebrew prophets undertook both roles; the Persian philosophers were also Magi and priests. The Egyptian priests were also mathematicians and metaphysicians. The Hindu Brahmins gave counsel both on nature and on purgation. 'The same custom prevailed in Greece under Linus, Orpheus, Musaeus, Eumolpus, Aglaophemus and Pythagoras.' Thus he linked together the early Greek sages and poets, combining the traditions of *prisci poetae* and *prisci theologi*. The Celts, Romans and the *prisci* Christian bishops also united the roles of philosopher and priest.

He bemoans the fact that they have become separated:

> O much too unhappy ages, when the separation and divorce of Pallas and Themis (that is wisdom and virtue) miserably occurred. For learning has for the most part been passed down to the profane with whom it has for the most part become an instrument of iniquity and lust, and it should be called malice rather than science. . . . The most precious pearls of religion, on the other hand, are often handled by the ignorant and are trampled by them as if they were swine. For the inert ministry of the ignorant and lazy ought to be called supersition rather than religion, it seems. Thus on the one hand those who are learned do not know the truth sincerely as something divine that might lighten the eyes of the pious alone. On the other hand the clergy, entirely ignorant of divine and human things, do not worship God and administer sacred things rightly as far as they are able. How long must we sustain this hard and miserable fate of the iron age?

This is Ficino's judgement on the relation of secular and religious truth and roles, in his own day, and a certain suggestion of his personal motivation and hope that a Platonic theology might simultaneously purify and elevate the clergy and return the philosophers to the service of the cure of souls. One can see in this a persistence of the same motivation that led Petrarch to condemn the Aristotelians of his day and put his trust in Ciceronian rhetoric and a revival of Plato—sight unseen. Ficino, however, as a humanist-turned-philosopher, did not despise all the help he could get from the scholastic philosophic and theological traditions. But he wished to transform religious thought so that it would enlighten the clergy and the minds of the Christians through his new philosophy. And he found his own purposes close to the humanistic conception of a poetic theology, so that those men who were praised as *prisci poetae* in the one tradition, in their role of bards and prophets, were taken over by Ficino as *prisci theologi*, or founders and early participants in a divinely inspired philosophical-religious tradition.

Ficino's *De religione Christiana* is, like Manetti's *Contra Iudeos et Gentes*, and apologetic work which seeks, on the one hand, to establish the supremacy and truth of Christianity over its rivals, which for Ficino included the Moslems as well as the Jews and Gentiles. On the other hand, it is a work which also seeks to establish the relationships and points of contact within the total plan of divine providence between the non-Christian religions and Christianity—the extent to which the pagans and infidel shared in revealed truth and the modes and sources of the transmission of the truth.

In keeping with his entire philosophy, this work is also centred about man though it deals with religion. But, as he titles chapter one, 'Religion is especially proper and genuine to man,' as he had argued in *Theologia platonica*, it was man's restless pursuit of infinity and immortality that most sharply separated him from the mortal animals, so here he reaffirms that while animals share many human talents, man alone is religious. Again it is as proper for us to raise our minds to the King of heaven as it is to walk erectly. If men do sometimes pay honours to animals as though they were divine [e.g. in Egypt, etc.] these men are either ignorant or the animals are disguised celestial beings. Man is the most perfect animal by that quality which most sharply distinguishes him from the lower animals and joins him to divinity. Man alone abstains from temporal goods for the sake of divine worship and celestial goods.

Add that the sting of conscience constantly pricks us alone and the fear of divine jealousy of lower beings sharply vexes us. Therefore if religion is vain, as we have argued, there is no animal more insane or unhappy than man.

Here he repeats the opening statement of the *Theologia platonica.* If man's religious faith is illusory he is the most imperfect of all, if true the most perfect. He must be most perfect since God, the highest truth and goodness, would not deceive his own progeny, mankind.

Moreover, his second chapter continues this demonstration and reiteration of the universality of religion. As Plato emphasised in the *Protagoras,* man alone participates in divinity by recognising God, for 'God without God is not known'. The soul is raised to God in so far as it is flooded with divine light. Man, in fact, is completely preoccupied with God. 'The human mind is constantly agitated about God, the heart daily burns with God, the breast sighs over God, the tongue sings Him, head, hand and knee adore Him, the works of man refer to Him'. If God was ignorant or deaf to these things He would be an ingrate. But the supreme wisdom and charity can be neither ignorant nor ungrateful. If the human mind attains to the divine mind, it is necessary that the human be understood and governed by divinity.

This means that religion is a universal and admirable characteristic of man. The problem then is how to discriminate between the true and the false, the good and the bad. How can one move from a philosophical view of man and God to a specifically revealed religion, in particular to Christianity? Ficino must devise an argument that all religions are true and all religions are good, but one is truer and better than the others. Indeed, he must show that it alone is specifically true and good. The first step in this dialectic occurs in chapter four, 'Every religion has some good, provided it is directed to God Himself, the Creator of all things, but the Christian is sincere.' Divine providence solves the problem for Ficino, in the traditional sense that providence is shown to have permitted a universal but partial revelation to all men, true and perfect revelation to a chosen few, all as a part of a design for the opening of ultimate revelation and the possibility of salvation to all.

But the details of the design, as Ficino reads it, are his own and necessarily related to his admiration of Plato and the Neoplatonists and to his need to place them in acceptable historical relationship to the sacred history of the Scriptures. Therefore 'divine providence did not permit there to be in any time any region of the world entirely without any religion; however, it permitted different rites of worship to be observed in different times and places.' God 'prefers to be worshipped, though it be ineptly or humanly, to not being worshipped at all due to human pride.' But in this universality of religion, only those who worship God by goodness of actions, truth of speech, clarity of mind and charity of spirit are truly sincere. These are those who adore God in the manner Christ and His disciples taught.

This introduces a defence of the truth of Christianity by the human evidence of a demonstration of its 'sincerity' as manifested in the spirit and sacrifices of the disciples and apostles. These used none of the methods of persuasion of Demosthenes or Cicero and nevertheless they won the hearts of mankind. This could only have happened if the religion that inspired them was founded on divine power, wisdom and hope. Moreover, the Scriptures themselves were of the greatest aid to these men, and indeed are a further demonstration of Christian truth because of their intrinsic power and sincerity.

For in them there is a new force, singular in its simplicity, sobriety, ardour, gravity, profundity and majesty. . . . These writers have an indescribable something pious and awesome, and there is something marvellous common to them all, not in the least shared with any others.

The next succeeding chapters supply further arguments to prove the divine authority of Christ, and the miraculous character of His mission. His advent was not predicted by astrologers but by prophets of the Hebrews and pagan sibyls. The moment of His death was accompanied by an eclipse and other celestial phenomena that have been widely attested. Though there are reports of contemporary miracles, there is no need to ask for new miracles to prove the divinity of Christ as some do. Many pagan rulers, writers and philosophers after the time of Christ testified to His divinity even when they did not discard their other beliefs. Some of the Neoplatonists engaged in bitter attacks on Christianity, which was defended by the Fathers, but others thought of it as something to imitate. The Moslems, as the Koran shows, thought of Jesus as divine, born of a virgin, the last of the prophets and the most sublime, the first of all men, as Mary was the first of all women. But they held to two errors: one that Christ was divine but of a lesser substance than the Father, which they derived from the Arians; and the other that Christ was snatched up to heaven and a substitute crucified in his place, which they learned from the Manichaeans. Thus the Gentiles, the Jews and the Moslems all agree that the Christian law is the best, though they all cling to their own heresy. They prefer Christianity to all other religions except their own.

From this rhetorical defence of Christianity by the attestation of human experience and human testimony Ficino turns to a philosophical defence which is intended to show that, just as representatives of other faiths admitted their admiration for the partial acceptance of Christian authority, so the philosophers gave a partial recognition to the same truths on which Christianity had to rest. Thus the Son is generated by God by an act of divine thought. The *prisci theologi* Orpheus, Plato, Hermes Trismegistus and Zoroaster all believe in the divine birth of the *logos.* 'They said, of course, what they were able, and that with the aid of God. Moreover God alone knows this and those to whom He wished to reveal it.' But they all agreed, that

In God, because essence and knowledge are the same, knowledge, which is God always knowing Himself, always generates as though a most exact image of Himself; and what is generated has the same essence as He who generated, although by a certain marvellous relationship as though the generated is distinguished from the generating.

Thus in a rough way they had a knowledge of the Trinity.

But there is need to go beyond these approximations to the more precise doctrine which Ficino proceeds to elucidate in the succeeding chapters. After outlining the hierarchies of the heavens, he moves towards and concentrates on the specifically Christian doctrine of the Incarnation. For the Incarnation is the revealed Christian form of the unification of the divine and the human, which he found in a general way in the Gentile philosophers, particularly in the so-called *prisci theologi,* and the later Platonists. Thus by this exposition he both demonstrates the superiority and preciseness of Christianity (as well as its supreme truth and authority), and establishes the grounds for partial contact with the Gentiles. The creation of individual men is itself a kind of incarnation, since by divine will a rational soul is joined to a fleshly foetus. This Platonic doctrine must, of course, be contrasted with a view such as Pomponazzi's which sees the human soul in an inseparable organic relationship with corporeal physiology. For Ficino the Platonic notion of the soul, not as the form of the body, but as the temporary inhabitant and animator, has obvious advantages, since it makes possible this analogy between human incarnation and the divine Incarnation.

The divine Incarnation occurred in time when not the nature of God, but the person of the Son, or Word, was united, not to the person of Jesus but to the human nature of Jesus. In this there is another analogy, for the Word become flesh is like a human thought which is insensible while in the mind but which becomes sensible when spoken or written. The divine Word, similarly, remained invisible in God from eternity, but was made visible with its assumption of humanity. Moreover, 'the divine sublimity was not depressed to the human as if through some defect, but the human rather was elevated to Him; and the infinite light of the divine sun never can become anything less by the union with man, but man is always illumined and perfected by it'. This idea of the Christian Incarnation as the specific way in which man can find his much sought-after immortality, which Ficino had lengthily discussed philosophically in the *Theologia platonica,* is developed here as the central demonstration of the Christian truth. Man as the composite of all powers, in the body, as he had proved in the other work, 'is the most harmonious image of heaven. Moreover it was fitting for a universal creature to be joined to God, the common leader of all. . . . Therefore it was necessary for God to be united to human nature in which are all qualities.' 'Moreover God in man renders man divine.'

The consequences of the Incarnation are then presented. Man's defects were reformed. It was not less for God, the effecter of all, to perfect what was defective, just as to be well is not less than simply to be. Divine power, wisdom and benevolence manifested themselves in the union also.

> Therefore God so declared and acted that nothing would be deformed in the world, nothing wholly contemptible, since the earthly was joined to the king of heaven and in such way that it was made equal to the celestial. . . . And there is no more apt way for this to have happened than that God should become man, so that man, who was made of the corporeal in corporeal things, might now desire God in a certain way and so that he would more clearly recognise the corporeal and human and more ardently love God and also more easily and diligently imitate Him and become blessed. Finally man could not be perfectly cured unless he recovered the innocence of mind and friendship of God and his own excellence, which he had when he was subject to God alone according to his nature at the beginning.

Besides the recovery of the lost perfection and the repair of the defect in man, there was added the new virtues of faith, hope and charity. We could not have faith if God had not become man, since it rises from a foundation of knowledge. Revelation and the Incarnation itself, then, were essential for faith to confirm philosophical speculation. The Incarnation also gave man the hope of being himself joined to God, of dei-

fication. Love which is the bliss of divine contemplation is impossible without faith and hope.

> Therefore let men cease now to doubt their own divinity, on account of which doubt they drown themselves in mortal things. They should revere themselves as though divine beings, and hope that they can ascend to God, since in a certain way it was worthy enough for divine majesty to descend to them.

Christ's Incarnation removed the burden and sufferings of sin, and Christ was a teacher sent to instruct man in virtue by His example of perfectly filling all offices. 'For actions are much more moving than words, especially in moral discipline whose most proper end is involved in action.' Christ also expelled all the errors that were rampant in the universe and manifested in the worship of demons and materialistic and obscene religious cults. Christ, not Hercules, conquered these foul monsters. In the centuries after Christ these horrible cults which raged everywhere were put down solely by the power of the Christian inspired by the virtue of Christ.

He is at this point concerned to show how Christ was the fulfilment of all which lacked in the Gentile philosophers, however great, as well as how these latter were able to come at all close to the insights that mankind received by the manifestation of Christ. 'What else was Christ but a certain living book of moral and divine philosophy, sent from heaven and manifesting the divine idea itself of the virtues to human eyes.' But some of these things were known through the Sibyls and the Hebrew prophets, and by the *prisci theologi*. But if they possessed any such knowledge before the time of Christ, it was usurped from the Hebrew Scriptures as very many pagan writers testify and prove.

> From this it appears that the Gentiles, as Clement of Alexandria, Atticus the Platonist, Eusebius and Aristobulus have proved, if they had any outstanding dogmas and mysteries, had usurped them from the Jews, but whatever was contained among the latter as simple history was transformed by the former into poetic fables. . . . Plato imitated the Jews so far that Numenius the Pythagorean said he was nothing but Moses speaking in the Attic tongue.

Plato attributed the knowledge of science itself to a certain barbarian from Syria. Judea or Galilee was always part of Syria and called Phoenicia by the ancients. Thus when Proclus revered Phoenician theology before all and Pliny called the Phoenicians the inventors of letters and astrology, they were referring to the Hebrews. When the Chaldeans are praised, these also were the Jews who, as Lactantius proved, were often called Chaldeans. When Orpheus said God was known solely by a certain Chaldean, he meant Enoch or Abraham or Moses. Zoroaster, according to Dydimus, was the son of Chan or Canham who lived at the time of Abraham. The Jews also mingled with the Egyptians and passed their gifts on to them. He adds many more examples of this rather outrageous misreading of history, but they are significant of his efforts not only to claim priority for the Scriptural tradition but to prove a Biblical origin for pagan philosophy. Even more specifically he believes that the Pentateuch was translated into Greek before the time of the Persian empire, and that at the time of Ptolemy Philadelphus the translation made possible the further dissemination of the pre-Advent revelation of Christian truth.

But the *prisca theologia,* which began Gentile philosophy on the basis of Hebrew prophecy and revelation, led up to post-Advent Neoplatonism which could borrow even more directly from the knowledge of Christ himself as spread by the Apostles.

> The *prisca theologia* of the Gentiles, in which Zoroaster, Mercury, Orpheus, Aglaophemus, Pythagoras agree, was all contained in the books of our Plato. Plato predicted in his letters that these mysteries could at length become manifest to men after many centuries. This, indeed, happened, for in the times of Philo and Numenius the mind of the *prisci theologi* first began to be understood in the pages of the Platonists, namely immediately after the preaching and writing of the Apostles and apostolic Disciples. For the Platonists used the divine light of the Christians for interpreting the divine Plato. This is what Basil the Great and Augustine have proved, the Platonists have usurped the mysteries of John the Evangelist for themselves. I certainly have found that especially the mysteries of Numenius, Philo, Plotinus, Iamblichus and Proclus were received from John, Paul, Hierotheus and Dionysius the Areopagite. For whatever they have said concerning the divine mind, and the angels and other things pertaining to theology, however magnificently, they manifestly usurped from them.

Having settled in this way the relationship of the manifestation of divine truth in the person of Christ and in the Biblical tradition to that pagan tradition which to his mind contained the closest approximation to the same truth, Ficino turned to meet the question of Judaism. First of all he shows in two long exegetical chapters how ample prefiguration of the coming of Christ and of the sacred events may be found by a careful reading of the Old Testament. To this the Jews are blind, as they were blind to Christ himself. Then he turns to the books of Jewish writers for confirmation of Christian truth, just as he had done with the Gentiles.

Ficino was, along with Manetti and his own disciple Pico, a student of Jewish theology and Biblical commentary. He was not an accomplished Hebraist as Manetti was, and his knowledge of medieval Jewish theology and of the Cabalistic tradition was far more limited than that of Pico. None the less it is of interest that he shows some knowledge here of writers other than Josephus, whom he could read in Latin and Greek. Using translations and compendia he cited the *Targumin*, the *Seder 'Olam,* the *Talmud,* the *Midrashim,* the Bible Commentaries of Rashi, Nachmanide, Levi ben Gereshom, the *Book of Things to Believe* of Sa'adia, Maimonides' *Directorium,* and *Letter to the Africans,* and the Cabalistic *Lucidus.* According to Umberto Cassuto his references are very inexact and his names are quite mixed up and approximate. Later he acquired a somewhat more direct knowledge of Hebrew scholarship through Pico. But in general Ficino's scholarship in Hebrew studies was limited.

Like Manetti, Ficino compares the Mosaic Law and the Christian Law. The former is civil and moral and the latter purgative, purifying the soul by the example of heavenly virtues and enabling it to move towards immortality. The Mosaic Law is vain in comparison to the Christian, but superior to all others. It is a preparation for the Christian. However, he also distinguishes between the moral and ritual aspects of the Mosaic Law, as Manetti did. The latter are superseded.

By far the greatest proportion of his polemic is directed against the Jews, who interpreted the same text of the Old Testament [in their own Hebrew version, of course, with certain variants] in terms of a very different theology, and without the necessity of viewing it as a prefiguration of the New Testament. His polemic against the pagans consisted mostly in trying to show that they were not original, and erroneous in clinging to the old gods. He has correspondingly little to say against the Moslems, mainly repeating what we reported earlier in the two short chapters near the end of his work.

This book, which is so clearly of a parallel character to Manetti's *Contra Iudeos et Gentes,* was not Ficino's only effort to render an account of Christianity in relation to the Gentile and Hebrew traditions. . . . The occasion of [Paul's *Epistle to the Romans*], he holds, was the need to counter the rival claims of Jewish and Gentile Christians at Rome to spiritual preeminence by pointing out the faults of both. Ficino approached the actual text, however, by first providing a theological explanation of Christianity which runs parallel to that of the **De religione Christiana.** Paul was called to bring all men to Christ, and it is the missionary role of Paul that is in the centre of Ficino's interest—as an instrument of divine providence, not as a fervent preacher. The Old and New Testaments respectively deal with the human and divine natures of Christ, as Christ was descended from David through the Jews. He must therefore briefly explain the Trinity. The divine nature cannot be double, so that Father and Son are of one nature, but in the relative opposition of the generating and generated, they may be seen as twin persons, not natures. Thus if any human mind knows perfectly and loves itself strongly, it has a sharper image of the Trinity.

Why also was there an Incarnation? Again, he answered, that it was necessary to overcome the limitations of human sense by providing a living figure of God that could be seen by human eyes. The sum of the *Epistle* is therefore to convince Jews and Greeks both that they are called by Grace alone, and not by either the Old Law of the Jews or the science of the Gentiles, both of which are superseded. Salvation is offered to the Jews first, not because there is any distinction or separation of persons with God, but, because the Jews had the privilege of having the Prophets and Christ, they ought to come to salvation first as an example to the others. The Greeks, on the other hand, represent and stand for all idolators.

Paul says that the just live by faith, and the justice of God is revealed in faith. This means that a double faith is necessary, in the prophets and in Christ and His apostles. And it must be a faith sustained by works as well as words, because accompanied by charity. So the justice of God does not rest on the external ceremonies and rules of the Jews but in Evangelical spiritual truth. He compares the Mosaic Law with its limited worldly provisions and the Greek philosophical conception of justice of rendering each his due. Plato made justice the harmony of all parts of the soul, which is closer to the Evangelic justice of Paul.

> This justice neither the Gentiles nor the Mosaic Law fully achieved. For while the Gentiles' was promulgated according to the opinions of men, the Mosaic was according to the nature and custom of the people. But the Evangelic law leads on to justice, that is universal virtue, not civil only, but purgatory and even that of the soul already purged.

So in this way Ficino accommodates his exposition to his own conception of the virtue that leads to purification and immortality.

He is again establishing a parallelism between the religious thought of the Jews and Greeks as preparatory to but short of Evangelical truth, which does correspond to Paul's argumentation. But he finds in Plato and Socrates a critical vision of the fault of the Greeks which allows him to place them almost on the same level as St. Paul. They, like the Lord in the Gospel, criticised the Greeks' vindictive conception of justice, which was similar to the Jews' insistence on punishment by equality of injury, as may be seen in *Crito, Gorgias, The Republic* and Plato's letters.

When Paul speaks of the virtue of God, Ficino interprets this as meaning that the Evangel is the virtue of God, which is Christ, the Word of God, dressed in humanity, sanctified by the Spirit. Here he unites the word of man religiously uttered with inspiration of the Spirit, with the Divine word. This is a passage of especial importance because it gives an almost sacramental character not only to the Scriptures, but to the religious speech and oratory and prayer of man, so that, almost like the Eucharist, Ficino says, the language of the Gospel bears in itself the Divine Word, or Son.

> The Evangel also, either in meditation, or in voice, or in writing, is the Word of God, delivered indeed by the inspiring Spirit, but dressed in human meditation, or voice, or writing; moreover the linking in this way of the Divine Word with the body seems to have existed not only in the Apostles but in the Prophets from the beginning, so that the entire Holy Scriptures speaking of Christ through the Holy Spirit, is as if it is Christ Himself, living everywhere and breathing into all who ever reads, hears, meditates by a more powerful affection. Therefore Paul seems secretly to warn that we should approach the Evangel with the highest reverence, almost as if to the Eucharist.

It was one thing for God to condemn the Jews, who possessed the oracles and prophecies, for their perfidy, but it was more difficult to argue that the Gentiles were inexcusable. And as Paul speaks of the anger of God towards all, Ficino engages in a long explanation of how the Greeks possessed a far-reaching natural knowledge of God but worshipped Him wrongly. Moreover, they had been shown the truth by Plato in the seventh book of the *Republic.* 'God manifested Himself through a common knowledge of divine things, just as He revealed Himself to the Jews through the Prophets so He made Himself manifest to the Gentiles through the Philosophers.' (pp. 734-46)

But the Gentiles 'were a Law unto themselves', and knew by conscience all that was revealed by prophecy to the Jews [*Rom.* ii:14-16]. According to Ficino the Jews received a double law from Moses, the Decalogue, comprehensive and enduring forever, to which the Gentiles also are subject, and the ceremonial laws, valid up until the time of the Gospel, to which the Gentiles are not subject. . . . Manetti criticised the second law even before the time of Christ, and Ficino himself made the same distinction in *De religione Christiana.* The first part of the Mosaic Law corresponds to natural law, and only its works are subject to the Last Judgement. 'Yet no law, either natural, or written, has efficacy for justice and salvation, unless divine grace, beyond the intellect, moves the affections also and so moves them that the precepts of the law are obeyed for the sake of God Himself.' In all of this discussion, which may seem to fall into a kind of legalism, as indeed it also seems to do in Paul himself, if the context is removed, Ficino does not forget Paul's stress, and his own, on grace.

As to the Pauline statement that the Gentiles 'are a law unto themselves'—this to Ficino is conscience. 'Certainly that true light illumining all men coming into this world infuses the light of truth into the mind.' This light, 'like a judge, sits in the soul and takes the place of God in man.' Through it all knowledge of right and wrong, both in doing and not doing, of the good, of the virtuous, of the fitting, of the just is made known internally to man. All of this should lead as an innate light to the worship of God, just as in his ***Theologia platonica,*** he showed the Platonic reasons for thinking so.

Ficino's comments on conscience have a special importance, apart from the Pauline context, which he proceeds to develop here. Although the question of grace is not cast aside by Ficino, he, like certain of the humanists, placed a significantly greater emphasis on human moral autonomy as implemented through the conscience than on the external formalities. We need to hear him here at slightly greater length. The conscience acts as a judge within, weighing the evidence for and against the soul. It has of course a close connection with the human will, but it sits in judgement over the will both before and after action.

> Now indeed the power of the conscience considering the case for the soul and against the soul in the heart by an internal light, as though a judge holding court, produces witnesses, thoughts, and frequent memories, which sometimes accuse us, objecting by a certain reason against something badly done. . . . And so often by a mutual kind of alternation, while recognising that these are matters under judgement, the conscience is divided. But accusation and defence and judgement cannot take place without a certain knowledge of the law. Through these therefore it is confirmed that a moral law is impressed into our minds. Through this some more prudent and temperate men carry on a just life in a certain way without any written laws. Written laws seem to be additional armaments for compelling the imprudent and the unwise who neglect the internal laws.

There thus seems to be in Ficino, also, the rejection of the formal, external modes of solving the problems of conscience which . . . Bruni and Valla rejected in the procedures of the regular clergy. We shall see how this leads him to a further deprecation of the legalistic formalism of Judaism.

The action of conscience, he claims, meant in Paul's argument the preparation of the soul in the daily forum for the two days of judgement at the moment of death, and the final judgement, when a total decision was made. The daily forum of the conscience considers doubts and alternations take place. These present self-judgements, Paul means, prove that in the next life souls will be damned by their own judgement; just as sick eyes avoid light, sick souls flee into evil and hide in its darkness. As Plato said in the Laws, 'The wicked by their own inclination seek a place suitable to their merits, just as fire is born upwards by a certain levity and earth downwards.'

That Ficino does regard the Jews more severely than the Gentiles because the Jews sought to live by a formal morality seems to appear from a comment to Paul's succeeding verses on the arrogance of the Jews in seeking to teach the Gentiles when they sin themselves. Ficino says, 'and he generally means that they are some way worse than the Gentiles. And, as it seems to me, he interrogates them with a certain indignation and rejects them almost with a certain invective.' And to Paul's invective against both Jews and Gentiles in iii:9-20, Ficino says, 'Therefore both seem to be blamed by the Apostle but especially the Jews.' But because he believes so strongly in the natural knowledge of good and evil, he interprets Paul's 'for by the law is the knowledge of sin' [*Rom.* iii:20] to mean that with the law we sin in a certain more serious damnation, rather than that by means of the imposition of external constraints of law, whether Mosaic or political, man develops the inner awareness of conscience. Ficino's ethical and philosophical naturalism is prominent here, as would follow from his Platonism.

But Ficino's naturalism does not carry so far that he believes man can be saved by his innate knowledge of righteousness without the aid of grace. His great emphasis on the Incarnation, as we saw it above, should make that plain. So he again alludes to his previous discussion that original sin must be removed by some infinite power given by God. 'Not through the merit of legal works but through Christian faith is the Gentile made just and saved as likewise the Jew.' Grace meant that the Jews were equally guilty and the Gentiles equally saveable. There is one law of works, the Mosaic, which is intended for disposing of external actions rather than removing the perturbations of the soul. The other law of faith, the Evangelic law, not only disposes actions but moderates and removes the disturbances of the soul.

> Faith certainly living, and operating through charity, revealed in Christ, brings about perfect justice to whomever believes in it even if he was not involved in the works of the law. Nevertheless it is necessary that the believer perform legitimate works so that faith will not be judged dead without works.

Moreover,

> From external works civil and human justice is acquired, giving glory among men indeed, but nothing similar with God, because external glory does not make man worthy unless a great affection of faith and charity, given by divine grace, is added to it and precedes it.

Indeed, his anti-nomianism goes so far that he seems predisposed to think the Gentiles had the greater possibility of salvation, depending on grace alone.

Grace, also, contrary to some interpreters who, like Anders Nygren, seek to impute an *eros* derived from man's own soul, rather than a charity infused from above in Ficino's 'pagan' thinking, was clearly descended from God in Ficino's thought. Faith, to him, was not the cause of grace but a gift of grace from which follows charity, joy and glory.

> For if our charity towards God has its beginning from the charity itself of God towards us, truly what is also necessary to charity, namely faith and hope, proceed from the same divinity. . . . That moreover the instinct towards the divine in us proceeds from divinity itself is also confirmed because everything mortal connected with the soul in earthly things generates the contrary instinct in us so that the soul is not able to be detached from the mortal things except through divinity.

Charity is kindled in us from the flame of divine charity as fire from a spark. The Apostle proves the firmness of our hope by a double argument. In the present life it is a gift to us from the Holy Spirit; in the future by the death of Christ.

> Meanwhile he touches both kinds of charity, that in the sense that God loves us and that in which we love God, and he shows that both are impressed into our wills through the Holy Spirit. We, moreover, as we speak with our Thomas, expound as follows: the Holy Spirit, which is the love of the Father and the Son, is given to us in order to lead us to the participation in His love which certainly is His Holy Spirit, and by this participation we are made into lovers of God Himself. Now indeed from the fact that we love Him, we have the proof that He loves us. Not as though we first loved God, but because He first loved us.

I have quoted this passage more fully specifically because it so patently contradicts not only Nygren's distorted Lutheran desire to misinterpret Ficino but also because it seems to be the exact opposite of Walter Dress' statement in *Die Mystik des Marsilio Ficinos.* Dress says,

> Indeed the love which draws man into the realm of the Seraphim is not once thought of as the work of the Holy Spirit; on the contrary the Spirit rather follows the love-instinct. It is identified with the knowledge of God which comes out of love—thus it is apparent how little Ficino understood Christian ways of thinking.

We need not carry this very far. Dress claims that Ficino has no understanding of Paul and treats him as on the same level as a pagan philosopher. I would not, on the contrary, want to argue that Ficino was a forerunner of Luther, which might perhaps be what Nygren and Dress would demand of him. What does seem quite clear is that a careful reading of Paul's *Epistle* did give Ficino a certain confirmation of his previously developed ideas that among certain pagan *prisci theologi,* and particularly in Plato, there was a grasp of the religious [or metaphysical] limitations of the civil law prevailing in their times. Ficino by no means claimed that man could attain through philosophy alone to salvation, although salvation was the goal of his philosophy, at least the demonstration of the immortality of the soul.

He was, however, too deeply immersed in the medieval Christian tradition, and especially in Augustinianism, from which Luther also derived much, to leave himself subject to the charge of 'paganism'. Nor would he, on the other hand, exclude the great insights of the Greek philosophers, and particularly those of Plato and the Neoplatonists, from the work of divine providence. He was an enlightened Christian, and despite his efforts to develop a 'spiritual magic', not an obscurantist. He was, it is true, by no stretch of the imagination a Lutheran of the sort, at least, that the early twentieth century sometimes produced. But in his concentration on the nature of the human soul and its strivings, he also gave an emphasis to the subjective side of philosophy and of man, as Luther in his own quite different way was to do. These remarks are in fact quite irrelevant to my purposes and necessary only because certain scholars seem to have found that the reaching towards greater universality in man's intellectual and religious traditions was a great crime in the Renaissance, and have seen in Marsilio Ficino one of its principal perpetrators. (pp. 748-53)

Charles Trinkaus, "Accommodation and Separation in the Destiny of Mankind: Manetti, Ficino and Pico on Christians, Jews and Gentiles," in his In Our Image and Likeness: Humanity and Divinity in Italian Humanist Thought, Vol. 2, The University of Chicago Press, 1970, pp. 722-60.

ARDIS B. COLLINS   (essay date 1974)

[An American educator, Collins wrote The Secular Is Sacred: Platonism and Thomism in Marsilio Ficino's "Platonic Theology" *(1974). In the following excerpt from that work, she demonstrates the inseparability of philosophy from religion in* Platonic Theology.]

The preface to *Platonic Theology* introduces the work as a search for God which uses the Platonic philosophy as a guide. Ficino chooses this guide in order to make manifest the inseparability of philosophy and religion and the special place which man holds in God's revelation of himself. Platonism recognizes that every intellectual enterprise, even physics and mathematics, is en route to the divine. It seeks to make its way through the levels of knowing to the point at which it touches God himself, and it does this, not in order to know a fact, but in order to contemplate and venerate a wondrous reality. But if he would know God, man must know himself, for the way to God inevitably leads to this place where God is revealed in a special way. Ficino gives this as a reason for focusing his Platonic theology on the immortality of the soul. In some way, the essential orientation of philosophy toward God becomes manifest in man's everlasting destiny.

Ficino opens the work with an argument for human immortality which sets the tone of the whole enterprise. The argument begins with a dramatic description of man's plight. What does this life offer him? Restlessness, dissatisfaction, the continual frustration of his longing for fulfillment. His body is weak, his mind hindered by the darkness of the earthly prison. Can he hope for nothing more than this? If not, then his situation is worse than that of any other animal on earth. Why? Other animals are doomed to live out their destiny in this place. Why should the same destiny be more tragic for man? Because man shows by his chronic dissatisfaction and restlessness that something in himself transcends the limits of what life on this earth can afford. His desire points beyond moral existence. If this desire is doomed to frustration, then man is indeed a tragic figure. Since such an absurdity cannot come from the hand of God, man must be destined for a life which overcomes the darkness and frustrations of mortal existence. (p. 105)

The *Platonic Theology* begins and ends with this theme—man's desire for something beyond the limits of his life on this earth taken as evidence that fulfillment awaits him in a life which breaks through these limits. Between the two developments of the theme, Ficino establishes a necessary connection between the desire and its fulfillment by showing that the desire springs from human nature itself and is implicit in all those acts, acts of knowing and acts of will, which manifest the nature of man. This justification rests on an analysis of being, first as a principle of reality and second as the proper object of human knowledge and desire.

Ficino's metaphysics is founded on the concept of causation or efficacy. This is what the word 'act' means. But causation is not merely one event following another according to a regular pattern. To be a cause is to be the power in virtue of which something stands in reality. The cause explains the effect, it answers the question 'Why?', because the effect takes its being out of the cause. Thus, causation involves influence, a flowing of originating power into the effect, a coming forth of the effect from the depths of that power. That is why causation, being and presence are so intimately and inevitably linked in Ficino's thought. Nothing can get closer to a thing than its own reality; nothing is more intimate than being.

Hence, the power which is the source of being enters the innermost regions of its effect. The more complete the dependence of the effect on its cause, the more intimate and pervasive is the presence of the efficacious power in and throughout the effect.

Although we may come to understand causation first as the relation between one thing and another, causation as Ficino understands it is derived from the efficacy which is being itself. To cause is to put a thing into being and thus to touch its innermost reality. Being is the originating power by which a thing holds itself in reality and by which it gives reality to another. 'Act' at first means to produce something, to impose influence, to put into being. But more fundamentally it means the power to be. This is the significance of the principle that being is act and that absolute being is absolute perfection in itself and absolute power in relation to possible effects.

In the service of this concept of causation, Thomistic metaphysics finds a most suitable place. Indeed, it is difficult to determine whether Ficino adopted Aquinas' thought because it was most appropriate to his own basic metaphysical principle or learned the principle itself from his reading of Aquinas. Aquinas understands being in the context of creation. To create is to produce a thing from nothing. This means that the agent is so completely the cause of the effect that nothing in the effect falls beyond its influence. Creation is perfection in the order of causing. The intrinsic principle by which a thing stands forth out of nothing is the act of being, an efficacious power belonging to the thing itself. Out of this power or act, all that the thing is exists. Therefore, to create is to cause the effect in its being or to give to it that innermost power which permeates all that it is and puts it in being. Only God can be a creator. Only one being can be pure and absolute being or act or efficacy, the perfection of casual power. Only one can be the originator of a perfect productive act and an all-pervasive, intrinsic causal principle. This one is infinite; he is God.

On this basic metaphysical position stands Ficino's whole doctrine of divine presence. Presence and union are explained in terms of being—the presence of the soul to the body, the presence of God in all his creatures, his special presence in the soul of man. Nothing can be more intimate to a thing than its being; being is the power out of which its whole self stands; being is its innermost region. Since being is the proper effect of God, God is most intimately present to his creatures. As the origin of their being, he pervades and surrounds them. He touches even the actions which flow up from their own originating power.

As creator God is not only the first origin of all things, but also their measure and ideal. Following Aquinas, Ficino distinguishes the way in which being is possessed by God from the way in which it belongs to his effects. A contingent thing is by nature and definition the kind of thing which depends upon a cause. Its essence, therefore, is a receptive principle, a potency or capacity for being. The act which fulfills this capacity must be distinct from the essence itself, since actual existence belongs to the thing not by nature but in virtue of its relation to a cause. God, however, originates being, and hence must possess it in virtue of himself alone. He does not receive being, but is being itself.

Since being as being is causal, since its proper function is to posit perfection, accounting for whatever *is* rather than *is not*, pure being is absolute, complete and infinite perfection. It is actually and all in one all the perfection which can be. This is God. Other things, the things we know, are not such. Each of them in some way is not. Its limits, however, do not come from being, for that which it lacks is also being. Limitation is established by the potency which can receive being only within the confines of its limited essence.

A capacity or potency, however, is nothing at all unless it is a capacity in an actually existing thing. Being comes first after nothing; there is no reality whatsoever without existence. Hence, all that a thing is, it is in virtue of its being, and this is the principle which relates it to its cause. As the first origin of being, God causes the effect in every aspect. Even the receptive principle to which being is given and whose capacity limits being to a finite mode is produced by God in the production of being. Ultimately, the being of creatures receives its limits from the divine cause, who, by knowing himself, knows and produces both the perfections and the limits of his effects. Being itself reveals what creatures are and what they fail to be. Both the act of existing and the essence refer to God, the first establishing the likeness, the second the unlikeness between creatures and the creator. Thus, the fundamental reality of things is their relation to God, and this is true not only because in him they have their origin, but also because in him they have their ideal. The fundamental reality of things is being in a finite mode, being determined by a limitation which is not proper to being itself. Thus, God who is being itself, infinite and perfect, is the absolute version of what things are imperfectly and incompletely.

Because being points to God and because being permeates all that is, it is impossible for man to turn anywhere without turning toward God. Being attracts the human will under the aspect of goodness or perfection. Everything we seek, we seek as a good, and goodness itself is God who is being itself and absolute perfection. Being is present in all our knowledge and brings to light all else. Our knowledge of different things is a knowledge of being in different modes. In all our knowing, being is the light which reveals everything else. All that a thing is has reality from its act of being; so all that we know about it has intelligibility from this act. But behind even this, and shining through it, is God, who is being itself continuously and efficaciously present in and through the being of creatures whose source he is. That aspect of things which reveals them to the human intellect, that aspect which makes them accessible to human knowledge is that aspect in which their whole reality is a reference to God. The human mind is by nature directed toward being and through this toward God.

We must distinguish, however, between direction and achievement. A human being is a finite thing with finite powers. Since man must receive existence from a cause, his nature is not being itself, but a capacity for being which limits being to a finite mode. His natural powers, therefore, cannot encompass the infinity of God. The human mind knows God only through a finite manifestation. By this means, it can know that God exists, arguing from the contingency of things to the necessity of God. It can distinguish God from creatures, denying of him the limits and imperfections proper to beings which depend upon a cause. It can know the relation between creatures and God, knowing God as the cause or origin of creatures. But it cannot know God as he is in himself. It does, nevertheless, desire this knowledge, for in this alone does it fulfill its natural inclination. Knowledge is complete only when it grasps the object in its true identity. If man has any knowledge of God, he expresses in that knowledge the

desire to know him completely and definitively. And all knowledge leads to God, since all knowledge is directed toward being and being refers to God and is filled with his presence. God is being itself and truth itself, beyond the natural limits of the mind and yet the completion of the mind in its own line, for God is intelligibility *par excellence,* so perfectly knowable that he can join with the mind through direct and substantial union.

The inclination and inadequacy of human nature are brought together in desire. Desire is that ambiguous situation in which the object is both present and absent. The desire implies some sense of the object, for we cannot want something if we are totally unaware of it. Yet this sense of the object does not yield possession and satisfaction, but rather reveals that something is missing. Thus, desire reveals the object only enough to create dissatisfaction with the present state of affairs. Man is by nature one who knows God, for all his knowledge is a knowledge of being and this is implicitly a knowledge of God. But this knowledge is only enough to reveal that there is more. Thus, man is by nature one who seeks God, but cannot find him.

It is no wonder, then, that man is frustrated, unhappy, and dissatisfied with his lot. His very nature thrusts him far beyond the human. His desire for God is intense and unavoidable; it is a necessity of nature. Yet he cannot by his own power achieve the object, since the object is beyond his nature. But natural desire cannot be frustrated without involving the creator in contradiction and absurdity. Therefore, Ficino, following Aquinas, concludes that man is destined for a perfect union with God in which God will carry the human soul beyond its limitations revealing himself not through an image or representation, but through direct presence. Thus, man's dissatisfaction with his present condition and his desire for a more perfect contemplation manifests his immortality and justifies the claim that philosophy cannot be separated from religion. All human knowledge is a search for God and hence is necessarily related to the worship of its object.

But if Ficino is to complete his project, he must provide not only evidence for a conclusion, but also a guide to the object which the conclusion asserts. Since man cannot comprehend the object he seeks, there must be some other guiding principle which keeps him to the right direction in spite of his blindness. At this point, Ficino, following Plotinus, introduces the love theme. A love or longing for God leads man to his goal without comprehension to guide him, for man's love transcends the limits of his knowledge. Ficino interprets this in Thomistic terms. The love which carries man beyond the limits of his knowledge is that same natural desire which gives evidence of his immortality and makes philosophy inseparable from religion.

Since natural desire is directed toward being, man moves toward God by seeking to understand all things in the light of being. This understanding begins with a reflection on the universal and evaluative character of our knowledge, a character which reveals that we know not only things themselves, but also the norm in relation to which the many share in one exemplar and are measured in value. The measure according to which a thing can be so judged is the divine idea which governs its production as a certain finite approximation of being itself. Ficino concludes, therefore, that there are in the human mind innate representations of the divine ideas. These representations inform the mind in such a way as to make its knowledge an act revealing the relation between God and creatures.

Just as the divine being has a certain priority over the divine ideas, so knowledge in the common light of being surpasses knowledge in the light of various norms and principles. The divine being is the one *ratio* or intention which governs the creation of all the diverse things of the universe. Hence, our knowledge reaches the peak of its natural capacity when it knows and judges all things according to that one norm which includes all others in its all-encompassing unity.

Man makes his way to God under the impetus and guidance of a blinded love springing from the depths of his being. This is the vision which dominates the ***Platonic Theology.*** This is the vision which fulfills the purpose outlined in the preface. The doctrine of being which Ficino develops under the influence of Thomistic theology gives to this vision a philosophical justification for assuming that the desire will be fulfilled. Knowledge is directed toward being and being refers to God as its origin and measure. Implicit in every act of human knowledge is the desire for God, for he alone can complete its natural inclination. Thus, man's proper activity reveals a desire for God which belongs to the very nature of man. Man is defined as the desire to transcend himself. This is the reason why it is absurd to think that the desire could be frustrated.

Important as this justification is, however, Ficino's vision remains Platonic. Ficino claims that love or desire guides man to God even though the human mind cannot comprehend the object it seeks. This aspect of his position he does not take from Aquinas. It is inspired by neo-Platonism. And it is the central issue for the purpose proposed in the preface of the ***Platonic Theology.*** Aquinas points to the desire for an adequate knowledge of God as evidence for a conclusion—that man is destined to know God as he is in himself. Ficino presents the desire not just as evidence for a conclusion, but as a light which shows us the way to the divinity we do not comprehend. Man can find God if he but know himself. His own desire to transcend himself reveals his own immortality and the way to God for whom he is destined. Thus, Ficino writes a work of Platonic theology on the immortality of the soul. Hidden away in every man's search for truth and goodness is the desire for God. All intellectual endeavors are at bottom attempts to find God, no matter what the more explicit object may be. He who would separate philosophy from holy religion separates the pursuit of wisdom from the honor and reverence of it, for philosophy seeks what religion worships.

Thus, Thomistic metaphysics serves the purpose of the ***Platonic Theology*** by giving a metaphysical foundation to the neo-Platonic vision which dominates it. But Ficino tries to give not only a philosophical justification for the claim that philosophy cannot be separate from religion or out of harmony with theology, but also a practical example of the unity of philosophy and theology. His own work is an attempt to show that Platonic philosophy and Thomistic theology are congruent in their grasp of basic truths about God's relation to the world. According to Aquinas, all creatures have in their basic constitution two principles—essence, a receptive potency, and being, the act of this potency. This composite character marks things as dependent on God for their reality. Ficino relates to this the Platonic claims that all things under the first principle are composites of the infinite and the limit, of matter and form, of possible and actual being. In Platonic philosophy itself, these compositions do not have exactly the same meaning and none of the three signifies the relationship

between essence and being as it is explained by Aquinas. But when Ficino juxtaposes them and points to their harmony, he suppresses the differences and points only to what they have in common.

He follows a similar procedure when he presents Platonic and Thomistic accounts of the beatific union between man and God. In the Platonic account, he describes this union as a union with the one and the good above being. This is contrasted to our ordinary knowledge which has as its object the second god, the first being *(ens)*. Being *(esse)* properly means the act of being which is limited to a certain mode by the finite capacity of the essence to which it belongs. In the Thomistic account, beatific union is described as a union with being itself and truth itself; it is contrasted to our ordinary knowledge of beings and true things. Being *(esse)* properly means the act of existing, which according to itself is infinite in perfection and power, and can only be limited by something other than being, i.e. potency. It is obvious that these two accounts are not exactly the same. Ficino himself mentions this. He does not accept two gods, a first being who is different from and subordinate to the one and the good above being. He introduces the Thomistic account as a more direct route to the truth leaving behind the ambiguities of the philosophers. What he does not say, but must have known, is that his interpretation of the Platonic position on the divine names is more Thomistic than Platonic. The Platonists do not relate essence and being in such a way as to make essence the limiting principle. What Ficino shows by juxtaposing the Platonic and Thomistic accounts is that both Platonic philosophy and Thomistic theology distinguish between knowing the divine in a finite light, i.e. the common light of being, and knowing the origin of the light by a mystical union with the First.

Ficino also presents two views of the world in terms of efficacious power, one influenced by Proclus with its emphasis on unity, and one influenced by Aquinas with its emphasis on being. But Ficino makes no attempt to show that these are fundamentally the same. He moves through the hierarchy of the universe in virtue of the dependence which each level has on the higher one for unity and the power to act. On the highest level he identifies unity and efficacious power. But the efficacy of the First Unity, Truth, and Goodness is teleological; it moves as an end. Following this comes a discussion of primary and secondary causality in which dependence in action rests on dependence in being, and the primary cause is the originating cause of being and through this of action. Ficino relates these two discussions implicitly by juxtaposing arguments for divine omnipotence identifying unity in one and being in another with absolute efficacious power.

It is difficult to determine how much Ficino wishes to claim when he points to the likeness between Platonism and Thomism. He has on occasion called attention to their differences and expressed his preference for the theological explanation. The most plausible view is that he intends to bring out the fundamental insights which Platonism shares with Christian theology, but recognizes that Platonism grasps these truths only vaguely and implicitly. In this way, he shows that philosophy follows the same direction as Christian theology, and Christian theology is explicitly joined to religion.

In all his searching after knowledge, man pursues perfect union with all-perfect being, a pursuit guided by a love relentlessly drawing him on beyond the limits of his comprehension. Thus, the pursuit of wisdom is the search for God; philosophy cannot be philosophy without seeking him who is the object of religious veneration. Being is the object of secular knowledge; but being is holy since God dwells within it. The secular is sacred. (pp. 106-13)

Ardis B. Collins, in his The Secular Is Sacred: Platonism and Thomism in Marsilio Ficino's "Platonic Theology," *Martinus Nijhoff, 1974, 223 p.*

MICHAEL J. B. ALLEN   (essay date 1975)

[*Allen is an English educator and the author of several studies, including the critical edition and translation* Marsilio Ficino: The "Philebus" Commentary *(1975) and* Marsilio Ficino and the Phaedran Charioteer *(1981). In the following excerpt from his introduction to the former work, Allen proposes the historical significance of Ficino's commentary on Plato's* Philebus *and touches on its contents.*]

[Marsilio Ficino's ***Philebus Commentary***] has received some notice from modern scholars. Giuseppe Saitta talks of "the extremely beautiful commentary on the *Philebus* in which the superiority of the good over the beautiful is vigorously affirmed. All beauty is good, but not all good is beautiful: this is the Platonic concept that Ficino is continually attempting to illustrate in his own way. However, a common bond exists between the good and the beautiful, and this is supplied by the appetite . . . etc." Later he talks of the "magnificent commentary on the *Philebus*" in which Ficino "had explicitly identified the universal act with the good." Paul Kristeller has frequently referred to it and Michele Schiavone has used it as a whipping boy while devoting careful attention to certain theses. It would be interesting to speculate on the influence the commentary has had in subsequent centuries; but, as Saitta says, Ficino was often robbed but rarely acknowledged. Much more work has to be done on specific ideas and theories in Ficino and Renaissance philosophy in general before anything can be said with accuracy about the influence of a particular commentary and this is true even of the *Symposium* commentary.

What we do know, however, is that the *Philebus,* more perhaps than any other Platonic dialogue, including the *Symposium,* seems to have dominated the early days of the Platonic revival, and it is important we take note of its popularity if we want to understand the genesis of Florentine Platonism. It was through the *Philebus* that the newly revived interest in Plato began to broaden into what was later to become a European movement. (p. 15)

Given the humanists' particular concern with ethical problems and that the standard topic of classical ethics was happiness or the supreme good for man, the designated theme of the *Philebus,* it was inevitable a humanist would write directly on the *Philebus* once it was made available. This humanist was to be Ficino himself. However, Saitta is not strictly correct when he says "the ethical interest in Ficino dominates over the speculative one." Although man occupies a central position in Ficino's thinking, Ficino has, as Kristeller observes, no real system of ethics; for in the Renaissance " . . . we do not find any system of ethics based primarily on Plato, as so many were on Aristotle. . . . The leading Platonists of the Renaissance . . . were interested in questions of metaphysics and cosmology rather than of ethics." This is mainly because the perfection of the soul " . . . is entirely bound up with its spiritual ascent and with the contemplative attitude." As in the case of the ancient Neoplatonists, Ficino's ethical

ideas are part and parcel of a metaphysical framework: as a humanist Ficino would be drawn towards an ethical dialogue, but as a Platonist he would be drawn towards it for metaphysical reasons.

Aristotle's *Ethics* had long been the classical source for ethical studies. In the thirteenth and fourteenth centuries we find not only the great editions and translations of Grosseteste, William of Moerbeke and Gerard of Cremona but also the extended commentaries of such eminent scholastics as St. Albertus Magnus, Giles of Rome, St. Thomas Aquinas and many others. But in the fifteenth century, after Bruni's new, controversial translation and Argyropoulos' lectures too had again stimulated interest in the *Ethics,* the commentaries began to shift their emphasis. In Eugenio Garin's words: "They . . . ceased to interpret this work in the narrow terms of social and political problems and of man seen as a political animal. They interpreted the *Nicomachean Ethics* as a final exaltation of the contemplative and separated intellect." There is much resulting controversy over the nature of the separation and the relationship between the soul's natural and supernatural powers, and the book becomes a touchstone in the battle with Latin Averroism. Many eminent thinkers were, therefore, involved in restating and reassessing the *Ethics*' arguments throughout the period, including Bruni, Donato Acciaiuoli, Ermolao Barbaro, Filelfo, Lefèvre D'Étaples, and Philip Melanchthon. But, since the principal Aristotelians were primarily interested in their master's ethical writings, their opponents were forced to become familiar with them too. Ficino himself had studied under a dedicated Aristotelian (Nicolò Tignosi, who had taught theoretical medicine and natural philosophy at the Studio in Florence) and he knew his Aristotle well, valuing him in particular for his work in logic and physics. In the May of 1455 he had copied out Bruni's translation of the *Ethics* and written his own notes in the margin; and, according to Eugenio Garin, his notes are even to be found in a copy of the first edition of Acciaiuoli's commentary on the *Ethics* (which was based on Argyropoulos' earlier lectures).

When Ficino started to write on the *Philebus,* he aimed to do three things: first, to counter the naturalist and activist ethics that had stemmed from the *Ethics*' commentators with new arguments drawn from Plato's counterpart to the *Ethics;* second, to reconcile and synthesize the two masters like the Neoplatonists before him. The first meant proving Aristotle had been betrayed by his commentators, the Alexandrists and Averroists; the second that he and Plato were not in real conflict, but concerned, rather, with different levels of moral experience (hence the *Philebus* was to subsume not supersede the *Ethics*—the appearance of the theory of the mean in both works was merely the most obvious instance of what Ficino saw as the absence of any "real conflict"). Third, apart from the two ethical aims there was a metaphysical aim. Ficino's own city had seen a prolonged controversy, in which the *Ethics* had played a central role, between the Aristotelians and the Platonists on the subject of Plato's Ideas. The *Philebus* lectures were Ficino's own initial contribution to the controversy, so he obviously felt the dialogue was specially suited to combat Aristotle's attack on Plato's metaphysics. (pp. 15-17)

Initially the commentary confronts us as a medieval work. Kristeller says of Ficino, "the strongly medieval, scholastic character which we notice in his works . . . consists not so much in specific philosophical ideas, but rather in the terminology and in the general method of arguing." But he goes on to say this scholastic element "was not due to an extensive reading of the scholastic authors of the twelfth and thirteenth centuries, but rather to the training which Ficino must have had in the current Aristotelianism of the schools as a student in the University of Florence." Kristeller maintains Ficino did not have any extensive firsthand knowledge of the medieval philosophers with the notable exception of Aquinas, but was able "to build his Platonism on the method and terminology of late medieval Aristotelianism." The result is daunting: the reader is confronted with chains of syllogistic reasoning which have the appearance of being tightly organized and utterly logical. But the logic frequently begs the very questions it is attempting to answer; in this it is reminiscent of much medieval philosophy, the texture of which more nearly resembles a row of mental walnuts than it does a series of Euclidean proofs.

The commentary is eclectic in its approach. This is typical not only of the Renaissance but of most medieval philosophy and, indeed, of patristic and Neoplatonic thinking. Ficino was not trying to be original; he was trying to synthesize, as Charles Trinkaus has recently reemphasized. Besides the many quotations and references to other Platonic dialogues in the commentary, there are references to other ancient authors, real and fictive, and to a few medieval ones; but Ficino rarely cites the specific works he is referring to. In addition to the acknowledged references, there are some which are unacknowledged. Most notable are the extensive borrowings from Aquinas in several of the chapters, which are in paraphrase rather than direct quotation. Marcel suggests in his new edition of the *Platonic Theology* that Ficino habitually reduced his quotations to the essential meaning and adapted them to his own context. Perhaps Ficino assumed some of his allusions were too familiar to need acknowledgment, but at times it seems as if he were deliberately concealing his authorities. Marcel observes: "It is almost as if he wanted to appropriate their thinking or [wanted] to constrain his readers to admit principles or arguments which they would have refused to examine on principle [a priori] if they had known the source." Ficino often groups his references by school and these group references are frequently taken *en masse* from later authorities: the list of ancient physicists and moralists, for example, he could have derived from Diogenes Laertius or Aristotle or Cicero or Augustine or Lactantius or Aquinas or from half a dozen medieval or contemporary sources. (pp. 22-3)

Structurally the commentary is confusing because it is cumulative rather than systematic in its approach. While it purports to follow the order of the *Philebus* itself . . . the *Philebus,* which it must be remembered is itself a multifaceted work, simply serves as the starting point for trains of thought which bear no organized relationship to it. While individual sections or paragraphs are systematic in their construction, the commentary itself follows a much more leisurely plan, gradually unfolding the central propositions of Ficino's metaphysics and epistemology with many repetitions and digressions (and in one instance a whole proof is repeated word for word). But the absence of structural rigour does not prescind from the philosophical unity of Ficino's system as a whole, nor does it detract from the ferocious rigour Ficino often applies to the individual parts. . . . The cumulative approach can make for difficulties. Before any one section can be understood, it is often necessary to understand the metaphysical principle involved. Since, in Trinkaus' words, Ficino's philos-

ophy is "to a very great extent a seamless garment," single propositions tend to stand or fall on the truth or adequacy of a few a priori assumptions. But this has one overwhelming advantage: the commentary is more than a series of scholarly notes for it explores propositions with endless ramifications—something it shares with other Neoplatonic and scholastic commentaries derivative in appearance but often containing truly original insights.

However, despite its medieval tone and texture, the *Philebus* commentary is a Renaissance document and in it we can hear echoes of numerous Renaissance themes and preoccupations. There are passages of interest to historians concerned with: the "dignity of man" theme; educational theory; aesthetics; psychology; the debate over the merits of the active or contemplative lives; the concepts of the intellect, the will and freedom; Pelagianism; Epicureanism; Averroism; Thomism; the inception of the idea of natural religion; iconography and myth, etc. Although the commentary is a piece of formal philosophical writing, it does spring directly from the imaginative and intellectual worlds of the humanists and reflects many of their obsessions. There are several suggestions, even, that it is more closely interwoven with Renaissance Hermetism and occultism than might appear feasible from its uncompromising facade. (pp. 24-5)

The *Philebus* commentary is also the work of the greatest Christian rationalist of the Renaissance. In his preface to the *Concerning the Christian Religion* Ficino talks of the intelligence and the will as the soul's two wings enabling it to fly back towards its home: "the intelligence illuminates the will" and "the will embraces the intelligence" and so philosophy, the activity of the intelligence, being a gift from God must be used to defend religion. In a letter to Pico della Mirandola, his "brother philosopher," he refers to Platonism (which for him is synonymous with philosophy) as the way which leads men to Christianity; it is the necessary first step which takes the unbeliever towards the concept of a natural religion and thence towards Christianity itself.

For a Christian the intelligence can be seen from two angles: either it is moved naturally by God towards the apprehension of a truth which the will does not yet believe in; or it is moved supernaturally towards the defense of a truth which the will already believes in. Ficino is writing in order to lead men towards faith: hence his insistence that "the intelligence illuminates the will" and his subordination here of the will to the intelligence, an aspect we shall return to. Consequently, certain fundamental Christian ideas associated with the will are absent: the fall of man and his consequent need for atonement and grace are never mentioned and the concept of sin is subsumed into that of error. Nevertheless, the Christian context is there. As Kristeller says, "the Platonic Academy of Florence was Christian in its tendency and a center of religious as well as of philosophical and of literary importance." More particularly, the *Philebus* lectures took place in a church and were part of a conscious programme to harness the "divine Plato" to Christianity. So the emphasis on the withdrawn, contemplative life in the lectures must have had religious—perhaps even specifically Augustinian—implications for Ficino's contemporaries. (pp. 25-6)

Michael J. B. Allen, in an introduction to The "Philebus" Commentary *by Marsilio Ficino, edited and translated by Michael J. B. Allen, University of California Press, 1975, pp. 1-58.*

JOHN WARDEN (essay date 1982)

[*Warden is an English educator and author. In the following excerpt, he details the philosophical, political, and aesthetic importance of the Orpheus myth to Ficino's thought.*]

Orpheus' voice and lyre are not only a metaphor to describe Ficino's teaching. They are meant literally too. As Corsi tells us in his biography, 'He set forth the hymns of Orpheus and sang them to the lyre in the ancient manner with incredible sweetness, so people say.' . . . Johannes Pannonius says much the same: 'You restored to the light the ancient sound of the lyre and the style of singing and the Orphic songs which had previously been consigned to oblivion.' . . . Cosimo de' Medici finishes a letter of invitation with the words: 'Farewell. And do not forget your Orphic lyre when you come.'(pp. 86-7)

There can be no doubt then that Ficino played an 'Orphic' lyre, emblazoned with a picture of Orpheus; and that as he played he sang 'antiquo more' the Hymns of Orpheus. What is more difficult to decide is how seriously all this should be taken. Is it an important ingredient in Ficino's philosophy, or is it mere metaphor and play? Poliziano . . . is nicknamed Hercules by Ficino for his skill at slaying the monsters of textual corruption. Landino is Amphion. It is hard to re-create the atmosphere of the Academy at Careggi, but the intense interest in and concern about man's soul and destiny was accompanied by a large ingredient of make-believe. The aesthetic and imaginative qualities of classical mythology provided a sense of 'detachment and joy'; but at the same time . . . the content of the myths was treated seriously not simply as allegory, but as a set of symbols which if correctly read offered an understanding of higher levels of reality. So too the festivals and hymn-singing—on one side a 'jeu erudit,' on the other a seriously intended religious ritual. So that our question was wrongly formulated—metaphor and play were taken very seriously by the Florentine Neoplatonists. At the most profound level the activities of the Academy were 'a game of symbols and forms' [André Chastel, *Marsile Ficin,* p. 74]. (p. 87)

Why was Orpheus so important to Ficino? Before attempting an answer we must be sure what we are trying to account for. The presence of references to and quotations from Orphic teaching in Ficino should occasion no surprise. One important ingredient in the unique hotchpotch that makes up Ficino's philosophy is of course the writings of the Greek Neoplatonists in general and Proclus in particular. It became an orthodoxy to the Neoplatonists that Plato was drawing on Orpheus in developing his own philosophy. (pp. 88-9)

But it is the whole figure of Orpheus, three-dimensional and real, not just his theoretical teaching, that is drawn into Ficino's thought. And this I believe is something one does not find in Proclus or in the later eastern Neoplatonic tradition. For the Byzantine artist the image is justified in that it raises the mind to God; for the Renaissance artist the image is also enjoyed and explored for its own sake. Myth grows from allegory into symbol, and as it grows it puts on flesh. One can see the process occurring by comparing the abstract moral allegorizing of Landino with the concreteness and plasticity of Poliziano, for whom the illustrative moment has its own autonomy, its own right to exist and be cherished [Chastel, *Marsile Ficin,* p. 144]. One can only guess how much is owed to Gemisto Pletho who brought his baggage of Byzantine Neoplatonism to Italy by way of Islam and Zoroastrianism,

giving it a new exoticism and a new paganism [B. Kieszkowski, *Studi sul Platonismo del Rinascimento in Italia* (1936), Chap. 2; Abbé R. Marcel, 'Le Platonisme de Petrarche à Léon l'Hebren,' *Congrès de Tours et Poitiers* (1954), p. 315; M. F. Masai, 'Le Platonisme italien et la problème des influences byzantins,' ibid. 321; P. O. Kristeller, *The Philosophy of Marsilio Ficino* (1954), p. 15; 'The Scholastic Background of Marsilio Ficino,' p. 259; D. P. Walker, 'Orpheus the Theologian,' p. 107ff.; Chastel, 'Le Platonisme et les arts à la Renaissance' (1954), p. 392 and *Marsile Ficin,* p. 9f.]. The gods of antiquity acquire again a significance as powers within the universe; nothing perhaps that was not already present in the Henads of Proclus, but introduced afresh into a Christian context. More important, however, is the continuity of the iconographic tradition through the western Middle Ages and its meeting with the rediscovery of ancient art. However much he is sucked bloodless by the allegory that spreads from Boethius and Fulgentius, Orpheus remains a person in the illustration of the manuscripts of the *De consolatione* or of *Ovide moralisé.* [J. B. Friedman, *Orpheus in the Middle Ages* (1970), Chap. v passim; Pierre Courcelle, *La Consolation de philosophie dans la tradition littéraire* (1967), p. 190f. and plates 107 and 108.2; Chastel, *Marsile Ficin,* p. 136ff.]. Pletho's use of pagan mythology, like his hymn-singing, is self-conscious and intellectual: for Ficino and his companions at Careggi it is rather a mixture of aesthetic delight and simple piety.

Perhaps the most familiar image of Orpheus to the Italian Renaissance is that of Orpheus the civilizer. The *locus classicus* is Horace *Ars Poetica* 391ff: Orpheus the first poet is the first to soften the hearts of the 'stony and beastly people' and set them on the path to civilization. His instrument is his eloquence (for Boccaccio the lyre is 'oratoria facultas'). (pp. 89-90)

This is a social and political programme. Orpheus is the statesman or legislator who with his *dolce parlare* brings men to live together in communities. This civil life is the essence of *humanitas*—man is a political being. In Ficino the emphasis is rather metaphysical and moral. The skillful speaker is replaced by the artist, who looks within himself to discover the harmony of the cosmos, and by artistry leads others to an understanding and beyond. (p. 90)

What is the song he sings? Not far behind Orpheus the civilizer comes Orpheus the theologian. Here we are dealing with a figure of a different order, not a mythical hero, redefined by allegory, but a historical personage (for such he undoubtedly was to the *quattrocento*), religious teacher, and author of a number of works (especially the *Rhapsodic Theogony,* the *Argonautica,* and the *Hymns*) which had a great influence on the period in general and on Ficino in particular. . . . Orpheus is the go-between in the liaison between Hebrew and Greek. The results of this doctrine are far-reaching: pagan religion is not something to be shunned and feared, but a source of truth, a partial evolution. Religion is treated not as a revelation, but as a natural evolutionary phenomenon depending for its development on a few individuals of superior knowledge and will-power. Christianity is a continuation of ancient theological thought. Whether it marks the end-point is a question never fully answered [Kieszkowski, pp. 84, 88]. (p. 91)

Orpheus, of course, is not just *theologus* but *theologus poeta.* He is the first poet to celebrate the mysterious principles that underlie the universe. It is because he is a poet, because he has skill and inspiration, that he is able to understand and is privileged to tell of these mysteries. He . . . is possessed with the *furor divinus.* He is an artist and this world, this 'bel tempio,' is a work of art; he has privileged access to its secrets and to the mind of its architect. . . .

The lyre, given, as Gafurio tells us, to Orpheus by Mercury and by Orpheus to Pythagoras, confers the divine right, like the sceptre of Agamemnon. It represents the harmony of the spheres, its seven strings standing for seven planets. And it is more than a symbol; mathematically the intervals of the Orphic lyre are the structural basis of the entire visible universe [Chastel, *Marsile Ficin,* p. 100]. and of the human soul. It offers an assurance on the relationship between microcosm and macrocosm. Man by exploring his own interior space finds a structure in the microcosm identical with that of the macrocosm. He finds the lyre within himself and 'explicates' it, as Cusanus put it. (p. 93)

For Ficino there are two types of music. First there is the divine music, which is itself divisible into two—the music in the mind of God and the music of the spheres. And then there are the *imagines* of the divine music in the human soul. This reflection of the divine music is expressed in various forms and at various levels—as reason, imagination, discourse, song, instrumental playing, and dance. 'We see then that the music of the soul gradually spreads to all the limbs of the body. And it is this that orators, poets, painters, sculptors and architects express in their works.' . . . It is not only the musicians in the narrow sense but all the artists who express this divine music of the soul.

God granted us these two types of music 'so that through the former [ie, the divine] we might imitate God himself in our thought and feelings [music is thus a paradigm of the mind of God], and through the latter we should celebrate the name of God for ever with hymns and instrumental music.' . . .

This then is the most obvious explanation for Ficino's own hymn-singing. But if we examine his analysis of the physical basis of music we can begin to understand what he thought was the precise effect of these hymns of praise. In his letter **De musica** to Canisianus he describes how singing and instrumental music start from the mind, the imagination, and the heart (of the player) and are translated into movements and controlled disturbances of the air; these impulses strike the *spiritus* of the listener, being itself composed of air. The *spiritus* is the *nodus* of soul and body—the meeting-point of the physical and the psychological. Thus the impulses can easily be translated back into psychological terms and reach the imagination, heart, and innermost mind of the listener. (p. 94)

What exactly is the *spiritus*? The simplest answer is found at **Convivium** 6.6. We consist of three parts, *anima, spiritus,* and *corpus. Anima* and *corpus* being very different in nature are held together by *spiritus,* which is 'a very fine and transparent vapour, generated from the subtlest part of the blood through the heat of the heart.' . . . It acts as a go-between transmitting the *animae vires* to the body, and transforming sense-experience into the purer perceptions of the imagination. As it is 'an airy vapour from the blood' . . . it is tempered and nourished 'by scents and sounds and songs that consist of air.' . . . (pp. 94-5)

What we have been talking of so far is the *spiritus humanus,* that which links the human body and soul. But there is also a *spiritus mundanus,* which 'interconnects the sublunary

world with the translunary' [E. Panofsky, *Studies in Iconology* (1939), p. 136]. *Spiritus* in its fullest sense is 'a divine influx, flowing from God, penetrating through the heavens, descending through the elements and finishing up in lower nature.' . . . It is 'an uninterrupted current of supernatural energy [which] flows from above to below and reverts from below to above, thus forming a *"circuitus spiritualis"*' [Panofsky, p. 132].

The musician plugs into this current. The aim of his hymns is to bring the *spiritus* of man into accord with the *spiritus mundi;* or more particularly to make man accessible to the *influence* of the *spiritus* of a particular astral body. This is brought about in the first instance by our own predisposition, by an act of love; and only then by the magical techniques of song, light, and scent. It is important that the music, perfume, etc be appropriate to the deity being invoked. 'Our *spiritus* is in conformity with the rays of the heavenly *spiritus,* which penetrates everything either secretly or obviously. It shows a far greater kinship when we have a strong desire for that life and are seeking a benefit that is consistent with it, and thus transfer our own *spiritus* into its rays by means of love, particularly if we make use of song and light and the perfume appropriate to the deity like the hymns that Orpheus consecrated to the cosmic deities . . . ' Ficino then gives a list of deities and the appropriate scents. 'For the *spiritus,* once it has been made more akin to the deity by emotional disposition, song, perfume, and light, draws a richer influence from it.' (p. 95)

Orpheus the self-conscious artist. The phrase brings together two themes which are of great importance for Ficino and his time. The notion of the dignity of man, which gets its best-known treatment from Pico della Mirandola, is already familiar to classical antiquity. 'There are many marvels,' says the Chorus of Sophocles' *Antigone,* 'but nothing is more marvellous than man.' And some 600 years later a similar sentiment is expressed in the Chaldaean Oracles: 'O man, invention of nature at her boldest.' . . . [Chastel, *Marsile Ficin,* p. 59ff.]. In the Hermetic writings there is a significant difference of emphasis. It is not so much man as a creation who is held up for our attention, but man the creator. Man's special status stems from the intermediary position of the human soul which can range from the bestial to the divine. 'Man is a great miracle, a creature fit to be worshipped and honoured. For he crosses over to the nature of a god, as though he were himself a god . . . God composed him out of both natures, divine and mortal, and thus it was arranged through the will of God that the constitution of man was superior even to that of the gods.' . . . And his privileges are manifested in his power to create; it is as 'artifex' that he is 'deus in terris.' The startling conclusion is reached that man shows these powers to the highest degree in the creation of the gods, ie, the bringing alive of statues. 'Just as the Lord and Father made the eternal gods so that they should both be like him, so let mankind fashion its gods in the likeness of its own face.' . . . Pico is not the first to present a strange and disconcerting mixture of humanism and occultism. Man's creative powers are shown best in the practice of theurgic magic.

Ficino is clearly drawing directly on this tradition. In Book 14 of the **Theologia Platonica** he cites both the passages from the oracles (Chapter 1) and from the *Asclepius* ('magnum miraculum' in Chapter 3). In Book 13, Chapter 3, where his object is to prove the immortality of the soul by showing the extent of its power, he deals at length with the notion of man the 'artifex.' 'It is a remarkable thing that the human arts fashion on their own whatever nature herself fashions, as though we were not the servants of nature but her rivals.' . . . Man controls the elements and the other animals that inhabit the world; in this respect, 'vicem gerit dei' (he stands in for God). But more than this, he creates for the pleasure of creation and for the delight in sense experience. 'Hence proceeds the unspeakable variety of pleasures which bring delight to the five bodily senses, pleasures which we ourselves devise by our own genius.' . . . (This aesthetic delight in the senses is something new that the Florentines gave to Neoplatonism; one cannot imagine Plotinus, for all his sense of beauty, saying anything like this.) This creativity manifests itself in textiles, paintings, sculptures, buildings, artistic activities which may not in themselves be functional or useful, or even pleasant; but they satisfy man's aesthetic need to create. Similarly 'musicae consonantia . . . oratorum facundia,' 'poetarumque furores' are activities we pursue even though they bring no material benefit, but are often hurtful ('sed plurimum noxiae'). We are imitating the activities of God the creator. We are equipped with an 'artifex interior' (the soul) which uses as its instruments the tongue and the hand. We are doing in our own way what God is doing: 'So our mind conceives within itself by thought as many things as God creates in the universe by thought. Just so many things does it express in the air by speaking, does it write with a pen on paper, does it fashion in matter by manufacturing. (pp. 99-100)

If we ask how this can be so, how the mind can conceive what does not already exist in nature, the answer is that everything that is possible, that has potential existence, already exists in the infinite mind of God. Now the human mind has the capacity to conceive possibilities that do not exist. It can proceed to infinity. . . . The mind in fact can conceive something 'which, as possible, is already real in God' [Kristeller, p. 53ff.]. Man the artist follows in the footsteps of God the artist. Man 'prolongs the divine act' [Chastel, *Marsile Ficin,* p. 66]. The motive in both cases is aesthetic.

Creation starts from within. 'Begin by considering thyself.' This emphasis on the inner life of man, on the importance of the will as a dynamic and creative force, is common in the Renaissance writers who precede Ficino, and of course owes much to St Augustine. For Petrarch 'man's inner life is a continual process of self-creation.' Orpheus-like, man through his studies softens his own spirit and tempers his own wrath. . . . We must start from within ourselves, . . . says Traversari; for within ourselves, . . . we will find the divine [A. Traversari, *Epistolae* 13.526, ed. Méhus (1759), II. 639]. 'The soul,' says Ficino, 'on its own through its own activity continually fashions itself and completes itself by the continual exercise of the intellect and the will.' . . . (pp. 100-01)

And lastly and above all, Orpheus the lover and prophet of love. Love is of course the overriding concept in the system of Ficino. It explains the relationship between the different levels of reality, between microcosm and macrocosm, between man and his fellows, between man and God. (p. 101)

Ficino's love is a composite of Plato's sublimated sexual love, of Aristotle's 'scala naturae' yearning for the Prime Mover, of Plotinus' lonely relationship with the One, of the Christian love of God for man and man for God. There are important additional ingredients: an emphasis on friendship and the social role of love from Aristotle and the Stoics, an elegiac quality from the Stilnuovisti and Petrarch [Kristeller, p. 287]. Orpheus as civilizer brings about a state of *humanitas,* which is defined as man's love for his fellows; Orpheus as theologian asserts the primacy of love as a cosmic force, as that which brings about creation, and thus acts as a go-between for Christian and Neoplatonist; as musician and artist he brings about a state of love by imposing order and shape; as one who loves and suffers he is privileged to be filled with the *furor amatorius* which leads the mind beyond understanding to the vision of divine beauty and to a state of joy. (pp. 102-03)

Orpheus has helped Ficino in many ways: to bridge the gap between pagan and Christian; to rescue Neoplatonic monism and restate it in Christian terms; to redefine the relationship between the first principle and the created world; to combine a sense of delight in the beauty of this world with an aspiration for the beauty that lies beyond; to be aware of both the joys and sadness of existence, its permanence and its evanescence [N. A. Robb, *Neoplatonism in the Italian Renaissance* (1935), p. 111]. Above all he enables Ficino to hold the balance between the ordered and stable cosmos of antiquity and the Middle Ages, and the new dynamic concept of man, the restless creator, Proteus and Chameleon [Kristeller, p. 184], ranging at will and creating his own space. He has contributed to this moment of equilibrium between two worlds.

And what has Ficino done for Orpheus? If the Middle Ages subjected him to *sparagmos,* Ficino has found his heart and brought him back to life—the musician, magician, and hierophant that he was in the beginning. (p. 103)

John Warden, "Orpheus and Ficino," in Orpheus: The Metamorphoses of a Myth, *edited by John Warden, University of Toronto Press, 1982, pp. 85-110.*

CHARLES TRINKAUS   (essay date 1986)

[*In the following excerpt, Trinkaus links Ficino's notions of human divinity and immortality with his vision of a comprehensive ideal of self-sufficiency.*]

A generation and a half ago no topic aroused a more intense interest among students of early European culture than the thesis of Max Weber deriving what he called *Der Geist der Kapitalismus* from the Protestant ethic. The inculcation of a routinized, goalless mode of behaviour by the Lutheran and Calvinistic injunctions to please God in one's calling and to prove one's election by a strict adherence to the rules of morality gave to the modern world a docile population of spiritless robots. Weber, elaborating on the earlier Marxian notion of alienated labour, repudiated the more ample vision of Jacob Burckhardt. Burckhardt, let us recall, hailed the birth of the self-conscious individualism in the Renaissance as the quality rendering Italians the 'first-born among the sons of modern Europe.' Burckhardt's conception of Renaissance individualism stressed the element of self-conscious search for the understanding of man and the universe and the uninhibited pursuit of the secular goals of power, fame, and wealth. The ideal of human autonomy is a post-Burckhardtian conception, fueled by Nietzsche's amplifications of Burckhardt, and developed, especially in the 1930s and 1940s, as a counter to the gloomy forebodings of Marx, Weber, and others. It is the vision of man commanding his environment with the resources of science, creating his own rules of personal behaviour, free from the restrictions imposed by theologians, and governing his relationships with his fellows in an open, psychically informed, and mutually tolerant discourse.

Certain ingredients of this ideal did indeed exist during the Renaissance. But the ideal was formulated ordinarily with a deep awareness of the limitations that God, the physical universe, and the human polity placed upon it. The theme of the dignity and excellence of man, derived though it was from a patristic and mediaeval Christian tradition, was the principal medium through which the status and powers of man in relation to divinity, cosmos, and polity were treated in a focused way. This occurred in works of this genre by Petrarch, Fazio, Manetti, Brandolini and other humanists, and was usurped by Pico as a fitting introduction and invitation to debate his *Conclusiones*. Other humanists, in a less formally thematic way, carried the assertion of human self-direction farther and more effectively—certainly Coluccio Salutati, Lorenzo Valla, Benedetto Morandi, and in political thinking Leonardo Bruni among them. It will be my claim in this paper that the philosopher and physician, Marsilio Ficino, developed the fullest and most far-reaching exposition of the ideal of human autonomy in the Renaissance, and that this was certainly one of the most important contributions of his philosophy to the future of human culture, alongside his great work of textual recovery and dissemination of Platonism and Neoplatonism.

Ficino attempted in his **Theologia Platonica** to demonstrate the divinity and immortality of man. What better way to do this than by showing how man, created in God's image and likeness, attained remarkable powers over himself and his natural environment, and in shaping his relations with his fellow men, provided he did not turn against and repudiate the very divinity within his soul? What better way of demonstrating man's dignity and autonomy than by proving his divinity and his immortality?

Just as Lorenzo Valla asserted that man was superior to the animals by his possession of immortality, so Ficino develops this theme of man's godlikeness in a variety of ways. Since God created the world by the very act of knowing the world, He does not despise man, one of whose chief characteristics is intelligence.

> Indeed if God does not in any way neglect the least parts of the world, certainly He will not despise mankind, which is such a precious part of the world that it is the mean between temporal and eternal things, since it receives the eternal and commands the temporal. So close to God is this His work that, sliding itself into the secrets of the divine mind, it actually knows the order of the world. Understanding of the world order is more excellent even than that order, since this kind of order is created and ruled through intelligence.

Critical for Ficino's conception of human autonomy is man's use of intelligence for shaping the world of nature. God, whose trinitarian nature of infinite power, absolute intelligence, and most blessed will is stressed, is the most perfect author who,

> does all things in that kind of action which is most perfect. Thus He is not led to action by a necessity of nature but rather by a certain purpose of the will. For what is done by freedom of the will is more excellent than what is dragged into action by a necessary instinct of nature. That action is happiest in which the author is in command of his own actions, so that he prescribes the manner, measure, and end of acting.

Such freedom and control of action is certainly the quality

of autonomy, here applied to God, but intended to describe man as well, since this statement is followed in his **Disputatio contra Iudicium Astrologorum** by a demonstration that God intended man so to act. 'If God is pleased with Himself, if He loves Himself, certainly He cherishes His own images [men] and His works. The smith loves his own works which he makes from external material.'

In order for man to act freely and to operate on nature, it becomes necessary for Ficino to show two things: that man's freedom is not restricted by divine foreknowledge, and that man's actions are not determinate as are the movements of nature, upon which men act; nor are they determined by nature. Man is distinguished from the divine, but he is not coerced by God in his actions; man is different from and above nature, which cannot act upon or determine man. It is therefore necessary for Ficino to define man as a rational soul, distinct from the body, which is also a part of nature which man can employ as an instrument and which he need not allow to influence or move his soul, though it can if he permits it.

The rational soul is a mean between the eternal and the temporal, the divine and the natural. It cannot be acted upon or compelled by natural things, else it could not rise above them in knowledge or emotion and direct itself toward the divine. Although there is no motion in divine things, there is some in the soul, namely changes in time and variation of the affects. The soul possesses primacy of movement which is supreme and efficacious in causing the movements of the body. Therefore, moving by its own nature and power, it is free and most comprehensive. The soul, thus, can transfer itself into anything, descend into corporeal forms and matter, ascend to the angels and God. It can be moved and not be moved into anything created by God. It can be moved into one thing or equally into another.

> It is not compelled by the divine, from whose providence it is free from the start, nor is it coerced by anything natural over which it widely rules, nor is it dependent upon them, for indeed they are moved and judged by it; . . . since it is not acted upon by any natural object, therefore it is not determined by it, thus it moves along freely.

God's foreknowledge does not circumscribe the freedom of man's will because 'just as He foresees *that* you will do this, so He foresees *how* you will do it, that is willingly and freely.' Ficino then explains that the will operates when the intellect presents two opposing alternatives of equal seeming goodness. The will cannot choose neither, or both, because it would become a mean or a contradiction. Choosing one, it does so freely. 'Hence when both are equally attractive, if the will leans toward one, it proceeds spontaneously and is not forced.' Then he repeats, concerning an act of the human will, exactly what he had said earlier concerning God's voluntary action: 'Hence a voluntary action is nobler than acting by necessity of nature because it adds intelligence above nature, is master of its own act, places a measure to the act, prescribes the end, makes a different act in a different manner.' A natural action is coerced because the matter is prepared and cannot happen otherwise. 'For fire unimpeded cannot not burn dry close-by material, a stone unimpeded cannot not descend to a lower level.' The property of a voluntary action is to act contingently and freely. 'Therefore when there is a voluntary principle in man, there will also be a principle of liberty.' There must be the contingency of choosing between two alternatives, otherwise it would not be a mean between the necessary and the impossible, thought by Ptolemy and others to be the condition requiring conjecture rather than knowledge. For Ficino it is also the condition for *consilium,* meaning intention, or deliberate decision. 'If everything happened by necessity, it would be in vain that we deliberate. We should remember that the proper function of any species cannot be entirely in vain.' No one would say that bees collect honey, spiders weave webs, ants assemble grain in vain. 'Therefore no one would dare to confess that the proper office of man, which is to deliberate and decide, is in vain. I would say, moreover, that this is the property of man in so far as he is man.' All men, always and everywhere engage in deliberation and choice; those who are above men do not need deliberation; those who are below are unable to choose.

Ficino continues to analyze the relationship of human, voluntary, purposive action to the condition of nature in his *Theologia Platonica* IX,4, a chapter which he inserts in the *Disputatio* at this point. First the quality of human autonomy is developed on the relationship of the intellect to the will. The intellect deals in conceptions of universal reason which hold to a common good. The will must apply the universal reason to particular circumstances and locate a choice between particular goods in order to will one or the other of them. In this range of choices of particular and contingent courses of action lies man's freedom. Other animate creatures do not have this choice. They make or eat one thing always. The character of nature is to obey certain innate laws and to be always the same. Men can err, but nature cannot. Animal actions are coercive, corporeal, unrepenting or unemending, always the same. (pp. 141-45)

As far as the will is concerned, since the things of nature are led to an end by determined means, and always get there in the same way, they are predetermined for some one end. 'The elections of man, however, reach an end by diverse ways both in morals and in the arts.' (p. 146)

Naming the realistic artistic creations of ancient artists, the paintings, flying doves, Hermes's talking idols, Ficino concludes that man imitates the works of divine nature and perfects and corrects those of lower nature.

This leads to what must be viewed as a threnody for *homo faber,* an ecstatic passage which should be repeated here as the most emphatic description of human autonomy.

> The power of man, therefore, is very similar to that of the divine nature, seeing that man by himself, that is through his own decision and art, rules himself without being in the least limited by his physical nature, and imitates individual works of the higher nature. And he has as much less need than the beasts for the aid of inferior nature as he is endowed by nature with fewer natural aids to bodily protection than the animals, but he himself provides his own supply of food, clothing, bedding, housing, furnishings, and arms. Hence he supports himself by his own capacity more richly than nature preserves the beasts. In connection with this an indescribable variety of pleasures are developed for delighting the five senses of the body which we invent for ourselves by our own talents. . . . Our soul is concerned not only with the necessities of the body like the beasts subjected to the rule of nature but with various delights of the senses as though a kind of food for the phantasy. And the soul not only flatters its phantasy with these various pleasures while daily seducing it with various games as if for jest, but meanwhile also the cogita-

tive reason acts seriously, and it comes out eager to propagate its own progency, and to show how strong its own inventive genius is through various silk and woolen textiles, paintings, sculptures, and buildings. In composing these works it often respects no bodily comforts, no pleasing of the senses, since it sometimes willingly undergoes hardship and trouble, but it also expands and proves its productive power. (p. 147)

But man is not only a consumer, producer, and industrial manager; he is also a governor, a superior office to that of *homo faber:* 'But the arts of this type, although they mould the matter of the universe and command the animals, and thus imitate God, the creator of the universe, are nevertheless inferior to those arts which imitating the heavenly kingdom undertake the responsibility of human government.' Man rules himself first, then his family, administers the state, and commands the world. He is impatient of servitude, but he will submit to death for the sake of the public good.

Yet beyond both the industrial and civil arts, Ficino places those that are not necessary for physical survival and existence, namely the liberal arts and sciences:

> The subtle computation of numbers, the meticulous description of figures, the most obscure movement of lines, the mysterious consonance of music, long observation of the stars, the study of natural causes, the investigation of enduring things, the eloquence of orators, the madness of poets—in all of these the soul of man despises the ministry of the body as though he would one day be able and now already begins to live without the aid of the body.

The ultimate achievement of man, to become God Himself, remains beyond the powers of the human species, so that man's autonomy is not complete. Yet Ficino so yearns for this total fulfillment of human autonomy that he speculates that, given the proper instruments and material, mankind could recreate the universe itself, as once Archimedes, and now some of Ficino's contemporaries, constructed working models thereof.

This is how Ficino built his vision of human autonomy and revealed thereby also his image of God. If in the slow process of western history human thought gradually replaced the God, whom mankind worshipped and endowed with humanly conceivable qualities, with a conception of man in which now man himself was to be worshipped because he was endowed with godlike qualities, Ficino's place in this process is a vastly important one. Thus the ancient ideal of *autarkeia* and self-sufficiency underwent a Renaissance metamorphosis. (pp. 148-49)

> *Charles Trinkaus, "Marsilio Ficino and the Ideal of Human Autonomy," in* Ficino and Renaissance Neoplatonism, *edited by Konrad Eisenbichler and Olga Zorzi Pugliese, Dovehouse Editions, 1986, pp. 141-53.*

THOMAS HYDE (essay date 1986)

[*In the following excerpt, Hyde explores the mythography of Cupid as it is reflected in Ficino's ideas on love.*]

In the Renaissance, mythography catches up with medieval poetry, focusing as medieval mythography had not on the divinity of Cupid and the other gods. It asks what it means to make Cupid a god, as well as what he may mean as a rhetorical figure. Yet Renaissance mythographers lag behind the most daring poetry because they must engage the problems of poetic theology more immediately than poets, who may evade this task, though at peril to their poetic longevity. A mythographer's explicit task is to recreate his figures from the *disjecta membra* of classical fables and then to reveal their meaning. His entry on Cupid will tend, therefore, to fall into a pattern like that of the most complex and profound *poetic* uses of Cupid, in which a deluded perception or belief about the god of love is followed by recognition of the less apparent truth. Poets could learn more than information from Renaissance mythographers.

Boccaccio is the first great Renaissance mythographer, and his *Genealogia deorum gentilium,* written between 1350 and 1370 and first printed in 1472, went largely without competition, except from older and less ambitious compendia, until the middle of the sixteenth century. Beginning in 1548, three major treatments of the ancient gods appeared in Italy and were quickly reprinted and distributed throughout Europe. These were Lilio Gregorio Giraldi's *De deis gentium varia et multiplex historia . . .* (1548), Vincenzo Cartari's *Le imagine colla sposizione degli dei degli antichi* (1556), and Natale Conti's *Mythologiae sive Explicationis fabularum libri decem* (1568). The essential development between Boccaccio and the later mythographers began toward the end of the fifteenth century with Marsilio Ficino's commentary on the *Symposium* (written 1474-75, first published 1484) and culminated at the beginning of the sixteenth in a remarkable profusion of commentaries, dialogues, and treatises passing under the name *trattati d'amore.* The most influential of these are Pietro Bembo, *Gli Asolani* (1505), Mario Equicola, *Libro di natura d'amore* (1525), Baldassare Castiglione, *Il Cortegiano* (1528), and Leone Ebreo, *Dialoghi d'amore* (1535). All of the *trattati* have threads of mythographical inquiry woven into their fabric, and the later mythographers adapt ideas from the *trattatisti.* Cupid, along with Venus, is probably the most important meeting place of these two strains of Renaissance thought.

For both the mythographers and the Neoplatonists, the chief question about Cupid is the same . . . : is Love a god or a passion of the mind? In the Neoplatonists, the question is resolved by the doctrine of emanations and the *scala amoris.* In the mythographers, it is often closely allied to another question: is there one Cupid (the god) or are Cupids as many and varied as the human desires they personify? Cupid's ambiguity is in no way lessened in the Renaissance, but it comes to be seen less as a dangerous potential for abuse and self-deception than as a reflection of the sacredness of love and of the dignity of man. (pp. 87-8)

Cupid regained his divinity at a stroke, we might say, on 7 November 1474 when the Florentine Platonic Academy observed the anniversary of Plato's birth and death by reenacting the banquet reported in the *Symposium.* Such, at least, is the purported origin of Ficino's *Commentarium in Convivium Platonis de amore,* which [according to Paul Oscar Kristeller in *The Philosophy of Marsilio Ficino* (1943)] "marks a turning point in the history of love speculation" and if not a turning point, at least a sudden acceleration in the evolution of the god of love. Before Ficino, Cupid was now a god, now a personification, but never, except by delusion or abuse, both at the same time. In Ficino, Cupid's equivocal double nature

becomes daemonic, simultaneously divine and human, and becomes in addition his most important attribute.

Ficino and his followers greatly expand the theory that ancient myths contain veiled mysteries of true divinity, but this theory of a *prisca theologia* is no longer, as in Petrarch, Salutati, and Boccaccio, merely a rejoinder to pious enemies of poetry. Cupid's divinity, too, is no longer a potentially dangerous side effect of a defense of poetry, but a consequence and expression of a novel philosophical system that comprises a theology, cosmology, psychology, and ethics, all centered on the idea of love. The system is most easily approached through its cosmology, which, following Plotinus's version of Plato, represents the universe emanating from "the One" or God in a hierarchy of four grades of being: *mens, anima, natura,* and *materia.* The "perpetual knot and binder" of this universe is love, because it is the motive force of both the downward emanation and the upward return: "There is one continuous attraction, beginning with God, going to the world and ending at last in God, an attraction which returns to the same place whence it began as though in a kind of circle." Love is always "desire of beauty" or, more precisely, "desire for the fruition of beauty." In whatever grade of the hierarchy it appears, Beauty is incorporeal— "the radiance of the Divine Goddness"—and so the ultimate object of love is God. When Ficino sent a copy of the **Commentary** together with his treatise **De Christiana religione** to a friend, his witticism in the accompanying letter was entirely just: "I send you my *Amor* as I promised; but I also send my *Religio* so that you will recognize that my love is religious and my religion amatory."

Ficino presents these doctrines, none too consecutively, in speeches by his reenactors expounding the speeches of the original *Symposium.* His originality should not be overestimated. His idea of love draws elements from Plato, Plotinus, Aristotle, Cicero, St. Paul, St. Augustine, the *stilnovisti,* and Petrarch. The Middle Ages knew a simpler version of his cosmology, visible for example in the *De planctu Naturae,* through Chalcidius's translation of the *Timaeus.* Even the doctrine of the ladder of love, which sanctified human love as a preliminary form of divine love, was medieval. But the synthesis Ficino made was new, as was the fact that its major vehicle was the mythology of Cupid and Venus. Plato's dinner guests, obligated to speak in praise of love, had presented and interpreted mythological themes, and Ficino's **Commentary,** therefore, consists in large part of mythographical interpretation.

The hierarchical cosmology is the basis of Ficino's mythography. Like Alain de Lille's simpler version, it allows the gods their circumscribed divinity, but it also serves Ficino in the same way that genealogy had served Boccaccio, permitting him to account for discrepancies among myths by distinguishing multiple gods of the same name. There is a Saturn, Jupiter, and Venus in each grade of the hierarchy, for example. Pausanias, the second speaker of the *Symposium,* had made a start on this type of explanation by distinguishing a celestial and an earthly Venus, each having different parents and accompanied by a different Cupid. Invoking his cosmology, Ficino explains that the celestial Venus is said to have been born without a mother because *mater* signifies *materia.* She is the immaterial beauty of the *mens angelica,* the realm of essences next below God. The second Venus is the "power of generation" (vis generandi) in the next lower grade, the *anima mundi.* Her Cupid is the desire that inspires her to translate the sparks of divine beauty into the bodies of the third grade of the hierarchy, *natura.* She is born from the principles of the *mens angelica* that the poets call Jupiter and Dione. The contradictory myths of the birth of Venus, then, no longer threaten the prestige of mythology, but conceal the nature of the cosmos that, in the Neoplatonic reading, mythology presupposes.

This multiplication of entities may seem obscurantist, but it allows Ficino not only to explain discrepancies that Boccaccio had been able only to acknowledge, but also to resolve them. As in Plato's parable of the cave, the entities in each grade of Ficino's hierarchy are shadows or simulacra of those in the superior grade, both representing and obscuring the higher realities. Properly speaking, then, Venus and Cupid are "duplex" (twofold) rather than double, for the first Venus and Cupid contain the second as potentials within themselves. The second pair are images of the first. The great merit of the Neoplatonic cosmology when applied to mythology is that it both multiplies and reassembles the gods, rationalizing their unity in multiplicity. There is not, for example, one Cupid who is older than the other gods and another who is younger, but one god, whose status is allusively assured by his." . . . (pp. 92-4)

These duplex Venuses and Cupids represent metaphysical processes entirely divorced from human experience, but, because the order of the universe repeats itself in the human soul, they have their shadows also in man. The ancient doctrine of the correspondence between macrocosm and microcosm brings Ficino's theology and cosmology down to earth where they become a psychology and an ethics, but do not lose their mythological features. Like the universe, the soul contains two Venuses accompanied by two Cupids: "When the beauty of the human body first meets our eyes, the mind, which is the first Venus in us, worships and adores the human beauty as an image of the divine beauty. . . . But the power of generation in us, which is the second Venus, desires to create another form like this. Therefore there is a Love in each case: in the former, it is the desire of contemplating Beauty; and in the latter, the desire of propagating it."

Physical beauty should be a road by which we ascend to the higher beauty, and therefore both loves are honorable and praiseworthy, for each is concerned with the divine image." "Desire for physical union," on the other hand, is "bestial love," not love at all because it is not desire of beauty. It is "madness" (insania), and to it "the sacred name of Love is given falsely."

The most important effect of Renaissance Neoplatonism on Cupid, then, is to shift the twin Cupids of the medieval mythographers upward so that no longer is one pair good and chaste and the other unchaste and evil. Both of Ficino's Cupids are divine; the second is a simulacrum of the first, and to both "the sacred name of Love" is given truly.

The correspondence of macrocosm and microcosm has another, more subtle effect on Cupid; it links Cupid the god to Cupid the personification. As a shadow or image of divine love, human love is no longer merely an "accident in a substance," but also a "prior and essential being in the intellectual world, and thence is extended to the corporeal." This extension becomes, in the sixth speech of the *Commentary,* an identity. Cupid is a daemon, half divine and half human. Ficino's enthusiasm for concord here leads him to neglect the dialectics of the original *Symposium,* in which Socrates pro-

claims Love a daemon in order to criticize rather than to fulfill the earlier speeches. For Ficino, following the ancient syncretist Dionysius the pseudo-Areopagite, Plato's daemons are our angels. The line of evolution that begins with Isidore of Seville's interpretation of Cupid as a *daemon fornicationis* and continues through the ironically angelic Amors of the *Roman de la rose* and the insidiously Biblical Amore of the *Vita Nuova* reaches its apogee in Ficino. Cupid has become a true Silenus, uniting in one figure the human effect with its divine cause. A clever transposition clinches the point. While in Plato Alcibiades had compared Socrates to a Silenus, the ugly exterior concealing a godlike interior (hence the name *Silenus Alcibiadis*), Ficino compares Socrates to Cupid. Both true lovers and personified love conceal divinity within themselves.

Ficino's reconciliation of the god of love with the passion he inspires puts an end to the tension that animated many of Cupid's appearances in the Middle Ages. While medieval poets dramatized the abuse of Cupid's unreal divinity, Ficino urges men to participate in his real divinity, to deify their own desires by ascending from desire for physical beauty to contemplation of God. Men may still descend the ladder of love and color their descent with "the sacred name of Love," but Cupid's real divinity makes these abuses, which had been inherent in his old ambivalence, mere contingencies. Ficino is vigorously orthodox in his approval of sex only for generation, dwells at length on the opposite of "Socratic love," and expels the profane from his "heavenly feast." But all these prohibitions do not touch upon Cupid. The divine potential figured in Cupid interests Ficino, not the dangers of abuse, and so he confidently develops the transvaluations that follow from Cupid's divinity. *Voluptas,* the daughter of Cupid and the consummation of love, becomes divine joy; *furor amoris* becomes the irrationality of holy rapture, transcending rather than rejecting reason. Ficino gives a generally positive reinterpretation to the odd collection of attributes that Eros has in Plato, and writers after Ficino regularly will reverse the ancient moralizations of Cupid's attributes to accord with his divinity. Pico della Mirandola, for example, maintains that love was blind "because he is above the intellect." The mythographers Cartari and Conti will give divine significations for his other attributes as if they were commonplaces.

Ficino affirms, then, what Boccaccio had only hinted—both Cupid's divinity and his unity in multiplicity. What is more, his *Commentary,* by neglecting the discontinuities of the original, mirrors in its form the doctrine it asserts. Alain de Lille, Dante, and Petrarch . . . proceeded from confusion to clarity by excluding misconceptions or abuses of Cupid's fictional divinity. Their final affirmations of Cupid followed recognition that he is merely a figure of speech. Ficino's *Commentary,* in contrast, proceeds by accretion of meaning, unfolding Cupid's unitary divinity into the multiplicities of his emanations and effects. The first three speeches deal with Love as he is in himself, but the later speeches are increasingly concerned with Love as he affects men. At the same time the hierarchy of being appears more and more in the aspect of a ladder. The *Commentary,* then, descends from the divine to the human, but at the close begins the return whose means it has explored. The last chapter, "How Thanks are to be Given to the Holy Spirit Which Has Illuminated and Inspired Us for this Discussion," gives thanks to the Love that was discussed: "The cause and teacher of this most fortunate discovery was the very same Love who has been discovered. . . . With the result that, aroused by love of finding Love, so to speak, we have sought and found Love, so that we must be thankful to Him equally for the question and its answer." The form of the *Commentary* itself and the wordplay of its conclusion reveal the self-reverting circuit of love which lies at the center of Ficino's system and which restored both divinity and singleness to Cupid. (pp. 94-6)

Thomas Hyde, "Renaissance Mythographers and Neoplatonists," in his The Poetic Theology of Love: Cupid in Renaissance Literature, *University of Delaware Press, 1986, pp. 87-110.*

FURTHER READING

Allen, Michael J. B. "The Absent Angel in Ficino's Philosophy." *Journal of the History of Ideas* XXXVI, No. 2 (April-June 1975): 219-40.

Investigates Ficino's modification of Plotinian ontology. Allen argues that the soul subsumes the angel's function in Ficino's universal hierarchy.

————. "Ficino's Theory on the Five Substances and the Neoplatonists' *Parmenides.*" *The Journal of Medieval and Renaissance Studies* 12, No. 1 (Spring 1982): 19-44.

Establishes the sources of Ficino's five ontological hypostases in *Platonica theologia.*

————. The Platonism of Marsilio Ficino: A Study of His "Phaedrus" Commentary, Its Sources and Genesis. Berkeley and Los Angeles: University of California Press, 1984, 284 p.

Presents the author in later years as a magus and exegete of the highest Platonic mysteries.

————. "Marsilio Ficino on Plato, the Neoplatonists and the Christian Doctrine of the Trinity." *Renaissance Quarterly* XXXVII, No. 4 (Winter 1984): 555-84.

Account of Ficino's accommodation of Platonism to Christianity and particularly his reconciliation of Platonic texts to the dogma of the Trinity.

Collins, Ardis B. The Secular Is Sacred: Platonism and Thomism in Marsilio Ficino's "Platonic Theology." The Hague: Martinus Nijhoff, 1974, 223 p.

Detailed exposition of *Platonica theologia* and its specific relation to Thomist thought. Collins maintains that the coupling of Thomism and Platonism in Ficino's work reflects the author's efforts to unite theology and philosophy.

Devereux, James A. "The Object of Love in Ficino's Philosophy." *Journal of the History of Ideas* XXX, No. 2 (April-June 1969): 161-70.

Delineates the interdependence of divine and human love in *Il libro dello amore.*

Eisenbichler, Konrad, and Pugliese, Olga Zorzi, eds. Ficino and Renaissance Platonism. Ottawa: Dovehouse Editions Canada, 1986, 202 p.

Collection of highly discursive essays on Ficino by various scholars.

Gombrich, E. H. "Botticelli's Mythologies: A Study in the Neo-Platonic Symbolism of His Circle." In his *Symbolic Images: Studies in the Art of the Renaissance,* pp. 31-81. Oxford: Phaidon, 1978.

Points to direct references to art in Ficino's work, claiming that the author's philosophy "provided the spiritual tools for the artists in their struggle for emancipation from the status of 'menial' craftsmen."

Hersey, George L. "Marsilio Ficino's Cosmic Temple." In *Collaboration in Italian Renaissance Art,* edited by Wendy Stedman Sheard and John T. Paoletti, pp. 91-7. New Haven: Yale University Press, 1978.

Extrapolates cosmic implications from Ficino's ideas on architectural design.

Jayne, Sears. "Ficino and the Platonism of the English Renaissance." *Comparative Literature* IV, No. 3 (Summer 1952): 214-38.

Traces Ficino's impact on the prose and poetry of the English Renaissance, most demonstrably through his conceptions of love and beauty.

————. John Colet and Marsilio Ficino. London: Oxford University Press, 1963, 172 p.

Postulates the influence of *Platonica theologia* and Ficino's letters on John Colet, fifteenth-century English theologian and scholar.

Kristeller, Paul Oskar. "Ficino and Pomponazzi on the Place of Man in the Universe." *Journal of the History of Ideas* V, No. 2 (April 1944): 220-26.

Finds Ficino's and Pietro Pomponazzi's philosophical attitudes towards man respectively representative of Platonic and Aristotelian traditions.

————. "The Dignity of Man." In *Renaissance Thought and Its Sources,* edited by Michael Mooney, pp. 169-81. New York: Columbia University Press, 1979.

Examines the Renaissance glorification of man in the views of Ficino, Pico della Mirandola, Pietro Pomponazzi, and Francesco Petrarch.

Levi, A. H. T. "Rabelais and Ficino." In *Rabelais in Glasgow,* edited by James A. Coleman and Christine M. Scollen-Jimack, pp. 71-85. Glasgow: n.p., 1984.

Proposes the indebtedness of sixteenth-century French satirist François Rabelais to Ficino's philosophies of human love and autonomy.

Moore, Thomas. The Planets Within: Marsilio Ficino's Astrological Psychology. Studies in Jungian Thought, edited by James Hillman. Lewisburg, Pa.: Bucknell University Press, 1982, 227 p.

Comprehensive study of planetary influence on the human psyche as represented in *De vita coelitus comparanda.*

Robb, Nesca A. "Marsilio Ficino and the Platonic Academy of Florence." In her *Neoplatonism of the Italian Renaissance,* pp. 57-89. New York: Octagon Books, 1968.

Outlines Ficino's philosophical principles and their relation to Florentine Neoplatonism.

Trinkaus, Charles. "Humanist Themes in Marsilio Ficino's Philosophy." In his *In Our Image and Likeness: Humanity and Divinity in Italian Humanist Thought,* Vol. 2, pp. 461-504. Chicago: University of Chicago Press, 1970.

Evaluates *Platonica theologia* according to the humanist vision of man in the image of God.

————. "Humanism and Greek Sophism: Protagoras in the Renaissance." In his *The Scope of Renaissance Humanism,* pp. 169-91. Ann Arbor: University of Michigan Press, 1983.

Regards Greek philosopher Protagoras's precepts in the interpretations of three Italian humanists: Leon Battista Alberti, Nicholas of Cusa, and Ficino.

Walker, D. P. Spiritual and Demonic Magic from Ficino to Campanella. Studies of the Warburg Institute, edited by G. Bing, vol. 22. London: University of London, 1958, 244 p.

Considers *De triplici vita* a forerunner of similar Renaissance treatises on magic. Walker discusses planetary worship, demons as mediums of planetary influence, and the link between music and celestial spirit—the last especially crucial to Ficino's theories.

Wind, Edgar. "Platonic Tyranny and the Renaissance Fortuna: On Ficino's Reading of *Laws,* IV, 709A-712A." In *The Eloquence of Symbols: Studies in Humanist Art,* edited by Jaynie Anderson, pp. 86-93. Oxford: Clarendon Press, 1983.

Asserts that Ficino's interpretation of Plato's *Laws* anticipates Niccolò Machiavelli's thoughts on political tyranny.

Italian Humanism

INTRODUCTION

The term "humanism" denotes a revival of classical letters that originated in Italy during the fourteenth and fifteenth centuries and later spread throughout Europe. This revival was accompanied by renewed emphasis upon the individual and a growing insistence upon secular values. In Italy, humanism permeated nearly every facet of life, informing a cultural movement widely considered one of the most significant in world history—the Renaissance.

The manifestation, flowering, and decline of Italian humanism have been documented and appraised in a number of critical and historical studies. Scholars agree that by the late fourteenth century, Italians were eager for emancipation from what they had come to perceive as medieval ignorance, superstition, and spiritual repression. Before this time, all but the most rudimentary knowledge rested chiefly with churchmen and logicians, who retained a considerable portion of the Latin classics yet nearly ignored those in Greek. Their very approach to the ancients, moreover, was characterized by a vague mistrust—as John Addington Symonds observed, an "odour of unsanctity clung around those relics of the pagan past." Many Renaissance scholars mark the beginning of humanist thought with Francesco Petrarch, whose poetry has been found to embody fundamental reverence for man's dignity and his earthly existence. Petrarch also stressed the inestimable value of classical letters. Numerous enthusiasts, subsidized by wealthy noblemen and merchant-princes, were dispatched as far as Byzantium to recover important manuscripts and thereby restore humanity to a long-neglected portion of its birthright. Hebrew and Oriental erudition were mastered along with Latin and Greek. So compelling was the pursuit of classical learning that the lecture halls of philologists and rhetoricians soon overflowed with diverse disciples where once only adherents of Scholasticism had convened. Printers, libraries, and museums helped further the dissemination of philosophies whose relevance had long been obscured. Tolerant papacies aided many humanist endeavors.

Historians have noted that the revival of classical tenets helped divest humanity of many nonprogressive elements of medieval thought. In theory and often in practice, a man's importance no longer depended on his birth but on personal merit. External life grew more refined as interest in the arts soared. However, as veneration for the pagan models of antiquity increased, religious feeling sometimes diminished in tandem. The loftiest ideals became tainted by corruption. Philosophy was often slavish to the vanities of style and rhetoric. The languages of ancient Greece and Rome threatened to submerge Italy's native tongue, all but abandoned by men of letters after Petrarch and Boccaccio.

Perspectives broadened toward the middle of the fifteenth century when such renowned classical scholars as Leone Battista Alberti began to write in their own vernacular. Humanists also found that they might reconcile ancient principles with modern sentiment. Uncritical absorption of the classics ripened into considered analysis, which weighed the knowledge of intervening centuries as well. Patrons established academies for classical studies and related subjects. The most famous of these was the Platonic Academy in Florence, founded by the elder Cosimo de' Medici and headed by Marsilio Ficino; other groups arose in Rome and Naples. The greatest minds of the day exchanged ideas, from which were generated seminal philosophical treatises. Elsewhere, rules governing the tragedies and comedies of antiquity were applied to modern dramatic pieces. Humanism supplanted medievalism in the celebrated epic romances of Ludovico Ariosto and Matteo Maria Boiardo, as well as in works by others.

Renaissance Italy experienced unparalleled heights in the plastic arts. Here, too, men took their stimulus for form and subject from antiquity. Classical grace and perspective informed the painting, sculpture, and architecture of the period. Unique employment of mythological elements and the harmonious blend of secular and religious details prevailed. Just as disciples of philosophy had been seasoned by their elders in Greece and Rome, talented youths were apprenticed to acknowledged masters. Wealthy patrons commissioned magnificent works for their homes or public display. Such individuals as Leonardo da Vinci, Michelangelo, Raphael, and Donatello sought to realize the capabilities of marble and canvas. As Symonds noted, "art of the Renaissance was an apocalypse of the beauty of the world and man in unaffected spontaneity."

Humanism altered the fabric of daily life. Awakened intelligence and diffused wealth led to a thorough refinement of social manners patterned after those of antiquity. While neighboring countries remained comparatively backward, Italy set standards for culture and conduct that were to influence the rest of Europe into the sixteenth century. This fascination with deportment reached its fullest expression in Baldassare Castiglione's *Il libro del cortegiano* (1528; *The Book of the Courtier,* 1561), in which are described the qualities of the ideal courtier. What has come to be called a classical education also originated in Renaissance Italy. By no means restricted to indoctrination in antique tongues and philosophies, it included a broad range of academic subjects as well as those physical disciplines favored by the ancients. Many humanist authorities were professors, whose reputations admitted them into chanceries of the republics and the council chambers of princes.

Historians agree that the humanist outgrowths of worldliness and materialism gradually dissolved Italy's cohesion. Beneath a polished surface of social culture and artistic refinement boiled passions that erupted in violence and lust. The eventual corruption of papal Rome and misplaced emulation of antique virtues by some of the ablest thinkers of the time resulted in widespread moral bankruptcy, scholars have argued. Political diplomacy bred license and intrigue throughout a network of divisive states, left vulnerable to French, German, and Spanish forces towards the close of the fifteenth century. As the Renaissance waned, ideals were compromised for the convenience of politics and epicurean ease.

When humanism ultimately passed from Italy into the several nations of Europe, it was not realized again, in kind or degree, as it had first been nurtured. As Symonds concluded, without "the sceptical and critical industry of the Italians; without their bold explorations in the fields of philosophy, theology and political science; without their digging round the roots of human knowledge; without their frank disavowal of past medieval transcendentalism; neither the German Reformation nor the advance of speculative thought in France, Holland and England, would have been possible."

ORIGINS AND EARLY DEVELOPMENT

F. FUNCK-BRENTANO

[*A native of Luxembourg, Funck-Brentano was an editor and historian who wrote widely on France of the pre-Revolutionary era. In the following excerpt, he outlines the historical background of Italian humanism.*]

It has rightly been said that humanism was the source of the Italian, and especially of the Florentine Renaissance. Florence remained the soul and inspiration of the Renaissance until her part was assumed by Rome, and . . . Cosimo and Lorenzo dei Medici . . . were in turn the inspiration of Florentine humanism.

To-day we should answer the question, "What is Humanism?" with some such definition as "The study of the humanities, that is, of literature, and particularly Greek and Latin literature". At its birth toward the end of the fifteenth century, it was essentially the study of those sciences which advanced the happiness and perfection of the human race, in contradistinction to theology (now become scholastic) which turned away from man to God. Humanism owes its name to this contrast with scholasticism. It received a decisive impulse from the Italian fourteenth-century cult of antiquity, which cult was in its turn advanced by humanism.

The humanists professed a deep and attractive faith, clearly enounced by Pico della Mirandola. Nothing which in the past has stirred and inspired the soul of man should or can perish, whether it be faith or language, customs, arts and letters, science or philosophy. All are products of human toil, faith and love. The labour of man is always admirable and must needs have left fertile seed for the future. The relics of the Romans, and of the Greeks who were the source of Roman civilization, naturally took first place among the sacred memorials of the past which the present piously collected and preserved.

Humanism, deeply influenced by classical culture, spread from the Italy of Rome and Florence over all the neighbouring lands.

The Middle Ages were certainly far from ignorant or contemptuous of the Ancients. Many of the Fathers of the Church, as St. Jerome, St. John Chrysostom and St. Gregory of Nazianza, had a good grounding in Greek. St. Ambrose set the Pandects beside the Gospel and Cicero beside St. Paul. Gregory the Great held the study of ancient philosophy and literature to be of great value for the understanding of the Scriptures. Plato's *Phædo* had been translated into Latin in the thirteenth century. It may even be maintained that Aristotle was better understood in the Middle Ages than since: does not Dante call him "the master of those who know"? At the same time the "subtle doctor", Duns Scotus, was subjecting the logic and metaphysics of the Peripateticians to his minute and thought-provoking analysis.

The Middle Ages wanted to make Virgil a saint, and Dante makes him his laurel-crowned companion on his travels to the nether world. But besides Virgil, the Middle Ages studied Ovid and Lucan, though except for Cicero, most of whose works they knew, they made little account of Latin prose.

As a matter of fact, when we draw up a list of the Latin authors known and appreciated in the Middle Ages, we find that only Tacitus and Lucretius, Quintilian and a part of Cicero are lacking of those we know to-day.

The Middle Ages, too, made constant use of their classics. The first support a thirteenth- or fourteenth-century writer seeks for an opinion he wishes to maintain is its agreement with the opinion of some classical author. The Latin of Frenchmen of the twelfth century was perhaps more vigorous and less slavishly Ciceronian than that of the Florentine author of the quattrocento, so that it served better to express their thought.

The monasteries, too, in the days of "Gothic barbarism" were the pious preservers of the philosophical and literary treasures of Antiquity. From the tenth century onwards the convent of Bobbio prided itself on its Greek and Latin manuscripts. The monks plumed themselves on possessing Demosthenes and Aristotle, but they had also most of the Latin poets and even the grammarians Adamantius, Papirius, Priscian and Flavian.

Passing to the thirteenth century, Petrarch and Boccaccio were both enthusiastic Latinists. Petrarch ransacked first Italy, then France, Germany, Spain and even Greece for manuscripts. Thus he brought to light the Institutions of Quintilian and some letters and a few distiches of Cicero. Certain Latin works, now lost, were known to him, among them a collection of letters and epigrams of Augustus.

Petrarch is the illustrious precursor of the Renaissance, as Erasmus was to be its Pontifex Maximus. He eschewed the conversation of the living, to talk with Cicero and Virgil. Antiquity, to him was a temple of beatific mediation. "The mere sight of the men of to-day offends me," he wrote, "but the memory, the shadow of the great deeds, even the names of the ancients fill me with delight." Even his beloved Laura existed only in his imagination.

His library, dearly bought in money and toil, was his greatest treasure. Through it he could converse with Virgil. Homer he had too, but knew no Greek. "My Homer," he says sorrowfully, "lies dumb beside me. I am deaf to his voice, but at least I can see and often embrace him." If he had occasion to visit a convent, he went into raptures at the thought of the classical texts there might be in its library. He valued his own *Africa* and *De Viris Illustribus,* which celebrate the heroes of Rome, far more highly than the *Canzoniere,* which contains his love poetry in the vulgar tongue. It was to him only "the follies of youth, which he desired might remain forever unknown to others as to himself ". The letters, both in prose and in verse, which he wrote to his friends, were all in Latin, and it was as their writer, and as the singer of Laura, that he attained the proud position as an intellectual leader of Europe that Erasmus was to obtain two centuries later by the same method. (pp. 64-7)

[Petrarch] had entered the Church in 1326, so that we can say that the three greatest of the humanists of the Renaissance, whose most marked characteristic is the cult of pagan antiquity, were churchmen: Petrarch, Ficino and Erasmus.

Boccaccio, like Petrarch, ransacked the monasteries, especially that of Monte Cassino. Like Petrarch, too, he was ashamed to be known as the author of the *Decameron,* and held only his Latin writings of any worth.

Petrarch, who loved the ruins as well as the literature of classical antiquity, travelled all through Italy, Greece, the Islands, and part of the Asiatic and African coasts in his search for inscriptions and coins and to make drawings. He was once asked why he took such trouble, and replied, "To bring the dead to life."

This was the Renaissance.

Gradually it spread with the spread of Latin and Greek, and in the most diverse quarters. We have seen, in the persons of the Medici and the Fuggers, how classical thought and classical languages conquered the minds of the great financiers, and it is interesting to note that this great movement in literature and philosophy began in the merchant class. It was only later that the great ones of the earth became converts.

There was more than a mere æsthetic curiosity behind this desire to recall antiquity to life. Men were weary of the dry and barren scholastic wrangles which had engulfed alike the thought of Gerbert and the science of the precursor of Descartes and Spinoza, Duns Scotus, the touching faith of St. Francis of Assisi, and the wholesome, living doctrines of Thomas Aquinas.

Erasmus took up the cudgels against the scholastic theologians:

> Their whole energy is given up to questioning, dividing, distinguishing, defining: the first part is split into three, the first of these three into four, and each of the four again into three. What could be further from the style of the prophets, of Christ and of the Apostles?

All this was true, but all the same, their thought must be assimilated as far as possible. At least it was not surrounded with that vague halo of mysticism which has formed round the scientific discoveries made since their day. Copernicus' disturbing revelation of a world rolling through space was yet to come. Everything was still fixed and definite, on earth and in the heavens as in the minds of men. They had the Scriptures, and the Scriptures had themselves been fixed and defined by the Fathers of the Church, by Popes and Councils. The Scriptures were Truth made absolute, an unshakable Truth which could neither be broken nor bent.

The processes of theology were like the processes of algebra or geometry to us. "The three angles of a triangle are together equal to two right angles" is a definite proposition, on which a man can find firm foothold. The truths of religion were at that time equally definite, and as a mathematician, starting from irrefutable axioms, proceeds by deduction to discover and demonstrate further truths, so did the scholiasts, by processes which seemed to them equally scientific, go forward to discover theological truths till then unknown.

To-day, when thought has been overlaid by a hundred new extravagances, such efforts do not seem utterly ridiculous, but in the dawn of the Renaissance, when Aristotle, Socrates and Plato burst anew on man's sight, they seemed dull and frigid, and the discovery, translation and circulation of each new masterpiece of classical literature seemed to the eager minds of that day the dawn of liberty, new life to a world in which life was almost extinct.

To this, quite apart from purely æsthetic and literary reasons, humanism mainly owed its triumph. There were, it is true, complementary causes, and among them the new order of society which arose when the leaders of the Middle Ages, feudal lords and patricians of the towns, had accomplished their appointed task and could find no place in the new order of things. In this new order there was a gulf fixed between aristocracy and commonalty, a gulf widened by the flow of wealth from the New World, by the spread of commerce and the fortunes that accrued therefrom. Though a Cosimo dei Medici might be leader of a "popular" party, though he might dress as a peasant and hold familiar converse with workmen, yet he was far removed from the people in the high place to which money had raised him. High finance was outside the orbit of the common people; they could only stare and marvel at its results.

The new class distinctions naturally produced a change in the ideas and tasks of the ruling class. "Humanism," says Imbart de la Tour, "rebelled against scholasticism and against the people." The vulgar tongue, the language of the Chansons de Geste, of popular lays and ballads, the language of Commines, of Gringoire and of Villon, was despised and rejected; anathema was the tongue in which Dante, Petrarch and Boccaccio wrote, the tongue which had sung the Nibelungs and Gudrun.

The humanists thus wrote only for a small and select public. As Erasmus, the best of them, puts it, "A good prince should admire nothing which the mob extols. He should disregard the opinions of the common herd. It would be unworthy of him to feel as do the people."

The same tendencies appeared in religious matters. Religion must be freed from the vulgar accretions of popular observance which had overlaid it for many ages. Away with the processional dancing round saintly relics, away with their motley bearers. Away with the candles lighted before the Virgin of the Via Larga, while her neighbour Virgin of the next quarter is not honoured with the raising of a hat. Away with the crowd of Saint Sebastians who ward off epidemics, and the still greater crowd of Christophers who shield their devotees from accident, so that even the troops paint them on their tents and pray to them as to God. Away with Saint Roch who vies with St. Sebastian as a protector against plague, and St. Apollina who cures toothache. St. Anthony of Thebes, his faithful pig by his side, can deal effectively with skin diseases, except that which affects Job, as he sits melancholy on his dunghill. St. Anthony of Padua finds that which is lost. Away with all these vulgar superstitions.

All this provided plentiful material for the Ciceronian jests of the humanists. This religion of charcoal-burners and old women seemed to them pitiable and nothing else. Religion should be based on the knowledge of man as an individual and of mankind as a whole.

Unmeasured was the zeal of the converts to this new faith. One would go hungry to buy his favourite author, Cicero or

Plato, Virgil or Epictetus. Another would do menial tasks for a teacher whose fees he could not hope to pay. The classics were their life as the religion of Christ was life to the early Christians.

Marsilio Ficino, a priest, wrote to a mother grieving for her dead son a letter which might have come from some Athenian rhetorician. Not one word does it contain of Christian comfort. Ficino preached on Plato from the pulpit of San Lorenzo in Florence, and tried to reconcile his teaching with that of the Gospel. (pp. 67-71)

[Ficino's] chief work, *De Religione Christiana,* is an attempt to reconcile religious and scientific truths, and in his commentaries on Plato's *Symposium* he stresses the points of contact between religion and philosophy. "Wise men are believers and believers are wise men." In his mind Platonism becomes a theology and Christ himself a Platonist. According to Ficino, Plato had made it clear that his teaching would only prevail at the coming of One from whom all truth should flow, and the ancient gods had foretold the coming of Christ, immortal like themselves and filled with religion and piety. "They spoke of him very kindly," he says.

University teaching stresses the Christian tendencies of the Aeneid, and the beauties of classical poetry in general, both Greek and Latin, are explained as allegories of divine truth. Pius II summarizes the general tendency in a letter to the Sultan. "Christianity is only a modern version of the 'supreme good' of the ancients."

Tyrannicide after the antique manner became a fashion. Boscoli, who tried to kill Giuliano dei Medici, believed himself possessed by the soul of Brutus, and Lorenzaccio boasted that when he murdered his cousin Alessandro his hand was guided by the spirit of antiquity.

Erasmus tells of a conversation on the immortality of the soul which he once had with an Italian priest. The priest could only allege in support of the Christian doctrine the testimony of Pliny the Elder. Filelfo, in his funeral oration on Francesco Sforza, proves this same immortality by reference to the Greek philosophers, adding that "the Old and New Testaments afforded additional evidence". Cardinal Pallavicini roundly declared that Christianity would be an untenable hypothesis were it not for Aristotle. (pp. 71-2)

The personages of Scripture were treated like heroes of Olympus, and in return, the great figures of antiquity became Christian saints. Virgil, as we have seen, became a precursor of the true faith, Aristotle and Plato were nearly canonized. A translator of Ovid takes pains to make clear his point of view by invoking the aid of the Trinity in his first line, a proceeding which would probably have caused some surprise to the author of the Metamorphoses and the Art of Love, whose copyist, a Parisian monk, would have amazed him more by dedicating it "to the honour and glory of the Virgin Mary".

Between 1433 and 1445 Antonio Averlino executed the carvings of the entrance to St. Peter's in Rome, the focal point of every Christian eye. But Averlino called himself "Philaretes"—lover of virtue—and his typically humanistic treatment of his task may be seen from the subjects he used. There were the Fables of Æsop, "which I have read in the Greek", as he proudly says, Mars, the Roman wolf with Romulus and Remus, and finally, a masterpiece of incongruity at the threshold of a Christian church, the sculptured fable of Leda and her amorous swan.

The Renaissance received a new impulse from the discovery of ancient statuary, which was recognized as the finest so far known. The soil of the Eternal City and the Roman Campagna, and even the bed of the Tiber, were meticulously searched for further examples. (pp. 73-4)

In Rome itself, the streets were grass-grown, filthy, tortuous. Ferdinand, King of Naples, confessed to the Pope his surprise at the state of the Eternal City, with its foul alleys, the lurking place of footpads. The paving of the squares was broken, shrubs sprouted from the cracks, heaps of garbage defiled them, for they served as common refuse-heaps. There was no street-planning and buildings jutted out haphazard into the streets. A visitor had to worm his way among vast dilapidated piles, often turned into fortresses, among the madly magnificent ruins, scattered by time with wayward hand, and covered with plants which at once adorned and destroyed them. (p. 75)

In Rome, life was lived in the open. Family history was enacted in the street. On the first of May, young lovers decorated the dwelling of their beloved, gilded its door, hung garlands and wreaths upon it and suspended from them a variety of gifts: bright fabrics, cages of singing birds. They fixed to it sonnets of their own making or purchased from poets, describing in mottoes their loves and their hopes. Every quarter of the city was alive with people going about to look, to criticize and to admire this lovers' exhibition.

At every wedding the streets must have the chance to admire the bride's trousseau; so she is marched through the streets and put on show in the squares. Even the chests— "cassone"—in which the wedding-gifts were arranged are works of art now much sought after by museums. Funerals vie with bridals as an occasion for display, and criers were sent about the streets to announce them to the populace.

This publicity in daily life extended to matters which the opinion of to-day banishes to decent obscurity. (p. 76)

Hand in hand with the discovery of works of art went on the search for lost works of classical authors. Gian-Francesco Bracciolini, called Poggio, deserves honourable mention among the searchers. He discovered in the monastery of St. Gall manuscripts of the *Institutions* of Quintilian, of a part of the *Argonautica* of Valerius Flaccus, and certain unknown speeches of Cicero. Later were discovered the *De Rerum Natura* of Lucretius, some *Odes* of Horace, the *De Re Rustica* of Columella and many more.

When but a simple monk, Pope Nicholas V had already run into debt in his search for copies of Greek and Roman authors. His elevation to the papacy was his opportunity to indulge his taste still further. The manuscripts he collected form the basis of the Vatican Library.

Niccolo Niccoli, a friend of Cosimo the Elder, carried on the same work with his own and with Medici money. He it was who first brought to light the complete works of Ammianus Marcellinus, Cicero's *De Oratore,* and the basic text of Lucretius, which, as we have said . . . was discovered by Poggio, as were the works of Pliny, bought from a monastery in Lübeck. There were in Venice and Florence days of rejoicing, comparable with the day of Laocoon in Rome, when Giovanni Aurispa or Filelfo or Guarino da Verona, home from Byzantium, laid before the eyes of the humanists some new fragment of Greek literature. And with reason, since these fragments contained Plato, Xenophon, Strabo and Dio Cassius.

The first five books of the *Annals* of Tacitus were disinterred from a Westphalian monastery and presented to the astonished eyes of Leo X. (pp. 78-9)

The idol of the humanists was Cicero, that prolix, pretentious, empty windbag. On him modelled themselves a host of slavish imitators and a few writers of worth. Bembo advised his friends to spend whole years on reading Cicero and nothing but Cicero and to eschew all words, both in writing and in conversation, which were not to be found in him. Some of them even followed his advice. Cicero's contemporaries shared his fame. "Cicero's century, immortal, half divine." He became a cult which had its own theologians. When Erasmus dared to write that, though Cicero was worthy of all praise, there were other sound writers and that some words and expressions were permissible beyond those found in his works. . . . (pp. 81-2)

Latin thus came to be the only language for the thinker and the scholar, and even for most ordinary writers. Niccolo Niccoli asks whether it is possible for a man to be a poet if he does not write in Latin. Poggio declares that the man who has no works in Latin to his credit has never lived, and laments that the *Divine Comedy* was not composed in Latin. It is stated that Dante had considered it, and had even begun to write in Virgilian Alexandrines. Fortunately he reverted to his native tongue. It must none the less be recognized that Latin was for the humanists at least a kind of Esperanto, understood all over Europe in countries which did not study merely "foreign" tongues. Filelfo said that Italian was only used in matters not destined for posterity, but even in Italy the diversity of dialects hampered the formation of a written language, before the sweet Tuscan dialect of Florence attained preeminence. Till that time, Latin was the language not only of the scholar and the philosopher, but of good society and of all with any pretensions to gentility. A gentleman used only Latin in his correspondence, and welcomed his guests in Latin. Even ladies delivered set speeches in that tongue. Latin epigrams, such as those of Pontano or Sannazaro, were more likely to wound their object than if they were in Italian. To all but her intimate friends Lucrezia Borgia's reputation was irretrievably destroyed by a single such epigram. Pius II demanded from his abbreviators and protonotaries a Ciceronian elegance in their writing. Latin too was used for an endless variety of purposes; lullabies, mottoes for wedding presents, and epitaphs on tombs. A Latin inscription may record the erection of a new fountain by a country squire or the dedication of a street-corner shrine by a pious townsman. The incisiveness of the Latin, so meet to be carved in stone, naturally made it more acceptable in practice. In this everyday use the idiom of Cicero, of Horace and of Virgil gained a suppleness and grace which it had lost in the Middle Ages. It was reborn. (pp. 82-3)

As Burckhardt has pointed out, while in the rest of Europe Latin and Roman literature remained of necessity the province of scholars and writers, one element only of an all-round education, in Italy they were part of the national life. Italy relived its own proud past in the tradition deeply implanted in the national consciousness and amid the imposing remains of its historic greatness. Life was lived in the classical manner. Christmas certainly remained Christmas, the anniversary of the birth of Christ, but the Romans honoured as highly the anniversary of the foundation of Rome.

A merchant like Niccolo Niccoli could live among his statues, his medallions and his cameos, having antique vases for his table service. Vespasiano has painted him thus, in a long toga-like robe, the very pattern of a Roman patrician of Cato's day. Pietro Pazzi, son of a colleague of Niccoli and an idle, pleasure-seeking youth, chanced one day to pass by the Podesta's palace. Niccoli hailed him:

> "What does thou with thy life?" "I take it as it comes." "Listen, and be ashamed that thou, the son of such a father, shouldst yet lack knowledge of the Latin tongue to grace thee. If thou hast no Latin, thy life will be as nothing, and, youth once past, thou wilt be but a poor miserable creature."

The young Pazzi took the hint, the more readily since Niccoli promised he should lack for nothing if he followed his sage counsels. Niccoli found teachers for him, and he developed a taste for study, going so far as to learn the whole *Æneid* by heart, and the speeches of Livy's heroes which he declaimed aloud all the way from his villa at Trebbio to Florence and back again. (pp. 84-5)

Humanism had many and important results. The first and most obvious was the tendency towards the abandonment of purely national tradition in letters and arts, and especially in architecture. The change in taste it produced had the effect of condemning the Gothic style as the futile refuge of a barbarous world. The second result was the accentuated gulf between the two classes of society, the "greater" and the "lesser", "majores et minores".

Humanism, like finance, was international. Pico della Mirandola corresponded with Reuchlin in Germany, Budé in Paris with Aldus in Venice, and Erasmus with all Europe, but always within their own class, never with the people. Great and small are no longer separated merely by wealth or social position, but by taste, that taste which is the prerogative of the leisured class.

The humanist shuts himself away in his study to pore over his manuscripts, his whole mind and soul taken up with the striving to assimilate the thought of Plato, the eloquence of Cicero, the dreams of Homer and Virgil. The people, on the other hand, living in the open, whether they follow the plough or work in the towns, sing their own songs, full of life, love, beauty and faith; they still gather round the strolling singers to hear the stories of Merlin, of the Four Sons of Aymon or of Fair Melusine. Two "ciompi" were known to come to blows in front of the Signoria in Florence, over the question of the relative merits of Roland and Renaud de Montauban, two heroes of their puppet plays.

Meanwhile, the humanists were deep in their Greek and Latin. The people clung to ancient beliefs and practices, old wives' tales, perhaps, but nevertheless penetrated with the beauty and strength of the past. The humanist had no longer lot or part in the ideas and feelings of the people; he wilfully shut himself off from communion with the vulgar, toiling mob, the "vulgum pecus".

The final result of humanism was the introduction of new ideas into religion itself. Ficino kept a lamp burning day and night before his bust of Plato, as if it were an image, and yet remained a good Catholic. Another equally good Catholic, Erasmus, once gave vent to the heartfelt murmur, "Saint Socrates, pray for us".

But time was to have its revenges on a society which exalted pagan wisdom above all others and foreign thought above that of its own ancestors, which preferred an ancient beauty far removed from Christian faith to all other forms of beauty, which gave to a civilization "where four thousand gods found not one unbeliever" an admiration it withheld from that of the One God. The studious humanist thought more of the loves of Jupiter, of wise Minerva and beauteous Venus, of fair Helen and the Siege of Troy, than of the preaching of John the Baptist, of the miracle of the Incarnation, and the faith of the martyrs. Mythology seemed to them vastly more attractive and interesting than the Gospel story.

It is not easy to envisage the enormous shock to the thought of mankind given first by the discoveries of Copernicus, who left the world unstable and far from the watchful eye of an imminent God, and then by the sudden dazzling view of the genius and thought of the ancients. Some historians take the view that the humanists were themselves the involuntary precursors of the Reformation. Erasmus and Ficino made the bed; it was Luther and Calvin who were to lie in it. (pp. 85-7)

> F. Funck-Brentano, "The Humanists," in his The Renaissance, *translated by F. C. Fletcher, Geoffrey Bles: The Centenary Press, 1936, pp. 64-87.*

ERNESTO GRASSI

[*Grassi is an Italian educator, editor, and author. In the following excerpt, he considers the Latin roots of Italian humanism, noting particularly the views of eighteenth-century Italian philosopher Giambattista Vico on this subject.*]

Does the Italian humanistic tradition have a philosophical or only a purely historical significance? If it has a philosophical importance, of what does it consist in our contemporary situation? Finally does this tradition have its origin in the Latin literature, and if so, where primarily?

In order to answer this question I must begin, if only briefly, with a consideration of today's general conception of scientific thought which, especially in the Anglo-Saxon world, is characterized by a certain formalism. Accordingly all "humanistic" thought and all metaphysics must be despised.

That thought is considered to be scientific which proceeds in the framework of a rational process, i.e., in the sphere of proof. This thesis is set forth in modern logical theory in a significant way in Wittgenstein's *Tractatus logicophilosophicus.* Assertion and contradiction are possible only in the context of a system. Outside the symbolic world of the system we have only silence and mystery. The presuppositions upon which the system is based cannot be founded upon the system itself. Hence in its scientific form language is and can be only the expression of objects in "states of affairs," i.e., the only acceptable language is the logical, since it alone puts the rationality in question into words. "The description of the most general propositional form is the description of the one and only general primitive sign in logic." The rejection of all passionate rhetorical language and at the same time all ordinary language as the expression of common sense is based on this. On the other hand this marks the emergence of the ideal of language as a calculus with a mathematical structure that is reduced to the function of formalizing symbols.

Can the Italian humanistic tradition still contribute something effective in opposition to such a view? I know how greatly Anglo-American philosophy is governed by the influence of formal logic, and I cannot claim to be in a position to make any critical commentary on this topic. I only want

to present you with my tradition as a beginning point for your own reflection. I believe that I can accomplish my task only if I begin with the thought of that philosopher who in my judgment saw most deeply and most fully the tradition of Italian Humanism in all of its implications. I am referring to Giambattista Vico. . . . (pp. 4-5)

(*a*) As we know, Vico takes the object of philosophy to be speculation about history and not nature, and he does this because, as he says, man makes history himself but he does not make nature.

> But in the night of thick darkness enveloping the earliest antiquity, so remote from ourselves, there shines the eternal and never failing light of a truth beyond all question: that the world of civil society has certainly been made by men, and that its principles are therefore to be found within the modifications of our own human mind. Whoever reflects on this cannot but marvel that the philosophers should have bent all energies to the study of the world of nature . . . and that they should have neglected the study of the world of nations, or civil world, which, since men had made it, men could come to know.

(*b*) From this results one essential conclusion. The range of Vico's thesis does not consist exclusively or even primarily—as is usually assumed—in the identity of *verum* and *factum*, but rather in the fact that scientific thought is liberated from all formalism. The problems that concern human beings—and these are the only kinds that can have scientific interest—are the ones that urge themselves upon us in the construction of the human world and therefore concern the realization of man as such. Hence we have the primacy of the question of the origin of history.

With this Vico rejects every a priori derivation of metaphysics. From this comes his constant polemic against Descartes and the attempt to derive scientific thought from original, independent, underived principles. Hence the rejection of "critical thinking."

(*c*) But how and where and in what form do the questions that urge themselves upon human beings arise? For Vico the main thing here is what in our contemporary terminology we would call the "humanization" of nature.

This refers to something of principal importance. Nature appears to us only in its meaning with reference to satisfying our existential needs. For this reason the decisive meaning of the function of work is given expression in Vico's interpretation of the myth of Hercules. The clearing of the primeval forest in order to delimit the first human place is the beginning of human history. No theory, no abstract philosophy is the origin of the human world, and every time that man loses contact with the original needs and the questions that arise out of them, he falls into the barbarism of *ratio*. "In this way, through long centuries of barbarism, rust will consume the misbegotten subtleties of malicious wits that have turned them into beasts. . . . Hence peoples who have reached this point of premeditated malice . . . are thereby stunned and brutalized. . . ."

(*d*) But how does this "humanization of nature" take place if not through *ratio*? We already said that nature possesses a meaning only in regard to human needs. This presupposes that we discover a relationship, a *similitudo,* between what the senses reveal to us and our needs. Already in classical Greek thought Pythagoras set forth the proposition that the similar can be grasped only through something similar [*similia similibus comprehendere*].

Insight into relationships basically is not possible through a process of inference, but rather only through an original *insight* as invention and discovery [*inventio*]. From this comes Vico's continual emphasis of *inventio* as primary over that which he calls "critical," i.e., purely rational thought.

Once again only insight into "common" or shared characteristics in the above-mentioned sense makes possible the lending of meanings that allow things to appear [*phainesthai*] in a way that is human. Since such a capacity is characteristic of fantasy, it is this, therefore, which lets the human world appear. For this reason it is expressed originally in metaphors, i.e., in the figurative lending of meanings. "Hence poetic wisdom, the first wisdom of the gentile world, must have begun with a metaphysics not rational and abstract like that of learned men now, but felt and imagined as that of these first men must have been, who, without power of ratiocination, were all robust sense and vigorous imagination." In another place Vico states: "The poetic characters of which we speak were certain imaginative genera . . . to which they reduced all the species or all the particulars appertaining to each genus." Along these lines he also says: "Fantasy collects from the senses and connects and enlarges to exaggeration the sensory effects of natural appearances and makes luminous images from them, in order to suddenly blind the mind with lightning bolts and thereby to conjure up human passions in the ringing and thunder of this astonishment."

The metaphor is, therefore, the original form of the interpretative act itself, which raises itself from the particular to the general through representation in an image, but, of course, always with regard to its importance for human beings. The Herculean act is always a metaphorical one and every genuine metaphor is in this sense Herculean work. (pp. 5-7)

As the fundamental result of this discussion we have (1) the primacy of "topical" philosophy ("topics" as the theory of the finding of arguments) over "rational" philosophy and (2) the primacy of rhetoric—as imagistic and effective speech and thereby dialogue—over rational speech and thereby over the monologue.

The question is now, in what tradition does Vico's view have its roots, his thesis of the priority of inventive, topical philosophy, of work as the source of the development of the human world through original ingenious activity? I want to answer this question with several references to Cicero, references through which the picture of Cicero as only a dilettantish popular thinker who repeated the ideas of Greek philosophers proves to be untenable and which bring to light his Roman-Latin originality.

Cicero conceives nature in two aspects. It is in its own way *mirabile*, hidden, and cannot be known in its most basic reality; it both excites our astonishment and puts before us tasks whereby it becomes the source of *invitamenta*. The second aspect of nature is that one that is revealed through human activity. Man transforms reality through his own capacities [*virtus*]. . . . (p. 8)

These human capacities [*virtutes*] arise from *ingenium*, which Cicero calls "*semina virtutum.*" Through this ingenious activity we surpass what lies before us in our sensory awareness. "*Ingenii specimen est quoddam transilire ante pedes positum.*" Or in another formulation Cicero says: "*Magni autem*

est ingenii sevocare a sensibus," a statement that we find again almost word for word in Salutati's *De laboribus Herculis.* The activity of *ingenium* consists in catching sight of relationships, of *similitudines* among things, "*Comparabile autem est, quod in rebus diversis similem aliquam rationem continet.*" This insight has no deductive character: "*Video summi ingenii causam esse, non ut id demonstretur, quod ante oculos est.*"

Cicero distinguishes in principle between the traditional art of proof, which is based upon deduction, and the art of invention. Since *ars demonstrandi* has no inventive character, "we find in this art no indication of how we are to find the truth [*nullum est praeceptum, quo modo inveniatur*], but only the way in which we are to judge [*sed tantum est quo modo iudicetur*]."

An essential characteristic of *ingenium* consists in its *celeritas,* which is manifested in discerning, ingenious speech. . . . Through what and in what form does nature make its appearance for man? It appears in the form of *res* as the carrier of human meanings, and it does this through work [*labor*]. By appearing as works within the limits that men have created, these *res* thereby are completed [*perfacere, perfectum*]. They receive their meaning in *usus.* (pp. 8-9)

Since the essence of *res* is revealed only in their ingenious utilization [*usus*] in the context of the social and political community, *res* proves to be *res publica,* and the state, in its concrete historical situation, turns out always to be its original horizon. Only with his efforts on the *res publica* does man grasp the deep meaning of his labor. In this way the "*magnus et sapiens vir*" raises the animal human being to something "new" within the limits of the community and unites him to a *populus.* . . . This means that the mind can be known exclusively through its own works. To accomplish this act is what Vico calls "the act of Hercules"; it means both work and the taking of pains, which is the double meaning of the term "labor."

The historical aspects of the realization of the mind are *never eternally valid,* never absolutely "true," because they always emerge within limited situations bound in space and time; i.e., they are probable and seem to be true [*verisimile*], true only within the confines of "here" and "now," in which the needs and problems that confront human beings are met. I refer you here to the concept of *verisimile* as Vico develops it in his *On the Study Methods of Our Time* and in *De antiquissima Italorum sapientia.*

Cicero's Latin thought is fundamentally different from the medieval conception of knowledge, which proceeds through the derivation from original principles. Cicero conceived the only philosophical problems to be those that lead to the perfection of man within the context of situations that are always new. In this way Cicero came to the primacy of rhetoric, whose scientific significance is so resolutely denied by every variety of a priori thought. For when the *res* show their objective meaning through their utilization or *usus* with regard to their usefulness for society—and not for the individual—it follows from this that the orator, who speaks only in the context of different, particular situations, attains and expresses the meaning of the *res.* This is possible only when the *res* also are seen always as problems of the *res publica.*

On this interpretation the theoretical contemplative task is identical with the discovery of those forces that lie at the basis of the human world. Because man is no longer anchored within nature like the animals, he must discover the powers that have torn him out of nature and that force him to construct a world of his own.

My task now would be to show how, on the basis of this tradition, the questions of the philosophical importance of philology, rhetoric, and jurisprudence are developed in the humanistic literature and how these come to be the basic structure of the human world. (pp. 9-11)

I do not refer here to the Italian humanistic tradition, but to a Spanish representative of this movement, whereby we see also the historical breadth of the consciousness of these problems. I am referring to Juan Luis Vives (1492-1540). In his work the *Fabula de homine,* we have a radical reversal of the medieval interpretation of metaphysics and a renunciation of the primacy of all speculation about nature, a disowning of every form of a priori or formal thinking—in line with the tradition that I have attempted to disclose here—as Vico formulated it, in order to look for the source of historicity in the modifications of the human mind.

Let me begin by noting that the traditional objects of *contemplatio* are the first principles and hence the eternal and unchanging from which we derive the meanings that we give to reality. In the *Fabula de homine* the object of thought is the changing, and from this the original and divine then are recognized. What is important here is the foundation. The mind—as the object of *contemplatio*—cannot show itself immediately, but only through different "masks," and it is here in fact that the principal similarity of man with the divine is revealed. Seeing this *similitudo,* the discovery of relationships between appearances as the foundation of the revelation of reality, is the task of the new ingenious philosophy.

Let us look at the *Fabula de homine* and the way it is written and how it reverses the concept of *contemplatio.* In it, according to a schema to which the Italian humanists turn again and again (it is enough to recall Giordano Bruno's *Spaccio della*

A humanist between two muses, by Francesco di Giorgio Martini.

bestia trionfante), we have a "fantastic" story of a festival on Olympus to celebrate Juno's birthday. A "theater performance"—let us not forget this—takes place. The aim of this undertaking is that man is invited to show or act out for the others his threefold nature: vegetable, sensitive, and intellectual. Man fulfills his task in such a perfected way that, as Vives puts it, the gods are filled with doubt, for possibly Jupiter himself is acting under the masks of these men. "When the gods first saw him, they were roused and upset at the thought that their master and father had stooped to the stage [*hunc simul ac dii conspicati sunt, primum animo commoti atque turbati dominum putarunt patremque suum in scenam descendisse*]." The amazement at this play which overcame the gods is so extreme that they check to see if Jupiter is still in the audience. "Soon, however, with composed minds, they glanced repeatedly at Jupiter's stall wondering whether he himself was still sitting there or whether he had appeared masked to play a part [*post vero, sedata mente, oculos identidem ad Iovis sellam tollebant, ut viderent sederetne illic ipse, an personatus prodiiset aliquid acturus*]."

According to the general opinion of interpreters, the parallelism between this elevation of man and that found in *De Hominis Dignitate* of Pico della Mirandola or Giannozzo Manetti's work of the same name is what must be taken into account. But de facto I do not believe that this exhausts the philosophical content of Vives's fable. I believe its accent comes from the fact that, when compared with the views of Pico and Manetti, it represents a complete reversal of interpretations concerning knowledge that is based upon *contemplatio.*

Let us remember that in Vives's text the concern is viewing not merely a theater performance, i.e., a *contemplatio,* but also a *fabula,* that is, a form which, according to humanist tradition, lays claim to revealing a truth in a disguise. With such an interpretation the fable no longer can be seen as merely a "game" of fantasy, as a purely literary jest. Let us remember here again that we also are dealing with *seeing* a theater performance (in Greek *theoria,* in Latin *contemplatio*) that is put on by gods and not men. Not only that, it takes place on the occasion of a celebration, that is, this *theoria* takes place at a time that represents the pinnacle of existence, the high point of joy, freedom, and perfection.

In the course of this "fabulous" story there is a *peristrophe,* to use a term from Aristotle's analysis of drama, that is of theatrical action [*drao*]. At the beginning of the fable the gods are *viewers,* but in the course of the play they recognize themselves as put into the play, that is, they no longer stand before the stage, before the drama. Instead it is the other way around; the play proves to be original reality. The play is performed and the gods recognize themselves in this human work. (pp. 11-12)

The gods recognize themselves in the acting, in man's concrete development, because his divinity becomes visible in this sphere. What was at first a play and fiction changes into "reality," and it is this *peristrophé* which in fact induces the gods to invite man to leave the scene, to put down his mask, and to sit with them. . . .

The fable, the fantastic representation of a truth, is the original form of man's self-realization in Vives's view. Here it is legitimized methodologically as the expression of a truth under a disguise (the human mask). At bottom here is a similarity [*similitudo*] between the community of man with what is primordial. "Man lay bare, showing the immortal gods his nature akin to theirs" [*ostendit agnationem illam quam habet cum diis*]. Vico's statement that man should not concern himself with the study of nature but rather ought to direct his study to history is anticipated here.

With respect to what we said at the beginning of our discussion about Vico, we must recall that we could point out fundamental ideas in Vives that we had emphasized in Cicero and in Vico. On the one hand the human world stands as the expression of needs that are to be fulfilled, and on the other hand it represents the efforts of an ingenious capacity. The noteworthy element here is the continuity of this basic theme and problem, a continuity which most of all comes from the nature of the question itself and its examination. For example we have no reason to assume that Vico knew the writings of Vives. (p. 13)

Justice has a slow, quiet power, while the word possesses a pressing and quick force that affects both the mind and the passions. . . . This is precisely the reason why the orator assumes such an important place in society, for Vives defines the word as "the living flow of the soul." . . . (pp. 13-14)

The origin of society, history, work, the arts, and metaphor, however, is the *inventio,* which overcomes man's difficult situation . . . . The fact is that the circumstances in which particular urgent needs arise are new and will not be repeated and, to use Vives's metaphor, "besiege us," they sharpen our inventive capacity. . . .

Vives defines *ingenium* precisely as that capacity in man which can meet urgent needs through its acumen. . . . Even the metaphor, that figurative transfer of meaning, stands in the service of satisfying urgent needs. (p. 14)

I have attempted to suggest how the humanistic tradition is rooted in the Latin tradition and is differentiated in a fundamental way from a priori thought on the one hand and every type of formalism on the other. This scholarly tradition is continued in Pontano, Landino, Poliziano, Valla, and Nizolio. The problems of this tradition were continued in modern thought in England with the theory of *ingenium,* wit, common sense, and the affirmation of rhetorical, metaphorical speech in Shaftesbury and then in Germany in the eighteenth century in the polemical, anti-idealistic thought of Hamann, Jean Paul, and Herder. (p. 17)

> *Ernesto Grassi, "Introduction: The Roots of the Italian Humanistic Tradition," in his* Rhetoric as Philosophy: The Humanist Tradition, *translated by John Michael Krois, The Pennsylvania State University Press, 1980, pp. 1-17.*

J. C. L. SIMONDE DE SISMONDI

[*Sismondi was a Swiss economist, historian, and literary scholar. In the following excerpt from his pioneering study* De la littérature du Midi de l'Europe *(1813;* Historical View of the Literature of the South of Europe, *1823), he examines early manifestations of humanism as evidenced in the works of Giovanni Boccaccio and comments upon succeeding humanist authors who shared Boccaccio's love of classical learning.*]

The fourteenth century forms a brilliant æra in Italian literature, highly honourable to the human intellect, and is distinguished, beyond any other period, for the creative powers of genius which it exhibited. The germ of literature also existed in other countries. The poetry of this epoch which has survived to us, possesses a charm, derived from the dawn of civilization, in its novelty, vigour, and freshness of imagination; but it belongs rather to the age which gave it birth than to any individual. The songs of the South of France, the chivalrous tales of the North of Europe, the romances of Spain, and the pastorals of Portugal, bear a national character, which pleasingly reminds us of the spirit and manners of the time; but they do not strike us as the work of a powerful genius, nor awake in us an attachment to any individual poet. It was not thus with Italy. The culture of the mind was, at least, as far advanced there, as in France and Spain; but in the midst of their numerous contemporaries, three writers, who, each in his own sphere, gave a new impulse to their native tongue, were especially remarkable. These men afforded models which were ardently followed in other countries, and raised to themselves memorials which the most distant posterity will regard with delight. At the opening of this century, Dante gave to Europe his great poem; the first which, since the dawn of letters, could bear a comparison with the ancient epic. The lyric muse again strung her lyre at the call of Petrarch; and Boccaccio was the creator of a style of prose, harmonious, flexible, and engaging, and alike suitable to the most elevated and to the most playful subjects. The last mentioned member of this illustrious triumvirate cannot, indeed, be ranked so high as his two contemporaries, since the prose style, of which he was the author, is not of so elevated a class as the efforts of the muse, and the formation of the language of common life seems less to require the higher powers of genius. His chief work, moreover, is sullied by immorality; and the eloquence of his expression is too frequently allied to an improper levity. Yet that energy of mind which enabled him to give birth to a style of prose at once so pure, so elegant, and so harmonious, when no model for it existed either in the Italian, or in any other language of the age, is not less deserving of admiration, than those inspirations of genius which awoke and gave rules to the higher strains of poetry. (pp. 293-94)

The Decameron, the work to which Boccaccio is at the present day indebted for his highest celebrity, is a collection of one hundred Novels or Tales. He has ingeniously united them, under the supposition of a party formed in the dreadful pestilence of 1348, composed of a number of cavaliers, and young, intelligent, and accomplished women, retired to a delightful part of the country, to escape the contagion. It was there agreed that each person, during the space of ten days, should narrate, daily, a fresh story. The company consisted of ten persons, and thus the number of stories amounted to one hundred. The description of the enchanting country in the neighbourhood of Florence, where these gay recluses had established themselves; the record of their walks, their numerous *fêtes,* and their repasts, afforded Boccaccio an opportunity of displaying all the treasures of his powerful and easy pen. These stories, which are varied with infinite art, as well in subject as in style, from the most pathetic and tender to the most sportive, and, unfortunately, the most licentious, exhibit a wonderful power of narration; and his description of the plague in Florence, which serves as an introduction to them, may be ranked with the most celebrated historical descriptions which have descended to us. The perfect truth of colouring; the exquisite choice of circumstances, calculated to produce the deepest impression, and which place before our eyes the most repulsive scenes, without exciting disgust; and the emotion of the writer, which insensibly pervades every part, give to this picture that true eloquence of history which, in Thucydides, animates the relation of the plague in Athens. Boccaccio had, doubtless, this model before his eyes; but the events, to which he was a witness, had vividly impressed his mind, and it was the faithful delineation of what he had seen, rather than the classical imitation, which served to develop his talent.

One cannot but pause in astonishment, at the choice of so gloomy an introduction to effusions of so gay a nature. We are amazed at such an intoxicated enjoyment of life, under the threatened approach of death; at such irrepressible desire in the bosom of man to divert the mind from sorrow; and at the torrent of mirth which inundates the heart, in the midst of horrors which should seem to wither it up. As long as we feel delight in nourishing feelings that are in unison with a melancholy temperament, we have not yet felt the overwhelming weight of real sorrow. When experience has, at length, taught us the substantial griefs of life, we then first learn the necessity of resisting them; and, calling the imagination to our aid, to turn aside the shafts of calamity, we struggle with our sorrow, and treat it as an invalid, from whom we withdraw every object which may remind him of the cause of his malady. With regard to the stories themselves, it would be difficult to convey an idea of them by extracts, and impossible to preserve, in a translation, the merits of their style. The praise of Boccaccio consists in the perfect purity of his language, in his elegance, his grace, and, above all, in that *naïveté,* which is the chief merit of narration, and the peculiar charm of the Italian tongue. Unfortunately, Boccaccio did not prescribe to himself the same purity in his images as in his phraseology. The character of his work is light and sportive. He has inserted in it a great number of tales of gallantry; he has exhausted his powers of ridicule on the duped husband, on the depraved and depraving monks, and on subjects, in morals and religious worship, which he himself regarded as sacred; and his reputation is thus little in harmony with the real tenor of his conduct. *The Decameron* was published towards the middle of the fourteenth century (in 1352 or 1353). . . . (pp. 296-97)

Many of the tales of Boccaccio appear to be borrowed from popular recitation, or from real occurrences. We trace the originals of several, in the ancient French *fabliaux;* of some, in the Italian collection of the *Centi Novelli;* and of others, again, in an Indian romance, which passed through all the languages of the East, and of which a Latin translation appeared as early as the twelfth century, under the name of *Dolopathos,* or the King and the Seven Wise Men. Invention, in this class of writing, is not less rare than in every other; and the same tales, probably, which Boccaccio had collected in the gay courts of princes, or in the squares of the cities of Italy, have been repeated to us anew in all the various languages of Europe. They have been versified by the early poets of France and England, and have afforded reputation to three or four imitators of Boccaccio. But, if Boccaccio cannot boast of being the inventor of these tales, he may still claim the creation of this class of letters. Before his time, tales were only subjects of social mirth. He was the first to transport them into the world of letters; and, by the elegance of his diction, the just harmony of all the parts of his subject, and the charm of his narration, he superadded the more refined gratifications of language and of art, to the simpler delight afforded by the old narrators.

A romance of Boccaccio, called the *Fiammetta,* is, after the Tales, the most celebrated of his works. Boccaccio may be considered as the inventor of the love romances. This species of composition was wholly unknown to antiquity. The Byzantine Greeks, indeed, possessed some romances, which have since reached us; but there is no reason to believe that Boccaccio had ever seen them, nor, if he had been acquainted with them, is it probable that he would have imitated works of imagination, invented so long after the decline of literature. The chivalric romances of the French, of which we have spoken, had, it is true, a connexion with that class of which Boccaccio may be considered the creator. But instead of having recourse to marvellous incidents, which might engage the imagination, he has drawn his resources from the human heart and passions. (pp. 297-98)

Boccaccio was the author, also, of another romance, longer than the Fiammetta, and more generally known, intitled *Filocopo.* In this, are narrated the adventures of Florio and Biancafiore, the heroes of an ancient chivalric romance, which Boccaccio has merely remodelled. The mixture of the ancient mythology with Christianity seems, there, to be effected in a more systematic manner than in the Fiammetta. Boccaccio speaks always of the religion of the moderns in the terms of the ancients. In alluding to the war between Manfred of Sicily and Charles of Anjou, he represents the Pope as high priest of Juno, and imagines him to be instigated by that goddess, who thus revenges herself on the last descendants of the emperors, for the ancient wrong which Dido suffered. He afterwards speaks of the incarnation of the son of Jupiter, and of his descending to the earth to reform and redeem it. He even addresses a prayer to Jupiter, and, in short, seems determined to confound the two religions, and to prove that they are, in fact, the same worship, under different names. It may be doubted, whether fastidiousness might lead Boccaccio to believe that he ought not to employ, in a work of taste, names which were unknown to the writers of the Augustan age; or whether, on the contrary, a religious scruple, still more eccentric, forbade him to mingle the name of the Deity, with the tales of his own invention. In either case, this system of poetical religion is not less extraordinary than profane. There are, in the Filocopo, many more adventures, and a greater variety of incident, but less passion than in the Fiammetta. The perusal is sometimes rendered fatiguing, by the pains which Boccaccio has taken to make the style harmonious, and to round his periods; and this measured prose betrays a laboured and sometimes an affected style.

Boccaccio has also left two heroic poems, *La Theseide* and *Filostrato,* neither of which has obtained any great reputation, and both are, at the present day, nearly forgotten. They deserve, however, to be mentioned, as being the first attempts at the ancient epic, since the fall of the Roman empire. Petrarch, it is true, had, in his Latin poem of *Africa,* attempted to rival Virgil; but he did little more than clothe an historical narration in frigid hexameters, nor has he invested his subject with any other poetic charm than that which arises from the regularity of the verse. Boccaccio, on the contrary, was sensible that a powerful imagination and feeling were essential to the epic. But he overreached his mark, and composed romances rather than poems; although, even here, he opened to his successors the route which they were to follow.

These two poems of Boccaccio, in another point of view, form an æra in the history of epic poetry. They are both composed in *ottava rima,* or in that kind of stanza of eight lines, which has since been employed by all the epic poets of Italy, Spain, and Portugal. Of this, Boccaccio was the inventor. He found that the *terza rima,* employed by Dante, imposed too great a constraint on the poet, and, by its close texture, held the attention of the reader too long suspended. All the other forms of versification were appropriated to the lyric muse; and any verses which were not submitted to a regular structure, did not seem sufficiently poetical to the refined ears of the Italians. The stanza which Boccaccio invented, is composed of six lines, which rhyme interchangeably with each other, and are followed by a couplet. There exist instances of the octave verse before his time, but under a different form.

The Latin compositions of Boccaccio are voluminous, and materially contributed, at the time they were written, to the advancement of letters. The most celebrated of these works, are two Treatises; the one on the Genealogy of the Gods, and the other on mountains, forests, and rivers. In the first he gave an exposition of the ancient mythology; and in the second, rectified many errors in geography. These two works have fallen into neglect, since the discovery of manuscripts then unknown, and in consequence of the facilities which the art of printing, by opening new sources, has afforded to the study of antiquity. In the age in which they were composed, they were, however, equally remarkable for their extensive information and for the clearness of their arrangement; but the style is by no means so pure and elegant as that of Petrarch.

But, while the claim to celebrity, in these great men, is restricted to the Italian poetry of Petrarch and to the novels of Boccaccio, our gratitude to them is founded on stronger grounds. They felt more sensibly than any other men, that enthusiasm for the beauties of antiquity, without which we in vain strive to appreciate its treasures; and they each devoted a long and laborious life to the discovery and the study of ancient manuscripts. The most valued works of the ancients were at that time buried among the archives of convents, scattered at great distances, incorrect and incomplete, without tables of contents or marginal notes. Nor did those resources then exist, which printing supplies, for the perusal of works with which we are not familiar; and the facilities which are afforded by previous study, or the collation of the originals with each other, were equally wanting. It must have required a powerful intellect to discover, in a manuscript of Cicero, for example, without title or commencement, the full meaning of the author, the period at which he wrote, and other circumstances, which are connected with his subject; to correct the numerous errors of the copyists; to supply the chasms, which, frequently occurring at the beginning and the end, left neither title nor divisions nor conclusions, nor any thing that might serve as a clue for the perusal; in short, to determine how one manuscript, discovered at Heidelberg, should perfect another, discovered at Naples. It was, in fact, by long and painful journies, that the scholars of those days accomplished themselves for this task. The copying a manuscript, with the necessary degree of accuracy, was a work of great labour and expense. A collection of three or four hundred volumes was, at that time, considered an extensive library; and a scholar was frequently compelled to seek, at a great distance, the completion of a work, commenced under his own roof.

Petrarch and Boccaccio, in their frequent travels, obtained copies of such classics as they found in their route. Among other objects, Petrarch proposed to himself to collect all the works of Cicero; in which he succeeded, after a lapse of many years. Boccaccio, with a true love of letters, introduced the study of the Greek to the Italians, not only with the view of

securing the interests of commerce or of science, but of enriching their minds, and extending their researches to the other half of the ancient world of letters, which had, till then, remained hidden from his contemporaries. (pp. 299-304)

Two poets of this age, shared with Petrarch the honours of a poetic coronation: Zanobi di Strada, whom the Emperor Charles IV. crowned at Pisa, in 1355, with great pomp, but whose verses have not reached us; and Coluccio Salutati, secretary of the Florentine republic, one of the purest Latinists, and most eloquent statesmen whom Italy in that age produced. The latter, indeed, did not live to enjoy the honour which had been accorded him by the Emperor, at the request of the Florentines. Coluccio died in 1406, at the age of seventy-six, before the day appointed for his coronation, and the symbol of glory was deposited on his tomb; as, at a subsequent period, a far more illustrious crown was placed on the tomb of Tasso.

Of the prose writers of Tuscany, Francho Sacchetti, born at Florence about the year 1335, and who died before the end of the century, after filling some of the first offices in the republic, approaches the nearest to Boccaccio. He imitated Boccaccio in his novels, and Petrarch in his lyric poems; but the latter were never printed, while of his tales there have been several editions. Whatever praise be due to the purity and eloquence of his style, we find his pages more valuable, as a history of the manners of the age, than attractive for their powers of amusement, even when the author thinks himself most successful. His two hundred and fifty-eight tales consist, almost entirely, of the incidents of his own time, and of his own neighbourhood; domestic anecdotes, which in general contain little humour; tricks, exhibiting little skill, and jests of little point; and we are often surprised to find a professed jester vanquished by the smart reply of a child or a clown, which scarcely deserves our attention. After reading these tales, we cannot help concluding that the art of conversation had not made, in the fourteenth century, an equal progress with the other arts; and that the great men, to whom we owe so many excellent works, were not so entertaining in the social intercourse of life, as many persons greatly their inferiors in merit.

Two poets of this time, of some celebrity, chose Dante for their model, and composed after him, in *terza rima,* long allegories, partly descriptive, partly scientific. Fazio de' Uberti in his *Dettamondo,* undertook the description of the universe, of which the different parts, personified in turns, relate their history. Federigo Frezzi, Bishop of Foligno, who died in 1416, at the council of Constance, has, in his *Quadriregio,* described the four empires of love, satan, virtue, and vice. In both of these poets we meet, occasionally, with lines not unworthy of Dante; but they formed a very false estimate of the works of genius, when they regarded the *Divina Commedia* not as an individual poem, but as a species of poetry which any one might attempt.

The passionate study of the ancients, of which Petrarch and Boccaccio had given an example, suspended, in an extraordinary manner, the progress of Italian literature, and retarded the perfection of that tongue. Italy, after having produced her three leading classics, sunk, for a century, into inaction. In this period, indeed, erudition made wonderful progress; and knowledge became much more general, but sterile in its effects. The mind had preserved all its activity, and literary fame all its splendour; but the unintermitted study of the ancients had precluded all originality in the authors. Instead of perfecting a new language, and enriching it with works in unison with modern manners and ideas, they confined themselves to a servile copy of the ancients. A too scrupulous imitation thus destroyed the spirit of invention; and the most eminent scholars may be said to have produced, in their eloquent writings, little more than college themes. In proportion as a man was qualified by his rank, or by his talents, to acquire a name in literature, he blushed to cultivate his mother tongue. He almost, indeed, forced himself to forget it, to avoid the danger of corrupting his Latin style: and the common people thus remained the only depositories of a language, which had exhibited so brilliant a dawn, and which had now again almost relapsed into barbarism.

The fifteenth century, so barren in Italian literature, was, nevertheless, a highly literary period. In no other age, perhaps, was the love of study so universal. Letters were powerfully supported by princes and by their subjects. All, who attached themselves to literature, were assured of fame; and the monuments of the ancient tongues, multiplied by the recently discovered press, exercised a great and lasting influence on the human mind. The sovereigns of Europe, at this brilliant period, rested their glory on the protection afforded to letters, on the classical education they had themselves received, and on their intimate knowledge of the Greek and Latin tongues. The popes, who, in the preceding times, had turned the whole weight of superstition against study, became, in the fifteenth century, the most zealous friends and protectors, and the most munificent patrons of men of letters. (pp. 304-07)

Two sovereign princes . . . , the Marquis Gonzaga, of Mantua, and the Marquis D'Este, of Ferrara, endeavoured to supply what was wanting to them in power, by their active zeal and by the constant protection which they afforded to literature. They sought for and collected together men of letters from every part of Italy, and seemed to rival each other in lavishing upon them the richest gifts and the most flattering distinctions. To them, they entrusted exclusively the education of their children; and we should probably, in the present day, search in vain, in our most learned academies, for men who wrote Greek verse with so much elegance and purity as many of the princes of Mantua and Ferrara. At Florence, a wealthy merchant, Cosmo de' Medici, had acquired a degree of power which shook the constitution of the state; and his descendants were destined to substitute, in that city, the will of an individual for that of the people. In the midst of his vast projects of ambition, master of the monied credit of Europe, and almost the equal of the kings with whom he negotiated, Cosmo accorded, in his house, an asylum to all the men of learning and artists of the age, converted his gardens into an academy, and produced a revolution in philosophy, by substituting the authority of Plato for that of Aristotle. (pp. 307-08)

The men who flourished at this period, and to whom we owe the revival of Greek and Latin literature, the preservation and correction of all the monuments of antiquity, the knowledge of its laws, manners, and customs, of its religion and its language, do not properly belong to Italian literature: and we shall not make a point of describing their writings, their persons, or their lives, which were continually agitated by disputes. It will be sufficient to impress a few names on the memory of the reader, in gratitude for the eminent services which they have rendered to Europe, and in recollection of a species of glory which has passed away. (p. 309)

The celebrated Lionardo Bruno d'Arezzo, better known under the name of Lionardo Aretino (1369-1444), was . . . a scholar of Emanuel Chrysoloras. He was apostolic secretary to four popes, and ultimately chancellor of the Florentine republic; and was not only one of the most learned, but also one of the most amiable, men of the fifteenth century, equally dignified and respectable in morals and in manners. He has left, besides a number of translations in Greek and Latin, some letters and Latin poems, and a History of Florence to the year 1404, written with correct judgment, and in an elegant and pure style, but with too evident an imitation of Livy. In consequence of this unreasonable fondness for relating the events of modern times in the style of antiquity, the historians of the fifteenth century deprived their works of all nature and originality.

Poggio Bracciolini (1380-1459) was the friend of Lionardo, and continued his history. He also was a pupil of John of Ravenna, and of Emanuel Chrysoloras. From the year 1402, and during more than fifty years, he was writer of the apostolic letters; an employ which brought him little fortune, but which did not require his residence in Rome. Poggio was thus enabled to travel frequently, not only in Italy, but in Germany, in France, and in England. In his journeys, he discovered a great number of manuscripts, in danger of perishing in the hands of the monks, who were insensible to their value, and who had banished them to the damp and obscure recesses of their convents. In this manner, he redeemed for posterity the works of Quintilian, Valerius Flaccus, Vitruvius, and others. He was tenderly attached to Cosmo de' Medici; and, when that illustrious citizen was recalled to Florence, he fixed his own residence there, in the year 1435. Florence, indeed, was his native place, but, until that period, he had always lived absent from it. He was appointed, in 1453, chancellor of the republic. Shortly afterwards, he was elected into the number of the *Priori delle arti,* or presidents of the trading companies; and he died, loaded with honours, in his native city, on the thirtieth of October, 1459. A monument was erected to his memory in the church of Santa Croce, near those of other great men, who form the boast of Florence.

Poggio was one of the most voluminous writers of his age, and united a profound genius, philosophy, fervour of imagination, and eloquence, to the most extensive attainments. Next to his History of Florence, which extends from 1350 to 1455, and which is, perhaps, his best work, may be ranked many of his philosophical dialogues and letters, in which the most noble and elevated sentiments prevail. His memory, indeed, derives less honour from his too celebrated Book of *Facetiæ,* which he published in his seventieth year; and in which, with a sarcastic gaiety, he outrages, without restraint, all good manners and decorum. Nor are the numerous invectives, which, in his literary quarrels, he addressed to Francesco Filelfo, to Lorenzo Valla, to George of Trebizond, and to many others, less exceptionable. In an age when literature was confined to scholastic erudition, taste exercised on it little influence. Society could not repress the malignant passions, nor could respect for the other sex inspire a sense of propriety. We are astonished and disgusted at the odious accusations, with which these scholastic champions attack each other; reproaching their opponents with theft and fraud, poisonings and perjury, in the most opprobrious language. In order to justify an insolent and gross expression, they did not consider whether it were consistent with a due observance of decorum, but merely whether it were authorized by its pure Latinity; and, in these calumnious aspersions, they were much less solicitous about the truth or probability of their charges, than about the classical propriety of their vituperative epithets.

The man, whose life was most agitated by these furious literary quarrels, was Francesco Filelfo (1398-1481), the rival in reputation, and the declared enemy, of Poggio Bracciolini. Born at Tolentino, in 1398, he early distinguished himself by his erudition, and, at the age of eighteen, was appointed professor of eloquence at Padua. He relinquished that situation to go to Constantinople, to perfect himself in the Greek language. He repaired thither, in 1420, with a diplomatic mission from the Venetians, and was afterwards employed on others, to Amurath II, and the Emperor Sigismund. Having married a daughter of John Chrysoloras, who was allied to the Imperial family of the Palæologi, this noble alliance intoxicated the mind of a man already too vain of his knowledge, and who considered himself to be the first genius, not only of his own, but of every age. On his return to Italy, his ostentatious disposition exposed him to numerous distresses, notwithstanding the liberality with which, in many cities, he was rewarded for his instructions. At the same time, the violence and asperity of his character procured him many bitter enemies. Not content with literary altercations, he interfered also in political disputes, although, in these, he was not actuated by any noble feelings. He pretended that Cosmo de' Medici had twice intended his assassination, and he, in his turn, attempted the life of Cosmo. He published his invectives in all the cities of Italy, loading, with the heaviest accusations, the enemies whom he had drawn on himself. After the death of his first wife, he married a second, and subsequently a third at Milan, where he resided a considerable time, at the court of the Sforza family. He died on the thirty-first of July, 1481, on his return to Florence, to which place he was recalled by Lorenzo de' Medici. In the midst of these continual disquiets, Filelfo, however, laboured with indefatigable activity for the advancement of literature. He left behind him a prodigious number of translations, dissertations, and philosophical writings and letters; but he contributed still more to the progress of study by his lectures, and by the treasures of his knowledge, which he displayed before four or five hundred scholars at a time, to whom he gave instruction on various subjects, four or five times repeated in the course of one day.

Lorenzo Valla is the last of these celebrated philologists whom we shall here notice. Born at Rome, at the close of the fourteenth century, he there completed his early studies. He was afterwards professor of eloquence at Pavia, until about the year 1431, when he attached himself to Alfonso V. He opened, at Naples, a school of Greek and Roman eloquence; but, not less irascible than Filelfo and Poggio, he engaged with them and others in violent disputes, of which the written invectives left us by these scholars form a lamentable proof. He composed many works, on history, criticism, dialectics, and moral philosophy. His two most celebrated productions are, a History of Ferdinand, King of Aragon, father of Alfonso, and the *Elegantiæ Linguæ Latinæ*. He died at Naples, in 1457.

The attention of the literary men of the fifteenth century was wholly engrossed by the study of the dead languages, and of manners, customs, and religious systems; equally extinct. The charm of reality was, of course, wanting to works which were the result of so much research and labour. All these men whom we have noticed, and to whom we owe the discovery and preservation of so many valuable works, present to our observation, boundless erudition, a just spirit of criticism, and nice sensibility to the beauties and defects of the great authors of antiquity. But we look in vain for that true eloquence, which is more the fruit of an intercourse with the world, than of a knowledge of books; and these philologists professed too blind a veneration for every thing belonging to antiquity, to point out what was worthy of admiration, or to select what was deserving of imitation. They were still more unsuccessful in poetry, in which their attempts, all in Latin, are few in number; and their verses are harsh and heavy, without originality or vigour. It was not until the period when Italian poetry began to be again cultivated, that Latin verse acquired any of the characteristics of genuine inspiration.

The first man to whom may, perhaps, be attributed the restoration of Italian poetry, was, at the same time, one of the greatest men of his own and succeeding ages. This was Lorenzo de' Medici, chief of the Florentine republic, and arbiter of the whole political state of Italy (1448-1492). Lorenzo the Magnificent had written his first poems, before he was twenty years of age. A whole century had elapsed since Petrarch and Boccaccio, renouncing subjects of love, had ceased to cultivate Italian verse; and, during this long interval, no poet worthy of commemoration had appeared. Lorenzo attempted to restore the poetry of his country, to the state in which Petrarch had left it; but this man, so superior by the greatness of his character, and by the universality of his genius, did not possess the talent of versification in the same degree as Petrarch. In his love verses, his sonnets, and *canzoni,* we find less sweetness and harmony. Their poetical colouring is less striking; and it is remarkable, that they display a ruder expression, more nearly allied to the infancy of the language. On the other hand, his ideas are more natural, and are often accompanied by a great charm of imagination. We are presented with a succession of the most delightful rural pictures, and are surprised to find the statesman so conversant with country life. His works consist of one hundred and forty sonnets, and about twenty *canzoni,* almost all composed in honour of Lucretia de' Donati. He has not, however, named her; and he seems to have chosen her only as the object of a poetical passion, and as the subject of his verse. He has celebrated her with a purity not unworthy of Petrarch, and with a delicacy which was not always observed in his other attachments. But Lorenzo did not confine himself to lyric poetry. He attempted all kinds, and manifested in all, the versatility of his talents and the exuberance of his imagination. His poem of *Ambra,* intended to celebrate the delicious gardens, which he had planted in an island of the Ombrone, and which were destroyed by an inundation of that river, is written in beautiful octave verse. In his *Nencia da Barberino,* composed in the rustic dialect of Tuscany, he celebrates, in stanzas full of natural simplicity, gaiety, and grace, the charms of a peasant girl. His *Altercazione* is a philosophical and moral poem, in which the most sublime truths of the Platonic philosophy are displayed with equal clearness and sublimity. Lorenzo has also left, in his *Beoni,* an ingenious and lively satire against drunkenness; and in his Carnival songs, couplets of extreme gaiety, that accompanied the triumphal feasts which he gave to, and shared with, the people. In his *Canzoni a ballo,* we have other verses, which he sung himself, when he took a part in the dances exhibited in public; and in his *Orazioni* we find sacred hymns, which belong to the highest order of lyric poetry.

Such was the brilliant imagination, and such the grace and versatility of talent, of a man to whom poetry was but an amusement, scarcely noticed in his splendid political career; who, concentrating in himself all the powers of the republic, never allowed the people to perceive that they had relinquished their sovereignty; who, by the superiority of his character and of his talents, governed all Italy as he governed Florence, preserving it in peace, and averting, as long as he lived, those calamities with which, two years after his death, it was overwhelmed; who was, at the same time, the patron of the Platonic philosophy, the promoter of literature, the fellow-student of the learned, the friend of philosophers and poets, and the protector of artists; and who kindled and fanned the flame of genius in the breast of Michael Angelo. (pp. 310-15)

> *J. C. L. Simonde de Sismondi, "Boccaccio.—Italian Literature, at the Close of the Fourteenth, and during the Fifteenth Century," in his* Historical View of the Literature of the South of Europe, *Vol. I, translated by Thomas Roscoe, second edition, Henry G. Bohn, 1846, pp. 293-315.*

REVIVAL OF CLASSICAL LETTERS

JACOB BURCKHARDT

[*Burckhardt was a Swiss historian whose best-known work,* Die Cultur der Renaissance in Italien *(1860;* The Civilization of the Period of the Renaissance in Italy, *1878), is a classic analysis of the period. In the following excerpt from that work, he offers sketches of several Italian humanists who greatly advanced classical studies.*]

We have here first to speak of those citizens, mostly Florentines, who made antiquarian interests one of the chief objects of their lives, and who were themselves either distinguished scholars, or else distinguished *dilettanti* who maintained the scholars. They were of peculiar significance during the period of transition at the beginning of the fifteenth century, since it was in them that humanism first showed itself practically as an indispensable element in daily life. It was not till after this time that the popes and princes began seriously to occupy themselves with it. (p. 128)

[Niccoló Niccoli] is described to us by Vespasiano as a man who would tolerate nothing around him out of harmony with his own classical spirit. His handsome long-robed figure, his kindly speech, his house adorned with the noblest remains of antiquity, made a singular impression. He was scrupulously cleanly in everything, most of all at table, where ancient vases and crystal goblets stood before him on the whitest linen. The way in which he won over a pleasure-loving young Florentine to intellectual interests is too charming not to be here described. Piero de' Pazzi, son of a distinguished merchant, and himself destined to the same calling, fair to behold, and much given to the pleasures of the world, thought about anything rather than literature. One day, as he was passing the Palazzo del Podestá, Niccoló called the young man to him, and although they had never before exchanged a word, the youth obeyed the call of one so respected. Niccoló asked him who his father was. He answered, 'Messer Andrea de' Pazzi'. When he was further asked what his pursuit was, Piero replied, as young people are wont to do, 'I enjoy myselfc' ('attendo a darmi buon tempo'). Niccoló said to him, 'As son of such a father, and so fair to look upon, it is a shame that thou

knowest nothing of the Latin language, which would be so great an ornament to thee. If thou learnest it not, thou wilt be good for nothing, and as soon as the flower of youth is over, wilt be a man of no consequence' (*virtù*). When Piero heard this, he straightway perceived that it was true, and said that he would gladly take pains to learn, if only he had a teacher. Whereupon Niccoló answered that he would see to that. And he found him a learned man for Latin and Greek, named Pontano, whom Piero treated as one of his own house, and to whom he paid 100 gold florins a year. Quitting all the pleasures in which he had hitherto lived, he studied day and night, and became a friend of all learned men and a noble-minded statesman. He learned by heart the whole *Æneid* and many speeches of Livy, chiefly on the way between Florence and his country house at Trebbio. Antiquity was represented in another and higher sense by Giannozzo Manetti (1393-1459). Precocious from his first years, he was hardly more than a child when he had finished his apprenticeship in commerce and became book-keeper in a bank. But soon the life he led seemed to him empty and perishable, and he began to yearn after science, through which alone man can secure immortality. He then busied himself with books as few laymen had done before him, and became . . . one of the most profound scholars of his time. When appointed by the government as its representative magistrate and tax-collector at Pescia and Pistoia, he fulfilled his duties in accordance with the lofty ideal with which his religious feeling and humanistic studies combined to inspire him. He succeeded in collecting the most unpopular taxes which the Florentine State imposed, and declined payment for his services. As provincial governor he refused all presents, abhorred all bribes, checked gambling, kept the country well supplied with corn, was indefatigable in settling lawsuits amicably, and did wonders in calming inflamed passions by his goodness. The Pistoiese were never able to discover to which of the two political parties he leaned. As if to symbolize the common rights and interests of all, he spent his leisure hours in writing the history of the city, which was preserved, bound in a purple cover, as a sacred relic in the town hall. When he took his leave the city presented him with a banner bearing the municipal arms and a splendid silver helmet.

For further information as to the learned citizens of Florence at this period the reader must all the more be referred to Vespasiano, who knew them all personally, because the tone and atmosphere in which he writes, and the terms and conditions on which he mixed in their society, are of even more importance than the facts which he records. Even in a translation, and still more in the brief indications to which we are here compelled to limit ourselves, this chief merit of his book is lost. Without being a great writer, he was thoroughly familiar with the subject he wrote on, and had a deep sense of its intellectual significance.

If we seek to analyse the charm which the Medici of the fifteenth century, especially Cosimo the Elder (d. 1464) and Lorenzo the Magnificent (d. 1492) exercised over Florence and over all their contemporaries, we shall find that it lay less in their political capacity than in their leadership in the culture of the age. A man in Cosimo's position—a great merchant and party leader, who also had on his side all the thinkers, writers and investigators, a man who was the first of the Florentines by birth and the first of the Italians by culture—such a man was to all intents and purposes already a prince. To Cosimo belongs the special glory of recognizing in the Platonic philosophy the fairest flower of the ancient world of thought, of inspiring his friends with the same belief, and thus of fostering within humanistic circles themselves another and a higher resuscitation of antiquity. The story is known to us minutely. It all hangs on the calling of the learned Johannes Argyropulos, and on the personal enthusiasm of Cosimo himself in his last years, which was such that the great Marsilio Ficino could style himself, as far as Platonism was concerned, the spiritual son of Cosimo. Under Pietro Medici, Ficino was already at the head of a school; to him Pietro's son and Cosimo's grandson, the illustrious Lorenzo, came over from the Peripatetics. Among his most distinguished fellow-scholars were Bartolommeo Valori, Donato Acciaiuoli, and Pierfilippo Pandolfini. The enthusiastic teacher declares in several passages of his writings that Lorenzo had sounded all the depths of the Platonic philosophy, and had uttered his conviction that without Plato it would be hard to be a good Christian or a good citizen. The famous band of scholars which surrounded Lorenzo was united together, and distinguished from all other circles of the kind, by this passion for a higher and idealistic philosophy. Only in such a world could a man like Pico della Mirandola feel happy. But perhaps the best thing of all that can be said about it is, that, with all this worship of antiquity, Italian poetry found here a sacred refuge, and that of all the rays of light which streamed from the circle of which Lorenzo was the centre, none was more powerful than this. As a statesman, let each man judge him as he pleases; a foreigner will hesitate to pronounce what in the fate of Florence was due to human guilt and what to circumstances, but no more unjust charge was ever made than that in the field of culture Lorenzo was the protector of mediocrity, that through his fault Leonardo da Vinci and the mathematician Fra Luca Pacioli lived abroad, and that Toscanella, Vespucci, and others remained at least unsupported. He was not, indeed, a man of universal mind; but of all the great men who have striven to favour and promote spiritual interests, few certainly have been so many-sided, and in none probably was the inward need to do so equally deep.

The age in which we live is loud enough in proclaiming the worth of culture, and especially of the culture of antiquity. But the enthusiastic devotion to it, the recognition that the need of it is the first and greatest of all needs, is nowhere to be found in such a degree as among the Florentines of the fifteenth and the early part of the sixteenth centuries. On this point we have indirect proof which precludes all doubt. It would not have been so common to give the daughters of the house a share in the same studies, had they not been held to be the noblest of earthly pursuits; exile would not have been turned into a happy retreat, as was done by Palla Strozzi; nor would men who indulged in every conceivable excess have retained the strength and the spirit to write critical treatises on the *Natural History* of Pliny like Filippo Strozzi. Our business here is not to deal out either praise or blame, but to understand the spirit of the age in all its vigorous individuality.

Besides Florence, there were many cities of Italy where individuals and social circles devoted all their energies to the support of humanism and the protection of the scholars who lived among them. The correspondence of that period is full of references to personal relations of this kind. The feeling of the instructed classes set strongly and almost exclusively in this direction.

But it is now time to speak of humanism at the Italian courts. The natural alliance between the despot and the scholar, each relying solely on his personal talent . . . [is well known]; that the latter should avowedly prefer the princely courts to the free cities, was only to be expected from the higher pay which he there received. At a time when the great Alfonso of Aragon seemed likely to become master of all Italy, Æneas Sylvius wrote to another citizen of Siena: 'I had rather that Italy attained peace under his rule than under that of the free cities, for kingly generosity rewards excellence of every kind.' Too much stress has latterly been laid on the unworthy side of this relation, and the mercenary flattery to which it gave rise, just as formerly the eulogies of the humanists led to a too favourable judgement on their patrons. Taking all things together, it is greatly to the honour of the latter that they felt bound to place themselves at the head of the culture of their age and country, one-sided though this culture was. In some of the popes, the fearlessness of the consequences to which the new learning might lead strikes us as something truly, but unconsciously, imposing. (pp. 129-32)

Among the secular princes of the fifteenth century, none displayed such enthusiasm for antiquity as Alfonso the Great of Aragon, King of Naples. It appears that his zeal was thoroughly unaffected, and that the monuments and writings of the ancient world made upon him, from the time of his arrival in Italy, an impression deep and powerful enough to reshape his life. With strange readiness he surrendered the stubborn Aragon to his brother, and devoted himself wholly to his new possessions. He had in his service, either successively or together, George of Trebizond, the younger Chrysoloras, Lorenzo Valla, Bartolommeo Fazio and Antonio Panormita, of whom the two latter were his historians; Panormita daily instructed the King and his court in Livy, even during military expeditions. These men cost him yearly 20,000 gold florins. He gave Panormita 1,000 for his work; Fazio received for the *Historia Alfonsi*, besides a yearly income of 500 ducats, a present of 1,500 more when it was finished, with the words, 'It is not given to pay you, for your work would not be paid for if I gave you the fairest of my cities; but in time I hope to satisfy you.' When he took Giannozzo Manetti as his secretary on the most brilliant conditions, he said to him, 'My last crust I will share with you.' When Giannozzo first came to bring the congratulations of the Florentine government on the marriage of Prince Ferrante, the impression he made was so great, that the King sat motionless on the throne, 'like a brazen statue, and did not even brush away a fly, which had settled on his nose at the beginning of the oration'. His favourite haunt seems to have been the library of the castle at Naples, where he would sit at a window overlooking the bay, and listen to learned debates on the Trinity. For he was profoundly religious, and had the Bible, as well as Livy and Seneca, read to him, till after fourteen perusals he knew it almost by heart. Who can fully understand the feeling with which he regarded the supposititious remains of Livy at Padua? When, by dint of great entreaties, he obtained an arm-bone of the skeleton from the Venetians, and received it with solemn pomp at Naples, how strangely Christian and pagan sentiment must have been blended in his heart! During a campaign in the Abruzzi, when the distant Sulmona, the birthplace of Ovid, was pointed out to him, he saluted the spot and returned thanks to its tutelary genius. It gladdened him to make good the prophecy of the great poet as to his future fame. Once indeed, at his famous entry into the conquered city of Naples (1443) he himself chose to appear before the world in ancient style. Not far from the market a breach forty ells wide was made in the wall, and through this he drove in a gilded chariot like a Roman Triumphator. The memory of the scene is preserved by a noble triumphal arch of marble in the Castello Nuovo. His Neapolitan successors inherited as little of this passion for antiquity as of his other good qualities.

Alfonso was far surpassed in learning by Federigo of Urbino, who had but few courtiers around him, squandered nothing, and in his appropriation of antiquity, as in all other things, went to work considerately. It was for him and for Nicholas V that most of the translations from the Greek, and a number of the best commentaries and other such works, were written. He spent much on the scholars whose services he used, but spent it to good purpose. There were no traces of a poets' court at Urbino, where the Duke himself was the most learned in the whole court. Classical antiquity, indeed, only formed a part of his culture. An accomplished ruler, captain, and gentleman, he had mastered the greater part of the science of the day, and this with a view to its practical application. As a theologian, he was able to compare Scotus with Aquinas, and was familiar with the writings of the old Fathers of the Eastern and Western Churches, the former in Latin translations. In philosophy, he seems to have left Plato altogether to his contemporary Cosimo, but he knew thoroughly not only the *Ethics* and *Politics* of Aristotle but the *Physics* and some other works. The rest of his reading lay chiefly among the ancient historians, all of whom he possessed; these, and not the poets, 'he was always reading and having read to him'.

The Sforza, too, were all of them men of more or less learning and patrons of literature. . . . Duke Francesco probably looked on humanistic culture as a matter of course in the education of his children, if only for political reasons. It was felt universally to be an advantage if a prince could mix with the most instructed men of his time on an equal footing. Lodovico il Moro, himself an excellent Latin scholar, showed an interest in intellectual matters which extended far beyond classical antiquity.

Even the petty rulers strove after similar distinctions, and we do them injustice by thinking that they only supported the scholars at their courts as a means of diffusing their own fame. A ruler like Borso of Ferrara, with all his vanity, seems by no means to have looked for immortality from the poets, eager as they were to propitiate him with a 'Borseid' and the like. He had far too proud a sense of his own position as a ruler for that. But intercourse with learned men, interest in antiquarian matters, and the passion for elegant Latin correspondence were necessities for the princes of that age. What bitter complaints are those of Duke Alfonso, competent as he was in practical matters, that his weakliness in youth had forced him to seek recreation in manual pursuits only! or was this merely an excuse to keep the humanists at a distance? A nature like his was not intelligible even to contemporaries.

Even the most insignificant despots of Romagna found it hard to do without one or two men of letters about them. The tutor and secretary were often one and the same person, who sometimes, indeed, acted as a kind of court factotum. We are apt to treat the small scale of these courts as a reason for dismissing them with a too ready contempt, forgetting that the highest spiritual things are not precisely matters of measurement.

Life and manners at the court of Rimini must have been a singular spectacle under the bold pagan Condottiere Sigismondo Malatesta. He had a number of scholars around him, some of whom he provided for liberally, even giving them landed estates, while others earned at least a livelihood as officers in his army. In his citadel— 'arx Sismundea'—they used to hold discussions, often of a very venomous kind, in the presence of the 'rex', as they termed him. In their Latin poems they sing his praises and celebrate his amour with the fair Isotta, in whose honour and as whose monument the famous rebuilding of San Francesco at Rimini took place—'Divæ Isottæ Sacrum'. When the humanists themselves came to die, they were laid in or under the sarcophagi with which the niches of the outside walls of the church were adorned, with an inscription testifying that they were laid here at the time when Sigismundus, the son of Pandulfus, ruled. It is hard for us nowadays to believe that a monster like this prince felt learning and the friendship of cultivated people to be a necessity of life; and yet the man who excommunicated him, made war upon him, and burnt him in effigy, Pope Pius II, says: 'Sigismondo knew history and had a great store of philosophy; he seemed born to all that he undertook'. (pp. 134-36)

Jacob Burckhardt, "The Revival of Antiquity: Propagators of Antiquity," in his The Civilization of the Renaissance: An Essay, *edited by L. Goldscheider, translated by S. G. C. Middlemore, revised edition, Phaidon Press Ltd., 1951, pp. 128-36.*

PAUL OSKAR KRISTELLER

[*Kristeller is a German-born American educator and author who has written extensively on the Renaissance. C. B. Schmitt has observed that "the influence exerted by Kristeller on the philosophico-intellectual side of Renaissance studies has been greater than that of any of his contemporaries." In the following excerpt from an essay originally published in 1943, Kristeller broadly addresses humanist contributions to Renaissance learning, commenting especially on the revival of classical letters in fifteenth-century Italy.*]

I do believe that classical humanism was, if not the only, certainly the most characteristic and pervasive intellectual current of [the Renaissance]. With its merits and with its limitations, humanism pervaded more or less all achievements and expressions of the fifteenth century. When its influence declined in the sixteenth century, its work had been already done. The influence of humanism on science as well as on philosophy was indirect, but powerful. The actual performance of the humanists in these fields was rather poor. But they popularized the entire body of ancient Greek learning and literature and thus made available new source materials of which the professional scientists and philosophers could not fail to take advantage. This was important, because at that time occidental science and thought had not yet reached or surpassed the results of classical antiquity, and hence had still something to learn from the ancients. Moreover, medieval science had developed in definite patterns, and the introduction of new sources and "authorities" eventually prepared the way for new methods and theories. Those who claim that ancient science was completely known to the Middle Ages are as mistaken as those who deny that it was known at all. At least some of the classical Latin authors became more widely known in the Renaissance, Lucretius, for example. Numerous Greek manuscripts were brought over from the East, and more men were able to read them in the original. Moreover, practically all the Greek texts were translated into Latin by the humanists, many for the first time. The question of how many were translated for the first time and whether the new translations were better or more influential than the extant earlier translations, cannot be settled by dispute, but only by a careful bibliography of the Latin translations from the Greek, which should include the manuscript materials. In the field of philosophy, humanism introduced most of the works of Plato, Plotinus, Epictetus, Diogenes Laertius, Plutarch, Lucian, as well as many works of the commentators on Aristotle and of the Greek Fathers, not to speak of the Greek poets, historians, and orators. In science the contribution may be less impressive, but it has still to be investigated. Archimedes and Hero came at least to be more widely known, and many of the minor mathematicians were translated for the first time. The Latin translations were followed by extensive commentaries, and by translations into the various vernacular languages which reached an even wider public.

The humanists were certainly not the only representatives of science and learning in the fifteenth century. On the one hand, there were the followers of the medieval traditions who carried on the work of their predecessors, especially at the various universities. On the other hand, there were the artists and engineers who through their practical work came face to face with mathematical and scientific problems and sometimes made important contributions, as has been recently emphasized. But in the fifteenth century both of these latter groups were influenced by humanism, as was the general public. If the humanists failed to make substantial contributions to the various fields of traditional learning, they did introduce source materials and problems which could be applied to those fields. By the end of the fifteenth century, humanism had not indeed replaced the traditional learning, but the representatives of traditional learning had absorbed the achievements of humanism. This accounts for the changes and progress which took place in the sixteenth century, just as the achievements of the artists and engineers were taken over by the professional scientists after the middle of that century. On the other hand, even the artists and engineers were subject to the influence of humanism. . . . The personal relations between the humanists and the artists need further investigation, especially as they appear from numerous letters and poems of the humanists which have not yet been utilized for this purpose. The number of artists and engineers who made active contributions to science was still comparatively small in the fifteenth century as compared with the sixteenth. But the case of Leon Battista Alberti shows that this scientific activity of the artists cannot be separated from, or opposed to, contemporary humanism.

I cannot agree with those who identify these artists with the general public of the unlearned or who make a sharp contrast between the "Academic" humanists who wrote in Latin, and the "popular" writers who used the vernacular language. Those artists who also wrote scientific treatises certainly had some learning beyond that of the general public, and drew something from the professional learning of their time, whether it was in the medieval or in the humanistic tradition. The humanists themselves, no less than these artists, impressed the popular imagination of their time, as many anecdotes show. Since this was a matter of fashion, no real understanding on the part of the public was required. If today many admire the achievements of modern science without understanding its methods, we may well grant that in the early renaissance many admired the humanists without understanding their Latin. Moreover, the question of language is less important for our problem than might be supposed. In the fifteenth century there is abundant evidence for the mutual influence between vernacular and Neo-Latin literature, and when the vernacular definitely won out in the sixteenth

Portrait of a woman, by Sandro Botticelli.

century, it had already absorbed the characteristic achievements of humanism, in style, terminology, literary form, and subject matter. Otherwise, it could not have replaced Latin.

To conclude, I should like to add . . . that by popularizing in the fifteenth century the works of classical antiquity, the humanists made an important, though indirect contribution to the development of science and philosophy, and that this contribution bore fruit not only in the work of the humanists themselves, but also in that of the professional scientists and artists of their time and of the following century. All these statements, however, are tentative rather than final, and subject to further revision. The only thing that really counts in Renaissance studies is the actual investigation of the extensive source materials which have not yet been included in any extant synthesis. This investigation must proceed with the cooperation of all scholars interested in the period, regardless of their point of view. In this study we should try to eliminate so far as possible our personal preference for or against this or that nation, language, class, current, or field, and to arrive at a fair evaluation of the contribution each of them has made to the whole of occidental civilization. Such an evaluation will not depend wholly on the influence, direct or distant, which each phenomenon has exercised on later developments, but will also acknowledge the inherent, "absolute" significance of many ideas and achievements which for some reason or other failed to have any visible influence. It is this significance, rather than any incidental sequence of changes or influences, which in my opinion should be the ultimate purpose of the history of ideas, if not of all history. (pp. 12-15)

Paul Oskar Kristeller, "The Place of Classical Humanism in Renaissance Thought," in his Studies in Renaissance Thought and Letters, *Edizioni di Storia e Letteratura, 1956, pp. 11-15.*

GEORGE SAINTSBURY

[*Saintsbury was a late nineteenth- and early twentieth-century English literary historian and critic. In the following excerpt from his historical survey of the quattrocento,* The Earlier Renaissance (*1901*), *he notes humanist achievements in classical studies.*]

That Italian Humanism, from which all other varieties were to spring more or less immediately, draws its fount and origin, as such things go, from Petrarch, is an accepted *datum* of literary history which need not be attacked or denied. It is, indeed, necessary here as elsewhere to repeat the warning (so constantly neglected by literary historians, yet so necessary for the literary historian to keep as a sign upon his hand and as a frontlet between his eyes) that such things never really come from an individual—that they are winds of the spirit blowing no man knows whence, dews of heaven sinking into the earth and reappearing as streams no man knows how. All that we can in such cases justly say is that one man seems to trim his sail before others to the breeze, to hold his pitcher before others to catch the stream. Petrarch certainly does appear to deserve this credit in the present instance. . . . Both Petrarch and Boccaccio] agreed in that eager and almost ferocious quest for the actual writings of antiquity, as to which all sane critics are agreed that it was the work which Humanism had to do, and the work which it is chiefly to be thanked for doing. And putting the points in which they agreed together with the points in which they differed—that is to say, Plutarch's quest for Latin style and Boccaccio's for Latin and Greek knowledge—they may be said between them to have very nearly exhausted all that Humanism had of good in germ if not in fulness, with the exception of the purely critical side, which neither shows. To recover and make sure of the riches of antiquity; to understand them; to copy them as far as was possible—these were the aims of these two great men. Petrarch at least showed something of the coming folly of despising his mother tongue, or affecting to despise it; but it was not really possible for the author of the *Rime* to do this seriously, and so long as he was the author of the *Rime* it did not much matter whether he was serious or not. He and Boccaccio between them gloriously continued the work of Dante in verse, while Boccaccio extended it in the direction of prose, so far as the vernacular was concerned. What they also did in reference to the learned languages was therefore pure gain in every respect.

Not so much can be said of their successors, the travelling scholars and lecturers who represent the first three-quarters of the Fifteenth century.

Although it has been generally admitted that these Humanists of the main body did not, as a rule, deserve very well of their mother tongue, yet their services in assuring, not merely to their own age but to all future time, the possession of the inestimable treasures of antiquity have been justly counted to them as more than counterbalancing righteousness. And they

have also appealed to the natural appetite for picturesque contrast, and to other appetites not quite so respectable. The notion of these scholars—wandering first over Italy and then over Europe; rising by their own efforts from the position of penniless nobodies, destitute in many though not in all cases of birth, breeding, or wealth, to that of the familiar and honoured companions of princes and prelates; marrying beautiful, rich, and well-born damsels; allured from state to state and city to city by golden bribes; setting out in quest of the buried treasures of learning like knights of adventure; helping to despatch generation after generation of neophytes, often from half-barbarous nations, to spread learning and the appreciation of beauty all over Europe; honoured in their deaths with stately monuments, and rewarded by posterity for no few generations not merely as good workers in their day and way, but as men of genius and public benefactors,—all this has excited interest neither unnatural nor ungenerous, though perhaps sometimes a little uncritical. Even their much more questionable virtues, and their quite unquestionable vices, have also made them interesting. The ludicrous vanity and the cat-like quarrelsomeness which distinguished most of them have not been disagreeable to that somewhat morbid taste for "curiosities of literature," "quarrels of authors," and the like, which undoubtedly does exist in many persons. It is to be feared that the licence, conventional or sincere, of their sentiments and language has not been without a certain attractive effect in some cases. And the devotees of free-thought have not failed to celebrate them as "champions of the modern spirit," as having "vindicated the rights of the human soul," and all the rest of the well-known cant of anti-cant.

We have here, fortunately, nothing to do with free-thought, or the rights of the spirit, or any other of the regalia and paraphernalia of this kind of craft or mystery. We have not much, but something (for it is a distinctly literary feature), to do with the peculiarities which make the lighter work of Beccadelli and Filelfo, of Politian and Pontanus, so exceedingly "curious," in the bibliographical sense of that adjective. With the position of the Humanists in literary history and the value of their work as literature, we have a very great deal to do.

It is admitted that till we come to the extreme end of the century, the intrinsic value of Humanist work, vernacular or Latin, is exceedingly small, while its critical attitude to literature shows no advance, and even some falling off, from that of the Middle Ages. In regard to the first head, the *Facetiæ* of Poggio and the *Euryalus and Lucretia* of Æneas Sylvius are not exactly great literature, yet it would be difficult to say what better things the early and middle divisions of the century produced. With regard to the second, Vittorino da Feltre, one of the best of the whole school, is admitted to have been the first, and was apparently for a long time almost the only, teacher who was himself alive, and who endeavoured to make his pupils alive, to the differences of style and kind in the writers of antiquity.

But, it is said, they gained the classics for us and made them known. If this were wholly, as it is partly true, and if it were the whole of the truth, there would be little or nothing more to say. But, in the first place, the actual recovery and publication of MSS. was a small part of the work of the Humanists of 1375-1475; in the second, a great deal more was previously known than is sometimes allowed; in the third, the credit is at least not less, perhaps more, due to the princes and merchant-princes who would have these things, than to the scholars, who were often little more than their commercial travellers or collectors; and in the fourth, considering the general trend of thought in all countries, the thing would pretty certainly have been done if these particular men had not done it. But let us grudge them no possible credit for what they did do in this way.

They cannot, it may be feared, be said to have done very much in others. Aided by, and aiding, the fashion, they were no doubt sometimes good, and always more or less useful, teachers; but there are good and useful teachers in all times, and the office, alas! is seldom more than that of the unprofitable servant, who does but what it is his duty to do. They were not, as a rule, good grammarians, and were scarcely ever good critics; and if it be said that it is ungenerous to blame them for this, let it be remembered that if they had spent on real study half the time that they wasted on vain jactation, and idle quarrelling, and the composition of indecent verses, they might have made themselves very good grammarians, and much better critics than they were.

But the chief mistake and the greatest error of the Humanists, when tried before the high court of serene historical criticism, is the enormous waste of their energies on Latin translation of Greek. It is true that it was the most paying work that they, as working men of letters, could undertake; but this excuse, though valid up to a point, is not valid beyond that point. It is true also that though, in the reluctant epigram extorted from a defender of theirs, these translations "were done for the most part by Greeks who had an imperfect knowledge of Latin and by Italians who had not complete mastery of Greek," it would be really ungenerous to lay much stress on this. The important point, from the literary point of view, is that a translation from Greek into Latin could at most do good to the man who made it by improving his own knowledge of the two languages, was but too likely to hinder the study of Greek itself, and could hardly fail to produce the impression that the matter of Greek, and not its literary beauty, was its title to greatness.

This process of translation from Greek, not into the vernacular but into Latin, and the concomitant use of Latin itself for original or quasi-original composition, not only could do little or nothing for the progress of the actual vernacular, but were even antagonistic to that progress. The process resembled in no whit the effect produced on English most of all, and on French and German to some extent, by the age-long practice of translation from Latin, and from modern languages, into the actual living tongue. It is to this process that English in particular owes its extraordinary wealth of vocabulary, and the unrivalled splendour and variety which, even more than mere wealth, distinguish it. But Italian remained unenriched by any contributions of the kind. Nor could the additional familiarity with Latin itself fail to weaken as well as to refine Italian. For it was a kind of process of "breeding in and in," of pouring in more water where the water had already choked. The wonderful effect of the blends of Latin and French, which were unceasingly poured into English between the eleventh and the sixteenth century, and which by the latter date had made it a not much more than recognisable descendant of the language of Caedmon and Cynewulf, is paralleled by nothing in Italian. On the contrary, the accomplished Italian of our present period is far thinner and weaker than Dante's own, though it may be more elegant; nor does the language seem ever to have fortified itself since. The Fifteenth century was the great time of this process of fortification in

all other European tongues, and the missing of the opportunity was, at least partly, the fault of the Humanists.

It may, however, be urged, with some show of reason, that at the end of the period immediately preceding our own, no small atonement was made. Most assuredly the great Florentines and Neapolitans, . . .—Æneas Sylvius, Sannazar, Pontanus, Alberti, Marsilio Ficino, Pico della Mirandula, and above all Politian,—whether they write entirely in Latin, or, like Sannazar and Politian, are masters of either instrument; they provide literature of an accomplished kind in both classes of writing; they advance, refine, reform the literary quality.

Once more we must not deny the truth of this; yet once more it will be difficult for even the greatest representatives of Humanism at this time to make good any very much higher claims than those secure and great ones, of having been the channels and the distributors of classical learning to countries and to individuals that could make better use of it than themselves.

For throughout—in the Utraquists as well as in the Monoglots, in Politian and Sannazar as in Piccolomini and Pontano—the fault and the mischief of the Humanist position are seen in the strange unrealities of many kinds, which mar their vernacular and their "regular" work alike. Everything is out of focus. The famous transference of the Pagan ecclesiastical dictionary to Christian use; the employment of Jupiter Optimus Maximus to designate the divinity whose worshippers, in the very towns where the words were written, had been cast to the lions for refusing to worship the said Jupiter; the fitting of the whole terminology of Latin ritual into the services of the Christian Church; the sincere horror, late in our own period, of an equally sincere Christian like Lilius Giraldus at the person who, *si Deo placet!* wanted of Sannazar *dictionem Christianam id est barbaram;* other well-known and often-quoted things, which it is not necessary to quote again, merely give the results of this mischief in one particular direction. The evil was, in fact, all-pervading in literature. The Latin poets themselves had gone beyond measure, and certainly far beyond the Greeks, in appropriating stock imagery, stock characters, stock phrases, to different literary kinds; but the Humanists out-aped them twenty-fold. To the practice of this time, and to its criticism a little later . . . are due the "pastoral" frippery which revolted even such a sturdy Latinist and neo-classic as Dr Johnson, and which, to make it quite tolerable, requires the superhuman poetry of a Milton or a Shelley,—the tawdry and tumbled finery of the "heroic poem," with its cut-and-dried exordia and invocations, its cut-and-dried supernatural interferences, its cut-and-dried revolutions, its cut-and-dried everything. In those who did not write Italian the principle and its practice produced at best *pastiche;* in those who wrote Italian as well, they produced something which was not only *pastiche* but patchwork. Even the great Politian, the man who really might, without much absurdity, have echoed Filelfo's absurd boast that he could write as well in Greek as in Latin, and as well in Italian as in either, suffers (at least in some judgments) terribly from this mixture, and from the sense of unreality, of the school exercise, of the copy of verses. And all the others suffer much more. (pp. 5-14)

George Saintsbury, "The Harvest-Time of Humanism," in his The Earlier Renaissance, *William Blackwood and Sons, 1901, pp. 1-102.*

HUMANISM AND OTHER PHILOSOPHIES

PAUL OSKAR KRISTELLER

[*In the following excerpt from an essay originally published in*
Byzantion *in 1944, Kristeller explores the relationship between
Italian humanism and philosophical currents of the Middle
Ages.*]

Ever since 1860, when Jacob Burckhardt first published his
famous book on the civilization of the Renaissance in Italy,
there has been a controversy among historians as to the
meaning and significance of the Italian Renaissance. Almost
every scholar who has taken part in the discussion felt it was
his duty to advance a new and different theory. This variety
of views was partly due to the emphasis given by individual
scholars to different historical personalities or currents or to
different aspects and developments of the Italian Renaissance. Yet the chief cause of the entire Renaissance controversy, at least in its more recent phases, has been the considerable progress made during the last few decades in the field
of medieval studies. The Middle Ages are no longer considered as a period of darkness, and consequently many scholars
do not see the need for such new light and revival as the very
name of the Renaissance would seem to suggest. Thus certain
medievalists have questioned the very existence of the Renaissance and would like to banish the term entirely from the
vocabulary of historians.

In the face of this powerful attack, Renaissance scholars have
assumed a new line of defense. They have shown that the notion embodied in the term *Renaissance* was not an invention
of enthusiastic historians of the last century, but was commonly expressed in the literature of the period of the Renaissance itself. The humanists themselves speak continually of
the revival or rebirth of the arts and of learning that was accomplished in their own time after a long period of decay. It
may be objected that occasional claims of an intellectual revival are also found in medieval literature. Yet the fact remains that during the Renaissance scholars and writers
talked of such a revival and rebirth more persistently than at
any other period of European history. Even if we were convinced that it was an empty claim and that the humanists did
not bring about a real Renaissance, we would still be forced
to admit that the illusion itself was characteristic of that period and that the term Renaissance thus had at least a subjective meaning.

Without questioning the validity of this argument, I think
that there are also some more objective reasons for defending
the existence and the importance of the Renaissance. The
concept of style as it has been so successfully applied by historians of art might be more widely applied in other fields of
intellectual history and might thus enable us to recognize the
significant changes brought about by the Renaissance, without obliging us to despise the Middle Ages or to minimize the
debt of the Renaissance to the medieval tradition.

Moreover, I should like to reexamine the relation between the
Middle Ages and the Renaissance in the light of the following
consideration. Scholars have become so accustomed to stress
the universalism of the medieval church and of medieval culture and also to consider the Italian Renaissance as a European phenomenon, that they are apt to forget that profound regional differences existed even during the Middle Ages. The
center of medieval civilization was undoubtedly France, and
all other countries of Western Europe followed the leadership
of that country, from Carolingian times down to the beginning of the fourteenth century. Italy certainly was no exception to that rule; but whereas the other countries, especially
England, Germany, and the Low Countries, took an active
part in the major cultural pursuits of the period and followed
the same general development, Italy occupied a somewhat
peculiar position. Prior to the thirteenth century, her active
participation in many important aspects of medieval culture
lagged far behind that of the other countries. This may be observed in architecture and music, in the religious drama as
well as in Latin and vernacular poetry in general, in scholastic philosophy and theology, and even, contrary to common
opinion, in classical studies. On the other hand, Italy had a
narrow but persistent tradition of her own which went back
to ancient Roman times and which found its expression in
certain branches of the arts and of poetry, in lay education
and in legal customs, and in the study of grammar and of
rhetoric. Italy was more directly and more continually exposed to Byzantine influences than any other Western European country. Finally, after the eleventh century, Italy developed a new life of her own which found expression in her
trade and economy, in the political institutions of her cities,
in the study of civil and canon law and of medicine, and in
the techniques of letter-writing and of secular eloquence. Influences from France became more powerful only with the
thirteenth century, when their traces appeared in architecture and music, in Latin and vernacular poetry, in philosophy
and theology, and in the field of classical studies. Many typical products of the Italian Renaissance may thus be understood as a result of belated medieval influences received from
France, but grafted upon, and assimilated by, a more narrow,
but stubborn and different native tradition. This may be said
of Dante's *Divine Comedy,* of the religious drama which
flourished in fifteenth century Florence, and of the chivalric
poetry of Ariosto and of Tasso.

A similar development may be noticed in the history of learning. The Italian Renaissance thus should be viewed not only
in its contrast with the French Middle Ages, but also in its
relation to the Italian Middle Ages. The rich civilization of
Renaissance Italy did not spring directly from the equally
rich civilization of medieval France, but from the much more
modest traditions of medieval Italy. It is only about the beginning of the fourteenth century that Italy witnessed a tremendous increase in all her cultural activities, and this enabled her, for a certain period, to wrest from France her cultural leadership in Western Europe. Consequently, there can
be no doubt that there was an Italian Renaissance, that is, a
cultural Renaissance of Italy, not so much in contrast with
the Middle Ages in general or with the French Middle Ages,
but very definitely in contrast with the Italian Middle Ages.
It appears from a letter of Boccaccio that this general development was well understood by some Italians of that period,
and we should keep this development constantly in mind if
we want to understand the history of learning during the Italian Renaissance.

The most characteristic and most pervasive aspect of the Italian Renaissance in the field of learning is the humanistic
movement. I need hardly say that the term "humanism",
when applied to the Italian Renaissance, does not imply all
the vague and confused notions that are now commonly associated with it. Only a few traces of these may be found in the
Renaissance. By humanism we mean merely the general ten-

dency of the age to attach the greatest importance to classical studies, and to consider classical antiquity as the common standard and model by which to guide all cultural activities. (pp. 553-57)

[The] Italian humanists were the ancestors of modern philologists and historians. Even a historian of science can afford to despise them only if he chooses to remember that science is the subject of his study, but to forget that the method he is applying to this subject is that of history. However, the activity of the Italian humanists was not limited to classical scholarship, and hence the theory which interprets the humanistic movement merely as a rise in classical scholarship is not altogether satisfactory. This theory fails to explain the ideal of eloquence persistently set forth in the writings of the humanists, and it fails to account for the enormous literature of treatises, of letters, of speeches, and of poems produced by the humanists.

These writings are far more numerous than the contributions of the humanists to classical scholarship, and they cannot be explained as a necessary consequence of their classical studies. A modern classical scholar is not supposed to write a Latin poem in praise of his city, to welcome a distinguished foreign visitor with a Latin speech, or to write a political manifesto for his government. This aspect of the activity of the humanists is often dismissed with a slighting remark about their vanity or their fancy for speech-making. I do not deny that they were vain and loved to make speeches, but I am inclined to offer a different explanation for this side of their activity. The humanists were not classical scholars who for personal reasons had a craving for eloquence, but, vice versa, they were professional rhetoricians, heirs and successors of the medieval rhetoricians, who developed the belief, then new and modern, that the best way to achieve eloquence was to imitate classical models, and who thus were driven to study the classics and to found classical philology. Their rhetorical ideals and achievements may not correspond to our taste, but they were the starting point and moving force of their activity, and their classical learning was incidental to it.

The other current interpretation of Italian humanism, which is prevalent among historians of philosophy and also accepted by many other scholars, is more ambitious, but in my opinion less sound. This interpretation considers humanism as the new philosophy of the Renaissance, which arose in opposition to scholasticism, the old philosophy of the Middle Ages. Of course, there is the well known fact that several famous humanists, such as Petrarch, Valla, Erasmus, and Vives, were violent critics of medieval learning and tended to replace it by classical learning. Moreover, the humanists certainly had ideals of learning, education, and life that differed from medieval modes of thinking. They wrote treatises on moral, educational, political, and religious questions which in tone and content differ from the average medieval treatises on similar subjects. Yet this interpretation of humanism as a new philosophy fails to account for a number of obvious facts. On one hand, we notice a stubborn survival of scholastic philosophy throughout the Italian Renaissance, an inconvenient fact that is usually explained by the intellectual inertia of the respective philosophers whom almost nobody has read for centuries and whose number, problems and literary production are entirely unknown to most historians. On the other, most of the works of the humanists have nothing to do with philosophy even in the vaguest possible sense of the term. Even their treatises on philosophical subjects, if we care to read them, ap-

pear in most cases rather superficial and inconclusive if compared with the works of ancient or medieval philosophers, a fact that may be indifferent to a general historian, but which cannot be overlooked by a historian of philosophy.

I think there has been a tendency, in the light of later developments, and under the influence of a modern aversion to scholasticism, to exaggerate the opposition of the humanists to scholasticism, and to assign to them an importance in the history of scientific and philosophical thought which they neither could nor did attain. The reaction against this tendency has been inevitable, but it has been equally wrong. Those scholars who read the treatises of the humanists and noticed their comparative emptiness of scientific and philosophical thought came to the conclusion that the humanists were bad scientists and philosophers who did not live up to their own claims or to those of their modern advocates. I should like to suggest that the Italian humanists on the whole were neither good nor bad philosophers, but no philosophers at all.

The humanistic movement did not originate in the field of philosophical or scientific studies, but it arose in that of grammatical and rhetorical studies. The humanists continued the medieval tradition in these fields, as represented, for example, by the *ars dictaminis* and the *ars arengandi,* but they gave it a new direction toward classical standards and classical studies, possibly under the impact of influences received from France after the middle of the thirteenth century. This new development of the field was followed by an enormous growth, both in the quantity and in the quality, of its teaching and its literary production. As a result of this growth, the claims of the humanists for their field of study also increased considerably. They claimed, and temporarily attained, a decided predominance of their field in elementary and secondary education, and a much larger share for it in professional and university education. This development in the field of grammatical and rhetorical studies finally affected the other branches of learning, but it did not displace them. After the middle of the fifteenth century, we find an increasing number of professional jurists, physicians, mathematicians, philosophers, and theologians who cultivated humanistic studies along with their own particular fields of study. Consequently, a humanistic influence began to appear in all these other sciences. It appears in the studied elegance of literary expression, in the increasing use made of classical source materials, in the greater knowledge of history and of critical methods, and also sometimes in an emphasis on new problems. This influence of humanism on the other sciences certainly was important, but it did not affect the content or substance of the medieval traditions in those sciences. For the humanists, being amateurs in those other fields, had nothing to offer that could replace their traditional content and subject matter.

The humanist criticism of medieval science is often sweeping, but it does not touch its specific problems and subject-matter. Their main charges are against the bad Latin style of the medieval authors, against their ignorance of ancient history and literature, and against their concern for supposedly useless questions. On the other hand, even those professional scientists who were most profoundly influenced by humanism did not sacrifice the medieval tradition of their field. It is highly significant that Pico, a representative of humanist philosophy, and Alciato, a representative of humanist jurisprudence, found it necessary to defend their medieval predecessors against the criticism of humanist rhetoricians.

Yet if the humanists were amateurs in jurisprudence, theology, medicine, and also in philosophy, they were themselves professionals in a number of other fields. Their domain were the fields of grammar, rhetoric, poetry, history, and the study of the Greek and Latin authors. They also expanded into the field of moral philosophy, and they made some attempts to invade the field of logic, which were chiefly attempts to reduce logic to rhetoric.

Yet they did not make any direct contributions to the other branches of philosophy or of science. Moreover, much of the humanist polemic against medieval science was not even intended as a criticism of the contents or methods of that science, but merely represents a phase in the "battle of the arts", that is, a noisy advertisement for the field of learning advocated by the humanists, in order to neutralize and to overcome the claims of other, rivaling sciences. Hence I am inclined to consider the humanists not as philosophers with a curious lack of philosophical ideas and a curious fancy for eloquence and for classical studies, but rather as professional rhetoricians with a new, classicist ideal of culture, who tried to assert the importance of their field of learning and to impose their standards upon the other fields of learning and of science, including philosophy.

Let us try to illustrate this outline with a few more specific facts. When we inquire of the humanists, it is often asserted that they were free-lance writers who came to form an entirely new class in Renaissance society. This statement is valid, although with some qualification, for a very small number of outstanding humanists like Petrarch, Boccaccio, and Erasmus. However, these are exceptions, and the vast majority of humanists exercised either of two professions, and sometimes both of them. They were either secretaries of princes or cities, or they were teachers of grammar and rhetoric at universities or at secondary schools. The opinion so often repeated by historians that the humanistic movement originated outside the schools and universities is a myth which cannot be supported by factual evidence. Moreover, as chancellors and as teachers, the humanists, far from representing a new class, were the professional heirs and successors of the medieval rhetoricians, the so-called *dictatores,* who also made their career exactly in these same two professions. The humanist Coluccio Salutati occupied exactly the same place in the society and culture of his time as did the *dictator* Petrus de Vineis one hundred and fifty years before. Nevertheless there was a significant difference between them. The style of writing used by Salutati is quite different from that of Petrus de Vineis or of Rolandinus Passagerii. Moreover, the study and imitation of the classics which was of little or no importance to the medieval *dictatores* has become the major concern for Salutati. Finally, whereas the medieval *dictatores* attained considerable importance in politics and in administration, the humanists, through their classical learning, acquired for their class a much greater cultural and social prestige. Thus the humanists did not invent a new field of learning or a new professional activity, but they introduced a new, classicist style into the traditions of medieval Italian rhetoric. To blame them for not having invented rhetorical studies would be like blaming Giotto for not having been the inventor of painting.

The same result is confirmed by an examination of the literary production of the humanists if we try to trace the medieval antecedents of the types of literature cultivated by the humanists. If we leave aside the editions and translations of the humanists, their classical interests are chiefly represented by their numerous commentaries on ancient authors and by a number of antiquarian and miscellaneous treatises. Theoretical works on grammar and rhetoric, mostly composed for the school, are quite frequent, and even more numerous is the literature of humanist historiography. Dialogues and treatises on questions of moral philosophy, education, politics, and religion have attracted most of the attention of modern historians, but represent a comparatively small proportion of humanistic literature. By far the largest part of that literature, although relatively neglected and partly unpublished, consists of the poems, the speeches, and the letters of the humanists.

If we look for the medieval antecedents of these various types of humanistic literature, we are led back in many cases to the Italian grammarians and rhetoricians of the later Middle Ages. This is most obvious for the theoretical treatises on grammar and rhetoric. Less generally recognized, but almost equally obvious is the link between humanist epistolography and medieval *ars dictaminis.* The style of writing is different, to be sure, and the medieval term *dictamen* was no longer used during the Renaissance, yet the literary and political function of the letter was basically the same, and the ability to write a correct and elegant Latin letter was still a major aim of school instruction in the Renaissance as it had been in the Middle Ages.

The same link between humanists and medieval Italian rhetoricians which we notice in the field of epistolography may be found also in the field of oratory. Most historians of rhetoric give the impression that medieval rhetoric was exclusively concerned with letter-writing and preaching, represented by the *ars dictaminis* and the somewhat younger *ars praedicandi,* and that there was no secular eloquence in the Middle Ages. On the other hand, most historians of Renaissance humanism believe that the large output of humanist oratory, although of a somewhat dubious value, was an innovation of the Renaissance due to the effort of the humanists to revive ancient oratory and also to their vain fancy for speech-making. Only in recent years have a few scholars begun to realize that there was a considerable amount of secular eloquence in the Middle Ages, especially in Italy. I do not hesitate to conclude that the eloquence of the humanists was the continuation of the medieval *ars arengandi* just as their epistolography continued the tradition of the *ars dictaminis.* It is true, in taking up a type of literary production developed by their medieval predecessors, the humanists modified its style according to their own taste and classicist standards. Yet the practice of speech-making was no invention of the humanist, of course, since it is hardly absent from any human society, and since in medieval Italy it can be traced back at least to the eleventh century.

Even the theory of secular speech, represented by rules and instructions as well as by model speeches, appears in Italy at least as early as the thirteenth century. Indeed practically all types of humanist oratory have their antecedents in this medieval literature: wedding and funeral speeches, academic speeches, political speeches by officials or ambassadors, decorative speeches on solemn occasions, and finally judicial speeches. Some of these types, to be sure, had their classical models, but others, for example, academic speeches delivered at the beginning of the year or of a particular course or upon conferring or receiving a degree, had no classical antecedents whatsoever, and all these types of oratory were rooted in very specific customs and institutions of medieval Italy. The humanists invented hardly any of these types of speech, but they merely applied their standards of style and elegance to a previously existing form of literary expression and thus satisfied a demand, both practical and artistic, of the society of their time. Modern scholars are apt to speak contemptuously of this humanistic oratory, denouncing its empty rhetoric and its lack of "deep thoughts". Yet the humanists merely intended to speak well, according to their taste and to the occasion, and it still remains to be seen whether they were less successful in that respect than their medieval predecessors or their modern successors. Being pieces of "empty rhetoric", their speeches provide us with an amazing amount of information about the personal and intellectual life of their time.

In their historiography, the humanists succeeded the medieval chroniclers, yet they differ from them both in their merits and in their deficiencies. Humanist historiography is characterized by the rhetorical concern for elegant Latin and by the application of philological criticism to the source materials of history. In both respects, they are the predecessors of modern historians. To combine the requirements of a good style and those of careful research was as rare and difficult then as it is at present. However, the link between history and rhetoric that seems to be so typical of the Renaissance was apparently a medieval heritage. Not only was the teaching of history in the medieval schools subordinate to that of grammar and rhetoric, but we also find quite a few medieval historiographers and chronists who were professional grammarians and rhetoricians. Even the Renaissance custom of princes and cities appointing official historiographers to write their history seems to have had a few antecedents in medieval Italy.

Most of the philosophical treatises and dialogues of the humanists are really nothing but moral tracts, and many of them deal with subject matters also treated in the moralistic literature of the Middle Ages. There are, to be sure, significant differences in style, treatment, sources, and solutions. However, the common features of the topics and literary patterns should not be overlooked either. A thorough comparative study of medieval and Renaissance moral treatises has not yet been made so far as I am aware, but in a few specific cases the connection has been pointed out. Again it should be added that the very link between rhetoric and moral philosophy which became so apparent in the Renaissance had its antecedents in the Middle Ages. Medieval rhetoric, no less than ancient rhetoric, was continually quoting and inculcating moral sentences that interested the authors and their readers for their content as well as for their form. Moreover, there are at least a few cases in which medieval rhetoricians wrote treatises on topics of moral philosophy, or argued about the same moral questions that were to exercise the minds and pens of their successors, the Renaissance humanists.

Less definite is the link between humanists and medieval Italian rhetoricians in the field of Latin poetry. On the basis of available evidence, it would seem that in the Italian schools up to the thirteenth century versemaking was less cultivated than in France. Throughout the earlier Middle Ages, historical and panegyric epics as well as verse epitaphs were composed abundantly in Italy, yet prior to the thirteenth century her share in rhythmical and in didactic poetry seems to have been rather modest. It is only after the middle of the thirteenth century that we notice a marked increase in the production of Latin poetry in Italy, and the appearance of the teaching of poetry in the schools and universities. This devel-

opment coincides with the earliest traces of Italian humanism, and it is tempting to ascribe it to French influences.

The same may be said with more confidence of the literature of commentaries on the Latin classics, which are the direct result of school teaching. It is often asserted that Italy throughout the Middle Ages was closer to the classical tradition than any other European country. Yet if we try to trace the type of the humanistic commentary back into the Middle Ages, we find hardly any commentary on a Latin poet or prose writer composed in Italy prior to the second half of the thirteenth century, whereas we find many such commentaries, from the ninth century on, written in France or in the other Western countries that followed the French development. Only after 1300, that is, after the earliest phase of humanism, did Italy produce an increasing number of such commentaries. Also of antiquarian studies there is very little evidence in Italy prior to the latter part of the thirteenth century. Whereas we have abundant information about the reading of the Latin poets and prose writers in the medieval schools of France and of other Western countries, and whereas such centers as Chartres and Orléans in the twelfth and early thirteenth century owed much of their fame to the study of the Latin classics, the sources for Italy are silent during the same period and begin to speak only after the middle of the thirteenth century. It was only after the beginning of the fourteenth century that the teaching of poetry and of the classical authors became firmly established in the Italian schools and universities, to continue without interruption throughout the Renaissance. Italian libraries, with the one exception of Monte Cassino, were not so well furnished with Latin classical poets as were some French and German libraries, and it has been noticed that the humanists of the fifteenth century made most of their manuscript discoveries not in Italy, but in other countries. The conclusion seems inevitable that the study of classical Latin authors was comparatively neglected in Italy during the earlier Middle Ages and was introduced from France after the middle of the thirteenth century. The Italian humanists thus took up the work of their medieval French predecessors just about the time when classical studies began to decline in France, and whereas the classical scholarship of the earliest humanists in its range and method was still close to the medieval tradition, that of the later Renaissance developed far beyond anything attained during the Middle Ages. Consequently, if we consider the entire literary production of the Italian humanists we are led to the conclusion that the humanistic movement seems to have originated from a fusion between the novel interest in classical studies imported from France toward the end of the thirteenth century and the much earlier traditions of medieval Italian rhetoric. (pp. 559-71)

If we care to look beyond the field of the humanities into the other fields of learning as they were cultivated during the Italian Renaissance, that is, into jurisprudence, medicine, theology, mathematics, and natural philosophy, what we find is evidently a continuation of medieval learning and may hence very well be called scholasticism. Since the term has been subject to controversy, I should like to say that I do not attach any unfavorable connotation to the term scholasticism. As its characteristic, I do not consider any particular doctrine, but rather a specific method, that is, the type of logical argument represented by the form of the *Questio*. It is well known that the content of scholastic philosophy, since the thirteenth century, was largely based on the writings of Aristotle, and that the development of this philosophy, since the twelfth century, was closely connected with the schools and universities of France and England, especially with the universities of Paris and of Oxford. The place of Italy is, however, less known in the history and development of scholastic philosophy. Several Italians are found among the most famous philosophers and theologians of the twelfth and thirteenth centuries, but practically all of them did their studying and teaching in France. Whereas Italy had flourishing schools of rhetoric, of jurisprudence, and of medicine during the twelfth and early thirteenth century, she had no native center of philosophical studies during the same period. After 1220 the new mendicant orders established schools of theology and philosophy in many Italian cities, but unlike those in France and England, these schools of the friars for a long time had no links with the Italian universities. Regular faculties of theology were not established at the Italian universities before the middle of the fourteenth century, and even after that period, the university teaching of theology continued to be spotty and irregular.

Aristotelian philosophy, although not entirely unknown at Salerno toward the end of the twelfth century, made its regular appearance at the Italian universities after the middle of the thirteenth century and in close connection with the teaching of medicine. I think it is safe to assume that Aristotelian philosophy was then imported from France as were the study of classical authors and many other forms of intellectual activity. After the beginning of the fourteenth century, this Italian Aristotelianism assumed a more definite shape. The teaching of logic and natural philosophy became a well established part of the university curriculum and even spread to some of the secondary schools. An increasing number of commentaries and questions on the works of Aristotle reflect this teaching tradition, and numerous systematic treatises on philosophical subjects show the same general trend and background. During the fourteenth and fifteenth centuries, further influences were received from Paris in the field of natural philosophy and from Oxford in the field of logic; and from the latter part of the fourteenth century on we can trace an unbroken tradition of Italian Aristotelianism which continued through the fifteenth and sixteenth century and far into the seventeenth century.

The common notion that scholasticism as an old philosophy was superseded by the new philosophy of humanism is thus again disproved by plain facts. For Italian scholasticism originated toward the end of the thirteenth century, that is, about the same time as did Italian humanism, and both traditions developed side by side throughout the period of the Renaissance and even thereafter.

However, the two traditions had their locus and center in two different sectors of learning: humanism in the field of grammar, rhetoric, and poetry and to some extent in moral philosophy, scholasticism in the fields of logic and of natural philosophy. Everybody knows the eloquent attacks launched by Petrarch and Bruni against the logicians of their time, and it is generally believed that these attacks represent a vigorous new movement rebelling against an old entrenched habit of thought. Yet actually the English method of dialectic was quite as novel at the Italian schools of that time as were the humanistic studies advocated by Petrarch and Bruni, and the humanistic attack was as much a matter of departmental rivalry as it was a clash of opposite ideas or philosophies. Bruni is even hinting at one point that he is not speaking quite in earnest. Such controversies, interesting as they are, were

mere episodes in a long period of peaceful coexistence between humanism and scholasticism. Actually the humanists quarreled as much among each other as they did with the scholastics. Moreover, it would be quite wrong to consider these controversies as serious battles for basic principles whereas many of them were meant to be merely personal feuds, intellectual tournaments, or rhetorical exercises. Finally, any attempt to reduce these controversies to one issue must fail since the discussions were concerned with many diverse and overlapping issues. Therefore, we should no longer be surprised that Italian Aristotelianism quietly and forcefully survived the attacks of Petrarch and his humanist successors.

But the Aristotelianism of the Renaissance did not remain untouched by the new influence of humanism. Philosophers began to make abundant use of the Greek text and of the new Latin translations of Aristotle, of his ancient commentators, and of other Greek thinkers. The revival of ancient philosophies that came in the wake of the humanistic movement, especially the revival of Platonism and of Stoicism, left a strong impact upon the Aristotelian philosophers of the Renaissance. Yet in spite of these significant modifications, Renaissance Aristotelianism continued the medieval scholastic tradition without any visible break. It preserved a firm hold on the university chairs of logic, natural philosophy, and metaphysics, whereas even the humanist professors of moral philosophy continued to base their lectures on Aristotle. The literary activity of these Aristotelian philosophers is embodied in a large number of commentaries, questions, and treatises. This literature is difficult of access and arduous to read, but rich in philosophical problems and doctrines. It represents the bulk and kernel of the philosophical thought of the period, but it has been badly neglected by modern historians. Scholars hostile to the Middle Ages considered this literature an unfortunate survival of medieval traditions that may be safely disregarded, whereas the true modern spirit of the Renaissance is expressed in the literature of the humanists. Medievalists, on the other hand, have largely concentrated on the earlier phases of scholastic philosophy and gladly sacrificed the later scholastics to the criticism of the humanists and their modern followers, a tendency that has been further accentuated by the recent habit of identifying scholasticism with Thomism.

Consequently, most modern scholars have condemned the Aristotelian philosophers of the Renaissance without a hearing, labeling them as empty squibblers and as followers of a dead past who failed to understand the living problems of their new times. Recent works on the civilization of the Renaissance thus often repeat the charges made against the Aristotelian philosophers by the humanists of their time, and even give those attacks a much more extreme meaning than they were originally intended to have. Other scholars who are not favorable to the humanists either include both scholastics and humanists in a summary sentence that reflects the judgments of seventeenth-century scientists and philosophers. (pp. 575-78)

The only way to understand the Renaissance is a direct and, possibly, an objective study of the original sources. We have no real justification to take sides in the controversies of the Renaissance, and to play up humanism against scholasticism, or scholasticism against humanism, or modern science against both of them. Instead of trying to reduce everything to one or two issues, which is the privilege and curse of political controversy, we should try to develop a kind of historical pluralism. It is easy to praise everything in the past which happens to resemble certain favorite ideas of our own time, or to ridicule and minimize everything that disagrees with them. This method is neither fair nor helpful for an adequate understanding of the past. It is equally easy to indulge in a sort of worship of success, and to dismiss defeated and refuted ideas with a shrugging of the shoulders, but just as in political history, this method does justice neither to the vanquished nor to the victors. Instead of blaming each century for not having anticipated the achievements of the next, intellectual history must patiently register the errors of the past as well as its truths. Complete objectivity may be impossible to achieve, but it should remain the permanent aim and standard of the historian as well as of the philosopher and scientist. (pp. 582-83)

> *Paul Oskar Kristeller, "Humanism and Scholasticism in the Italian Renaissance," in his* Studies in Renaissance Thought and Letters, *Edizioni di Storia e Letteratura, 1956, pp. 553-83.*

WILLIAM J. BOUWSMA

[*Bouwsma is an American educator and author. In the following excerpt, he delineates the impact of Stoicism and Augustinianism on Italian humanism.*]

Recent emphasis, stemming primarily from the work of P. O. Kristeller, on the central importance of rhetoric for Renaissance humanism, has enabled us to understand the underlying unity of a singularly complex movement; and it has proved singularly fruitful for Renaissance scholarship. At the same time, since this approach depends on the identification of a kind of lowest common denominator for humanism, it may also have the unintended effect of reducing our perception of its rich variety and thus of limiting our grasp of its historical significance. I should like, accordingly, to begin with Kristeller's fundamental insight, but then to suggest that rhetoric, for reasons closely connected with the circumstances under which the rhetorical tradition was appropriated in the age of the Renaissance, was also the vehicle of a set of basic intellectual conflicts crucial to the development of European culture in the early modern period. For there were divisions within Renaissance humanism which, since they were perennial, seem hardly incidental to the movement and which can perhaps be explained more persuasively than by the familiar suggestion that, as "mere rhetoricians," humanists felt comfortable in invoking any set of ideas that seemed immediately useful for their purposes, a notion that is in any case psychologically not altogether persuasive. The humanists were not inclined, I think, to invoke simply *any* set of ideas but tended rather to be divided by a fairly constant set of issues.

From this point of view humanism was a single movement in much the sense that a battlefield is a definable piece of ground. The humanists, to be sure, were often engaged in a conscious struggle with the schoolmen, but this was an external conflict in which the opposing sides were more or less clearly separated. But the struggle within humanism which I shall discuss here, though related to that external struggle, was subtler, more confused, and more difficult, though possibly of greater significance for the future of European culture. Often scarcely recognized by the humanists themselves, more frequently latent than overt for even the most acutely self-conscious among them, and never fully resolved, this internal struggle also helps to explain the adaptability of Renaissance humanism to changing needs, and hence its singular durability.

The two ideological poles between which Renaissance humanism oscillated may be roughly labeled "Stoicism" and "Augustinianism." Both terms present great difficulties, and neither, as an impulse in Renaissance intellectual culture, is yet susceptible to authoritative treatment. I will employ them here in a rather general sense, to designate antithetical visions of human existence, though both are rooted in concrete movements of thought that invite more precise analysis. But any effort to deal with the ideological significance of Renaissance humanism must now grapple with their confrontation.

It seems curious that historians have been so slow, until quite recently, to recognize the importance of the opposition between these impulses in humanist thought. One reason for this, perhaps, has been the persistent notion that Renaissance culture was centrally preoccupied with the recovery of an authentic classicism; and the classical world of thought has been ultimately brought into focus through the issues raised by ancient philosophy. Thus it has been assumed that the two greatest philosophers of classical antiquity, Plato and Aristotle, must represent, however distantly, the essential options available to the thinkers of the Renaissance. This approach to the Renaissance problem may still be encountered in the familiar notion of a medieval and Aristotelian scholasticism confronted by a Platonic humanism.

Whether because or in spite of its neatness, almost everything in this formula is misleading, if not wrong. In the first place it is wrong in fact. Medieval philosophy, even in the thirteenth century, was by no means entirely Aristotelian, and on the other hand the culture of Renaissance humanism probably owed at least as much to Aristotle as to Plato. But it is equally wrong in principle, for it seeks to comprehend the eclectic and non-systematic culture of the Renaissance in overtly systematic terms. It seems to be based on the quaint but durable notion that every man must, in his deepest instincts, be either a Platonist or an Aristotelian. In fact the conflict between Plato and Aristotle is, for the understanding of the Renaissance, a false scent, especially if we are primarily concerned with the tensions within humanism. Neither Plato nor Aristotle was closely connected with the rhetorical tradition, for whose ancient sources we must look instead to the Sophists and the less overtly philosophical pronouncements of the Latin orators. Furthermore, though Renaissance thinkers (including some humanists) sometimes disputed the relative merits of Plato and Aristotle, this rather academic debate was not a major or a regular concern of humanism; hence it can hardly be expected to illuminate its central concerns. More seriously, when compared with the humanists of the Renaissance Plato and Aristotle seem more to resemble than to differ from one another, not only because both were systematic philosophers but also because, however serious their disagreements, they came out of the same cultural world. By the later fifteenth century this was commonly observed by the humanists themselves, and Raphael, in an early representation of the division of labor, celebrated their complementarity by placing Plato and Aristotle side by side in the Stanza della Segnatura. Finally, the attempt to understand the polarities of Renaissance culture in terms of Plato and Aristotle seems to be based on the common but mistaken identification of antique thought with classical hellenism. It ignores the rich variety of the ancient heritage, and above all the significant fact that the earliest and probably the most influential ancient sources on which Renaissance humanism was nourished were not hellenic but hellenistic.

Thus although it is useful, both for the longer historical perspectives the exercise affords and for the deeper resonances it releases, to associate the impulses at work in Renaissance humanism with the various resources of the western cultural tradition, we must locate these resources first of all in the hellenistic rather than the hellenic world of thought. Stoicism and Augustinianism both meet this requirement, but they are also closer to Renaissance humanism in other respects. Both were bound up with the ancient rhetorical tradition, Stoicism through the ethical teachings of the Latin orators and essayists particularly beloved by the humanists, Augustinianism through the rhetorical powers of Augustine himself and, more profoundly, the subtle rhetorical quality of his mature theology. Furthermore the tension between Stoicism and Augustinianism was a perennial element in the career of Renaissance humanism, and indeed persisted well beyond what is conventionally taken as the end of the Renaissance; the ambiguous confrontation between the two impulses is still as central for Antoine Adam's distinguished Zaharoff Lecture on the thought of seventeenth-century France as it is in Charles Trinkaus's rich studies of fourteenth and fifteenth-century Italian humanism. Finally, Stoicism and Augustinianism represented, far better than Plato and Aristotle, genuine alternatives for the Renaissance humanist to ponder. (pp. 3-6)

The notion of the compatibility and even the affinity between Stoicism and Christianity goes back to the yearning of early Christian converts for some bridge between the old world of thought and the new. Stoic elements in the expression (if not the thought) of the Apostle Paul tended to obscure their radical differences, and the apocryphal correspondence between Paul and Seneca confused the issue further. The affinities, indeed, might seem immediately impressive, as they did in the Renaissance. The Stoics were commendably pious; they spoke much about the gods and even about God, praising his wisdom, his power, and his love for mankind. Their emphasis on divine providence and its ultimate benevolence seemed a particular point of contact with Christianity, and the idea of a single providential order led in turn to an ostensibly Christian ethic of absolute obedience and acceptance of the divine will. The Stoics displayed a singular moral seriousness; and their emphasis on virtue, through their famous contrast between the things that are within and those that are not within human control, recognized its inwardness; they acknowledged the problem of sin and stressed man's moral responsibility. They preached the brotherhood of man as well as the universal fatherhood of God, and they had much to say about the immortality of the soul.

But at a deeper level Stoicism and Augustinian Christianity were in radical opposition. The issue between them, in its most direct terms, was the difference between the biblical understanding of creation, which makes both man and the physical universe separate from and utterly dependent on God, and the hellenistic principle of immanence which makes the universe eternal, by one means or another deifies the natural order, and by seeing a spark of divinity in man tends to make him something more than a creature of God.

This fundamental difference has massive implications, and from it we may derive the major issues on which Stoicism and

The Colleoni Monument.

Augustinianism would be in potential opposition within Renaissance humanism. The anthropological differences between the two positions were of particular importance. The Stoic view of man attributed to him a divine spark or seed, identified with reason, which gave man access to the divine order of the universe, from which the existence, the nature, and the will of God could be known. Stoicism therefore pointed to natural theology; and since reason was seen as a universal human attribute, which meant that all men have some natural understanding of God, Stoic anthropology virtually required a religious syncretism. As the distinctive quality of man, reason also gave him his specifically human identity; a man was most fully human, best realized the ends of his existence, and became perfect, through the absolute sovereignty of reason over the other dimensions of the human personality. Virtue consisted, accordingly, in following the dictates of reason, to which the rebellious body and its passions were to be reduced by the will. But the will was not perceived as an independent faculty; it was the faithful and mechanical servant of reason, and therefore Stoicism rested on the assumption that to know the good is to do the good. Through rational illumination and rational control man was capable of reaching perfection. The body presented problems, but these could be solved through a disciplined *apatheia*, a cultivated indifference to physical needs and impulses, to the affections, and to external conditions. But since only man's reason was divine, immortality was reserved for the soul. Conversely Stoicism had a typically hellenistic contempt for the body.

Augustinianism contradicted this view at every point. Seeing man in every part of his being as a creature of God, it could not regard his reason (however wonderful) as divine and thus naturally capable of knowing the will of God. Such knowledge was available to man only in the Scriptures, particular revelations from God himself, which spoke not to mankind as a general category but to the individual. And because neither reason nor any other human faculty was intrinsically superior to the rest, Augustinianism tended to replace the monarchy of reason in the human personality with a kind of corporate democracy. The primary organ in Augustinian anthropology is not so much that which is highest as that which is central; it is literally the heart (*cor*), whose quality determines the quality of the whole. And that this quality is not a function of rational enlightenment is seen as a matter of common experience. The will is not, after all, an obedient servant of the reason; it has energies and impulses of its own, and man is a far more mysterious animal than the philosophers are inclined to admit. Human wickedness thus presents a much more serious problem than the Stoics dream of, and the notion that man in his fallen condition can rely on his own powers to achieve virtue is utterly implausible. Nor, in any event, is there virtue in withdrawal from engagement with the non-rational and external dimensions of existence. The physical body and the emotional constitution of man were created by God along with man's intellectual powers, and their needs too have dignity and are at least equally worthy of satisfaction. For the same reason immortality cannot be limited to the soul; man must be saved, since God made him so, as a whole.

The contrasts are equally significant in respect to the position of man in society. Although the self-centeredness in the Stoic ideal of individual existence was often uneasily and joylessly combined with a Roman concern for civic duty, the Stoics generally left the impression that social existence was a distraction from the good life, which could be satisfactorily pursued only by withdrawal from the world of men. Despite his recognition of the basic equality of man, the Stoic was also persuaded that the good life based on the contemplation of eternal verities was possible only for a few select souls; he was therefore contemptuous of the vulgar crowd. By contrast the mature Augustine, though still yearning for a contemplative life, insisted unequivocally on the obligations of the individual to society, obligations at once of duty, prudence and love; and at the same time the conception of the blessed life opened up by his less intellectual vision of man was not for the few but accessible to all.

Stoicism, again, had little use for history. Its conception of a rational and unchanging law of nature underlying all things led to a peculiarly rigid notion of cyclical recurrence that denied all significance to discrete events, which in any case belonged to the uncontrollable outer world irrelevant to the good life, just as it precluded the idea of a direction and goal for history. Its cultural values were not the products of particular experience in the world of time and matter but eternal, perennially valid, and so perennially recoverable. Thus its only remedy for present discontents was a nostalgic return to a better past. But Augustine vigorously rejected the eternal round of the ancients. He brooded over the mystery of time as a creature and vehicle of God's will and proclaimed that history was guided to its appointed end by God himself and therefore, expressing his wisdom, must be fraught with a mysterious significance.

But underlying all these particular contrasts was a fundamental difference over the order of the universe. For the Stoics a single cosmic order, rational and divine, pervaded all things, at once static and, through a divine impulse to achieve perfection planted in everything, dynamic, its principles operative alike in physical nature, in human society, and in the human personality. The existence of this order determined all human and social development; and the end of man, either individually or collectively, could not be freely chosen but consisted in subjective acceptance and conformity to destiny. The perfection of that order meant that whatever is right, however uncomfortable or tragic for mankind; at the heart of Stoicism is that familiar cosmic optimism which signifies, for the actual experience of men, the deepest pessimism. Against all this Augustinianism, though by no means denying in principle the ultimate order of the universe, rejected its intelligibility and thus its coherence and its practical significance for man. The result was to free both man and society from their old bondage to cosmic principles, and to open up a secular vision of human existence and a wide range of pragmatic accommodations to the exigencies of life impossible in the Stoic religious universe. In this sense Augustinianism provided a charter for human freedom and a release for the diverse possibilities of human creativity. (pp. 9-12)

Stoicism addressed itself to the problems of modern Europe, as to those of later antiquity, by reaffirming the divine, harmonious, and intelligible order of nature and drawing appropriate conclusions, practical as well as theoretical. The Stoicism of the Renaissance, perhaps especially when it was least aware of its Stoic inspiration, was based, like ancient Stoicism, on natural philosophy and cosmology, a point of some importance in view of the common supposition that Renaissance thinkers only drew isolated, practical ethical precepts from Stoic sources. Valla's Epicurean (in this case made, perhaps deliberately, to sound like a Stoic) declared nature virtually identical with God. Vives from time to time elaborated on the meaning of this proposition. The universe, he wrote, was governed "by the divine intelligence which commands and forbids according to reason." Calvin, for all his concern to maintain the distinction between God and nature, drew on the same conception. "This skillful ordering of the universe," he argued, "is for us a sort of mirror in which we can contemplate God, who is otherwise invisible." For Charron nature was "the equity and universal reason which lights in us, which contains and incubates in itself the seeds of all virtue, probity, justice."

And man is also a part of this rational order of nature. Montaigne found this humbling: "We are neither superior nor inferior to the rest. All that is under heaven, says the sage, is subject to one law and one fate. . . . Man must be forced and lined up within the barriers of this organization." Others saw in it some justification for glorifying man. "This is the order of nature," wrote Vives, "that wisdom be the rule of the whole, that all creatures obey man, that in man the body abides by the orders of the soul, and that the soul itself comply with the will of God." Another way to coordinate man with the universe was the notion of man as microcosm in Pomponazzi and even Calvin. Calvin was willing, too, to acknowledge the influence of the rational order of the heavens on the human body.

Implicit in these passages, and sometimes more than implicit, is the assumption that this divinely-ordered universe is accessible to the human understanding, that man's perception of the rational order of the universe tells him a good deal about the nature and will of God, and that man's reason is thus the link between himself and God. This conception of nature leads us accordingly to the notion of man as essentially an intellectual being. As Aeneas Sylvius declared, the mind is "the most precious of all human endowments;" and Petrarch's definition of man as a rational animal is enthusiastically developed, in the *Secretum,* by Augustinus: "When you find a man so governed by Reason that all his conduct is regulated by her, all his appetites subject to her alone, a man who has so mastered every motion of his spirit by Reason's curb that he knows it is she alone who distinguishes him from the savagery of the brute, and that it is only by submission to her guidance that he deserves the name of man at all. . . . when you have found such a man, then you may say that he has some true and fruitful idea of what the definition of man is." As this passage suggests, this view of man requires the sovereignty of reason within the personality. For Pomponazzi human freedom depended on the subservience of will to intellect, and for Calvin this had been the situation of Adam in Paradise, the consequence of his creation in God's image: "In the mind [of Adam] perfect intelligence flourished and reigned, uprightness attended as its companion, and all the senses were prepared and molded for due obedience to reason; and in the body there was a suitable correspondence with this internal order." Before the fall, apparently, Adam had been a model of Stoic perfection. "The understanding," he wrote more generally, "is, as it were, the leader and governor of the soul" and the instructor of the will.

On the other hand this elevation of reason was often likely to be accompanied by a denigration of other dimensions of the personality, especially the passions and the body with which they were regularly associated, which threatened to challenge the sovereignty of reason. From this standpoint the body and the rational soul could be seen as radically opposed. Petrarch claimed to have learned from his own body only "that man is a vile, wretched animal unless he redeems the ignobility of the body with the nobility of the soul." He saw his soul as imprisoned in and weighed down by the body, the one "an immortal gift, the other corruptible and destined to pass away." With Vives attack on the body achieved an almost pathological intensity. But happily the rational soul, however threatened by the body and the affections, was in the end clearly superior to them. As Lipsius remarked, "For although the soul is infected and somewhat corrupted by the filth of the body and the contagion of sense, it nevertheless retains some vestiges of its origin and is not without certain bright sparks of the pure fiery nature from whence it came forth." (pp. 17-20)

[The] formation men most required in a brutal and disorderly world was training in morality, and it was in this area that Stoic doctrine seemed most relevant to contemporary needs, most immediately prescriptive. The rational order of nature was to be the foundation for the orderly behavior of men; this was its practical function. Stoic moralists were attractive, then, because of their emphasis on the supreme value of virtue, sometimes, as Augustinus tells Franciscus, because it is the only basis for human happiness, sometimes, as Petrarch wrote elsewhere, because virtue, "as the philosophers say," is "its own reward, its own guide, its own end and aim." Pomponazzi, who had clearer reasons, agreed that virtue could have no higher reward than itself and praised it as the most precious quality in life; and Calvin recognized the peculiar emphasis of the Stoics on virtue. Guarino applied the conception directly to education, seeing "learning and training in virtue" as the peculiar pursuit of man and therefore central to *humanitas.*

This concern with virtue reflects also the persistence of the intellectual conception of man so closely bound up with the rational order of the Stoic universe. This is apparent in two ways. In the first place Stoic virtue is acquired through the intellect; it is a product of philosophy, absorbed from books. Thus Erasmus believed that even small children could absorb it through beginning their education by reading ancient fables. He particularly recommended the story of Circe, with its lesson "that men who will not yield to the guidance of reason, but follow the enticements of the senses, are no more than brute beasts." "Could a Stoic philosopher," he asked rhetorically, "preach a graver truth?" But in the second place, as this passage also suggests, the practice of this Stoic virtue depended on the sovereignty of reason and its powers of control over the disorderly impulses arising out of other aspects of the personality. Alberti's Uncle Lionardo made the point clearly. "Good ways of living," he declared, "eventually overcome and correct every appetite that runs counter to reason and every imperfection of the mind." Vives identified this ethics of rational control with the teaching of Christ:

> Our mind is a victim of its own darkness; our passions, stirred by sin, have covered the eyes of reason with a thick layer of dust. We need a clear insight, serene and undisturbed. . . . All the precepts of moral philosophy can be found in the teachings of Christ. In his doctrine, and in his words, man will find the remedy to all moral diseases, the ways and means to tame our passions under the guidance and the power of reason. Once this order has been secured man will learn proper behavior in his relations with himself, with God, and with his neighbor; he will act rightfully not only in the privacy of his home but also in his social and political life.
>
> (pp. 22-3)

The Stoic model for the order of society, like its model for the order of the individual personality, was also derived from the order of the cosmos. An authentic and durable social order that would properly reflect the stability of the cosmos had thus to meet two basic requirements. It had to be a single order, and it had to be governed by reason. This meant in practice that the human world must be organized as a universal empire, and that it must be ruled by the wise, by men who are themselves fully rational and in touch with the rational principles of the cosmos.

Thus the Stoic type of humanist tended, from Petrarch in some moods to Lipsius in the waning Renaissance, to admire imperial Rome. The conquest of the Roman Empire, Petrarch once remarked, had been "actuated by perfect justice and good will as regards men," however defective it may have been in regard to God. Castiglione's Ottaviano Fregoso found an earlier example of the universal model to admire; he praised Aristotle for "directing Alexander to that most glorious aim—which was the desire to make the world into one single universal country, and have all men living as one people in friendship and in mutual concord under one government and one law that might shine equally on all like the light of the sun." Erasmus decried any attachment to a particular community; he had succeeded himself, he said, in feeling at home everywhere. Lipsius similarly attacked love of country as an expression of the lower demands of the body and of custom rather than nature, which commands us to regard the whole world as our true fatherland. (pp. 23-4)

The idealism in this conception of government generally makes it appear singularly unsuited to the actualities of political life, but in at least one respect it helped to meet genuine practical needs. By its conception of a rational law of nature, it assisted in the rationalization of law and social relations. The problem is suggested by Salutati's confrontation between law and medicine, in which the latter offers a kind of diagnosis of the human scene: here, without the stability of some eternal principle, all things would belong "to the realm of the accidental." Law, "based upon eternal and universal justice," placed government upon a more secure foundation than the whims of the ruler or the accidents of custom. It seems likely that the Stoic conception of a natural law governing all human intercourse and authenticating all particular laws gave some impetus, perhaps most powerful when the cosmic vibrations in the conception were least felt, to the systematic codification of the chaos of existing legislation, to the general rule of law, and to more equal justice. Yet we may sense something equivocal, however opportune, even here. This is apparent in the impersonal rationality in the Stoic idea of social virtue based on law, which corresponded to the increasing legalism and impersonality of the new urban scene. It tended to base social order not on the unreliable vagaries of personal ties, personal loyalties, and personal affection, but on abstract and general social relationships: in a word, on duty rather than on love. The social thought of Stoic humanism thus reflected and probably helped to promote the rationalization of society on which large-scale organization in the modern world depended. But it also made the human world a colder place.

On the other hand the Stoic conception of social improvement was diametrically opposed to the actual direction in which European society was moving. Its ideal, like Seneca's, was nostalgic. As the retrospective prefix in the familiar Renaissance vocabulary of amelioration attests—*renascentium, reformatio, restoratio, restitutio, renovatio,* etc.—it could only look backward for a better world. Petrarch chose deliberately to live in spirit in the ancient past; one of the participants in an Erasmian colloquy deplored the disappearance of "that old time equality, abolished by modern tyranny," which he also associated with the Apostles; Castiglione thought men in antiquity "of greater worth than now." Even the improvement Renaissance writers occasionally celebrated was regularly conceived as the recovery of past excellence, and hope for the future usually was made to depend on some notion of revival. Petrarch found strength in the greatness of Rome. "What inspiration," he exclaimed, "is not to be derived from the memory of the past and from the grandeur of a name once revered through the world!" Lorenzo de Medici's motto in a tournament of 1468 was *le tems revient.* Machiavelli's chief ground for hope, when he deplored the decadence of contemporary Italy, was that "this land seems born to raise up dead things, as she has in poetry, in painting, and in sculpture." Giles of Viterbo applied the conception to ecclesiastical renewal: "We are not innovators. We are simply trying, in accordance with the will of God, to bring back to life those ancient laws whose observance has lapsed."

All of this suggests the lack of a sense of the positive significance of change in Stoic humanism. Since excellence was associated with the divine origins of all things, change could only mean deterioration; and improvement necessarily im-

plied the recovery of what was essentially timeless. The static character of this ideal was reflected in its vision of the good society which, once it had achieved perfection, could not be permitted to change. So Erasmus hoped that the conflicting interests of human society might "achieve an eternal truce" in which proper authority and degrees of status would be respected by all. One of the essential duties of the Erasmian ruler is to resist all innovation. The central virtue in the Stoic ideal of society is thus peace, which is not simply the absence of war but ultimately dependent on the correspondence of social organization to the unchanging principles of universal order. (pp. 25-7)

Stoicism, then, had both attractions and weaknesses as the basis for accommodation to the conditions of Renaissance life, and these were not unrelated to one another. It identified the major problems of modern existence, often vividly and concretely, as the schoolmen did not. It reaffirmed in a new form a traditional vision of universal order which seemed an attractive prescription for the practical evils of a singularly disorderly society. It affirmed personal responsibility, its inwardness corresponded to the growing inwardness of later medieval piety, and it promised consolation for the tribulations of existence. But the structure of assumptions that enabled Stoic humanism to perform these services was not altogether adequate to the changing needs of a new society. Its conception of a universal order was singularly contradicted by the concrete world of familiar experience, and its idealism, however plausible in theory, ran the risk of seeming as irrelevant to life as the great systems of the schoolmen. Its intellectual vision of man was hardly adequate to a world in which men constantly encountered each other not as disembodied minds but as integral personalities whose bodies could not be ignored, whose passions were vividly and often positively as well as dangerously in evidence, and whose actions were profoundly unpredictable. The Stoic idea of freedom was too elevated to have much general application, and also severely limited by the large area of determinism in Stoic thought. And Stoicism appeared often to ignore or to reason away rather than to engage with and solve the practical problems of life; its disapproval of cities, of political particularity and individual eccentricity, of change, demonstrated the high-mindedness of its adherents, but it did not cause these awkward realities to go away. And it was scarcely helpful, especially since even the Stoic had no remedy for the misery of the overwhelming majority of mankind, to deny that suffering was real because it belonged to the lower world of appearances, or to direct the attention of wretched men from mutable to eternal things, or to insist that the world ought to be one and to be ruled by the wise. Like ancient Stoicism, therefore, the Stoic humanism of the Renaissance was ultimately hopeless. It is thus hardly surprising that, like the Stoicism of the hellenistic world, it was contested, within humanism itself, by another and very different vision of man, his potentialities, and his place in the universe. The great patron of this vision was Saint Augustine. (pp. 33-4)

Augustinian humanism saw man, not as a system of objectively distinguishable, discrete faculties reflecting ontological distinctions in the cosmos, but as a mysterious and organic unity. This conception, despite every tendency in his thought to the contrary, is repeatedly apparent in Petrarch, in the *Secretum* and elsewhere, and it explains Melanchthon's indifference to the value of distinguishing the various faculties of the human personality. One result was a marked retreat from the traditional sense of opposition between soul and body.

Bruni found support for the notion of their interdependence in Aristotle, and Valla, as Maffeo Vegio, vigorously rejected the possibility of distinguishing the pleasures of the soul from those of the body; Pomponazzi's notorious refutation of the soul's immortality must be understood against this background. A corollary of this position is that the soul cannot be seen as a higher faculty in man, a spark of divinity which is intrinsically immune from sin and can only be corrupted from below. Petrarch confessed that, in the end, his troubles came rather from his soul than his body; and Calvin was only applying this insight in his insistence that the fall of Adam had its origins in deeper regions of the personality. "They childishly err," he wrote against a hellenistic understanding of Christianity, "who regard original sin as consisting only in lust and in the disorderly motion of the appetites, whereas it seizes upon the very seat of reason and upon the whole heart." It follows, therefore, that the distinctive quality of man cannot be his reason. Valla identified it with his immortality, Calvin with his capacity to know and worship God. It also follows that the abstract knowledge grasped by reason is not sufficient to make men virtuous and therefore blessed, a point made with considerable emphasis by Petrarch in praising oratory above philosophy; thus Aristotle suffered as a moralist in comparison with Cicero, whom Petrarch now exploited in his less Stoic mood. Since to know the good could no longer be identified with doing the good, it might also now be necessary to make a choice between knowledge and virtue, and the Augustinian humanist regularly came out on the side of virtue.

Despite their underlying belief in the integral unity of the personality, the Augustinian humanists accepted and argued in terms of the old vocabulary of the faculties; but the faculties they chose to emphasize implied a very different conception of the organization of man from that of the Stoics. They spoke above all of the will. Petrarch recognized clearly that Augustine's own conversion had been a function of his will rather than his intellect, and Calvin was similarly Augustinian in recognizing the crucial importance of the will in the economy of salvation. But the essential point in this conception of the will was its separation from and its elevation above reason. "It is safer," Petrarch declared, "to strive for a good and pious will than for a capable and clear intellect. . . . It is better to will the good than to know the truth." Melanchthon was developing the implications of this view in saying that "knowledge serves the will. . . . For the will in man corresponds to the place of a despot in a republic. Just as the senate is subject to the despot, so is knowledge to the will, with the consequence that although knowledge gives warning, yet the will casts knowledge out and is borne along by its own affection." One consequence was a new degree of freedom for the will, always severely restricted by the Stoic conception of the will as the automatic servant of reason. Salutati recognized this with particular clarity. Nothing, he wrote, could "even reach the intellect without the consent or command of the will," and once knowledge had penetrated the intellect, the will could freely follow or disregard it. Valla saw in the freedom of the will the only conception of the matter consistent with the evident reality of sin, which would be impossible, and man would be deprived of responsibility and moral dignity, if reason in fact ruled will.

The will, in this view, is seen to take its direction not from reason but from the affections, which are in turn not merely the disorderly impulses of the treacherous body but expressions of the energy and quality of the heart, that mysterious organ which is the center of the personality, the source of its unity and its ultimate worth. The affections, therefore, are intrinsically neither good nor evil but the essential resources of the personality; and since they make possible man's beatitude and glory as well as his depravity, they are, in Augustinian humanism, treated with particular respect. Thus even when Augustinus recommended Franciscus to meditate on the eternal verities, he called on him to invest his thought with affect, as a necessary sign that he has not meditated in vain. Valla was especially emphatic about the positive quality of the passions, a primary consideration both in his perception of the particular importance of oratorical as opposed to philosophical communication and in the understanding of Christianity. "Can a man move his listeners to anger or mercy if he has not himself first felt these passions?" he asked. "It cannot be," he continued; "So he will not be able to kindle the love of divine things in the minds of others who is himself cold to that love." For Valla religious experience was not intellectual but effective; the love of God is to be understood as man's ultimate pleasure. (pp. 36-8)

[There was an] insistence, within Augustinian humanism, on man's absolute dependence on his creator, which contrasted sharply with the Stoic tendency to emphasize man's sufficiency. This sense of human dependence is especially apparent in the Augustinian attitude to virtue, the supreme good of the Stoic. Valla thought the Stoic ideal of the sage a contradiction in terms, if only because the triumph of virtue implied constant struggle; Stoic serenity was therefore unattainable. Brandolini doubted that virtue could overcome suffering. The examples of ancient virtue adduced as models by the Stoic humanist thus required some analysis. It might be remarked in general, as Petrarch and Erasmus did, that "true" virtue could not be attributed to any pagan, since his actions were obviously not done in the love of Christ. Valla went beyond such generality to suggest that pagan virtue was vitiated by its concern for glory, a point the young Calvin also emphasized. "Remove ambition," he wrote, "and you will have no haughty spirits, neither Platos, nor Catos, nor Scaevolas, nor Scipios, nor Fabriciuses." He saw the Roman Empire as "a great robbery", a notion also bearing on the Stoic ideal of a universal state. Melanchthon viewed the virtues that enabled Alexander to conquer an empire simply as evidence that he loved glory more than pleasure. These humanists did not deny the practical value of the alleged virtues of the pagans, but they insisted on distinguishing between the restraint of human nature and its purification, which only grace could accomplish. From this standpoint the Stoic ideal was shallow and therefore, in the end, unreliable. Christianity, as Melanchthon remarked, was not primarily concerned with virtue, and the pursuit of instruction on this topic in the Scriptures "is more philosophical than Christian."

In fact a deeper knowledge of the self revealed that, like his knowledge of God, man's virtue and happiness also come entirely from God. To realize this was the goal of self-knowledge. Such knowledge, Calvin declared, "will strip us of all confidence in our own ability, deprive us of all occasion for boasting, and lead us to submission;" and Petrarch's own spiritual biography may be understood as a prolonged search for this kind of knowledge. It taught man, for example, the precise opposite of Stoic wisdom. Against the Stoic notion that blessedness can be founded only on the things that are man's own, Petrarch argued directly that in fact the only things that are a man's own are his sins; thus "in what is in one's own power" there is chiefly "matter of shame and fear."

There is an obvious connection between this interest in self-knowledge and the Pauline teaching on the moral law as the tutor of mankind, a conception again quite at odds with the Stoic notion of the function of law. If Petrarch's self-knowledge brought him to despair, he could take hope if only "the Almighty Pity put forth his strong right hand and guide my vessel rightly ere it be too late, and bring me to shore." God was the only source of his virtues (these are clearly not his own), of his blessedness, of his very existence: "In what state could I better die than in loving, praising, and remembering him, without whose constant love I should be nothing, or damned, which is less than nothing? And if his love for me should cease, my damnation would have no end." Peace itself, the essence of Stoic beatitude, could only be the consequence, not of "some human virtue", Brandolini contended, but of grace.

But there are, for the general development of European culture, even broader implications in the sense, within Augustinian humanism, of man's intellectual limitations. It pointed to the general secularization of modern life, for it implied the futility of searching for the principles of human order in the divine order of the cosmos, which lay beyond human comprehension. Man was accordingly now seen to inhabit not a single universal order governed throughout by uniform principles but a multiplicity of orders: for example, an earthly as well as a heavenly city, which might be seen to operate in quite different ways. On earth, unless God had chosen to reveal his will about its arrangements unequivocally in Scripture, man was left to the uncertain and shifting insights of a humbler kind of reason, to work out whatever arrangements best suited his needs. Hence a sort of earthy practicality was inherent in this way of looking at the human condition. (pp. 43-5)

In the same way Augustinian humanism attacked the spiritual elitism of the Stoic tradition, both in its loftier forms and in its application to government; and it was thus more sympathetic to those populist movements that found religious expression in the dignity of lay piety, political expression in the challenge of republicanism to despotism. For it was obvious that if rational insight into cosmic order could not supply the principles of either religious or political life, neither the church nor civil society could be governed by sages. This conviction had deep roots in Italian humanism. Charles Trinkaus has presented at least one group of humanists as lay theologians who were concerned to assert the religious competence of ordinary men by their emphasis on Christianity as a religion of grace accessible to all. Valla contrasted the exclusiveness of Stoicism with the popularity of Epicureanism, and he rested his case for eloquence against philosophy largely on the fact that it employed the language of ordinary men rather than the specialized vocabulary of an elite who "teach us by an exquisite sort of reasoning both to inquire what illiterates and rustics do better than philosophers transmit." There is a hint of this attitude even in Castiglione, who was willing to leave the evaluation of his *Courtier* to public opinion "because more often than not the many, even without perfect knowledge, know by natural instinct the certain savor of good and bad, and, without being able to give any reason for it, enjoy and love one thing and detest another." Augustinian humanism denied any privileged position to a philosophically enlightened class. (p. 48)

So the willingness to accommodate human institutions to the varieties of circumstance also implied a willingness to ac-

knowledge the significance of change in human affairs. "Now we know," Calvin declared, "that external order admits, and even requires, various changes according to the varying conditions of the times." The historicism of the Renaissance, to which recent scholarship has given much attention, was distinctly not a function of the Stoic tendencies in humanism, which could only view mutability with alarm, but rather of the Augustinian tradition, in which God's purposes were understood to work themselves out in time. Thus for Salutati God "foresaw all that was and will be in time entirely without time and from eternity, and not only did he infallibly foresee and wish that they occur in their time, but also that through contingency they should be produced and be." Contingency was no longer a threat to order but the fulfillment of a divine plan, and discrete events thus acquired meaning. This repudiation of Stoic stasis opened the way to the feeling for anachronism that we encounter not only in Valla's analysis of the Donation of Constantine and Guicciardini's attack on Machiavelli's rather Stoic application of the repetition of analogous situations but also in a more general relativism that left its mark on Calvin's understanding of church history and on his exegetical methods. He saw the rise of episcopacy, for example, as a practical response to the problem of dissension in the early church, an "arrangement introduced by human agreement to meet the needs of the times;" and he noted that there are "many passages of Scripture whose meaning depends on their [historical] context." For Calvin fallen man seems to confront God in history rather than in nature.

At the same time these tendencies in Augustinian humanism also suggest the repudiation of the Stoic vision of peace as the ideal toward which man naturally aspires. This too was an expression of the greater realism in the Augustinian tradition; it had no conflict in principle with the acceptance by Renaissance society of warfare as a normal activity of mankind. Within the Renaissance republic conflict had been institutionalized by constitutional provisions for checks and balances among competing social interests; the Stoic ideal, on the contrary, would have sought to eliminate conflict by submitting all interests to the adjudication of reason, settling for nothing less than final solutions to human problems. And the restlessness of human society was paralleled, in the vision of Augustinian humanism, by the inescapable restlessness of individual existence. The Augustinian conception of man as passion and will implied that he could only realize himself fully in activity, which inevitably meant that life must be fraught with conflict, an external struggle with other men, but also an inner struggle with destructive impulses in the self that can never be fully overcome. For Valla virtue was only ideally a goal; practically it was an arduous way. And the Calvinist saint, unlike the Stoic sage, could by no means expect a life of repose; on the contrary he must prepare himself "for a hard, toilsome, and unquiet life, crammed with numerous and various calamities. . . . in this life we are to seek and hope for nothing but struggle." The ideal of earthly peace, from Calvin's standpoint, was a diabolical stratagem in which the struggle with sin was left in abeyance and God's will went undone. Here too it was apparent that Stoicism tended to confuse earthly with heavenly things.

Yet, far less equivocally than Stoic humanism, the vision of Augustinian humanism was social; and, based on the affective life of the whole man, its conception of social existence was animated not by abstract duty but by love. Augustinus reproved the anti-social sentiments of Franciscus by pointing out that life in society is not only the common lot of mankind but even the most blessed life on earth: "Those whom one counts most happy, and for whom numbers of others live their lives, bear witness by the constancy of their vigils and their toils that they themselves are living for others." Salutati found in charity, understood in an Augustinian sense as a gift of divine grace, a way to reconcile—that there should have been a problem here testifies to the strength of the contrary Stoic impulse—his religious values with his love of Florence and his other attachments to the world. Love alone, he wrote, "fosters the family, expands the city, guards the kingdom, and preserves by its power this very creation of the entire world." Thus Stoic withdrawal was countered by Augustinian engagement, which offered not the austere satisfactions of Stoic contemplation but the warmer and more practical consolations of a love applied to the needs of suffering mankind. (pp. 49-51)

At least two general conclusions emerge from this contrast between Stoic and Augustinian humanism. The first comes out of the fact that we can illustrate either with examples drawn indiscriminately from anywhere in the entire period of our concern, and this suggests that the tension between them found no general resolution in the age of the Renaissance and Reformation. But it is equally striking that we have often cited the same figures on both sides. Neither pure Stoics nor pure Augustinians are easy to find among the humanists, though individual figures may tend more to one position than the other. Erasmus, for example, seems more Stoic than Augustinian: Valla appears more Augustinian than Stoic. A closer study of individuals may reveal more personal development, from one position to another, than has been possible to show here. Petrarch, Erasmus, and Calvin may especially invite such treatment. But the general ambivalence of humanists makes clear the central importance for the movement of the tension between the two positions. It was literally in the hearts of the humanists themselves. At the same time this ambiguity also reveals that Stoicism and Augustinianism do not represent distinguishable factions within a larger movement but ideal polarities that help us to understand its significance as a whole. (p. 52)

> *William J. Bouwsma, "The Two Faces of Humanism: Stoicism and Augustinianism in Renaissance Thought," in* Itinerarium Italicum: The Profile of the Italian Renaissance in the Mirror of Its European Transformations, *edited by Heiko A. Oberman with Thomas A. Brady, Jr., E. J. Brill, 1975, pp. 3-60.*

PAUL OSKAR KRISTELLER

[*In the following excerpt from an essay originally published in* Il Rinascimento: Interpretazioni e Problemi *(1979), Kristeller sees humanism, Aristotelianism, and Platonism as intellectual components of Italian Renaissance thought.*]

The first signs of Italian humanism can be found in the early trecento, and even as far back as the late duecento, when its grammatical and rhetorical (more than philosophical) connections to the Middle Ages were still visible. Although the first full blossoming took place in the quattrocento, it should not be forgotten that the movement remained active, especially in the disciplines of rhetoric, Latin poetry, historiography and classical philology, straight through the entire cinquecento and into the early seicento. Bembo, Vida, Vettori and Sigonio were only four representatives of a movement which was still lively and productive. On the other hand, al-

though the origins of humanist culture were Italian, the movement was by no means limited to Italy. As early as the fourteenth century, it had spread to France, Germany and Bohemia; in the next century, it reached the rest of Europe. It was in the sixteenth century that the great non-Italian humanists worked: Reuchlin, Erasmus, Budé, Vives and Sir Thomas More were only a few of the most illustrious of these. There were variations in style, and there were contrasts due to the different countries and moments in time, but the same fundamental traits existed: a deep classical culture, a sense of criticism and history, a literary elegance, eclecticism, an interest not only in moral and pedagogic problems but in political and religious ones as well, an aversion to scholasticism and an indifference to the professional traditions of the university disciplines. By the end of the century, we find Lipsius, the great renovator of Stoic philosophy, and Montaigne, the vibrant, cultured moralist, whose classical references and highly personal style combined the best features of humanist culture, despite the fact that he wrote his *Essais* in French rather than in Latin, which he had learned well as a youth. And finally we come to the great French and Dutch scholars such as Turnèbe and Scaliger, who developed the classical philology of the humanists and transmitted it to successive centuries.

I cannot share the opinion which has occasionally claimed that humanist culture was suppressed by the religious movements of the sixteenth century, or that the humanists, as a group, favoured one religion, whether Protestant or Catholic. Humanist culture as such was neutral with regard to certain theological or even philosophical doctrines, and each humanist was free to formulate his opinions according to his own convictions and inclinations. We find humanist scholars and men of letters, as well as men reared in the humanist culture, among the Catholics, Protestants and heretics of the sixteenth century. Perhaps Luther, certainly Melanchthon, Calvin and many Jesuits were well steeped in the humanist culture of their time, and it was thanks to them that the humanist school became so firmly established in all the Catholic and Protestant countries that it managed to survive until the first decades of our own century.

Although it is true that humanism was probably the most lively and novel element in Renaissance intellectual culture, especially in fourteenth- and fifteenth-century Italy, and although its influence gradually spread out to touch every area of the culture of the period, it would none the less be an error to think that the intellectual life of the period could be reduced to humanism alone. The fact is that there were many traditions and movements with differing origins and interests, and every one of them either rivalled or simply coexisted alongside humanism. Our picture of the period would be incomplete—even distorted—if we were to repeat the oft-committed error of ignoring the existence and the importance of these other movements, or even of treating them as the mere residue of a medieval tradition which had run dry. Humanist culture managed to conquer the secondary schools and to take over the university instruction of grammar, rhetoric, poetry, Greek, and often moral philosophy. However, at the same time, instruction continued in the other disciplines, whose origins went back to the twelfth and thirteenth centuries, when the universities were founded; the scholastic, i.e. university, tradition of these subjects was never interrupted during the period in question, but was merely modified by the influence of humanism. This phenomenon has been more clearly understood in the past few decades, but much research should still be carried out on university documents and learned literature in both printed and manuscript forms. The same problem exists with regard to theology, jurisprudence, medicine and mathematics, but we must limit ourselves here to the philosophical disciplines which, at that time, also included the physical and biological sciences.

Consideration of these rather fundamental facts is essential to the comprehension of the importance and vitality of Aristotelianism, whose position in Renaissance thought was distinct from that of humanism. Whether we assign more importance to Aristotelianism or to humanism depends on our criteria. If we choose to emphasize the technical and professional, i.e. university, tradition of philosophy, then it must be acknowledged that this tradition was represented during the Renaissance by Aristotelianism, and that the humanists' contributions to philosophy, however interesting and influential, were essentially those of dilettanti and outsiders. This does not detract from the importance of those contributions, just as it cannot be denied that there were other moments in the history of philosophy when philosophical thought was modified or transformed by external impulses which were extraneous to the technical and professional tradition of the preceding period. But historians of Renaissance thought would be committing an error of judgement if they were to take the humanists' invectives against contemporary scholasticism at face value, without examining the other side of the coin, as many historians of literature and even of philosophy have in fact done. As Renan and then Duhem both remarked, the late medieval Aristotelians adopted a rationalistic method, studying many problems of logic and physics in such a way that they appeared to be the predecessors of free thought and modern science. From this angle, the humanists' contributions appear less illustrious; it is occasionally written that the progress of the sciences was delayed at least a century by the movement. The only way to escape from this dilemma is to realize that it is not only in our own century that there have been two, or rather, several cultures, and that we cannot expect the scholars of one culture to contribute to the progress of another; throughout the ages, there have always been many differing opinions with regard to the same problem and, what is more, there have always been competition and rivalry between the scholars of different themes and problems.

The vast Aristotelian literature produced from the thirteenth century to the seventeenth and beyond, is rooted in university and scholastic teaching. It includes commentaries on the writings of Aristotle and on some of the complementary texts, such as the logical works of Porphyry, Gilbertus Porretanus and Peter of Spain and Averroes's treatise of physics, *De substantia orbis;* these commentaries reflect the practice of the *lectura.* Only some of these texts have survived to the present day; a large number, at least of those from the later period, have still not been studied. Often they only exist in the form of lecture notes, which were occasionally edited by the professors themselves, but were usually the exclusive work of students who had attended the lectures. They usually begin with a general introduction, one issue of which includes an analysis of to which part of philosophy the text in question belongs. This type of commentary, based on the study of the text chosen for instruction, gradually appeared in all the other disciplines taught at the universities, from theology to jurisprudence, medicine and mathematics. Each of these had its pre-scholastic tradition, which may be traced back through the grammatical commentaries of the twelfth centu-

ry and of the early Middle Ages to the ancient Latin commentaries of Servius and Boethius and finally to the Greek commentaries on Aristotle and other writers. The other literary form of Aristotelian philosophy and the other scholastic disciplines is the *quaestio,* or the collection of questions. The *quaestio* has its own precise, almost schematic structure, which corresponds to another important practice in university instruction, the *disputatio.* The collections, and the questions themselves, were often edited by the professor and it was rare for a student to edit them directly. (pp. 135-39)

Like humanism and Aristotelianism, Platonism, the third great movement of the Renaissance, is still in need of much research and a great deal of clarification. Quattrocento Florentine Platonism has often been interpreted as a mere part or appendix of humanism, because its representatives were in fact steeped in humanist culture, and because they studied and translated the Platonic and neo-Platonic texts. It is true that they did attempt to revive ancient Platonism, albeit with different ancient elements, just as other humanists had tried, or would try, to resuscitate the Stoic, Epicurean, sceptic and other doctrines. On the other hand, Renaissance Platonism often opposed late medieval scholastic Aristotelianism, and this contrast was accentuated by the reference to the anti-Aristotelian Platonism of Pletho and his Byzantine followers. None the less, . . . there was a strong Platonic and neo-Platonic movement in the Middle Ages, based upon the translations of several texts from Plato and Proclus, on Boethius and other Latin Platonists, and above all on St Augustine and on the extremely widespread texts which circulated under the name of Dionysius the Areopagite. Moreover . . . , Aristotelianism in the Renaissance was possessed of remarkable strength, making it anything but a barren residue of the late Middle Ages. And finally, . . . the Platonism of both Ficino and Pico was in no way anti-Aristotelian; it was profoundly permeated with and influenced by scholastic philosophy. It gave great space to cosmological and metaphysical problems which never attracted the thought of the humanists. As compared to the sources and influences of the past, it must be acknowledged that its synthesis was original, in its entirety and in many of its separate elements. These reasons make it imperative to consider and treat Renaissance Platonism as a movement unto itself, distinct from Aristotelianism and humanism.

Renaissance Platonism did not take its strength from the tradition of instruction, as did Aristotelianism, which dominated the teaching of philosophy and the sciences in the universities and religious colleges, or humanism, which dominated the secondary-school and the university instruction of the *studia humanitatis.* In the late sixteenth century, Francesco Patrizi occupied chairs of Platonic philosophy in Ferrara and Rome, where he tried in vain to replace Aristotelian philosophy with the Platonic in university teaching. For several decades, Pisa hosted courses of Platonic philosophy held by scholars who also taught Aristotelian philosophy and were thus willing to search for compatibility in the two schools. The Platonic Academy of Florence, under Ficino, was certainly an influential nucleus for the discussion and divulgation of Platonist-related doctrines, but its organization was loose and it lasted a mere three decades. In the sixteenth century, when academies began to spring up in all the Italian cities as extra-university centres of literary culture, Platonic love became a frequent subject of lectures and conferences which dealt with some of the sonnets of Petrarch and Bembo. But this cannot be called a real teaching of Platonic philosophy. Renaissance Platonism owed its strength not to the schools, but to the fact that the three most important quattrocento thinkers—Nicholas of Cusa, Ficino and Pico—were, if not pure Platonists, then at least highly affected by Platonism. Like the texts of Plato and the neo-Platonists, the works of these three men were widely read in the late fifteenth century and in the sixteenth century, in both manuscript and printed form. Their many interested readers were not only professional philosophers; they were poets, men of letters, scientists, theologians, scholars and dilettantes.

In speaking of Platonism, it is important to understand that this is not the tradition of the pure doctrine of Plato, as modern scholars after Schleiermacher have tried to construe it. It is a wide and complex movement which combines the most authentic Platonic doctrines with neo-Platonic and pseudo-Platonic ideas from various periods and origins.

Every thinker who is called Platonic represents his own synthesis of Platonic, extraneous and original elements, which must all be carefully examined; it is quite possible to find two thinkers who are correctly identified as Platonic or Platonizing, but who share no common doctrine. It cannot be postulated that the earlier of two thinkers called Platonic must have influenced the later, unless there are clear connections in doctrine, terminology or text. In this case, as in many others, the labels written by modern doxographers do not lend themselves to an algebra or alchemy of ideas.

Nicholas of Cusa, probably the most original and profound fifteenth-century thinker, has been the object of many recent studies, particularly in Germany, but the critical edition of his works is still incomplete. The sources of his thought and culture include scholastic philosophy—Scotism and nominalism in particular—and the mystic and neo-Platonic movement of the Middle Ages, plus a deeper familiarity with Plato, Proclus, the (pseudo-)Dionysius and others, both in the original Greek and in many new humanist translations. His interests in mathematics and astronomy have attracted the attention of historians of science. His language is extremely difficult; his themes and terminology change from one work to the next, and it is not always easy to decide if this is due to differing development or accentuation, or if it derives from more fundamental changes in doctrine. In treating the general and specific concepts of reason as simple abstractions, he discloses nominalist tendencies. But when he defines God as an infinite essence and the coincidence of opposites, and interprets the world and all of its parts as distinct manifestations and contractions of a simple divine archetype, explaining our knowledge of God as the continual approximation of our intellect to the infinite, this clearly shows Platonic and neo-Platonic overtones, and in particular, the influence of St Augustine and the Areopagite. Nicholas of Cusa was closely associated with the humanist world, but the roots of his thought are different, and the influence of his works was felt less in his own times than in the sixteenth century, when it reached its peak, for example in Lefèvre d'Etaples, Charles de Bovelles and Giordano Bruno.

Marsilio Ficino and his Platonic Academy represent the most important centre of Renaissance Platonism. By publishing the first complete Latin translation of the works of Plato, and the first version of Plotinus, Ficino made these central texts available to all western readers; the addition of an introduction and commentaries also determined the way these texts would be read and understood for several centuries to come. Ficino's *Theologia Platonica,* presented as an authoritative

synthesis of Plato's metaphysics, was accepted as such both in its day and later. In fact, although his synthesis included many elements which were extraneous to Plato, i.e. neo-Platonic, Aristotelian and Epicurean, Augustinian, Thomist and others, it none the less was able to leave its successors a rich and solid metaphysical alternative to conventional Aristotelianism. Ficino's acceptance of the apocryphal writings of Hermes Trismegistus, Zoroaster, Orpheus and Pythagoras as documents attesting to an ancient and pre-Platonic wisdom, gave him the means to present the Platonic tradition as an almost unbroken chain, a form of perennial philosophy which was distinguished from Hebrew and Christian religious tradition, but in fundamental agreement with it. Encouraged by his neo-Platonic and Hermetic sources, but also by his familiarity with medical literature, he accepted and propagated certain forms of astrology and magic. Many sixteenth-century thinkers liked his central ideas on the contemplative life, on the immortality of the soul, on natural religion, on Platonic love, on the innate ideas of man which derive from the archetypal ideas of the divine intellect, on a universe permeated by the Soul of the World and unified by the thought and appetite of the rational and human soul; the influence of these ideas was reinforced by the Platonic, neo-Platonic and Hermetic authority which seemed to support them.

While it is true that Ficino's young friend Giovanni Pico della Mirandola, who tragically met with an early death, felt the influence of his friend and of his Platonism, he cannot be characterized as merely Ficinian or even Platonic. Pico's humanist education was enriched by a masterful familiarity with the scholastic philosophy he had acquired in Padua and Paris; he always tried to absorb numerous scholastic doctrines into his own thought and to defend the scholastic philosophers from the attacks of the humanist Ermolao Barbaro. As a youth, Pico also studied magic, but in his last and longest book he firmly attacked judiciary astrology, supporting his position with arguments from astronomy, philosophy and theology. One of the first western scholars to learn Hebrew and Arabic, he took an interest in the untranslated writings of Averroes, in the rabbinical commentaries on the Bible and, most of all, in cabalistic literature, which he believed he could reconcile with Christian theology. The Christian cabalist movement of the sixteenth century, which includes Reuchlin and many others, originates in Pico's works, as does the cabalistic element in late Renaissance syncretism. In the same way the Hermetic, Chaldaic and magic element can be traced back to Ficino. (pp. 143-46)

Like the philosophy of other periods, Renaissance philosophy contains many ideas of an intrinsic and permanent worth and interest. If we insist upon trying to show that these thinkers were the predecessors or precursors of certain modern or contemporary movements, their importance will never be demonstrated. What seemed modern yesterday is no longer so today, and what seems modern today might not be so tomorrow. A thinker who belongs to the past does not seem to gain much by association with a modernity which is *passé* or outmoded. It would seem safer to treat the thought of the past, whether that of the Renaissance or of some other period, as a treasure trove of ideas which are always fruitful when studied, even though they may not lend themselves to repetition without some modification, and even though they merely contribute to the themes and alternatives of the philosophical and human discourse, which we adopt and perpetuate, and which we hope our successors will continue as long as our culture manages to retain the tiniest breath of authentic life—a thing which at this moment is not beyond doubt, but also not beyond hope. (p. 148)

> Paul Oskar Kristeller, "The Renaissance in the History of Philosophical Thought," translated by Kristin Jarratt, in The Renaissance: Essays in Interpretation by André Chastel and others, Methuen & Co. Ltd., 1982, pp. 127-52.

HUMANISMS AND HUMANISTS

ERNEST HATCH WILKINS

[Wilkins was an American educator and scholar of Italian literature. In the following excerpt from his A History of Italian Literature (1954), he sketches the achievements of several Italian men of letters who were, he argues, "militant in their assertion of the importance of their own studies and their own services."]

Within the first sixty years of the fifteenth century the Sforza family succeeded the Visconti as rulers of Milan; Venice greatly enlarged her dominion on the mainland; Cosimo de' Medici became in 1434 the *de facto* ruler of Florence; and the House of Aragon came into possession of the Kingdom of Naples. Two important ecumenical councils were held: the Council of Constance (1414-1418) put an end to the Great Schism, and the Council of Basel, Ferrara, Florence, and Rome (1431-1443) led to a short-lived union of the Greek and Roman Churches. Both councils were of great cultural importance, the first because it brought together Northern and Italian scholars, and the second because it brought several Greek scholars to Italy. A new Islamic thrust resulted in 1453 in the fall of Constantinople. A good many Greek scholars came to Italy as refugees, but Greek studies were already so well established in Italy that the contribution of the newcomers was of secondary importance. Other events, taking place outside of Italy, were of world-wide significance: overseas exploration began with the Portuguese rediscovery of the Madeiras and the Azores; and German printers, about the middle of the century, invented the process of printing from movable type.

These same decades witnessed an extraordinary outburst of genius in the fine arts. In architecture Brunelleschi, reacting from the outworn Italian Gothic tradition and turning again to the monuments of ancient Rome, established concepts and patterns that were to endure, with various modifications, for centuries. His own work culminated in the superb dome of the Florentine cathedral. In sculpture Jacopo della Quercia, medieval in certain limitations, was modern in his tremendous vigor; Ghiberti's "gates of Paradise" combined grandeur and supreme grace; Donatello, greatest of them all, entering to some extent into the Roman tradition, was yet more concerned with vigor and with realism, especially in the rendering of character; and Luca della Robbia, companion to the others in the dignity of his marbles, created in his terra cottas a new medium for pure loveliness. Painting, which had no clear Roman tradition to resume, though it borrowed certain decorative elements from Roman art, saw the last perfect flowering of the medieval spirit in Fra Angelico; surged forward into vigorous modernity with Masolino and Masaccio; and found a new human charm with Fra Lippo Lippi.

Comparable in its profusion to the simultaneous development in the fine arts was the very great development of humanism, which now so fired the ambitions and absorbed the energies of Italian men of letters in general that few authors, and none of them of the highest order of ability, devoted themselves exclusively to writing in the vernacular.

To call the typical writers of this period "humanists" is to recognize their community in the enthusiastic and scholarly study of the classics, in the undertaking of extensive philological and editorial labors, and in the writing of Latin works of their own in classicizing form and style. Most of them were employed either as teachers, or as secretaries or chancellors in papal or princely courts or in city governments. And they were militant in their assertion of the importance of their own studies and their own services. But their several patterns of life and work were by no means identical. (pp. 123-24)

Leonardo Bruni (1374-1444) was born in Arezzo, and was often called, accordingly, Leonardo Aretino; but he became a Florentine by education and by choice. For some years he served as a papal secretary, and in that capacity he attended the Council of Constance. Thereafter he made his home in Florence, busied primarily with his writing, but taking a wise and honorable part in the public life of the city. He served as its Chancellor from 1427 to his death. The most important of his many and varied Latin works was his *History of Florence*, which covers the history of the city from its Roman origins to 1402. He is careful as to facts, judging his sources critically and supplementing them by the use of documents; he seeks the causes of the events he narrates; and he tries to see those events in due perspective—characteristics which, in their combination, entitle him to be considered as the first modern historian. He sought to achieve a classic dignity of style; and he enlivened his pages, in the classic fashion, by the introduction of numerous imaginary harangues, many of which are devoted to the exaltation of liberty. Bruni first, among the humanists, translated from the Greek, making Latin versions of the *Nicomachaean Ethics* and the *Politics* of Aristotle, several of the dialogues of Plato, and several works by other authors. He wrote in Greek a treatise on the political constitution of Florence. In Italian he wrote lives of Dante and of Petrarch, and one *novella* (on a classic theme).

The career of Poggio Bracciolini (1380-1459) was similar to that of Bruni in that Poggio, born in Southern Tuscany, became a Florentine by education and by choice, served for some years as a papal secretary, attended the Council of Constance, and toward the end of his life served as Chancellor of Florence. At one time he spent four lonely years in England. His distinctive contribution to the cause of humanism was his persistent and repeatedly successful effort to discover missing classic works. In the years 1415-1417 he found, in various Burgundian, Swiss, and German monasteries, manuscripts of Lucretius, the *Silvae* of Statius, a complete Quintilian, several orations of Cicero, and missing works or portions of works by other authors. He wrote voluminously, always in Latin, and almost always with vivacity and brilliance. Of all the thousands of humanist letters and hundreds of humanist dialogues his are easily the best. His long dialogue *De varietate fortunae*, moving from reflection upon the ruins of ancient Rome, and Stoic in its spirit, is his ablest single work. His wit ran to uncurbed excesses in his fierce polemics, directed usually against other humanists. He wrote an *Historia florentina* covering the period from 1350 to 1455, and a very famous *Liber facetiarum*, a collection of jests and amusing anecdotes.

Francesco Filelfo (1398-1481), born near Ancona, served in his youth as a subordinate in the Venetian foreign service, spending some time in Constantinople, where he studied Greek, and visiting Hungary and Poland. After his return to Italy he taught for a few years in the University of Florence; but he made enemies there, and left the city in hostility and fear. He soon established himself in Milan, where he remained for most of the rest of his arrogant and extravagant life, patronized first by the Visconti and then by the Sforza. Utterly unprincipled, he used his verbal facility in venomous invectives against his rivals and his enemies, or as a means of extracting favors or gratuities either from those to whom he paid fulsome tribute or from those whom he threatened with insult if they did not buy him off. His literary output was enormous, but pedestrian. He alone among the humanists of this period wrote extensively in Latin verse: his poems include odes, satires, epigrams, and an epic on the rise of the Sforza family. His excellent knowledge of Greek served him for several translations, and for the writing of some Greek verse. Unwillingly, at the desire of a Visconti duke, he wrote in Italian a perfunctory and incomplete commentary on the *Canzoniere* of Petrarch.

The Roman Lorenzo Valla (1407-1457) taught in his youth in Pavia and elsewhere in Northern Italy; served for ten years as secretary to King Alfonso of Naples; and then, returning to Rome, spent the rest of his life there as a papal secretary. Keenly critical in his thinking, he attacked what seemed to him to be undue assumptions of authority or of tradition in the fields of philosophy, religion, law, and philology. In his first work, the dialogue *De voluptate,* he maintains that the desire for pleasure is the central human motive; that man, being both body and spirit, naturally and rightfully seeks, as body, the normal human pleasures and, as spirit, the eternal blessedness; and that the two types of pleasure are perfectly compatible. In a later dialogue, the *De libero arbitrio,* he wrestles with the perpetual problem of free will, concluding that the will is free in that it is not conditioned by divine foreknowledge, and that its relationship to the will of God remains a mystery that reason cannot solve. With essentially modern methods of historical and textual criticism he proved that the document asserting the Donation of Constantine was unauthentic; and that the Apostles' Creed was the work not of the Twelve, but of the first Nicene Council. He compared St. Jerome's translation of the New Testament with its Greek original, and dared to attack the infallibility of the Latin version. The best known of all Valla's writings is the *De linguae latinae elegantia.* In this work his scorn for medieval barbarisms, his enthusiasm for classic Latin, and his determination to find authority not in the grammarians but in the best classic practice enabled him to establish standards of linguistic and stylistic excellence still higher than those attained by the other humanists of his own day. His philosophical and religious works, highly esteemed by Erasmus, Luther, and Calvin, served in the following century to give aid and comfort to the Protestant cause: it was Erasmus who first published Valla's work on St. Jerome's translation of the New Testament. But Valla himself, for all his criticism, was loyal to the Church.

Enea Silvio Piccolomini of Siena (1405-1464), often called Aeneas Sylvius, began his active life as a highly gifted youth, interested in everything he saw, much amused by mankind, and unscrupulously ambitious. He came first into prominence at the Council of Basel, which sent him on a mission to James I of Scotland. He then spent several years beyond the Alps, serving first an antipope and then the Emperor Frederick III, whose court, thanks to the presence of Piccolomini, became the seedbed of humanism in Germany. In these early years he indulged in Latin love poems, and wrote, in Latin, both a disreputable Plautine comedy, the *Chrisis,* and the most undeservedly famous of his writings, the *Historia de duobus amantibus,* a Boccaccesque *novella* of some length, which gained wide circulation not only in its original form but also in Italian, French, German, and English versions. In the very next year, however, seeing the political error of his ways, he made submission to the Pope in Rome, took orders, and embarked upon an ecclesiastical career in which he advanced swiftly through bishopric and cardinalate to the papacy, which he achieved, as Pius II, in 1458. Throughout this longer portion of his life he wrote extensively, seriously, and very well indeed. The most notable of all his works is his long autobiography, wide-ranging in its experiences, its descriptions, and its comments. Its first Book includes a very interesting account of his early adventures in Scotland and England. His letters and dialogues are picturesque and lively. He was the leading orator of his day. The most spectacular scenes of his life are recorded by Pinturicchio in frescoes that still glow convincingly on the walls of the library of the Cathedral of Siena.

Leon Battista Alberti (1404-1472), born of a prominent Florentine family, held a papal secretaryship and lived in Rome for the greater part of his mature life, but spent the years 1434-1443 chiefly in Florence. He was primarily a humanist; but he was atypical both in his extraordinary versatility and in his championship of the Italian language as a worthy literary medium. He was an athlete (he excelled in racing, jumping, vaulting, climbing, ball playing, fencing, archery, and horsemanship), a great architect, a sculptor, a painter, a musician, a mathematician, a scientist and inventor (he experimented in the field of optics, and developed several measuring devices), and an engineer (he tried to raise one of the sunken Roman ships in the Lake of Nemi); and he was skilled in astronomy and the law. He was, indeed, a preincarnation of Leonardo.

In his architecture he made eager, scholarly, and imaginative use of Roman principle and Roman design. The three structures that chiefly evidence his greatness are the so-called Malatesta Temple in Rimini, the Rucellai palace in Florence, and Sant' Andrea in Mantua. In Sant' Andrea the traditional Gothic columnar piers and groined vaults are replaced by massive rectangular piers and barrel vaults, suggested by those of the great Roman baths, the whole so ordered and so proportioned that the resulting structure is one of the noblest churches of the Italian Renaissance, perhaps the noblest of them all. It represents the initiation of the architectural system that was ultimately to find its most grandiose embodiment in the new St. Peter's.

Alberti wrote voluminously, both in Latin and in Italian. The most extensive of his Latin works is his very scholarly, very personal, and very influential treatise *De re aedificatoria.* Based upon a thorough and precise examination of extant monuments of Roman architecture and upon a critical study of Vitruvius, the work benefits by Alberti's experience as a successful innovating architect, and embodies confidently his firm convictions as to the nobility of a creative art concerned at once with scientific perfection and with the attainment of beauty. His *Intercoenales,* "Dinner Entertainments," is a collection of about twenty dialogues and other short pieces, largely in the mood and the manner of Lucian, which treat various aspects of life, sometimes with sympathy, oftener with satire, and always thoughtfully. Other Latin writings include an early allegorical comedy; an expert and enthusiastic treatise on the nature and the care of the horse; and a treatise on justice which inveighs impressively against pettifoggery and against cruelty in punishment, and argues that punishment should be designed not to crush but to amend.

The most important of Alberti's writings in Italian is his long dialogue *Della famiglia,* written during his stay in Florence. The conversation, which is carried on chiefly by men of the Alberti family, who evince a just appreciation of their honorable family tradition. The first Book, an educational classic, discusses the responsibilities of the old to the young and of the young to the old, and in particular the education of children. That education is to be physical and social as well as mental. Great stress is laid upon bodily discipline, exercise of many kinds, and the maintenance of health—all this in order that the *corpus sanum* may then serve its mature master well for activities of a higher order. The youth is to be initiated into architecture, sculpture, painting, and music, and is to be led into the love of nature, animate and inanimate. He is to gain much from association with men, growing thus in obedience, prudence, honor, self-control, and self-reliance. He is to be moderate, and never idle, and he is to be prepared, even to the extent of learning the rudiments of a trade, to withstand the onslaughts of ill-fortune. More formally, he is to be trained in the reading and writing of Italian, Latin, and Greek. Alberti's educational theory, like his architectural theory, is derived in the first instance from ancient sources, but is developed freely in accordance with his own personal experiences and convictions.

The second Book of the *Famiglia* discusses marriage, exalted as a union of minds and wills; the third, on the general management of the household, affirms, but in no miserly spirit, the excellence of thrift, and becomes eloquent in its praise of villa life; and the fourth deals with friendship.

Among Alberti's other writings in Italian the most interesting are two early treatises, one on sculpture and one on painting, which are the first Renaissance treatments of these themes, and his last and mellowest work, the *De iciarchia,* "On the Headship of a Family." In this he goes over again some of the ground he had covered in the *Famiglia;* but he now has in mind in particular the training of men who are to exercise power in the state, and are therefore to be responsible for the liberty and dignity of the state itself, and for the welfare of its citizens. He exalts the family as the pattern for the state, and self-mastery as the chief excellence of the individual man. In some respects, even in some details, he anticipates ideas that were to be set forth by Castiglione, a century later, in his *Book of the Courtier.*

Alberti's most dramatic gesture in his championship of the Italian language as a literary medium was the *certame coronario,* the "contest for the crown," which he devised and carried through, the costs being borne by Piero de' Medici, son of Cosimo. Alberti's purpose was to prove that Italian verse could treat worthily of worthy themes. The theme chosen for the contest was Friendship. On the appointed day, October 22, 1441, the contest was held in the crowded Cathedral. The Council was then in session in Florence, and the judges were ten papal secretaries, all of them humanists, and generally disposed to scorn the vulgar tongue. The prize was to be a sil-

ver crown in the form of a laurel-wreath. Eight poets, including Alberti, presented their poems, in Italian, on the stated theme. . . . At the close of the contest the judges, alleging that four of the competitors had shown equal merit, refused to award the crown, and directed that it be given to the Cathedral. The decision was ill received: it was generally believed that the judges had been moved by envy.

Many other men engaged with some distinction in humanistic activities, most of them combining scholarship with writing in Latin. Of the few whose humanism manifested itself chiefly in ways other than those of the pen, the two most eminent were the two great educators, Guarino of Verona (1374-1460), who taught chiefly in Ferrara, and Vittorino da Feltre (1373-1446), who taught chiefly in Mantua. Their careers were very similar: both maintained schools under court patronage in North Italian cities; both based their teaching upon Greek principles; both were concerned with physical, moral, and religious education as well as with mental education; both lived with their pupils; both were men of lovable and democratic personality; and both had great influence upon those whom they taught, and upon later educational theory and practice.

During these years many Greek scholars came to Italy, either to attend the second Council, or for other reasons; and several of them stayed on. The two who won greatest distinction and had greatest influence were Gemistus Pletho, a philosopher, and in particular an exponent of Neo-Platonism; and Bessarion, who transferred his ecclesiastical allegiance to the Roman Church, in which he became a cardinal.

The greatest of the several patrons of the period were Cosimo de' Medici, Pope Nicholas V (who in his early days had drawn up a plan of library classification for Cosimo), and, for the Greeks, Cardinal Bessarion. All three of these men, as well as others—some of them rulers, such as Federigo di Montefeltro, Duke of Urbino, and some of them private citizens—assembled fine collections of manuscripts. Under Nicholas V the Vatican Library grew from almost nothing to a collection of over a thousand volumes; and Bessarion's collection, bequeathed to the city of Venice, became the nucleus of the Venetian Library of St. Mark's.

Within this period humanism was introduced into England. Humphrey, Duke of Gloucester, the first English patron of the new learning, called three or four of the lesser Italian humanists to England, and corresponded with some of the greater ones. Toward the end of the period five Oxford men went to Italy to gain humanistic knowledge at first hand: all of them studied with Guarino, or were in some way associated with him. The most learned of the five, John Free, stayed on in Italy, where he was known among humanists as Phreas. The four who returned, and Free through his writings, did much to further the acceptance of humanism in England. (pp. 124-30)

Ernest Hatch Wilkins, "The Militant Humanists,"
in his A History of Italian Literature, *Cambridge,*
Mass.: Harvard University Press, 1954, pp. 123-30.

MARGARET L. KING

[*King is an American educator and author who has written widely on Venetian humanism. In the following excerpt, she regards conflicts between Venetian humanism and Christian virtue.*]

The fusion of learning and virtue was an objective named frequently in humanist culture. But virtue was a term richly ambiguous in the fifteenth century. It connoted, on the one hand, the moral ideal of the Christian religion as comprehended in the Middle Ages; on the other, a renewed classical ideal, secular and modern, proud and aggressive, destined for embodiment in Machiavelli's hero. In Venice, concepts of antique virtue were welcomed and adopted into humanist culture. But Venice's humanists—and their culture—remained staunchly pious, and humanist learning at times joined the battle of the medieval Church against passion and instinct.

Francesco Contarini, Zaccaria Trevisan the Younger, and Domenico Grimani were all commended . . . for having as youths resisted the seductions of lust and amusement and devoted their energies instead to studies. That topos is frequently encountered. Cristoforo Moro also, according to Bernardo Bembo, "passed all the years of his adolescence in the study of theology," and by his Christian virtue had earned not only the highest position in the republic (he had just been elected doge), but a place in heaven. Such youthful asceticism humanist authors also discerned and esteemed in those whose virtue was not linked to the new learning: Marco Corner, according to Pietro Contarini, rescued his youth from sensuality and devoted it to hard work; Giorgio Loredan, according to Leonardo Giustiniani, fled the passions that beset him in adolescence to take refuge in labors by which his body and mind were prepared for civic and military obligations. Yet even when corseted, the passions of youth were suspect. The very young were barred from government in Venice, while the most respected offices were reserved for the old whose experience *in se* bore fruit of wisdom: "There are no wise men who are not old," wrote Domenico Morosini, adding sourly, "and even then, very few."

Did the adolescents of Venice's patriciate in fact avoid as a class the intense passions peculiar to that age? Few would find that claim wholly credible. But the ideal of adolescent self-restraint seems to have been generally respected. And certainly, in their maturity many among the Venetian humanists, however they had weathered the turbulent years of youth, were pious by profession and in practice. Perhaps, since piety is expected of ecclesiastics, the examples of Pietro Barozzi and Marco Barbo are not compelling. Yet these humanist clerics, at a time when the moral corruption of the clergy was widespread and notorious, appeared to have given to the poor abundantly of their own substance. Barozzi, habitually generous, had in a year of particular need supplied the Paduan population with grain and money in quantities sufficient to save many from death. Barbo died in Rome, the "most honored" of the cardinals, clothed in a hair shirt, rich in books, poor in ducats—for he had given all his wealth to the poor. But not all the pious among Venice's humanists were clerics. Laymen as well found in established Christianity solace for the soul and hope for their city.

About to embark on the journey to Crete, to which island-colony he had been elected doge, Candiano Bollani put the final words to his commentary on Genesis and asked his friend, a Carthusian monk of no particular stature, to pray for him. Here is indeed a case of the blending of active and contemplative lives, when a nobleman of impeccably orthodox conviction devotes his leisure to reflection on Scripture, and pauses for the aid of prayer before assuming office! Ludovico Foscarini consulted a battery of spiritual advisers. To Matteo Contarini he spoke bravely of how the bodily pain he suffered aroused him to love of God. To Moro Lapi—a simple monk, prolific of pious works in the vernacular yet with but limping competence in Latin, correspondent of several highly placed patricians—he confessed his fear of demons, and of sin. To the saintly Patriarch Lorenzo Giustiniani, he deplored the immorality of conspicuous display and lamented the brutality of his own—not the enemy's—soldiers. With Francesco Trevisan, who had also the confidence of the doge, he shared his grief at the death of his father, a pious layman who wished to be buried in the habit of a Franciscan friar.

Francesco Barbaro, Venice's arch-humanist, was active in monastic reform and, like Foscarini, an intimate of holy men who could proffer advice and consolation. Poised to set out from Zoppola to Venice, he anxiously wrote two monks—one Carthusian, one Camaldulensian—for their prayers and their advice: should he travel when there was danger of the plague? He wooed the monk Giovanni Capistrano, inviting friendship in a letter accompanied by a generous gift of wine. That wealthy and powerful man who had taken under his protection learned commoners, poor noblemen, whole cities, implored Giovanni in the name of God to "receive me in your faith and your protection." No casual Christian, Barbaro was one of many Venetians fascinated by the preaching friar San Bernardino, whose cult of veneration of the holy name of Jesus he joined. Poggio Bracciolini, a humanist of a different stripe, bemoaned Barbaro's custom of heading manuscript pages with the radiant IHS of the holy name: "I rejoice that at last you have become a Christian," he mocked, then grieved that a wise and learned man should engage in such vulgar folly.

Barbaro's veneration of the holy name suggests more than conventional acquiescence to the credos of his age; it suggests profound conviction. His friend Leonardo Giustiniani also underwent a process of spiritual deepening akin, in his case, to conversion. The love poems of his youth for which he was justly famed he renounced, and devoted later years to religious *laudi* of great sensitivity. In his prose works, as well, urged by his brother the Patriarch Lorenzo, he progressed from secular to religious concerns. "For daily you urge me with your incredible piety," Leonardo wrote his brother in the dedicatory letter to the life of Nicholas of Myra he had translated from the Greek, "that I direct my studies and my thoughts above all to attaining the blessed life and [my] soul's immortality, and after sailing so long that I finally seek a harbor." The seriousness of his spiritual concern is evident elsewhere than in communications with the heroically ascetic patriarch. To the preacher Francesco of Rimini whose words had inspired many, Leonardo expressed gratitude for the liberating consolation he had received. Francesco was his "harbor," in which he found peace. Leonardo urged the monk and humanist Ambrogio Traversari to have his busy scribes provide vernacular books on sacred subjects so that less-educated readers might have access to them, and reproved his friend for devoting too much time to the study of secular authors.

The tension between secular and sacred studies was also felt by Gregorio Correr, a pupil of the humanist pedagogue Vittorino da Feltre, and in his youth an author of secular verse and an enthusiast of Virgil. For two years he had wavered between his life of civilized studies and a life devoted to God. Swayed finally by the example of his holy uncle, he renounced secular for sacred learning. Years later, though, the writings of the ancient pagans still tempted him. Exhorting a Carthu-

Cloisters of Santa Maria delle Grazie, Milan.

sian novice to read only holy books, Correr admitted his weakness. "Let no literature delight you other than that written in the name of our Lord. This will be easy for you; it was harder for me. I had loved the foolish learning of the world, and the seductions of secular letters—and even now, I have not ceased to love them." Like Correr, Ludovico Foscarini urged the young Jacopo Foscari to love not the pagan authors, but "ours," and to find truth in the gospel of Christ. Like Correr, too, Pietro Dolfin abandoned the secular studies he had loved when he entered the religious life, and mourned his former devotion to them in a long autobiographical letter to his friend, later abbot, Pietro Donato.

Though the religious experience of these Venetian humanists was sometimes intense and personal, they saw religion as a civic as well as a private concern. Pietro Contarini believed that no quality was more highly valued in Venice than piety, of which the witnesses were "the frequent ceremonies, the elaborate ornaments of prelates, the bones of saints brought from all over the world." The whole city could benefit from communal expressions of piety. Domenico Morosini recommended public preaching as a cure for the plague and argued that the devoutness of senators would assure the benevolence of God to the city.

Nothing was so likely, however, to win divine indulgence

than the presence of relics, hundreds of which Venice proudly possessed. The respect for these relics invades even the official language of the Senate, as in this passage from an act by which 10,000 ducats were allotted to purchase a garment worn by Christ. "In that our ancestors strove and sweated continually for the honor of God and the increase of the Christian religion and of our city's devotion, not considering the risks, labors and expenses which they might face, and brought to this city from every part of the world . . . the bodies and various relics of the saints . . . our city has been adorned with many holy and devout and venerable bodies and many relics of the saints by whose merits and prayers it must be believed that this city has been often saved and every day is saved and protected from many adversities, by the grace of God." Bernardo Giustiniani appealed for the city's welfare not only to God, to Mary, and the evangelist Mark, but to the relics of seventy saints which Venice housed; for he firmly believed that relics protected the city. By the "vigilance and patronage" of Saint Mark above all, the city's protector and almost her founder, Venice was rendered "unconquerable and impregnable." Ermolao Barbaro (the Elder) concurred: adorned with "so many and such saints," the city, become God's particular joy, would never perish.

If the humanists, along with other Venetians, trusted in the relics that protected their city, they feared those outsiders whose denial of Christianity—in their eyes, perverse—threatened the cohesion of the community. The cleric Pietro Bruto devoted two of his works and much of his energy to combatting the Jews of Vicenza where he was vice-regent and lieutenant to the Bishop Giovanni Battista Zeno. Paolo Morosini wrote a famous apology for Christianity against the Jews—the first book published in Padua. Ludovico Foscarini vigorously testified—against others who had doubted them—of atrocities committed by Jews. Concurring with Fantino Dandolo, who had denounced Jewish doctors who both killed the bodies of Christian patients and damned their souls, he praised Ermolao Donato, who had chosen to suffer from his wounds rather than be treated by a Jewish doctor. (pp. 31-7)

Margaret L. King, "The Humanists: 'Ordo litteratorum'," in her Venetian Humanism in an Age of Patrician Dominance, *Princeton University Press, 1986, pp. 3-91.*

E. R. CHAMBERLIN

[Chamberlin is a Jamaican-born author and historian. In the following excerpt, he looks at the lives of four Florentine humanists: Coluccio Salutati, Niccolò Niccoli, Poggio Bracciolini, and Leonardo Bruni.]

'Humanism' as a definition is as amorphous, as protean as 'Renaissance', and its current twentieth-century use, applied to a vaguely defined atheism and individualism, obscures its meaning even further. The first humanists were anything but atheists. The term itself did not come into general use until the late fifteenth century, nearly a century after the founders of the movement, when it came to be applied to those engaged in the teaching of the humanities—specifically, grammar, rhetoric, history and moral philosophy. But this definition errs in the opposite direction, turning the 'humanist' into something little different from a grammar school master, transforming what was essentially an explorer into a pedant.

However the term is defined, the inescapable point of departure for the study of humanism is the life and career of Francesco Petrarch. Despite the crowded stage, despite the sheer numbers of his brilliant followers, it is worth looking at that career . . . for it is literally archetypal, containing in itself the seeds of all that followed. Born in 1304 and dying in 1374, his life acts as a chronological bridge between the old and new worlds. He was seventeen years old when his great precursor, Dante, died and Giotto, his innovating equal in the world of art, died when he was thirty-three. At the end of his life, those of his disciples who were to influence the thinking of his next generation were already established in positions of authority. Indeed, the historian rash enough to assign an exact date of birth to the Renaissance could do worse than choose 6 April 1341, the day upon which Petrarch was crowned Poet Laureate upon the Capitol in Rome. Doubtless the ceremony was a fusty antiquarian revival; doubtless he owed the honour to his ceaselessly canvassing for it; doubtless his major work still lay ahead of him. Nevertheless, the ceremony on the Capitoline Hill marks a moment of vital change in Europe's intellectual climate: secular scholarship was again respectable. (pp. 50-2)

Carlyle, who condemned Petrarch's sonnets, might not be the best judge of lyric poetry but his opinion that Laura's main function was to spark off a sonnet sequence bears a ring of truth. Certainly her death in 1348 coincided with the exhaus-tion of Petrarch's lyrical vein. Thereafter follows the relentless work of the experimental scholar, curiously blind to visual art but acutely conscious of all other manifestations of existence, more truly the Complete Man than some of the lauded figures of the High Renaissance, aware of change when change was inchoate and so guiding the new impulses at a vital stage.

Petrarch's very originality serves to obscure the immense extent of his contribution to the new world. The poet endures, but much of the scholar was fated to be overshadowed by men who used, with the greater skill born of familiarity, techniques that he laboriously fashioned. As Latinist, for example—the skill upon which he prided himself most—he was surpassed by his followers, but their Ciceronian elegancies owed everything not merely to his written work but to his actual, physical discovery and transmission of the lost classical texts which were now beginning to serve as models—tasks which absorbed an immense part of his time and money.

The failure of his epic poem *Africa* is index at once to his originality and to his goal, pointing the contrast between his own 'modern' approach and that of the medieval world, barely a generation away. Infused with classicism, he attempted to recreate it, actually challenging Virgil on the Roman's own ground with an epic poem, in Latin, on a great Roman hero, Scipio Africanus. Dante, still immersed in the medieval tradition which was untroubled by anachronism, merely forced Virgil to copy Dante.

Again, the endless flow of quotations from the classics that made of Petrarch's works priceless anthologies for his contemporaries became an irritant for generations granted direct access to the quoted works themselves. So, too, his *Lives of Illustrious Men* became a museum piece as other writers first plundered it, then followed up and improved on its once novel approach.

But his letters retain all their immediacy of impact. Consciously, he intended them for posterity but the bulk of them were written to friends such as Laelius and Socrates and so bear—not spontaneity certainly, for each was a literary exercise—an undying freshness born of the knowledge that each was intended for a unique, living mind. Through them posterity gains a priceless view, at once wide and detailed, into a vanished world. Unlike most of his contemporaries he had a lively eye for nature: indicative of his approach is the fact that he climbed a mountain out of sheer curiosity to see what was at the top when his contemporaries regarded it merely as a larger lump of rock. Unlike so many of his followers, he avoided literary conceits, writing vividly, directly of what he saw and felt. He shared with Chaucer the dawning awareness that the humdrum and humble were as legitimate literary subjects as the noble and extraordinary. Unlike Chaucer, he did not process the material into poetry or fiction so that the peasant and the fisherman, the prelate and the pilgrim remain in reality, but in a single paragraph he can better portray the result of endless warfare in Italy than do pages of polemics from other men, for he writes of what he sees.

And it was as much through his letters, as through his formal work, that the 'new learning' was disseminated. Their fortunate recipients copied them out to send on to distant friends, or formed clubs to read them aloud to each other, acting as informal publishers. 'I stand as a man between two worlds, looking both forward and backwards,' he once wrote. He had little love for the new world; light lay only in the classic past.

Nevertheless, he was most vividly aware of living at a climacteric and it was this awareness that paradoxically made of him, supreme recreator of the past as he was, an authentic voice of the future.

Petrarch's scholarship, though bold in so many of its innovations—its techniques of observing the real world instead of taking it for granted—was still medieval in the sense that it was a private affair, something to be conducted in study or cloisters or between friends for their delectation. But like a leaven in the lump, it began to work when some of those friends and disciples took up public appointments. One of those disciples was Coluccio Salutati. Born in 1331, he studied law and was appointed Chancellor of Florence at the age of forty-four in 1375.

Salutati held that office until his death in 1406. The holding of such an appointment for thirty-two years in a city where hatred of the single ruler was elevated into a political principle speaks much for his skill and probity as a civil servant. But the Florentine merchants who approved his appointment, together with its comfortable salary of 100 florins per annum tax free, were less interested in his honesty and his commonplace qualifications as a notary than in the power of his pen. In his hands, the Latin prose he had absorbed direct from the great masters of Latin became a superb instrument of propaganda. During Florence's long drawn out war with Milan, the Milanese lord, Gian Galeazzo Visconti, ruefully admitted that a single letter of Salutati's did him more damage than a thousand Florentine horsemen. (pp. 53-5)

Among the members of the informal group around Salutati was a certain rich man, Niccolò Niccoli. Born in 1364, he was not only some thirty years younger than Salutati—becoming in effect a transmitter from one generation to another—but, unlike Salutati, he was freed from the necessity of earning a living. His father was one of the men who had made a fortune during the boom years of the Florentine woollen industry and had insisted that his son should at least learn the rudiments of the trade. As soon as the old man died, however, Niccoli promptly abandoned the business to his four brothers and devoted himself entirely to scholarship. So total was that devotion that, by the end of his life, Niccoli was dependent upon the Medici for the necessities of life, having spent his all on acquiring manuscripts and encouraging young scholars.

Vespasiano da Bisticci, the gossiping bookseller, left a vivid portrait of Niccoli.

> He was of handsome presence, lively, with a smile usually on his face and pleasant manner in conversation. His clothes were always of fine red cloth down to the ground; he never took a wife so as not to be hindered in his studies, and was accustomed to have his meals served to him in beautiful old dishes. His table would be covered with vases of porcelain, and he drank from a cup of crystal or of some other fine stone. It was a pleasure to see him at table, old as he was. All the linen that he used was of the finest.

A fastidious hedonist who delighted in the civilised pleasures of life, unlike most of his circle he opted out of active life even to the extent of allowing interference in his own domestic life. He had a beautiful but arrogant mistress, a young woman called Benvenuta, who so enraged his brothers with her high-handed attitude that one of them dragged her into the street and spanked her in public while Niccoli looked on, wringing his hands.

Niccoli's fastidiousness extended to his own attempts at literature: nothing he wrote pleased him and therefore he wrote little or nothing—certainly only two or three minor pieces can be attributed to him. The real reason for his restraint is probably the fact that his grasp of Latin, the only possible medium for a scholar, was something less than ideal. Despite, or because, of this limitation, he emerged as the foremost critic of his day. On one occasion, when an author demanded Niccoli's opinion of his newly finished work, Niccoli replied crushingly, 'I already have to deal with several hundred volumes of authors of repute before I shall be able to consider yours.' No visitor of any standing who came to Florence failed to call in upon him with the result that this stay-at-home, according to Bisticci 'had a great knowledge of all parts of the world, so that if anyone who had been in any particular region, and asked him about it, Niccoli would know it better than the man who had been there, and he gave many instances of this'.

But all Niccoli's activities were of decidedly lesser importance compared with his one abiding passion, the desire to possess books. At one stage, he directly employed more than forty copiers, and was accustomed to spend a certain amount of time each day in pursuing the craft himself, evolving a beautiful script which eventually provided the model for the modern italic script. Before the invention of printing, the survival of a book depended in large part on the accident of a scholar desiring a copy, and arranging for it to be made. It was only too easy for a book first to go out of fashion, and then to disappear altogether. Niccoli's contribution to that mysterious phenomenon known as the revival of learning was the location, copying and circulation of such lost texts. However, before they could be copied, they had to be found, tracked down like deposits of some rare mineral. Nobody in his senses travelled for pleasure and there was neither professional nor personal reason for the sedentary Niccoli to stir out of the comforts of Florence. He needed an agent, and found one in the person of Poggio Bracciolini.

Born in Terranova near Florence in 1380, Poggio Bracciolini was an excellent example of the new race of humanists who were bringing scholarship into the market-place—a man who had a deep and genuine love of learning, but was fully prepared to make money out of it. And Poggio's career was to show that there was quite a lot of money to be made. It was said that he arrived in Florence as a young man with just five soldi in his pocket. But, in the fullness of time he, too, became Chancellor of Florence, and on the way 'became very rich at the court of Rome' by employing the golden skills of language.

Apart from their mutual love of learning, Poggio and his patron Niccolò Niccoli differed from each other at every point. Where Niccoli was neat, restrained, gentlemanly, Poggio was large, expansive, rumbustious, 'given to strong invective' and a liking for even stronger drink. He was a born raconteur, and his collection of highly dubious stories, the *Facetiae*, was received with an enthusiasm in the Florentine equivalent of smoking rooms. He began his career, as did so many of his kind, as a notary and it was through the good offices of Salutati that he found a job in Rome as 'scrivener' at the papal court. It was a humble enough post, part copier, part writer of the innumerable letters that went out all over Christendom from Rome, but his outstanding gifts as Latin writer, combined with his easy bonhomie, took him out of the humble ranks of Chancery clerks. Pope Martin sent him to England as a courier 'where he found much to censure in the way of life of the country, how the people were fain to spend all their time in eating and drinking'—a curious criticism from Poggio Bracciolini with his passionate fondness for the white wines of Crete.

In 1414 Poggio was in the entourage of the bizarre figure of Baldassare Cossa, one of the three claimants of the papal tiara known to his adherents as John XXIII, when he was summoned to the Council of Constance. The Council had been called to end the scandal of the Schism and, unsurprisingly, 'John XXIII' was not only deposed but imprisoned, accused of an interesting variety of crimes ranging from piracy to rape. The Florentines had been among the few who recognised him as pope and it was through this link that Niccoli asked Poggio to keep an eye open for interesting manuscripts while they were in the barbaric land of Switzerland. After the pope's deposition, Poggio was unemployed and gladly devoted his time, at Niccoli's expense, to the hunting down of books. He had a remarkable flair, an instinct for the kind of place that would yield the treasure they sought. At the monastery of St Gall near Constance he stumbled immediately upon a rich vein, a collection of manuscripts some of which had been copied more than 800 years before. Among them was a veritable treasure, the complete book of Quintilian's *The training of an orator,* whose existence was known from a series of tantalising hints in other authors but of which Niccoli had despaired of ever finding a copy. (pp. 57-60)

The remarkably eclectic nature of the library Poggio assembled bears testimony to the almost mystic veneration in which the classical world was held. Books on cookery or astronomy, on agriculture or history—all were swept into the bag, regardless of the intrinsic value of the subject; they were in the Latin that Cicero wrote and that was good enough for Poggio. Greek was, for him, a closed book although, in 1396, the Greek scholar Manuel Chrysoloras had settled in Florence at the direct invitation of Coluccio Salutati.

There is something deeply poignant about the passionate desire to acquire Greek manifested by the first humanists. Petrarch, the greatest scholar of his age, could read only a few words of it and he went into partnership with his friend Boccaccio to set up a Greek-speaking monk, Leontius Pilatus, as translator of Homer in Florence in 1360. Pilatus was a repulsive old man—dirty, cantankerous, grasping. But to Boccaccio and Petrarch from his mouth there came only gold; admittedly an impure gold for the Greek he spoke was the bastard dialect spoken in a few monasteries in southern Italy. The experiment came to nothing: Pilatus took himself off to the Middle East leaving Petrarch to kiss his copy of Homer in frustrated substitution for reading it.

Chrysoloras, unlike the wretched old Pilatus, was a genuine scholar whose mother tongue was Byzantine Greek, and from the tiny little coterie that gathered round him in Florence during the three years he taught in the city, there developed the beginnings of a genuine school of Greek. Again, as with the Latin classics, it was not simply the language itself that magnetised the Florentine students as the fact that it was a vehicle, opening up a direct vision into the past—in particular, that segment of time which saw the fall of the Roman Republic. It was probably in response to this all-pervading interest of his hosts that Chrysoloras chose to lecture on Plutarch as representative of Greek culture rather than on one of the great dramatists or orators. Plutarch lived and taught in Rome in the last decades of the first century AD and, as the

Greek-speaking biographer of Roman heroes, was an ideal link between the two ancient cultures whose fusion had created the culture of Western Europe. Centring his lectures upon Plutarch's *Lives* Chrysoloras added a potent ingredient to the intellectual brew in Florence.

Among those who attended Chrysoloras' lectures was another young man from a small town who had come to Florence to make his fortune. He was Leonardo Bruni, born in Arezzo in 1370. Like Poggio, ten years his junior, he too owed his start in life to the generosity of Coluccio Salutati for it was through the Florentine Chancellor that, in 1405, he gained a position in the papal chancery in Rome. Again like Poggio, he found that learning yielded gold in comfortable quantities. After ten years' residence in Rome, Bruni too had amassed enough capital to return to his beloved, adopted city of Florence as a private citizen.

There he began his *History of the Florentine people,* a work which Poggio was to complete and of which the bookseller Vespasiano da Bisticci made the penetrating observation, 'Among the other singular obligations which the city of Florence owes to Messer Leonardo and to Messer Poggio is this: that except the Roman Republic no republic or free state in Italy has been so distinguished as the town of Florence, in having had two such notable writers to record its activities as Messer Leonardo and Messer Poggio: for up to the time of their histories everything was in the greatest obscurity . . . ' Machiavelli was to criticise them both for dwelling too exclusively upon Florence's wars and foreign affairs, at the cost of the description of the true inner life of the city: posterity might well find them almost intolerably mannered. 'We meet with frigid limitations and bombastic generalities, where concise details and graphic touches would have been acceptable . . . striving to rival Cicero and Livy (they) succeeded only in becoming lifeless shadows of the past,' is the judgement of J. A. Symonds. All this is true enough but it obscures one vital fact: through their work the Florentines became the first Italians to obtain a view of their past which, though distorted in detail, was true in perspective.

Salutati, Niccoli, Bruni, Poggio—they formed a species of apostolic succession stretching over a century from the first stirrings of self-consciousness in the mid-fourteenth century with its flowering at the end of the fifteenth. They are only four out of a dozen or more like-minded men in the city but, through them, it is possible to see the impulse being transmitted until it came to be amplified by the Medici bankers. (pp. 62-5)

E. R. Chamberlin, "Florence: The Search for the Past," in his The World of the Renaissance, *George Allen & Unwin, 1982, pp. 41-81.*

THE PLASTIC ARTS

PAOLO PINO

[*Pino was a sixteenth-century Venetian painter and art theorist. In the following excerpt from his* Dialogo di Pittura *(1548; Dialogue on Painting), Pino's viewpoint on art is conveyed through the remarks of two speakers: Lauro, the needy Venetian painter, and Fabio, his more successful Tuscan mentor and Pino's critical spokesman.*]

LAURO. Just a moment! How do you like a charming painter?

FABIO. He pleases me most, and I tell you that charm is the relish of our works. I do not, however, mean by charm the ultramarine blue at sixty scudi an ounce or fine lacquer, because paints are also beautiful by themselves in their boxes, and a painter can not be praised as charming for giving pink cheeks and blond hair to all his figures, for making serene expressions, or for coating the earth with beautiful green; but true charm is nothing else than grace, which comes from a harmony or just proportion of things, so that, while the pictures have decorum, they also have charm and bring honor to the master.

LAURO. How badly off I would be, if they did not sell those beautiful paints, which bring me credit and profit!

FABIO. This just dazzles the ignoramuses. I do not blame you for using beautiful colors in your work, but I would like *you* to enhance the colors, and not the colors to serve you.

LAURO. This is your wish and my desire, but we do not know how. Please, tell me: how do you like one who paints fast?

FABIO. Promptness is successful in all things, but speed in a man is a natural disposition and almost an imperfection. The artist does not deserve any praise for it, because it was not acquired by him, but given to him by Nature. Besides, in our art one does not judge by the time spent on one work, but only the perfection of that work, through which one can tell the master from the hack. It is true that both extremes are to be blamed, and, for example, we are told that Apelles scolded himself because he was too diligent and never stopped searching and perfecting his works, which is very harmful to one's intellectual power. And the contrary is told about another painter who showed a work of his to Apelles, boasting that he had done it very fast; whereupon Apelles answered: "You do not have to tell me, the work itself shows it." And also, this practice of smearing, as does your Andrea Schiavone, is a shameful thing, and painters like that show how little they know, since they don't reproduce but only vaguely suggest the effect of life, and for that reason they don't have to take much care, because they do not care to spend much time. On the other hand, ancient artists—and this should be practiced as a good method—used to put aside all their pictures when they were finished, and after a while they would look at them again and they would improve them. This method is used by writers for their compositions and it is very useful.

LAURO. And when would we get paid? Poverty is murderous, I tell you; and one work is not paid enough for the money to last until the next is completed. One goes as fast as one can, and, worse, sometimes one has to paint even furniture, not being able to keep oneself busy with the other application, because our art is not of vital use.

FABIO. And why don't you paint pictures, and not such hackwork which with us is considered shameful and improper?

LAURO. Because if a Titian were offered for sale they would say it is cheap stuff; and to our confusion they would offer us ten farthings or worse, for each house has its painter; and if I waited to be asked, I would paint less often than I see comets.

FABIO. To tell you the truth, I think you are trying to fool me. And because I am as soft as wax, you think you can easily print with the seal of disfavor on me, in order to clear the scene, fearing that I might steal your trade away. I believe so, because all these Venetian lords seem munificent to me, and partial to men of talent. (pp. 58-60)

Paolo Pino, in an excerpt in Italian Art: 1500-1600, Sources and Documents *by Robert Klein and Henri Zerner, Prentice-Hall, Inc., 1966, pp. 58-60.*

ANDRÉ CHASTEL

[*Chastel is a French educator and noted art historian. In the following excerpt, he discusses the influence of three distinct humanisms on the visual arts of Renaissance Italy.*]

Several aspects of the humanist movement need to be distinguished and localized. There was the epigraphical and archaeological humanism, with its principal centre in the North, at Padua; there was the philological and philosophical humanism, which developed in Florence; and the mathematical humanism, most brilliantly represented at Urbino. The last of these was most closely bound up with the arts. The second appeared to keep at the greatest distance from them by virtue of its abstruse speculations and its literary connections, but there nonetheless emerged from it ideas that proved fascinating to the more sophisticated artists, and a kind of climate of aestheticism. But the type of humanism which exercized the greatest influence on the imagination and repertory of artists was the first. It is through these three modalities of humanism that we can come to understand how closely the visual arts shared in the new formulation of culture: no conclusion can be reached without their aid.

There is a strange document—still worth attention—which shows the connection between the visual artists and the 'antiquaries' of Northern Italy. Its title is *Jubilatio,* and it is the account, by the epigraphist and archaeologist Felice Feliciano, of a walk by Lake Garda, in which Marcanova and Mantegna, and Feliciano himself took part, '*sub imperio faceti viri Samuelis de Tridate.*' This little expedition has about it an atmosphere of truancy and dressing-up, of joy and even of deep emotion. The friends took a boat ride on the lake, wore crowns of flowers, sang, gathered inscriptions, invoked the memory of Marcus Aurelius, and visited the Temple of the Blessed Virgin at Garda—where they addressed prayers and thanksgivings to the 'sovereign Thunderer and His glorious Mother.' This was in October 1464—if the account is to be taken literally as preserving the memory of an actual excursion, a forerunner of those in which the young members of the Pléiade delighted. Mantegna was then at the height of his glory, in Mantua. His companions were men of learning and talent: Marcanova in particular was well-known for his collections of inscriptions, such as the one that was to be compiled in 1465 and edited by Felice Feliciano himself. In it we find Rome with its great names and monuments, viewed in a somewhat fantastic light and mingled with the remains of ancient Verona, Mantua and Padua, with outlines of statues, notes on marble fragments, epigrams and emblems—antiquity seen from the Patavian point of view. For all this stems from Padua: the book begins by mentioning the epitaph of Gattamelata and makes much of *Patavium regium,* the ideal palace of the author's dreams. We are here at the heart of a strong tradition of archaeological humanism, which derived from Cyriacus of Ancona and leads to the most important of the archaeologist-epigraphists, to Fra Giocondo da

Verona, engineer, *pontifex* and architect, the key personality of that region at the end of the century.

The painter drew and emphasized what the archaeologist pointed out to him. The exchange of services is clear. A single example will show how far this went: in the fresco of the *Judgment of St James* (1454) in the Eremitani a conspicuous inscription—T. PVLLIO T. L. LINO—turns out to be a copy of a Roman inscription which Marcanova said he had seen at Monte Buso. Since the same inscription was used, independently of Mantegna, by Jacopo Bellini in one of his architectural drawings, it is clear that the documentation was passed from hand to hand. A slight error in transcription (Mantegna has written III IIII V[iri], *septemviri,* instead of *severi*) shows that these are not altogether archaeological abstracts, but rather 'motifs,' elements that are both significant and plastic. There is a preference for exploiting a fragment or inscription found in the province. This was the source of what became an imposing fashion: Mantegna started it, but it was continued far beyond the Mantua-Venice-Padua triangle.

Venice, towards the end of the century, attracted publications on pure archaeology, such as the *De amplitudine de vastatione et de instuaratione urbis Ravennae* by D. Spreti (1489). The name of Jacopo Bellini is worth mentioning in this connection: it is enough to remember those extraordinary documents, his great studies of perspective and architecture, to see the source—as early as 1450-1460—of that stream which would triumph in the great Aldine publications, and have its crowning glory in the *Hypnerotomachia Polyphili* (1499). The enthusiasm that fills this laborious and obscure masterpiece derives from the *Jubilatio* of Felice Feliciano, yet must be seen also as the culmination of a certain school of humanism and of a certain kind of taste which had not, as yet, their equivalent anywhere.

It is true that Rome, meanwhile, had again become a centre of study. Flavio Biondo's book, *Roma instaurata* (finished in 1446), had had an effect; but when, in 1471, Alberti took Donato Acciaiuoli, Giovanni Rucellai and Lorenzo the Magnificent round the ruins of Rome, what they mainly saw was how much would have to be done if so many scattered fragments were to be drawn and interpreted. And it is still a fantastic impression of Rome that the anonymous author of the *Antiquarie prospettiche romane* (a small compilation dating from the end of the century) seems to be trying to create. In the fifteenth century Rome was not yet the great centre of antiquarianism and of the trade in antiques (genuine or imitations); nor was Florence, nor was Milan. It was more in Padua and Venice that—as already in the Trecento—samples of *Kleinkunst* 'in the ancient style' were to be found: they were becoming more and more fashionable, with repercussions both on collecting and on neo-classical imitation. It was from Venice that Cardinal Pietro Barbo, when he became Pope Paul II, brought his famous series of Roman medals. And Boldi, another Venetian, was one of the first to delight in supplying his own medals with learned inscriptions imitated from antiquity. The small plaque, the medal and the statuette were to dominate taste in the north of Italy for a long time: through them, that taste was to leave a pronounced mark on the Renaissance.

The Florentine innovators had proclaimed with assurance, as a profession of faith, that the visual arts must be closely related to the *ordo mathematicus.* The idea made its way slowly—with Alberti, for instance, at the very beginning of his *De pictura* (1435), and with Brunelleschi; it took on its full meaning only when mathematical knowledge itself was set apart as a privileged discipline and began to detach itself from the traditional body of the 'liberal arts'. The translators of Plato, particularly in their commentaries on the *Timaeus,* produced attractive arguments in support of this 'intellectual' conception of art. In his commentary on the *Philebus,* Marsilio Ficino says: 'The sciences that operate manually are called arts; these owe their penetration and perfection chiefly to the mathematical faculty, that is to say to the particularly "mercurial" and rational ability to count, measure and weigh.' This faculty is regarded as rescuing the arts from uncertainty and from the merely approximate, as can be seen clearly in the case of architecture. What makes propositions of this kind interesting is that they show how one type of speculative humanism helped to steer the plastic arts in the direction of an 'absolute' conception, made explicit through mathematics. (pp. 41-5)

Humanism, whether archaeological or mathematical, . . . tended to give culture and taste a Mediterranean flavour. The fine lapidary inscriptions now so eagerly reproduced by the frontispieces of the manuscripts, the triumphal arches and the porticoes, with the solemn proportions that had taken hold of men's imaginations—these must live again because they ought never to have died. In this way humanism intervened as a stimulant to creation. It was not retrospective. Its aims were practical. And Alberti defined very well what he expected of an architect: 'In the study of his art I would have him follow the example of those who apply themselves to letters. For no one considers himself sufficiently instructed in any science if he has not read and studied all the others . . . So by a continuous study of the best creations . . . he can exercise and sharpen his own invention . . . ' (*De re aedificatoria,* IX, 10). The Florentines wished to have the formidable support of an ancient Italian culture now recovered, in order to face up to the modern tasks of which they had a more precise awareness than anyone. This gave rise to the methodical publications and critical studies carried out within the Accademia at Careggi, which were paralleled by the efforts of Giuliano da Sangallo to establish a kind of corpus of architecture in his monumental *Libro;* but it also led to the revolutionary application of all these resources to literature in the vulgar tongue—in the shape of the masterpieces of Politian, the *Stanze* and the *Orfeo,* and to philosophy—in the shape of Ficino's *Theologia platonica* (already written in 1474 and published in 1482) and of Pico's *Oratio de hominis dignitate* (1496), to mention only the best known. In a few years the whole tone of literature and culture was modified. The compositions of Politian bring together in a curious way the *all'antica* style and the courtly tradition—the comparison with Botticelli's *Primavera* is irresistible. Characters borrowing their language from Ovid or Virgil are engaged in adventures unknown to antiquity; and, inversely, the speeches of Orpheus take on the rhythm of a Tuscan lyric.

In philosophy the apparatus of scholasticism was still used for the purpose of demonstration; but it was now invaded by Platonic formulae, references to the ancient gods and quotations from the poets. The ancient world lay beyond history. The literary and philosophical humanism of the Florentines was led to a precocious awareness of the paradoxical quality of the period. In the mind of a Politian the permanent part of the ancient heritage was essentially poetry, in that of a Ficino a philosophical arcanum. 'In the second half of the fifteenth century, Hermes was the fashion' (E. Garin). It was this supra-historical viewpoint—the viewpoint of a universal

1522 portrait of a student at his desk, by Franciabigio.

doctrine and symbolism—that imposed order on that crushing accumulation of texts and ideas to which the humanists proceeded. Poetry, theology and mythology pointed to one and the same end. And no one who was not carried away by a certain enthusiasm could see this at all. The man of superior quality, the ideal man, was a magus, sensitive to the degrees of being. Nature was looked on as a concert, a 'demonic' edifice, tending towards an invisible harmony, and accomplishing itself through the intervention of man, who deciphered and proclaimed it. The success of this doctrine was immense, both in Italy and in the whole of the West. It is all the more necessary to replace it within the horizon of the Quattrocento, since it helps us to understand the mood of veneration in which men considered both the mother-forms, or mathematical principles, and the symbols of religion. It also enables us to gauge the breadth of the ambitions of that period,—the kind of great gulf, or wide intellectual difference, produced by the new knowledge of the ancient world, in which for the first time symbolical thinking was allowed as great an intensity as the historical vision.

Archaeology, science and doctrine were all present, demanding fresh means of expression. The result was a remarkable development of the preoccupation with symbols. This soon left its mark on architecture, now searching after new forms. At the same time men's image of man and nature was being changed by the rapid progress of naturalism: it became one of the tasks of the studios and workshops to supply a version of the traditional themes that would be modern, articulated, complex and supported by living and convincing details. Art-

ists had acquired such assurance that they soon returned of their own free will to the hieratic themes, disengaging, for instance, the *Holy Face* of the icons from its inert form: one may observe, round about 1480-1490, many variations on this devotional theme, to which the Flemish painters also restored all its old interest, and in which the fascination of the frontal image makes itself clearly felt. Similarly, the Entombment was re-interpreted, being either amplified to a great dramatic scheme or concentrated into a formula of presentation (following Donatello, the Paduan artists gave currency to the theme of Christ supported by two angels). The very development of the traditional themes produced, by the multiplication of picturesque details, a phenomenon of hypersymbolism, in other words, a tendency to summon up in some original way motifs taken from nature in order to harmonize them with the theme: thus in Carpaccio's *Meditation on the Dead Christ* everything, even minerals, seems to take on a precise value. The resources of the image were now such that everything seemed representable. The great astrological cycles, like the one in Ferrara, were continued by mythological series, such as those painted for Lorenzo de' Medici in the Villa of Spedaletto, and by allegorical series like the (lost) decorations of the library of Pico da Mirandola. All aspects of human activity and every type of emotion found a form, a symbol giving them authenticity; art offered consciousness the support that would exalt it. It was destined to be the age, *par excellence,* of cross-fertilizing meanings: Signorelli modelled his image of Pan on the *sacre rappresentazioni.*

By association with the ruin of the Temple—associated with the *Templum Pacis,* or with the triumphal arch, that symbol of antiquity—the Epiphany became a festival of architecture. Vanished works of art were reconstructed from the ancient texts about them: Botticelli arranged the agitated figures of his *Calumny of Apelles* in an original setting. Even ornamentation became 'speaking'. (pp. 50-5)

> *André Chastel, "Italy and Culture," in his* The Flowering of the Italian Renaissance, *translated by Jonathan Griffin, The Odyssey Press, 1965, pp. 27-56.*

ANDRÉ CHASTEL

[*In the following excerpt, Chastel asserts the importance of ancient mythology to the plastic arts of the Italian Renaissance.*]

In an eloquent passage, a minor Lombard humanist writing a eulogy of Pomponius Laetus describes him roaming the hills of Rome, fascinated by the things that met his eye at every turn. "Often he would wander by himself among the ancient monuments, yearning to recapture the spirit of the past. There was nothing in Rome so well concealed, so difficult of access, that he failed to discover it. Ancient sites, gates, hills, streets, districts, edifices, temples, altars, dwelling-houses, sanctuaries, pools, baths, basilicas, gardens, granaries, mills, tenements, halls, obelisks, libraries, squares, forums, bridges, thermae, byways, waters, rocks, amphitheaters, colossi, columns, slaughterhouses, theaters, stadia, shrines of the nymphs, bronze or ivory horses, pictures, emblems, arches, brothels, latrines, banners, barracks—all things sacred, all things profane he was familiar with, and he had the knowledge of them at his fingertips. Sometimes when seen roving among the ashes and graves of the ancients, he was taken for a ghost" (Michele Ferno). Lactus had come to Rome shortly after 1450 to join Lorenzo Valla, and he was perhaps the first of the new intellectual elite to search out concrete links between the world of antiquity as described by the classical authors and the relics strewn along the Tiber. Having read, digested and methodically annotated Columella and Varro, he collated the technical terms used by the authors with the vestiges found in the countryside or underground. Other dedicated humanists, Callimaco and Platina, joined forces with him—archaeology was being discovered. This new sodality even explored the catacombs, where a record of their activities has survived in the form of a rather odd inscription, describing them as *Sacerdotes Achademiae Romanae.* This was the group that in 1468 incurred the wrath of Pope Paul II; some, like Laetus, fled to Venice; the others, among them Platina, were harshly treated and flung into prison. (p. 176)

It is not too much to say that the fabric of culture was profoundly modified once the ancient fables, with their great figures and wealth of anecdotes and symbols, ceased to be regarded merely as pleasing illustrations of this or that branch of knowledge, and came to be viewed as an organic whole, at once poetic and scientific, dominating all knowledge and qualified to guide its course. This was brought about by the fascinating notion of a poetic theology implicit in the teaching of Politian, Ficino and their friends, who needless to say harked back to the authorities of late antiquity, such as Servius and Macrobius.

There is no need to insist on the artificial nature of this unified conception of ancient mythology; only on its consequences. It involved a drastic syncretism, a lumping together (without regard to historical considerations) of all the very different aspects of a god or hero through the ages. Plato and Pausanias, Hesiod and Apuleius were ransacked for details, with the result that the compilers soon lost their way in a jungle of facts. Yet they were led to spread their nets ever wider, to survey all the exotic Oriental cults of which something was known (those of Egypt, for example) and to discover curious equivalences. The Renaissance thus assembled and centered on the ancient gods an essential part of its resources. On the one hand, Fable provided a remarkably vivid and detailed analysis of human emotions and the order of nature: *potius physiologia aut etnologia quam theologia,* as Boccaccio said (*De genealogia deorum,* XV, 8); on the other hand, it guided the questing mind towards the loftiest arcana of spiritual and cosmic reality, key to a *docta religio.*

True, this was only an episode in the history of ideas, in which for the time being Italy drew ahead of the rest of Europe. But a parallel development was taking place in the arts, in which the forms of antiquity, both in architecture (hence in decorative settings as well) and in figural art, acquired an ever-increasing authority. Greatly simplifying it, we may describe this development as follows. Certain artists sought to regenerate the current iconographic formulas by the use of antique motifs and, above all, antique compositional schemes. A typical example is Donatello's Sant'Antonio altar in Padua: its *tempietto* structure, indeed its whole style, is intensified by the use of forms taken from sarcophagi and statuettes. Ghiberti did the same thing. His panels on the third door of the Baptistery contain many adaptations of the antique, even direct borrowings: the figure extracting a thorn, draperies, nudes, attitudes. This practice was not confined to a single group or a single style. Pisanello's drawings, for example, reveal his keen interest in figures in movement, a motif he had studied on reliefs and medals. A different repertory

was available at Padua, a center of epigraphy and archaeology, where Squarcione became the dominant figure; at Florence, where motifs were chosen for their elegance and distinction; and at Rome, where powerful effects were the desideratum. Generally speaking (except at Padua), painters felt less strongly impelled to change their methods than did the sculptors and decorators, who had so many antique models before their eyes.

Thus the stage was set for the momentous change which took place in Italy around 1460: "the re-integration of classical form and classical subject matter" (Fritz Saxl and Erwin Panofsky). Its mechanism was simple: antique motifs transmitted to the Middle Ages had been taken up by Romanesque, then by Gothic artists, but with a "transvaluation of values." A funerary genius became an angel, Hercules an embodiment of Fortitudo. Pallas, Achilles and Cupid survived in poetry and miniature painting, but in altered guise; they were given quaint costumes, whimsical attitudes, even new personalities, as when in Villon, by a *lapsus linguae,* the courtesan Archipiada steps into the place of the handsome Alcibiades. The idea of ancient Fable which had now come to prevail made it not merely optional but imperative to find out how to represent correctly Hercules, Venus and Minerva. On all planes alike artists had to use their imagination. For no illustrated manuals of mythology existed. They made their appearance only in the mid-sixteenth century, a very different phase of the Renaissance, when the old Gothic interpretations of these motifs had been superseded, not without many false and fanciful *rifacimenti.*

Thus the period from the 1460s to the 1520s was one in which all types of representation co-existed. The differences between one art milieu and another are often quite surprising. Things evolved slowly because (except in miniature painting) the illustration of antique scenes, stories of the gods and so forth was long limited to a few type figures: Venus, Hercules, Orpheus and of course the planetary deities; in other words, precisely those most affected by the deformations due to the moralizing and modernizing of the ancient myths. The need carefully to select a special type of figure and attitude made itself felt only in the case of the images used for a new edition of a text revised by humanist critics, or for a tale containing references to specific rites and well-documented incidents. But this need arose only at the close of the fifteenth century. The popular illustrations of famous episodes in the Iliad or Hercules' exploits that figure on *cassoni* long reveal a singular disregard for the historical context, the *realia* of mythology. This explains why Botticelli and Signorelli felt free to invent—without regard to archaeological constraints and mindful only of a certain literary climate—a neutral, almost otherworldly realm in which the heroes of the ancient myths could, provisionally, feel at home.

There was, however, one domain in which close attention had to be given to the exactitude of the imagery. This was sculpture, medals and reliefs—the domain, in fact, in which Mars, Hercules, Apollo and Venus were more often represented than in any other. It was here that Padua and Venice played a decisive role, determined by the formalism of the Riccios and the second generation of the Lombardi. Their art had that sedative, not to say paralysing effect that always follows the triumph of a full-fledged neoclassicism. But it would be wrong to see in it the last word of the Renaissance movement. Its interest lies mainly in the way in which it often overstepped its goal. For figures deriving from the past are constantly

The Marriage of the Virgin, *by Raphael.*

placed in modern contexts, such as the villa of Pierfrancesco de' Medici (Botticelli's patron), the *studiolo* of Isabella d'Este, the Stanza della Segnatura. But the initiative of the painters is evident above all in the reconstruction of ancient works described by Pliny and Pausanias, no models of which—or at best mere vestiges—were available. Such reconstructions were attempted by Antonio Pollaiolo, Botticelli and Mantegna, then by Dürer and Cranach. In this development an important part must have been played by Jacopo de' Barbari, who worked at the court of Margaret of Austria at Malines. There, from 1505 to 1517, he decorated the Busleyden House with scenes in the antique manner (destroyed in 1914 but known from Hannotiau's copies). And at Wittenberg he painted another mythological sequence, on an unusually ambitious scale, which no longer exists but there is a lengthy description of it by an art-loving humanist: it comprised an almost unbelievable number of scenes illustrating both obscure and famous episodes in the legends of the ancient gods and heroes.

This reintegration of form and notion, of image and text, abruptly and durably related visual data, drawn from experience and wide reading, to the fund of recorded knowledge. But in fact this was but one of the operative illusions of the period in so far as this reintegration was carried through in terms of poetic imagery and in answer to the needs of art; in

other words—and for this we have every reason to be grateful—it was shaped and guided by the artist's intuitions, his personal preferences and the inspiration of the moment. (pp. 177-78)

> *André Chastel, "Gods and Their Realm," in his* The Myth of the Renaissance: 1420-1520, *translated by Stuart Gilbert, Skira, 1969, pp. 176-78.*

ANDRÉ CHASTEL

[*In the following excerpt from a work originally published in French in 1965, Chastel touches on Renaissance perceptions of craftsmanship and culture.*]

By setting aside systematic categories that are either too sweeping or too narrow, one tends to substitute a problem for a definition. The Renaissance, seen as a problem—its own problem—becomes full of fascination; one finds in it the currents and accidents of history, instead of a facile story that gives a poor reconstruction of the real movement of the arts. From the details of historical analysis there emerges finally an essential characteristic of the period, which may be called *the power of style.* That last phase of the Quattrocento abounded in signs that people were beginning to recognize the authority of the artist—but not in the sense of any quasi-mystical prestige of genius. What the fifteenth-century Italian public, of every level and class, liked to feel and was eager to admire, was creative aptitude, the ability to produce complete and powerful works—that is to say, masterpieces. In the light of this concept it is possible to bring out more clearly two somewhat elusive aspects of the spiritual life of the period: the relations of artist to craftsman; and those between art and culture.

In the general enterprise of what Nietzsche described as the 're-Mediterraneanizing' of art and culture, the most modest craftsman, obliged as he constantly was to adapt his stock of forms and ornamental devices, found himself with a part to play. One is struck by the quality of the detail—even when it shows no particular research or pretention—that occurs on the buildings and decoration of the years around 1470 or 1480: not only quality that speaks of the workman's care, but quality that includes inspirations. . . . [There was a distinction] between the studios that went in for large output and the original studios . . . ; but the original studios did not restrict the scope of the craftsmen—quite the contrary. The mason had to learn to execute deep-cut fluting of a kind that had gone out of fashion; the stone-cutter to assimilate new cornice outlines; the painter, new folds of drapery and a whole gamut of details that to him were strange and unprecedented. High-level problems were resolved on the lower level, in terms of forms to be worked out. Everything became significant and precious, as soon as men were bent on recovering whatever was Mediterranean which they found even in the singularities of the Ottoman world or Hebraic epigraphy.

The Italian craftsmen held their own keenly against their Northern colleagues, letting none of the exceptional resources manifested by the sculpture and graphic art north of the Alps escape them. The circulation of motifs was extremely rapid and lively. It was probably at Nuremberg that Jacopo de' Barbari learned the astonishing skill in engraving which enabled him to produce in 1500 his wonderful panorama of Venice. The ceaseless vigilance and activity of its studios, finding a solution to every new problem, gave Italy the exceptional position as intermediary which it had won by 1500. In this context the artist, as we now call him, appears only as the superior—sometimes widespread—version of the craftsman. The Quattrocento artist, whatever his temperament, did not begin by being an intellectual: he was there to demonstrate by his actual output that culture is fulfilled in art.

This concept required time to ripen, and its rise was slow. True, for the first time in centuries the outlook of the sciences—in particular, the attitude to philosophic problems that found expression in an aestheticizing Platonism—was far from excluding such a concept, as it had formerly done. But this applied chiefly to certain advanced circles, and it would be wrong to believe that the men of letters, humanists, rhetoricians and poets were in general concerned to exalt the world of the arts. Most often they reacted as craftsmen of letters: what they sought from the arts—to which their period was becoming attentive—was a support for their own line of activity, an occasion for demonstrating its validity and interest. And there persisted, among the intellectuals, a distrust of those whose *ingenium* found its exercise in manual skill. This comes out clearly in a passage from a recently rediscovered treatise, written between 1450 and 1460, by a humanist of the court of Ferrara. Its author, Decembrio, puts into the mouth of Leonello d'Este arguments for the view that painting is inferior to poetry: *poetarum ingenia quae ad mentem plurimum spectant longe pictorum opera superare quae sola manus ope declarantur.* What is most surprising is that the man of letters reproaches painting for being unable to render nature: the painters, he says, try in vain to evoke what the poet succeeds in describing—storms, the winds, birds, twilight, the night sky. These assertions went against the facts of contemporary development in the arts, and they are not free from a sense of professional rivalry (which of, course, to be reckoned with, in a world of courts, clans and independent cities). During the half-century that followed, they were to be given the lie. Decembrio, as a good humanist, had taken his impressive list of phenomena not representable in painting from the very passage in which Pliny praises Apelles for having been able to represent them (such inconsistencies were common in the fifteenth century). It was now up to the painters to revive the aims and successes of Apelles, so as to deserve the praise given to him and turn the tables on the poets. And this Leonardo and the Venetians did. By the end of the fifteenth century painting had triumphed over the taunts of the men of letters. It was equipped to evoke *storie* of every kind and to represent nature. It had acquired a dominant position, though this was not yet recognized by all. Leonardo, refusing any compromise, maintained that a poet's description of a battle, a storm or a beautiful person was nothing in comparison with the painter's ability to represent such things: intelligible reality—that reality which was the domain of true culture and the goal of modern activity—was of the order of the visible. And by a bold, decisive stroke (which of course not everyone, even at the court of Lodovico il Moro, was prepared to go along with) Leonardo put forward the painter, suddenly, as a new intellectual hero—before the poet, or the musician, or the philosopher. This exaggeration must be taken as polemical, but it did reflect an order of values closely bound up with the development of the Quattrocento in Italy.

Italy was about to establish itself throughout the West not only as the privileged intermediary between the world of the present and Antiquity, but also as having mastered certain principles of renewal which would come through culture: the Italian artists seemed to possess the secret of style. Foreign-

ers, astonished and sometimes fascinated by the works now revealed to them, were no less beguiled and astonished by the comments and discussions in the circles of the cultivated. The clear articulation of forms had brought out a power of precise statement, a spiritual capacity, which irradiated the style. Growing awareness of the novelty of contemporary aims in art led to the discovery of a necessary reform of culture. And as political events became more confused and disquieting, as the religious situation grew darker, as problems of science or technique began to appear insoluble, people were more inclined to believe that the best reply to these difficulties was, in a sense, to multiply artistic experiments and to begin the reform of the present time by the renovation of style. The French, in particular, clung to this idea—from the time of Louis XII onwards, but especially with Francis I, who had in mind a real programme of intellectual and artistic reform. In the years about 1500 there emerged the conviction that culture was one of the means of saving humanity; and the culture in question was Mediterranean and Graeco-Roman in form. The West looked to Italy for the system of forms, the panoply of concepts, which was to enable men to take possession of a new world full of difficulties and surprises. (pp. 323-25)

André Chastel, "Conclusion—The Power of Style," in his Studios and Styles of the Italian Renaissance, *translated by Jonathan Griffin, Odyssey, 1966, pp. 321-25.*

ANDRÉ CHASTEL

[*In the following excerpt, Chastel links cosmological theory to architectural styles of Renaissance Italy.*]

Among the most powerful currents throughout . . . [the Renaissance] was a wholly original and to some extent compulsive awareness of nature as a living reality. The steady advance of cosmological speculation ran parallel to and sometimes overshadowed metaphysics. In its attempt to be both descriptive and comprehensive, it encountered the traditional affinities of philosophy: God and the World, Spirit and Nature, Invisible and Visible. It applied a strictly cosmological system to the natural species—mineral, vegetable and animal—and above all to the relationship between heaven and earth, which had become the chief concern of "physicists" as a result of the facts observed by Copernicus and his successors. In all this speculation there was a notable tendency to break the existing affinities, which were generally, like all philosophical categories, of Aristotelian and Scholastic origin: to break them, that is, extensively, by stressing the infinite diversity of phenomena, and comprehensively, by insisting on the connexity between all orders of phenomena and levels of existence.

Although the most startling consequence of Copernicus' discovery was the collapse of official geocentric dogma, a number of general philosophical inferences were likewise drawn from it. Men could more easily apprehend the harmonic structure of the planetary system and thereby the perfection and permanence of the natural order. Canon Kepler, moreover, advanced two memorable theories. Firstly, he believed that the connection between the "guiding angels" and the planetary orbits was now more apparent than ever, and that the solar system was indeed an analogue of the divine world and its unseen hierarchies. In the second place, the riddle of the *mysterium cosmographicum* could be answered not merely in terms of the musical scale, familiar to Platonic and Orphic tradition, but also by means of the interlocking of the "pure bodies," which themselves were related to musical tonality. It therefore became easier and more instinctual than ever to make a visual and graphic projection of the universe. The only change was that greater stress was laid on the thrust and rotation of energy. Finally, it should be remembered, this representation of a living cosmos was supplemented and reinforced by the mythological description of the zodiac and of the deities who symbolized the celestial powers.

Giordano Bruno was the first philosopher to adopt, or at any rate to follow up the implications of Copernican theory. In his dialogue *De l'Infinito, Universo et Mondi* he described an "infinite" universe made up of finite systems. In this he was doubtless employing an idea of Lucretius in order to convey the infinite expansion of reality and the coherence of each component unity (A. Koyré). He was thus led into a fundamental ambiguity due to his insistence on reconciling Platonism with naturalism; for he clung both to the Platonic concept of different levels of existence broadening through love into the Idea, and to that of an unlimited expansion of the energy inherent in nature. He seems often to have approached a pantheistic conclusion. His stellar universe, consisting of suns and earths, involved both a fascinating contraction in the scale of our own world and far greater proximity, amounting to downright fusion, of heaven and earth.

Bruno's attempt, however, cannot be summed up in terms of the usual dilemmas. "His vision could not be fully expressed by such antitheses" (P. O. Kristeller), except through the operation of a paradox whereby reason would be driven, from one extreme to another, towards an intuitive process of great intensity and, in the eyes of the twentieth century, extreme confusion. To the sixteenth century there was a correlation between the two concepts of a living natural order and of symbolic analogies or, in modern parlance, correspondences. (pp. 133-34)

Some of the finest creations of the sixteenth century consisted in the improvement of natural sites by means of architecture and gardens. They were ambitious compositions which have often lasted better than any others and can most vividly reveal to us at a glance the character of the period. Everything is to be found in them. The social status conferred by luxury is associated with landscaping and the novel employment of vegetation, which themselves are made more spectacular by terracing and ornamental water. There is complete freedom of architectural design, which can thus adapt itself to the whims of the exalted owner. Nothing stands in the way of his vagaries of taste, which can find expression in symbolic devices, pseudo-classical settings or allegories reflecting and befitting his zest for life. No more eloquent introduction to this subject can be found than the villas of Latium about the middle of the century: Caprarola, a fortress surmounted by a park; the Villa d'Este, composed by Pirro Ligorio of rich, mossy cadences for the Cardinal of Ferrara; the gardens of Bomarzo, where the bent for *capriccio,* so essential to these productions, resulted in a riot of fantastic clowning. In France there is no end of striking examples, among which one may mention Anet, Fontainebleau and the Tuileries as restored by Du Cerceau.

They all had something of the prodigy about them. It set them apart from normal dwellings and we shall try to define it shortly by resorting to the concepts of festivity and display. This quality was achieved by a skillful combination of effects and, so to speak, with the connivance of Nature, tamely submitting to the whims of the great. In other words, the novelty and charm of these creations depended to a great extent on the original bringing together of natural and social factors, whereby a grandiloquent ensemble was laid out on a commanding or well-disposed site.

Within the general context of this fashion there developed a curious motif in the shape of artificial caves and buildings imitating the wilderness of a rocky landscape. The architectural use of this imitative theme says a good deal about the naturalism of the Renaissance and its predilection for evocative organisms. No one has yet written a history of the subject, as regards Italy, France or western Europe as a whole. Poems and romances contain innumerable references to caves, either as earthly paradises or as retreats of sanctity and bliss, or sometimes as dread abodes of savagery. In the fifteenth century they still played a humble part in painting and decoration; yet one can perceive a dawning awareness of these natural phenomena in a famous passage where Leonardo da Vinci alludes to the fascination of caverns, with their overpowering mixture of curiosity and terror. Subsequently, however, the main interest is to be sought in the layout of parks and villas rather than in painting. The villa of Giulio de' Medici, built by Raphael and Giulio Romano, left unfinished and completed after 1527 by the daughter of the Emperor Charles V, includes a suite of rooms imitating those of Roman baths and laid out on different levels: the terraced effect produced here, on the slopes of Monte Mario, has much in common with the extraordinary terraced site of Palestrina. The result was a sort of mixture of villa, landscape-garden and thermal grotto. There came a succession of great villas designed in the same spirit: the Villa Farnese on the Palatine, the Villa Medici on the Pincio, etc. In these, however, the Roman bath was reduced to an architectural or, more simply, artificial grotto. Such fanciful structures called for fanciful decorations.

A particularly good example is the garden laid out by Buontalenti in 1583 for the Grand Duke Francesco, with its grottoes full of surprise effects, its automata, its fountains often calculated to start playing when the visitor least expected it; on each level of the garden was some new allegory of the nymphs or Cupid (description by Richard Lassels, 1670, utilized by John Shearman, 1967). At Saint-Germain-en-Laye, at the end of the century, the Château Neuf was fitted out by the Francini with an even bolder succession of fairy-like grottoes.

The taste for such constructions spread all over Europe. The court architect of every prince and princeling was expected to create new landscapes. One man alone seems in the plans of his villas to have stood out against the vogue for naturalism in architecture. The stately Palladio was content with the geometrical dignity of masses placed against the sky and the proper ordering of his surfaces. To him, as he said in so many words in his *Treatise,* cosmic harmony was reflected in the nobility of abstract form. But the man who built the Rotunda and Villa Maser did not confine himself to this lofty aim. He so orientated his houses that they lay along the axes of the sky, and he extended their vistas by a meticulous alignment of statues and objects. His structural purism, moreover, did not prevent him from frequently resorting to the use of bossage and rustic masonry, suggesting, in the consummate order and balance of this art, a lurking allusion to the geological origin and natural crudeness of the materials which he dominated and fashioned into architecture. (pp. 134-35)

*André Chastel, "Cosmos and Architecture," in his
The Crisis of the Renaissance: 1520-1600, translated by Peter Price, Skira, 1968, pp. 133-35.*

JOHN ADDINGTON SYMONDS

[*Symonds was an English poet, historian, and critic who wrote
extensively on Greek and Italian history and culture. He also
rendered authoritative translations of Greek poetry and literature of the Italian Renaissance. In the following excerpt from
the third volume,* Renaissance in Italy: The Fine Arts *(1877),
of his multi-volume study of the Italian Renaissance, he traces
the development of the fine arts in Renaissance Italy.*]

It has been granted only to two nations, the Greeks and the
Italians, and to the latter only at the time of the Renaissance,
to invest every phase and variety of intellectual energy with
the form of art. Nothing notable was produced in Italy between the thirteenth and the seventeenth centuries that did
not bear the stamp and character of fine art. If the methods
of science may be truly said to regulate our modes of thinking
at the present time, it is no less true that, during the Renaissance, art exercised a like controlling influence. Not only was
each department of the fine arts practised with singular success; not only was the national genius to a very large extent
absorbed in painting, sculpture, and architecture; but the
æsthetic impulse was more subtly and widely diffused than
this alone would imply. It possessed the Italians in the very
centre of their intellectual vitality, imposing its conditions on
all the manifestations of their thought and feeling, so that
even their shortcomings may be ascribed in a great measure
to their inability to quit the æsthetic point of view. (pp. 1-2)

It lies beyond the scope of this work to embrace in one inquiry the different forms of art in Italy, or to analyse the connection of the æsthetic instinct with the manifold manifestations
of the Renaissance. Even the narrower task to which I must
confine myself, is too vast for the limits I am forced to impose
upon its treatment. I intend to deal with Italian painting as
the one complete product which remains from the achievements of this period, touching upon sculpture and architecture more superficially. Not only is painting the art in which
the Italians among all the nations of the modern world stand
unapproachably alone, but it is also the one that best enables
us to gauge their genius at the time when they impressed their
culture on the rest of Europe. In the history of the Italian intellect painting takes the same rank as that of sculpture in the
Greek. Before beginning, however, to trace the course of Italian art, it will be necessary to discuss some preliminary questions, important for a right understanding of the relations assumed by painting to the thoughts of the Renaissance, and
for explaining its superiority over the sister art of sculpture
in that age. This I feel the more bound to do because it is my
object in this volume to treat of art with special reference to
the general culture of the nation.

What, let us ask in the first place, was the task appointed for
the fine arts on the threshold of the modern world? They had,
before all things, to give form to the ideas evolved by Christianity, and to embody a class of emotions unknown to the
ancients. The inheritance of the Middle Ages had to be appropriated and expressed. In the course of performing this
work, the painters helped to humanise religion, and revealed
the dignity and beauty of the body of man. Next, in the fifteenth century, the riches of classic culture were discovered,
and art was called upon to aid in the interpretation of the ancient to the modern mind. The problem was no longer simple.

Christian and pagan traditions came into close contact, and
contended for the empire of the newly liberated intellect.
During this struggle the arts, true to their own principles,
eliminated from both traditions the more strictly human elements, and expressed them in beautiful form to the imagination and the senses. The brush of the same painter depicted
Bacchus wedding Ariadne and Mary fainting on the hill of
Calvary. Careless of any peril to dogmatic orthodoxy, and
undeterred by the dread of encouraging pagan sensuality, the
artists wrought out their modern ideal of beauty in the double
field of Christian and Hellenic legend. Before the force of
painting was exhausted, it had thus traversed the whole cycle
of thoughts and feelings that form the content of the modern
mind. Throughout this performance, art proved itself a powerful co-agent in the emancipation of the intellect; the impartiality wherewith its methods were applied to subjects sacred
and profane, the emphasis laid upon physical strength and
beauty as good things and desirable, the subordination of
classical and mediæval myths to one æsthetic law of loveliness, all tended to withdraw attention from the differences between paganism and Christianity, and to fix it on the goodliness of that humanity wherein both find their harmony.

This being in general the task assigned to art in the Renaissance, we may next inquire what constituted the specific quality of modern as distinguished from antique feeling, and why
painting could not fail to take the first place among modern
arts. In other words, how was it that, while sculpture was the
characteristic fine art of antiquity, painting became the distinguishing fine art of the modern era? No true form of figurative art intervened between Greek sculpture and Italian
painting. The latter took up the work of investing thought
with sensible shape from the dead hands of the former. Nor
had the tradition that connected art with religion been interrupted, although a new cycle of religious ideas had been substituted for the old ones. The late Roman and Byzantine manners, through which the vital energies of the Athenian genius
dwindled into barren formalism, still lingered, giving crude
and lifeless form to Christian conceptions. But the thinking
and feeling subject, meanwhile, had undergone a change so
all-important that it now imperatively required fresh channels for its self-expression. It was destined to find these, not
as of old in sculpture, but in painting.

During the interval between the closing of the ancient and the
opening of the modern age, the faith of Christians had attached itself to symbols and material objects little better than
fetishes. The host, the relic, the wonder-working shrine,
things endowed with a mysterious potency, evoked the yearning and the awe of mediæval multitudes. To such concrete actualities the worshippers referred their sense of the invisible
divinity. The earth of Jerusalem, the Holy Sepulchre, the
House of Loreto, the Sudarium of Saint Veronica, aroused
their deepest sentiments of aweful adoration. Like Thomas,
they could not be contented with believing; they must also
touch and handle. At the same time, in apparent contradistinction to this demand for things of sense as signs of supersensual power, the claims of dogma on the intellect grew
more imperious, and mysticism opened for the dreaming soul
a realm of spiritual rapture. For the figurative arts there was
no true place in either of these regions. Painting and sculpture were alike alien to the grosser superstitions, the scholastic subtleties, and the ecstatic trances of the Middle Ages; nor
had they anything in common with the logic of theology. Votaries who kissed a fragment of the cross with passion, could
have found but little to satisfy their ardour in pictures painted

by a man of genius. A formless wooden idol, endowed with the virtue of curing disease, charmed the pilgrim more than a statue noticeable only for its beauty or its truth to life. We all know that *wunderthätige Bilder sind meist nur schlechte Gemälde.* In architecture alone, the mysticism of the Middle Ages, their vague but potent feelings of infinity, their yearning towards a deity invisible, but localised in holy things and places, found artistic outlet. Therefore architecture was essentially a mediæval art. The rise of sculpture and painting indicated the quickening to life of new faculties, fresh intellectual interests, and a novel way of apprehending the old substance of religious feeling; for comprehension of these arts implies delight in things of beauty for their own sake, a sympathetic attitude towards the world of sense, a new freedom of the mind produced by the regeneration of society through love.

The mediæval faiths were still vivid when the first Italian painters began their work, and the sincere endeavour of these men was to set forth in beautiful and worthy form the truths of Christianity. The eyes of the worshipper should no longer have a mere stock or stone to contemplate: his imagination should be helped by the dramatic presentation of the scenes of sacred history, and his devotion be quickened by lively images of the passion of our Lord. Spirit should converse with spirit, through no veil of symbol, but through the transparent medium of art, itself instinct with inbreathed life and radiant with ideal beauty. The body and the soul, moreover, should be reconciled; and God's likeness should be once more acknowledged in the features and the limbs of man. Such was the promise of art; and this promise was in a great measure fulfilled by the painting of the fourteenth century. Men ceased to worship their God in the holiness of ugliness; and a great city called its street Glad on the birthday-festival of the first picture investing religious emotion with æsthetic charm. But in making good the promise they had given, it was needful for the arts on the one hand to enter a region not wholly their own—the region of abstractions and of mystical conceptions; and on the other to create a world of sensuous delightfulness, wherein the spiritual element was materialised to the injury of its own essential quality. Spirit, indeed, spake to spirit, so far as the religious content was concerned; but flesh spake also to flesh in the æsthetic form. The incarnation promised by the arts involved a corresponding sensuousness. Heaven was brought down to earth, but at the cost of making men believe that earth itself was heavenly.

At this point the subject of our inquiry naturally divides into two main questions. The first concerns the form of figurative art specially adapted to the requirements of religious thought in the fourteenth century. The second treats of the effect resulting both to art and religion from the expression of mystical and theological conceptions in plastic form.

When we consider the nature of the ideas assimilated in the Middle Ages by the human mind, it is clear that art, in order to set them forth, demanded a language the Greeks had never greatly needed, and had therefore never fully learned. To over-estimate the difference from an æsthetic point of view between the religious notions of the Greeks and those which Christianity had made essential, would be difficult. Faith, hope, and charity; humility, endurance, suffering; the Resurrection and the Judgment; the Fall and the Redemption; Heaven and Hell; the height and depth of man's mixed nature; the drama of human destiny before the throne of God: into the sphere of thoughts like these, vivid and solemn, tran-

scending the region of sense and corporeity, carrying the mind away to an ideal world, where the things of this earth obtained a new reality by virtue of their relation to an invisible and infinite Beyond, the modern arts in their infancy were thrust. There was nothing finite here or tangible, no gladness in the beauty of girlish foreheads or the swiftness of a young man's limbs, no simple idealisation of natural delightfulness. The human body, which the figurative arts must needs use as the vehicle of their expression, had ceased to have a value in and for itself, had ceased to be the true and adequate investiture of thoughts demanded from the artist. At best it could be taken only as the symbol of some inner meaning, the shrine of an indwelling spirit nobler than itself; just as a lamp of alabaster owes its beauty and its worth to the flame it more than half conceals, the light transmitted through its scarce transparent walls.

In ancient art those moral and spiritual qualities which the Greeks recognised as truly human and therefore divine, allowed themselves to be incarnated in well-selected types of physical perfection. The deities of the Greek mythology were limited to the conditions of natural existence: they were men and women of a larger mould and freer personality; less complex, inasmuch as each completed some one attribute; less thwarted in activity, inasmuch as no limit was assigned to exercise of power. The passions and the faculties of man, analysed by unconscious psychology, and deified by religious fancy, were invested by sculpture with appropriate forms, the tact of the artist selecting corporeal qualities fitted to impersonate the special character of each divinity. Nor was it possible that, the gods and goddesses being what they were, exact analogues should not be found for them in idealised humanity. In a Greek statue there was enough soul to characterise the beauty of the body, to render her due meed of wisdom to Pallas, to distinguish the swiftness of Hermes from the strength of Heracles, or to contrast the virginal grace of Artemis with the abundance of Aphrodite's charms. At the same time the spirituality that gave its character to each Greek deity, was not such that, even in thought, it could be dissociated from corporeal form. The Greeks thought their gods as incarnate persons; and all the artist had to see to, was that this incarnate personality should be impressive in his marble.

Christianity, on the other hand, made the moral and spiritual nature of man all-essential. It sprang from an earlier religion, that judged it impious to give any form to God. The body and its terrestrial activity occupied but a subordinate position in its system. It was the life of the soul, separable from this frame of flesh, and destined to endure when earth and all that it contains had ended—a life that upon this planet was continued conflict and aspiring struggle—which the arts, insofar as they became its instrument, were called upon to illustrate. It was the worship of a Deity, all spirit, to be sought on no one sacred hill, to be adored in no transcendent shape, that they were bound to heighten. The most highly prized among the Christian virtues had no necessary connection with beauty of feature or strength of limb. Such beauty and such strength at any rate were accidental, not essential. A Greek faun could not but be graceful; a Greek hero was of necessity vigorous. But S. Stephen might be steadfast to the death without physical charm; S. Anthony might put to flight the devils of the flesh without muscular force. It is clear that the radiant physical perfection proper to the deities of Greek sculpture was not sufficient in this sphere.

Again, the most stirring episodes of the Christian mythology involved pain and perturbation of the spirit; the victories of the Christian athletes were won in conflicts carried on within their hearts and souls—'For we wrestle not against flesh and blood, but against principalities and powers,' demoniac leaders of spiritual legions. It is, therefore, no less clear that the tranquillity and serenity of the Hellenic ideal, so necessary to consummate sculpture, was here out of place. How could the Last Judgment, that day of wrath, when every soul, however insignificant on earth, will play the first part for one moment in an awful tragedy, be properly expressed in plastic form, harmonious and pleasing? And supposing that the artist should abandon the attempt to exclude ugliness and discord, pain and confusion, from his representation of the *Dies Iræ,* how could he succeed in setting forth by the sole medium of the human body the anxiety and anguish of the soul at such a time? The physical form, instead of being adequate to the ideas expressed, and therefore helpful to the artist, is a positive embarrassment, a source of weakness. The most powerful pictorial or sculpturesque delineation of the Judgment, when compared with the pangs inflicted on the spirit by a guilty conscience, pangs whereof words may render some account, but which can find no analogue in writhings of the limbs or face, must of necessity be found a failure. Still more impossible, if we pursue this train of thought into another region, is it for the figurative arts to approach the Christian conception of God in His omnipotence and unity. Christ Himself, the central figure of the Christian universe, the desired of all nations, in whom the Deity assumed a human form and dwelt with men, is no fit subject for such art at any rate as the Greeks had perfected. The fact of His incarnation brought Him indeed within the proper sphere of the fine arts; but the religious idea which He represents removed Him beyond the reach of sculpture. This is an all-important consideration. It is to this that our whole argument is tending. (pp. 4-12)

To sculpture in the Renaissance, shorn of the divine right to create gods and heroes, was left the narrower field of decoration, portraiture, and sepulchral monuments. In the last of these departments it found the noblest scope for its activity; for beyond the grave, according to Christian belief, the account of the striving, hoping, and resisting soul is settled. The corpse upon the bier may bear the stamp of spiritual character impressed on it in life; but the spirit, with its struggle and its passion, has escaped as from a prison-house, and flown else-whither. The body of the dead man, for whom this world is over, and who sleeps in peace, awaiting resurrection, and thereby not wholly dead, around whose tomb watch sympathising angels or contemplative genii, was, therefore, the proper subject for the highest Christian sculpture. Here, if anywhere, the right emotion could be adequately expressed in stone, and the moulded form be made the symbol of repose, expectant of restored activity. The greatest sculptor of the modern age was essentially a poet of Death.

Painting, then, for the reasons already assigned and insisted on, was the art demanded by the modern intellect upon its emergence from the stillness of the Middle Ages. The problem, however, even for the art of painting was not simple. The painters, following the masters of mosaic, began by setting forth the history, mythology, and legends of the Christian Church in imagery freer and more beautiful than lay within the scope of treatment by Romanesque or Byzantine art. So far their task was comparatively easy; for the idyllic grace of maternal love in the Madonna, the pathetic incidents of martyrdom, the courage of confessors, the ecstasies of celestial joy in redeemed souls, the loveliness of a pure life in modest

virgins, and the dramatic episodes of sacred story, furnish a multitude of motives admirably pictorial. There was, therefore, no great obstacle upon the threshold, so long as artists gave their willing service to the Church. Yet, looking back upon this phase of painting, we are able to perceive that already the adaptation of art to Christian dogma entailed concessions on both sides. Much, on the one hand, had to be omitted from the programme offered to artistic treatment, for the reason that the fine arts could not deal with it at all. Much, on the other hand, had to be expressed by means which painting in a state of perfect freedom would repudiate. Allegorical symbols, like Prudence with two faces, and painful episodes of agony and anguish, marred her work of beauty. There was consequently a double compromise, involving a double sacrifice of something precious. The faith suffered by having its mysteries brought into the light of day, incarnated in form, and humanised. Art suffered by being forced to render intellectual abstractions to the eye through figured symbols.

As technical skill increased, and as beauty, the proper end of art, became more rightly understood, the painters found that their craft was worthy of being made an end in itself, and that the actualities of life observed around them had claims upon their genius no less weighty than dogmatic mysteries. The subjects they had striven at first to realise with all simplicity now became little better than vehicles for the display of sensuous beauty, science, and mundane pageantry. The human body received separate and independent study, as a thing in itself incomparably beautiful, commanding more powerful emotions by its magic than aught else that sways the soul. At the same time the external world, with all its wealth of animal and vegetable life, together with the works of human ingenuity in costly clothing and superb buildings, was seen to be in every detail worthy of most patient imitation. Anatomy and perspective taxed the understanding of the artist, whose whole force was no longer devoted to the task of bringing religious ideas within the limits of the representable. Next, when the classical revival came into play, the arts, in obedience to the spirit of the age, left the sphere of sacred subjects, and employed their full-grown faculties in the domain of myths and Pagan fancies. In this way painting may truly be said to have opened the new era of culture, and to have first manifested the freedom of the modern mind. When Luca Signorelli drew naked young men for a background to his picture of Madonna and the infant Christ, he created for the student a symbol of the attitude assumed by fine art in its liberty of outlook over the whole range of human interests. Standing before this picture in the Uffizzi, we feel that the Church, while hoping to adorn her cherished dogmas with æsthetic beauty, had encouraged a power antagonistic to her own, a power that liberated the spirit she sought to enthral, restoring to mankind the earthly paradise from which monasticism had expelled it. (pp. 15-17)

The Church imagined art would help her; and within a certain sphere of subjects, by vividly depicting Scripture histories and the lives of saints, by creating new types of serene beauty and pure joy, by giving form to angelic beings, by interpreting Mariolatry in all its charm and pathos, and by rousing deep sympathy with our Lord in His Passion, painting lent efficient aid to piety. Yet painting had to omit the very pith and kernel of Christianity as conceived by devout, uncompromising purists. Nor did it do what the Church would have desired. Instead of riveting the fetters of ecclesiastical authority, instead of enforcing mysticism and asceticism, it really restored to humanity the sense of its own dignity and beauty, and helped to prove the untenability of the mediæval standpoint; for art is essentially and uncontrollably free, and, what is more, is free precisely in that realm of sensuous delightfulness from which cloistral religion turns aside to seek her own ecstatic liberty of contemplation.

The first step in the emancipation of the modern mind was taken thus by art, proclaiming to men the glad tidings of their goodliness and greatness in a world of manifold enjoyment created for their use. Whatever painting touched, became by that touch human; piety, at the lure of art, folded her soaring wings and rested on the genial earth. This the Church had not foreseen. Because the freedom of the human spirit expressed itself in painting only under visible images, and not, like heresy, in abstract sentences; because this art sufficed for Mariolatry and confirmed the cult of local saints; because its sensuousness was not at variance with a creed that had been deeply sensualised—the painters were allowed to run their course unchecked. Then came a second stage in their development of art. By placing the end of their endeavour in technical excellence and anatomical accuracy, they began to make representation an object in itself, independently of its spiritual significance. Next, under the influence of the classical revival, they brought home again the old powers of the earth—Aphrodite and Galatea and the Loves, Adonis and Narcissus and the Graces, Phœbus and Daphne and Aurora, Pan and the Fauns, and the Nymphs of the woods and the waves.

When these dead deities rose from their sepulchres to sway the hearts of men in the new age, it was found that something had been taken from their ancient bloom of innocence, something had been added of emotional intensity. Italian art recognised their claim to stand beside Madonna and the Saints in the Pantheon of humane culture; but the painters re-made them in accordance with the modern spirit. This slight touch of transformation proved that, though they were no longer objects of religious devotion, they still preserved a vital meaning for an altered age. Having personified for the antique world qualities which, though suppressed and ignored by militant and mediæval Christianity, were strictly human, the Hellenic deities still signified those qualities for modern Europe, now at length re-fortified by contact with the ancient mind. For it is needful to remember that in all movements of the Renaissance we ever find a return in all sincerity and faith to the glory and gladness of nature, whether in the world without or in the soul of man. To apprehend that glory and that gladness with the pure and primitive perceptions of the early mythopoets, was not given to the men of the new world. Yet they did what in them lay, with senses sophisticated by many centuries of subtlest warping, to replace the first free joy of kinship with primeval things. For the painters, far more than for the poets of the sixteenth century, it was possible to reproduce a thousand forms of beauty, each attesting to the delightfulness of physical existence, to the inalienable rights of natural desire, and to the participation of mankind in pleasures held in common by us with the powers of earth and sea and air.

It is wonderful to watch the blending of elder and of younger forces in this process. The old gods lent a portion of their charm even to Christian mythology, and showered their beauty-bloom on saints who died renouncing them. Sodoma's Sebastian is but Hyacinth or Hylas, transpierced with arrows, so that pain and martyrdom add pathos to his poetry of youthfulness. Lionardo's S. John is a Faun of the forest, ivy-

crowned and laughing, on whose lips the word 'Repent' would be a gleeful paradox. For the painters of the full Renaissance, Roman martyrs and Olympian deities—the heroes of the *Acta Sanctorum,* and the heroes of Greek romance—were alike burghers of one spiritual city, the city of the beautiful and human. What exquisite and evanescent fragrance was educed from these apparently diverse blossoms by their interminglement and fusion—how the high-wrought sensibilities of the Christian were added to the clear and radiant fancies of the Greek, and how the frank sensuousness of the Pagan gave body and fulness to the floating wraiths of an ascetic faith—remains a miracle for those who, like our master Lionardo, love to scrutinise the secrets of twin natures and of double graces. There are not a few for whom the mystery is repellent, who shrink from it as from Hermaphroditus. These will always find something to pain them in the art of the Renaissance.

Having co-ordinated the Christian and Pagan traditions in its work of beauty, painting could advance no farther. The stock of its sustaining motives was exhausted. A problem that preoccupied the minds of thinking men at this epoch was how to harmonise the two chief moments of human culture, the classical and the ecclesiastical. Without being as conscious of their hostility as we are, men felt that the Pagan ideal was opposed to the Christian, and at the same time that a reconciliation had to be effected. Each had been worked out separately; but both were needed for the modern synthesis. All that æsthetic handling, in this region more precocious and more immediately fruitful than pure thought, could do towards mingling them, was done by the impartiality of the fine arts. Painting, in the work of Raphael, accomplished a more vital harmony than philosophy in the writings of Pico and Ficino. A new Catholicity, a cosmopolitan orthodoxy of the beautiful, was manifested in his pictures. It lay outside his power, or that of any other artist, to do more than to extract from both revelations the elements of plastic beauty they contained, and to show how freely he could use them for a common purpose. Nothing but the scientific method can in the long run enable us to reach that further point, outside both Christianity and Paganism, at which the classical ideal of a temperate and joyous natural life shall be restored to the conscience educated by the Gospel. This, perchance, is the religion, still unborn or undeveloped, whereof Joachim of Flora dimly prophesied when he said that the kingdom of the Father was past, the kingdom of the Son was passing, and the kingdom of the Spirit was to be. The essence of it is contained in the whole growth to usward of the human mind; and though a creed so highly intellectualised as that will be, can never receive adequate expression from the figurative arts, still the painting of the sixteenth century forms for it, as it were, a not unworthy vestibule. It does so, because it first succeeded in humanising the religion of the Middle Ages, in proclaiming the true value of antique paganism for the modern mind, and in making both subserve the purposes of free and unimpeded art. (pp. 23-6)

John Addington Symonds, "The Problem for the Fine Arts," in his Renaissance in Italy: The Fine Arts, *1877. Reprint by Capricorn Books, 1961, pp. 1-28.*

ACHIEVEMENT AND SIGNIFICANCE

CHARLES TRINKAUS

[*Trinkaus is an American educator and the author of several studies of the Italian Renaissance. In the following excerpt from one of these,* In Our Image and Likeness: Humanity and Divinity in Italian Humanist Thought *(1970), he finds unity and diversity in the philosophical conceptions of several Italian humanists.*]

The Renaissance was a complex civilisation and full of individual variation. If individuals alone were regarded, a disconnected episodic chaos would emerge. But this is true of all but the simplest primitive societies. The historian's duty is to discover interpretative abstractions that make sense of the evidence he has uncovered, arranged and reported. Never mind that his selection of what to uncover, and his arranging and reporting, already impose an organisation and pattern. This is unavoidable and not necessarily arbitrary beyond endurance; the available evidence itself can frequently show him the way. Therefore, whatever the situation, the following is my version of the unity of discoverable humanist ideas of human nature and divinity amidst a plurality we all know is there.

It is obvious that the humanists were religious and Christian; the religious ideas and practices they knew were those that awaited them when they were born, and were guarded, promulgated, promoted and operated by a well-organised international body of professional administrators or 'ministers' of religion and a numerous body or bodies of men professionally dedicated to leading a religious life, the 'religious', monks and friars. It is equally obvious that no humanist was born a humanist, but had to become one by encountering the ideas and practices of a pre-existing group of men who, if at one point they were not 'humanists' were rapidly becoming humanists. As humanists they were involved through their writings with the moral problems and religious outlooks of their contemporaries, and were imbued with a knowledge of ancient moral thought. As a consequence of this situation, which varied greatly according to whether it was early or late fourteenth century, early, middle, or late fifteenth century, and so on, a task of self-justification of their literary activities and mode of life in relation to the religious establishment was inescapably imposed on the humanists.

Now this self-justification has often been regarded as directed primarily towards the natural philosophers, or the physicians, or the lawyers (though more ambivalently because of certain professional interrelationships). It has also at times been regarded as directed in a critical way against the clergy generally, or in a more limited way towards some group such as the Fraticelli or the Observant Franciscans. Because the humanists have been so obviously part of a secular, if not an entirely lay, movement, less attention has been focused on their theological notions, or on their turning of their humanistic skills towards religious tasks. But . . . a significant number of the more influential humanists entered the realm of religious thought and counselling both as an inseparable part of their general activities and in works of a specifically religious character. (pp. 761-62)

The humanists may have felt that they could handle the religious theme well because of their skill in writing, their rhetorical or poetic talents; or they might use it as a convenient and popular subject on which to discourse in a letter or dialogue, or on an appropriate oratorical occasion, such as in a funeral oration, or in a speech of consolation; or as something they could do effectively by dressing up ideas that were taken over completely from popular and established sources. In plain fact this unthinking conventional utilisation of religious notions was certainly apparent. . . . The frequency, however, with which certain points of view have come to the fore and the peculiarly, though not exclusively, humanist quality of these views suggests at the same time that they tried also to say something on their own account and of a special nature about man and his relationship to God, if not to their contemporaries, at least to themselves. That the form and content of humanist anthropological and religious thought was itself characteristic and important is, in short, an inescapable conclusion.

I have found in looking at the humanists' ideas of human nature in conjunction with their religious ideas that it is practically impossible to separate the two areas. Even where they are not completely integrated and identical, whenever the humanists single out certain theories as having a secular, or a pagan, or a philosophical or a rhetorical character separate from either religion or Christianity, they are immediately at pains to establish between the two what should be to their mind the proper relationship. Those ideas that seem clearly opposed to religion, or to Christianity, they sincerely reject. Or else they find by a process of reinterpretation either the common ground between the two spheres or the hidden harmony in the pagan or secular with the true faith.

Now this practice, or rather state of mind, seems to be a definite characteristic of the Renaissance, or of Renaissance humanism. It was not medieval, although in some ways resembling medieval practices, because it was far more self-conscious than the medieval procedures, where medieval writers sometimes even accept the pagan images and ideas wholesale and naïvely, unaware of the possible discrepancy. (pp. 762-63)

At the same time, this attitude and practice could by no means be called modern, or it would not have made so many modern historians, Catholic, Protestant, non-religious alike, uncomfortable and apologetic. It is indeed the source of much of the confusion and controversy about the Renaissance. From a religious point of view—modern Protestant or Catholic—the humanists and Platonists went much too far in secularising, classicising, stressing the oneness of spirit of the Christian traditions and revelation with the pagan and secular traditions and ideas. From the non-religious, or even anti-clerical and anti-religious point of view, which has been fairly endemic among modern historians, the humanists obviously did not go far enough in rejecting the peculiarly and traditionally Christian and revelational. (pp. 763-64)

Possibly today when the slogans of 'Ecumenism' have so much support, a look at what the humanists and Platonists were trying to do in this respect would be helpful, for it seems quite clear that the ideal of the brotherhood of mankind, if it can ever become concrete, cannot become so if the vast cultural and historical divergences among the peoples of the world were compressed into one homogeneous totalitarian mass, but due recognition must be given to a unity in the midst of plurality. One cannot forget in this connection the influence of the Conciliar movement in the Renaissance which, though it might have staved off the Protestant schism, certainly failed to do so, and which certainly surrendered the ideal of unity within plurality to the curial centralists. The relationships between humanists and clergy in the history of the conciliar movement and its demise needs a major historical study.

A further question is that of the specific influence of the humanist movement on subsequent religious developments both Protestant and Catholic. It is certainly true that the tendency towards philological exactness of the Italian humanists greatly furthered, through their northern and German humanist successors, an Evangelical literalism which was ahistorical in its attempts to purge itself of the excrescences of tradition. Valla is the humanist who went farthest in this respect. Some of his ideas may have contributed to a new rigorism of historical and Scriptural interpretation limiting the movement towards universality amid plurality. Valla, however, despite his fiery polemics aimed sharply against the historical misinterpretations embedded in ecclesiastical tradition, including the Donation of Constantine, the interpretation of the Creed and the translation of the New Testament, must be recognised as a staunch Catholic and a Romanist. He is very much distrusted by Catholic scholars today, and Father Garofalo is a good example. Yet he did not wish for a Protestantism, but a more historically responsible and at the same time liberal Catholicism under the leadership of the Roman curia and the Pope. I believe neither that he was cynical in his labours for Nicholas V or Calixtus IV, nor that they were naïve in supporting him.

Valla had many ideas which in the light of Post-Tridentine Catholicism were alien and even dangerous, but he was a Romanist before all. Believing in the sanctity of the Word and in the sacred trust with which the human word, embodied in the Latin language should be regarded, he looked upon the Roman Church as the providentially appointed guardian of human civilisation embodied in the great Latin tradition of European culture. His inaugural oration in the last year of his life makes this clear. Thus, though he was probably a very irritating and unorthodox Catholic, and even at one point knowingly supported a heretical dogma of the schismatic Greek Church on the procession of the Holy Spirit, he was basically a Roman Christian who found the rhetorical and philological values of Roman civilisation embodied in the Roman Church. It needed to be purged of philosophy, particularly the alien Greek Aristotelianism and Stoicism, and this judgement obviously created for him an automatic opposition from the Scholastic establishment. But Protestant he cannot be imagined.

Valla represents the extreme of a humanist statement of position both on religion and human nature. But in his extremity much is revealed about humanism generally. Valla's positivism and philologism points up most sharply the affinity that the humanists felt between a rhetorical, anti-metaphysical approach to the world and the tradition of a Scriptural, revelational approach to the Christian religion. It was inevitable, and it would seem inevitable once it is realised how central was the concern of the humanists with rhetorical force and philological precision, that they would seek to unify the secular with the religious, historical and literary traditions. But again they wished to do this with a sharp eye for historical and textual accuracy. (pp. 764-66)

Manetti also belongs to the literalist school of interpretation, perhaps making up in erudition for his total inability to compete in analytical acuteness with Valla. Yet Manetti was an equally pious Catholic, just as bold as Valla in his actual literary activities but as timid in the way he talked and thought

about what he was doing as Valla was defiant and boastful. Then there was Aurelio Brandolini, who challenged the doctors of theology but ended up as an Augustinian Hermit; Poggio, whose attacks on the Observants did not lessen his religious orthodoxy and conservatism; and the fervently pious and loyal Salutati who looked for new ways to interpret man's actual and desirable freedom of will in relation to the providence and power of God; and the indescribably subtle Petrarch who bared the depths of his religious feeling.

All of these men, and the others, were a challenge to the old order of considerable significance and proportion, and if their influence had become dominant, there is no doubt that at least the tone and manner of the practice of the Christian religion would have changed drastically. But none of these men were reformers in the sense of the Protestant Reformers. They represent a certain ideal of human life within a Christian framework in the age of the Renaissance. The outlook that they expressed became a characteristic of the Renaissance, but they were not reformers, nor even 'Pre-Reformers', nor do they succeed in changing the course of events in the history of religion.

This suggests that the humanists were lost in the Renaissance in some in-between or truly 'middle' age that was overwhelmed by a far more powerful course of events. But this would be an exaggeration, or rather a minimisation, of their influence. . . . If it was not to be their destiny to shape the major events of European history, they nevertheless did contribute markedly to a new view of human nature and a new attitude towards man's place in the world.

Frescoes in the Sala degli Angeli of the Palazzo Farnese.

Thus the major historical role of the humanist movement was in the shaping of the values of European culture rather than in their impact on economic and political events and institutions or on ecclesiastical history. They had far more to do with the civic attitudes and the religious attitudes of their contemporaries and of the succeeding centuries than they had to do with the behaviour of the rich, the powerful, the prestigious. Although I do not subscribe to the materialist interpretation of history, I am ready to concede the power of those who were in a position to manipulate wealth or authority or military force. But already with the humanists, if this had not been always true for the great mass of mankind, these activities were regarded almost like the intrusions of the weather, as meteorological events, as most truly those kinds of actions that were under the sway of the stars and out of the control of man, except as they could be interpreted as fulfilling God's divinely providential purpose in some way.

Yet paradoxically, the humanists offered through their writings a new affirmation of the possibility and value of human action. They presented a vision of man controlling and shaping his own life and the future course of his history and they stressed a new conception of human nature modelled on their own image of the Deity. There is no need to attempt here a condensed version of the medieval conception of human nature and man's role in the world, since this would result in caricature. In the closing medieval centuries, however, there was a great deal of frantic anxiety either present or deliberately inculcated by the popular literature and the arts concerning the minutiae of human behaviour which might determine one's destiny in the Last Judgement. The medieval God may have been a quiescent one, as Valla and later Calvin charged, but it is certain that to the scholastics and the canonists he was a finicky, hair-splitting one, intimately concerned with all the minute details of the circumstances, motivation, timing, internal attitudes, external manifestations of individual human behaviour. And a conviction was present among the scholastic theologians and the canonists of all schools that these infinite distinctions counted, were in fact crucial, that there was a one right way of interpreting religion and guiding human behaviour, even though there might be infinite disagreement as to what that way was.

I can agree with the Lutheran criticism of this procedure and attitude as a vain and fruitless producer of needless anxiety, whatever the merits of the doctrine of salvation *sola fide*. But it can also be seen how this great challenging insight of the Reformation was rather too quickly swamped in a new kind of scriptural literalism which insisted on the minutely accurate interpretation of the divine word, or in the more Calvinistic anxiety of a casuistic examination of one's conscience and behaviour in order to determine whether one had 'made his election'.

Coming from the rhetorical tradition, the humanists offered the first great challenge and the first great alternative to this fixation on the practical detail and on the over-refined distinction. This was a major historical contribution. It is true that they contributed in some way to the later Protestant casuistries and to the Counter-Reformational Jesuit ones too, but this was after their own day had passed and certain of their scholarly procedures had been taken up and misapplied in an exaggerated way.

Beginning with Petrarch, the humanists broke free from the bonds of religious externalism and objectivism that resulted from the application of the dialectical procedures of scholastic philosophy and theology to ordinary Christian life. The humanist turned back to man as a living, feeling subject. He found him frightened and overwhelmed with despair at the impossibility of believing that such a finicky deity could have any interest in the salvation of such a disorganised, loosely behaving, though well-intentioned Christian. It was Petrarch who grasped the psychological untenability of this version of man's relationship to God. There came from his writings . . . a vision of an all-merciful, loving Father who, far above and beyond the limits of our understanding and of our capacity to master-mind His judgements about our salvation or damnation, had offered His grace freely to all. Running consistently through all of his work was this new conception of man and of God.

Much too much time has been wasted wondering about Petrarch's doctrinal inconsistencies, his eclecticism and inclination to mix the philosophies from all the classical schools with each other and with Christianity. For the very point of his whole position was that these were merely diverse human ways of trying to make sense out of something that was too complicated and turbulent and constantly changing to be grasped for long by any one such point of view. God Himself had to be viewed by Petrarch as majestically free and moved more by his outpouring of love or anger than by any attempt to sit down and make precise calculations. And man in his image and likeness would share these qualities on a lesser and weaker scale, over-timorous and over-bold, needing to find the balance between elation and despair, aware of the limitations of his capacity and the strength of the vicissitudes with which his life was beset, but equally aware of his position within the creation and encouraged by it, created in the image and likeness of God, destined to be the master of all the world, and the replica in this of God and the universe.

Will comes to the fore with Petrarch, since intellect can be so betraying. But he does not dispense with intellect. Rather he feels it should not be misapplied to a vain attempt either to calculate man's own destiny or to manipulate the physical world in ways that are beyond man's capacity. Sometimes he sounds anti-intellectual, anti-scientific, but it is because he trusts to the insights of literature and poetry and history more than to those of dialectic and natural philosophy. The former reveal the actualities of human life and feeling, the latter deal in false abstractions. Moreover action, which is the consequence of the human word used in discourse to direct and influence the feelings of others, is more in keeping with the image of man dealing with his own human world and with the sub-human animal and vegetable and mineral worlds. Man's dignity lies in his acting in a providential way as he believed his God was doing, but not as though he were not a subordinate part of the divine providence itself and subject to it.

One can see how this stress on will continues through Salutati and Valla and influences many other humanists. One can also see the compatibility of such an image of man with the rhetorical approach to existence. We need to remind and to stress again just how far Salutati and Valla went in this, and how much more explicitly they applied it to a conception of man created in the image of God. But it is also necessary to be aware constantly that some of these statements of the humanists were exaggerations and that they did not abandon the intellect or reject the value of theory and philosophy altogether. Through the intellect man acquired the knowledge that was essential to his shaping of his affairs within the world. The intellect was, as Salutati and Valla as well as Petrarch claimed, the minister or agent of the will. Men did not and should not act blindly. It was not a case of 'Blind Eros' as it was later depicted in classical Renaissance artistic treatments of the theme. Salutati strove valiantly to create a new synthesis of divine providence, natural physical order, and human free will. A philosopher might judge it as probably not very successful, although it has its merits. The point is, Salutati was fearful not of philosophy in general, but of the kind of philosophy and science that would by implication give man a false image of himself.

Man was by nature volitional and operative. He was involved in the world in managing his individual and his communal affairs through business, politics and family life. But he needed not to forget what his nature was in his pursuit of more and more efficient means of accomplishing subsidiary purposes. Both Petrarch and Salutati had a strong impulse to glorify man and his achievements, if not of their contemporaries, then of the ancients. But they never forgot the perils with which human life was beset and the danger that man, in his emulation of the providential activist, volitional deity, would imagine he was himself truly a god and not see that he had to wait for his deification in the next world. Man's triumph was to act as though he truly were made in the image and likeness of God, but not to act as though he was God and therefore lose his dignity. For man to be God meant for man to become beast-like to other men and to God's creation and find in himself the image of the beast and not of God.

All of these ideas came better from the pen of a humanist than from the sermons of a preacher, though the latter was not to be scorned. For the humanist might be able to help his contemporaries see the larger image. The humanist sought to join together the functions of the theoretical theologian and the practical preacher in what I have called *theologia rhetorica*. The one was far too above and the other too far below the spiritual needs and level of the educated ruling classes of the Renaissance cities. Salutati and Petrarch had many clerical friends and were most respectful of them, but never feared to disagree. The popular preacher and the scholastic theologian they both disliked. Humanism did not espouse a cause that was exclusively its own but one that was shared by contemporaries and certainly many members of the clergy, as the associations of the humanists make very clear.

Now Valla moved from the comparatively moderate vision of volitional and operational man to what I have called a 'passional' view of human nature. Regardless of the value of his epistemological and philosophical notions, of his construction of a philologically based 'non-philosophy' which was a philosophy, certainly this conception of human nature is remarkable in both its insight and its modernity. . . . [Its] roots are Augustinian and patristic Christian, as were those of Petrarch and Salutati, but Valla went far beyond the bounds of previous speculation on the dynamics and power of the affects, of the will, of the emotions in human nature. Man became an emotional force, imbued with love and hate, fearless of the consequences in enacting his purposes, not completely blind, since he had the intellect at his disposal, but careless of the voice of the intellect when his passions were sufficiently powerful to sweep him beyond it. As a description of human behaviour as it can be observed in history, literature and experience, this is a profound and magnificent insight. Whether it is in the final analysis a true one, or one that does not need to be tempered by the realisation of the power

of man's sheer fascination with the kinds of orderliness his mind leads him to perceive in the world, is another question. We are not examining its validity but only its historical significance, which to me seems enormous both for its early statement of a later romantic and twentieth-century psychological point of view and for its expressiveness of so much of the behaviour of individuals in the Renaissance. The Stendhalian, Burckhardtian, Nietzschean image of the Renaissance is epitomised in this theory.

But with it go his epistemology and his religious ideas. It was a psychology of man acting, impelled by the power of his loves and his hates, and these were mediated to him by the meanings he perceived through language and words. Words to Valla were quite literally actions since they pronounced a view of reality which helped to shape the direction of the passions. God revealed the world through his Word in the Scriptures, whereupon this became the reality with which man had to live and deal. And man, cast in the image and likeness of God, moved towards ultimate union with Him in the next world if powerful enough verbal images urged him on his way. Valla's 'Epicureanism' was all psychological and non-material. Man loved and hated, not according to material or physical realities, either the external or internal physiological ones. In fact the emotions could suppress physiological reactions and sensual perceptions easily. Man's loves and actions were according to his images mediated by the words he used to describe his perceptions. Man was, in fact, like God, constantly creating his own world through his words in literature and art and in personal life.

Manetti, influenced more by the civic tradition of Florence and the high estimation of Aristotle after Bruni's new translation, was none the less equally eclectic in his outlook, and equally emphatic in his emphasis on action. Will is important but not to the exclusion of the intellect. What seems most important in his thinking was his projection of the character of man's striving in the third book of his treatise on the *Dignity and Excellence of Man*. Man wishes to be, and this is a matter of will underlying his nature, or rather God wished to produce in man, who is made in His own image and likeness, the most beautiful, the most ingenious, the most wise, the most opulent and the most powerful of creatures. This image of the five qualities that men in the Renaissance seemed to strive after is central in Manetti's conception of man, along with his operative conception of the intellect.

Manetti's Aristotelianism is a functional and not a hieratic one. It is not necessary that there be complete doctrinal congruity between these thinkers, for us to see the kinship of these ideas to those of his predecessors. But close to Manetti in his operational Aristotelianism, and in his emphasis on the creative and inventive powers of human industry, and the goodness of human labours and even hardships and sufferings, not for the inheritance of a heavenly recompense but for their this-worldly advantages to the human species, was the Bolognese Benedetto Morandi. What is interesting is the way in which these humanist Aristotelians gave forth a far more optimistic and operational conception of man than Pomponazzi, even, did. The latter, despite his also operational Aristotelianism, could not help being overwhelmed by the pessimistic implication of the more Stoic, universal, natural determinism he saw everywhere. The humanist tradition, on the other hand, with its adherence to Providence and Revelation, had a larger vision of the possibility of man managing his affairs, and this was in good part the consequence of the rhetorical attitude of directing and influencing men as individuals and groups that stimulated this kind of thinking. Philosophic naturalism, hierarchical and static in its traditional aspects, as Pomponazzi well saw, tended also, even when viewed operationally, to paralyse by its commitment to a purely theoretical stance. (pp. 766-73)

[There is also] an underlying consistency between the humanists and the Platonists, particularly with Ficino, but with Pico as well in a more complicated way. The fashion of thinking of Ficinian Platonism as a departure from the civic and operational spirit of humanist Florence is an erroneous one to my mind. Ficino was a true Florentine, and in his yearnings for immortality did no more than Manetti did in describing the great earthly achievements of man as part of his striving towards immortality. If man did not have the possibility of becoming immortal it would be senseless for him so to strive in emulation of the qualities of God. Ficino also retained a stress on the superiority of the will, though more hesitantly than the earlier humanists, as Kristeller has demonstrated.

What significantly distinguishes Ficino from the humanists is his elaboration of a metaphysics. One cannot say whether a Valla would regard this with equal disdain to his contempt for scholastic metaphysics. But in general I believe it is wrong to intepret the hostility of many of the humanists towards the inherited metaphysical systems either of the natural philosophers or the theologians as an absolute hostility towards philosophy of all sorts. . . . Salutati, in fact, attempted to elaborate a philosophy in his *De fato*. And Valla, as a matter of fact, did also, though he preferred to think of it as its opposite. By and large the humanists did not wish to be sectarians and isolated from the mainstreams of intellectual life, which meant university learning. Their various efforts to elaborate theological ideas, as well as moral philosophies are evidence of this. Ficino was able to offer the humanists the kind of interpretation of the Platonic tradition that might seem compatible with their own emphasis on the internal, psychological side of man, on an emotional-moral dialectic, on will and love. It is ridiculous to argue as to whether Ficino was the philosophical fulfilment of humanism or not. The point is that contemporary humanists flocked to his ideas and his 'academy' with no hesitation and great approval, understanding his philosophy or not.

Thus, just as in their conception of the relation between the various parts of mankind and the various religious and intellectual traditions the humanists and the Renaissance Platonists sought a unity amidst plurality, so in their conceptions of man—manifesting in his own trinitarian nature of memory, intellect and will, the image and likeness of the divine Trinity—they reveal a remarkable degree of homogeneity in their ideas with a plurality of variations and borrowings from various schools of ancient and Christian moral philosophy and theology. In each instance there is an absence of any kind of doctrinal purity, an eclecticism among the humanists or an attempt at syncretism among the Platonists, allowing them to build out of a variety of sources and traditions a new homogeneous view of man knowing, willing and acting in the image and likeness of God. (pp. 773-74)

> *Charles Trinkaus, in his* In Our Image and Likeness: Humanity and Divinity in Italian Humanist Thought, Vol. 2, *The University of Chicago Press, 1970, 985 p.*

CECIL GRAYSON

[*Grayson is an English literary historian and critic of Italian literature. In the following excerpt from an essay originally published in 1979, he characterizes chief developments in Italian Renaissance literature.*]

It has long been debated whether Dante should or should not be included within the Renaissance. Much of the argument has rested in the past on the supposition that there exist qualifications for entrance possessed by the majority of those living in a certain period of time. I shall not attempt to define such qualifications either on literary or other grounds, because that would imply pre-empting the issue; and in any case it is an anti-historical way of posing the problem. It is better to approach from another angle, and to study (along the lines of two excellent studies by Garin and Dionisotti) the varied fortunes of Dante and his works in the centuries after his death. Here we find that his fame as a poet reached its apogee (with reference to the *Comedy, Rime* and *Convivio*) in the age of Lorenzo de' Medici, only to go into progressive decline and be overtaken by Petrarch by the turn of the century. It is not so material, therefore, to establish when a hypothetical Renaissance begins, and whether with Dante or not: there is absolutely no doubt that the great Italian literary tradition begins with him. It is more important to know how and why Dante's works survive up to a certain point, and then fail to pass the barrier of a literary criticism nurtured on the Latin Ciceronianism of the late fifteenth century. If we follow the same exercise for Petrarch, we find the fame of his vernacular and of some of his Latin works unbroken throughout; which would seem to prove what is commonly believed, that the Renaissance begins and continues with him. But I prefer not to play with such general terms. There is no doubt about the novelty of Petrarch's philological activity, from which humanism in the true and strict sense starts (and here Dante has no part). There is also no doubt about Petrarch's different poetic sensibility, even though it is expressed through traditional forms and language. Yet there are other aspects of Petrarch's work which no longer corresponded by the end of the fourteenth century to the interests of his successors, who were quite differently involved in affairs and teaching. His unfinished Latin epic *Africa* had virtually no following; the religious sensitivity which at times dictated renunciation of this world, the dissatisfaction with himself and his age which made him look back to the past or upwards towards heaven, seems to find no echo in humanist circles. There are no imitations of the *Segretum* or *De remediis* (though this work enjoyed wide circulation for a long time). This is not the Petrarch who continues at this cultural level into the fifteenth century, even though some of the questions he raised, such as that of the active and contemplative lives, continued to be debated and differently resolved. On the literary plane too, that inner conflict which was the moving force of his poetry has no true imitators before the sixteenth century: fifteenth-century Petrarchism is superficial and external. Bembo was the first to appreciate and recreate the spirit as well as the form of Petrarch's poetry. This brief sketch of the fortune of Petrarch, like that for Dante, reveals assimilations, rejections, imitation and disagreement throughout the fourteenth and fifteenth centuries according to the knowledge, tastes and understanding of readers. Yet the presence of both Dante and Petrarch, however incomplete or reinterpreted, dominates the literature of the following centuries, so that any history of Renaissance literature has no alternative but to start from Dante. The question whether he is or is not a Renaissance writer (in some broad sense) seems an idle one. It is obvious that Dante is different from Petrarch; not so obvious perhaps, but no less true that the so-called Renaissance is crammed full of differences and contrasts.

It used to be fashionable in the wake of De Sanctis's criticism to contrast the *Divine Comedy* with Boccaccio's 'human comedy' in his *Decameron,* and to interpret it as the clearest indication of the passage from Middle Ages to Renaissance: the *Comedy* severe, menacing, based on faith and aimed at salvation; the *Decameron* light, pleasurable, based on human nature and aimed at entertainment, especially of women. One can certainly make such a contrast, and it tells us a lot about the differences between the two writers. Whether it demonstrates a transition to a new age is another matter. Twenty years ago Vittore Branca published some of his essays under the title *Boccaccio medievale* with the intention of stressing not so much the novelty of Boccaccio's works as those elements in them which relate to past traditions of a cultural level totally different from those frequented by Dante and Petrarch. So, without losing any of its stylistic or human originality, the *Decameron* can be seen as the apotheosis of a long popular narrative tradition in which Boccaccio celebrates the actions of merchants, the middle class and court society of the early fourteenth century—an epic, therefore, in content and structure no less 'medieval' than the *Comedy,* despite its different sense of values. Furthermore, whatever his antecedents in translation and adaptation of medieval French romances and in the works of *cantastorie,* Boccaccio certainly gave, through his minor works, tremendous impulse to the chivalric tradition which, in a verse form possibly invented by him (*ottava rima*), runs right through the following centuries. The debt to Boccaccio of the *novella* from Sacchetti onwards is plain to see: less evident but equally significant is the debt to him of the romance in prose and verse, of pastoral and mythological poetry. In these sectors the relatively minor works of Boccaccio (*Filocolo, Filostrato, Teseida, Ameto, Ninfale*) are all in some ways linked to traditions which were alive in Dante's time or before and unconnected either with the new humanism or with most of the Italian literature which precedes them. The question arises as to how and why works with such distant medieval origins could exercise so much influence and determine for so long the form and spirit of what we call Renaissance literature.

Of the three major fourteenth-century writers Boccaccio is the one most changed by modern studies. In all three the autobiographical element constitutes a problem, but in Boccaccio's case it had for a long time led critics on a false trail. Shorn of the legends of exotic birth and aristocratic loves, Boccaccio's biography and biographical myths now appear (thanks largely to Billanovich and Branca) in their true light. His origins and formation now look even more different from those of Dante and Petrarch. But they had something in common; all were exiles of a kind: Dante, resentful of his expulsion but attached for ever to Florence and her language, while he roamed in spirit over and under the world; Petrarch, born in Arezzo, but a citizen of the republic of letters and of no city in particular; Boccaccio, reared in Naples on the margins of the court society, but compelled to return to Tuscany and thereafter ever nostalgic for his golden youth. Each of them was destined, because of these varied backgrounds, to be the mouthpiece of a different literary tradition. While Petrarch alone opened up the possibilities of a new or at least renewed Latin eloquence, all three in their different ways offered examples of a new literature in the vernacular potentially valid,

like Latin, for the whole of Italy. The choice between the two roads, Latin and vernacular, and the resolution of the problems as models implicit in the very different works of these three writers, constitute the central issues to be faced by later literature. In this sense Dante, Petrarch and Boccaccio are the key to understanding the literature of the fifteenth and sixteenth centuries. This is evident not only from the frequent and varied imitation of their works, but from the central position they occupy in the discussions of both humanist and vernacular writers from the early fifteenth century onwards. This, therefore, will be our starting-point for considering what I have termed the inner problem of the Renaissance.

In the last twenty-five years one particular discussion of these three authors has received a great deal of attention, viz. that represented by the *Dialogi ad Petrum Histrum* of Bruni, which is undoubtedly a very important text for understanding the outlook of a group of Florentine humanists at the beginning of the fifteenth century. We must be careful, however, not to attribute to it motives and significance of a political-cultural character which it may not possess. One of the many merits of the historian Hans Baron has been to draw attention to the dating and interpretation of the *Dialogues* in the context of the attempt by Gian Galeazzo Visconti to extend his rule, not only over Lombardy and Emilia, but over Tuscany as well. Whilst one can fairly readily agree with Baron's demonstration of separate composition of the two dialogues with the *Laudatio Florentinae urbis* in between, there seem less grounds for accepting his explanation of the contrasting judgements in them, one negative, the other positive, of the achievements of Dante, Petrarch and Boccaccio, in terms of a radical revaluation of fourteenth century culture provoked in Bruni by the political situation. According to this view the Visconti crisis caused a volte-face in Florentine humanist circles, particularly in relation to fourteenth-century vernacular traditions, constituting a new attitude on the part of this élite more sympathetic to the city's contemporary interests and her recent and past traditions; and this would mark the beginnings of that Florentine civic humanism typical of the first half of the fifteenth century. It seems unlikely, however, that the pessimistic judgement of the first dialogue was meant by the author to be final: it must surely be seen (as in some rhetorical works of Antiquity) as the point of departure for a positive celebration in the second. The interval of time between them may well have a practical, political explanation, but not necessarily an ideological one. None of which detracts from the important fact that precisely at the moment Bruni and his colleagues chose to review the cultural balance sheet in relation to both ancients and moderns, evidently in order the better to determine their own direction; and this historical-cultural awareness of the *Dialogues* seems far more significant than any possible political or ideological implications.

At the same time these *Dialogues,* together with the *Laudatio,* may be seen as an affirmation of Florentine traditions and their past and present superiority over the rest of Italy. Baron was right, therefore to stress those opening years of the fifteenth century as a turning-point in Florentine humanism, which from then on asserts itself in the vanguard of Italian culture, and in contrast with the old imperial tradition, forges a new link between ancient republican Rome and republican Florence in terms of culture and civic institutions. But if such an attitude inspired the Florentine humanists at that time, it was a local phenomenon without special impact on other centres, which were influenced by Florentine historical, philological and philosophical activities, not by her civic example. It is right to take account of the republican element in Florentine humanism at that time, but wrong to exaggerate that civic factor in relation to the development of humanist studies elsewhere. Hans Baron's works have stimulated many other useful studies in Florentine history of the period; to the neglect, in consequence, of other centres, where without the benefit of the political stimuli experienced by Florence, important contributions were made to humanism and the development of education. I am referring particularly to the Veneto, to Padua and Mantua, and to Guarino, Barzizza, and Vittorino; and whereas much has been done for Padua and its university in recent years, other cities and people have been less studied because they seem off-centre in relation to Florence, and because they were less or not at all involved in political conflicts of the same kind. For these the Florentine yardstick is not applicable: it will not explain, for example, Valla or Flavio Biondo. In any comprehensive view of the Renaissance we need to reduce this Florentine angle of vision, and especially not to exaggerate, in relation to the culture of the age, the apparent contrast between republican and princely rule. (pp. 207-11)

In the past much emphasis has been placed on humanist opposition to the vernacular on the evidence of a few invectives and defences. Baron has rightly stressed the more positive evaluation of the vernacular by Bruni in the works already quoted and in his later *Lives* of Dante and Petrarch; but that did not justify for Bruni or others the use for serious purposes of a language considered to be different and distinct from Latin and of inferior capabilities. It was not a case, then, so much of hostility to the vernacular, as of a quite understandable belief at that time that the future lay with the renewed and stable Latin, not with the multiform, unstable vernacular. Against the large and growing corpus of classical texts, the relatively recent tradition of the modern vernacular could hardly compete as guide and model, especially since it was either serious or amorous in verse (. . . Bruni's generation was not much for poetry), or lightweight or amorous in prose. At that time, too, and against that background, the Latin of the trecento did not impose itself: Dante's Latin works were mostly forgotten, Petrarch's only partially influential, and Boccaccio's even less so. This is why—and Bruni's *Dialogues* seem to prove it—we have the impression that humanists at the beginning of the fifteenth century felt themselves to be starting almost *ex novo*. It should not surprise us, therefore, to find Alberti in the 1430s, when attempting to write a serious, learned vernacular prose, starting virtually from scratch and without reference to the fourteenth-century writers. It is true that in his amorous prose and verse there are echoes of Dante, Petrarch and Boccaccio, and that in these genres (though not among humanists) these writers functioned as masters and models; but for the expression of higher thought which preoccupied humanists, they offered little or no help or precedent. The only way in which the vernacular could compete with Latin was through a writer like Alberti who deliberately set out to use it for learned subjects, and to defend it, not on the basis of its past achievements, but on its intrinsic merits and by a demonstration that it possessed grammatical regularity similar to the Latin from which it descended. Hence the character of his prose, which owes so much to Latin in its vocabulary and syntax. The absence of Dante, Petrarch and Boccaccio from Alberti's use and defence of the vernacular in the 1430s and 1440s shows how little the fourteenth-century tradition then counted at that level of culture. At lower levels—in amorous, moral and political verse, and

in narrative prose—that tradition had remained uninterrupted. Such literary stratification is typical of the cultural situation of the first part of the fifteenth century.

The situation in Florence changed completely in the last thirty years or so of the century in the age of Lorenzo de' Medici, when times were ripe for the renewal of interest in the Tuscan tradition, especially in Tuscan poetry. It began with Alberti's young friend and admirer Cristoforo Landino, and was promoted by the neo-Platonic revival of Ficino and his circle, which gave new dignity to poetic expression and brought Dante, Petrarch and other Florentine poets to the forefront of learned attention. At this point, when the political circumstances had also changed, taking the form of a kind of *Signoria* not very different from the rest of Italy (and certainly different from the Florentine situation at the opening of the century), the cult of Florentine writers became almost a deliberate programme; there then came to the surface not only the great writers of the past but also the tradition of popular verse, which had hitherto remained more or less in the shadows. In Lorenzo's time we see a democratization of culture, and simultaneously a mixing of the vernacular and classical traditions which had so far largely remained apart. The result is that eclecticism typical of the late fifteenth century, with conspicuous contrasts not only between writers but within writers themselves—a clear indication that Dante, Petrarch and Boccaccio had not yet become established as the dominant guides and models, but were confused with the rest of the vernacular tradition. Some signs of historical perspective and critical awareness of the relative merits of Tuscan poets are evident in the *Epistola a Federigo d'Aragona* and the *Commento* of Lorenzo to some of his *rime;* but perhaps more significant, because it transcends the limits of local traditions, is the criticism of Landino (most recently studied by Cardini), which poses the problem basic to understanding certain aspects and debates of late fifteenth-century literature, of the relationship between nature and art, between free expression and tradition—the problem, that is, of imitation, which Landino resolves in general terms, stressing the need for the discipline of art learned from the classical as well as vernacular traditions. In his well-known formula: 'è necessario essere latino chi vuole essere buono toscano' ('you have to know Latin to write well in Tuscan'), which has literary as well as linguistic implications, he gives explicit expression to the concept, exemplified in Alberti's practice, of deliberate fusion of the two traditions. This concept was to produce very varied results in Florence and elsewhere, from the *Stanze* and *Orfeo* of Poliziano to the *Arcadia* of Sannazzaro, and even the *Hypnerotomachia Polyphili.* These works take us to the linguistic crisis of the late fifteenth century (studied by Folena and Dionisotti), which involves both Latin and the vernacular, and concerns not simply languages but literature and style.

The last decades of the fifteenth century from a literary point of view are a time of infinite possibilities and uncertain standards. Ever since Petrarch and Boccaccio there had been much discussion of poetry and imitation, but it had little effect on literary practice outside the field of Ciceronian Latin prose. While Italian and Latin remained two distinct media and levels of culture, the question seems to have had little actuality and substance, but the more they came together, the more urgent became the need to resolve the problem for both. They had been brought closer for one thing by the important recognition in the 1430s that Latin had also had a vernacular existence, and was not, as had hitherto been thought, an artificial medium divorced from speech: furthermore, Latin had

The Triumph of Bacchus and Ariadne, *by an anonymous Florentine artist.*

given rise to the modern language by a process of corruption. As the century advanced, the patrimony of Latin literature had been enriched by new discoveries, and there developed, especially with Valla, a new historical sense of the language even more evident in the wider knowledge of texts and keener linguistic sensitivity of Poliziano (cf. the important publication by Branca and Pastore Stocchi of his 'lost' *Seconda Miscellanea*, 1960). But this new philology and the new texts do not altogether explain that widening of interest and change of taste, towards the end of the century, for late Latin, so different in its vocabulary and style from the Ciceronian. This tendency, followed but kept under control by Poliziano, reached extravagant proportions in some lesser writers. Against this background are to be seen the discussions about imitation between Poliziano and Cortese, Bembo and G-F. Pico, and other lesser-known documents of the time studied by Dionisotti. As for the vernacular, the literary tradition of the fourteenth and fifteenth centuries offered a variety of choice almost as rich as that of Latin, and more accessible to all for being in the live, modern idiom. The literary works of Lorenzo and his circle illustrate this point in their amazing diversity from the lowest to the highest level in content, form and language. Here there was novelty and freshness as well as continuity with the earlier traditions, and a kind of experimentalism which inspired writers to try out, often with remarkable felicity, every sort of poetry from rustic, bucolic verse to sacred drama, from the mythological poem to the chivalric romance, from the carnival song to amorous lyrics in *stilnovo* fashion. It was an experimentalism not only of a technical and thematic nature (without prejudices as to the relative legitimacy of this or that genre), but also of intellectual origin in a generation of men of restless temperament, in whose works it is difficult to pinpoint the central core of their thought or to follow some definite line of development (Lorenzo himself was perhaps the best example). The contrasts to which I have referred are not explicable, therefore, solely in the historical and literary terms so far indicated; they correspond also to a certain social and cultural situation which was both happy and flourishing and at the same time complex and full of uncertainties. Poliziano was, of course, a case apart. In exquisite Latin and Italian verse he celebrated fleeting feminine beauty in settings of classical myths and reminiscences; even in his popular poetry he had an elegance all his own. All this he produced on the margins, or, in his *sylvae,* in the midst of humanistic, philological activities of great consequence for European scholarship. If in his *Giostra* he seems to meet Pulci on common ground, it is only to depart in a totally different direction. Only in Lorenzo's Florence can the coexistence of the *Stanze* and *Morgante* be appreciated and explained. Pulci took up the tradition of the Carolingian tales, and continued it in a completely different spirit and style, using it as basic material for his own extravagant comic imagination and linguistic exuberance, in which there is something of everything from Dante to the neo-Platonists, from Florentine slang to Petrarchan phrases: not a trace of nostalgia for the age of chivalry, but a hilarious take-off of events and figures seen not as history, but as stories for entertainment. It is a curious fact that in this Florentine context no one took up the prose tradition of Boccaccio, preference going to his verse, to the *ottava rima* and themes of the *Ninfale* and *Teseida,* and the *terza rima* of *Ameto* and the *Caccia.* All these works enjoyed great popularity also outside Tuscany; but only there do we find imitation of Boccaccio's prose works, especially the *Decameron.*

So far I have tried to characterize the literary production of the area which dominates the Italian cultural scene for a great part of the fourteenth and fifteenth centuries. It is time to transfer attention to those regions which appear to produce little of note before the mid-fifteenth century, and from then on prepare to supplant the Tuscan hegemony and take over its language and literature, calling it Italian. Speaking generally, one might say that up to the end of the fifteenth century humanist culture evolved on a national plane, and that the vernacular developed more on a regional one while pursuing in different ways the leads given by the works of Dante, Petrarch and Boccaccio. From the early sixteenth century on, coinciding with the political crisis of the French wars, vernacular literature began to shed its local characteristics and moved in a national direction. It is certainly possible to identify some local characteristics in some humanist groups—Florentine civic humanism, Paduan educational ideas, Roman antiquarianism—but for the most part humanistic activity developed on a supra- or inter-regional level, dealing with general moral historical and philological matters, not simply ones of local interest. This inter-regionalism was fostered by the disposition of scholars to travel from one city to another, from one teaching-post to another, from one patron to another; and these movements increased as patronage grew and humanistic studies penetrated the universities. Latin was their universal language, valid everywhere within and outside the boundaries of Italy. On the other hand, by saying that vernacular literature was regional in the fifteenth century I am not meaning to underrate the influence from the fourteenth century onwards of Tuscan language and literature on the rest of Italy both through the diffusion of written works and the presence of Tuscans in many parts of the peninsula. In consequence a rich tradition of amorous and moral verse arose, especially in northern Italy, which imitated the themes, style and language of the great (and the lesser) Tuscan poets. But not all these versifiers succeeded like Francesco di Vannozzo (nor perhaps even strove to do so) in shedding all their regional features: whilst following the content and metrical form of the Tuscans, they stopped, as it were, half-way linguistically and wrote in a kind of northern *koine*. A similar phenomenon occurred elsewhere: if the origins of the Roman Giusto de' Conti are not apparent in his poetry, one cannot say the same about Giustinian, even though he did not write in pure Venetian; or about Boiardo, whose fine Petrarchan verse is full of Emilianisms. In lyric poetry, therefore, whether or not in Tuscan metrical forms, there was a strong Tuscan influence; but this did not preclude a certain linguistic hybridism, which persisted and grew throughout the fifteenth century down to the courtly lyric of Tebaldeo and Serafino Aquilano, around whom the key questions of imitation, of nature and art, of free expression and discipline based on tradition, were to arise. The position outside lyric poetry was no different, in other poetic genres (e.g. the chival-

ric poems of Boiardo and others) and in prose, where hybridism is more marked and complicated by a large dose of Latinisms, as in the *novelle* of two imitators of Boccaccio, Sabbadino degli Arienti and Masuccio Salernitano. The regional character of vernacular literature can, therefore, be said to be largely linguistic, with strong tendencies towards a mixed literary idiom, combining local, Tuscan and Latin elements. It is this development, particularly evident in the last decades of the quattrocento, which was to constitute the practical background to the defence in the early sixteenth century of the concept of a courtly language in opposition to Tuscan. The phenomenon is well documented from early in the fifteenth century in northern Italy and Emilia; it appears later, but is certainly present in the south, in Naples in the circles of Pontano's 'academy'—the first redaction of Sannazzaro's *Arcadia* reflects very clearly the literary-linguistic situation of the turn of the century. (pp. 211-16)

By this time Italy had been involved in war for several years and the most flourishing branch of modern poetry had been broken with the deaths of Lorenzo and Poliziano. After 1494 Florence's position in literature as in politics changed dramatically. The cultural scene came to be dominated instead by the northern courts, Rome and Naples. Italian literature was all courtly lyric, eclogues, mythological poems and chivalric romances (though, as Dionisotti has shown, there were some indications of a sense of disquiet at the contrast between this literature of fantasy and the often bloody reality of war). Two major factors, therefore, helped to throw into relief the critical situation of vernacular literature: the awareness of the distance between contemporary poetry and the great poetry of the past both vernacular and classical, and a sense of the widening abyss between literature and life. In these circumstances the problem arose acutely of how to create a serious and disciplined vernacular literature comparable with that of the ancients. The problem was not altogether new. Dante had posed and resolved it in his own way; Alberti consciously faced it for vernacular prose. But with very few exceptions fifteenth-century literature offers no examples of like determination. In consequence the writer who was to attempt to solve it in the early sixteenth century, and look back in search of models, virtually ignored the entire quattrocento. Before solving it in theory with his *Prose della volgar lingua* (1525), Bembo faced it in practice with *Gli Asolani* (1505), showing how, on the subject of the nature of love, it was possible to achieve gravity and gracefulness of expression in prose and verse by following the language and style of Dante, Petrarch, Boccaccio and *stilnovo* poets. (p. 218)

Between 1494 and 1530 the political future of Italy was decided largely by foreign powers. During those same years Italy also passed through a cultural crisis, and emerged with a clearer, quasi-national linguistic and literary identity. During those years Trissino (and others, but not Bembo) began to talk of an Italian language, and the debate known as the 'questione della lingua' was launched. Whatever the precise stages of evolution of this debate between 1502 and 1530 (a subject much to the fore in recent studies), we know enough to appreciate its fundamental importance for understanding the literature of the time. While the writers and supporters of an Italian 'courtly' language offered some resistance to Bembo's theories, others began to accept them and to conform more and more to the older Tuscan norm. Even Castiglione turned out to be more of a Tuscan writer in this sense than his own declarations and the discussions of *Il Cortegiano* suggest. Other authors, who had no direct part in the debate, like Sannazzaro and Ariosto, corrected their works, removing Latinisms and regionalisms. Grammar and orthography, hardly considered in the fifteenth century, became the subject of discussions and publications. Florentines and other Tuscans reacted strongly against what seemed to them the robbery of their language and their literary patrimony, and the disputes continued throughout the century, culminating in the writings and Dictionary of the Florentine Academy and the Crusca. But this is another story, or rather another chapter of the same story, written in different historical circumstances from those of the earlier sixteenth century, with which we are at present concerned. It is true that the great literary works of this period are not explicable only in the terms of the problems outlined above. But the *Arcadia* would not be the pastiche it is without the prevailing eclecticism and Tuscan linguistic influence of those years, nor would *Il Cortegiano* have dealt with questions of society, language and love, if these had not been related themes in the forefront of everyone's minds at that time (there is a good dose of neo-Platonism in Bembo's aesthetic-linguistic theory as well as in the *Asolani*). It is perhaps more difficult to explain why Ariosto should take up, at a time when the genre was in decline, the threads of Boiardo's *Innamorato* which had been broken off at the first clash of real arms in 1494. As Dionisotti has shown, Ariosto must have made his decision in full awareness of the situation and of his purpose to create something quite new. The fact that he used the chivalric legends as fable rather than as history, enriching them with classical elements, does not mean that he was taking refuge in a dream-world purely for artistic satisfaction. It cannot be called escapist literature, unless one is prepared to ignore the very serious human and moral substance within and behind the tales of the paladins. The intricate, interwoven adventures, brilliantly handled and elegantly expressed, illustrate the constant mutability of fortune and emotions, the joys and tragedies of human life. Classical in its spirit and equilibrium of form, *Orlando Furioso* is the finest expression of the new vernacular humanism. (pp. 219-20)

In the first thirty years of the sixteenth century the main cultural focus is in northern Italy, and literature and language, from local and provincial, move towards becoming national and Italian. Florence was not wholly outside or indifferent to these developments, though more out of defensive reaction than positive initiative. Machiavelli was certainly an exception in his own field of history and political thought. But as a writer he was clearly tied to the habits of the late fifteenth century, expressing himself vigorously in modern Florentine larded with Latinisms of vocabulary and syntax. He stood, at least in practice, outside the contemporary question of an Italian language. In his *The Prince* and *Discourses,* however, he went beyond any local limits to embrace the problems of Italy, basing his reflections on continual comparison of ancient and modern times: he was a humanist, therefore, in spirit if not in form. Among his literary works his comedies, partly but not entirely explicable in terms of the new genre begun shortly before by Ariosto, stand out well above the rest, especially the incomparable *Mandragola*. In comparison his poems seem to belong more to the history of his political thought than to the history of literature. As a literary figure Machiavelli appears an exception even in relation to his immediate Florentine background, being more provincial in a certain sense than some of his friends of the *Orti,* who aspired like Trissino to a more Italian literature. They were difficult years in every respect for Florence. In those who remained there, like Machiavelli, it is not surprising to find oscillations

between optimism and pessimism as the city's fortunes changed. When the Republic fell in 1530, it marked the beginning of an entirely different era in politics and culture. Guicciardini, who had lived through it all on both the Florentine and Italian levels, had no optimism, no faith either in men or the lessons of history. His great *Storia d'Italia* might be said to represent the consciousness and the epitaph of a national reality which did not materialize.

In the circumstances Italy had to be content with her cultural pre-eminence in a Europe of which war had made her too well aware. In the field of scholarship this pre-eminence rested on the achievements of distinguished humanists of the late quattrocento—Poliziano, Pico, Barbaro, Pontano—and on the editorial activities of men like Aldo Manuzio (as well as, of course, the entire Italian tradition of published texts and commentaries of Latin and Greek authors); but it began to decline around the mid-sixteenth century as that older generation was not replaced, and eminent thinkers and philologists emerged in other countries. The great tradition of Italian humanists came to an end with Vettori. In literature it had given its best with the Latin poetry of Poliziano, Sannazzaro, Pontano, Mantovano (and finally Vida). After them, despite attempts at revival, Latin came to be regarded more and more as a dead language, for the schoolroom not for real life. From the fourth decade of the sixteenth century on, and outside the classroom, another activity of great importance began—the divulgation of ancient and also modern works through Italian translations in prose and verse, significant for the general enrichment of culture and the education of the vernacular in broader fields of expression. The object and the effect of Bembo's *Asolani* and *Prose* had been to direct Italians towards the making of a serious vernacular literature based on the best writers of the trecento (which in practice meant Petrarch for poetry and Boccaccio for prose). Generally speaking, this lesson was accepted. But it was particularly valid for certain kinds of composition, outside which writers managed as best they would and could by following the examples of modern Tuscan or Tuscanizing authors. It is not true, therefore, to say that Bembo put the Italian language into a fourteenth-century straitjacket; nor is it correct to believe, as critics did until not long ago, that his imitation of Petrarch dictated to the cinquecento a single type of slavish Petrarchism which can be dismissed en bloc for its servility and insincerity. In its best exponents the sixteenth-century lyric shows how rich and flexible such imitation could be. On the other hand, Bembo had ruled Dante out of court because he had tried to be more than a poet (with consequent grave damage to his language and style); and since no one in the cinquecento seemed to have had similar ambitions, Dante withdrew among his fellow Florentines who zealously defended him and illustrated his work in their academy speeches. Echoes and explicit imitation of Dante can be found in Michelangelo, Ariosto and others, but they became rarer as the century advanced. Alongside Petrarch, modern poets were favoured as models—Bembo, Sannazzaro, Della Casa. In prose Boccaccio was the major model for writers of love treatises, and naturally for the newly flourishing genre of the *novella* (Lasca, Firenzuola, Bandello, Giraldi); but in general Boccaccio cannot be said to dominate as model of language and style (as Petrarch did for poetry) the far wider, more varied and less disciplined field of prose. In their *Vocabolario* the Crusca academicians, guardians of the language of the trecento (the 'buon secolo') and defenders of good modern Tuscan, arrived at the compromise of reinforcing the former with the latter, and thereby ratified a process which was in effect well under way—to the great satisfaction of the Tuscans, for whom the dictionary was the culmination of a long grandducal campaign to affirm the linguistic predominance of Tuscany. But by that time the door was already wide open. Writers of every part of Italy no longer thought of composing in a regional or hybrid language, or they did so on purpose, and conscious dialect literature was born.

While Italy had been engaged in war in the first thirty years of the sixteenth century, the Reformation had begun in Germany and elsewhere. The measures taken by the Church to suppress its manifestations in Italy were at first moderate, but became more severe after 1540. After the Council of Trent the Counter-Reformation made itself felt through censorship and the prohibition of books. The intellectual climate changed and moved towards religious and moral conformity. The confidence in man and nature which had characterized and inspired writers and men of action in the fifteenth and early sixteenth centuries dwindled away. Those who felt oppressed or persecuted fled to Venice or abroad. Doubts and suspicions invaded individuals and society at large. While the abbé Bandello could still decline responsibility for the moral content of his *novelle* (ed. 1554), only a few years later Giraldi presented his collection of stories, *Hecatommithi* (1565), with the precise intention of 'condemning vice, teaching morals and good conduct, honouring the papal authority and the dignity of the Roman Church'. In 1573 Boccaccio's *Decameron* was published in the version corrected by a Florentine committee, purged in its content and language, and partly rewritten to satisfy the ecclesiastical authorities. This change in climate had already begun to produce a rich tradition of sacred verse, in which everyone joined—even the author of the scurrilous *Ragionamenti*, Pietro Aretino, in whom one can observe in extreme form the typical contrasts of the mid-sixteenth century between aspirations to liberty (or even to licence) and the desire to submit or conform to the dictates of religious conscience and authority.

The last great poet of the sixteenth century, Torquato Tasso, responded to these developments in his own particular way, but not at the outset of his literary career. His early romance *Rinaldo* and his pastoral fable *Aminta* seem far from being preoccupied with great moral or spiritual concerns. In the chorus to *Aminta* he could celebrate Nature and Love according to the formula: 's'ei piace, ei lice' ('if it gives pleasure, it is permissible'), while many of his early amorous and occasional lyrics are free from any spiritual anxiety. In his *Gerusalemme Liberata,* on the other hand, we can observe a more conscious sensuality and a characteristic, often sombre awareness of the limitations imposed on human desires and ambitions by external and internal forces, which make life mysterious, unpredictable and tragic. When it appeared without his consent, Tasso's personal crisis had already begun, and from this there followed his religious preoccupations, the defence of his poem against the critics and its eventual rewriting under the new title, *Gerusalemme Conquistata,* which changed its character and tone in so many ways. Even his earlier lyrics were then submitted to revision, in general for the worse. As an exquisite poet who used Italian with great freedom and boldness, and at the same time a tormented, unhappy soul, he ended up as a victim of his own conscience and of the times in which he lived. Their spirit was summed up by the reverse of Tasso's formula in *Aminta,* as it appears in Guarino's pastoral drama *Il pastor fido:* 's'ei lice, ei piace' ('if it is permissible, it gives pleasure'). The parabola of Tasso's

life and literary production seems to reflect exactly the cultural development of the sixteenth century. (pp. 221-24)

Cecil Grayson, "The Renaissance and the History of Literature," in The Renaissance: Essays in Interpretation by André Chastel and others, Methuen, 1982, pp. 201-26.

J. C. L. SIMONDE DE SISMONDI

[*In the following excerpt, Sismondi appraises numerous writers in surveying Italian humanist literature.*]

In tracing the history of the literature of Italy, it is important to distinguish the most remarkable of that body of orators, scholars, and poets, who flourished in the sixteenth century, and, more particularly, during the pontificate of Leo. X.; and who gave to Europe an impulse in letters, the influence of which is felt to the present day.

The study of the ancients, and the art of poetry, had been universally encouraged during the fifteenth century. All the free cities, as well as the sovereigns of Italy, endeavoured to assume to themselves the glory of extending their protection to literature. Pensions, honours, and confidential employs, were bestowed on men who had devoted themselves to the study of antiquity, and who best knew how to expound and to contribute to the restoration of its treasures. The chiefs of the republic of Florence, the Dukes of Milan, of Ferrara, and of Mantua, the Kings of Naples, and the Popes, were not merely friends of science. Having themselves received classical educations, they were, almost all, better acquainted with the ancient languages, with the rules of Greek and Latin poetry, and with all relating to antiquity, than the greater part of our scholars of the present day. This universal patronage of letters was not, however, of lasting duration. The rulers of states even pursued, in the sixteenth century, a contrary course; but it was not sufficient to arrest the impression which had been made, and to check the impulse already given.

The first persecution, which letters experienced in Italy, dates from the middle of the fifteenth century. It was short-lived, but violent, and has left melancholy traces in the history of literature. The city of Rome was desirous, after the examples of other capitals, of founding an academy, consecrated to letters and to the study of antiquity. The learned popes, who had been elevated to the chair of St. Peter, in the fifteenth century, had beheld with satisfaction, and encouraged this literary zeal. A young man, an illegitimate son of the illustrious house of San Severino, but who, instead of assuming his family appellation, embraced the Roman name of Julius Pomponius Lætus, after having finished his studies under Lorenzo Valla, succeeded him, in 1457, in the chair of Roman eloquence. He assembled around him, at Rome, all those who possessed that passion for literature and for ancient philosophy, by which the age was characterized. Almost all were young men; and, in their enthusiasm for antiquity, they gave themselves Greek and Latin names, in imitation of their leaders. In their meetings, it is said, they declared their predilection for the manners, the laws, the philosophy, and even the religion of antiquity, in opposition to those of their own age. Paul II. who was then Pope, was not, like many of his predecessors, indebted to a love of letters for his elevation to the pontificate. Suspicious, jealous, and cruel, he soon became alarmed at the spirit of research and enquiry which marked the new philosophers. He felt how greatly the rapid progress of knowledge might contribute to shake the authority of the

Detail of Benozzo Gozzoli's 1459 Procession of the Magi.

Church, and he viewed the devotion of these scholars to antiquity, as a general conspiracy against the state and the holy faith. The academy, of which Pomponius Lætus was the chief, seemed particularly to merit his attention. In the midst of the Carnival, in 1468, whilst the people of Rome were occupied with the festival, he arrested all the members of the academy who were then to be found in the capital. Pomponius Lætus alone was absent. He had retired to Venice, the year after the elevation of Paul II. to the pontificate, and had resided there three years; but, as he held a correspondence with the academicians at Rome, the Pope beheld in him the chief of the conspiracy, and procured his apprehension, through the favour of the Venetian Senate. The academicians were then imprisoned and consigned to the most cruel tortures. (pp. 404-05)

The persecution of Paul II. was a direct attack upon literature. But the public calamities which succeeded, overwhelmed all Italy, and reached every class of society, at the same moment. They commenced in the year 1494, with the invasion of Italy by Charles VIII. The sacking of cities, the rout of armies, and the misfortunes and death of a great number of distinguished men; evils, always accompanying the scourge of war; were not the only fatal consequences of this event. It was a death-blow to the independence of Italy; and, from that period, the Spaniards and the Germans disputed the possession of her provinces. After a series of ruinous wars and numberless calamities, fortune declared herself in favour of Charles V. and his son. The Milanese and the kingdom of Naples remained under the sovereignty of the house of Austria; and all the other states, which yet preserved any independence, trembled at the Austrian power, and dared to refuse nothing to the wishes of the Imperial ministers. All feeling of national pride was destroyed. A sovereign prince could not afford an asylum, in his own states, to any of his unfortu-

nate subjects, whom a viceroy might choose to denounce. The entire face of Italy was changed. Instead of princes, the friends of arts and letters, who had long reigned in Milan and Naples, a Spanish governor, distrustful and cruel, now ruled by the aid of spies and informers. The Gonzagas of Mantua plunged into pleasures and vice, to forget the dangers of their situation. Alfonso II., at Modena and Ferrara, attempted, by a vain ostentation, to maintain the appearance of that power which he had lost. In place of the republic of Florence, the Athens of the middle ages, the nurse of arts and sciences, and in the place of the early Medici, the enlightened restorers of philosophy and letters, three tyrants, in the sixteenth century, succeeded each other in Tuscany: the ferocious and voluptuous Alexander; Cosmo I., founder of the second house of Medici, who rivalled his model and contemporary, Philip II., in profound dissimulation and in cruelty; and Francis I., his son, who, by his savage suspicion, carried to its height the oppression of his states. Rome also, which, at the commencement of the century, had possessed, in Leo X., a magnanimous pontiff, a friend of letters, and a generous protector of the fine arts and of poetry, was now become jealous of the progress of the Reformation, and only occupied herself in resisting the dawning powers of the human intellect. Under the pontificates of Paul IV., Pius IV., and Pius V., (1555-1572), who were elevated by the interest of the Inquisition, the persecution against letters and the academies was renewed, in a systematic and unrelenting manner.

Such, notwithstanding, had been the excitement of the human mind in the preceding century, and so thickly were the germs of literature scattered from one end of Italy to the other, by an universal emulation, that no other country can be said to have raised itself to a higher pitch of literary glory. Among the numbers of men who had devoted themselves to letters, Italy produced, at this glorious epoch, at least thirty poets, whom their contemporaries placed on a level with the first names of antiquity, and whose fame, it was thought, would be commensurate with the existence of the world. But even the names of these illustrious men begin to be forgotten; and their works, buried in the libraries of the learned, are, now, seldom read.

The circumstance of their equality in merit, has, doubtless, been an obstacle to the duration of their reputation. Fame does not possess a strong memory. For a long flight, she relieves herself from all unnecessary incumbrances. She rejects, on her departure, and in her course, many who thought themselves accepted by her, and she comes down to late ages, with the lightest possible burthen. Unable to choose between Bembo, Sadoleti, Sanazzaro, Bernardo Accolti, and so many others, she relinquishes them all. Many other names will also escape her; and we perceive the blindness of our presumption, when we compare the momentary reputations of our own day with the glory of the great men of antiquity. The latter, we behold conspicuous through a succession of ages, like the loftiest summits of the Alps, which, the farther we recede from them, appear to rise the higher.

But what most contributed to injure the fame of the illustrious men of the sixteenth century, was the unbounded respect which they professed for antiquity, and the pedantic erudition which stifled their genius. Their custom, also, of writing always after models, which were not in harmony with their manners, their characters, and their political and religious opinions; and their efforts to revive the languages in which the great works which they admired were composed, materially tended to this result. It has long been said, that he who only translates will never be translated; and he who imitates, renounces at the same time the hope of being imitated. Still, the noble efforts of these studious men in the cause of letters, the recollections of their past glory, and the celebrity which yet attaches to them, merit an enquiry, on our part, into the history of their most distinguished scholars. (pp. 406-08)

The most just title to fame possessed by [Gian-Giorgio] Trissino, is founded on his *Sofonisba,* which may be considered as the first regular tragedy since the revival of letters; and which we may, with still greater justice, regard as the last of the tragedies of antiquity, so exactly is it founded on the principles of the Grecian dramas, and, above all, on those of Euripides. He wants, it is true, the genius which inspired the creators of the drama at Athens, and a more sustained dignity in the character of the principal personages; but, to a scrupulous imitation of the ancients, Trissino had the art of uniting a pathetic feeling, and he succeeded in moving his audience to tears. (p. 409)

It would, doubtless, be easy to multiply criticisms on this piece, written, as it was, in the infancy of the dramatic art, and without a knowledge of stage effect. It is unnecessary to animadvert either on the narrative, in which Sophonisba recounts to her sister the history of Carthage, from the reign of Dido to the second Punic war; on the improbability of a chorus of female singers always occupying the stage, even when the soldiers of the enemy enter the city as conquerors; on the entire want of interest in the characters of Syphax, Lælius, Cato, and Scipio himself; on the weakness of Sophonisba, who, on the day that her husband is made prisoner, marries her enemy; or, in short, on the contemptible part assigned to Massinissa. It is easy to any one to urge these defects, and there is no fear of their being imitated. But it is to be regretted that the modern stage has not profited more by the Greek model which Trissino has given. His chorus, above all, is in the true spirit and character of antiquity. With the ancients, their whole lives were public; their heroes lived in the midst of their fellow citizens, and their princesses amongst their women. The chorus, the friends and comforters of the unhappy, transport us to the ancient times and ancient manners. We cannot, and ought not to introduce them into pieces, of which the subject is modern; but, in excluding them from those dramas which are founded on the history and mythology of the ancients, and substituting in their stead, the presence of modern confidants, we ascribe to the Greeks the customs and language of our own age and of our own courts.

The poetry of Trissino is equally deserving of praise. He had remarked that the Greeks, in their best works, did not confine tragedy to the style of a dignified conversation; but lavished on it the richness of their numerous metres, applying them to the various situations in which their actors were placed; sometimes confining them to iambics, which contributed only to a somewhat loftier expression; and sometimes raising them to the most harmonious lyric strophes. He saw also that they proportioned the flight of their imagination to the metre which they employed; speaking, by turns, as orators or poets, and rising, in their lyric strophes, to the boldest images. Trissino alone, among their modern imitators, has preserved this variety. The usual language of his heroes is in *versi sciolti,* blank verse: but, according to the passions which he wishes to express, he soars to the most varied forms of the ode, or *canzone,* and by this more poetical language he proves that the pleasure of the drama consists not wholly in the imitation of nature, but also in the ideal beauty of that poetic world which the author substitutes for it. (pp. 410-12)

A friend of Trissino, Giovanni Rucellai, laboured with not less zeal, and often with more taste, to render the modern Italian poetry entirely classical, and to introduce, into every class of it, a pure imitation of the ancients. . . .

His most celebrated production is a didactic poem on Bees, of about fifteen hundred lines, which receives a particular interest from the real fondness which Rucellai seems to have entertained for these creatures. There is something so sincere in his respect for their virgin purity, and in his admiration of the order of their government, that he inspires us with real interest for them. All his descriptions are full of life and truth. (p. 415)

But it was as a tragic poet that Rucellai attempted to tread in the footsteps of his friend Trissino, although in this respect he appears to be much inferior to him. Two dramas of Rucellai remain, written in blank verse, with a chorus, and as much resembling the Grecian pieces in their distribution, as a learned Italian could make them, at an epoch when the study of antiquity was the first of sciences. One of these is entitled *Rosmonda,* and the other, *Orestes. Rosmonda,* the wife of Alboin, the first king of the Lombards, who, to avenge her father, destroyed her husband, was a new subject for the stage. Rucellai altered historical facts sufficiently happily, in order to connect events which a long space of time had in reality separated; to unite more intimately causes and effects; and to describe the former relation of his characters to each other. But *Rosmonda* is only the sketch of a tragedy. The situation is not marked by any developement; time is not given for the exhibition of the passions; nor are they at all communicated to the spectators. Conversations and long dialogues usurp the place which ought to be reserved for action; and the atrocity of the characters and events, which are rather related than shewn, forbids all sympathy. The other tragedy of Rucellai is an imitation of Euripides, and is called *Orestes,* although the subject is that known under the name of Iphigenia in Tauris. But the example of the Greek poet has not availed Rucellai. His piece is deficient in interest, in probability, and, above all, in action. The Italian dramatists of the sixteenth century, seem to have aimed at copying the defects rather than the beauties of the Greeks. If there chance to be, in the dramas of the Greeks, any unskilful exposition, or any recital of overwhelming tediousness, they never fail to take it for their model. It would almost appear to have been their intention that Sophocles and Euripides should be received with hisses; and they seem to wait, at the conclusion of the piece, to inform us that the part which has so wearied us is from the ancients. Euripides had the fault of multiplying moral precepts, and philosophical dissertations; but one of his maxims is only like the text to a commentary in Rucellai. (pp. 417-18)

The early Italian drama comprises a considerable number of pieces. But the pedantry which gave them birth, deprived them, from their cradle, of all originality, and all real feeling. The action and the representation, of which the dramatic poet should never for an instant lose sight, are constantly neglected; and philosophy and erudition usurp the place of the emotion necessary to the scene. (p. 418)

The inferiority of the Italians to the Spaniards, in dramatic invention, is remarkable; and particularly at the epoch of their greatest literary glory. These pretended restorers of the theatre conformed, it is true, to all the precepts of Aristotle, from the time of the sixteenth century, and to the rules of classical poetry, even before their authority was proclaimed. But this avails little when they are wanting in life and interest. We cannot read these tragedies without insufferable fatigue; and it is difficult to form an idea of the patience of the spectators, condemned to listen to these long declamations and tedious dialogues, usurping the place of the action, which ought to be brought before their eyes. The Spanish comedies, on the contrary, although extravagant in their plots, and irregular in their execution, always excite our attention, curiosity, and interest. It is with regret that we suspend the perusal of them in the closet, and they are not less adapted for the stage, where the dramatic interest is throughout maintained, and the spectator is always interested in the events passing before him.

Even the names of the dramatic pieces of Italy, in the sixteenth century, are scarcely preserved in the records of literature. But posterity seems to have paid a greater respect to the memory of some of the lyric and pastoral poets. Many of these have retained great celebrity, even after their works have ceased to be read. Such, amongst others, was the case with Giacomo Sanazzaro. . . . He was early remarkable for his proficiency in Greek and Roman literature; but his love for a lady of the name of Carmosina Bonifacia, the rest of whose history is wholly unknown, engaged him to write in Italian. He celebrated this lady in his *Arcadia,* and in his sonnets; and, when death deprived him of her, he renounced the Italian muses for Latin composition. From that time, he was devoted to religious observances, which had before held little place in his thoughts. (pp. 419-20)

The *Arcadia* of Sanazzaro, on which his reputation principally depends, was begun by him in his early youth, and published in 1504, when he was forty-six years of age. A species of romantic pastoral, in prose and without action, serves to connect twelve romantic and pastoral scenes, and twelve eclogues of shepherds in Arcadia. Each part commences with a short recital in elegant prose, and ends with an eclogue in verse. In the seventh, Sanazzaro himself appears in Arcadia; he recounts the exploits of his family, the honours they obtained at Naples, and how love had driven him into exile. Thus, the ancient Arcadia is, to Sanazzaro, nothing more than the poetical world of his own age. He awakes, in the twelfth eclogue, as from a dream. The plan of this piece may be subject to criticism, but the execution is elegant. Sanazzaro, inspired by a sentiment of tender passion, found, in his own mind, that reverie of enthusiasm that belongs to pastoral poetry. The sentiments, as in all idyls, are sometimes trite and affected, though sometimes, also, breathing warmth and nature. The thoughts, the images, and the language, are always poetical, except that he has too frequently introduced Latin words, which were not then naturalized into the Tuscan dialect. The stanzas, with which each eclogue terminates, are generally under the lyric form of *canzoni.* (pp. 420-21)

A new description of poetry arose in Italy, under Francesco Berni, which has retained the name of the inventor. The Italians always attach the appellation of *bernesque* to that light and elegant mockery, of which he set the example, and which pervades all his writings. The gaiety with which he recounts serious events, without rendering them vulgar, is not confounded by his countrymen with the burlesque, to which it is so nearly allied. It is, above all, in the *Orlando Innamorato* of the Count Boiardo, remodelled by Berni in a free and lively

style, that we perceive the fulness of his genius. His other works, imbued, perhaps, with more comic wit, trespass too frequently on the bounds of propriety. (pp. 423-24)

Berni had diligently studied the ancients, and wrote himself elegant Latin verse. He had purified his taste, and accustomed himself to correction. His style possesses so much nature and comic truth, that we can easily imagine the enthusiasm with which it is to this day adopted as a model. But, under his hand, every thing was transformed into ridicule. His satire was almost always personal; and when he wished to excite laughter, he was not to be restrained by any respect for morals or for decency. His *Orlando Innamorato* is ranked, by the Italians, among their classical poems. Berni, even more than Ariosto, treats chivalry with a degree of mockery. He has not, indeed, travestied the tale of Boiardo. It is the same tale sincerely narrated, but by a man who cannot resist indulging in laughter at the absurd suggestions of his own genius. The versification is carefully formed; wit is thrown out with a lavish hand; and the gaiety is more sportive than that of Ariosto; but the two poems will not bear a comparison in respect to imagination, colouring, richness, and real poetry. The other works of Berni are satirical sonnets, and *Capitoli,* in *terza rima,* among which the eulogy on the Plague, and that on Aristotle, are conspicuous. They were prohibited, and, indeed, not without very good reason.

Few men were more admired and obtained a greater share of fame, in the sixteenth century, than Pietro Bembo. . . . He was the admiration of his own age, which placed him in the first rank of classic authors. His fame, however, has since materially declined. Bembo, who had professedly studied the Latin and the Tuscan languages, and composed, in both, with the utmost purity and elegance, was, all his life, too exclusively occupied with words to support the brilliancy of his fame, after the Latin was no longer cultivated with ardour, and custom had introduced many alterations in the Tuscan. The style of Bembo, which was highly extolled in his lifetime, appears, at the present day, affected and greatly laboured. We are aware of his imitations in every line, and seek in vain for an expression of genuine sentiment. Neither is he distinguished by depth of thought, or by vivacity of imagination. He has aspired to rank himself with Cicero in Latin prose, and with Petrarch and Boccaccio in Italian poetry and prose; but, however great the resemblance may be, we instinctively distinguish the original from the copy, and the voluminous writings of Bembo now find few readers. His History of Venice, in twelve books, his letters, and his dialogues, in the Italian language, are among the best of his prose works. His *Canzoniere* may bear a comparison with that of Petrarch. His conversations on love, which he entitled *Asolani,* and which are interspersed with poetry, approach to the style of the tales of Boccaccio. The singular purity of style, on which he prides himself, and which his contemporaries acknowledged, has not, on all occasions, preserved him from *concetti* and affectation. Occasionally, however, we find in him not only imagination, but real sensibility. His Latin poems are in high esteem, and he was sufficiently master of the modern tongues to have also attempted Castilian verse.

The same age gave the name of *Unico* to Bernardo Accolti, of Arezzo, born before 1466, and who died after the year 1534. Whenever this celebrated poet announced his intention of reciting his verses, the shops were shut up, and the people flocked in crowds to hear him. He was surrounded by prelates of the first eminence; a body of Swiss troops accompanied him; and the court was lighted by torches. But, as Mr. Roscoe has justly remarked, there wanted but one circumstance to crown his glory—that his works had perished with himself. Their style is hard and poor; his images are forced, and his taste is perverted by affectation. He has left us a comedy, *La Virginia;* some octaves and *terza rima;* some lyric poetry; and some *strambotti,* or epigrams.

It is not by the side of these evanescent poets that we must rank the illustrious secretary of the Florentine republic, the great Nicolo Machiavelli, whose name is in no danger of being buried in oblivion. This celebrity is his due, as a man of profound thought, and as the most eloquent historian, and most skilful politician that Italy has produced. But a distinction less enviable, has attached his name to the infamous principles which he developed, though probably with good intentions, in his treatise, entitled *Il Principe;* and his name is, at the present day, allied to every thing false and perfidious in politics. (pp. 426-29)

[In *Il Principe,* it is not] probable that he only proposed to himself, to expose to the people the maxims of tyranny, in order to render them odious; for an universal experience had, at that time, made them known throughout all Italy, and that diabolical policy, which Machiavelli reduced to a system, was, in the sixteenth century, that of all the states. There is, in his manner of treating the subject, a general feeling of bitterness against mankind, and a contempt of the human race, which induces him to address it in language adapted to its despicable and depraved condition. He applies himself to the interests, and selfish calculations of mankind, since they do not deserve an appeal to their enthusiasm and moral sense. He establishes principles in theory, which he knows his readers will reduce to practice; and he exhibits the play of the human passions with an energy and clearness which require no ornament.

The *Principe* of Machiavelli is the best known of his political works, but it is neither the most profound, nor the most considerable. His three books of discourses on the first Decade of Livy, in which he investigates the first causes of the power of the Romans, and the obstacles which have impeded other nations in a similar career, discover an extensive knowledge, a great perspicacity in judging of men, and a powerful talent of mind in abstracting and generalizing ideas. The most profound political observations, which have been written since this epoch, in any language, have been derived from these early meditations of Machiavelli. As in this work he goes much more directly to his object, and as he did not write either for a tyrant or for a free people, but for every honest mind which loves to reflect on the destinies of nations, this book is, in consequence, more moral in principle, though containing lessons not less profound; nor has it incurred, on the part of the church or of society, the same anathema which some time after the death of Machiavelli was pronounced against his treatise of the *Principe.*

It was also at this period of his life that Machiavelli wrote his History of Florence, dedicated to Pope Clement VII., and in which he instructed the Italians in the art of uniting the eloquence of history with depth of reflection. He has attached himself, much less than his predecessors in the same line, to the narration of military events. But his work, as a history of popular passions and tumults, is a masterpiece, and Machiavelli has completed, by this noble example of his theories, his analysis of the human heart. (pp. 430-31)

Machiavelli might have rendered himself illustrious as a comic writer, if he had not preferred political fame. He has left three comedies, which, by the novelty of the plot, by the strength and vivacity of the dialogues, and by their admirable delineation of character, are far superior to all that Italy had then, or has, perhaps, since produced. We feel sensible, in perusing them, of the talent of the master who conceived them, of the elevation from which their author judges the beings whom he has depicted with so much truth, and of his profound contempt for all the duplicity and hypocrisy which he so faithfully exposes. Two monks in particular, a brother Timoteo, who appears in the two first, and a brother Alberico, protagonist of the third, are represented with a vivacity and accuracy which have left nothing to the invention of the author of the *Tartufe.* It is to be regretted, that public manners authorized, at that time, such an extreme license in theatrical representations, that it is impossible to give even an analysis of these comedies. His tale of *Belfagor,* or the devil, who takes refuge in hell to avoid a scold, has been translated into all languages, and remodelled in French by La Fontaine. His poems are more remarkable for vigour of thought, than for harmony of style, or grace of expression. Some are composed of historical facts versified, and others, of satirical or burlesque fragments. But the pleasantries of the author are generally mingled with gall, and when he indulges his humour, it is always in derision of the human race. It was thus that he wrote the Carnival Songs, to be recited by different troops of masks; each dance having a song or an ode, appropriated to its character and to its disguise. In the streets of Florence there were successively seen, on the triumphant cars, despairing lovers, ladies, the spirits of the blest, hermits, fruit-sellers, and quacks. They were connected by a kind of dramatic action, but Machiavelli contrived that they should be preceded by a chorus of demons; and we seem to recognize the writer of the *Principe* in the morose manner in which he introduces this annual and popular feast. (pp. 431-32)

Some similitude may, perhaps, be remarked between Machiavelli and a man of this time, Pietro Aretino, whose name has acquired an infamous celebrity. Those who are not acquainted with the works of either the one or the other, regard them both with equal horror; the first, as the abettor of political crime, and the other, as having made a boast of his impiety, immorality, and profligacy. A comparison, however, cannot be admitted between them. Aretino was a man of infamous character; Machiavelli was, at the worst, only a culpable writer. . . . [Aretino] composed, during a considerably long life, (1492 to 1557) a great number of works, which are scarcely read at the present day. Some of these owed their reputation to their extreme licentiousness; others, to the caustic satire with which he attacked his powerful enemies; many, which were purchased at an extraordinary price by reigning sovereigns, are filled with the most base and degrading flatteries; and others, in no small number, are devotional pieces, which the author, an enemy to every religious faith and to all morals, wrote only because they brought him a larger sum of money. Notwithstanding this profligacy of mind and heart, Aretino received from his contemporaries the epithet of *Il Divino.* Possessed of assurance of every description, he adopted this title himself, repeated it on all occasions, and attached it to his signature as a person attaches a title to his name, or takes an addition to his arms. (pp. 433-34)

The dramatic pieces of Aretino are the only works of his which can be said to have contributed to the advancement of letters in Italy; and it must be allowed that they are sometimes singularly attractive. In spite of all the disgust which the character of the author inspires; in spite of the effrontery with which, even in these comedies, he by turns sets himself above all the laws of decency in speaking of others, and those of modesty in speaking of himself; in spite of the gross faults in the conduct, and, almost always, of the want of interest in his characters, of perspicuity in the plot, and life in the action; we still find in his comedies a genuine dramatic talent, an originality, and often a gaiety, rarely met with in the early dramatic writers of Italy. Aretino probably owed his merit in great part to the absence of all imitation. He had neither the Greek nor Latin models before his eyes; he depicted human nature merely as he saw it, with all its vices and all its deformity, in a corrupted age; and, inasmuch as, like Aristophanes, he confined himself to the manners of his own time, he bears a greater resemblance to the Athenian dramatist than they who have taken him for their immediate model. In his comedies, Aretino makes continual allusions to local circumstances; he paints undisguisedly the vices of the great as well as those of the people; and, at the same time that he mingles his satires with the lowest flattery, in order to procure for himself the protection of the great, or to remunerate them for the money he had obtained from them, he always preserves the picture of the general dissoluteness of manners, and the loose principles of the age, with singular truth and vivacity of colouring. From no other source can we obtain a more correct insight into that abandonment of all morals, honour, and virtue, which marked the sixteenth century. This age, so resplendent in literary glory, prepared at the same time the corruption of taste and of genius, of sentiment and of imagination, in destroying all that Italy had hitherto preserved of her ancient laws.

As we are compelled to pass over many illustrious authors, lest we should fatigue the reader by a barren enumeration of names, we shall conclude this list by a short notice of Teofilo Folengi, better known by the name of Merlino Coccajo. He was the inventor of the macaronic poetry, a species not less below the burlesque, than the *Bernesque* is above it. It is difficult to say whether these poems are Italian or Latin. The words and phrases are chosen from the most vulgar of the low Italian dialects; but the terminations are Latin, as is also the measure of the verse; and the wit consists in lending to a composition and to ideas already burlesque, the language and the blunders of an ignorant scholar. This ridiculous style, supported by great vivacity, but often by pleasantries of very bad taste, had a prodigious success. Merlino Coccajo had many imitators; and macaronic verses have been written, formed of Latin and French, as his partook of Latin and Italian. (pp. 435-36)

We shall not speak at length of Baldassare Castiglione, the celebrated author of the *Cortegiano,* who exhibits in his verses both grace and sensibility; of Francesca Maria Molza of Modena, whose whole life was consecrated to love and the Muses, (1487–1544), and whom many critics have placed in the first rank of the lyric poets of the age; of Giovanni Mauro, a burlesque poet, a friend and imitator of Berni; nor of Nicolo Franco, who, after having been brought up in the school of Aretino, had a furious quarrel with him, but attacked at the same time, with not less effrontery than his rival, both the government and public morals, in such a manner that Pius V., to put an effectual stop to his pasquinades, caused him to be hanged in 1569. Nor shall we pause to notice the Latin poets of this period. Sadoleti, Fracastoro, Pontano, and Vida, all of whom, by the purity of their language, by the elegance

of their taste, and often by their classic genius, have approached the authors of antiquity whom they had taken for models. The greater part of these have written poems on didactic subjects. This kind of composition appears, in fact, to suit better than any other with authors who submitted their genius to prescribed rules, and who, wishing to restore a nation and a literature which would not harmonize with their own age and manners, have in their poems studied more the form than the substance. Nor shall we further speak of several distinguished historians of this epoch, Giovio, Nardi, and Nerli; nor of a man more celebrated and universally read, Francesco Guicciardini, whose history is quoted, even at the present day, as a school of politics, and a model of judicious criticism. In works of this nature, the literary merit, that of expression, is only secondary. It is from their profoundness of thought, and their vivacity, that we assign a rank to historians; and, in order to pass an opinion on Guicciardini, we should be obliged to go beyond the bounds which we have prescribed to ourselves, on a subject already too extensive in itself. (pp. 436-37)

> *J. C. L. Simonde de Sismondi, "State of Literature in the Sixteenth Century," in his* Historical View of the Literature of the South of Europe, Vol. I, *translated by Thomas Roscoe, second edition, Henry G. Bohn, 1846, pp. 404-39.*

JACOB BURCKHARDT

[*In the following excerpt, Burckhardt treats the decline of humanism in sixteenth-century Italy.*]

After a brilliant succession of poet-scholars had, since the beginning of the fourteenth century, filled Italy and the world with the worship of antiquity, had determined the forms of education and culture, had often taken the lead in political affairs and had, to no small extent, reproduced ancient literature—at length in the sixteenth century, before their doctrines and scholarship had lost hold of the public mind, the whole class fell into deep and general disgrace. Though they still served as models to the poets, historians and orators, personally no one would consent to be reckoned of their number. To the two chief accusations against them—that of malicious self-conceit, and that of abominable profligacy—a third charge of irreligion was now loudly added by the rising powers of the Counter-reformation.

Why, it may be asked, were not these reproaches, whether true or false, heard sooner? As a matter of fact, they were heard at a very early period, but the effect they produced was insignificant, for the plain reason that men were far too dependent on the scholars for their knowledge of antiquity—that the scholars were personally the possessors and diffusers of ancient culture. But the spread of printed editions of the classics, and of large and well-arranged handbooks and dictionaries, went far to free the people from the necessity of personal intercourse with the humanists, and, as soon as they could be but partly dispensed with, the change in popular feeling became manifest. It was a change under which the good and bad suffered indiscriminately.

The first to make these charges were certainly the humanists themselves. Of all men who ever formed a class, they had the least sense of their common interests, and least respected what there was of this sense. All means were held lawful, if one of them saw a chance of supplanting another. From literary discussion they passed with astonishing suddenness to the fiercest and the most groundless vituperation. Not satisfied with refuting, they sought to annihilate an opponent. Something of this must be put to the account of their position and circumstances; . . . the age, whose loudest spokesmen they were, was borne to and fro by the passion for glory and the passion for satire. Their position, too, in practical life was one that they had continually to fight for. In such a temper they wrote and spoke and described one another. Poggio's works alone contain dirt enough to create a prejudice against the whole class—and these *Opera Poggii* were just those most often printed, on the north as well as on the south side of the Alps. We must take care not to rejoice too soon, when we meet among these men a figure which seems immaculate; on further inquiry there is always a danger of meeting with some foul charge, which, even if it is incredible, still discolours the picture. The mass of indecent Latin poems in circulation, and such things as ribaldry on the subject of one's own family, as in Pontano's dialogue *Antonius,* did the rest to discredit the class. The sixteenth century was not only familiar with all these ugly symptoms, but had also grown tired of the type of the humanist. These men had to pay both for the misdeeds they had done, and for the excess of honour which had hitherto fallen to their lot. Their evil fate willed it that the greatest poet of the nation, Ariosto, wrote of them in a tone of calm and sovereign contempt.

Of the reproaches which combined to excite so much hatred, many were only too well founded. Yet a clear and unmistakable tendency to strictness in matters of religion and morality was alive in many of the philologists, and it is a proof of small knowledge of the period, if the whole class is condemned. Yet many, and among them the loudest speakers, were guilty.

Three facts explain and perhaps diminish their guilt: the overflowing excess of fervour and fortune, when the luck was on their side; the uncertainty of the future, in which luxury or misery depended on the caprice of a patron or the malice of an enemy; and finally, the misleading influence of antiquity. This undermined their morality, without giving them its own instead; and in religious matters, since they could never think of accepting the positive belief in the old gods, it affected them only on the negative and sceptical side. Just because they conceived of antiquity dogmatically—that is, took it as the model for all thought and action—its influence was here pernicious. But that an age existed which idolized the ancient world and its products with an exclusive devotion was not the fault of individuals. It was the work of an historical providence, and all the culture of the ages which have followed, and of the ages to come, rests upon the fact that it was so, and that all the ends of life but this one were then deliberately put aside.

The career of the humanists was, as a rule, of such a kind that only the strongest characters could pass through it unscathed. The first danger came, in some cases, from the parents, who sought to turn a precocious child into a miracle of learning, with an eye to his future position in that class which then was supreme. Youthful prodigies, however, seldom rise above a certain level; or, if they do, are forced to achieve their further progress and development at the cost of the bitterest trials. For an ambitious youth, the fame and the brilliant position of the humanists were a perilous temptation; it seemed to him that he too 'through inborn pride could no longer regard the low and common things of life'. He was thus led to plunge into a life of excitement and vicissitude, in which exhausting studies, tutorships, secretaryships, professorships,

offices in princely households, mortal enmities and perils, luxury and beggary, boundless admiration and boundless contempt, followed confusedly one upon the other, and in which the most solid worth and learning were often pushed aside by superficial impudence. But the worst of all was, that the position of the humanist was almost incompatible with a fixed home, since it either made frequent changes of dwelling necessary for a livelihood, or so affected the mind of the individual that he could never be happy for long in one place. He grew tired of the people, and had no peace among the enmities which he excited, while the people themselves in their turn demanded something new. Much as this life reminds us of the Greek sophists of the Empire, as described to us by Philostratus, yet the position of the sophists was more favourable. They often had money, or could more easily do without it than the humanists, and as professional teachers of rhetoric, rather than men of learning, their life was freer and simpler. But the scholar of the Renaissance was forced to combine great learning with the power of resisting the influence of ever-changing pursuits and situations. Add to this the deadening effect of licentious excess, and—since do what he might, the worst was believed of him—a total indifference to the moral laws recognized by others. Such men can hardly be conceived to exist without an inordinate pride. They needed it, if only to keep their heads above water, and were confirmed in it by the admiration which alternated with hatred in the treatment they received from the world. They are the most striking examples and victims of an unbridled subjectivity.

The attacks and the satirical pictures began . . . at an early period. For all strongly marked individuality, for every kind of distinction, a corrective was at hand in the national taste for ridicule. And in this case the men themselves offered abundant and terrible materials which satire had but to make use of. In the fifteenth century, Battista Mantovano, in discoursing of the seven monsters, includes the humanists, with many others, under the head 'Superbia'. He describes how, fancying themselves children of Apollo, they walk along with affected solemnity and with sullen, malicious looks, now gazing at their own shadow, now brooding over the popular praise they hunted after, like cranes in search of food. But in the sixteenth century the indictment was presented in full. Besides Ariosto, their own historian Gyraldus gives evidence of this, whose treatise, written under Leo X, was probably revised about the year 1540. Warning examples from ancient and modern times of the moral disorder and the wretched existence of the scholars meet us in astonishing abundance, and along with these, accusations of the most serious nature are brought formally against them. Among these are anger, vanity, obstinacy, self-adoration, a dissolute private life, immorality of all descriptions, heresy, atheism; further, the habit of speaking without conviction, a sinister influence on government, pedantry of speech, thanklessness towards teachers, and abject flattery of the great, who first give the scholar a taste of their favours and then leave him to starve. The description is closed by a reference to the golden age, when no such thing as science existed on the earth. Of these charges, that of heresy soon became the most dangerous, and Gyraldus himself, when he afterwards republished a perfectly harmless youthful work, was compelled to take refuge beneath the mantle of Duke Ercole II of Ferrara, since men now had the upper hand who held that people had better spend their time on Christian themes than on mythological researches. He justifies himself on the ground that the latter, on the contrary, were at such a time almost the only harmless

Casino della Grotta, Mantua, designed by Giulio Romano.

branches of study, as they deal with subjects of a perfectly neutral character.

But if it is the duty of the historian to seek for evidence in which moral judgement is tempered by human sympathy, he will find no authority comparable in value to the work so often quoted of Pierio Valeriano, *On the Infelicity of the Scholar.* It was written under the gloomy impressions left by the sack of Rome, which seems to the writer, not only the direct cause of untold misery to the men of learning, but, as it were, the fulfilment of an evil destiny which had long pursued them. Pierio is here led by a simple and, on the whole, just feeling. He does not introduce a special power, which plagued the men of genius on account of their genius, but he states facts, in which an unlucky chance often wears the aspect of fatality. Not wishing to write a tragedy or to refer events to the conflict of higher powers, he is content to lay before us the scenes of everyday life. We are introduced to men who, in times of trouble, lose first their incomes and then their places; to others who, in trying to get two appointments, miss both; to unsociable misers who carry about their money sewn into their clothes, and die mad when they are robbed of it; to others, who accept well-paid offices, and then sicken with a melancholy longing for their lost freedom. We read how some died young of a plague or fever, and how the writings which had cost them so much toil were burnt with their bed and clothes; how others lived in terror of the murderous threats of their colleagues; how one was slain by a covetous servant, and another caught by highwaymen on a journey,

and left to pine in a dungeon, because unable to pay his ransom. Many died of unspoken grief for the insults they received and the prizes of which they were defrauded. We are told how a Venetian died because of the death of his son, a youthful prodigy; and how mother and brothers followed, as if the lost child drew them all after him. Many, especially Florentines, ended their lives by suicide; others through the secret justice of a tyrant. Who, after all, is happy?—and by what means? By blunting all feeling for such misery? One of the speakers in the dialogue in which Pierio clothed his argument, can give an answer to these questions—the illustrious Gasparo Contarini, at the mention of whose name we turn with the expectation to hear at least something of the truest and deepest which was then thought on such matters. As a type of the happy scholar, he mentions Fra Urbano Valeriano of Belluno, who was for years a teacher of Greek at Venice, who visited Greece and the East, and towards the close of his life travelled, now through this country, now through that, without ever mounting a horse; who never had a penny of his own, rejected all honours and distinctions, and after a gay old age, died in his eighty-fourth year, without, if we except a fall from a ladder, having ever known an hour of sickness. And what was the difference between such a man and the humanists? The latter had more free will, more subjectivity, than they could turn to purposes of happiness. The mendicant friar, who had lived from his boyhood in the monastery, and never eaten or slept except by rule, ceased to feel the compulsion under which he lived. Through the power of this habit he led, amid all outward hardships, a life of inward peace, by which he impressed his hearers far more than by his teaching. Looking at him, they could believe that it depends on ourselves whether we bear up against misfortune or surrender to it. 'Amid want and toil he was happy, because he willed to be so, because he had contracted no evil habits, was not capricious, inconstant, immoderate; but was always contented with little or nothing.' If we heard Contarini himself, religious motives would no doubt play a part in the argument— but the practical philosopher in sandals speaks plainly enough. An allied character, but placed in other circumstances, is that of Fabio Calvi of Ravenna, the commentator of Hippocrates. He lived to a great age in Rome, eating only pulse 'like the Pythagoreans', and dwelt in a hovel little better than the tub of Diogenes. Of the pension which Pope Leo gave him, he spent enough to keep body and soul together, and gave the rest away. He was not a healthy man, like Fra Urbano, nor is it likely that, like him, he died with a smile on his lips. At the age of ninety, in the sack of Rome, he was dragged away by the Spaniards, who hoped for a ransom, and died of hunger in a hospital. But his name has passed into the kingdom of the immortals, for Raphael loved the old man like a father, and honoured him as a teacher, and came to him for advice in all things. Perhaps they discoursed chiefly of the projected restoration of ancient Rome, perhaps of still higher matters. Who can tell what a share Fabio may have had in the conception of the School of Athens, and in other great works of the master?

We would gladly close this part of our essay with the picture of some pleasing and winning character. Pomponius Lætus, of whom we shall briefly speak, is known to us principally through the letter of his pupil Sabellicus, in which an antique colouring is purposely given to his character. Yet many of its features are clearly recognizable. He was a bastard of the House of the Neapolitan Sanseverini, princes of Salerno, whom he nevertheless refused to recognize. . . . An insignificant little figure, with small, quick eyes, and quaint dress, he lived, during the last decades of the fifteenth century, as professor in the University of Rome, either in his cottage in a garden on the Esquiline hill, or in his vineyard on the Quirinal. In the one he bred his ducks and fowls; the other he cultivated according to the strictest precepts of Cato, Varro, and Columella. He spent his holidays in fishing or bird-catching in the Campagna, or in feasting by some shady spring or on the banks of the Tiber. Wealth and luxury he despised. Free himself from envy and uncharitable speech, he would not suffer them in others. It was only against the hierarchy that he gave his tongue free play, and passed, till his latter years, for a scorner of religion altogether. He was involved in the persecution of the humanists begun by Pope Paul II, and surrendered to this pontiff by the Venetians; but no means could be found to wring unworthy confessions from him. He was afterwards befriended and supported by popes and prelates, and when his house was plundered in the disturbances under Sixtus IV, more was collected for him than he had lost. No teacher was more conscientious. Before daybreak he was to be seen descending the Esquiline with his lantern, and on reaching his lecture-room found it always filled to overflowing. A stutter compelled him to speak with care, but his delivery was even and effective. His few works give evidence of careful writing. No scholar treated the text of ancient authors more soberly and accurately. The remains of antiquity which surrounded him in Rome touched him so deeply that he would stand before them as if entranced, or would suddenly burst into tears at the sight of them. As he was ready to lay aside his own studies in order to help others, he was much loved and had many friends; and at his death, even Alexander VI sent his courtiers to follow the corpse, which was carried by the most distinguished of his pupils. The funeral service in the Aracœli was attended by forty bishops and by all the foreign ambassadors.

It was Lætus who introduced and conducted the representations of ancient, chiefly Plautine, plays in Rome. Every year, he celebrated the anniversary of the foundation of the city by a festival, at which his friends and pupils recited speeches and poems. Such meetings were the origin of what acquired, and long retained, the name of the Roman Academy. It was simply a free union of individuals, and was connected with no fixed institution. Besides the occasions mentioned, it met at the invitation of a patron, or to celebrate the memory of a deceased member, as of Platina. At such times, a prelate belonging to the academy would first say mass; Pomponio would then ascend the pulpit and deliver a speech; someone else would then follow him and recite an elegy. The customary banquet, with declamations and recitations, concluded the festival, whether joyous or serious, and the academicians, notably Platina himself, early acquired the reputation of epicures. At other times, the guests performed farces in the old Atellan style. As a free association of very varied elements, the academy lasted in its original form down to the sack of Rome, and included among its hosts Angelus Coloccius, Johannes Corycius and others. Its precise value as an element in the intellectual life of the people is as hard to estimate as that of any other social union of the same kind; yet a man like Sadoleto reckoned it among the most precious memories of his youth. A large number of other academies appeared and passed away in many Italian cities, according to the number and significance of the humanists living in them, and to the patronage bestowed by the great and wealthy. Of these we may mention the Academy of Naples, of which Jovianus Pontanus was the centre, and which sent out a colony to Lecce, and that of Pordenone, which formed the court of the Condottiere Alviano. (pp. 162-69)

About the middle of the sixteenth century, these associations seem to have undergone a complete change. The humanists, driven in other spheres from their commanding position, and viewed askance by the men of the Counter-reformation, lost the control of the academies: and here, as elsewhere, Latin poetry was replaced by Italian. Before long every town of the least importance had its academy, with some strange, fantastic name, and its own endowment and subscriptions. Besides the recitation of verses, the new institutions inherited from their predecessors the regular banquets and the representation of plays, sometimes acted by the members themselves, sometimes under their direction by young amateurs, and sometimes by paid players. The fate of the Italian stage, and afterwards of the opera, was long in the hands of these associations. (p. 170)

Jacob Burckhardt, "The Revival of Antiquity: Fall of the Humanists in the Sixteenth Century," in his The Civilization of the Renaissance in Italy: An Essay, *edited by L. Goldscheider, translated by S. G. C. Middlemore, third edition, Phaidon Press Ltd., 1951, pp. 162-70.*

FURTHER READING

Berenson, Bernard. *The Italian Painters of the Renaissance.* London: Phaidon Press, 1952, 488 p.
Covers artists of Venice, Florence, and central and northern Italy. Berenson examines the individual conditioning of these artists, as well as their mutual grounding in humanist ideals.

Blunt, Anthony. *Artistic Theory in Italy, 1450-1600.* Oxford: Clarendon Press, 1940, 168 p.
Marks the influence of humanist doctrine on the works of Leonardo da Vinci, Michelangelo, and lesser-known artists.

Burke, Peter. *The Italian Renaissance: Culture and Society in Italy.* Cambridge, Eng.: Polity Press, 1986, 287 p.
Regards manifestations of humanism in the learning, literature, and plastic arts of Renaissance Italy.

Caponigri, A. Robert. "The Timelessness of the *Scienza Nuova* of Giambattista Vico." In *Italian Literature: Roots and Branches: Essays in Honor of Thomas Goddard Bergin,* edited by Giose Rimanelli and Kenneth John Atchity, pp. 309-32. New Haven: Yale University Press, 1976.
Finds Vico's noted work a distinct departure from the humanist philosophies of his contemporaries.

Chastel, André. *The Age of Humanism: Europe, 1480-1530.* Translated by Katherine M. Delavenay and E. M. Gwyer. London: Thames and Hudson, 1963, 347 p.
Addresses wide-ranging effects of humanism on European, and particularly Italian, culture and the arts.

Gilmore, Myron P. "Italian Reactions to Erasmian Humanism." In *Itinerarium Italicum: The Profile of the Italian Renaissance in the Mirror of Its European Transformations,* edited by Heiko A. Oberman and Thomas A. Brady, Jr., pp. 61-115. Studies in Medieval and Reformation Thought, edited by Heiko A. Oberman, Vol. XIV. Leiden: E. J. Brill, 1975.
Chronicles the impact of Dutch scholar Desiderius Erasmus's philosophies on Italian humanism.

Greene, Thomas M. "Petrarch and the Humanist Hermeneutic." In *Italian Literature: Roots and Branches: Essays in Honor of Thomas Goddard Bergin,* edited by Giose Rimanelli and Kenneth John Atchity, pp. 201-23. New Haven: Yale University Press, 1976.
Indicates broad humanist approaches to self-discovery and self-expression in Francesco Petrarch's verse.

Grendler, Paul F. "Five Italian Occurrences of *Umanista,* 1540-1574" and "The Concept of Humanist in Cinquecento Italy." In his *Culture and Censorship in Late Renaissance Italy and France,* pp. 317-25, 447-63. London: Variorum Reprints, 1981.
Cites varying uses of the term *umanista* ("humanist") from sixteenth-century texts and attempts to define the humanist's role as it evolved in cinquecento Italy.

Hay, Denys. "Historians and the Renaissance during the Last Twenty-Five Years." In *The Renaissance: Essays in Interpretation,* edited by André Chastel and others, pp. 1-32. London: Methuen, 1982.
Surveys Renaissance scholarship from Jacob Burckhardt on, with attendant perspectives on Italian humanism.

Kristeller, Paul Oskar. "Philosophical Movements of the Renaissance." In his *Studies in Renaissance Thought and Letters,* pp. 17-31. Rome: Edizioni di Storia e Letteratura, 1956.
Ranks Italian humanism with major currents of Renaissance thought.

———. "The Humanist Movement" and "Italian Humanism and Byzantium." In his *Renaissance Thought and Its Sources,* edited by Michael Mooney, pp. 21-32, 137-50. New York: Columbia University Press, 1979.
Overview of Italian humanism and the importance of Byzantine scholarship to its growth.

Plumb, J. H. *The Horizon Book of the Renaissance,* edited by Richard M. Ketchum, pp. 20ff. New York: American Heritage Publishing, 1961.
Overall view of the Italian Renaissance, with commentary on the achievements of better-known humanists.

Symonds, John Addington. *Renaissance in Italy: The Revival of Learning.* 1877. Reprint. Gloucester, Mass.: Peter Smith, 1967, 399 p.
Traces Italian humanism from its inception to its decline.

———. "History and Philosophy" and "Conclusion." In his *Renaissance in Italy: Italian Literature,* Part II, pp. 376-425, 426-63. 1881. Reprint. London: Smith, Elder, & Co., 1904.
Evaluates the cultural contributions of several prominent humanists and notes the importance of humanist objectives to the Italian Renaissance.

Trail, Florence. *A History of Italian Literature,* Vol. I. New York: Vincenzo Ciocia, 1903, 292 p.
Wide-ranging chronicle offering brief critical sketches of major and minor Italian humanists.

Trinkaus, Charles. "Italian Humanism and the Scriptures" and "From *Theologia Poetica* to *Theologia Platonica.*" In his *In Our Image and Likeness: Humanity and Divinity in Italian Humanist Thought,* Vol. 2, pp. 563-614, 683-721. Chicago: University of Chicago Press, 1970.
Details two significant facets of Italian humanism: assimilation of the Scriptures to particular humanist disciplines and the consolidation of allegorical interpretation with Christian tradition.

Vasari, Giorgio. *Lives of the Artists.* Translated and abridged by E. L. Seeley. New York: Noonday Press, 1957, 325 p.
Selections from the 1550 work by Vasari, a painter, architect, and the contemporary of many whose biographies he recorded. *Lives* provides a colorful, often intimate, glimpse into the artistic careers of leading and lesser-known Italian humanists.

Vittorini, Domenico. "Leonardo Bruni Aretino and Humanism." In his *High Points in the History of Italian Literature,* pp. 90-100. New York: David McKay Co., 1958.
Links the aesthetics of Aretino's philosophy to the humanist concern for the beauty of form.

Wilkins, Ernest Hatch. "Contemporaries of the Militant Humanists" and "Florentine Humanists." In his *A History of Italian Literature,* 2d ed., pp. 131-35, 148-57. Cambridge: Harvard University Press, 1974.
Regards humanist influence on minor Italian writers and the major achievements of four Florentine humanists: Cristoforo Landino, Marsilio Ficino, Politian, and Pico della Mirandola.

Yates, Frances A. "The Italian Academies." In her *Renaissance and Reform: The Italian Contribution,* pp. 6-29. London: Routledge & Kegan Paul, 1983.
Explores the development of intellectual circles throughout fifteenth- and sixteenth-century Italy that were instrumental to the humanist spirit.

Lo Kuan-chung

1330?-1400?

(Also known as Lo Kuan, Lo Pen, Lo Tao-pen, and Ming-ch'ing) Chinese novelist, dramatist, and editor.

Acclaimed as the father of the Chinese historical novel, Lo is one of the most popular writers of the Orient. He has been credited with two of China's most treasured historical novels, *San-kuo chih t'ung-su yen-i* (*Romance of the Three Kingdoms*) and *Shui-hu ch'üan-chuan* (*The Water Margin*), though much controversy surrounds his role in producing these and other works attributed to him. Yet despite such questions of authorship, Lo has been heralded throughout the centuries as an exceptional storyteller and as the creator of beloved landmarks in Chinese literature.

Almost nothing is known about Lo's life. Aside from a brief biographical notice in a 1422 registry, no other extant contemporary documents mention him. It is likely that he was born in 1330 in Taiyuan and lived in Hangchow, an important cultural center. Lo was apparently a scholar and a wanderer who led a somewhat solitary existence. In addition, at least one sixteenth-century writer has suggested that he was a revolutionary who participated in an unsuccessful revolt against Mongolian rule. Most sources concur that he died around 1400.

In the six centuries since Lo's lifetime, scholars have vigorously debated which novels and dramas belong in his literary canon. He has been credited with up to nine works, but for every scholar who has ascribed a text to him, another has disputed it. Moreover, none of the novels assigned to him was published during his lifetime, and no irrefutable testimony exists concerning his role in producing any work. Indeed, evidence linking him to such novels as *San sui p'ing-yao chuan, Sui T'ang liang-ch'ao chih-chuan, Ta-t'ang ch'in-wang tz'u-hua,* and *Ts'an-t'ang wu-tai-shih yen-i,* is slim. Lo's role in creating *Romance* and *Water Margin,* however, has been more firmly established. His signature appears on the oldest extant copy of the former as well as on early editions of the latter. Although the novels were written sometime during the Yüan (1260-1368) or Ming (post-1368) periods of the fourteenth century, editions that have survived were not published until two centuries later, long after they had undergone numerous revisions and redactions. Thus, some scholars debate whether Lo deserves credit for the texts as they exist today. In addition, a second author, Shih Nai'an, is sometimes credited with writing *Water Margin.* It is possible that Lo either jointly produced *Water Margin* with Shih, or used Shih's text as a primary source. Today scholars generally concur that Lo played an important role in producing both *Romance* and *Water Margin.* Disagreement continues, however, as to whether he wrote, compiled, redacted, or edited them.

Lo modeled his narratives upon tales and legends developed over centuries of Chinese history. Both *Romance* and *Water Margin* evolved from oral traditions of Chinese folklore and are based upon actual or legendary historical events. Although not the first to borrow from traditional literature, Lo was one of the earliest writers to produce a unified, coherent narrative written in polished prose—a marked departure from the unrefined literary techniques used in earlier written examples of Chinese lore. *Romance* recounts the closing years and eventual collapse of China's longest and most powerful empire, the Han dynasty (206 B.C.-A.D. 220). The narrative, which contains more than 700,000 words and includes over four hundred characters, vividly records fierce military campaigns that were waged between three feudal kingdoms, Shu, Wei, and Wu, from A.D. 168 to 265. Consulting well-known third- and fifth-century texts by Ch'en Shou and P'ei Sung-chih, Lo described the unsuccessful efforts of Liu Pei and his sworn brothers Kuan Yu and Chang Fei to restore the failing regime to its former prominence. While incorporating characteristics of native folklore, Lo eschewed discernible falsehoods, creating what is considered a fairly accurate account of the Three Kingdoms period.

In contrast, the events depicted in *Water Margin* are almost entirely fictional. Only a few of the characters appear to have been modeled upon historical figures. Based upon the anonymous early Yüan work *Historical Anecdotes of the Hsüan-ho Period,* the loosely structured text of *Water Margin* recounts the legendary adventures of a group of twelfth-century Shantung bandits. The narrative is divided into cycles that portray the events leading the 108 outlaws first to unite against and then later to swear allegiance to the existing regime. Each cycle chronicles the life of one of the bandits and the reasons for his exile. Central to the plots of both *Romance* and *Water Margin* are questions of moral righteousness and legitimacy in issues of political rule and class struggle.

Literary studies in English on the dramas and novels attributed to Lo vary widely in critical conclusion. Of the three dramas referred to in the 1422 registry, *Chung-cheng hsiao-tzu lien-huan chien, San p'ing-chang ssu-k'u fei-hu tzu,* and *Sung-t'ai-tsu lung-hu feng-yun-hui,* only *Sung-t'ai* is extant and is rarely performed. Scholars agree that the work has little literary value and that Lo is but a minor dramatist. He has been called an outstanding prose writer, however. *Romance* and *Water Margin,* both prototypes of Chinese popular history and fiction, are considered crucial in the development of the prose narrative in China. Scholars have particularly praised Lo's dramatic heroes, his elegant use of language, and his refined narrative technique. At the same time, critics have identified structural weaknesses, stylistic incongruities, and stereotyped or underdeveloped characters in Lo's work. Nevertheless, both novels have long been immensely popular among readers of virtually every social stratum. According to Moss Roberts, *Romance* is "a popular classic, the foremost work of semifictional history in China, and one of the greatest Chinese literary masterpieces." *Water Margin* has been accorded equally high praise. As Li Hsi-fan has acclaimed, "The influence of this novel is inestimable. No other of our Classics has exercised a comparable influence. We are therefore justified in saying that this is a great epic of peasant revolt, a splendid work of classical realist literature, and the most treasured part of our cultural heritage."

Today Lo is best remembered for the historical narratives *Ro-*

mance of the Three Kingdoms and The Water Margin, two masterpieces that have appealed to readers for over five hundred years. As one of the first authors to record the oral folklore and legends of Chinese history in elegant prose narratives, Lo has been accorded a unique place in Chinese literature.

*PRINCIPAL WORKS

†Sung-t'ai-tsu lung-hu feng-yun-hui   (drama)   1400
‡San-kuo chih t'ung-su yen-i   (novel)   1522
    [San kuo; or, Romance of the Three Kingdoms, 1925]
§Shui-hu ch'üan-chuan   (novel)   1954
    [All Men are Brothers, 1933; also translated as The Water Margin, 1937; also translated as Outlaws of the Marsh, 1981]

*Establishing composition and initial publication dates for Lo's works has proved extremely problematic to scholars. Additionally, two dramas believed to be by Lo, Chung-cheng hsiao-tzu lien-huan chien and San p'ing-chang ssu-k'u fei-hu tzu, are no longer extant and little is known about them.

†The date given here is the last possible composition date.

‡The date given here is of the earliest extant edition of this work.

§Several widely varying editions of this work, some of them undated or fragments, were published in the sixteenth and seventeenth centuries. Scholars have been unable to determine conclusively which, if any, of these editions exactly reflects the author's intent. The date given here is of the most complete modern Chinese version of the text.

TA-CH'I CHIANG   (essay date 1494-1522)

[In the following excerpt from the preface to the earliest surviving version of San-kuo, the Chia-ching edition published sometime between 1494 and 1522, Chiang emphasizes the historical merits of the text.]

The former dynasties saw the rise of p'ing-hua based on unreliable history and recited by blind storytellers. Such p'ing-hua, characterized by their contemptible and erroneous language and their retelling of wild fiction, were detested by gentlemen-scholars. Lo Kuan-chung of Tung-yuan, however, basing his account on Ch'en Shou, consulted official history and carefully adapted and expanded its chronicle of events from the first year of the Chung-p'ing reign of Han Ling-ti to the first year of the T'ai-k'ang reign of the Chin dynasty. He called it **An Explanation of the San-kuo-chih, Done in the Popular Style.** Its language is neither too difficult nor too vulgar. It records events truthfully so that it should be properly deemed history.

Ta-ch'i Chiang, in an excerpt in The Classic Chinese Novel: A Critical Introduction by C. T. Hsia, Columbia University Press, 1968, p. 38.

IMPERIAL MANDATE OF CHIA CH'ING   (essay date 1799)

[During the eighteenth century, Chinese emperor Ch'ien Lung expressed great interest in literature and scholarship and thus commissioned the monumental compilation and cataloging of all rare books in China. Upon Ch'ien's abdication in 1796, this massive task was assumed by his son Chia Ch'ing. Over twenty-six hundred of the texts collected were deemed critical either of the existing dynasty or of earlier empires. As a result, most were banned as revolutionary works unfit for public consumption. Indeed, many scholars were put to death and the general public was threatened with severe consequences for reading such works. In the following excerpt, the total suppression of Shui-hu chuan is ordered by official decree.]

All bookshops which print the licentious story **Shui Hu Chuan** must be rigorously sought out, and the work prohibited. Both the wood blocks and the printed matter should be burned. In case (it is discovered that) this book is being made, and the local official is not acting to find out and prevent it, then shall he lose six months' pay. In case bookstores are permitted to lend this book with the knowledge of this official, then shall he be demoted two ranks and removed elsewhere. Should (an official) himself engrave it he shall be stripped of office entirely. In case he buys a copy and reads it, his punishment shall be the loss of a year's pay. (pp. vi-vii)

An excerpt in All Men Are Brothers (Shui hu chuan), Vol. I, translated by Pearl S. Buck, 1933. Reprint by The John Day Company, 1968, pp. vi-vii.

PEARL S. BUCK   (essay date 1933)

[Buck is probably the most acclaimed twentieth-century writer on China and its culture. Her novel The Good Earth, for which she won the Pulitzer Prize in 1932, did much to unlock the interior of China and to clarify for the Western world many of its misconceptions about life in that country. In her works, Buck stressed the need for a total human community and a sympathy toward all nations. For her humanitarian efforts, she was awarded the Nobel Prize in Literature in 1938, becoming the first woman to achieve that honor. In the following excerpt from the introduction to the 1933 translation of Shui-hu chuan, she justifies her method of translating and addresses the question of Lo's authorship of the work.]

This translation of one of China's most famous novels, **Shui Hu Chuan,** does not pretend to be a scholar's effort, meticulous in explanation and documentation. Indeed, in translating this novel I have had no academic interest at all, and no purpose beyond my delight in the original as an excellent tale excellently told. I have translated it as literally as possible, because to me the style in Chinese is perfectly suited to the material, and my only effort has been to make the translation as much like the Chinese as I could because I should like readers who do not know that language to have at least the illusion that they are reading an original work. I say effort, for although I do not pretend to have succeeded, I have attempted to preserve the original meaning and style even to the point of leaving unenlivened those parts which are less interesting in the Chinese also. For it is inevitable that so long a book should be uneven in quality. Certain of the verses at the ends of chapters are examples of this, and those which are doggerel in the original are doggerel in translation also. . . . (p. v)

The English title is not, of course, a translation of the Chinese title, which is singularly untranslatable. The word SHUI means water; the word HU, margins or borders. The word CHUAN is the equivalent of the English word novel. The juxtaposition of these words in English is so nearly meaningless as to give, in my opinion at least, an unjust impression of the book. I have chosen arbitrarily, therefore, a famous saying of Confucius to be the title in English, a title which in amplitude and in implication expresses the spirit of this band of righteous robbers. . . . (pp. v-vi)

The story of the growth of *Shui Hu Chuan* into its present form is an interesting one. Like many of the Chinese novels it developed rather than was written, and to this day its final author is unknown. It is said to be written by one Shih Nai-an, but little is known of him except that it is said that he was a native of Huai-an in Kiangsu province, and became an official in Ch'ien-t'ang in Chekiang province, after graduating as *chin shih* in the Yüan Dynasty. Many Chinese scholars believe Lo Kuan Chung, the author of *The Three Kingdoms*, wrote *Shui Hu Chuan* also, and it seems fairly sure that at least he revised it and perhaps made substantial changes and additions, whether or not it be true that he wrote the whole, using Shih Nai-an merely as a pen name. One Chinese scholar at least gives as authority for Lo Kuan Chung's authorship the fact that *Shui Hu Chuan* is so evil a book that the curse was laid upon the author that for three generations his descendants were to be deaf and dumb and since for three generations Lo Kuan Chung's descendants were deaf and dumb therefore he must be the author.

But the discussion is scarcely of general importance here, since the fact remains that whoever wrote *Shui Hu Chuan* performed an eclectic rather than a wholly creative role. . . . (p. vii)

Today the newest and most extreme party in China, the Communist, has taken the *Shui Hu Chuan* and issued an edition with a preface by a leading Communist, who calls it the first Communist literature of China, as suitable to this day as to the day it was written.

There can be no sounder proof of the living quality of a novel than this, that it stands still great and full of the meaning of humanity in spite of the passing of centuries. (p. ix)

> *Pearl S. Buck, in an introduction to* All Men Are Brothers (Shui hu chuan), Vol. I, *translated by Pearl S. Buck, 1933. Reprint by The John Day Company, 1968, pp. v-ix.*

MAO TSE-TUNG   (essay date 1938)

[*A political writer, philosopher, and poet, Mao was the founder and Chairman of the Communist party in China. He is generally considered the greatest twentieth-century Chinese revolutionary. With over one billion copies printed, his* Little Red Book *became the Chinese guide to life. In the following excerpt from* Red Star Over China, *a biography containing interviews with Mao by Edgar Snow, the Chairman recalls his childhood pleasure in reading* San-kuo *and* Shui-hu chuan.]

What I enjoyed were the romances of Old China, and especially stories of rebellions. I read the *Yo Fei Chuan (Chin Chung Chuan)*, *Shui Hu Chuan, Fan T'ang*, *San Kuo,* and *Hsi Yu Chi*, while still very young, and despite the vigilance of my old teacher, who hated these outlawed books and called them wicked. I used to read them in school, covering them up with a Classic when the teacher walked past. So also did most of my schoolmates. We learned many of the stories almost by heart, and discussed and rediscussed them many times. We knew more of them than the old men of the village, who also loved them and used to exchange stories with us. I believe that perhaps I was much influenced by such books, read at an impressionable age. (pp. 115-16)

> *Mao Tse-tung, in an interview with Edgar Snow, in* Red Star Over China *by Edgar Snow, revised edition, 1938. Reprint by Garden City Publishing Co., 1939, pp. 115-16.*

RICHARD GREGG IRWIN   (essay date 1953)

[*In the following excerpt from* The Evolution of a Chinese Novel: 'Shui-hu-chuan,' *Irwin traces possible plot origins and examines evidence of authorship.*]

How far removed are the novel in its most complete form and the meager historical references to Sung Chiang and his band! With the exception of the campaign against Fang La, *Shui-hu-chuan* is not even a romanticized version of history, but merely a collection of tales, some of them legendary, which deal with supposed associates of this one notorious figure. What, then, was the origin of these tales? (p. 23)

There is ample evidence that *Shui-hu-chuan,* like other novels which appeared at about the same time, derives from earlier *tz'u-hua.* In the first place, one of the *tz'u* escaped the deletion which was their common fate in later editions of all the early novels and is still found in Chapter 48. After an initial attack on the Chu Family Village had been repulsed, Sung Chiang himself led a second assault. When his force approached it, they saw, in the words of the *tz'u,*

> Single Dragon Hill before Single Dragon Mount,
> Chu Family Village atop Single Dragon Hill.
> Circling the hill a flowing stream,
> Girdling the whole a line of trailing willows.
> Within the wall swords and halberds bristle,
> Before the gate wait serried ranks of spearmen.
> Confronting the foe, valiant stalwarts all,
> The vanguard comprised of men in their prime.
> Chu Lung in combat is hard to oppose,
> Chu Hu's lance none can withstand,
> And Chu Piao to boot, replete with martial skill,
> Bellowing in anger like a king.
> A Croesus, Lord Chu, and wily strategist,
> Whose wealth a thousand chests contain.
> White flags stand paired before the gate,
> On which is writ for all to see:
> "Fill in the marsh and seize Ch'ao Kai,
> Trample Liang-shan, capture Sung Chiang."

Since this forwards the narrative instead of paralleling it, it must come directly from a *tz'u-hua.* In transposing from this form to one intended for a reading public, editors usually rewrote such passages in prose, since to drop them entirely would leave gaps in the story. Such was the case with this *tz'u* in the revision which cut the novel to seventy chapters, but in the 100- and 120-chapter versions it was retained as originally sung. In style as well as function, it differs from the balanced composition of poems which are elsewhere used as "evidence," for the abrupt ending betrays unwonted lack of care. Unquestionably, it was originally employed by a storyteller and was but one of many, though the others have long since been paraphrased in prose.

Elsewhere, too, the *tz'u-hua* have left their imprint on the novel. In Sung and Yüan times it was customary, when single episodes were narrated in public, for the raconteur to identify each by its title both at the beginning and end of the session. At least two such titles are still imbedded in the text of *Shui-hu-chuan,* one in Chapter 16: "This is known as stealing the birthday gifts by a ruse," and the other in Chapter 40: "This is known as the small assembly at White Dragon Temple."

Finally, the numerous devices forced upon the novelist as a means of incorporating various earlier and independent series of stories into his work are readily visible. Sung spends a period as a fugitive so that the events following the murder of Yen P'o-hsi and preceding his capture may be included. He must suffer arrest so that his imprisonment in Chiang-chou, the friendships to which it led, and the dramatic rescue from the execution ground may be described; hence his abrupt withdrawal from the group he is leading to Liang-shan-po, and the trip home precipitated by the uncharacteristic duplicity of his father. In order that the tale of his hiding in the temple where he receives the Heavenly Writ may be included, he must make another such trip after being rescued at Chiang-chou and taken safely to the lair. The second trip was completely unnecessary, for his father could be and was brought to Liang-shan-po by others; it merely resolves the dilemma of a compiler who cannot bring himself to reject a good tale.

The foregoing evidence clearly demonstrates that the novel was derived from more than one *tz'u-hua*. Portions of the story similar or identical to those recounted in it by *Hsüan-ho i-shih* were subsequently adapted from it by a *tz'u-hua* which appears to have been compiled in the South late in the Yüan period. Features in which *Shui-hu-chuan* differs from both *Hsüan-ho i-shih* and the autobiographical statements of Sung in the *tsa-chü* are the peculiar contribution of this southern *tz'u-hua*. (pp. 39-41)

The assumption of southern origin is further strengthened by instances in which Chekiang colloquialisms are employed in passages of *Shui-hu-chuan* whose action is laid in the North and whose dramatis personae are Northerners. One of these occurs when the men sheltered by Liu Shih-ch'üan, to whom Kao Ch'iu turned for aid early in his career, are dismissed as "*kan-ke-lao han-tzu. . . .*" Here "*kan-ke-lao,*" the colloquial designation of a skin disease, is combined with a term of contempt to form what appears a metaphor for those whose behavior is as loathsome as the sores. A second colloquialism is found in a conversation between Hsi-men-ch'ing and old Mistress Wang, who tells him she is able to perform "*ma-po-liu*" . . . , that is, bring man and woman together. After she has succeeded in arranging his clandestine meetings with P'an Chin-lien, the wife of Wu Ta, the affair is discovered by Yün Ke, who informs the injured husband by likening him to a duck, which in Chekiang parlance means a cuckold.

Since none of these passages occurs in a section previously identified as derived from the southern *tz'u-hua*, its scope must either be enlarged to include them or they must fix the locale in which the novel itself was compiled. As a matter of fact, such a short time elapsed between the writing of the missing *tz'u-hua* and the drafting of the novel that they may have been done by the same group of men. (p. 42)

We may briefly summarize our conclusions concerning this phase in the evolution of *Shui-hu-chuan* as follows: Much of what was incorporated in the novel existed previously in various *tz'u-hua*. The most comprehensive of these stemmed in part from one of Southern Sung origin adumbrated in *Hsüan-ho i-shih,* in part from a similar, hypothetical text current in the North during the mid-Yüan period and reflected in the *tsa-chü*; but it was, by virtue of its own contributions, more inclusive than a mere combination of these two. Its compilation was the work of a *shu-hui* which existed in or near Hang-chow at the end of the Yüan period.

We have traced the *Shui-hu-chuan* stories from their historical beginnings through a long formative period, during which they at first existed separately, then came together in geographical cycles, and were finally combined in lengthy *tz'u-hua* or story-chains. The transition from the *tz'u-hua* to what we may term the original novel involved no change in form, and was largely a matter of increased length and superior craftsmanship.

The feature which chiefly distinguished the novel from the southern *tz'u-hua* was the presentation of a unified account of the gradual assembling of 108 heroes at Liang-shan-po and their subsequent dispersal, one by one. Some had previously led a nameless existence as members of the subsidiary group of seventy-two referred to in the *tsa-chü*. Others had been named, but never individualized. Still others were characterized in the episodes of the southern *tz'u-hua,* but it remained for the novelist to characterize the remainder. Furthermore, there is no evidence that any earlier version had attempted to carry the story to a mechanically perfect close. Such a close provided an obvious challenge which could equally result in the success which one associates with inspiration or the failure which one often associates with deliberate contrivance. Some of the finest and poorest writing in the novel results from the acceptance of this challenge; the best writing includes the story of Lin Ch'ung, the revision by which Yang Chih is matched against the "date merchants" in the theft of the birthday gifts, and the tragic finale, while the worst is exemplified by the campaign against Fang La. (pp. 43-4)

From the standpoint of literary craftsmanship, the novel's greatest advance comes in character portrayal, notably in the handling of the relationship between Sung Chiang and Li K'uei. The *tsa-chü, Liang-shan-po Li K'uei fu-ching,* vividly contrasts the two: one in the role of a cool disciplinarian, the other as his hot-headed, guileless underling, but there is no hint of any special bond between them setting Li apart from other members of the band. From the time of their first meeting, they are attracted to each other by their disparity in temperament, and the development of their relationship throughout the course of the novel is a manifestation of psychological insight deserving the highest praise. The change in Sung is less noticeable than that in Li, who develops immeasurably; Li finally accepts death with understanding and humility, concerned lest the very demonstration of his loyalty injure the good name of the band. Chin Sheng-t'an called attention to the manner in which the two were set off against each other, interpreting it as a device to emphasize Sung's treacherousness by contrasting it with Li's forthrightness. I cannot concur in this highly colored judgment, but I do consider the handling of the relationship between the two of major significance, both as an index of the genius of the novelist, and for the underlying unity it gives to what is in many respects a heterogeneous series of events. (pp. 45-6)

No problem in connection with the history of *Shui-hu-chuan* has occasioned more speculation than its authorship. Beginning with the earliest bibliographical reference to the novel, two men have been constantly associated with its composition, Shih Nai-an . . . and Lo Kuan-chung. . . . Sometimes, as in this citation, they have been linked with Lo in a secondary role. But often as not sole authorship has been attributed to one or the other. Recent discoveries afford more information about them than was previously available; in order to test the validity of their claims, we must examine this with reference to the chronological and geographical requirements established by internal evidence.

Contemporary Chinese writers are generally agreed that the original version of the novel appeared at the turn of the Yüan and Ming dynasties. One of them, Hsieh Wu-liang, goes further by insisting that because of its revolutionary tenor it must be a Yüan work. Certainly the early years of the Ming, when an energetic leader of humble origin occupied the throne, provided no atmosphere of popular discontent such as that which might be expected to produce such a work. And by the time the decadence of later rulers became apparent, *Shui-hu-chuan* had not only appeared but was undergoing its initial alteration. While it may have been written slightly later than 1368, the year in which Chu Yüan-chang . . . (*reg.* 1368-98) was invested as the first emperor of the Ming, the rancor of its author must spring from personal experience of the harsh and inept rule of the crumbling Mongol line. We may be confident that he lived at the end of the Yüan, and perhaps into the Ming period.

It has already been pointed out that there is good reason to believe that the novel was written in the vicinity of Hangchow. It is possible, of course, that the author, so accustomed to using the Chekiang dialect that he failed to note the incongruity of its appearance in the conversation of northerners, resided elsewhere at the time of composition. But this is unlikely since Hangchow was then the center of dramatic activity, and drama and fiction were closely allied. A man who tried his hand at both would certainly be there. Birth or residence in Chekiang is, then, the second qualification demanded of the writer, and ideally he should be the author of other works which establish his literary talent.

From what is reported of him, Lo Kuan-chung satisfies all these requirements. (pp. 47-8)

In addition to the *tsa-chü,* only one of which, *Lung-hu feng-yüan-hui,* is still extant, Lo is credited with the authorship of four novels: *Shui-hu-chuan, San-kuo-chih yen-i, Sui-T'ang liang-ch'ao chih-chuan* . . . , and *San-Sui p'ing-yao chuan.* He may also be responsible for *Ts'an-T'ang wu-tai-shih yen-i.* . . . It is significant that every one of his extant writings has some basis in fact, though this is not apparent from the titles of three: *Lung-hu feng-yün hui* concerns Chao K'uang-yin . . . (*reg.* 960-65), first emperor of Sung; *San-Sui p'ing-yao chuan* centers on the sixty-six day rebellion of Wang Tse . . . in 1047; *Shui-hu-chuan,* as we have seen, deals with events of the following century.

Until a few years ago, the nearest approach to an identification for Shih Nai-an was the suggestion that "Nai-an" might be the pseudonym of Shih Hui . . . (*fl. ca.* 1295), a native of Hangchow, author of *Yu-kuei-chi* . . . , and a friend of Chung Ssu-ch'eng. But no definite evidence could be adduced to support this hypothesis. (p. 49)

[That] other novels claimed for Shih—*San-kuo-chih yen-i, Sui-T'ang chih-chuan, San-Sui p'ing-yao chuan*—were actually the work of Lo is attested by every known bibliographical notice and reprint edition. To all appearances, the Shih family, not content with the qualitative superiority of the work in which their alleged kinsman collaborated, simply padded the record with three of Lo's titles to make it more imposing.

Because of the stylistic superiority of *Shui-hu-chuan* to *San-kuo-chih yen-i,* it has been argued they cannot be the work of the same author. Other critics, noting analogies between

the two, have agreed on their common origin while reaching contradictory conclusions as to chronological priority. Hsieh Wu-liang, writing before the publication of the Shih family documents, attributed the superiority of *Shui-hu-chuan* to the technical progress made by Lo in the course of his career. I am convinced of its later origin, but ascribe the advance it represents to a fortunate association in which the ripe experience of Lo was challenged by the fresh insight of Shih (whether or not he is the putative ancestor of the Po-chü-chen family), resulting in their joint triumph.

Sun K'ai-ti maintains that *Shui-hu-chuan* was the product of a *shu-hui,* and that any contribution by Shih and Lo came simply as members of a group. Li Ch'ang-tung goes still further by suggesting that neither was actually involved in its composition, their names having been borrowed by the original publisher in order to protect the author of such "dangerous thoughts" and, at the same time, capitalize on the established reputation of men no longer living. However, the weight of tradition, together with what is known of Lo, tends to vindicate his title to authorship. (p. 51)

> *Richard Gregg Irwin, "Evolution of the Novel, Part I," in his* The Evolution of a Chinese Novel: Shui-hu-chuan, *Cambridge, Mass.: Harvard University Press, 1953, pp. 23-60.*

LI HSI-FAN (essay date 1959)

[*Li is a twentieth-century Chinese critic. In the following excerpt, he cites the author's portrayal of Lin-chung's life and hardship in* Outlaws of the Marshes *as indicative of Lo's delineation of character.*]

[*Outlaws of the Marshes* reflects the peasant revolt led by Sung Chiang] by relating the adventures of many different characters, giving us a panorama of the whole society in all its complexity. The life-like portraits of widely differing men who were driven to become outlaws in Liangshan include many who were not peasants; for fishermen, vagabonds, the city poor, artisans, hunters, small shop-keepers, impoverished scholars, mendicant friars, wandering priests, low-ranking officials and military officers and even some minor landlords joined the outlaws. The novel presents us with many profoundly depicted, vivid and typical characters. (p. 63)

Of course, if *Outlaws of the Marshes* were made up only of stories of different heroes, it would not be the masterpiece it is. These stories are used to show how men of different classes and different temperaments gathered at Liangshan and formed a mighty peasant force to wage a brave struggle against the rulers.

It has been said with truth that one of the good features of classical Chinese novels is that they tell dramatic stories, and that it is this which endears them to Chinese readers. But a really great work of any nation, one which lives for hundreds of years to move and influence generations of readers, does not achieve this entirely by the story but rather because the typical characters in the work are alive, alive on paper, on men's lips, in their hearts. When we say that a novel tells a good story, we actually mean that the story is alive thanks to the profound delineation of character. Among Chinese classics, the *Outlaws of the Marshes* is an outstanding example of this.

Lin Chung is one of the most successfully drawn characters

in the novel. His dramatic adventures, his banishment to Tsangchou, his actions at the temple during the snowstorm, his fight with the brigand leaders in the stronghold at Liang-shan and many other episodes all help to make this hero vividly alive.

The portrayal of Lin Chung's character—and this applies to the characterization throughout the novel—is done by depicting the man in action. In describing Lin Chung's mental conflict and how he joins the outlaws only when there is no other way out, the author does not tell us what this hero is thinking but, from the beginning when Lin Chung meets Lu Chih-shen in the monastery, he unfolds his character through action.

Of course it is most humiliating for Lin Chung to have his wife insulted, and he grows indignant: The author describes this scene as follows:

> Lin Chung quickly took his leave of Chih-shen. . . . He leaped through the gap in the wall and raced with Chin Erh back to the temple. . . . Lin pushed forward, seized the young man by the shoulder and spun him around. "I'll teach you to insult a good man's wife," he shouted, raising his fist. . . .

The reader at this point expects the young reprobate to receive a thorough beating, but: "After spinning him around, when Lin Chung saw that he was Young Master Kao, the strength left his arms."

This episode describing his indignation and his timidity bring out two salient facets of Lin Chung's character. Of course one incident is not enough to present a character, and the author's description of Lin Chung does not stop here. We see him ill-treated on his way to exile, begging Lu Chih-shen in the forest to spare his escorts' lives, settling down to serve his prison sentence in Tsangchou. All these incidents help us to visualize Lin Chung clearly. When we read of his hardships on the road we sympathize with him, but when we see how meekly he submits to his escorts and later to the gaoler we cannot help regretting his timidity. This could only be Lin Chung: Wu Sung or Li Kuei would never behave in this way.

When the writer describes what is passing in Lin Chung's mind, again it is done not by direct analysis but through action. One very fine, telling description occurs in the passage where Lin Chung bids farewell to his wife. Only the incident itself is related, with no dramatic comment. We are not told how Lin Chung looked or what he felt—nothing but this moving act. But what an insight that gives us into his mind! What mental anguish lies hidden in his simple words! He is about to part from his dearly loved wife. On her account he has been unjustly sentenced to a banishment in a remote, unfriendly region, and his life hangs by a thread. Yet his first concern is not to let his wife waste her youth for his sake—rather than this he will divorce her. Of course, he hopes to win through to a reunion. All his natural instincts encourage him to hope. But not until after he reaches Liang-shan does he confide his heart's desire to Chao Kai: "Ever since I came up the mountain I've been wanting to fetch my wife here, but because Wang Lun was unreliable and things were uncertain, I hesitated and left her in the eastern capital. I don't know whether she is alive or dead!" Not till he hears of his wife's death does this hero at last shed tears, and long for her no more. But this intensifies his hatred for the rulers.

These passages in *Outlaws of the Marshes* describe true love between a man and a woman. This abiding, tragic love is not expressed by means of detailed descriptions but is implicit in Lin Chung's behaviour and this brings it out more powerfully. Hence the strong emotional impact of these scenes.

The *Outlaws of the Marshes* not only creates Lin Chung's character vividly but also gives a convincing picture of its development.

To achieve this, certain special devices are used.

First of all, the author clearly indicates Lin Chung's special family and class background and faithfully mirrors the contradictions in his character. The author does not idealize his character in an unrealistic way. He uses Lin Chung's actual behaviour in specific circumstances to express the submissiveness which characterizes him at the start. But this does not mean that he overlooks the rebellious streak in Lin Chung, for at the same time he indicates his standard of values and the sense of justice and mutiny always just below the surface. Lin Chung's complaints of "dirty treatment," his determination to avenge himself on Steward Lu makes it evident that this instructor who pockets an affront today will sooner or later come to the end of his tether. It is precisely these touches that make Lin Chung such a vivid, convincing figure and show that he is no obedient slave but a hero submitting for a time to humiliation.

The second thing to notice is that the development and changes in Lin Chung's character are closely linked with the direct influence of the environment. By environment we do not mean simply the mental climate in which each individual lives, but the most important setting for his actions—the historical and social background. Generally speaking, only an author with a deep understanding of and ability to describe the historical and social background can give profound pictures of men and truthfully reflect reality. It is only because *Outlaws of the Marshes* gives a faithful picture of the main features and social relations of feudal society in the Sung and Yuan dynasties that it can create so many typical heroes from different classes and with different characters.

Although Marshal Kao, who represents the oppressors, appears only once in the plot against Lin Chung, his henchmen dog the latter's footsteps. Steward Lu and Fu An do the Marshal's bidding, while Tung Chao and Hsueh Pa in Wild Boar Forest and the warden and head keeper in the Tsangchou prison are simply executioners sent by him. This host of executioners large and small around him weighs heavily upon the law-abiding Lin Chung, while the tragedy of his banishment and separation from his wife shatter his dream of a comfortable life. Anyone reading of this bitter parting for life must hate the tyrants responsible. But desperate as is Lin Chung's plight, the author does not force him to rise at once in revolt. In accordance with the laws of actual life he lets this character formed in a special social environment continue to be tested by life itself. Lin Chung changes by degrees as a result of one happening after another. His situation grows steadily more insupportable on his way to banishment and in the Tsangchou prison where he is rudely treated by the head keeper, till the reader suffers vicariously and longs impatiently for him to change. In all these episodes, the author brings out clearly the effect of the environment on Lin Chung. But none of these things are enough to shatter his acquiescence to fate and bring about a decisive change in him. Not till Lin Chung is driven to the point where he must either perish or resist, do we get the chapter "Lin Chung in the Temple in a

Snowstorm," in which the long-suffering Lin Chung takes the path of revolt. In this chapter the author links closely together the environment and the character, and achieves a high level of artistic synthesis by the way in which he conjures up the grim atmosphere. The howling north wind, the snow whirling down in great eddies, the blazing conflagration in the fodder depot are closely linked with the changes in Lin Chung and powerfully reflect his passionate desire for revenge and his courageous spirit. Amid these warring elements Lin Chung slays his enemies—Steward Lu, Fu An and the head keeper.

This brilliant craftsmanship gives profound expression to the actions and truthfulness of the characters, holds the attention of readers and moves them deeply.

There is no more weakness in Lin Chung after this. From now on he is one of the bravest leaders of the heroes of the marshes, the firmest, the most daring in all battles against the tyrants.

These changes in Lin Chung conform completely to the rules of character development and leave the reader with a strong, unforgettably vivid impression. They deepen our understanding of how it was that a law-abiding arms instructor who had grown up in the feudal court could be driven by savage oppression to take the path of revolt.

The foregoing is, of course, not simply a question of the art of writing, but is inseparable from the deeply "popular" nature of *Outlaws of the Marshes,* from the deep knowledge and understanding of the heroes shown by the authors—both those who handed on the story orally and those who wrote it up. From our analysis of the creation of a character like Lin Chung we can see that the reason why his story moves us is not because it contains exciting adventures but because the author has given a truthful, specific historical account of the social environment of the time and of men's development according to objective laws in this specific environment. It should be said that this is the main feature of realist characterization, and it is the reason for the unsurpassed success of *Outlaws of the Marshes* among China's classical works.

Outlaws of the Marshes, with its magnificently drawn characters and tremendous artistic power, has moved and influenced countless generations in China. After it was written down it circulated very widely and has been used in many literary forms. These tales of heroes are today known to all, so that virtually everyone in China, whether old or young, can tell you about certain figures in this novel.

What is more significant is that these heroic figures served as examples and weapons in the peasants' struggle. China's millions throughout the centuries have drawn inspiration and strength from this book. The leaders of many later peasant revolts took the names of the Liangshan heroes or used slogans from the Liangshan revolt such as "Mete Out Justice for Heaven!" "Kill the Rich to Relieve the Poor!" "Loyalty and Justice!" These watchwords helped to organize the masses and deal severe blows at the feudal system and the feudal rulers.

The influence of this novel is inestimable. No other of our classics has exercised a comparable influence. We are therefore justified in saying that this is a great epic of peasant revolt, a splendid work of classical realist literature, and the most treasured part of our cultural heritage. (pp. 65-71)

Li Hsi-fan, "A Great Novel of Peasant Revolt," in Chinese Literature *No. 12, December, 1959, pp. 62-71.*

CHEN MIN-SHENG (essay date 1962)

[*In the following excerpt, Chen investigates why* Romance *is regarded as "a source-book of life and history."*]

The *Romance of the Three Kingdoms,* by Lo Kuan-chung of the fourteenth century, is the first long novel in classical Chinese literature. Its rich content, brilliantly constructed plot and masterly characterization marked a new departure in the development of Chinese fiction. The book depicts the political and military struggle between feudal rulers of China and reflects the historical conditions of nearly a hundred years from the end of the second to the end of the third century. (p. 62)

Chen Shou's history [*The History of the Three Kingdoms*], and these various anecdotes, legends and prompt books . . . were the basis and raw material of the *Romance of the Three Kingdoms,* one of the world's great novels. (p. 63)

Based to a large extent on historical fact, this novel reflects all the ramifications of the contest for power among various ruling cliques during the Three Kingdoms period, vividly bringing out the sharpness of these conflicts. The fierce struggles for selfish interests left a mark on all those involved, affecting every aspect of their life—family, friends and marriage. Those in power showed unparalled cruelty and ferocity. The whole country was in a turmoil and the lot of the common people was wretched indeed. It was against such a vast and complex background that this epic work was written. Chinese readers, comparing this book with a later masterpiece, *Water Margin,* have passed this verdict: "*Water Margin* teaches courage, while the *Romance of the Three Kingdoms* teaches wisdom." In other words, men down the ages have always regarded this novel as a source-book of life and history.

The author in this novel created more than four hundred characters with different personalities and the work embodies his own political ideal—benevolent rule and opposition to despotism. The struggle between the two factions of Liu Pei and Tsao Tsao is treated, with a wealth of human documentation, as a struggle between a kindly ruler and a despot, a good man and a tyrant. So the conflict in the story unfolds and deepens through the struggles between these two groups, while the conflict with Sun Chuan's faction is described as secondary; sometimes Sun Chuan allies with Liu Pei against Tsao Tsao, at others he helps Tsao Tsao against Liu Pei. By this treatment the complex struggle among these political factions comes to possess a typical significance; stress is laid on its main features, while a clear and logical picture and one of absorbing interest is presented.

The author shows his hatred for treacherous schemers and warlords whose ambition knew no bounds in his successful portrait of Tsao Tsao. All that is evil and hateful in rulers of the feudal society is epitomized in him. Hypocritical and crafty, willing to stoop to the basest machinations, Tsao Tsao adopts a pose of humanity and justice to win men to his side. After wantonly murdering an innocent man, he laments bitterly and gives his victim a sumptuous burial to show his fairness and benevolence. Once escaping from the capital, he is well treated by an old friend of his father called Lu, but he suspects that Lu is going to betray him and kills the man's whole family; later he discovers his mistake, but to prevent Lu from taking revenge he kills the old man too. His motto in life is "It is better for me to injure others than to let any other man injure me." However, Lo Kuan-chung does not simply make Tsao Tsao an out-and-out villain. His penetrating portrayal of Tsao Tsao's wickedness and cruelty is supplemented by equally vivid descriptions of the man's extraordinary ability and courage, so that Tsao Tsao as a character appears both complex and thoroughly authentic. The remarkable character of Tsao Tsao will live as long as Chinese literature.

The author shows a partisan spirit too when it comes to presenting Liu Pei, Kuan Yu, Chuko Liang, Chang Fei and others whom he endows with such qualities as loyalty, patriotism, courage and wisdom.

Liu Pei, for instance, is a humane, enlightened ruler who loves the people, helps those in distress and works untiringly to pacify the state. Of course, in this respect the author was influenced by the orthodox view of history of that time. Liu Pei, a descendant of the House of Han, wants to restore the Han empire and therefore he represents the side of right; whereas Tsao Tsao, prime minister to the Han emperor, has contrived to usurp the throne and is therefore disloyal and a traitor. Historians and critics today hold divergent views on this question, but it is perhaps worth pointing out that the ideas expressed in the stories about the Three Kingdoms came into being over a long period of time and were the outcome of very real problems. The Han people had suffered for long years from foreign aggression as well as from despotic rule. The common people's own experience and their deep observation of life made it natural that they should champion Liu Pei and condemn Tsao Tsao for his many evil deeds. This was actually a reflection of the people's patriotism, their demand for a better and more stable government and their opposition to despotism and oppression. Obviously, in that historical period it was, to a certain extent a reflection of the people's aspirations.

Liu Pei's adviser Chuko Liang and his sworn brother Kuan Yu, both of whom stand highly in the author's regard, have also had a very strong influence on later generations owing to the skill with which they are presented.

Chuko Liang's extraordinary wisdom and foresight and Kuan Yu's conspicuous courage and dignity have won the admiration and love of readers through the centuries. More important still are the moral qualities which they symbolize: Chuko Liang's selfless devotion and loyalty and Kuan Yu's unswerving sense of justice and goodness to Liu Pei. Many unforgettable episodes in the novel lay stress on these moral attributes, and by so doing add to the stature of Liu Pei.

The author's view of these men was naturally conditioned by his age. For example, in the Battle of the Red Cliff he regards Kuan Yu as gallant and kind because he lets Tsao Tsao go, while Chuko Liang is described as a man who has powers to summon the wind at will. But these instances of prejudice and superstition are after all unimportant and cannot seriously detract from the greatness of this masterpiece.

The hundred and twenty chapters of the *Romance of the Three Kingdoms,* totalling over seven hundred thousand words, deal mainly with various campaigns, battles and skirmishes; but these are described and treated differently, without any repetition. In the course of describing these fierce and involved battles, the author also depicts complex human rela-tionships between the ruler and his ministers, between father and son, between brothers, friends, or husband and wife, while there are passages presenting the life of hermits in the hills, feasts and celebrations, marriages, the writing of poems and so forth. In this way the spirit of the characters is more profoundly revealed, and a rich picture of historical reality is given. The story revolves around wars, which are dealt with to show a host of characters. The descriptions of war in this novel are outstanding in classical Chinese literature, while the characters in the book are known throughout China.

The section dealing with the Battle of the Red Cliff is one of the finest in the book for its detailed, profound portrayal of the complexity and sharp contradictions in a campaign. It takes eight chapters, starting with Chuko Liang's argument with Sun Chuan's advisers and ending with Kuan Yu's release of Tsao Tsao. It deals not merely with fighting but with the tact and wisdom of Chuko Liang. Tsao Tsao is attacking Sun Chuan and Liu Pei, but this section is concerned largely with the secondary conflict between Liu Pei and Sun Chuan; and Chuko Liang's decisive role throughout the whole campaign and at the crucial moment is emphasized. One subtle and interesting episode after another brings out his extraordinary wisdom. He joins in the campaign alone and uses Sun Chuan's forces to achieve a great victory for Liu Pei.

The author's skill is shown above all by the way in which he uses these episodes to draw character. When Tsao Tsao is advancing on the Yangtse Valley at the head of eight hundred and thirty thousand men, the officers of the south are alarmed and cannot decide whether to make peace or fight. Chuko Liang has a clear idea of the situation, however; he analyses the strength and weakness of the three sides and takes the initiative, never worrying because Liu Pei's force is weak. Sun Chuan hesitates, on the other hand, feeling unequal to resisting so powerful an enemy. Chou Yu has a good grasp of the situation; while treating different factions politely, he despises those who have panicked and makes careful plans to worst the enemy; yet when he pits his wits against Chuko Liang, his limitations, pettiness and over-confidence are revealed. Again, Tsao Tsao is shown as a proud man who despises his enemy and counts on his superior strength to win the war and conquer the whole empire; but his weakness is utilized and he falls repeatedly into his enemy's traps until he is badly defeated. As this dramatic story develops, all the characters in it spring to life.

Although the *Romance of the Three Kingdoms* covers such a vast range of political and military struggles, the author shows discrimination in his choice of episodes and great attention to detail in his characterization. For example, in the Battle of the Red Cliff, Chuko Liang, Chou Yu and Lu Su all have political acumen; but Lo Kuan-chung contrasts the attitude of these three men to the main conflict—the attack on Tsao Tsao's forces—to reveal their different characteristics. Lu Su is used to bring out his two friends' wisdom and foresight, while the description of Chou Yu reveals the broadmindedness and shrewdness of Chuko Liang. Again, the pretended defection of Tsai Chung and Tsai Ho, which appears to take Chou Yu in, but which he actually uses for his own purpose, is followed by that of Huang Kai and Kan Tse, which at first arouses Tsao Tsao's suspicions but eventually fools him; the scene in which Chou Yu fools Chiang Kan by pretending to be asleep is followed by that in which Chiang Kan falls into Chou Yu's trap by trying the same trick. These similar actions have such different results that they shed light on the mood, temperament and situation of the different characters involved. Then there are many fine touches of detail exemplifying the skill with which the author handles his plot. For instance, Huang Kai's loyalty is first suggested during Chuko Liang's debate with the advisers, to be emphasized later in the crucial scenes when he is beaten and when he takes his fire-boats up the river. All this throws Huang Kai's character into sharp relief. This attention to detail undoubtedly strengthens the artistic impact of the work.

The *Romance of the Three Kingdoms* exerted a tremendous influence on the novels which followed it and many later writers modelled their historical novels on this work, which also supplied the theme for other forms of literature and drama.

All the tactics and strategy described in this novel, the offensive and defensive measures employed, the reasons for the rise and fall of kingdoms and the other historical experience embodied in it have much influenced later generations. It is said that Li Tzu-cheng and Chang Hsien-chung who led the seventeenth-century peasant revolt at the end of the Ming dynasty learned much from this novel, as did some leaders and generals of the Taiping revolution. And countless others have admired the heroes of this novel or used the characters in it as a yardstick for behaviour in real life. The *Romance of the Three Kingdoms* can without exaggeration be described as a textbook on life in feudal China. (pp. 64-9)

> Chen Min-sheng, "On the 'Romance of the Three Kingdoms'," in Chinese Literature *No. 2, February, 1962, pp. 62-9.*

JACK WU (essay date 1963)

[*In the following excerpt, Wu challenges Pearl S. Buck's humanistic interpretation and, as he labels it, "watered down" portrayal of the outlaws in her 1933 translation of* Shui-hu chuan.]

It is nearly impossible for a novel of any large influence to pass through this discordant world of ours without being variously labeled with conflicting morals. The glorious but unrealistic title of *All Men Are Brothers* is adopted by Pearl Buck for her translation of the Chinese novel, *Shui Hu Chuan,* and constitutes but the latest of a series of misreadings into this famous book about a hundred and eight outlaws supposed to have lived in thirteenth-century China.

Although the story of *Shui Hu Chuan* has long been a favorite among the Chinese people, the book has been strictly forbidden until the beginning of the present century. As quickly as it assumed the leading position in popular Chinese literature, it was variously interpreted to favor different interests.

Red China calls it the first communist literature of China. On the other hand, most humanitarian critics are eager to conclude that it is a tribute to the brotherhood of man, as Pearl Buck clearly signified in her arbitrarily chosen title, *All Men Are Brothers,* and in the concluding sentence of her introduction, "It stands still great and full of the meaning of humanity" [see excerpt dated 1933].

Pearl Buck states that she has attempted to preserve the meaning and style of the original. I cannot but doubt her success in this extremely difficult task, not primarily because she hastily translated while a Chinese scholar read the book to her, but mainly because of internal textual evidences of general carelessness and occasional errors.

We can only conjecture that the Chinese scholar's moralistic spirit as well as Miss Buck's love for humanity may have unconsciously influenced her interpretation of a book that is actually pessimistic in its views. This cannot be definitely proved without involving the language of the original text. However the general brutality of the heroes and their total unconcern in murdering innocent victims, the bitterness of their protests, and the thoroughness of their vengeance, hardly indicate that they can be considered "humanitarian." Instead, these men are a group of outcasts from the evil society they live in; they are active reactionaries ready to remove anyone that stands in their way.

This uncompromising and unforgiving attitude would seem to bring them nearer to the communist idea of class struggle. However, a closer look at their conduct discloses the fallacy of this conclusion. It is true that the heroes are more likely to kill men of property and power than negligible and helpless commoners. But "class struggle" hardly accounts for their practice of drugging travelers and fixing them up to sell as cow or buffalo meat (depending on the fatness or the leanness of the victims). Most of the heroes have at one time or another been badly dealt with, and cheated by other "heroes" until they come to respect the prowess of each other. Is this the communist idea of equality among comrades? Perhaps it is. If so, the communist explanation of the text would be curious indeed. The lust for wealth that is universal among the characters of the novel, and the respect for position and authority—carried to the extreme of assigning seats of priority among the robbers—would seem to contradict the communist ideology for a classless society.

Fortunately the essence of the book's popularity goes far deeper than the propagandist labels that might be read on the surface. What angers these outlaws is what angers every human heart: the threat to its individual identity. The outlaws revolt against society because their individualism is suppressed. They kill their foes without hesitation and treat their friends with generosity; and this embracing of extremes shows them to be neither followers of selfless virtue nor slaves to senseless evil, but egoistic and passionate average people capable alike of love and hate.

It is a corrupt society that the author describes; yet there is also immense good in that society. Through the world of villians moves a group of courageous fighters. In the midst of treachery, adultery, and bribery we see a group of heroes whose faults are varied but whose common virtues are loyalty, friendship, and generosity.

Double-dealing and disloyalty are always avenged, and many examples are given. Treachery is indeed the major theme of the novel; and personal loyalty may be said to be the outstanding moral. In response to an exhortation to join the gang, three heroic brothers say: "We will sell this hot blood of ours to that one who knows us for what we are." And this is the typical attitude of the heroes. Thus the bloody acts of the outlaws are sanctified by their rare loyalty and compare favorably with the actions of their opponents. (pp. 86-7)

Since the traditional tea-house narration form is adopted, and the story is aimed at holding the momentary interest of talkative tea drinkers, breathtaking and exaggerated actions are essential; and eye-opening, meticulous descriptions are helpful. Thus interest and realism are often found to be the dual virtues of this book. The idea of all men being brothers appealed very little to the oppressed and ignorant commoners of that age, and it was duly neglected, if not even disbelieved in, by the author. It is hard to conceive that a book of such obvious fury could be the work of a disinterested philosopher who loved all mankind as brothers, and that he spent his time to adorn a purely moralistic tale or fable. If this is a moralistic tale or fable, it is certainly not a conventional one.

Although double standards of conduct among the heroes greatly mar their virtue, we are at least presented with greater realism. Enough love for all humanity is indeed a hard proposition, even in this modern age and even with Christian guidance; in-group love is much more common. If we are not presented with the purest ideas and actions, we are at least exhorted to loyalty and friendship. Let us consider how isolated and friendless modern men are, before we demand the absolute good from those that have gone before us. Surely it is not an easy thing to sacrifice one's life for another man, and the courage and devotion of these heroes deserve our respect.

To have a true appreciation of the virtues of these heroes, we should not cover up their shortcomings, and the translation of Pearl Buck is watered down—it does not give the deep pathos of bitterness and revenge which is found in the original. (pp. 87-8)

> *Jack Wu, "The Morals of 'All Men Are Brothers',"*
> in Western Humanities Review, *Vol. XVII, No. 1,*
> *Winter, 1963, pp. 86-8.*

C. T. HSIA   (essay date 1968)

[*Hsia is considered one of the foremost scholars of classical Chinese literature. In the following excerpt from* The Classical Chinese Novel, *he examines the advancements made by Lo in literary techniques and his portrayal of the Three Kingdoms period.*]

The Romance of the Three Kingdoms is by design a historical narrative rather than a historical novel as we understand the term in the West. Hardly a single character in the book is ahistorical, and there is no plot to speak of beyond the plot of history. Though it borrows from the oral tradition of storytelling, it is clearly far more an epic than a romance (to borrow the distinction maintained in W. P. Ker's still useful book, *Epic and Romance*), in that its drama of human motivation is rarely adulterated by other independent kinds of narrative interest to be found in knightly and amatory adventure, in pageantry and fantasy. Finical scholars from the Ch'ing historian Chang Hsüeh-ch'eng to Hu Shih, it is true, have complained that it is neither sufficiently truthful to be good history nor sufficiently fictionalized to be good literature. To complain so, however, is to disregard the peculiar strengths and limitations of the *yen-i* type of fiction of which *The Romance of the Three Kingdoms* is the first and greatest example: it attains the condition of good literature precisely because its slight fictional elaboration of history has restored for us the actuality of history. The work contains, to be sure, occasional minor episodes patently fictitious and unworthy of the name of history. Yet in comparison with a great many other Chinese historical novels or with the pseudohistorical epics of the Renaissance, *The Romance of the Three Kingdoms* is remarkably chaste in its supernaturalism and restrained in its use of folk material. By and large it is a sober drama of political and military contention of about a hundred years' duration (A.D. 168-265) among rival power groups bidding for control of the Chinese empire.

Long before Lo Kuan-chung (*ca.* 1330-1400) compiled *The Romance of the Three Kingdoms* in the late Yuan or early Ming period, its major characters and events had been romanticized by poets, storytellers, and playwrights so that their influence could not but be felt in his work. Yet Lo's main intention was to abide by history as he knew it and to reject palpable fiction. Though for the earlier attempts at historical fiction, which are nothing but inept compilations of oral material, we should properly emphasize their popular, folk quality rather than their individual authorship, *San-kuo-chih yen-i* represents a major breakthrough for the Chinese novel in that it is a unified piece of work by a single author which is intentionally corrective of the narrative crudities and superstitious excesses of the storytellers. The Three Kingdoms period had been a major subject for historical storytellers at least since the late T'ang. Though they followed the main events of the period, in catering to their unlearned audience they must in time have exaggerated the traits of certain beloved and detested characters and added a wealth of fanciful and interpretative fiction until the retold cycle of stories departed quite far from official history. There is an extant compilation of such stories dating from the Yuan period entitled *San-kuo-chih p'ing-hua*. This version is atrocious in style and often transcribes the names of places and persons in wrong characters. Events are narrated most sketchily and history itself is reduced to a contest in magic, cunning, and prowess. Insofar as other preserved *p'ing-hua* are less illiterate, it is possible that the publishers in this instance had entrusted the task of compilation to a hack of little learning and less writing ability. Based on promptbooks of provincial storytellers, it could not have represented the art of storytelling among its famous practitioners in the capital cities. But with all its uncharacteristic crudities, this version must have conformed to their repertoire in one respect at least: the application of the theory of moral retribution to the workings of history. (pp. 34-6)

Lo Kuan-chung does away with all this kind of didactic nonsense. In fact, he is so intent on retelling history that the earliest preserved version of his *San kuo* (the so-called Hung-chih edition, actually published in the Chia-ching period, 1522-66) begins without rhetorical flourish of any kind:

> Upon the death of Huan-ti of the Later Han, Ling-ti succeeded to the throne. He was then twelve years old. At court Grand General Tou Wu, Grand Tutor Ch'en Fan, and Minister of Public Instruction Hu Kuang gave him counsel and assistance. The ninth month of that autumn, the palace eunuchs Ts'ao Chieh and Wang Fu arrogated power. Tou Wu and Ch'en Fan plotted their death, but their plot leaked out and they themselves were killed by Ts'ao Chieh and Wang Fu. From then on the palace eunuchs became powerful.

In its complete independence of the oral conventions, the passage recalls the terse style of official dynastic history and makes few concessions in the direction of a more popular narrative. (p. 36)

Lo Kuan-chung was writing in conscious departure from the tradition of the storytellers rather than in imitation of them. His novel was popular literature with a difference, compiled by a scholar and carrying forward the historiographical tradition of Ssu-ma Ch'ien and Ssu-ma Kuang. As a matter of fact, several Ming publishers of *San kuo* and other *yen-i* novels announce these works as adaptations from Ssu-ma Kuang's comprehensive history, with the phrase *an Chien* (According to *Tzu-chih t'ung-chien*) duly incorporated in their titles.

Lo Kuan-chung is extremely fortunate in that his source, Ch'en Shou's *San kuo chih,* is rich in historical and biographical detail. One is used to the idea of the voluminousness of Chinese dynastic histories; yet, with all the records at their disposal, most official historians are actually too concise to fully capture the personalities of the historical figures they are dealing with. Though superior to later histories, Ch'en Shou's *San kuo chih* is less copious in detail and less dramatic in style than Ssu-ma Ch'ien's *Records,* but its relative terseness is early complemented by a lengthy commentary by P'ei Sung-chih of the Liu Sung period (420-78), who sees as his task the inclusion of all relevant passages from other sources to illuminate the text. Drawing upon some 210 titles, most of which have long since been lost, P'ei Sung-chih therefore preserves twice the amount of material included in the history proper; most of this material dates from Ch'en Shou's time (the third century) and has as much claim to reliability. Some of these sources are written from a definite point of view; thus, the biography of Ts'ao Ts'ao known as *Ts'ao Man chuan* includes many interesting episodes that are derogatory in intention though their maliciousness does not necessarily preclude their truth. In compiling his novel, Lo Kuan-chung draws as much from P'ei as from Ch'en, apparently proceeding on the assumption that all this material is worthy of elaboration. It may appear as a weakness that he does not have the modern historian's sophistication or passion for consistency. Yet, whereas a modern biographer like Lytton Strachey inevitably introduces a note of falsity in his ironic concern for a consistent image, Lo Kuan-chung, in his apparent failure to discriminate among his sources, ultimately attains a remarkably impersonal objectivity in his recreation of a complex age.

In compiling his novel, Lo Kuan-chung had also to accept certain myths that were too well entrenched in the popular mind to be rejected, such as the sworn brotherhood of Liu Pei, Kuan Yü, and Chang Fei; the extraordinary nobility of Kuan Yü; and the supernatural wisdom of Liu Pei's chief counselor, Chu-ko Liang. These myths, however, were themselves developed from hints in the official history, and their inclusion in the novel dramatizes the history without falsifying it to any serious extent. Thus the sworn brotherhood of Liu, Kuan, and Chang confirms rather than contradicts the genuinely fraternal relations between the Shu leader and his comrades-in-arms; Kuan Yü's undoubted nobility lends poignancy to his folly and arrogance; and, with the possible exception of one important episode, Chu-ko Liang's supernatural powers only embellish his career without contributing to the impression that his wizardry is essential to his success.

Because of the compiler's eclectic inclusion of a diversity of materials, it is very easy to misread *The Romance of the Three Kingdoms.* Careless readers would form their impression of the major characters, say Ts'ao Ts'ao and Kuan Yü, on the strength of a few dramatic and unambiguous scenes and then maintain that it is indeed the compiler's conscious intention to vilify one and ennoble the other. While agreeing with this simplistic view of the major characters, more careful readers would notice scenes where they are presented in a different light. Thus Hu Shih, who, incidentally, subscribes to the view that the novel came about through a slow process of evolution, maintains that *San kuo* is an inconsistent narrative:

The authors of *San-kuo yen-i,* its revisers and final

editor were all provincial Confucians of ordinary intelligence; they were not literary geniuses or exceptional thinkers. They did their level best to portray Chu-ko Liang. But they had a preconceived notion that Chu-ko Liang's great forte lies in his "resourceful plotting and strategy"; so in their hands he eventually became a Taoist magician of divine intuition and wonderful calculation who could summon winds and propitiate the stars. They further wanted to portray Liu Pei as a man of benevolence and righteousness but ended in making him a coward of no ability. Again, they wanted to portray a Kuan Yü of divine prowess, but he was reduced to an arrogant and stupid warrior.

What Hu Shih seems to be doing here is testing the book against the popular conceptions of three beloved characters and deploring its lack of success in embodying these conceptions. While, in line with Chu Hsi and the succeeding historians, Lo Kuan-chung shows evident sympathy for the cause of Shu and regards it as the legitimate successor to the Han dynasty, it would be extremely naïve to suppose that he had indeed preconceived its founding heroes in a simple-minded fashion. For most Chinese, of course, it is very easy to misread the novel since they have been conditioned by the popular theater and the storytellers to accept unquestioningly the benevolence of Liu Pei, the wizardry of Chu-ko Liang, and the divine bravery of Kuan Yü. Furthermore, in the version then available to Hu Shih—the standard version edited by Mao Tsung-kang—minor stylistic changes have been introduced to ensure the reader's sympathy for these heroes. But even in that edition the version of Lo Kuan-chung has remained substantially intact and no one should have been misled by the thin veneer of flattery.

Take Kuan Yü, a most misunderstood character. To any unbiased reader it must be quite apparent that Lo Kuan-chung has adopted, not inadvertently or perfunctorily but deliberately, Ch'en Shou's view of the hero as a haughty warrior deficient in generalship. Lo Kuan-chung was writing at a time when Kuan Yü was already an object of national veneration (he was to become a god in Ch'ing times) and so he accords him all the reverence merited by a saint. He duly notes his imposing looks and martial stature, his long beard and mighty sword, and, whenever justified, impresses us with his surpassing bravery and extreme nobility. But at the same time he gives history its due by noting in instance after instance his sheer ignorance of policy, his childish vanity and unbearable conceit. And this conceit, abetted by general credulity, eventually brings about his downfall. He dies a shattered idol deserving some pity because of his invincible belief in his own sagacity and prowess.

Far from producing a discordant impression, as Hu Shih would suggest, the mythical and historical strands of Kuan Yü's character are consistently interwoven to produce an impression of organic unity. The author makes it quite clear that both his strengths and his weaknesses stem from his extreme pride and self-confidence. He underscores this point in describing Kuan Yü's initial deed of valor that so impresses the assembled nobles and rebel leaders in their expedition against their common enemy, Tung Cho. They are temporarily at a loss before the unexpected might of Tung Cho's general, Hua Hsiung. . . . (pp. 39-42)

In this scene the author has refrained from describing the actual encounter between the two warriors so that Kuan Yü's celerity in making good his boast may make a deeper impression upon the leaders assembled at the tent, as it does upon the reader. Initially, the leaders are divided in their reactions to his boast: his impressive features and carriage are definitely in his favor but his humble position speaks for his extreme insolence. The exchange of words among three of these leaders—Yuan Shao, Yuan She, Ts'ao Ts'ao—may not seem impressive until one realizes that each speaks entirely in character and that it is these small scenes of dialogue that build up the cumulative impression of the realness of the major characters. A vain aristocrat, Yuan She shows his utter contempt for the plebeian upstart. Yuan Shao is not as rude as his younger brother; in fact, he has always cultivated an image of hospitality so that, until he suffers utter defeat in the hands of Ts'ao Ts'ao many years later, he enjoys the reputation of a great leader with a following of distinguished counselors and generals. In the present scene his characteristic weakness is shown in the fact that, while he himself is willing to try Kuan Yü, he fears the ridicule of the opponent. Ts'ao Ts'ao eventually vanquishes the Yuan brothers, and in this scene his superior judgment is already apparent in his confidence in a man of ability, whatever his origin.

But Ts'ao Ts'ao may have been overimpressed. If in the present scene the author secures for his hero a strong impression of self-confidence and bravery, he at the same time may have hinted at a possible weakness in his eagerness to impress people. As we read on, we are introduced to more tableaux of this sort, with Kuan Yü keeping night vigil outside the bedchamber of Liu Pei's wives to avoid any hint of a scandal, charging down a hill to kill a general who under normal circumstances would have been his superior in armed combat, swiftly dispatching another enemy general to prove his innocence before the incredulous Chang Fei, and calmly playing a game of *go* while a physician operates on his poisoned arm. With his undoubted courage and his long streak of good luck, he acts with increasing arrogance and haughtiness to sustain his public image, not realizing that even in his prime there are at least a dozen generals who are his equal in armed combat and that in military strategy and statesmanship he is a mere bungler. It is his tragedy that he eventually takes his appearance for his reality. (pp. 43-4)

Kuan Yü's downfall and death are recounted in some of the finest chapters of the novel (chaps. 74-77). An aging warrior, he is reaching the pinnacle of his fame but also exhibiting the most impossible haughtiness and folly. Luck once more prevails in his vanquishment of P'ang Te, a fierce Wei general determined to destroy his reputation and expose it as a lie, and in his capture of P'ang Te's cowardly commander, Yü Chin. But Kuan Yü proves no match for a man of true cunning, the Wu commander Lü Meng. His forces disintegrate under the combined attack of Wei and Wu, but he remains a hero of desolate grandeur as for the last time he breaks out of the enemy's encirclement to face his capture and death.

In my presentation of Kuan Yü's character, I have tried to demonstrate the care with which Lo Kuan-chung has used his sources to compile his novel. It is simply not true, as Hu Shih has alleged, that he conceived a Kuan Yü of "divine prowess" and then bungled the job by turning him into an "arrogant and stupid" warrior. The arrogance and simple-mindedness are essential to Lo's concept of a hero cursed with the tragic disease of hubris; without this flaw, a storybook hero of divine prowess would have been insufferable. By the cumulative use of telling detail, Lo Kuan-chung has

blended the historical and folkloristic concepts of the hero and made him into something truly memorable. (p. 48)

I have presented *San kuo* primarily as a novel of character with its continual preoccupation with human motivation. Yet a young Chinese reading the work for the first time will inevitably be engrossed in the story itself, in its countless military campaigns and political intrigues. But for the mature reader even the cleverest stratagems of Chu-ko Liang, however they may overawe the young, are nothing beside the cunning of a Western detective, and few scenes of armed combat are as vivid as those in *The Iliad,* where the duel of champions is inevitably presented in sharp and grim detail. Like most other Chinese historical novelists, Lo Kuan-chung is often merely content with summary narration, giving us the number of strokes exchanged between two generals until one flees or is killed. (p. 63)

In like manner, the battles and intrigues in *San kuo* are interesting to the extent that they are informed with human purpose. As in the *Tso Commentary,* the first major Chinese chronicle to describe battles in detail, human interest resides far more in the preparation for battle than in the battle itself. This is true of the most celebrated long episode in the novel—the Battle of Red Cliff, during which the combined forces of Sun Ch'üan and Liu Pei smash Ts'ao Ts'ao's ambitious design to cross the Yangtze River and subdue the Wu kingdom. It is the pivotal event upon which hangs the eventual equilibrium of power of the three kingdoms, and Lo Kuan-chung rises to the occasion by giving it the most elaborate fictional treatment of any event in the novel. (p. 64)

After calling attention to the childishness of some of the most celebrated scenes in the account of the Battle of Red Cliff, Hu Shih draws the conclusion that, if these most fictionalized scenes are obviously weak, then the rest of the novel which is little fictionalized must enjoy even less literary success. But Lo Kuan-chung, at least while he was composing *The Romance of the Three Kingdoms,* had no pretension to being a novelist. Occasionally he rises to the challenge of fiction, but his habitual strength lies in his role as a popular historian. He exhibits little talent for that full-bodied kind of fiction which calls for the invention of character and plot in the absence of historical documentation. Where his sources have misled him—as in some of the episodes in the Battle of Red Cliff—his further elaboration of these sources only enhances their naïveté.

The habitual strength of the work is therefore far more impressively present in the little fictionalized battle at Kuan-tu between the armies of Ts'ao Ts'ao and Yuan Shao than in the battle at Red Cliff. In hewing to the line of the historical chronicle, Lo Kuan-chung has preserved intact a gripping story that could have been fitting material for Greek tragedy. Yuan Shao's indecisiveness and lack of leadership, his passionate partiality for one of his sons, his failure to make use of a group of individually brilliant but feuding counselors—these are some of the factors in the easy victory scored by Ts'ao Ts'ao over an amply provisioned army of numerical superiority. Lo Kuan-chung does not elaborate on any of the episodes building up to the battle at Kuan-tu and the subsequent rapid disintegration of Yuan Shao's forces, but the reader nevertheless feels caught in the web of a weighty historical event fraught with deep human significance. (pp. 70-1)

Because in *San kuo* history is no longer broken up into a series of individual and collective biographies, the ultimate sense of fate as heaven's design emerges with even greater clarity. Not only the battle at Kuan-tu but scores of other weighty and little fictionalized events contribute to the impression that, while heaven's design is inscrutable, it is at the same time the sum total of men's conscious endeavor. From the meanest general who makes a brief appearance only to forfeit his life in the battlefield to the sagacious Chu-ko Liang whose prolonged attempt to rectify the design of heaven ends in failure, the crowded stage of *San kuo* is enkindled with this sense of earnest endeavor. However small his role in history, each candidate for fame enacts a personal drama which is the impingement of his endeavor upon his fate. (p. 74)

> C. T. Hsia, " 'The Romance of the Three King-doms'," in his The Classic Chinese Novel: A Critical Introduction, *Columbia University Press, 1968, pp. 34-74.*

MOSS ROBERTS   (essay date 1976)

[*Roberts is an American essayist and academic. In the following excerpt, he explores issues of political legitimacy and governmental rule addressed by Lo in* Romance of the Three Kingdoms.]

From the ruins of the Han (206 B.C.-A.D. 220), longest and mightiest of China's dynasties, three smaller states emerged and began warring for sovereignty. Lo Kuan-chung's *Three Kingdoms* portrays this fateful moment in Chinese history, when it was uncertain whether the empire could be made whole again. The book is a popular classic, the foremost work of semifictional history in China, and one of the greatest Chinese literary masterpieces. Though it was written six centuries ago, its heroes and legends are still vivid for the Chinese, whose intense consciousness of their history has always been central to their culture. Mao Tsetung has said:

> What I enjoyed were the romances of old China, and especially stories of rebellions. I read . . . the *San Kuo* [*Three Kingdoms*] while still very young and . . . so did most of my schoolmates. . . . We learned many of the stories almost by heart, and discussed and rediscussed them many times. We knew more of them than the old men of the village, who also loved them and used to exchange stories with us. [See excerpt dated 1939].

The vast canvas of *Three Kingdoms* is crowded with stories and peopled with kings and courtiers, peasants, soldiers, sorcerers, scholars. Its themes of power, loyalty, and social obligation appear and vanish, only to surface again in a different context and with ironically altered significance. Its scale of time is dynastic rather than individual: men's acts overtake them, but then run beyond their personal destinies until the flow of history absorbs them all. In much the way that Shakespeare fashioned the English chronicles into drama, Lo Kuan-chung collected tales that had been treasured for centuries by the Chinese people and then transformed them into a sophisticated and panoramic work of art. (pp. xix-xx)

Among the primary questions posed by *Three Kingdoms* is the basic issue of government: What is the source of political legitimacy? Is it geographic advantage—possession of the sacred northern heartlands? Is it genetic right, sanctioned by the principle of continuity within the dynastic patronym? Or is it some higher virtue—a moral charisma that affects both the inner circle of advisers, officers, and officials, as well as the people at large?

At first, *Three Kingdoms* appears to counterpose the first two types of legitimacy through the conflict between the Emperor Tributor and his Chancellor Ts'ao Ts'ao. But in the course of the action Liu Pei validates himself as a contender because he is a moral force, becoming true heir to the Han by his virtue rather than his blood right.

Confucius had sought to idealize clan right by projecting a potential brotherhood of men, although of "noble" men rather than men in general. The Peach Garden Oath, by making strangers brothers in a cause, poses a similar challenge to clan rules for the transmission of position and property. These rules were the mainstays of feudal order. In one episode not included in this translation, Chang Fei, the third brother, presents himself to Liu Pei to atone with his life, thinking he has lost Liu Pei's land and family. Liu Pei comforts him: "A brother is a limb. Wives and children are but clothes, which torn can be mended. But who can restore a broken limb? We linked our destinies in the Peach Garden when we vowed to die as one. My land, my family, I can spare, but not you, midway in our course."

Liu Pei's moral virtue is at full strength when, in flight, with neither land nor titles to bestow, his brothers, advisers, and a human sea all follow him into adversity. By contrast, after he has taken power in his kingdom of the Riverlands, he attempts to reward his followers with choice estates in the newly conquered land. But a loyal general, Chao Yün, stops him: "Military disaster has befallen these people again and again. The deserted fields and homesteads should revert to the local people and not be appropriated for your personal bounty." Liu Pei is dissuaded, but the danger of his ultimate corruptibility should he reign over a restored Han is suggested.

Liu Pei is established as a model, however flawed, against which any Emperor could be tested. Lo Kuan-chung probes the relation between kinship and kingship and the ethics pertaining to each sphere. When the two spheres are in harmony, social order is assured. When they conflict, the consequences may be tragic.

The tragedy of Lo's epic arises from Kuan Yü's imperfect commitment to the brotherhood, followed by Liu Pei's too-perfect commitment. Liu Pei will be brother before king. Breaking with K'ung-ming to fulfill the oath and avenge Kuan Yü, Liu Pei shows the same noble ardor and generosity of spirit that ruined Kuan Yü when he reciprocated the kindness of Ts'ao Ts'ao.

But at his crucial moment Kuan Yü meets with no reciprocity from Ts'ao Ts'ao. When the Southland sends Kuan Yü's head north, Ts'ao Ts'ao mocks the dead visage with the very words he used to beg for mercy after the battle of the Red Cliffs: "You have been well, I trust, general, since we parted?" Unlike Liu Pei, Ts'ao Ts'ao has ambition unrestrained by conscience.

One Chinese scholar [Mao Tsung-kang] has said: "The artful chessplayer in a casual move [ten moves ago] gains the desired response ten moves ahead. The method of narration in *Three Kingdoms* is like this." But in the course of the epic a larger theme is asserted. Through the accumulation of ironies a karmic pattern of retribution develops—history's "law of obligations." In the ever-lengthening perspective of historical movement, the major events and characters are canceled out.

The flow of history, like the flow of the mighty Yangtze,

sweeps heroes off the stage and clears the way for their successors. The effect of individual purpose on the future is small and uncertain.

The law of retribution that flickers through the narrative as irony (the faint indication of retribution's ultimate force) is not something metaphysical or independent. It arises dialectically from the concrete character or event. This is the dramatic reality of *Three Kingdoms.* The ultimate ground of the law of retribution is the will and the judgment of the people. This is the historical reality of *Three Kingdoms.* In the first chapter the popular rebellion that initiates the fall of the Han is described as the result of corruption in the Court. And when Liu Pei is fleeing Ts'ao Ts'ao, he refuses to abandon the human sea following him, remarking: "Any undertaking must be based on the people."

However, the retributive power of the people is rarely manifested overtly in feudal China; it is shown through charms, cures, jingles, omens, and the like. However potent, mass sentiment is largely latent and may manifest itself as a supernatural force. This crucial theme is established in the case of the magician Yü Chi. Executed by a feudal lord for "seducing" the masses, Yü Chi returns to haunt the murderer and eventually drives him to his death. Magic, retribution, and the moral force of the masses are intertwined, preparing the way for the exploits of K'ung-ming, Liu Pei's principal adviser and architect of his restorationist cause. K'ung-ming's phenomenal powers of insight and natural magic rise to apparently supernatural heights, but only when based on the moral force of Liu Pei's virtue. The taproot of that virtue is Liu Pei's link to the masses and to the transcendence of clan right. The ultimate power of history is the people. (pp. xxii-xxiv)

> *Moss Roberts, in an introduction to* Three Kingdoms: China's Epic Drama *by Lo Kuan-chung, edited and translated by Moss Roberts, Pantheon Books, 1976, pp. xix-xxv.*

PETER LI (essay date 1977)

[*Li is an American essayist and academic. In the following excerpt, he analyzes structural patterns in Lo's work, concentrating upon the author's use of a "conflict-resolution" model in* San-kuo *and a "cyclical chain" in* Shui-hu.]

San-kuo yen-i and *Shui-hu chuan* are the earliest examples of extended prose-fiction . . . in China. The appearance of these works in the latter part of the fourteenth century is an unprecedented literary event that deserves our special attention. This essay, however, will not be concerned with the long period of "gestation" that must have preceded their appearance, but will present only some preliminary reflections on the organizational patterns of these narratives. No attempt is made to relate these patterns to sociopolitical and ideological structures, or to other cultural complexes that lie outside these works. My main concern will be to examine *San-kuo* and *Shui-hu* together, side by side, to see how these long prose-narratives, though diverse in nature, are held together as unified, coherent wholes. Although limited in its purview, such an approach is justified on the ground that too often studies of these works have tended to dwell on the portrayal of unforgettable heroes and their historical counterparts, the exploration of these works as manifestations of class struggle and intra-class rivalry, or detailed argumentation on their historical developments, but have not focused sufficient attention on the problem of overall structure and organization.

In one of the most critical and thorough studies of *Shui-hu chuan,* Richard G. Irwin remarked, "*San-kuo yen-i* and *Shui-hu chuan* suffer from the structural weakness and rudimentary characterization typical of such pioneering efforts. The limitations of *San-kuo yen-i* derive from its factual basis and from a lack of selection, while the demands of an artificial mold make for the uneven narrative quality found in *Shui-hu chuan.*" In this statement Irwin has pointed out the crucial issues in *San-kuo* and *Shui-hu* criticism. How should the critical matter of the tension and division between the whole and its parts be handled? How should the critic deal with *San-kuo*'s extensive reliance on historical facts? Chang Hsüch-ch'eng's now famous line, "*San-kuo yen-i* is seven parts fact and three parts fiction . . . " has plagued students of Chinese literature who wish to treat *San-kuo* as literature rather than as popular history. *Shui-hu,* on the other hand, according to Irwin, "is not even a romanticized version of history, but merely a collection of tales, some of them legendary . . . " [see excerpt dated 1953]. It has been rejected from the genre of the historical novel by another critic [Y. W. Ma; see Further Reading]. There is enough disturbing truth in these statements to cause concern. Therefore, this essay will examine some of the methods and principles of organization used in these works; it will contrast these works with the short story, to determine whether they can truly be regarded as extended prose-fiction, or whether they are merely a number of short stories linked together mechanically.

In considering the organization and structure of traditional Chinese fiction, we cannot afford to neglect the two great masters of traditional criticism, Chin Sheng-t'an and Mao Tsung-kang. Their observations on the fine structure of *San-kuo* and *Shui-hu* have given us many insights for understanding these works. On the other hand, it seems that they have in general taken for granted the overall structure and have dwelled only on the fine structure, or, to borrow a term from Chinese drama criticism, "textural linkages." Some examples of these are the art of planting narrative threads, various methods of emphasis by contrast, techniques of creating suspense, ways of building up and rounding out a high point, etc. In other words, their observations have been mostly on the level of the smaller units of narration, such as the single event or incident, the structure of the incident, and occasionally the interconnection between incidents. Their overall approach can be summarized in this succinct statement of Chin Sheng-t'an: "What is the essence of good writing? It is the careful selection of words, construction of sentences, arrangement of the composition, and organization of sections." . . . The traditional Chinese critics have brought to our attention the importance of the small scale logical connection between events, and the close interweaving of narrative strands. These we cannot afford to lose sight of in our search for larger structural patterns. (pp. 73-5)

Perhaps too obvious to need mentioning, the traditional Chinese critics did not point out the three principal lines of action centered about the three protagonists in *San-kuo,* Ts'ao Ts'ao, Liu Pei, and Sun Ch'üan, which form the central narrative threads in *San-kuo.* (pp. 75-6)

The interrelationship between events and sequences are numerous and intricate. Let me cite one example; the royal hunt at Hsü-t'ien leads to the emperor's issuing of the secret "sash-belt" decree that leads to Liu Pei's signing of the decree that commits him to opposing Ts'ao Ts'ao; this adversary relationship between the two then leads to Ts'ao Ts'ao's numerous subsequent attempts to eliminate Liu Pei, and so on. (p. 78)

The major points of conflict follow a pattern of development that I have labeled a conflict-resolution model. There are four stages in this model: (1) a point of contention, (2) confrontation among the opposing parties, (3) open conflict, and (4) the resolution. The first major conflict is between Yüan Shao and Ts'ao Ts'ao at Kuan-tu. The point of contention is the imperial capital at Hsü-tu, which has been the envy of Yüan Shao for some time. As early as Chapter 18, Ts'ao Ts'ao has known of Yüan Shao's designs, and Kuo Chia (one of Ts'ao Ts'ao's advisers) has predicted his master's ultimate victory over Yüan Shao. But the major outbreak does not take place until after several intermediate stages in which the four other major contenders for power have been put out of action: Lü Pu, Yüan Shu, Sun Ts'e, and Liu Pei. . . . Even though the death of Yüan Shao ends the conflict, it is not the final resolution. With his position secure, Ts'ao Ts'ao now plans his southward expansion.

The second major conflict is the battle at Ch'ih-pi, in which the combined forces of Liu Pei and Sun Ch'üan face Ts'ao Ts'ao. With Yüan Shao out of the way, Liu Pei becomes Ts'ao Ts'ao's prime target. In the meantime, Liu Pei has enlisted the help of Chu-ko Liang. But even with the aid of Chu-ko Liang, Liu Pei must make a series of strategic retreats and the huge force of Ts'ao Ts'ao advances southward threatening Wu, which then becomes the point of contention in this new conflict. As Ts'ao Ts'ao's huge army approaches, Sun Ch'üan is first provoked and then threatened by Chu-ko Liang into forming an alliance with Liu Pei to resist Ts'ao Ts'ao. Then preparations for the battle take eight chapters, although the battle itself is short. In the final outbreak, Ts'ao Ts'ao's force of nearly a million men is quickly defeated by a much smaller allied force of Liu Pei and Sun Ch'üan. Ts'ao Ts'ao's defeat marks the end of the conflict, but again the resolution is not complete. His thirst for revenge persists.

The third major conflict is between Sun Ch'üan and Liu Pei over Ching-chou. After Ts'ao Ts'ao's defeat, Liu Pei stakes his claim over the strategic region of Ching-chou, which is equally coveted by Sun Ch'üan. Sun Ch'üan tries repeatedly to take it away but without success. This on-and-off confrontation over Ching-chou continues for twenty-six chapters. The decisive open conflict occurs when Ts'ao Ts'ao decides to ally his forces with Sun Ch'üan, on the one hand to ward off Kuan Yü, and on the other to help Sun Ch'üan recover Ching-chou. Kuan Yü, who has been enjoying repeated victories and growing overconfident, suddenly finds himself confronted with shrewd and scheming opponents who bring about his defeat, death, and loss of Ching-chou.

The fourth and final major conflict is between Liu Pei and Sun Ch'üan over the death of Kuan Yü. Liu Pei mobilizes a force of 750,000 men to avenge his sworn brother's death. The campaign lasts over one and a half years, with many initial victories for Liu Pei. But Sun Ch'üan's newly appointed commander Lu Hsün waits patiently for Liu Pei's tactical error before launching the fatal attack. Again Liu Pei with his superior forces is defeated and he retreats to Pai-ti Ch'eng to die. This is the last major conflict in the narrative, but it does not mark the end of the story. Liu Pei's grander mission of restoring the Han dynasty is carried forward by his worthy military counselor and generals.

These four major events in the central section of *San-kuo* are closely linked together in a series of conflict situations. The point of contention is different in each case, and there usually follows a long confrontation period during which schemes and stratagems are made, minor clashes take place, and tensions mount. These lead up to the final show of force when the major battle is fought, usually short and straightforward. After the decisive battle, the conflict is temporarily—but never completely—resolved. In fact, it is the incomplete resolution of the preceding conflict that leads into the subsequent one.

In contrast to *San-kuo yen-i,* which roughly follows the conflict-resolution model both in its overall pattern and internal structure, the internal structure of *Shui-hu chuan* is markedly different. Instead of having lines of action that follow the career of individual heroes, the fundamental pattern in *Shui-hu* is a cyclical chain or, more accurately, a sequence of cycles in each of which a different hero is featured. There is much controversy over the organization and unity of *Shui-hu.* While Cheng Chen-to, who has written a detailed textual study of the evolution of *Shui-hu chuan,* says that the close-knit organization of this work is water-tight, Richard Irwin believes, as mentioned earlier, *Shui-hu* is "merely a collection of tales. . . ." Perhaps the most balanced view is that of Patrick Hanan, who has characterized the cycles noted above as systems of linked plots, which are further linked together to form the story of *Shui-hu chuan.* Then, above all this, there is a "superstructure" that governs the operation of these systems. Hanan discusses this pattern in detail with regard to the Wu Sung cycle: "But although the Wu Sung chapters form a system of linked plots, they are themselves linked to other systems, for example the chapter that deals with Sung Chiang. There is a master link between the two systems, in this case the recurring motif of the chance confrontation that ends in firm friendship. Therefore, in the *Shui-hu chuan* and in certain other works, there is a level of organization above the kind we have been speaking of [the system of linked plots], a superstructure . . . in this work the assembling of the heroes, the birth and death of the rebellion . . . which controls the various systems of linked plots."

The first seventy chapters of *Shui-hu chuan* are dominated by eight story cycles each with its own system of linked plots: (1) Lu Chih-shen (Chapters 3-7), (2) Lin Ch'ung (Chapters 7-12), (3) Yang Chih (Chapters 12-13, 16-17), (4) Ch'ao Kai (Chapters 14-15, 18-20), (5) Sung Chiang (Chapters 21-22, 32-42), (6) Wu Sung (Chapters 23-32), (7) Hu-yen Cho (Chapters 54-58), and (8) Lu Chün-i (Chapters 60-70). This cyclical chain is interspersed with collective raids, rescue missions, and organized campaigns. It must be acknowledged, however, that the system of linked plots is fundamentally a weaker and looser form of organization than that of the interweaving of narrative strands, even though these cycles are part of a larger process of "the assembling of the heroes." The overall unifying elements must be sought on a higher level.

Let us for the moment turn to the cycles themselves. The individual cycles, besides displaying the aristeia of a particular hero, follow this general pattern. The hero first demonstrates his gallantry with a feat of bravery that, unfortunately, is a violation of the law, and he takes flight. But his flight is shortlived; he is captured and branded. Then he is sentenced and exiled to a distant region to serve his term. Usually, being sent into exile is the beginning of the hero's adventures. He is escorted by two incompetent and unscrupulous guards who invite trouble. But the hero does arrive at his destination and begins to serve his sentence. Soon, however, unbearable conditions force him to escape again, and this time he becomes a permanent fugitive from the law. These permanent fugitives eventually and inevitably gravitate towards Liang-shan-po, the geographic center that serves as the rallying point for all those whose actions and thoughts run counter to the government. In these story cycles then, each of the individual heroes proves his manhood and moral worth.

This cyclical pattern ends at the high point in the work in Chapter 71. All 108 heroes have gathered on Liang-shan-po, and they receive the Heavenly Tablet with the inscription of their names and the phrases "Carry out the Will of Heaven" and "Fidelity and Loyalty Complete." This tablet consolidates the heroes' relationship as a group, gives them a common goal, and, above all, reveals that they have been banded together not merely by chance but by heavenly predestination.

The six middle chapters (75-80) have a different structure; the cyclical chain dissolves into a quick succession of five battles. In the first, there is a magnificent display of the collective prowess of the band in their "Nine Palaces and Eight Trigrams Maze," which totally overwhelms its enemies. If there exists a second high point in the work, this must be it. In the remaining battles, individual heroes display their skill and prowess until the opposing forces, along with their specially recruited members, are completely subdued. In Chapter 82, Sung Chiang surrenders voluntarily to the throne after his triumphant victory over the two evil ministers.

The forty odd chapters that follow Sung Chiang's surrender revert to a cyclical pattern. These chapters describe an interminable number of battles in four major campaigns in which the heroes fight against (1) the Liaos (Chapters 83-90), (2) T'ien Hu (Chapters 91-100), (3) Wang Ch'ing (Chapters 101-110), and (4) Fang La (Chapters 111-119). The pattern follows no particular logic other than that of repetition. One more or one less campaign does not make much difference, except for the last one in which 81 of the 108 heroes die. In the final chapter Sung Chiang and Lu Chün-i, the leader and the second in command, both die. This is essentially a tragic ending, but it is precisely Sung's tragic death that preserves his heroic stature after his surrender to the government; for it is as a rebel leader with moral righteousness on his side that he has acquired his reputation, and this he retains when he dies as a victim of the immorality of his time.

Although the conflict-resolution model is not applicable to the internal structure of *Shui-hu chuan,* it does seem to fit the overall pattern well. The opposing groups in the conflict are the righteous fugitives from the law, on the one hand, and the morally corrupt and abusive government, on the other. Chapters 1-70 make up the long period of confrontation in which tensions build as the number of outlaws grows and their organization becomes strong. The group achieves "critical mass," as it were, when its number reaches 108. Shortly after this, the government forces, first under T'ung Kuan and then under Kao Ch'iu, force the issue and large-scale conflict breaks out. In Chapters 75-80, the Liang-shan band deals two defeats to T'ung Kuan and three defeats to Kao Ch'iu, both leading major forces (the former 100,000 and the latter 130,000 men). A resolution of the conflict is reached in Chapter 82, when Sung Chiang decides to surrender to the throne. But the story does not end here. Poetic justice demands that the heroes revel a bit longer in their new-found glory, and there follows an aftermath in which the heroes wage four

major campaigns against various rebel groups. The final resolution comes when Sung Chiang himself succumbs to the evil machinations of Kao Ch'iu and T'ung Kuan.

In this analysis we have briefly considered *San-kuo* and *Shui-hu* on different narrative levels, beginning with the basic literary unit of the event or incident and moving on to the larger unit of sequences of events or lines of action that form the narrative strands in the works; then we have examined the interaction among the narrative strands that gives the text its intermeshing quality. Moreover we find in *Shui-hu* that the narrative strands form only a system of linked plots within a cycle and do not run through the entire narrative. This led us to go beyond the level of interrelationship between strands to seek a superstructure that gives direction to the shorter systems of linked plots.

In *San-kuo yen-i,* after tracing the three main narrative strands, we examined the interaction among the strands at four major points of conflict: Kuan-tu, Ch'ih-pi, Ching-chou, and Hu-t'ing. . . . [The] conflict-resolution model is useful at this level of interpretation to enable us to see the interlocking of conflict situations. This model is roughly applicable to the external pattern also, though not with the same forcefulness. The conflict is among the three contenders for the throne. There is a long and colorful period of confrontation that does not end until the very end of the narrative in Chapter 120 when a fourth party resolves the conflict by overcoming the others and uniting the country again. The application is not ideal because the stages in the conflict are not clearly defined.

In the case of *Shui-hu chuan* the cyclical chains and repetitive sequences give it a rather weak internal structure. The system of linked-plots is basically loose compared to the unitary plot structure and the interweaving of numerous narrative strands. Therefore, we turn to other unifying elements. We find that Liang-shan-po serves as a geographic center for rallying the fugitives from the law. Common motivation of the heroes is another unifying theme. The conflict-resolution model also serves formally as a mold for holding the work together. Most important, probably, is the bond that holds the 108 heroes together as symbolized by their receiving the Heavenly Tablet on Liang-shan-po in Chapter 71. This point serves as a "nucleus" from which the action can proceed in both directions, backward to the very beginning of the narrative with Commander Hung's releasing of the evil spirits, and forward to the end of the story with the dissolution of the Liang-shan band.

In these two earliest examples of extended prose-fiction in China, we find that unity and continuity are achieved with a variety of devices on different levels of narration. The author or authors were conscious of the fact that they were creating works of great length and complexity, and they must have had at their command a variety of narrative techniques and conventions to which they can turn. To the exclusion of many other alternative approaches, I have focused my attention only on a combination of an internal structure and an overall external pattern. *San-kuo yen-i* has a tightly knit internal structure made up of a number of interrelated conflict situations. But its overall pattern is comparatively weak because the period of confrontation is disproportionately drawn out and the final resolution is cursory and anticlimactic. On the other hand, the systems of linked plots in *Shui-hu chuan* give it a comparatively weak internal structure that is compensated for by a strong external pattern brought about by a combination of elements. Thus, it is the combination of, among other things, an internal structure and overall pattern that gives these works their sense of unity and coherence. (pp. 78-84)

> Peter Li, "Narrative Patterns in 'San-kuo' and 'Shui-hu,'" in Chinese Narrative: Critical and Theoretical Essays, *edited by Andrew H. Plaks, Princeton University Press, 1977, pp. 73-84.*

WINSTON L. Y. YANG, PETER LI, AND NATHAN K. MAO (essay date 1978)

[*Yang, Li, and Mao are American essayists and academics. In the following excerpt from their collaborative text* Classical Chinese Fiction, *the critics identify and assess the achievements of* Romance of the Three Kingdoms *and* The Water Margin.]

Romance of the Three Kingdoms and **The Water Margin** are important landmarks in the history of Chinese fiction. Popular in China, they represent significant achievements of Chinese literature. They are often treated together or compared with each other by scholars because of their obvious similarities. Despite their differences in design and in other areas, the two are grouped together for discussion in this essay.

Romance of the Three Kingdoms, probably the most popular historical narrative in China, has been widely read not only by scholars and officials but by the less educated as well. In the West it is one of the few Chinese novels of which there are complete translations. It was first translated into English by C. H. Brewitt-Taylor more than fifty years ago. Even though a more accurate English translation of the title should be the **Popular Elaboration of the Chronicle of the Three Kingdoms,** the novel has long been known in the West by its familiar name, **Romance of the Three Kingdoms,** adopted by Brewitt-Taylor.

The **Romance** has been attributed to Lo Kuan chung . . . , of whom little is known. He was probably a playwright and fiction writer of the late Yüan or the early Ming period. Many other works, such as **The Water Margin,** have also been attributed to him. Of all the works attributed to Lo Kuan-chung, scholars generally agree that the **Romance** bears the closest resemblance to what might have been his original version. In addition, of the works attributed to him in whole or in part, only the **Romance** can be reasonably accepted as his own compilation, for Lo Kuan-chung's name appears not only in its earliest surviving edition but also in nearly all subsequent ones. Also, later bibliographical sources almost unanimously attribute the work to him.

The evolution of the **Romance** can be divided into three periods. The first period began with the T'ang dynasty (618-907) when oral tales about the events of the Three Kingdoms period became popular and ended at the beginning of the Ming (1368-1644). This period's major work was no doubt the *San-kuo chih p'ing-hua* (A P'ing-hua of the History of the Three Kingdoms). The second period started with the compilation of the **Romance** in the early years of the Ming. But no handwritten copies of the novel's original version have survived. The earliest surviving and probably the first printed edition, entitled *San-kuo chih t'ung-su yen-i* (Popular Elaboration of the *Chronicle of the Three Kingdoms*), was issued in the Chia-ching period (1522-1567). Numerous editions based on the Chia-ching version were published during the second half of the Ming dynasty. Most scholars believe that the Chia-ching edition was not derived from or based on the *San-kuo chih p'ing-hua* version but was an entirely different creation. The destruction of the Ming empire ended the second period of the history of the **Romance.** The third period began when Mao Tsung-kang (*fl.* 1679) produced a revised version and a commentary on the novel in the early years of the Ch'ing dynasty. The Mao edition has since become the standard version of the *Romance* and is still widely used today.

Many scholars, notably Hu Shih, believe that the **Romance** came about through a slow process of evolution, even though it reflects very limited influences of the folk tradition. In fact, it reveals in some respects an obvious departure from the storyteller's tradition. Capitalizing on the old Three Kingdoms story cycle, Lo Kuan-chung has refined its narration and reduced its falsification of history. Adding new elements to the cycle, he has created a small number of fictional episodes and a few ahistorical characters in accordance with known historical facts. Despite its extensive use of sources, the **Romance** is more likely the work of a single author.

Of all the sources used by Lo Kuan-chung, the most important is Ch'en Shou's (233-297) *Chronicle of the Three Kingdoms* (San-kuo chih), a reliable official history of the Three Kingdoms period (220-280), when China was divided into Wei, Shu (also known as Shu-Han), and Wu. Lo has also utilized much of the information found in P'ei Sung-chih's (*fl.* 400-430) lengthy commentary on the official history. Lo shares many of Ch'en's views on history. But Ch'en, for political reasons, regards the Wei as the legitimate successor to the Han, whereas Lo considers the Shu as the sole heir to the Han Empire. Although they share the same orthodox Confucian didactic views on history, Lo obviously has adopted a cyclical interpretation of the rise and fall of dynasties.

In his presentation of historical episodes Lo, in most instances, follows the official history fairly closely. Because of the framework of the official history, Lo could not freely create fictional characters and episodes from imagination. Nevertheless, even within such limitations, Lo had managed to present many remarkable and fascinating accounts of historical events.

Lo Kuan-chung's views on the three states are amply revealed in his character portrayals. For example, in contrasting Liu Pei (162-223) of the Shu with Ts'ao Ts'ao (155-220) of the Wei, and Chu-ko Liang (181-234) of the Shu with the Wu general Chou Yü (174-218), Lo makes Liu and Chu-ko come out as much more positive characters than Ts'ao Ts'ao and Chou Yü. It should also be noted that Lo has extended his own predilections beyond character portrayals. To him the rivalry between the Shu and the Wei, like that between the Shu and the Wu, is a contest between legitimacy and illegitimacy; the forces of legitimacy, in his view, should rightly defeat those of illegitimacy. Therefore, he portrays most leaders of the Shu as heroes and those of the Wei or the Wu often as villains. This bias is seen in his portrayals of many major and minor characters.

Although he intends, in general, to glorify Liu Pei and his followers and to vilify Ts'ao Ts'ao, Sun Ch'üan (181-252) and their associates, Lo also painstakingly presents them as complex beings. For instance, his Ts'ao Ts'ao has many of the virtues as recorded in the official history; similarly, his portrait of the much admired Kuan Yü includes many of Kuan's character flaws. Successfully blending popular views with historical facts, he has produced many memorable portrayals. Even though he uses Ch'en Shou's official history *Chronicle of the Three Kingdoms* as his main source to develop his characters, he adheres to it or deviates from it as he sees fit. It is a generally accepted view that the *Romance* excels in its character portrayals, particularly in its descriptions of those obsessed with ambition. Several of his important characters will be examined to illustrate his portrayals.

Lo Kuan-chung has given much attention to Chu-ko Liang, the Prime Minister of the Shu Kingdom. In the novel, Chu-ko is portrayed as a military genius, scoring triumphs at the Battle of Ch'ih-pi, in the campaigns against the southern Man tribes, and in his numerous battles with Ssu-ma I. Lo stresses Chu-ko as a military commander without peer, a master of tactics and strategy who often defeats his enemy through strange plans and even through the use of magic; Lo places less emphasis on Chu-ko Liang's administrative abilities. However, in the official history, Chu-ko is a prudent and cautious administrator and a less-than-spectacular military commander. It is obvious that Lo has added new elements to the portrayal of Chu-ko Liang as found in the official history. To Chu-ko's high intelligence and organizational ability Lo has added the heroic qualities of wizardry and invincibility in war. Thus the fictional Chu-ko Liang possesses powers that the historical Chu-ko did not have. These include his magic powers, martial prowess, and a penchant for successfully executing strange and deceptive plans. In short, the difference between the historical and fictional Chu-ko is that the former is a cautious, orthodox, and politically oriented Legalist administrator whereas the latter is a Confucian statesman and invincible general with superhuman strategic abilities and Taoist magical powers. Having deviated significantly from his main historical source in his portrayal of Chu-ko Liang, Lo has transformed a historical figure into an essentially different fictional character. But a more careful scrutiny of Chu-ko in the novel will demonstrate the historicity of this character.

First of all, there are Chu-ko Liang's superhuman wisdom and magical powers. Throughout the novel superhuman elements play only a very minor part. Major Three Kingdoms figures, especially Chu-ko Liang, are rationalists who emphasize human efforts. Chu-ko Liang's superhuman powers fail to make significant differences in the final outcome of the military struggles. Also, some of his fictional contraptions and schemes, such as "wooden oxen" and "flying horses," are actually elaborations of hints from the official history or from P'ei Sung-chih's commentary.

Moreover, although Lo occasionally presents Chu-ko as a military commander of superhuman powers, he in the main has kept Chu-ko as a mortal and made him realistically human. It is true that Chu-ko's preternatural intelligence and wizardry often enable him to defeat almost any human adversary, but he is not immune from miscalculations and misjudgments. While stressing Chu-ko's noble qualities, Lo also shows Chu-ko's human weaknesses, such as his cruelty and cunning. In the novel he dies as a mortal despite his elaborate, almost mystical, efforts to prolong his own life. Since Lo intends the *Romance* to be essentially a human drama, he has no intention of portraying Chu-ko as a supernatural or divine being. What Lo has done is to weave together the historical image and popular views of Chu-ko into a complex and fascinating character. (pp. 39-42)

In the *Romance* there are many other heroes. But no matter

how brilliant and talented they may be, most of their efforts are foredoomed to failure because the time is not propitious. It is under these circumstances that their actions must be judged. They make their choices and stand by them even though they know that the odds against their success are formidable. Their ambition is to help their respective chosen masters fulfill their ambitious designs. In fact, ambition is one of the most important themes of the novel. Nearly all the major characters are ambitious in one way or another. Some, like Ts'ao Ts'ao, dream of national unification through the annihilation of rivals; others, like Liu Pei, hope to restore the Han empire. Without exception, generals, ministers, counselors, strategists, and even minor officials all intend to serve their respective princes faithfully and play important roles. But in the end nearly all fail to reach their life-long goals, and many die in bitter disappointment. Stressing their ambitions, failures, and deaths, Lo Kuan-chung dramatically reveals, often at the deathbed, their helplessness, their inability to challenge fate, and their ultimate failure. Even though most of them know that the times are against them, and that it is unlikely that they will ever fulfill their ambitious goals, they would not give up their ambitions or admit their failures until the very end of their lives. (p. 43)

The *Romance* cannot be considered a historical novel in the Western sense of the term, because of its fairly close adherence to historical facts, its emphasis on historical figures rather than fictional characters, its attention to historical events rather than fictional episodes, and its lack of imagistic or symbolic structure. It bears little resemblance to such historical novels as those by Sir Walter Scott. In addition, unlike the Western historical novel which generally concentrates on one or two characters, the *Romance* emphasizes the exploits of multiple heroes and villains and a rapid sequence of dramatic events within a historical period. Like a Chinese scroll painting of enormous length, as pointed out by Roy Andrew Miller, the *Romance* presents "a long, continuous spectacle, but only a single episode and a few characters are visible at any one time." The novel is "caught up in carefully placed foci of excitement and emotion from time to time, giving articulation and structure to what otherwise might have been simply an interminable assembly of anecdotes and narrative clichés."

With its close adherence to history and its retelling of history in a plain language, the *Romance* should probably be regarded as a popular history. In fact, Lo Kuan-chung's intent, as reflected in the title of his work and in Chiang Ta'ch'i's preface to the Chia-ching edition, is to retell the official history in plain language and to make its meaning more comprehensible to the common people. Identifying himself essentially as a popular historian, Lo has adhered closely to a strict chronological sequence and created relatively few patently fictional episodes. In short, with his strength primarily as a popular historian, he has created a single continuous narrative of the major events of the Three Kingdoms period. It is not a haphazard collection of anecdotes, rambling episodes or fictional biographies but a coherently structured narrative. He has greatly popularized the history of the Three Kingdoms period for the common people of China who otherwise might not have a chance to learn about it. Moreover, unlike the official historical account, Lo's version, in humanizing historical figures, enables the reader to see the cause and effect of historical events.

Harold Toliver says that "whereas fiction moves toward history in presenting an assumed historical reality, history writing moves toward fiction in its storied coherence and embellishments." This statement aptly describes the *Romance,* a unique mixture of history and fiction. While some critics reject the book as creative historical fiction, arguing that it is not fully fictionalized with historical imagination, few, if any, historians accept it as authentic history because they do not consider it sufficiently truthful or objective. But many critics and historians fail to realize that, despite its slightly fictional elaborations and some episodes with little historical basis, the *Romance* is fairly reliable, because its elaborations and episodes seldom contradict recorded history; in fact, they tend to confirm historical facts. In dramatizing history, they have injected new vitality and vividness into the facts of history.

To summarize, Lo Kuan-chung's main contribution lies in his success in instilling a new life into the old Three Kingdoms cycle; he rejected vulgar elements common among folk speech and introduced a more elegant language. Embellishing the main thread of history without seriously contradicting historical facts and rejecting most of the sensational and supernatural elements found in oral tales and popular legends, he produced a fairly reliable and extremely popular and interesting historical account, superior to the official history in terms of readability and literary interest. Lo created a new genre of fiction: the *yen-i* type of popular historical narrative, a uniquely Chinese contribution to world literature.

At about the time of the appearance of the earliest surviving version of the *Romance of the Three Kingdoms, The Water Margin* (also known in the West as *All Men Are Brothers,* the title of Pearl Buck's translation) became available. Written in a far more colloquial language than the *Romance, The Water Margin* deals with the exploits of a band of outlaws of the early twelfth century. Even though some of its characters are historical, and the setting in the present Shantung province is geographically correct, *The Water Margin,* unlike the *Romance,* is a fully fictionalized account of history. With little historical basis, most of its episodes, derived from oral and legendary sources, are fictional and its heroes ahistorical. In short, while the *Romance* can be read as a type of popular history, *The Water Margin* is essentially fiction. (pp. 45-6)

The textual history of *The Water Margin* is complex and its authorship especially puzzling. It has been attributed to various writers, including Lo Kuan-chung and Shih Nai-an. The attribution to Lo has never been firmly established, and the identity of Shih has been seriously questioned. Since the book is essentially a compilation of different hands at different times, a knowledge of its authorship is not crucial to its appreciation.

A Western reader may be disturbed by the novel's many inherent flaws, such as authorial digressions, contradictory views, stock phrases, gratuitous sadistic activities, narrative inconsistencies, loose structure, and episodes with little bearing on its central themes. He may also be disturbed by its large cast of characters, many of whom are undeveloped or stereotyped. Most are either heroes or villains, and the heroes' actions often contradict their declared sense of justice and righteousness.

In considering these apparent weaknesses, however, one should not evaluate *The Water Margin* by the same standards as he would in dealing with a modern novel. A proper appreciation of *The Water Margin* requires the consideration of its long evolutionary process, its multiple authors, and its folk and oral origins. Its folk origin is such that some scholars suggested that it be approached as a folk epic or saga. If one can accept some characteristics of the novel as conventions, one is able to see its strengths in other areas. For example, although most heroes are stereotypes, some are well developed individuals. In addition, the novel is noted for its smooth and expressive colloquial style, exciting episodes, effective dialogue, vivid imagination, limited dependence on historical sources, and realistic descriptions of the common people.

Among the many exciting episodes in the novel, the description of Wu Sung's barehand killing of a tiger is outstanding. One of the one hundred and eight heroes of the band, he is intensely loyal to his brother Wu Ta and to his comrades. A man of principle and imbued with a strong sense of justice, he does what he considers to be right and he would rather go to jail or die than to yield. Even though his rough appearance and brute strength may suggest a lack of intelligence, he has enough moral fiber to resist the temptations of his seductive sister-in-law. Violent toward his enemies but generous and loyal to his friends, he is one of the most popular fictional heroes in China. (pp. 47-8)

If *The Water Margin* is compared with the *Romance of the Three Kingdoms,* a number of differences become apparent. *The Water Margin* covers a far shorter period of time than the *Romance* does. More importantly, *The Water Margin*'s multiple authors of different periods were not interested in historical accuracy but merely in creating a narrative of popular heroes and exciting episodes developed from their own imagination or popular legends. On the other hand, the author of the *Romance* was seriously interested in historical substance, and his work is essentially a type of popular historical narrative based mainly on the official history of the Three Kingdoms period. Lastly, while *The Water Margin* may appear more creative than the *Romance* because of the former's creation of ahistorical characters and fictional episodes, each of the two has its own strengths. One may view *The Water Margin* as imaginative literature and the *Romance* as a type of popular history. While *The Water Margin* is unreliable as history but fascinating as fiction, the *Romance* appears to be fairly reliable and extremely interesting as a popular history.

In structure the two reveal even more dissimilarities. In contrast to the *Romance of the Three Kingdoms,* which has a tightly knit internal structure based on the interweaving of narrative strands, *The Water Margin* is composed of a sequence of cycles, each of which features a different hero. The first seventy chapters of *The Water Margin* are dominated by eight story cycles centering around eight important heroes, such as Lu Chih-shen, Lin Ch'ung, Wu Sung, and Sung Chiang. This cyclical chain is interspersed with descriptions of raids, rescue missions, and campaigns against the government. But it must be recognized that the system of linked plots is fundamentally a looser form of organization than that of the interweaving of narrative strands. In spite of this weakness in internal structure, the overall pattern of conflict and resolution in *The Water Margin* seems impressive. The opposing groups in the conflict are the "righteous" fugitives from the law on the one hand and the corrupt, despotic government on the other. In Chapters 1-70, a pattern of confrontation emerges; tensions increase as the number of outlaws grows and their organization strengthens. The group reaches its full strength when the number hits 108. Shortly afterwards, in Chapters 75-80, the government sends T'ung Kuan and Kao Ch'iu on separate occasions to suppress the band, but the band is too strong. It defeats T'ung Kuan twice and Kao Ch'iu thrice. However, in Chapter 82, a resolution of the confrontation is reached, when Sung Chiang surrenders to the government. Meanwhile, the plot continues to unfold. Poetic justice demands that the outlaws score greater and more impressive triumphs. They wage four successful campaigns against various rebel groups. And the final resolution takes place when Sung Chiang himself succumbs to the machinations of Kao Ch'iu and T'ung Kuan.

Even though the **Romance** has a tightly-knit internal structure of interrelated conflict situations and the interweaving of narrative strands, its overall pattern is comparatively weak because of its emphasis on a disproportionately long period of conflicts among the major parties and its cursory and anticlimactic resolution of the conflicts. On the other hand, while the system of linked-plots gives *The Water Margin* a relatively weak internal structure, the novel has a strong external pattern achieved through the combination of the following factors: unity of theme, an overall conflict and resolution situation, a geographic focus, and the band's common goals. In short, the **Romance** has a good internal structure but a weak overall pattern; *The Water Margin,* weak internally, is strong in its overall pattern. Each novel has its own specific structural features.

Notwithstanding differences in style, plot and theme, the *Romance* and *The Water Margin* marked the coming of age of the Chinese novel. While the former is concerned with a tripolar struggle for power in the last years of the Han dynasty and following Han's collapse, the latter deals mainly with the exploits of a band of Sung outlaws. In the former one finds generals, warlords, strategists and princes guided by Confucian political ideals, and in the latter, outlaws motivated primarily by righteousness and justice. The authors of the two works created different types of popular narrative, but very few later works patterned after them achieved the level of artistry as found in either the *Romance* or *The Water Margin,* both landmarks in the development of Chinese prose fiction. (pp. 49-50)

> *Winston L. Y. Yang, Peter Li, and Nathan K. Mao, "'Romance of the Three Kingdoms' and 'The Water Margin',"* in their Classical Chinese Fiction: A Guide to Its Study and Appreciation, *G. K. Hall & Co., 1978, pp. 39-50.*

WILLIAM F. WU (essay date 1984)

[*In the following excerpt, Wu briefly examines* Romance of the Three Kingdoms *and comments on Moss Roberts's 1976 translation of the text.*]

One of China's classic novels is **Three Kingdoms** by Lo Kuan-chung, who wrote it during the early Ming Dynasty, six centuries ago. In 1976, Moss Roberts of N.Y.U. translated and edited this work into a very readable English version. It is fantasy, full of heroes, magicians, and ghosts. While it is obscure in the United States, it is one of China's most important literary works, and its characters and events have much the same kind of general recognition among the Chinese that King Arthur and the Knights of the Round Table have in the English-speaking world. Again like the story of King Arthur, **Three Kingdoms** is a highly fictionalized and embellished historical tale with a bit of fact at its core, and it is a tragedy.

Other English translations have been published, but this novel presents two serious problems that Roberts has handled most effectively. One problem is that the author, Lo, created it by compiling centuries-old folktales and weaving them into a sophisticated, highly-complex drama. He includes a large number of historical and cultural details, many of which would seem to clutter the plot for American readers. On the other hand, many of those details are crucial to an understanding of the society in which the novel takes place. Roberts has deleted a number of long sections in the novel, reducing it as much as possible to its central plot. At the same time, footnotes and summaries of deleted sections provide the information that is essential to an understanding of significant details. In length, only about a quarter of the novel is actually represented by Roberts's translation, but the full course of the plot is here and plenty of adventure, mysticism, and heroism.

The story begins in the waning years of the Han Dynasty (206 B.C.-220 A.D.), the longest and most important dynasty in China's history. The Han gave China the political, cultural, and geographical identity it would have until the twentieth century. When it collapsed, however, China split into three separate kingdoms which began to vie for supremacy. No one knew if China would be made into a cohesive empire once again or if the former empire would remain splintered forever, as happened to the Roman Empire a few centuries later. *Three Kingdoms* tells the story of three men who join together to restore the Han to prominence. (p. 33)

Be warned, however: *Three Kingdoms* bears little resemblance to contemporary American fantasies set in old Asian countries. This is the real thing. (p. 50)

> *William F. Wu, "Three Kingdoms," in* Fantasy Review, *Vol. 7, No. 1, January, 1984, pp. 33, 50.*

FURTHER READING

Irwin, Richard G. "Water Margin Revisited." *T'oung Pao Archives* XLVIII (1960): 393-415.
> Examines the historical and textual differences of various editions of *Shui-hu ch'üan-chuan.*

Ma, Y. W. "The Chinese Historical Novel: An Outline of Themes and Contexts." *Journal of Asiatic Studies* XXXIV, No. 2 (February 1975): 277-93.
> Briefly explores the place of *San-kuo* in the development of the Chinese historical novel, noting as well the literary merits of the work.

Ts'un-yan, Liu. "Lo Kuan-chung and His Historical Romances." In *Critical Essays on Chinese Fiction,* edited by Winston L. Y. Yang and Curtis P. Adkins, pp. 85-114. Hong King: Chinese University Press, 1980.
> Textual comparison of several works attributed to Lo.

Yang, Winston, L. Y. "The Literary Transformation of Historical Figures in the 'San-kuo chih yen-i': A Study of the Use of the 'San-kuo chih' as a Source of the 'San-kuo chih yen-i.' In *Critical Essays on Chinese Fiction,* edited by Winston L. Y. Yang and Curtis P. Adkins, pp. 47-84. Hong Kong: Chinese University Press, 1980.
> Detailed comparison of Lo's *San-kuo* with its primary source,

Ch'en Shou's *San-kuo chih* (*The Chronicle of the Three Kingdoms*).

Michelangelo

1475-1564

(Born Michelangelo di Lodovico di Lionardo di Buonarroto Simoni; also Michelagnolo; also Michael Angelo; also Michelangelo Buonarroti) Italian poet and epistler.

Michelangelo is recognized as a leading creative genius of the Italian Renaissance. Although best known as a painter, sculptor, and architect, he was also an accomplished poet, madrigalist, and letter writer. His works in the visual arts are highly esteemed. They include a colossal figure of young David carved out of a single marble block, the Vatican *Pietà*, and ceiling decorations in the Sistine Chapel of the Vatican. Throughout his adult life, Michelangelo carried on an extensive correspondence and wrote lyrics, religious verse, and philosophical poems. These works are valued today as a rich source of information about the artist's emotions and ideals and as a mirror of Renaissance life. According to sixteenth-century critic Pietro Aretino, "the world has many kings but only one Michelangelo."

Michelangelo was born in Caprese, near Arezzo, in 1475. His father was then *podestà*—resident magistrate—of Caprese and Chiusi. His mother died when the boy was six. In 1488 Michelangelo was apprenticed to Florentine painter Domenico Ghirlandajo, in whose workshop he was introduced to fresco and panel painting. Early on, however, Michelangelo discovered that his first love was sculpture. In 1489 he joined the "School of Sculpture" founded by Lorenzo de' Medici in the Medici gardens in Florence. There, under the tutelage of Bertoldo di Giovanni, Michelangelo studied ancient marbles and executed the bas-relief *Madonna of the Stairs*. He was befriended by Lorenzo, through whom he met the celebrated humanists Marsilio Ficino, Pico della Mirandola, and Angelo Poliziano. These men helped spur Michelangelo's interest in Christian Platonism, a matter that later colored much of the artist's poetry. Recognizing that the advancing French army would soon take Florence, Michelangelo fled to Bologna in 1494. In 1495 he briefly returned to Florence. The city was then under the rule of Girolamo Savonarola, a Dominican reformer whose advocation of an ideal Christian state impressed Michelangelo deeply. By June 1496 Michelangelo was in Rome. He accepted several commissions for sculpture, most notably the Vatican *Pietà*, which he completed early in 1499 at age 24. Michelangelo had promised French cardinal Jean de Villiers de la Groslaye that this sculpture would be "the finest marble work of today in Rome, such as no living master could do better." By all accounts, Michelangelo kept his word.

Michelangelo returned to Florence, now a republic under Pietro Soderini, in 1501. In August he signed the contract for his colossal *David*. Three years later he began work on his *Cartoon of the Battle of Cascina*. In 1505 he was called to Rome by Julius II, who commissioned him to design and sculpt his tomb. Work continued sporadically on this monumental project for decades, but it was never completed to original plan and proved an abiding torment to the artist. This failure, brought about chiefly by Michelangelo's unwillingness to delegate sculpturing responsibilities to subordinate members of his workshop, is regarded as the principal trage-

dy of the artist's life. During the next decade, Michelangelo executed some of his most celebrated works, including the frescoes of the Sistine Chapel ceiling. Following the election of Guilio de' Medici as Pope Clement VII in 1523, Michelangelo undertook several projects for the Medici in Florence: the Medici tombs, the Laurentian Library, and the New Sacristy of San Lorenzo. These and other works helped spread his reputation far beyond the borders of his native land.

Michelangelo moved back to Rome in 1534 and lived there for the rest of his life. He formed a deep friendship with young nobleman Tommaso de' Cavalieri, to whom he addressed many poems, and met Vittoria Colonna, widow of the Marquis of Pescara, who was to inspire much of the artist's poetry. Scholars have been puzzled by the artist's relationship with Tommaso and Vittoria. To Tommaso, who was renowned for his physical beauty, Michelangelo wrote in 1533: "I could as easily forget the food which only nourishes my body miserably, as your name, which nourishes both body and soul, filling the one and the other with such sweetness that neither weariness nor fear of death is felt by me while memory preserves you in my mind. Think, if the eyes could also enjoy their portion, in what condition I should find myself." This and other apparent declarations of love have been variously interpreted as platonic or markedly sexual. In either case, few commentators have viewed the relationship as essentially physical, and only a handful have suggested consummated pederasty. Michelangelo's love for Vittoria was almost certainly chaste. By his own declaration, the artist admired the marchioness for her wit, intellect, and Christian devotion. The latter quality particularly impressed Michelangelo, whose poems to Vittoria often concern spiritual matters.

During the 1530s and 1540s Michelangelo wrote most of his surviving poems, all the while executing commissioned projects at an almost feverish pace. Having been appointed chief sculptor, painter, and architect to Pope Paul III, Clement VII's successor, in 1535, Michelangelo was thereafter responsible for major works in the Vatican. He decorated Paul's private chapel and began planning St. Peter's. The death of Vittoria in 1547 was a bitter blow to him. According to Ascanio Condivi, who published a biography of the artist in 1553, Michelangelo "often remained dazed, as one bereft of sense" in recalling Vittoria's death. Evidently he found consolation in his friend Tommaso and through a growing interest in Christian spirituality. During the same year, 1547, Michelangelo was much honored by an address delivered by critic Benedetto Varchi before the Accademia Fiorentina—the Florentine Academy—on Michelangelo's sonnet "Non ha l'ottimo artista alcun concetto." This lecture was the first public declaration of Michelangelo's talent as a poet. By the year 1550 Michelangelo was already well into his seventies. Most of his time was spent performing his duties as architect of St. Peter's, yet he corresponded extensively with his nephew Lionardo di Buonarroto Simoni and with eminent artist and biographer Giorgio Vasari. He also continued to write poetry, though apparently with less fervor than in the 1530s and 1540s. Michelangelo kept working until days before his death; his last project, left uncompleted, was a pietà. He died on February 18, 1564. Pope Pius IV wished him to be buried in St. Peter's, but by order of his nephew and heir Lionardo, he was buried at Santa Croce in Florence.

Michelangelo's literary canon consists of about 300 surviving poems and nearly 500 letters. Sonnets and madrigals make up almost all of the verse, though there are a few stanzas in terza rima and a small number of epigrams. Most of the poems focus on one or more of four themes: art, beauty, old age, and God. Critics have noted that Michelangelo apparently wrote with effort and much self-correction. A few of the poems went through five or more drafts, while others were abandoned in progress. Still others were dashed off on scraps of paper and evidently forgotten by the poet. Variant readings are commonplace. Whether Michelangelo approached his poetry with the same degree of seriousness as his sculpture is not known, but commentators have sensed a complementary energy and impetuosity in Michelangelo's labors in both media. Many of the verses are infused with a strong strain of Platonism, especially the love sonnets addressed to Cavalieri and Colonna. According to twentieth-century critic George Bull, "Michelangelo's verse was an instinctive way for him to turn his experiences, where they did not fit into one form of art or craft, into yet another—nothing wasted—never without some flash of originality of thought and language, and sometimes with results approaching the splendour of his pictures and statues." Michelangelo's letters, like his poems, provide insight into the artist's mind and creative process. Most of the surviving correspondence is addressed to members of his family. These letters are most valued for information they supply about the artist's ongoing nonliterary projects, especially the Julius tomb, the Medici tombs, and St.

Peter's. Others, written to patrons, friends, and fellow-artists, treat religious feelings, sexual issues, and the philosophy of art. Michelangelo's letters are generally matter-of-fact in tone. "Unlike many Renaissance letters, those of Michelangelo were not stylistic exercises, but intimate communications addressed to his family and to his friends, often written in a hurry and sometimes under physical and mental stress," wrote E. H. Ramsden in the introduction to *The Letters of Michelangelo* (1963). They thus provide a mirror of the artist's mind and thoughts—one that has surprised critics for the brilliance and clarity of its reflection.

Michelangelo has long been esteemed for his verse. Although his poems were not published in his lifetime, they were well known in Italian literary circles before the artist's death. The earliest major work of criticism is Benedetto Varchi's 1547 address before the Accademia Fiorentina, published in 1549 as *Due lezzioni di Messer Benedetto Varchi*. In this work Varchi explicated at length Michelangelo's sonnet "No ha l'ottimo artista alcun concetto," focusing on the poet's interior vision of love and offering definitions of "concetto." For Varchi, the fundamental meaning of *concetto* is intention, but he isolated additional shades of meaning ranging from a Platonic idea to an internal image founded upon artistic creativity. Michelangelo himself often commented on his own poems. In one letter, written in 1554 to Vasari, he defended his literary endeavors against detractors. "You will say rightly that I am old and foolish in wishing to write sonnets, but because many people say that I am in my second childhood I've tried to fulfil my part," he stated. In another letter, written in 1533 to Sebastiano del Piombo, he expressed intense pleasure upon learning that two of his madrigals had been set to music and successfully performed. The second edition (1568) of Vasari's *Lives of the Most Eminent Architects, Painters, and Sculptors of Italy* included an early evaluation of Michelangelo's technical skills as litterateur. Vasari wrote: "[He] distrusted his ability to write, although in his letters he expressed himself well and tersely. He enjoyed reading our Italian poets, particularly Dante. Like Petrarch, he was fond of writing madrigals and of making sonnets."

Encouraged by close friends, Michelangelo once chose 105 of his poems for publication, but the project went no further in his lifetime. In 1623 the poet's grandnephew—known as Michelangelo Buonarroti junior—issued the first collection of his granduncle's poems, *Rime di Michelagnolo Buonarroti*. In the preface to *Rime* he wrote: "Since several poems of Michelagnolo Buonarroti, both published and unpublished, go around with many mistakes, we inform our readers that, having compared the text of his compositions which is kept in the Vatican Library . . . with all those poems of his which are the property of his heirs and of other persons in Florence, we have chosen the most adequate and definitive variants." Additionally, Michelangelo junior polished lines he considered rough and altered texts in an effort to draw attention away from the poet's freely expressed admiration of the male body. This collection remained the only text of Michelangelo's poems until 1863, when Cesare Guasti published the first critical edition of *Rime*. Scholars have noted that all textual and aesthetic commentary written between 1623 and 1863 is therefore unreliable, based as it is on faulty texts that do not reflect the author's intentions.

Since 1863, critics of Michelangelo's verse have concentrated primarily on aesthetic, historical, and biographical issues. Most commentators have ranked the poet high among Renaissance lyricists and sonneteers, and a few have classified him among the most original of Italian poets. Among nineteenth-century critics writing in English, John S. Harford treated the Platonic and Christian bases of Michelangelo's poems; Walter Pater viewed the verses as mirrors of the author's mind and temper; T. A. Trollope favorably appraised the poems addressed to Vittoria Colonna; and John Addington Symonds—an early biographer of the poet—examined the thoughts and images that gave rise to Michelangelo's sonnets and madrigals. In 1895 John Jay Chapman wrote: "[Each of the sonnets] seems to be the bearer of some deep harmony, whose vibrations we feel and whose truth we recognize." Twentieth-century critics have refined views expressed in earlier studies. In his 1921 biography of the artist, Georg Brandes treated the poetry in detail. The poems "startle us with their blending of deep human passion and sophisticated reflection," he determined. Later, in 1954, Ernest Hatch Wilkins considered the intellectual foundation of the verses: "Michelangelo's poems are in general heavily freighted with deeply meditative thought." Commenting on the relationship between the visual and literary arts, Wilkins added: "[The best of Michelangelo's poems]—and there are many in which he finds perfect expression for his demanding thought—attain a nobility quite comparable to that of his greatest creations in sculpture and in painting." Other twentieth-century critics have considered the Petrarchan and Christian influences that helped shape the poems, offered close analyses of stylistic elements, expounded upon form and imagery, and further related Michelangelo's growth as a poet to his work in the visual arts. Nearly all critics have agreed that Michelangelo was a poet of high achievement, and some have found him peerless. Wrote Heinz Norden in 1967: "In sheer force of expression he remains to this day the most compelling poet Italy ever produced."

Michelangelo is known as a thinker and craftsman of astonishing range and ability. He fashioned artworks recognized as among the best of their kind, and his literary works are celebrated both for their originality and as seminal documents of Italian Renaissance cultural history. As Brandes wrote: "The fine arts which Michelangelo pursued in the forms of sculpture and painting were not sufficient to contain all the passion and emotion that dwelt in his soul, his need to admire, his irony and humor. His surging feelings often transcended chisel and brush, required an outlet in another creative medium, burst forth in forms that could be captured only by the pen."

*PRINCIPAL WORKS

Rime di Michelagnolo Buonarroti   (poetry)   1623
  [*The Sonnets of Michael Angelo Buonarroti,*   1897]
†*Le rime di Michelangelo Buonarroti*   (poetry)   1863
Le lettere di Michelangelo Buonarroti   (letters)   1875
  [*The Letters of Michelangelo, Translated from the Original Tuscan,*   1963]

*Michelangelo's poems were not published in his lifetime, though many of them circulated in manuscript.

†This work is the first critical edition of Michelangelo's poems.

MICHELANGELO   (letter date 1533)

[*In the following letter to his friend Sebastiano del Piombo, Michelangelo expresses his sentiments upon learning that two of his madrigals have been publicly performed. Both pieces had been set to music, one by Constanzo Festa of Piedmont (1490-1545), a member of the Sistine Choir, the other by Giacomo Concilion (?-1535), a French musician and member of the Papal Choir.*]

I have received the two madrigals and Ser Giovan Francesco has had them performed several times; according to what he tells me, they are considered wonderful things to sing; the words didn't merit such a setting. It's what you wanted and has been a source of the greatest pleasure to me. Please will you let me know what I should do for the master who wrote the music, so that I may not appear more ignorant and ungrateful than need be.

As to the work here [the Medici Tombs at San Lorenzo], I'll say no more for the moment, as I think I've said enough about it recently, but I've done my best to imitate Figiovanni's manner and style in every particular, as it seems to me well suited to anyone who wants to have a say in everything. Don't show this letter.

You tell me you have given a copy of the above-mentioned madrigals to Messer Tommao [Tommaso de' Cavalieri]. I'm very grateful to you for having done so. If you see him, I beg you to commend me to him a thousand times, and when you write to me tell me something about him to put me in mind of him, because if he were to fade from my memory I think I should instantly fall dead.

> *Michelangelo, in a letter to Sebastiano del Piombo in August, 1533, in* The Letters of Michelangelo: 1496-1534, Vol. 1, *edited and translated by E. H. Ramsden, Stanford University Press, 1963, p. 185.*

PIETRO ARETINO   (letter date 1537)

[*Aretino was a sixteenth-century Italian dramatist, satirist, and letter writer. Described by Ludovico Ariosto as the "Scourge of Princes," he wrote audacious and biting indictments of powerful men. He was also an ardent and skilled literary blackmailer, mercilessly pillorying patrons who failed to reward him to his satisfaction. Aretino apparently often sought Michelangelo's friendship through letters, but there is no evidence that the artist ever offered it to him. Critics have questioned the sincerity of Aretino's overtures charging that he was more interested in obtaining Michelangelo's working sketches than his friendship. In the following letter, written in 1537 just after Michelangelo had begun work on the* Last Judgment *on the altar wall of the Sistine Chapel, Aretino proposes that "the world has many kings but only one Michelangelo."*]

Sir, just as it is disgraceful and sinful to be unmindful of God so it is reprehensible and dishonourable for any man of discerning judgement not to honour you as a brilliant and venerable artist whom the very stars use as a target at which to shoot the rival arrows of their favour. You are so accomplished, therefore, that hidden in your hands lives the idea of a new kind of creation, whereby the most challenging and subtle problem of all in the art of painting, namely that of outlines, has been so mastered by you that in the contours of the human body you express and contain the purpose of art. These things are so difficult to bring to perfection that they baffle art itself, since the outline, as you know, must both encompass itself and then be brought to completion in such a way as to bear witness to things which it cannot show, as the figures in the Chapel do for those who really know how to judge and not merely look at them.

I have never hesitated to praise or scorn the merits and demerits of many people and so now, in order not to diminish what worth I have, I salute you. Nor would I dare to do so, save that my name is now acceptable to all our rulers and so it has shed a great deal of its ill-repute. And it is surely my duty to honour you with this salutation, since the world has many kings but only one Michelangelo.

And what a miracle it is that Nature, in whom nothing is so exalted that your skill cannot seek it out, does not know how to imprint on her works the majesty contained in the immense power of your brush and your chisel: wherefore he who sees you does not care that he has never seen Phidias, Apelles and Vitruvius, whose spirits were but the shadows of your spirit.

In fact, I maintain that it is fortunate for Parrhasius and the other ancient painters of the ancient world, that time has not allowed what they did to survive to our own day; for this is the reason why we who give credit to what the written page claims for them refrain from conceding you the palm which they would give you if they could judge with our eyes and hail you as the supreme sculptor, supreme painter and supreme architect.

In view of this, however, why are you not content with the glory you have already acquired? I believe it should be enough for you to have vanquished the others with the works you have already done. But I hear that with the *Last Judgement* which you are painting at present, you intend to outdo the *Creation of the World* which you have already painted, so that vanquishing with your own paintings what you have painted, you will triumph over yourself.

Now who would not be terrified to apply his brush to so awesome a subject? I see Antichrist in the midst of the rabble, with an appearance only conceivable by you. I see terror on the faces of all the living, I see the signs of the impending extinction of the sun, the moon and the stars. I see, as it were breathing their last, the elements of fire, air, earth and water. I see Nature standing there to one side, full of terror, shrunken and barren in the decrepitude of old age. I see Time, withered and trembling, who is near to his end and seated upon a dry tree-trunk. And while I hear the trumpets of the angels setting all hearts astir, I see Life and Death in fearsome confusion, as the former exerts himself to the utmost in an effort to raise the dead, while the latter goes about striking down the living. I see Hope and Despair guiding the ranks of the good and the throng of evil-doers. I see the amphitheatre of the clouds illuminated by the rays which stream from the pure fires of Heaven and on which Christ sits enthroned among His legions, encircled by splendours and terrors. I see His countenance refulgent with brightness, and as it blazes with flames of sweet and terrible light it fills the children of good with joy and those of evil with fear.

Then I see the guardians of the infernal pit, who are dreadful to behold and who to the glory of the martyrs and the saints are taunting all the Caesars and Alexanders, who may have conquered the world but did not therefore conquer themselves.

I see Fame, with her crowns and her palms scattered beneath her feet, crushed under the wheels of her own chariots. At the last I see coming from the mouth of the Son of God his awesome sentence: it is in the form of two flights of arrows, the one bringing salvation and the other damnation; and as I see them descending, I hear His fury shake the fabric of the universe, shattering and reducing it to its elemental parts with tremendous peals of thunder.

I see the lights of Paradise and the furnaces of the abyss which pierce the shadows cast on the vault of the empyrean; and my thoughts on seeing this vision of the ruin of Doomsday prompt me to exclaim:

'If we are in fear and trembling on contemplating the work of Buonarroti, how much more will we fear and tremble when we are being judged by the One who must judge us?'

But now, Sir, you must realize that the vow I made never to see Rome again will have to be broken because of my desire to see this great painting. I would rather make a liar of myself than slight your genius, which I hope will approve the desire I have to spread its fame through the world. (pp. 109-11)

> *Pietro Aretino, in a letter to Michelangelo on September 15, 1537, in* Aretino: Selected Letters, *translated by George Bull, Penguin Books, 1976, pp. 109-11.*

BENEDETTO VARCHI   (lecture date 1547)

[The following excerpt is from the peroration of Florentine scholar and critic Benedetto Varchi's 1547 address delivered before the Accademia Fiorentina—the Florentine Academy—on Michelangelo's sonnet "Non ha l'ottimo artista alcun concetto." In the address, Varchi praised the poem highly and at great length. Here, he extols Michelangelo as "most excellent poet."]

[From the sonnet by Michelangelo beginning "I saw no mortal beauty with these eyes"], I think that any man possessed of judgment will be able to discern to what extent this angel, or rather archangel, in addition to his three first and most noble professions of architecture, sculpture, and painting, wherein without dispute he not only eclipses all the moderns, but even surpasses the ancients, proves himself also excellent, nay singular, in poetry, and in the true art of loving; the which art is neither less fair nor less difficult, albeit it be more necessary and more profitable than the other four. Whereof no one ought to wonder: for this reason; that, over and above what is manifest to everybody, namely that nature, desirous of exhibiting her utmost power, chose to fashion a complete man, and (as the Latins say) one furnished in all proper parts; he, in addition to the gifts of nature, of such sort and so liberally scattered, added such study a diligence so great that, even had he been by birth most rugged, he might through these means have become consummate in all virtue: and supposing he were born, I do not say in Florence and of a very noble family, in the time too of Lorenzo the Magnificent, who recognised, willed, knew, and had the power to elevate so vast a genius; but in Scythia, of any stock or stem you like, under some commonplace barbarian chief, a fellow not disdainful merely, but furiously hostile to all intellectual ability; still, in all circumstances, under any star, he would have been Michelangelo, that is to say, the unique painter, the singular sculptor, the most perfect architect, the most excellent poet, and a lover of the most divinest. For the which reasons I (it is now many years ago), holding his name not only in admiration, but also in veneration, before I knew that he was architect already, made a sonnet; with which (although it be as much below the supreme greatness of his worth as it is unworthy of your most refined and chastened ears) I mean to close this present conference; reserving the discussion on the arts (in obedience to our Consul's orders) for another lecture.

> Illustrious sculptor, 'twas enough and more,
> Not with the chisel and bruised bronze alone,
> But also with brush, colour, pencil, tone,
> To rival, nay, surpass that fame of yore.
>
> But now, transcending what those laurels bore
> Of pride and beauty for our age and zone,
> You climb of poetry the third high throne,
> Singing love's strife and peace, love's sweet and sore.
>
> O wise, and dear to God, old man well born,
> Who in so many, so fair ways, make fair
> This world, how shall your dues be duly paid?
>
> Doomed by eternal charters to adorn
> Nature and art, yourself their mirror are;
> None, first before, nor second after, made.

(pp. 177-79)

> *Benedetto Varchi, in an excerpt in* The Life of Michelangelo Buonarroti, Vol. 2 *by John Addington Symonds, second edition, John C. Nimmo, 1893, pp. 177-79.*

MICHELANGELO   (letter date 1547)

[Michelangelo was flattered and pleased by the honor done him by Benedetto Varchi in his 1547 lecture before the Accademia Fiorentina. In the excerpt below, he expresses his pleasure to Luca Martini, a member of the Accademia and an active patron of the arts.]

Through Messer Bartolomeo Bettini I have received a letter of yours, together with a treatise—a commentary on a sonnet by my hand. The sonnet is indeed by me, but the commentary is from Heaven and is really admirable, I do not say in my judgment but in that of learned men and of Messer Donato Giannotti in particular, who can't put it down. He commends himself to you.

As regards the sonnet, I know it for what it's worth; but be that as it may, I cannot pretend that I do not feel a little vainglorious in being the subject of so fine and learned a commentary [see excerpt by Varchi dated 1547]. And as I perceive from his words of praise that I appear to its author to be what I am not, I beg you to express my acknowledgments to him in terms befitting such devotion, affection and courtesy. I beg you to do this, because I feel myself to be of little worth and he who is well esteemed ought not to tempt fortune. It is better to remain silent than to fall from on high.

I am an old man and death has robbed me of the dreams of youth—may those who do not know what old age means bear it with what patience they may when they reach it, because it cannot be imagined beforehand.

Commend me, as I've said, to Varchi, as being enamoured of his gifts and at his service wherever I am.

> *Michelangelo, in a letter to Luca Martini in March, 1547, in* The Letters of Michelangelo: 1537-1563, *Vol. 2, edited and translated by E. H. Ramsden, Stanford University Press, 1963, p. 72.*

MICHELANGELO   (letter date 1547)

[Although extremely pleased by the attention Varchi's 1547 address before the Accademia Fiorentina brought him, Michelangelo was apparently somewhat miffed that the scholar did not communicate with him directly. He wrote to Varchi in March 1547, acknowledging receipt of a transcript of the lecture through a third party. According to E. H. Ramsden, Michelangelo's letter—the full text of which appears below—"betrays, unwittingly, a certain impatience with the amount of time and thought spent upon the resolution of problems which, in face of the anomalies of destiny and of the unresolved mysteries of life and death with which he was overtaken, must necessarily, and despite his gratitude, have seemed to him not only purely academic, but altogether trivial and unreal."]

So that it may indeed be evident that I have received your treatise, as I have, I will make some attempt to reply to the question asked of me, unlearned though I am.

I admit that it seems to me that painting may be held to be good in the degree in which it approximates to relief, and relief to be bad in the degree in which it approximates to painting. I used therefore to think that painting derived its light from sculpture and that between the two the difference was as that between the sun and the moon.

Now, since I have read the passage in your paper where you say that, philosophically speaking, things which have the same end are one and the same, I have altered my opinion and maintain that, if in face of greater difficulties, impediments and labours, greater judgment does not make for greater nobility, then painting and sculpture are one and the same, and being held to be so, no painter ought to think less of sculpture than of painting, and similarly no sculptor less of painting than of sculpture. By sculpture I mean that which is fashioned by the effort of cutting away, that which is fashioned by the method of building up being like unto painting. It suffices that as both, that is to say sculpture and painting, proceed from one and the same faculty of understanding, we may bring them to amicable terms and desist from such disputes, because they take up more time than the execution of the figures themselves. If he who wrote that painting is nobler than sculpture understood as little about the other things of which he writes—my maidservant could have expressed them better.

There are an infinite number of things, still unsaid, which could be said of kindred arts, but, as I've said, they would take up too much time, and I've little to spare, because I am not only an old man, but almost numbered among the dead. I therefore beg you to have me excused. I commend me to you and thank you to the best of my ability for the too great honour you do me, of which I am undeserving.

> *Michelangelo, in a letter to Benedetto Varchi in March, 1547, in* The Letters of Michelangelo: 1537-1563, *Vol. 2, edited and translated by E. H. Ramsden, Stanford University Press, 1963, p. 75.*

MICHELANGELO   (letter date 1550)

[In the excerpt below from a 1550 letter to Giovan Francesco Fattucci, Michelangelo acknowledges the compliment paid him by Benedetto Varchi in his 1547 address to the Accademia Fiorentina, recently published under the title Due lezzioni di Messer Benedetto Varchi. *The sonnets by Varchi to which Michelangelo refers in the last line of the letter are one in praise of Michelangelo, "Ben vi devea bastar chiaro scultore," and*

one in praise of Tommaso de' Cavalieri, "Quel ben, che dentro informa, e fuor reluce."]

Messer Tommaso de' Cavalieri has recently asked me to thank Varchi on his behalf for a certain admirable small book of his that has been published, in which he says he speaks of him in the most honourable terms and of me no less [see excerpt by Varchi dated 1547]. He [*Cavalieri*] has given me a sonnet I wrote for him at that time, begging me to send it to him as a justification; the which I am sending you with this. If you like it, give it to him; if not, consign it to the fire, reflecting that I contend with death and that my mind is on other things. However, one sometimes has to do things like this. Please thank the said Messer Benedetto for the honour he does me in his sonnets, and offer him my services, poor though they are.

> *Michelangelo, in a letter to Giovan Francesco Fattucci on February 16, 1550, in* The Letters of Michelangelo: 1537-1563, Vol. 2, *edited and translated by E. H. Ramsden, Stanford University Press, 1963, p. 118.*

ASCANIO CONDIVI (essay date 1553)

[*The following excerpt is from Ascanio Condivi's 1553* Life of Michelangelo Buonarroti, *one of the earliest biographies of the poet. Condivi knew Michelangelo well and personally discussed with him many of the matters treated in the* Life. *According to George Bull, who edited a 1987 translation of the text, Condivi's* Life *constitutes "a critically important source for Michelangelo's life and, carefully interpreted, for Michelangelo's vision of himself." Here, Condivi offers an account of Michelangelo as a man of letters.*]

Now Michelangelo, when he was young, gave himself not only to sculpture and painting, but also to all those branches of study which either belong or are close to them; and he did this so zealously that for a while he came near to cutting himself off completely from the fellowship of men, except for the company of a very few. For this, he was held to be proud by some, and by others very touchy and temperamental, though he had neither one or the other of these faults. Rather (as has been the case with many men of excellence) it was the love of virtuosity, and the continuous practice of the fine arts, that made him solitary; he took so much delight and pleasure in them that the company of others not only did not bring him contentment but positively gave him displeasure, since it diverted him from his meditation, and he (as the great Scipio used to say himselfc) was never less alone than when alone. Yet he has willingly kept the friendship of those from whose virtuous and learned conversation he could gather some fruit, and in whom there shone forth some ray of excellence: for instance, of the most reverend and illustrious Monsignor Pole, for his rare talents and singular goodness; and likewise of my reverend patron, Cardinal Crispo, since he found in him, along with many other good qualities, rare and outstanding judgement. And he felt great affection for the most reverend Cardinal Santa Croce, a very grave and prudent man, of whom I have many times heard him speak with the greatest esteem; and for the most reverend Maffei, of whose goodness and learning he has always spoken well. And without exception he loves and honours all the persons of the Farnese house, for the lively memory he still has of Pope Paul, recalled by him with the utmost reverence, and continuously mentioned by him as a good and holy old man; and also the most reverend Patriarch of Jerusalem, formerly Bishop of

Cesena, with whom he has long had a warm relationship, finding great pleasure in his open and generous nature. He also enjoyed a close friendship with my most reverend patron, Cardinal Ridolfi, of happy memory, the refuge of all talented men.

There are some others whom I shall leave out, not to be too prolix; such as Monsignor Claudio Tolomei, Messer Lorenzo Ridolfi, Messer Donato Giannotti, Messer Lionardo Malespini, Lottino, Messer Tommaso Cavalieri and other esteemed gentlemen, about whom I shall not write at any greater length.

Finally, he has become very fond of Annibale Caro, and he has told me that he regrets not having been familiar with him sooner, since he has found him much to his taste. In particular, Michelangelo greatly loved the Marchioness of Pescara, with whose divine spirits he fell in love, and by whom in return he was himself loved utterly and tenderly; he still has many of her letters, full of pure and most tender love, such as used to pour forth from her heart. And he correspondingly wrote for her many, many sonnets, full of innocent and tender longing. Many times she made her way from Viterbo or other places where she had gone for recreation or to pass the summer; and she would come to Rome for no other reason than to see Michelangelo; and he in return loved her so much that I remember having heard him say that what grieved him above all else was that when he went to see her as she was passing from this life, he did not kiss her brow or her face but simply her hand. Through her death, he many times felt despair, acting like a man robbed of his senses.

At the request of his lady he made a naked Christ being taken down from the cross; as His dead body is let go, if Christ were not supported under the arms by two little angels, He would fall at the feet of His holy Mother. But she, seated beneath the cross with tearful and sorrowful countenance, with open arms is raising both her hands to heaven, and utters this sentence, which we see written on the stem of the cross: 'They do not realize how great the cost in blood!' The cross is similar to the one which, at the time of the pestilence of 1348, was carried in procession by the Bianchi, and which was then put in the church of Santa Croce in Florence. For love of her, he also made a drawing of Jesus Christ on the cross, not in the semblance of death, as is commonly done, but in a godlike attitude, raising his countenance to the Father, and appearing to say 'Eli, Eli': and thus the body does not fall as if slumped in death but is seen as a living being, wracked and contorted by a bitter torment.

And just as he has delighted in the conversation of learned men, so he has found pleasure in studying the writers of prose, and equally so of verse, among whom he has especially admired Dante, delighted by the marvellous genius of that man, whose work he knows almost all by heart; though he thinks perhaps just as highly of Petrarch.

Then he has taken delight not only in reading but also in sometimes composing verse himself, as witness some of his existing sonnets, which give a very good example of his great inventiveness and judgement. And on some of them certain discourses and observations have been published by Varchi [see excerpt by Varchi dated 1547]. But he has attended to these matters more to give himself pleasure than to make a profession of them, and he has always denigrated himself and alleged his ignorance in these things.

Michelangelo has similarly with great diligence and attention

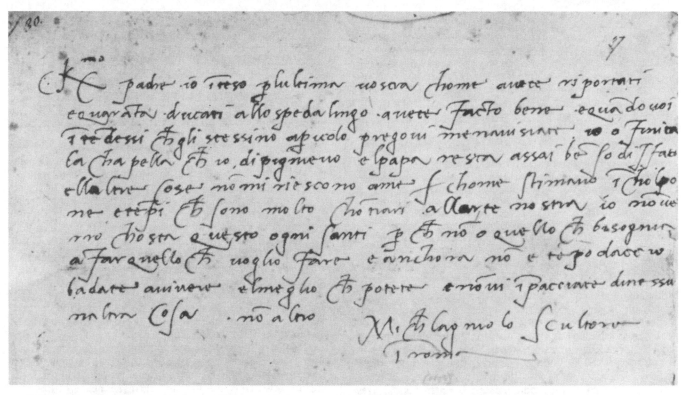

1512 letter from Michelangelo to Lodovico di Buonarrota Simoni. Here, Michelangelo discloses that he has finished painting the ceiling of the Sistine Chapel.

read the holy scriptures, both the Old Testament and the New, as well as the writings of those who have busied themselves with their study, such as Savonarola for whom he has always had a strong affection, and the memory of whose living voice he still carries in his mind. He has loved, too, the beauty of the human body, as one who knows it thoroughly and well. And he has loved it in such a fashion that among certain lewd men, who do not know how to understand the love of Beauty unless it is lascivious and impure, there has been occasion to think and talk evil of him: as if Alcibiades, a most handsome young man, had not been loved most chastely by Socrates; from whose side, when he lay with him, it used to be said that he did not get up otherwise than as from the side of his father.

I have many times heard Michelangelo talk and argue about love; and I have heard later from those who were present that he did not speak otherwise of love than is to be found written in the works of Plato. For myself, I do not know what Plato said on the subject: I well know, having been close to him for so long and so intimately, that I have never heard his mouth utter other than the purest words, which had the power to extinguish in youth every indecent and unbridled desire that could come along. And that he conceives no filthy thoughts can also be recognized from the fact that he has loved not only human beauty but universally every beautiful thing, a beautiful horse, a beautiful dog, a beautiful landscape, a beautiful plant, a beautiful mountain, a beautiful wood, and every place and thing beautiful and rare after its own kind, looking at them all with marvellous feeling and admiration and so selecting what is beautiful from nature, as bees gather honey from the flowers, to make use of it later in their works, and

as do all those who have made some name for themselves in painting.

That ancient master when he wanted to paint a Venus was not content just to see one virgin but wished to contemplate many; and then he took from each one the most beautiful and perfect feature to use for his Venus. And truly anyone who thinks he can reach some degree of excellence without following this path (which leads to the correct theory of beauty) deceives himself very badly. (pp. 66-9)

> *Ascanio Condivi, "Life of Michelangelo Buonarroti," in* Michelangelo: Life, Letters, and Poetry, *edited and translated by George Bull, Oxford University Press, Oxford, 1987, pp. 1-73.*

MICHELANGELO   (letter date 1554)

[*In the following letter to fellow-artist Giorgio Vasari, sent from Rome on September 19, 1554, Michelangelo defends his literary endeavors against detractors. This letter accompanied the sonnet "Giunto è già'l corso della vita mia."*]

You will say rightly that I am old and foolish in wishing to write sonnets, but because many people say that I am in my second childhood I've tried to fulfil my part.

From your letter I realize the love you bear me and you may be sure that I should be glad to lay my feeble bones beside my father's, as you beg me. But if I were to leave here now, it would be the utter ruin of the fabric of St. Peter's, a great disgrace and a greater sin.

But when the structure has completely taken shape, so that it cannot be altered, I hope to do as you suggest, unless of course it be a sin to keep a few sharks waiting who anticipate my early departure. (pp. 146-47)

> Michelangelo, in a letter to Giorgio Vasari on September 19, 1554, in The Letters of Michelangelo: 1537-1563, Vol. 2, edited and translated by E. H. Ramsden, Stanford University Press, 1963, pp. 146-47.

GIORGIO VASARI (essay date 1568)

[*Vasari was a sixteenth-century Italian painter, architect, art historian, and biographer. Best known for his biographies of Italian artists, he is considered the founder of modern art criticism. Vasari and Michelangelo were close friends: they corresponded extensively with each other and shared advice on art projects. In the following excerpt from his biography of Michelangelo, first published in the second (1568) edition of his* Lives of the Artists: Biographies of the Most Eminent Architects, Painters, and Sculptors of Italy, *Vasari explores Michelangelo as litterateur.*]

Michelangelo loved the society of artists, especially of Jacopo Sansovino, Il Rosso, Pontormo, Daniele da Volterra, and the Aretine, Giorgio Vasari, to whom he showed infinite kindness. Those who say he would not teach others are wrong. I have been present many times when he assisted his intimates or any who asked his counsels. It is true he was unfortunate in those whom he took into his house. His disciples were wholly unable to imitate their master. Even in his old age, had he found a disciple to his mind, he would have written a treatise on anatomy, in his desire to help artists, who are frequently misled by a lack of knowledge of anatomy. But he distrusted his ability to write, although in his letters he expressed himself well and tersely. He enjoyed reading our Italian poets, particularly Dante. Like Petrarch, he was fond of writing madrigals and of making sonnets. Michelangelo sent a large number of these verses to the most illustrious Marchesana di Pescara, and received replies both in verse and prose from that lady, of whose genius he was as much enamored as she of his. Michelangelo designed for her a Pietà with two angels of infinite beauty, a figure of Christ on the Cross, and one of Our Saviour at the Well with the Woman of Samaria. He delighted in the reading of the Scriptures, like the good Christian that he was, and honored the writings of Fra Girolamo Savonarola. He was an ardent admirer of beauty for art, and knew how to select the most beautiful, but he was not liable to the undue influence of beauty. This his whole life has proved. In all things he was most moderate. He ate frugally at the close of the day's work. Though rich, he lived like a poor man and rarely had a guest at his table. He would accept no presents for fear of being under an obligation. (p. 293)

> Giorgio Vasari, "Michelangelo Buonarroti," in his Lives of the Artists: Biographies of the Most Eminent Architects, Painters, and Sculptors of Italy, edited by Betty Burroughs, translated by Mrs. Jonathan Foster, George Allen & Unwin Ltd., 1960, pp. 258-301.

R. DUPPA (essay date 1806)

[*Duppa was an eighteenth- and nineteenth-century English artist, essayist, and literary critic. In the following excerpt from a work first published in 1806 as* The Life and Literary Works of Michel Angelo Buonarotti, *he briefly appraises Michelangelo's poetry and character as an artist.*]

[Of the sonnets of Michel Angelo], religion and love are the prevailing subjects. In the former Michel Angelo is sometimes very successful; in the latter he is either monotonous or quaint; a jargon of Platonism and crude metaphysical divinity, acquired from the prevailing taste of the times, with little mind and no sensibility, supply the place of real feeling. He who only imagines that he loves is sure to be mistaken; and that which is worthless to himself, is still more cold and insipid to others. (p. 163)

[It] would be useless to multiply words in summing up the character of this great man. All short modes of defining complicated powers are fallacious, however dexterously language may be employed to give antithesis the force of wit or the air of profound sagacity. By studying his works alone Michel Angelo is thoroughly to be known. His genius was vast and wild, by turns extravagant and capricious, rarely to be implicitly followed, but always to be studied with advantage. Those who have hitherto taken him for their guide, seized what came within the sphere of gross representation, and caricature was the only result of their feeble efforts. Eccentricity, not borrowed from nature, nor the result of feeling, may for a time astonish vulgar minds; but that which is like nothing that can be seen or understood, will perish with the author, by whatever ingenious means it may be made to assail the public taste. Sprangher and Goltzius have been long dead; and wherever such artists may arise, they will now no longer serve to disgrace the genius of Michel Angelo, who has been but too often censured for their extravagance. (p. 164)

> R. Duppa, "Life of Michel Angelo Buonarotti," in Lives of the Italian Painters: Michel Angelo by R. Duppa, Raffaello by Quatremère de Quincy, translated by W. Hazlitt, David Bogue, 1846, pp. 133-64.

JOHN S. HARFORD (essay date 1857)

[*Harford was one of the first major English-language biographers of Michelangelo. In the following excerpt from his 1857* Life of Michael Angelo Buonarroti, *he treats the Platonic and Christian foundations of Michelangelo's poems.*]

The poetry of Michael Angelo is deeply interesting from the light which it reflects upon his character and opinions, as well as from its intrinsic beauties. It chiefly consists of small poems, some of which are light, airy effusions of sportive fancy, whilst the greater part are of a graver character, and are replete, like his art, with original and lofty thought, and pure and noble sentiment, conveyed in language concise, vigorous, and elegant.

"I mentioned Michael Angelo's poetry" (says Mr. Wordsworth, in one of his letters) "to you some time ago; it is the most difficult to construe I ever met with, but just what you would expect from such a man, showing abundantly how conversant his soul was with great things. There is a mistake in the world concerning the Italian language; the poetry of Dante and Michael Angelo proves, that if there be little majesty and strength in Italian verse, the fault is in the authors, and not in the tongue. I can translate, and have translated, two books of Ariosto, at the rate, nearly, of one hundred lines a day; but so much meaning has been put by Michael Angelo into so little room, and that meaning sometimes so excellent in itself, that I found the difficulty of translating him insurmountable. I attempted, at least, fifteen of the sonnets, but could not anywhere succeed. I have sent you the only one I was able to finish: it is far from being the best, or most characteristic, but the others were too much for me."

Such a declaration from so eminent a poet as Wordsworth will, it is hoped, procure indulgence for the present writer in those instances in which, in the course of this chapter, he has endeavoured to versify some of these pieces in the legitimate sonnet metre; while it will justify the course he has pursued with respect to many more, of presenting them to the reader in the form of blank verse; the object being to give full and faithful expression to the sentiment which they embody.

The poems of Michael Angelo were first published at Florence in the year 1623, by his nephew, Michael Angelo the Younger, himself an elegant poet. They were reprinted by Manni in 1726.

The original manuscript in his own hand-writing, very clearly and carefully transcribed, is among the literary treasures of the Vatican Library.

These poems have since passed through various editions (some of which are accompanied by comments on the text), both in Italy and France.

The collection includes sixty-two small poems, under the name of Madrigals, and sixty-four sonnets, besides a few pieces of somewhat greater compass,—the most interesting among which is an elegy, in which he deplores the death of a brother, and describes, in a touching strain of devotion and tenderness, how much this stroke had revived his feelings of grief for the loss of his father.

The madrigals are in general light, elegant effusions in a lyrical form, or in more measured numbers, the favourite topic being the charms of some nameless fair whose favour it is his object to propitiate. Others of the same class are imbued with a lofty strain of philosophical or religious sentiment.

The sonnets comprehend the most beautiful and finished of his poems—those which are most read and oftenest recurred to, and upon which his reputation as a votary of the Muses chiefly depends.

Of these some are interesting from the noble or profound sentiments which pervade them, or from their felicitous illustrations of, or allusions to, artistic principles; or from keen observations on life and manners; but the distinctive feature of no small portion of them is their Platonic sentiment and tendency. On this topic we shall presently have occasion to touch at some length, but it will suffice to add that this was, no doubt, a consequence of the early bent in this direction imparted to his mind by his intimate connexion with the Platonic Academy of Florence, and of his having become familiar with some of the finest parts of Plato's writings in the translation, probably of Marsiglio Ficino.

In the decline of life he ceased to blend Platonism with his religious sentiments, and wrote many beautiful sonnets and other pieces, in the spirit of a humble and enlightened Christian. Some of these rank among the most exquisite and impressive examples of devotional poetry to be found in any language. (pp. 107-10)

[In many of his] sonnets we behold Michael Angelo indulging the fanciful theories of Platonism, and wrapped up in its abstractions. A character of grandeur, highly gratifying to the pride of the human intellect, no doubt, distinguishes these theories; they address the soul as immortal, and invite it as

such (spurning the objects and the bounds of time) to ascend by means of rigid self-discipline, and on the wings of contemplation, to intimate union with God as the first Perfect and the first Fair. But however elevated in themselves such sentiments may be, it is a philosophy wholly unsuited to the condition and the real wants of mankind as a fallen race; needing, therefore, mercy and restoration, before they can thus aspire to a consummation so glorious. The distinguishing feature of Christianity, as opposed to Platonism, is, that while its end and aim are transcendantly sublime, it opens the way of access to God, in a mode revealed by Himself, bearing upon it the stamp of infinite wisdom, goodness, and love. "In this was manifested the love of God towards us, because that God sent his only begotten Son into the world, that we might live through him." (1 John, iv. 9.) The advent of Christ was a merciful response to the groans of nature, which for ages had, in various ways, been inviting the coming of a Deliverer, a Restorer, a Redeemer.

> In his blest life
> We see the path, and in His death the price,
> And in His great ascent the proof supreme,
> Of Immortality.
>
> YOUNG.

Michael Angelo wrote his Platonic Sonnets not without knowledge and love of these glorious truths; but his early initiation into Platonism appears in no small degree to have overlaid his Christianity; and it was not till he reached the decline of life, that he became fully convinced that, as far as this was the case, he had been grasping at shadows, and admiring the baseless fabric of a vision. The proofs of this conviction, and of his new views of Religious Truth consequent on it, are furnished by himself. In . . . his latter Sonnets, the lofty Platonist will be found transmuted into the humble Christian, who on a review of the past is deeply smitten with a sense of his unworthiness, and can find no ground for present peace, or immortal hope, but that of penitential faith in the merits of his Redeemer. (pp. 145-47)

The great change in his religious views and sentiments . . . may be traced, upon his own authority, in no small degree, to the influence of a friendship which he had the happiness of forming, in the year 1537, with one of the most illustrious and accomplished ladies of the sixteenth century, the celebrated Vittoria Colonna, Marchioness of Pescara. Her name has come down to us encircled with all the honours, which the poets and men of letters of the golden age of modern literature, could pay to rank, talent, and virtue, enshrined in a form of surpassing loveliness. (pp. 148-49)

[What Michael Angelo's] real feelings towards her were, he has himself recorded in no less than five poems inscribed with her name; and they prove, that the influence she exerted over him was indeed great, but that it pointed to that brighter world and to those immortal objects, in which her affections supremely centred. His poetic addresses to her, though marked by the highest admiration of the great qualities of her mind and heart, are throughout expressive of the most deferential respect. They gratefully acknowledge her condescending courtesy, and the beneficial influence of her piety and wisdom upon his principles and opinions; but he presumes not even to glance at her personal attractions, or to quit the ground of almost ceremonious homage. It was not till her eyes were sealed in death, that he allowed himself to expatiate, in a closing sonnet, upon her beauty; and he then does it, in terms of sacred affection, far elevated above the sphere of earthly love. He describes in strong terms the fluctuating nature of his religious opinions, and the doubts and difficulties which harassed his mind; he entreats her to be his spiritual guide, and adds that her example and influence have already shed a bright ray upon his steps in the way to heaven. How well she was qualified to respond to these earnest appeals, is attested by her sacred poetry, which, while it rivals in style the beauties of Petrarch, is marked by enlightened piety and elevated devotion. (pp. 152-53)

[Any lengthened comment upon the poems addressed to Vittoria Colonna] is needless; they speak, we conceive, for themselves. Here there is no approach to the language of love. All is admiration of the rare talents and Christian virtues of the lady, whom the writer addresses, conveyed in the most deferential manner. Their friendship, it is obvious, had taken a religious turn. . . . He addresses her in the most grateful terms, as having been the instrument of remodelling his opinions, and of making him almost feel, as it were, a new man. The tenor of the poems of his latter days . . . leave, we conceive, no doubt as to the nature of the change that had ensued. In them, he bids a final adieu to all false philosophy; he is become a humble learner in the school of Christ, and the consequence is, peace with God, and peace in his own conscience. (p. 158)

John S. Harford, in his The Life of Michael Angelo Buonarroti, *Vol. II, translated by John S. Harford, Longman, Brown, Green, Longmans, and Roberts, 1857, 367 p.*

JACOB BURCKHARDT   (essay date 1860)

[*Burckhardt was a nineteenth-century Swiss historian of art and culture. He is best known for* Die Cultur der Renaissance in Italien: Ein Versuch (*1860:* The Civilisation of the Period of the Renaissance in Italy, *1878), an authoritative study of the Italian Renaissance. In the following excerpt from this work, Burckhardt remarks upon strains of religious feeling in Michelangelo's sonnets.*]

[During the time of the Renaissance in Italy, the] attitude of the educated classes toward Mariolatry is more clearly recognizable than toward the worship of images. One cannot but be struck with the fact that in Italian literature Dante's *Paradise* is the last poem in honour of the Virgin, while among the people hymns in her praise have been constantly produced down to our own day. The names of Sannazaro and Sabellico and other writers of Latin poems prove little on the other side, since the object with which they wrote was chiefly literary. The poems written in Italian in the fifteenth and at the beginning of the sixteenth century, in which we meet with genuine religious feeling, such as the hymns of Lorenzo the Magnificent and the sonnets of Vittoria Colonna and of Michelangelo, might have been just as well composed by Protestants. Besides the lyrical expression of faith in God we chiefly notice in them the sense of sin, the consciousness of deliverance through the death of Christ, the longing for a better world. The intercession of the Mother of God is mentioned only by the way. The same phenomenon is repeated in the classical literature of the French at the time of Louis XIV. Not till the time of the Counter-Reformation did Mariolatry reappear in the higher Italian poetry. Meanwhile the plastic arts had certainly done their utmost to glorify the Madonna. It may be added that the worship of the saints among the educated classes often took an essentially pagan form. (p. 468)

Jacob Burckhardt, "Morality and Religion: Religion in Daily Life," in his The Civilization of the Renaissance in Italy, *Vol. II, edited by Dr. Ludwig Geiger and Professor Walther Götz, translated by S. G. C. Middlemore, 1929. Reprint by Harper and Brothers, Publishers, 1958, pp. 444-72.*

WALTER PATER   (essay date 1871)

[*A nineteenth-century essayist, novelist, and critic, Pater was the first major English writer to formulate an explicitly aesthetic philosophy of life. He advocated the "love of art for art's sake"—a belief exemplified in* Studies in the History of the Renaissance (*1873*) *and in the novel* Marius the Epicurean (*1885*). *In the following excerpt from an essay originally published in 1871 in the* Fortnightly Review *and later included in* Studies in the History of the Renaissance, *he discusses Michelangelo's poems as mirrors of the author's mind and temper.*]

Critics of Michelangelo have sometimes spoken as if the only characteristic of his genius were a wonderful strength, verging, as in the things of the imagination great strength always does, on what is singular or strange. A certain strangeness, something of the blossoming of the aloe, is indeed an element in all true works of art: that they shall excite or surprise us is indispensable. But that they shall give pleasure and exert a charm over us is indispensable, too; and this strangeness must be sweet also—a lovely strangeness. And to the true admirers of Michelangelo this is the true type of the Michelangelesque—sweetness and strength, pleasure with surprise, an energy of conception which seems at every moment about to break through all the conditions of comely form, recovering, touch by touch, a loveliness found usually only in the simplest natural things—*ex forti dulcedo.* (p. 60)

[Michelangelo's] genius is in harmony with itself; and just as in the products of his art we find resources of sweetness within their exceeding strength, so in his own story also, bitter as the ordinary sense of it may be, there are select pages shut in among the rest—pages one might easily turn over too lightly, but which yet sweeten the whole volume. The interest of Michelangelo's poems is that they make us spectators of this struggle; the struggle of a strong nature to adorn and attune itself; the struggle of a desolating passion, which yearns to be resigned and sweet and pensive, as Dante's was. It is a consequence of the occasional and informal character of his poetry, that it brings us nearer to himself, his own mind and temper, than any work done only to support a literary reputation could possibly do. His letters tell us little that is worth knowing about him—a few poor quarrels about money and commissions. But it is quite otherwise with these songs and sonnets, written down at odd moments, sometimes on the margins of his sketches, themselves often unfinished sketches, arresting some salient feeling or unpremeditated idea as it passed. And it so happens that a true study of these has become within the last few years for the first time possible. A few of the sonnets circulated widely in manuscript, and became almost within Michelangelo's own lifetime a subject of academical discourses. But they were first collected in a volume in 1623 by the great-nephew of Michelangelo, Michelangelo Buonarroti the younger. He omitted much, re-wrote the sonnets in part, and sometimes compressed two or more compositions into one, always losing something of the force and incisiveness of the original. So the book remained, neglected even by Italians themselves in the last century, through the influence of that French taste which despised all compositions of the kind, as it despised and neglected Dante. "His reputation will ever be on the increase, because he is so little read," says Voltaire of Dante.—But in 1858 the last of the Buonarroti bequeathed to the municipality of Florence the curiosities of his family. Among them was a precious volume containing the autograph of the sonnets. A learned Italian, Signor Cesare Guasti, undertook to collate this autograph with other manuscripts at the Vatican and elsewhere, and in 1863 published a true version of Michelangelo's poems, with dissertations and a paraphrase.

People have often spoken of these poems as if they were a mere cry of distress, a lover's complaint over the obduracy of Vittoria Colonna. But those who speak thus forget that though it is quite possible that Michelangelo had seen Vittoria, that somewhat shadowy figure, as early as 1537, yet their closer intimacy did not begin till about the year 1542, when Michelangelo was nearly seventy years old. Vittoria herself, an ardent neo-catholic, vowed to perpetual widowhood since the news had reached her, seventeen years before, that her husband, the youthful and princely Marquess of Pescara, lay dead of the wounds he had received in the battle of Pavia, was then no longer an object of great passion. In a dialogue written by the painter, Francesco d'Ollanda, we catch a glimpse of them together in an empty church at Rome, one Sunday afternoon, discussing, indeed, the characteristics of various schools of art, but still more the writings of Saint Paul, already following the ways and tasting the sunless pleasures of weary people, whose care for external things is slackening. In a letter still extant he regrets that when he visited her after death he had kissed her hands only. He made, or set to work to make, a crucifix for her use, and two drawings, perhaps in preparation for it, are now in Oxford. From allusions in the sonnets, we may divine that when they first approached each other he had debated much with himself whether this last passion would be the most unsoftening, the most desolating of all—*un dolce amaro, un sì e no mi muovi.* Is it carnal affection, or, *del suo prestino stato* (of Plato's ante-natal state) *il raggio ardente?* The older, conventional criticism, dealing with the text of 1623, had lightly assumed that all, or nearly all, the sonnets were actually addressed to Vittoria herself; but Signor Guasti finds only four, or at most five, which can be so attributed on genuine authority. Still, there are reasons which make him assign the majority of them to the period between 1542 and 1547, and we may regard the volume as a record of this resting-place in Michelangelo's story. We know how Goethe escaped from the stress of sentiments too strong for him by making a book about them; and for Michelangelo, to write down his passionate thoughts at all, to express them in a sonnet, was already in some measure to command, and have his way with them—

> La vita del mia amor non è il cor mio,
> Ch' amor, di quel ch' io t' amo, è senza core.

It was just because Vittoria raised no great passion that the space in his life where she reigns has such peculiar suavity; and the spirit of the sonnets is lost if we once take them out of that dreamy atmosphere in which men have things as they will, because the hold of all outward things upon them is faint and uncertain. Their prevailing tone is a calm and meditative sweetness. The cry of distress is indeed there, but as a mere residue, a trace of bracing chalybeate salt, just discernible in the song which rises like a clear, sweet spring from a charmed space in his life.

This charmed and temperate space in Michelangelo's life,

without which its excessive strength would have been so imperfect, which saves him from the judgment of Dante on those who "wilfully lived in sadness," is then a well-defined period there, reaching from the year 1542 to the year 1547, the year of Vittoria's death. In it the lifelong effort to tranquillise his vehement emotions by withdrawing them into the region of ideal sentiment, becomes successful; and the significance of Vittoria is, that she realises for him a type of affection which even in disappointment may charm and sweeten his spirit.

In this effort to tranquillise and sweeten life by idealising its vehement sentiments, there were two great traditional types, either of which an Italian of the sixteenth century might have followed. There was Dante, whose little book of the *Vita Nuova* had early become a pattern of imaginative love, maintained somewhat feebly by the later followers of Petrarch; and, since Plato had become something more than a name in Italy by the publication of the Latin translation of his works by Marsilio Ficino, there was the Platonic tradition also. Dante's belief in the resurrection of the body, through which, even in heaven, Beatrice loses for him no tinge of flesh-color, or fold of raiment even; and the Platonic dream of the passage of the soul through one form of life after another, with its passionate haste to escape from the burden of bodily form altogether; are, for all effects of art or poetry, principles diametrically opposite. Now it is the Platonic tradition rather than Dante's that has molded Michelangelo's verse. In many ways no sentiment could have been less like Dante's love for Beatrice than Michelangelo's for Vittoria Colonna. Dante's comes in early youth: Beatrice is a child, with the wistful, ambiguous vision of a child, with a character still unaccentuated by the influence of outward circumstances, almost expressionless. Vittoria, on the other hand, is a woman already weary, in advanced age, of grave intellectual qualities. Dante's story is a piece of figured work, inlaid with lovely incidents. In Michelangelo's poems, frost and fire are almost the only images—the refining fire of the goldsmith; once or twice the phœnix; ice melting at the fire; fire struck from the rock which it afterwards consumes. Except one doubtful allusion to a journey, there are almost no incidents. But there is much of the bright, sharp, unerring skill, with which in boyhood he gave the look of age to the head of a faun by chipping a tooth from its jaw with a single stroke of the hammer. For Dante, the amiable and devout materialism of the middle age, sanctifies all that is presented by hand and eye; while Michelangelo is always pressing forward from the outward beauty—*il bel del fuor che agli occhi piace,* to apprehend the unseen beauty; *trascenda nella forma universale*—that abstract form of beauty, about which the Platonists reason. And this gives the impression in him of something flitting and unfixed, of the houseless and complaining spirit, almost clairvoyant through the frail and yielding flesh. He accounts for love at first sight by a previous state of existence—*la dove io t' amai prima.*

And yet there are many points in which he is really like Dante, and comes very near to the original image, beyond those later and feebler followers in the wake of Petrarch. He learns from Dante rather than from Plato, that for lovers, the surfeiting of desire—*ove gran desir gran copia affrena,* is a state less happy than poverty with abundance of hope—*una miseria di speranza piena.* He recalls him in the repetition of the words *gentile* and *cortesia,* in the personification of *Amor,* in the tendency to dwell minutely on the physical effects of the presence of a beloved object on the pulses and the heart. Above all, he resembles Dante in the warmth and intensity of his political utterances, for the lady of one of his noblest sonnets was from the first understood to be the city of Florence; and he avers that all must be asleep in heaven, if she, who was created "of angelic form," for a thousand lovers, is appropriated by one alone, some Piero, or Alessandro de' Medici. Once and again he introduces Love and Death, who dispute concerning him. For, like Dante and all the nobler souls of Italy, he is much occupied with thoughts of the grave, and his true mistress is death—death at first as the worst of all sorrows and disgraces, with a clod of the field for its brain; afterwards, death in its high distinction, its detachment from vulgar needs, the angry stains of life and action escaping fast.

Some of those whom the gods love die young. This man, because the gods loved him, lingered on to be of immense, patriarchal age, till the sweetness it had taken so long to secrete in him was found at last. Out of the strong came forth sweetness, *ex forti dulcedo.* The world had changed around him. The "new catholicism" had taken the place of the Renaissance. The spirit of the Roman Church had changed: in the vast world's cathedral which his skill had helped to raise for it, it looked stronger than ever. Some of the first members of the *Oratory* were among his intimate associates. They were of a spirit as unlike as possible from that of Lorenzo, or Savonarola even. The opposition of the Reformation to art has been often enlarged upon; far greater was that of the Catholic revival. But in thus fixing itself in a frozen orthodoxy, the Roman Church had passed beyond him, and he was a stranger to it. In earlier days, when its beliefs had been in a fluid state, he too might have been drawn into the controversy. He might have been for spiritualising the papal sovereignty, like Savonarola; or for adjusting the dreams of Plato and Homer with the words of Christ, like Pico of Mirandola. But things had moved onward, and such adjustments were no longer possible. For himself, he had long since fallen back on that divine ideal, which above the wear and tear of creeds has been forming itself for ages as the possession of nobler souls. And now he began to feel the soothing influence which since that time the Roman Church has often exerted over spirits too independent to be its subjects, yet brought within the neighborhood of its action; consoled and tranquillised, as a traveller might be, resting for one evening in a strange city, by its stately aspect and the sentiment of its many fortunes, just because with those fortunes he has nothing to do. So he lingers on; a *revenant,* as the French say, a ghost out of another age, in a world too coarse to touch his faint sensibilities very closely; dreaming, in a worn-out society, theatrical in its life, theatrical in its art, theatrical even in its devotion, on the morning of the world's history, on the primitive form of man, on the images under which that primitive world had conceived of spiritual forces. (pp. 67-74)

Walter Pater, "The Poetry of Michelangelo," in his The Renaissance, *The Modern Library, 196-? pp. 60-80.*

T. A. TROLLOPE (essay date 1877)

[*Trollope was a nineteenth-century English essayist, biographer, and travel writer. In the following excerpt from an essay first published in* Belgravia *in 1877, he favorably appraises Michelangelo's poems addressed to Vittoria Colonna.*]

Of all the names which Italy has so abundantly contributed to the roll of those of our race who have elevated, ennobled,

and benefited humanity, there is perhaps no other one which has become a household word among our insular selves to the same degree as that of Michelangelo. And it is reasonably intelligible that such should have been the case. Of all the otiose, if ingenious, speculation, with which cultivated minds are wont to amuse themselves, there is none more futile or more surely condemned to issue in mere logomachy than the question of the comparative "greatness" of great men. But it is, as I have said, intelligible enough that he whose greatness has been displayed in pursuits and capacities very diverse, and appealing to the admiration and sympathies of several differently constituted orders of mind, should become the favourite of a very general hero-worship. Among ourselves, however, Michelangelo has always been very much better know as a sculptor and a painter than as an architect or a poet. He has been better known, too, as an architect than a poet. Of course, to a certain degree, this had been the case also in his own land. For it is unquestionable that, be comparative estimates as between him and others what they may, he approached the topmost summit of art as a sculptor and a painter very much more nearly than as a poet. But in speaking, writing, or thinking of him his countrymen never forget that he was all these; and it is in the latter capacity that we have here to consider him.

In contemplating a human mind simply with reference to its capacity for manifesting the extent of the powers of the wondrous instrument, versatility should perhaps be considered as the surest mark of superior power. Of course it is generally the case that what the individual gains by the development of many-sided activity and diverging capabilities, the world loses. The faculties of the man whose life is devoted to the making of pins will be stunted and all but destroyed by such limitation; but the world will get better pins than would have been in any other way attainable. Nevertheless, it may be questioned whether Michelangelo would have given any better painting to the world than the vaults of the Sistine Chapel, if he had never touched a chisel; any better sculpture than the Moses, if he had never handled a brush; any grander architectural conception than the dome of St. Peter's, if he had never meddled with sculpture or painting; or any sweeter poetry than the sonnets addressed to Vittoria Colonna, had he never used any other medium for the manifestation of his thought than the pen. I doubt whether the same thing could be said with equal security of any other of the exemplars of marvellous versatility which have commanded the admiration of the world. (pp. 257-59)

[One chapter of Michelangelo's eventful life] very mainly influenced him as a poet. I mean, of course, his friendship for Vittoria Colonna. It is unnecessary to say anything of her, or of the nature and circumstances of that truly noble and pure friendship. . . . It may suffice to advert to the fact, that his intimacy with her coloured altogether the style and tone of thought of his poetry, some seventy sonnets and eighty or so of "Madrigals," and the choice of his subjects, mainly religious. It was not till he was far advanced in life that Michelangelo solaced himself with poetry; and it is evident that the character of his mind, grave and serious at all times, became deeply tinged with religious feeling after his acquaintance with Vittoria. It is well known that her religious feelings leaned strongly towards the doctrines of the reformers, which prevailed in Italy at that day to a degree that has never been the case since. And there are many passages in the sonnets and madrigals, the purely Calvinistic sentiment of which might have obtained a guarantee of orthodoxy from Newton or Toplady. The sincerity and earnestness of them is unmistakable, and they differ in this respect very remarkably from his love poetry, which in truth consists of little else than the cold, make-believe, Platonic conceits so dear to the academies of that period. Nevertheless, I may well end, as I began, this notice of Michelangelo as a poet, by saying that he is, to the best of my knowledge, the only writer of verses of those days who never wrote a line that in his eighty-ninth year he need have wished to blot! (pp. 294-96)

T. A. Trollope, "Michelangelo Buonarroti," in The Homes and Haunts of the Italian Poets, *Vol. 1 by Frances Eleanor Trollope and T. Adolphus Trollope, Chapman and Hall, Limited, 1881, pp. 255-96.*

EDNAH D. CHENEY (essay date 1885)

[*In the following excerpt, Cheney surveys the critical history of Michelangelo's poems and comments on the poet's treatment of love and beauty in his literary works.*]

To the triple crown of Sculptor, Painter, and Architect, to which Michelangelo's claim is undisputed, must be added that of Poet, which has been accorded to him by the finest critics of his own time and of ours; yet to many readers of scholarship and taste his poems are still almost unknown. This neglect is partly due to the intrinsic difficulty in the poems themselves, which usually treat of lofty themes in condensed language, and partly to the fact that not until twenty-one years ago were his works properly edited and published in Italy. These poems contain such wealth of thought and feeling, touching upon the deepest questions of philosophy and the tenderest experiences of the human heart, that he who once tastes of their sweetness will never cease to thirst for this fountain of refreshment and strength. The epitaphs on Cecchino Bracci Fiorentino, for instance, may, on the first reading, seem quaint and formal, reiterating trite thoughts of death and immortality; but a fuller acquaintance with them recognizes the expression of every form and thought of grief, and they lie in the memory as a treasure-house of sympathetic utterance which matches the changing phases of one's own experience.

Condivi, Michelangelo's personal friend, says: "He devoted himself to poetry rather for his own delight than because he made a profession of it, always depreciating himself and accusing his ignorance" [see excerpt dated 1553].

His poems were scribbled upon the backs of old letters, drawings, or other chance papers; sometimes copied and sent to his friends, but as often left unfinished and unknown. Yet the corrections and various readings of many of the sonnets show that he did give them much thought, and was careful in his choice of words and form. Although urged by his friends, he never consented to make any collection of his poems during his lifetime; yet in such esteem were they held that Varchi delivered a full commentary on the sonnet beginning "Non ha l'ottimo artista alcun concetto," before the Florentine Academy; analyzing it line by line, and bestowing upon it unbounded praise [see excerpt by Varchi dated 1547]. But even more precious is the brief eulogium of Berni, "Others say words, but he speaks things,"—which must have pleased him far more than the lavish adulation of the sycophant Aretino, who "wished to place every word of Michelangelo in an urn of emerald" [see excerpt dated 1537]. Nor was popular recognition wholly wanting. Three, at least, of his madrigals were set to music by distinguished composers, and were favorites with

the people, who had only lately found good melody married to anything but the hymns of the Church. But through all the sixteenth century only a few of his sonnets and madrigals were to be found. These were in a collection of verses in the *Life of Michelangelo* by Vasari, and in Varchi's lectures. Mario Giudicci gave two fine lectures upon the first edition of his works.

During the latter part of the eighteenth century the French taste then prevalent led the hearts of Italians somewhat away from Dante and Michelangelo, and the poems of the latter did not escape sharp criticism.

Four years after Michelangelo's death, a son was born to his favorite nephew, Lionardo, and named for his great ancestor. Although this child became a well-known writer, the world honors him most for his devotion to the memory of the great artist. He built a noble gallery, which he adorned with collections of his uncle's works, and pictures of the scenes of his life. He also recognized the value of the poems, and for the first time collected the scattered leaves and carefully revised and edited them.

But, unfortunately, his care was not satisfied with ascertaining what Michelangelo really wrote, and giving it to the public; but he thought his duty required him to make his poems acceptable to a newer and more enlightened age. He therefore *reduced* the poems to the level of his own taste; filling up gaps in the verses, adding others, softening harsh expressions, and omitting many strong peculiarities. He seems to have feared their free expression in religion; and, as Guasti says, "he kept an eye on the fiscal auditor and the theologian of Santa Croce." This work, published in 1623, was the basis of all the editions and translations for more than two hundred years. Yet even in this garbled form the poems attracted the attention and won the hearts of scholars and lovers of poetry, so that several editions were published in Italy, and translations made in Latin, German, French, and English. In 1858 the Counsellor Cosimo Buonarroti, with patriotic generosity, gave to the city of Florence all the treasures received from his great ancestor, including many of the original manuscripts of the poems. Signor Guasti, having access to these remains, and also to other manuscripts preserved in the Vatican, has prepared and published an edition of the poems which for clear arrangement of the text and for thoroughness and beauty of execution is eminently satisfactory. He has given every aid needed by a foreigner moderately acquainted with the Italian language to read intelligently these masterpieces of thought; while he has carefully preserved all the various readings of the originals, giving first the one to which he himself assigns the preference as probably the final form satisfactory to the poet himself.

The English translators, Wordsworth, Taylor, and Harford, did not have the inestimable benefit of his work, and yet they have enriched our language with noble versions of some of the poems. Since Guasti's work was completed, Mr. John Addington Symonds has published a full set of translations of the sonnets. His work is of the greatest value to English students. He is as faithful to the text as the exigencies of translation will permit, and has given the historical sonnets with great spirit and energy. His versions differ in merit, it may be, from the greater obscurity of the original, or from less sympathy on his part with the thought of the poem; and a harsh expression sometimes destroys the harmony of the poetic diction. It is often difficult to render a terse Italian expression into English without using a homely word which approaches to coarseness.

The modern reader misses in these poems the constant reference to Nature's outward works which forms so large a part of the poetry of our own time. Michelangelo seldom alludes to special appearances in Nature, and then only slightly, to illustrate an abstract thought; yet those argue superficially who believe him to have been insensible to natural beauty. The sonnets on Night show his feeling for one of the most mysterious and exciting phases of Nature, and the thirty-eighth sonnet refers to the common beauties of fount and rill and wave with freshness of tender feeling. We cannot accept the judgment of even so accomplished a critic as Pater, that "the world of natural things has almost no existence for him" [see excerpt dated 1871]. He wrote a long pastoral poem in which he celebrates the peace and happiness of a shepherd's life. It begins simply, and even playfully; but as he proceeds he quits this unfamiliar style for metaphysical speculation, and for a weird and powerful allegory, difficult to interpret. This poem recalls the style of Poliziano, as his madrigals and sonnets remind one sometimes of Petrarch, but more often of Dante. (pp. xiii-xvii)

[Few of Michelangelo's] early writings remain, and it is not easy to assign the date of all his love poems. Probably many are lost; most of those which we possess were written after his sixtieth year, and given to various friends. Among these were Sebastian del Piombo, the well-known artist; Luigi del Riccio, of whom Michelangelo said that he had the spirit of poesy; Donato Giannotti, whose criticisms he valued greatly; and Tommaso dei Cavalieri, a young man of talent and beauty. His friends were very anxious to obtain these gems of poetry, and often sent him some little present of fruit or game, which he playfully acknowledges in a note appended to a sonnet or madrigal. The greater part of his poems are referred by Pater to the period between 1542 and 1547,—the latter being the year of Vittoria Colonna's death,—or from his fifty-eighth to his sixty-third year. We have, however, the sonnet to Giorgio Vasari, dated 1554, and the lines to Cardinal Beccadelli, 1556, when he was eighty-two years old.

The personal relation of greatest importance in this connection is with his beautiful and truly noble friend Vittoria Colonna. It is probable that Michelangelo first met this congenial spirit in 1536 or 1538. She was already a widow, whose poetic muse was employed in a constant tribute of love and grief to the memory of her husband. She was the idol of her own sex in Italy, who adored her as a saint and sought her counsels in doubt and distress. She was indeed admired by men of all classes; but she preserved the purity and modesty of her spirit, and was only prevented by the commands of the Pope from seeking the retirement of a cloister. The high themes of Patriotism, Philosophy, Art, and Religion engaged her thoughts, as they did those of Michelangelo; and on them they exchanged letters and poems, and he dedicated to her some of his noblest works in sculpture. He lived to mourn over her grave, and henceforth to find life robbed of its sweetest joy. The burden of old age and approaching death, with a deep sense of his own imperfections, lay heavy upon his heart, and found expression in those sonnets so full of deep struggle and suffering. Fully to understand them requires an intimate knowledge of the heart of man, as well as of the circumstances of the age and country which surrounded him.

It is common to speak of this relation as one of love, and ex-

pressions in the sonnets referring to his passion are taken literally. But to understand his words, we must remember the Platonic philosophy which filled his mind and gave color to all his thoughts. This high and dignified friendship was undoubtedly made sweet and tender by the delicate reverence which every true man feels for woman; but it was free from the folly of passion, which would have been alike unbecoming his high tone of thought and her unswerving devotion to her husband's memory. Such seems to have been the opinion of his contemporaries, who say "he was enamoured of the divine spirit of Vittoria Colonna."

In the early part of their acquaintance, he wrote to Tommaso dei Cavalieri some poems which are supposed to have covert reference to Vittoria. It is possible that he may thus have spoken to this friend before he dared to address her personally; but the whole tone of their intercourse is frank, friendly, and thoughtful. Patriotism, Love, Art, and Religion are the themes of his verse, and in all of them he struggled with passionate longings and bitter regrets. The city of his birth was degraded and enslaved; and in the visible Church, which he never forsook, he had been obliged to recognize the foe of his country. We know nothing of the outward history of his love; but that he had felt the shock and recoil of passion, and that he had hungered and thirsted for affection, is but too evident. And yet there is no personal allusion or recognition of a want of the natural domestic ties dear to the heart: all is veiled in dim, solemn imagery which hides even while it reveals.

Michelangelo's philosophy, based upon Platonism, is pure idealism. Human life, all mortal forms, are but the outward expression of spiritual life. He never rests in the outward and material, but sees it only as now concealing, now revealing, the inward idea,—

The more the marble wastes, the more the statue grows.

Death is a constant theme; but it is never a final end—always a step to higher life. He feels deep grief when it bears away his beloved ones, but he recognizes it as a sure friend which is to end all sorrows: "It could defend one from all other miseries, even those of love." This philosophy was blended with his religious ideas, and the influences of the newly revived love of antiquity and of Christian teachings are both apparent in his poems. It is therefore possible to draw very varying inferences from his expressions in regard to his religious convictions. The more definite allusions to Christian theology in his later poems may be attributed to the influence of his friends Vittoria Colonna and the Cardinal Beccadelli; while the boldness and freedom of his thought in the poem on the death of his father recalls his early admiration for the prophet Savonarola.

That Michelangelo was truly an idealist in Art is evident: it is not the outward form, but the inward image, that he is ever seeking. The Beautiful is always an image of the Divine, and the only reason for loving it in outward form is that it brings us near to the eternal fountain of Love. So closely were Religion, Art, and Love blended in his thought that it is sometimes impossible to tell to which he refers in his poems. The remorse which often oppresses him for the false love which has deluded him is that keen sense of unworthiness which haunts every sensitive soul worshipping the ideal, and by no means implies any moral fault in his life. His contemporaries, especially Condivi, bear emphatic testimony to the temperance and purity of his thought, speech, and life. His love of poetry was fostered, if not awakened, by his early residence in Bologna with Aldovrandi, who delighted in his Tuscan accent, and often engaged him to read to him from Petrarch, Dante, and Boccaccio. How highly he reverenced the great poet of his country is shown by his noble sonnets to Dante, and by his illustrating the *Divina Commedia* with designs which—alas for us!—are forever lost.

But no biography gives us so intimate an acquaintance with the heart and life of this man as the poems, which were the delight, solace, and relief of his lonely days. The many different readings show that they were dear to him; and we can often trace his efforts to give the exact shade of thought which he longed to express. They prove how utterly superficial is the judgment which denies to him tenderness and piety, and the most intense longing for the love and communion of his fellow-beings; yet too often solitude and loneliness were his lot,—how keenly felt, is shown in these poetic revelations.

Life was very serious to him; and in an age so luxurious and frivolous, solitude seemed the only fitting companionship. And yet Donato Giannotti, who knew him well, makes him say, in his *Dialogues:* "Know that I am the man the most inclined to love persons that ever was born in any time. Whenever I see any one who has any virtue, or shows any quickness of mind, or can do or say anything more fittingly than others, I am constrained to fall in love with him; and I give myself up as a prey to him, so that I am no more my own, but all his." Does not this explain many passages in his poems where he complains of the empire of love over him? His sympathies were so profound and intense that he felt obliged to hold himself aloof from men, lest his own power of free creation should be lost.

Greatness and goodness are nearly allied; the more closely we study the life of this artist, whose colossal intellect and stern will give him rank among the very highest names in history, the more do we find the purity and truth of his moral nature and the depth of his affections; and we learn anew the great truth that intellectual development alone may make monsters, but only when heart and head work together can we have a true artist. (pp. xvii-xxii)

> *Ednah D. Cheney, in an introduction to* Selected Poems from Michelangelo Buonarroti, *edited by Ednah D. Cheney, Lee and Shepard, Publishers, 1885, pp. xiii-xxii.*

[W. P. KER]   (essay date 1888)

[*A Scottish scholar of medieval literature, Ker was an authority on comparative European literature and the history of literary forms. In the following excerpt from a review of Cesare Guasti's 1863 critical edition of Michelangelo's* Rime, *he offers a favorable appraisal of Michelangelo's poetry.*]

Michael Angelo, like Dante, seems to have a special attraction for the Northern mind. His genius is in some ways ascetic and puritanic, and appeals to those who seek rather for edification than for artistic beauty. The ingenuous barbarian in Italy is taken at once with the noble aspect of Michael Angelo's 'David;' he is impressed by the passionate resolve shown in the knit brows. The spiritual emotion in the face he can understand, because he has been brought up on dramas, novels, and religious and reflective works, which treat of emotions and passions. But appreciation of the story of a picture or a statue may be possible without any real appreciation of painting or sculpture, and perhaps many people admire the

'David' or the 'Moses' of Michael Angelo—on account of the expression in their faces—who find it difficult to see much in the Parthenon marbles. It may be suspected that, in a similar way, of the many English students of Dante more are attracted by the religion, the mysticism, the prophesyings, than by the verse, the imagery, or the characters of the *Divine Comedy*. A great deal of the poetry of Michael Angelo resembles the more abstract and mystical parts of Dante. Michael Angelo studied Dante zealously, as is proved by his own poems and the evidence of his friends, and notably by the Florentine petition to Leo X. in 1519 to have the ashes of Dante brought back to his native land. 'Michelagniolo schultore' does not only sign his name, but breaks in upon the decent Latin of the document, and says, in his Tuscan, that he offers himself 'to the Divine poet to make his tomb in a seemly manner, and in an honourable place in this city.' It is from this love for Dante, perhaps, that Michael Angelo takes his antique Florentine character; for in many ways he seems to belong rather to the older narrower Florentine state, represented by Villani, than to the confused and heavily labouring Florence of the times following on the first French invasion of Italy. The mysticism in Michael Angelo's sonnets is like that of the *Vita Nuova*, or of Guido Guinicelli, still earlier. It is a sort of recovery of the genius of the first simple outburst of Italian idealistic poetry, after generations of Petrarchians had done their worst to spoil everything by their endless iteration of the same tune, and their monotonous variations. This is one of the greatest charms of Michael Angelo's poetry; this is what makes the sonnets an all but unique production in literature—that in an age of literary conventionality and incipient decadence, a great genius, working at literature as a pastime, struck back instinctively to forms of thought long ago out of fashion, and produced verses unfashionably sincere. One remembers how Blake reinvented the Elizabethan mode of lyric poetry, in the days of the mechanical utterers of heroic couplets. There is this great difference, however, between the two cases, that Blake was a thoroughgoing antagonist of the established and accepted school of poetry, and paid his reverence to a quite distinct older one. Michael Angelo did what was much more singular, though much less obviously remarkable. He did not go into direct opposition. He kept within the limits of the contemporary school, and yet freed himself in a miraculous way from the vices of that school—at all events in his best poems—and reproduced the original wild type which had been obliterated by a long course of artificial cultivation, by gardeners' varieties of gaudy and sterile blossoms.

There is no explanation to be found of this, except the perfectly satisfactory one, that Michael Angelo was Michael Angelo. He could hardly, if he tried, talk or write, paint or carve, without putting his whole strength into it. The Petrarchians differed from the early Tuscan sonnetteers chiefly in not believing what they wrote, nor even seriously making believe. Michael Angelo had difficulty in being insincere, and his sincerity brought back to him the tone of Dante's *Vita Nuova*. The intensity of feeling, which strikes even the inartistic and uninstructed in the presence of the 'David' or the 'Moses,' found a literary expression in the sonnets and madrigals, by means of which his great and lonely genius gave voice to its complaint, its *desiderium* of a land that is very far off.

It would be a daring and rather foolish thing to say that the poems are as valuable in themselves, apart from all thought of the author, as they are when regarded as his confessions—his own personal words. It may be true enough, that as anonymous compositions they would still be unparalleled and wonderful. Only very serious students, however, will give themselves the trouble of going through the necessary process of abstraction in order to get rid of the personal bias. Most people will be content to be thankful for the poems, first and chiefly, because their author—he and no other person—wrote them.

Not that they are of much value to the biographer on the search for picturesque details. The dates of most of them are vague; the certain dates belong for the most part to the latter years, when the adventures of Michael Angelo among popes, cardinals, politicians, and rivals generally, were pretty nearly at an end. Most of the poems are rather abstract; Michael Angelo did not bring the plastic individualising faculty much into use in his verse. Dante is more of a painter and sculptor than Michael Angelo when it comes to rhyming. Emotions and ideas there are in plenty, but few concrete images. The great artist found a relief in getting away into a vaguer region of intelligence, from the bondage of line and colour in which his working days were passed. (pp. 1-4)

Michael Angelo never published his verses, further than to his own friends, yet in his lifetime they were well known and appreciated. He was not careless about them either, and evidently took a great interest in poetical composition; though—or perhaps because—'writing was not his trade,' as he wrote once to Vasari. In many of his letters he shows anxiety about the correctness of his poems, and entrusts them to the judgement of Luigi del Riccio or Donato Giannotti. 'Messer Luigi, you have the poetic genius; mend me one of these two madrigals, for I want it to give to a friend of ours.' 'Choose the one which Messer Donato judges to be the less wretched (*il manco tristo*).' And again he sends greeting 'to Messer Donato, mender of things ill-made.' Criticism, at that time, it should be remembered, exercised the minds of artists almost as much as their own proper work. There was an immense and continuous production of opinion on general and particular artistic matters. Michael Angelo read Varchi's treatise on the comparative merits of painting and sculpture, and gave judgement in his own manner—authoritatively enough. He had a certain finite amount of respect for the literary man's point of view. It was not for nothing that he had walked in the garden of Lorenzo the Magnificent, along with the philosophers and scholars. He could talk on abstract questions of æsthetics as well as the best of them. 'Let Painting and Sculpture be at peace with one another, and leave wrangling,' he says, 'for there goes more time to that than to the making of figures.' Varchi had before this given a remarkable indication of the importance of Michael Angelo's poems in the estimation of the doctors of literature. On the second Sunday in Lent, 1546, he had read before the Florentine Academy a discourse on Michael Angelo's sonnet, **"Non ha l'ottimo artista alcun concetto"** [see excerpt by Varchi dated 1547]; and this Lent sermon was printed afterwards by its author, and published along with the essay on painting and sculpture, and was greatly admired. Michael Angelo himself used very courteous language about it, and wrote to the author that Donato Giannotti could not have enough of reading it. Thus it is plain that the sonnets, even though unpublished in the ordinary sense of the word, were fully recognised and appreciated by the literary tribunals, and that the author of them, however lightly he may have spoken of his rhymes, did not keep them to himself or refuse the praise that was accorded them by those instructed in such things. His best friends were men of letters; the society in which he lived was

occupied quite as much with philosophy and literature as with art. There were other ways also in which his poems became known outside the circle to which he communicated them. His madrigals were set to music by different composers. And there was one poem which at once struck the imagination and was remembered. That poem is the quatrain belonging to the statue of Night—**"Caro m' è 'l sonno, e più l' esser di sasso."** It is this, and not any more philosophical poem, that keeps alive, in the general reader and the general tourist, a knowledge that Michael Angelo wrote poetry. It is printed in Baedeker, and the custodian of the sacristy of San Lorenzo recites it to the passing generations. (pp. 4-5)

There is a very natural prejudice among artists against any theory which magnifies the unseen idea at the expense of the sensible antitype of it. Instinctively, it is felt that the pursuit of the pure idea of the beautiful is fatal to arts, which are busied for the most part with the senses and matter belonging to the senses. Platonism, like all modes of belief that make a divorce between the soul and the body, the unseen and the seen, might be expected to be incompatible with art, as inducing distrust of the means employed by the artist. A theory which offers a general idea as an object of pursuit, which encourages contempt of bodily details, is not likely to be favoured in any art school where the masters wish their pupils to be modest, painstaking, and accurate. Idealism may be an easy refuge for the bungler and the impostor, or for innocent foolish persons. The 'Platonic' manner of poetising has a fatal fascination for people who never ought to be allowed to write a verse—who have no imagination, except in the belief that they are artists; or passion, except in hankering after unattainable powers of poetry. Its abstract character commends itself to minds that are destitute of the artistic faculty. Those who have failed in art retain the consolation that they have been inspired by a divine universal idea. When one has been baffled by the intricate particular details of execution in any art, it may be a relief to decide that those details are unimportant, irrelevant, and shadowy in comparison with the idea. That is the worst of this sort of idealism: it is far too easily imitated.

Michael Angelo stands separate from the crowd. He, at any rate, is not open to the reproach of choosing the easier way—he who, according to his own humorous description of his Sistine experiences, had bowed and cramped himself out of all human likeness, through years of a daily contest with those same despised particular details—the terrene paint and plaster in which his ideas were expressed. With Michael Angelo the idealistic way of thinking is not a short cut, a bypath meadow to escape the heartbreaking labour of the highway of art. It comes after the labour, after the victory, not before it. His mystical language proceeds out of the depth of a long experience, and is weighted with the solemnity of his noble and devoted life. That gives his poetry its incomparable force of character. There are not many artists who can use the language of idealism with perfect sincerity, having accomplished their apprenticeship, and mastered all the real difficulties of their craft. Among those few are Dante and Michael Angelo. (pp. 8-9)

[That Michael Angelo sent Vittoria Colonna poems] of his own is proved by a sonnet in his own hand, followed by a letter of thanks for presents—presents, whatever they may have been, which, when they came into his house, came, he says, not as guests but as lords, and turned the place into a heaven. The sonnet is only an occasional poem, on the same subject as the letter, arguing the baseness of those people who try to

The Vatican Pietà, *by Michelangelo.*

show their gratitude by repaying favours, as if they found it burdensome to be indebted to any benefactor. It is a courteous message, sent probably near the beginning of their friendship by the hands of the faithful Urbino. It is not easy to say which of all the other extant poems were addressed to Vittoria. It is certain enough that none of the later poems, many of which are definitely religious in subject, can have been independent of the friendship for Vittoria. But of only a small number of poems can it be affirmed that they were written for her, and for no imaginary and no less noble lady. Of these the finest and most significant is that in which he describes himself in his present nature and condition, as a mere rough sketch or model, from which the lady, an artist of virtue, will fashion him into perfection. . . . (p. 23)

Metaphors drawn from painting and sculpture—especially sculpture—recur frequently in the poems, and always seem to bring with them an increase of passion and insight. The great sonnet on which Varchi commented may or may not have been written for Vittoria—there is no evidence; but, at any rate, it stands naturally by the side of that poem of the model, as another poem in which the processes of art are transferred by a mystical analogy to the way in which the soul is influenced, as if by some plastic artist. Here the idea is that all the shapes of art are potential in the matter from which the artist extricates them; and that, in a similar way, it lies with the lover, as artist, to bring out of the soul of the beloved the image corresponding to his desire. (pp. 23-4)

[Michael Angelo's] poetical work can never be widely popular, even among those who read old books. It is impossible that it should ever be forgotten: it is a different thing from the 'flattery and fustian' of decadent Italian literature. Its ideas and style may often be hard to understand, and may in many

cases be derived from a bad school of artificial and affected poetry. There is little danger, however, that Michael Angelo will ever come to be confounded with the unendurable Petrarchist rhetoricians. After the labours of the editor of the poems and of the other eminent scholars who since the beginning of the century have illustrated the history of Michael Angelo, very little study is needed to get rid of the accidental hindrances to proper comprehension. But it may be that the best security for Michael Angelo's poetical fame is the popular recollection of the four lines of the 'Night,' which are the key to almost all the verses he ever wrote. (p. 34)

[W. P. Ker], "The Poems of Michael Angelo," in The Edinburgh Review, Vol. CLXVIII, No. CCCX-LIII, July, 1888, pp. 1-34.

JOHN ADDINGTON SYMONDS   (essay date 1893)

[*Symonds was a major nineteenth-century English writer on the Italian Renaissance. In the following excerpt from his 1893 biography of Michelangelo, he explores the thoughts and images that gave rise to Michelangelo's sonnets and madrigals.*]

The value of Michelangelo's poetry is rather psychological than purely literary. He never claimed to be more than an amateur, writing to amuse himself. His style is obscure, crabbed, ungrammatical. Expression only finds a smooth and flowing outlet when the man's nature is profoundly stirred by some powerful emotion, as in the sonnets to Cavalieri, or the sonnets on the deaths of Vittoria Colonna and Urbino, or the sonnets on the thought of his own death. For the most part, it is clear that he found great difficulty in mastering his thoughts and images. This we discover from the innumerable variants of the same madrigal or sonnet which he made, and his habit of returning to them at intervals long after their composition. A good fourth of the Codex Vaticanus consists of repetitions and *rifacimenti.* He was also wont to submit what he wrote to the judgment of his friends, requesting them to alter and improve. He often had recourse to Luigi del Riccio's assistance in such matters. I may here adduce an inedited letter from two friends in Rome, Giovanni Francesco Bini and Giovanni Francesco Stella, who returned a poem they had handled in this manner:

> We have done our best to alter some things in your sonnet, but not to set it all to rights, since there was not much wanting. Now that it is changed or put in order, according as the kindness of your nature wished, the result will be more due to your own judgment than to ours, since you have the true conception of the subject in your mind. We shall be greatly pleased if you find yourself as well served as we earnestly desire that you should command us.

It was the custom of amateur poets to have recourse to literary craftsmen before they ventured to circulate their compositions. An amusing instance of this will be found in Professor Biagi's monograph upon Tullia d'Aragona, all of whose verses passed through the crucible of Benedetto Varchi's revision.

The thoughts and images out of which Michelangelo's poetry is woven are characteristically abstract and arid. He borrows no illustrations from external nature. The beauty of the world and all that lives in it might have been non-existent so far as he was concerned. Nor do his octave stanzas in praise of rural life form an exception to this statement; for these are imitated from Poliziano, so far as they attempt pictures of the country, and their chief poetical feature is the masque of vices belonging to human nature in the city. His stock-in-trade consists of a few Platonic notions and a few Petrarchan antitheses. In the very large number of compositions which are devoted to love, this one idea predominates: that physical beauty is a direct beam sent from the eternal source of all reality, in order to elevate the lover's soul and lead him on the upward path toward heaven. Carnal passion he regards with the aversion of an ascetic. It is impossible to say for certain to whom these mystical love-poems were addressed. Whether a man or a woman is in the case (for both were probably the objects of his æsthetical admiration), the tone of feeling, the language, and the philosophy do not vary. He uses the same imagery, the same conceits, the same abstract ideas for both sexes, and adapts the leading motive which he had invented for a person of one sex to a person of the other when it suits his purpose. In our absolute incapacity to fix any amative connection upon Michelangelo, or to link his name with that of any contemporary beauty, we arrive at the conclusion, strange as this may be, that the greater part of his love-poetry is a scholastic exercise upon emotions transmuted into metaphysical and mystical conceptions. Only two pieces in the long series break this monotony by a touch of realism. They are divided by a period of more than thirty years. The first seems to date from an early epoch of his life:—

> What joy hath yon glad wreath of flowers that is
> Around her golden hair so deftly twined,
> Each blossom pressing forward from behind,
> As though to be the first her brows to kiss!
>
> The livelong day her dress hath perfect bliss,
> That now reveals her breast, now seems to bind:
> And that fair woven net of gold refined
> Rests on her cheek and throat in happiness!
>
> Yet still more blissful seems to me the band,
> Gilt at the tips, so sweetly doth it ring,
> And clasp the bosom that it serves to lace:
>
> Yea, and the belt, to such as understand,
> Bound round her waist, saith: Here I'd ever cling!
> What would my arms do in that girdle's place?

The second can be ascribed with probability to the year 1534 or 1535. It is written upon the back of a rather singular letter addressed to him by a certain Pierantonio, when both men were in Rome together:—

> Kind to the world, but to itself unkind,
> A worm is born, that, dying noiselessly,
> Despoils itself to clothe fair limbs, and be
> In its true worth alone by death divined.
>
> Would I might die for my dear lord to find
> Raiment in my outworn mortality:
> That, changing like the snake, I might be free
> To cast the slough wherein I dwell confined!
>
> Nay, were it mine, that shaggy fleece that stays,
> Woven and wrought into a vestment fair,
> Around yon breast so beauteous in such bliss!
>
> All through the day thou'd have me! Would I were
> The shoes that bear that burden! when the ways
> Were wet with rain, thy feet I then should kiss!

I have already alluded to the fact that we can trace two widely different styles of writing in Michelangelo's poetry. Some of his sonnets, like the two just quoted, and those we can refer with certainty to the Cavalieri series, together with occasion-

al compositions upon the deaths of Cecchino and Urbino, seem to come straight from the heart, and their manuscripts offer few variants to the editor. Others, of a different quality, where he is dealing with Platonic subtleties or Petrarchan conceits, have been twisted into so many forms, and tortured by such frequent re-handlings, that it is difficult now to settle a final text. The Codex Vaticanus is peculiarly rich in examples of these compositions. Madrigal lvii. and Sonnet lx., for example, recur with wearisome reiteration. These laboured and scholastic exercises, unlike the more spontaneous utterances of his feelings, are worked up into different forms, and the same conceits are not seldom used for various persons and on divers occasions.

One of the great difficulties under which a critic labours in discussing these personal poems is that their chronology cannot be ascertained in the majority of instances. Another is that we are continually hampered by the false traditions invented by Michelangelo the younger. Books like Lannan Rolland's *Michel-Ange et Vittoria Colonna* have no value whatsoever, because they are based upon that unlucky grand-nephew's deliberately corrupted text. Even Wordsworth's translations, fine as they are, have lost a large portion of their interest since the publication of the autographs by Cesare Guasti in 1863. It is certain that the younger Michelangelo meant well to his illustrious ancestor. He was anxious to give his rugged compositions the elegance and suavity of academical versification. He wished also to defend his character from the imputation of immorality. Therefore he rearranged the order of stanzas in the longer poems, pieced fragments together, changed whole lines, ideas, images, amplified and mutilated, altered phrases which seemed to him suspicious. Only one who has examined the manuscripts of the Buonarroti Archives knows what pains he bestowed upon this ungrateful and disastrous task. But the net result of his meddlesome benevolence is that now for nearly three centuries the greatest genius of the Italian Renaissance has worn a mask concealing the real nature of his emotion, and that a false legend concerning his relations to Vittoria Colonna has become inextricably interwoven with the story of his life.

The extraordinary importance attached by Michelangelo in old age to the passions of his youth is almost sufficient to justify those psychological investigators who regard him as the subject of a nervous disorder. It does not seem to be accounted for by anything known to us regarding his stern and solitary life, his aloofness from the vulgar, and his self-dedication to study. In addition to the splendid devotional sonnets addressed to Vasari . . . , I may corroborate these remarks by the translation of a set of three madrigals bearing on the topic.

> Ah me, ah me! how have I been betrayed
> By my swift-flitting years, and by the glass,
> Which yet tells truth to those who firmly gaze!
> Thus happens it when one too long delays,
> As I have done, nor feels time fleet and fade:—
> One morn he finds himself grown old, alas!
> To gird my loins, repent, my path repass,
> Sound counsel take, I cannot, now death's near;
> Foe to myself, each tear,
> Each sigh, is idly to the light wind sent,
> For there's no loss to equal time ill-spent.
>
> Ah me, ah me! I wander telling o'er
> Past years, and yet in all I cannot view
> One day that might be rightly reckoned mine.
> Delusive hopes and vain desires entwine

My soul that loves, weeps, burns, and sighs full sore.
Too well I know and prove that this is true,
Since of man's passions none to me are new.
Far from the truth my steps have gone astray,
In peril now I stay,
For, lo! the brief span of my life is o'er.
Yet, were it lengthened, I should love once more.

Ah me! I wander tired, and know not whither:
I fear to sight my goal, the years gone by
Point it too plain; nor will closed eyes avail.
Now Time hath changed and gnawed this mortal veil,
Death and the soul in conflict strive together
About my future fate that looms so nigh.
Unless my judgment greatly goes awry,
Which God in mercy grant, I can but see
Eternal penalty
Waiting my wasted will, my misused mind,
And know not, Lord, where health and hope to find.

After reading these lamentations, it is well to remember that Michelangelo at times indulged a sense of humour. As examples of his lighter vein, we might allude to the sonnet on the Sistine and the capitolo in answer to Francesco Berni, written in the name of Fra Sebastiano. Sometimes his satire becomes malignant, as in the sonnet against the people of Pistoja, which breathes the spirit of Dantesque invective. Sometimes the fierceness of it is turned against himself, as in the capitolo upon old age and its infirmities. The grotesqueness of this lurid descant on senility and death is marked by something rather Teutonic than Italian, a "Danse Macabre" intensity of loathing; and it winds up with the bitter reflections, peculiar to him in his latest years, upon the vanity of art. "My much-prized art, on which I relied and which brought me fame, has now reduced me to this. I am poor and old, the slave of others. To the dogs I must go, unless I die quickly." (pp. 168-76)

John Addington Symonds, in his The Life of Michelangelo Buonarroti, Vol. 2, *second edition, John C. Nimmo, 1893, 449 p.*

JOHN JAY CHAPMAN   (essay date 1895)

[*Chapman was an American lawyer, poet, playwright, and essayist. In the following excerpt, he examines Michelangelo's character as it is revealed in his sonnets, commenting as well on the problems posed by reading the poems in English translation.*]

Michael Angelo, as a man, is chiefly revealed to us in his sonnets. Although he wears the triple crown of artist, poet and sculptor, although his genius was worshipped with a kind of awe even while he lived, and has left his name unique, yet we know the man best through these little pieces of himself which he broke off and gave to his friends, not for publication, but out of courtesy and because it was the custom of the times. The fragments were so vibrating with the life of the man that they were instantly recognized as wonderful things. In his lifetime they were treasured and collected by his friends, and at a later day they were seized upon by the world at large.

As is well known, the first published edition of the sonnets was prepared for the press many years after the death of the author by the artist's grand-nephew, who edited the poems to suit the taste of the seventeenth century. The extent and atrocity of his emendations can be realized by a casual comparison of texts. The sonnets survived the improvements, however, and indeed made headway under them; and when,

in 1863, Guasti gave the original readings to the public, the world was prepared for them. The bibliography of editions and translations which Guasti gives is enough to show the popularity of the sonnets, their universal character, and, as it were, their international currency. (p. 175)

It would not be just to class all the poems in one category, for they are exceedingly various, some being rough and some elegant, some obvious and some obscure, some humorous, some religious. Yet they have this in common, that each seems to be the bearer of some deep harmony, whose vibrations we feel and whose truth we recognize. It is curious to note that from the very beginning they seem to have had a provocative and stimulating effect upon others; ever since they were written cultivated people have published essays about them. One of them has been the subject of repeated academical disquisition. They absorb and reflect the philosophy of the times; they appeal to and express the individual; they have done this through three centuries and throughout who shall say how many different educational conditions? Place them in what light you will, they gleam with new meanings. This is their quality. It is hard to say whence the vitality comes. They have often a brilliancy that springs from the juxtaposition of two thoughts, a brilliancy like that produced by unblended colors roughly but well laid on. They have, as it were, an organic force which nothing can render. The best of them have in a marked degree the reflective power above alluded to, which gives back light from the mind of the reader. The profounder ones appear positively to change and glow under contemplation; they re-echo syllables from forgotten voices; they suggest unfathomable depths of meaning. These sonnets are, indeed, themselves protean in character; they represent different things to different people—religion to one, love to another, philosophy to a third.

It is easy to guess what must be the fate of such poems in translation. The translator inevitably puts more of himself than of Michael Angelo into his version. Even the first Italian editor could not let them alone. He felt he must dose them with elegance. This itching to amend the sonnets results largely from the obscurity of the text. A translator is required to be, above all things, comprehensible, and, therefore, he must interpret, he must paraphrase. He is not at liberty to retain the equivocal suggestiveness of the original. The language of a translation must be chastened, or, at least, grammatical, and Michael Angelo's verse is very often neither the one nor the other.

It is not the intention of this paper either to render the sonnets or to write an adequate account of them, but to call attention to the fact, perhaps it will be said, sufficiently known already, that there is nothing else just like them in the world. (pp. 176-78)

The Italian sonnet is, indeed, both in its form and spirit a thing so foreign to the English idea of what poetry should be that no cultivation can ever domesticate [it] into our tongue. The seeds of flowers from the Alps may be planted in our gardens but a new kind of flower will come up; and this is what has happened over and over again to the skilled gardeners of English literature in their struggles with the Italian sonnet. In Italy, for six hundred years, the sonnet has been the authorized form for a disconnected remark of any kind. Its chief aim is not so much to express a feeling as an idea—a witticism—a conceit—a shrewd saying—a clever analogy—a graceful simile—a beautiful thought. Moreover, it is not primarily intended for the public; it has a social rather than a literary function. Such is [the] ideal of the Italian sonnet.

The English with their lyrical genius have impressed the form as they have impressed every other form into lyrical service, and with some success it must be admitted. But the Italian sonnet is not lyrical. It is conversational and intellectual and many things which English instinct declares poetry ought not to be. The remark may be hazarded that we feel throughout the poetry of the Latin races a certain domination of the intelligence which is foreign to our own poetry. But in the sonnet form at least we may sympathize with this domination. Let us read the Italian sonnets, then, as if they were prose; let us seek first the thought and hold to that, and leave the eloquence to take care of itself. It is the thought after all which Michael Angelo himself cared about. He is willing to sacrifice elegance, to truncate words, to wreck rhyme, prosody and grammar, if he can only hurl through the verse these thoughts which were his convictions.

The platonic ideas about life and love, and art, which lie at the bottom of most of these sonnets are familiar to us all. They have been the reigning commonplace ideas of educated people for the last two thousand years. But in these sonnets they are touched with new power; they become exalted into mystical importance. We feel almost as if it were Plato himself that is talking. I am not sure that the interest is lessened when we remember that it is Michael Angelo. It is necessary to touch on this element in the sonnets, for it exists in them; and because while some will feel chiefly the fiery soul of the man, others will be most struck by his great speculative intellect.

It is certain that the sonnets date from various times in Michael Angelo's life; and, except in a few cases, it must be left to the instinct of the reader to place them. Those which were called forth by the poet's friendship for Vittoria Colonna were undoubtedly written toward the close of his life. While he seems to have known Vittoria Colonna and to have been greatly attached to her for many years, it is certain that in his old age he fell in love with her. The library of romance that has been written about this attachment has added nothing to Condivi's simple words [see excerpt dated 1553]:

> He greatly loved the Marchesana of Pescara, with whose divine spirit he fell in love, and was in return passionately beloved of her; and he still keeps many of her letters, which are full of most honest and tenderest love, such as used to issue from a heart like hers; and he himself had written her many and many a sonnet full of wit and tenderness. She often left Viterbo and other places, where she had gone for pleasure, and to pass the summer, and came to Rome for no other reason except to see Michael Angelo. And in return he bore her so much love that I remember hearing him say that he regretted nothing except that when he had gone to see her on her death-bed he had not so kissed her brow and her cheek as he had kissed her hand. He was many times overwhelmed at the thought of her death and used to be as one out of his mind.

It seems, from reading the sonnets, that some of those, which are addressed to women, must belong to a period anterior to his friendship with Vittoria. This appears from the internal evidence of style and feeling, as well as by references in the later sonnets.

One other fact must be mentioned—both Vittoria and Mi-

chael Angelo belonged to, or at least sympathized with, the Piagnoni, and were in a sense disciples of Savonarola. Now, it is this religious element which makes Michael Angelo seem to step out of his country and out of his century and across time and space into our own. This religious feeling is of a kind perfectly familiar to us; indeed, of a kind inborn and native to us. Whether we be reading the English prayer-book or listening to the old German Passion Music, there is a certain note of the spirit which, when we hear it, we perfectly recognize as a part of ourselves. What we recognize is in fact the Protestantism which swept over Europe during the century of Michael Angelo's existence; which conquered Teutonic Europe, and was conquered, but not extinguished, in Latin Europe; and a part of which survives in ourselves. If one wishes to feel the power of Savonarola one may do so in these sonnets. We had connected Michael Angelo with the Renaissance, but we are here face to face with the Reformation. We cannot help being a little surprised at this. We cannot help being surprised at finding how well we know this man.

Few of us are familiar enough with the language of the plastic arts to have seen without prompting this same modern element in Michael Angelo's painting and sculpture. We might, perhaps, have recognized it in the Pieta in St. Peter's. We may safely say, however, that it exists in all his works. It is in the Medicean statues; it is in the Julian marbles; it is in the Sistine ceiling. What is there in these figures that they leave us so awestruck, that they seem so like the sound of trumpets blowing from a spiritual world? The intelligence that could call them forth, the craft that could draw them, have long since perished. But the meaning survives the craft. The lost arts retain their power over us. We understand but vaguely, yet we are thrilled. We cannot decipher the signs, yet we subscribe to their import. The world from which Michael Angelo's figures speak is our own world after all. That is the reason they are so potent, so intimate, so illimitably significant. We may be sure that the affinity which we feel with Michael Angelo, and do not feel with any other artist of that age, springs from experiences and beliefs in him which are similar to our own.

His work speaks to the moral sense more directly and more powerfully than that of any one—so directly and so powerfully, indeed, that we whose physical senses are dull, and whose moral sense is acute, are moved by Michael Angelo, although the rest of the *cinque cento* culture remain a closed book to us.

It is difficult this conjuring with the unrecoverable past, so rashly done by all of us. Yet we must use what light we have. Remembering, then, that painting is not the reigning mode of expession in recent times, and that in dealing with it we are dealing with a vehicle of expression with which we are not spontaneously familiar, we may yet draw conclusions which are not fantastic, if we base them upon the identity of one man's nature some part of which we are sure we understand. We may throw a bridge from the ground in the sonnets, upon which we are sure we stand firmly, to the ground in the frescoes, which, by reason of our own ignorance, is less certain ground to us, and we may walk from one side to the other amid the elemental forces of this same man's mind. (pp. 178-83)

John Jay Chapman, "Michael Angelo's Sonnets," in The Bachelor of Arts, *Vol. I, No. 2, June, 1895, pp. 175-89.*

THOMAS B. REILLY (essay date 1897)

[In the following essay, Reilly explores elements of religion and morality in Michelangelo's verse.]

Everything is beautiful to the one whose soul is susceptible to pleasures that spring from works of art and the fairer forms of human life and nature. A man thus fashioned does not live on an earth of commonplace existence; he stands aside from busy throngs, in a vague sort of twilight, catching from behind the material veil ideals of the world beyond. He drifts out into the ways of contemplation, forgetting the dust of the journey, remembering only the scent of the wild-rose that drifted upward from the wayside. He looks at the red-barred sunset, which burns above the green sea-marsh or flames behind the blue hills, and he sees, as few men ever do, that half-retreating spirit of the beautiful which lurks in the glowing depths of light. Many of us have never seen a sunset. The arrowed light that glances from a sea-bird's wing, or glistens along the whitening wave, silvering the line of snow on gray sands; the star on fire in the west; the low fluting of a bird among the reeds—all of these have for him a subtle charm and beauty which few men understand.

Such a man is not sentimental; he makes wings of material types, that he may soar through the deeps of spiritual order. He writes, and around the thought plays a halo, drawing us away from the noise and glare of city streets; leading us out to the hillsides flecked with sheep, along the winding brook where wearied cattle stand knee-deep in the cool water, up through the meadow-land and pasture, into the depths of shady woodlands, there to lie and dream of ideal worlds and ideal men and women. He catches the fragrance of the past; but he also plants new shrubs along his foot-path, watching them break into blossom, knowing that the scent thereof will be the richest burden on time's drifting breeze. His woof is made from the hearts of men, and from the loom of imagination he weaves the story of their dreams.

Such a man was Michelangelo Buonarroti. His life was nearly full, for its better qualities were rounded out under the touch of time. Some natures never unfold; for want of care, like withered buds, they sink to the roadside, sere and brown—unopened spheres that might have been the fairest flowers of all. The Florentine, however, was strong and sturdy, as the pure of heart must be; like those yellow flowers of autumn, his life was golden in its purity, its work, and its purpose.

As a painter and sculptor he is the one solitary figure standing between us and the golden age of Greece. With a mind far beyond his hour, he knew and felt that the highest object of art for thinking men was man. The masterpiece of God gave inspiration to his brush, life and warmth to the chiselled forms, a depth of purity, thought, and beauty to the work of his pen.

Angelo is best known as an artist, yet it seems to me are we to know him fully, to see the color, space, and shape of his world, we must read his verse. It is there especially that we find his aspirations and his fears. Some writers have charged him with obscurity of thought; Angelo simply went beyond their depth. Power and ingenuity are perhaps the two most striking marks of his poetry. Now and then the form is bold and rugged, but vitality, fervor, and a hidden sweetness permeate every line. Just as his half-emergent forms are held to the cold block by a few uncut edges of stone, so do we often find his words and thoughts, ready at a touch to spring into life and action. We find in his poems a wealth of beauty, spiri-tual not human, which for years has withstood the extravagant drain of criticism. We of the younger generation, perhaps, may see the full development of his worth; but even those who are now at life's turn can partly understand the depth of his ideals, his keen perception of the beautiful, and some of the innate truths of his bold, lofty nature.

Some one has said that style is "all that makes for the form in which thought of any kind is cast." I think it is greatly determined by the tendencies of one's nature, and the influences with which one may be surrounded. Style must, above all else, be a reflection of the writer's character. For Michelangelo this shadow of self increased in clearness and strength, springing as it did from his association with the pious Vittoria Colonna, who was for him "quella luce che fu guida della sua vita e lo trasse ad operar grandi cose" (that light which was the guide of his life, and which drew him on to the accomplishment of nobler works). Her love for art and letters, together with her deep-grounded faith, served to draw the soul of the poet under her influence; giving rise to a friendship, I am tempted to say to love, that became stronger as the lives of each turned into the sere and yellow leaf. Religion, art, and philosophy were subjects dear to both; they tasted, as Pater says, "the sunless pleasures of weary people whose hold on outward things is slackening."

The restless activity of the poet's heart and mind was stilled by the power of woman's soul, just as a child is soothed by the cradle song of its mother. A calm and thoughtful spirit seized him, and his powerful emotions were drawn towards the realm of idealism, whose charm and potency were discovered in the higher affection of his friend.

It was during those quiet talks behind the white walls of San Silvestro that Angelo sounded the depths of Plato and of Dante. It was there he reached out beyond the material veil and caught up the high ideals contained in life and death. Dante must have fashioned the mould of his verse, yet a Platonic touch is seen in many of his thoughts. He did not seek the color, form, nor composition of beauty, but he loved to catch the subtle spirit that moved behind it. His half-emergent forms in marble beautifully show to us this same spirit, chained and complaining, ready at a touch of his fingers to stand forth a breathing personality. The same strange element drifts through his poetry; "where the brooding spirit of life itself is and where summer may burst out in a moment."

If we would see Michelangelo's nature struggling to attune itself aright, we must read the verse rather than gaze at the material work. There are moments when he comes so near Dante that we imagine it is the latter himself who speaks. This is especially felt when he sings of love and death, or when speaking of Florence and the political life of his country.

In the vigor and boldness of his lines is a hidden sweetness, as one critic aptly calls it, "ex forte dulcedo." We can almost see the poet's soul in the expression of his thoughts; it lingers for a moment, vanishes, comes stealing out from the black type, retreats into darkness, and leaves us standing in a sort of twilight, uncertain of our thoughts and powerless to fathom his greatness. Not Art alone, as some one has said, but especially Poetry was the ladder upon which the "angels of his fancy were ever ascending and descending."

We should know that at the time in which the poet lived nearly all educated persons in Italy wrote in verse; the sonnet was the favorite form. What could be more natural than for a soul that saw beauty in everything to set free in words the drifting thoughts and cares, and the thousand longings of a human life? He seemed to feel that he could never express in material work what he felt and saw in his mental conception. He could not bring himself to things of earth: "Non abassava gli occhi alle cose mortali" (he did not bend his eyes to mortal things).

Michelangelo nourished himself with readings from Dante and Savonarola; yet through all his work we see only himself, for in the light of his own personality, which streamed through all he said or did, no other presence could live. He lingered in a dream-world of thought, and his work is shot through with contemplations of a high ideal. He was not simply an artist, not a mere dreamer of dreams, but a man whose heart was eager in sympathy and love for his fellow-man. A brooding twilight of melancholy, sorrow, and sadness clung to him throughout his whole life. His brighter self was always in shadow; peace was seldom his. I doubt if the light of contentment ever broke upon his soul; if it did, he saw it only as through a mist, as sometimes we see the burning west veiled by the downpour of summer showers. The fact that he suffered gives a charm to his verse, for it makes us feel that he was after all a man; and who of us will deny that from lips that have tasted sadness the sweetest and purest songs of life shall fall?

I like to think of a poet as one who dwells among the people of his own land, singing the song of their lives, and dreaming in glow of their hearthstone. I would have him draw from the vibrant strings of his art such melody and charm as would lead me beyond the confines of material life, open for me a higher sphere, where the contemplation of a soul's tumult, the pangs of regret, and the nameless longings of a thousand hearts may come in the peace and quiet of an infinite world. Let him draw from the gloom and darkness, from the suffering and misery of human life, ideals of faith and love which may, in the calm light of hope, reach out into eternity. From his hand must come the storm and lightning, the rain and thunder of our lives; even the silent touch of an atmosphere should be present; but he must suggest also the blue of summer skies, the greening spring, and the sunshine that is again to come.

Shakspere did this, but he did more, for he seemed to have held in his hand a living heart; he felt its weakest beat, he breathed upon it, bruised it with love, crushed it with despair, tore it apart with passion—making of its life a transcription, at all times wonderful, now and then rising to the sublime. He was a child of nature; Michelangelo was a lover of mysticism. The creator of Lear took love as a theme and sounded every key; touched weird chords in minors, or rang out the full, deep tone of major strains. The hand that fashioned the "Pietà" sometimes struck such chords as might have come from "sweet bells out of tune," for they were made up of the philosophy of the *Commedia,* the dreams of Plato, and the vagaries of a four-fold genius. The truest and most touching strains came from notes of piety, melancholy, and an intense love of art. How truly has it been said that Angelo stands like his own grand Jeremias, "bowed down with the contemplation of human wickedness and woe"—weary, sad, patient, sublime!

The echoes of that so-called Reformation had drifted across the Alps, and had given rise to religious talks between the poet and her whom he calls "the force" that urged him on to heaven—Vittoria Colonna. The result of these conversa-

tions was the budding of his thoughts into blossoms of poetry. The fires of youth had long since been chilled, yet as an argument in many of his poems we find the sort of spiritual love which comes only from a holy affection, and to those alone who are pure of heart.

In Italy they call him "Uomo di quattro alme"—the man of four souls. The nation dearly reveres his name, for he proved to be a worthy son; and I think it is a characteristic of his people to love with a strength as deep as the bitterness of their hate; and still they allowed his reputation as a poet to rest for over two centuries on the work of an inferior mind. This is due to the classical spirit that came stealing out of the twelfth century.

That ever-recurring period of the Renaissance, so complex, so interesting, and so little understood, gave rise, by its tendencies and achievements, to a rapid movement in every walk of life. Art became beautiful in the concrete, strange individualities arose, and intelligence and imagination strode forward into the gloom of the future. The law that seemed to govern all work was the search for æsthetic charm. People were elevated to and supported by those higher planes of thought and existence that sprang from a closer realization of ideals. The culture of the day had gathered itself into one complete and almost faultless type. The products of that movement, whether material or spiritual, were dignified and unique; and we find them, even in our age, exercising a direct influence upon the world of fine arts.

Men felt, in the subtle touch of a classic atmosphere, a keen sense of the beautiful, and this feeling served to bind them closer in the relations of life. One art drifted into the realm of another, and from the diffusion of many excellences a more perfect type of civilization stood forth. The dreams of the philosopher were echoed in the songs of the poet; new lights and shadows flitted across the canvas sheet; the sculptured form took to itself fresh lines of grace; the influence of the Germans, the Lombards, and the Franks wore away, and the spirit of Greece and Rome again directed the hand of genius. The bold thought and rugged line were rounded off until they became refined and polished, even as Horace would have them—*ad unguem facta.*

Men, looking on life with clearer minds and with a more liberal spirit, sought hidden sources of intellectual enjoyment. The narrow channels of Art and Poetry were broadened, allowing the tide of revival to sweep into other ages, catching in its current the loosened work of genius.

It was owing to this spirited movement, which shone through the Italian nature, that the great-nephew of Angelo deemed a reformation of his ancestor's literary work an absolute necessity. "He rewrote," says Pater, "the sonnets in part, and sometimes compressed two or more compositions into one, always losing something of the force and incisiveness of the original." Indeed, the true lines are to the false what diamonds are to broken quartz; the one flashes with all the lights of a setting sun, the other scarce reflects the subdued glow of twilight. In the two texts there is a great difference of expression, strength, and boldness of thought. In one we see a rugged, stern, manly touch; the expression of ideas is personal, the flashing thought is caught and held. The false lines are weak, shallow productions, moulded to suit the sentimentalism of the age; they are soft and over-elegant, and all thoughts that might offend politically are left out. We see the poet as through a heavy mist; we can never fully know him, for the work is not consistent with his character. We must look at Angelo in the light of sun-touched mountains, not in an atmosphere that is burdened with the scent of exotic plants or loaded with the heavy odor of the locust-tree. He loved the pure, fresh air of his native hills; his thoughts were drawn from the blue deeps over his head, and were as bold and rugged as the white cliffs of the quarry wherein he worked.

In one of his early sonnets Angelo says:

> L'amor mi prende, e la beltà mi lega,
> La pietà, la mercè con dolci sguardi
> Ferma speranz' al cor par che ne doni.

> Love takes me captive; beauty binds my soul;
> Pity and mercy with their gentle eyes
> Wake in my heart a hope that cannot cheat.

This love, however, was far from the worldly type; it was the enchantment of an ideal which dwelt in the sheer depths of his soul. The beauty that bound his heart with its golden chains was not of the sensual order; it was above all orders, it was infinite. Love and Beauty were for him a blending of truth with perfected goodness, and from this union sprang Art. He thought, as Guasti says, that the beautiful was nothing more than "a flowing out of the Eternal Beauty, as a river from a fountain." He felt that the nearer man approached God, the closer he was to perfection; the more intimate his knowledge of the Creator, the better would he understand the scattered beauty of the material world. As Angelo became more sensitive and responsive to those higher forms of human life and nature, his mind soared upward in search of the infinite, which alone could quench its thirst. The accidents of nature bound down his spiritual self to things of earth, vainly trying to satisfy its cravings by feeding it with reflections of that "eterna belleza" which Guasti calls the fountain head of beauty.

The spiritual natures of some men are so highly strung that a single strain of music will draw them away from all that is human, make them forget their surroundings, place them amid fields of snow and ice, or in the luxuriant growth of a Southern clime: sunrise and morning light; the heat of day, the cooling showers; sunset and starless night,—all these come stealing across such souls, when trembling notes from a master-hand ring out the song of life, or cry in the agony of death. Other natures, whose susceptibility to impressions has been deep and varied, catch the gleam and gloom of a lifetime, the joys and sorrows of a day, to send them out again after many years in some work of art. It was to both classes that Angelo belonged. He saw beauty everywhere, his soul seemed to lean out into eternity that it might feed itself with contemplations of the infinite.

What Michelangelo thought of Art may be found in this sonnet, which is the only one that has not suffered from the touch of a lesser mind:

> Non ha l' ottimo artista alcun concetto,
> Ch' un marmo solo in sè non circonscriva
> Col suo soverchio; e solo a quello arriva
> La man che ubbidisce all' intelletto.
> Il man ch' io fuggo, e' l ben ch' io mi prometto,
> In te, donna leggiadra, altera e diva,
> Tal si nasconde; e perch' io più non viva,
> Contraria ho l' arte al disiato effetto.

> Amor dunque non ha, nè tua beltate,
> O durezza, o fortuna, o gran disdegno,
> Del mio mal colpa, o mio destino o sorte;

> Se dentro del tuo cor morte e pietate
> Porti in un tempo, e che 'l mio basso ingegno
> Non sappia, ardendo, trarne altro che morte.

> The best of artists hath no thought to show
> Which the rough stone in its superfluous shell
> Doth not include: to break the marble spell
> Is all the hand that serves the brain can do.
> The ill I shun, the good I seek, even so
> In thee, fair lady, proud, ineffable,
> Lies hidden: but the art I wield so well
> Works adverse to my wish, and lays me low.

> Therefore, not love, nor thy transcendent face,
> Nor cruelty, nor fortune, nor disdain,
> Cause my mischance; nor fate, nor destiny:
> Since in thy heart thou carriest death and grace
> Enclosed together, and my worthless brain
> Can draw forth only death to feed on me.

There is music, thought, and feeling in every line. Varchi, in speaking of this work before the Academy at Florence [see excerpt by Varchi dated 1547], said: "Per maggiore e più agevole intelligenza del soggetto di questo grave e dotto Sonetto, avemo a sapere, nobilissimi uditori, che niuno affetto, o vero accidente (qualunche egli sia), è tanto universale, e tanto comune a tutte le cose, quanto l' Amore."

The lines addressed to Dante are as rich in poetic thought and beauty as any in the literature of Italy. It may be interesting to note the difference in the two texts. The first quatrain of the original is:

> Dal ciel discese, e col mortal suo, poi
> Che visto ebbe l' inferno giusto e 'l pio,
> Ritornò vivo a contemplare Dio,
> Per dar di tutto il vero lume a noi.

> From Heaven his spirit came, and, robed in clay,
> The realms of justice and of mercy trod,
> Then rose, a living man, to gaze on God
> That He might make the Truth as clear as day.

Condivi has it thus:

> Dal mondo scese ai ciechi abissi, e poi
> Che l' uno e l' altro inferno vide, e a Dio,
> Scorto dal gran pensier, vivo salio,
> E ne diè in terra vero lume a noi.

It is in this sonnet that the poet says:

> Nè sare' 'l premio tutto 'l mondo rio:
> Tu sol, che la creasti, esser quel puoi.

> Not all the wicked world reward could be:
> Alone canst Thou who hast created him.

Some critic has justly compared this thought with the one found in Saint Augustine's works: "Tu fecisti nos ad te; et inquietum est cor nostrum donec requiescat in te." The idea is also found in the *Imitation:* "I am able to reward thee above all measure and degree."

Michelangelo, like his great countryman Dante, sang in exile. Both men loved their native city. When the siege of Florence was raised by the treachery of Baglioni; when Alessandro de' Medici marched through the Roman gate, and enemies had conquered, then it was that the poet, brooding in silence over the wrongs of his city, turned wholly to Art and Poetry, seeking rest and finding none. If you would fully know him, gaze at his *Thinker of San Lorenzo,* and repeat with its creator:

Ohimè, ohimè! pur reiterando
Vo 'l mio passato tempo, e non ritrovo,
In tutto, un giorno che sia stato mio.
Le fallaci speranze e 'l van desio,
Piangendo, amando, ardendo e sospirando,
(Ch' effetto alcun mortal non mi è più nuovo)
M' hanno tenuto; ond' il conosco, e provo.

Alas, alas! when I, retracing,
O'er the drifting past bewildered go,
I do not find in all one day my own,
False hopes and vain desires enchained me so.

Weeping, loving, burning, sighing,
No mood upon a human heart can call
That will to mine appear an utter stranger,
Since I, for long, have known and felt them all.

Turn to his *Day,* upon the sarcophagus below, and watch, in the spirit of a chiselled form, the undying energy of a genius struggling against despair. Stand before the figure of *Night,* that seems asleep in dreams—for its maker thought:

'Tis well to slumber, best to be of stone,
While shame endures and Florence is not free—

and see therein the longing of a soul to be at rest. And still we read:

Destala, se nol credi, e parleratti;
Wake it, if still in doubt: 'twill speak to thee;

as though the poet longed for Florence as he once knew her, longed for his youth, his steady hand, and the brighter dreams; but in vain, for the flowers of one year die for ever, and the thrush that now sings in the tangled copse will never return. We feel that in those days, for him, sunshine never fell; and that already the creeping shadows of night were lengthening out into the blackness of death.

It was not in Art alone that the exile left his thoughts; all the regrets, indignations, hopes, and fears that touched his heart found an outlet in the trembling song that passed his lips. His madrigals are tinged with the sufferings of a human soul.

Ritorni a' nostri pianti
Il sol degli occhi tuo', che par che schivi
Chi del suo dono in tal miseria è nato.

Give back to streaming eyes the daylight of thy face,
That seems to shun those who must live defrauded of their
     bliss.

Such was the plaintive appeal that his heart made to its lost Florence.

The music of the Italian tongue is almost denied to our ear. We can no more catch the full strain of a *terza rima* in the *Divina Commedia* than we can justly appreciate the full harmony of a Ciceronian period. The English language is strong and expressive, and wonderful effects have been produced by it in the hands of Shelley, Keats, and Shakspere. It is full of life and motion. Dante, who completed the work of Saint Francis of Assisi in the formation of a national language, uses the Italian tongue more like a sturdy Goth of the North than a native of Florence. Michelangelo is equally as strong, though at times less clear and polished. His mind outstrips his pen, leaving the thought to be rounded out by the reader himself.

In speaking of the death of his father the poet says:

Non è, com' alcun crede, morte il peggio

A chi l' ultimo di tranciende al primo,
Per grazia, eterno appresso al divin seggio;
Dove, Die grazia, ti prossummo e stimo,
E spero di veder, se 'l freddo core
Mie ragion traggie dal terrestre limo.

This poem is especially beautiful for its Christian thought and belief. It may be freely translated:

No. Death is not, as some think, the worst of evils, if, by God's goodness, our last day on earth goes to join itself to eternal life in heaven; where I believe you are by the mercy of God, and where I hope to see you once again, if reason draw from the mud of earthly passions my chilled heart.

The mind of the poet often turned to religious subjects, and his thoughts, drifting out into the ways of God, filled his soul with aspirations, loaded his heart with sorrow, and lifted his mind from things of earth to changeless dreams of eternity. "Touching and beautiful," says one writer, "are the religious sonnets of Angelo, for they show how, in the light which streamed from the other world as he neared its confines, he judged rigorously of the failings and imperfections of a life which, in its purity and austerity, appeared to his contemporaries severe and holy and exemplary, as indeed it was." What is there more touching than this prayer, coming from a once strong and sturdy nature, which is now broken beneath the weight of sorrowing years?

Non basta, Signor mio, che tu m' invogli
Di ritornar là dove l' alma sia,
Non come prima di nulla, creata.
Anzi che del mortal la privi e spogli,
Prego m' ammezzi l' alta e erta via,
E fie piu chiara e certa la tornata.

Even in the translation, which rubs off much of the pristine beauty, the thought is high and noble, worthy of the heart from which it came:

'Tis not enough, dear Lord, to make me yearn
For that celestial home, where yet my soul
May be new made, and not, as erst, of naught;
Nay, ere Thou strip her mortal vestment, turn
My steps toward the steep ascent, that whole
And pure before thy face she may be brought.

When old age had come upon him, and the gales of a stern life had wrenched the spars, and had torn in shreds the sails of his little bark, then it was that he turned to his Maker to find protection and a peaceful harbor:

Scarco d' un' importuna e grave salma,
Signor mio caro, e dal mondo disciolto,
Qual fragil legno, a te stance mi volto
Dall' orribil procella in dolce calma.

Freed from a burden sore and grievous band,
Dear Lord, and from this wearying world untied,
Like a frail bark I turn me to Thy side,
As from a fierce storm to a tranquil land.

The prayer that trembled on his lips in old age was:

Teach me to hate the world, so little worth,
And all the holy things I once did prize,
That endless life, not death, may be my wage.

When his hold on outward things was loosened, and he drew nearer the light of another world, he said:

The impassioned fantasy that, vague and vast,

Made Art an idol and a king to me,
Was an illusion, and but vanity
Were the desires that lured me and harassed.

It is while studying the works of such a genius as Michelange-lo that the reader feels the flight of time, and understands the expressionless formula of beauty. He is drawn aside from the pushing, surging crowds in commonplace life, and stands in a world of dreams, where the silent touch of atmosphere is no more; where thought alone can live; where all types are gathered into one being; where all beauty rests in a single point—the centre of the rose of Dante—where "all the good that will may covet there is summ'd; and all, elsewhere defective found, complete."

Although living in an age of moral dissolution and religious apostasy, Angelo kept his heart pure and clean; a man of charity and piety, mindful of his last end, for he often said: "Bisogna pensare alla morte. Questo pensiero è solo quello che ci fa riconoscere noi medisimi, che ci mantiene in noi uniti" (We ought to think of death. This thought is the only one that makes us remember what we are, that keeps us at unity with ourselves). He was like to Euphranor, of whom Quintilian writes: "Admirandum facit, quod et ceteris optimis studiis inter præcipuos et pingendi fingendique idem mirus artifex fuit." Angelo, however, was more than this; he was, in the words of Guasti, the "grandi assertori del domma cattolica nella poesia, nella scienza, e nell' arte." He was a Christian philosopher and poet, to whom beauty and excellence were things of another sphere; a man that rose by means of material agencies, which are but steps, to the contemplation of the great Ideal Himself—the Changeless God. (pp. 802-14)

> *Thomas B. Reilly, "Michelangelo Buonarroti as a Poet," in* The Catholic World, *Vol. LXV, No. 390, September, 1897, pp. 802-14.*

WILLIAM EVERETT   (lecture date 1904)

[*In the following excerpt from a 1904 lecture delivered at the Lowell Institute in Boston, Everett describes Michelangelo's poetry as self-contained.*]

Michael Angelo was born in the same year as Ariosto, and died in 1563, the year before the birth of Shakespeare. A course on Italian poetry must never omit his name, though it is no place for a survey of his works. His poetry, like that of so many Italians, is founded on the model of Petrarch, in sonnets and madrigals, a somewhat indefinite name for short poems in lines of varying length and combination of rhyme. But Michael Angelo could not be a copyist of Petrarch, or, indeed, of anybody. His poetry has much the same traits as his sculpture: loftiness of design, an intense love of beauty, somewhat injured by the artist's absorption in his own skill, so that we rather admire the craft of the designer than the result of his labor, and sometimes find that result obscure; and, more than all, a prevailing air of withdrawal from the crowd, of self-contained contemplation, for which I could almost bear to use the detestable modern word "aloofness." This air is, of course, wholly alien to Petrarch or Ariosto or Chaucer or Spenser; Michael Angelo derived it from Dante and passed it on to Milton, though its first and greatest exponent is Æschylus. (pp. 96-7)

> *William Everett, "Vittoria Colonna—Michael An-*

gelo—Tasso," in his The Italian Poets since Dante, *Charles Scribner's Sons, 1904, pp. 90-122.*

GEORGE McLEAN HARPER   (essay date 1920)

[*Harper was an American biographer and scholar who wrote widely on Italian literature. In the following excerpt, he explores the spirituality of Michelangelo's verse.*]

The depth and scope of Italian thought in the Middle Ages are adequately reflected in Dante. The only Italian poet of the Renaissance who can compare with him for greatness of soul is Michelangelo. What then though Michelangelo's poetry be small in quantity and hard to comprehend? If it is an authentic utterance of his mighty spirit, it is more likely to represent the serious feeling of the time than a dozen "Orlandos." These rough verses are the only Italian poetry, after Dante, which is of the same order of greatness as his, until the mantle falls on Leopardi.

Dante, Michelangelo, Leopardi are the Italian poets who utter the deepest note, each in his own age; the first mediaeval, the second of the Renaissance, the third in modern times. The note grows less rich and full as we descend the centuries. In Dante it is re-enforced with overtones and undertones innumerable; in Leopardi it is pathetically thin. But it is the same note, deep, mournful, austere. It is a note of yearning for divine love, a cry for spiritual help against the allurements of sense and the world's deceptions. Reading Michelangelo and Leopardi after Dante—and they are the only Italian poets who will bear reading immediately after him—we perceive that the unity of the three ages is more remarkable than the diversity. Dante maintains, in its fulness, the Catholic ideal and celebrates its triumph in the wide field of human destiny. Michelangelo abstracts from the Catholic ideal just so much as is necessary for his own support and consolation. Leopardi ponders it, rejects it in form, and re-admits part of it in substance, under the guise of an agnostic stoicism. Dante touches and illumines the whole sphere of relations between faith and the world. Michelangelo grapples with the central problem only. Leopardi seems to reject both faith and the world. And now that his voice too is silent, it would appear, in the words of Sir Philip Sidney, that "an over-faint quietness should seem to strew the house for poets."

Michelangelo's sonnets number seventy-seven in all and there are, besides, a few madrigals, canzoni, stanzas, epitaphs, and epigrams. One of these last is of profound significance, as showing the great master's weariness of the evil times in which he lived. It helps us understand those enigmatical figures of his on the tomb of the Medici, in the sacristy of San Lorenzo in Florence. Through contempt or fear he left that work unfinished. The republic of Florence had been abolished. Tyranny, magnificent it is true, and enlightened, but none the less tyranny, had throttled the free life of the city. Throughout Italy wickedness was enthroned in high places, and at Rome in the highest place of all. Beside the sarcophagus in Michelangelo's famous composition, recline two statues, of Day and Night. Beneath the latter, a lighthearted admirer, alluding to the name Angelo, wrote four lines, which I venture to translate as follows:

> Night, whom thou seest in this fair attitude
> Sleeping, was by an angel graven in stone,
> And, though asleep, she is with life imbued.
> Dost thou believe not? Wake her; she will speak.

The aged sculptor, deeming an eternal sleep preferable to a life without honor, replied in an epigram, of which we fortunately possess a translation from the hand of Wordsworth:

> Grateful is Sleep, more grateful still to be
> Of marble; for while shameless wrong and woe
> Prevail, 'tis best to neither hear nor see.
> Then wake me not, I pray you. Hush, speak low.

Many of the sonnets were inspired by Michelangelo's love for Vittoria Colonna. He seems to have made her acquaintance in his sixty-third year, when she was in her forty-seventh. Born of the great house of Colonna, she had already been for eight years the widow of the Marquess of Pescara, a renowned soldier of fortune. She was celebrated for her beauty, her piety, her serious learning, and her gifts as a poet. In that age of unbridled passion, another quality that added not a little to her fame was her acknowledged purity of life. Michelangelo was the most illustrious of living artists. Popes and temporal despots had vied with one another to obtain and reward his services. Amid them all he had kept the jewel of his soul, his kingly independence. It was said of him that he braved Pope Julius II as the King of France would not have done. He had preserved, too, a childlike simplicity. His manners were plain. He was pious, hard-working, and of a naturally kind disposition, though, when exasperated by deceit, he was terrible in his anger. Long acquaintance with some of the greatest and wickedest of mankind had begun to make him weary of the world and scornful of its honors. In early manhood a deep impression had been made on him by the preaching of Savonarola. Roman Catholic writers are probably justified in rejecting the suggestion that Michelangelo was tainted with Protestant heresy. They fail, however, in attempting to prove that Vittoria Colonna did not lay more stress on the doctrine of justification by faith than was compatible with orthodoxy. She was interested in the Protestant movement, though perhaps not implicated in it. One might safely say that the same process of criticism which produced an Erasmus, north of the Alps, and even a Luther, had begun to affect some of the noblest minds of Italy.

A distinct stage in every revolution is a longing for simplicity, a longing prompted by disgust with the complexities and artificialities, the injustice and absurdity, that accumulate around a successful system. The Catholic ideal had lost simplicity. Vittoria Colonna is the most conspicious example, after Savonarola, of an Italian who perceived this with regret. Michelangelo loved her for her beauty, the comfort of her kindness, and above all for her character. Her spiritual insight confirmed his own. She too was weary of the world. She too was unable to accept those official methods of dealing with the world which the Church recommended. He would not accept the world; his conscience revolted, though he saw that the most eminent churchmen really did accept it. Neither could he embrace a purely ascetic life; the largeness of his nature forbade this, though he studied with keen interest the discipline of hermits. He might have fought out the battle in solitude and inconclusively, a lonely soul, distracted, baffled, embittered. But cheered by the society of such a woman as Vittoria Colonna, animated by her example, refreshed by her hope, rewarded with her encouragement, he rose above despair.

Walter Pater appears to me to use singularly inapt terms when he says that in reading Michelangelo's poems we are spectators of "the struggle of a desolating passion, which yearns to be resigned and sweet and pensive, as Dante's was"

[see excerpt dated 1871]. Merely sweet and pensive Dante's passion was not, nor can Michelangelo's love for Vittoria Colonna be properly called "desolating."

The chief subjects of Michelangelo's sonnets are Beauty and Death. He looked upon life, and lo! it was good. Earth, sun, moon, and stars, their forms, their colors, and the laws that govern their motions were beautiful. Men and animals were beautiful. The best works of men were beautiful, and their best thoughts. He, Michelangelo, whose brain had conceived and whose hand had wrought so many brave inventions, could not deny this. Yet none of these things live forever. Their life is but a moment in the vast abyss of time, a flash in the limitless void of space. Is there not something that endures, that binds all things together, that gives continuance to beauty? Strange to say, the word that for most of us darkens the mystery gave forth light to Michelangelo. This word is Death. In Death he saw not the end of this world and all its beauty, but the possibility, nay the promise, of eternal life. From the decay of a flower or the withering of a lovely human face, he saw, in the words of a quaint old English poet, "bright shoots of everlastingness." Death is the door through which the Divine Artist re-admits to the fulness of His embrace those images of Beauty, Goodness, and Truth which came forth from Him as examples of His handiwork. In them we apprehend Him here below. Through Death we follow them into His presence.

Michelangelo was not the first man, any more than he was the last, to argue that, in the divine economy, beauty, goodness, and truth must be imperishable, and that Death must mean their revival in the bosom of God. As Mr. W. S. Lilly has pointed out in his thoughtful essay, "the leading ideas of Michael Angelo's poetry, often vaguely and obscurely expressed, may be found in Dante, writ large and duly formulated." Here again we have occasion to observe the unity of spirit that pervades the greatest Italian poetry, a unity too deep to be affected by the Zeit-geist. Whenever a poet ventures to express the hope, so natural to a poet, that the beauty of this world may after all be a promise rather than an illusion, it is customary to speak of his "Platonism." In the present instance I see no reason to infer that Michelangelo would not have thus ventured, even had he never heard of Plato; and quite agree with Mr. Lilly that "there is as much and as little reason for attributing Platonism to Michelangelo as to the most distinctly Christian of poets."

When his dear friend died, in 1547, after their spiritual communion had lasted ten years, he little realized that he should long survive her. He had thought of her as the consolation of his end. Her death confirmed his faith in Immortal Love. And for sixteen years more, his conversation was in heaven.

This, in brief, is the story of Michelangelo's sonnets. They are love-poetry, and of such a kind as might be inferred from the characters of the two lovers. But I have said that they interpret the Catholic ideal and apply it in a peculiar manner to the problem of how to exist in the world. They recognize the world and distinguish in it two elements, the one evil, the other divinely good and fair. For salvation from the evil they suggest no help from sacraments nor yet from works, but only the simplest faith in Christ. They do not advocate withdrawal from the world, but a brave endeavor to seek its divine essence.

The spirit of Michelangelo's poetry is grandly sad. His is no private grief, but the tragic sorrow of a soul that feels its greatness and its bounds. This mortal would put on immortality. As one reads the sonnets, so hard, so impenetrable at first, so abstract always, so lacking in references to known things, events, and persons, one at length is lifted from the historical, the concrete, the personal, to the contemplation of pure beauty and eternal love.

There have been and are millions of men and women, even in modern times, to whom religion means other-worldliness. To lives merely monastic, it was and is nothing else. To Dante, and to Michelangelo, it meant something more: the selection of an eternal element in this world, which through its affinity with the divine nature will survive death. The souls whose destinies are bound up with this element are saved. I cannot see that the great Italian poet of the Renaissance differed in this respect from the great Italian poet of the Middle Ages. He was, however, repelled by the excesses of overgrown and too grossly triumphant Catholicism into a reaction against what I make bold to call religious superfluities; his faith was simpler than Dante's; he approached God directly, not asking for sacramental or sacerdotal intervention. (pp. 38-44)

Michelangelo's fiftieth sonnet, using Symonds's translation, shows us a touching picture of the grave old man comforting himself with the thought that if he had found his love sooner he might not have adored her so perfectly:

> Had I but earlier known that from the eyes
> Of that bright soul that fires me like the sun
> I might have drawn new strength the race to run,
> Burning as burns the Phoenix ere it dies;
>
> Even as the stag or lynx or leopard flies
> To seek his pleasure and his pain to shun,
> Each word, each smile of her would I have won,
> Flying where now sad age all flight denies.
>
> Yet why complain? For even now I find
> In that glad angel's face, so full of rest,
> Health and content, heart's ease and peace of mind.
>
> Perchance I might have been less blest,
> Finding her sooner: if 'tis age alone
> That lets me soar with her to seek God's throne.

The fifty-second recalls to memory more than one poem of the English Renaissance, more than one sonnet of Shakespeare, Spenser's four Hymns in Honour of Love and Beauty, Heavenly Love and Heavenly Beauty, and, above all, the sonnet in which Sidney, remorseful at having written so much in praise of his Lady, tremblingly lays a new song at the feet of Love Divine. We see that not in Italy alone were there religious poets, and not in Italy alone did the two ideals clash. In Michelangelo's sonnet we observe three thoughts interwoven: his love for his lady is above sensual passion; this kind of love raises the soul to heaven; death is the lover's friend:

> I saw no mortal beauty with these eyes
> When perfect peace in thy fair eyes I found;
> But far within, where all is holy ground,
> My soul felt Love, her comrade of the skies:
> For she was born with God in Paradise;
> Else should we still to transient loves be bound;
> But finding these so false, we pass beyond
> Unto the Love of Loves that never dies.
> Nay, things that die cannot assuage that thirst
> Of souls undying; nor Eternity
> Serves time, where all must fade that flourisheth.
> Sense is not Love, but lawlessness accurst:
> This kills the soul, while our love lifts on high

> Our friends on earth—higher in heaven through death.

Sir Philip Sidney's poem is much simpler and because of its directness appears more heartfelt:

> Leave me, O love! which reachest but to dust;
> And thou, my mind, aspire to higher things:
> Grow rich in that which never taketh rust:
> Whatever fades but fading pleasure brings.
> Draw in thy beams, and humble all thy might
> To that sweet yoke where lasting freedoms be,
> Which breaks the cloud and opens forth the light
> That doth both shine and give us light to see.
> O take fast hold! let that light be thy guide,
> In this small course which birth draws out to death,
> And think how evil becometh him to slide
> Who seeketh heaven and comes of heavenly breath.
> Then farewell, world, thy uttermost I see;
> Eternal Love, maintain thy life in me.

Michelangelo's effort to reconcile the two ideals, the worldly and the other-worldly, is shown in sonnet LVII:

> Swift through the eyes unto the heart within
> All lovely forms that thrall our spirit stray;
> So smooth and broad and open is the way
> That thousands and not hundreds enter in
> Of every age and sex: whence I begin,
> Burdened with griefs, but more with dull dismay,
> To fear; nor find mid all their bright array
> One that with full content my heart may win.
> If mortal beauty be the food of love,
> It came not with the soul from heaven, and thus
> That love itself must be a *mortal* fire.
> But if love reach to nobler hopes above,
> Thy love shall scorn me not nor *dread* desire
> That seeks a carnal prey assailing us.

The sixtieth sonnet is so like one of Shakespeare's that we might be tempted to think our English poet had read it, were we not checked by remembering that Shakespeare's sonnets were printed in 1609, fourteen years before Michelangelo's:

> Sometimes my love I dare to entertain
> With soaring hope not over-credulous;
> Since if all human loves were impious,
> Unto what end did God the world ordain?
> For loving thee what license is more plain
> Than that I praise thereby the glorious
> Source of all joys divine, that comfort us
> In thee, and with chaste fires our soul sustain?
> False hope belongs unto that hope alone
> Which with declining beauty wanes and dies,
> And, like the face it worships, fades away.
> That hope is true which the pure heart hath known,
> Which alters not with time or death's decay,
> Yielding on earth earnest of Paradise.

Shakespeare's one hundred and sixteenth sonnet is like a development of the last five lines of the sonnet just read. It is as follows:

> Let me not to the marriage of true minds
> Admit impediments. Love is not love
> Which alters when it alteration finds,
> Or bends with the remover to remove:
> O, no! it is an ever fixéd mark.
> That looks on tempests and in never shaken;
> It is the star to every wandering bark,
> Whose worth's unknown, although his height be taken.
> Love's not Time's fool, though rosy lips and cheeks
> Within his bending sickle's compass come;
> Love alters not with his brief hours and weeks,

But bears it out even to the edge of doom.
If this be error and upon me proved,
I never writ, nor no man ever loved.

In the sixty-fifth sonnet, written after the death of Vittoria Colonna, Michelangelo, thinking his own departure at hand, makes the painful declaration that even the pure and exalted toils of his life, even painting and sculpture, which he had never degraded to a base use, were an impediment to his soul, which now turned to Christ alone:

Now hath my life across a stormy sea
Like a frail bark reached that wide port where all
Are bidden, ere the final reckoning fall
Of good and evil for eternity.
Now know I well how that fond phantasy
Which made my soul the worshipper and thrall
Of earthly art, is vain; how criminal
Is that which all men seek unwillingly.
Those amorous thoughts which were so lightly dressed,
What are they when the double death is nigh?
The one I know for sure, the other dread.
Painting nor sculpture now can lull to rest
My soul that turns to His great love on high,
Whose arms to clasp us on the cross were spread.

How inward and profound is the religious feeling in the seventy-second! Beauty is still his theme, but regarded now as a danger to the soul, which God alone can avert, by an act of sovereign grace:

Oh, make me see Thee, Lord, where'er I go!
If mortal beauty sets my soul on fire,
That flame, when near to Thine must needs expire,
And I with love of only Thee shall glow.
Dear Lord, thy help I seek against this woe,
These torments that my spirit vex and tire;
Thou only with new strength canst re-inspire
My will, my sense, my courage faint and low.
Thou gavest me on earth this soul divine;
And Thou within this body weak and frail
Didst prison it—how sadly there to live!
How can I make its lot less vile than mine?
Without Thee, Lord, all goodness seems to fail.
To alter fate is God's prerogative.

Finally an overwhelming world-weariness weighs him down in the seventy-fourth:

What though strong love of life doth flatter me
With hope of yet more years on earth to stay,
Death none the less draws nearer day by day,
Who to *sad* souls *alone* comes lingeringly.
Yet why desire long life and jollity,
If in our *griefs* alone to God we pray?
Glad fortune, length of days, and pleasure slay
The soul that trusts to their felicity.
Then if at any hour through grace divine
The fiery shafts of love and faith that cheer
And fortify the soul, my heart assail,
Since nought achieve these mortal powers of mine,
Straight may I wing my way to heaven; for *here*
With lengthening days good thoughts and wishes fail.

It was not until his ninetieth year that his desire was granted, and death opened the way, if his hope was well founded, to new activities.

Milton, a kindred, though less devout and loving soul, nourished his genius at these breasts. With his subtle understanding of the Italian language, it is strange that he did not render some of Michelangelo's sonnets into English. They were first printed only fifteen years before Milton's Italian journey, and he must have seen them. But no translation can convey a true sense of the weight and seriousness of Michelangelo's poetry. It is massive, grave, and pure. We close the book thinking with Wordsworth "how conversant his soul was with great things." (pp. 45-50)

George McLean Harper, "Michelangelo's Sonnets," in his John Morley and Other Essays, *Princeton University Press, 1920, pp. 26-50.*

GEORG BRANDES (essay date 1921)

[*Brandes was a distinguished Danish literary historian. He is best known for his* Main Currents in Nineteenth-Century Literature *(1872-90), a pioneering study valued for its insight and lucidity. In the following excerpt from his 1921 biography of Michelangelo, he closely examines a selection of Michelangelo's poems and letters, commenting on the works as expressions of the author's conception of love and beauty.*]

The fine arts which Michelangelo pursued in the forms of sculpture and painting were not sufficient to contain all the passion and emotion that dwelt in his soul, his need to admire, his irony and humor. His surging feelings often transcended chisel and brush, required an outlet in another creative medium, burst forth in forms that could be captured only by the pen. His wry wit and self-detachment, particularly, called irresistibly for the epigram as a mode of expression.

Despite his role as a statesman, Lorenzo de' Medici, the protector of Michelangelo's youthful years, had dabbled in verse, love lyrics and other poetic forms, defending and glorifying the Italian idiom, then still waging a hard battle against the much more highly esteemed Latin. Lorenzo called Italian a beautiful and mellifluous tongue, legitimized as a vehicle for poetry by Dante, Petrarca and Boccaccio. Angelo Poliziano, who thought highly of the young Michelangelo, was no less bent upon breathing new life into vernacular poetry, and through his good offices the youth was soon initiated into the mysteries of prosody. So strong an influence did Poliziano's verse exert on Michelangelo that in his stanzas in praise of the rustic life (*in lode della vita rusticale*) the young artist followed the paean to nature Poliziano indited in stanzas 17 to 21 of his poem *Giostra*.

Even in these verses Michelangelo's native self soon went beyond mere imitation, displaying his distaste of everything that did not harmonize with nature. Yet they are scarcely rewarding for the modern reader, since they consist largely of allegories strung together. Vainly Michelangelo tries to make generalizations come to life. In one passage, speaking of doubt, he says that the word "why" is lean and jingles many keys at its belt, fiddling with all the locks since none of the keys fits.

Other members of Lorenzo's circle, like Cristoforo Landino, commentator of the *Divine Comedy,* and Pico della Mirandola, served to introduce him to Dante's poetry. And here he found a spirit worthy of his own, the same pride and austerity, the same love of beauty and virtue, the same tendency to damn personal enemies and other contemptibles to the nethermost depths of hell. He read Dante over and over and in the end became a recognized Dante expert. He made an offer to the city of Florence to erect a worthy monument to the great poet, provided Ravenna would, as was hoped, surrender his remains to his ancestral city; and he wrote one of his finest sonnets in honor of Dante:

> From heaven he came, in mortal clothing, when
> All that was worst and best had been observed.
> Living, he came to view the God he served
> To give us the entire, true light again.
>
> For that bright star which with its vivid rays
> Picked out the humble place where I was born—
> For this, the world would be a prize to scorn;
> None but its Maker can return its praise.
>
> I speak of Dante, he whose work was spurned
> By the ungrateful crowd, those who can give
> Praise only to the worthless. I would live
>
> Happy were I but he, by such men scorned,
> If, with his torments, I could also share
> His greatness, both his joy and exile bear.

The sonnet form, however much of a straitjacket to sentiment, was popular in sixteenth-century Italy, on the one hand, because it lent itself to the traditional cerebral style of verse with its more or less barbed points; and on the other because theoreticians and practitioners of the muse, like Lorenzo il Magnifico, had expressly declared it the finest poetic form of all. Its brevity seemed to preclude even a single superfluous word; hence it was suited to lofty statement or polished thought, compelled the utmost clarity while avoiding volubility.

A predilection for conciseness leads logically from the sonnet to the epigram, and we note indeed that Michelangelo, in addition to writing a large number of sonnets, also composed a great many epigrams, including no less than forty-eight on a single occasion, when Luigi del Riccio lost his fifteen-year-old nephew, dearly beloved on account of his grace. Responding to his friend's request, Michelangelo in these epigrams rang many changes on the theme of sorrow that death should have cheated the world of so much beauty. No one at the time took offense at the passionate love Riccio felt for Cecchino Bracci. Michelangelo had known the youth but briefly, but he too had warmed to him and in his first access of feeling promised to design a fine marble tomb. The pledge was redeemed only with a rough sketch, which served as a model for the marble sarcophagus and bust, executed by Michelangelo's assistant, Francesco Urbino (in the church Santa Maria in Araceli).

Of the many poems Michelangelo wrote about Cecchino, the sonnet to Riccio is probably the finest, yet even it is labored. It mourns the fact that the handsome lad, so soon after Michelangelo had first beheld his beautiful eyes—those eyes that meant paradise to Riccio—opened them in heaven to behold God. And Michelangelo adds that if he, as a sculptor, were

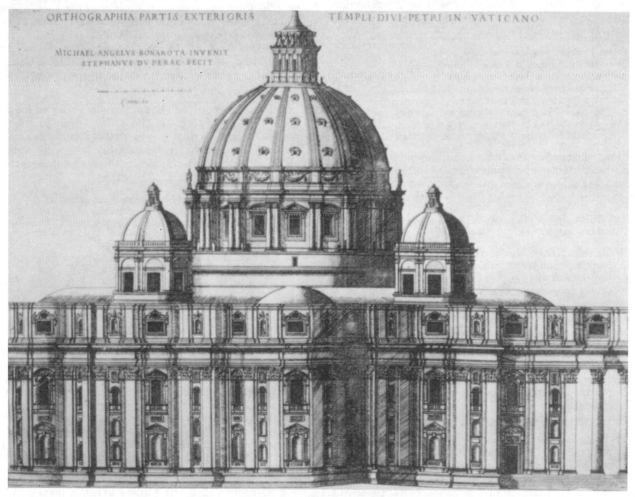

Exterior view of St. Peter's, engraved by Dupérac.

to immortalize Cecchino in stone he would have to create a statue of Riccio, since the lover was one with the beloved.

In a manner no less affected, the epitaphs insist that Cecchino Bracci was asleep rather than dead; for he lived on in the weeping Luigi del Riccio, the beloved ever living in the lover. The letters accompanying the verses include acknowledgments of various delicacies Riccio had sent when asking Michelangelo for further poems.

Thus epigram No. 18 bears the note: "In appreciation of the pickled mushrooms, since you desire further verses." No. 23: "Thus speak the trout, not I; if the verses do not please you, then do not again pickle it without pepper." No. 28: "With this slip I send you back the melons, but the drawing is not finished. I shall, in any event, do the very best I can." No. 29: "This is for the turtledove; as for the fish, Urbino [a servant and assistant of Michelangelo] will have to write you an epigram, for he ate them."

One element in Michelangelo's character that never found expression in his works of art comes to the fore in his letters no less than his poetry—a penchant for mockery, especially self-mockery, but also scorn of others. The humor in his verses, with himself as the butt, is usually bitter, though at times he asserts himself in a vein of broad irony. Michelangelo never commanded the wit the French call *esprit,* but like his later compatriot Napoleon he occasionally shows a streak of farce—what the Italians call *buffo,* a coarse variety of humor, not always in the best of taste. Here, for example, is a stanza in a parody on rhymed declarations of love:

> When I behold your pointed dugs, I see
> Two ripe cucumbers in a sack of gunny
> And soon go up in flame, like a fusee.
> The hoe has bent my back—'tis scarcely funny;
> But were I still just as I used to be,
> I'd chase you like a cur. You draw me as honey
> Does draw the bee. How easy then it seemed—
> What would today quite marvelous be esteemed.

Most surprising perhaps is that in one of the epitaphs for Cecchino Bracci Michelangelo puts words in the youth's mouth that unadornedly reveal the true nature of his relationship with Riccio:

> Tan fede a quel ch'i'fu gratia nel lecto.
> Che abbracciava, e'n che l'anima vive.

Ordinarily Michelangelo was very far from jesting at, let alone accepting such relationships, as seen from an undated letter to Niccolò (Quaratesi) in Florence, in which he indignantly rejects a handsome apprentice, whose father had cynically told the master he was certain to keep him, in his bed if not his house, if he but laid eyes on him. "I shall forego such solace," he wrote, "and do without the boy."

Characteristic of his bent toward barbed satire is the reply Michelangelo made when Clement VII, through the priest Fatucci, asked him to do a marble colossus 40 ells high, to be composed of smaller blocks and set up at a street corner in Florence. (pp. 325-29)

The clear-cut and consistent irony with which a foolish plan is here rejected is characteristic of Michelangelo's cast of mind, even though the bizarre touches of whimsy that so often mark his style are missing. Another of his letters hints at a quarrel between him and his wealthy friend Luigi del Riccio, who was employed in the Strozzi bank, apparently over Riccio's refusal to destroy a poem, or perhaps several,

which Michelangelo had sent him, and for which he had refused a proffered fee. "You give me what I decline to accept," he wrote, "while balking at what I ask." And in a passage utterly typical of his irrepressible self-deprecation, he adds under his signature: "Neither painter nor sculptor nor architect, but what you will, except a drunkard, as I told you in your house."

In a similar vein, scoffing at his lack of influence, compared to his worth, he began a letter of recommendation in 1520 to Cardinal Bibbiena, on behalf of Sebastiano del Piombo, asking that the Venetian rather than Raphael's disciples be given the decoration of the Hall of Constantine in the *stanze:*

> Monsignor: I beg Your Right Reverend Magnificence, not as a friend or servant, neither of which I deserve to be, but as a poor, worthless, half-crazed person, to give the painter Bastiano from Venice a share of the work in the palace, now that Raphael is dead.

Not only was this recommendation, couched in tones of such bitter humility, ignored; it served merely to make the cardinal guffaw and later passed from hand to hand in the papal circle, creating merriment wherever it went. None perceived the poignant frustration behind the mock humility.

A memorable example of how this bitter self-irony took poetic form is seen in a sonnet describing his physical ordeal while painting the frescoes under the ceiling of the Sistine Chapel. Another, showing his passionate scorn, is the sonnet against the Pistoians (*contro a' Pistoiesi*). While lacking in wit, it testifies to the depth of his ire. The Pistoians, Michelangelo writes, show clearly that they are descended from Cain, and he invokes Dante's judgment of the town (*Inferno,* 24 and 25).

In still another poem Michelangelo enumerates all the tribulations his long life brought him. Offal of every kind was deposited outside his door day in, day out, while age ravaged his body and health. Deliberately he chooses the strongest and most picturesque expressions, often approaching the baroque, with never a polished word:

> Grape-munching behemoths my doors beleaguer,
> Takers of purges, hulking apparitions,
> Their piles of ordure to deposit eager.
>
> I am familiar with their micturitions,
> Hissing through hairy vents, as they forever
> Arouse me with matutinal emissions.

(pp. 331-32)

Except for Tommaso Cavalieri, we know little of the young men who—to judge from the well-known letter of invective by Pietro Aretino—wielded such influence over Michelangelo that he readily made them gifts of his magnificent drawings.

The first one to whom Aretino points was a young Florentine, Gherardo Perini. A brief and courteous note from him has survived, beginning: *Honorandissimo et damme amato singolare.* It says the writer is well and hopes the same of the master. He is at his disposal, hopes to see him again soon, sends his own regards and those of Master Giovan Francesco (Fatucci) and Michelangelo's other friends. May God protect him!

Michelangelo replied with a brief and highly mannered letter from Florence, dated February 1522, addressed to *al pru-*

dente giovane (the prudent youth) Gherardo Perini in Pesaro. It merely expressed pleasure at having heard from him. He was well. It was unnecessary to write at length now, since they would soon meet. *Non mi sento però soffiziente a farla,* he wrote—he felt unable to reply to the letter, barely hinting at a warmer feeling, also evident from the plaintive signature, *vostro fedelissimo e povero amico.* Vasari reports that Michelangelo presented this young man with three splendid drawings in chalk (now in the Uffizi, Florence).

That is all we know of Perini.

We know little more about Febo di Poggio, to whom Michelangelo twelve years later, in September 1534, addressed [a] . . . letter from Florence. . . . (pp. 340-41)

[Under the] letter the great artist wrote six lines of verse, the fourth version of a longer poem apparently written to a woman in 1524, but here addressed to a man. Their meaning may be rendered approximately as follows: "Nothing but my death will satisfy you. . . . The more I suffer, the less you show pity on all my woe. . . . Oh, Febo, Phoebus, Sun, who gives warmth and light to all the world, why are you dark and cold to me and to no one else?"

Apparently Michelangelo sang the praises of Febo di Poggio in a fragment from another sonnet. It is addressed to the eagle and the word *poggio* (height) is used in a double meaning: "Oh, happy bird! You fly up to the sun (Phoebus, Febo) and see his beautiful face; you safely soar from the hill (*poggio*) where we come to fall."

A third poem, again playing on the name Febo, begins: "When Phoebus still sent all his rays over the hills, I was to have soared aloft into the air. His wings would have borne me, and death would have been sweet for me." The imagery continues with similar hyperbole: "Pen became wing, the hill a stair, Phoebus a light for my foot."

In all this labored effusiveness an altogether baroquelike air emanates from the letter in which Febo di Poggio, writing on January 14, 1535, from Florence, sought to dispel Michelangelo's apprehensions:

> Most noble Michelangelo, whom I honor like a father! I arrived here yesterday from Pisa, whither I had gone to visit my father. Directly upon my return, through your friend who is employed at the bank, I received your letter, which I read with the greatest pleasure, since I learned from it that you are well. I see from it further that you believe I am angry with you. Surely you must know I could never entertain such feelings toward you, since I look upon you like a father, nor has your conduct toward me ever been of such a nature as to give rise to such feelings. You must also know that on the night before your departure I was unable to get away from Messer Vincenzo, though I felt a great desire to see you. The next morning I went to your home, but you had already left and I was most unhappy not to be able to meet you again.

Quite plausible and fair enough; but then we read: Michelangelo had told him he could turn to one of the artist's friends, if he needed anything. Unfortunately, the friend happened to be away and Febo needed money for clothes to attend the races at Monte. Would Michelangelo be kind enough to see to it that he got the funds?

The only young man of breeding and stature among the sev-

eral young men Michelangelo admired was the Roman nobleman, Tommaso de' Cavalieri. There are astonishing accesses of admiration in the master's letters to young Cavalieri. In a letter from Rome, dated December 1532, we read, for example:

> If I lack the skill to sail that ocean formed by your mighty genius, that genius will pardon me and neither despise me on account of my inequality with you nor demand of me what I cannot do; for he who, in every way, stands alone cannot find fellows. Your Magnificence, sole light of the world in our century, hence can find no satisfaction in the work of another, since you are peerless and nonpareil. If nonetheless one or the other of my works, which I hope and pledge to do, may find your favor, I should call the work fortunate rather than good. And if indeed I had the certainty, as I have been told, to please Your Magnificence in this way or that, I should offer you as a gift my presence with all the future may bring me. I am grieved exceedingly not to be able to regain the past, the better to serve you, having toward that end but the future, which cannot long endure, since I am even now too old.

When Cavalieri wrote Michelangelo he felt as though reborn since he had come to know the master, Michelangelo replied from Rome on January 1, 1533: "On my part, I should feel unborn, still-born, or bereft of heaven and earth, but for having gained from your letters faith that Your Magnificence will agree to accept a few of my works. . . ." In a letter to Sebastiano del Piombo half a year later, he sent greetings to "Messer Tommaso," adding: "I believe I should instantly fall dead, were he no longer in my thoughts."

To be sure, this Platonic love must be viewed in the light of the sixteenth and early seventeenth centuries. Montaigne's friendship for Estienne de la Boëtie, Languet's passionate tenderness toward young Philip Sidney are instructive examples. Some remarks on friendship in Sir Thomas Browne's *Religio Medici* (1642) closely mirror Shakespeare's sentiments and those of Michelangelo: "I love my friend before myself, and yet, methinks, I do not love him enough. Some few months hence, my multiplied affection will make me believe I have not loved him at all. When I am from him, I am dead, till I be with him."

Note this passage from a letter by Michelangelo to Cavalieri of late July 1533: "I would far easier forego food, which nourishes but the body, and even that imperfectly (*infelicemente*), than your name, which sustains my body and soul, filling both with such great joy (*dolcezza*) that I feel neither sorrow nor fear of death so long as I carry it in my thoughts."

The drawings of figures from Greek mythology—Phaëthon, Tityus, Ganymede—which Michelangelo presented to Cavalieri were accompanied by sonnets. One of them carries an allusion to Cavalieri's name:

> Why, more than ever, do I give such vent
> To my desire, when neither tears nor words
> Can change the destiny I move towards?
> Nothing I do can my own fate prevent.
>
> Why does the weary heart make death appear
> Desirable, since every man must die?
> There is no consolation for me here
> Where joy is far outweighed by misery.
>
> Yet if the blows must come decreed by fate

And I am powerless, there's comfort in
The thought that nothing now can intervene.

If to be blest I must accept defeat
It is no wonder if, alone and nude,
I am by one in arms chained and subdued.

It is the last line of the original that alludes to Cavalieri: *Resto
prigion d'un cavalier armato.*

There are other poems of stature that were evidently addressed to Cavalieri, though by modern standards they are
all somewhat mannered. One senses in them an awe of beauty, an unfulfilled yearning for love, a vague metaphysics of
beauty and love. (pp. 341-44)

Michelangelo's verses cost him immense effort. Most of them
he polished over and over again, sometimes at intervals of
many years. We know as many as eight versions of some of
them. As in the case of his sculpture, he left many of them
unfinished. He expressed what was close to his heart, what
he felt at the moment; but he lacked the patience and will to
finish it when inspiration ebbed or some poem had miscar-
ried.

To be rated highest are the several poems in which images
and similes are taken from the art that was closest to him,
sculpture. Here he moved in a sphere where he was at home,
yet even these poems are never quite unambiguous and unequivocal in their imagery. Here Michelangelo's intellectualism was a handicap. There is a dearth of sensual richness in
these poems. Take the famous sonnet on which Benedetto
Varchi in Michelangelo's lifetime held an entire lecture before the Florentine Academy (February 25, 1547) [see excerpt by Varchi dated 1547]. Beginning *Non ha l'ottima artista alcun concetto,* it is addressed to a fair and fickle
lady. . . . (pp. 351-52)

In time the thought of death became a constant refrain in Michelangelo's poetry. The years went by, his solitude grew, his
chances for finding love had dwindled. Reaction against the
great ideas of the Renaissance grew in strength. In many
ways, especially through his liaison with Vittoria Colonna,
the great artist's mind was increasingly haunted by doubts
over the worship of beauty and hopes of salvation by God's
grace.

Of much significance is this fine sonnet from 1554, plainly influenced by Petrarca:

> Already now my life has run its course,
> And, like a fragile boat on a rough sea,
> I reach the place which everyone must cross
> And give account of life's activity.
>
> Now I know well it was a fantasy
> That made me think art could be made into
> An idol or a king. Though all men do
> This, they do it half-unwillingly.
>
> The loving thoughts, so happy and so vain,
> Are finished now. A double death comes near—
> The one is sure, the other is a threat.
>
> Painting and sculpture cannot any more
> Quieten the soul that turns to God again,
> To God who, on the cross, for us was set.

Deeply felt as is this sonnet, the thought that this is how the
poet Michelangelo is to end is even sadder. There is a touch
of the spirit of the Council of Trent in this sonnet. All the fire

that once meant the grandeur of the Renaissance is dead and
only the ashes remain.

The reformers had shouted so long about the corruption of
the Roman Church and especially the immorality among the
clergy, that the Council of Trent resolved to restore the strictest discipline. The divine streak in the Renaissance, its exuberance and irreverence, its mighty espousal of the essential
rights of humanity, its faith in the beauty of ancient art and
indeed, its worship of all art—all this was crushed by censorship, killed by the Inquisition. Cynicism was supplanted by
hypocrisy. Freedom of thought and freedom to write were re-
voked. The human body was banished from the fine arts.

Strangest of all, the creative artist who in youth and manhood
seemed to be the Renaissance incarnate was to end as an instrument of the trend that unseated and finished the Renaissance. (pp. 352-54)

> *Georg Brandes, in his* Michelangelo: His Life, His
> Times, His Era, *translated by Heinz Norden, revised
> edition, Frederick Ungar Publishing Co., 1967, 434
> p.*

ERNEST HATCH WILKINS (essay date 1954)

[*Wilkins was a distinguished American authority on Italian
Renaissance literature. In the following excerpt, he examines
the forms and themes of Michelangelo's poetry.*]

Most of the many men and women who wrote lyric verse
[during the time of the Italian Renaissance] were docile Petrarchists, in the Bembist sense, with little of their own to say;
but the one great lyric poet of the period, Michelangelo Buonarroti, was too powerfully individual to be subservient to
Bembo or to anyone else, and was in spirit more closely akin
to Dante than to Petrarch.

Born in 1475, he had in his teens been taken by the discerning
Lorenzo into the Medici household; and his thought and his
art were indelibly impressed with the influences of Laurentian thought and Laurentian art. In particular, he came to
share with firm conviction the current Florentine admiration
for Dante; he stored in his mind the Platonic lore of Ficino;
and the examples of Lorenzo and of Politian gave to him or
reënforced in him the impulse to write lyric poetry.

In the years just before and just after the turn of the century
the already recognized greatness of his work as sculptor won
him many commissions in Florence and elsewhere. The series
of his monumental enterprises began in 1505, when Julius II
called him to Rome, employing him first to design and execute the pope's own tomb—a project which, shrinking gradually in its scope and attended by tragic frustrations, pursued
the sculptor for forty years. Rome shocked him. A sonnet
written probably soon after 1505 begins thus:

> Here helms and swords are made of chalices:
> The blood of Christ is sold so much the quart:
> His cross and thorns are spears and shields; and short
> Must be the time ere even His patience cease.

Presently Julius diverted him, much against his will, to the
painting of the Sistine ceiling. The physical difficulties he encountered, high on his scaffolding, are listed in a humorous
sonnet which contains this quatrain:

> My beard turns up to heaven; my nape falls in
> Fixed on my spine; my breast-bone visibly

> Grows like a harp: a rich embroidery
> Bedews my face from brush-drops thick and thin.

For some years after the death of Julius, Michelangelo worked mainly on the ill-fated tomb. About 1523 Clement VII employed him to add to the church of San Lorenzo in Florence a new sacristy which should contain the tombs of Lorenzo the Magnificent and other members of the Medici family. This project, also, was only partly carried out: the only tombs that Michelangelo brought close to completion were those of the younger Giuliano and the younger Lorenzo. The tomb of Giuliano bears the reclining allegorical figures of Day and Night, that of Lorenzo the similar figures of Dawn and Evening. It must have been while his thoughts were busy with this work that he wrote, in rhythmic prose, these lines:

> The Day and the Night speak, and say:
> "We with our swift course have brought
> Duke Giuliano to his death.
> It is but just that he should take vengeance upon us as he
> does.
> And his vengeance is this:
> That as we have slain him,
> So he by his death has taken the light from us, and by the
> closing of his eyes has sealed our eyes, which shine no
> more upon the earth.
> What, then, would he have done with us, if he had lived?"

Heartsick over the state of Florence after the siege, Michelangelo in 1534 left his city, never to return, and went to Rome. Some ten years later, when the sacristy of San Lorenzo was at last opened to the public, an insignificant poet wrote, of the figure of Night, a quatrain of which the meaning is:

> Night, whom you see so sweetly sleeping, was
> carved by an Angel in this stone, and because she
> sleeps, she lives: wake her, if you believe it not, and
> she will speak to you.

To which Michelangelo, from Rome, replied:

> 'Tis sweet to sleep, sweeter of stone to be,
> While ruin and dishonor hold their sway.
> To see nought, to hear nought, is gain to me.
> Wake me not, therefore: speak you softly, pray!

In the years immediately following his return to Rome he painted, again in the Sistine Chapel, his "Last Judgment," Dantesque in its general inspiration and in some of its details. In 1547 he was made architect of St. Peter's, whose unequalled dome is his crowning achievement. He died in 1564.

In the course of his life he completed about two hundred poems, and he left many poetic fragments, some of them written on sheets on which he had made drawings. Some of the poems are early; but most of them seem to have been written after his return to Rome, from about his sixtieth to perhaps his eightieth year. Most of the completed poems are sonnets or madrigals: a few are in other forms.

Michelangelo's poems are in general heavily freighted with deeply meditative thought. His approach to poetry was sculptural. Within the untouched block of marble he felt the presence of an imagined statue that his strong and patient chisel must release: within an inchoate mass of thoughts and words he felt the presence of an imagined poem that he must similarly release—and at times he wrought for that release as if he were working with a chisel rather than a pen. Yet with all their difficulties his poems constitute a unique and varied treasure: the best of them—and there are many in which he finds perfect expression for his demanding thought—attain a nobility quite comparable to that of his greatest creations in sculpture and in painting.

His experience in the practice of those other arts enters into the making of his poems, giving them their most distinctive imagery—as in the sonnet that begins

> The best of artists hath no thought to show
> Which the rough stone in its superfluous shell
> Doth not include: to break the marble spell
> Is all the hand that serves the brain can do.

They are enriched also—but never through mere imitation—by evidences of the love and understanding with which he had read the poetry of Dante, of Petrarch, and of Lorenzo de' Medici.

He was the one true Platonist among the Italian poets of his century—the only one, that is, to whom love meant specifically the searching for the divine immanence and the ascent to the divine that had been set forth by Ficino. Michelangelo's Platonism appears most clearly in poems written chiefly after 1534 to a Roman youth, and in other poems written still later to Vittoria Colonna. These three short passages, from three different sonnets, are typical:

> Love wings and wakes the soul, stirs her to win
> Her flight aloft, nor e'er to earth decline;
> 'Tis the first step that leads her to the shrine
> Of Him who slakes the thirst that burns within.

> Lo, all the lovely things we find on earth
> Resemble for the soul that rightly sees
> That source of bliss divine which gave us birth.

> True love is that which the pure heart hath known,
> Which alters not with time or death's decay,
> Yielding on earth earnest of Paradise.

Perhaps the most perfectly poetic expression of his Platonism is to be found in this sonnet:

> This heart of flesh feeds not with life my love:
> The love wherewith I love thee hath no heart;
> Nor harbours it in any mortal part,
> Where erring thought or ill desire may move.
> When first Love sent our souls from God above,
> He fashioned me to see thee as thou art—
> Pure light; and thus I find God's counterpart
> In thy fair face, and feel the sting thereof.
>
> As heat from fire, from loveliness divine
> The mind that worships what recalls the sun
> From whence she sprang, can be divided never:
> And since thine eyes all Paradise enshrine,
> Burning unto those orbs of light I run,
> There where I loved thee first to dwell for ever.

Two fine late sonnets are devoted to impassioned praise of Dante. One begins:

> From heaven his spirit came, and robed in clay,
> The realms of justice and of mercy trod:
> Then rose a living man to gaze on God,
> That he might make the truth as clear as day.

And the other:

> No tongue can tell of him what should be told,
> For on blind eyes his splendour shines too strong.

The coming of old age brought no slackening in the vigor of

Michelangelo's thought or of his feeling. Many of the late poems express the tension between his continuing power of heart and mind and the impairment of his bodily strength. The last poems of all are deeply and nobly religious. One of them ends with this tercet:

> Painting nor sculpture now can lull to rest
> My soul, that turns to His great love on high,
> Whose arms to clasp us on the cross were spread.

The poems of Michelangelo have found great favor with English and American translators of the nineteenth and twentieth centuries—among them Wordsworth, Southey, Symonds, Emerson, Longfellow, Norton, and Santayana. (pp. 196-200)

> Ernest Hatch Wilkins, "Michelangelo and Other Poets," in his A History of Italian Literature, 1954. Reprint by Cambridge, Mass.: Harvard University Press, 1962, pp. 196-207.

JOSEPH TUSIANI   (essay date 1959)

[In the following excerpt from the 1959 introduction to his translation of The Complete Poems of Michelangelo, Tusiani reviews Michelangelo's career as a poet.]

Michelangelo's poems did not pass unnoticed in his lifetime. They "sounded" utterly different from the general poetic trend of the century—an over-musical current of Platonism and Petrarchism. Composers such as Arcadelt and Tromboncino had set them to music; men of letters such as Benedetto Varchi [see excerpt by Varchi dated 1547] and Francesco Berni had praised them. Yet those madrigals and sonnets lacked the sonority of Bembo's verse and seemed to envy the fluency of Vittoria Colonna's spiritual rhymes and the refinement of Molza's, or Alamanni's, descriptive ease. Both Varchi and Berni had understood, almost instinctively, that the new voice, though rude and rugged, was almost Dantesque in the vastness of its echoes.

> Enough of you, sweet pallid violets,
> And liquid crystals, and fair beasts astray:
> You babble words, but only *he* writes thoughts.

These lines, part of a *capitolo* which Berni sent to Sebastiano del Piombo, are typical of the half-humorous, half-sneering nature of their author. But in their succinctness they give an impeccable portrayal of the literary situation of the Renaissance in Italy.

With Ariosto the language had achieved its greatest significance, for every word had been filtered through the magic of his genius. After the *Orlando Furioso* there was the heritage of a glorious idiom without another magician who could give it new life and new resonance. In the years that followed (until Tasso) many wrote verse but few wrote poetry. The latter was relegated, it seemed, to the accessible realm of felicitous sound and pictorial detail. The soul was missing, for even man's soul had been lent easy wings by Ficino's reinterpretation of Plato which had started in Florence around Lorenzo the Magnificent. The humanistic breath had become too violent a storm not to sever all human links with the earth and its deepest conflicts. Because of political disasters Italy was bleeding from innumerable wounds, yet countless sonneteers found joy, and perhaps refuge, in the remembrance of Laura's golden tresses. Petrarch became a god while Dante was neglected or only remembered as a stern moralist of the

past. The reason was simple: the boisterous exaltation of the former and the silent condemnation of the latter explained the very soul of the Renaissance. The *Canzoniere* and the *Comedy* could not meet for Laura and Beatrice could never become one. And there was more than that. Dante had left a city and lost "all things most dearly loved" to force open all sounding heavens and capture an echo of them; Petrarch had to meet princes and popes to find out none was worth his splendid page. To Dante life was love to live and fight for; to Petrarch it was love to write about. Thus the *Canzoniere* was rediscovered by many who had learned to imitate Petrarch's voice, though not his soul. Imagine now a deluge of sonnets in which recur green, sweet hills, solitary shores, desperate tears, burning darts, fresh waters, stars and nightingales. To all this add Plato and his concept of love and beauty, and you will understand the meaning of Berni's lines and the sincerity of his praise of Michelangelo's "thoughts."

Even when honored by inclusion in the Florentine Academy, Michelangelo did not consider himself a poet, for he knew his verse to be "unprofessional, rude and rough." It was exactly the awareness of his lack of musical feeling that kept him apart from those who deemed music the only poetry possible, and made him find a friend in Dante. A scene from Longfellow's *Michael Angelo* shows our Titan reading the *Comedy* and conversing with the great Florentine he loved. More than the coincidence of the "same nest," other factors strengthened that spiritual kinship. Michelangelo had the same power of vision, the same consciousness of sin and human frailty, the same need of God, the same concept of life and death, and the same understanding of art and love. The fiery sermons of Savonarola, which he had heard in his youth, had kept Dante's sublime song of penance alive in his mind and, more, in his heart. Something in him had remained medieval for something in him was Dantesque.

Yet he too had to burn his grain of incense on the altar of Petrarch; he too was, then, at times, artificial and fond of conceits and preciosities. Surrounded as he was by Petrarchists, he could not escape their influence. He even asked them to polish this or that of his sonnets, to retouch this or that of his madrigals; a very common thing, this candid admission of incompetence, among the writers of the Renaissance. Even Cellini, for instance, will want to submit the manuscript of his *Vita* to Benedetto Varchi. But Michelangelo's poems could neither be polished nor retouched. Even when on the brink of the commonplace, or lost in the dry meanderings of imitation, Michelangelo could not be called a perfect Petrarchist, for he lacked the very secret of Petrarchism— musicality and smoothness. His verse was at times too ungrammatical to be aided and sped toward the gentle fashion of love poetry. Yet it was not dismissed. It had strength and massiveness. To soften it was to kill it. His madrigals, for example, said more or less what Petrarch had sung, but they had, in the conclusive couplet, a marmoreal quality that made one forget the weakness of their poetic nucleus. It was as though impersonal emotions became suddenly personal and acquired a marble rigidity or, rather, a monumental solemnity. Neither Bembo nor Della Casa had ever been capable of so powerful a voice as this:

> And loss eternal does not scare at all:
> One moment cannot make two decades fall;

or

> Great happiness can bear great misery;

or

> A future bliss makes present sorrows light;

or

> Weak virtue dies at fortune's lavish touch.

Michelangelo's handling of the couplet in most of his madrigals prefigures Shakespeare. Was it such strength that tempted more than one composer, or perhaps the fact that music could do more with roughness than it could with elegance of verse which in itself was music? Michelangelo's fame cannot be the answer, for there was hardly an artist of the Renaissance who, in moments of *otium,* did not exchange the pain of the brush for the pleasure of the pen.

Even in the case of Michelangelo, as of all poets, there is a high and low tide of inspiration. He is at his worst when he uses tools that are not his own, or re-echoes Dante's *Vita Nuova* and Petrarch's *Canzoniere.* The flame of his inspiration depends, then, on another flame; his images cannot take wing but are linked to the old imagery of Love's bow and arrows, of the phoenix, of the salamander, and similar devices. Though often on the verge of true poetry, he is not himself yet.

But when Michelangelo forgets arrows and bow, salamander and phoenix, his poetry is titanic and unique and he is once more the Michelangelo we know. This happens, that is, whenever his own heart becomes the subject of his poems and the fetters of erudition are broken loose by the hammer of his individuality. The expression may sound baroque but is not. Hammer and stone become the new, powerful image of Renaissance poetry, into which Michelangelo's soul enters not as song but as sense of Greek fate and Christian faith. To understand how Michelangelo finds himself in the world of his own heart, one has but to read his poems for Vittoria Colonna, the Marquise of Pescara. They range from embarrassing imitation to sheer sublimity. When Michelangelo sees his lady through the eyes of Petrarch or Dante, he only says what a Bembo could express with greater felicity of mood and accent:

> Love, when my spirit did from God depart,
> Made *me* pure glance, and *you,* light's destiny:
> That is the reason *God* I seek and see
> In what of you, alas, time wears apart.

This is true even of his madrigals for the Marquise of Pescara. Michelangelo can say of her:

> My only will is in your will alone,
> My very thoughts are born within your heart,
> And only in your breath my words can be.
> If left alone, I am just like the moon:
> Of all its light our eyes can see a part—
> Only that much the sun grants us to see.

But he is not himself until he finds inspiration within, not around, him. When he does, he writes these lines:

> Just as an empty form
> Awaits its gold or silver liquefied,
> And, broken, then reveals
> The perfect work; thus, I can only fill
> With inner fire of love my void and need
> Of the immortal beauty of my lady,
> Both mind and heart of these my fragile days.
> Through such a narrow space
> Her gentleness and love pour into me,

> That, to draw forth her perfect image, I
> Must agonize and die.

The very death of Vittoria is the subject of both a celebration and a tragedy. The celebration is done in terms of Petrarchan fashion: triumph of fame over death, of time over fame, and of eternity over time. That Michelangelo was not satisfied with these echoes that failed to convey the sorrow of his loss, is proved by the fact that he even repeated a thought with which, ten years earlier, he had celebrated young Cecchino Bracci's death. He knew that no Petrarchan image, either from the second part of the *Canzoniere* or from all *I Trionfi,* sufficed to express his colossal suffering. So, one day, he forgot Petrarch and Petrarchists and wrote this sonnet:

> If my rough hammer gives a human face
> To this or that of all hard blocks that wait,
> It is another smith makes me create,
> Controlling each my motion, each my pace.
> But that high hammer beyond stars and space
> Makes self, and others, with each stroke, more great
> And bright; and since the first must generate
> All hammers, *that* gives life to all, always.
>
> And since the most effective is that blow
> Which falls from highest in the smithy, mine
> Shall fall no more—my hammer having flown.
> Now here am I, unskilled, and do not know
> How to go on, unless the smith divine
> Teaches me how, who am on earth alone.

This vision of death, snatching the happy hammer from the uplifted hand of a smith, is new. And this *is* Michelangelo for no one else could have written such a powerful poem.

We know now what to look for in the production of this poet—that unmistakable force of vision and emotion which is to the Renaissance what a sudden thunderstorm is to the monotony of a dry summer. And we do not have long to wait for such violence of ideas, for Michelangelo's nature, though tender at its core, can only reveal itself through a gigantic explosion of moods. After poems in which inspiration seems to drag, we shall once more find the poet who becomes his own poem. It can be in the bitter description of the physical torture during and after his work in the Sistine Chapel. It can be in the monstrosity of the giant who, with his one eye beneath the heel, sees the past flow underground and is breastfed by a huge, lurid hag who tosses seas and mountains into her stomach. Or we find Michelangelo whenever the word "night" is mentioned. This is another of his new, great images. He calls himself "son of the night," his art, "fruit of the night." Darkness to him is not the termination of light, but life itself. We walk, he says, from dark into dark, yet this creates our greatness, for, though vast and frightening, night is, in turn, frightened by our deeds of splendor.

> Wrong are all those who praise her qualities:
> She is so dark, lost, lonely, that the birth
> Of one small firefly can make war on her;

and

> The *night* they gave to me and to my art
> That very day my body met my soul.
> Now like the one who blames his destiny,
> As night grows darker since it has begun,
> I, darker with the night, bemoan my fate.
> And yet, one thought is dear and comforts me—
> To warm my darkest hour within that sun
> Which on your birth was given you as mate.

The fundamental notes in Michelangelo's poetry are four—love of beauty, art, old age, and God. The four motifs seem to constitute the rational development of his personality, yet they are intermingled, so much so that any attempt at a chronological analysis will prove futile. Much has been written about Michelangelo's *loves*. It would be better, and certainly more cautious, to speak of his *love,* for it is possible to reconcile his ardent admiration for Tommaso Cavalieri, Febo del Poggio, Gherardo Perini, and Cecchino Bracci, with his equally ardent adoration of Vittoria Colonna. To Michelangelo beauty was one, whether he caught a glimpse of it in Vittoria's "sweet and holy eyes" or whether he found it in the ephebic harmony of a male body. Love to him was therefore a state of grace, an exaltation of all his energies, spiritual and physical, a path of light, like that of his firefly, in the vast darkness of life. But even in that state of grace he was still linked to his human, conventional terms of flesh and hunger, wood and fire. Other poets were able to control both struggle and elevation by their sense of literary proportion; Michelangelo could not, for his deepest feelings were always immense.

> Now with your splendor printed on my face,
> I go like one who, dressed with every kind
> Of amulets and arms, can dare all wars.
>
> I can walk on the ocean, brave all blaze,
> Give in your name the light to all the blind,
> And my saliva heals all poisonous sores.

Love has become religion and the one in love yearns for Christ's miraculous power to feel complete. It does not matter, then, whether these lines were written for Tommaso Cavalieri or Vittoria Colonna. We must expect far more than this, for Michelangelo the poet and Michelangelo the painter of the "Last Judgment" are exactly the same person. That *terribilità* of which Vasari spoke is to be found even in his best poems. Take, for instance, the sonnet in which the simile of the silkworm turns immediately into something apparently monstrous and macabre.

> Would that I were—my hairy skin alone—
> The skin that makes with its soft hairs a plate
> (O happy dress!) around his handsome breast
> All day! Were I two slippers he could own
> And use as base to his majestic weight!
> I would enjoy two snowy feet at least.

What seems torrid sensuality is only violence of thought and emotion, for, even when he paints, Michelangelo remains a sculptor.

Sculpture is the second main note in his poetry. He reminds Giovanni, "the one from Pistoia," of the fact that he, Michelangelo, is not a painter. More than once he likes to add to his signature the qualification, "scultore." Sculpture is "the first of the arts" because God was a sculptor, not a painter, when he created Adam. Michelangelo will consequently associate with painting all the minor manifestations of his intellect, but only with sculpture the major activities of his soul. In the moving poem on the death of his father, in which he also mourns the loss of a younger brother, he writes:

> My brother is now painted in my mind,
> But you are sculpted in my deepest heart,
> And on my face is weeping all mankind.

It is mostly in his poems to Vittoria Colonna that he reveals the secret of his art:

> After the divine part has well conceived

> Man's face and gesture, soon both mind and hand,
> With a cheap model, first, at their command,
> Give life to stone. . . .

Her image he wants to bring, engraved in his soul, to the angels in heaven, so that they learn to make for the world another face as beautiful as hers. And of Vittoria Colonna he says in a superb line:

> No iron chisel carves me—one of gold.

Michelangelo was sixty-three years old when he met Vittoria Colonna. His greatest poetry therefore was written in his old age. On September 19, 1554 (he was close to his eightieth birthday) he sent this note to Vasari [see excerpt dated 1554]: "Messer Giorgio, dear friend, you too perhaps will say that I am an old fool for wanting to write sonnets; but since many people accuse me of senility, it is my duty to write." With these words he accompanied one of his greatest poems. His "duty" was then to show that he was not usurping life, as if his work as papal architect were not enough to justify his presence among the living. Those who saw him ride to Saint Peter's almost every day, even when he was eighty-nine, could not guess the struggle of his soul with fear of death and hell. Old age was to him the most tragic period of man's life. Deeply religious, he was tormented by the terror of two deaths—of the body and of the soul. A retrospective glance on his life made him discover with horror a long existence "full of puppets" and spent for others, not for his God. Even art seemed futile and, worse yet, sinful.

> Painting no more, nor sculpture, can now quiet
> My soul, turned to that Love divine that, here,
> To take us, opened its arms on a cross and bled.

The question whether the Council of Trent with all its implications might have brought Michelangelo's consciousness of sin to its deepest exacerbation is of little import. Michelangelo was colossal even in his conversation with death and God. Unlike Dante he was not a theologian. Though he "read and read" the Holy Scriptures, his knowledge of religion was limited and intransigent. He knew and believed what his father had known and believed: that man is born in sin and must cling to the Cross of Christ to obtain eternal salvation, and that he who loses his soul, loses all. Death, fear of hell, temptations of the flesh, cross, redemption—these are the themes of Michelangelo's last poems, in which one hears both a wounded lion roaring in the night and a child crying for his mother. A blade of grass withers unnoticed; an oak falls with a thunder. Michelangelo could not surrender to death without a fierce, long struggle:

> This is the way Daedalus arose,
> This is the way the sun rejects the shadow.

It was the afternoon of February 18, 1564. (pp. 3-12)

> *Joseph Tusiani, in an introduction to* The Complete Poems of Michelangelo, *edited and translated by Joseph Tusiani, The Noonday Press, 1960, pp. 3-17.*

CHARLES SPERONI (essay date 1960)

[*In the excerpt below, Speroni enumerates characteristic features of Michelangelo's letters.*]

Michelangelo's letters fall conveniently into two groups: those to his family, and those to "others." The 495 letters can be subdivided as follows: 45 to his father Lodovico; 78 to his brother Buonarroto; 12 to his brother Giovansimone; 206 to his nephew Lionardo, and 154 to "others." We see, then, that the letters to his family far outnumber the others: 341 against 154. This, to a large extent, explains the personal tone of the artist's correspondence. Outside his family, Michelangelo's correspondents are numerous: Pope Clement VII, King Francis I, Duke Cosimo de' Medici, the artists Giorgio Vasari and Sebastiano del Piombo, the poet Vittoria Colonna, his friend Luigi del Riccio, Don Francesco Fattucci priest of Santa Maria del Fiore in Florence, the handsome young artist Tommaso Cavalieri, representatives of banking firms, and even simple workers such as Maestro Domenico, called Topolino, a stonemason. Especially significant in this group are the letters addressed to Giorgio Vasari, one of the few artists who can be called a true friend of Michelangelo. His first surviving letter, which was written on the 2nd of July, 1496, soon after Michelangelo's arrival in Rome where he had been called by Cardinal di San Giorgio, was not addressed to the artist's family but to Lorenzo of Pier Francesco de' Medici; his last surviving letter is of December 28th, 1563, also from Rome, and was addressed to his nephew Lionardo.

The largest part of the letters were written from Rome, where after all Michelangelo spent most of his life away from Florence, and the last thirty years of his long life; but there are many letters from Florence, while he was working on the Medici chapel and on the plans for the never finished façade of San Lorenzo; from Bologna, where he was casting the large bronze statue of Pope Julius II; from Carrara and Pietrasanta, where he went on various occasions to direct the quarrying of marble; and from a few other places where his travels took him.

There are several breaks in Michelangelo's correspondence which are easily explained: the most significant occurs between 1534 and 1541, when he was completely absorbed in painting the Last Judgment in the Sistine Chapel, which was unveiled on Christmas Day 1541.

In general, the frequency of Michelangelo's correspondence increases as he grows older; between 1542 (after the completion of the Last Judgment) and 1563 Michelangelo wrote more than twice the number of letters he wrote between 1496 and 1542. Most of those written in his old age are addressed to his nephew.

Some of the letters—mainly the ones connected with his work—are long; the majority, however, are rather short. Several are very brief: these are mostly receipts, covering letters, and the like.

In the preface to his [1910 edition of the letters, Giovanni Papini] does not hesitate to state that in some of Michelangelo's letters there is more "force" and "sincerity" than in all of his poems: a statement with which it is easy to find oneself in agreement. I wonder, however, how many readers would agree with him when he states that in every Italian family there ought to be a copy not only of the *Divine Comedy* but also of the poems and letters of Michelangelo.

Force and sincerity are undoubtedly two main characteristics of Michelangelo's letters; but there is another: naturalness. Force, sincerity and naturalness are indeed the characteristics that distinguish most of Michelangelo's letters from the countless others that were written and published by the Italian stylists of the sixteenth century. Letter-writing, which had a long tradition in Italy (was it not one of the main activities of the Humanists, from Petrarch on down, even if they expressed themselves in the nobler Latin rather than in the vulgar tongue?), had reached its height in Michelangelo's time. Montaigne was completely awed by the epistolary activity of Italians in the sixteenth century, and declared that he had acquired over one hundred volumes of Italian letters. But while, as even Montaigne's statement implies, the Italian literati of the Renaissance wrote with an eye to a vast public of readers—some collections of letters went through several editions within a few years—Michelangelo wrote strictly out of necessity, and was totally unfamiliar with the numerous treatises on letter-writing, the *ars dictandi,* then available to the stylist. We may be sure that if telegraphy—let alone telephony—had been invented by his time, Michelangelo would have left us only a handful of the longer letters. For, whereas the letters of his contemporaries, such as Aretino, Bembo, and even Machiavelli, read almost like essays, some of his own have rather the air of a night-letter.

Michelangelo was usually not concerned with style: he wrote as he spoke, so that most of his letters have an immediacy, a spontaneity that we would seek in vain in other letters of the time. His letters are of the "newsy" sort, and although it is true that some of his contemporaries must on occasion have written similar letters, they were not the kind that would be published and thus transmitted to posterity. Stylists were after effect, polish, the well-rounded phrase, the balanced composition, structurally sound, and linguistically as pure as possible. They were highly conscious of style and language. Michelangelo, who in this instance was the pot of crockery travelling in the midst of pots of iron, was usually not after rhetorical effect: his prose is straightforward and energetic. Michelangelo became conscious of his style only when he was obliged to write to some important person: a Cardinal, Duke Cosimo, the King of France, Vittoria Colonna, and a few others. Then his style becomes ceremonious and cumbersome; the artist is aware of his shortcomings, and while putting his best phrase forward, he admonishes his correspondent that writing is not his profession: "Writing is very grievous to me, for it is not my profession;" "When I write to you, if I should not write as correctly as one should . . . forgive me." But if Michelangelo's style lacks polish—as do his poems, for that matter—it is not impersonal like the style of many of the professionals; it is rich in psychological insight. *Le style c'est l'homme;* his letters abound in naturalness and candor, both in the language and in the feelings expressed.

Haste is another characteristic of Michelangelo. It is evident especially at the beginning and at the end of his letters. He begins with no rhetorical circumlocutions or preambles: he fairly jumps *in medias res:* "I inform you that on Friday Buonarroto arrived here;" "Michele the stonemason came to live with me here;" "I received the contract, and it looks all right to me;" "I have seen the drawings of the rooms painted by Messer Giorgio." The endings are often also abrupt: "I have nothing else to say. The Pope left Rome, and the rumor is that he is coming there;" "Nothing else;" "Pray God that my things come out all right;" "I can't think of anything else, nor do I have time to write;" "I had no more paper;" "I'm well. I hope you are too. Say hello to my friends."

Sometimes the artist is so pressed for time, or so anxious to finish writing and to return to his work, that he forgets to date or even to sign his letters. Other times he wants to date them, but cannot remember what day of the month it is: "October . . . ;" "I do not know the date, but I know that

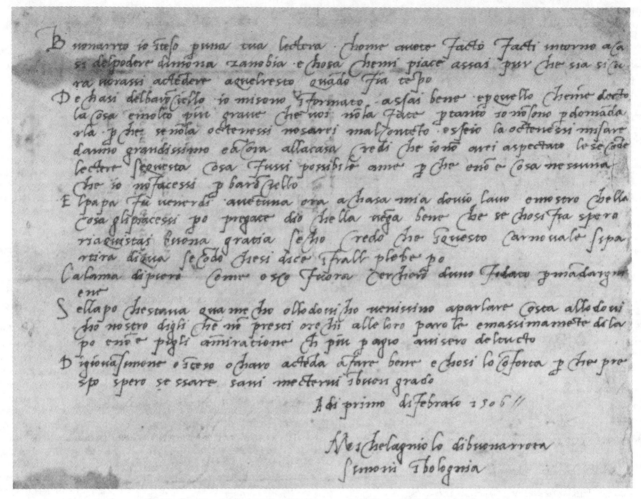

1507 letter from Michelangelo to Buonarroto di Lodovico di Buonarrota Simoni.

tomorrow is the Epiphany;" "Some day in February, according to my housemaid;" "I do not know what day of April, 1554." But, then, of course, in those days insurance and airline companies did not provide their clients with calendars.

The reader who picks up Michelangelo's letters full of expectations, since, after all, they are the letters of a great artist, is soon disappointed. This is because he fails to find what he may well have expected: the artist immersed in his grandiose conceptions; the artist about to attack a blocked out piece of marble to extract from it a David or a Pietà; the artist who, while protesting that painting is not his profession, reveals his secret plan for covering the vast vault of the Sistine Chapel with the supreme moment of God's creation of the world and of man, or the altar wall with the bliss of eternal salvation and the agony of eternal doom.

No: this aspect of his genius Michelangelo revealed to his contemporaries and to posterity only through the magic of his chisel and his brush. To his pen he entrusted another aspect of his complex personality: his innermost human feelings towards the members of his family and towards those in whose midst he lived and worked; in short, Michelangelo the man. His letters reflect his intimate joys and sorrows, his struggles with powerful men who wanted his services, and his squabbles with inefficient and unreliable workers. Michelan-

gelo's letters reveal the whole man with his frailties, his problems, his fears, his hopes, and his disappointments. They are candid and intimate.

Michelangelo's letters tell us a great deal about his anxieties over his family; his sincere interest in setting up a business for his brothers; his constant desire to acquire real estate, especially farms (a concern that grew with the years, for he was looking forward to returning to Florence and to having enough to live upon for the rest of his days); his pride in his ancestry; his interest in finding a good wife for his nephew Lionardo. It is evident that Michelangelo loved and respected his father, in spite of the latter's orneriness. He loved his brothers, who were so different from him in their lack of purpose. He loved his nephew as a father. He loved and helped them all financially throughout his long life. But how many times they made him lose his patience, with their greed, their shiftlessness, their lukewarmness towards him, who surely needed their affection. "Go on shouting and saying what you will of me, but stop writing to me, since you keep me from working," he wrote on one occasion. Michelangelo loved his servants, who became part of his family, especially one named Urbino, who for many years took good care of him; when he died, the broken-hearted artist helped his wife and children. Michelangelo, however, was not "a shin of a saint," as the saying goes in Italian, and if something went wrong, he lost his temper; but his anger was like a summer squall, and soon died down. This is borne out by some of the post-scripts he appended to a particularly "hot" letter. In the body of the letter he boils and gives full vent to his feelings; after hastily signing it, however, he cools off and adds a P.S.: he feels he has been too harsh, too outspoken, and so he adds a conciliatory note.

Like his father, whom he criticized for being too suspicious, Michelangelo was suspicious himself. When it was a matter of trusting a banker, or someone who had property for sale, or a father who offered his daughter in marriage to his nephew Lionardo, or the honesty of certain laborers, Michelangelo never grew weary of preaching prudence and caution. He was not, though he might easily have been, the inventor of that old Italian adage "to trust someone is all right, but not to trust him is even better." Like his compatriot Machiavelli, Michelangelo had a pessimistic view of human nature.

And like his father, Michelangelo was easily offended. When his feelings were hurt, he minced no words, and he was as hard to stop as a runaway mule. He was not afraid of anyone, not even of Julius II, who, with all his threats, was unable to convince young Michelangelo to return to Rome. This explains the so-called "terribilità" of the artist. Once Sebastiano del Piombo wrote Michelangelo a letter in which he plainly told him: "You frighten everyone, even Popes."

In Michelangelo's letters there is a notable lack of tenderness and sentimentality. There is no fond remembrance of places or things, such as may be experienced by a man as he grows older, especially if he has been away for many years from his birthplace and family. Somehow he retained the rough surface of the *pietra serena* he learned to chisel as a boy under the guidance of the stonemasons of Settignano. It was against his rough-hewn nature to express himself in tender terms. On one occasion he says in a letter: "Read my heart, not my words." We do know that he loved Florence; and had he not been kept in Rome by the long work of St. Peter's cathedral, he probably would have returned there to spend his old age; but he could not tear himself away in spite of the repeated invitations and pleas of Duke Cosimo, of Cellini, and others.

Also, in Michelangelo's letters there is a real dearth of references to the contemporary scene. His letters make only vague mention of the tumultuous political events of the day; and this cannot but surprise us, for we recall that in his time, not to mention the mishaps of his Florence, now a republic, now ruled by the Medici, Italy was invaded by the French kings and by the armies of Charles V, Rome was cruelly sacked, and with the treaty of Cateau-Cambrésis Spain secured a lasting strangle hold on almost the whole peninsula. What the letters do reveal is the great fear, for himself and his family, of becoming involved in anything dangerous. Typical is the advice he gave his brother Buonarroto during the Medici's struggle to get back into Florence in 1512: "Regarding the events in our city, do not get involved either in word or in deed." The artist himself fled from Florence on two different occasions when danger threatened from within or from without.

What Michelangelo cherished was tranquility and peace of mind to concentrate on his work. He wanted to be left alone. This is clearly shown by several of his letters in which he finds one excuse or another to discourage his brothers or his nephew from coming to visit him. He tells them that this is not a good time to come, that he is especially busy and would not be able to receive them properly, or that his quarters are crowded and lack the comforts to which they are accustomed. There is no doubt that Michelangelo always lived like a pauper: his quarters were very simple, and his food and drink Spartan. He was generous, however, and whenever he received wine, cheese, or fruit from his family, he invariably gave most of it to the Pope and to his friends. But he liked solitude and in many ways he was not easy to live with: this partly explains why he left no school like his more sociable and urbane contemporary Raphael.

As the years passed Michelangelo became even more unsociable and solitary than he had been in his youth. The twilight of his life was characterized even more poignantly by a phrase he had written in his early days in Rome: "I have no friends, and I seek none." His father and all his brothers had died one after the other, and he concentrated his deep-seated love for his kin on his nephew Lionardo who lived far away in Florence. He wrote him often, and he often asked him to distribute goodly sums of money from his own funds to impoverished Florentine noble families, to families with girls desiring to enter a convent, and also for the recitation of prayers for the repose of the dead and for the salvation of his own soul. The thought of death came to mind with increasing frequency: "Not a single thought is born in me which does not have death graven in it," he wrote Vasari in 1555. He found consolation in religion.

The reader of Michelangelo's letters is struck time and again by his insatiable appetite for work down to his last days and by his reluctance to give up a single moment of his time for the necessities, let alone the niceties, of daily existence. When he found it impossible to carry out a request of the king of France, he wrote him in all earnestness: "If death should interrupt this desire of mine (to please you), and if it is possible to paint and to sculpture in the next life, I shall not fail to do so then, for in the next life man does not grow old." If eternal bliss for Dante consisted in the vision of God, which implied immediate knowledge of the mysteries of the universe, for Michelangelo it probably consisted in the hope of an eternity of tranquil work in a vast quarry of flawless marble with no contracts to worry him.

We have said that Michelangelo's letters reveal little of the artist; there are, however, many letters that are important, even if only tangentially, to a full picture of Michelangelo's activities in connection with his work. Among these are the letters from Bologna that tell us of his prolonged difficulties in casting the statue of Julius II and the letters from the marble quarries that describe his troubles with the stonemasons, the building of a road from the quarry to the seashore, the anguish over imperfect blocks of marble, the quarrels with shippers, his despair over the drought which kept the waters of the Arno river at a low level and prevented the shipping of quarried blocks. Then there is a group of letters which reveal his concern and anguish over his inability to fulfill the contract for Julius's tomb, and the litigations in trying to break the contract. Further, there are several letters which touch upon his activity as a poet.

Without going further into a general analysis of Michelangelo's letters, it is evident that they are indispensable for a full understanding of the man, and also, though to a lesser degree, of the artist. It is hardly surprising, therefore, that Michelangelo's biographers from H. Grimm to A. Gotti, from J. A. Symonds to G. Papini, and more recently, from M. Saponaro to D. L. Finlayson, Sydney Alexander, Charles H. Morgan, and Irving Stone (whose biography of the artist will be published early in 1961) have made ample use of his letters. What is surprising is that both in Italy and abroad, Michelangelo's letters have not been studied as fully as they deserve, and that as yet there is no complete English translation of his letters other than my own unpublished version. (pp. 5-13)

Charles Speroni, "Michelangelo's Letters," in Italian Quarterly, *Vol. IV, No. 15. Fall, 1960, pp. 3-29.*

GLAUCO CAMBON   (essay date 1962)

[*In the following excerpt, Cambon relates Michelangelo's work in the visual arts to his achievement as a poet.*]

As Joseph Tusiani has remarked in the introduction to his complete translation of Michelangelo's verse, the frequent roughness of diction is likely to enhance rather than impair the versatile artist's poetry [see excerpt dated 1959]. The sculptor's chisel makes itself felt in that roughness no less than in the "unfinished" *Captives,* and that is where the smoothness of Petrarchan convention is broken by the sharp edge of a rugged style which makes Michelangelo an Italian Metaphysical, a forerunner of John Donne and Andrew Marvell.

It is only natural to expect this kind of stylistic behavior signally in the poems which take their cue from the art of sculpture. Rather than the inherited elegance of formalized lyricism common to many Renaissance versifiers, we find here the transposed experience of wrestling with the reluctant medium of stone, to which Michelangelo bore the same fierce love Dante expressed for his tameless language when he said that " . . . a risponder la materia è sorda." The "deafness" or opacity of matter is what provokes the artist to his strongest performance, whether in words or stone; and when Michelangelo talks of this, he is always memorable. The experience is so seminal to him that it will recur again and again.

Thus Sonnet XIV, Sonnet XV and the madrigal **"Sì come per levar, Donna, si pone"** (numbered LXXXIV by Ceriello) all develop the concrete image of a block of stone to be hewn into a life-like shape, but in such a way as to make it a metaphor of the soul's rebirth from the grossness of flesh through purifying love, thereby fusing the personal experience of the craftsman with the Platonic idea of form and maieutic. In Sonnet XV it is the artist who strives unsuccessfully to draw the imaged good from the person of his beloved Vittoria Colonna, whose divine haughtiness (*altera e diva*) and hardness (*durezza*) parallel the imperviousness of the monolith defiantly awaiting the assault of his chisel:

Non ha l'ottimo artista alcun concetto
Ch'un marmo solo in sé non circoscriva
Col suo soverchio, e solo a quello arriva
La man che ubbidisce all 'intelletto.

Il mal ch'io fuggo e 'l ben ch'io mi prometto,
In te, Donna leggiadra, altera e diva,
Tal si nasconde; e perch 'io più non viva,
Contraria ho l'arte al disiato effetto.

[The best artist has no image in mind
That one marble block will not circumscribe
With its excess part: and it is only to be attained
By the hand which obeys the intellect.

The evil I flee and the good I strive for,
Just in that way, O fair Lady haughty and divine,

Are hidden in you; and so that I may no longer live
My art refuses the desired effect.]

The verb *circoscrivere* (to circumscribe), always basic in Michelangelo as a comparison with Sonnets XXXIV and XLII will show, reverberates on *si nasconde* (hides) five lines below to emphasize the maieutic act of bringing forth the hidden form from an enveloping, and fiercely resistant sheath; there is something stony in the beautiful lady's impenetrability which defeats her lover's effort, causing him to burn himself to death, and there is something feminine in the marble block which contains the potential shape to be hewn out by the sculptor's virility. The whole poem dramatizes, in terms of two such different experiences as art and love, the crucial passage of form from latency to actuality. Since the analogy by which the poet unifies his twofold experience is counterpointed by a symmetric contrast of hard-won artistic success with utter failure in love, and of a transition from idea to reality with the reverse transition from visible existence to invisible spirit, we can consider the whole sonnet an extended metaphysical conceit.

Its archetypal value shines out more vividly if we think of Sonnet XLII, which likens the enveloping protection of the house to the sheltered fruitfulness of the womb, Day to fiercely destructive masculinity and Night to the creative female principle, so much superior because " . . . l'ombra sol a piantar l'uomo serve." (only in darkness can man be sowed). The first three lines of this sonnet exhibit a telling variation on the initial motif and wording of Sonnet XV:

Ogni van chiuso, ogni coperto loco,
Quantunque ogni materia circoscrive,
Serba la notte, quando il giorno vive, . . .

[Each closed room, each sheltered place,
Whatever is by matter circumscribed,
Preserves night during daylight's fierce life . . .]

The *materia* here, as sensitized by progenitive imagery of the context, clearly evokes the related words *matrix* and *mater,* which denote indeed a "circumscribing" function par excellence; and the focal use of *circoscrivere* reflects back on the earlier poem, where this verb by itself may be said to create the image of a stone womb. Instead of constructing his form, Michelangelo reaches inward for the latent archetype.

But in the two versions of Sonnet XIV it is Vittoria who works maieutically on our artist, and he becomes her child as well as the provisional model for the finished statue she will make of him. Thus the elevating influence a long Platonic tradition in love poetry had attributed to woman, from Dolce Stil Nuovo to the Renaissance, is here envisaged in utterly unconventional terms by a threefold conceit: the model stands to the statue as old Adam (*primo parto,* first birth) to new Adam (*pietra viva,* living stone, in Version I, *dà vita ai sassi,* gives life to stones, in Version 2, *da voi rinasce po',* from you to be then reborn, ibidem); and this rebirth is what Michelangelo has undergone at the hand of Vittoria, who has been to him both a second mother and a chiseler in endeavoring to raise him above his original stature:

Simil di me; model di poca stima
Mio parto fu, per cosa alta e perfetta
Da voi rinascer po', Donna alta e degna.

[The same with me; a model of no account
Was my original birth, and to become lofty and perfect

I had then to be reborn from you, o high and worthy Lady.]

The artist's faith in his own power to eternize both his beloved and himself in a marble likeness which will survive its creator asserts itself, instead, in Sonnet XVII:

> Com'esser, Donna, può quel ch'alcun vede
> Per lunga esperienza, che più dura
> L'immagin viva in pietra alpestra e dura,
> Che 'l suo fattor, che gli anni in cener riede?
>
> La causa all 'effetto inclina e cede,
> Onde dall'arte è vinta la natura.
> I' 'l so che 'l provo in la bella scultura, . . .
>
> [How can it be, Lady, what everybody sees
> Through long experience, that more endures
> The life-like image in hard mountain stone
> Than its own maker, whom years reduce to ash?
>
> The cause, overwhelmed, yields to its own effect,
> So that nature is conquered by art.
> I know it, who prove it in delectable sculpture . . .]

The identic rhyme between *dura* as a verb (lasts, endures) and *dura* as an adjective (hard) is a telling etymological wordplay based on an awareness of the positive quality of the sculptor's indocile material, which insures endurance for the living form; we find the same metaphoric linkage heightened to identity in Sonnet XXXIV:

> E se 'n fornace dura, estate e verno
> Vince, e 'n più pregio che prima s'ascrive,
> Dunque, s'i' vivo, fatto fumo e polve,
> Eterno ben sarò, s'induro al foco; . . .
>
> [And if it endures the furnace, it will outlast
> Summer and winter, and acquire greater worth . . .
>
> Then, if I live though turned to smoke and dust,
> I shall eternal be, if fire hardens me; . . .]

And in the madrigal to Vittoria we have again the *pietra alpestra e dura* (hard mountain stone) from which a living image (*viva figura*) has to be drawn by the chisel's work; what the sculptor thus does to his resistant material, his lady alone will be able to do to him, since she alone has the strength to draw (*levare*) his pure self, his invisible form, from the cumbersome flesh:

> Sì come per levar, Donna, si pone
> In pietra alpestra e dura
> Una viva figura,
> Che là più cresce, u' più la pietra scema,
> Tal alcun'opre buone,
> Per l'alma, che pur trema,
> Cela il soverchio della propria carne
> Con inculta sua cruda e dura scorza.
> Tu pur dalle mie streme
> Parti puo' sol levarne,
> Ch'in me non è di me voler né forza.
>
> [Just as by sheer subtraction, Lady, one puts
> Into a hard mountain rock
> A life-like shape
> Which grows there most, where most the stone is dwindling,
> Just so the few good works
> That spell salvation for the trembling soul
> Are hidden by the excess of one's own flesh
> With its unworked, gross and hard shell.
> You alone from my outermost
> Part can thus unsheathe me,

For on my own self I have myself no power.]

This poem, thematically close to Sonnet XIV, has the exactitude and finality of great art. Once again, the equation between stone and flesh, artist and regenerating lady, life-like shape and invisible soul, aesthetic creation and the operation of love, affords the highest tension within a rigorous geometry of images. The initial antithesis of *levar* (to take away) and *si pone* (puts in) is charged with the whole meaning of Michelangelo's effort as a sculptor. He has to bring forth the figure latent in the marble block, but he can only do so by eliminating the excess matter: the potential shape can be made actual at the price of chipping off the redundant parts of the encasing stone, and in this process the figure itself will proportionally *grow* (cresce) as the stone *dwindles* (scema). The verb "cresce" acquires from the epithet *living* of "viva figura" an organic quality of growth which enhances the magic illusion of art.

The reiterated antithesis (*levar . . . si pone, cresce . . . scema*) brings home the paradox of creation, that only through the negative can the true positive be attained; and in the first line the exalted lady ("Donna") occupies, syntactically as well as spiritually, the position of mediator between the two contrary phases. When in the second part of the poem the artist himself becomes in his turn the raw material for his lady's reshaping spirit, the negative verb *levare* reappears, but resolved in its affirmative implications: to raise, to elevate, to deliver, to unsheathe. Dante in *Par.* I uses this verb in the same heightened way when he describes as "mi levasti" the action by which the Divine Power made him light (Latin *levis*) enough to *lift* him into the sky, away from the physical and moral pull of sin-burdened earth. Another striking affinity to such archetypal usage would clearly be that much quoted ending of Goethe's *Faust*, which makes the Eternal Feminine (*das Ewig Weibliche*) tirelessly elevate us through its attraction (*zieht uns hinan*).

Since Vittoria as a sculptress of the soul is really maieutic to Michelangelo as he was maieutic to the stonebound form, we can even read in "levare" an obstetric overtone, for *levatrice* after all means "midwife" and a metaphoric "delivery" is in question. Conversion of negativity into the highest positive through subtraction of matter: this is the structural conceit from which the whole poem arises just as the Pietà Rondanini took ascetically shape from within its towering monolith.

In Michelangelo's language, *levare* is akin to *trarre,* another sculptural-maieutic term to be found in several sonnets, and ideally translatable into Goethe's *hinanziehen,* or at least *herausziehen.* Sonnet XV for instance ends with the line: "non sappia, ardendo, trarne altro che morte" (consumed by fire, I can only draw death from it) where *trarre* equals "to extract", but sculpturally heightened in the context by the initial reference to the marble block from which the mallet will release the implicit shape by removing whatever is "soverchio" (superfluous). Then we have Sonnet XXXIV ("Sì amico al freddo sasso è 'l foco interno," "so friendly to the cold stone is its inner fire"), one of the most striking, where *trarre* is said at first literally, of the spark drawn by attrition from the stone, and after that metaphorically, of the poet who may be "extracted, brought forth, delivered" from himself by his own inner fire. *Trarre* here has to do with the *levare* of the madrigal just discussed, and also with the *attraction* exercised upon Michelangelo's soul by his hermetic lady's power.

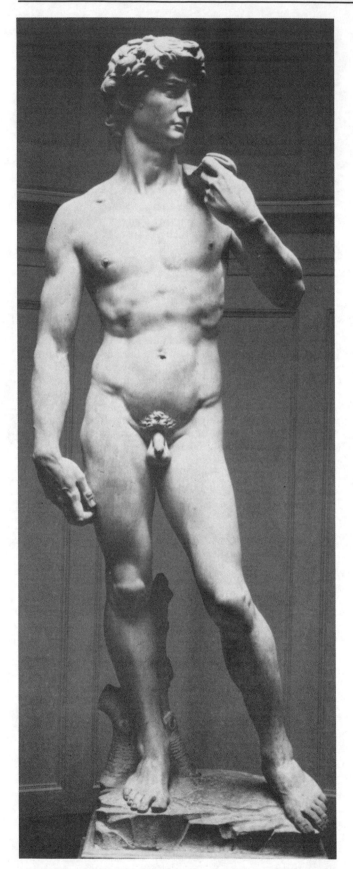

Michelangelo's colossal David, *sculpted between 1501 and 1504.*

A delightful surprise meets us in the last line, "Da tale oro e non ferro son percosso" ("By such gold, not iron, am I struck"), introducing Vittoria in a purely emblematic form, as the precious metal that strikes the consuming-renewing fire out of his own metaphoric stone. One kind of hardness— that of the sin-ridden soul—is thereby melted by the fire which "lo circonscrive", just as limestone is melted in the kiln, only to bring about another (and transparent) kind of hardness: that of the fire-tempered spirit, ready for eternity. Up to the last line, the spiritual event seemed to take place only within Michelangelo's own self; the oblique reference to his lady in the last line redirects our perception by making her finally appear as the elicitor of his higher powers. These, imagined in Michelangelo's favorite symbol of the fire, are both destructive and creative, and thus the conceit of a phoe-nix-soul tempered by hellfire to rise to heaven,

> Come purgata, infra l'altre e dive
> Alma nel ciel tornasse da l'inferno,

> > [As if a soul were to return from hell, purified, into the company of the saintly ones.]

has its demonic appropriateness.

If Vittoria Colonna can be spark-striking metal to our artist's ideal flint, we need not founder in astonishment when the em-blem-sonnet written in 1547 on her death (numbered LXI by Symonds) identifies her, on account of her soul-shaping action, with the sculptor's hammer. The master fashioner of durable forms expected to be fashioned by her ethereal hammer, and is now left "unfinished" by her death, like one of his own *Captives:*

> Se 'l mio rozzo martello i duri sassi
> Forma d'uman aspetto, or questo or quello,
> Dal ministro, che 'l guida, iscorge e tiello,
> Prendendo il moto, va con gli altrui passi.

> Ma quel divin, che in cielo alberga e stassi,
> Altro, e sé più, col proprio andar fa bello;
> E se nessun martel senza martello
> Sì può far, da quel vivo ogni altro fassi.

> E perché 'l colpo è di valor più pieno
> Quant'alza più se stesso alla fucina,
> Sopra 'l mio, questo al ciel n'è gito a volo.

> Onde a me, non finito, verrà meno,
> S'or non gli dà la fabbrica divina
> Aiuto a farlo, ch'al mondo era solo.

> > [If my rough hammer hews the hard rocks into sundry human shapes, it takes its motion from the ministering hand, which holds, wields and guides it, so that it moves with alien steps.

> > But the divine one, which permanently dwells in heaven, with its own movement beautifies others, and itself even more; and if no hammer can be made without a hammer, from that living one any other takes shape.

> > And since a hammer stroke is the more powerful the higher it rises above the anvil, this one hammer rising above mine has flown to heaven.

> > Hence it will fail me in my unfinished state, unless the divine workshop helps it now in its task, for it was the only one of its kind in this world.]

The baroque audacity of that conceit, by which Vittoria's rise to heaven is equated with the infinite rise of a hammer from its unaccomplished work, is a match for the wildest flights of Marino, Quarles or Crashaw. Somehow we are left in suspense, waiting for the last inconceivable blow of that heaven-hammer, which will be a lightning of death and transfiguration—what else? For only in death perhaps our lonely artist will shed his residual "soverchio" and acquire himself the purified spiritual shape he had managed to impart to so much marble. (pp. 155-63)

Glauco Cambon, "Sculptural Form as Metaphysical Conceit in Michelangelo's Verse," in The Sewanee Review, *Vol. LXX, No. 1, Winter, 1962, pp. 155-63.*

JOHN ARTHOS (essay date 1963)

[*In the following excerpt, Arthos explores the underlying concepts of artistic and divine creation in Michelangelo's poetry.*]

In his own time it was said that Michelangelo's work rivalled God's, and his force and authority are still overpowering. Sometimes he hardly seems to care about beauty, but the *terribilità,* the power and glory—this is everywhere his touch and his sign.

In what he has written he never speaks of this—what he does speak of is the work of the artist and the urgency and aspiration of love. His poems are as much a philosophy of art as they are the praise of anything, or anyone, and from them one would gather that his whole life was ridden with the torment of ambition, with the passion to achieve not merely the grandiose and monumental but the divine, as if indeed he did mean to rival God. A contemporary reported, one supposes rather faithfully, that he said substantially that: 'This sort of painting is a great undertaking', proceeded Michelangelo;

> in order to imitate to some extent the venerable image of our Lord it is not sufficient merely to be a great master in painting and very wise, but I think it is necessary for the painter to be very good in his mode of life, or even, if such were possible, a saint, so that the Holy-Spirit may inspire his intellect . . . And even in the Old Testament God the Father wished that those who only had to ornament and paint the *arca foederis* should be masters not merely excellent and great, but also touched by His grace and wisdom, God saying to Moses that He would imbue them with the knowledge and intelligence of His spirit so that they might invent and do everything that He could invent and do . . . Frequently images badly painted distract and cause devotion to be lost, at least in those who possess little; and, on the contrary, those that are divinely painted provoke and lead even those who are little devout and but little inclined to worship to contemplation and tears, and by their grave aspect imbue them with reverence and fear.

In the Middle Ages there was an aphorism that the inspiration of the Holy Ghost brought peace, and the Muses fury. The dove and the raven became the opposing symbols of Christian and pagan art. The Creation of Adam in the Sistine Chapel has the freshness of the Earthly Paradise and perhaps even of the first cantos of the *Paradiso* although it may not express the serenity of 'e la sua volontade è nostra pace'. But in the turmoil of the rest of the great panel there is the sublimity of passion and suffering and little enough of the peace of God. The inspiration is twofold. Now the claim of one subdues the other, and always the claim is final.

Michelangelo developed a philosophy of art that was as coherent as Dante's, and the philosophy was always part of the subject of his art. In it he sought out the authority for his ambitions, and he attempted to unite his perfect orthodoxy with the convictions of the nature of reality his Neo-Platonism certified. The *terribilità* is in part his greatness, and in part the strength of his effort to reconcile Christian and pagan truth. His poetry tells us much that helps characterize all his achievements, and it may help us determine to what degree his greatest works in their *terribilità* deserve to be thought of as sublime.

That the achievement is of the greatest order is certain. That Michelangelo's religion as well as his Neo-Platonism affects his work differently than Dante's is equally evident, as evident as the difference between his system of ideas and that of Longinus. To what degree these differences indicate a different kind of excellence is determined, I think, by the very fact that Michelangelo was inextricably committed to philosophy as such.

The Neo-Platonism of the Renaissance is generally characterized by irresponsibility, it too often accepts conclusions that are more accountable to a suffused eroticism than to reason. It begins, as all Platonism, in the most serious engagements of deductive philosophy, and it is consequently led into comprehensive and in many instances rewarding systematizing. But even at its best—in Pico and Ficino and Bruno—too often the love of truth is taken as the truth itself, and much turns out to be a mere ringing of changes on the theme of self-indulgence, an elaborate complication of egotism presented as epistemology and metaphysics.

However ridiculous and enervating at its worst, one must always take account of its value—the perfected zeal for a beautiful if not a holy life, and an enthusiasm that enthralled one noble spirit after another—Cosimo, Lorenzo, Botticelli, Michelangelo—the list never ends. And more than its influence upon lives, one must exalt its power to determine and create styles of expression for the most ambitious artists, and to inspire particular works of superlative quality—the New Sagresty in San Lorenzo, the Primavera, the Virgin of the Rocks. What Garin says of Ficino must be said of the movement, it changed the tone of religion and morality in the sixteenth and seventeenth centuries and it renewed and redefined the sense of the beauty of the inner life.

As philosophy it can be used to support religion and religiousness, and Christianity itself, but, uncontrolled, it would supplant the uniquely Christian dogmas. Sooner or later it promises immortality for certain if not all souls independently of the acts of a Creator who, incarnate as a man, offers the means of external felicity; and in the reverse, the distinctive exigencies of Christian dogma cannot tolerate the Platonists' arrogance. . . . (pp. 50-2)

Michelangelo seems to have lived at the crisis of highest tension in the contrast. His work shows that from his earliest days his mind had been molded by the habits, the idiom, the tenor and limitations of the Neo-Platonic cult, and it is at the same time equally certain that from the beginning to the end of his anguish-ridden life he preserved the strictest and most passionate orthodoxy, a conservatism in faith and observance to which the Counter-Reform presented no stress even of the slightest novelty. In drawing and in sculpture he made relatively few representations of the Crucifixion, and yet there is hardly any work of his whose subject is not intrinsically the fact and nature of it, the divine incarnated, mangled and humiliated, glorious and wasted and merciful. It is as if he thought of nothing else. The lines might have been spoken at almost every moment of his life.

> Né pinger né scolpir fie più che quieti
> l'anima, volta a quell 'amor divino
> c'aperse, a prender noi, 'n croce le braccia.

> Painting nor sculpture now can lull to rest
> My soul that turns to His great love on high
> Whose arms to clasp us on the cross were spread.

The Resurrection, which he seldom represents, and, I think, never mentions in his verse, is, so to speak, in the offing. Sometimes it seems rather far distant from his immediate subject, sometimes quite close. A Neo-Platonist whose reasonings were less complicated would have had little difficulty in making it part of the background, in feeling, or in a detail of representation, and to have excluded it from the great wall paintings shows the extent of the preoccupation with the idea of the Crucifixion, the Sacrifice. But this is Michelangelo's form, as a Neo-Platonist and as a Christian—he will represent life up to the point of death, and death, and not the moment after: the conflict, the suffering, the sacrifice, all those images of the using up and devouring of life which he presents so fully, and egotistically, and beyond that the most he will do is to affirm, often in verse, and often in the Pietàs, the need of the Resurrected God and his faith in Him, but not the fact in itself. Even the Rondanini Pietà shows no abrogation of the faith though it seems to confront a life as horrible as Belsen—

> Già fur gli occhi nostri interi
> con la luce in ogni speco;
> or son voti, orrendi e neri . . .

> Once our eyes were full of light throughout the
> pupil; now they are empty, hideous and black—this
> is what time has done.

And wonderfully enough, in him it is also the faith of the Neo-Platonist—the faith of the pagan helps the Christian consolidate his strength.

A man who had seen Michelangelo working said that 'He went at the marble with such an impetus and fury as to make me believe that the entire work was going to pieces. With a single stroke he would split off morsels of three or four inches in thickness.' Cellini's comment was that 'he was often seized by many awesome furies that came over him as he worked', and one would judge this to be his temperament in everything he did. And in the poems one judges that the character of his love was much as the character of his approach to stone and paint and verse.

He himself speaks of the relationship between an artist and his material in terms that are parallel to those that describe the way of love:

> Se ben concetto ha la divina parte
> il volto e gli atti d'alcun, po' di quello
> doppio valor con breve e vil modello
> dà vita a' sassi, e non è forza d'arte.

> Né altrimenti in più rustiche carte,
> anz'una pronta man prenda 'l pennello,
> fra ' dotti ingegni il più accorto e bello
> pruova e rivede, e suo storie comparte.

> Simil di me model di poca istima

> mie parto fu, per cosa alta e prefetta
> da voi rinascer po', donna alta e degna.

> Se 'l poco accresce, e 'l mie superchio lima
> vostra mercé, qual penitenzia aspetta
> mie fiero ardor, se mi gastiga e 'nsegna?

> When that which is divine in us doth try
> To shape a face, both brain and hand unite
> To give, from a mere model frail and slight,
> Life to the stone by Art's free energy.

> Thus too before the painter dares to ply
> Paint-brush or canvas, he is sent to write
> Sketches on scraps of paper, and invite
> Wise minds to judge his figured history.

> So, born a model rude and mean to be
> Of my poor self, I gain a nobler birth,
> Lady, from you, you fountain of all worth!

> Each overplus and each deficiency
> You will make good. What penance then is due
> For my fierce heat, chastened and taught by you?
>
> (Symonds—*second reading*)

Such working of art and love, if not described as fury or the onset of demons, is nevertheless compared to the consuming of fire, at once a devouring and a purification:

> Sol pur col foco il fabbro il ferro stende
> al concetto suo caro e bel lavoro,
> né senza foco alcuno artista l'oro
> al sommo grado suo raffina e rende;

> né l'unica fenice sé riprende
> se non prim'arsa; ond'io, s'ardendo moro,
> spero più chiar resurger tra coloro
> che morte accresce e 'l tempo non offende.

> Del foco, di ch'i' parlo, ho gran ventura
> c'ancor per rinnovarmi abbi in me loco,
> sendo già quasi nel numer de' morti.

> O ver, s'al cielo ascende per natura,
> al suo elemento, e ch'io converso in foco
> sie, come fie che seco non mi porti?

> It is with fire that blacksmiths iron subdue
> (*translating a different first line*)
> Unto fair form, the image of their thought:
> Nor without fire hath any artist wrought
> Gold to its utmost purity of hue.

> Nay, nor the unmatched phœnix lives anew,
> Unless she burn: if then I am distraught
> By fire, I may to better life be brought
> Like those whom death restores nor years undo.

> The fire whereof I speak, is my great cheer;
> Such power it hath to renovate and raise
> Me who was almost numbered with the dead;

> And since by nature fire doth find its sphere
> Soaring aloft, and I am all ablaze,
> Heavenward with it my flight must needs be sped.

As any Neo-Platonist, and any Christian, he wants to assert the primacy of love, in God, in God the Creator, in the Created, and he has the need to assert of his own work that it shares in and derives from divinity. His thought will take many directions in supporting the analogy, and at times he will explore ideas that do more to confuse than certify it, but the intensity of his love, for the meaning of his art as for those he loves, the wholeness of the dedication, the concentration of his egotism, all require the reasoning that will justify the wholeness of the effort and the sacrifice of life to its effects. The affirmations that follow his commitment are almost obsessional. The act of loving, in every sphere, becomes an act either of engendering or conceiving, the life of the artist is a life of gestation. In love as in art, the lover loses himself in what he loves or makes; his gestation, his creation, is a dying to himself and a rebirth in another, a newly created and immortal life—in the Platonic way:

> model di poca istima
> mie parto fu, per cosa alta e prefetta
> da voi rinascer po', donna alta e degna.

> born of a model of little worth, I am reborn through you, O noble and virtuous Lady, through so lofty and perfect a thing.

Nevertheless, it is the purpose and the intention that he tries never to forget, however much the idea of travail absorbs him—all is hopefully for the sake of a new creation.

Longinus's idea that the poet and his readers, in a state of elevation, suppose for a while they are taking part in the creating processes of Nature itself seems more a figure of speech than a belief when one confronts it with Michelangelo's argument to demonstrate that the process of engendering in nature is also the process of the imagination itself in bringing its works into being.

In one of his greatest poems Michelangelo says that the labour of a lifetime finally resulted in an achievement that was true to his intention. And he says that what was such long travail with him was the same as the process with Nature herself who, after so many ages, fashioned 'you'. 'And as I look on your face', he said (I am paraphrasing), 'I do not know whether to be sad or joyful, seeing that it is at the end of my life that this perfection is attained—whether to be sad or joyful because this is the end; or whether to be sad at the sight of such perfection; or to be filled with joy at it.'

> Negli anni molti e nelle molte pruove,
> cercando, il saggio al buon concetto arriva
> d'un'immagine viva,
> vicino a morte, in pietra alpestra e dura;
> c'all'alte cose nuove
> tardi si viene, e poco poi si dura.
> Similmente natura,
> di tempo in tempo, d'uno in altro volto,
> s'al sommo, errando, di bellezza è giunta
> nel tuo divino, è vecchia, e de' perire:
> onde la tema, molto
> con la beltà congiunta,
> di stranio cibo pasce il gran desire;
> né so pensar né dire
> qual nuoca o giovi più, visto 'l tuo 'spetto,
> o 'l fin dell'universo o 'l gran diletto.

> After searching many years and after many trials, only when he is near death is the artist on the point of giving life, through rough, hard stone, to the lofty idea that is in his mind; for he comes late to new and lofty ideas and when but little of life remains to him. So nature, too, in its wanderings through time, passing from one countenance to another, comes finally to the making of thy face, the very perfection of beauty, but by then nature, too, is old and ready to die.

> This is why the fear of death, so closely bound to beauty, feeds my great yearning with strange food,

and, watching you, I neither know how to think or to say what gives me the greatest pleasure—the feeling of the approaching end of the world, or my great delight in the sight of you.

The artist who has arrived at the conception of a living image communicates its very life to the stone he is working with, just as Nature in her creation gives life to her children.

What is at issue is what Vasari speaks of in praising Donatello:

> For the Guild of Armourers, Donatello executed a most animated figure of St George, in his armour. The brightness of youthful beauty, generosity, and bravery shine forth in his face; his attitude gives evidence of a proud and terrible impetuosity; the character of the saint is indeed expressed most wonderfully, and life seems to move within that stone.

(pp. 52-8)

The idea of the artist as creator, by the terms of the Neo-Platonic paradox, is also the idea that creation is merely the discovery of the self. The love of God is identical with the love of self, and the process of creating, as of loving, is the same as the act of knowing. The fact that this is paradox absorbs Michelangelo quite as much as the doctrine it embodies.

Michelangelo so strongly felt the attraction of the beautiful that his mind and all his being seemed to move immediately to possess it. 'It was not only the beauty of human beings that he loved, he loved every beautiful thing, "con maraviglioso affetto".' And in what are reported to us as his own words:

> Whenever I see someone who possesses virtue, who displays an agile mind, who knows how to do or say something better than others, I am forced to fall in love with him.

As always with Michelangelo, philosophy could be used to support the authority of love, for it could be shown to lead to the love of God and to the love of God within the self. Arrogating to itself the quality of divinity, it would turn even defeat into victory. And religion also was brought to its support. There is an interesting letter which a certain Frate Lorenzo delle Colombe wrote to Michelangelo in 1516 in words that might have been the artist's own:

> Thou knowest that neither time nor place can put an end to love, least of all God's love; and more, too, love transforms one into the other, the lover into what he loves, and makes a mutual interpenetration of souls. And therefore, from the love I bear thee, being within thee, I penetrate thy inmost parts and I understand what thou art thinking and saying and writing . . . Let us love each other then, in the Lord, as we have done heretofore, and we shall know and understand all things, and truth itself, and we shall see it face to face, if we live well and as Christians. Meanwhile, prepare to sculpture within thy soul, with the hammer of good and virtuous works, the imprint of Christ who was crucified for us, all which should be done in faith and through faith inspired by holy charity . . .

This is indeed the old Platonic and Petrarchan doctrine in Christian terms, 'l'amante ne l'amato si transforme', the lover is transformed into the loved one. The idea is in the *Phaedrus,* and wherever there is the doctrine that where your heart is, there will your treasure be; it is in the Aristotelian psychology

Dante uses at almost every point where the sinner or the virtuous soul becomes transformed into the likeness of his adulation. But there is a particular bent to the idea in Michelangelo that is specially Petrarchan as well as religious, the changing of the lover into the very person of the beloved—'l'immedisimarsi dell'amante nella persona amata'.

F. M. Bongianni does better than the Freudians, I think, in referring this matter of the identification with the beloved to Michelangelo's religion. [In his 1935 *Rivista di Sintesi Letteraria* article "Sul travaglio religioso di Michelangelo," he] remarks, for example, that Michelangelo's love for Tommaso de' Cavalieri and Vittoria Colonna is for him a means of rediscovering the destiny of his own soul, even though, paradoxically, he speaks of it as a loss of his own identity in theirs.

> D'altrui pietoso e sol di sé spietato
> nasce un vil bruto, che con pena e doglia
> l'altrui man veste e la suo scorza spoglia
> e sol per morte si può dir ben nato.
>
> Così volesse al mie signor mie fato
> vestir suo viva di mie morta spoglia,
> che, come serpe al sasso si discoglia,
> pur per morte potria congiar mie stato.
>
> O fussi sol la mie l'irsuta pelle
> che, del suo pel contesta, fa tal gonna
> che con ventura stringe sì bel seno,
>
> ch'i' l'are' pure il giorno; o le pianelle
> che fanno a quel di lor basa e colonna,
> ch'i' pur ne porterei duo nevi almeno.

> Kind to the world, but to itself unkind,
> A worm is born, that dying noiselessly
> Despoils itself to clothe fair limbs, and be
> In its true worth by death alone divined.
>
> Oh, would that I might die, for her to find
> Raiment in my outworn mortality!
> That, changing like the snake, I might be free
> To cast the slough wherein I dwell confined!
>
> Nay, were it mine, that shaggy fleece that stays,
> Woven and wrought into a vestment fair,
> Around her beauteous bosom in such bliss!
>
> All through the days she'd clasp me! Would I were
> The shoes that bear her burden! When the ways
> Were wet with rain, her feet I then should kiss!

Michelangelo speaks of a worm becoming a butterfly and of a serpent's changing its skin as a preparation for the expression of his desire that his own skin should become the skin of his beloved. This is more than the Petrarchan metaphor, for it also signifies salvation: '. . . renewed through the experience of another's individuality, and all the while still most intimately conscious of his own being, the poet believes that the labour of his love promises to achieve that satisfaction, and indeed that masterpiece, that he despairs of in his present life and by the very fact of his individuality . . . We do not achieve our work as mere individuals engaged in serving our ordinary interests, but through serving the Good that joins us to itself.' Bongianni means to say that we are to think of all such ideas of metamorphosis as conversion.

What gives all this such extraordinary intensity is the actuality of the process as Michelangelo conceives it, the transformation of the body as well as of the soul. There is in the very idea an urgency that distinguishes Michelangelo's thought from all gentlemanly Neo-Platonizing, and even from the

most responsible Platonists. It may be true, as Garin says, that Ficino's Platonism is an elaborate answer to a despair he cannot endure, and that for him therefore beauty is also a means of conversion, a conversion of the soul to divine existence. But the despair that is part and parcel of Michelangelo's faith I think is more appropriately to be compared with Pascal's than Ficino's. In at once seeking and fleeing solitude he seeks and flees annihilation as well as God. As Bongianni says, he thinks of his life as part of the history of humanity, always awaiting the Apocalypse that will never come because it is outside history. The Apocalypse and the Resurrection.

But the poems do not always express the violence and desperation of the desire, sometimes there is something much more like peace, as if there were at least a sight of fulfilment. So it is, I think, in the beautiful and moving sonnet in which the poet imagines he succeeds in seeing with the beloved's eyes:

> Veggio co' be' vostr'occhi un dolce lume
> che co' mie ciechi già veder non posso;
> porto co' vostri piedi un pondo addosso,
> che de' mie zoppi non è già costume.
>
> Volo con le vostr'ale senza piume;
> col vostro ingegno al ciel sempre son mosso;
> dal vostro arbitrio son pallido e rosso,
> freddo al sol, caldo alle più fredde brume.
>
> Nel voler vostro è sol la voglia mia,
> i miei pensier nel vostro cor si fanno,
> nel vostro fiato son le mie parole.
>
> Come luna da sé sol par ch'io sia,
> ché gli occhi nostri in ciel veder non sanno
> se non quel tanto che n'accende il sole.

> With your fair eyes a charming light I see,
> For which my own blind eyes would peer in vain;
> Stayed by your feet the burden I sustain
> Which my lame feet find all too strong for me;
>
> Wingless upon your pinions forth I fly;
> Heavenward your spirit stirreth me to strain;
> E'en as you will I blush and blanch again,
> Freeze in the sun, burn 'neath a frosty sky.
>
> Your will includes and is the lord of mine;
> Life to my thoughts within your heart is given;
> My words begin to breathe upon your breath:
>
> Like to the moon am I, that cannot shine
> Alone; for lo! our eyes see nought in heaven
> Save what the living sun illumineth.

The idea of becoming what one loves, of reaching forth to take on another's identity, is a significant paradox for the Neo-Platonists, committed as they also are to the cultivation of the inner self, to finding God and truth within themselves, and in their very psychology of the imagination committed to adoring the image that is within them:

> Amore è un concetto di bellezza
> immaginata o vista dentro al core,
> amica di virtute e gentilezza.
>
>> Love is an idea of beauty, imagined or seen within
>> the heart, friend to virtue and nobility.

Looking into the eyes of the beloved, Michelangelo said he found perfect peace, 'intera pace'; and in the same breath, that he felt love in the very likeness of his own soul, deep within and all holy

dentro, ov'ogni mal dispiace,
chi d'amor l'alma a sé simil m'assale.

> Within, where every impure thought displeases, I
> beheld Him who clothes my soul with the love that
> makes it like unto Him.

The conceit and the paradox are meant to be a solution to explain how it is one may love another than oneself.

And there were, one supposes, rare instants where the peace, the attainment of what he strove for so furiously, came beneficently, seeking him out, and leaving him with the conviction that he had come to rest in truth itself.

In a certain fragment Michelangelo wrote of his original sight of absolute beauty, speaking of it as something the soul received through the eyes. (He may be saying that this beauty first appeared to him as he looked at his beloved, but this is not the necessary condition of the statement.) The power of the beauty was such that the image of it that was formed in his mind grew to such brightness it quite overpowered the soul.

The next thought of the fragment prepares for a conclusion that we cannot now certainly anticipate: the god of love saw his amazement and smiled; and then the god returned (I suppose, from occasioning this event) to the side of the lover, meaning to see to it that the lover should not undo what had been effected.

The complexity of possibilities is now such that one hardly knows who is on whose side—the lover's, love, beauty, the soul, but there seems to be an implication that the soul in partnership with love possesses an excellence that cannot tolerate ravishment even by absolute beauty:

> Mentre c'alla beltà ch'i' vidi in prima
> appresso l'alma, che per gli occhi vede,
> l'immagin dentro cresce, e quella cede
> quasi vilmente e senza alcuna stima.
>
> Amor, c'adopra ogni suo ingegno e lima,
> perch'io non tronchi 'l fil ritorna e riede.

In saying that the image can grow until it takes possession of all one's being, the poet seems to be rejecting the authority of the imagination, and to insist upon the nobility of other phases of his life, perhaps in particular, the necessary relation of the soul to truth and goodness, and thus is insisting on the authority of reason and virtue. The final emphasis is on the marriage of the mind with truth.

The idea of the artist as creator naturally leads to the consideration of the distinctions that are to be made between what goes on within the mind and what goes on outside. In one aspect Michelangelo approaches the problem whenever he opposes *concetto* and *imagine* on the one side—the glorious or, as the case may be, blinding ideal itself—and on the other, that which has a concrete and living existence in the mind of the beholder of the ideal, its image.

He uses the same word for the image within his mind and the representations of his painting and sculpture, and it does not seem that he considers there to be a radical difference in the nature of the two kinds of image. He is as much absorbed in the mystery of his imagination as in that of art, although the latter as a subject for meditation often leads him into more elaborate analysis. The analogy of the artist with the creating God in particular brings out his fullest and clearest state-ments as he tries to show the likeness of the creation that takes place in the mind with that outside it. Michelangelo is consistent in maintaining that the key factor is the operation of divine power, and he will even speak of it as 'grace', in painting and in sculpture as well as in the forming of the image in the mind:

> Se 'l mie rozzo martello i duri sassi
> forma d'uman aspetto or questo or quello,
> dal ministro che 'l guida, iscorge e tiello,
> prendendo il moto, va con gli altrui passi.
>
> Ma quel divin che in cielo alberga e stassi,
> altri, e sé più, col propio andar fa bello;
> e se nessun martel senza martello
> si può far, da quel vivo ogni altro fassi.

> When my rude hammer to the stubborn stone
> Gives human shape, now that, now this, at will,
> Following his hand who wields and guides it still,
> It moves upon another's feet alone:
>
> But that which dwells in heaven, the world doth fill
> With beauty by pure motions of its own;
> And since tools fashion tools which else were none,
> Its life makes all that lives with living skill.

The power of the artist at another place is spoken of as deriving from the artist's contemplation of heavenly beauty, a power which is itself inadequate without grace:

> Per fido esemplo alla mia vocazione
> nel parto mi fu data la bellezza,
> che d'ambo l'arti m'è lucerna e specchio.
> S'altro si pensa, è falsa opinione.
> Questo sol l'occhio porta a quella altezza
> c'a pingere e scolpir qui m'apparecchio.
>
> S'e' giudizi temerari e sciocchi
> al senso tiran la beltà, che muove
> e porta al cielo ogni intelletto sano,
> dal mortale al divin non vanno gli occhi
> infermi, e fermi sempre pur là d'ove
> ascender senza grazia è pensier vano.

> The beauty that gives me light and is the model of
> both the arts I practise was given me at birth as the
> faithful guide for my vocation. If anyone thinks
> otherwise of my work he is wrong, for it is beauty
> alone that can raise the sight to those lofty concep-
> tions that I labour to paint and carve. If bold, fool-
> ish men think that beauty, which moves every sane
> intellect and transports it to heaven itself, is born
> of the senses, let them know that our weak vision
> cannot of itself ascend from the mortal to the di-
> vine, but remains always below. For it is vain to
> think that it can be raised without the help of grace.

Michelangelo is here saying that beauty exists in potentiality in the inmost spirit and after that in the actualization of the artist's work—beauty which comes to be part of the soul, is made concrete there, as an image, and later it is embodied in things that can be seen and touched and heard. And all this, depending upon the mind's being carried up to heaven, would come about, and no fulfilment of the desire to create would be granted—indeed the thought itself would be vain—if it were not that grace permitted the ascent.

He might have left it at this, using the idea of grace as a mere metaphor for light, or taking up with any of the other devices of the Neo-Platonists that ascribe divinity to the processes of the mind. But in the very sonnet in which he speaks of his mallet as being guided by a divine hand, he presents a Christian idea that goes beyond anything a Platonic theory would assert, where he declares that an angel, and no mere spirit, but the angelic being of a once mortal person, Vittoria Colonna, is the instrument of God's use of him. In almost anyone else one would speak of this as preciosity, but here the very particularity of the Christian idea relates the idea of creation by an artist to the most mysterious phase of all in the theory of creation, the creating of the individual and the concrete.

> E perché 'l colpo è di valor più pieno
> quant'alza più se stesso alla fucina,
> sopra 'l mie questo al ciel n'è gito a volo.
>
> Onde a me non finito verrà meno,
> s'or non gli dà la fabbrica divina
> aiuto a farlo, c'al mondo era solo.
>
> Now, for that every stroke excels the more
> The higher at the forge it doth ascend,
> Her soul that fashioned mine hath sought the skies:
>
> Wherefore unfinished I must meet my end,
> If God, the great artificer, denies
> That aid which was unique on earth before.

The claim to create as God does, giving life, and even fashioning individuals, is one thing if it is thought to be within the comprehension and justification of philosophy, but it is quite another when it includes the claim of being able to create what is corporal and unique. It is the particular work of art, at the particular time of its creation, that is taken as the demonstration of the justice of the analogy with God, but the claim falters badly when the artist claims that the material of his work—the stone, words, colour—are also his creation. And yet there is no part of the aspiration Michelangelo clings to more tenaciously.

He was supported in this, of course, by his temperament. It was well remarked [by Arturo Farinelli in *Michelangelo e Dante* (1918)] that 'his whole soul drew whatever was bodily and corporal to it as to its own'. One might well believe that it is this disposition that caused him to put aside the reasoning of Ficino and Diacceto, his own teacher, whereby one conceived of love as a series of steps leading to the ultimate absorption: 'for this he substituted the idea of the closest relationship between lover and loved one, a relationship so close it would itself be conceived of as the hammer that gave new form to the substance, otherwise inert, of the lover'. This would be part and parcel of his famous *senso delle cose* which as much as anything accounts for the peculiar characteristics of his language. And it is this trait that has been said to explain how he can substitute the figure of the angel, who was Vittoria Colonna, for the Platonic schematization. He went contrary to the dominant expression of the problem in Neo-Platonism by this very concreteness, not forgetting or suppressing in the process of abstraction the reality of the individual, whose peculiar function it could be, in being loved, to transform the lover. And it is this trait, signally defined in the sonnet 'se 'l mie rozzo martello', that helps provide the interpretation for his most famous and possibly most profound statement on the nature of artistic and divine creation.

> Non ha l'ottimo artista alcun concetto
> c'un marmo solo in sé non circonscriva
> col suo superchio, e solo a quello arriva
> al man che ubbidisce all'intelletto.
>
> Il mal ch'io fuggo, e 'l ben ch'io mi prometto,
> in te, donna leggiadra, altera e diva,

> tal si nasconde; e perch'io più non viva,
> contraria ho l'arte al disïato effetto.
>
> Amor dunque non ha, né tua beltate
> o durezza o fortuna o gran disdegno
> del mio mal colpa, o mio destino o sorte;
>
> se dentro del tuo cor morte e pietate
> porti in un tempo, e che 'l mio basso ingegno
> non sappia, ardendo, trarne altro che morte.
>
> The best of artists hath no thought to show
> Which the rough stone in its superfluous shell
> Doth not include: to break the marble spell
> Is all the hand that serves the brain can do.
>
> The ill I shun, the good I seek, even so
> In thee, fair lady, proud, ineffable,
> Lies hidden: but the art I wield so well
> Works adverse to my wish, and lays me low.
>
> Therefore not love, nor thy transcendent face,
> Nor cruelty, nor fortune, nor disdain,
> Cause my mischance, nor fate, nor destiny;
>
> Since in thy heart thou carriest death and grace
> Enclosed together, and my worthless brain
> Can draw forth only death to feed on me.

The gist of the poem is that even the best artist is dedicated to failure, and failure means death. Neither the work of his making—the obedience of the hand to the mind, like the obedience of God's hand to His mind—nor the love of duty, will secure the immortality he so much desires. The effort of his life works to conflicting ends—he aspires to eternal life even when he is making matter into beauty, the beauty does not give him satisfaction, and the desire that drives him to create it subsides before the greater desire to unite himself with God.

He is thus as it were committed to failure, a failure that is rooted in his nature, and he asks to be pardoned. God can pardon him, and so also can a living saint, Vittoria Colonna, his friend, in her love and pity.

So much, I think, is the apparent beginning to the complexity of the thought in this poem, and only the beginning. The main point is the idea of failure, and if one asks if there is some explanation for its necessity, I think the answer that is implied is that the work of the artist does not participate fully in the harmony of ideas that are latent in the material itself with which he works. Benedetto Varchi insisted that the *concetto* of the first line was to be defined in Aristotle's terms as 'the active cause, the form that exists in the soul of the artist . . . Art is nothing other than the form, that is, the model of the art object existing in the soul, which is to say, the imagination of the artist, and this form or model is the principal agent in the forming of the object' [see excerpt by Varchi dated 1547]. (pp. 61-73)

[Michelangelo] speaks of Vittoria Colonna in words that might be beautifully applied to the Virgin—'leggiadra, altera e diva'—this beautiful lady all purity and fire, and the connection with what has gone before seems to be that just as in stone there is a truth he seeks and that seeks him, so in this mortal woman there is a parallel relation. But here, as a saint and as a woman, who inspires and also forgives, and more than that, who confers the last gift, the fulfilment of his aspiration, she has the very power of Christ, mercy and redemption.

This way of combining the ideal with the real, the spiritual with the mortal, Michelangelo speaks of as the way of chaste love. The terms he uses are important. It seems that the passions for Vittoria Colonna and for Tommaso de' Cavalieri are of the same intensity as those for his father and brothers, where also he clings to the flesh as to life itself:

> L'un m'era frate, e tu padre di noi;
> l'amore a quello, a te l'obrigo strigne:
> non so qual pena più mi stringa o nòi . . .
>
> Nostro intelletto dalla carne inferma
> è tanto oppresso, che 'l morir piu spiace
> quanto più 'l falso persuaso afferma.

> > One was brother to me, and you, our father; love bound me to him, duty to you. I do not know which burden afflicts or troubles me more . . . Our intellect is so much oppressed by our frail flesh that death displeases by so much the more as the flesh draws us to what is false.

Condivi remembered hearing Michelangelo say that nothing grieved him so much after Vittoria Colonna passed away from this life than that he did not kiss her on the brow or face as he did kiss her hand [see excerpt dated 1553].

What all this has to do with sexuality I do not think anyone can say, and certainly Adrian Stokes in his most discerning analysis in Freudian terms rejects all observations of a simple kind. Just as in the sonnet to Tommaso de' Cavalieri, where one feels that this is as much in the tone of a Christian offering his soul to God as it is a poem of friendship, one insists that the power and integrity of the thought, the dignity and nobility of the passion, are such that the reader is required to accept the religious affirmations seriously:

> Tu sa' ch'i' so, signor mie, che tu sai
> ch'i vengo per goderti più da presso,
> e sai ch'i so che tu sa' ch'i' son desso:
> a che più indugio a salutarci omai?
>
> Se vera è la speranza che mi dai,
> se vero è 'l gran desio che m'è concesso,
> rompasi il mur fra l'uno e l'altra messo,
> ché doppia forza hann' i celati guai.
>
> S'i' amo sol di tc, signor mic caro,
> quel che di te più ami, non ti sdegni,
> che l'un dell'altro spirto s'innamora.
>
> Quel che nel tuo bel volto bramo e 'mparo
> e mal compres' è dagli umani ingegni,
> chi 'l vuol saper convien che prima mora.

> > Thou knowest, love, I know that thou dost know
> > That I am here more near to thee to be,
> > And knowest that I know thou knowest me:
> > What means it then that we are sundered so?
> >
> > If they are true, these hopes that from thee flow,
> > If it is real, this sweet expectancy,
> > Break down the wall that stands 'twixt me and thee;
> > For pain in prison pent hath double woe.
> >
> > Because in thee I love, O my loved lord,
> > What thou best lovest, be not therefore stern:
> > Souls burn for souls, spirits to spirits cry!
> >
> > I seek the splendour in thy fair face stored;
> > Yet living man that beauty scarce can learn,
> > And he who fain would find it, first must die.

Again, the Petrarchan paradox, in itself absurd, and equally absurd if referred to Freudian meanings, is anything but that if referred to the artist's faith in the absolute.

And if one relates all these intricate affirmations to his respect and passion for the physical and material, one must nevertheless not suppose that there is any weakening of the Neo-Platonic commitments. This hand or this face that is to be kissed is also in another light the embodiment of the divine. The limbs, the *belle membre,* are the reflection of something celestial:

> Spirto ben nato, in cu' si specchia e vede
> nelle tuo belle membra oneste e care
> quante natura e 'l ciel tra no' può fare,
> quand'a null'altra suo bell'opra cede:
>
> spirto leggiadro, in cu' si spera e crede
> dentro, come di fuor nel viso appare,
> amor, pietà, mercè, cose sì rare,
> che ma' furn'in beltà con tanta fede:
>
> l'amor mi prende e la beltà mi lega;
> la pietà, la mercè con dolci sguardi
> ferma speranz' al cor par che ne doni.
>
> Qual uso o qual governo al mondo niega,
> qual crudeltà per tempo o qual più tardi,
> c'a sì bell'opra morte non perdoni?

> > Choice soul, in whom, as in a glass, we see,
> > Mirrored in thy pure form and delicate,
> > What beauties heaven and nature can create,
> > The paragon of all their works to be!
> >
> > Fair soul, in whom love, pity, piety,
> > Have found a home, as from thy outward state
> > We clearly read, and are so rare and great
> > That they adorn none other like to thee!
> >
> > Love takes me captive; beauty binds my soul;
> > Pity and mercy with their gentle eyes
> > Wake in my heart a hope that cannot cheat.
> >
> > What law, what destiny, what fell control,
> > What cruelty, or late or soon, denies
> > That death should spare perfection so complete?

Michelangelo is not alone among the Neo-Platonists in the vitality of his *senso delle cose,* not all are like Bembo in Castiglione's *Courtier,* devoted to the etherealizing of the senses. Ficino himself speaks of love and friendship in the most concrete way and with an intensity that betrays any argument he might ever offer that the flesh is but the veil of the spirit. Friendship, he wrote, 'is the enduringly honourable communion of wills. Its end is a united life. Its beginning is in knowledge, and its means is love'. And again: 'The knowledge that leads to friendship is concurrence in ideas, in the stars, in the genius, and indeed in love and the affection of the body.'

Michelangelo recognizes love as a power or a demon or a god—his personifications represent a sure faith. He as plainly and consistently recognizes that love moves him by the motions of the senses as much as through the soul, senses which, if they could, would captivate the soul. But he is not, I think, particularly interested in regarding the senses as the mortal enemies of the soul even though he may acknowledge their capacity to make vile. They too possess their own purity and clarity, and in the service of a 'chaste will' are themselves chaste. (pp. 76-80)

In following his vocation Michelangelo had come to know, he said, that beauty had been given to him as an ideal. It was

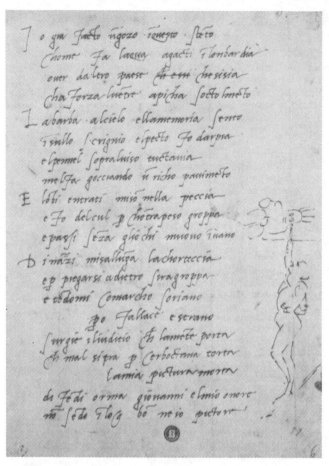

Autograph manuscript of Michelangelo's sonnet on the painting of the Sistine Chapel.

both a light and a mirror, leading his intellect to the very gate of heaven. All this, he concluded, was in the nature of things, and yet grace, too, was necessary to his success, in art as in contemplation—what one might take to be the nature of things was in fact so only through God's bounty:

> dal mortale al divin non vano gli occhi
> infermi, e fermi sempre pur là d'ove
> ascender senza grazia è pensier vano.

> Our feeble eyes cannot raise themselves from what is mortal to that which is divine and remain firmly there where it is vain to think of mounting without grace.

The artist, by the nature of his devotion to the ideal, is caught up in the process of perfection the ideal engenders in him. The work that follows, and as a consequence of his devotion, is the work of Nature, and it is also the work of grace. It is the evidence and embodiment of his dedication.

Because the artist does think of himself as part of Nature, he likes to think of his work as Nature's way of creating life, and of abjuring death. Like Nature, the artist, too, creates something that lives—the 'immagine viva'. But whether or not this is so for Nature, for the artist the completed work does not give peace, the creation is followed by despair. Having done what he set out to do, nothing remains but death.

He counters the despair by even greater ambition. He puts

aside the idea of himself as the artist alone with his work, 'l'ermite esthétique', to take on another role, the ruler and creator of the world itself. (pp. 81-2)

Dante's conception of the nature of love, which is ultimately the determining element in his attitude towards the work of the poet, involves an attitude towards the particular and the individual that is alien to Michelangelo. . . . (p. 87)

There is a certain easiness in Dante's way of seeing things, and of writing them down. He appears not to feel the necessity that Michelangelo does of marrying everything to the ideal, and although allegory and symbol are obviously his continuous concern, it is also obvious that the simply literal has for him a most serious authority. God is unique, not least in the manner of creation.

Michelangelo understood this and was in fact committed to the importance of such a view, but the extent of his commitments to Neo-Platonic assumptions prevented him from a comparable respect for the concrete. He must concentrate on the tension in the relationship of the particular and the ideal. He will never present the thing for its own sake, the man, the armour, the veil over the face, without expressing also the mirror in which all these are the images, of ideas, of God, of himself.

In his poetry the tension shows itself in the gnarled and tortured language, the twisted conceits, the syntax that wrenches every normal procedure of reasoning in order to fashion an all but incomprehensible complexity—a word, a song of praise, a meditation, must always be identified with the self-absorption that comments on it. Yet it *is* comprehensible, the control is ultimately perfect, though the mastery is never, or perhaps never, so free and all-conquering as in his work in the other arts. But there, too, sooner or later we turn our eyes away from the David or Moses to look at the image he is giving us of himself, and of his truth—his passion and understanding and labouring. Even at his greatest he is not letting us love for its own sake the work he has made—he seems to say that even love distracts us from being ourselves and from being at peace.

Despite all he writes about the likeness of the artist to God, peace is not a state he can ever know. By all rights he ought to have known how to come to rest in the Ideas, as Ficino said one should, 'quiescere in ideis', but the nearest thing he does know to that is what happens when he thinks about death:

> And I tell you that to rediscover and to enjoy yourself it is necessary not to seek delight and joy, but rather to think on death. It is only such thought that helps us come to know ourselves again, that holds us as it were, together, instead of letting ourselves be pillaged by relations and friends, by the powers that be and ambition and avarice and all the other vices and sins that rob a man of himself and cause him to be dispersed and dissipated.

As for the bliss of solitude, this, too, turns out to be anguish. He lacks the peace of the Christians and the peace of the Platonists alike.

It has been said [by Raymond Bayer in *Leonard de Vinci, La Grâce* (1933)] that 'il fut un moment où le platonisme fut intensément, profondément vécu, mêlé au rêve de tous les jours, en une tension presque douloureuse, dont l'effort n'était rien moins que de l'incorporer au sang et à la chair du christianisme médiéval'. Such a moment was Michelangelo's life. Longinus thought of the divine vistas as joyful and serene, and I think this was possible for him because, as he saw it, the Nature he shared with all things existed in harmony and order, and he took only the slightest thought of the process in Nature that brought that order into being: Nature *was* order. He might merely say more simply, with William Blake, that all great art is praise. He was separated from the later developments of Platonism which worked together with Christianity to turn the mind inward, to see the drama of the universe within the soul, and separated also from the intolerable mystery of the Incarnation—intolerable for Michelangelo, if nearly ninety years of rivalry with God are sufficient witness of what is not to be borne. And yet his greatest works may be thought to communicate vistas as vast as those Longinus supposed the gods looked on.

For Longinus wisdom and comprehension were ennobling and sustaining, as they were for Michelangelo, for whom, however, every manifestation of the peace that truth and wisdom give was inescapably accompanied by the idea of its transience. The reasoning of Longinus appeared not to entertain the idea that anything so splendid could pass away so quickly and fearfully; he must have rested secure in the promises of his philosophy. (pp. 87-9)

> John Arthos, "Michelangelo," in his Dante, Michelangelo, and Milton, *The Humanities Press, 1963, pp. 50-89.*

CHANDLER B. BEALL   (lecture date 1964)

[*In the excerpt below from a lecture delivered at Portland State College in April 1964, Beall views Michelangelo's poems as intensely personal.*]

It has been said that Michelangelo is a magnificent artist and a good poet, i.e., his literary output is *not* his greatest contribution to the arts. In painting and in sculpture and, to a slightly lesser degree in architecture, Michelangelo Buonarroti created a multitude of powerful forms and figures which, taken together, may be said to constitute a world of almost cosmic and overwhelming dimensions, in which the materiality of our human condition is ideally depicted, constantly transcended, and brought into visible relationship with the superhuman and the divine. Or, to put it another way, an invisible Logos is materialized by the artist in noble pigment and stone so that it may the more readily dwell among us. The poetry of Michelangelo has a less sublime function; its scope is limited to the more local and personal concerns of a very human, and deep, and constantly tormented man. I do not mean that the poems are to be read as purely occasional poems, or rhymed notations in a diary. They have literary pretensions which are fully justified, they are meant to be works of art, not sublime but broadly human; the personal concerns tend to be universalized, as in all good poetry. The poems, then, are on a level considerably below the paintings and the statues; they present, not a cosmic world, but a private, individual world, depicted not plastically but in Italian words shaped into a poetic language stemming from an old tradition. All I can hope to do here is to give an overall characterization, and to present a few typical examples of his poetry. I have added translations that claim no literary qualities of their own, or have used poetic translations from the nineteenth century.

I shall not discuss Michelangelo's letters, which are on a still humbler level, have virtually no artistic pretensions in their practical prose, and are almost wholly circumstantial, dealing with business and family matters, and the endless problems of a harried existence. They are fascinating biographical documents, but they do not, for the most part, fall within my subject. (p. 235)

[Many of Michelangelo's] poems exist in numerous versions, proving that he attacked the resistant medium of words with the same furious tenacity as stone, many of them remain unfinished, like some of the statues; the smaller fragments and single lines are often preliminary sketches, or left-over chips, or isolated details. Many poems doubtless were not preserved at all, especially from the youthful period. Michelangelo always claimed that he was not a professional poet; nevertheless, he seems to have realized early that poetry was also an art in which he might develop a talent and a style of his own.

Unlike most Renaissance poets, Michelangelo does not seem to have been widely read in the writings of the Ancients. But he was deeply familiar with the poetry of Dante and of Petrarch, both of whom he admired greatly. And he knew, of course, the innumerable imitators of Petrarch in the intervening two centuries who had made of the Italian lyric a limpid, musical, elegant, highly polished, and somewhat academic composition, filled with well-worn imagery and rhetorical figures—Cupid and his darts, the grief and joys of love, often expressed as living death and dying life of fire and ice, allusions to classical mythology, and more recently, the stylish jargon of the Platonic or Neoplatonic theories of love. All this he inherited, experimented with, adapted to his own use. What he rejected was the smooth academic finish, the limpid clarity, the flowing musicality of the sonneteers of his day. He preferred a harsher, more energetic language, an uneven rhythm, a distorted syntax, a difficult and even obscure phrasing. Like his sculptured *Captives,* his poems often twist and writhe from inner tensions, hidden forces, or, at times, mere experimental word-juggling. Strong feeling comes out, but we usually learn nothing of its occasion or circumstances.

We know that Michelangelo would often work at a statue in his room at night, to calm his nerves and to relieve tension. His friend Vasari once visited him late at night and found him thus at work by lamp-light. Not wishing to be spied on, Michelangelo dropped the lamp, saying: "I am so old that death often pulls me by the cloak, that I may go with him, and one day this body of mine will fall like the lamp, and the light of my life will be quenched." This is a precious glimpse of a lifelong habit of the artist. He often worked in the same fashion with his poems, jotting down a thought, or a line, or a rough draft on whatever paper was at hand; and always struggling to shape the form to his own serious thought, his own feeling, and his private concern with Love, with Beauty, with Death, and with God. Such a struggle may be taken as a prerequisite of originality, and Michelangelo is indeed the most original lyric poet of his time. Not in the sense that he tries to be different or to invent novelties, but in the sense that he deals with the great eternal commonplaces of the human condition—which are the subjects that all poets must treat—in an intensely personal manner.

This intensity is tantalizingly evident even in the chips and fragments he discarded. We have a sheet of paper which shows two sketches, one of the bronze David and one of the right arm of the marble David; on the right side of the paper is the single hendecasyllabic line:

> Davitte colla fromba e io coll'arco.

Michelagniolo
David with the sling and I with the bow.

and a little below, a line from one of Petrarch's sonnets:

Rott'è l'alta colonna e 'l ver(de lauro).
Broken is the tall column and the green laurel.

We know that Petrarch's line announces in an emblematic fashion the death (1348) of Petrarch's friend, Cardinal Colonna, and of his beloved French lady, Laura, and so we are led to speculate on the meaning of Michelangelo's emblematic line and the symbolism of the sling and the bow—none of the explanations thus far proposed are satisfying. . . . He doubtless intended to use this line in a sonnet or madrigal which would develop and contrast the two images and give them significance. But he never completed the poem. This is the earliest scrap of poetry we have by Michelangelo, and it remains a powerful and haunting enigma.

In another fragment he rephrases the ancient adage that art is long and life is fleeting:

Non ha l'abito intero
prima alcun, c'a l'estremo
dell'arte e della vita.

No one has complete skill
Before he is at the end
Of his art and his life.

And he says the same thing later on in two lines:

Chi non vuol delle foglie
non ci venga di maggio.

If you don't want just leaves,
don't come in May.

A rough draft for a sonnet he never finished condenses into six terse lines a typical Renaissance theme—the instability of man's estate, the reversals of fortune, and the inevitable triumph of death:

Molti anni fassi qual felice, in una
brevissima ora si lamenta e dole;
o per famosa o per antica prole
altri s'inlustra, e 'n un momento imbruna . . .

Cosa mobil non è che sotto el sole
non vinca morte e cangi la fortuna.

This is so compact that a translation must also be an interpretation; it goes about as follows:

A man, happy for many years, may in a brief hour come to grief and woe; and another, illustrious through fame or nobility, in a single moment fall into oblivion. There is nothing mutable under the sun that death does not vanquish or fortune change.

This was written on the back of a sheet of sketches when Michelangelo was still in his twenties. It is a fragment of a sonnet, but it makes complete sense. And it is a typical piece. The lines are difficult, rough-hewn; they do not flow smoothly. The thought is concentrated into three compact statements which are interrelated like the facets of a small statue one turns in one's hands. The words are forceful, as if solidified. The whole effect is sculptural. Michelangelo tends to work words as he works stone; he has a sense of the weight and mass and density of language, and of the lyrical possibilities

of these physico-verbal properties. The point has often been made, and is corroborated by the sculptural tendencies to be observed in his painting. He rarely narrates or describes; he is less interested in fixing in words the spectacle of our existence than in expressing its abstract meaning in the form of general truths. The brief pieces that I have quoted thus far have this maxim-like character, this lapidary quality, as if chiseled in stone.

The topics that the poems deal with are, as I have said, Love, Beauty, Death, and God. Not that these are separate and distinct concerns; they are rather the larger aspects of the intense inner life of an extraordinary individual who was constantly and painfully evolving toward a deep spirituality. Michelangelo was one of the very few religious poets of the Renaissance. At the same time he was literally overwhelmed by the beauty of the human form and face as well as by the beauty of the intellect and the soul. This is obvious in all he painted, or sculptured, or sketched, or wrote. His heart was pure and in some ways childlike. He had a religious conception of love, part Christian and part Platonic, and extremely idealistic. He had been impressed by the preaching of Savonarola, and had been caught up in the Florentine Academy's enthusiasm for Plato's doctrines of the soul and of love. Religion for him was never mere outward show, and his Platonism was not mere jargon but an integral part of his philosophic outlook. He was never married except, as he said, to Art, and his works were his children. But there was nothing cold or literary about his Platonic idealism. His mind could be set aflame by whatever was beautiful. He was aware of this, and wrote in a letter declining an invitation from his friend Giannotti:

Whenever I see a man who has some talent or some intellectual gift, a man who can do or say something better than other people, I am irresistibly attracted to him and give myself so completely over to him that I no longer belong to myself . . . You are all so talented that if I accepted your invitation I would lose my freedom; each of you would steal from me a portion of myself. Even the dancer and the lute-player, if they were outstanding in their art, would do with me as they pleased! Instead of being rested, strengthened, and calmed by your company, I would have my mind torn and scattered to the winds, so that, for days thereafter, I would not know in what world I was moving.

He was conquered by the beauty of thoughts, words, music—and still more so by physical comeliness, in which he saw, as time went on, a manifestation of spiritual harmony and of the Divine:

La forza d'un bel viso a che mi sprona?
C'altro non è c'al mondo mi diletti:
ascender vivo fra gli spirti eletti
per grazia tal, c'ogni altra par men buona.

Se ben col fattor l'opra suo consuona,
che colpa vuol giustizia ch'io n'aspetti,
s'i' amo, anz'ardo, e per divin concetti
onoro e stimo ogni gentil persona?

To what am I not driven by the power of a beautiful face? For nothing else on earth delights me but to ascend alive among those spirits who are blest by virtue of a grace superior to any other. Since the creature is similar to its creator, if I love and burn with love, and honor and esteem each noble person because of the divine stamp upon him, what blame can justly be attached to me?

He has left us a charming, youthful poem describing a pretty blond girl with a garland of interwoven flowers on her hair, her hair held in place by a gold filigree snood that touches her cheek and neck, a gold-tipped ribbon lacing the bodice tightly, and a simple sash tied with a knot around her waist—as if she had stepped out of a picture by some other painter—and, like Tennyson in "The Miller's Daughter," he envies the flowers, the ribbon, the bodice, and the belt, thinking that his own arms could encircle her still better. But such detailed sensuous notations are rather rare in his poetry. I shall quote a later one which is more closely connected with his art and interests us more. It shows a flirtatious model admiring herself in her mirror and teasing the artist by contrasting her youthful beauty with his aging features:

> La si gode e racconcia
> nel suo fidato specchio,
> ove sé vede equale al paradiso;
> po', volta a me, mi concia
> sì, c'oltr'all'esser vecchio,
> in quel col mie fo più bello il suo viso,
> ond'io vie più deriso
> son d'esser brutto; e pur m'è gran ventura,
> s'i' vinco, a farla bella, la natura.

>> She loves to primp before her trusted mirror, in which she sees herself as pretty as Paradise. Then turning to me, manages so that her face is reflected along with mine, and besides being old I am still further humiliated by being made uglier: but I am fortunate nevertheless, since by making her look more beautiful, I outdo nature herself.

Michelangelo was indeed, from all accounts, an ugly man, and he felt it and suffered from it. And it is meager consolation he gets from this clever twisting of words, when he thinks he is in love with the girl. The beauty-ugliness antithesis is a constant motif in his aesthetics, and in his sentimental life (about which we do not know as much as we should like to), and in his poetry, which is nearly always a hymn to beauty, and very often a lament on growing old.

Usually Michelangelo refrains from mentioning his specific works of art in his poems. But there is one famous four-line epigram we ought to quote. During the most somber years of his life, the artist made the sculptures for the tombs of Julian and Lorenzo de' Medici in Florence—stylized statues of the two princes and four figures which furnish a commentary on them: Dawn and Twilight, and Day and Night, figures that express the wearisome suffering of living and contempt for the things of this world. These great symbols of human grief were finished in 1531, but not put into place and shown to the public until years later. Ironically, no one understood them. Giovanni Strozzi, a minor poet, wrote what he thought was a clever epigram on the statue of Night. It said:

> Night, whom you see sleeping in such
> graceful posture, was sculptured by an
> Angel in this stone; and since she sleeps,
> she is alive. Awaken her, if you don't
> believe it, and she will speak to you.

Michelangelo, now in Rome and deeply unhappy with his personal woes and the wretched state of affairs in Florence and in Italy, was in no mood for such a precious conceit; but he accepted it in order to reply in an epigram of his own, simple, forceful, and clear. Moreover, he invented a new, politi-

cal allegory for his Night, and he let her speak, without being awakened, as follows:

> Caro m'è 'l sonno, e più l'esser di sasso,
> mentre che 'l danno e la vergogna dura;
> non veder, non sentir m'è gran ventura;
> però non mi destar, deh, parla basso.

>> Dear to me is sleep, but more dear to be of stone,
>> So long as ruin and dishonour reign;
>> Not to see, not to feel, is my great good fortune;
>> Therefore do not wake me, oh, speak low.

He is expressing his bitterness over the fall of the Florentine republic and the tyranny of the ignoble Duke Alessandro de' Medici, who had taken over in 1530.

Michelangelo has left two fine appreciative sonnets on Dante, a few passionate and disillusioned poems to a lady or ladies unknown; one or two sardonically humorous poems about himself or his patrons (he did have a sense of humor, without it he could not have lived so long!). He composed a number of strange great sonnets couched in Platonic language and addressed, like some of Shakespeare's, to a young gentleman of handsome mien and noble soul, Tommaso Cavalieri, who felt puzzled, embarrassed, honored, and touched by the aging artist's admiration and effusive affection. Whatever else it may have been, this affection was above all an enthusiasm for the perfect creations of God, a token that the friend or lover can transcend the humanness of his feeling, grasp the essence of it, and make it a way of worship, of progress towards God. The kinship of souls here on earth is a promise and a foretaste of a higher communion. And Michelangelo implores his readers not to be like the stupid and evil crowd, "il vulgo malvagio, isciocco e rio," who out of baseness, ignorance, and malice, misinterpret his affection. Here is a sonnet to Tommaso Cavalieri expressing his ideal of spiritual kinship in the Neoplatonic conceit of one soul that can function fully only in and through the kindred soul:

> Veggio co' be' vostr'occhi un dolce lume
> che co' mie ciechi già veder non posso;
> porto co' vostri piedi un pondo addosso,
> che de' mie zoppi non è già costume.
>
> Volo con le vostr'ale senza piume;
> col vostro ingegno al ciel sempre son mosso;
> dal vostro arbitrio son pallido e rosso,
> freddo al sol, caldo alle più fredde brume.
>
> Nel voler vostro è sol la voglia mia,
> i miei pensier nel vostro cor si fanno.
> nel vostro fiato son le mie parole.
>
> Come luna da sé sol par ch'io sia,
> ché gl occhi nostri in ciel veder non sanno
> se non quel tanto che n'accende il sole.

>> I see with your beautiful eyes a sweet light
>> which with my blind eyes I cannot see;
>> with your feet I carry a burden
>> which with my lame feet I cannot carry.
>> Deprived of pinions, I fly with your wings;
>> with your intellect I always strive towards heaven;
>> At your whim I become pale, or blush,
>> am cold in the sunshine, warm in the cold fog.
>> In your will only is my will,
>> my thoughts spring from your heart,
>> in your breath are my words.
>> When alone I am like a moon by itself
>> for our eyes see nothing in the sky
>> except what the sun illuminates.

This poem was greatly admired in the sixteenth century when this kind of language was more in fashion, and it was published during Michelangelo's lifetime in Vasari's *Lives of Architects, Painters, and Sculptors.* It presents a series of concrete images, none of which can be taken literally; but each is effective in its figurative fashion, and the fervent enumeration generates the overall spiritual attitude the author wishes to create, or re-create. The simple wonderful line, "nel vostro fiato son le mie parole" greatly impressed the late Thomas Mann as a sublime acknowledgment of the interrelationship between enslavement to beauty, affection, and productivity—a line, he says, "which I have locked so deep in my heart," "den ich so tief in mein Herz geschlossen habe."

But Michelangelo's finest poems, and the happiest, were written for Vittoria Colonna, one of the noblest—by birth and by her character—of the women of the Italian Renaissance. Michelangelo met her when he was in his sixties. Their common interest in artistic, intellectual, and religious matters, the fact that both were poets, and that both were lonely despite many interesting acquaintances—these were the basis of a mutual respect and affection, a grave and serene friendship in which the artist found intelligent understanding, comfort, gentle guidance, and growth. One of the fascinating aspects of the poetry of this period is a new use of imagery derived from sculpture. Here is a fine, brief example in the form of a madrigal:

> Sì come per levar, donna, si pone
> in pietra alpestra e dura
> una viva figura,
> che là più cresce u' più la pietra scema;
> tal alcun'opre buone,
> per l'alma che pur trema,
> cela il superchio della propria carne
> co' l'inculta sua cruda e dura scorza.
> Tu pur dalle mie streme
> parti puo' sol levarne,
> ch'in me non è di me voler né forza.

> As when by sculpting, Lady, one models
> Within the hard mountain rock
> A living figure
> Which grows as the stone decreases,
> Just so in the case of the trembling soul
> A few good works
> Are hidden by the excess of one's own flesh
> With an uncouth gross hard shell.
> You alone from my outer
> Portions can remove the excess.
> For of myself I have no will nor power over me.

For Michelangelo true sculpture meant to remove, "levare," directly from the block of marble; "pone" from "porre," means to do sculpture not by taking away but by adding clay or wax. But these technical terms receive a new and deeper meaning here, as the poet utilizes one of those Platonic concepts he so loved. If the sculptor removes the outer shell and reveals the image by freeing it from its matrix of marble, the image is conceptually assumed to be pre-existent; it is therefore one of those perfect or divine ideas which are incorporated in the imperfect material form; and to reveal it one needs not only art (i.e., technique) but also intellect, which enables the artist to discern its sublime outlines. The sculptor "pone," puts, or composes, or creates the living figure through removing the outer covering ("per levar"). The figure grows, takes shape, as the stone diminishes and is chipped away. Not only are we given here an insight into the sculptor's method and theory of his art, but he has it function here as a splendid met-

aphor of the liberation of a human soul trembling under the weight of its materiality. Note that it is the lady who is now the sculptor, and the living figure that she thus brings to birth is the spiritual personality of the poet.

The same image is repeated with variations in other poems. I have transcribed the most famous of these. In it the poet imagines that in the heart of his lady rather than in himself he may discover the best part of himself:

> Non ha l'ottimo artista alcun concetto
> c'un marmo solo in sé non circonscriva
> col suo superchio, e solo a quello arriva
> la man che ubbidisce all'intelletto.

> Il mal ch'io fuggo, e 'l ben ch'io mi prometto,
> in te, donna leggiadra, altera e diva,
> tal si nasconde; e perch'io più non viva,
> contraria ho l'arte al disïato effetto.

> Amor dunque non ha, né tua beltate
> o durezza o fortuna o gran disdegno
> del mio mal colpa, o mio destino o sorte;

> se dentro del tuo cor morte e pietate
> porti in un tempo, e che 'l mio basso ingegno
> non sappia, ardendo, trarne altro che morte.

The translation is by Longfellow:

> Nothing the greatest artist can conceive
> That every marble block doth not confine
> Within itself; and only its design
> The hand that follows intellect can achieve.

> The ill I flee, the good that I believe,
> In thee, fair lady, lofty and divine,
> Thus hidden lie; and so that death be mine,
> Art, of desired success, doth me bereave.

> Love is not guilty, then, nor thy fair face,
> Nor fortune, cruelty, nor great disdain,
> Of my disgrace, nor chance nor destiny,

> If in thy heart both death and love find place
> At the same time, and if my humble brain,
> Burning, can nothing draw but death from thee.

This poem was the subject of a public lecture by Benedetto Varchi before the Florentine Academy which was printed and widely discussed [see excerpt by Varchi dated 1547]. The striking sculptural metaphors used in these last two poems are of the sort that we call metaphysical or baroque, and Michelangelo is indeed an authentic representative of this European school of poets which seems to express the spirit of the Counter-Reformation, and includes St. Teresa (born forty years after Michelangelo), Marino, Richard Crashaw, John Donne, and even John Milton. Nothing is more baroque than the sonnet which Michelangelo wrote, it seems, on the death of Vittoria Colonna in 1547. The opening lines describe the use of the sculptor's mallet working the hard stone and guided by his inspiration. In like manner, God in Heaven is a divine hammer, the model and the shaping instrument of all lesser hammers. And Vittoria was a hammer that had begun to shape him, Michelangelo, but has now been raised high above, and into heaven itself, by death; and he will be left incomplete, "non finito," like some of his own statues, unless help comes from the divine workshop:

> Se 'l mie rozzo martello i duri sassi
> forma d'uman aspetto or questo or quello,
> dal ministro che 'l guida, iscorge e tiello,

prendendo il moto, va con gli altrui passi.

Ma quel divin che in cielo alberga e stassi,
altri, e sé più, col propio andar fa bello;
e se nessun martel senza martello
si può far, da quel vivo ogni altro fassi.

E perché 'l colpo è di valor più pieno
quant'alza più se stesso alla fucina,
sopra 'l mie questo al ciel n'è gito a volo.

Onde a me non finito verrà meno,
s'or non gli dà la fabbrica divina
aiuto a farlo, c'al mondo era solo.

When my rude hammer to the stubborn stone
Gives human shape, now that, now this, at will,
Following his hand who wields and guides it still,
It moves upon another's feet alone:

But that which dwells in heaven, the world doth fill
With beauty by pure motions of its own;
And since tools fashion tools which else were none,
Its life makes all that lives with living skill.

Now, for that every stroke excels the more
The higher at the forge it doth ascend,
Her soul that fashioned mine hath sought the skies:

Wherefore unfinished I must meet my end,
If God, the great artificer, denies
That aid which was unique on earth before.

(J. A. Symonds)

If, as some scholars suspect, this stupendous sonnet was written, not for the death of Vittoria Colonna, but much earlier, for the death of his brother, Buonarroto Buonarroti, in 1528, the meaning of this extended metaphysical conceit would remain psychologically the same; but Michelangelo would then stand as an early and important forerunner of the Counter-Reformation period-style.

After the death of his beloved friend, Vittoria Colonna, Michelangelo moves painfully and majestically into his old age. He is still wonderfully alive and alert, planning and beginning the dome of Saint Peter's, and skirmishing with envious rivals and political enemies. But despite the admiration and the glory that surround him, he is increasingly sad and lonely. His was a desolate grandeur, in the ninth decade of his life. He lived meagerly in one of the poorer sections of Rome, continuing as always to work alone at night. His sculptures and drawings of this period depict mainly the Passion and Crucifixion. The old sculptor of tombs is more and more haunted by the idea of approaching death. I have already quoted his remark to Vasari about death plucking at his cloak. And in a letter he writes this startling sentence: "No thought comes to me that does not have death sculptured within it"—"Non nasce in me pensiero che non vi sia dentro sculpita la morte." That statement itself is sculptured in words. His soul, he says, converses with death: "l'anima mia che con la morte parla." His thought more and more turns inward, and upward; and his poems are often moving prayers addressed to Christ. I have transcribed a beautiful heart-felt one, a first form of which may well have been addressed orally to one of his own drawings of the Crucifixion before he reworked it on paper. It is the prayer of a very old and very tired man, eager to turn from the horrible storm of life to a sweet repose, "da l'orribil procella in dolce calma."

Scarco d'un'importuna e greve salma,
Signor mie caro, e dal mondo disciolto,

qual fragil legno a te stanco rivolto
da l'orribil procella in dolce calma.

Le spine e' chiodi e l'una e l'altra palma
col tuo benigno umil pietoso volto
prometton grazia di pentirsi molto,
e speme di salute a la trist'alma.

Non mirin co' iustizia i tuo sant'occhi
il mie passato, e 'l gastigato orecchio;
non tenda a quello il tuo braccio severo.

Tuo sangue sol mie colpe lavi e tocchi,
e più abondi, quant'i' son più vecchio,
di pronta aita e di perdono intero.

This sonnet was admired and translated by Wordsworth:

Eternal Lord! eased of a cumbrous load,
And loosened from the world, I turn to Thee;
Shun, like a shattered bark, the storm, and flee
to thy protection for a safe abode.
The crown of thorns, hands pierced upon the tree,
The meek, benign, and lacerated face,
To a sincere repentance promise grace,
To the sad soul give hope of pardon free.
With justice mark not Thou, O Light divine,
My fault, nor hear it with thy sacred ear;
Neither put forth that way thy arm severe;
Wash with thy blood my sins; thereto incline
More readily the more my years require
Help, and forgiveness speedy and entire.

The inward look involves also a backward look. In the last poem that I shall quote, Michelangelo, having reached, as he supposes, the threshold of the hereafter, surveys rapidly the long course of his career. This sonnet marks, symbolically if not chronologically, the culminating moment of his evolution as a spiritual personality and as a literary figure. It deals with all his most intimate concerns—Love, Beauty, Death, and God—as an erring and passionate man has had to experience them in his daily living, and must now re-order them in a new perspective:

Giunto è già 'l corso della vita mia,
con tempestoso mar, per fragil barca,
al comun porto, ov'a render si varca
conto e ragion d'ogni opra trista e pia.

Onde l'affettüosa fantasia
che l'arte mi fece idol e monarca
conosco or ben com'era d'error carca
e quel c'a mal suo grado ogn'uom desia.

Gli amorosi pensier, già vani e lieti,
che fien or, s'a duo morte m'avvicino?
D'una so 'l certo, e l'altra mi minaccia.

Né pinger né scolpir fie più che quieti
l'anima, volta a quell'amor divino
c'aperse, a prender noi, 'n croce le braccia.

Again I take the translation from Longfellow:

The course of my long life hath reached at last,
In fragile bark o'er a tempestuous sea,
The common harbor, where must rendered be
Account of all the actions of the past.

The impassioned phantasy, that, vague and vast,
Made art an idol and a king to me,
Was an illusion, and but vanity
Were the desires that lured me and harassed.

The dreams of love, that were so sweet of yore,
What are they now, when two deaths may be mine,—
One sure, and one forecasting its alarms?

Painting and sculpture satisfy no more
The soul now turning to the Love Divine,
That oped, to embrace us, on the cross its arms.

The first lines, which state the point the poet has reached, evoke in their phrasing and imagery his Petrarchan beginnings. Now he confronts two deaths: the death of his body—he is sure that will come—and the death of his soul—he is not sure that will not come. This great poem is fraught with a double sadness. A life intensely lived is drawing to its close, and the verses conjure up the long, rich, and well-filled years and savor once more their acrid, intoxicating taste. But now the poet looks at his life, at all human life, from a great distance and under the aspect of eternity; and he sees the vanity, the emptiness of it all, as he turns for refuge to the Love Divine. Even painting and sculpture, which had been his deepest passions and his *raison d'être,* he freely sacrifices now and offers to the Lord; and, for this moment at least, only poetry remains for the enacting of this supreme renunciation. (pp. 236-50)

> Chandler B. Beall, *"The Literary Figure of Michelangelo," in* Italica, *Vol. XLI, No. III, September, 1964, pp. 235-51.*

JOHN CHARLES NELSON   (lecture date 1964)

[*In the following lecture, originally delivered at Columbia University in 1964 and later read at the State University of New York at Binghamton in 1968, Nelson discusses the background of Michelangelo's poetry and considers the Platonic, Petrarchan, and Christian influences that affect it.*]

Much can be learned about Michelangelo's poetry from the analysis of even a single representative poem. Let us consider, for example, the following sonnet, chosen from his 302 extant poems, and translated as literally as possible.

Non so se s'è la desïata luce
del suo primo fattor, che l'alma sente,
o se dalla memoria della gente
alcun' altra beltà nel cor traluce;

o se fama o se sogno alcun produce
agli occhi manifesto, al cor presente,
di sé lasciando un non so che cocente
ch' è forse o quel c' a pianger mi conduce.

Quel ch' i' sento e ch' i' cerco e chi mi guidi
meco non è; né so ben veder dove
trovar mel possa, e par c' altri mel mostri.

Questo, signor, m' avvien, po' ch' i' vi vidi,
c' un dolce amaro, un sì e no mi muove:
certo saranno stati gli occhi vostri.

> I do not know whether my soul feels the longed-for light of its Maker [that is, the light to which it wishes to return], or whether some other source of beauty seen among people, remaining in memory, now shines in my heart, or whether fame or dreams give back to me the image of someone manifest to my eyes and present in my heart, leaving an unspecifiable ardor which is, perhaps, what leads me now to weep. Neither that which I feel and see nor he who might guide me is with me; nor can I see where to find my goal, though it seems that someone is show-

ing me the way. This has happened to me, my lord, since the day I first saw you. I am moved by bitter-sweetness, by yes and no: certainly the fault belongs to your eyes.

In many of Michelangelo's poems we find images so striking that we feel at once that they are spontaneous expressions of the poet's feeling, deriving, as the case may be, from a cherished recollection of things seen; from the sculptor's meditation; from wry reflection on life's paradoxes. But there are even more poems, where, if we look for the mark of originality or spontaneity, we will either find it lacking, or, as in the sonnet we have just read, find that it consists in Michelangelo's manner of juxtaposing and rethinking elements of the poetic tradition inherited by all cinquecento poets. While Dantean and Bernesque flashes appear throughout his *Rime,* it comes as no surprise to find Petrarchism and Platonism woven strand-by-strand through the majority of his poems.

Let us identify these elements in the poem we have just read. In the opening quatrain, the soul's desire to return to the light of its Maker has strongly Platonic overtones. The return journey of the soul to its patron god or its parent star, retracing in the upward path of love and knowledge the downward thrust of divine creation, was a frequent theme of prose theorists and poets following Marsilio Ficino's monumental translations and interpretations of the complete works of Plato and Plotinus in the latter part of the fifteenth century. Generally this theme and others taken over from Plato were couched in Christian, or at least nonpagan, terms. The less philosophically oriented Platonizing writers, among whom we should include Michelangelo, easily blend Platonic and Christian spirituality without even noticing the points of conflict that troubled Girolamo Benivieni and the proverbially erudite Giovanni Pico della Mirandola and which were to spell trouble a century later for the professional philosophers, Francesco Patrizi and Giordano Bruno.

Now, one might disagree with our labeling as specifically Platonic the opening thought of this sonnet—the soul's desire for the light of its Maker. One might observe that if there had never been a Platonic revival in Florence in the fifteenth century, continuing until well after Michelangelo's death, the idea of the soul's return to the Divinity, as Christian as it is Platonic, here coupled with the metaphor of light, might well have reached Michelangelo through Dante's *Paradiso.* Certainly it is the case with Michelangelo, as it is with almost every other important Italian Renaissance poet, that Dantean and *stilnuovo* motives, often themselves ultimately of Neoplatonic derivation, are inseparably intermingled with elements of the later Platonic revival initiated by Petrarch and carried to fruition by Ficino. The second idea of this sonnet, beauty as a memory cherished in the heart, might convince us, associated as it is with the first idea, of their common Platonic inspiration. We must observe that the memory is not Socrates' reminiscence of an eternal essence glimpsed in the soul's previous life in the empyrean, but the memory of a human face or form seen in the society of men. Even so, it is just the sight of such beauty that starts the soul on the restless search which Michelangelo describes in the remainder of this sonnet and which Plato details in the *Phaedrus.* Yet here, also, the motive of remembered beauty shining in the lover's heart could be a reflection of *Rime* written by Dante and other poets of the *dolce stil nuovo.* Again, we are faced with a multiple derivation.

In the second quatrain the irrepressible sensuality expressed

The Dying Slave, *sculpted by Michelangelo for the tomb of Julius II.*

by the words "un non so che cocente" is too forceful to be restrained by the bonds of Platonism as interpreted by the Italian Renaissance. The struggle of flesh against spirit, the hallmark of Petrarch's poetry, familiar to all Christians from personal experience if not from Augustine's *Confessions,* asserts itself.

In the first tercet (ll. 9-11), the author feels that disoriented, restless dissatisfaction which, according to the Platonic Socrates and his later disciples, characterizes all earthbound loves. In the concluding tercet the ascent to the higher world envisioned by the Platonists fails to occur, though it does in some other sonnets by Michelangelo, and the poet is left in that state of bittersweet reverie made so familiar to everyone by Petrarch.

In the following sonnet the Platonism is even more unmistakable:

> Veggio nel tuo bel viso, signor mio,
> quel che narrar mal puossi in questa vita:
> l'anima, della carne ancor vestita,
> con esso è già più volte ascesa a Dio.
>
> E se 'l vulgo malvagio, isciocco e rio,
> di quel che sente, altrui segna e addita,
> non è l'intensa voglia men gradita,
> l'amor, la fede e l'onesto desio.
>
> A quel pietoso fonte, onde siàn tutti,
> s'assembra ogni beltà che qua si vede
> più c'altra cosa alle persone accorte;
>
> né altro saggio abbiàn né altri frutti
> del cielo in terra; e chi v'ama con fede
> trascende a Dio e fa dolce la morte.

> I see in your handsome visage, my lord, something which is hard to imagine in this earthly life: your soul, still united with your flesh, has already several times, with your visage, made the ascent to God. And if the vicious crowd, foolish and guilty, attributes to others its own ignoble sentiments, yet not even so are my intense cravings, my love and faith and honorable desire, any less dear to me. Every beautiful thing which is seen on earth, in the judgment of the wise resembles more than any other thing that divine fount from which we all derive; nor do we have on earth any other example or other fruits of heaven; and he who loves you faithfully rises up to God and thinks death sweet.

Here we see at once the Platonic scheme of two worlds—the essential and divine realm above us and the shadowy corporeal world around us—where man must reject what is vicious and merely material in order to see and experience the beauty which can lead the soul in Diotiman ascent to the source of all beauty, triumphant over death and evil and the flesh.

The derivation of Michelangelo's Platonism is as easy to explain in a general way as it is difficult to pinpoint in specific detail. According to an anonymous, unpublished, Renaissance biographer of Girolamo Benivieni, quoted by Giovanni Papini in his *Life of Michelangelo,* Benivieni predicted a brilliant future for the artist, such as to retain for Florence her primary in art, when Michelangelo was a thirteen-year-old novice in the workshop of Ghirlandaio. Incredible? Perhaps. But it is certain that Michelangelo, at fifteen, was received by Lorenzo il Magnifico into the Medici household, perhaps as a result of Benivieni's praise. In the palace on the Via Larga Michelangelo inevitably came under the influence of other

Platonizing humanists and poets—Marsilio Ficino, Angelo Poliziano, Giovanni Pico della Mirandola, and others who either were members of the Medici circle or who were frequent visitors to Lorenzo. The Platonic coloration of his poetry can be explained by this fact alone.

Thus it comes as no surprise to us that Michelangelo, who knew everyone in the Medici circle in his youth, whose character was deeply spiritual, and who read the poetry of other contemporary Petrarchizing and Platonizing poets, should employ Neoplatonic motives in his poems, now clearly, now vaguely. This does not mean that we can put our finger on a line of his poetry and say, "This concept was taken from Marsilio Ficino," but we can affirm that his poetry is imbued with a Platonic spirit. Indeed, if there is one characteristic of Michelangelo's Platonism which distinguishes it from that of other poets of his time, it is his unmistakable sincerity. For Michelangelo Buonarroti, Platonism was not lip service to a current literary fashion as it was for so many of his contemporaries—such as Lorenzo, Bembo, and Castiglione, to name three; it was the expression of a deeply felt affinity for spiritual concerns. The same genuineness characterizes his somber religious sonnets to Vittoria Colonna. Even his *scherzi* in the manner of Burchiello and Berni bear the imprint of his strong personality—the hallmark, ultimately, of all his poetry— which sets him apart from the many lesser poets of his age whose literary preparation far exceeded his own.

Let us return to the first sonnet that we read, **"Non so se s'è la desïata luce."** It is written and rewritten several times by Michelangelo. The autographs are still extant. Two of the redactions are translated by John Addington Symonds; the second of these is the one which we have read. In the earlier draft Michelangelo employed, in line 12, the word *donna* ("lady") instead of *signore*. It appears from the several texts collated by Enzo Girardi that Michelangelo originally composed this sonnet for a lady, and then decided to send it to his friend Tommaso Cavalieri.

Symonds's translation of the concluding tercet of the earlier redaction, to the lady, reads as follows:

> This, since I saw thee, lady, makes me weak:
> a bitter-sweet sways here and there my mind;
> and sure I am thine eyes this mischief breed.

It is no accident that his translation of the same lines in the later redaction, where the word *signore* is used instead of *donna,* is identical (that is, even the word *signore* is translated "lady" instead of "lord"). It was Cesare Guasti's opinion, when he published the first critical edition of Michelangelo's **Rime** (Florence, 1863) that Michelangelo had intended for the poetess Vittoria Colonna the poems which we now know were written to Cavalieri. Much earlier, in 1623, the artist's grand-nephew, Michelangelo Buonarroti the younger, in the earliest edition of the **Rime,** had purposely altered a few of his granduncle's expressions, changing some masculine words to their feminine counterparts.

Later editors and interpreters of Michelangelo's **Rime** were reluctant to believe that some of his finest poems had been inspired by a handsome young Roman nobleman; yet Benedetto Varchi, a prominent cinquecento man of letters, had stated in a public lecture apropos of a certain sonnet by Michelangelo, without the slightest suspicion of scandal [see excerpt dated 1547]:

> [This sonnet is] addressed to Messer Tommaso

Cavalieri, a most noble Roman youth, in whom I found, when I met him in Rome, besides his incomparable beauty of body, such charming behavior, such excellent intelligence and gracious ways that he indeed deserved, as he still does, that the better one knew him, the more one loved him.

There is, however, another possible reason for the later reluctance to see what Varchi saw and accepted. In early Tuscan poetry, as before it in Provençal poetry, masculine designations such as "lord" instead of their feminine counterparts were employed in poems written to ladies. The reason for this strange custom is not hard to find: it is well known that with the sudden appearance of the poetry of courtly love in Southern France around the year 1100 and its novel, not to say revolutionary, way of celebrating women as objects of romantic love, the lady was placed upon a pedestal, giving her the same position of command over her lover as the feudal lord exercised over his vassal. Hence she was his lord and could be so addressed.

There also remained, from the Platonic dialogues, translated by Ficino, the male-oriented picture of love which Plato had painted. Love in these dialogues, however lofty its ultimate goal, begins as the love of two men (generally a mature man and a younger man) for each other. In their interpretations of Platonic myth and doctrine, the Renaissance Platonist philosophers employed abstract terms such as "beloved" and "object of love" which avoided reference to the sex of the persons involved, or else attributed to the lovers only a moral and intellectual fervor. Giuseppe Betussi said of love between two persons of the same sex, "It can be true and most perfect while it is concerned with the beauties of the soul and it is licit; just as it becomes illicit when it tends toward another end." To Marsilio Ficino, who first used the term "Platonic love," the words signified an intellectual love between friends based on the individual's love of God. Such relationships, as Professor Kristeller has demonstrated [in *The Philosophy of Marsilio Ficino* (1943)], were the foundation of his Platonic Academy. Almost all of the Platonists, both in Ficino's generation and later, were very explicit in their condemnation of the vice of homosexuality, with which men of letters had been taxed at least from the time of Dante's *Commedia:*

> In somma sappi che tutti fur cherci
> e litterati grandi e di gran fama,
> d'un peccato medesmo al mondo lerci.
> [*Inferno, canto* XV, 106-108]

These are Brunetto Latini's words to Dante ("In short, know that all were great and renowned clerks and men of letters, stained on earth by one same sin").

Michelangelo's second biographer, Ascanio Condivi, writing in direct competition with Giorgio Vasari's famous, though inaccurate, biography, could vaunt his close association with the master. Indeed, it is quite probable that Michelangelo himself encouraged Condivi in his task. Thus Condivi's account of Michelangelo's view of love and beauty may be accepted as authoritative [see excerpt dated 1553]:

> He [Michelangelo] has also loved bodily beauty, as one who knows it very well. Thus he has given occasion to certain carnal men, who are unable to understand the love of beauty in any but a lascivious and unchaste way, to think and speak evil of him— as though Alcibiades, a very handsome youth, had not been loved most chastely by Socrates. . . . I have several times heard Michelangelo talk about

love; and then heard it said by those who were present that he spoke about it not otherwise than as Plato wrote. I never heard from his mouth any but the most chaste words. . . . [Furthermore,] he not only has loved human beauty, but universally every beautiful thing, a beautiful horse, a beautiful dog, a beautiful town, a beautiful plant, mountain, woods, admiring every beautiful thing and place with marvelous affection, thus taking beauty from nature as bees gather honey from flowers in order to use it in their work.

A recent biographer, Giovanni Papini, one of Italy's best known literati in this century, goes to some length to refute the crude charge of pederasty levelled by Pietro Aretino, himself morally unblemished of course, and more recently repeated by such unbiased observers as Havelock Ellis and André Gide. Papini quotes these lines from Michelangelo:

S' i' amo sol di te, signor mie caro,
quel che di te più ami, non ti sdegni,
chè l'un dell'altro spirto s'innamora.

Quel che nel tuo bel volto bramo e 'mparo,
e mal compres' è dagli umani ingegni,
chi 'l vuol saper convien che prima mora.

If I love only that in you, my dear Lord, which you yourself most love, do not feel disdainful, for one spirit becomes enamored of the other. He who would know that which I crave and learn in your handsome face and which is poorly understood by human intellects, needs must first die.

Papini concludes with an animated defense of the "absolute purity" of Michelangelo's and Cavalieri's reciprocal affection, which he sees as "completely spiritual and almost sacred."

However, a careful reading of Michelangelo's **Rime** in the context of what passed for Platonism in his times cannot support Papini's view. Contemporary writers widely repeated Ficino's classification of three kinds of love: divine, human, and bestial. Divine love advances from the visual appreciation of the object of love to the contemplation of divine essences. Human love, also accepted as a moral pursuit and frequently identified in the sixteenth century with Petrarch's love of Laura, is that which continues to delight in seeing and conversing with the person loved. Bestial love, on the other hand, plunges from sight into what Ficino calls the "concupiscence of touch." Platonizing interpreters of Petrarch were embarrassed by Petrarch's more sensual expressions, which seemed to break the bounds of moral, human love:

Con lei foss'io da che si parte il sole,
E non ci vedess'altri che le stelle,
Solo una notte! e mai non fosse l'alba. . . .
            [*Rime sparse* XXII, 31-33]

Would that I were with her from the setting of the sun, and that none saw us but the stars, one sole night, and it were never dawn.

Neither Condivi's nor Papini's defense of the spirituality of Michelangelo's passion will stand up when we read the following lines written by Michelangelo to Cavalieri, which Papini conveniently ignores:

O felice quel dì, se questo è certo!
Fermisi in un momento il tempo e l'ore,
il giorno e 'l sol nella su' antica traccia,
acciò ch' i' abbi, e non già per mie merto,

il desïato mie dolce signore
per sempre nell'indegne e pronte braccia.

If this [your compassion toward me] is certain, how happy that day! May time and the hours, the day and the sun stop suddenly in their ancient track, so that, even if not by my own merit, I may hold forever in my undeserving and ready arms, my sweet, desired lord.

These lines, echoing Petrarch's most openly sensual utterance, are clearly not susceptible of Platonic interpretation in the sixteenth-century sense—nor, for that matter, in ours.

My own conclusion on this much-debated point is that Michelangelo wrote poems replete with overtones of Platonic philosophy to a handsome young man for whom he felt a passionate ardor, the intensity and sensuality of which were considerably greater than that allowed by his age to one who would call himself a Platonic lover. Some of Michelangelo's letters to Cavalieri tend to confirm this fact.

There was another way, besides the intellectualization of love, in which the Renaissance Platonists could avoid the idea of homosexuality. Was it not possible that the passion of love, the dynamic for the ascent of Diotima's ladder, could be sparked not by a young man, but even by a young woman, someone not unlike Petrarch's golden-haired Laura? It could indeed! The first post-Ficinian Platonist clearly to choose this path was Pietro Bembo, eventually a Cardinal in the Roman Catholic Church—the same Bembo who canonized Petrarch and Boccaccio as the models for vernacular poetry and prose. Pietro Bembo, the immensely prestigious classicist from Venice who defended the literary excellence of the Tuscan vernacular, was soon to count many followers in the transformation of the philosophic love dialogue of Ficino and Leone Ebreo into a primarily literary topic of wide public appeal. During the sixteenth century the interpretation of Platonic myth and theory and the illustration of Platonic love by quotations from Petrarch were to become suitable subjects for Sunday afternoon lectures in Italian academies. The marriage of Neoplatonism with Neopetrarchism was celebrated—one cannot say "consummated" in this case—in Bembo's *Asolani,* published in 1505.

Thereafter the writing of sonnets and canzoni after the manner of Petrarch assumed epidemic proportions. I use the word advisedly; it was a disease. No one was to achieve in lyric poetry the Olympian heights of the master of Vaucluse. In the long century that runs from the appearance of Bembo to the tragic death of Giordano Bruno in 1600, only a few names stand out in the realm of the lyric: Torquato Tasso, Luigi Tansillo, Gaspara Stampa, perhaps Giovanni della Casa, Annibal Caro, Vittoria Colonna, and several others, but certainly also Michelangelo Buonarroti. None of them even remotely approach the level of excellence achieved in narrative poetry by Ariosto and Tasso. Those who stand out from the crowd do so by virtue of a rare, but unmistakable afflatus. Poetry is after all, as Plato said it was, a divine madness; and that divine madness was in Michelangelo Buonarroti.

Michelangelo's poems are not easy to read. Their texture is as rough as that of his unfinished *Prisoners* in the Accademia delle Belle Arti in Florence. I have not seen the autographs of his sonnets, but Girard, who studied them carefully for his recent critical edition, tells us they sometimes show evidence of the haste with which he wrote down his first draft—

frequently on a corner of some sketch, now on the back of a letter, now in the margin of a financial account. But to finish them—ah! that was another matter. Sometimes they were left unfinished. Sometimes a given line was rewritten as many as five or ten times. Even in their final state, one misses the even flow, the perfect diction of Petrarch and his most accomplished followers. The verbal energy comes out in irregular jets, so to speak, giving us for an instant the stark beauty and the incisiveness of a line from Dante, but resulting ultimately in flawed splendor. If we range through the volume of Michelangelo's poetry, picking a line here and a tercet there, we can easily delude ourselves into thinking that we have found a master poet. Perhaps this fact accounts for the awe and enthusiasm which his verse has inspired among foreign readers, notably in Germany. To find poems which are excellent in their entirety is more difficult. Compared with his sculptures and paintings, his poems have only a marginal importance. The very fact that he wrote them at all may be seen as an expression of the humanists' ideal of the universal man, which called forth verses of sorts even from the totally untrained Benvenuto Cellini. Michelangelo himself clearly separated his verse writing, wherein he was an amateur, from his professional activity as an artist. His biographer Condivi, a younger contemporary, wrote,

> Since he takes great delight in the discussions of learned men, he has also derived pleasure from reading writers of both prose and verse, among whom he especially admires Dante, delighted by the wonderful intelligence of that man, whom he knows almost in his entirety. Yet he knows perhaps as much of Petrarch. And not only does he take pleasure in reading them, but in writing as well sometimes, as may be seen from some of his sonnets, which give excellent evidence of his great inventiveness and discernment. . . . But he does this more for his own pleasure than because he would make a profession of it, always disparaging himself and accusing his ignorance in these matters.

The contortions and imperfections of Michelangelo's verses have been interpreted somewhat romantically as the same internal struggle between form and matter, spirit and flesh, which found expression in his sculpture and painting. A more realistic view of these imperfections would consider them simply the inevitable result of an inadequate literary education.

When Michelangelo began writing sonnets and letters to Vittoria Colonna, some time after their initial meeting, he was in his sixties and the famous poetess in her late forties. She replied to his letters, but despite the fact that she addressed verses to other poets of her time, she did not answer Michelangelo's sonnets. The overall picture of their relationship which one derives from their correspondence and from the poems that Michelangelo addressed to her is that of two ageing people "tied," as Vittoria says, "by a Christian knot of surest affection," engaged in a religious dialogue. For Michelangelo, Vittoria plays the role of a mediatress between himself and the Divinity, not unlike that of the *donna angelicata,* or "angel-lady," of *stilnuovo* poetry. The following madrigal may be taken as typical:

> S'egli è che 'l buon desio
> porti dal mondo a Dio
> alcuna cosa bella,
> sol la mie donna è quella,
> a chi ha gli occhi fatti com'ho io.
> Ogni altra cosa oblio

> e sol di tant'ho cura.
> Non è gran maraviglia,
> s'io l'amo e bramo e chiamo a tutte l'ore;
> nè proprio valor mio,
> se l'alma per natura
> s'appoggia a chi somiglia
> ne gli occhi gli occhi, ond'ella scende fore.
> Se sente il primo amore
> come suo fin, per quel qua questa onora:
> c'amar diè 'l servo chi 'l signore adora.

> If it is true that good desire brings a thing of beauty from the world to God, only my lady can be *that,* to one who has eyes made like mine. I forget every other thing and care only for this. It is no great wonder if I love and desire and invoke her at every hour; nor is it my merit if my soul by nature finds support in her who in her eyes reflects the eyes through which my soul issues forth. If my soul feels primal Love as its end, it therefore honors her [on earth] this lady: for he who adores the lord must love the servant.

Michelangelo wrote many love poems that are addressed neither to Cavalieri nor to Vittoria Colonna. Some of them are excellent, and the show a fairly wide variation of tone. It would be interesting to know for whom they were intended, and whether some of them were merely literary exercises. We shall probably never know.

How moving, in another sonnet, is his tribute to Dante:

> Di Dante dicco, che mal conosciute
> fur l'opre suo da quel popolo ingrato
> che solo a iusti manca di salute.

> Fuss'io pur lui! c'a tal fortuna nato,
> per l'aspro esilio suo, co' la virtute,
> dare' del mondo il più felice stato.

> I speak of Dante, whose greatness was insufficiently recognized by that ungrateful people [the Florentine people] who denies its favor only to just men. O, would that I were he! Born as he was to such fortune, I would give up the happiest condition in the world in order to have his *virtù* [ability], and with it, face his harsh exile.

Here one great artist, fully conscious of his creative power, pays heartfelt homage to another, who was equally conscious of his own greatness. It would be rewarding to trace Michelangelo's debt to Dante—not only in his great paintings such as the Last Judgment, as German scholars did in the nineteenth century, but in his verses as well. But here we must be content with the mere observation that there are few if any poets in cinquecento Italy in whom Dante's presence is felt more strongly than in Michelangelo.

There remains yet another thread to mention in the tapestry of Michelangelo's *Rime:* those violent and bizarre poems of humor and ill humor in which, even when we least expect it, serious echoes resound. Consider these lines:

> I' sto rinchiuso come la midolla,
> de la sua scorza, qua pover e solo,
> come spirto legato in un'ampolla:

> e la mia scura tomba è picciol volo,
> dov'è Aragn' e mill'opre e lavoranti,
> e fan di lor filando fusaiuolo.

> D'intorn' a l'uscio ho mete di giganti,
> chè chi mangi' uva o ha presa medicina

non vanno altrove a cacar tutti quanti.

> I am enclosed here like the wood inside its bark, poor and alone; like spirits imprisoned in a vial; and my dark tomb is so small that there is little room for flight. In it are Arachne and a thousand works and workers [in other words, a thousand spiders with their webs] and they turn with their threads like so many spinners. Around my door there is the excrement of giants, for all those who eat grapes or take some medicine go nowhere else to defecate.

That is just the beginning. And so he continues for another forty-six lines with "gatti, carogne, . . . la tosse, il freddo, . . . dilombato, crepato, infranto e rotto, . . . la maniconia, . . . un calabron in un orciuolo, . . . in un orecchio un ragnatelo, . . . " (" cats, carrion, . . . a cough, the cold, . . . broken-backed, cracked, shattered, and broken, . . . melancholy, . . . a hornet in a jug, . . . in an ear a cobweb, . . ."). He concludes:

> L'arte pregiata, ov'alcun tempo fui
> di tant' opinion, mi rec' a questo,
> povero, vecchio e servo in forz'altrui,
> ch i' son disfatto, s' i' non muoro presto.

> The prized art for which I once had so much fame has brought me to this, poor, old and a slave to the will of others, so that I am finished, if I don't die soon.

This *capitolo,* if formally it is humorous, contains a very grim humor. Stark misery in old age, the feeling of neglected greatness—who has expressed them better? And what pathos in the last line, "ch' i' son disfatto, s' i' non muoro presto" ("for I am finished, if I don't die soon")!

This is indeed a somber note on which to end our brief discussion of Michelangelo's poetry. We might have ended on the high note of the heaven-wafted flame of love. Yet it is not inappropriate to conclude with a note of contrast which will once again remind us of the overpowering humanity of Italy's greatest artist and of the variegated, ever-changing richness which characterizes the Italian Renaissance. (pp. 15-33)

> *John Charles Nelson, "The Poetry of Michelangelo," in* Developments in the Early Renaissance, *edited by Bernard S. Levy, State University of New York Press, 1972, pp. 15-35.*

ROBERT J. CLEMENTS (essay date 1965)

[*Clements is a leading twentieth-century authority on Michelangelo's life and creative career. In the following excerpt from his 1965 study* The Poetry of Michelangelo, *he discusses Platonism in Michelangelo's poetry.*]

When Lorenzo de'Medici took the boy Michelangelo into his garden, it was not merely to furnish him with the necessities of his craft mentioned in Alberti's *De Statua* or to give him casual instruction on mimesis (e.g., "old fauns, like old men, have not retained all their teeth"). It was equally to give the unschooled boy some of the learning necessary that his art might have substance. This explains why the Magnifico admitted the boy also to his home, just as Cosimo before him had taken in the eighteen-year-old Marsilio Ficino. Michelangelo would not otherwise have come into direct commerce with the greatest of the early Platonists. Ficino had recently terminated the *Theologia Platonica* and Pico completed his commentary on the *Enneads* in 1491, precisely when Michel-

angelo was living in the home of Lorenzo. The boy was thus a witness to the excitement caused by the arrival of Plotinus's work in Italy. If there are constant evocations of Plato in Michelangelo's work, there are also some passages which would indicate that he knew Plotinus. Unschooled in Latin, he could nevertheless avail himself of the Platonic discussions in the Medici household. These discussions made of him (for the efforts to make Michelangelo an Etruscan seem endless) a "platonico etrusco." As time went on he could read the Italian versions of Ficino's commentary, and such Platonic works as his patron Lorenzo's poetry, Benivieni's *Canzona di amor celeste e divino,* Diacetto's *Libri d'amore,* Bembo's conversations, and the poetry of his friend and counselor Poliziano, whose octave "Costei ha privo il ciel d'ogni bellezza" is, in Nesca Robb's words, "prophetic of Michelangelo." If many pages have been devoted to the Platonic interpretation of Michelangelo's works of art—especially the Medici Chapel, which has inspired at least three books dwelling on its Platonism—the poetry remains no less Platonic. Miss Robb wrote [in *Neoplatonism of the Italian Renaissance* (1935)], "It was left for Michelangelo to inform the Petrarchan-Neoplatonic lyric with something of the fire and vigour that distinguishes his art." The success of Lorenzo's immersion of the young sculptor into the atmosphere of the Platonic Academy is nowhere better measured than by Berni's perceptive comment on Michelangelo's artistic and poetic Platonism:

> Ho visto qualche sua compositione:
> Sono ignorante e pur direi d'havelle
> Lette tutte nel mezzo di Platone.

> [I have seen some of his compositions;
> I am ignorant, and yet could claim
> To have read them all in the middle of Plato.]

Berni, with his usual sagacity, localised in this *capitolo* the one element of Platonism most exploited by Michelangelo as a poet: the *kalakagathon*—the idealistic system expounded by Platonists and Neo-Platonists. This area of Platonism—involving the ideal world above zones and spheres/perception and reminiscence of that world/the meteorisis of the soul—informs a major segment of his **Rime.** It is applied to his outpourings of love, his pieces on art, his theorising on beauty, and even his sonnets anticipating death. . . . To complete the inventory of imagery which Neo-Platonism placed at the disposal of the Renaissance poets, we might mention those which Michelangelo as poet rejected. There is no mention in the **Rime** of such familiar Platonic elements as the ladder of love (though the ascents to Febo's *poggio* are suggestive of it), the androgyne, the unchecked steed, the four furies, demons, the Great Year, or the torches that light the path to heaven. (pp. 228-29)

[The] concept of prototypical form which exists and remains in heaven but whose reflection or imitation may be perceived on earth by those endowed with a special vision is at the basis of most Renaissance Platonism. It was particularly appealing to Michelangelo, engaged in the mimetic arts. The archetypal art-form, which Michelangelo called *idea, concetto, immago,* or *immagine,* existed by God's grace on earth within the very materials of art. This is best expressed in the famous quatrain "Non ha l'ottimo artista alcun concetto" . . ., which Varchi first discovered and which launched Michelangelo's fame as a philosophic poet. (It is an amusing irony that Varchi's labored commentary on the quatrain views it continually as essentially Aristotelian [see excerpt by Varchi dated 1547], no doubt a surprise to Michelangelo, who . . . hailed the commentary nevertheless as "coming from God.")

The four words describing the prototypical art-form crop up throughout the **Rime,** always in a Platonic sense: "il buon concetto," "un concetto di bellezza," "l'immagine vera," "l'immagine uiua in pietra alpestre e dura," "d'un'immagine uiua," "l'immagine del cor," "ho concetto alcun immago," etc. The *concetto* then becomes the artistic objective, the perfect coupling of form and content, which the talented artist knows is possible for him to achieve. It is as true for the goldsmith as it is for the painter and sculptor:

> Only with fire does the smith bend iron
> Into his cherished *concetto* and fine work.

And it is true even for the writer, as we suggested earlier. The sonnet **"Si come nella penna e nell'inchiostro"** assumes that artistic creations exist within the ink of his inkwell. Tityus, Orlando, Panurge, all preexisted in the ink of their creators.

The perception of the *concetto* is restricted to those with a special endowment of vision. The eye in Plato and Plotinus may have an inner, intellectual power as well as the outer vision given to all. The elite which possess this inner vision are called *accorti:*

> Every beauty which is to be seen here below
> Resembles that merciful source whence we are all come
> More than anything else, if one is a person of perception.

The object perceived by the outer eye passes through the retina and becomes lodged in the heart; here it grows into a larger image corresponding to the *typos* in heaven of which heretofore it has been the mere reflection. The image swelling within the heart may grow to such size that it occupies the entire body, an idea which could explain Michelangelo's curious thought:

> Make of my entire body one single eye, nor let there be
> Then any part of me not taking pleasure in thee.

In the very Platonic sonnet, **"La uita del mie amor',"** God transforms the poet into a whole eye: "Me fe' san ochio e te luc' et splendore." This mechanism is best explained in the dialogue between the poet and Love, **"Dimmi di gratia, Amor, se gli ochi mei."** Like Phaedrus interrogating Socrates, the poet asks if true beauty is contained in the object or person before his eyes or whether it is something within him. Love replies with [a lesson in Platonism] . . . , explaining how beauty is converted into something finer as it passes from the outer to the inner eye. This conversion of the outer into an inner vision is again described:

> As I draw my soul, which sees through the eyes,
> Closer to the beauty which I saw at first,
> The image therein grows, and the other recedes
> As though unworthy and without any value.

The implication seems to be that whereas the earthly image makes the poet tender, the heavenly archetype makes him feel greatness and possibly more power. This expanded inner image has a tremendous effect, even against death, when the image is of a loved one:

> But the true image.
> Which keeps me alive, then rises to the heart
> So that love might not be vanquished by death.

When Michelangelo looked upon the beauty of Tommaso

Cavalieri, the image of this patrician was converted into that of his lofty *typos,* already known through anamnesis.

> That, friend, which in thy gracious face I see
> Scarce in this present life may man express;
> The spirit, wearing yet its fleshly dress
> By this upborne has looked on deity.
> And though the throng, malign and brutish, free
> Its gibes and scoffs at what the few possess,
> There fails no joy from this warm eagerness,
> This chaste desire, this love, this fealty.
> For every beauty that we look on here
> Brings, to wise souls, in recollection clear
> The merciable fount whence all things flow;
> Nor other pledge nor other fruit have we
> Of heaven on earth. Who loves thee faithfully
> To God ascends, and makes death precious so.
> (Nesca Robb)

Within this idealistic context . . . , the poet manages to revile those slanderers who gave Tommaso concern. Of this particular sonnet, **"Veggio nel tuo bel uiso"** [J. H. Whitfield claims in *A Short History of Italian Literature* (1960)]: "It is of Shakespeare rather than of Bembo that he reminds us." Once the eyes have transformed the earthly image to the heavenly one, the soul itself ascends to its source of origin:

> The soul, the whole and sound intellect,
> Through the eyes ascends more free and loose
> To thy lofty beauty . . .

The eyes themselves begin to long for the heavenly beauties, for the *accorti* weary easily of mere earthly beauties, which arrive accompanied by thoughts of death rather than everlasting life:

> Ravished by all that to the eyes is fair,
> Yet hungry for the joys that truly bless,
> My soul can find no stair
> To mount to heaven; save earth's loveliness.
> For from the stars above
> Descends a glorious light
> That lifts our longing to their highest height
> And bears the name of love.
> Nor is there aught can move
> A gentle heart, or purge or make it wise,
> But beauty and the starlight of his eyes. . . .
> (George Santayana)

[Splendid sonnets to Cavalieri extol] the union of two perfect lovers, with their fusion of wills. **"Veggio co be uostr'ochi"** implies that a fused vision is best able to give the weaker lover the acuity needed to witness the sweet splendors ("dolce lume") of heaven.

The special Neo-Platonic conception of vision espoused by Michelangelo gives deeper meaning to two seemingly banal lines of the **Rime.** "Nessun uolto fra noi è che pareggi/L'immagine del cor" would seem at first glance to mean that a person's face seems handsomer to those who love him; Platonically, it portends that the expanded image in the heart is metamorphosed from that captured by the outer eye. Similarly, the curious single line: "Che mal si puo amar ben chi non si uede" carries not only its apparent, superficial meaning, "out of sight, out of heart," but implies also that love comes not with the outer vision but after the conversion of the inner vision. This same tribute to the power of the *visus interior* is contained in a madrigal probably addressed to Vittoria Colonna:

> Since man's thought falls late in love

1532 drawing by Michelangelo of his friend Andrea Quaratesi.

Through that eye which cannot see
[Divine things] through its own power.

Let us turn now to the theme of the winged soul longing to return to the paradise from which it descended. Imprisoned in the body, its wings weakened, it remembers the joys of the empyrean, and this makes it impatient. As Francesca sighed to Dante and Vergil, "Nessun maggior dolore."

Because the half of me which comes from heaven
Thereto with great longing wings its way back.

The wings which Plato assigned to the soul are viewed by Ficino not as plumes but actually as lights, one innate and one divine, which carry the soul about as though they were wings. "Lumen igitur habet geminum; naturale alterum, sive ingenitum; divinum alterum et infusum, quibus una conjunctis ceu duabus alis per sublimen pervolare valeat regionem." Michelangelo, like most of the Cinquecento poets, knows Ficino's special view of these wings, but favors the traditional view of Plato himself.

One of the poems best illustrating this theme was probably inspired by Cavalieri. **"Non uider gli occhi miei"** does not exist in manuscript form, but appeared in the *Due lezzioni* of Varchi, who explicated it before the Florentine Academy. The sonnet expresses a conviction that an ideal love will spur the soul's return to heaven. Having shown the heights to which true love can carry us, the poet dispatches with three lines the tawdry imitation of sensual love:

Mine eyes beheld no thing of mortal shape,
When the first gleam of thy serene regards
Shone on me, and the soul, that aye ascends
To its end, had hoped to find in them its peace.
Stretching its wing toward Heaven, from whence it came,
It aims not only at the beauty which
Pleases the eyes; since that is frail and weak,
It passes on to universal form.
(John E. Taylor)

The rise of the earthly image to its archetypal phase is the transition from a particular to a universal. In this sonnet the wings which operate the ascension, as is often the case, are not specifically mentioned. An excellent example (1536-42) of the wingless soul is found in the following quatrain referring to the descent and imprisonment of a soul (wingless as the angels of the Sistine Vault):

The immortal soul, aspiring to that height
It stooped from, to your earthly prison came,
An angel of compassions infinite
To heal all hearts and bring our earth good fame.
(Nesca Robb)

When the fusion of two lovers is achieved, their souls, like their wills, are joined and may wing their way back to heaven as one:

One soul in two bodies is made eternal,
Raising both to heaven with equal wings.
I fly with your wings and without plumes,

Lofty thoughts are precursors of the *ascensio*. As in Bernardino Daniello's "Se 'l viver nostro è breve giorno oscuro" and Du Bellay's "Si nostre vie est moins qu'une journèe" the poet eyes heaven longingly; such thoughts spur the soul's wings to spread:

Now, weary, I raise my thought on wings, and spur
Myself on to a more secure and noble place.

The winged soul may return not only to the empyrean but also to its own star of origin:

But since the liberated spirit
Returns to its star . . .

When the lofty thoughts are missing, the soul no longer has the will to ascend on its wings:

My soul is plucked and shaved of its plumes.

The general idea of the ascent of the soul was known to Michelangelo from a host of sources both Christian and Platonic. At times it is uncertain whether his use of the image is Christian or Platonic, or a fusion of the two, as in its occurrence in poetry of his idol Petrarch (in "Quel antico mio dolce mio Signore"):

Anchor, e questo è quel che tutto avanza,
Da volar sopra 'l ciel le avea dat' ali,
Per le cose mortali,
Che son scala al Fattor, chi ben l'estima.

The staircase mentioned in Petrarch was also a Dantean image, for his St. Thomas Aquinas speaks of the ray of grace as leading only upward: "quella scala/U' senza risalir nessun discende." Other writers known to Michelangelo used the image of the stair: Pico, Lorenzo de' Medici, Ficino, Giambattista Lapini, and Leo the Jew. Michelangelo, despite his preoccupation with the stairs of the Laurentian Library, of the Capitoline, and so on, does not associate his image of ascent with *scale* or *gradi.* The idea of soaring ascent, a preoccupation of his art, is most evident in his drawings: the several resurrections of Christ, the more limited rearising of Lazarus. He did not portray Daedalus, but mentions him in [a] two-line fragment. . . . (We omit Michelangelo's interest in the soarings of angels, visible in the drawings of the *Sogno* and the *Sacrifice of Isaac* or in the *Conversion of Paul* and the Sistine *Creations.*) If the lofty elevations of the soul describe an ideal love or one going well, the inability to soar (the phoenix, the apathetic soul) or the plunging fall describe an unhappy or disastrous love. Thus, the three drawings of the *Fall of Phaeton* (who wished to fly with Phoebus) symbolise the fall of Michelangelo after the break with Febo di Poggio ("Onde io rouino e caggio"). The casting of Tityus into hell has a similar personal meaning. . . . (pp. 229-34)

The idea of soaring and plunging, Christian and Platonic and mythical in origin, comes thus to have a principally psychological meaning in Michelangelo's love poetry. This is an easy transition, in any case, for most of the Ficinian reasoning on Plato was centered in the context of love, and Neo-Platonism's re-emergence in Renaissance literature was principally in amorous poetry.

Two minor themes will conclude our passing discussion of Platonism. The concept of Eros and Anteros which was picked up by Renaissance literature and art was so closely affiliated with Platonism that Antoine Héroët held it to be "aultre invention extraicte de Platon." If Plato never told the tale of the sibling loves popularized by Héroët, he did use the word *anteros* in the sense of reciprocated affection. By the Cinquecento the notion had evolved to one of two conflicting loves, one divine and one carnal. It is in this sense only that the Eros-Anteros concept found its way into Michelangelo's **Rime:**

> The love of which I speak aspires to the heights—
> Too unlike that for a woman; it ill befits
> A heart wise and virile to burn for a woman.
>
> The one draws you to heaven, the other down to earth;
> The one inhabits the soul, the other the senses,
> Aiming its bow at base and vile things.

Eros or Cupid has by now become the god of passion, while Anteros symbolises the pure love which elevates one as do the wings of the soul.

The other development of the Anteros, entirely different, is the *Contr'-amour,* the poem emphasising the ugly or ridiculous features and characteristics of a mistress or ex-mistress. Poliziano's "Una vecchia mi vagheggia" is a perfect example. Such poems, a product of the antifeminine viewpoint expressed in Boccaccio's *Corbaccio* and become common coin in the misogynistic literature of the Renaissance, frequently bore the title of "Anteros." It is inevitable that Michelangelo should have been interested in this vogue of misogynistic verse. Michelangelo's two parodies of love poetry (**"Io crederrei, se tu fussi di sasso"** and **"Tu ha' 'l uiso"**) may contain one or two misogynistic touches ("Perchè non basta a una donna bella/Goder le lodi d'un amante solo,/Che sua belta potre' morir con ella"), but in general they mock love poetry rather than mocking the woman addressed.

The Platonic (and Pythagorean) doctrine of metempsychosis makes a brief appearance in the **Rime.** Like so many of the Renaissance poets, Michelangelo availed himself of this theme variously described in the *Republic* and the *Phaedrus:*

> If it is true that the soul, from its body freed,
> In some other person may return,
> For a short and brief sojourn,
> To live and die another time . . .

And, as with the Pléiade poets in France and the Platonists in Italy, his adaptation is fitted into a love poem. Michelangelo seemed to feel that beauty and form are kept in the storehouse of nature; they are given prodigally to men and women at youth, but slowly taken back with the passage of time.

> I believe that nature takes back unto itself
> All that which day by day disappears from thee,
> That it may serve for the birth from a greater womb
> With a better fate and with more extreme care
> To form anew another person
> Who will have thy angelic and serene face.

There is no hint of the time which will elapse before the beauties are utilised again in a reincarnation, although Ficino had associated the doctrine of transmigration with the Platonic Great Year. Platonic and Ficinian thought on palingenesis varies from Michelangelo's treatment, for in Plato and his exegete the emphasis is on the transmigration of the soul, not of the body. Michelangelo evokes the reincarnation of souls on the Day of Judgement, a repeated theme of the epitaphs to Cecchino Bracci.

There is in addition . . . another, clearer suggestion of the Platonic doctrine of reminiscence. Just as the individual's soul may recall prenatal experience, so may one experience racial memory, the "déjà vu." Michelangelo senses that it may be some primeval beauty out of racial memory which so affects him:

> I know not if it is the desired light
> Of its primordial maker which the soul feels,
> Or whether out of the memory of the race
> Some other beauty shines within the heart . . .

(pp. 234-36)

Robert J. Clements, in his The Poetry of Michelangelo, *New York University Press, 1965, 368 p.*

J. H. WHITFIELD   (lecture date 1967)

[*In the following excerpt, Whitfield notices parallels between the sonnets of Michelangelo and William Shakespeare, noting as well Christian and Platonic elements in Michelangelo's poetry.*]

Michelangelo died in 1564. It was the date of Shakespeare's birth. His poems were first printed (garbled) in 1623, the year of the First Folio; and Shakespeare's *Sonnets* had been printed also in 1609. Now these dates exclude the possibility of influence (unlikely also, since Shakespeare had less Italian than either Latin or Greek, presumably). Yet it is not only the consonance of time, and fame, which brings Shakespeare and Michelangelo together. Out of all the lyric tradition, here are the two who verge on homosexual love: Mr W. H. stands opposite the Dark Lady of the *Sonnets,* as Tommaso de' Cavalieri alongside Vittoria Colonna. Not only that, but for both of them the answer is different from that of the permissive society. For this, see in Shakespeare the sonnet

> A woman's face with Nature's own hand painted,

and in Michelangelo (*inter alia*)

> Non vider gli occhi miei cosa mortale

(My eyes have seen no mortal thing),

with its later line

Voglia sfrenata el senso è, non amore

(Sense is unbridled lust, it is not love),

which may remind us of a celebrated sonnet of Shakespeare,

The expense of spirit in a waste of shame
Is lust in action

The consciousness, too, which Shakespeare has, of words (his words) outriding time,

Not marble, nor the gilded monuments
Of princes, shall outlive this powerful rhyme . . .

Since brass, nor stone, nor earth, nor boundless sea,
But sad mortality o'ersways their power . . . ,

is matched by Michelangelo's knowledge that his art can outlast Nature and life itself (***"Com'esser, donna, può quel c'alcun vede"***), where man turns to ashes, and his image lasts in stone,

onde dall'arte è vinta la natura

(Thus Nature's overcome by art.)

Yet both Shakespeare and Michelangelo can come together in an image of Man confronted with the ruthless hand of Time:

Time doth transfix the flourish set on youth,
And delves the parallels in beauty's brow,
Feeds on the rarities of nature's truth,
And nothing stands but for his scythe to mow.

Against the elaboration of which fascinating rhetoric (recalling T. S. Eliot's awareness of the contrast between Dante's and Shakespeare's poetry) we may set the bare bones of Michelangelo's lament:

Muovesi 'l tempo, e compartisce l'ore
al viver nostr'un pessimo veleno;
lu' come falce e no' sian come fieno

(Time moves, a bitter poison marks the hours out of our life; Time like a scythe and we like hay).

I must not stay too long among these casual, though interesting, parallels with Shakespeare. Nor must I mislead you into thinking Michelangelo unsophisticated. Certainly, however good your Italian, you will be grateful for the paraphrases which Girardi (as Guasti before him in 1863) has added in elucidation of the poems. And sometimes the elaboration of a conceit may remind us of Donne rather than of Shakespeare. You will remember that little poem called "A Feaver," in which his mistress's fever becomes, by hyperbole, the fire that is the essence of the world's end:

O wrangling schooles, that search what fire
Shall burn this world, had none the wit

Unto this knowledge to aspire,
That this her feaver might be it?

Now turn to Michelangelo **"Negli anni molti e nelle molte pruove,"** in which all achievement is late, the greater the later, and so can least last. What then of Nature, which has reached its utmost in your beauty, and therefore must end soon, so that I can neither think nor say which hurts or helps

the most, in seeing you, either my great delight, or the world's end:

né so pensar né dire
qual nuoca o giovi più, visto 'l tuo 'spetto,
o 'l fin dell'universo o 'l gran diletto.

That being said, the nineteenth century swept aside, as an historic curiosity, Donne and Shakespeare being left, as accidental encounters in adjacent time, we are left with Michelangelo. Now there are two simple, though opposite, propositions that must come first. We may not take it that because his **Rime** have been so long neglected, therefore they cannot have poetic worth. But on the other side, we must not say, Michelangelo's genius as an artist is supreme, therefore his poetry has equal rank. For his art is his art, and his poetry, his poetry, and we cannot merely presume a judgment equal on both sides. Next, we must look (as some recent Italian criticism has done) to the areas of catchment, the influences which predetermine the nature of his poetry. And here the date of Michelangelo's birth is a basic and significant factor. 1475: it leaves him mainly open, in spite of his longevity, to the currents of fifteenth-century Florence: the neo-platonism of Marsilio Ficino, the austere Christianity of Savonarola. And behind these, of course, are the great exemplars of Florentine (or Italian) poetry, Dante and Petrarch. Now for the first of these we have some salient connections. There is the presumption of equal stature in differing fields; there are the sonnets specifically addressed to Dante (which Southey and others translated), with the explicit homage of Michelangelo:

Fuss'io pur lui! c'a tal fortuna nato,
per l'aspro esilio suo, co' la virtute,
dare' del mondo il più felice stato

(Would I were he! for born so fortunate,
for his sharp exile, with his worth,
I'd give the happiest condition in the world)

—which recalls the proud line of Dante himself (*l'esilio che m'è dato onor mi tegno*). And two sonnets away, a closing line,

simil uom né maggior non nacque mai

(neither a like nor else a greater man was ever born)

In one who feels so strongly the weight of Dante, and who writes in Tuscan verse, there will be obvious places where he echoes Dante. And half a dozen, at least, of these will be discoverable to the reader of Michelangelo's **Rime**. It is not enough to make them seem in any way dantesque.

Indeed, though Michelangelo never expresses for Petrarch the reverence he has for Dante, or ever mentions him by name, yet his **Rime** can be more easily explained in juxtaposition with those of Petrarch. Here again I must issue the caveat which attaches to that birth-date of Michelangelo. For Petrarchism will flower with Bembo after the first quarter of the sixteenth century, but there is no sign that Michelangelo is ever aware of Bembo, nor does he attempt the orthodox imitation of Petrarchan themes which Bembo and his many followers bring back to artificial life. Perhaps the only influence from the sixteenth-century fashion, quite different, and so far unclaimed, is that of Ariosto. This is in the composition in *ottava rima* (the metre of the *Orlando furioso*), **"Nuovo piacere e di maggiore stima,"** written before 1534 (the definitive edition of the *Furioso,* which took all Italy by storm, is 1532), where echoes of Politian and of the *Nencia* of Lorenzo have been seen for the opening stanzas. But the last two verses are pure Ariosto, written under the strong imprint of those personifications which are the engine-power of the *Orlando furioso:*

> Cogli occhi onesti e bassi in ver 'la terra,
> vestito d'oro e di vari ricami,
> il Falso va, c'a iusti sol fa guerra;
> ipocrito, di fuor par c'ognuno ami;
> perch'è di ghiaccio, al sol si cuopre e serra;
> sempre sta' n corte, e par che l'ombra brami;
> e ha per suo sostegno e compagnia
> la Fraude, la Discordia e la Bugia.
>
> L'Adulazion v'è poi, ch'è pien d'affanni,
> giovine destra e di bella persona;
> di piú color coperta di piú panni,
> che 'l cielo a primavera a' fiori non dona:
> ottien ciò che la vuol con dolci inganni,
> e sol di quel che piace altrui ragiona;
> ha 'l pianto e 'l riso in una voglia sola;
> cogli occhi adora, e con le mani invola.

You will forgive me if here I do not pause to translate, since this is a sidetrack in Michelangelo's verse. But I cannot refrain from adding the celebrated stanza from Canto XIV of the *Furioso,* of which this is a palpable echo. In this Canto, to make assurance sure, you will find pictured both Fraud and Discord, but it is Fraud which has always stolen the picture:

> Avea piacevol viso, abito onesto,
> Un umil volger d'occhi, un andar grave;
> Un parlar sí benigno, e sí modesto,
> Che parea Gabriel, che dicesse, Ave.
> Era brutta, e deforme in tutto il resto,
> Ma nascondea queste fattezze prave
> Con lungo abito, e largo; e sotto quello
> Attossicato avea sempre il coltello.

That we may take as Michelangelo's return for the celebrated lines of praise which Ariosto gave him in the same *Furioso,*

> quel che a par sculpe e colora,
> Michel, piú che mortale, Angel divino.

But from this marginal point, let us go back to the central links with Petrarch. In the *Secretum* Petrarch wrote of Laura as the hook of salvation, which saved him from the turpitude of youth. But in the *Canzoniere* he remains uncertain whether she is this, or a temptation. Hence the hesitations which make the pattern of the *Canzoniere.* Now with Michelangelo the terms are not precisely the same, since this time there is no Laura. But they are precisely similar, when we have put for Laura the concept of *beauty* itself. *La bellezza:* is this the divine spark which carries Michelangelo upwards, or is it a temptation which lures him downwards, and at the last an irrelevancy, to be forgotten? On the one side there is his conviction, stated in two poems of *c.* 1520:

> Amore è un concetto di bellezza
> immaginata o vista dentro al core,
> amica di virtute e gentilezza.
>
> (Love is an idea of beauty, imagined or seen
> within the heart, the friend of virtue and
> of gentleness).

And on these grounds Love can speak to him:

> I' son colui che nc' prim'anni tuoi
> gli occhi tuo infermi volsi alla beltate

> che dalla terra al ciel vivo conduce.
>
> (I am he who in your youth turned your
> weak eyes to beauty, beauty which takes
> you though alive from earth to heaven).

And on the strength of those two statements there can follow, some time after 1528, the line which sums them up:

> l'amor mi prende e la beltà mi lega
> (Love takes hold of me, and beauty binds).

It is on the fringe of this first attitude that the rare note of sensual appetite appears. You will find it in a sonnet of 1507 . . . : the garland in which each flower seems to wish to be the first to kiss her head, the dress which clasps her breast, and then pours down, the ribbon on her breast, and the belt which seems to say: here will I always press.

> E la schietta cintura che s'annoda
> mi par dir seco: qui vo' stringer sempre.
> Or che farebbon dunche le mie braccia?
>
> (What would my arms do then?)

Nor is this desire to seize and to enjoy unjustified. In a fragment of *c. 1511,* which starts from an obvious dantesque echo, we can see the answer to the unspoken question:

> Colui che 'l tutto fe', fece ogni parte
> e poi del tutto la piú bella scelse,
> per mostrar quivi le suo cose eccelse,
> com'ha fatto or colla sua divin'arte.
>
> (He who made all, made every part,
> and then from all chose out the best,
> to show in you his highest things,
> as he has done with godlike art).

That is to say, the miracle of feminine beauty is the highest act of creation. And even when Michelangelo, at the age of 50, feels the need to write of himself as 'old', yet he can still claim there is no shame in using divine things:

> E se motteggia o finge,
> chi dice in vecchia etate esser vergogna
> amar cosa divina, è gran menzogna.
>
> L'anima che non sogna,
> non pecca amar le cose di natura,
> usando peso, termine e misura.
>
> (And if men jest or jibe, saying that in old age
> it is shameful to love divine-created things,
> it is a lie. The soul which does not dream
> sins not in loving natural things, if it keeps
> weight, bounds and measure).

Nevertheless, it is here that there intrudes the note for which I have recorded already the consonance between Michelangelo and Shakespeare.

> And Time that gave doth now his gift confound.
> Time doth transfix the flourish set on youth,
> And delves the parallels in beauty's brow,
> Feeds on the rarities of nature's truth,
> And nothing stands but for his scythe to mow.
>
> lu' come falce e no' sian come fieno.

And following immediately that line (which I quoted before) there comes the lament,

> La fede è corta e la beltà non dura.

(Faith is brief, and beauty does not last).

It brings Michelangelo to a short composition . . . which seems to me to have one congener in Italian sixteenth-century poetry. This is the final chorus of Tasso's rather unhappy tragedy, *Il re Torrismondo* (though, as you will see when we come to Michelangelo's poem, Hamlet and the gravediggers are not out of sight). Here is Tasso, for once splendidly, and wholly, tragic:

> Ahi lacrime, ahi dolore!
> Passa la vita, e si dilegua, e fugge,
> Come giel che si strugge,
> Ogni altezza s'inchina, e sparge a terra,
> Ogni fermo sostegno,
> Ogni possente Regno
> In pace cadde al fin, se crebbe in guerra;
> E come raggio il verno imbruna, e more
> Gloria d'altrui splendore;
> E come alpestro, e rapido torrente,
> Come acceso baleno
> In notturno sereno,
> Come aura, o fumo, o come stral repente
> Volan le nostre fame, et ogni onore
> Sembra languido fiore.
>
> Che piú si spera, o che s'attende omai?
> Dopo trionfo, e palma
> Sol qui restano a l'alma
> Lutto, e lamenti, e lagrimosi lai.
> Che piú giova amicizia, o giova amore?
> Ahi lagrime, ahi dolore!

So Tasso on the universal theme of the brevity of human lot, and barer and less harmonious, but equally insistent, Michelangelo:

> Chiunche nasce a morte arriva
> nel fuggir del tempo; e 'l sole
> niuna cosa lascia viva.
> Manca il dolce e quel che dole
> e gl'ingegni e le parole;
> e le nostre antiche prole
> al sole ombre, al vento un fummo.
> Come voi uomini fummo,
> lieti e tristi, come siete;
> e or siàn, come vedete,
> terra al sol, di vita priva.
> Ogni cosa a morte arriva.
> Già fur gli occhi nostri interi
> Con la luce in ogni speco;
> or son voti, orrendi e neri,
> e ciò porta il tempo seco.

> (All who are born arrive at death,
> with flight of time; the sun leaves
> nothing live. The sweet, the painful
> fails, and wits and words; our ancient
> race are shadows in the sun, mist in the wind.
> We like you were men, happy and sad, like you;
> Now as you see we are, earth in the sunlight,
> lost from life.
> All things arrive at death.
> Our eyes were whole, with light in every cavity;
> now they are empty, fearsome, black,
> and time brings this about).

But it is here, of course, that there springs to Michelangelo's mind the superiority of his art. You will be aware of those accounts, first of the opening of his coffin in Florence, when he was three weeks dead, and when he seemed still as one who slept, with no corruption, and no corpse-like smell; then of

a similar adventure in the eighteenth century, when his body still appeared intact. We should not have a similar expectation today. But his sculpture? And to Michelangelo also this phenomenon, of the lesser power outbidding the greater one, appealed. You will find in one of the sonnets for Vittoria Colonna **"Com'esser, donna, può quel c'alcun vede"**, where the image lasts, while its owner dies,

> onde dall'arte è vinta la natura

> (Thus Nature's overcome by art),

and he adds in the next line,

> I 'l so, che 'l pruovo in la bella scultura,

while the close of the sonnet foresees, a thousand years after the death of Vittoria Colonna the proof of her beauty, and the reason of his love, in what he carves. *La bella scultura:* the ideas of Michelangelo, on the primacy of sculpture over painting, are to be found scattered in the **Rime.** Here, close by, it is *la prim'arte;* and these confirm the conclusion to the most celebrated *sonetto caudato,* the best-known of what we may call Michelangelo's occasional poetry, the one which grotesquely particularises the consequences for his person of the twenty months labour, as a painter, in the Sistine Chapel (**"I' ho già fatto un gozzo in questo stento"**). It ends:

> La mia pittura morta
> difendi orma', Giovanni, e 'l mio onore,
> non sendo in loco bon, né io pittore.

> (Defend my dead painting now, Giovanni,
> and my honour, for I am not in a good place,
> nor I a painter).

After what you have heard, and seen, you will have views of your own on such a judgment. But the important fact is, that it is Michelangelo's own. And it gives tremendous relief to certain attitudes. One of those is his indignation against the corruption of papal Rome, and the warlike nature of Julius II, his turbulent patron. You will find it first in the sonnet that immediately follows the one on his cramped labours on the Sistine scaffolding, which is addressed to Julius II himself,

> Signor, se vero è alcun proverbio antico,
> questo è ben quel, che chi può mai non vuole

> (No proverb truer than this ancient one,
> That he who can, will never will);

and it takes fire in that nearby sonnet (signed Vostro M. in Turchia 1512), which has always been paralleled to the invectives of Dante, or the Babylonian sonnets of Petrarch (against the papal court of Avignon). Its strength, naturally, does not derive from those, respectable, literary connections, but from the convictions of Michelangelo. From his convictions, and his pride: the necessary corollary to those two sonnets on the Rome of Julius II, and the commentary on all Michelangelo's grappling with the temporarily great who were perforce his patrons, you will find in a late fragment:

> Con tanta servitú, con tanto tedio
> e con falsi concetti e gran periglio
> dell'alma, a sculpir qui cose divine.

> (In so much servitude, with so much weariness,
> and with false thoughts, great danger to my soul,
> carving things here that are divine).

A sculpir qui cose divine: it is the one lightning-flash, the sole

The tomb of Julius II in San Pietro in Vincoli, Rome, engraved by Antonio Salamanca.

place where the veil of modesty which Michelangelo interposes between himself and the world lifts for a moment, and he claims consciously what none of us would dare dispute, the splendour of his own genius.

And still in this context, you would not forgive me if I passed over what Michelangelo has to say, within the **Rime,** of the nature of his art. And here, since I did not say it before, I may throw in an experience. In my desire to read the relevant, I sought a famous book which I had read long ago, but of which my memory was blandly (blankly) innocent: Walter Pater, *The Renaissance.* And in a row beneath the copy on the shelf in stack were the works of Stephen Phillips, with the title *Paolo and Francesca* staring me in the face. I had come for Pater, but I had also then to feed my students on *Inferno* V, and so I took both books away. Now Stephen Phillips' poetic drama was played in 1899, printed in 1900, and if you are lucky in your copy you will find what all the critics said about the greatness of his poetic achievement in the advertisement section at the end. They are written over some respectable academic names still not quite out of sight; but the play, that great achievement which was to resurrect poetic drama, is the feeblest wish-wash piffle-wiffle. Oh yes, you will say, but Walter Pater? Well, of course, I shall not speak so slightingly of him, especially as I only re-read the essay specifically enti-

tled *The Poetry of Michelangelo* [see excerpt dated 1871]. But I can tell you now, in case your own homework on Michelangelo is still to do, and will be inspired or directed by what we tell you here, that in twenty-six pages you will find perhaps half a page which speaks directly of the poetry; and in the rest nothing more nutrient than what you might have found in Stephen Phillips. And now you will wonder why I dragged them in at all: it is just because, though you will find nothing whatever in Pater, who professed to speak of Michelangelo's poetry, you will find a good deal in Sir Anthony Blunt, who only volunteered to write on artistic theory. There you will find what, in the **Rime,** is specifically concerned with art. And having said that, it may be enough for our purpose if I look to the one sonnet which you will all feel I must not fail to quote, **"Non ha l'ottimo artista alcun concetto".** There is somewhere in Vasari the illustration of the waxen image in a bath of water. As the water-level sinks, so do the features emerge. Or, as Michelangelo puts it in the next composition, it is by subtraction from the hard stone that the living image within appears. It was Mario Praz who observed that, by a curious coincidence, Donne in *The Crosse* has the same image:

> As perchance, Carvers do not faces make,
> But that away, which hid them there, do take.

And in noting other affinities in the religious lyrics, Praz added that the dates allowed no influence. And here, in this most famous of all Michelangelo's sonnets, the idea both in the mind and in the marble, and if the hand obeys the brain, it can come forth at command. Remember, though, this is not a poem on art theory, but Michelangelo, as artist, can not forget his art when he writes love-poetry. And plainly, this sculpture image is stronger than the other, out of painting, also in a composition for Vittoria Colonna **"S' egli è, donna, che puoi",** where the final appeal is to her to draw on him as he on stone or on blank paper, where there is nothing, but yet there is what I choose to put:

> Disegna in me di fuora,
> com'io fo in pietra od in candido foglio,
> che nulla ha dentro, e èvvi ciò ch'io voglio.

By now you will be feeling that, like Hamlet, I have mislaid a somewhat blunted purpose: the parallel I proposed with Petrarch. But there is still another, obvious, side to the relationship of Michelangelo with the beautiful, and you will find it best expressed in the poems for Tommaso de' Cavalieri. Tommaso de' Cavalieri is, as I have hinted, the Mr W. H. of Michelangelo's poetry, and you may feel that we are with him entering the danger zone. That is not true. The lure of the senses, for Michelangelo, is where we saw it first, in that early sonnet on the garland and the belt; and if there is any offence to be given by his poetry it will be found in the attempt to reject the senses at this point. You will find it in . . . one of the poems written for Tommaso de' Cavalieri, **"Non è sempre di colpa aspra e mortale"** . . . in which the first tercet is a rejection of woman, because love for her brings down to sense a lover who would soar up:

> L'amor di quel ch'i' parlo in alto aspira;
> donna è dissimil troppo; e mal conviensi
> arder di quella al cor saggio e virile.
>
> (The love of which I speak aspires on high;
> woman is too unlike; it ill befits
> a wise and virile heart to burn for her).

The expense of spirit in a waste of shame: it was for Tommaso also that the earlier sonnet was written from which I instanced the parallel with Shakespeare:

> Non vider gli occhi miei cosa mortale
> allor che ne'bei vostri intera pace
> trovai, ma dentro, ov'ogni mal dispiace,
> chi d'amor l'alma a sé simil m'assale;
>
> e se creata a Dio non fusse equale,
> altro che' l bel di fuor, c'agli occhi piace,
> piú non vorria; ma perch'è sì fallace,
> trascende nella forma universale.
>
> Io dico c'a chi vive quel che muore
> quetar non può disir; né par s'aspetti
> l'eterno al tempo, ove altri cangia il pelo.
>
> Voglia sfrenata el senso è, non amore,
> che l'alma uccide; e 'l nostro fa perfetti
> gli amici qui, ma piú per morte in cielo.
>
> (My eyes saw no mortal thing when I found full peace
> in your beauteous eyes, but within, where all ill
> displeases, Him who assaults my soul with love like
> to Himself; and if the soul had not been made akin
> to God, it would not seek for more than for
> the outward forms which please the eyes; but since
> these are deceitful, it transcends them to gaze
> on universal form. I say that for those who live,
> what dies can not fulfil desire; nor does it seem
> eternity belongs to time, where hair turns white.
> The senses are unbridled appetite, which kills the soul,
> not love; but ours makes perfect friendship here,
> and more, with death, in heaven above.)

There is nothing in the whole series of poems for Tommaso de' Cavalieri which belies the plain statements of that sonnet. This is not homosexuality in action, but the process by which beauty is taken upwards to its source; and this impetus gives an afflatus to the poems for Tommaso which is not equalled in the colder exchanges with the pious, and middle-ageing, Vittoria Colonna. Let me just refer you here to two sonnets of the series, **"Veggio co' bei vostr' occhi un dolce lume"** and **"I' mi son caro assai piú ch'i' non soglio."**

Meanwhile, however, there is riding up an attitude which is Christian rather than platonic, to remind us that the High Renascence, in its highest representative, is not the pagan movement dreamed up by nineteenth-century thought. The prelude is in a sonnet of 1534, **"Vorrei voler, Signor, quel ch'io non voglio"**:

> Vorrei voler, Signor, quel ch'io non voglio:
> tra 'l foco e 'l cor di ghiaccia un vel s'asconde
> che 'l foco ammorza . . .
>
> I' t'amo con la lingua, e poi mi doglio
> c'amor non giunge al cor . . .
>
> (I would I would, Lord, what I do not will:
> between heart and fire a film of ice is hid
> which damps the fire . . .
>
> I love Thee with my tongue, and then lament
> love does not reach the heart . . .)

So we pass to the moving, and eloquent, closing sequence of Michelangelo's *canzoniere*. The apprehension of beauty (and I need not labour for you the Sappho-Leopardian contrast of his own graceless form) is the breath of his being.

> Che poss'io altro che cosí non viva?
>
> (What can I do, but live like this?)

To which the answer comes two lines later, in the last line of the same sonnet,

> il cangiar sorte è sol poter divino
>
> (only the power of God can change one's lot).

Thus though there crowd about us at this point in the *Rime* the attestations of his responsiveness to beauty (which is to say, as you will know, to human beauty, for Michelangelo's awareness is all of Man, and little of Nature), we know that we are bound to pass through them, to what for Michelangelo at least must cancel them. On the one side, then, the full confession of his susceptibility:

> Passa per gli occhi al core in un momento
> qualunche obbietto di beltà lor sia,
> e per sí larga e sí capace via
> c'a mille non si chiude, non c'a cento,
> d'ogni età, d'ogni sesso . . .
>
> (Whatever beauteous object meets my eyes
> passes at once into my heart,
> and by so broad commodious a way,
> it is not shut, not to a hundred
> or a thousand such; of every age, of every sex.)

Or alongside that:

> La forza d'un bel viso a che mi sprona?
> C'altro non è c'al mondo mi diletti
>
> (What may the strength of a fair face spur me to?
> For nought else pleases me in all the world),

with its claim that beauty is the work of God, so that no guilt attaches to the love of it,

> Se ben col fattor l'opra suo consuona,
> che colpa vuol giustizia ch'io n'aspetti,
> s'i' amo, anz'ardo, e per divin concetti
> onoro e stimo ogni gentil persona?
>
> (For if indeed creation and Creator are akin,
> what fault can justice find in me,
> who love, or rather burn, and for their
> godlike qualities honour and esteem
> all gentle souls?)

And, of course, what I quoted earlier, the flash of resentment against the conditions of Rome under which he works, with the flash of revelation, that his own assessment of himself is the same as ours, comes in this late period:

> Con tanta servitú, con tanto tedio
> e con falsi concetti e gran periglio
> dell'alma, a sculpir qui cose divine.

This is Michelangelo the lightning-conductor, transmitting the beauty that comes from God in the forms of godlike art. Then equally logically he turns away,

> Piú l'alma acquista ove piú 'l mondo perde;
> l'arte e la morte non va bene insieme
>
> (The soul gains most where the world's most lost;
> art and death do not go well together.)

So Petrarch had turned from Laura,

> Che quanto piace al mondo è brevè sogno
>
> (All that pleases in the world as brief as is a dream),

so Michelangelo, in a substantial, not an imitative gesture, for this is life, not literature, renounces art, the idol and the monarch of his life (**"Giunto è già 'l corso della vita mia"**), with its specific

> Né pinger né scolpir fie piú che quieti

> (To paint or sculpt can bring no comfort now),

and its appeal, instead, to the Christ, who had been the centre of all Michelangelo's late art, and who now replaces it in his own person. All Michelangelo's dazzling career he now enters in the chronicle of wasted time:

> Carico d'anni e di peccati pieno

> (Laden with years and full of sin),

he asks only to hate the world, and have the earnest of eternity:

> Mettimi in odio quanto 'l mondo vale
> e quante suo bellezze onoro e colo,
> c'anzi morte caparri eterna vita.

For those who still hanker for those old views on the pagan nature of the Renascence world there is no better antidote than the last *Rime,* or the last works, of Michelangelo. (pp. 105-21)

> *J. H. Whitfield, "The Poetry of Michelangelo," in* Collected Essays on Italian Language & Literature Presented to Kathleen Speight, *Giovanni Aquilecchia, Stephen N. Cristea, Sheila Ralphs, eds., Manchester University Press, 1971, pp. 101-21.*

ALMA B. ALTIZER (essay date 1973)

[*In the following excerpt, Altizer relates Michelangelo's growth as a poet to his work in the plastic arts.*]

Michelangelo was not a consistently "good" poet. He was an extraordinary poet, whose best poems embody a unity and power of vision which make them seem at once rugged and sophisticated, archaic and contemporary, obscure and startlingly clear. What is the vision that informs these poems? It is the same vision that many of his less successful poems struggle and fail to formulate fully—an intuition into a fundamental dialectic of human consciousness. Recurring throughout the 302 poems and fragments which comprise the body of his poetic work is a preoccupation with problems of imagination and reality: relationships between perception and creation, tensions between subject and object, spirit and matter, lover and beloved, interior and exterior, beauty and ugliness. A passionate desire to give poetic form to the creative, life-giving process and its opposite, death or destruction, is what seems to motivate Michelangelo's endeavors as a poet.

As the poems devote themselves increasingly to the exploration of these tensions and antitheses, particularly within the context of love, the poet comes to understand that the basic relationship between the apparent opposites is dialectical. Gradually he develops a metaphoric language capable of evoking the simultaneous interplay of several of these relationships, so that an integrated vision finally emerges, one in which the *substance* of experience appears as a continuous dialectical movement, while the ultimate yearning, the final *goal* of experience, is for infinite, timeless ecstasy and the cessation of all movement or human process. It is his experience of the dialectic of imagination and reality in the creation of

works of art which provides Michelangelo with both the insight and the language with which to create the complex, compact "concetto" that characterize his most original poems.

Instead of beginning with Michelangelo's earlier poetry, in which the conceits tend to be derivative and conventional, let us plunge directly into one of his later and most original poems, the madrigal **"Non pur d'argento o d'oro,"** which is entirely structured upon a single extremely complex insight or "concetto." Here is the complete poem, written for Vittoria Colonna sometime between 1538 and 1544:

> Non pur d'argento o d'oro
> vinto dal foco esser po' piena aspetta,
> vota d'opra prefetta,
> la forma, che sol fratta il tragge fora;
> tal io, col foco ancora
> d'amor dentro ristoro
> il desir voto di beltà infinita,
> di coste' ch'i' adoro,
> anima e cor della mie fragil vita.
> Alta donna e gradita
> in me discende per sì brevi spazi,
> c'a trarla fuor convien mi rompa e strazi.

> • • • • •

> Not only with silver or gold
> Conquered by fire waits then to be filled,
> Empty of finished work,
> The mould, which only broken can be drawn out;
> So I, with fire still
> Of love inside refill
> The empty desire of infinite beauty
> With the one I adore,
> Soul and heart of my fragile life.
> The high and welcome lady
> Descends in me through such narrow spaces,
> That to draw her out I must be broken and torn apart.

The central image of this poem is that of an artist's mold being filled with liquefied gold or silver which will be formed into a precious art object and then removed by breaking the mold which formed it. The mold is a metaphor of the poet himself; the silver or gold which will become the art object is a metaphor of the beloved lady; the metaphoric fire of love within the poet melts or "conquers" her just as fire melts the silver or gold to be poured into the waiting mold. But the mold and the molded objects become one; the beloved cannot be extracted from the poet's interior unless he be broken up. Thus the underlying "concetto" which makes possible the whole poem's complex network of meaning and imagery is the broad insight that creation and destruction are interdependent, no less so in love than in art, and that to experience love is truly to be creative and created—to be fulfilled and destroyed in the process, to be at once the fire, the mold, and the completed work, which cannot be fully realized or created without breaking apart that which has given it form.

The first four lines, with their twisted syntax, grammatic license, compact imagery and deceptively simple vocabulary, manage to condense three separate and distinct acts into one moment and one movement: it is implied that the artist melts the silver, fills the mold, and withdraws the finished work by breaking the mold. This entire process is sketched out in one thought, one "concetto." But the first four lines, after once being grasped as a whole, come to life only when joined with the interiorized love imagery in the rest of the poem. This imagery can now afford to be extremely abstract since its dynamic principle has already been established in the concrete imagery of the opening lines. Once the syntax and grammar have been unraveled, the poignancy and clarity of the poem derive from the aptness of the image of the receptive, yearning lover welcoming the hot, molten substance—the very being of his beloved *as he experiences her* and gives her form, *his* form. It enters him slowly through "narrow spaces" (probably an allusion to the Neoplatonic convention of love entering through the eyes) and creates his own inner being, thus giving value, beauty and wholeness to what was once a mere form burning only with the "empty desire of infinite beauty."

Paradoxically, however, this image seems so vivid precisely because the opening lines are so "obscure": the artist who would presumably be performing the actions is alluded to only at the end of the fourth line ("il tragge fora"); there is no antecedent for "il," contrary to what one would normally expect. Instead, a dramatic suspension of imagination and thought is created by the unusual placing of the subject "la forma" down at the fourth line, where it is appropriately hidden by all the preceding imagery. Its position, then, emphasizes its passive yet fervent nature, while making it the focal point at which the acts of waiting and filling have ended and the act of breaking is anticipated. The only verb in the whole poem that is *actively* and immediately in the present tense is "discende," which comes toward the end of the poem. Only here is the infinite yearning finally fulfilled, accompanied by the realization that self-annihilation is inevitable. (pp. 1-4)

Most of Michelangelo's earliest poetic endeavors remain unfinished, as if the effort were usually more frustrating than fruitful. Here one can clearly see an "oscillation" between artificiality and emotional or moral intensity, with the tone of each poem or fragment differing drastically from the one preceding or following it. One could compare, for example, #1 and #3, both written in 1503 or 1504. The first is a rough draft of an unfinished sonnet, discursive in mode, gravely moralizing in tone, and completely conventional in its theme of the fragility of earthly life:

> Molti anni fassi qual felice, in una
> brevissima ora si lamenta e dole;
> o per famosa o per antica prole
> altri s'inlustra, e'n un momento imbruna.
>
> Cosa mobil non è che sotto el sole
> non vinca morte a cangi la fortuna.

· · · · ·

> After being happy many years, one short
> Hour may make a man lament and mourn,
> Or one whose ancient famous family line
> Illumined him, will fade out in a moment.
> Under the sun there's not a thing that's transient
> Not overcome by death and changed by fortune.

In complete contrast with the verses above is the finished sonnet #3, **"Grato e felice, a' tuo feroci mali."** It overflows with the most frivolous kind of Petrarchan imagery—snares and meshes and arrows of love—and ends with a weakly formulated metaphor of the poet as a little bird evading for many years the snares of love, only to die more harshly of love in old age. An exceptional early poem, however, is the bitingly satiric sonnet #10, **"Qua si fa elmi di calici e spade,"** which is about the corruption of religion in Rome. Written in 1512, it contains such imaginative conceits as that of Christ's blood spurting up to the stars if he should ever come again, "poscia c'a Roma gli vendon la pelle," now that in Rome they sell His skin. In this mode the formal irregularities actually contribute to the effect of righteous indignation, and the far-flung imagery seems appropriate.

By 1524, which is still a very early stage in Michelangelo's avocation as a poet, already he tends to take Petrarchan images out of their conventional setting, abstractly isolating them and then recombining them either to express an intensely personal feeling or to develop a generalized idea related to his own experience. By 1534, Michelangelo is able to write relatively polished, witty poems, most of which are based on conventional ideas and imagery handled skillfully and with a keen sense of syllogism, antithesis, and paradox. In fact, many of the verses written at the peak of his poetic creativity (1536-1545) are self-consciously witty and clever, sometimes to the extent of seeming superficial and facile. Such poems demonstrate that he has indeed learned how to manipulate conventional imagery and ideas as well as any "professional" poet of his time.

Even in many of the most self-consciously witty poems, however, there is a tendency to abstract and interiorize the imagery. In fact, . . . it is the very process of intellectually juggling and reworking conventional conceits which gradually reveals new metaphoric possibilities and leads to a genuinely dialectical perspective. And this is what finally transforms recurring imagery into genuine "concettos." In a similar process, Michelangelo's habitual use of irregular meter and syntax and his predilection for an archaic vocabulary become transformed in the "concetto" poems into a positive, indeed essential, part of the poem's structure. In these poems, instead of being held captive by conventional formulations of inner psychology (mostly Neoplatonic), the poet has found a paradoxical kind of freedom by identifying with the unfinished work of art. For example, he is a block of stone to be given life by the artist, who becomes a metaphor of his beloved lady (#63 and #152); or, as we saw in **"Non pur d'argento o d'oro,"** he is the mold to be transformed into a finished work of art by receiving her love.

Two basic developments can be discerned which lead to the creation of Michelangelo's "concetto" poems. His self-consciously witty poetry turns increasingly to art imagery and to problems of artistic perception and creation. And in the process of exploring the relationships between subject and object, imagination and reality, the wit becomes less self-conscious and more concerned with evoking the dynamics of the relationships themselves. As the dynamics appear in clearer focus, their application to a fully positive love experience becomes ever more appropriate, so that finally the analogies between artist and lover seem to crystallize into metaphors revealing an underlying dialectical experience common to both art and love. The second development involves the concentration on a few key images, which evolve into tools enabling the poet to evoke rapidly and succinctly his fundamental insights. These images, some nouns and some verbs, are "circonscrivere," "trarre," "superchio," "concetto," "pietra," and "fuoco." (pp. 5-7)

In the most rhetorical, self-consciously witty madrigals, it is less the desire to express a personal feeling that structures and motivates a given poem than the desire to explore the mechanisms governing complex relationships between conflicting states of being or between the self and the beloved. Almost invariably, these relationships are evoked in terms of an opposition between an exterior appearance and an interior reality (such as her beauty versus her cruel heart, his pain versus her beauty, her happy face contrasting with his sad heart, or his inner passion versus her cold heart). Such antitheses are the stock-in-trade of Renaissance love poetry, with its fascination for the "belle dame sans merci" which dates back to the troubadours. What distinguishes even the most conventional poem of Michelangelo from those of other love poets is his treatment of these oppositions as part of a larger and problematic phenomenon—the role of the creative imagination in the perception and experience of beauty and love, and the complex analogy between the lover and the artist as subjects or centers of consciousness, both of whom are transformed, in various ways, by the objects they perceive and create.

In the madrigals to "la donna bella e crudele," most of the tensions between subject and object, as well as those between conflicting states of being, resolve themselves into a paradox of pleasure-pain. One of the simplest examples, in terms of the mechanics involved, and also one of the most contrived, is #136, **"L'alma, che sparge e versa."** It also serves to illustrate Michelangelo's typical abstraction and interiorization of Petrarchan motifs:

> L'alma, che sparge e versa
> di fuor l'acque di drento,
> il fa sol perché spento
> non sie da loro il foco in ch'è conversa.
> Ogni altra aita persa
> saria, se 'l pianger sempre
> mi resurge al tuo foco, vecchio e tardi.
> Mie dura sorte e mie fortuna avversa
> non ha sì dure tempre,
> che non m'affligghin men, dove più m'ardi;
> tal ch'e' tuo accesi sguardi,
> di fuor piangendo, dentro circumscrivo,
> e di quel c'altri muor sol godo e vivo.

• • • • •

> The soul has poured and spouted
> Its inner waters out
> Only so they will not
> Put out the fire to which it is converted.
> Your fire has always started
> Tears in me, so, though tired
> And old, I could not get other assistance.
> My destiny is hard, my fortune thwarted,
> Yet they are not so hard
> But that their sting, where more you burn, decreases.
> And so your burning glances,
> Outwardly weeping, I shut up within me,
> And what most die of only enjoy and live by.

Here the conventional plays on tears-fire imagery have been concentrated within the soul of the poet, where the "waters are converted into fire." At first, there is no explicit mention of tears, which appear only as the inner waters of the soul. Then the tears are directly related to the fatigue of old age which is unable to deal more effectively with "tuo foco," *her* fire within *him*. It is deliberately unclear whether she is also experiencing "her" fire (reappearing in "tuo accesi sguardi") or whether it exists only in his soul and in his perception of her. The formulation of the final paradox of pleasure-pain so as to involve two other paradoxes tends to reinforce both the abstraction (living on death) and the interiorization of the imagery (by focusing on what is "circumscribed" or enclosed within). The central movement described here is that of emptying the soul of all elements that might inhibit the intensely destructive and creative fever contained within it. Although

the verb "circumscrivere" lacks here the full suggestive force it will attain in some of the other poems, it emphasizes the image of the soul as a circular, self-contained enclosure, whose life-in-death experience will go on forever, with fire regenerating itself eternally. Thus, what started out as a play on conventional love-paradoxes evolves into an evocation of an intensely personal state of being. (pp. 7-9)

[Images] drawn from Michelangelo's experiences as an artist appear in increasing numbers of poems written between approximately 1538 and 1545. Since the dating of many of his poems remains a point of controversy, it is impossible to trace an exact chronological evolution of the way in which he uses these images. We cannot be absolutely certain that the intellectual juggling we see in madrigals such as #123 and #242, or the groping attempt at synthesis and new insight we found in #173, leads directly to the discovery of the authentic and successful "concettos" informing Michelangelo's most original poems. On the other hand, there is nothing to disprove the thesis. Likewise, there is no evidence to indicate that the combination of art imagery and wit, found in so many poems between 1538 and 1545 (such as #'s 62, 162, 239, 240 and 243), does *not* represent an attempt to explore certain analogies between artist and lover—analogies based on a similar experience of the self as both agent of creation and object to be created. Perhaps some of these poems were written *after* those in which a unifying "concetto" had been discovered and evoked. It is difficult, however, to believe that *most* of them came later.

The crucial point, regardless of the inevitable ambiguity concerning precise data, is that many of his wittiest poems explore—by juggling, juxtapositioning, and playing with conceits—the very relationship which will be synthesized, in a few poems, into coherent yet extremely complex "concettos." . . . [The] wit is dispersed and located in an interplay of conceits involving an apparent antithesis often resolved by paradox. The basic preoccupation is almost always with the inter-related problems of subject and object, exterior and interior, creation and destruction. It is only in the "concetto" poems that these dichotomies appear as fully dialectical in nature and as part of Michelangelo's insight into the human experience of being and becoming.

Before discussing in detail the "concetto" poems, it is necessary to take note of the second process which seems to lead to their creation. Stated most simply, it is the recurrence of certain key terms already mentioned ("circumscrivere," "trarre," "concetto," "superchio," "pietra," and "fuoco"), which become powerfully suggestive when used in combination with each other. Then they are able to evoke a complex movement-image-idea that is raised to a symbolic level, which is in fact a good way to describe the "concettos" themselves. One can see that each of these key terms lends itself easily to imagery describing an artistic endeavor; but none of them belong necessarily or even normally to the world of art. Fire and stone are conventional images in Italian Renaissance poetry; but . . . Michelangelo tends to transform them into metaphors of a particular state of being. This tendency reaches its peak when "fire" and "stone" are united with the other terms. [Charles de Tolnay points out in *The Art and Thought of Michelangelo* (1964)] that the notion of "superchio" or "surplus" was common to Aristotle, Plotinus, and the ancient Neo-platonists, who described the method of creation in plastic work as the removal of the superfluous. But for Michelangelo, the word had a psychological connotation as well. The notion is central to a poem such as #149, **"Non posso non mancar d'ingegno e d'arte,"** but it appears as an adjective ("tal superchia aita") and retains only its usual meaning, quite literal, of "too much." With all of these key terms, however, it is only when the poet synthesizes them into metaphors of a state of being that they become poetically original expressions of experiences at once intensely personal and symbolic in scope. (pp. 14-16)

The famous sonnet, **"Non ha l'ottimo artista alcun concetto"** (#151) has been widely commented upon ever since Varchi's "lezione" to the Academy of Florence in 1546 [see excerpt by Varchi dated 1547]. The disproportionate attention it has received (compared with the rest of the *Rime*) is largely due to the first quatrain's apparent expression of what has been called Michelangelo's "theory of art." Yet in many respects this sonnet is less complex than some of his other "concetto" poems, and it actually reveals less about his notion of artistic creativity than some of his less explicitly theoretical verses. Nevertheless, it provides an important example of how his experience as an artist helps him formulate poetic "concettos" capable of evoking complex human relationships. Of course, it also illuminates Michelangelo's attitudes toward art and reality, as its numerous commentators have pointed out. To counteract the usual tendency to interpret the first quatrain out of context, we shall start by giving the sonnet in its entirety, followed by as literal a translation as possible:

> Non ha l'ottimo artista alcun concetto
> c'un marmo solo in sé non circonscriva
> col suo superchio, e solo a quello arriva
> la man che ubbidisce all'intelletto.
> Il mal ch'io fuggo, e 'l ben ch'io mi prometto,
> in te, donna leggiadra, altera e diva,
> tal si nasconde; e perch'io più non viva,
> contraria ho l'arte al disïato effetto.
> Amor dunque non ha, né tua beltate
> o durezza o fortuna o gran disdegno,
> del mio mal colpa, o mio destino o sorte;
> se dentro del tuo cor morte e pietate
> porti in un tempo, e che 'l mio basso ingegno
> non sappia, ardendo, trarne altro che morte.

. . . . .

> The best artist has not any concept [idea]
> Which a single marble block in itself does not circum-
>   scribe
> With its surplus, and to this arrives only
> The hand that obeys the intellect.
> The pain that I flee and the good that I promise myself,
> In you, gay lady, high and divine,
> Likewise hide themselves; and so I may not live any lon-
>   ger,
> Since I have art contrary to the desired effect.
> Love therefore is not to blame, nor your beauty
> Or hardness or fortune or great disdain,
> For my pain, or my destiny or fate;
> If within your heart death and pity
> Are present at the same time, and if my low understanding
> Does not know, burning, how to draw from it other than
>   death.

If . . . in #241 (**"Negli anni molti e nelle molte pruove"**) . . . the "concetto" did not exist only in the mind of the poet-artist, in this sonnet it is necessary to emphasize that it does not exist only in the single marble block. The "best artist," in this case a sculptor, can create a work of art only when his "intelletto" grasps the ideal or essential form which is circumscribed by the "surplus" or exterior of the marble block,

and when his "hand" or technical skill is able to realize the intellect's desires. "Intellect" refers here to all aspects of artistic creation which are not simply technical or of the "hand"—imagination, intuition, perception, understanding, soul. The "concetto" is clearly a result of the coming together of "intellect" and inner reality, the interior form of the stone and the interior force of the artist. Although there are obvious traces of Neoplatonism in the first quatrain, there is no indication that the "concetto" originates in a supra-terrestrial sphere, as Neoplatonism would have it. In fact, as [Erwin Panofsky shows in *Idea: A Concept in Art Theory* (1923)], there are also elements of Aristotelianism in Michelangelo's use of "concetto." Other critics have demonstrated how Michelangelo's "concetto" differs from Leonardo's "invention," and from both the Renaissance and the sixteenth-century or Mannerist interpretations of "idea." And Varchi's erudite "lezione" compared Michelangelo's "concetto" to the Latin "exemplum" and to the Greek "eidos."

One thing seems clear: Michelangelo's "theory of art," as evoked in this and other poems, transcends Neoplatonism or any other system of thought. It is not just a question, as Tolnay puts it, of an artistic Idealism that identifies "the subjective intention of the artist" with the "objective intention of nature," or which represents things as they are according to their Idea. His theory of art (which is virtually nonexistent, unless one counts a few lines of his poetry such as those in the sonnet above), like his complicated "concept" of love, was something he arrived at independently and gradually, probably by a "profondo colloquio con se stesso nell' atto di operare," as Mariani puts it, by a profound conversation with himself in the midst of the action and experiences themselves. For Michelangelo was primarily interested in "making art," not in theorizing about it. As for Varchi's elaborate commentary, Michelangelo thanked him for it politely, and, with typical sixteenth-century amplification aimed at flattering his well-meaning commentator, wrote that if the sonnet came from him, the commentary came rather from Heaven.

Two observations will help to clarify the vision evoked in the first quatrain: Michelangelo chooses the word "concetto" instead of "Idea," which would inevitably be associated with Neoplatonism and would necessarily entail a transcendent meaning; he is less interested in the origin of the "concetto" than in how its realization requires the bringing together of imagination and reality, subject and object. Thus, in the rest of Sonnet #151, love (a transcendent force) is not to blame for the poet-artist's inability to draw from his lady's heart pity instead of death; the blame is placed on his low "ingegno" (here encompassing both skill and understanding) which is unable to experience or realize all of the potential hidden within her heart. Her potential depends upon his potential; both "il mal" and " 'l ben" lie latently within her, but since *he* is fragmented and incomplete (having "arte" contrary to the desired effect), *she* appears fragmented and only partially realized. Once again, the question of who is transforming or influencing whom remains ambiguous, primarily because it is irrelevant, just as the question of the precise origin of the artistic "concetto" is irrelevant for Michelangelo. What matters to him is that great works of art can be created only when the artist's "concetto" merges with the "concetto" circumscribed by matter, just as a genuine love relationship can be created only when each partner's inner being or soul is wholly realized by the other and transformed into the other.

The poetic "concetto" on which this poem is structured is a positive one—an intuition of the ideal creative process—yet the love situation described is basically negative. As in other poems we have discussed, the poet-artist is still trying to create himself by creating his beloved. The love situation becomes more fully positive in the next poem we shall discuss, because the poet lets his lady play the role of artist and identifies himself with the work of art to be created. The movement toward self-surrender augments the potential of "concettos" based on artistic creativity to evoke the creative love experience. And a new poignancy is created when the art imagery is thoroughly interwoven with love imagery, as it is in the following brief but splendid madrigal (# 152) written to Vittoria Colonna between 1538 and 1544:

Sì come per levar, donna, si pone
in pietra alpestra e dura
una viva figura,
che là più cresce u' più la pietra scema;
tal alcun' opre buone,
per l'alma che pur trema,
cela il superchio della propria carne
co' l'inculta sua cruda e dura scorza.
Tu pur dalle mie streme
parti puo' sol levarne,
ch'in me non è di me voler né forza.

• • • • •

Just as by removing, lady, one puts
Into stone rough and hard
A living figure,
Which there grows more where more the stone decreases;
So any good works,
By the soul that still trembles,
Are hidden by the surplus of its own body
With the roughness of its coarse and hard hide [exterior].
Yet you alone from my outer
Parts can remove this,
For in me there is neither my will nor my force.

The rough, hard block of stone has become a metaphor of the poet himself. His body is described by the term "superchio," previously applied to the stone itself, and his soul's "good works" must be created by his beloved, who will "put" them into his soul by "removing" his coarse "outer parts." Although antitheses seem to dominate the poem (body-soul, exterior-interior), they are in fact synthesized perfectly by the paradoxical "coincidentia oppositorum" of the opening lines, where the apparently contrary acts of removing and putting into can only be performed simultaneously. Notice that the verb "puts" appears in reflexive form; there is no active subject of the action. The "living figure" is put there by the sculptor, of course; but in a sense it is also pre-existent to his skillful removing of the superfluous outer stone. The figure can appear to "grow" within the stone because its ideal form has been discovered, "conceived" by the sculptor's imagination. It is his hand that is now giving life to the figure by making the stone fall away from the "concetto" that seems hidden within the stone, just as the poet's "good works" lie hidden within his trembling soul.

Why is his soul trembling? "Trema," with its connotation of fear and trepidation, ties together all aspects of the "concetto" at the base of this poem. Fear, throughout Michelangelo's poetry, is associated both with beauty (whether it be the beauty of art or that of the beloved) and desire, which for Michelangelo is ultimately a desire for infinite beauty. And the desire for infinite beauty is inextricably connected to a yearning for self-liberation—liberation of the soul from the body, and of the spirit from matter. Loss of self and perfect self-realization through infinite expansion: this is both the hope and the fear underlying this madrigal as well as many other poems in the *Rime*. In most of the poems, this desire for liberation appears quite explicitly in the form of conflict and tension between the matter that circumscribes or limits and the spirit struggling to break through its confines. However, in this madrigal, with its tone of subdued resignation, the tension is visible only through the gentle interplay of the imagery, which evokes with utter simplicity what Mariani calls a "dialectic between stereometric form and 'live' form." . . . The "concetto" poems, including the madrigal presently under discussion, tend to evoke this dialectic between matter and spirit primarily through a synthesis of imagery, without the dramatic urgency of tone or the clash of antitheses that we found in the self-consciously witty poems. This is because in the "concetto" poems the dialectic has found its true embodiment in the metaphor of the poet as unfinished work of art, most often as a rough block of stone to be sculpted by love. In the poems discussed earlier, the opposition between stereometric form and live form appeared as conflict and antithesis struggling for resolution. In poems such as the madrigal above, the resolution has been achieved not only by the poetic conceit bringing together the stone and the poet (who is at once the figure emerging from the stone and the superfluous rock to be chipped away), but also, and more fundamentally, by the underlying intuition or "concetto" that grasps the dialectical process of artistic creation. However, the poetic success of both kinds of "concetto" depends on the metaphor of the beloved lady as artist and on the implicit assumption that artistic creativity is at least a divine gift, if not itself divine. It is only then that human love, evoked via metaphors drawn from art, can hold out the hope of rebirth and redemption. (pp. 18-24)

It might be well to contrast briefly the simplicity and unity of this madrigal with the equally famous sonnet #236, **"Se ben concetto ha la divina parte,"** which is similar in theme, but lacks the former's extreme synthesis of imagery and fails to achieve an absolute unity of poetic structure and "concetto." Yet this sonnet can be considered one of Michelangelo's finest poems because of the poignant suggestiveness of the tercets, in which the art imagery has indeed been interiorized and incorporated into the poet's own self-image.

Se ben concetto ha la divina parte
il volto e gli atti d'alcun, po' di quello
doppio valor con breve e vil modello
da vita a' sassi, e non è forza d'arte.

Né altrimenti in più rustiche carte,
anz'una pronta man prenda 'l pennello,
fra 'dotti ingegni il più accorto e bello
pruova e rivede, e suo storie comparte.

Simil di me model di poca istima
mie parto fu, per cosa alta e prefetta
da voi rinascer po', donna alta e degna.

Se 'l poco accresce, e 'l mie superchio lima
vostra mercé, qual penitenzia aspetta
mie fiero ardor, se mi gastiga e 'nsegna?

• • • • •

If our divine part has imagined well
Therefrom, with only a crude and rapid sketch,
Makes the stones live; it's not the power of skill.

With rougher papers it is parallel;
Someone's gestures and face, then double strength
Before a ready hand can take the brush,
The finest, most alert of learned wits
Checks and reviews, and has composed his tale.

Likewise with me, a sketch when I was born,
Of no account, to be reborn from you,
High worthy Lady, a thing high and perfect;

If you in mercy trim my surplus down
And build my little, what is my fierce fire due
As penance, when you punish and correct?

The quatrains present a relatively explicit, detailed, concrete perspective of the same process of artistic creation described in #'s 151 and 152 (**"Non ha l'ottimo artista . . ."** and **"Si come per levar . . ."**). The first quatrain refers to the sculptor, the second to the painter. The main point of both examples is that the genuinely artistic work is performed by the intellect ("la divina parte") as it formulates the fundamental "concetto" of the work and captures it in a small model without much value. The sculptor is able to give "life to stone" by capturing well the "face and gestures of someone," just as the best painter makes a "rustic" design of the "storia" he wishes to paint, testing and revising his "concetto" before actually taking up the brush. Even these rough models of the future work of art are not created by "arte" (here meaning primarily "skill" or "technique"), but rather by the intellect which partakes of the divine. The sketch of little esteem then becomes a metaphor of the poet, who hopes to be given a new life of genuine worth by his lady-artist, who, being "alta e degna," likewise partakes of the divine. It is not until the final tercet, however, that the metaphors come to life and the process of artistic creation merges with the poet's longing for transformation through love. Now he identifies himself completely with the stone to be sculpted, and the language finally takes on the force of Michelangelo's most original verses, as the lady's mercy makes grow his "little" and files down his "surplus" in an act at once creative and destructive, charged with explicitly religious meaning. She castigates him and instructs or corrects him, with both words ("gastiga" and " 'nsegna") containing their full etymological meanings of "chastise" and "build." (pp. 25-7)

The dialectical vision of the "concetto" poems would seem to be contradictory to the quest for grace, which calls for denial of the world, the flesh, and the willful imagination. Michelangelo's most original vision as poet-artist transcends both Neoplatonism and Christian doctrine in its insistence on the active imagination's ability to create and be created by its own forms of reality. This mode of imagination or consciousness is essentially willful, proud, and self-affirming. With the desire for grace and spiritual redemption comes an emphasis on the worthlessness of the soul and the inability of the imagination to create and participate in its own "truest" reality, accompanied by an emphasis on the need for receptive passivity. Gradually, the poet-artist abandons his dialectical vision and returns to a more thoroughly Neoplatonic mode of imagination, one which is complementary to his quest for Christian redemption.

In #161, for example, the sculptor's file has become a metaphor of time, and the stone is a metaphor of the poet's "sick soul" and "tired carcass." But the metaphors no longer evoke a "concetto" that informs the whole poem. They serve rather as a point of departure for an intensely personal self-analysis:

Head of Michelangelo, by Daniele da Volterra.

Per qual mordace lima
discresce e manca ognor tuo stanca spoglia,
anima inferma? or quando fie ti scoglia
da quella il tempo, e torni ov'eri, in cielo,
candida e lieta prima,
deposto il periglioso e mortal velo?

• • • • •

Amore, a te nol celo,
ch'i' porto invidia a' morti,
sbigottito e confuso,
sì di sé meco l'alma trema e teme.
Signor, nell'ore streme,
stendi ver' me le tuo pietose braccia,
tomm'a me stesso e famm'un che ti piaccia.

• • • • •

What kind of biting file
Makes your tired carcass shrivel and decrease,
Sick soul, forever? When will time release
You from it, back to where you were in Heaven,
Earlier bright and joyful,
Your dangerous and mortal veil thrown down?

• • • • •

To you, Love, I must own
My envy of the dead.
I am frightened and confused,
Such, for myself, my soul's convulsive fear.

Lord, in the final hour,
Stretch out thy pitying arms to me, take me
Out of me, make me one that pleases Thee.

This madrigal for Vittoria Colonna, like the two which follow, bears no definite date, but may well have been written round 1545-46, toward the end of Michelangelo's relationship with her. In both #162 and #163, Vittoria is presented as the embodiment of divine grace and as a spiritual guide, a kind of mediator between earth and Heaven, sin and redemption:

Ora in sul destro, ora in sul manco piede
variando, cerco della mie salute.

• • • • •

Porgo la carta bianca
a' vostri sacri inchiostri,
c'amor mi sganni e pietà 'l ver ne scriva . . .

• • • • •

Now on my right foot, now upon my left one,
Toward my salvation shifting in my searches,

• • • • •

I offer a clean sheet
To take your sacred inks:
Let love inform me, truth be inscribed by pity; . . .
(#162)

The soul becomes increasingly its own object, as the desire for salvation leads to moral self-scrutiny:

Quante più fuggo e odio ognor me stesso,
tanto a te, donna, con verace speme
ricorro; e manco teme
l'alma di me, quant'a te son più presso . . .

• • • • •

While still I shun and hate myself the more,
The more, Lady, with proper hope I call
On you; in me the soul
Is less afraid, as I to you draw near . . .
(#163)

Indeed, most of the poems of this period affirm and reaffirm the capacity of terrestrial love and beauty to bring grace and salvation. But as the perspective becomes more subjective and personal, and the language more explicitly Christian, an element of doubt creeps into the affirmation of the senses as stepping stones to grace. The recurring attempts to conjoin Neoplatonism and Christianity begin to suggest an element of uncertainty, as in the first quatrain of #259, one of the few poems of the period which refers directly to "god," rather than to "divine beauty" or "il cielo."

Ben può talor col mie 'rdente desio
salir la speme e non esser fallace,
ché s'ogni nostro affetto al ciel dispiace,
a che fin fatto arebbe il mondo Iddio? . . .

• • • • •

My hope now and again can climb indeed
With my inflamed desire, and not be false;
For if our feelings all leave Heaven displeased,
To what end was the world then made by God?

Sonnet #260 attempts to prove that "violent passion for tremendous beauty" is not always a "bitter mortal error" if it

can leave the heart melted so that a holy dart ("un divino strale") can penetrate it quickly. In the earlier poems it was taken for granted that such passion was not only guilt-less, but also an experience of the sacred. Love of a "divine woman" can still bridge the gap between earth and Heaven; but it appears increasingly to be a desperate, wild hope for the future, rather than an immediate experience, or at least a potentially real human experience. Furthermore, whereas the "concetto" poems did not even mention a dichotomy between earth and Heaven, since their underlying vision transcended such a distinction, the two realms are frequently contrasted in the poems dating from 1546.

With the death of Vittoria Colonna in February, 1547, Michelangelo is bereft of his spiritual guide, his bridge between earth and Heaven, and his faith that love can be at once human and divine. At the age of 72, as his own death seems imminent, he has lost his hope for rebirth and salvation through platonic love. Now his primary preoccupation concerns the state of his soul and the quality of his faith in relation to a purely Christian concept of redemption and rebirth. In Sonnet #274, written in the spring and summer of 1547, the old inner fire, which cannot even now be quenched, yearns for transformation into a holy flame capable of renewing the poet "fuora e drento," within and without.

Deh fammiti vedere in ogni loco!
Se da mortal bellezza ardër mi sento,
appresso al tuo mi sarà foco ispento,
e io nel tuo sarò, com'ero, in foco . . .

• • • • •

Oh make me so I'll see you everywhere!
If ever I feel by mortal beauty burnt,
Set beside yours I'll think it fire that's spent,
And as I was I'll be, in yours on fire.

For the first time, the relationships between imagination and beauty, and between earthly beauty and divine beauty, become problematic. The role played by the artist's will is now considered crucial, as the last stanza of Sonnet #276, written between 1547 and 1550, makes clear:

S'un ardente desir mortal bellezza
ferma del tutto, non discese insieme
dal ciel con l'alma; è dunche umana voglia.

Ma se pass'oltra, Amor, tuo nome sprezza,
c'altro die cerca; e di quel più non teme
c'a lato vien contr'a sì bassa spoglia.

• • • • •

If mortal beauty stops a passionate flame
Completely, it did not come down together
From Heaven with the soul; it's human will.

But if, Love, it moves on, it jeers your name,
Seeking another God, fearful no longer
You'll come to grapple with a prey so vile.

Truly platonic love, capable of leading the soul to perfection, seems to have died with Vittoria Colonna; and the imagination's ability to discriminate between ordinary beauty and divinely-inspired beauty is no longer taken for granted. (pp. 33-7)

In the period 1550-1554, the *Rime* reflects an ever-increasing desire to transcend the realities of material human existence and to love earthly beauty only insofar as it can become a means of achieving grace. Having already abandoned his proud vision of the imagination's ability to create its own reality, he tries to focus his imagination and his art on purely spiritual realities. For example, in the following fragment (#282) the sculpture of "divine things" appears as an attempt to concentrate evermore fully on spiritual realities, in order to overcome and transcend the realities of human existence:

> Con tanta servitù, con tanto tedio
> e con falsi concetti e gran periglio
> dell'alma, a sculpir qui cose divine.

• • • • •

> With so much bondage, with so much tedium
> And with false notions and great danger
> Of the soul, here to be sculpting divine things.

As Leo Steinberg points out, at the time this fragment was written (1552-1554), Michelangelo was working on the "Pietà del Duomo," the group of four figures that he undertook as a "pastime," that is, for himself and without a commission. "A sculpir qui cose divine": this is what Michelangelo tries to do ever more intensely as he feels his death draw nearer.

His task, however, proves harder and more frustrating than he had anticipated. In several sonnets written between 1552 and 1554 (most of which are incomplete), art appears as the very antithesis of redemption and grace; for the creative imagination cannot function without the senses, which, for Michelangelo, can only rejoice in earthly beauty:

> Più l'alma acquista ove più 'l mondo perde;
> l'arte e la morte non va bene insieme:
> che convien più che di me dunche speri? (#283)

• • • • •

> The soul gains more the more it's lost the world,
> And death and art do not go well together.
> What should I of myself then hope for still?

> S'a tuo nome ho concetto alcuno immago,
> non è senza del par seco la morte,
> onde l'arte e l'ingegno si dilegua . . . (#284)

• • • • •

> If, in your name, I have conceived some image,
> It is not without death joined onto it,
> So that my art and understanding flee . . .

And the famous Sonnet #285, **"Giunto è già 'l corso della vita mia,"** which has often been interpreted as a "farewell" to art, contains the following verses:

> . . . Onde l'affettüosa fantasia
> che l'arte mi fece idol e monarca
> conosco or ben com'era d'error carca . . .

> Né pinger né scolpir fie più che quieti
> l'anima, volta a quell'amor divino
> c'aperse, a prender noi, 'n croce le braccia.

• • • • •

> . . . So that the passionate fantasy, which made
> Of art a monarch for me and an idol,
> Was laden down with sin, now I know well,
> Like what all men against their will desired . . .

> There's no painting or sculpture now that quiets

> The soul that's pointed toward that holy Love
> That on the cross opened Its arms to take us.

This is by no means a rejection of art *per se,* but the rejection of a proud, willful art which is now clearly an obstacle to grace. But more fundamentally, this sonnet expresses Michelangelo's feeling that his art is no longer able to embody the intensity of his spiritual hunger and intuitions. Even the sculpting of "holy things" is unable to calm a soul that is totally absorbed in the quest for its salvation through Christ love. Steinberg's convincing article ["The Metaphors of Love and Birth in Michelangelo's *Pietàs*" in *Studies in Erotic Art* (1970), edited by Theodore Bowie and Cornelia V. Christenson] notes that the date of this sonnet falls within the year during which Michelangelo destroyed the "Pietà del Duomo" on which he had been working for eight or nine years. Steinberg speculates that the demolition occurred out of despair, that Michelangelo "felt himself crossing the limit of what seemed expressible in his art."

After 1554, the **Rime** are purely religious in theme. Many of them are Christ-centered pleas for grace, a few are relatively rational attempts to reconcile past, present and future, and many are combinations of prayerfulness and intellectualization. Most of them are heavy with the consciousness of an overwhelming sinfulness, rather vaguely related to the senses and their willful, inordinate love of beauty:

> Penso e ben so c'alcuna colpa preme,
> occulta a me, lo spirto in gran martire;
> privo dal senso e dal suo propio ardire
> il cor di pace, e 'l desir d'ogni speme . . . (#291)

• • • • •

> I think, I know, some sin, to me a secret,
> Is driving my spirit to great grief.
> My senses and their own fire have bereft
> All hope from my desire, peace from my heart . . .

And they are permeated with the fear that grace will never come, that faith is not strong enough to climb "l'alta e erta via," the high and steep way leading to God. Perhaps #295 evokes this frustrated state of mind better than any other single sonnet:

> Di morte certo, ma non già dell'ora,
> la vita è breve e poco me n'avanza;
> diletta al senso, è non però la stanza
> a l'alma, che mi prega pur ch'i' mora.

> Il mondo è cieco e 'l tristo esempro ancora
> vince e sommerge ogni prefetta usanza;
> spent'è la luce e seco ogni baldanza,
> trionfa il falso e 'l ver non surge fora.

> Deh, quando fie, Signor, quel che s'aspetta
> per chi ti crede? c'ogni troppo indugio
> tronca la speme e l'alma fa mortale.

> Che val che tanto lume altrui prometta,
> s'anzi vien morte, e senza alcun refugio
> ferma per sempre in che stato altri assale?

• • • • •

> Certain of death, but not when it will be,
> Life's short, and I have little of it left,
> Joy to the senses, but no resting place
> For the soul only begging me to die;

> The blind world and its bad example, though,

Leave all right practice swallowed and suppressed.
The light is spent, and with it all assurance,
The false is king, the truth cannot break through.

When will it be, O Lord, what we await,
Your true believers? All the great delay
Cuts off our hope, making the soul be mortal.

What good to promise men so great a light
If death comes first, pinning us just the way
We are attacked, with no escape at all.

All in sonnet form, the last verses contain no clever conceits, no difficult syntax, almost no obscurities either of grammar or meaning, and as little artifice as possible. The metaphors which appear at all are drawn from conventional Christian symbolism. Never does the soul find *its* perfect metaphor, as it once did in the stone to be sculpted or in the art object to be created by love. Not once does the poet's consciousness or imagination truly merge with its objective reality, and thus release the spirit from its limited confines. There are no original "concettos" in these sonnets; the gap between the soul and its truest reality, between earth and heaven, appears enormous and unbridgeable, except through the grace that will not come.

The only image which seizes the aged poet's weary imagination time and again is that of Christ's blood. It not only symbolizes and draws together all of the traditional Christian paradoxes involving death and rebirth; it also negates the old yearning for infinite beauty and expansion by transforming it into a sense of infinite sin and worthlessness, and it negates the old vision of a dialectic of imagination and reality by transforming the willful, active imagination into a passive receptacle of grace. Yet the power of the symbol exists only in potential form, as one sees in Sonnet #302, one of the last poems that Michelangelo tried to write, and, at the age of 85, left unfinished. Even now, the artist's imagination struggles to free itself from its bondage to earth, beauty, and passion:

Non più per altro da me stesso togli
l'amor, gli affetti perigliosi e vani,
che per fortuna avversa o casi strani,
ond'e' tuo amici dal mondo disciogli,

Signor mie car, tu sol che vesti e spogli,
e col tuo sangue l'alme purghi e sani
da l'infinite colpe e moti umani . . .

• • • • •

In no way else you take out of myself
My love, my dangerous and vain emotion,
Than by strange happenings or adverse fortune,
Whereby you loose your chosen from the earth.

Dear Lord alone, who dresses and strips off
Each soul, your blood its healing, its purgation
From infinite sin and from the human motion . . .

It is only with the "Pietà Rondanini" that Michelangelo achieves a new synthesis of imagination and reality, a perfect fusion of matter and spirit, in which the stone itself seems informed by grace. This is a work of art that transcends all concepts or canons of "art," and whose "unfinished" state could hardly seem more final, perfect, and complete. Michelangelo probably began it shortly after the destruction of the "Pietà del Duomo" in 1554, and worked on it right up to his death in 1564. But it is only with the last, drastic revisions that the effect of absolute fusion is realized. According to Tolnay [in *Michelangelo* (1947)], Michelangelo cut away the whole

upper portion of the completed Christ figure, and hewed the "new body of Christ directly from the part of the block belonging to the Virgin: the new head of Christ is carved from the right shoulder of the Virgin, the new arms of Christ from the sides and thighs of the Virgin's body." The two figures arise out of the same core of stone, almost out of the same body. In a gesture embodying a love at once erotic and mystical, the figures are reborn together, and absorb into their ecstatic union the very stone from which they emerge.

How different this vision is from the one embodied, twenty years earlier, in the best poems of the *Rime*! The dialectical relationships between matter and spirit, reality and imagination, creation and destruction, have all been negated in the last work of Michelangelo, in which only one pole remains—spirit and rebirth. The imagination has been totally subsumed into the ultimate reality of grace. One is left to wonder: did Michelangelo's earlier poetic vision of the imagination's power to create its own reality prompt an enormous self-fear leading to its own negation? Or would his consciousness of self have developed with the same threatening intensity, evolving toward the same thirst for grace and redemption, even if he had not articulated in poetic "concettos" his intuitions as an artist? It is difficult to believe that his artistic-poetic "concettos" did not play a crucial role in Michelangelo's self-understanding, perhaps by making concrete and real the capacity of the individual imagination to acquire such autonomy and power that it might no longer participate in traditional modes of self-understanding and symbolization. The thought of death, first made real by the passing of Vittoria Colonna, would then have provided the impetus toward reintegration of the isolated self with the community of Christian faith. (pp. 38-43)

Alma B. Altizer, "Michelangelo," in her Self and Symbolism in the Poetry of Michelangelo, John Donne, and Agrippa D'Aubigné, *Martinus Nijhoff, 1973, pp. 1-43.*

GEORGE BULL   (essay date 1987)

[*A well-known American writer and journalist, Bull has translated the works of such Italian Renaissance authors as Benvenuto Cellini, Niccolò Machiavelli, and Giorgio Vasari. In the following excerpt, from the introduction to his translation of a selection of Michelangelo's works, Bull considers the range of Michelangelo's verse and appraises English translations of the sonnets.*]

Michelangelo was one of the most original of Italian poets, giving to the forms he inherited, especially the Petrarchan sonnet, fresh verbal freedom and inventiveness, and a deep spiritual and emotional intensity. The *Rime* of Michelangelo, who loved music and the human voice, have attracted composers from contemporary madrigalists to Hugo Wolf and Benjamin Britten in our own time. He was held to be a luminous poet by his contemporaries, and after a long period of neglect (in Italy especially) his poetry has come into its own as literature worthy of study, intellectually and emotionally challenging and expressive, and pleasurable to read. It is immensely variegated, ranging from black humour, surrealism, and obscenity in verses of agonized complaint or self-parody to the baroque imagery, Platonic fervour, and lyricism of his amorous and religious stanzas. As with the letters, Michelangelo's poems sometimes shed light on his artistic thinking and techniques, the subject of art being one of the overarching themes of his poetry, along with sacred and secular love, illness and death, and his native land. He used verse, constantly varying in tone and pace, as a vehicle for an amazingly wide range of purposes: from fleeting thoughts on the theme of Night or Fire, to messages of anger, self-mockery, or consolation.

Michelangelo's verse was an instinctive way for him to turn his experiences, where they did not fit into one form of art or craft, into yet another—nothing wasted—never without some flash of originality of thought and language, and sometimes with results approaching the splendour of his pictures and statues. Interweaving with his work as an artist and with his letters, strengthening the impression of his intellectual cohesion, his poems shift our view of Michelangelo's spiritual and mental landscape, omitting some subjects covered by his art, such as the classical nudes, extending the observation of others, such as death and resurrection. They cluster in several distinct groups and show poetical skill in several demanding forms, from sonnets (chiefly) to madrigals, stanzas in *terza rima,* and epigrams. Following the verses inspired successively by the personalities of Tommaso de' Cavalieri, Vittoria Colonna, and Cecchino Braccio (and the autobiographical and burlesque material) in the last decades of his life, Michelangelo's poetry grew more deeply and poignantly religious, like his sculpture and painting. (pp. xiv-xv)

There are interesting parallels between themes and phrases in the poetry of Shakespeare and that of Michelangelo (who died in the year that Shakespeare was born) though direct influences seem to be ruled out. The sonnets translated by Wyatt from Petrarch's *Rime,* with their anticipations of Donne, point to the receptiveness in Renaissance England for the kind of conceits and verse forms which influenced Michelangelo. But though he was less neglected as a poet in England than (till recently) in Italy, Michelangelo has received only spasmodic and often exasperated attention from English-speaking poets. For Richard Duppa's *Life and Works of Michel Angelo Buonarroti* at the beginning of the nineteenth century [see excerpt dated 1806], Southey translated two of the sonnets, those on Dante, and Wordsworth translated a 'fragment' from the ingenious half-pastoral, half-allegorical octave stanzas in praise of rustic life; the quatrain spoken by the statue *Night;* and two of the religious sonnets. (Four, possibly five, depending on attribution, of Wordsworth's translations of the sonnets are extant, one of them in two versions.) The combination of Wordsworth and Michelangelo inevitably produced some memorable lines, such as the conclusion of the sonnet *Ben può talor col mie 'rdente desio:*

> But, in chaste hearts uninfluenced by the power
> Of outward change, there blooms a deathless flower,
> That breathes on earth the air of paradise.

Wordsworth, however, abandoned his original thought of translating fifteen of the sonnets, after he had already written in a letter of 1805 that Michelangelo's poetry was 'the most difficult to construe that I have ever met with, but just what you would expect from such a man, showing abundantly how conversant his soul was with great things . . . '. He added that Michelangelo packed so much excellent meaning into so little room, that he found the problem of translating 'insurmountable'. Later, John Addington Symonds, Longfellow, and Emerson were the most distinguished nineteenth-century poets to produce selective translations of the sonnets which, though honest and well-intentioned, were coloured by Victorian sentiment and terminology whose rhetoric could not ex-

press Michelangelo's range of religious and erotic feeling, or reproduce the force and muscularity of his language and syntax. In our own century, the challenge has been bravely taken up by a few poets ranging from Robert Bridges to Elizabeth Jennings. (pp. xv-xvii)

> *George Bull, in an introduction to* Michelangelo: Life, Letters, and Poetry, *edited and translated by George Bull, Oxford University Press, Oxford, 1987, pp. ix-xvii.*

FURTHER READING

Carden, Robert W. *Michelangelo: A Record of His Life As Told in His Own Letters and Papers.* London: Constable & Co., 1913, 535 p.
>   Biography of Michelangelo, with extensive quotation from the artist's correspondence.

Carne-Ross, Donald. "The Poetry of Michelangelo." *The Times Literary Supplement,* No. 3718 (8 June 1973): 639-40.
>   Attempts to establish the role of poetry in Michelangelo's "total economy," noting that Michelangelo " 'wasted' less of his total experience than any man we know of."

Clements, Robert J. "Eye, Mind, and Hand in Michelangelo's Poetry." *PMLA* LXIX, No. 1 (March 1954): 324-36.
>   Discusses the contrast between nature and art expressed in Michelangelo's poetry.

——. "Michelangelo As a Baroque Poet." *PMLA* LXXVI, No. 3 (June 1961): 182-92.
>   Discusses the baroque character of Michelangelo's sonnets, madrigals, canzoni, stanze, and fragments.

——. "Prayer and Confession in Michelangelo's Poetry." *Studies in Philology* LXII, No. 2 (April 1965): 101-10.
>   Examines Michelangelo's personal relationship with Christ and God as it is reflected in his sonnets and prayers.

——, ed. *Michelangelo: A Self-Portrait, Texts and Sources.* New York: New York University Press, 1968, 193 p.
>   Annotated collection of Michelangelo's own thoughts about his life and creative works. The material is arranged under seven headings: "Art and Letters," "Religion and Philosophy," "Love," "Family and Friends," "Government and Society," "Self-Portrait, Physical and Moral," and "Old Age and Death."

Craven, Thomas. "Michael Angelo." In his *Men of Art,* pp. 111-60. New York: Simon and Schuster, 1931.
>   Biographical sketch, with brief commentary upon "two strong sources" of poetic inspiration in Michelangelo's old age, his friends Vittoria Colonna and Tommaso de' Cavalieri.

De Tolnay, Charles. *Michelangelo: Sculptor, Painter, Architect.* Princeton: Princeton University Press, 1975, 283 p.
>   Biographical and critical study focusing on Michelangelo's principal achievements in the plastic arts.

Hibbard, Howard. *Michelangelo.* New York: Harper & Row, Publishers, 1974, 347 p.
>   Copiously illustrated profile of Michelangelo as artist and thinker.

Hope, Charles. "The Real Leonardo." *The New York Review of Books* XXXVI, No. 13 (17 August 1989): 16-18.

Examines the creative processes of Michelangelo and Leonardo da Vinci.

Labriola, Albert C. "Sculptural Poetry: The Visual Imagination of Michelangelo, Keats, and Shelley." *Comparative Literature Studies* 24, No. 4 (1987): 326-34.

Compares Michelangelo's descriptions of sculpture and sculpturing in his poetry with those of John Keats and Percy Bysshe Shelley.

Liebert, Robert S. *Michelangelo: A Psychoanalytic Study of His Life and Images.* New Haven: Yale University Press, 1983, 447 p.

Comprehensive biography, with extensive commentary on Michelangelo's psyche as it is revealed in his paintings and sculptures.

Lucente, Gregory L. "Lyric Tradition and the Desires of Absence: Rudel, Dante, and Michelangelo ('Vorrei uoler')." *Canadian Review of Comparative Literature* 10 (September 1983): 305-32.

Explores themes of confidence, assurance, and absence in Michelangelo's sonnets.

Moses, Gavriel. "Philosophy and Mimesis in Michelangelo's Poems." *Italianistica* X, No. 2 (May-August 1981): 162-77.

Contends that the best evidence concerning Michelangelo's poetic philosophy is to be found in the testimony of the author himself.

Musser, Benjamin F. "The Creator and the Carver of Sonnets." In his *Franciscan Poets,* pp. 67-81. New York: The Macmillan Co., 1933.

Considers Michelangelo's role in the development of the Italian sonnet.

Ramsden, E. H. Introduction to *The Letters of Michelangelo, Translated from the Original Tuscan,* by Michelangelo, edited and translated by E. H. Ramsden, Vol. I, pp. xxiii-lvii; Vol. II, pp. xv-lviii. Stanford: Stanford University Press, 1963.

Concise biography of Michelangelo, emphasizing events treated in his correspondence.

Summers, David. "Non ha l'ottimo artista alcun concetto." In his *Michelangelo and the Language of Art,* pp. 203-33. Princeton: Princeton University Press, 1981.

Close study of Benedetto Varchi's 1547 lecture on Michelangelo's sonnet "Non ha l'ottimo artista alcun concetto," focusing on the meaning of *concetto* in Renaissance Italy.

"Talking of Angels: Michelangelo in His Letters." *The Times Literary Supplement,* No. 3205 (2 August 1963): 585-86.

Discusses possible motives behind Michelangelo's carefully worked portrayal of himself in his letters.

Leonardo da Vinci

1452-1519

Italian essayist, treatise writer, and fabulist.

Leonardo is universally acclaimed as the archetype Renaissance man. Although best known for such artistic masterpieces as the *Mona Lisa* and *The Last Supper,* he was also a writer and a scientist who excelled in virtually every discipline he pursued. His *Notebooks* are diverse in both content and style, containing observations and inventions that reveal an intellect centuries ahead of its time. Today, he continues to represent an ideal of mankind. American author and art critic Thomas Craven has called Leonardo "perhaps the most resplendent figure in the history of the human race. In person, distinguished and strong; in bearing, generous and gentle; in intellect, a giant; in art, the most perfect painter who ever held a brush, he stands so far above the ordinary mortal that his name, for centuries, has signified less a man than a legend, less an artist than a magician."

Leonardo was born in the village of Vinci in 1452, the illegitimate son of a well-to-do Florentine notary. He was educated at home, where he also received instruction in music and art. Although he excelled in academia, he had avowedly little regard for traditional scholarship. "My subjects are to be dealt with by experience rather than by words," he wrote. This interpretation of learning as a process predominantly of observation and experience is clearly evidenced in the *Notebooks.*

In approximately 1467, Leonardo was apprenticed to Andrea del Verrocchio, a prominent Florentine painter, sculptor, and goldsmith. Verrocchio tutored him in painting and sculpture, though more often than not, according to legend, the student corrected the master. In 1472 Leonardo was inducted into the Florentine guild of painters. During the decade that followed he became one of the most sought-after artists in Florence. Only one negative incident mars his early career. In 1476 he was anonymously accused of homosexuality and was brought to trial on charges of offending public morality. The allegations, repeated less than a year later, were dismissed as unsubstantiated. That he never married and found physical intimacy extremely distasteful has only heightened speculation concerning his personal life.

Leonardo's interests were not limited to the plastic arts. Sometime between 1481 and 1483 he became a military and civil engineer for the duke of Milan, Ludovico Sforza. Leonardo flourished in the intellectual atmosphere of Milan. He enjoyed contact with prominent artists and scholars, and the two decades of his residence there were the most productive of his career. He pursued studies in several disciplines and began keeping the first of his voluminous notebooks. In addition to painting such masterpieces as the *Virgin of the Rocks* and *The Last Supper,* he completed a substantial portion of a treatise on painting and laid the groundwork for texts on anatomy, architecture, and mechanics as well. Because most scientific and philosophical literature was not available in Italian, he taught himself Latin. This enabled him to study the works of authors, particularly Archimedes, whose scholastic methodology he believed paralleled his own. When Milan fell to French forces in 1499, Leonardo returned to

Florence. From 1502 to 1503 he was chief architect and engineer for Cesare Borgia, designing weapons and drawing strategic maps: early examples of modern cartography. Returning to Milan in 1506, Leonardo enjoyed a prominent position at the court of French governor Charles d'Amboise. In 1517 he was invited by Francis I to join his court at Amboise. The new French king greatly admired the Italian, honoring him with the title "Premier peintre, architecte, et méchanicien du Roi." In France, Leonardo was revered as much for his philosophy and knowledge as for his technical or artistic skills. He was provided with a château at Cloux near Amboise (the king's summer residence), where he lived until his death in 1519. The legend advanced by sixteenth-century biographer Giorgio Vasari that Leonardo died in the arms of Francis I is unfounded.

For over three decades Leonardo kept detailed written records and illustrations of his work. Believing the individual must "understand how to see," he considered his eyes his most valuable asset and acquired knowledge chiefly through observation. The diversity of his interests as well as his apparent passion for recording in minute detail virtually all of his perceptions, resulted in writings on a multitude of subjects. According to twentieth-century English historian Kenneth Clark: "It is a miracle that any man should have observed, read, and written down so much in a single lifetime." The *Notebooks* contain preliminary notes and outlines for treatises on art, architecture, and engineering, as well as studies in several branches of science, notably anatomy, zoology, physiology, geography, and astronomy. During the early years of his career, Leonardo was chiefly interested in mechanics and engineering. His desire to understand not only how an object works, but also why, led him to make several discoveries. Included among his inventions are the helicopter, submarine, and armored tank. Later, he concentrated almost exclusively upon his scientific studies, particularly human anatomy. Leonardo performed over thirty dissections, documenting in detail the circulatory system and internal structure of the human body. These writings are considered among the most important scientific studies of the Italian Renaissance. Leonardo also wrote a small amount of fiction. Fascinated with allegory, he borrowed from Pliny and Aesop to compose several fables and a bestiary. Many of these tales have pessimistic outlooks, and most are intended to instruct the reader by revealing fatal flaws in human nature. Isabel Quigly has theorized that these stories represent their author's "search for truth in every form, including poetic forms in which parables and fables tell us hidden truths."

Throughout the centuries, the task of collecting, editing, and publishing the mass of undated notes accumulated in Leonardo's journals has proved complex. Leonardo left all of his writing to his favorite pupil, Francesco Melzi. Melzi organized some of the manuscripts, and his efforts helped in the eventual publication of *A Treatise of Painting* in 1651. Despite his attempts to preserve the notebooks, Melzi's heirs allowed the journals to be separated, selling some and discarding others. As a result, Leonardo's work is scattered throughout Europe, and scholars can only surmise at the number of pages that are lost or have been destroyed. Aside from logistic difficulties, editors were hindered by several factors including inherent problems in transcription and organization. Leonardo wrote in a mirror script from right to left with a unique orthographic style. There is no other known instance of this method of writing in the history of handwriting. In addition, his handwriting remained essentially unchanged during his entire writing career. This has made attempts at chronologizing the texts through handwriting analysis impossible. While Leonardo's scholastic and scientific methodology reveals a structured approach to learning, rarely do his journals as a whole reflect any system of order. To prevent possible refutation of his theories, he repeated many of his arguments, approaching and developing each from a variety of angles. Only rarely did he complete studies on any given topic.

The depth and diversity of Leonardo's scholarly achievements have been admired and acclaimed by commentators throughout the centuries. His contemporaries recognized his genius and sought his expertise in a number of disciplines. Fifteenth-century Italian mathematician Luca Pacioli, whose *De divine proportione* Leonardo illustrated, called his artistic friend "one endowed with all perfections." Leonardo's work, not only as an artist and sculptor, but also as an engineer, scientist, and philosopher, was deemed exceptional. Sixteenth-century biographer Giorgio Vasari's impression that Leonardo had "such a power of intellect that whatever he turned his mind to he made himself master of with ease" epitomizes the general tenor of critical opinion of the artist's life and work. Less than two centuries later an anonymous critic in the *Spectator* echoed Vasari's sentiments, extolling Leonardo as "the most singular Instance of an Universal genius I have ever met

with." Leonardo's reputation with the general public has remained virtually unchanged throughout the centuries. While the artist and his technical work received much scholastic attention, little or no criticism of his writings exists prior to the publication of the *Notebooks* during the late nineteenth century. Commentators concur that had the notebooks been published during the sixteenth century, they would probably have had a decided effect upon the development of several fields Leonardo investigated.

Twentieth-century studies of the *Notebooks* have touched upon many subjects. Most scholars concur that Leonardo's observations and inventions were in advance of their time and that his scientific methodology anticipated the techniques of future generations of scientists as well. Some scholars have criticized the diverse range of subjects covered in the manuscripts, claiming that Leonardo would have made a greater contribution had he focused exclusively upon one or two fields. Other critics counter that he successfully integrated the various disciplines he pursued, thereby achieving a more universal perspective. Because Leonardo rarely completed anything, assessing his ability as a writer has proved difficult. As a whole, his writing has received mixed reviews. While some commentators agree with Emilio Goggio's opinion that Leonardo was "an accomplished writer who will always hold a place of prominence in the history of Italian literature as a champion of the vernacular and a master and precursor of Italian scientific prose," others question the quality of his literary accomplishments. More than one critic has deemed the manuscripts a jumbled mass of information unworthy of publication in their entirety.

Leonardo's life and scholarly achievements have fascinated readers throughout the centuries. Today his manuscripts are considered among the best representatives of the transition from Renaissance to Modern scholasticism and are highly valued for the insight they provide into the Italian Renaissance. Ernest Hatch Wilkins considers the *Notebooks* "such, in their incredible wealth and novelty, as to command an amazed admiration, whether for their revelation of facts, their assertion of great possibilities, their exposition of fine techniques, their insight into the ways of mankind, or the fascination of their fragmentary philosophy."

*PRINCIPAL WORKS

Trattato della pittura di Lionardo da Vinci nuoamente dato in luce, con la vita dell' istesso autore   (treatise) 1651
  [*A Treatise of Painting,* 1721]
Tabula anatomica Leonardi da Vinci . . .e bibliotheca . . . Magnae Britanniae Hannoveraeque Regis deprompta, venerem obversam e legibus naturae hominibus solam convenire, ostendens   (treatise) 1830
†*Les manuscrits de Léonard de Vinci . . . Fac-similés . . . avec transcription littérale, traduction française, préface et table methodique.* 6 vols.   (notebooks) 1881-1891
The Literary Works of Leonardo da Vinci. 2 vols.   (treatises and notebooks) 1883; revised and enlarged, 1939
Il Codice de Leonardo da Vinci nella biblioteca del principe Trivulzio in Milano   (treatise) 1891
‡*Il Codice Atlantico di Leonardo da Vinci nella biblioteca Ambrosiana di Milano*   (notebooks) 1894-1904

---

*The various manuscripts by Leonardo collectively known as the *Notebooks* are scattered in libraries throughout Europe.

†This publication contains facsimiles of the manuscripts housed in the Institut de France.

‡The *Codice Atlantico* contains Leonardo's writings from approximately 1483 to 1518. It comprises 1222 pages and almost 400 designs and is considered the most important single manuscript in the *Notebooks*.

GIOVANNI DI FRANCESCO NESI   (poem date 1501?)

[*In the following excerpt, Francesco Nesi pays tribute to Leonardo.*]

In carbon vidi già con arte intera
Imago veneranda del mio Vinci
Che in Delo e in Creta e Samo me' non era,

Tal che se col pennel ritrahi di quinci
Qualcunche tu ti sia che di colore
Pinga non però lei superi et vinci

Perchè più degna et di maggior valore
Fa l'arte quella, in cui par che s'infonda
Quanto in sè cape il suo primo valore.

(In a charcoal drawing, I saw with complete art depicted
The venerable image of my Vinci
Than which there was no better in Delos, Crete, or Samos,

So much so that though thou may'st portray with brush
   hereafter
Whoever thou may'st be painting with color
Never wilt thou surpass or vanquish him in skill.

For more to be esteemed and of greater value
Does art render that which is infused
Through and through with his supreme worth.)

> *Giovanni di Francesco Nesi, in an excerpt from a poem in* Leonardo da Vinci, *Reynal & Company, 1956, p. 11.*

ANTONIO DE BEATIS   (letter date 1517)

[*A sixteenth-century Spaniard, Beatis was secretary to Cardinal Louis of Aragon. From 1517 to 1518, he kept a journal of the cardinal's travels through England, France, Belgium, Holland, and Italy. It was during their sojourn in France that he became acquainted with Leonardo and his work. In the following excerpt from a letter written in 1517, he outlines the artist's career and accomplishments.*]

[On the 18th of October 1517], we went from Tours to Amboise. In one of the suburbs, we went with the cardinal to visit Messer Leonardo Vinci, the Florentine, more than seventy years old, the most excellent painter of the time. He showed his Excellency three pictures: one, drawn from the model, is of a certain Florentine Lady [this picture has not been identified], executed at the request of the late Giuliano de' Medici the Magnificent; the other of Saint John Baptist; young; and the third of the Madonna and the Son who rest in the lap of Saint Anne; all the three very perfect, although from him, since he has been stricken with a certain paralysis of the right hand, no more masterpieces can be expected. He has been the benefactor of a Milanese disciple [Melzi] who works very well. Although the said Messer Leonardo cannot paint any longer with the suavity (dolcezza) which was natural to him,

he can still make drawings and teach others. This gentleman has written on anatomy in its relations to painting in an admirable fashion, describing the bones, members, muscles, nerves, veins, joints, intestines—and all that one can study in the body of man or woman—as none has done before him. We have seen it with our eyes: and he told us that he had dissected more than thirty bodies of men and women of all ages. He has also written on the nature of water. With various machines and other things he has filled an infinity of volumes, all written in the vulgar language, which, published, would be of the greatest utility and the greatest charm. (pp. 92-3)

> *Antonio de Beatis, in an excerpt from a letter dated October 18, 1517, in* Leonardo da Vinci *by Clifford Bax, D. Appleton and Company, 1932, pp. 92-3.*

LEONARDO DA VINCI   (essay date 1519?)

[*In the following excerpt from the general introduction to* A Treatise of Painting, *Leonardo anticipates negative criticism of his methodology.*]

I am fully concious that, not being a literary man, certain presumptuous persons will think that they may reasonably blame me; alleging that I am not a man of letters. Foolish folks! do they not know that I might retort as Marius did to the Roman Patricians by saying: That they, who deck themselves out in the labours of others will not allow me my own. They will say that I, having no literary skill, cannot properly express that which I desire to treat of; but they do not know that my subjects are to be dealt with by experience rather than by words; and [experience] has been the mistress of those who wrote well. And so, as mistress, I will cite her in all cases.

Though I may not, like them, be able to quote other authors, I shall rely on that which is much greater and more worthy:—on experience, the mistress of their Masters. They go about puffed up and pompous, dressed and decorated with [the fruits], not of their own labours, but of those of others. And they will not allow me my own. They will scorn me as an inventor; but how much more might they—who are not inventors but vaunters and declaimers of the works of others—be blamed.

And those men who are inventors and interpreters between Nature and Man, as compared with boasters and declaimers of the works of others, must be regarded and not otherwise esteemed than as the object in front of a mirror, when compared with its image seen in the mirror. For the first is something in itself, and the other nothingness.—Folks little indebted to Nature, since it is only by chance that they wear the human form and without it I might class them with the herds of beasts.

Many will think they may reasonably blame me by alleging that my proofs are opposed to the authority of certain men held in the highest reverence by their inexperienced judgments; not considering that my works are the issue of pure and simple experience, who is the one true mistress. These rules are sufficient to enable you to know the true from the false—and this aids men to look only for things that are possible and with due moderation—and not to wrap yourself in ignorance, a thing which can have no good result, so that in despair you would give yourself up to melancholy. (pp. 14-15)

Leonardo da Vinci, in his The Notebooks of Leonardo da Vinci, Vol. I, *edited by Jean Paul Richter,*
translated by Mrs. R. C. Bell, Dover Publications,
Inc., 1970, pp. 1-24.

GIORGIO VASARI (essay date 1568)

[*Vasari was a sixteenth-century Italian architect, artist, and bi-*
ographer. His most important work, Le vite de' piu eccellente
pittori, scultori, e architettori *(1550; revised edition, 1568;*
The Lives of the Most Eminent Painters, Sculptors, and Architects, *1850-85), has been considered a primary biographical*
source on early Italian artists. In the following excerpt from
that work, he recounts Leonardo's life and career.]

[The greatest of all Andrea del Verrocchio's] pupils was Lionardo da Vinci, in whom, besides a beauty of person never
sufficiently admired and a wonderful grace in all his actions,
there was such a power of intellect that whatever he turned
his mind to he made himself master of with ease.

Marvellous and divine, indeed, was Lionardo the son of Ser
Piero da Vinci. In erudition and letters he would have distinguished himself, if he had not been variable and unstable. For
he set himself to learn many things, and when he had begun
them gave them up. In arithmetic, during the few months
that he applied himself to it, he made such progress that he
often perplexed his master by the doubts and difficulties that
he propounded. He gave some time to the study of music, and
learnt to play on the lute, improvising songs most divinely.
But though he applied himself to such various subjects, he
never laid aside drawing and modelling in relief, to which his
fancy inclined him more than to anything else; which Ser
Piero perceiving, he took some of his drawings one day and
carried them to Andrea del Verrocchio, with whom he was
in close friendship, and prayed him to say whether he
thought, if Lionardo gave himself up to drawing, he would
succeed. Andrea was astounded at the great beginning Lionardo had made, and urged Ser Piero to make him apply himself to it. So he arranged with Lionardo that he was to go to
Andrea's workshop, which Lionardo did very willingly, and
set himself to practise every art in which design has a part.
For he had such a marvellous mind that, besides being a good
geometrician, he worked at modelling (making while a boy
some laughing women's heads, and some heads of children
which seem to have come from a master's hand), and also
made many designs for architecture; and he was the first,
while he was still quite young, to discuss the question of making a channel for the river Arno from Pisa to Florence. He
made models of mills and presses, and machines to be worked
by water, and designs for tunnelling through mountains, and
levers and cranes for raising great weights, so that it seemed
that his brain never ceased inventing; and many of these
drawings are still scattered about. Among them was one
drawn for some of the citizens then governing Florence, to
show how it would be possible to lift up the church of S. Giovanni, and put steps under it without throwing it down; and
he supported his scheme with such strong reasons as made
it appear possible, though as soon as he was gone every one
felt in his mind how impossible it really was.

He delighted much in horses and also in all other animals,
and often when passing by the places where they sold birds
he would take them out of their cages, and paying the price
that was asked for them, would let them fly away into the air,
restoring to them their lost liberty.

A face amidst a list of words, by Leonardo.

While, as we have said, he was studying art under Andrea del
Verrocchio, the latter was painting a picture of S. John bap-
tizing Christ; Lionardo worked upon an angel who was holding the clothes, and although he was so young, he managed
it so well that Lionardo's angel was better than Andrea's figures, which was the cause of Andrea's never touching colours
again, being angry that a boy should know more than he.
(pp. 144-46)

There was great ill-feeling between [Lionardo] and Michael
Angelo Buonarroti, on which account Michael Angelo left
Florence. But when Lionardo heard this, he set out and went
into France, where the king, having already some of his
works, was well affectioned towards him, and desired that he
should colour his cartoon of S. Anne; but he, according to his
custom, kept him waiting a long time. At last, having become
old, he lay ill for many months, and seeing himself near
death, he set himself to study the holy Christian religion, and
though he could not stand, desired to leave his bed with the
help of his friends and servants to receive the Holy Sacra-
ment. Then the king, who used often and lovingly to visit
him, came in, and he, raising himself respectfully to sit up in
bed, spoke of his sickness, and how he had offended God and
man by not working at his art as he ought. Then there came
a paroxysm, a forerunner of death, and the king raised him
and lifted his head to help him and lessen the pain, where-

upon his spirit, knowing it could have no greater honour, passed away in the king's arms in the seventy-fifth year of his age.

The loss of Lionardo was mourned out of measure by all who had known him, for there was none who had done such honour to painting. The splendour of his great beauty could calm the saddest soul, and his words could move the most obdurate mind. His great strength could restrain the most violent fury, and he could bend an iron knocker or a horseshoe as if it were lead. He was liberal to his friends, rich and poor, if they had talent and worth; and indeed as Florence had the greatest of gifts in his birth, so she suffered an infinite loss in his death.   (pp. 156-57)

> *Giorgio Vasari, "Lionardo da Vinci," in his* Lives of the Artists, *edited and translated by E. L. Seeley, The Noonday Press, Inc., 1957, pp. 140-61.*

BENVENUTO CELLINI   (essay date 1571?)

[*Cellini was a sixteenth-century Italian autobiographer, essayist, and poet who was also a highly acclaimed sculptor and goldsmith. In the following excerpt, he recalls his discovery of a portion of the notebooks and Francis I's favorable opinion of Leonardo.*]

[I discovered] a book written in ink, copied from one by the great Leonardo da Vinci. . . . This book was of great excellence, and beautifully made, with the marvellous genius of the said Leonardo (no greater man than he, I believe, has been born into the world), concerning the three great arts of sculpture, painting, and architecture. And because he abounded in great genius, and had some knowledge of Latin and Greek literature, King Francis, being deeply fascinated by his virtues, took such pleasure in hearing him converse that few were the days in the year when he could bear to be separated from him; which was the cause of his not being able to carry out the remarkable studies over which he took such infinite pains. I must not fail to repeat the words spoken of him by the king, who said to me in the presence of the Cardinal of Ferrara, the Cardinal of Lorraine, and the King of Navarre, that he believed no other man had been born into the world who knew as much as Leonardo—not so much speaking of sculpture, painting, and architecture, as saying that he was a very great philosopher.

> *Benvenuto Cellini, from an excerpt in* Leonardo da Vinci, *Reynal & Company, 1956, p. 11.*

THE SPECTATOR   (essay date 1712)

[*In the following excerpt from* The Spectator, *the anonymous critic extols Leonardo, calling him a universal genius.*]

I am obliged for the following Essay, as well as for that which lays down Rules out of *Tully* for Pronunciation and Action, to the Ingenious Author of a Poem just Published, Entitled *An Ode to the Creator of the World, occasioned by the Fragments of* Orpheus.

It is a Remark made, as I remember, by a celebrated *French* Author, that *no Man ever pushed his Capacity as far as it was able to extend.* I shall not enquire whether this Assertion be strictly true. It may suffice to say, that Men of the greatest Application and Acquirements can look back upon many vacant Spaces, and neglected Parts of Time, which have slipped away from them unemployed; and there is hardly any one considering Person in the World, but is apt to fancy with himself, at some time or other, that if his Life were to begin again, he could fill it up better.

The Mind is most provoked to cast on itself this ingenuous Reproach, when the Examples of such Men are presented to it, as have far outshot the generality of their Species, in Learning, Arts, or any valuable Improvements.

One of the most extensive and improved Genius's we have had any Instance of in our own Nation, or in any other, was that of Sir *Francis Bacon* Lord *Verulam.* This great Man, by an extraordinary Force of Nature, Compass of Thought, and indefatigable Study, had amassed to himself such Stores of Knowledge as we cannot look upon without Amazement. His Capacity seems to have grasped All that was revealed in Books before his Time; and not satisfied with that, he began to strike out new Tracks of Science, too many to be travelled over by any one Man, in the Compass of the longest Life. These, therefore, he could only mark down, like imperfect Coastings in Maps, or supposed Points of Land, to be further discovered, and ascertained by the Industry of After-Ages, who should proceed upon his Notices or Conjectures.

The Excellent Mr. *Boyle* was the Person, who seems to have been designed by Nature to succeed to the Labours and Enquiries of that extraordinary Genius I have just mentioned. By innumerable Experiments He, in a great Measure, filled up those Plans and Out-Lines of Science, which his Predecessor had sketched out. His Life was spent in the Pursuit of Nature, through a great Variety of Forms and Changes, and in the most rational, as well as devout Adoration of its Divine Author.

It would be impossible to name many Persons, who have extended their Capacities so far as these two, in the Studies they pursued; but my learned Readers, on this Occasion, will naturally turn their Thoughts to a *Third,* who is yet living, and is likewise the Glory of our own Nation. The Improvements which others had made in Natural and Mathematical Knowledge have so vastly increased in his Hands, as to afford at once a wonderful Instance how great the Capacity is of an Human Soul, and how inexhaustible the Subject of its Enquiries; so true is that Remark in Holy Writ, that, *tho' a wise Man seek to find out the Works of God from the beginning to the End, yet shall he not be able to do it.*

I cannot help mentioning here one Character more, of a different kind indeed from these, yet such a one as may serve to shew the wonderful Force of Nature and of Application, and is the most singular Instance of an Universal Genius I have ever met with. The Person I mean is *Leonardo da Vinci,* an *Italian* Painter, descended from a noble Family in *Tuscany,* about the beginning of the Sixteenth Century. In his Profession of History-Painting he was so great a Master, that some have affirmed he excelled all who went before him. It is certain that he raised the envy of *Michael Angelo,* who was his Contemporary, and that from the Study of his Works *Raphael* himself learned his best Manner of Designing. He was a Master too in Sculpture and Architecture, and skilful in Anatomy, Mathematicks, and Mechanicks. The Aquaeduct from the River *Adda* to *Milan,* is mentioned as a Work of his Contrivance. He had learned several Languages, and was acquainted with the Studies of History, Philosophy, Poetry, and Musick. Tho' it is not necessary to my present Purpose, I cannot but take Notice, that all who have writ of him mention likewise his Perfection of Body. The Instances of his Strength are almost incredible. He is described to have been of a well-formed Person, and a Master of all genteel Exercises. And lastly, we are told that his moral Qualities were agreeable to his natural and intellectual Endowments, and that he was of an honest and generous Mind, adorned with great Sweetness of Manners. I might break off the Account of him here, but I imagine it will be an Entertainment to the Curiosity of my Readers, to find so remarkable a Character distinguished by as remarkable a Circumstance at his Death. The Fame of his Works having gained him an universal Esteem, he was invited to the Court of *France,* where, after some Time, he fell sick; and *Francis the First* coming to see him, he raised himself in his Bed to acknowledge the Honour which was done him by that Visit. The King embraced him, and *Leonardo* fainting at the same Instant, expired in the Arms of that great Monarch.

It is impossible to attend to such Instances as these without being raised into a Contemplation on the wonderful Nature of an Human Mind, which is capable of such Progressions in Knowledge, and can contain such a Variety of Ideas without Perplexity or Confusion. (pp. 245-47)

> *An excerpt in* The Spectator, Vol. 4, *by Addison & Steele and others, edited by Gregory Smith, J. M. Dent & Sons Ltd., 1907, pp. 245-48.*

WALTER PATER   (essay date 1873)

[*A nineteenth-century essayist, novelist, and critic, Pater is regarded as one of the most famous proponents of aestheticism in English literature. Distinguished as the first major English writer to formulate an explicitly aesthetic philosophy of life, he advocated the "love of art for art's sake" as life's greatest offering, a belief he exemplified in his influential* Studies in the History of the Renaissance *(1873) and elucidated in his novel* Marius the Epicurean *(1885). In the following excerpt from* The Renaissance, *a revision of an essay originally published in 1869 in the* Fortnightly Review, *he investigates Leonardo's philosophy and the legends put forth by Giorgio Vasari (see excerpt dated 1568).*]

In Vasari's life of Leonardo da Vinci as we now read it [see excerpt dated 1568], there are some variations from the first edition. There, the painter who has fixed the outward type of Christ for succeeding centuries was a bold speculator, holding lightly by other men's beliefs, setting philosophy above Christianity. Words of his, trenchant enough to justify this impression, are not recorded, and would have been out of keeping with a genius of which one characteristic is the tendency to lose itself in a refined and graceful mystery. The suspicion was but the time-honoured mode in which the world stamps its appreciation of one who has thoughts for himself alone, his high indifference, his intolerance of the common forms of things; and in the second edition the image was changed into something fainter and more conventional. But it is still by a certain mystery in his work, and something enigmatical beyond the usual measure of great men, that he fascinates, or perhaps half repels. His life is one of sudden revolts, with intervals in which he works not at all, or apart from the main scope of his work. By a strange fortune the pictures on which his more popular fame rested disappeared early from the world, like the *Battle of the Standard;* or are mixed obscurely with the product of meaner hands, like the *Last Supper.* His type of beauty is so exotic that it fascinates a larger number than it delights, and seems more than that of any

other artist to reflect ideas and views and some scheme. (p. 846)

The science of that age was all divination, clairvoyance, unsubjected to our exact modern formulas, seeking in an instant of vision to concentrate a thousand experiences. Later writers, thinking only of the well-ordered *Treatise on Painting* which a Frenchman, Raffaelle du Fresne, a hundred years afterwards, compiled from Leonardo's bewildered manuscripts, written strangely, as his manner was, from right to left, have imagined a rigid order in his inquiries. But this rigid order would have been little in accordance with the restlessness of his character; and if we think of him as the mere reasoner who subjects design to anatomy, and composition to mathematical rules, we shall hardly have that impression which those around Leonardo received from him. Poring over his crucibles, making experiments with colour, trying, by a strange variation of the alchemist's dream, to discover the secret, not of an elixir to make man's natural life immortal, but of giving immortality to the subtlest and most delicate effects of painting, he seemed to them rather the sorcerer or the magician, possessed of curious secrets and a hidden knowledge, living in a world of which he alone possessed the key. What his philosophy seems to have been most like is that of Paracelsus or Cardan; and much of the spirit of the older alchemy still hangs about it, with its confidence in short cuts and odd byways to knowledge. To him philosophy was to be something giving strange swiftness and double sight, divining the sources of springs beneath the earth or of expression beneath the human countenance, clairvoyant of occult gifts in common or uncommon things, in the reed at the brook-side, or the star which draws near to us but once in a century. How, in this way, the clear purpose was overclouded, the fine chaser's hand perplexed, we but dimly see; the mystery which at no point quite lifts from Leonardo's life is deepest here. (p. 849)

> *Walter Pater, "Leonardo da Vinci," in* An Oxford Anthology of English Prose, *edited by Arnold Whitridge and John Wendell Dodds, Oxford University Press, 1937, pp. 846-57.*

CHARLES CHRISTOPHER BLACK   (essay date 1874)

[*Black was a nineteenth-century English essayist and art historian. In the following excerpt, he traces the history of the manuscripts of Leonardo's works and illustrates the diversity of Leonardo's interest and talent.*]

In all branches of literature and science [Leonardo's] universal genius loved to test its powers; in all he added line upon line, precept upon precept, at first with little care for practical ends, and enjoying discovery merely for its own pleasure, till he seems to have been startled by the immense bulk of his own accumulated observations. When, therefore, he undertook the task of classifying and reducing to order his manuscripts, it is little wonder that Time overtook him with his work yet incomplete, and that in science as in art, his place must be judged, not merely by the few complete works now existing, but by the numerous hints, plans, and sketches filling the fourteen great volumes which, dying at the comparatively premature age of 67, he bequeathed to his friend and scholar, Francesco Melzi.

Did we, in fact, possess all these volumes, we might, by painful and reverent search, carry out the work which he proposed to himself, and thus by degrees trace out in its true proportions the mighty image of the universal inventor. But this has been denied us. Various have been the vicissitudes to which this valuable legacy has been exposed; and it is with no small indignation that we find the family of Melzi, within 70 years of Leonardo's death, so utterly ignorant of its value as to allow thirteen volumes to be abstracted, and when (so Mazenta informs us) he managed to restore them to the original owners, the then chief of the family "wondered he had taken so much trouble, informed Mazenta he might keep them, and added that there were many more which had lain for years in the garrets of his villa."

It does not enter into the scope of this notice to follow minutely the various fortunes of the different parts of Leonardo's legacy. An Italian author (Gilberto Govi) has traced with reverent accuracy the course of many volumes, till, like the pilgrims on the bridge of Mirza, they suddenly disappear from sight. The Earl of Arundel and Consul Smith of Venice appear in Govi's pages among the accidental possessors of uncertain portions; and so numerous have been their casualties, that the reader is rather surprised to find thirteen volumes still remaining in the Ambrosian Library of Milan in 1796. So rich a prize was not likely to escape the plundering hands of the French, and, seemingly through negligence of the Austrian Commissioner in 1815, one only of the fourteen was restored to Milan. Happily this one was the most important, being that long known by the title of **Codice Atlantico,** having been compiled by mounting near 400 designs from the master's hands upon drawing paper, many of which contain notes of explanation written, as was his ordinary habit, with the left hand, and from right to left, so as to require the aid of a mirror to render them legible. The volumes which still remained at Paris were subject, so Govi states, to further mutilations; but we do not propose to carry this narrative further, our object being simply to point out the difficulties inevitably accompanying any attempt to reconstruct from such imperfect materials a true and correct image of their author. Nor, even could the depredations of centuries be restored, would a simple reprinting of this huge mass of notes do anything like justice to Leonardo's memory. Frequently a first idea, remarkable for its originality, and destined in the hands of future discoverers to produce rich fruits, appears in these pages, is developed so far as to show how clearly its capabilities were foreseen by the author, and then breaks off short without any reason which we can even conjecture.

On the other hand, we find suggestions carefully noted down, and deductions drawn which the author's better judgment disavows, and which some few pages onwards are overthrown by their original construction. Of these a notable instance is to be found in the treatise **On the Motion and Power of Water,** in which Leonardo has devised an ingenious instrument for perpetual motion, a chimæra which he afterwards abandons, and the impossibility of which he demonstrates with the clearest logic. But nothing can more plainly show the author's sense of the imperfect character of these notes than his own "Codicetto," or preface, the original of which is among the treasures of the British Museum, part of which we commend to the notice of our readers:—

> Cominciato in Firenze in casa di Piero di Braccio Martelli, addì 22 di marzo 1508; e questo fia un raccolto senza ordine, tratto di molte carte, le quali ho qui copiate, sperando poi di metterle alli lochi loro, secondo le materie che di esse tratteranno; credo che avanti ch' io sia al fine di questo, io ci avrò a replicare una medesima cosa più volte, sicchè, let-

> tore, non mi biasimare, perchè le cose son molte, e la memoria non le può riservare, e dire: questa non voglio scrivere, perchè dinanzi la scrissi: e s' io non volessi cadere in tale errore, sarebbe necessario che per ogni caso ch' io ci volessi copiar sù, che per non replicarlo, io avessi sempre a rileggere tutto il passato, e massime stando con lunghi intervalli di tempo allo scrivere da una volta a un' altra.

> Begun at Florence in the house of Piero di Braccio Martelli, on the 22nd March, 1505; and this can be a collection without order, extracted from many papers which I have copied, hoping hereafter to arrange them in their proper order, according to the subjects of which they treat. I expect that before concluding this task I shall have to repeat the same thing more than once; wherefore, reader, do not blame me, seeing that the things are many, and I cannot keep them in my memory and say, 'This I will not write because already I have written it.' Were I anxious to avoid falling into such an error, it would be necessary for me whenever I proposed to copy anything, for fear of repetition to read over all previous matter; particularly considering that long intervals of time exist between my times of writing.

Bearing, therefore, in mind the fragmentary nature of the evidence on which alone we have to rely, we proceed to show from his own manuscripts how many were the varied branches of knowledge in which he had made actual progress, how few those in which he had not at least pointed out to others the true road to useful discovery. It was especially fortunate for Leonardo that his early dedication to the fine arts left his mind free from the foolish talk of schoolmen, his inquiring spirit untrammeled by the unreasoning deference then paid to the great names of Aristotle and Plato. Then and long afterwards, as the well-known history of Galileo demonstrates, a wish to learn from nature rather than from any master, however great, was held the height of insupportable presumption. All honour then to one who so far anticipated both the Tuscan astronomer and the "eagle spirit" of Bacon, as to originate and inculcate such maxims as we shall now proceed to place on record:—

> Experience never deceives; only man's judgment deceives when promising effects which are not supported by experiment.

> Speculators, do not trust authors who wish to interpret between nature and man through their own imaginations, but trust only those who have exercised their understandings upon the results of their own experiments.

Having laid down carefully the rules by which experiments should be conducted, he observes:—

> If then you ask me, 'What fruit do your rules yield, or for what are they good?' I reply that they bridle investigators, and prevent them from promising impossibilities to themselves and others, and so being rated as fools or cheats.

> Many will think themselves warranted in blaming me, alleging that my proofs are contrary to the authority of certain men whom they hold in high reverence. . . . not considering that my facts are obtained by simple pure experiment, which is our real mistress.

But these doctrines, however simple and manly they may

seem to us, were little likely to find favour with the age in which they were uttered. The warning (uttered probably rather to himself than to any reader) that "patience against injustice is as a garment against the cold, and that as the cold increases there is no other remedy than to don additional wraps, and so bid defiance to your assailant," was not wrung from a tranquil mind; nor can we wonder that when Savonarola was proclaiming Christ King of Florence, and calling, not vainly, upon the citizens to offer in his honour a holocaust of books, paintings, rich tapestries, and all the luxuries of the sinful world, a man like Leonardo should be deemed a heretic or even an atheist. Vasari, after referring to his "caprices" relative to natural philosophy, adds that by these methods he had brought his mind into so heretical a state as to be unable to attach himself to any form of religion, and indeed seemed to care more for being a philosopher than a Christian. A dangerous man, truly!

Nor were the following speculations as to mind and matter likely to find favour in priestly councils. "Spirit has no voice, for where there is voice there is body, and where there is body there is occupation of place. . . . There can be no voice where there is no movement and percussion of air, no percussion of air without some instrument, no instrument incorporeal. A spirit cannot have either voice, form or force. . . . Where there are neither nerves nor bones, no force can be exerted in movements made by the imagined spirits." Maxims such as these—not out of place even in the enlightened nineteenth century—seemed greatly so in the fifteenth, and a marginal note found in the *Codicetto Trivulziano*:—"Pharisees, that is to say, Friars"—was not made by a favourite of the priestly order. Indeed, it is not unlikely that the artist alludes to some actual persecution when we find him writing: "When I made the Lord God an infant, you imprisoned me; now if I make him grown up, you will treat me worse." Throughout the whole of his life, indeed, the comments which it continually pleased him to make are brief but comprehensive evidences of the many painful thoughts that could not but fill the mind of an earnest man, frequently sorrowful yet never cankered, zealous to gather from all events some fruitful precepts for future self-guidance, till, conscious, as no doubt he was, that the end was approaching too soon for what he had hoped to achieve, he utters the regretful cry, "When I thought I was learning to live, I was but learning to die." (pp. 117-22)

Some attention should be given to the unsatisfactory condition of the Italian language at this epoch. The same struggle which the English tongue had to sustain against the preponderating reverence for Latinity implanted in the minds of learned men was fought out in Italy; and while Spenser was sorely tempted to leave posterity, instead of his nobly rhythmic Faerie Queen, a mountainous mass of barbarous hexameters, so Petrarch, thinking lightly of his sonnets, rested his hopes of fame on the dreary Latin epic of "Africa." No wonder, therefore, that in the mere elementary paths of orthography and grammar Leonardo found his own native tongue woefully defective. There, as elsewhere, he had to lay down rules and establish principles; there, as elsewhere, whatever his hands found to do, he began to do with all his might. In one of the Ambrosian manuscripts now detained at Paris, we find a chapter on grammatical conjugations. In the *Codice Trivulziano* frequent evidences exist that the writer felt the need of a dictionary of his native tongue, and was preparing to supply the want; and while his own orthography in its tentative character shows how unfixed his ideas on that matter

were, with the true strength of genius he accepted the responsibility of inventing new words whenever the need for doing so was clearly obvious.

Of the songs which, as we are told, he used to accompany on his lyre, we possess no specimens, nor, perhaps, is the loss great; they were probably easy improvisations, owing their reputation rather to the good-natured judgments prevalent in that age than to any sterling thoughts which the world would not willingly let die. A few sonnets he wrote—would he have been Italian had he not done so?—but they are of the dogmatic, self-anatomizing character common to that age, and closely copied by our own sonnetteers of Elizabethan times. Two detached lines—

> Deh! non m' aver a vil, ch' io non son povero;
> Povero è quel che assai cose desidera—

> *Hold me not vile, for lo! I am not poor;*
> *The poor is he who over much desires—*

seem as though they might be expanded into a Shakespearian sonnet.

It is, however, more pleasing to meet Leonardo in a field of which he was surely master [the history of art]. (pp. 122-24)

Our limits will not permit us more than a glance at sundry humourous and satirical remarks of Leonardo to which he chose to affix the pompous title of prophecies. Playful allegory, descending even to the level of punning—tell it not in the halls of the Della Cruscans—characterizes most of these maxims, among which his old foes the "Pharisees" come in for many a sly hit. It is easy to recognize who are the "numerous crowd that heap up great riches, paying for the same in invisible coin;" nor can we doubt "those who avoid hard work and poor living, that they may inhabit rich palatial edifices, clearly demonstrating that by so doing they exalt the glory of God;" or who "sell publicly things of great value which never were theirs, nor in their power, without any license from the real owner." Such keen satire as this—and his writings abound in such—sufficiently explain the charges of naturalism, rationalism, and, to crown worthily the edifice of calumny, of atheism, to which Leonardo was exposed. Before quitting this part of our subject, allusion must be made to the fables with which he seems to have occupied his leisure moments, one of which, in a slightly abbreviated form, is here presented to our readers, who may possibly trace in the old Florentine somewhat of the playfulness which, in our own time, has enabled Hans Andersen to anatomize the emotions of darning needles and morocco slippers.

> A razor having come out of the sheath in which it was usually concealed, and placed itself in the sunlight, saw how brightly the sun was reflected from its surface. Mightily pleased thereat, it began to reason with itself after this fashion: 'Shall I now go back to the shop which I have just quitted? Certainly it cannot be pleasing to the gods that such dazzling beauty should be linked to such baseness of spirit! (What a madness it would be that should lead me to shave the soaped beards of country bumpkins!) Is this a form fitted for such base mechanical uses? Assuredly not; I shall withdraw myself into some sheltered spot, and in calm repose pass away my life.' Having therefore concealed himself for some months, on leaving his sheath one day, and returning to the open air, he found himself looking just like a rusty saw, and totally unable to reflect the glorious sun from his tarnished surface.

He lamented in vain this irreparable loss, and said to himself, 'How much better had I kept up the lost keenness of my edge by practising with my friend the barber! What has become of all my brilliant surface? This abominable rust has eaten it all up.' If genius chooses to indulge in sloth, it must not expect to preserve the keen edge which the rust of ignorance will soon destroy.

(pp. 125-26)

It cannot be expected that a genius so restless, so divergent in its pursuits, should never err; and no doubt sometimes Leonardo wastes precious time in pursuit of scientific chimæras. Of these, we have already alluded to the perpetual motion as one which he himself soon rejected as fit only for the lunar limbo of Astolfo. Perhaps—for we cannot even now speak with certainty—we may dismiss to the same region the numerous schemes for winged men, aërial chairs, and flying ships, which crowd the pages of the *Codice Atlantico,* testifying to the marvellous fecundity of the designer, to his unwillingness to accept defeat at the hands of Nature; but not so practically useful as the numerous humble implements of which we have just given a very incomplete list. Nor have we cause to regret that so keen an intellect should have been exercised upon the somewhat barren fields of air, remembering the remark of Bacon, "that if a proposition be wholly rejected, yet that negative is more pregnant of direction than an indefinite; as ashes are more generative than dust." (p. 169)

A few—far too few—mighty works still surviving while many are known to have perished, a bewildering mass of plans, sketches, maps, and manuscript notes, testifying to the all-embracing, over-discursive intellect of their author; such is the monument of Leonardo's life. After all, truth surpasses fiction; and all the array of qualities, to which Juvenal in bitter mockery represents his hungry Greek as laying claim,

> Grammaticus, rhetor, geometres, pictor, aliptes,
> Augur, schœnobates, medicus, magus: omnia novit,—

can, with more than common accuracy, be maintained as belonging, in simple truth, to Leonardo da Vinci. (pp. 179-80)

Charles Christopher Black, "Leonardo da Vinci in Science and Literature," in Leonardo da Vinci and His Works *by Mrs. Charles W. Heaton and Charles Christopher Black, Macmillan and Co., 1874, pp. 113-80.*

JEAN PAUL RICHTER   (essay date 1883)

[*Richter was a nineteenth-century German essayist who completed one of the first English translations of Leonardo's writings,* The Literary Works of Leonardo da Vinci, *in 1883. In the following excerpt from the preface to this collection, he characterizes Leonardo's works, tracing the history of the text as well.*]

Vasari says, and rightly, in his *Life of Leonardo,* "that he laboured much more by his word than in fact or by deed", and the biographer evidently had in his mind the numerous works in *Manuscript* which have been preserved to this day. To us, now, it seems almost inexplicable that these valuable and interesting original texts should have remained so long unpublished, and indeed forgotten. It is certain that during the XVIth and XVIIth centuries their exceptional value was highly appreciated. This is proved not merely by the prices which they commanded, but also by the exceptional interest

which has been attached to the change of ownership of merely a few pages of *Manuscript.* (p. xiii)

Leonardo's literary labours in various departments both of Art and of Science were those essentially of an enquirer, hence the analytical method is that which he employs in arguing out his investigations and dissertations. The vast structure of his scientific theories is consequently built up of numerous separate researches, and it is much to be lamented that he should never have collated and arranged them. His love for detailed research—as it seems to me—was the reason that in almost all the *Manuscripts,* the different paragraphs appear to us to be in utter confusion; on one and the same page, observations on the most dissimilar subjects follow each other without any connection. (p. xiv)

As I am now, on the termination of a work of several years' duration, in a position to review the general tenour of Leonardo's writings, I may perhaps be permitted to add a word as to my own estimate of the value of their contents. I have already shown that it is due to nothing but a fortuitous succession of unfortunate circumstances, that we should not, long since, have known Leonardo, not merely as a Painter, but as an Author, a Philosopher, and a Naturalist. There can be no doubt that in more than one department his principles and discoveries were infinitely more in accord with the teachings of modern science, than with the views of his contemporaries. For this reason his extraordinary gifts and merits are far more likely to be appreciated in our own time than they could have been during the preceding centuries. He has been unjustly accused of having squandered his powers, by beginning a variety of studies and then, having hardly begun, throwing them aside. The truth is that the labours of three centuries have hardly sufficed for the elucidation of some of the problems which occupied his mighty mind.

Alexander von Humboldt has borne witness that "he was the first to start on the road towards the point where all the impressions of our senses converge in the idea of the Unity of Nature." Nay, yet more may be said. The very words which are inscribed on the monument of Alexander von Humboldt himself, at Berlin, are perhaps the most appropriate in which we can sum up our estimate of Leonardo's genius:

> Magestati naturae par ingenium.

(pp. xviii-xix)

Jean Paul Richter, in a preface to The Notebooks of Leonardo da Vinci, *Vol. I, edited by Jean Paul Richter, Dover Publications, Inc., 1970, pp. xiii-xix.*

PAUL VALÉRY   (essay date 1894)

[*A prominent French poet and critic, Valéry was one of the leading practitioners of nineteenth-century Symbolist aestheticism. His work reflects his desire for total control of his creation, while his absorption with the creative process forms the method of his criticism. His critical writings are collected in the five volumes of* Variété (*1924-44;* Variety) *as well as in his personal notebooks, the* Cahiers (*1894-1945*). *In the following excerpt from* An Introduction to the Method of Leonardo da Vinci, *originally published in 1894 and later reprinted in* Variety, *he characterizes various facets of Leonardo's thought.*]

Of a man there remain the dreams which his name inspires, and the works which make that name a symbol of admiration, hate, or indifference. We think that he once thought, and can rediscover among his works a thought which really derives from us; this thought we can remake into the image of our own. It is easy to represent an ordinary man; our own simple memories restore his motives and elementary reactions. The indifferent acts which constitute the exterior of his life, and those which form the semblance of ourselves, are linked by the same causation. We can serve as the bond of these acts as well as he; and the circle of activity which his name suggests is no wider than ours. On the other hand, if we choose an individual who excels in some respect, we shall find it more difficult to imagine the paths and labours of his mind; and, in order not to be restricted to a confused admiration, we shall be forced to expand our conception of his dominating quality, which we doubtless possess only in the germ. However, if all the faculties of the chosen mind are widely developed at the same time, or if considerable traces of its activity are to be found in all fields of endeavour, then the figure of our hero grows more and more difficult to conceive in its unity, and tends to escape our efforts. From one extreme to the other of this mental territory, there are such great distances which we have never travelled. Our understanding fails to grasp the continuity of this whole—just as it fails to perceive those formless rags of space which separate known objects and are subject to the chance of intervals; and just as it loses myriads of facts from moment to moment, perceiving only the small number which can be evoked by speech. However, we must delay over the task, become inured to its difficulties; and, if our imagination suffers from its efforts to grasp this combination of apparently heterogeneous elements, we must learn to withstand the pain.

In this process, all our intelligence is applied to conceiving a unique order and a single motive force. We desire to place a creature in our likeness at the heart of the system we impose on ourselves. We struggle to form a decisive image. And our mind, with a violence proportionate to its lucidity and breadth, ends by reconquering its own unity. As if by the action of a machine, an hypothesis takes shape; it proves to be the individual who performed all these deeds, the central vision where all must have taken place, the monstrous brain or strange animal which wove thousands of pure bonds between so many forms. Those enigmatic and diverse constructions were the labours of this brain, its instinct making an abode. . . . The production of such an hypothesis is a phenomenon which admits of variations, but not of chance. Its value is the same as that of the logical analysis whose object it should be. And it is the basis of the method which will occupy and serve us.

I propose to imagine a man who shall have performed actions so thoroughly distinct that, if I succeed in postulating the general purpose which lies behind them, none could be more universal. And I should like this man to possess an infinitely keen perception of the difference of things, the adventures of which perception might well be called analysis. All the world is his objective and his guide; he thinks of the universe continually, and of rigour. He is so formed as to forget nothing which enters into the confusion of things; not the least shrub. He descends into the depths of that which exists for all men; he wanders apart and examines himself. He learns to know the habits and structures of nature, works on them from every angle, and finally it is he alone who constructs, enumerates, sets in motion. He builds churches and fortresses; he fashions ornaments full of harmony and grandeur; he makes a thousand curious engines, and performs the rigorous calculations of many a research. He abandons the debris of nobody knows what grandiose games. In the midst of these pastimes,

which are mingled with his science, which in turn cannot be distinguished from a passion, he has the charm of always seeming to think of something else. . . . I shall follow him as he moves through raw unity and the substance of the world, where he will become so familiar with nature that he will imitate in order to touch it, and will end in the difficulty of conceiving an object which it does not contain.

This creature of thought requires a name, to limit the expansion of terms too far removed from ordinary usage, too difficult to grasp. I can find none more suitable than that of *Leonardo da Vinci.* (pp. 224-28)

Within the mind, there is a drama. Drama, adventure, agitation, all words of this category can be employed on condition that several are used, and are corrected one by the other. Such dramas are generally lost, like the plays of Menander. However, we preserve the manuscripts of Leonardo and Pascal's illustrious notes. These fragments demand our attention. Having examined them, we can guess by what starts and snatches of thought, by what strange suggestions from human events or the flow of sensations, and after what immense moments of lassitude, men are able to see the shadows of their future works, the ghosts which precede. (p. 231)

We arrive at the conception that parts of the world can be reduced to intelligible elements. Sometimes our senses suffice; at other times the most ingenious methods must be employed; but always there are voids. The attempts remain imperfect. And here is the kingdom of our hero. He has an extraordinary sense of the symmetry which makes him regard everything as a problem. He introduces the creations of his mind into every fissure of the understanding. It is evident how extraordinarily convenient he can be. He is like a scientific hypothesis. We should have to invent him, but he exists; the universal man can now be imagined. We have reached the point where a Leonardo da Vinci can exist as a concept in our minds, without immeasurably dazzling them. Our dream of his power need not be too quickly lost in a fog of the great words and magnificent epithets which are so friendly to inconsistent thought. Do you believe that Leonardo himself would be satisfied with such mirages?

This *symbolic* mind preserved an immense collection of forms, a treasure always rich with the attitudes of nature, a potentiality always ready to be translated into action, and growing with the extension of its domain. A host of concepts, a host of possible memories, the power to choose an extraordinary number of distinct things from the world at large, and to arrange them in a million ways—these elements composed the mind of Leonardo. (pp. 252-53)

He made sport of difficulties; and growing bolder, he translated all sentiments into the clarity of his universal language. The abundance of his metaphorical resources made these feats possible. His desire utterly to probe the slightest fragment, the least splinter of the world, renewed the force and cohesion of his being. His joy can be read in his decorations for fêtes and in other charming inventions; when he dreamed of constructing a *flying man,* he would have him rise to seek snow on the mountaintops and, returning, scatter it over the streets of cities which pulse with the heat of summer. His emotion delighted in pure faces touched by a pouting shadow, and in the gesture of a silent god. His hate employed all weapons: all the artifices of the engineer, all the stratagems of the general. He established terrible engines of war, and protected them with bastions, caponiers, salients, and with moats which he provided with water gates, so as suddenly to transform the aspect of a siege; and I remember—meanwhile enjoying this fine Italian wariness of the *cinquecento*—that he built donjons in which four flights of stairs, independent round the same axis, separated the mercenaries from their leaders, and the troops of hired soldiers one from the other.

He worshipped the human body, which measures and is measured by all things. He was aware of its height—that a rose can come to its lips, and a great plane-tree surpass it twenty times, while dropping a spray of leaves to the height of a man's head. He knew that a radiant body will fill a given room, or the concavity of a vault which is deduced from the human form, or a landscape which counts the steps of man. He overheard the light fall of a foot; and he spied on the skeleton silent in its flesh, on the accidents of the human walk, on all the superficial play of heat and coolness over nudities—perceiving them as a diffused whiteness or a sheet of bronze, welded to a mechanism. And the face, that enlightening and enlightened thing; of all visible things the most individual, the most magnetic, the most difficult to regard without reading therein—the face would always haunt him. In each man's memory, there are a few hundred faces with their vague variations. In his, they were classified and proceeded consecutively from one physiognomy to another, from one irony to another, from one wisdom to a lesser, from kindness to divinity—by symmetry. About the eyes—fixed points of variable brilliance—he adjusted the mask which hides a complex structure of bones and distinct muscles under a uniform skin; drawing the mask taut, he made it reveal all.

Among the multitude of minds, that of Leonardo impresses us as being one of those *regular combinations* which were mentioned above. Unlike most of the others, he need not be attached, in order to be understood, to a particular nation, a tradition, or a group exercising the same art. His acts, by virtue of their number and intercommunication, together form a symmetrical object—a sort of *system complete in itself,* or completing itself incessantly.

He lived to be the despair of those modern men who, since youth, have been turned aside into a specialized activity, in which they think to become superior because they are confined to it. The variety of methods is invoked, and the quantity of details, and the continual addition of facts and theories; with the result that the patient observer, the meticulous accountant of existence, the individual who reduces himself, not without merit—if this word has any meaning!—to the minute habitudes of an instrument, is confused with the man for whom this labour is performed—the poet of the hypothesis, the builder with analytical materials. (pp. 256-59)

I can see Leonardo da Vinci delving into mechanics, which he called the paradise of the science, with the same natural resources he devoted to the invention of pure and misty faces. And the same luminous territory that he peopled with the docile tribe of possible constructions, is the scene of those actions which, by losing their velocity, become distinct works. In all his studies his passions remained the same; and, on the last page of that slender notebook, scored with his ciphered writing and adventurous calculations, in which he gropes toward his favourite research, aviation, he exclaims—thundering against his imperfect labour, illuminating his patience and its obstacles by the apparition of a supreme spiritual view, an obstinate certainty:—

The great bird will take its first flight on the back

of its great swan, and filling the universe with stupor, filling all writings with its renown, and eternal glory to the nest where it was born! *Piglierà il primo volo il grande uccello sopra del dosso del suo magno cecero e empiendo l'universo di stupore, empiendo di sua fama tutte le scritture e gloria eterna al nido dove nacque.*

(pp. 282-83)

Paul Valéry, "An Introduction to the Method of Leonardo da Vinci: Introduction," in his Variety, translated by Malcolm Cowley, Harcourt Brace Jovanovich, 1927, pp. 224-83.

[JULIA MARY ADY]   (essay date 1899)

[Ady was an English essayist and art historian. In the following excerpt, she creates an idealistic image of Leonardo's life, writings, and philosophy.]

The place which Leonardo da Vinci holds in the history of art must always be unique. He stands alone among the painters of the Renaissance, by reason not only of the rare perfection and high intellectual qualities of his art, but of the extraordinary influence which he exerted upon his contemporaries, and the universal character of his genius. Never before or since in the annals of the human race has the same passionate desire for knowledge been combined with the same ardent love of beauty, never have artistic and scientific powers been united in the same degree as in this wonderful man. Painting, as we all know, was only one of the varied forms in which his activity was displayed, and occupied a comparatively small portion of his time and thoughts. As sculptor, architect, and engineer Leonardo was alike illustrious in his day; as a philosopher and man of science he has been justly hailed as the precursor of Galileo, of Bacon and Descartes. Alexander von Humboldt proclaimed him to be the greatest physicist of the fifteenth century, the one man of his age who 'united a remarkable knowledge of mathematics with the most admirable intuition of nature'; and scholars of our own day have recognised in him—to use the words of Hallam—a thinker who anticipated the grander discoveries of modern science, and a master of literary style who knew how to clothe his lofty thoughts in noble and eloquent language.

It is only during the last twenty years that the writings of Leonardo have been fully made known to the world. Although it was his practice, during more than thirty years, to write down his thoughts and observations daily, he never published a single line during his lifetime. After the master's death in France his manuscripts, consisting of thirty *libretti,* containing as many as five thousand sheets, were brought back to Italy by his favourite scholar, Francesco Melzi, who kept them as a sacred treasure until his own death about 1570. His heirs proved unworthy of the trust reposed in them, and the precious writings were gradually dispersed and scattered abroad. Loose pages were often detached, and were either given away as relics of the great master or stolen by unscrupulous hands. Thus, for instance, one page of the treatise on Motion is at Venice, others are in Paris and London, while the remaining portion is preserved in the Ambrosian Library at Milan. The two volumes formerly in the Ashburnham Collection consisted entirely of separate sheets which had been torn out of manuscripts in the Institut de France, but which have now been restored to their original places. In spite, however, of the great value attached to Leonardo's manuscripts and the high prices which they commanded in the sixteenth

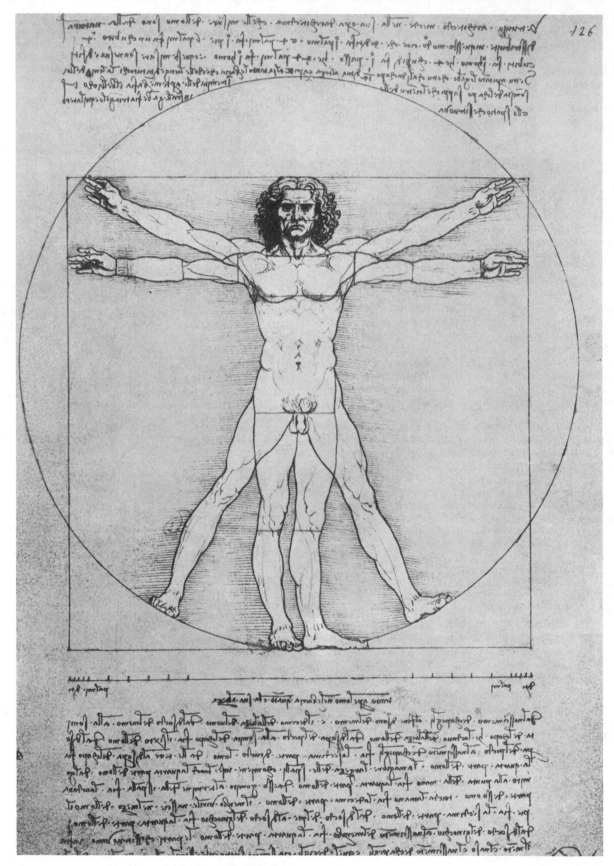

The canon of proportions, by Leonardo.

and seventeenth centuries, no attempt was made to publish any of his writings, except the ***Treatise on Painting,*** for more than three hundred years after his death. (pp. 381-82)

Leonardo's writings afford the best explanation of his life, and supply the key to many of the problems that meet us in his works. From these scattered sayings, written down in odd moments at all stages of his career, on loose sheets and scraps of paper, on the backs of drawings, or in the corners of plans, we can reconstruct a whole philosophy of life. In his ***Treatise on Painting,*** he writes:—

> When a work satisifies a man's judgment, it is a bad sign, and when a work surpasses his expectation, and he wonders that he has achieved so much, it is worse. But when an artist's aim goes beyond his work, that is a good sign, and if the man is young, he will no doubt become an excellent artist. He will compose but few works, but they will be such that men will gaze in wonder at their perfection.

There we have the secret of Leonardo's long ponderings and delays, of the doubts and hesitation which vexed the soul of his employers and excited the scorn of smaller minds. 'When he sat down to paint,' says Lomazzo, 'he seemed overcome with fear. And he could finish nothing that he began, because his soul was so full of the sublimity of art, and he only saw faults in works which others hailed as miraculous creations.'

One golden thread runs through all the volumes that he has left us, and recurs at almost every page in one form or another. Knowledge is the supreme good, the only possession that endures, the true reward of its owner, for it can never be lost. As for earthly riches, let a man hold them with trembling, for they often depart and leave us to the scorn of men. Again, knowledge of past times and of this earth is at once the ornament and the food of the human mind. The acquisition of knowledge is always of use to the intellect, which learns to reject what is useless and to keep what is good. Time, which destroys all things, respects thought. Sensual pleasures, he tells us, degrade the dignity of man, while sentiment, on the other hand, is a fruitful cause of suffering. 'Where there is much feeling, there will be great martyrdom.' Work, in his eyes, is the one source of happiness, the one enduring satisfaction. 'I am never weary when I am useful,' is one of Leonardo's favourite mottoes. 'In serving others I cannot do enough.' Fortune, he says elsewhere, is of no avail to the man who will not toil. So Dante writes: 'The master says: lying down on feathers or under the quilts will never bring thee to fame: without which, he who lets his life burn to waste, leaves no more track of his name on earth than the wind-blown smoke or the foam upon the sea' . . . . (pp. 399-400)

In Leonardo's eyes, the noblest lot of all is to work for the good of humanity, to bring beauty and joy into the lives of men, to water the desert places and make the wilderness rejoice and blossom as the rose. Leonardo, it must be remembered, was not a scholar. His education had been desultory and irregular. He had, as Vasari tells us, begun many things and then abandoned them. 'I know,' he says himself, 'that I am not a man of letters; an impertinent person might even call me illiterate.' He never learnt Latin in his youth, although in middle life he worked hard to remedy this defect, and in spite of his love of history and geography, he is often guilty of curious blunders and anachronisms. In one place, for instance, he talks of the part played by Archimedes of Syracuse in the wars between the English and the Spaniards, and in another he confuses Cato with Cicero.

But his genius broke through all trammels, and his very want of education stood him in good stead. It is just because he was not encumbered with the learning of the schools and did not strive after rhetorical effects that his language is so natural and forcible. He sets down his ideas in the simplest words, and here and there rises to unconscious eloquence. His descriptions of a tempest, of the deluge, for instance, are full of grandeur and poetry, while nothing can surpass the charm of such a phrase as this—'Cosa bella mortal passa e non arte.' 'Mortal beauty passes away, but not art.' His love of knowledge led him to form a small but choice library, in which the Bible and the Psalms, the works of Albertus Magnus and Marsilio Ficino, Pliny and Ovid, Æsop and Livy, Pulci and Filelfo, John of Mandeville's travels, and Petrarch's sonnets, were included. In his daily records he notes down where a Dante or a Vitruvius can be borrowed, and where he can obtain the loan of a French edition of Roger Bacon's works, a volume of Euclid, the works of Avicenna, or a map of India. But, as M. Müntz has pointed out, it is worthy of note that, while he quotes Aristotle constantly, there is only one mention of Plato in the whole of the twelve volumes published by M. Ravaisson-Mollien. In his eagerness for information, Leonardo frequently jots down such notes as the following:—

> Speak to Pietro Monti of these methods of throwing spears.
>
> Learn the multiplication of roots from Messer Luca.
>
> Messer Guiliano Marliano has a fine herbal. He lives opposite the carpenter.
>
> Ask the wife of Biagio Crivelli how the capon hatches the eggs of the hen.
>
> Get the teacher of arithmetic to show you how to square a. . . .
>
> Ask Benedetto Portinari how men run on ice in Flanders.
>
> Ask Giovannino the gun-founder why . . .

This boundless curiosity lies at the root of all his speculations. Beauty in his eyes was a divine thing, both that natural loveliness which leads men to forsake the city where their friends dwell to roam among lonely mountains and valleys, and that beauty of the human form which Leonardo valued even more highly; and it is the painter's privilege not only to enjoy, but to create and multiply loveliness in all its varied forms. But art alone could not satisfy this mighty intellect. Nature must yield up her secrets to him, and Leonardo early took her for his teacher and guide.

What strikes us most, when we turn to Leonardo's scientific writings, is the infinite variety of subjects which excited his interest. All forms of life attracted him; every kind of science invited his attention. Certain fields of study, it is true, he put deliberately aside. 'I leave alone the sacred writings,' he says, 'for they are the supreme truth'—*somma verità*. Neither will he attempt to define the existence of God or the nature of the soul. These seem to him *cose improvabili,* things unfathomable, concerning which it is idle to speculate. Rather will he confine himself to facts which can be proved by human experience. Dreamer as Leonardo was, he showed himself in some respects the most practical of men. Avoid all labour that is useless and unprofitable, never attempt the impossible, are among his favourite axioms. Mechanics, he declares, is the paradise of mathematicians: consequently, all forms of scientific industry appealed to him with peculiar attraction. He studied the flight of birds during five-and-twenty years in the hope of learning how to construct a flying machine. In the different departments of hydraulics, astronomy, and geology, he went further than any thinker of his age, and in more than one instance anticipated the triumphs of modern science. He discovered the motive force of water, and tried to move a boat by steam. He was already conscious of the circulation of the blood, and long before Copernicus he proclaimed that the sun does not move. Again, he was the first to recognise the power of water on the formation of the earth, and boldly declared that mountains were made and destroyed by the currents of rivers. In his botanical researches the artist and the man of science are never separated, and his drawings of brambles and flowers are both accurate studies of plant life and beautiful works of art. As for anatomy, it was the continual object of his thoughts and labours, from the day when he wrote his first treatise on the subject, in 1489, to that when he finished the last, in 1515.

In conclusion, we must point out two common fallacies regarding Leonardo's beliefs and practice which still need to be refuted. One is the accusation of dabbling in occult science, which has been brought forward by more than one writer, and has lately been revived by the clever Italian novelist, Gabriele d'Annunzio. That the grotesque and fantastic had a strong attraction for Leonardo from his boyhood, and that he occasionally found amusement in painting hideous and unnatural figures, may be true. But that he was such a would-be magician as some writers would have us believe, is a notion as absurd as it is groundless. Leonardo's intellect was too lucid, his mind too sane, to be led astray by the deceits or self-delusions of magic. We have only to look at the passages in which he denounces alchemists and necromancers, and 'those other quacks and charlatans who grow rich at the expense of credulous and ignorant men,' to see that this accusation is utterly without foundation. It is perfectly true, as M. Müntz remarks, that astrology flourished at the Court of Milan, and that Lodovico Sforza trusted implicitly in the prognostications of his favourite seer, Ambrogio da Rosate. But the Duke's astrologer was the very man on whose false and venal science Leonardo poured contempt, and whose name we find held up to scorn in one of his epigrams at Windsor.

There is hardly more foundation for the heretical notions which Vasari imputed to the great master, and for the supposed recantation of these errors on his death-bed. This accusation, it is worthy of note, was omitted in the second edition of Vasari's works which he published before his death. Leonardo lived and died a good Christian, and conformed to the rites of the Catholic Church both in life and death. But, like many other Renaissance scholars, he handled sacred subjects with a freedom displeasing to theologians, and was fearless in his condemnation of superstitious abuses. He shows no mercy to bad priests or lazy friars; he derides the traffic of indulgences, and pities silly women who pour out the tale of their frailties in the ear of a confessor. The spirit of Luther, we feel, is already in the air: but, in the words of M. Séailles, 'Where Luther thunders, Leonardo only smiles.' Along with the vein of subtle irony which runs through his remarks on these matters, we trace a current of deeper thought. 'Many hold the faith of the Son,' he observes in one place, 'but only build temples to the Mother.' True religion, in his eyes, consists in the knowledge and love of God. Great love is born of great knowledge, and the best way to know God is to study

the universe which He has made. In speaking of those foolish persons who find fault with a painter for working on holy days, he says: Let them hold their tongues for this is the true way to know the Workman who has made such admirable things, and, by knowing, to learn to love the great Inventor.' Deep at the root of all his beliefs lay a profound reverence for the great First Cause, that infinite unfathomable God whose nature is beyond the range of all human thought—a reference which finds frequent expression in his writings, and occasionally breaks forth in such passages as this: *'O mirabile giustitia di te!'* 'O how admirable is Thy justice, O great First Cause! Thou hast not allowed any force to be lacking in the order and quality necessary to produce the effects that are desired.'

So the master's scientific knowledge and his artistic sense of the beauty and dignity of the human frame lead him on to the love of humanity, and lift his thoughts from earth to heaven. Both in his life and in his works we find him loftier than the world suspects. The last word has not yet been said: we still await the coming of the biographer who will show us the figure of Leonardo in all his majesty and completeness. Meanwhile we may welcome each fresh discovery that throws light upon the character and personality of one of the greatest men of a great age. (pp. 400-03)

> *[Julia Mary Ady], in a review of "Leonardo da Vinci: Artist, Thinker, and Man of Science" and others, in* The Quarterly Review, *Vol. CXC, No. CCCLXXX, October, 1899, pp. 381-403.*

THE BOOKMAN, LONDON   (essay date 1910)

[*In the following excerpt, the anonymous critic evaluates Leonardo's* Notebooks.]

Few personalities have had more fascination for the minds of men than that of Leonardo da Vinci. From his own day to ours he has exacted a tribute of almost superstitious admiration. To Morelli he was "perhaps the most richly gifted by nature among all the sons of men." Francis I., Leonardo's friend—might they not be called the outward and visible sign and the inward and spiritual grace of the Renaissance?—considered him pre-eminently a philosopher. Ruskin might call him "the slave of an archaic smile," but we know what Walter Pater made of that smile in a piece of creative criticism the greatness of which should not be forgotten in contempt for the mechanical worship of Monna Lisa which has been its fruit. R. L. S., who cared more for life than for art, thought Leonardo the only man certainly worthy to inspire a woman's love. Michelet thought him a brother of Faust. And all these opinions find their justification in the pages of those *Note-books* which the great artist filled with his tiny, left-handed writing. Leonardo's mind was a diamond of many facets. We think of him most readily as the supreme painter. But he was much more than that. He was certainly no nebulous æsthete. A dreamer of strange dreams, his thought was curiously concrete. His dicta on painting are precise and practical. Much of his writing was scientific, and his great mind apprehended dimly many a truth which was not for many a generation to be brought to light. He was an insatiable seeker after knowledge, which he calls the "natural desire of good men." . . . Much of what, to Leonardo, was new truth or daring conjecture, is to us chimera or old fable or platitude. Also it must be remembered that though Leonardo wrote for publication, many of his notes are the unrevised jottings of the moment's thought. Here and there pure, unconditioned gold glows forth, but it is when viewed in relation to the whole that each part takes on its full value, recreating for us the man with all his varied activities, his restless energy, his great desire, his great beauty of spirit. (pp. 137-38).

A review of "Leonardo Da Vinci's Notebooks," in The Bookman, *London, Vol. XXXVIII, No. 225, June, 1910, pp. 137-38.*

EMIL LUDWIG   (essay date 1925)

[In the following excerpt from an essay originally published in German in 1925, Ludwig compares the accomplishments and natural endowments of Leonardo with those of Johann Wolfgang von Goethe.]

> Once I have learned how to die,
> then I shall know how to live.

His life was a dialogue with nature.

Often this dialogue may have been obscured by the silence of his eternal loneliness; at other times it was revealed in brief notes, in comparisons, deductions, observations, and notations. Frequently it attained expression in formal works—yet with a few exceptions these too remained fragmentary or soon lost their power of survival. Since he valued things purely as experiments, and since neither ambition nor jealousy nor the sheer feel of mastery could induce him to mirror himself in his works, nothing now is left but a few tables, a painted wall, a few dozen drawings, and the diaries with their 5000 pages or so of notes.

These papers, the documents of an essayist, were soon as thoroughly enshrouded in legend as the works of a mystic. Mystery seemed latent in these reliques of a creative life—and the less tangibly his life was revealed, the more readily it took on the compensatory veil of mystery, as with the life of a prophet. Later generations told of his riding through the streets like a prince, on a white, gold-bridled horse, wrapped in flowing silks, and preceded by the laughter of beautiful boys, his pupils and minions: a symbol of the artist in the heyday of that era.

The truth is simpler and deeper. The life-long dialogue between himself and nature exacted of him a profound loneliness—for this sort of dialogue is not only a dialogue; it is also a monologue. In these countless musings of his *Note-books,* which almost seem as though they had been washed up from alien shores and which whole centuries have labored to decipher, he admonishes himself repeatedly: "Remember . . . wrong! right! mistake! . . . That is a beautiful possibility, worth further investigation! . . . How then would you account for the presence of gravel on high mountains? . . . And do you have all the necessary anatomical data?" And in order that his dialogue with himself and nature might be made less accessible, he resorted to mirror writing.

For Leonardo was both a student of nature and a prophet—and this duality of his character produced marked contrasts which had an important effect upon his work. Without his scientific eye—his observation—he would never have become the greatest pathfinder of the Occident. Without his mystical gaze—his vision—he could not have used his knowledge to make himself, we might say, the prehistoric discoverer of all that a later era worked out patiently and laboriously. For a thousand years, there has been no other prophetic tempera-

ment except Goethe so richly endowed with this intellectual duality, this pliant realism. Leonardo occupies the relatively easier position of groping prophetically into regions not yet explored. Goethe, likewise an observer and an essayist, but with the mania of the genuine collector, was better able to coördinate his discoveries. And although he too left very little finished work behind him, the thousands of pages of notes have rounded themselves off into a consistent interpretation, so that his results become more tangible. Goethe produced more, and carried more of his works through to completion. In many-sidedness Leonardo remains unmatched.

But as his work was never assembled or completed, his endowments were much greater than his results. He did plan to collect his notes into books, arranging them by subject, such as a treatise on water, on mechanics, on painting, and so forth. The whole was to be called: On the Things of Nature. But his curiosity drove him restlessly on from decade to decade; a roving and vigorous pioneer, he had none of Goethe's resignation, restraint, and punctiliousness. Thus the tangible results were few, everything remaining in the stage of theme and hypothesis. Like a sportive god, this genius took up the works of nature one by one, looked at them, and laid them down again—and thus Leonardo himself remained hardly more than a sport of nature, almost without predecessors, and wholly without successors. (pp. 151-53)

Emil Ludwig, "Leonardo da Vinci," in his Genius and Character, *translated by Kenneth Burke, Harcourt Brace Jovanovich, 1927, pp. 151-81.*

LUDWIG H. HEYDENREICH   (essay date 1928)

[Heydenreich is a German art historian and academic. In the following excerpt from a work originally published in German in 1928, he offers an analysis of Leonardo's various theories on painting and drawing.]

In studying the scientific works of Leonardo we must always keep in mind that they are the mental achievement of a man who was, first and foremost, an *artist.* Consciously and with pride, he described himself as such throughout his life, and it was in this capacity that he made his first contacts with science. This first encounter of art and science in the service of a project which partook of each, but transcended both, finds its clearest expression in Leonardo's ***Treatise on Painting.***

This famous book is not, in the form in which it is known and disseminated today, the original work of the master, but a compilation from various of Leonardo's manuscripts, brought together by anonymous copyists under the supervision of his pupil and heir, Francesco Melzi, in the middle of the sixteenth century. It is the ***Codex Urbinas*** lat. 1270, preserved in the Biblioteca Vaticana. So that, whilst this compilation represents a faithful rendering of many single notes as they were found in Leonardo's notebooks, it is the work of its editors as regards the sequence of its contents. We know Leonardo intended to write and publish a treatise on painting, both from his own words and from Luca Pacioli, who wrote in the foreword of his book *On Divine Proportion* (dated February 9, 1498): "With painstaking care Leonardo had completed a book on painting and human movement." This can, however, only refer to a part of the whole work, as we find preparatory notes done much later for the book, which, however, Leonardo never finally completed. Similarly, a manuscript "in mirror script" containing a treatise on painting and the technique of drawing and colouring, that Vasari saw around 1560 in the possession of an artist in Milan, can only have been—like the manuscript seen by Paolo Lomazzo about 1580—a fragment of the whole.

We can reconstruct how Leonardo planned his treatise from three different sources: the Melzi compilation, which contains many notes which cannot today be traced in the original manuscripts; original notes by Leonardo in addition to those in Melzi's compilation, intended for the *Treatise;* and finally two further collections of excerpts from the sixteenth century, one of which has been made known to us by Cellini, and another, which is highly instructive, and for which we have the original: the **Codex Huygens** in the Pierpont Morgan Library of New York.

From these sources we can gain some idea of the contents as visualized by Leonardo for his *Treatise on Painting.* We can appreciate how comprehensive and far-reaching was his conception of its subject matter. For it covers, within the framework of the innumerable directions concerning the technique of painting and drawing, all those fields dealing with practical science that are necessary for a painter's education. There are three principal problems which form the structural skeleton around which the imposing work is built:

1. The definition of painting as a science.

2. The theory of the mathematical foundations of painting, i.e. geometry, perspective, and optics.

3. The theory of forms and functions in organic and inorganic nature.

In the draft for his introduction to the *Treatise on Painting,* Leonardo gives an unusually comprehensive and penetrating new formulation to the contemporary doctrine of "*Art as Science.*" He explicitly affirms that painting is "the queen of all sciences," and attempts to prove her supremacy over the other arts.

With the almost poetic persuasiveness which is characteristic of his style, he transfers painting from the *artes mechanicae,* to which as a mere craft it had belonged in the intellectual system of the Middle Ages, and places it amongst the *artes liberals*—the sciences—by stressing its spiritual element as the primary factor.

> It is said that a particular field of knowledge is mechanical when it proceeds from experience or sensory experiment, and that another is scientific if it begins and ends in the realm of the spirit; those which have their birth in knowledge and their expression in manual work, however, are classified as only half mechanical. But to me it seems plain that knowledge is vain and full of errors unless it proceed from sensorial experience, the Mother of all knowledge, and be proved by experiment . . .
>
> The true and scientific beginnings of painting first establish the following: what is the shadow-producing body, and which shadows are primary and which secondary; what is lighting, that is darkness, light, colour; what is mass, figure, pose; what is nearness and distance; what is motion and quiescence. These things can only be grasped by the spirit, without manual performance, and this is the science of painting as it persists in the spirits of those who study it; these things are fundamental to its execution . . .

And then he continues:

> That knowledge whose fruits are the most communicable is the most useful, and vice versa, the less communicable is the less useful.
>
> Painting has for its ultimate end something which can be communicated to all the generations of the world, in as much as it is subject only to the faculty of sight for its effect; and it is a fact that that which is admitted to the consciousness through the ear is not as forceful as that which comes through the eye.
>
> Thus it does not depend on accuracy of the translators of various languages, but immediately reveals its content to human beings, in exactly the same way as nature does . . .

Thus, with regard to the aims of science—the acquisition and imparting of knowledge—painting was placed by Leonardo above all other sciences, because it dispenses with language and, exactly like Nature herself, reveals itself not by words but directly to the sight. Experience through sight—that is perception—is the work of the eye. For Leonardo the eye is the most infallible, and therefore the most important, of the sensory organs. (pp. 95-7)

No other artist, before or after Leonardo, has . . . equated artistic perception with scientific comprehension; but above all none other has rated art so highly as a means of knowledge. It is in this that Leonardo's greater significance as a theorist lies, when compared with his predecessors Alberti, Filarete and Piero della Francesca. A critical analysis of the theories of High and Late Scholasticism led him to define sight as the noblest of all senses, and to assert, therefore, that the painter is the most reliable intermediary of true knowledge, providing he masters and follows the laws of the "science of painting." For these laws make possible not only the correct and true reproduction of things perceived; they also allow him to comprehend and represent Beauty, which as "quality" is inherent in "quantity" and is to be seen in the shapes and proportions of the world of substance. For Leonardo there was in the artistic creative process a unique example: the painter as twice-blessed, with the gifts of seeing and of giving form, is called upon to acquire knowledge and to "communicate it to all the generations of the world."

Only a genius was capable of such thoughts: they are self-revelations which shed a new light upon the task which Leonardo set himself. An outstanding, all-embracing, and penetrating intelligence, filled with a passionate impulse for discovery, endowed with a unique gift for artistic expression, approaches Nature—the Cosmos—as a seeker after knowledge, as an explorer. To comprehend the forms and laws of Nature and Life, as they reveal themselves to his keen and lively perceptions, and to capture these forms and laws in a work of art, was the task and aim of Leonardo's artistic life.

After such a lofty description of painting as "the queen of all sciences," Leonardo proceeds to his teaching concerning its practice. He first defines its *mathematical foundations: geometry, perspective* and *optics* are the presuppositions of recognition, understanding, and reproduction of all visible forms. In addition to linear perspective, based on the laws of geometry, whose value as well as limitations he clearly appreciated and used systematically (cf. the carefully studied pictorial construction of the *Adoration of the Magi* and the *Last Supper,* as well as the ingenious application of perspective in his maps), Leonardo developed a perspective of colour and atmosphere based on optics. In a passage of his **Treatise on Painting** he expressly differentiates between the three perspectives:

> Perspectives are of three kinds. The first has to do with the causes of the diminution or, as it is called, the diminishing perspective of objects as they recede from the eye. The second, the manner in which colours are changed as they recede from the eye. The third and last consists in defining in what way objects ought to be less carefully finished as they are further away.

Leonardo seems to have avoided giving a detailed account of mathematical linear perspective, presumably because Alberti and Piero della Francesca had already dealt thoroughly with its theory and practice in their treatises. In any case, apart from giving the basic principles relating to it, Leonardo's notes concentrate on the deliberate use of perspective in representing space and substance, as a means of obtaining especially strong, even bold effects—for example "to paint on a wall which is 12 ells high a figure that appears to have a height of 24 ells." From copies and original documents that have come down to us (Cellini, Codex Huygens and Lomazzo), it seems that Leonardo used this specific application of the laws of linear perspective to demonstrate a definite "system of diminution" which, looked at historically, paved the way for the illusionist painting from the Mannerists to the Baroque. (pp. 97-8)

Leonardo's theories of perspective form the most comprehensive statement on vision that an artist has ever presented, or anyway intended to present. Linear perspective had certainly been thoroughly dealt with by his predecessors and contemporaries, and there are also indications that Alberti was interested in colour perspective. But the methodical presentation of colour and aerial perspective was Leonardo's own personal achievement. Its value lies in the ingenious summarization of all matters pertaining to optical perception; each problem that presented itself was solved theoretically, defined, and then applied practically to the requirements of art. Leonardo was also well aware of problems of physiological or the so-called "correcting" vision, and a note in the **Codex Atlanticus** emphasizes the limitations of rules of perspective when considering the artistic contents of a work of art: "These rules should be used merely to adjust the object. For everybody makes mistakes in his first composition, and he who does not recognize these mistakes cannot correct them . . . But if you were to apply these rules to your composition (meaning the artist's design), you would never attain your aim and only bring about confusion in your work" (**Codex Atlanticus**).

We shall investigate later how far Leonardo's "Theory of Vision" is concerned with the problems of optical physics and thus takes him into the field of pure scientific research. For the present we shall demonstrate the use made of the knowledge contained in the **Treatise on Painting** in the field of artistic activity, and the initial relationship of theory and practice.

Thus is Leonardo's famous *sfumato* built upon his knowledge of aerial and colour perspective. It is no more than the pictorial representation of the atmosphere which, as a transparent but nevertheless modifying medium, lies between the eye and the object, so that we perceive only its "image". . . . (p. 100)

We have previously indicated how highly Leonardo valued modelling in light and shade as the decisive ingredient of good and accurate painting. More clearly than his teachers, who had a predilection for the *relievo* of the Old Tuscan tradi-

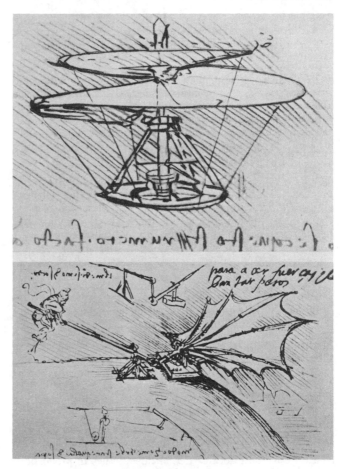

Leonardo's helicopter.

tion, he recognized that every optical impression is built mainly on the results of light and shade, and that line and colour are essentially secondary in the field of vision, that is phenomena dependent upon light and shade. He shows such a coordination of the perspectives of air, colour and line that the picture comes as close as possible to the natural visual impression and indeed to its most ideal form. He investigates and then records exactly which lighting conditions give the most effective interpretation of nature, warning against harsh lighting, and always recommending an even, diffuse light, whether the north light of the studio, or late daylight in the open air.

"If you paint objects in an open field, do not let the direct rays of the sun shine upon them, but pretend that some sort of mist or translucent cloud formation lies between the object and the sun . . .". "Notice the faces of men and women in the streets towards evening, or when the weather is bad, to see how much grace and softness they display . . .".

Leonardo's theory concerning atmospheric and colour perspective, which he so brilliantly illustrated in practice by his *sfumato* technique, had a tremendous influence on subsequent painting. Although Vasari's statement that Giorgione took his softness of style direct from Leonardo may be exaggerated, it is certainly probable that especially in Venice, the centre of pure colour painting, Leonardo's work could not have been disregarded. We trace his influence clearly on the great masters of the *cinquecento,* especially on Raphael, Andrea del Sarto, and Correggio. Besides, Leonardo's "Theory of Vision" which combines so uniquely the keen perception of a creative artist and the great abilities of a theorist, maintained its influence throughout the following centuries.

The "Theory of Vision," being based equally upon nature and mathematics, is, to Leonardo's mind, the factor which enables the painter to perceive, understand, and represent nature in its forms and functions—that is, the forces at work in the forms.

Leonardo's *Theory of Forms* with its many subdivisions, covers the entire field of animate and inanimate nature. Here again he begins with mathematics, namely with studies of *proportion*—that is, of the sizes of bodies and of their relationships. The treatise proper contains only a few notations on the subject; there are, however, many single drawings and texts, which indicate that Leonardo had intended to devote considerable attention to this subject within his project as a whole. . . . (pp. 100-01)

"Make sure that every portion of a whole is well-proportioned in relation to that whole," writes Leonardo, adding that this rule holds good not only for human figures, but "for all animals and for plants" as well.

Naturally the greatest stress is laid on the proportions of man. The sizes of the human body and its members are examined in numerous studies, as well as the differences in proportion between children and adults, male and female bodies. Here already the anatomy acquires a special importance; Leonardo indicates that the bone and muscle structure of the body are subject to various laws of growth, which are thus a determining factor for the development of the proportions.

Within the framework of Leonardo's studies in proportions belong the investigations in which, from the size relationships of the various parts of the physiognomy—forehead, nose, mouth, chin,—he sought to establish definite categories of human facial types, and thereby make it possible to classify all possible variants thereof. For example, "in order to make the impression of faces easier," he drew up tables of the differing shapes of noses. Starting with three basic types, the straight, the pug, and the hooked nose, he describes eight, eleven, and thirteen sub-types respectively. The study of proportion thus led Leonardo to the investigation of normal and abnormal forms; first, in order to exercise the memory for forms, but further, in order to define exactly the differences between the typical and beautiful on the one hand, and the atypical and ugly on the other. (pp. 101-02)

Leonardo's *Treatise on Painting* was essentially and entirely intended as a practical handbook for painters. In it the study of nature—the "scientific" study—is still subordinated to aims of the artist:

> You, o painter, who long for the greatest perfection, must understand that if you do not achieve it on the solid basis of the study of nature, you will produce many works with little honour and less gain.

Leonardo presents his observations in the form of advice on how things might be represented. His theory of forces in nature also appears in the *Treatise on Painting,* as we have seen, as a series of rules for painters. But the manner and style in which these theories are given expression indicates that his scientific studies were no longer being pursued only to perfect the education of the painter, but were beginning to assume

importance in their own right. One often finds references to purely scientific studies, such as the *Treatise on Anatomy,* or the *Book of Mechanics,* which Leonardo cites as independent works.

When in the paragraphs on the growth of trees and plants is simultaneously produced a whole series of observations on new scientific knowledge; when in his instructions on expressions and movements in man and animal Leonardo discusses anatomical and physiological matters far beyond the simple practical needs of the painter; when, finally, he begins to develop a whole theory of the creation and destruction of the earth, the boundaries of a practical handbook are shattered.

The enduring value and unequalled fascination of Leonardo's *Treatise on Painting* is above all due to the fact that he was as much a master of language as of artistic representation. A unique and perfected "intuitive judgement" expresses itself with such clearness and beauty, that knowledge and performance both reach the same high degree of perfection. The strength of conviction conveyed by Leonardo's words is compelling, for behind each thought lies the genius of a practising artist whose theory is constructed out of his own experience, and is confirmed in every one of his artistic works. This treatise includes a completely new and valid "Theory of Vision"; it developes the principles of aerial and colour perspective, and thus discusses problems of representation in painting which lead us to the work of a Rembrandt and the painters of the nineteenth century; further, it offers a complete—technical as well as aesthetic—theory of colour; and, finally, gives a multitude of practical directions, ranging from details such as the construction of a well-lighted studio, or the education of an apprentice, to general rules for a painter's way of living. Only a lofty, poetic imagination like Leonardo's could transform practical rules for artists into ethical rules of living which seem to explain his whole activity in an allegorical way. Leonardo states that the artist should take a mirror for instruction in learning about light and shade, and perspective, since the surface of the mirror reflects "true painting," just as a completely successful painting will resemble the surface of a mirror, and he transforms this "practical" rule into a wonderful metaphor.

> The painter should dedicate himself to solitude in order to weigh and consider everything which he sees, and to choose the best parts thereof. He should accomplish this in the manner of a mirror, which changes itself into as many colours as are contained in the objects placed before it. And if he does this, he will be like a second Nature.
>
> (pp. 107-08)

Ludwig H. Heydenreich, in his Leonardo da Vinci, *The Macmillan Company, 1954, 210 p.*

CLIFFORD BAX   (essay date 1932)

[Bax was an English critic, dramatist, novelist, and editor. In the following excerpt from his 1932 biography of Leonardo, he appraises the artist's literary skill.]

[Leonardo] developed, very early, a marked talent for music, modelling, drawing and arithmetic. He seems, in youth, to have had little Latin and no Greek, but in later life he improved his Latin, principally for the purpose of reading scientific treatises. We also know that he read Ovid with some appreciation and that he was a keen student of Dante's poem, but in general he shows little respect for literature and none for scholarship. Most of us have known men, highly gifted in many directions, who somehow cannot bring themselves to admit the value of a talent which they do not possess: and I doubt whether any expert would maintain that Leonardo reveals much literary skill. True, we sometimes hear that, in addition to everything else, he was also a poet. Addington Symonds, indeed, presents us with a translation of one chilly sonnet—about the wisdom of willing to do what you can rather than trying to do what you cannot. (pp. 16-17)

> *Clifford Bax, in his* Leonardo da Vinci, *D. Appleton and Company, 1932, 159 p.*

HUNTINGTON CAIRNS, ALLEN TATE, AND MARK VAN DOREN (conversation date 1941)

[*An American lawyer and literary critic, Cairns is the author of* Law and the Social Sciences *(1935) and* Legal Philosophy from Plato to Hegel *(1949). Tate, a prominent American man of letters, is associated with two critical movements, Agrarianism and New Criticism. Van Doren, perhaps best known as a poet, was also a respected critic. His criticism is aimed at the general reader, rather than the scholar or specialist, and is noted for its lively perception and wide interest. Their guest, Radin, was a Polish-born American academic and well-known essayist. In the following excerpt from a radio broadcast aired in 1941, the critics attempt to define Leonardo's concept of the universe as expressed in the* Notebooks.]

The creator of Mona Lisa and the Last Supper was not only one of the greatest of painters; he was a great sculptor, architect, musician, engineer, and scientist as well. He has been called the universal genius, and those who study him in any of his phases come away convinced that he is without his peer. His drawings, which survive in profusion among the libraries of the world, are the despair of anyone who has tried to explain their inexhaustible variety and their impeccable skill. Leonardo was that rare if not unique thing, a man equally gifted in art and in science. The two for him were not opposed or unrelated; his curiosity concerning the secrets of life, being unlimited, took him without prejudice into both precincts, where in the solitude of his genius he embraced the most difficult of problems and at least suggested the most brilliant of answers. It is only of late that he has been known as an author. His manuscripts, surviving in the fragmentary form of notes, have gradually been explored and edited, and now his *Notebooks* are available to those who wish to see how he conversed with himself in words rather than by line and color. Here as elsewhere he reveals a tireless and beautiful mind to which nothing in nature is alien. His reports of experiments, his generalized observations, his apothegms, even the turns of his phrases are those of a secret master. The *Notebooks* of Leonardo are not the least monument he erected to himself without the thought that it would some day be standing in the marketplace. (pp. 359-60)

• • • • •

Cairns: It is customary to put Leonardo forward as a universal man, and it is certainly true that he went into many fields. He explored mathematics and geology, art, anatomy, aviation, mechanics, music and many other departments of knowledge. There was hardly a field of interest at his time that he did not explore, and to which he did not make contributions. Mr. Tate, do you think we are apt to get more from

such a man, or would you say that we are likely to receive more from a man who studies just one aspect of nature?

Tate: There are two points involved in such a question. We have first to define an aspect of nature, and then see what it is that we expect to get from any field of study. Take Leonardo's own practice. He was a painter and he was also a student of anatomy. For him—for all artists—the two fields are connected: he used his knowledge of anatomy in his painting. But I do not believe the two fields are equal or on the same level. For example, the painter encompasses, it seems to me, a great deal more than the anatomist—the artist more than a scientist pursuing any one field.

Cairns: Are you assuming that art and science can be separated?

Tate: Separated in a sense. They certainly are connected, insofar as the artist has to rely upon the common sense of scientific knowledge. I can illustrate that, I believe, with another point. Take Dante's universe. The ancient mathematicians could express it mathematically, but we needed Dante to show the experience of the human race within that universe. In that sense, by the way, it seems to me that Dante is far more the universal man than Leonardo.

Van Doren: Dante was a scientist too, was he not? Science means knowing, and for Dante knowledge was a very important thing. He assumed, as any good poet would assume, that knowledge is necessary to poetry. But the relation between the thing known and the poem written is a subtle relation, one that you cannot state by saying merely that a man is a poet and a scientist. A good poet's science becomes a part of his poetry.

Tate: Exactly, and they are not separable. We might put it this way: While you can abstract the science from the poetry, you cannot abstract or separate the poetry from the science.

Cairns: I would not agree with that. In Leonardo's case there is a fusion of science and art; he was not a scientist who became an artist, nor an artist who became a scientist. There is a single word that covers both aspects of his life and his consideration of them: he was a naturalist.

Van Doren: Would it not be true to say that for him his painting and his scientific investigations were both forms of the same exploration? He was always curious about the world.

Tate: Don't you believe that the fact that Leonardo did not succeed in bringing all the results of his investigations together into any great design would indicate that his vision was not actually universal? Probably he did it in painting; that is, the fusion of anatomy and the art of painting represents what you are talking about better than anything else. But he did not use his other knowledge that way.

Radin: That would assume that Leonardo really believed that you must have a unified vision of the world. It may very well be that Leonardo definitely saw the world, not as a unified thing but as one of very separate and only partially related facets.

Cairns: Do you find anything in the *Notebooks* to support that point? Would you not say rather that Leonardo was intensely interested in the universe, in the world as a totality, and that art was to him merely one method of exploring that universe, and that science was another method. It has always appeared to me that he regarded the universe, if I may speak abstractly, as continuous rather than discontinuous, if any man ever did. Yet he saw it whole.

Van Doren: He thought of it, if you like, as one thing. From the famous paragraph which is called a "hymn to force," the reader can form the impression that for Leonardo the universe was a living thing, a creature, an animal breathing and using its muscles. I was interested in what Mr. Radin said about Leonardo's vision of a world which cannot be easily known as a single thing, but can be known only in terms of facets that present themselves from time to time. If that is true—if Leonardo did see the world as something that can never be seen all at once—he may not deserve the epithet "universal" as a great painter like Rembrandt, a great scientist like Darwin, a great statesman like Julius Caesar deserves it. Those men, though in the beginning limited, or apparently limited, ended by seeming to cover the world and to unify experience.

Tate: There is still another question involved. Perhaps Leonardo is the modern, multiple man. He believed in "multiplicity," as Henry Adams would have expressed it. He was not concerned with the unified vision, and we inherit, I think, the Leonardo tradition, or the tradition of his age. We are still men of the Renaissance.

Radin: It seems to me to be only partially correct to say that Leonardo was a man of the Renaissance. We must remember that he emphatically rejected the return to Plato and that he stressed experiment and measurement, both of them traits not characteristic of the Renaissance.

Van Doren: I am glad to hear you mention Henry Adams, Mr. Tate, because Henry Adams writes hymns to force also, and they sound very much like Leonardo. Force for both men is something explosive and destructive; it tends to make the universe fly apart.

Cairns: We should seek a guiding thread for his scientific approach. The modern scientific mind, that is, the mind that has had the benefit of seventeenth-century science, is a product of two streams—legalism and naturalism. By legalism I mean the theory of order in the universe; that is to say, the notion that the universe operates in accordance with certain immutable laws.

Van Doren: You mean natural laws?

Cairns: The laws of nature. Their perception and formulation was the great contribution of seventeenth-century science. That influence is something that extended even to literature; Bunyan, for example, had it. He shared the world view of the seventeenth-century scientists. It is clear that he belongs in the school of Newton and the other seventeenth-century scientists as a legalist. In my opinion Leonardo anticipated the seventeenth-century scientists both as a legalist and as a naturalist. I find many instances throughout the *Notebooks* of a belief in the omnipresence of law throughout the universe.

Tate: Purely natural law. It is not the divine law of the medieval church. It is something else.

Cairns: Laws of this sort: Here is one of his statements: "Nature never breaks her own laws." Here is another statement: "Oh marvelous necessity, thou with supreme reason constrainest all efforts to be the direct result of their causes and by a supreme and irrevocable law every natural action obeys thee by the shortest possible process."

Tate: There is a very interesting quality in that statement, and you find it, I think, all through the *Notebooks.* Although Leonardo is talking about natural law, he expresses it in something like rhetoric. The vocabulary is not scientific and exact unless he is doing some precise piece of observation, or giving us a diagram. When he talks about science in general, it turns into a kind of pseudo-poetry; for example, his deification of force, which becomes, as Mr. Van Doren was saying, a personal and living thing. In other words, is he not on one side still a little medieval and religious? He has not made a clean break over into a strictly rational and scientific conception.

Radin: There was not any proper scientific vocabulary in existence then and we cannot hold him too responsible for expressing himself in what seems to us rhetoric and pseudo-poetry. Despite verbal inadequacies his was a strictly rational and scientific conception. As I see it, he knew the essential parts of the scientific practice of today: the observation of a phenomenon, artificial reproduction if possible, the discovery of some relationship between its various features, the measurement of these relationships and the deduction of a law.

Tate: I did not mean to hold him responsible, or to say that he was at fault. I thought it was an interesting fact that he was so placed historically that he spoke ambiguously.

Cairns: That is true, but at the same time I do not know anyone who was further on the modern side than Leonardo. Mr. Radin's point that Leonardo was without a proper scientific vocabulary undoubtedly accounts for the vagueness of many of his remarks. He suffered, moreover, from another disability: he lacked modern instruments. In estimating his work, we should always bear in mind that not until the seventeenth century were the microscope, telescope, thermometer, barometer, air pump and pendulum clock invented.

Van Doren: Mr. Cairns, I failed to understand something you said a minute ago, a distinction you were making between legalism and naturalism in scientific thought. Which of those things do you mean to say that Leonardo anticipated?

Cairns: Leonardo was the first man to represent or to embody to a really full degree both aspects. My point is that the modern scientific mind is the product of both of those streams; first, of naturalism in the sense that nature is the primary object of study; and secondly, of legalism. Bunyan, although he lived in the seventeenth century, represented only one aspect. He was a legalist and not a naturalist.

Tate: But in his conception of a world order, Bunyan is closer to the medieval conception of the divine order. It is very hard to separate Bunyan from that tradition. He is in a period in which the ideas can go in either direction.

Cairns: He lived in a period, of course, when the natural legalistic order was dominant in men's minds. All his contemporaries were thinking those thoughts.

Tate: But Bunyan's own education, which was almost wholly Biblical, must have been such that he was not very conscious of the new discoveries in science.

Cairns: Probably not. But it was part of the climate of opinion of the time, and it would have been difficult for him to escape it.

Van Doren: Would Bunyan have been capable either of writing or of understanding this sentence of Leonardo? "A bird is an instrument working according to mathematical law." I should say that would be completely unintelligible to Bunyan, for whom a bird would be—well, what I should say a bird is.

Cairns: Bunyan would not have understood that sentence if he had ever heard it, and he certainly would not have written it; Bunyan would have thought of the bird in a religious sense. What Leonardo is doing in that sentence is making an assertion about a natural object, a bird, and he is also bringing in the element of legalism.

Van Doren: But your language itself is interesting. "To him a bird is a natural object." Why is it clear that a bird is a natural object? Why is the bird not one of God's creatures? That is another way of speaking of a bird, is it not?

Radin: That is what makes Leonardo definitely the naturalist. But this does not prevent his thinking of a bird as one of God's creatures. However, I should be inclined to disagree with Mr. Cairns that he had this other facet to his nature, I mean, legalism. (pp. 361-66)

Cairns: I should like to explore a little bit more why Mr. Radin thinks Leonardo was not a legalist. I derived such a strong impression to that effect from my reading of the *Notebooks.* Let me give you, Mr. Radin, one further sentence which seems to me to go to the heart of Leonardo's scientific theory, insofar as you can say he worked out a general scientific theory, as to which I have a considerable doubt. He makes this statement: "My intention is to give first place to experience and then by means of reason to demonstrate why the experience was as it was. This is the true rule according to which the investigators of natural phenomena must proceed." Now I can shorten that. What he is saying there is that experience is the point of departure and mathematical form is the point of arrival, which seems to me solidly to embrace legalism.

Radin: My objection is to the term "legalistic."

Cairns: I do not want to quarrel over a word, particularly when it is not even mine.

Radin: It seems to have certain implications that I do not think fit into this particular context. I, for one, always think the term legalism implies something mechanically rigid and static.

Cairns: It is a customary word in the history of science. All I mean is the conception of the universe as subject to general laws.

Radin: Clearly Leonardo was definitely interested in that, and he would have had no interest in his observations unless he could at the end of them have deduced certain laws. If you mean that, I certainly would agree with you, but that is part, of course, of the naturalist.

Cairns: You don't think they can be separated?

Radin: I do not think so.

Van Doren: I do not see the separation clearly.

Cairns: Don't you agree that you can study the natural object without attempting to generalize your observations? That is to say, the natural object can be studied by itself—as by a painter; but in that study there is no necessary implication about an order of nature.

Tate: By legalism in the seventeenth century, Mr. Cairns, do you mean the unique development of the science of physics? That was the special form that the development of science took at that time. If we take the physical view of the universe, we can think of it in terms of a very strict mechanical order, governed by "law," but certainly beyond an interest in mechanics. Leonardo probably was not much interested in the general science of physics. Or do you think he was?

Cairns: He did not arrive, of course, at a general physics, as Newton did.

Radin: He was a practical man, was he not?

Cairns: He was a wonderful inventor. And the real question is: How much more was he than an inventor?

Tate: I should judge that he was much more than that. He was a great artisan, let us put it.

Van Doren: He was a man who had a great natural curiosity as to how things worked. His tendency when he saw anything was to want to take it apart. When he saw a human being he wanted to cut him in two, so he could see his blood vessels and his nerves. He once said that he would like to saw the whole earth in two, so that he could see it in cross section.

Cairns: That is the naturalistic element that I had in mind. It has nothing to do with an order of nature or general laws.

Radin: I would agree with you then, if you meant that he liked to analyze and take apart. But that was generally for a purpose: namely, to put together again.

Van Doren: You throw light, then, upon the meaning of your term. I am still interested in the epithet "universal" which has been applied to Leonardo. I take it that we are faced with a legend about him, and Leonardo surely is one of the most interesting of men. But I agree with Mr. Tate that the method of Leonardo, the method which consists in adding always one more field to the number of fields already explored, will leave the student in the end somehow behind nature, behind the world. It will keep regularly ahead of him.

Tate: Perhaps the legend of Leonardo is largely due to our sympathy with his diffusion of interest. He has an interest in mechanics, an interest in anatomy, an interest in hydraulics. Well, in those scattered interests he becomes a symbol of our modern state of mind. It is merely an aggregation of interests and not a unity of purpose or a unity of vision.

Van Doren: You can say that he studied twenty-five things, but of course there are twenty-five million things to study; there is no end to the number of things. Whereas if you do happen to be fortunate enough to believe that there is one thing to study, perhaps you can study that with something like completeness, before you die.

Cairns: That may satisfy you personally as an individual, but I do not see that there is any guarantee it will lead to a full comprehension of the world unless the world is continuous.

Tate: I think a full comprehension of the world is possible only to a man who sees it all his life from one point of view. Comprehensiveness is not the same thing as a statistical completeness. For example, if you look at the world from Leonardo's point of view, you must conclude that before you can have a unity of conception, you have to get the complete aggregation of all the scientific facts; and that is clearly impossible.

Van Doren: We are speaking of science. Perhaps we should say knowledge. Shakespeare knew the world. When you have finished reading his plays you have no sense that you are ignorant of the world. You know much more about it, indeed, than you did before.

Cairns: You know human beings but not nature.

Van Doren: Not nature? I doubt that. I have the sense, as I read Shakespeare, that I know nature too.

Radin: But not in certain formulations of interest to the scientist and just as complete and fundamental as those of the poet.

Van Doren: I am not talking about knowing formulations of nature. I am talking about knowing nature, which is a very different thing.

Radin: Well, if you can make valid formulations of nature, you know nature.

Cairns: Does Shakespeare add anything to our knowledge of the ultimate substance of the world? What is the nature of matter as Shakespeare sees it?

Van Doren: Does science add anything?

Tate: Science is always pushed on from one position to another.

Cairns: But science is closer. At least science attempts to answer such questions and Shakespeare does not even attempt to do that.

Tate: Maybe Shakespeare knows better than to attempt it.

Van Doren: That is quite right. In the long run, the poet knows more about the world than the scientist does, because he keeps his eye on the world. The poet is not interested in statements that can be made *about* the world. He is interested *in* the world.

Tate: May we say, Mr. Van Doren, that one thing that the poet knows is the scientist himself?

Van Doren: Yes.

Tate: And the scientist does not know the poet.

Van Doren: That may be.

Radin: I doubt that very much. I suspect he may know the poet better than the poet knows himself, or the poet the scientist.

Cairns: Mr. Tate and Mr. Van Doren are using "world" in a different sense. Mr. Radin and I are talking about the world of matter; they are talking about the world of human beings.

Van Doren: At any rate, we have in Leonardo a man who, whenever he drew a bird, and in my opinion he was the great draftsman of history, drew a bird which is a bird, which has the life of a bird as well as the looks of one. When he is a scientist he talks in that curious language which makes it possible for him to say that a bird is an instrument working according to mathematical law. I maintain that that is one of the most fantastic statements which can be made. Mr. Tate once complained that most people these days could not look at a horse and see simply a horse. They see it as a beast of burden, as something which ought to be saved from its misery, as a quadruped, as almost anything except what it is.

Tate: What Leonardo says about the mechanics of a bird is

probably true, but suppose we look at the bird from the point of view of the ornithologist. He is not interested in mathematics. He is classifying birds according to shape, color, their phylogenetic habits and so on. But when you put all those different scientific pictures together, do you ever get the real bird?

Cairns: Perhaps Mr. Van Doren can help settle this matter of the bird. Leonardo, when he wanted to draw a bird as an artist, drew it. There is no greater European draftsman than Leonardo. Let me ask: What chapter in the *Notebooks* is that sentence in? What question is Leonardo trying to answer? What is the title of the chapter containing that sentence?

Van Doren: It is the first sentence of the chapter called "The Flying Machine." He is interested in adapting such knowledge as he can get of the mechanics of bird flight to the making of a machine with which a man can fly.

Radin: That is quite true.

Cairns: We can understand Leonardo's intention in that sentence when he approaches the bird from that point of view.

Tate: He is interested in the flying aspect of the bird.

Van Doren: These *Notebooks* are not a treatise, and it is unjust to Leonardo to give the impression that he thought so.

Cairns: It is not only unjust to Leonardo, but it is also hard on the reader. There is an old saying that all Leonardists in the end go mad.

Van Doren: All I want to say is that a reading of these remarkable notes does not leave me with a sense that Leonardo knows the whole world in anything like the way in which the legend makes him out to know it. He knows a great many things about the world, if you like. It is my belief that he did not know the world, and there are gaps even in his cursory knowledge which are astonishing. For instance, music seems to him contemptible and mean because it is an art of repetition. He thinks there is something unworthy about repetition.

Tate: Then as to poetry, his conception of it is extremely naive. For example, he says that if you put an image of God before a person he is much more moved than he is moved by the word God written on a piece of paper. Well, that is by no means a fair comparison of sculpture or painting with poetry. A poem is not isolated words.

Cairns: The explanation might be that the book is heavily weighted on the side of physics. It is largely natural science as Leonardo understood it.

Tate: Practical physics, let us say. It is not speculative physics, is it?

Cairns: No. It is largly technology. Occasionally you run across a sentence such as "Truth is the only daughter of time," which has a poetic element in it.

Van Doren: Here is one sign to me that he is not the effective mind he might have become. There is frequently in him, if not always, an element of the fantastic. He did not submit himself to that discipline which any art, if a man marries the art, makes him submit to, correcting each work that he does so that the next work becomes better. He tends to fray, to spread out, and is often-times childish.

Cairns: You mean he tends to the extraordinary and the extravagant in his speculation?

Van Doren: He tends to be extravagant, even trivial.

Cairns: You were not making the point that he had a naturalistic interest in ugliness as such?

Van Doren: No, although ugliness interested him as it interests anybody.

Cairns: As a painter, he was particularly interested in it.

Van Doren: There is a paragraph in the section of this book called "Philosophy" which I consider highly characteristic of Leonardo, for it expresses that man in him who saw the world as a creature.

> Behold now the hope and desire of going back to one's own country or returning to primal chaos, like that of the moth to the light, of the man who with perpetual longing always looks forward with joy to each new spring and each new summer, and to the new months and the new years, deeming that the things he longs for are too slow in coming; and who does not perceive that he is longing for his own destruction. But this longing is in its quintessence the spirit of the elements, which finding itself imprisoned within the life of the human body desires continually to return to its source. And I would have you to know that this same longing is in its quintessence inherent in nature, and that man is a type of the world.

(pp. 367-73)

Huntington Cairns, Allen Tate, and Mark Van Doren, "Leonardo da Vinci, 'Notebooks'," in their Invitation to Learning, *Random House, 1941, pp. 359-73.*

FRED GLADSTONE BRATTON   (essay date 1943)

[*An American cleric, Bratton was an editor, essayist, and academic. In the following excerpt from* The Legacy of the Liberal Spirit, *he sketches Leonardo's career and personality.*]

The example par excellence of [the] eclectic, universal vitality which was the Renaissance is Leonardo da Vinci, "the most resplendent figure in the history of the human race," as Thomas Craven calls him. When Leonardo died, his faithful disciple, Melzi, said: "It is not in the power of Nature to produce such another man" (the chances physiologically speaking are, for that matter, probably one in ten billion). Long remembered as the painter of a dozen pictures, he has emerged from the last half century of research as the finest product of the Renaissance, the most versatile and capacious mind in all history. Here was a man who saw the whole world as his province and yet could penetrate to the utmost point of specialization and spectroscopic analysis.

Leonardo was both skeptic and mystic. In him were combined the scientific and aesthetic, qualities rarely present in one personality. Challenged by the potentialities of mechanical invention, he directed his attention to the release and multiplication of power. He invented the first self-propelling vehicles with differential gear. His *Notebooks* contain drawings of cranes, boring machines, armored tanks, and flying machines. He was always haunted by the dream of men flying in the air. He left many pages of specifications for airplane construction. Most of the designs call for wings or sails that can be beaten, birdlike, up and down on the air. Following the laws of avian flight, he indicated that the relation between the weight to be borne and the span of the wings must be the same as in birds.

He was the first to make records of the internal structure of the body in drawings not excelled in accuracy for centuries. Having dissected some thirty corpses, he was able to describe death by arteriosclerosis and tuberculosis. He made drawings of embryos at different stages; also skulls, muscles, and various organs. He anticipated Harvey in the discovery of the circulation of the blood. He planned cities with sewage systems, underground sanitation and air conditioning. He experimented with steam and recorded his use of this new power; helped to design the Milan Cathedral and Saint Peter's in Rome; constructed a camera; organized festivals and staged great theatrical productions; designed a spinning machine and looms; surveyed Italy from coast to coast and made relief maps of the country; erected an astronomical observatory; discovered the laws of inertia; and wrote a volume on the anatomy of the horse. He drained marshes, built canals, devised locks to control water; established the laws of petrifaction; invented roller bearings, the diving bell, the dulcimer, and the submarine.

Even in his painting his approach was that of experimentation. With Leonardo came the earliest independent landscape in western art and the first use of chiaroscuro. He was interested not in making a photographic likeness but in studying and portraying emotional states, optical phenomena, atmospheric effects, divisions of tones, and colors of shadows. He was attracted by unusual heads and searched the city for the oddest, ugliest and most grotesque faces, which he reproduced in caricature form.

Much has been made in recent studies of Leonardo's inventions and scientific observations but his biographers have never done him justice as a philosopher. His *Notebooks* reveal him to be the same prophetic spirit in the philosophic world as in the realm of science. Thoroughly religious, he was opposed to fanaticism, superstition, and magic. As an enemy of clericalism and dogma, he may well be considered a precursor of modern liberal thought. His interest in religion was ethical rather than mystical. "Whoever in discussion," he wrote, "adduces authority uses not his intellect but rather memory." Following the implications of humanism more critically than his fellow Italians, he anticipated Erasmus and Luther in his denunciation of ecclesiasticism, and he disapproved strongly of such practices as the sale of indulgences, worship of saints, Mariolatry, and confession. He was vehemently opposed to astrology, witchcraft, and alchemy.

The conflict between freedom and authority finds Leonardo always on the side of freedom. "When besieged by ambitious tyrants," he wrote, "I find a means of defense in order to preserve the chief gift of nature which is liberty." His recognition of the "cultural lag" sounds strangely appropriate for our day: "How by an appliance many are able to remain for some time under water. How and why I do not describe my method for remaining under water; for this I do not publish or divulge on account of the evil nature of men who would practice assassinations at the bottom of the sea by breaking the ships in their lower parts and sinking them together with the crews who are in them."

The clue to Leonardo's religious liberalism is discovered in the nature of the opposition. His clash with Thomism and Scholasticism provoked the enmity of both ecclesiastical authorities and orthodox scientists. The Church, for instance, placed a ban on his anatomical studies on the grounds that the human body is a sacred mystery and dissection is a sacrilege. Using the empirical method before Copernicus, Galileo,

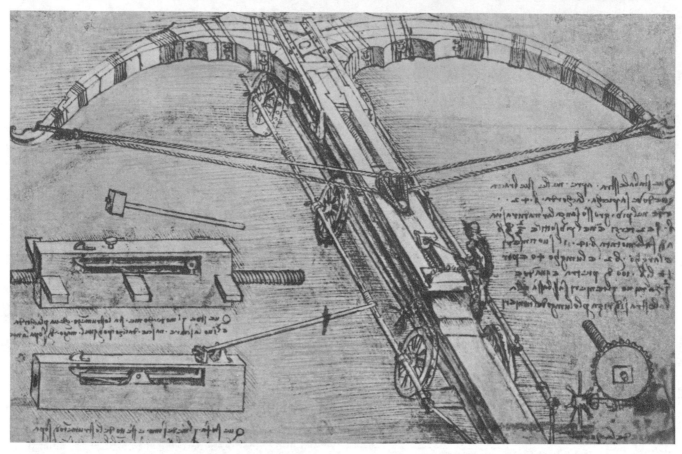

A giant crossbow mounted on a carriage, an example of Leonardo's work as a military engineer.

and Bacon, he can be considered, to use a phrase from Emil Ludwig, "the greatest pathfinder of the new occident." "Those sciences are vain and full of errors," wrote Leonardo, "which are not born of experience, mother of all certitude, and which do not terminate in observation; that is, whose origin or middle or end does not come through one of the five senses. . . . I will make experiment before I proceed because my intention is first to set forth the facts and then to demonstrate the reason why such experience is constrained to work in such fashion. And this is the rule to be followed by the investigators of natural phenomena: while nature begins from causes and ends with experience, we must follow a contrary procedure, that is, begin from experience and with that discover the causes."

Leonardo was the Renaissance. His life is the story of Florence and Rome, Milan and Venice, Lorenzo the Magnificent and Michelangelo, Leo X and the Borgias, Mirandola and Ficino, political intrigue and ecclesiastical corruption, city rivalries and foreign invasions—a kaleidoscopic scene, dominated by the titanic figure of Leonardo da Vinci. His life is the story of a mind that grew with the world in the most pregnant period of human history. (pp. 61-4)

Fred Gladstone Bratton, "Renaissance Humanism," in his The Legacy of the Liberal Spirit: Men and Movements in the Making of Modern Thought, *Charles Scribner's Sons, 1943, pp. 59-85.*

A. DIDIER GRAEFFE   (lecture date 1952)

[In the following excerpt from a 1952 lecture delivered at a Southern Illinois University symposium on "The Resources of Leonardo da Vinci," Graeffe contends that the humanist and idealist perspectives expressed by Leonardo are unique among Renaissance thinkers.]

As a painter, Leonardo contributed more than anybody else to the philosophies of naturalism and idealism in art—problems which, under different labels, pre-occupy our artists today. As engineer, he anticipated the trends of modern technology by at least two centuries. More than that, he put technical invention on the one philosophic basis that permitted it to prosper as incredibly as it has done and is still doing. That basis is, of course, the philosophy of pragmatism. As a scientist, he found more keys to open Nature's locked doors than all of his contemporaries put together, and more perhaps than any single scientist after him, although he failed to see the implications of the most effective of those door openers, namely, the experimental method.

But all these are contributions of a specialized nature. Leonardo was more than a painter, an engineer, a scientist, and a dozen other things. In fact, he cannot be understood as a sum of talents. There is not enough time and strength in any one man's life to do the things that Leonardo did, unless they are all done in the light of a unifying principle. Such a principle must be simple if it is to explain the confusing variety of apparently unconnected pursuits. Once we understand the principle, the details of Leonardo's incredible career should fall together like the pieces of a puzzle.

That central light is Leonardo's *humanism.* Leonardo lived in the midst of the Humanist movement that flourished during the fifteenth century all over Italy. Being a Florentine and an artist and a many-talented man put him as close to the origin of that movement as he could have wished. But Leonardo's humanism is not at all like that of the other Humanists. It is original, unique, and radically different. To some extent this is owing to the difference in training and background between Leonardo and his Humanist contemporaries. Partly it must be attributed to an indefinable something in the depth of Leonardo's personality, something almost identical with what we regard as his specific greatness. . . .

How does Leonardo's humanism differ from that of the Renaissance in general—from the movement that began with Dante, Petrarch, and Boccaccio, that attained a climax in Leonardo's vicinity, namely, in the famous Platonic Academy presided over by one of Leonardo's own patrons, Lorenzo the Magnificent of Medici, and that finally produced figures like Erasmus of Rotterdam and the writer of the *Anatomy of Melancholy?*

All these men were scholars. Leonardo was not. Their humanism was part of a revival of classical antiquity in which Leonardo showed little interest. It centered in the study of the classical languages, which Leonardo hardly bothered to learn, and it was intimately connected with the *readings of books* on which, often, Leonardo vented his scorn and his ridicule. (p. 1)

His humanism is *naturalistic* and *pragmatic.* Pragmatism and naturalism are attitudes we expect to be drawn from an unprejudiced scientific investigation of Nature. We rightly do not connect them in our minds with the Humanist movement. In fact, from the Renaissance to the present time, there has been mutual misunderstanding between the humanities and the natural sciences—a misunderstanding that is about to become fatal inasmuch as both these philosophies claim man as their exclusive property. In Leonardo they are intimately fused and interlocked. (p. 2)

The true humanist is he who does not lose his aims in the process of realizing them; he who can specialize and yet remain conscious of the whole; he whose insight can be the fruit of subjectivity and intuition without becoming a mere cloud of dust; he who can adhere to pure truth without being simpleminded; he who can observe with detachment, not harming his powers of love and tenderness; he who can see himself without abrogating the finesse of scientific reasoning.

Leonardo, more than any classical scholar, and more than any exponent of science alone or of the arts alone, was this true humanist. Whether he observed angles of reflection on glittering surfaces or the facial expression of one sentenced to be hanged; whether he discovered the geometric formula for the most pleasing subdivision of a rectangle or the aerodynamic laws of bird flight; whether he mused upon the life that once inhabited a fossil fish or indulged with gusto in riddles, paradoxes, allegories, and fanciful prophecies; his apparent absorption in detail is never more than one step removed from the center of things, i.e., from man in his wholeness and in the strange tensions that characterize man's existence.

In Leonardo's work, form is *confession;* form is the self, petrified. As the soul of man submits in humility to the absolute,

the absolute attains form in man's soul. Silence is the preparation for the feast of confession, humility is its consummation, form its fruit. (p. 3)

In Leonardo, alone among the masters of the Renaissance, the strange fusion of Platonic idealism and new scientific naturalism is real and convincing. His naturalism does not stay at the surface, and his idealism is not a pretense.

What is Leonardo's idealism like? One of his aphorisms recalls the superstition that the ermine would rather die than soil itself. The implication is not that a white coat makes puritans but that white is an *ideal* color. White is not the absence of color, or purity the absence of impurity. As white is the perfect equilibrium of all colors, purity is the perfect balance of all impurities. The difference between disgust and pleasure is one of degree, not one of essence.

All art is synthesis; the artist rejects nothing; negligence is his cardinal sin. Satisfaction results not from matters, but solely from the proportion in which they are put together. We eliminate disturbance not by destruction of the disturbing, but by fitting it into the whole that attains greater perfection thereafter.

It takes no more than pure linear melody to say all things.

"Small rooms or dwellings," says Leonardo, "set the mind in the right path, large ones cause it to go astray."

The largest room is the unwalled, inarticulate primeval waste world, a disorder of smells and acoustic danger signals, mere bait for dim sense organs, the chaos, the limitless biblical abyss as yet unpenetrated by the Great Spirit who merely hovers above in blind self-abandon, the raw matrix from which form is to emerge.

Formlessness is non-existence; disorder is emptiness; the eternity of the shapeless is uncreated. Beginning is attaining form; attaining form is becoming conscious; consciousness is man.

These are the premises of Leonardo's idealism. They identify his exact location in our past. Intuitively, Leonardo himself discovers his own place and function in Western history with far greater accuracy than did the historians who afterwards were to place him. It takes the researches of modern historic philosophy to confirm Leonardo's insight. To understand him fully requires our present-day knowledge of a remoter past than Leonardo was in a position to investigate. (p. 4)

Leonardo's humanism and our discovery of it may remind us of the tale of the map that falls from heaven, in response to a child's prayer for a kingdom that has been promised him. Disappointed, the child starts unfolding the map. As he unfolds, he discovers highways and bridges, fields, cities, and a castle; they expand and grow until the kingdom is complete.

As Leonardo's work is unfolded before our eyes in its rhythmical order and symmetry, and in its strange fragmentary and aphoristic form, it is Nature herself that is unfolded and revealed; not a particle of nature but Nature the whole; not an object in nature but that Nature indivisible, intangible, that is the ground from which objects draw their existence.

In all of his wisdom and maturity, Leonardo shows in his work a gay spirit of wonder and enthusiasm. When he guides Mona Lisa's emotions and thereby her facial expression during her long sittings by means of storytelling and of musical entertainment, he may appear to us a calculating engineer.

But flowers and tunes were not invented by introverts. The healthy workman of the Renaissance was not as implacable an eliminator of sweetness for naive senses as the solemn critic of today likes to assume.

We do well to remember Leonardo's childlike delight in the new visual conquests of the painters, transparent bodies and luminous bodies, shining bodies such as mirrors and like things of ambiguous definition, mists, dull weather, accidental spots on old walls, and an infinite number of new things to delight in.

He never forgets that the artist is there to glorify and that glorification is indulgence in delight. Praise is the artist's dearest profession and his very homeland and origin. Not only the geometrical praise of concentric circles, but everything— the exalted sternness of stylized posture, the impersonal placement of the venerated in the exact center, the rhythmical symmetry, and the severe significance of spatial relationships, reveal common descent with frame and pedestal, pageant and ritual, rhyme and meter.

Leonardo manages to carry this temperamental addiction of the artist into his scientific researches and his feats of technological invention. Exultation never appears to him an obstacle to sober reckoning and measurement. His scientific humanism is like a diamond that *enchances* the light which falls into it, while breaking it up and analyzing it into its components.

His observations are impregnated with this constant readiness for wonder and delight. Thus, in formulating his pragmatic approach to mathematical reasoning, he calls mechanics a "paradise of the mathematical sciences," inasmuch as through mechanics one comes to the *fruits* of mathematics; in defining an architectural arch, he calls it "a strength caused by two weaknesses"; in his attempt to anticipate what was later to become Newton's First Law of Motion, he finds "inequality" to be the cause of all local movements: "there is no rest without equality"; in his famous research into biological function of emotions, he calls *lust* "the cause of generation," *appetite* "the stay of life," *fear* and *timidity* "the prolongation of life," *deceit* "the preservation of the instrument."

Among his inventions, we find not only the monumental experiments in pragmatic technology, his universal joint, his harbor dredge, his alarm clocks, drilling machines, mud sledges, concrete mixers, magnifying glasses, movable bridges and drainage pumps, but also the bizarre tricks of drawing black lines on paper by means of saliva, of adding water to white wine and thereby causing it to become red, and of scissors that open and shut with a single movement of the hand.

One of the most lovable examples of Leonardo's spirit of childlike wonder paired with the most earnest sense of scientific responsibility is the following memo in his notebooks:

> Make to-morrow out of various shapes of card-board figures descending through the air, falling from our jetty; and then draw the figures and the movements made by the descent of each, in various parts of its descent.

We must understand that in this experiment there is not only an anticipation of the inquiries into the falling of bodies which Galileo pursued with grim determination a century afterward, but also an essential complement to Leonardo's other researches in aerodynamics, and, curiously, an investi-

gation of accidental curves quite similar to those studies conducted both by contemporary physicists and by the most recent movement in contemporary art. The aesthetics of such curves would remind us of Alexander Calder's mobiles as well as of Pollock's graphic work. (pp. 5-6)

The portrait of modern man is a home with a short frontage, but with many rooms behind. As the natural limits of our age expand into the limitless vastness of possibilities, self-imposed classical measure becomes again necessary. This necessity of restraint connects us directly with the Renaissance and its spirit.

In our search for a teacher in the humanities we discover that we have to go back five hundred years. There we find Leonardo, the man from Florence who was a universal man, the artist who was a scientist, the great teacher who *was* what he *taught*. (p. 7)

> *A. Didier Graeffe, "Leonardo's Humanism and Our Time," in* The Resources of Leonardo da Vinci: Papers Delivered at Southern Illinois University, *edited by George Kimball Plochmann, Southern Illinois University, 1953, pp. 1-7.*

GEORGE KIMBALL PLOCHMANN   (lecture date 1952)

[*Plochmann is an American editor, short story writer, essayist, and academic. In the following excerpt from a lecture delivered in 1952 as part of a symposium on "The Resources of Leonardo da Vinci," he investigates Leonardo's approach to scholarship in an attempt to determine the author's philosophical perspective.*]

Just as men who see the tattered remains of *The Last Supper* feel certain that behind its hopeless flakes was once a dominant form, so may readers of the **Notebooks** be sure that looming over the miscellany is an integral system of ideas in which part with part make a catena, and in which every part is an intimate subdivision of an articulated whole. The philosophical interpretation of Leonardo should exhibit his work as a limning, at least, of a set of self-expanding coherent ideas which intend the real world.

An interpreter is unlikely to be more than partly wrong about Leonardo's crisp sentences, and almost never can he be wholly and comprehensively right, because the original is so spotty. This sketchiness applies chiefly to the middle range of magnitude, however: of the system as a whole, I do not believe Leonardo was in doubt, and in the single assertions he was usually quite abundantly clear. But in connecting principles with discreet subject matters he left much undone. The making apparent of these hidden connections is surely the first task of the philosophical interpreting of Leonardo da Vinci.

He was the inheritor of extremely subtle philosophic traditions, and he neither garbled them nor made use of them in a particularly subtle way. He was not like Duns Scotus or William of Ockham, and his finesse, when it appears, was either borrowed or arose out of the occasionally unresolved conflict of pairs or groups of his statements.

A new Plato and a new Aristotle erupted into Florentine intellectual society during the fifteenth century. It is customary to say that these Greeks were both humanized at this time; perhaps it is more correct to say that greater emphasis was now placed upon rhetoric than upon dialectic (reversing

Plato) or than upon analytic (reversing Aristotle). But here Leonardo ran counter to the tendency of his day: abjuring the somewhat hortatory bearing of his contemporaries Marsilio and Pico (whom he virtually ignored), he preferred to make different use of the earlier masters. If he took anything directly or indirectly from the Greeks (and he did), he at least treated their principles much as they would have enjoyed having them treated—cavalierly, a little dogmatically, yet employing these bald principles as starting-points, not so much for debate as for meticulous exploration of the world. Certain assumptions and a considerable vocabulary in the *Notebooks* derive from Plato's *Timaeus* and from Aristotle's smaller physical treatises, plus the Hellenistic writers on mechanics. Surprisingly little seems to have stemmed from the emanation theory of Plotinus, who more than Plato and Aristotle, was ascendant in Florence in the days of Leonardo's young manhood and whose distant disciples made his hierarchies the scaffolding upon which the reader was exhorted to climb to the One.

Though not a scholar of any particular range, Leonardo apparently felt himself continuous with the past—there is little talk of a Baconian or Kantian reform of knowledge or of the society based upon knowledge. The several dozen authors Leonardo quotes are mentioned with some respect, a few of their more metaphysical pronouncements emerging in his jottings so unaltered as to sound like common coin, their value taken for granted because already in circulation. One soon feels that Leonardo stood at an advantage over his contemporaries not through his superior use of books but by reason of his wonderful eyes and hands.

About fifteenth-century Florence there must have been a little of Transcendentalism, wordy, humanity-inspirited, heady. If so, then remote, effulgent, and infinitely more fertile in his intellectual expedients than the others was Leonardo da Vinci, standing to his own time somewhat as Charles Sanders Peirce stood to nineteenth-century America. Leonardo was evidently something of a controversialist, living in an epoch when debate blew fresh air over Italy and the worth of a man was oftenest judged by the vigor of prosecution of his disputes. Yet the solitude of his *Notebooks* shows that Leonardo's debating oftenest took place in himself: in a time of symposia and of person-to-person antinomy, Leonardo was both demonstrator and respondent, orator and auditor. Apostrophes contribute the only slight heft that the otherwise sparse notebooks possess, for their leaves are hardly tricked out with prefaces, transitions, and summaries; and cross-references are brief to the point of uselessness. So Leonardo is set over against his rather easy and deceptively systematic time, and he must have preferred talking to himself, though not in the thorough and meditative fashion of Descartes or Kierkegaard.

So we have, then, this discrepancy between Leonardo's remoteness from his contemporaries and his tolerable continuity with traditions of scientific and humane letters. Much as Leonardo did, the other writers of the day were struggling to identify themselves with a notable past, although this identification of the Humanists had a quite different impulse from that of Leonardo. I think this teasing sameness and difference between him and his contemporaries arose out of his own duality—his emotional introversion and his intellectual extroversion; surely this must have been the cause. The introversion could account for his Parnassian hauteur, but the externalizing of his mind brought about his great passion for demonstrating the works of nature and his unceasing alertness and curiosity—alertness to the effects of nature, curiosity about the causes. However, the hauteur was personal. The natural desire of good men, he said, is knowledge (Aristotle would have put it *all* men.) The worst intellectual evil, for him, was not error but sloth; the lazy, as he remarked, leave nothing to posterity but "filled privies," and this simple *ad hominem* sums up the feeling of his divergence from ordinary efforts.

Again, my supposal resolves the paradox that Leonardo is gathering glory in our own century, in which his impact is mental because it is now altogether conveyed through books and drawings. In his own day, he was neither obscure nor famous, but a little of both, depending chiefly upon currents of political favor. There was a contradiction in the way he affected other men, and their standards, even more than ours, must have shifted frequently as these men transferred their attention from his creations to his personality and back again.

Leonardo shows little interest in laying down distinction after distinction in a summating display of all human values and divine laws, as did certain earlier Italians like Thomas Aquinas. But he left distinct clues to the way he would organize knowledge: sequential propositions rather like those of Euclid and Archimedes, built into short treatises which were to receive titles that occasionally crop up in his extant notes— *The Flight of Birds, Movements of Water, Treatise on Shadows, The Geometrical School,* and so forth. (*The Treatise on Painting* was brought closer to completion.) Evidently the plan of these was based upon single topics within a science, not upon the science as a whole, such as aerodynamics, hydraulics, optics, or more broadly, physics. At least Leonardo had a potent impulse *toward* organization of his work.

Whether he intended these demarcations to be final or temporary is a steeper question. Occasionally he speaks of science in general, or of art in general, but never, so far as I know, does he absolutely differentiate between science and art. Where he mentions individual sciences, it is nearly always to join them with others: mechanics, he says, is the fruit of mathematics, mathematics is the entrance-door, the beginning of knowledge, painting is the highest of the sciences. Paradoxically, I think he intended to cut across the lines of the sciences by his topical treatment of separate problems. If the reader of the *Notebooks* sticks too rigidly to the conception of divided sciences, he soon meets passages unintelligible by his interpretation, for the passages assume a connection between disciplines which *approaches* a thoroughgoing unification of knowledge:

> Therefore painting is philosophy, because philosophy deals with the increase and decrease [of bodies] through motion [as does painting] . . . .

and again, we have the implied marriage of optics and mathematics:

> . . . That which is not a part of anything is invisible, as is proved by geometry.

So the subject matters, at least, of the sciences are not cut off; but in the procedures of sciences we do find differences:

> Astronomy and the other sciences also entail manual operations although they have their beginning in the mind, like painting, which arises in the mind of the contemplator but cannot be accomplished without manual operation.

No doubt the "beginning" is a beginning in temporal order. (pp. 28-30)

[Art] and science are both concerned with intelligible necessities and causes, and both deal with the same world of quantified and qualified bodies; but art is not altogether continuous with science for the art proceeds from that which is known to that which is to be made, and hence forms a propaedeutic for the act of insight, of inspiration, of making whole. If we can believe this, it is not impossible to see how Leonardo can say (in the *Trattato della Pittura*) that the science of painting is the mother of perspective, which is in turn the science of visual rays: as mother, painting may give birth either to works or else to principles worth while in the formulation of additional sciences.

Although mathematics is continuous with mechanics and optics, and optical science is continuous with painting, mathematics is related to painting in another way, for it is the "foundation." Histories of ideas sometimes put it that Leonardo ranked the sciences in dignity according to their certitude, not according to their objects. This construction is not wholly wrong, for painting (as a mode of knowledge) is as certain as is hydraulics or mathematics, even though mathematics, with its comparative simplicity, may serve as the underpinnings of other knowledge. I think Leonardo intends that painter and mathematician and physicist deal with a common world, but vary in their emphases and in the order in which they should step forward to instruct the beginner. (pp. 30-1)

The world for Leonardo reveals itself to us progressively, and although phenomena can be isolated for study, every part tries to unite with the whole, to overcome its own incompleteness. Not only has the world a real togetherness, but so has knowledge: more and more light is thrown upon the part as the context of knowledge about the part becomes wider. This widening is not entirely a matter of experience. It is true that we must augment and enhance our system of thoughts by constant reference to what the senses report, yet to *know*, we must reason:

> You who speculate on the nature of things, I praise you not for knowing the processes which nature ordinarily effects of herself, but rejoice if so be that you know the issue of such things as your mind conceives.

Knowledge is not self-knowledge in any moral, Socratic sense, but the examination of the consequences of ideas. This conception helps illuminate a troublesome passage attesting to Leonardo's virtual identification of the principles of things with ideas:

> Experience . . . always proceeds from accurately determined first principles, step by step in true sequences, to the end; as can be seen in the elements of mathematics founded on numbers and measures. . . .

The world moves according to its own laws, the mind grows in contiguity (or should we say union?) with the world, and yet the growth of the mind is not the growth of the world: it is rather the logical self-expansion of the consequences of principles grasped after sensuous contact with the world, but going far beyond that contact. "The thing," says Leonardo, "is known with our intellect." For these and other reasons, it is difficult to say whether Leonardo was a speculative man or not. Perhaps we are seduced by the sheer simplicity of his

instruments of reasoning into believing he was a naive trundler after facts—the kind of observer that Jevons and, to some extent, Mill deluded us into thinking is the true man of science.

But beyond this intellectualism there is another, perhaps more significant aspect of Leonardo's philosophy, certainly one which has suffered neglect at the hands of most of his commentators. The absolutely radical fact, for him, is that there are *two* ultimate, and, I think, irreconcilable categories of existence and explanation, the rational and the irrational. What Leonardo consciously seeks is a particular effect brought about reasonably enough by a limited cause; yet at any point he is inclined to give way to a feeling that the categories of necessity and nature cannot wholly account for the world, and that outside these is an unknowable realm which for Leonardo assumes various guises—goodness, nothingness, creativity, and so on, depending upon the context. Over and over again, there is the injection of this mystery right into the heart of the analysis. (p. 31)

[We] must draw attention to some features of Vincian logic which are not so much stated as illustrated in the writings. In his frequent directions to himself Leonardo usually reminds himself to look for, or write of, effects—*that* a phenomenon is—rather than causes—*why* it is. *That* a thing exists can ordinarily be told by the eye; *what* it is is given by essential qualities or quantities, mentally discriminated. The mind penetrates to the *why* beyond existence, to causes, and since causes are necessarily related to phenomena, they, the causes, may be said to be universal—they always operate. The mind sees universally the law of the object which was seen by the eye as particular and as subject to birth and decay. Leonardo says that truth, as soon as it is known, is incontrovertible, again an annoying remark to those who would make him out a simple empiricist, who erases all distinctions between sense and intellect, and who thinks of causes as being merely sensible particulars.

Leonardo's reason-guided eye and vision-nourished brain, however, were admittedly insufficient to his scientific purposes, for he urged experiment upon his readers. In his philosophy, an experiment seems to be either a sequence of like observations to determine whether experience produces the same effect, or else mechanical devices to aid in the elimination that he requires to insure that the relations between causes and phenomena are necessary and are correctly stated.

The experiments Leonardo thought essential to the unfolding of knowledge are interpreted by him in the light of a multitude of principles, some of them physical, some logical, some moral, some mechanical—and, of course, some of them related to the ineffable realm which cannot be causal in any ordinary sense but which nevertheless makes itself felt. Because of this multitude of principles, whose applications are limited to specific types of phenomena (Leonardo never claims to find any single postulate at the bottom of all knowledge), the method seems to demand elaborate cross-classifications. But what we find in the *Notebooks* is rather different. The whole problem is avoided. Leonardo rarely attempts, for example, to use successive dichotomies in a subject matter. He often classifies, it is true . . . , but these classifications are very simple and remain "horizontal," every subdivision being coordinate with its neighbors. He avoids the hierarchies dear to his Neoplatonic contemporaries, falling back instead upon literal statements of permanent diagnostic features of kinds of things. If he distinguishes primary and secondary illumina-

Allegory of a dragon overcoming a lion, by Leonardo.

tions in his notes on optics, it is in terms of physical sources and effects, not metaphysical perfections. So, too, he uses analogies sparingly. In order to rank levels into ladders, one must show how the lower is vaguely, the higher clearly, expressive of perfection, else there would be no reason for this ranking. One must say the low is like the high in order to make plain the correspondence and order. I think it fair to claim that Leonardo never sets up a hierarchy to which he adheres throughout; many different things are accorded highest place, and comparisons hold in narrow contexts only. Exceptionally, he analogizes certain things to water, but even in such cases, there are careful delineations which reduce the correspondences and which preclude the possibility of saying that water is an essence of all other things, that it is in water and its movements that other things find their manifest exemplifications.

There was for him no single master science. Because he eschewed analogies, seeking instead limited causes of disparate effects, Leonardo was little given to the kind of Cartesian generalization that casts into mathematical form the study of nature and art. No doubt Leonardo was a second rate mathematician; but I submit that this may well have been an effect rather than a cause, may easily have been owing to a pull away from mathematizing that his various physical methods, including the experimental, exerted. This is only one instance

of the point that highly generalized principles, supreme sciences or highest things, and all-mastering methods (often mathematical), frequently go hand in hand—but not quite in Leonardo.

We should not be persuaded to believe that Leonardo's science universally rests upon inductions. Much of his writing merely *seems* inductive and empirical, e.g. his description of raindrop formation, which, with the instruments lying at his hand, could only have been a shrewd guess. Or take the passage:

> When mountains fall headlong over hollow places
> they shut in the air within their caverns, and this
> air, in order to escape, breaks through the earth,
> and so produces earthquakes.

Such accounts would be tales of the marvellous but for the fact that Leonardo makes a strenuous effort always to use natural laws as bases of his explanations. But a remark like this about terrestrial catastrophes can hardly be set down as the immediate result of inductive reasoning.

We have seen that Leonardo often mentions mathematics or mechanics or the science of painting, but that when he projects treatises, each one is planned to deal with one topic, albeit from several points of view. The very splitting up implied by the treatises involves carrying certain quite general concepts over from one set of problems to another. "Nature," "quantity," "force," "movement"—these and a few others—pervade every discussion. This gives each work a family resemblance to every other, making the treatise on painting look like a book on nature and mathematical notes look like both. (pp. 31-3)

> Among the great things which are found among us the existence of Nothing is the greatest. This dwells in time, and stretches its limbs into the past and the future, and with these takes to itself all works that are past and those that are to come, both of nature and of the animals, and possess nothing of the indivisible present. It does not however extend to the essence of anything.

So Leonardo might preface his account of the system of the world. Things begin in non-entity, just as knowledge commences in nescience. Yet in a way which only a Hegelian would have troubled to explain, the mirror image of nothing is everything, and it is from everything, says Leonardo, attempting to paraphrase Anaxagoras, that everything comes—"Because whatever exists in the elements is made out of the elements." The flux of existents stems from a series of limited changes all based upon the four elements, which, in Platonic fashion, are mainly relegated to four typical regions, each portion of the element always tending towards its own proper region. For example:

> Water is by its weight the second element that encompasses the earth, and that part of it which is outside its sphere will seek with rapidity to return there. And the farther it is raised above the position of its element the greater the speed with which it will descend to it.

These concentric spherical regions are contiguous one to the next, and each one is a plenum furthermore. The whole universe is filled, and there is no vacuum. Characteristically the natural changes taking place are regular fluxes and refluxes, not cyclic movements. The motions Leonardo describes so painstakingly—of falling bodies, of water, of shot and shell, of blood—are fundamentally rectilinear in his view, modified here and there by other forces acting, like externally imposed weights, upon the bodies. Leonardo evidently does not wish to affirm a heavenly sphere essentially different from the other four; there is no Aristotelian *aither* which could account for the seeming incorruptibility of the stars. Nor does Leonardo distinguish things on the earth's surface as being specifically terrestrial, from things aloft, except to note variations of degree. (pp. 33-4)

So much of Leonardo's metaphysics as did not advert to principles of nature is little more than a collection of tasteless commonplaces. And such, too, is his moral philosophy. In the ethical apothegms, the vestiges of his scientific method disappear. He is concerned chiefly with the condition of man, how man finds himself situated in a strange world, rather than with the precise specification of good habits, promptings of inner moral sense, or the purifications of man's soul through crisis. Leonardo was no doubt a stern moralist; but two things, his self-confessed inability to write comprehensively of human nature and life, and the preoccupations of his abstracted temperament, made him both weak in moral theory and maddening in his dealings with other men. Especially in his financial arrangements was he like the mighty Beetho-

ven, indulgent toward self and harsh toward others in this department of ordinary life.

There appear to be two positive clues to Leonardo's attitude toward human life—I do not call it a theory, the tracings are so faint. One is the passion for freedom, the other, his ontological grounding of the world in crude nothingness. If, in the first place, there is any humane justification for Leonardo's virtual obsession with engines of war, it lies in the fact that he sought to preserve peace and liberty for his princes; we may take as perfectly sincere his characterization of war as a most bestial frenzy. In the second place, Leonardo was evidently filled with a dread consciousness of the bivalence of nature—it constructs all, but it destroys all. The works of nature are shot through with shortages. Leonardo's famous caricatures, mainly of the aged, show the ugliness of man, stripped of everything but the grimaces of vapid pretensions. And the animal tales abound in the cruelties of beasts, the fruitless struggle for perduring safety. Towards the end of his life, in Rome, when he was still vibrantly alive intellectually but giving way before Michelangelo and Raphael in his reputation as an artist, Leonardo drew a series of apocalyptic visions of the destruction of the world—the total inundation of all habitable places; and he wrote hair-raising descriptions of the effect of this catastrophe upon human life.

In our own day, no doubt Leonardo would be the greatest of existentialists, attentive to bare existence, and facing, in vacuous liberty, choices of infinite consequence. The barbed drawings of degraded humanity, the plaint against "fillers of privies"—are these not the Renaissance analogue of today's philosophical dread and nausea confronted by the order of nature and the human ordeal? If this seems to emphasize a negative side of Leonardo's moral life, still the interpretations harking back to Vasari that make Leonardo's personal generosity rotund and his companionship genial, must be set off by some plain and disturbing evidences of another side. The complex, brilliant, independent intellect was hardly supported by a sanguine temperament.

Much has been offered to prove Leonardo's religiosity, much more to confute. His written words are noncommittal, and I am inclined to believe that in his great pursuits Leonardo was content to neglect a supreme being. It would be a begging of the question even to inquire what secret word transpired when Leonardo was alone with his God, at midnight.

We have reviewed certain fundamentals of Leonardo's work, that, in a Greek phrase, "have philosophy." No matter whether any particular idea was copied, altered, or newly created by him: these presuppositions pivot the sweep of his system. It is impossible, I think, to find any single guiding principle for the whole of his philosophy, and the postulates I have rehearsed in this essay have been chosen for their heuristic value, not for their constituting a full-dress theory, although one feels that the system was never far away from Leonardo's thoughts. Leonardo has shared with Leibniz and with our own Charles Sanders Peirce the character (and fate) of men whose brilliant ideas have been thrown out to the world as scintillating suggestions, and whose books have not been worked up in systematic completeness. Because the rushing fountain of his genius never abated from pouring out fresh discoveries, it was in his attempts to bring order into his thoughts that Leonardo continually failed. Hence to seek to outline his system in any rigid codification, using the familiar artifices of modern formalisms, would result in a distorting reduction. Doubtless the system is there, but it must be approached cautiously, on foot, and using only the principles Leonardo himself supplies. And even the system as he sketched it has this pervading element of irrationality—the nothingness, the creative imagination, the tight-lipped tantalizing smile.

Leonardo is broader and bolder than most attempts to codify his thought would suggest. In the twentieth century, when experimental procedure has hardened from a brave epistemic decision into a technical dogma, it is quite easy for us to take Leonardo's practices in philosophy for granted. Although the Middle Ages was a good deal more reliant upon experience than is commonly supposed, still Leonardo, coming at its final end, stands out with a peculiar eminence, because of the fantastic variety and precision of his observations, the great dexterity of his hands, which one feels must have guided him almost as often as did his eyes.

Leonardo's reluctance to arrange and narrow his findings is given his own sanction. "Abbreviations," he says, "do harm to knowledge." The mind is a free-loving spirit, for him, and like the eye which serves as a magnet for light, intellect and the object it properly knows are drawn together by similar total attraction. "Abbreviations," he goes on, "do harm to knowledge and to love, seeing that the love of anything is the offspring of this knowledge, the love being the more fervent as the knowledge is the more certain." And in turn, love stimulates the growth of the mind. In Leonardo's superb extroversion, this is the generous and capable love that ever moves the intellect and all the other faculties. (pp. 38-9)

> George Kimball Plochmann, "Leonardo da Vinci as Philosopher," in The Resources of Leonardo da Vinci: Papers Delivered at Southern Illinois University, edited by George Kimball Plochmann, Southern Illinois University, 1953, pp. 28-39.

GIORGIO DE SANTILLANA (essay date 1953)

[An Italian-born American, de Santillana is an essayist, editor, and historian. In the following excerpt from an essay originally published in French in 1953, he debates whether Leonardo can be called a Platonist.]

I have heard Leonardo accused of having been a scientific failure because he was a Platonist. Now Leonardo remains for us a strangely ineffectual genius, at times even a perverse nature, but of all strictures that could be leveled at him, that of "Platonism" seems to me the most wildly unfair. I have been wondering why the artist and geometer Leonardo actually had so little of the "Platonist bias" common to the artists and geometers of his day, and with which he has been rather unjustly reproached.

Alexandre Koyré has shown us Galileo the Platonist, and we are entirely in agreement. Galileo was a Platonist, not only in his manner of explaining the concrete by means of the abstract but also in the Socratic method of his *Dialogue,* and especially in his tendency, here and there avowed, toward pan-mathematicism. But nevertheless there is the fact that Galileo was thought to be a Platonist by order and obedience, so to speak; for the mathematical sciences were under the aegis of Plato, and Galileo's friends and followers were Platonists—much better Platonists, actually, than he ever was. There is no doubt at all that the entire group of the Accademia dei Lincei was Platonistic before it was anti-Aristotelian, and in a vividly militant manner. With Ciampoli, the young prelate

who heroically sacrificed his career in order to allow the *Dialogue* to be printed, one glimpses Platonistic insights that border on heresy.

Galileo, then, had good reason to belong to the "sect," as it was called; but more significant is it that he insisted on holding explicit reservations about Platonism as a philosophy. For, as Koyré has very ably proved, he was first and above all an Archimedean. It is Archimedes who was his master in the new science, and Democritus as well; Plato is merely his guarantor, so to speak, in the world of philosophy. What is most "Platonistic" in Galileo is his Pythagoreanism.

But, it might be said, is not Archimedes, again, in the spirit of Plato? I wonder. There is a whole pious tradition, created by Plutarch and other orthodox thinkers, which can be discounted. Archimedes himself was, perhaps, somewhat in Galileo's position. Among the great Greek scientists after Plato, there is actually a visible tension between the accepted philosophy and the necessities of their craft that impels them toward physics, technology, indeed raw operationalism. In the work of Ptolemy, which has been rather fully preserved for us, this struggle is explicit. It is inevitable and as old as time. Daedalus could not, I daresay, be as much of a "Platonist" as Pythagoras (if you don't mind my inverting the times) because he had to manage the Research and Development Center for the National Defense of the Cretan Empire.

Well, there you are: Leonardo is much more of a Daedalus than a Pythagoras. If we pause a moment over this idea, we shall see that, despite his technical advancement, his counterparts were not Heron of Alexandria and Polycletus but rather those half-fabulous, Palamedean figures, the first great artist-craftsmen, the *technitai:* Rhoecos and Theodoros of Samos, Harpalos, Hicetas, and Eupalinos. I am well aware that this is not a new idea; it was present in the mind of Valéry when he wrote the dialogue *Eupalinos* and the *Introduction à la méthode de Léonardo de Vinci* [see excerpt dated 1894]. But since I am trying to establish reference points as an historian, I cannot but be happy to find myself at his side. I am well aware, also, that I am making mythic comparisons. But Leonardo is, precisely, an irreducibly mythic personality. That is what he was to his contemporaries; he escaped their understanding in spite of their attention to his work. No one, outside of Shakespeare and possibly Rembrandt, is more mythic than he.

When we come closer to the historical person, the impression persists. At that time, metaphysical Platonism was in sway among artists: consider Paolo Uccello, Piero della Francesca—his direct predecessor—Leon Battista Alberti, Botticelli. Leonardo remains outside of all that: Leonardo, the "man without letters," the solitary man of incomprehensible fantasies, he of whom Michelangelo scornfully said that he had found no one to work his bellows for him.

Similarly, he is far less a Platonist than his teacher of mathematics, Luca Pacioli, whose *Divina Proportione* he nevertheless helped to edit.

And yet, it will be said, what about the Divine Proportion and his studies concerning the symmetries of the human body? But these things were in the air; they came out of Vitruvius and were common parlance. Ictinus, too, had been thinking of them twenty centuries before, when he built the Parthenon; and he could not have borrowed them from the yet-unborn Plato. One might, in that case, think instead of the influence of the Pythagorean Philolaus, whom modern criticism insists upon reducing to the status of a character in some dialogue—for it is well understood among the Right People that there could not have been any truly philosophic ideas before the Academy and the Academicians began giving regular courses in it (for the first time). But that is another story.

The Platonists firmly believed in the mystery of numbers, whereas Leonardo developed a rather special notion of mathematics, one closer to the spirit of his old practical teacher, Benedetto dell' Abaco, than to that of Copernicus. The mathematical instrument that he indefatigably pursued was, for him, really an instrument, a means of construction, a way—as Valéry would put it—of making himself an equerry of his own ideas. It is not the contemplation of a suprasensible world but the study of the geometrical skeleton of the real one.

His style reveals to us the same distance. Had I the time to do so, I could show through stylistic analysis that Leonardo has nothing in common with the robed and lettered brood of his time or even with Leon Battista Alberti. His language is, essentially, spoken Tuscan, such as it continues among the peasants of his region, with its rich pungency, its simplicity, its artlessly graceful turns of phrase, its countless anacolutha. Obviously he knows how to organize it, but then that develops from Machiavelli. It is his friend Machiavelli who is the closest to him as far as style is concerned—Machiavelli, whom elsewhere I have tried to show to be a born physicst, a *physiologos* searching his way among what we call today the social sciences—and also the tough-minded Guicciardini, as he is in the *Ricordi*. In various other places, in some of Leonardo's flights of lyricism, there is a hint of Ariosto, another man of no great learning. That is the intellectual pedigree.

But then, it will be said, all that famous reading, all those authors cited in the Notes, all those influences reconstructed by Duhem and many others? Well, that is the point. I simply ask that one page of manuscript be looked at with an open mind. We are immediately struck by the neat, practiced handwriting, sure and rapid; the handwriting of a notary's son, whose graphic formation fits in so well with the drawings. But when we read, the spelling proves to be a pure chaos, one that far exceeds the irregularities of the day.

The words are severed and broken and also amalgamated. Leonardo writes exactly as the peasants of his century wrote and as they still write today. The spelling is that of the servant maid or the recruit. The phonetization is the same. They, too, cut and combine in the effort of spelling out syllable after syllable, thus breaking the cadence of the spoken word. Leonardo writes rapidly and knows how to retain the cadence, but he remains bound up by his little world's way of writing. He uses archaic verbal forms which had disappeared from contemporary literature: thus *laldare* for *lodare, altore* for *autore.* Doubtless he must have spoken in the same way. If Dante shaped the "illustrious vernacular," one might almost say that Leonardo clung to expressing himself in High Demotic, creating the language of learned ignorance. "Savage is he who saves himself." He will never write in the style of *messieurs de la ville,* as Rousseau would say. This is a rejection that extends to their concepts, their logic, and their values.

This man without letters is not illiterate, but as a mistrustful, suspicious, and captious artist-peasant, he examines letters from without. He takes and he leaves. Thus in Pico della Mirandola and his Florentine elders he finds a whole subtle Pythagoreanism which might seem to be cut out for him. His friend Botticelli will let himself be taken up with it; Leonardo rejects it categorically, all the while taking his idea of man from Pico—or perhaps rediscovering it there. His own Pythagorean ideas will be taken from Ovid: the plurality of worlds, the community of the living, even vegetarianism. This is the doctrine of the *Hieros Logos,* the true and the ancient doctrine that he has identified as if by instinct. (pp. 1-4)

> *Giorgio de Santillana, "Leonardo, 'Man without Letters'," translated by Starr Atkinson and Jim Atkinson, in his* Reflections on Men and Ideas, *The M.I.T. Press, 1968, pp. 1-19.*

ERNEST HATCH WILKINS (essay date 1954)

[*In the following excerpt from* A History of Italian Literature, *Wilkins extols Leonardo's notes.*]

[The *Notebooks* of Leonardo da Vinci] are such, in their incredible wealth and novelty, as to command an amazed admiration, whether for their revelation of facts, their assertion of great possibilities, their exposition of fine techniques, their insight into the ways of mankind, or the fascination of their fragmentary philosophy. In form their outstanding general qualities are lucidity, pungency, and grace. Those that are most extended are magnificently pictorial, especially his detailed descriptions of possible paintings of a tempest, a flood, and a battle. Many quiver with a sense of the marvelousness of the world and of man; some were written in moods of depression; some are triumphant in their assurance of truth attained; and some are exalted prophecies of achievement still to come. The most obsessing of all his prophecies was his prophecy of human flight—a prophecy that he himself strove vainly to fulfill. (p. 165)

> *Ernest Hatch Wilkins, "Luigi Pulci and Other Florentine Writers," in his* A History of Italian Literature, *Cambridge, Mass.: Harvard University Press, 1954, pp. 158-66.*

GIOVANNI GENTILE (essay date 1956)

[*In the following excerpt, Gentile postulates that Leonardo successfully integrated his skills as a scientist, artist, engineer, and philosopher, thereby gaining a more comprehensive scholastic perspective.*]

Leonardo, the "divine" Leonardo of the writers of the sixteenth century (like the "divine" Ariosto or the "divine" Michelangelo), is one of the most complete expressions of the Renaissance personality. His contemporaries felt vaguely that there was divinity in the creative power of Leonardo's artistic genius, a typical embodiment of the humanist ideal which was the most exquisite fruition of that marvelous age of poetry, intelligence, and indomitable energy of character. This ideal took form within life itself, after humanism had freed the most gifted individuals from every prejudice and arbitrary presupposition, and given them an unlimited confidence in their own powers and in the freedom of the spirit as capable of building its world for itself. But through life this ideal came to the light of consciousness, and became a meditated doctrine, a philosophy, a great faith that could direct life. Not only in art and the exercise of intelligence, but also in warfare and the winning of wealth and the building of the state by craft and force, things worthy of being called *virtù* (as they were in fact called), since they were truly a plenitude of human activity for ends transcending the individual, man idolized himself in a wondrous representation of a conscious power, as a creature able to solve the problem of his life and to be what he ought to be, starting from himself alone and relying only on himself. This was Machiavelli's faith as it was that of Leonardo. It was a faith in man, who is spirit, who is that being which is not naturally, but makes itself what it is by rising from itself by means of study, by means of will power, by means of persevering in study and will until it reaches the plane on which it wills to live, to conquer fortune, to establish itself, to gain honor.

It was a faith that multiplied the native vigor of the human individual and instilled into him an acute and persistent need for making the most of all his energies, for testing all his capabilities, for mastering all the instrumentalities that could add to his powers, for trying all the ways that opened out before him or that he could open up by his ingenuity and his determination to engage in every battle and win every victory over the surrounding hostile forces of nature and men. From this sprang an unquenchable thirst for knowledge and a proud dissatisfaction with all particular and limited knowledge, along with an irresistible desire to break down every barrier between theory and practice, science and art, thought and action. For this man, the child of humanism and the creator of the Renaissance, every action had to be a trial of thought in reality, in which it was to unfold and prove its worth; thought could be no mere impotent and inert contemplation shutting the mind within the narrow confines of the individual personality. Science was man's tool for founding that dominion of man over nature (*regnum hominis*) which Francis Bacon was to proclaim throughout all Europe as the great task of modern times. For man can never be at ease in his belief in his own liberty if he does not feel himself altogether as a being that cannot be split up in the dichotomy of theory and practice, which only an abstractly intellectualist and hence at least in tendency materialist philosophy can differentiate as two effectively distinct and divergent forms of human activity.

Unity of theory and practice—a Herbartian philosopher would call it many-sidedness of interests, and the writers of the Renaissance spoke of universality. The complete artist is not only a painter, not only a sculptor, not only an architect. He is if possible a poet, or at least a writer with a feeling for art. At the same time he is an engineer, whose point of departure is geometry, and who studies mechanics and hydraulics and propounds problems of every kind—in agriculture, in regard to soil improvement, in the art of war. The mathematical and physical sciences were just taking form at that time; their individual contours were not yet firm, and their distinction and connections both inchoate. He who took up one of them as a guiding light for his practical functioning became interested in all of them. All the arts and all the sciences, if they are to be learned deeply or touch the ideal, are intertwined inextricably and endow man's soul with a complex of varied interests, at that point in history bringing together in the breast of a single individual various urges which in more advanced and more analytical ages might reflect the spirits of artists and scientists of differing tempers and orientations. (pp. 163-64)

Leonardo's universality can be better understood if we go on from the threshold of the Renaissance, over which he towers like a colossal boundary statue set in the vestibule of those

times, and compare him with one of the great figures which tragically conclude that age—with Giordano Bruno or Tommaso Campanella, who likewise were universal geniuses, but oriented in a direction opposite to that in which Leonardo looks. He was artist principally, and a scientist in so far as he was an artist, by virtue of the problems to which the exercise of art gave rise in his restless and powerful intelligence. They were philosophers, constrained by the direction of their philosophizing to interest themselves in the most vital scientific problems of their times. At the same time, however, they were artists and poets; in their treatises, as in their poetry, there vibrates the intense emotion deriving from a certain deep mysterious sense of an immanent divinity that is their own very essence—a sense of Nature as divine, of Wisdom as absolute, of Truth as infinite. Just as in Leonardo the thinker (the scientist and philosopher) is contained in the artist, so in Bruno and Campanella there is, within the thinker, the poet. This is one of the characteristics of the epoch, and explains such a large part of Leonardo's mind as epitomizing the spirit of that glorious civilization.

There is a famous letter of Leonardo's calling to mind all those missives which Campanella wrote to popes, cardinals, and emperors during his imprisonment in the castles of Naples to ask their intercession in his favor, in order that he might at last, after so many tortures and sufferings, obtain his freedom and devote himself to their service with the ability and the enormous learning acquired in so many years of solitary meditation. And he makes long lists of the marvelous things he is able to do. Campanella's promises comprise great plans for religio-political action—a field that Leonardo does not enter. The difference between these documents of the Renaissance at its rise and at its decline is as significant historically as their similarity: for the passage of the Renaissance spirit from contemplation of nature to contest with historical (politico-religious) reality marks the beginning of the tragic end of that era.

The letter of Leonardo, to be found in the ***Codex Atlanticus,*** dates from 1483, when he had already taken up residence in Milan and wanted to have a settled place in the service of Ludovico il Moro. It presents the credentials of the candidate:

> Having now, Most Illustrious Lord, sufficiently seen and considered the proofs of all those who proclaim themselves masters and inventors of instruments of war, and finding that their inventions and use of the said instruments are nothing different from common practice, I am emboldened, without prejudice to anyone else, to put myself in communication with Your Excellency, in order to acquaint you with my secrets.

Finally, Leonardo recalls that he also has some ability applicable in times of peace:

> In time of peace I believe that I can give you as complete satisfaction as anyone else in architecture pertaining to the construction of buildings both public and private, and in conducting water from one place to another. Also, I can execute sculpture in marble, bronze, or clay, likewise painting, in which my work will stand comparison with that of anyone else, whoever he may be. Moreover, I would undertake the work of the bronze horse, which is to endue with immortal glory and eternal honor the auspicious memory of the Prince your father and the illustrious house of Sforza.

In the last sentence the writer's return to the center of his own personality, in which he feels his true greatness, lifts him to a loftier style, to a heightened self-consciousness. And the applicant does not hesitate to set himself above the potentate to whom he is addressing himself, and above his "illustrious house," from whom he does not expect honor, but upon whom rather he intends to confer it—eternal honor and immortal glory, such as only art can bestow. But in painting, as in every other art or technique to be used in war or peace, Leonardo is proudly aware that his work "will stand comparison with that of anyone else, whoever he may be." He knows that he can do everything in this field as no one else can.

Able to do everything—the effect of study, for no one believes in technique as much as he does, and in his *Treatise on Painting,* which does not even bring together everything that his reflection on his art suggests by way of precepts, there is the general theme of the science in his art. It is a logical corollary of the thoroughly humanistic and Renaissance notion of the divine nature of thought, which is identical in God and in the man who studies in order to rise above his immediate humanity; thus it is possible for man to investigate and reproduce within himself the secret processes by which the divine thought creates living nature, which man prompts and urges to live the outer life of art.

But Leonardo knows that study, reflection, and technique by themselves can only prepare art, not generate it: they are the condition of the creative process, which requires that more strictly and directly divine thing which moderns call genius, while Leonardo, using a no less suitable term, calls it *naturale,* which is in fact nature.

"Anyone who argues by referring to authority," he says, "is not using his mind but rather his memory. Sound learning is born of a sound spirit [*naturale*], and since the cause is more to be praised than the effect, I shall praise a sound spirit without learning more than someone well lettered but without spirit." And, being a man "without letters," he was content to be looked on as such, as long as the men of letters did not proceed from this to accuse him of not being able to say well that which he had to present. "Foolish folk! Do they not know what I am capable of, so that I might retort as Marius did to the Roman patricians by saying: 'They who deck themselves out in the labors of others will not allow me my own.'" Leonardo's manuscripts frequently wage a polemic against the bookish learning of erudite men content to be wise at second hand, strangers to the custom and desire of those who write well to return to the source, which is experience, namely, nature itself.

When he comes to speak of the power of his painting, he boasts as one who possesses a divine power:

> If the painter wishes to see beauties to fall in love with, he is master of producing them; and if he wishes to see monstrous things to terrify, or clownish and ridiculous things, or things that are truly moving, he is lord and god thereof. And if he wishes to produce desert places, groves shady and dark in hot seasons, he represents them, and likewise warm places in cold seasons. If he wants valleys, if he desires to disclose a great plain from the high summits of mountains, and if he desires thereafter to look on the horizon of the sea, he is the master, and likewise if from the low valleys he wishes to see the high mountains, or if he wants to view the low valleys and beaches from the high mountains. And what the universe contains by essence, presence, or

> imagination, he has first in his mind and then in his hands; and these are of such excellence that in equal time they generate a proportionate harmony in a single glance, as things themselves do.
>
> (pp. 164-67)

There are many such pages, both in the *Treatise on Painting* and in other writings of Leonardo's, in which the artist lends a helping hand to the thinker, as in this case, where it almost seems that in order better to convince himself and feel that deity characteristic of his science as a painter able to raise before the astonished eyes of men spectacles no less marvelous and sublime than those that nature offers us when it unleashes the fury of its elements, he is not content with theoretical assertions but exemplifies them and thus passes over to practice, and paints in broad strokes, even with the simple means of the ready word—whatever theories he may form in the abstract—no less powerfully than with the brush, receiving and remolding in eternal forms the fluid wave of his mighty fantasy. And the burning word dramatizes its own nature, and becomes a picture, which the painter, in a frenzy of his *naturale,* unfolds before us as seen and imaged by his inner eye. The eye that he endeavors to praise as the privileged organ of the art of arts—which for him is, above music and poetry, painting—is not really the material eye, but the eye of the mind, the divine fantasy in which the eye sees and in general the soul feels. Thus painting (and Leonardo knows this well) first evokes within the mind its figures and their movements and their expressions, and the landscape and the light and shade bathing it all with the art whose secret Leonardo possesses, because it can make itself hand and brush, and become a painting evoked in the fullness of its life and set down on the canvas or the wall.

This divinity of art which Leonardo feels within himself does not inhere in technique or reflection, although the richness of his experience in art and the reflective and speculative quality of his spirit led him to lay great weight on technique; it is rather a prerogative of that fortunate *naturale* which passes beyond study and every kind of knowledge to turn to nature itself. This is the world of Leonardo, as it was in general that of the man of the Renaissance, for the Neoplatonism of Ficino and the other Florentine thinkers had made familiar the idea that man is of a piece with nature, which is also possessed of a soul, since it is all divine, and essentially spiritual, as man surprises it in the inner pulsing of its consciousness, where it is concentrated and revealed.

This eternal and infinite nature is before the eyes of our senses and is in fact present in sense; from it all the normal life of the human spirit begins, although that spirit then goes forward with the mind, or reason, or judgment, which Leonardo well realizes is necessary for the completion of the cognitive act, into which sensation itself enters and in which it is reflected in the light of consciousness. But Leonardo mistrusts this judgment which, working on what is felt, is a source of error whenever it departs from the sensible datum; and above all he distrusts the argumentation of reason in the void, giving rise to empty sciences that start and finish in the mind, as Leonardo says, or a priori sciences, as we should say. For that which has to be known is not in the mind, but out there in nature, which to be sure is internally reason, as is found in the end, once it is known by means of our reason, with which natural reason converges. Hence the definitive form of knowledge, the end point aimed at, which is constructed by means of attentive examination of the effects of natural operation, derived from sensible experience, is rational knowledge.

Allegory of a boat, a wolf, and an eagle, drawn by Leonardo.

But reason, which is the starting point for nature, is the end point for us, who have first, to open our eyes, and observe, scrutinize, discover. Once the reason of the natural fact is understood, Leonardo says, experience is no longer required. But in order to arrive at the point where the reason is understood, we must open our eyes, and see, see.

He was indignant at those philosophers who consider much seeing as a distraction of thought, which calls for withdrawal.

> And if you will say that seeing hinders fixed and subtle mental cognition, which is the means of penetrating into divine sciences, and that this impediment led one philosopher to deprive himself of sight, the answer to this is that the eye, as master of the senses, does its duty in impeding false and confused, not sciences, but talk, the discussions that are always carried on with loud cries and gesturing with the hands. . . . And if that philosopher put out his eyes to remove the impediment to his discourses, the fact is that this action was a worthy companion to the brain and the discourses, for everything there was madness. Could he not have closed his eyes when he entered upon this frenzy, and kept them closed until the paroxysm had passed? But the man was mad and mad the discourse, and most idiotic was putting out his eyes.

Theology, metaphysics (as we should say), sciences of crotchets and authorities, sciences of "enthroned letters," as Leo-nardo calls them, are all stuff for friars—holy friars, but pharisees, as he says in a phrase that breaks from him at one point, to be lumped together with the astrologers, the alchemists, and the speculators on perpetual motion, and perhaps as well with the many who "trade in deceits and feigned miracles, deceiving the stupid multitude: and if anyone proves to have uncovered their deceit, they beat him."

There is irony in a note in the Quaderni di Anatomia: "I leave the definition of the soul in the minds of the friars, the fathers of the people, who know all secrets by instigation. Let enthroned letters alone, for they are highest truth." This parallels the disdain with which, in the ***Codex Atlanticus,*** Leonardo compares the originality of inventors and direct interpreters of nature with the mechanical relations of the "reciters and trumpets of the works of others." There is as great a difference, he exclaims, "as between the object outside of the mirror and the image of that object appearing in the mirror: the one is something in itself, and the other is nothing. Men who owe little to nature, since it is only by accident that they wear clothing, and otherwise could be classed among the herds of beasts."

As an admonition he writes: "O wretched mortals, open your eyes."

His assiduous uninterrupted labor of observation every day, even on festival days, scandalized some people. And he reacted with bitter sarcasm:

There is among the number of the foolish a certain sect called hypocrites, who constantly strive to deceive themselves and others, but others more than themselves: yet actually they deceive themselves more than others. It is they that reprove painters who study on holy days, on matters concerning the true knowledge of all figures that the works of nature have, and eagerly strive to acquire that knowledge so far as they are able.

He rises up against this brood of hypocrites with all his proud awareness of the religious nature of his tireless study of nature:

> But let these reprovers be silent, for this is the way of knowing the performer of so many wonderful works, and this is the way of loving so great an inventor! For in truth great love is born of great knowledge of the thing loved: and if you did not know it, you could not love it, or could love it but little. And if you love it for the good you expect to get from it, and not for its sublime virtue, you are acting like a dog that wags his tail and fawns before someone who can give him a bone. But if the virtue of that man were known, he would love him much more, if that virtue served his designs.

This was the religion of the Renaissance, which sought God in nature. Hence, to fix his glance on natural things was Leonardo's perpetual longing and joy. It was an anxious longing, as he expressed it in a symbolic representation of nature and in the trembling, careful scrutiny with which he explored it:

> The stormy sea does not roar so loud when from the north Aquilo strikes it with foaming waves between Scylla and Charybdis, nor Stromboli or Mongibello when the sulphurous flames shut up within them break forth and open up the great mountain, and throw into the air rocks and earth, together with the flame they vomit; nor when the glowing caverns of Mongibello, vomiting forth again the ill-contained element and urging it to its own region, furiously drive before them every obstacle that comes in the way of their impetuous fury. . . . Drawn by my eager wish, desirous of seeing the great confusion of the various strange forms created by ingenious nature, I wandered for some time among the shadowed cliffs, and came to the entrance of a great cavern. I remained before it for a while, stupefied, and ignorant of the existence of such a thing, with my back bent and my left hand resting on my knee, and shading my eyes with my right, with lids lowered and closed, and often bending this way and that to see whether I could discern anything within; but this was denied me by the great darkness inside. And after I had stayed a while, suddenly there arose in me two things, fear and desire—fear because of the menacing dark cave, and desire to see whether there were any miraculous thing within.

This is religious terror. The keenness of that marvelous eye which Leonardo, whether writing or painting, casts on nature cannot suffice to quench his insatiable thirst for knowledge. His glance lights on all the surfaces of living things, perceives their constant motion, catches every vibration, adhering to and moving with the object, almost merging with it. Whether the object be near or far, in an unending perspective, in a living light that also moves and trembles and plays with the shadow, he takes advantage of the circumstance to illuminate it by veiling it with gradations of shading that are light and shadow at once, in a velvety delicacy of surface. When we

read the minute and yet vivid description of trees moved by the wind, and of the branches, and of the leaves and the flowers, and of the ground in which they are planted, and of the rocky background against which they stand out in a complex which the words analyze and embrace and hold close in a living nexus, we behold the restless mind and the anguish of the artist who strives by means of his numberless sketches and drawings and notes to retrace the infinite path that nature has run to attain any one of its slightest effects. And on this path, what man ever labored as much as Leonardo? But he knew well that there is one thing "that is not given, and if it were given would not be," namely, the infinite, "which would be limited and finite if it were given, for that which can be given has a boundary with the thing that surrounds it at its ends, and that which cannot be given is that thing which does not have ends."

Untiringly he follows up the unattainable idea. "O Leonardo, why do you labor so?" he says on a folio of the *Codex Atlanticus.* And in a prayer he turns to God with these sad words: "Thou, O God, sellest us all good things at the price of labor." His motoes are of this sort: *Sine lassitudine;* "Death before weariness. No work shall tire me. I do not grow weary of serving." And his warning runs: "A life well spent is long. Just as a day well spent gives grateful sleep, so a life well employed gives grateful death." Campanella's great imperative, "Think, man, think," is anticipated in Leonardo's severe judgment, "He who thinks little errs much." Thinking—this is "serving" as one should, up to death. And not sleeping; for "sleep resembles death," and one should act "in such a way that after death you resemble one completely alive" rather than "living make oneself by sleep like unto the gloomy dead." Memory conquers time, and the glory of imperishable works conquers death.

But what works are imperishable? Do not perfect works also require an infinity that will assure them immortality? And is this infinity at least given? Even if Leonardo had not expressed his thought in a single note, there could be no doubt that his answer would be negative. But in fact he has written memorable words on the inevitable dissatisfaction of every excellent author with respect to his own work. Every master, it is known, must be surpassed by his disciple: "It is a sorry disciple that does not go beyond his master." But the master himself, if he realizes what art is—how can he help feeling sadness in face of his work, when he sees it falling below his ideal? "It is a sorry master whose work surpasses his judgement; and that master tends toward the perfection of art whose work is surpassed by his judgment." At bottom such a man will always retain a doubt, a discontent, a desire for something better. "The painter who does not doubt achieves little. When the work surpasses the judgment of the worker, that worker achieves little; and when the judgment surpasses the work, that work never ceases to improve, if injury does not supervene."

This discontent was therefore not flightiness, as Leonardo's contemporaries sometimes whispered among themselves, nor was it a result of "caprices," as Vasari says. Rather, it was due to that divergence between idea and hands to which Vasari himself refers: "It is obvious that Leonardo, because of his knowledge of the art, began many things, and never finished any, for it seemed to him that the hand could not attain the perfection of art in the things that he imagined—since in his idea he formed certain subtle difficulties so marvelous that hands, no matter how excellent, could never have expressed them." This was the necessary consequence of the conception that Leonardo had, and had to have, of art, of human thought, and of nature, which he followed so closely. This is the secret cause of his travail ("O Leonardo, why do you labor so?"), and hence of the dispersion of the powerful vigor of his activity, as well as of the shadow of melancholy that suffuses the creations of his art.

It is a mysterious melancholy rising from the soul of the artist anxious for light and fascinated by mystery, divided between the sense of the divine in nature, which is unity and life and is essentially spirit, as nature was felt to be by the man of the Renaissance, once Ficinian Platonism had enlarged the capacity of his breast, with its boldness and its faith in human freedom, to a sense of the infinite life in which his individual soul expands into the breast of nature—and the concept of the unattainability in concepts of that universal unity, since nature is known only by way of sense experience. And this is shown through a numerable multiplicity, susceptible of mathematical treatment, which Leonardo was among the first to proclaim, anticipating the canons of Galilean science, which is modern science. It is a multiplicity that can be ordered in a closed and fixed system, necessary and mechanically invariable, according to causal relationship, which is nothing but the factual connection between the condition and the conditioned, capable of endowing the totality with the mechanistic character proper to the single elements—the character of the fact that exists, though we do not know how or why. Science grows and the unknown grows.

The little facts, whose number is infinite, become an enormous fact enveloped in the same darkness as each minutest object of the initial observation. Why? How? Questions without a reply.

Science must silence these questions. From Galileo's day on, rigorous scientific method has rejected such questions as undue and illegitimate, and limited itself consciously to what are called appearances, or phenomena (as they were later to be termed) of nature—that is, to the surface. But Leonardo, while looking to such an ideal of scientific knowledge, cannot be satisfied with the surface. His keen unsleeping eye penetrates deeper; and when observation, the experience that is so greatly praised and exalted, no longer serves him, he intuits or evokes the inner life, the secret soul setting in motion the great machine that he has taken apart and studied piece by piece, watching, espying, scrutinizing, by means of mathematics, mechanics, anatomy, and every instrument that might enable him to follow the operations of nature step by step.

The painter, the artist, seeks and glimpses the infinite from afar; the scientist, who would wish to introduce into painting the certainty of facts and of the external manifestations of the All, and rigorously measure and count—*pondere numero et mensura*—whatever can be observed, strives to confine himself within limits. The unity of the inward illuminates the fantasy; and the intellect comes to break up this unity into the endless multiplicity of sensible appearances.

Hence the anguish and the innermost tragedy of this universal man, divided between two irreconcilable worlds. Hence the desperate lifelong labor of this implacable self-torturer, whose marvelous work of gleaming phantasms of art, spread from full hands day by day on paper, on canvas, and on storied walls, and of precise concepts and inspired researches which in many fields of scientific knowledge are portentous

anticipations of the future, leaves in the mind an infinite longing, made up as it were of regret and sadness. It is the longing for a Leonardo different from the Leonardo that he was, one who could have gathered himself up at each phase and remained closed himself off either altogether in his fantasy or altogether in his intelligence, in order to taste the pure joy of divine creation. It is an anguished longing such as always welled up in Leonardo's heart each time that he put down his brush, his charcoal, or his rod, or had to break off setting down his secret thoughts.

Secret thoughts—and on this account entrusted to that most singular handwriting which Leonardo was pleased to use, as if in despite of anything easy and usual, that mirror writing which was to hinder the profane from setting eyes at once on his thoughts. He felt that he was thinking for himself, to bring together bit by bit the materials for the works that, once they had come to maturity in the fullness of their being, and hence in the logical and persuasive coherence of their elements, could come to light like the bodies generated by nature that are brought to birth when their time has come. (pp. 168-74)

> *Giovanni Gentile, "Leonardo's Thought," in* Leonardo da Vinci, *Reynal & Company, 1956, pp. 163-74.*

MARK J. TEMMER   (essay date 1966)

[*Temmer is an American essayist and academic. In the following excerpt, he explores Leonardo's polemical attacks on poets, appraising the poetic nature of the prose in the* Notebooks *as well.*]

Admittedly, the subject-matter cannot be sharply defined, for the very universality of Leonardo's genius precludes the use of clear-cut categories. It is, to be sure, permissible to approach his character and achievements from the viewpoints of the arts and sciences in which he excelled, be they anatomy, engineering, painting, sculpture or literature. However, the latter, chosen as a point of departure in our appreciation of the artist, is a discipline which he held to be secondary in importance. Were this contempt expressed by a lesser man, it would be ignored, inasmuch as indictments of this kind often conceal weakness and prejudice. But in the case of Leonardo the flaws are not apparent, and his scorn for poets must therefore be likened to that of Plato whose writings abound with invectives against the fancies of poetry. Yet, it is well known that the *Dialogues* live on not only by virtue of their perennial truth, but also because of the excellence of their form. And whereas for most artists, Buffon's critical principle, *le style c'est l'homme,* has a restrictive value, that is, delineates the limits of their talents, this criterion becomes in the case of Plato and Leonardo a possible means to venture hypotheses concerning universal minds whose thoughts are not limited by stylistic or formal impediments. Thus, an analysis of Leonardo's attitude concerning literature might shed some light on the proverbial mystery of his personality as well as stress the extraordinary self-sufficiency of his psyche, seemingly untroubled by turbid emotions and disordered thoughts. This, at least, is Valéry's conclusion:

> What could be more alluring than a God who repudiates mystery, who does not erect his authority on the troubles of our nature, nor manifest his glories to what is most obscure, sentimental, sinister in us? Who forces us to agree rather than to submit, whose mystery is self-elucidation, whose depth an

admirable calculated perspective. Is there a better sign of authentic and legitimate power than that it does not operate from behind a veil? Never had Dionysus an enemy more decided, or one so pure or so armored with lights as this hero, who was less concerned to rend and destroy dragons than to examine the springs of their activity; disdaining to riddle them with arrows when he could riddle them with questions: their superior rather than vanquisher, he represents less an assured triumph over them than perfect comprehension of them—he understood them almost to the point of being able to reconstruct them; and once he had grasped the principle at work, he could leave them, having mockingly reduced them to the mere category of special cases and explained paradoxes.

This admirable analysis, probably inspired by Valéry's youthful confrontation with Kant's philosophy, stresses the lucidity of Leonardo's supposedly impersonal genius, but fails to discover the heart of the matter by neglecting Leonardo, the experimentalist, and above all, Leonardo the poet. True, one may assert that his use of language is *instrumental,* that his words are functions of his mind. However, they are also essences, having value in and for themselves—a fact abundantly stressed by Fumagalli and Momigliano. Thus, while concerning himself to some degree with belletristic effects, he describes everything—muscles, vertebrae, the nature of water, thunderbolts, the structure of the walnut tree—with a passionate precision and intellectual elegance that has only been equaled by Pascal. Paradoxically, Leonardo holds that the picture is superior to the word, since the former embodies the eternal form of things, while the latter, that is, the word, is limited in its usefulness by the linguistic borders of any given language. Such are the views expounded in his *Comparison of the Arts*. . . . (pp. 34-6)

Leonardo's comparision . . . lauds the unchanging aspects of pictorial form at the expense of the descriptive and supposedly transitory nature of poetry, making no references whatsoever to the moral, esthetic and metaphysical themes of the great Italian poets. Thus, the *Divine Comedy* tells the story of the soul, which from form to form, from appearance to appearance finds itself and recognizes itself in God, in pure intelligence and in pure love. Similarly, Petrarch's *Canzoniere,* the first great work of the Renaissance, attempts to immortalize the poet's love for Laura. Indeed, it is this very act of symbolic transcendence—the essence of the poetic act—which Leonardo transforms into a pretext for a pun: "If Petrarch loved the laurel so much it was because it is good with sausages and thrushes; I don't attach any value to their [poets'] trifles." His interest focuses on experience and he disregards ostensibly though not actually the spiritual transfiguration of human activities. Love, a major theme of fifteenth century Italian literature, art and metaphysics, is reduced to its bare anatomy, to a series of preposterous and monstrous acts. "Love in its fury," he states, "is a thing so ugly that the human race would die out—*la natura si perderebbe*—if those engaged in it were to see themselves." His notebooks make no mention of Dante, save for one quotation, or Boccaccio, nor do they quote Lorenzo the Magnificent, whose poem "The Triumph of Bacchus and Ariana" (Quant'é bella giovinezza / che si fugge tuttavia!) suggests a conception of time quite similar to da Vinci's evocations of the temporal flow. There is no reference to the songs of Poliziano and an understandable silence concerning the sonnets written by his rival Michelangelo. Since Leonardo was acquainted with major lit-

erary figures of his age, such as Bramante and perhaps Poliziano, and surely aware of the existence of the others, his disinterest and, more important, his polemical attacks against poets in general—he refers to them as braggarts (*trombetti*)—are as significant as they are baffling.

Before attempting to account for Leonardo's "poetic refusal" of poetry, one should cast a glance at the milieu in which he spent his formative years. Brought up in Florence during the second part of the fifteenth century, Leonardo decides to look at things the way they are, "le cose come sono," poetically, pictorially and scientifically, initiating as well as reinforcing naturalistic and experimental trends in European thought. Disdainful of Neoplatonic dreams, he returns, as it were, to Plato, maintaining a viewpoint that is both Idealist and Positivist. In the words of Momigliano, the intent of his entire artistic prose is spiritual; his naturalistic studies, a part of the experimental current of his age. In order to recognize relationships of Leonardian thoughts with Neoplatonism, it is not necessary to trace them in detail, but to mind the mood of his poetic prose, which reveals his need of transcendence in his most careful consideration of the reality of nature. "There is in his prose," writes Momigliano, "a mysterious quality which makes us sense his affinities with the Neoplatonists as well as with the followers of the occult sciences whom he despised (cf. his essays on alchemy and necromancy) which, although censorious of such activities, betray a fantasy avid of what is marvelous."

In view of his poetico-scientific inclinations, how is one to explain his polemical attacks against poets? In the first place, his attack against poetry stems from his desire to give painting the same status as that enjoyed by the humanities. (pp.37-9)

Where there is soliloqy, there is silence, the *sine qua non* of *poésie pure* or pure poetry so admirably defined by Baudelaire in his "Invitation au Voyage" as being the "mother tongue of the soul." Incited by his musical inclinations, Leonardo animates his prose with a pulsating rhythm. However, his gift to sense what is supernatural, marvelous, reveals itself solely when he observes nature, or when he imagines miracles conceived by his love of nature, or, when this attraction to, and predilection of, the supernatural, quasi surrealistic modalities of life, express themselves in intellectual terms: the texture, the solidity, the complexity of matter, and the sure mastery he enjoys over it, enjoin him to seek expressions that are fresh and spontaneous instead of having to have recourse to the rigid patterns of the Petrarchistic school and of classical prose writers. In the words of Momigliano: "The perfect literary achievements of Leonardo may be found in the circle of his thoughts and *pensieri.*" Fumagalli has analyzed subtly their syntactical structure which reflects the living process of his reflections: "Elliptical and anacoluthic phrases abound, . . . phrases, propelled by the impetuous motion of his thoughts that are impatient to be translated into words and yet hostile towards formalism." Consideration of this kind may help to discover the unity in his disparate prose—a unity whose formulation must remain as problematical as that of Pascal's *Thoughts.* Certain it is that whenever his observations of natural phenomena assume artistic form, one senses a corresponding *élan* or aspiration that invests "these things" with a radiance characteristic of his drawings. However, to assert like Fumagalli that he is more of a poet in his prose than in his paintings seems to us both ambiguous and exaggerated. More just, and more relevant, it would appear, are Momigliano's remarks concerning the effects and "consequent defects" of this extraordinary discrepancy. He speaks of "strident oscillations between systematic observation and caressing design brought about by moments of poetic temptations." Commenting on this supposedly unresolved dichotomy, Momigliano allows himself the pleasure of prudent criticism behind which lurk the spectres of Vasari and Croce: "Here we approach the very limits of Leonardo's writings. All that we said in his favor, need be defined in a precise manner. Much of his prose, or at least part of it, is arrested in its thrust at the auroral moment of the concession, perhaps because Leonardo, the observer, was impeded and diverted by the poet just as the poet was hindered by the observer."

Regardless of whether or not one subscribes to this view, it is fitting to recall Jean Guéhenno's admonition "On ne critique pas un chef-d'oeuvre." Bearing it in mind, we shall examine some of his prose passages in a manner which, in view of the synoptic nature of this essay, can only be exemplary. Thus, one of his finest combinations of creative analysis and style in language is his definition of Force in which the invisible activity of a cosmic power is uniquely visualized:

> Force I define as an incorporeal agency, an invisible power, which, by means of unforeseen external pressure, is caused by the movement stored up and diffused within bodies which are withheld and turned aside from their natural uses; imparting to these an active life of marvelous power, it constrains all created things to change of form and position, and hastens furiously to its desired death, changing as it does according to circumstances. When it is slow, its strength is increased, and speed enfeebles it. It is born in violence and dies in liberty; and the greater it is, the more quickly it is consumed. It drives away in fury whatever opposes its destruction. It desires to conquer and slay the cause of opposition, and in conquering destroys itself.

Thus, in his method of representation, Leonardo utilizes words and imagery to relate abstract ideas to concrete experience in a manner that foreshadows the tumultuous prose of the German Idealists. Like Hegel, Leonardo invests his world-view with a dramatic and at times ironic mood: all is conquest and defeat and the impersonal fury of primordial powers, awesome to behold.

His genius for correlating prose, drawing, and experimental science is well illustrated by two drawings dating from between 1513 and 1515, which are complemented by a passage of the same period intended for the *Treatise on Painting* in which Leonardo explains how to paint the picture of the Deluge. The description falls into two parts: on one side of the page he evokes a visionary account of the annihilation of all creatures in a desperate struggle with the elements; on the other, an equally masterly piece of objective prose one finds a scientific account and physical explanation of the various natural phenomena to be portrayed. . . . These visions of total destruction find equally strong expression in Leonardo's meditations on time, an Italian version of Ovid's *Metamorphoses:*

> O time, thou that consumest all things! O envious age, thou destroyest all things and devourest all things with the hard teeth of the years, little by little, in slow death! Helen when she looked in her mirror and saw the withered wrinkles which old age had made in her face, wept, and wondered to herself why ever she had twice been carried away.

Here, Leonardo achieves perfect style, whose beauty does not depend on improvisation, but on a syntax, whose articulations are governed by feeling, by a driving and tragic design that points to aspirations engendered by melancholy. "Nor are we led astray," writes Momigliano, "by the fascination of that voice which speaks with profound sentiment and high dignity, yet devoid of romantic languor and pomp, of the sadness of life"—of a life that escapes us, intangible, leaving nonetheless in our souls a residue of meaning and regret.

Such depth of feeling is unusual for Leonardo, whose will tends to circumvent or resolve the problem of emotions that lead to sorrow, affliction, and intellectual stagnation: "Where there is the most power of feeling, there of martyrs is the greatest martyr." His proverbial impassivity appears even more enigmatic if one considers the emotional contrast between his pictorial art and his prose. While one encounters suppressed emotion in the latter, his drawings and paintings reveal overt and tender understanding of man and his world. Could it be that his tenderness did not surge from his passions, but from his intellect, that the source of his love was not the womb, but the mind? (pp. 40-4)

In addition to his essays in poetico-scientific prose, Leonardo cultivated the genre of the allegory. He compiled a bestiary, one of his largest pieces of organized prose, in which he draws on Pliny as well as on fanciful medieval authors to whom natural history was but a pretext for moral allegory. His crocodile, symbol of hypocrisy, exemplifies the curiously impersonal quality of his allegorical imagination.

> This animal seizes a man and instantly kills him and after he is dead, it mourns for him with a piteous voice and many tears, and having ended its lament it cruelly devours him. It is thus with the hypocrite, whose face is bathed in tears over every slight thing, showing himself thus to have the heart of a tiger, he rejoices in his heart over another's misfortunes with a face bedecked with tears.

Closely allied to this bestiary, and inspired by similar sources, are the fables scattered throughout the *Codice Atlantico.* Although most of them appear to be derivative, they have, when interpreted as a whole, a certain unity in terms of mood and ideas. Almost all are pessimistic and Freud comments with unwitting humor that they are "to a striking degree" devoid of humor. Objects, plants, and animals, which assume the roles of protagonists, are no sooner confident of success than then are destroyed by some superior and implacable agent. Whenever they escape misfortune, they immediately fall victim to a far greater disaster that results from previous cunning. The fable of the mirror (a talisman in Leonardo's thought) tells of such vainglory and ensuing disenchantment. "The mirror bears itself proudly, holding the queen mirrored within it, and after she has departed, the mirror remains abject."

Few of these fables, writes Momigliano, are successful. And the critic goes on to observe: "Often the choice of motives is not felicitous, especially whenever Leonardo abandons the subject-matter of animals and attempts to attribute to them characteristics belonging to another reign or to things themselves. . . . Too often, his fables remain unfinished or formulated according to a plan that is too sketchy and which does not do justice to his melancholic or dramatic intent." The critic could have added that Leonardo's love of silence necessarily impedes the development of dialogue so essential to this *genre mineur.* Generally speaking, one might also consider the possibility that Leonardo shared the Italian reluctance to "reduce" man to the level of animals, that the humanistic passion that permeates the Renaissance prevented the development of the apologue on a high literary level although, to be sure, medieval fabulistic trends manifest themselves occasionally on the regional level. Viewing the problem historically, one could speculate that the collapse of the Hohenstauffen dynasty diminished possible interaction with, and borrowing from, the Franco-German fabular tradition exemplified by *Le Roman du Renart* which finds classical expression in La Fontaine's *Fables.* One could add parenthetically as well as paradoxically that the best fabulist of the *Cinquecento* is Bassano just as in our age, regardless of poets like Saba, Supervielle, and Thurber, the loveliest metamorphoses have been wrought by the magic of Picasso and Chagall.

The most personal of Leonardo's emblematic writings is a series entitled **Prophecies.** They are cast in a form popular among the wits of Milan, and we are told that these prophecies were written in competition with those of Bramante. Everyday happenings are worded to sound like appalling disasters. Thus, "The masters of estates will eat their own laborers," to which the author supplies the explanation "Of oxen which are eaten". Another example, more bitter in it sense, bears the title "Of Sculpture": "Alas! whom do I see? The Savior crucified again." Other prophecies, neither ironic nor witty, foreshadow times to come. The one entitled "Of Dreaming" is apocalyptic in mood, and the poetic power of its vision, manifest. Leonardo, derider of poets, reveals himself a *vates,* a seer, who, unable or unwilling to engage in dialogue with his fellow-men, forsakes the present in favor of fantastic dimensions to exhaust his anguish and dreams:

> It shall seem to men that they see new destructions in the sky, and the flames descending therefrom shall seem to have taken flight and to flee away in terror; they shall hear creatures of every kind speaking human language; they shall run in a moment, in person, to divers parts of the world without movement; amidst the darkness they shall see the most radiant splendors. O marvel of mankind: What frenzy has thus impelled you.

(pp. 46-8)

Mark J. Temmer, "Leonardo da Vinci's Poetic Prose," in Italian Quarterly, *Vol. 10, Nos. 36 & 37, Winter-Spring, 1966, pp. 34-50.*

AUGUSTO MARINONI   (lecture date 1966)

[*Marinoni is an Italian essayist and academic. In the following excerpt from a lecture delivered in 1966 as part of an international symposium on "Leonardo's Legacy," he distinguishes variations in Leonardo's writing style.*]

The fame of Leonardo as a writer—if we can speak of real fame—remained for some centuries limited to the **Treatise on Painting,** which was in great demand and deeply appreciated by the artists of the sixteenth and seventeenth centuries. A medal struck about the middle of the eighteenth century can be considered a symbol and synthesis of this fame; it bears Leonardo's head on the obverse and a crown, a pen, and the words *scribit quam suscitat artem* on the reverse. This means that Leonardo was considered as great a writer and theorist on art as he was an artist. Yet when real men of letters, not artists, set about examining Leonardo's original writings with the intention of publishing them, their disappointment was

keen. At first Ludovico Antonio Muratori and Antonio David, and later the professors of the University of Pavia, after examining Leonardo's papers, expressed their dismay at that chaotic mass of fragmentary notes which they judged absolutely unfit for publication. Antonio David, though convinced that Leonardo had written books and treatises, refused to identify them with those manuscripts. Muratori declared them "a barren field." Apart from the wonderful drawings, he considered the notes to be too few and, besides, not sufficiently explanatory. Later on, Padre Fontana, in his unfavorable report on Leonardo's writings, complained again of the lack of proof. In other words, if language is an instrument of communication, it cannot be said that Leonardo's language is so, according to Fontana, because it fails to communicate the author's thought. And this seems to be a completely negative judgment.

In the nineteenth century Venturi, Bossi, Manzi, Libri, and others showed greater confidence and even enthusiasm, but for the novelty of Leonardo's scientific thought more than his literary expression. Only in our century has Leonardo been held in increasing esteem as a writer, after the great romantic revolution had destroyed many formal prejudices and had predisposed men's minds to accept even a splintered and fragmentary work. The situation has even been reversed at times, because at the very point where Leonardo's expression fails to communicate his thought many have yielded to the fascination of the riddle and abandoned themselves to the most arbitrary conjectures.

Leonardo's "The Condottiere," believed by some scholars to be a self-portrait.

The generation that lived in the last years of the nineteenth century and the first years of the twentieth bequeathed us a mythological image of Leonardo. Both the enthusiasm aroused by the discovery of the manuscripts, which had lain hidden and unpublished for so many centuries, and the ignorance of the actual state of medieval scientific thought contributed to the creation of this image. A deeper knowledge of the cultural environment in which Leonardo lived and worked, together with a deeper and more analytical scrutiny of the actual contents of Leonardo's writings, has brought about a revision of that myth. This revision, instead of destroying Leonardo's greatness, has freed it from many ridiculous misconceptions. If it is true, as Leonardo says, that love derives from knowledge, we think we love Leonardo more than he was loved by his blind admirers of the past, especially because, having a deeper knowledge of the man and his limits, we can base our admiration on surer foundations. Even from the literary point of view, Leonardo as a writer has been judged in different ways; some critics maintain he was the founder of Italian scientific prose, while others deny this. Some are inclined to consider him one of the greatest Italian writers, while others put him among the minor ones. I think it is possible to clear up this problem by carrying out an analytical examination of Leonardo's style.

We may consider as a starting point for our research the *Codex B,* which is the oldest of Leonardo's *Codici* that can be dated. In this Leonardo piles up, without any order, drawings of arms, machines, fortifications, civil and sacred buildings, accompanied by some short explanations and others less short; or he transcribes, with a summary, certain passages from the *De Re Militari* of Valturio. In all these writings there are very scanty traces of an attempt at style, of any particular attention to rhythm, to the sound of words, to their position in the sentence, or even to the syntactical structure of the period. The practical and utilitarian purpose of this type of writing, which aims at fixing rules and standards for the activity of an artist, only requires brevity and conciseness, and not always clarity since it is not intended for the common reader. The more usual form of expression is the independent clause, which is as simple as possible: "Il pié dalla punta al calcagno, entra due volte"; "A la Fama si de' dipigniere tutta la persona. . . ." The verb often has the peremptory form of the imperative or of the commanding future. The main clause is often connected with a subordinate conditional one which expresses the circumstance in which one must execute the order given. And this is precisely one of the most frequent syntagma used. . . . There is a prevalence of simple propositions, sometimes accompanied by one subordinate proposition. Generally no care has been taken to compose these simple periods into a harmonic whole. When the speech exceeds the usual limits of brevity, Leonardo does not think of varying the phrasing in order to avoid monotony, but, following the rhythm of oral speech, directed to a practical end, he links one proposition to the other with a sequence of "ands." . . . . We can say that the typical phrasing of Leonardo in this sort of writing is generally linear, but disharmonious, that is, it is made up of one or more straight segments, one after the other, which do not join together so as to form any design. The extremely simple vocabulary, too, is made up of the usual names of the objects described and of their parts, a language that, unaided by the imagination, remains purely technical. It is used by a craftsman who is writing for himself what are absolutely private notes.

Yet there are at least two points where Leonardo's words have an unusual depth and energy. In folio 4*r* he fights against the belief in *spiriti* or ghosts, and he sums up in a few lines a speech that will be developed more fully in another paper. Here we can trace unusual stylistic care. The sentences are simple and short, of the usual rectilinear type. Yet they are repeated three times, identical at the beginning and varied at the end, with a concentration of energy that shows itself in the rapid conclusion: "non pò essere voce dove non è movimento e percussione d'aria; non pò essere percussione d'aria dove non è strumento, non pò essere strumento incorporeo. Essendo così, uno spirito non pò avere né voce, né forma, né forza; e piglierà corpo, non potrà penetrare né entrare dove li usci sono serrati." In this way the few uniform sentences have a unitary rhythmic and musical structure, which derives from insistent repetition and from parrellelism of the opposed parts. Instead of developing the thread of his thought on a wide canvas with subtle and progressive argumentations Leonardo arrives at a vigorous and definite conclusion immediately. But, to tell the truth, he does nothing but fix the most important subjects of a theme which he intends to develop more widely. Therefore even here he is writing for himself.

The second point concerns one of the deepest themes of Leonardo's cosmology: the definition of Force. The definition is so solemn as to require the use of latinizing forms. . . . The same concepts are developed in the *Codex Atlanticus* in a still more interesting page. Force is defined in a series of bare sentences grammatically detached, yet connected by so insistent a rhythm as to transform them into a kind of biblical hymn, almost like the verses of a psalm.

> Tardità la fa grande e prestezza la fa debole.—Vive per violenza e more per libertà.—Trasmuta e costrigne ogni corpo a mutazione di sito e di forma.—Gran potenza le dà desiderio di morte.—Scaccia con furia ciò che s'oppone a sua ruina.—Trasmutatrice di varie forme.—Sempre vive con disagio di chi la tiene.—Sempre si contrapone ai naturali desideri.—Da piccola con tardità s'amplifica, e fassi d'una orribile e maravigliosa potenza.—E costrignendo se stessa ogni cosa costrigne.

It is not a logical discourse, but the enunciation of experimental facts that have, however, the solemnity of an epic poem and the strength of dogmatic truths. The impression is one, not of scientific prose, but of a sudden lyrical outburst.

In many pages of the *Codex B* Leonardo transcribes or summarizes certain parts of the *De Re Militari* of Valturio, which he read in Ramusio's bad translation. The quickening spirit of this book is clearly humanistic. Though the author intends to turn the military experience of the ancients to his contemporaries' advantage, the admiration and love for the classical world is so striking as to take the reader back through the centuries, as if the world had stopped its course in that age. In every line the author talks of ancient writers and figures as if they were alive: Quintilian, Caesar, Vitruvius, Plutarch, Xenophon, and even the smallest facts concerning their lives and sayings are mentioned with eager curiosity. Leonardo read the book from a different point of view. In his letter to Ludovico il Moro he said he knew every aspect of military engineering, both on land and sea. Each paragraph in that letter corresponds to parts or chapters of the *De Re Militari,* and this may be sufficient to demonstrate with what deep interest Leonardo consulted that book. When Valturio speaks of a weapon he dwells on the etymology of its name, on the passages of the authors who give us information about it, on when and how it was invented, but he fails to describe the weapon itself in detail. On the contrary, Leonardo's first concern is to make a drawing of it, so taking the first step toward its concrete realization. Yet the immense humanistic vitality of that book is not completely lost. In no other manuscript of Leonardo do we find the quotations from ancient authors so numerous and so detailed; which leads us to suspect that at least for once Leonardo wanted to try the method of contemporary men of letters and "allegare gli altori" or adorn himself with other men's labors. (pp. 57-60)

Leonardo already had the intention of becoming a writer himself, and, while reading that book, he must have realized the insufficiency of his own vocabulary, rich in technical words but poor in those abstract ones that all writers with a deep knowledge of Latin were continually transferring from the ancient language of Rome to their own vulgar tongue, so enriching and ennobling it. Leonardo thought it possible to obtain directly from these books, translated from the Latin, that lexical wealth which others were able to draw directly from the Latin language. And he began transcribing from these books thousands and thousands of words, which were in those days called *vocaboli latini* and which are Latinisms. The technical terminology that he had learned in the artisan shops was rich but tied to the everyday things. The *vocaboli latini* that Leonardo learned to "derive," as he called it, were more flexible and more suited to the expression of ideas and sentiments, that is to say, the objects of thought. A few years later he attempted a more radical solution of the problem, studying Latin directly from Perotti's grammar. He filled several pages of the **Codices H** and **I** with verbal conjugations, declensions, and syntactical schemes. But this attempt, which was soon interrupted, did not have any visible results.

The **Codex Trivulziano,** in which Leonardo made copious lists of about nine thousand *vocaboli latini,* was written a short time after the **Codex B** and shares a common characteristic: it contains a confused mass of personal notes, devoid of any literary value. Yet on folio 6*r* it gives us a famous evocative and enigmatic passage:

> Muovesi l'amante per la cos'amata come il senso e la sensible e con seco s'unisce e fassi una cosa medesima.—L'opera è la prima cosa che nasce dell'unione.—Se la cosa amata è vile, l'amante si fa vile.—Quando la cosa unita è conveniente al suo unitore, li seguita dilettazione e piacere e sadisfazione.—Quando l'amante è giunto all'amato, lì si riposa.—Quando il peso è posato, lì si riposa.—La cosa cogniusciuta col nostro intelletto.

The meaning of these seven propositions is not immediately clear. They are preceded by three words, which probably belong to this passage: "Sugietto colla forma." I think that the whole passage deals with the Aristotelian relationship between substance and form, that is, between power and act, from which motion derives. But it also deals with the Neoplatonic concept of "appetite," which, said Ficino, is an "inclinatio ab indigentia quadam adnitens ad plenitudinem." The appetite which drives the lover toward his beloved and the heavy object to come to rest is the same as that which drives the mind toward the joyful completeness of knowledge. This theory of ours has been formulated because we consider it to be implicit in the seven sentences of Leonardo; it is a theory that, were it actually developed by Leonardo, would involve the reader in the coils of his dialectics. But Leonardo, who is only speaking for himself, is not concerned with clearing up logical connections: he is only enunciating certain transparent truths with linear and parallel statements. But the parallelism and the symmetry of each part constitute a rhythmic, resonant, and musical link. Three consecutive

sentences begin with the same word "when"; two end in the same way, with an undulating movement; and at once a sudden inversion of rhythm indicates that the conclusion has been reached. The dynamic contents are fixed and almost frozen in the rigid and categorical formulation of scientific laws. (pp. 60-1)

Leonardo is perfectly consistent with his logical principles. He avoids all metaphysical discussion. It is not possible to give a definition of the elements; only their effects are known. And since the soul (or mind) is made up of the fifth element, it is compared with the other four and included in a scale that goes from the most solid and inert to the most mobile and ethereal. From this very simple comparison the nature of the soul can be clearly seen as pure activity, energy, and very rapid and unseizable motion. Here, too, Leonardo's real aims are implicit. If he were speaking to a reader, Leonardo would be more diffuse; but speaking to himself, he limits himself to registering certain indisputable physical phenomena, and says nothing about the deductions he wishes to draw from them. Yet the direction of his concealed thought, which hides itself behind these simple aspects of the natural world, is revealed by the rhythm of the sentences, which gets gradually faster to the point where it relaxes and finds its rest in the final conclusion.

So far we have examined how Leonardo put down on paper personal notes, which were not intended for a reader, notes which range from the most disordered and hurried to the deepest and most intense. They have a characteristic in common: the brief, concise, linear sentence, like the segment of a straight line. When the thought broadens out and is more deeply felt, these rectilinear sentences are set out parallel to each other, and join together to form one rhythmical, unitary group, charged with compressed energy. Their structure is no longer that of a continuous, logical discussion, but the musical structure of a poetic creation. However, even in Leonardo's manuscripts there are many pages that were evidently written for a reader to come. He decided to write several treatises on painting, on water, on anatomy, which unfortunately he was never able to finish. **The Codex A,** which was written a short time after the **Codex B** and **Trivulziano,** contains many passages of the **Treatise on Painting.** Many of them are bare rules for the painter, but many set out the reasons for those rules. Here Leonardo talks with his reader-pupil, without the strong conciseness of scientific definitions, and without the carelessness of hurried notes, but with an average tension, which neither avoids the anacoluthons of everyday speech nor leaves out those contemplative pauses when he dwells upon the most suggestive aspects of beauty. At those moments the rhythm of the word acquires a particular purity, which accompanies the trepidation of the soul. The words join together in uniform, rhythmical entities, which often coincide with lines from the Italian poetical tradition. "Poni mente per le strade,—sul fare della sera,—i volti d'omini e donne,—quando è cattivo tempo,—Quanta grazia e dolcezza—si vede in loro!"

Afterward, too, Leonardo happens to insert verse into his prose unconsciously. Some passages begin and end with resonant hendecasyllables. When in a moment of fervid enthusiasm he sees—unfortunately only with his imagination—the first aeroplane built by him rise and fly like a big bird from a hill in Florence, he expresses his joy in a series of hendecasyllables. "Piglierà il primo volo il grande uccello sopra del dosso del suo magno Cecero, empiendo l'universo di stupore, empiendo di sua fama tutte le scritture, a gloria eterna al nido dove nacque."

The *Codex C* has a particular interest for us. The perfection of its drawings and the care of the writing are certain proof that Leonardo intended to present his notebook to an important reader. Here the literary form must have received special attention, and it probably represents Leonardo's ideal at that moment. In fact we can see that all traces of hurry and improvisation have disappeared, and the style reveals a sustained confidence, which can only be seen at intervals in the preceding manuscripts. A peculiarity that strikes the reader is the frequent use of indirect constructions, which were adopted chiefly by Latin scholars. To give only a few examples, instead of writing "la quale fia causata dal lume più alto che largo," Leonardo writes "la qual dal lume più alto che largo causato fia;" instead of "del corpo ombroso piramidale posto contro a sé," he writes "del contr'a sé posto piramidal corpo ombroso." The affectation of putting the adjective before the noun is frequently repeated even in those cases where common usage prescribes the contrary. Consider also the use of latinizing words: *propinquo* instead of *vicino, circundare* instead of *circondare, conducere* instead of *condurre,* etc. The use of these latinizing devices reveals Leonardo's purpose: he wants to attain to a nobler and more dignified style by slackening the rhythm. In fact the rhythm is no longer rapid and broken, as it is in the passages we have already examined, but calm, solemn, and above all "legato." This term is used deliberately in its musical sense because we can clearly see Leonardo's predilection for a particular type of melody: "la piramidal pura ombra dirivative," "Quel corpo parrà più splendido, il quale da più oscure tenebre circundato fia." The syntax of the periods remains extremely simple, but the modulation of the sentences, prolonged and amplified, takes on a sense of grandeur. The language is also ennobled by coupling the nouns with particular adjectives: "le usate tenebre," "le ombrose cose," "la pupilla tenebrata," "lo sopravenente splendore." Adjective and noun are musically joined in one ample modulation which echoes the sonorous sound of the great poetry of the fourteenth century. His long practice in the choice and derivation of words from the books of men of letters had certainly helped him in refining his language, which has now become nobler and more sensitive.

If in these passages of the *Codex C* Leonardo enlarges and ennobles his sentences with various devices, yet still retaining a very simple syntax, in the Fables, on the other hand, he makes strenuous efforts to abandon the linear form and to arrive at that complex articulation of periods which is obtained by employing many subordinate propositions, hierarchically arranged (according to their importance) around the main proposition. By adopting this structure writers such as Boccaccio and, later on, Bembo established the so-called round period. Yet in Leonardo's Fables we see a great number of subordinate propositions, but not the "round period." In fact these subordinate propositions are mostly of the same degree and of a simple type. The verb has the gerund form or is a past participle, and the propositions are joined together as if they were coordinate clauses. Consequently the structure of the sentences remains linear. . . . We can conclude, therefore, that Leonardo's effort to arrive at more dignified literary forms is restricted to the simple proposition and is never realized within the complex structure of the period.

It is well known how writers at the time of the Renaissance were led by preference to use certain literary forms when ex-

pounding a scientific subject, forms such as the Treatise, the Discourse, the Dialogue, the Epistle. It is very interesting to notice how Leonardo tried to use each of these forms. (pp. 61-3)

All we have said so far confirms the intention of the *omo sanza lettere* to devote himself to a vast literary activity. He tried to enrich his language with a mass of learned words taken from books. He tried without any great success to learn Latin. He introduced into his style some of the devices frequently used by the men of letters of his day. He experimented with almost every type of literary production then in fashion. But it is evident that these attempts were not made according to any organic plan or firm decision. His literary projects had ripened in Milan, at the court of Ludovico il Moro. After the fall of the duke the environment in which Leonardo had cherished his projects changed greatly. He began to live an unsettled way of life, frequently moving from one prince to another. Besides, the more he devoted himself to the study of nature, the more the matter of his observation grew in volume, and consequently the length of his treatises. He continued to collect thousands of preparatory notes, but, perhaps unconsciously, he gave up writing his book, whatever book it was to have been, and even the idea of a complete series of chapters. Neither his exacting nature nor the adverse events of his life can give a sufficient explanation of this renunciation. The real reasons are the very ones that establish his position in the history of science. J. H. Randall so sums them up: "Science is not oracular utterances, however well phrased: it is not bright ideas jotted down in a notebook. Science is systematic and methodical thought" and Leonardo "has no interest in working out any systematic body of knowledge." The real reasons derive from his cultural formation. In the artisan shops he learned, together with manual skill, the cult of experimental research, and he sharpened his spirit of observation. He realized, and openly declared, that the progress of science could not be guaranteed without the experimental method, and, polemicizing with men of letters and philosophers, he asserted the superiority of the painter above all other artists and scientists. He thought that his anatomical drawings not only surpassed but could eliminate and take the place of any treatise. He was convinced that it was not permitted for man to discover the nature of the soul or of the natural elements, but only to describe their behavior and mode of functioning in the physical world. But the men of letters and philosophers, whom he opposed and despised, knew how to set up and bring to an end a discussion, and how to write a book—something that Leonardo appears never to have learned.

In the *Treatise on Painting* Leonardo exhorts: "Se vuoi aver vera notizia delle forme delle cose, comincierai dalle particole di quelle, e non andare alla seconda, se prima non hai bene nella memoria e nella pratica la prima." Even when writing he always composed the *particole,* the very small parts of his books, going over them again and again, always unsatisfied and incapable of ever putting them together. He thought of his books as of his final aim, but meanwhile he wrote only for himself, even neglecting certain attentions to style which we saw in the *Codex C.* It is significant that certain latinizing forms (such as the verb placed at the end of the sentence) are very frequent in the last ten years of the fifteenth century, but are very rare and almost disappear in the later manuscripts (*G, E*). This habit of writing "by particles" certainly influenced Leonardo's style. Think, for instance, of the famous description of the Deluge, which is rich in splendid details, but without any central core, and not conceived as a whole, but developed only within short, interchangeable periods. This is a characteristic of a great number of Leonardo's pages, where the propositions, even in the longest periods, follow one another, but are not strongly linked together.

Nevertheless, his style has become much more refined in comparison with the **Codex B** and **Trivulziano.** He still piles up series of short, linear, parallel sentences, but sometimes he is able to link them together with a very lively rhythmic cadence, as when he describes the aspects of water, where his style reproduces the extremely changeable forms of water. . . . Even simple lists of titles appear musically linked, as in the "Partizioni" of the Deluge: "Tenebre, vento, fortuna di mare, diluvio d'acque, selve infocate, piogge, saette dal cielo. . . . Rami stracciati da' venti, misti col corso de' venti, con gente di sopra. . . ." The adjectives have become richer and more sensitive, and the phrasing solemn due to the nobility of the words and the purity of rhythm. Long and suggestive modulations, often easily divisible into rhythmical entities corresponding to the lines of Italian poetry, alternate with the excited energy of brief and concise sentences. . . . And often we are astonished at the precision with which the words adhere to the most complex objects of reality.

Leonardo's visual qualities, even as a writer, have always been praised. But he does not only grasp the proportion of forms, the splendor of surfaces, and the sweetness of shadows in the natural world. Beauty does not exist only in the harmonious correspondence of the parts but also in the quickness of actions, "la prontitudine delle azioni," as he states, translating Marsilio Ficino's words, "actus vivacitas et gratia quaedam in fluxu ipso refulgens." Leonardo differs from the writer of his time because of his deeper, inner adherence to the dynamism of universal life, which he feels in every place and in every being as a longing and a passion, as sorrow and happiness, triumph and tragedy. Let us read one last and not very well-known fragment. "La setola del bue, messa in acqua, morta, di state, piglia senso e vita e moto per sé medesima; e paura e fuga, e sente dolore. E prova ne é che stringendola, essa si storce e si divincola. Rimettila nell'acqua. Essa, come di sopra dissi, piglia fuga e levasi dal pericolo." A sense of continuous wonder at almost every word arrests the movement of the phrase to propel it forward again only after the pause. The movement of the hair in water is followed with such wonder because it reveals a mysterious world of invisible forces that give life both to man and nature. Leonardo's poetry derives from this immense and harmonious vision of the universe.

We have tried to demonstrate here that Leonardo's poetry did not find a full and orderly expression in his writings, as he did not submit himself to a complete literary discipline. Therefore those who considered him as the founder of scientific prose or as a great writer used inexact terms. I think that the opinion of Attilio Momigliano is right: "Leonardo's fragments are for the most part the puffs of poetry, which arise and die out suddenly . . . he remained for the most part a poet in potential." But Leonardo was not only a writer, and if we catch these sudden puffs of poetry in his writings and connect them to those which burst forth from his pictures and drawings, we shall easily recognize the greatness of his spirit and receive the incomparable gift of his poetry. (pp. 64-6)

Augusto Marinoni, "Leonardo as a Writer," in Leo-nardo's Legacy: An International Symposium, ed-ited by C. D. O'Malley, University of California Press, 1969, pp. 57-66.

JAMES ACKERMAN   (lecture date 1966)

[Ackerman is an American editor, essayist, and academic. In the following excerpt from a lecture delivered in 1966 as the concluding remarks of an international symposium on "Leonardo's Legacy," he examines Leonardo's personality, humanism, philosophy, and art.]

[We] should admit that while Leonardo's learning was more integrated than ours is it was far short of being "universal." He had little or no interest in history, moral philosophy, theology, law, economy and trade, politics, classical literature, or, except as a practitioner, music—a list that includes practically everything that was believed in his time to be the province of the educated man. It was for this reason that he was called *omo sanza lettere*—"a man without learning"—as he himself proudly confessed in counterattacks on the pedants of his time. The accusation was not strictly true because Leonardo picked up masses of disconnected facts and ideas in his reading, but he tended to poke at rather than to chew on books, and he preferred popular manuals with excerpts to the original sources. Probably he learned more of the achievements of ancient and medieval science by ear than by poring over manuscripts and the few printed books available in his time; his Latin was weak, and he knew no Greek. But he knew whom to listen to and how to listen.

For Leonardo, however, reading, listening, and other paths to knowledge always were integrated with observation; he distrusted learning that could not be supported by visual evidence and, by that token, recorded in drawings. When he did tackle an abstract problem such as the nature of force and resistance, it was usually because he wanted to find reasons for what he had found by observation. Let's hear what he said of his investigations:

> First I make a certain experiment before proceeding farther, because my intention is first to present the experiment and then by reasoning to demonstrate why that experiment is compelled to behave as it did. And this is the true rule according to which speculations on natural effects must proceed. Since nature begins in reason and ends in experiences, we have to follow the opposite route, beginning with experiences and on that basis investigating the reason.

That statement, similar to one quoted by Professor Marinoni, might be called the first law of empirical science. But before saying any more about Leonardo's significance as a scientist or as an artist, we ought to consider what science and art meant in the Renaissance.

"Scientia" and "ars" are words of pure Latin derivation which, so long as Latin was alive, frequently were used together, but not in the sense in which we understand them today. What was meant by *ars* was simply manual proficiency or technique, and what was meant by *scientia* was knowledge or theory. Whether one spoke about anatomy or about painting, the art was the technical skill needed for designing an excavating machine or laying in a glaze, and the science was the body of principles and the tradition of learning that gave the activity some meaning. This is the distinction that Leonardo made when he said "those who fall in line with practice without *scientia* are like pilots who board a ship without a rudder or compass, who are never certain where they are going"; I regret to say that the standard English edition of the **Treatise on Painting** translates *scientia* as "science," when Leonardo meant "theory." The concept of *scientia* as the philosophy guiding creative activity offered the possibility of a true unity of knowledge in the Middle Ages and Renaissance because it was on a level sufficiently generalized to encompass all disciplines.

But the union of *ars* with *scientia* which Leonardo thought was essential was as difficult to achieve in those days as it is in ours. Most of the scholars and philosophers trusted only abstract book learning, and most of the artists and technicians only shop practice. When Leonardo came of age there was a young and growing intellectual movement, Humanism, which gradually had gained ascendancy over the scholastic, theological case of late medieval thought. The humanists were not necessarily preoccupied with humans; it was their achievement to have brought to life the knowledge and the languages of the ancient world by discovering and editing the surviving Greek and Roman manuscripts and by reformulating philosophy, science, and the arts on ancient models. Humanism might better have been called Hellenism or something of the sort. Its achievements and influence were increased greatly by the fortuitous perfection of printing just at this time—not only the printing of words, which usually comes to mind in this connection, but the printing of images by the process of engraving.

According to the traditional description, the Humanist Renaissance was an age of rediscovery of man and of the world around him, a time in which the superstitions and abstractions of the Middle Ages were cast aside to make way for modern thought. To call this generalization a half-truth would be generous; if Humanism were the measure, then we should have to confess that in some respect the Renaissance held back invention and discovery by directing attention to a distant and sanctified past. From the very start the majority of scholars then, like the majority now, got involved in parochial preoccupations. Stimulating as it was to have Greek science made available in well-edited and translated volumes, it soon proved that what was stimulated in that atmosphere was a love of books. For many humanists, the world of the ancient scientists was not just a guide to the study of nature, it was an article of faith. A lecture on anatomy in the university, for example, would involve the reading or reciting of passages by the professor from the ancient Roman authority, Galen, while the actual dissection was performed by a servant, whose discoveries cannot have conformed exactly to the text, since the taboos of Galen's time compelled him to use monkeys and other animals as a clue to human anatomy.

The lesser humanists scorned Leonardo for his undignified ways of getting information: he did his own dissections and got his hands dirty. And he replied with biblical fervor: "O human stupidity, do you not perceive that you have spent your whole life with yourself and yet are not aware of that which you have most in evidence, and that is your own foolishness? And so with the crowd of sophists you think to deceive yourself and others, despising the mathematical sciences in which is contained true information."

But not all of the humanists were pedants; some, like Leon Battista Alberti and Nicholas of Cusa, and Marsilio Ficino, formulated concepts and provided tools without which Leonardo would not have been able to work. And it must be admitted that the criticisms leveled at Leonardo by the human-

ists were not unfounded. In the vast range of his investigations he rarely achieved the ideal fusion of *ars* and *scientia* that was his stated goal. His observations had a way of leading him to more observations rather than to principles or laws of nature, and he seldom arrived at the mathematical description of phenomena . . . which he regarded as the only path to certainty in science. (pp. 206-09)

In one sense Alberti came closer to Leonardo's goals than Leonardo did himself; Alberti was not as adept professionally as Leonardo in mathematics, painting, architecture, cartography, and other mechanical arts, but he was an earnest practitioner, as well as a scholar, one of those Professor Marinoni referred to whose powers of theorizing were not inhibited; he arrived at formulations in many fields and got them into print, which Leonardo never did. Alberti was the embodiment of the new Renaissance ideals, ideals to which Leonardo was never fully attuned. Yet Leonardo remains for us the more appealing ancestor, partly because he anticipated the age of empirical science, but even more because his empiricism never shadowed his vigorous poetic prose and his mysterious and fantastic imagination—that air of the Magus and prophet reminiscent at once of the Middle Ages and (as Santillana has observed) of the pre-Socratic Greeks, which permeates his investigations and gives them a spiritual unity that later science lost.

The contrast suggests the rough generalization that while Alberti embraced Renaissance ideals in both his *ars* or practice and his *scientia* or theory, Leonardo owed only his practice to the age of Humanism; his theories were often arcane, an amalgam of elements from the entire corpus of Western thought. The great difficulty of achieving a compromise between fantasy and mathematical description helps to explain Leonardo's failures at synthesis and, on the other hand, his eminent success in one *scientia* that admits and even welcomes a fusion of empirical observation, mathematical order, and imagination: painting. Only as a *painter* did Leonardo effectively alter the evolution of Western culture. But I do not mean "only as an artist," because Leonardo was uniquely successful in elevating painting to the level of natural philosophy; much of what was lost when his manuscripts disappeared was preserved in his pictures.

What we have heard and seen in the course of this symposium demonstrates the extent to which Leonardo's method as a scientist in the modern sense was rooted in the technical innovations of the Renaissance artist's studio. While the scholars who practiced the liberal arts stayed in the library, the artists who were considered lowly practitioners of the mechanical arts were inventing ways to represent rationally the things they saw. This involved two processes which were the cornerstones of Renaissance art and science: first, observation of the world about with the intention of describing its appearance, which implies a certain conviction in the validity of worldly experience and in the educational value of experiment; second, giving a rational order to this visual data, which means fitting the individual subjective experience into a generalized structure that is more permanent and valid. (pp. 209-10)

Professor Gombrich showed us how, as Leonardo's interest in the vital forces of nature continued, its scope became more cosmic; he was fascinated and obsessed with catastrophic destruction—by wind, by flood, and even by the kind of all-annihilating explosion we might think of as a peculiar nightmare of the atomic age. Out of this passion for cataclysm came some of the most splendid and moving achievements of his draftsmanship. This vision may be set to an equally vivid text from Leonardo's hand which will serve to illustrate the sense in which Leonardo is universal. The man who inspired Walter Pater to literary arabesques on the mysteries of the smile or glance in a lady's portrait could write for us, the grandsons of Pater:

> The rivers will remain without their waters; the fertile earth will put forth no more her branches; the fields will be decked no more with waving corn. All the animals will perish, failing to find fresh grass for fodder; and the ravening lions and wolves and other beasts that live by prey will lack sustenance; and it will come about after many desperate shifts that men will be forced to abandon their lives and the human race will cease to be . . . Then the surface of the earth will remain burnt to a cinder and this will be the end of all terrestrial nature.

Such visions of the powers of nature gone awry did not emerge from the rational philosophy of the early Renaissance, nor from the empirical techniques of the studio. Yet they are, I believe, the key to Leonardo's unique *scientia*. Searching for the *ragioni*, the causes underlying the phenomena he observed, Leonardo continually found himself facing the necessity and his inability to define the forces operating on things. He called them "spiritual." For a scientist whose experiments were penetrating enough to overthrow the accepted views of the order of nature, and who could not bring himself to assign the realm of the unknown to the province of a rational God, chaos must have seemed as probable a condition as order. I do not mean, however, that Leonardo deduced the probability of chaos from his experiments. Rather, by virtue of his visionary and poetic disposition, he was attracted to a tradition outside of classical science and humanistic philosophy: the tradition of myth and saga, which is filled with cataclysmic finales, the wild unleashing of spiritual forces. (p. 224)

> *James Ackerman, "Concluding Remarks: Science and Art in the Work of Leonardo," in* Leonardo's Legacy: An International Symposium, *edited by C. D. O'Malley, University of California Press, 1969, pp. 205-25.*

KENNETH CLARK (essay date 1967)

[*A twentieth-century English essayist, historian, and autobiographer, Clark wrote extensively on artists and the history of art. Today he is best remembered for "Civilisation," a television series in which he chronicled the development of Western art and culture over a 1300-year period. In the following excerpt from a 1967 revision of his 1939 study* Leonardo da Vinci: An Account of His Development as an Artist, *he identifies elements of Leonardo's personality in* A Treatise of Painting.]

The *Trattato della Pittura* is not an easy book to read. In the Vatican MS. it consists of eight books and 935 'chapters', some no more than a few lines, some covering several pages. Although the compiler has tried to arrange the entries under their subjects, very few have any sequence, and many repeat each other in slightly varying form. In a short summary we may say that the contents are valuable in four different ways. First, they give Leonardo's general views on the nature of art; secondly, there are notes on the science of painting; thirdly, there are notes on studio practice; and fourthly, there are entries scattered through the *Trattato,* in which Leonardo expresses, sometimes half-unconsciously, his personal tastes and feelings as a painter.

Leonardo's general views on the art of painting are found for the most part in the first book of the *Trattato,* where he compares it to the arts of poetry, music, and sculpture. These comparisons, or *paragoni* as they were called, were a standard form of critical literature at the time, and something of what they contain is derivative; but the presentation of the argument and, above all, the illustrative examples quoted are characteristic of Leonardo and of immense interest, since nowhere else does he allow himself to write in such generalized or such personal terms of the things which concerned him most deeply.

Since classical times painting had been classed among the mechanical arts, and Leonardo, like Sir Joshua Reynolds in his *Discourses,* is concerned to establish its respectability by proving that it is a mental activity and a science. The destruction of such an artificial premiss naturally involves him in some artificiality himself, but above these sophistries, which are harmless enough if judged by the standards of contemporary literature, there towers a noble and thrilling conception of what painting should be. In the first place, it is a recreation of the visible world. Leonardo always insists on this godlike quality of the painter's imagination. From the divine element in the science of painting it follows that the mind of the painter is transformed into the likeness of the mind of God. It is this view of art as creation which makes him insist that the painter must be universal, must neglect no aspect of nature; and for the same reason he must be a scientist, that is to say, must understand the inner nature of what he paints almost as if he had created it himself. 'If you despise painting,' he says, 'which is the sole means of reproducing all the known works of nature, you despise an invention which with subtle and philosophic speculation considers all the qualities of forms: seas, plants, animals, grasses, flowers, all of which are encircled in light and shadow.' But the painter must not only recreate the semblance of things seen: he must select and dispose them with harmonious intention. Painting, he says, depends on 'l'armonica proporzionalita delle parti che compongono il tutto, che contenta il senso'. Here Leonardo shows himself touched by the predominant Platonism of his time, for the idea that the visual arts were a sort of frozen music was familiar to many theorists of the Renaissance, and had been given superb expression by Leon Battista Alberti, to whose treatise on painting, written in 1435, Leonardo was greatly indebted. But in his enthusiasm for painting, Leonardo goes farther and claims that painting is superior to music in so far as it *is* frozen, since its sequences are not fleeting sounds or images, *si volece nel nascere come nel morire,* but can be apprehended immediately and contemplated indefinitely. This exposition of the relative immediacy and permanence of the sensations aroused by the arts, anticipating to some extent the theories of Lessing, is, from a critical point of view, the most valuable part of the *Trattato.* But strict logic was no part of Leonardo's equipment, and when he comes to compare painting with sculpture his personal prejudices rush in, to the confusion of his aesthetic theories, but to the vast enrichment of our knowledge of his character.

For that side of painting which consists in the harmonious composition of proportionate parts Leonardo gives no rules, though in one abstruse passage he hints at a means of establishing an equivalent to certain musical intervals. The academic advice and instruction which fill a great part of the

Trattato are concerned with painting as the science by which visible objects are recreated in permanent shape. And since the exact sciences must be stated in mathematical terms, Leonardo insists that the student of painting must be grounded in mathematics. This union of art and mathematics is far from our own way of thinking, but it was fundamental to the Renaissance. (pp. 73-6)

In addition to defining the principal aims of painting, Leonardo gives us practical hints as to how they can be achieved, interesting to us as indications of his own studio practice. He tells the student to avoid above all light which casts a dark shadow, so that even if he is painting in the open air he must do so as if some mist or transparent cloud was between his object and the sun. In sunlight it is better to paint in a courtyard with high walls painted black and a linen curtain stretched over it. The ideal light falls on the object at an angle of 45 degrees. This last shows Leonardo at his most academic, and is a contrast to the Rembrandtesque figure looking out of a dark interior, described above. More sympathetic are his numerous instructions as to how to catch that degree of animation in figures which he valued so highly. 'When you are out for a walk,' he tells the painter, 'see to it that you watch and consider men's postures and actions as they talk, argue, laugh, or scuffle together: their own actions, and those of their supporters and onlookers: and make a note of these with a few strokes in your little book which you must always carry with you. This book should be of tinted paper so that you cannot rub out, but always go on to a new page.' He also gives the very sound advice that any student drawing a detail of a figure should first sketch in the figure as a whole, so that the real meaning of the finished part should not be lost sight of. Good examples of his own practice are the studies of the nude at Windsor. These practical hints show how far he was in revolt against the decorative style of the *quattrocento*. Painters are warned not to surround their figures with dark outlines; rows of frescoes one above the other, the time-honoured Italian way of telling a story in pictures, is blamed on grounds of reason (*ragionevolmente biasimato*), and as an alternative Leonardo suggests putting several scenes in the same composition, but cutting them off from one another by 'large trees, or angels if they are suitable to the story, or birds or clouds or similar devices'. Scorn is reserved for mere decorators. 'There is a certain race of painters,' he says, 'who from their lack of science have to live by the beauty of blue and gold—*vivano sotto la bellezza dell'oro e dell'azzuro*. With supreme folly these men allege that they cannot do anything good except at a high cost.' I think there can be little doubt that Leonardo was actually thinking of Pintoricchio, who was notoriously extravagant—*Consuma,* said the papal secretary of him, *troppo vino, troppo oro e troppo azzuro.* In any case, these maxims foreshadow that great stride in the history of art which the visitor to the Vatican can take by climbing the stairs from Pintoricchio's Borgia Apartments to Raphael's Stanze.

Interesting as are the theories and precepts propounded in the *Trattato,* and important in their bearing on Leonardo's painting, it contains entries of a far deeper significance. These are the passages in which he reveals his own preferences, prejudices, and the real colour of his imagination. His manuscripts, for all their enormous bulk, so seldom contain the least expression of personal feeling that the passages preserved by the unknown editor of the *Trattato* are worth examining at length. In the first place, Leonardo makes fairly frequent reference to the sort of subject the painter might wish to treat. Here is one of them, the 65th chapter of the *Trattato,* headed 'Piacere del Pittore'.

> The painter can call into being the essences of animals of all kinds, of plants, fruits, landscapes, rolling plains, crumbling mountains, fearful and terrible places which strike terror into the spectator; and again pleasant places, sweet and delightful with meadows of many-coloured flowers bent by the gentle motion of the wind which turns back to look at them as it floats on; and then rivers falling from high mountains with the force of great floods, ruins which drive down with them uprooted plants mixed with rocks, roots, earth, and foam and wash away to its ruin all that comes in their path; and then the stormy sea, striving and wrestling with the winds which fight against it, raising itself up in superb waves which fall in ruins as the wind strikes at their roots.

The rest of the passage is a description of the struggle between wind and water, in which the water takes the form of rain to assault the sea from above, but finally 'pressed back it turns into thick clouds, and these become the prey of the conquering winds'. Here is Leonardo carried away by his true feelings. He begins to enumerate the subjects that delight a painter, and instead of compositions of figures, classical and religious legends, beautiful faces and draperies, all the subjects which pleased the patrons and artists of his time, he describes this combat of the elements, a subject for Turner, in the language of Herman Melville. Nor was this an isolated freak. All his longest and fullest descriptions of pictorial subjects are of great battles, storms, and deluges and, as we shall see, he carried out these subjects in the most personal of all his designs. Unfortunately, we have no hint of how he would have executed another subject, which he describes with equal pleasure, a night piece with a fire, and when we try to picture it our eye cannot rid itself of the strong images created by an artist at the farthest remove from Leonardo, the night pieces of Rembrandt.

> The figures which are seen against the fire look dark in the glare of the firelight; and those who stand at the side are half dark and half red, while those who are visible beyond the edges of the flames will be feebly lighted by the ruddy glow against a black background. As to their gestures, make those which are near it screen themselves with their hands and cloaks, to ward off the intense heat, and some with their faces turned away as if drawing back. Of those further off, represent some of them with their hands raised to screen their eyes, hurt by the intolerable splendour of the flames.

These descriptions not only show the deeply romantic colour of Leonardo's imagination: they imply a sense of form completely at variance with that of his contemporaries. Instead of the firmly defined forms of the *quattrocento* or the enclosed forms of the high Renaissance, the subjects he describes could only be treated with the broken, suggestive forms of romantic painting. That Leonardo felt the full evocative power of such forms is proved by a famous passage in the *Trattato:*

> I shall not refrain [he says] from including among these precepts a new and speculative idea, which although it may seem trivial and almost laughable, is none the less of great value in quickening the spirit of invention. It is this: that you should look at certain walls stained with damp or at stones of uneven colour. If you have to invent some setting

Drawing of a cannon foundry, an example of Leonardo's work as a military engineer.

you will be able to see in these the likeness of divine landscapes, adorned with mountains, ruins, rocks, woods, great plains, hills, and valleys in great variety; and then again you will see there battles and strange figures in violent action, expression of faces, and clothes, and an infinity of things which you will be able to reduce to their complete and proper forms. In such walls the same thing happens as in the sound of bells, in whose strokes you may find every named word which you can imagine.

Later he repeats this suggestion in slightly different form, advising the painter to study not only marks on walls, but also 'the embers of the fire, or clouds, or mud, or other similar objects from which you will find most admirable ideas . . . because from a confusion of shapes the spirit is quickened to new inventions.' 'But,' he adds, 'first be sure you know all the members of all the things you wish to depict, both the members of animals and the members of landscapes, that is to say, rocks, plants and so forth.'

I have quoted this passage at length, familiar as it is, because it is profoundly characteristic of Leonardo. Nothing could be farther from the precepts of academic classicism than the use of stains in walls as a stimulus to the imagination. This procedure was followed by Goya, one of the most anti-classical of all painters; and Victor Hugo, whose name is the first to come to mind when we read Leonardo's descriptions of a deluge, made many of his strangely exciting drawings out of accidental blots and smears of coffee. Yet although Leonardo would admit such aids to the imagination, his conception of art as a science forced him to add a warning that the painter must understand the detailed structure of all that he wished to represent.

Before leaving the *Trattato* I will take the opportunity of quoting from it a few of the passages which throw some light on Leonardo's character apart from his ideas on painting. First of all, we have some first-hand confirmation of those early authorities who tell us that he was elegant, solitary, and calmly aware of his superiority to the average of mankind. This is apparent in his perfectly illogical attacks on sculpture. Sculpture, he says, is not a science, but an *arte meccanicissima,* for

> the sculptor in creating his work does so by the strength of his arm by which he consumes the marble, or other obdurate material in which his subject is enclosed: and this is done by most mechanical exercise, often accompanied by great sweat which mixes with the marble dust and forms a kind of mud daubed all over his face. The marble dust flours him all over so that he looks like a baker; his back is covered with a snowstorm of chips, and his house is made filthy by the flakes and dust of stone. The exact reverse is true of the painter (taking the best painters and sculptors as standards of comparison); for the painter sits before his work, perfectly at his ease and well dressed, and moves a very light brush dipped in delicate colour; and he adorns himself with whatever clothes he pleases. His house is clean and filled with charming pictures; and often he is accompanied by music or by the reading of various and beautiful works, which, since they are not mixed with the sound of the hammer or other noises, are heard with the greatest pleasure.

We are reminded of the description by Jusepe Martinez of El Greco in a great house with twenty-four rooms and a band of musicians to play to him while he took his meals. But with

Leonardo (as, indeed, with El Greco) this elegant way of life was combined with great austerity. 'In order that the prosperity of the body,' he says, 'shall not harm that of the spirit the painter must be solitary, especially when he is intent on those speculations and considerations, which if they are kept continually before the eyes give the memory the opportunity of mastering them. For if you are alone you are completely yourself but if you are accompanied by a single companion you are only half yourself.' And we know that Leonardo showed that perfect contempt for riches which he counsels so eloquently in chapter 62 of the *Trattato.*

Leonardo's description of the sculptor has a further significance for us. It is an unmistakable reference to his hated rival, Michelangelo. The very hardships which Leonardo describes in derision are recorded with a kind of sardonic pride in Michelangelo's letters and sonnets. We see that the antipathy, the *sdegno grandissimo* as Vasari calls it, which existed between the two men was something far more profound than professional jealousy; sprang, in fact, from their deepest beliefs. In no accepted sense can Leonardo be called a Christian. He was not even a religious-minded man. It is true that he allowed himself an occasional reference to superstitious observances: thus he writes 'of Worshipping the pictures of Saints. Men will speak to men who hear not. . . . They will implore favours of those who have ears and hear not; they will make light for the blind.' Here and in a few other passages he seems to associate himself with the precursors of the Reformation. But these protests spring from his dislike of mumbo jumbo and loose thinking in general rather than from any real religious conviction. Michelangelo, on the other hand, was a profoundly religious man, to whom the reform of the Roman Church came to be a matter of passionate concern. His mind was dominated by ideas—good and evil, suffering, purification, unity with God, peace of mind—which to Leonardo seemed meaningless abstractions, but to Michelangelo were ultimate truths. No wonder that these ideas, embodied in a man of Michelangelo's moral, intellectual, and artistic power, gave Leonardo a feeling of uneasiness thinly coated with contempt. Yet Leonardo held one belief, implicit in his writings, and occasionally expressed with a real nobility: the belief in experience. Such an expression is to be found in chapter 29 of the *Trattato,* in which Leonardo denies with passion the old scholastic belief that only those sciences which have their origin in abstract intellectual speculation can escape the charge of being 'mechanical'.

> To me it seems that those sciences are vain and full of error which are not born of experience, mother of all certainty, first-hand experience which in its origins, or means, or end has passed through one of the five senses. And if we doubt the certainty of everything which passes through the senses, how much more ought we to doubt things contrary to these senses—*ribelli ad essi sensi*—such as the existence of God or of the soul or similar things over which there is always dispute and contention. And in fact it happens that whenever reason is wanting men cry out against one another, which does not happen with certainties. For this reason we shall say that where the cry of controversy is heard, there is no true science, because the truth has one single end and when this is published, argument is destroyed for ever. But true sciences are those which, impelled by hope, have been penetrated by the senses so that the tongues of argument are silenced. They are not nourished on the dreams of investigators, but proceed in orderly sequence from the first

true and established principles through successive stages to the end; as is shown by the elements of mathematics, that is to say number and measure, called arithmetic and geometry, which with complete truth treat of quantities both discontinuous and continuous. In them one does not argue if twice three makes more or less than six, or that the angles of a triangle are less than the sum of two right angles: all argument is reduced to eternal silence, and those who are devoted to them can enjoy them with a peace which the lying sciences of the mind can never attain—*con eterno silenzio resta distrutto ogni arguizione, e con pace sono fruite dai loro devoti il che far non possono le bugiarde scienze mentali.*

(pp. 79-85)

> Kenneth Clark, in his Leonardo da Vinci: An Account of His Development as an Artist, *revised edition, Penguin Books, 1967, 185 p.*

CHARLOTTE F. JOHNSON (essay date 1972)

[*In the following excerpt, Johnson cites Dante's* Divine Comedy *as the literary source from which Leonardo drew in describing a childhood dream.*]

Leonardo da Vinci's dream about the kite, which Freud called the "vulture phantasy," has been the subject of much study and analysis—its relation to science and literary tradition, its unconscious content, and the precipitating factor that might have elicited the dream.

The dreams of a person endowed with enormous gifts, one would assume, are more richly associative than those of an ordinary man. The extraordinary scope of Leonardo's gifts was acknowledged even in his own time. Vasari, a younger contemporary, says of him: "There was such a power of intellect that whatever he turned his mind to, he made himself the master of it" [see excerpt dated 1550]. Freud, in his treatise, *Leonardo da Vinci and a Memory of His Childhood,* speaks of him as a universal genius. Not only was he one of the world's greatest artists; he applied his enormous creative energy to sculpture (the lost Sforza monument of a horse), architecture, and hydraulic engineering, to anatomy, optics and mathematics.

In his *Notebooks,* Leonardo writes,

> In the earliest recollection of my infancy it seemed to me when I was in the cradle that a kite came and opened my mouth with its tail, and struck me within upon the lips with its tail many times.

It is a strange image and a striking one. (p. 177)

The precipitating factor in Leonardo's recollection of the kite is that he was doing research on the flight of birds. (The dream, in fact, was recorded in Leonardo's *Notebooks* on the obverse of the page on which he discussed the flight of the kite.) The study of bird flight, done with the consuming hope of discovering the technique that would enable men to fly, has been acknowledged as a topic that most aroused Leonardo's zeal. In this connection, Freud sets forth the psychoanalytical principle that the dream of flying, reaching back through folk lore into antiquity, has always symbolized the longing for the ability to accomplish sexually, and that the image of the bird is associated with the male genital. He also speaks of Leonardo's "life of abstinence" and his homosexuality, or at least asexuality. There must have been a personal need, therefore,

as well as scientific interest, in Leonardo's investigation of the kite, which he describes in a virile image as "descending, turns itself right over and pierces the air head downwards, bending the tail swiftly according to the direction in which it wishes to turn." Indeed, he regards as inevitable the relationship of his interest in birds to his dream of the kite: "To write thus clearly of the kite is my destiny" is the sentence which introduces his "recollection" of the bird opening his mouth with its tail. Still, what contributed to the dream taking this particular form?

Scholars have discussed whether Leonardo, conforming to mythological and historical examples, used a literary convention in which to couch the report of his phantasy. However, there is another possibility: that the vivid recollection was a transmutation of some actual literary source. Freud speaks vaguely of the possibility that when Leonardo was once reading a book of the Church Fathers or a work of natural history, a memory sprang to mind which became transformed into a phantasy. Eissler says, "That Leonardo used an ancient model at all—a hypothesis I personally doubt—may be an important finding for the historians."

I believe that I have found the model, not in antiquity, but in Dante's *Inferno,* in the fourth and fifth cantos.

The question of what books Leonardo actually read is still in dispute. It cannot therefore be said with certainty that he read *The Divine Comedy,* but considering the fact that the work received immediate and continuous attention in Italy as well as elsewhere, the assumption is not unreasonable. By the end of the fourteenth century, a public lectureship on *The Divine Comedy* had been established in Florence; Boccaccio was the appointee to this chair. Six hundred manuscripts of the poem were copied before the invention of printing. Vasari speaks of the delight of his friend Michelangelo, a contemporary of Leonardo's, in "reading the poets, particularly Dante and Petrarch." Serious efforts were made, before and during Leonardo's lifetime, and culminating later with Galileo, to determine the exact location, shape and measurements of Dante's Hell. In the light of such prevailing contemporary familiarity with *The Divine Comedy,* the startling verbal parallel between Leonardo's kite dream and the fourth and fifth cantos of the *Inferno* commands attention.

In *Inferno* (V), Dante, guided by Virgil, has descended to the second circle, the proper beginning of Hell, and encounters Minos, the famed king of Crete, now the Infernal Judge.

> There Minos sits horrific . . . examines the crimes upon the entrance; judges, and sends according as he girds himself. / I say that when the ill-born spirit comes before him, it confesses all; and that sin-discerner / sees what place in Hell is for it, and with his tail makes as many circles round himself as the degrees he will have it descend.

Dante is moved by the plight to which the spirits are condemned by the motion of the fateful tail. "Now begin the doleful notes to reach me; now I am come where much lamenting strikes me."

The words *tail* (coda) and *strike* (percuotere) appear here as in the kite dream, and in the same order. Images of birds follow close upon the line "where much lamenting strikes me." The spirits are depicted as vexed by a hellish storm: "As their wings bear along the starlings, at the cold season . . . so that blast, the evil spirits . . . and as the cranes go chanting their

428

lays . . . so I saw the shadows come, uttering wails." Other spirits come, at Dante's cry, "like doves called by desire."

Here the image of the tail striking, is accompanied by images of Leonardo's obsessive interest, that of birds flying. Birds of prey, suggesting kites, have already been presented in *Inferno* IV:

> Mark him with sword in hand, who comes . . . /
> That is Homer, the sovereign poet; the next who
> comes is Horace the satirist; Ovid is the third, and
> the last is Lucan. / . . . Thus I saw assembled the
> goodly school of those lords of highest song, which,
> like an eagle, soars above the rest. / . . . I saw . . .
> Caesar armed, with the falcon eyes.

I believe that this combination of clearly visualized images, compactly placed together in the *Inferno,* is the heretofore undiscovered literary model, worked upon by Leonardo's long harbored memory of oral trauma until it became incorporated in his dream, and surfaced as the "vulture phantasy."

Further, there is also the strong possibility that the impact of this set of images upon Leonardo may have been reinforced by his further reading in the *Purgatorio.* Here (IX), Dante recounts a dream of an eagle, comparable in context with the image of the descending kite:

> In a dream methought I saw an eagle poised in the
> sky . . . with wings outspread, and intent to
> swoop. / . . . Then meseemed that, having
> wheeled awhile, terrible as lightning, he descended
> and snatched me up as far as the fiery sphere. /
> There it seemed that he and I did burn, and the vi-
> sionary flame so scorched that needs was my slum-
> ber broken.

Vultures, kites, perhaps eagles—birds of aggression—are frequently found in Leonardo's work. Harry Slochower points out that the artist embodies his phantasy in particular concrete objects, thereby setting limits to the phantasy. Thus the many birds, clearly visible, half hidden, or in puzzle pictures, which abound in Leonardo's sketches, notebooks and known masterpieces, may be seen as a "curative ingredient." . . . (pp. 178-82)

I maintain that the obsession with birds and their sexual symbolism, born out of Leonardo's particular sexual situation, and brought into focus by the kite dream, can be seen clearly, half hidden or in shorthand, in many of his works that on the surface have nothing to do with kites or sex. And the "vulture phantasy," I believe, was given its particular form by Leonardo's reading the kindred passages in Dante's *Inferno* and *Purgatorio.* (p. 185)

> *Charlotte F. Johnson, "Leonardo and Dante," in*
> American Imago, *Vol. 29, No. 2, Summer, 1972, pp.*
> *177-85.*

MARGARET MEEK (essay date 1973)

[*Meek is a Scottish journalist, editor, and essayist. In the following excerpt, she evaluates Leonardo's fables.*]

These are the stories of a great storyteller who liked nothing better than to put what he thought about things into the form of fables and legends. A fable is usually very short, and the author seems to say to his listener or his reader: "You'll see what I mean if I put it this way", and then he explains a complicated idea with an easily remembered example. Most peo-

ple know Aesop's fables—the lion and the rat, the fox and the grapes, for example. Certainly Leonardo did and he used them as his models because they seemed a good way to please people and to instruct them. He knew that if his readers were to learn the lesson of the story he had to make the point quickly and well, just as you tell a joke, in terms which they could associate with their everyday lives.

Legends are stories people have known for a long time and are handed down through many generations. While the outline and plot usually remain the same, the person who tells them changes the details to fit the situation in which he finds himself. There is less need to make them short as the pleasure comes from the way in which the new version is told. Leonardo used these two well-known forms to show a number of things in a new light.

Leonardo was a very great genius whose extraordinary gifts enabled him to tackle almost everything that men could do. He lived in Italy in the fifteenth century, a time thronged with new ideas and discoveries. His many distinguished and powerful contemporaries, some of whom commissioned work from him, included Lorenzo de' Medici, Ludovico Sforza, Duke of Milan and Francis I, king of France. He was an artist, a sculptor, a musician, a stage designer as well as an engineer who made canals. We know from his *Notebooks* that he explored the workings of the human body, studied rocks and fossils, and was fascinated all his life by the movement of water and the flight of birds. His curiosity was insatiable and he differed from his contemporaries in that he took nothing for granted and trusted only what he had actually seen. In his drawings he wanted to copy that abundant beauty of nature which he loved: animals, fish, birds, flowers, stones, grass and trees, all of which occur in these stories. He looked for the ideally beautiful—the portrait of the Mona Lisa is the most famous example—and contrasted such things with the ugliness and distortions he also saw around him. Above all, he was passionate about freedom. We are told that he bought caged birds in order to have the pleasure of setting them free.

Such a man, so intense about life and so full of ideas, found it difficult to explain to his contemporaries how he felt, so he told them stories in which his observations of fig trees, cranes, grapes, lilies and, above all, water, are linked to his passions. Read the stories of the goldfinch, the flames, the razor. As you read you will feel you come to know Leonardo, as he is concerned to make his listener look at things in his way, and you will recognise him as the eagle in the final story.

Because Leonardo's mind was restless and searching and his concerns were so like those of our day, we are sometimes surprised when he presents ideas which are more typical of his own period. Death was very near to people who lived when war and pestilence were common and violence could be seen everyday in the streets. Leonardo was outspoken about the corruption of courts and cities because he saw so much of it and contrasted it with the beauty of nature. But he was no sentimentalist; the animals are quite as ferocious in the stories as in real life. Sometimes the morals at the end of the tales seem a little far-fetched ('Falsehood, like the mole, can live only if it remains hidden') but we must remember that these are not lessons for children only, but also for grown men who prided themselves on their wordly wisdom. They had probably never before heard greed described in terms of the clematis and that made the lesson all the more memorable.

All his life and in all his work Leonardo aimed at perfection and often saw faults in things with which others were quite content. Even in the shortest fable we feel we have been looked into by a searching eye and we hear him say:

> At last, very suddenly, there flashed forth a spark which lit a marvellous fire, with the power to do marvellous things.

(pp. 9-13)

Margaret Meek, in an introduction to Fables of Leonardo da Vinci *by Leonardo da Vinci, edited and translated by Bruno Nardini, Hubbard Press, 1973, pp. 9-13.*

EMERY KELEN (essay date 1974)

[*A Hungarian-born American journalist and television newscaster, Kelen was an essayist, children's writer, and artist. In the following excerpt from* Leonardo da Vinci's Advice to Artists, *he ponders the varied impressions on art and artists expressed by Leonardo in the* Notebooks.]

When we read Leonardo's random notes reflecting on his profession, it is entertaining to sense the various moods in which he scribbled them. Sometimes he is being the stern preceptor, counting rules on his fingers, sometimes the compassionate master of a young pupil who is horrified by what he has put on canvas, or the self-examiner, or the poet. Now and then we find him bursting into a great exultation about his art, placing it in the very lap of Mother Nature and the artist within a breath of God. Remembering that he was a poor man, with no stature in his society, who walked among lords in a fancy coat, we can only admire his thundering pride as an artist. Of course, artists must have such pride; they cannot draw without it, or without the feeling of being somehow set apart.

All the same, though he was not a polished writer, he was choosy about his words and did not use the expressions *creative art* or *artistic creations* which are commonplace today; he considered them arrogant and preferred the word *generate.* God creates. Man is only the energy that arranges, according to his ability, the created objects that are placed before him, and thus passes them on to the understanding of others. (pp. 21-2)

Emery Kelen, "Art and the Young Artist," in Leonardo da Vinci's Advice to Artists *by Leonardo da Vinci, edited by Emery Kelen, Thomas Nelson Inc. Publishers, 1974 pp. 21-6.*

ISABEL QUIGLY (essay date 1976)

[*Quigly is a Spanish essayist, translator, and film critic. In the following introduction to* Leonardo da Vinci's Fantastic Animals, *she assesses the author's storytelling ability.*]

The *Notebooks* of Leonardo da Vinci make wonderful reading, whether you dip into them for immediate excitement or pore carefully over one of their sections. What they contain has been called "the records of the mightiest machine perhaps that has ever been a human brain." Leonardo wrote down much of what he observed, thought and imagined, and he illustrated his ideas and observations with detailed sketches.

He wrote about nature in all its forms—in the working of the human body, in animals, in plants and in the earth. Every-

thing that lived and grew or had lived and grown in the past excited him: the movement of birds or water or wind, the anatomy of the brain, the behaviour of the weather, flight, weight, geology, geography, botany, astronomy. He wrote about man-made things as well: architecture, canals, warfare, the techniques of painting. And, more extraordinarily perhaps, he wrote about what might happen in the future.

Leonardo was able to imagine, in a remarkably detailed way, all kinds of inventions that only appeared hundreds of years after his death—machines that would bring both progress and destruction, like the aeroplane and the tank. He foresaw what would happen not just in the case of mechanical inventions but in all sorts of fields of knowledge, in physics and optics, for instance, and he understood far better than anyone else in his day or for a long time after it, things which only much later became clear to scientists, things like the circulation of the blood.

But although he was such a careful investigator, and so passionately interested in the minutest detail of things in nature, he was an artist as well, which means he interpreted that world and did not just record what he saw there. His imagination was able to create not just an exact and likely future, but worlds of fantasy in which strange creatures lived and fabulous things happened.

These worlds were never separate from the world he actually observed and touched. Leonardo believed in the unity of all things. His scientific investigations were touched with fantasy, his most fantastic stories are filled with a sense of the truth of the imagination.

One of the most remarkable drawings in the *Notebooks* is a "study for a monster." It is of a human foot showing every vein and muscle with perfect exactness, but with bear's claws in place of toes. This shows the method he used in telling many of his stories. The creatures he describes may be mythical beasts like the phoenix, which is burnt to death yet always rises from the ashes, or the basilisk, which kills whatever looks at it or comes near it. They are products of his search for truth in every form, including poetic forms in which parables and fables tell us hidden truths. And even his most fantastic creatures are wonderfully vivid and easy to imagine.

Most of the stories are not about monsters and legends, though, but about everyday animals that can teach lessons of patience and faithfulness and love, sometimes of cunning and cruelty: owl, hawk and turtle-dove, pigeon, falcon and goldfinch, cocks and hens, bats, bees, spiders, snakes like the asp and the viper, impressive beasts like the lion and the panther, homely ones like the mouse, the duck and the donkey. All of them and their brief stories, which Leonardo took mostly from ancient sources, tell us something of the workings of nature.

Some of them are funny, some sad, some realistic and some fabulous. These divisions do not matter. All are minutely observed by an artist and thinker who saw all aspects of life as one, who longed to unite the worlds of fact and fantasy, of the mind and the imagination, the man-made and the natural.

Even Leonardo's own gifts overlapped. Although known chiefly as a painter and sculptor, he believed strongly in the power of the written word and spent much of his life writing down his ideas. In his day, pens were made out of quills—the feathers of birds with one end sharpened into a nib. "Feathers shall raise men as they do birds, towards heaven," he wrote, "that is, by letters written with their quills." (pp. 9-14)

Isabel Quigly, in an introduction to Fantastic Animals *by Leonardo da Vinci, edited and translated by Bruno Nardini and David Grant, William Collins Sons and Company Limited, 1976, pp. 9-14.*

ROGER SHATTUCK   (essay date 1984)

[*Shattuck is an American essayist, editor, translator, and academic. In the following excerpt, he compares the perceptions of Sigmund Freud and Paul Valéry on Leonardo's psyche.*]

Valéry wrote six different texts on Leonardo at approximately even intervals throughout his career. The first two are the most important, *Introduction à la méthode de Léonard de Vinci,* begun in 1894 soon after his detachment from poetry, and *Note et digression,* added to the previous work when it was republished in 1919. In 1929-30 he wrote extensive marginal notes to these two early texts and to a third written in 1928, so that today they appear as a palimpsest, the apt representation of a mind that could endlessly develop and transform any subject by bringing attention to bear on it.

Valéry opens the *Introduction* by stating flatly that neither the biography nor the personality of Leonardo concerns him [see excerpt dated 1894]. Rather, he will examine a method of thinking or a "creature of thought" to whom, because it appears the most appropriate, he assigns the name Leonardo. In prose so dense that one can feel the sustained cerebration that formed it, Valéry describes an elevated, universal, and perpetually self-correcting Mind. Its secret is to grasp "relations . . . between things whose principle of continuity escapes the rest of us." Thus, for both Leonardo and Napoleon, "at the crucial moment they had only to act." This hypersensitive ability to see connections is rendered bearable by a compensatory mechanism of "foresight" that carries every train of thought instantaneously to its limit, a heightened capacity for compression and comparison. Valéry is somewhat hard put to explain the operation of this form of consciousness. What he says about how thought organizes undifferentiated impressions resembles Taine's theory of *hallucination vraie.* He seems to be on firmer ground in considering the two complementary faculties of universal thought: to identify with individual things—a strong sense of particularity in the world—and to recognize regularities in the world: continuity, similarity, periodicity. The truly great mind exercises these faculties at a speed so high as to appear instantaneous, yet remains at least partially conscious of the mental operation taking place within it.

Valéry's undulating reflections on the nature of thought and subjectivity make difficult reading. In a curious way, though Valéry's theory of mind is diametrically opposed to that of biologically oriented behaviorists and sociologists, what he writes often sounds like an elaborate restatement of the dictum: "Mind is minding." But the crosshatch and chain stitch of his style convey Valéry's perpetual refinement of such an equivocation. The pure activity, the mere free play of mind is as exciting and as productive as any externally imposed purpose or special discipline. This in fact is the point with which he begins the later essay *Note et digression.* He swoops back down on Leonardo as the "leading actor in the intellectual comedy which never to this day has found its poet." In a less clotted, more transparent prose, Valéry reaffirms this judgment of the "integrity" of Leonardo as a mind, never

torn between a naturalistic and a spiritualistic sense of man. But another, more subtle division lurks within, for which Valéry offers the expression "presence of mind." He illustrates the delicate circular equilibrium of this self-awareness with two metaphors: first, the swirling drafts that form a smoke ring, and second, the stage of a theater surrounded by a hidden but distinctly real audience. (pp. 85-6)

In these two texts and the later ones, Valéry has composed variations on a single theme: the miraculous variety of Leonardo's work springs from a highly developed singleness of mind or unity of thought. Examined in itself, apart from the works it strewed along its path, this astonishing mind reveals the nature of the self, not personality or biography but pure consciousness beholding an infinity of relations in what it sees and perpetually backing away from what it sees in the very act of beholding. (p. 87)

The disclaimer with which Freud begins [*Leonardo da Vinci and a Memory of His Childhood*] differs from Valéry's. The fact that he is studying Leonardo, Freud tells us, does not suggest that the great Italian genius was a pathological case or even represent any desire to detract from his fame. Freud affirms he is concerned with "laws which govern normal and pathological activity with equal cogency." The problem Freud first poses is the apparent interference that occurred between Leonardo's investigative activities and his painting, between scientist and artist. The first and longest of the six sections advances the thesis that Leonardo's truly exceptional capacities as an experimental investigator, unimpeded by the authority of either church or antiquity, can be traced in great part to his childhood, through the theory of sublimation. "After his curiosity had been aroused in infancy, he succeeded in sublimating the greater part of his libido into an urge for research." His notes and his behavior show that he felt compelled "to love in such a way as to hold back the affect, subject it to the process of reflection." This instinct for knowledge, though it channeled his genius, in the end affected the free play of his artistic expression. What was left of his childhood sexuality, Freud supposes, expressed itself as sublimated homosexuality.

The remaining pages flesh out this hypothesis with a brilliant, though often factually unsupported, demonstration. (pp. 89-90)

This would seem a long way to come if these two highly individual books have no more in common than their subject and their total inadequacy as systematic biographies. But the reason for the comparison should begin to assert itself. Valéry, whom we think of as an artist, gives most of his attention to Leonardo's notebooks and to his methodology as a thinker. Freud, whom we think of as a scientist, at least by training, refers briefly to the notebooks and then elaborates the greater part of his argument on the basis of the painting and the life. Valéry cites no historical persons, dates, or places, and attempts only to illustrate a theory of self-consciousness; Freud obviously believed he could contribute to Leonardo's biography and to biographical method by bringing to bear on an enigmatic and eminent life the new science of analysis. Yet by the time we reach the end of Freud's study, Leonardo's personality interests us less than the process that permitted him to come to terms with himself and the world. Not the individuality but the generality of his case emerges from these pages. His personality has melted away into a set of carefully described responses.

Why, then, if neither author wrote a biography but was really concerned with something quite apart from Leonardo's individual life, did they compose these two books nominally aimed in his direction? The first answer is quite easy. They both identified with Leonardo—admired him, understood something of him, and could understand something of themselves in examining him. Though Valéry's first article was commissioned, the subject was far from new to him. He makes little effort to hide the fact that what he writes of Leonardo is in effect the fruit of introspection. And he wrote at far greater length on Leonardo than on any other person, including his master, Mallarmé. Freud's interest in Leonardo went back at least a dozen years and probably more, and the work remained one of his favorites. Ernest Jones tells us that Freud particularly admired two historical figures: Moses, the wise leader who guided his people to a new land and a full life, and Leonardo, who combined the talents of an artist and the knowledge of a scientist in creating some of the greatest artifacts of Western culture. There is nothing very rash in saying that both Valéry and Freud felt in themselves the double temperament, the twin genius that tradition attributes to Leonardo. Furthermore, Leonardo's apparent irresolution and perpetual shift of focus in his work probably struck a responsive chord in each of them. Valéry had just gone through a personal crisis that was to divert the channel of his writing for many years: he came to value a completed work less than the state of mind that permits creation. Freud, though well established in his central field of inquiry when he wrote on Leonardo, had been very much at loose ends for a time about what calling to follow. After deciding against law, a slow and somewhat erratic progress had carried him through physiology, medicine, teaching, neurology, and psychopathology to psychoanalysis. He was always profoundly attracted to literature and the arts, and wrote to the novelist Schnitzler that he felt their temperaments were very similar.

But more important than any personal reasons for writing of Leonardo, the conclusions of their studies show more similarity than we might have expected. I have suggested earlier that the books contribute to a discernible pattern that reveals Leonardo as a culture hero for the era. Yet these two works, weak as they are biographically, help us understand why so many other authors were studying Leonardo without shedding much new light. From their very different cultural vantage points, Valéry and Freud glimpsed something behind Leonardo they could approach through him. For both of them, Leonardo stood for a form of consciousness they admired—a new equilibrium of faculties that could be fully recognized and appreciated only four hundred years after the fact, and on slender evidence. Their essays describe a case that has particular relevance to our modern situation, like Eliot writing of Donne, or Baudelaire writing of Poe. I feel that in the end, for Freud as much as for Valéry, the name Leonardo is reduced to an exemplary case, a convention, a pure symbol, a term like "Socrates" as traditionally used in the syllogisms that start "Socrates is a man." Someone has to represent humanity, if possible at its best. But subtracted from his life, what does Leonardo stand for? Does anything remain beyond Vasari's appealing myth of a restless genius releasing birds, blowing up bladders, and painting an occasional picture? (pp. 91-3)

Valéry and Freud do not indulge in any suggestion that the superiority of Leonardo's mental organization, his power to perceive relations and find pleasure in experiment, removed him from humanity. On the contrary, an image they both use

The head of a soldier, a study prepared by Leonardo for Battle of Anghiari.

displays their awareness of the risks run by so powerful a mind if aware of its own power. Valéry's exposition never withdraws from the dilemma of self-consciousness, so that every metaphor for thought or attention ("the dreams of the waking sleeper," "detachment," "repulsion") signifies a perpetual spiraling out of the self in order to see the self—which is no longer there to be seen. Throughout his poetic production, Valéry reverted to the figure of Narcissus to express this problem of the fugitive self: and narcissism is precisely the psychoanalytic concept to which Freud gave one of its earliest elaborations in the Leonardo text. The metaphor does not serve the same purpose for the two of them; but in both cases its meaning reaches far into the ambiguous area where the mind, trying to catch sight of itself in action, discovers that nothing is there but a perpetual movement of recoil or afterthought. Narcissus attests not to a division but to a contortion of mind. Freud points out very shrewdly that nothing seemed to escape the notice of Leonardo's investigations. "Yet his urge for knowledge was always directed to the external world; something kept him far away from the investigation of the human mind. . . . There was little room for psychology."

In other words, Leonardo would never have written either Valéry's or Freud's book. (pp. 96-7)

For one very elementary lesson, then, we may look back a medium range of sixty-odd years to the turn of the century.

Amid the surprisingly large number of writers in Europe devoting their attention to Leonardo da Vinci, two thinkers discovered the opportunity to approach the most universal subject of all: the nature of the human mind. A little distance beyond the place where their explicit commentary stopped, one can discern a significant agreement. The division we have begun to lament publicly between two climates of thinking, scientific and humanistic, between opposed methods of inquiry, cannot be traced to any corresponding division between regions or faculties in the mind. At the origin is unity; we have imposed the separation upon ourselves, possibly to lighten our burden. For it is an onerous responsibility to live both inside and alongside the thoughts that we are—almost.

There is more than we ever knew in the story of the tortoise and the hare. Just look again. You will see not two animals but one, traveling at different speeds. (p. 101)

> Roger Shattuck, "The Tortoise and the Hare: Valéry, Freud, and Leonardo da Vinci," in his The Innocent Eye: On Modern Literature & the Arts, *Farrar Straus Giroux, 1984, pp. 82-101.*

PIETRO CORSI   (essay date 1988)

[Corsi is an Italian historian of science. In the following excerpt, he assesses discoveries concerning Leonardo's life and work.]

Painter and sculptor, technologist and inventor, botanist and anatomist, engineer and architect, for centuries Leonardo has appeared to embody all the virtues of the Renaissance man. Scholars and graduate students, as well as enraptured crowds of tourists, have turned the easy admiration for the enigmatic smile of the "Mona Lisa" or the enchanted landscape of "The Annunciation" into a litany of platitudes that in the summer season make the Louvre and the Uffizi unbearable places to visit. To a large extent, admiration and wonder have been Leonardo's worst enemies. Everything he did, and even things he attempted but was unable to accomplish, have been taken so seriously that industrial concerns have adopted some of his drawings of machines as symbols of their technological ingenuity without realizing that the machines were often impossible dreams.

After centuries of worship, in the last 60 years, and particularly in the last three decades, scholars have turned Leonardo upside down; they have examined sheet after sheet of his vast manuscript legacy and at long last have reassessed his contribution to Renaissance and modern culture (at times not without acrimonious self-satisfaction). Indeed, for a long time commentators used the myth of Leonardo the genius as an excuse for not even looking into the documents at their disposal, the 6,000 or so manuscript pages that make up roughly one-third of the papers Leonardo bequested to his pupil Francesco Melzi at the time of his death in 1519.

As is well known, Leonardo's works of art and papers have always attracted the attention of conquerors and other kinds of thieves. They have often disappeared for decades, some never to surface again. Yet no conquering army or private collector has done more to disrupt Leonardo's legacy than Pompeo Leoni, the sculptor who at the end of the 16th century felt he had to spend some time rearranging the Leonardo notebooks he had acquired. He divided the drawings and manuscript pages in his possession into various headings. The material relating to machines and inventions, for instance,

was put together in what became known as the ***Codex Atlanticus*** (an atlas-size miscellany), whereas artistic exercises, naturalistic observations and anatomical drawings became the core of the precious Windsor Castle collection. The view of Leonardo's mind at work which the original notebooks offered was thus lost, and all trace of his intellectual development disappeared with it. (p. 11)

At the end of the 1460's Leonardo came to Florence and started his apprenticeship in the workshop of Andrea del Verrocchio, the versatile artist who was then working on the lantern, the top of the dome. Brunelleschi's machines, built at considerable expense, were most probably still on the site, to allow the lifting of the heavy components of the lantern. There is no doubt that Leonardo was extremely impressed by Brunelleschi's work, as were many of his senior colleagues then active in Florence and Siena. Following a well-established trade practice, Leonardo's early technological work in fact consisted of a close study of Brunelleschi's machines, and of the work of engineers like Francesco di Giorgio Martini (1439-1501) and Jacopo Mariano, called Taccola (c. 1382-1458). From them Leonardo learned the secrets of the trade, including the art of drawing fantastic pieces of equipment—and of attracting the attention of patrons with his grandiose projects.

The fact that the roots of many of what were thought to be original ideas of Leonardo have thus been uncovered does not mean that historians have become blind to his merits and achievements. It simply means that research done in the last 30 years has allowed the identification of a series of points of departure for reconstructing the intellectual development of Leonardo as well as tracing how his accomplishments transformed the work of engineer-technologists.

It is the outstanding merit of the Montreal Museum of Fine Arts to have organized in 1987 an exhibition attempting a critical reconstruction of Leonardo's career as engineer and architect, set within the intellectual and social context of his time. It is now the merit of the catalogue of this exhibition, *Leonardo da Vinci: Engineer and Architect,* edited by Paolo Galluzzi, director of the History of Science Museum in Florence, to propose again the central themes of the show, and to make us wish that other museums or institutions, in the United States as well as in Europe, will host this exhibition for a wider public.

Already known to a limited number of experts, the portrait of Leonardo that emerges from this catalogue is sure to be a startling novelty for the general public. It is clear that Leonardo was not well understood by his contemporaries, and that he was not much loved either except during his last years at the court of the King of France. Nature and nurture made him a secretive man. Yet he was capable of displaying all the charms of a courtier. As was typical of Renaissance engineers, he excelled in building marvelous machines for the amusement of the courts in which he lived. But he was also expelled from the Santo Spirito hospital in Rome for his experiments in dissecting bodies; he was suspected of practicing necromantic arts. The idea of dissection he carried over to machines; he drew them as if they were organisms seen in cross section and thus he single-handedly transformed the art of technical design. He also dreamed up machines that the technology of his time would never have allowed to work (indeed, some of them violated his own theories). And yet he was fully confident that his impossible flying machine would have made him more famous than any man who ever lived.

The abandonment of myth now allows us to look at Leonardo's career with new eyes, and to appreciate the distance he covered from his early days in Verrocchio's shop to his last in the French court at Amboise. The various essays of this catalogue, written by the very men who have transformed Leonardo studies, tell us of his training in the practical arts and trade secrets of Renaissance engineers, of his shaky Latin and of his slow maturing into an ambitious reformer of his profession. Success, travel, frequenting various sophisticated courts and meeting intellectuals like the mathematician Luca Pacioli gave new dimensions to Leonardo's ambition. In time he developed the idea that technology had to be grounded in an understanding of natural laws and processes. He promised himself he would write basic treatises on the power of water and winds and on the general principles holding the universe together from the smallest organism to the orbits of stars—but in the end he never wrote them. The man who died in Amboise was four decades away, and several social classes above the young bastard apprentice in Verrocchio's shop. By the time of his death he was held in high esteem not only as a painter and architect, but also, and foremost, as a man of wide philosophical attainments versed in all subjects of natural and physical investigation. The copious illustrations of this elegant volume will allow readers to follow step by step the development of Leonardo's projects, dreams and failures. A new Leonardo—a man of more human, but not less amazing ingenuity and inventiveness—emerges from this outstanding contribution to Renaissance studies. (pp. 11-12)

> *Pietro Corsi, "The Beauty of His Machines," in* The New York Times Book Review, *July 24, 1988, pp. 11-12.*

CHARLES HOPE (essay date 1989)

[*In the following excerpt, Hope disputes commentators who label Leonardo's perceptions universal and unique, offering what he considers a more realistic portrait of the artist.*]

The idea that Leonardo was a universal man, committed to mastering the entire range of human knowledge and equally creative in every aspect of his activity, emerged in the nineteenth century with the gradual publication of the notebooks. The growth of his fame was almost inevitable, since nothing has survived from the period that is comparable in the accomplishment of the illustrations, the range of topics addressed, and the sheer bulk of the text. But Leonardo's reputation was made more by the mere existence of this material than by any real understanding of its character, because it has taken a century and more to establish in general terms just what the notebooks contain. His comments on individual subjects often have to be assembled from passages on different pages and in different volumes. Once collected, they have to be put into some chronological sequence. And finally, because much of what he wrote was copied or paraphrased (often inaccurately and without acknowledgment) from books, his sources have to be identified.

Many of the larger claims that were once made for Leonardo no longer seem tenable. Anyone who has looked at the notebooks will soon be struck by the fact that he was no more systematic at note-taking than the rest of us, and that he was certainly not good at bringing any of his ideas to a conclusion—or indeed to anything resembling publishable form. What has also become much clearer is the extent of his dependence on earlier writers. Seen in this light, his protestations against

those who blindly follow received authority rather than experience take on a defensive tone, simply because he was well aware that his lack of Latin excluded him from the higher learning of his day. Indeed, in other strictly practical matters, such as ability at arithmetic, Leonardo was by no means remarkable.

Just as Leonardo's originality as a speculative thinker now seems less marked than it once did, so too is it difficult to maintain that he was wholly exceptional in the variety of his interests and activities. On the contrary, the areas in which he was engaged—principally painting, sculpture, civil and military architecture, mechanical and hydraulic engineering, cartography, geometry, and anatomy—were all subjects in which men trained as artists often became involved. The Sienese painter and architect Francesco di Giorgio, for instance, has left us a manuscript filled with drawings of machines not unlike those illustrated by Leonardo, whom he knew personally; Piero della Francesca wrote treatises on perspective and commercial arithmetic; and, most conspicuously, Brunelleschi, having trained as a goldsmith, was apparently a pioneer in the use of linear perspective and successfully carried out one of the greatest feats of engineering since antiquity, the construction of the dome of Florence Cathedral.

Leonardo's interests may well have been wider than those of his fellow artists—though how much wider it is impossible to say in the absence of their notebooks—but the record of his achievements in applying his knowledge in a practical way is very meager. There is surprisingly little evidence of his various architectural and engineering projects being put into effect, and at least one important instance in which his ideas were apparently rejected. In short, there is a question mark over Leonardo's competence, which perhaps should not surprise us given his uniquely poor record at bringing paintings and sculptures to completion. In the field of technology, too, it is clear that he was less original than was once supposed—a point made eloquently in the London exhibition by the inclusion of a model of the crane built by Brunelleschi for the construction of the cupola in Florence, of which drawings are preserved in Leonardo's notebooks. Indeed, in the history of technology there is not a single invention with which he can confidently be credited. In anatomy, by contrast, there is no doubt about his brilliance in dissection and observation; but here too it is clear that where observation conflicted with his preconceived ideas, the latter often took precedence.

The development of Leonardo scholarship, then, has transformed him from an isolated genius into a more plausible figure. Even now we cannot fail to be astonished by his curiosity and his intelligence. But the purpose of Leonardo's entire enterprise is unclear, if indeed it had a single purpose at all. Yet the seductive notion of Leonardo the universal man dies hard, and scholars have been reluctant to abandon it. . . . (pp. 17-18)

[Even] if we cease to think of Leonardo as a superman there remain two reasons for investigating his thought. The first is that the survival of the notebooks gives us a unique body of evidence about important fields of activity of Renaissance artists and engineers. Leonardo has left the fullest group of studies of technology of the period, and his writings even provide an ideal case study (though they do not seem to have been much used for that purpose) of just how much—or, in this case, how little—Renaissance artists were able to pick up of the Latin-based culture of their day, without direct access to the texts. The other reason why the notebooks deserve the closest scrutiny is that Leonardo was a remarkable painter. It is this that gives a focus and purpose to many of his speculations and observations.

The one aspect of Leonardo's thought that was valued after his death was his comments on painting. These are far more extensive than those of anyone else writing in Italy up to that time, and in the sixteenth and seventeenth centuries they had the reputation of being original and useful. Leonardo was certainly planning to compose a treatise on painting, but characteristically he never managed to assemble or organize his many scattered remarks on the subject. Already in the sixteenth century some of them were collected in a volume called the **Codex Urbinas.** Using this and other sources, Martin Kemp and Margaret Walker [in *Leonardo on Painting*] have now tried to compose the ordered treatise that Leonardo never managed to produce. Although their work necessarily gives a false coherence to his typically unsystematic ideas, the result is certainly easier to read and in many ways more convenient than previous compilations.

If we assume that Kemp and Walker are true to Leonardo's intentions, most of his treatise would have been of an essentially practical kind, similar in character to his observations on other subjects in the notebooks. Leonardo, in short, was chiefly concerned with creating an art that would be true to natural appearances. This is why so many pages of the notebooks are devoted to the study of perspective, the fall of shadows, and the visual appearance of natural features like trees and distant mountains. Even in his writings on the *paragone*, the comparison of painting with sculpture, poetry, or music, again and again it is in the ability of painting to bring the real world before the eye of the spectator that provides the principal argument for its superiority over the other arts.

Leonardo's ideas were very different from those of the next generation of Italian painters. In particular, he did not share their belief that the principal task of the artist was to improve on nature. This is probably why he did not strongly advocate that painters develop a personal style and why he did not have much to say about the process of creation. Evidently he regarded the business of representation as far more onerous than that of conception. That, at least, is the message of the notebooks. Martin Kemp has argued, however, in the London catalog and elsewhere, that Leonardo did come to believe that "the painter needed to forge a new kind of union between *intelletto* and *fantasia*—between rational understanding and imaginative recomposition." His claim, which has been well received by other scholars, fits so well the familiar notion of Leonardo as universal man, combining in a wonderfully original way the diverse demands of art and science, that it needs to be treated with some suspicion; and I do not think it can be sustained.

Leonardo, like everyone else at that time, accepted the Aristotelian idea of mental faculties, and like most people he located these in the cavities or "ventricles" of the brain. Although various authorities differed on details, there was general agreement that memory was located in the rear ventricle and the rational intellect (*intelletto*) in the central ventricle, while the two front ventricles were the seat of the *sensus communis* (the confluence of the senses) and the *fantasia,* which can roughly be translated as imagination. Until long after Leonardo's time it was accepted that painters principally dealt with sense impressions, using the *fantasia.* In this respect they were fundamentally different from poets, whose

activity, involving language and intellect, was concentrated in the central ventricle.

Leonardo, according to Kemp, challenged this notion, by shifting the *sensus communis* to the central ventricle, and giving the front ventricles a new function as receptors of data from the eyes alone. The effect, he argued, was to place the *sensus communis* and so also the *fantasia* in the same ventricle as the intellect. Unfortunately, this attractive hypothesis cannot be proved. In none of his various drawings of the brain does Leonardo explicitly indicate the location of the *fantasia;* only once does he indicate the seat of the *intelletto,* and then it is in the front ventricle, whereas the *sensus communis* is in the middle ventricle. Nowhere does he explicitly link imagination and intellect, and there is no good reason to suppose that in this respect he was challenging conventional ideas of creativity—or indeed that he gave much thought to the workings of the imagination at all. His revision of the traditional ventricular scheme, such as it was, may as well have been due to a misunderstanding of Latin texts, which he could not read, as to any fundamental rethinking of the problem.

Even though Leonardo's views on painting, and in particular his stress on the importance of truth to natural appearances and his indifference to self-expression, now seem disappointingly prosaic, he himself clearly did not consider it an anodyne activity. On the contrary, he thought that painting was uniquely effective because it addressed the highest of the senses, sight. Painters can move spectators more effectively than poets, because of the vividness with which they can depict figures or landscapes. Painters can also instruct, because art can show things better than words.

It is this last idea that is Leonardo's chief claim to fame as a theorist of art. He was not, of course, the first Italian artist to try to represent the natural world; but we do not know that any of his predecessors undertook this task with such energy or commitment. And what distinguishes, for example, Leonardo's drawings of machines from others of this period is the information they contain and the powerful representation of force and motion. Leonardo was technically the most innovative draftsman of his age, as the drawings in London so beautifully illustrated. But the motive behind his innovations was not some internally generated desire for self-expression, but a wish to perfect the technical resources of his craft. Leonardo drew things, not ideas, even if, as David Rosand has recently argued [in *The Meaning of the Mark: Leonardo and Titian* (1988)], his understanding of natural phenomena reflected the ways in which he chose to represent them.

Today the notion of art as illustrative, as being a means of conveying information, hardly seems very exciting. Hence the low status of scientific illustration and the stress on spontaneity and fluency in drawings. Here Leonardo's drawings ought to give us pause for thought. More generally, the history of Leonardo studies, and likewise of the connoisseurship of Michelangelo drawings, ought also to remind us how hard it is to avoid modern values in investigating the artists of the past, not least our modern notion of genius. This has led generations of scholars to search in Leonardo's writings for the brilliance that he displayed in his drawings and paintings, and to judge Michelangelo's drawings on the premise that everything he touched must have turned to artistic gold. We may like to be dazzled by their work, but it is surely better to see their achievements clearly. (p. 18)

Charles Hope, "The Real Leonardo," in The New York Review of Books, *Vol. XXXVI, No. 13, August 17, 1989, pp. 16-18.*

FURTHER READING

Barzun, Jacques. "Truth and Biography: Leonardo and Freud." In his *Critical Questions: On Music and Letters, Culture and Biography, 1940-1980,* edited by Bea Friedland, pp. 183-92. Chicago: The University of Chicago Press, 1982.
> Questions Sigmund Freud's interpretation of Leonardo's psychosexual motivations.

Freud, Sigmund. *Leonardo da Vinci and a Memory of His Childhood.* Translated by Alan Tyson. New York: W. W. Norton & Co., 1964, 101 p.
> Cites Leonardo's recollection of a childhood dream as evidence that he sublimated his sexuality into artistic creations and scientific research.

Goggio, Emilio. "Leonardo the Man and the Writer." *University of Toronto Quarterly* XXIII, No. 1 (October 1953): 26-34.
> Favorable overview of Leonardo's writing.

Goldstein, Laurence. "Leonardo da Vinci and the Modern Century." In his *The Flying Machine and Modern Literature,* pp. 14-40. Houndmills, England: Macmillan, 1986.
> Traces theories concerning the source of Leonardo's fascination with flight and inventions of flying machines.

Heydenreich, Ludwig H. Introduction to *Treatise on Painting,* by Leonardo da Vinci, pp. xi-xliii. Princeton: Princeton University Press, 1956.
> Discusses the development and compilation of *A Treatise of Painting.*

Jaspers, Karl. "Leonardo as Philosopher." In his *Three Essays: Leonardo, Descartes, Max Weber,* pp. 3-58. New York: Harcourt, Brace & World, 1964.
> Characterizes Leonardo's philosophical perceptions and method of acquiring knowledge.

McCurdy, Edward. *The Mind of Leonardo da Vinci.* New York: Dodd, Mead & Co., 1928, 360 p.
> Critical biography of Leonardo that includes a discussion of the history of the *Notebooks.*

Maelsaeke, D. van. "Goethe and Leonardo: A Comparative Study." *Theoria* XXXIV (May 1970): 21-49.
> Detailed comparison of Leonardo and Johann Wolfgang von Goethe that treats such issues as their religious persuasions, world views, and fascination with human existence.

Mumford, Lewis. "Leonardo's Premonitions." In his *Interpretations and Forecasts: 1922-1972,* pp. 313-19. New York: Harcourt Brace Jovanovich, 1973.
> Describes various predictions made by Leonardo and their impact upon his life.

Papini, Giovanni. "Leonardo da Vinci." In his *Four and Twenty Minds,* translated by Ernest Hatch Wilkins, pp. 15-25. New York: Thomas Y. Crowell Co., 1922.
> Attempts to transform Leonardo's image so he will "live on as something more than a subject for theses and for lantern slides."

Philipson, Morris, ed. *Leonardo da Vinci: Aspects of the Renaissance Genius.* New York: George Braziller, 1966, 438 p.
> Collection of essays on Leonardo by such scholars as Paul Valéry and Kenneth Clark.

Reti, Ladislao, ed. *The Unknown Leonardo.* New York: McGraw-Hill Book Co., 1974, 319 p.
> Anthology treating various facets of the author's life and work.

Taylor, Rachel Annand. *Leonardo the Florentine: A Study in Personality.* London: Richards Press, 1927, 580 p.
> Romantic biography focusing upon Leonardo's aesthetic nature.

Zubov, V. P. *Leonardo da Vinci.* Translated by David H. Kraus. Cambridge, Mass.: Harvard University Press, 1968, 335 p.
> Critical biography of Leonardo originally published in Russian.

ISBN 0-8103-6111-6

90000

9 780810 361119